THE ROUGH GUIDE TO

Malaysia, Singapore and Brunei

Written and researched by

David Leffman and Richard Lim

with additional contributions by

Kiki Deere, Joanna James and Charles Young

roughguides.com

Contents

INTRODUCTION 4

Where to go	5	Things not to miss	14
When to go	12	Itineraries	24

BASICS 26

Getting there	27	Festivals	45
Getting around	30	Sports and outdoor activities	46
Accommodation	35	Culture and etiquette	47
Food and drink	37	Shopping	49
Health	42	Travel essentials	50
The media	44		

THE GUIDE 60

1 Kuala Lumpur and around	61	6 Sarawak	306
2 The west coast	112	7 Sabah	382
3 The interior	180	8 Brunei	444
4 The east coast	210	9 Singapore	466
5 The south	260		

CONTEXTS 552

History	553	Wildlife	583
Religion	570	Books	587
Peoples	574	Language	591
Development and the environment	579	Glossary	601

SMALL PRINT & INDEX 603

Introduction to

Malaysia, Singapore and Brunei

Populated by a blend of Malays, Chinese, Indians and indigenous groups, Malaysia, Singapore and Brunei boast a rich cultural heritage, from a huge variety of annual festivals and wonderful cuisines, to traditional architecture and rural crafts. There's astonishing natural beauty to take in too, including gorgeous beaches and some of the world's oldest tropical rainforest, much of which is surprisingly accessible. Malaysia's national parks are superb for trekking and wildlife-watching, and sometimes for cave exploration and river rafting.

As part of the Malay archipelago, which stretches from Indonesia to the Philippines, Malaysia, Singapore and Brunei share not only similarities in their ethnic make-up but also part of their **history**. Each became an important port of call on the trade route between India and China, the two great markets of the early world, and later became important entrepôts for the Portuguese, Dutch and British empires. Malaysia has only existed in its present form since 1963, when the federation of the eleven Peninsula states was joined by Singapore and the two Bornean territories of Sarawak and Sabah. Singapore left the union to become an independent country in 1965; Brunei, preferring to remain outside the federation in Borneo, only lost its British colonial status in 1984.

Since then, Malaysia, Singapore and Brunei have been united in their **economic predominance** among Southeast Asian nations. While Brunei is locked into a paternalistic regime, using its considerable oil wealth to guarantee its citizens a respectable standard of living, the city-state of Singapore has become a giant in commerce, having transformed itself from a strategic port. Malaysia, always competitive with its southern neighbour, is pursuing a similarly ambitious goal, to

ABOVE PULAU PERHENTIAN **OPPOSITE** ORANG-UTANS, SEPILOK, BORNEO which end the country is investing heavily in new infrastructure, from highways to ports and factories.

Today, the dominant cultural force in the region is undoubtedly **Islam**, adopted by the Malays in the fourteenth century, though in Chinese-dominated Singapore, **Buddhism** and **Taoism** together hold sway among half the population. But it's the religious plurality – there are also sizeable Christian and Hindu minorities – that is so attractive, often providing surprising juxtapositions of mosques, temples and churches. Add the colour and verve of Chinese temples and street fairs, Indian festival days and everyday life in Malay kampungs (villages), and the indigenous traditions of Borneo, and it's easy to see why visitors are drawn into this celebration of ethnic diversity; indeed, despite some issues, both Malaysia and Singapore have something to teach the rest of the world when it comes to building successful multicultural societies.

Where to go

Malaysia's capital, **Kuala Lumpur** (usually referred to as KL), is the social and economic driving force of a nation eager to better itself, a fact reflected in the relentless proliferation of air-conditioned shopping malls, designer bars and restaurants in the city, and in the continuing sprawl of suburbia and industry around it. But KL is also firmly

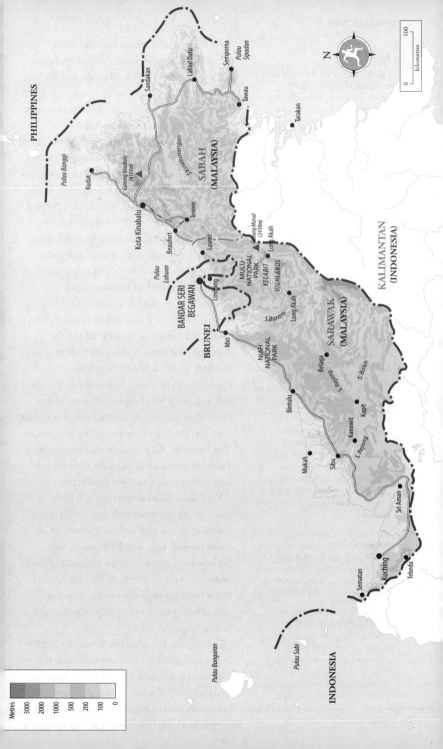

FACT FILE

• **Malaysia** is a federation of nine **sultanates**, plus the states of Penang, Melaka and, on the island of Borneo, Sabah and Sarawak.

• **Peninsular Malaysia**, where the federal capital Kuala Lumpur is located, and **East Malaysia**, the northern section of Borneo, are separated by more than 600km of the South China Sea.

• In terms of **population**, Malays make up just over half of Malaysia's thirty million people, ethnic Chinese around 22 percent, indigenous Orang Asli and Borneo tribes together 12 percent, and ethnic Indians 7 percent.

• Tiny **Singapore**, just 700 square kilometres in size, is a wealthy city-state cramming in 5.5 million inhabitants, including a sizeable minority of expats.

• Made up of two enclaves in eastern Sarawak, **Brunei** is nearly ten times the size of Singapore, but holds less than one tenth of the population.

• Both Malaysia and Singapore are British-style **parliamentary democracies**, the former with a ceremonial head of state known as the Yang di-Pertuan Agung (the post rotates among the sultans of the federation). Brunei is ruled by its **sultan**.

• The world's largest flower, **Rafflesia**, is a Malaysian rainforest plant measuring a metre across and smelling of rotten meat. It's named after the naturalist and founder of Singapore, Sir Stamford Raffles.

• Malaysia's **economy**, historically dominated by agriculture and mining, now features a healthy manufacturing sector, as does Singapore, where shipping and financial services are also key industries. Brunei profits handsomely from its reserves of oil and gas.

rooted in tradition, where the same Malay executives who wear suits to work dress in traditional clothes at festival times, and markets and food stalls are crowded in among high-rise hotels and bank towers, especially in older areas such as Chinatown and Little India.

Just a couple of hours' drive south of the capital lies the birthplace of Malay civilization, **Melaka**, its historical architecture and mellow atmosphere making it a must on anybody's itinerary. Much further up the **west coast**, the island of **Penang** was the site of the first British settlement in Malaysia. Its capital, **Georgetown**, still features beautifully restored colonial buildings and a vibrant Chinatown district, and is, together with Melaka, recognized for its cultural and architectural diversity as a UNESCO World Heritage Site. For a taste of Old England, head for the hill stations of **Fraser's Hill** and the **Cameron Highlands**, where cooler temperatures and lush countryside provide ample opportunities for walks, birdwatching, rounds of golf and cream teas. North of Penang, Malay, rather than Chinese, traditions hold sway at **Alor Star**, the last major town before the Thai border. This far north, the premier tourist destination is **Pulau Langkawi**, an island with international-style resorts and picture-postcard beaches.

The Peninsula's **east coast** is much more rural and relaxing, peppered with rustic villages and stunning islands such as **Pulau Perhentian** and **Pulau Tioman**, busy with backpackers and package tourists alike. The state capitals of **Kota Bharu**, near the northeastern Thai border, and **Kuala Terengganu**, further south, showcase the best of Malay traditions, craft production and performing arts.

Crossing the Peninsula's mountainous **interior** by road or rail allows you to venture into the majestic tropical rainforests of **Taman Negara**. The national park's four thousand square kilometres hold enough to keep you occupied for

OPPOSITE FROM TOP STREET MARKET, KUALA LUMPUR; KELABIT HIGHLANDS

SHOPHOUSES

A standard feature of local townscapes is rows of **shophouses** – two- or three-storey buildings traditionally containing a shop at street level, with residential quarters behind and above. For visitors, their most striking feature is that at ground level the front wall is usually set back from the street. This creates a so-called "**five-foot way**" overhung by the upper part of the house, which shelters pedestrians from the sun and pelting rain.

Shophouses were fusion architecture: facades have **Western** features such as shuttered windows and gables, while inside there might be an area open to the sky, in the manner of **Chinese** courtyard houses. Some, especially from the early part of the last century, are bedecked with columns, floral plaster motifs and beautiful tilework, while later properties feature simpler Art Deco touches. Sadly, shophouses went out of favour in the 1980s, and recent ones tend to be bland, functional affairs; older buildings, however, have won a new lease of life as swanky restaurants and boutique hotels.

days: trails, salt-lick hides for animal-watching, aerial forest-canopy walkways, limestone caves and waterfalls. Here you may well also come across the **Orang Asli**, the Peninsula's indigenous peoples, a few of whom cling to a semi-nomadic lifestyle within the park.

Across the sea from the Peninsula lie the east Malaysian states of Sarawak and Sabah. For most travellers, their first taste of **Sarawak** comes at **Kuching**, the old colonial capital, and then the Iban **longhouses** of the Batang Ai river system. **Sibu**, much further north on the Rajang River, is the starting point for trips to less touristed Iban, Kayan and Kenyah longhouses. In the north, **Gunung Mulu National Park** is the principal destination; many come here to climb up to view its extraordinary razor-sharp limestone Pinnacles, though spectacular caves also burrow into the park's mountains. More remote still are the **Kelabit Highlands**, further east, where the mountain air is refreshingly cool and there are ample opportunities for extended treks.

The main reason for a trip to **Sabah** is to conquer the 4095m granite peak of **Mount Kinabalu**, set in its own national park, though the lively modern capital **Kota Kinabalu** and its idyllic offshore islands, Gaya and Manukan, have their appeal, too. Beyond this, Sabah is worth a visit for its **wildlife**: turtles, orang-utans, proboscis monkeys and hornbills are just a few of the exotic residents of the jungle and plentiful islands. Marine attractions feature in the far east at **Pulau Sipadan**, pointing out towards the southern Philippines, which has a host of sharks, other fish and turtles, while neighbouring **Pulau Mabul** contains hip, but often pricey, diving resorts.

An easy entry-point for first-time visitors to Southeast Asia, **Singapore** is exceptionally safe, organized and accessible, thanks to its small size, excellent modern infrastructure, and Western standards of hygiene – and despite prices that are likewise at Western levels. The island has fascinating Chinese and Indian quarters, excellent historical museums and a smattering of colonial architecture as well as great shopping, all of which will keep you occupied for several days. Singapore also rightly holds a reputation as one of Asia's **gastronomic capitals**, where you can just as readily savour fantastic snacks at simple hawker stalls or an exquisite Chinese banquet in a swanky restaurant.

For those who venture into the tiny kingdom of **Brunei**, enveloped by Sarawak's two most northerly divisions, the capital **Bandar Seri Begawan** holds the entrancing Kampung Ayer, a sprawling stilt village built out over the Brunei River, plus a handful of

Author picks

Our authors traversed every corner of Malaysia, Singapore and Brunei, from KL's shopping malls and Sarawak's longhouses to the jungles of Taman Negara and the summit of Mount Kinabalu. Here are some of their favourite experiences.

Wildlife-spotting See elephants and tapir at Taman Negara (p.185), orang-utans at Kinabatangan (p.431) and proboscis monkeys near Bandar Seri Begawan (p.451).

Tastiest laksa Compare famous variations of the region's signature seafood soup in Penang (p.155), Singapore (p.542) and Kuching (p.325).

Shadow puppets Experience the magical Malay tradition of *wayang kulit* at Kota Bharu's Cultural Centre (p.218).

Amazing caves Sarawak has major cave systems which are both spectacular – especially at Mulu National Park (p.366) – and of archeological significance, as in the case of Niah (p.361).

Eccentric desserts Satisfy your sweet tooth with ABC – a shaved ice drenched in condensed milk and luridly coloured fruit syrups (p.41).

Turtle beaches Stay up late to catch marine turtles digging nests and laying eggs at Cherating (p.250) and Penang National Park (p.156).

Glittering cityscapes Admire the night lights from atop Menara KL (p.78) and *Marina Bay Sands*' SkyPark in Singapore (p.504).

Rowdiest festival You can't beat the crowds and slightly gory celebrations surrounding the Hindu festival of Thaipusam at KL's Batu Caves (p.106).

Bizarre blooms Discover the weird *Rafflesia* flower, whose scent mimics rotting meat, at the Royal Belum State Park (p.134), Gunung Gading (p.337) or Tambunan (p.401).

> Our author recommendations don't end here. We've flagged up our favourite places – a perfectly sited hotel, an atmospheric café, a special restaurant – throughout the guide, highlighted with the ★ symbol.

FROM TOP ABC; SHADOW PUPPETS

interesting museums and mosques. In the sparsely populated Temburong district, you can visit unspoiled rainforest at the **Ulu Temburong National Park**, where abundant wildlife roams and the rivers are clear.

When to go

Temperatures vary little in Malaysia, Singapore and Brunei, hovering constantly at or just above 30°C by day, while humidity is high year-round. Showers occur year-round too, often in the mid-afternoon, though these short, sheeting downpours clear up as quickly as they arrive.

The major distinction in the seasons is marked by the arrival of the northeast monsoon (ushering in what is locally called the **rainy season**). This particularly affects the east coast

WILDLIFE

Peninsular Malaysia, Borneo and Singapore are a paradise for wildlife-spotters, harbouring over 600 types of birds and 200 mammal species – including Asian elephants, sun bears, tigers, tapirs, barking deer, gibbons, hornbills and pythons. Borneo's speciality is the **proboscis monkey**, so-called because of its bulbous, drooping nose. The island is also one of only two natural habitats (with Sumatra) for **orang-utans** – indeed, the name is Malay for "man of the forest". **Marine life** is equally diverse: divers can swim with white-tip sharks, clown fish and barracuda, not to mention green and hawksbill **turtles**, which drag themselves ashore in season to lay their eggs by night. Even cosmopolitan Singapore maintains a pocket of primary rainforest that's home to long-tailed macaques and snakes.

of Peninsular Malaysia and the western end of Sarawak, with late November to mid-February seeing the heaviest rainfall. On the Peninsula's west coast and in Sabah, September and October are the wettest months. Monsoonal downpours can be heavy and prolonged, sometimes lasting two or three hours and prohibiting more or less all activity for the duration; boats to most islands in affected areas won't attempt the sea swell at the height of the rainy season. In mountainous areas like the Cameron Highlands, the Kelabit Highlands and in the hill stations and upland national parks, you may experience more frequent rain as the high peaks gather clouds more or less permanently.

The **ideal time** to visit most of the region is between March and early October, when you will avoid the worst of the rains and there's less humidity, though both ends of this period can be characterized by a stifling lack of breezes. Despite the rains, the months of January and February are rewarding, and see a number of significant **festivals**, notably Chinese New Year and the Hindu celebration of Thaipusam. Visiting just after the rainy season can afford the best of all worlds, with verdant countryside and bountiful waterfalls, though there's still a clammy quality to the air. Arrive in Sabah a little later, in May, and you'll be able to take in the Sabah Fest, a week-long celebration of Sabahan culture, while in Sarawak, June's Gawai Festival is well worth attending, when longhouse doors are flung open for several days of rice-harvest merry-making, with dancing, eating, drinking and music.

OPPOSITE ASIAN ELEPHANTS **ABOVE** PULAU PERHENTIAN

23

things not to miss

It's not possible to see everything that Malaysia, Singapore and Brunei have to offer in one trip – and we don't suggest you try. What follows is a selective taste, in no particular order, of the countries' highlights: natural wonders, stunning buildings and a colourful heritage. Each entry has a page reference to take you straight into the Guide, where you can find out more. Coloured numbers refer to chapters in the Guide section.

1

1 LANGKAWI
Page 163

Luxurious resorts on sublime beaches pretty much sums up these west coast islands, close to the border with Thailand.

2 GEORGETOWN
Page 136

A bustling Chinese-dominated haven with elaborate temples, colonial-era mansions and beaches galore.

3 ULU TEMBURONG NATIONAL PARK
Page 464

A beautiful approach by longboat brings you to Brunei's only national park; treks and a canopy walkway will keep you busy during your stay.

7

4 KAMPUNG AYER
Page 453

Take a boat ride around this wooden village in the middle of the Brunei River.

5 TAMAN NEGARA
Page 185

Malaysia's premier national park, Taman Negara, is one of the world's oldest rainforests, with hides for wildlife-spotting, treetop walkways and treks lasting from an hour to a whole week.

6 ADVENTURE TOURISM
Page 47

Whitewater rafting, caving and paragliding are among activities widely available in Malaysia.

7 SINGAPORE'S ARTS SCENE
Page 546

As befits the largest city in the region, Singapore offers a dynamic range of artistic activity – catch anything from Chinese street opera to indie rock gigs.

8 KELABIT HIGHLANDS
Page 373

These remote uplands offer excellent walks and hikes, plus encounters with friendly tribal communities along the way.

8

9 LITTLE INDIA, SINGAPORE

Page 485

On Serangoon Road you can almost believe you're in downtown Chennai – the area has all the sights, sounds and smells of the Indian subcontinent.

10 THE PERHENTIAN ISLANDS

Page 227

A popular pair of islands off the east coast, with beautiful beaches, great snorkelling and accommodation for all budgets.

11 GUNUNG MULU NATIONAL PARK

Page 366

A view of razor-sharp limestone pinnacles reward the challenging haul up Gunung Api, and the park also boasts underground caves that teem with wildlife.

12 MELAKA

Page 268

The city's complex historical heritage is evident in its Portuguese, Dutch and British buildings and Peranakan ancestral homes.

13

13 THE PETRONAS TOWERS
Page 74

KL's iconic towers not only hold your gaze from all angles but also house one of the city's best shopping malls.

14 SUNGAI KINABATANGAN
Page 431

Cruise through pristine jungle along this spectacular river, spotting proboscis monkeys and, occasionally, orang-utans.

15 CAMERON HIGHLANDS
Page 171

Misty tea plantations, afternoon tea and jungle trails in cool mountain air.

16 SHOPPING IN KL
Page 101

Malaysia's capital boasts a host of excellent malls, as well as vibrant street markets where bargaining is de rigueur.

17 TRADITIONAL CRAFTS
Page 49

Malaysia boasts a wide range of crafts, from batik and *songket* (brocade) to rattan baskets and *labu*, gourd-shaped ceramic jugs.

18 FOOD
Page 37

Simple stalls in markets and malls and on the street serve up mouthwatering noodles, snacks and desserts.

14

21

22

19 LONGHOUSES IN SARAWAK
Page 340

Large communal dwellings, home to members of indigenous tribes, are found along rivers and in remote mountain locations.

20 PROBOSCIS MONKEYS, BAKO
Page 332

These odd-looking creatures roam *kerangas* forest and mangrove swamps in the national park, not far from Kuching.

21 RAINFOREST MUSIC FESTIVAL
Page 332

Held annually near Kuching, this world music festival is an opportunity to see indigenous performers alongside musicians from across the globe.

22 MOUNT KINABALU
Page 414

Watch dawn over Borneo from the summit of Southeast Asia's highest mountain.

23 DIVING AT PULAU SIPADAN
Page 438

The spectacular islands off Sabah offer the thrill of swimming with sharks and turtles.

Itineraries

Malaysia, Singapore and Brunei cover such a spread-out area that it would be impossible to see everything, but each of the following routes makes a great way to spend two or three weeks in the region. While the Peninsula Circuit is the most varied, head east to Borneo if you prefer an outdoor-focused option. Singapore is obviously more of a long-weekend destination, but a stay here could easily be tacked on to a wider trip north up into Peninsular Malaysia.

PENINSULA CIRCUIT

For a straightforward taster of everything the region has to offer, try this three-week circuit.

❶ Kuala Lumpur Malaysia's capital offers shiny malls, showcase architecture and a mix of Muslim, Chinese and Hindu districts, with some of the best street food in the country. **See p.66**

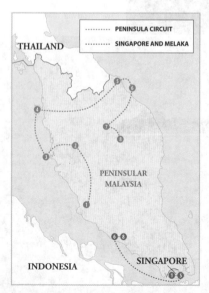

PENINSULA CIRCUIT
SINGAPORE AND MELAKA
THAILAND
PENINSULAR MALAYSIA
INDONESIA
SINGAPORE

❷ Cameron Highlands This former retreat for colonial administrators is now a rural idyll of tea plantations and forest walks. **See p.171**

❸ Pulau Pangkor Kick back at this low-key resort island that's a favourite with Malaysian families. **See p.122**

❹ Penang Packed with historic guildhalls and streets, eccentric temples and surprisingly wild gardens and national parks. **See p.134**

❺ Kota Bharu One of the last places in this Muslim country that allows shadow-puppet performances of the Hindu epics. **See p.215**

❻ Perhentian islands Superb tropical hangouts with gorgeous beaches and splendid snorkelling and scuba diving. **See p.227**

❼ Jungle railway This slow-moving commuter train chugs past languid towns, tiny kampungs and market gardens along the way. **See p.201**

❽ Taman Negara One of the world's oldest rainforests features superlative wildlife-spotting and jungle treks lasting up to a week or more. See p.185

SINGAPORE AND MELAKA

You can pack this round-up of great food and a centuries-old history into a week.

❶ Little India, Singapore Charismatic area of temples and shops selling gold and sari with the liveliest market in Singapore. **See p.485**

❷ **Chinatown, Singapore** Amid the modern shophouses, restaurants and markets, don't miss the Buddha Tooth Relic temple, full of dynamic statuary and the tooth itself. **See p.490**

❸ **Night Safari, Singapore** The highlight of what is already a superbly displayed collection of native wildlife, the night safari lets you see nocturnal creatures such as tigers, leopards, elephants and rhinos. **See p.511**

❹ **Bukit Timah, Singapore** The last patch of real rainforest left in Singapore offers an easy, leech-free introduction to jungle trails and colourful birdlife. **See p.509**

❺ **Eating, Singapore** Indulge in one of the world's gastronomic capitals, with varied menus of Indian, Chinese and Malay dishes. **See p.534**

❻ **Istana, Melaka** An exquisite Malay palace, built without nails and founded during the fifteenth century. **See p.271**

❼ **Baba-Nyonya Heritage Museum, Melaka** An elegant row of traditional houses decorated in tiling, lanterns and woodcarvings of the Chinese-Malay Peranakan culture, now – aside from its cuisine – virtually extinct. **See p.273**

❽ **Bukit China, Melaka** Hilltop covered in many crescent-shaped Chinese graves, some dating to the seventeenth century. **See p.275**

SARAWAK AND MT KINABALU

Allow at least three weeks for this adventurous trip into Malaysia's least-developed corners.

❶ **Kuching** Find your bearings at Sarawak's small, likeable capital: the museum's ethnological collection is worth a browse, and the Semenggoh orang-utan sanctuary makes a rewarding day-trip. **See p.315**

❷ **Bako** Sarawak's oldest national park, this small patch of well-preserved coastal forest is home to waterfalls, proboscis monkeys and bizarre pitcher plants. **See p.332**

❸ **Batang Ai** Take a boat through spectacular riverine forest in this often overlooked national park, and visit traditional longhouse communities such as Nanga Sumpa. **See p.338**

❹ **Gunung Mulu National Park** Spectacular jungle scenery, particularly the three-day trek out to a "forest" of limestone towers, and a network of rugged caverns. **See p.336**

❺ **Miri** A stepping stone to the more remote corners of Sarawak and to Sabah. Don't miss the caves at Niah National Park, inhabited by humans over 40,000 years ago. **See p.355**

❻ **Bario** Set out on some demanding multiday trekking via remote Kelabit longhouses or up Mount Murud. **See p.374**

❼ **Kota Kinabalu** Sabah's capital has lively markets, a district of traditional houses built over the water on piles, and an interesting indigenous museum. **See p.388**

❽ **Kinabalu National Park** This small reserve surrounds wind-seared Mount Kinabaulu, one of the toughest hikes in Malaysia. **See p.414**

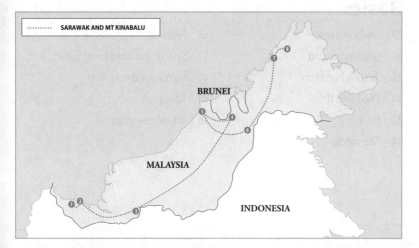

SARAWAK AND MT KINABALU

BRUNEI

MALAYSIA

INDONESIA

TRISHAWS

Basics

27   Getting there

30   Getting around

35   Accommodation

37   Food and drink

42   Health

44   The media

45   Festivals

47   Sports and outdoor activities

48   Culture and etiquette

49   Shopping

50   Travel essentials

Getting there

Located at the heart of Southeast Asia, on the busy aviation corridor between Europe and Australasia, Malaysia and Singapore enjoy excellent international air links. Singapore is served by many more flights than Kuala Lumpur (KL), but can also be slightly more expensive to fly into. Of Malaysia's regional airports, those in Kota Kinabalu, Kuching and Penang have the most useful international connections, albeit chiefly with other cities in East Asia. If you're flying long-haul to East Malaysia or, for that matter, Brunei, you may well have to transit in Kuala Lumpur or Singapore.

During the **peak seasons** for travel to Southeast Asia – the Christmas/New Year period, typically from mid-December until early January, and July and August – fares can be up to twice the price at other times of year, though you can often avoid the steepest fares by booking well in advance. Fares also rise at weekends and around major local festivals, such as Islamic holidays and the Chinese New Year. Sample fares given here include taxes and current fuel surcharges.

From the UK and Ireland

London Heathrow has daily **nonstop** flights to KL, with Malaysia Airlines, and to Singapore with British Airways, Virgin Atlantic and Singapore Airlines; these all take around thirteen hours. Flying with any other airline involves a change of plane in Europe or the Middle East, and possibly an additional stopover elsewhere. If you're flying from UK regional airports or from **Ireland**, you'll have to change planes at London or a hub elsewhere in Europe. The very best **fares** to KL or Singapore are around £500/€450 outside high season – though it's not uncommon to pay twenty percent more.

From the US and Canada

In most cases the trip from North America, including a stopover, will take at least twenty hours if you fly the **transatlantic** route from the eastern seaboard, or nineteen hours minimum if you cross the **Pacific** from the west coast.

The quickest route isn't always the cheapest: it can sometimes be cheaper to fly westwards from the east coast, stopping off in Northeast Asia en route. **Fares** start at around US$1100 or Can$1200 for flights from a major US or Canadian airport on either coast.

Plenty of airlines operate to East Asia from major North American cities. If your target is Borneo, it's worth investigating the possibility of connecting with one of the east Asian airlines – Kota Kinabalu, for example, has flights from Hong Kong operated by Malaysia Airlines and at least one other carrier.

From Australia and New Zealand

There's a particularly good range of flights from Australia and New Zealand into Malaysia, Singapore and Brunei, including a useful link between Melbourne and **Borneo** with Royal Brunei Airlines, plus **budget flights** from Australia and New Zealand to KL with AirAsia X and to Singapore with Tiger Airways, Jetstar and Scoot.

If you're flying from, say, Perth to Singapore or KL, **fares** start at Aus$550 return in low season, while Melbourne to KL will set you back at least Aus$750. Christchurch to KL generally starts at NZ$1300 return on AirAsia X.

From South Africa

The quickest way to reach Malaysia or Singapore from South Africa is to fly with **Singapore Airlines**, which offers nonstop flights to Singapore from Johannesburg, with connections from Cape Town; reckon on around ten hours' flying time. That said, it's often cheaper to book a ticket that involves changing planes en route, usually in the Middle East. If you're lucky you may land a fare of around

---

A BETTER KIND OF TRAVEL

At Rough Guides we are passionately committed to travel. We feel that travelling is the best way to understand the world we live in and the people we share it with – plus tourism has brought a great deal of benefit to developing economies around the world over the last few decades. But the growth in tourism has also damaged some places irreparably, and climate change is exacerbated by most forms of transport, especially flying. All Rough Guides' trips are carbon-offset, and every year we donate money to a variety of charities devoted to combating the effects of climate change.

R6000 return, including taxes, though it's not uncommon to have to pay R1000–2000 more.

From elsewhere in Southeast Asia

Budget airlines make it easy to explore Malaysia, Singapore and Brunei as part of a wider trip through Southeast Asia. The most useful no-frills carriers for the three countries covered in this book are Malaysia's AirAsia and Firefly, and Singapore's Jetstar Asia and Tiger Airways. Though fuel surcharges and taxes do take some of the shine off the fares, prices can still be keen, especially if you book well in advance.

You can, of course, reach Malaysia or Singapore from their immediate neighbours by means other than flying. There are **road** connections from Thailand and from Kalimantan (Indonesian Borneo), **ferries** from the Indonesian island of Sumatra and from the southern Philippines, and **trains** from Thailand. Below is a round-up of the most popular routes.

From Thailand

There are two daily express **train** services between Thailand and Malaysia – one between the southern Thai city of **Hat Yai** and **KL**, run by the Malaysian rail company KTM, and the other between **Bangkok** and the Malaysian west coast city of **Butterworth** (close to Penang island), run by State Railway of Thailand. The KTM service leaves Hat Yai at 4pm, taking just over thirteen hours to reach KL; the Bangkok train leaves Hualamphong Station at 2.45pm, calling en route at (among others) Hua Hin, Surat Thani, Hat Yai and Alor Star in Kedah, and arriving in Butterworth 24 hours later. Also useful is the Thai rail service from Hat Yai across to **Sungai Golok** on the east coast of the Kra isthmus, close to the Malaysian border crossing at Rantau Panjang, from where buses run to Kota Bharu. Hat Yai–KL

fares start at RM48 in an ordinary seat, rising to RM60 in a lower-berth sleeper.

As regards **flights**, plenty of services connect Bangkok, Chiang Mai and Thai resort destinations with Malaysian airports and Singapore. Some are run by the low-cost airlines, while others are provided by Bangkok Airways and Singapore Airlines subsidiary SilkAir.

A few scheduled **ferry** services sail from the most southwesterly Thai town of Satun to the Malaysian west coast town of Kuala Perlis (30min) and to Pulau Langkawi (1hr 30min). Departing from Thailand by sea for Malaysia, ensure your passport is stamped at the immigration office at the pier to avoid problems with the Malaysian immigration officials when you arrive. Another option is the ferry from the southern Thai town of Ban Taba to the Malaysian town of Pengkalan Kubor, where frequent buses run to Kota Bharu, 20km away. Buses connect Ban Taba with the provincial capital, Narathiwat (1hr 30min).

The easiest road access from Thailand is via Hat Yai, from where **minivans** and a few share taxis run to Butterworth (4hr) and nearby Georgetown on Penang island. From the interior Thai town of Betong, there's a road across the border to the Malaysian town of **Pengkalan Hulu**, from where Route 67 leads west to Sungai Petani; share taxis serve the route. You can also get a taxi from Ban Taba for the few kilometres south to Kota Bharu.

From Indonesia

Plenty of **flights**, including many operated by the low-cost airlines, connect major airports in Java and Sumatra, plus Bali and Lombok, with Malaysia and Singapore. There's also a service between Manado in Sulawesi and Singapore with Singapore Airlines' subsidiary SilkAir. As for Kalimantan, AirAsia operates between Balikpapan and KL, and Malaysia Airlines' subsidiary MASwings operates between

THE EASTERN & ORIENTAL EXPRESS

Unlike some luxury trains in other parts of the world, the **Eastern & Oriental Express** isn't a re-creation of a classic colonial-era rail journey, but a sort of fantasy realization of how such a service might have looked had it existed in the Far East. Employing 1970s Japanese rolling stock, given an elegant old-world cladding with wooden inlay work and featuring Thai and Malay motifs, the train travels from Bangkok to Singapore and back at least monthly. En route there are extended stops at Kanchanaburi for a visit to the infamous bridge over the **River Kwai**, and at Butterworth, where there's time for a half-day tour of **Georgetown**. An observation deck at the rear of the train makes the most of the passing scenery.

The trip takes four days and three nights (three days if done from Singapore) and costs around £1700/US$2700 per person in swish, en-suite Pullman accommodation, including meals, though alcohol costs extra. For **bookings** contacts in various countries and more details of the trip, see ⓦorient-express.com.

Pontianak and Kuching, and also between Tarakan and Tawau in southeastern Sabah.

It's possible to reach Sarawak from Kalimantan on just one **road route**, through the western border town of Entikong and onwards to Kuching. The bus trip from the western city of Pontianak to Entikong takes seven hours, crossing to the Sarawak border town of Tebedu; stay on the same bus for another three hours to reach Kuching.

As for **ferries**, Dumai, on the east coast of Central Sumatra, has a daily service to Melaka (2hr), with more sailings from Dumai and Tanjong Balai further south to Port Klang near Kuala Lumpur (3hr). There are also a few services from Bintan and Batam islands in the Riau archipelago (accessible by plane or boat from Sumatra or Jakarta) to Johor Bahru (30min) or Singapore (30min); and a minor ferry crossing from Tanjung Balai to Kukup (1hr), just southwest of Johor Bahru. Over in Borneo, daily ferries connect Nunakan in Kalimantan with Tawau in Sabah (1hr).

From the Philippines

Despite the proximity of Sabah to the southern Philippines, few transport links connect the two, though a ferry service operates between Zamboanga and Sandakan. As for **flights**, there are low-cost options from Clark to KL and Kota Kinabalu (both AirAsia), and from Cebu and Davao to Singapore (Tiger Airways) and Manila. Other connections are provided by full-cost airlines as well as some Philippine budget operators, including Manila to Bandar Seri Begawan (Royal Brunei Airlines).

AIRLINES

AirAsia Ⓦ airasia.com
AirAsia X Ⓦ airasiax.com
Bangkok Airways Ⓦ bangkokair.com
British Airways Ⓦ britishairways.com
Firefly Ⓦ fireflyz.com.my
Jetstar/Jetstar Asia Ⓦ jetstar.com
Malaysia Airlines (MAS) Ⓦ malaysiaairlines.com
MASwings Ⓦ maswings.com.my
Royal Brunei Airlines Ⓦ flyroyalbrunei.com
Scoot Ⓦ flyscoot.com
Singapore Airlines (SIA) Ⓦ singaporeair.com
Tiger Airways Ⓦ tigerair.com
Virgin Atlantic Ⓦ virgin-atlantic.com

RAIL CONTACTS

Eastern & Oriental Express Ⓦ orient-express.com
KTM Ⓦ www.ktmb.com.my
Man in Seat Sixty-One Ⓦ seat61.com
State Railway of Thailand Ⓦ www.railway.co.th

TRAVEL AGENTS AND TOUR OPERATORS

Adventure Center US ☎ 1800 228 8747, Ⓦ adventurecenter.com. A good range of packages, mainly focused on East Malaysia.
Adventure World Australia ☎ 1300 295049, Ⓦ adventureworld .com.au; New Zealand ☎ 0800 238368, Ⓦ adventureworld.co.nz. Short Malaysia tours, covering cities and some wildlife areas.
Allways Dive Expedition Australia ☎ 1800 338239, Ⓦ allwaysdive.com.au. Dive holidays to the prime dive sites of Sabah.
Asia Classic Tours US ☎ 1800 717 7752, Ⓦ asiaclassictours.com. Malaysia tours, lasting ten days or more, taking in various parts of the country and sometimes Singapore, too.
Asian Pacific Adventures US ☎ 1800 825 1680, Ⓦ asianpacific adventures.com. A handful of Malaysia packages, dominated by Borneo.
Bestway Tours US & Canada ☎ 1800 663 0844, Ⓦ bestway.com. A handful of cultural tours featuring Malaysia and Singapore.
Borneo Tour Specialists Australia ☎ 07 3221 5777, Ⓦ borneo .com.au. Small-group, customizable tours of all of Borneo, covering wildlife, trekking and tribal culture.
Dive Adventures Australia ☎ 1800 222234, Ⓦ diveadventures .com.au. Sabah and Labuan dive packages.
Eastravel UK ☎ 01473 214305, Ⓦ eastravel.co.uk. A small range of Malaysia and Singapore trips.
Emerald Global UK ☎ 0207 312 1708, Ⓦ etours.co.uk. A good range of Malaysia packages based in cities or resorts; Singapore too.
Explore UK ☎ 01252 883686, Ⓦ explore.co.uk. Adventure trips to Malaysia, plus Singapore.
Explorient US ☎ 1800 785 1233, Ⓦ explorient.com. Short tours, focused on major cities and with a cultural emphasis, which can be combined with one another.
Golden Days in Malaysia UK ☎ 0208 893 2941, Ⓦ goldendays .co.uk. A good range of Malaysia itineraries emphasizing Borneo and the main cities of the Peninsula, with some Singapore and Brunei add-ons.
Intrepid Travel US ☎ 1800 970 7299, Canada ☎ 1855 299 1211, UK ☎ 0808 274 5111, Australia ☎ 1300 797010, New Zealand ☎ 0800 600 610; Ⓦ intrepidtravel.com. Several Malaysia offerings, mainly focused on Borneo or taking in Thailand and Singapore as well.
Jade Tours US ☎ 212 227 0061, Canada ☎ 905 787 9288; Ⓦ jadetours.com. Borneo and Peninsular Malaysia trips.
Lee's Travel UK ☎ 0800 811 9888, Ⓦ leestravel.com. Far Eastern flight deals, including discounted Malaysia and Singapore Airlines tickets.
Pentravel South Africa ☎ 087 232 3000, Ⓦ pentravel.co.za. Flight deals plus KL and Malaysian Grand Prix holidays.
Peregrine Adventures UK ☎ 0207 408 9021, Australia ☎ 03 8601 4444; Ⓦ peregrineadventures.com. Experienced operator with a handful of East Malaysia packages.
Premier Holidays UK ☎ 0844 493 7531, Ⓦ premierholidays.co .uk. Tours of East Malaysia and Brunei, plus resort-centred holidays in Peninsular Malaysia and Singapore.
Reef & Rainforest US ☎ 1800 794 9767, Ⓦ reefrainforest.com. Sabah dive packages based in resorts or a liveaboard.
Rex Air UK ☎ 020 7439 1898, Ⓦ rexair.co.uk. Specialist in discounted flights to the Far East, with a few package tours to boot.
Sayang Holidays US ☎ 1 888 472 9264, Ⓦ sayangholidays.com. City-based Peninsular Malaysia and Singapore tours, plus Borneo.

ADDRESSES AND PLACE NAMES

Place names in Malaysia present something of a linguistic dilemma. **Road signage** always uses Malay names, and some colonial-era names have been deliberately changed to Malay ones, but **English** is widely used in much of the country – which means local people are just as likely to say "Kinta River" as "Sungai Kinta", or talk of "Northam Road" in Georgetown rather than "Jalan Sultan Ahmad Shah", and so on. In the text of this Guide we've used English names where it feels appropriate and they are most commonly used, but our maps show Malay names in line with official usage. Our "Glossary" includes terms for geographical features like beaches, mountains and so forth (see p.601).

STA Travel US ☎ 1800 781 4040, ⓦ statravel.com; UK ☎ 0333 321 0099, ⓦ statravel.co.uk; Australia ☎ 134782, ⓦ statravel.com.au; New Zealand ☎ 0800 474400, ⓦ statravel.co.nz; South Africa ☎ 0861 781781, ⓦ statravel.co.za. Worldwide specialists in low-cost flights for students and under-26s; other customers also welcome.

Symbiosis US ☎ 1 866 723 7903, UK ☎ 0845 123 2844; ⓦ symbiosis-travel.com. Diving, trekking and longhouse stays in various Malaysian locations.

Tour East Canada ☎ 1 877 578 8888, ⓦ toureast.com. Singapore, plus a couple of extended Malaysia excursions.

Trailfinders UK ☎ 020 7368 1200, ⓦ trailfinders.com; Ireland ☎ 01 677 7888, ⓦ trailfinders.ie. Efficient agent selling flights and a few Malaysia tours, including Malacca, Penang and Borneo.

Travel Masters US ☎ 512 323 6961, ⓦ travel-masters.net. Dive packages at Sipadan, Mabul and Kapalai.

USIT Ireland ☎ 01 602 1906, ⓦ usit.ie. Student and youth travel.

Getting around

Public transport in Malaysia, Singapore and Brunei is reliable and inexpensive. Much of your travelling, particularly in Peninsular Malaysia, will be by bus, minivan or, occasionally, long-distance taxi. Budget flights are a good option for hopping around the region, especially given that no ferries connect Peninsular and East Malaysia. The Peninsula's rail system remains behind the times but is finally being upgraded, slashing journey times.

Sabah and Sarawak have their own travel peculiarities – in Sarawak, for instance, you're reliant on boats, and occasionally planes, for some long-distance travel. The chapters in this Guide on Sarawak, Sabah, Brunei and Singapore contain detailed information on their respective transport systems; the emphasis in this section is largely on Peninsular Malaysia.

The transport system is subject to heavy pressure during any nationwide **public holiday** (see p.57) – particularly Muslim festivals, the Chinese New Year, Deepavali, Christmas and New Year. A day or two before each festival, whole communities embark upon **balik kampung**, which literally means a return to home villages (and towns) to be with family. Make bus, train or flight reservations at least **one week in advance** to travel at these times; if you're driving, steel yourself for more than the usual number of jams.

And finally, bear in mind that **chartering** transport – longboats, or cars with drivers – to reach some off-the-beaten-track national park or island, is always an expensive business.

By bus

Malaysia's **bus network** is fairly comprehensive, at least in terms of serving major cities and towns. However, buses rarely stray off main roads to reach rural sites of the kind that tourists might want to get to – nature reserves, caves, hill resorts and so forth. In such instances, the best you can do is to ask the driver if you can get off at the start of the turning for your destination, after which you're left to your own devices.

Long-distance (express) buses

The **long-distance bus network** borders on the anarchic: a largish town can have a dozen or more express bus companies operating to and from it.

BUS COMPANIES

A handful of well-established bus companies give reliable service in Peninsular Malaysia. The largest is **Transnasional** (ⓦ transnasional.com.my) and its slightly pricier subsidiary Plusliner (ⓦ plusliner.com.my), whose services have the entire Peninsula pretty well covered. Alternatives include **Sri Maju** (ⓦ srimaju.com) and **Konsortium Bas Ekspres** (ⓦ kbes.com.my), both strong on the west coast.

Timetabling is a mess, too: every bus station has signs above a zillion ticket booths displaying a zillion routes and departure times, but these may be out of date, as may even the websites of the biggest bus companies. Given this, the route details in this Guide are a general indication of what you can expect; for specifics, you will need to call the bus company's local office (stations do not have central enquiry numbers) or ask in person.

At least the plethora of companies means you can often find **tickets** at the station for a bus heading to your destination within the next two hours. However, it can be worth booking a day in advance for specific departures or on routes where services are limited (in between, rather than along, the west and east coasts for example). **Online booking** is possible, either on the websites of the biggest operators or on recently launched umbrella websites (such as ⓦeasybook.com) representing multiple firms, but there is nothing as reliable as buying a ticket at the bus station itself.

Most intercity buses are comfortable, with **air conditioning** and curtains to screen out the blazing sun, though seats can be tightly packed. There are rarely toilets on board, but longer journeys feature a rest stop every couple of hours, with a short meal stopover if needed. On a few plum routes, notably KL–Singapore and KL–Penang, additional **luxury** or "executive" coaches charge up to twice the regular fares and offer greater legroom plus on-board TVs and toilets.

Local buses

In addition to express buses, the Peninsula has a network of simple **local buses** serving small towns on routes that can stretch up to 100km end to end. Local buses are organized at the **state level**: every state has its own handful of companies, and this means that many services do not cross into adjacent states even when the same firm is active on both sides of the border. **Tickets**, usually bought on board from the driver or conductor, cost a few ringgit, reaching RM10 only on the longest routes. Note that services typically run only during **daylight hours**, winding down by 8pm if not earlier.

By train

The Peninsula's intercity train service is operated by **KTM** (short for Keretapi Tanah Melayu, literally "Malay Land Trains"; ⓦktmb.com.my). The network is shaped roughly like a Y, with the southern end anchored at Singapore and the intersection inside Malaysia at the small town of Gemas. The northwest

THE MALAYSIAN RAIL NETWORK

BANGKOK (International Express)
Hat Yai (Thailand)
Padang Besar
Arau
Alor Setar
Gurun
Sungai Petani
Butterworth
Bukit Mertajam
Nibong Tebal
Parit Buntar
Bagan Serai
Taiping
Kuala Kangsar
Sungai Siput
Ipoh
Batu Gajah
Kampar
Tapah Road
Sungkai
Slim River
Tanjung Malim
Rawang
Sungai Buloh
KL SENTRAL
Kajang
Seremban
Rembau
Tampin

Tumpat (Kelantan coast)
Wakaf Bharu (for Kota Bharu)
Pasir Mas
Tanah Merah
Kuala Krai
Dabong
Gua Musang
Kuala Lipis
Jerantut
Kuala Krau
Mentakab
Triang
Bahau

Gemas
Segamat
Labis
Paloh
Kluang
Kulai
Kempas Bahru
Johor Bahru
SINGAPORE (Woodlands)

Malaysian long-distance rail services

Express
KL–Hat Yai
KL–Singapore
KL–Tumpat
Singapore–Tumpat
Singapore–Butterworth
Butterworth–Bangkok (International Express)

This map shows stations served by most express trains. There are also local services on stretches of the Singapore–Tumpat line, calling at minor stations. Details of the Komuter rail services in the KL area are detailed in Chapter One.

Local trains call at virtually every station on the network. This map shows only stations served by most express trains.

branch travels into Thailand via KL, Ipoh and Butterworth, crossing the border at Padang Besar; the northeast branch cuts up through the interior to terminate at Tumpat, beyond Kota Bharu on the east coast. KTM also runs a useful **Komuter** rail service in the Kuala Lumpur area (see p.86).

Unfortunately, much of the network only has a handful of services each day. That's because a lot of the infrastructure is antiquated, which also means that not even express trains can keep up with buses where modern highways exist alongside. The 370km journey from Kuala Lumpur to Johor Bahru, for example, takes 5hr 30min; on a good day, buses are an hour faster. Services to the east coast via the **interior** are especially numbing, but trains can be the quickest way to reach some settlements here, and the **Jungle Railway** stretch is entertaining (see p.201).

The exciting news is that new stations have been built and, more importantly, new track has belatedly been laid **north of KL**. This has allowed a genuinely fast, frequent **Express Train Service (ETS)** to run between KL and Ipoh, shaving an hour off journey times. Even better, there is every prospect of the ETS being extended all the way to the Thai border by 2016.

There are three main classes of train. **Express** services call mostly at major stations and are generally modern, air-conditioned and well maintained; **local** trains, often not air-conditioned and of variable quality, operate on various segments between the interior and the east coast, and call at most towns, villages and hamlets en route. **Sleeper** services – named **senandung** in timetables – run on all legs of the network, not to mention the international service from Butterworth to Bangkok, and can save on a night's accommodation.

Seats and berths

On express trains, seats divide into **premier** (first), **superior** (second) and **economy** (third) class, though not all are available on all services. However, there are no seat classes on the ETS.

Sleeper berths come in **deluxe**, **2plus and superior**. Deluxe and 2plus are private cabins (deluxe has its own washroom); superior offers capsule-like bunks in an open carriage, with a curtain for privacy.

Tickets and timetables

You can buy **tickets** at stations, by phone on ☎ 1300 885 862, or online at ⓦ ktmintercity.com .my; **timetables and fare tables** are available online. It's worth booking in advance for sleeper berths and first-class seats.

Long-distance taxis

Long-distance taxis are fading away somewhat, but still run between some cities and towns. They can be a lot quicker than buses, but the snag is that they operate on a **shared** basis, so you have to wait for enough people to show up to fill the vehicle. In practice you're unlikely to make much use of them unless travelling in a group or because you want to charter a taxi to reach a less obvious destination. **Fares** usually work out at double the corresponding bus fare; official prices are usually chalked up on a board at the taxi rank or listed on a laminated tariff card (*senarai tambang*), which you can ask to see.

Some taxi operators assume any tourist who shows up will want to charter a taxi; if you want to use the taxi on a shared basis, say "*nak kongsi dengan orang lain*".

Ferries and boats

Regular **ferries** serve all the major islands, from Penang to Labuan off the coast of Sabah. Within Sarawak, there are scheduled boat services between Kuching and Sibu and up the Rejang River to Belaga. Vessels tend to be narrow, cramped affairs – imagine being inside an aircraft, only on water – and some may be no more than speedboats or motorized *penambang* (fishing craft). It's best to book in advance where there are only a few sailings each day; otherwise just turn up and buy tickets at the jetty. Boat travel also comes into play at **national parks** and in a few rural areas, where you may need to charter one to travel between coastal beaches or to reach remote upriver villages. Details are given in the text of the Guide where relevant.

KERETA SAPU AND MINIVANS

In rural areas of Malaysia, notably in Sarawak, private cars, minivans and (on rough roads) four-wheel-drives fill in handily for the lack of buses along certain routes. Sometimes called **kereta sapu** in Malay, or "taxis" as a shorthand, they may not be as ad hoc as they sound, even running at fixed times each day in some places.

Minivans also operate on a more formal level: travel agencies run them to take backpackers to destinations such as the Perhentians and Taman Negara, or just across the border to Hat Yai in Thailand.

By plane

It's easy to fly within Malaysia, Singapore and Brunei. Most state capitals have **airports** (though some have only one or two flights a day) and there are also regional airports at Langkawi, Labuan, Redang and Tioman islands, and scattered around Sabah and Sarawak – for example, at Mulu for Mulu National Park. You can fly either with the established national airlines or with a variety of low-cost operators, though there may be little to choose between them pricewise if you book late – in which case you might prefer to forgo the stingy luggage allowances and inflated meal charges of the budget airlines.

Fares can be remarkably keen, especially for early-morning or late-night departures, or when booked some way in advance. The ninety-minute flight from KL to Kuching, for example, can cost as little as RM100 one way including tax with a budget airline, though two or three times that is more typical. Note also that any trip involving Singapore or Brunei will be more expensive than the distance might suggest because it will involve an international flight.

DOMESTIC AIRLINES AND ROUTES

AirAsia Ⓦ airasia.com. The airline that pioneered the local low-cost market offers a comprehensive service throughout Malaysia and also serves Singapore and Brunei.

Berjaya Air Ⓦ berjaya-air.com. Malaysia's Berjaya leisure conglomerate runs a few weekly flights out to Redang and Tioman islands from KL and also between Singapore and Redang.

Firefly Ⓦ fireflyz.com.my. Malaysia Airlines' discount subsidiary has some useful flights out of KL's Subang airport, Penang and Ipoh, serving other Peninsula cities and Singapore.

Jetstar Asia Ⓦ jetstar.com. Budget flights from Singapore to KL and Penang.

Malindo Air Ⓦ malindoair.com. Part-owned by the Indonesian budget airline Lion Air, this new competitor already has a good range of flights throughout Malaysia and also serves Singapore.

MASwings Ⓦ maswings.com.my. A subsidiary of Malaysia Airlines, MASwings operates on many routes, both urban and rural, within Borneo, some using propeller-driven Twin Otter planes that are a lifeline for isolated communities.

Malaysia Airlines (MAS) Ⓦ malaysiaairlines.com. Flies between KL and many state capitals, plus Langkawi, Labuan, Singapore and Brunei.

SilkAir Ⓦ silkair.com. Singapore Airlines subsidiary that operates between Singapore and KL, Penang, Langkawi, Kuching and Kota Kinabalu.

Tiger Airways Ⓦ tigerair.com. Budget airline flying from Singapore to KL, Penang and Langkawi.

Driving and vehicle rental

The **roads** in **Peninsular Malaysia** are good, making driving a viable prospect for tourists – though the cavalier local attitude to road rules takes some getting used to. It's mostly the same story in **East Malaysia** and **Brunei**, though minor rural roads may be unpaved and susceptible to flash flooding. **Singapore** is in another league altogether, boasting modern highways and a built-in road-use charging system that talks to a black-box gizmo fitted in every car. All three countries **drive on the left**, and wearing seat belts is compulsory in the front of the vehicle (and in the back too, in Singapore). To **rent a vehicle**, you must be 23 or over and need to show a clean driving licence.

The rest of this section concentrates on **Malaysia**. For more on driving in Singapore and Brunei, see the respective chapters in the Guide.

Malaysian roads

Malaysian highways – called **expressways** and usually referred to by a number prefixed "E" – are a pleasure to drive; they're wide and well maintained, and feature convenient **rest stops** with toilets, shops and small food courts. In contrast, the streets of major cities can be a pain, regularly traffic-snarled, with patchy signposting and confusing one-way systems. Most cities and towns boast plenty of **car parks**, and even where you can't find one, there's usually no problem with parking in a lane or side street.

Speed limits are 110km per hour on expressways, 90km per hour on the narrower trunk and state roads, and 50km per hour in built-up areas. For intercity journeys, expressways are almost always quicker than using a trunk road, even if the latter passes through the town where you're starting out while the expressway is a little way away. Whatever

---

FARE COMPARISONS

Prices below are for ordinary express buses, superior (second-class) rail travel and budget airlines, without early-booking discounts.

Journey	By bus	By train	By plane
KL–Penang	RM40; 4hr 30min	RM22; 6hr	RM90; 45min
KL–Kota Bharu	RM45; 7hr 30min	RM34; 12hr	RM120; 50min
Ipoh–Johor Bharu	RM60; 8hr	RM46; 13hr	RM150; 1hr 20min

MALAY VOCABULARY FOR DRIVERS

The following list should help decipher road signage in Peninsular Malaysia and parts of Brunei, much of which is in Malay.

Utara	North	**Jalan sehala**	One-way street
Selatan	South	**Kawasan rehat**	Highway rest stop
Barat	West	**Kurangkan laju**	Reduce speed
Timur	East	**Lebuhraya**	Expressway/
Di belakang	Behind		highway
Di hadapan	Ahead	**Lencongan**	Detour
Awas	Caution	**Pembinaan di**	Road works
Berhenti	Stop	**hadapan**	ahead
Beri laluan	Give way	**Pusat bandar/**	Town/city centre
Dilarang meletak kereta	No parking	**bandaraya**	
Dilarang memotong	No overtaking	**Simpang ke…**	Junction/turning
Had laju/jam	Speed limit/per		for…
	hour	**Zon had laju**	Zone where speed
Ikut kiri/kanan	Keep left/right		limit applies

road you're on, keep to the speed limit; speed traps are not uncommon and fines hefty. If you are pulled up for a traffic offence, note that it's not unknown for Malaysian police to ask for a bribe, which will set you back less than the fine. Never offer to bribe a police officer and think carefully before you give in to an invitation to do so.

All expressways are built and run by private concessions and as such attract **tolls**, generally around RM20 per 100km, though on some roads a flat fee is levied. At toll points (signed "Tol Plaza"), you can pay in cash (cashiers can dispense change) or by waving a stored-value **Touch 'n Go** card (ⓦ touchngo.com.my) in front of a sensor (see p.86). Get in the appropriate lane as you approach the toll points: some lanes are for certain types of vehicle only.

Once out on the roads, you'll rapidly become aware of the behaviour of quite a few Malaysian motorists, which their compatriots might term *gila* (Malay for "insane"). Swerving from lane to lane in the thick of the traffic, overtaking close to blind corners and careering down hill roads are not uncommon, as are tragic press accounts of pile-ups and road fatalities. Not for nothing does the exhortation "*pandu cermat*" (drive safely) appear on numerous highway signboards, though the message still isn't getting through.

If you're new to driving in Malaysia, the best approach is to take all of this with equanimity and drive conservatively; concede the right of way if you're not sure of the intentions of others. One confusing local habit is that some drivers flash their headlights to claim the **right of way** rather than concede it.

Car and bike rental

Car rental rates with the national chains start at around RM200 per day for a basic 1.2-litre Proton, although you may find better deals with local firms. The rate includes unlimited mileage and collision damage waiver insurance; the excess can be RM1500 or more, but can be reduced by paying a surcharge of up to ten percent on the daily rental rate. Both petrol and diesel were unusually cheap at the time of writing, costing less than RM2 per litre.

Motorbike rental tends to be informal, usually offered by Malaysian guesthouses and shops in more touristy areas. Officially, you must be over 21 and have an appropriate driving licence, though it's unlikely you'll have to show the latter; you'll probably need to leave your passport as a deposit. Wearing helmets is compulsory. Rental costs around RM20 per day, while **bicycles**, useful in rural areas, can be rented for a few ringgit a day.

LOCAL CAR RENTAL AGENCIES

Hawk ⓣ 03 5631 6488, ⓦ hawkrentacar.com.my.
Mayflower ⓣ 1800 881 688, ⓦ mayflowercarrental.com.
Orix ⓣ 03 9284 7799, ⓦ orixauto.com.my.

City and town transport

The companies that run local buses in each state also run city and town buses, serving urban centres and suburbs. Fares seldom exceed RM5, though schedules can be unfathomable to visitors (and even locals). KL also has an LRT metro system, plus local rail and monorail systems.

Taxis are not metered in general, except in a few major cities, notably KL and Singapore; instead drivers negotiate the fare before setting out, so it's worth asking locals what a fair price to your destination would be. At a few taxi ranks, notably at airports and train stations, you buy a voucher for your destination at a sensible price.

Outside the largest cities, taxis do not ply the streets looking for custom. In these places, head to a taxi rank or look for taxis parked outside big hotels and malls. In some cities, you can now book a taxi using the **MyTeksi app**. It's also possible to charter a taxi rather like a chauffeur-driven car, for which you will pay at least RM35 an hour. Your accommodation might be able to do this for you, or at least provide an idea of the going rate in the area.

Trishaws (bicycle rickshaws), seating two people, are seen less these days, but they're still part of the tourist scene in places like Melaka, Penang and Singapore. You're paying for an experience here, not transport as such; details are given in the relevant sections of the Guide.

Accommodation

Accommodation in Malaysia is good value: mid-range en-suite rooms can go for as little as RM100 (£20/US$32), including breakfast. Details of accommodation in Brunei and Singapore are given in the relevant chapters of the Guide.

The cheapest form of accommodation is offered by hostels and guesthouses and lodges, which usually have both dorms and simple private rooms, sharing bathrooms. These places exist only in well-touristed areas, whether urban or rural. Elsewhere, you'll need to rely on hotels, which range from world-class luxury affairs to austere concrete blocks with basic rooms.

Advance reservations are essential to be sure of securing a budget or mid-range room during major festivals or school holidays (see p.56). The East Asian accommodation specialist **Ⓦagoda.com** has a wide selection of hotels in all three countries.

Air conditioning is standard in all but the cheapest hotels, and is fairly common at guesthouses too; **wi-fi** is also becoming widespread, and in the Guide we have tended only to mention it in accommodation reviews where it does not exist. Note that a single room may contain a double bed, while a double can have a double bed, two single beds or even two double beds; a triple will usually have three doubles or a combination of doubles and singles. Baby cots are usually available only in more expensive places.

Guesthouses, hostels and lodges

The mainstay of the travellers' scene in Malaysia are **hostels** and **guesthouses** (also called **backpackers** or **lodges** – all these terms are somewhat interchangeable). These can range from basic affairs to smartly refurbished shophouses with satellite TV and games consoles. Almost all offer **dorm beds**, starting at around RM20, though you can pay double that in fancy establishments. Basic double rooms are usually available for RM40 to RM80 a night, often with mere plywood partitions separating them from adjacent rooms. **Breakfast** is usually available – a simple self-service affair of coffee or tea and toast.

Hotels

Malaysia's **cheapest hotels** tend to cater for a local clientele and seldom need to be booked in advance. Showers and toilets may be shared and can be pretty basic. Another consideration at cheap and even some mid-range hotels is the **noise** level, as doors and windows offer poor sound insulation. Note that some of the hotels at the cheaper end of the scale also function as brothels, especially those that allow rooms to be paid for by the hour.

ACCOMMODATION PRICING

Most mid-range hotels in Malaysia have a published tariff or rack rate and a so-called **promotional rate**, generally around a third less. What's important to realize is that the promotional rate is the de facto price, applying all year except, perhaps, during peak periods such as important festivals. To be sure of getting the promotional rate, either book online or call in advance of your arrival.

Top-bracket hotels have a different strategy: their online booking engines constantly adjust prices according to demand – in general it pays to book early, although some last-minute discounts may also be available.

Finally, note that mid-range and pricey hotels levy a **service charge** and **government tax** (see p.52). Unless otherwise stated, the accommodation prices **quoted in the reviews** in this Guide include such surcharges and are based on promotional rates or, at luxury hotels, typical rates.

Mid-range hotels can be better value than a well-kept budget place. Prices start at around RM100 in cities, less in rural areas and towns, for which you can expect air conditioning, en-suite facilities and relatively decent furnishings, as well, sometimes, as a telephone and refrigerator. In these places, too, a genuine distinction is made between single rooms and doubles.

High-end hotels are as comfortable as you might expect, and many have state-of-the-art facilities, including a swimming pool, spa and gym. Some may add a touch of class by incorporating grand extrapolations of kampung-style architecture, such as saddle-shaped roofs with woodcarving. Although rates can be as low as RM250 per night, in big cities they can rocket above the RM400 mark.

In the major cities, look out for **boutique hotels**, usually set in refurbished shophouses or colonial-era office buildings. They are the most characterful places to stay, offering either retro-style decor or über-hip contemporary features – although never at budget prices.

Hotel **breakfasts**, where available, are either Asian/Western buffets with trays of noodles next to beans and eggs, or simpler affairs where you order off a menu. They're usually included in the rate except at four- and five-star places, where the spread is so elaborate you pay for it separately.

Camping

There are few official opportunities for **camping** in Malaysia, perhaps because guesthouses are so reasonably priced, and because the heat and humidity, not to mention the copious insect population, make camping something only strange foreigners would willingly do. Where there are **campsites**, typically in nature parks, they are either free to use or entail a nominal fee; facilities are basic and may not be well maintained. A few lodges and camps have tents and other equipment for rent, but you generally need to bring your own gear (see box, p.47).

If you go trekking in very remote regions, for example in the depths of Taman Negara and the Kelabit Highlands in Sarawak, camping is about your only option. Specialist tour operators or local guides can often provide gear.

Longhouses

A stay in a **longhouse**, de rigueur for many travellers visiting Sarawak, offers the chance to experience tribal community life, do a little trekking and try activities such as weaving and using a blowpipe. It used to be that visitors could simply turn up and ask the tuai rumah (headman) for a place to stay, paying only for meals and offering some gifts as an additional token of thanks. While some tourists still try to work things like this, these days most longhouse visits are invariably arranged through a **tour operator**; details are given in the Sarawak chapter of this Guide (see p.307). Gawai (see p.46) is the most exciting time to stay.

More expensive packages put visitors up in their own section of the longhouse, equipped with proper beds and modern washing facilities; meals will be prepared separately rather than shared with the rest of the community. More basic trips generally have you sleeping on mats rather than beds, either in a large communal room or on the veranda, and the main washing facilities may well be the nearest river. For meals the party will be divided up into smaller groups, each of which will eat with a different family.

Homestays

In many rural areas especially, **homestay programmes** offer the chance to stay with a Malaysian family, paying for your bed and board. The arrangement is an appealing one on paper, giving you a chance to sample home cooking and local culture. In practice, however, hosts may not be able to speak much English, a situation that effectively cuts foreign guests off from them and the community. As a result, homestays often end up being used by Malaysian travellers rather than foreigners. Tourist offices can usually furnish a list of local homestays on request, but be sure to raise the above issues if pursuing the idea.

CHALETS

Banish all thoughts of Alpine loveliness from your mind: Malaysian **chalets** are guesthouse and resort rooms in the form of little self-contained wooden or concrete cabins. They're mostly to be found in rural areas, especially at nature reserves and beaches. Chalets range from cramped, stuffy A-frame sheds named for their steeply sloping roofs, sometimes with a tiny bathroom at the back, to luxury en-suite affairs with a veranda, sitting area, minibar and the like; prices vary accordingly.

Food and drink

One of the best reasons to come to Malaysia and Singapore (even Brunei, to a lesser extent) is the food, comprising two of the world's most venerated cuisines, Chinese and Indian, and one of the most underrated – Malay. Even if you think you know two out of the three pretty well, be prepared to be surprised: Chinese food here boasts a lot of the provincial diversity that you don't find in the West's Cantonese-dominated Chinese restaurants, while Indian food is predominantly southern Indian, lighter and spicier than the cuisine of the north.

Furthermore, each of the three cuisines has acquired more than a few tricks from the other two – the Chinese here cook curries, for example – giving rise to some distinctive fusion food. Add to this cross-fertilization a host of regional variations and specialities, plus excellent seafood and unusual tropical produce, and the result can be a dazzling gastronomic experience.

None of this need be expensive. From the ubiquitous food stalls and cheap street diners called **kedai kopis**, the standard of cooking is high and food everywhere is remarkably good value. Basic noodle- or rice-based one-plate meals at a stall or *kedai kopis* rarely cost more than a few ringgit or Singapore dollars. Even a full meal with drinks in a fancy restaurant seldom runs to more than RM50 a head in Malaysia, though expect to pay Western prices at quite a few places in Singapore. The most renowned culinary centres are Singapore, Georgetown, KL, Melaka and Kota Bharu, although other towns have their own distinctive dishes too.

Food stalls and food courts

Some of the cheapest and most delicious food available in Malaysia and Singapore comes from **stalls**, traditionally wooden pushcarts on the roadside, surrounded by a few wobbly tables with stools. Most serve one or a few standard **noodle** and **rice dishes** or specialize in certain delicacies, from oyster omelettes to squid curry. One myth to bust immediately is the notion that you will get food poisoning eating at stalls or cheap diners. Standards of hygiene are usually good, and as most food is cooked to order (or, in the case of rice-with-toppings spreads, only on display for a few hours), it's generally pretty **safe**.

Many stalls are assembled into user-friendly **medan selera** (literally "appetite square") or **food courts**, also known as **hawker centres** in Singapore. Usually taking up a floor of an office building or shopping mall, or housed in open-sided market buildings, food courts feature stall lots with menus displayed and fixed tables, plus toilets. You generally don't have to sit close to the stall you're patronizing: find a free table, and the vendor will track you down when your food is ready (at some Singapore food centres you quote the table number when ordering). Play it by ear as to whether you pay when ordering, or when the food is delivered.

Stalls open at various times from morning to evening, with most closing well before midnight except in the big cities. During the Muslim fasting month of **Ramadan**, however, Muslim-run stalls don't open until mid-afternoon, though this is also when you can take advantage of the **pasar Ramadan**, afternoon food markets at which stalls sell masses of savouries and sweet treats to take away; tourist offices can tell you where one is taking place. Ramadan is also the time to stuff yourself at the massive fast-breaking buffets laid on by most major hotels.

Kedai kopis

Few downtown streets lack a **kedai kopis**, sometimes known as a *kopitiam* in Hokkien Chinese. Although both terms literally mean "coffee shop", a *kedai kopis* is actually an inexpensive diner rather than a café. Most serve noodle and rice dishes all day, often with a *campur*-style spread (see p.38) at lunchtime, sometimes in the evening too. Some *kedai kopis* function as miniature food

---

EATING ETIQUETTE

Malays and Indians often eat with the **right hand**, using the palm as a scoop and the thumb to help push food into the mouth. **Chopsticks** are, of course, used for Chinese food, though note that a spoon is always used to help with rice, gravies and slippery food such as mushrooms or tofu, and that you don't pick up rice with chopsticks (unless you've a rice bowl, in which case you lift the bowl to your mouth and use the chopsticks as a sort of shovel). **Cutlery** is universally available; for local food, it's best to eat mainly with a spoon, using a fork to get food on to it.

markets, housing a handful of vendors – perhaps one offering curries and griddle breads, another doing a particular Chinese noodle dish, and so on.

Most *kedai kopis* open at 8am to serve breakfast, and don't shut until the early evening; a few stay open as late as 10pm. Culinary standards are seldom spectacular but are satisfying all the same, and you're unlikely to spend more than small change for a filling one-plate meal. In some Malaysian towns, particularly on the east coast, the Chinese-run *kedai kopis* are often the only places where you'll be able to get **alcohol**.

Restaurants, cafés and bakeries

Sophisticated **restaurants** only exist in the big cities. Don't expect a stiffly formal ambience, however – while some places can be sedate, the Chinese, especially, prefer restaurants to be noisy, sociable affairs. Where the pricier restaurants come into their own is for **international food** – anything from Vietnamese to Tex-Mex. The chief letdown is that the service can be amateurish, reflecting how novel this sort of dining experience is for many of the staff.

Most large Malaysian towns feature a few attempts at Western **cafés**, serving passable fries, sandwiches, burgers, shakes and so forth. It's also easy to find **bakeries**, which can offer a welcome change from the local rice-based diet – though don't be surprised to find chilli sardine buns and other Asian Western hybrids, or cakes with decidedly artificial fillings and colourings. For anything really decent in the café or bakery line, you'll need to be in a big city.

Cuisines

A convenient, cheap way to get acquainted with local dishes is to sample the spreads available at many *kedai kopis*, particularly at lunchtime. The concept is pretty much summed up by the Malay term **nasi campur** ("mixed rice"), though Chinese and Indian *kedai kopis*, too, offer these arrays of stir-fries, curries and other savouries in trays. As in a cafeteria, you tell the person behind the counter which items you want, and a helping of each will be piled atop a mound of rice. If you don't like plain rice, ask for it to be doused with gravy (*kuah* in Malay) from any stew on display.

Nasi campur is not haute cuisine – and that's precisely its attraction. Whether you have, say, *ikan kembong* (mackerel) deep-fried and served whole, or chicken pieces braised in soy sauce, or bean sprouts stir-fried with salted fish or shrimp, a *campur* spread is much closer to **home cooking** than anything served in formal restaurants.

Nasi campur and noodle dishes are meals in themselves, but otherwise eating is generally a **shared** experience – stir-fries and other dishes arrive in quick succession and everyone helps themselves to several servings of each, eaten with rice, as the meal progresses.

Breakfast can present a conundrum in small towns, where rice, *roti canai* and noodles may be all that's easily available. If you can't get used to the likes of rice porridge at dawn, you'll find that many a *kedai kopis* offers *roti bakar*, toast served with butter and **kaya**. The latter is a scrumptious sweet coconut curd jam, either orange or green, not unlike English lemon curd in that egg is a major ingredient.

Malay food

In its influences, **Malay cuisine** looks to the north and east, most obviously to China in the use of noodles and soy sauce, but also to neighbouring Thailand, with which it shares an affinity for such ingredients as lemongrass, the ginger-like galangal and fermented fish sauce (the Malay version, *budu*, is made from anchovies). But Malay food also draws on Indian and Middle East cooking in the use of spices, and in dishes such as *biriyani* rice. The resulting cuisine is both spicy and a little sweet. Naturally there's an emphasis on **local ingredients**: *santan* (coconut milk) lends a sweet, creamy undertone to many stews and curries, while *belacan*, a pungent fermented prawn paste (something of an acquired taste), is found in chilli condiments and sauces. **Herbs**, including curry and kaffir lime leaves, also play a prominent role.

The cuisine of the southern part of the Peninsula tends to be more *lemak* (rich) than further north, where the Thai influence is stronger and *tom yam* stews, spicy and sour (the latter by dint of lemongrass), are popular. The most famous Malay dish is arguably **satay** (see opposite), though it can be hard to find outside big cities. Also quintessentially Malay, **rendang** is a dryish curry made by slow-cooking meat (usually beef) in coconut milk flavoured with galangal and a variety of herbs and spices.

For many visitors, one of the most striking things about Malay food is the bewildering array of **kuih-muih** (or just *kuih*), or sweets, on display at markets and street stalls. Often featuring coconut and sometimes *gula melaka* (palm-sugar molasses), *kuih* come in all shapes, sizes and colours (often artificial nowadays) – rainbow-hued layer cakes of rice flour are about the most extreme example.

Chinese food

The range of **Chinese cooking** available in Malaysia and Singapore represents a mouthwatering sweep through China's southeastern seaboard, reflecting the historical pattern of emigration from **Fujian**, **Guangzhou** and **Hainan Island** provinces. This diversity is evident in dishes served at hawker centres and *kopitiams*. Cantonese *char siew* (roast pork, given a reddish honey-based marinade) is frequently served over plain rice as a meal in itself, or as a garnish in noodle dishes such as *wonton mee* (*wonton* being Cantonese pork dumplings); also very common is Hainanese chicken rice, comprising steamed chicken accompanied by savoury rice cooked in chicken stock. Fujian province contributes dishes such as *hae mee*, yellow noodles in a rich prawn broth; *yong tau foo*, from the Hakka ethnic group on the border with Guangzhou, and comprising bean curd, fishballs and assorted vegetables, poached and served with broth and sweet dipping sauces; and *mee pok*, a Teochew (Chaozhou) dish featuring ribbon-like noodles with fishballs and a spicy dressing.

Restaurant dining tends to be dominated by **Cantonese** food. Menus can be formulaic, but the quality of cooking is usually high. Many Cantonese places also offer great **dim sum**, at which small servings of numerous savouries such as *siu mai* dumplings (of pork and prawn), crispy yam puffs and *chee cheong fun* (rice-flour rolls stuffed with pork and drenched in sweet sauce) are consumed. Traditionally, these would be served in bamboo steamers and ordered from waitress-wheeled trolleys, but these days you might well have to order from a menu.

Where available, take the opportunity to try **specialities** such as **steamboat**, a sort of fondue that involves dunking raw vegetables, meat and seafood into boiling broth to cook, or **chilli crab**, with a spicy tomato sauce. A humdrum but very commonplace stomach-filler is **pow**, steamed buns containing a savoury filling of *char siew* or chicken, or sometimes a sweet red bean paste.

Nyonya food

Named after the word used to describe womenfolk of the Peranakan communities (see p.575), **Nyonya food** is a product of the melding of Penang, Melaka and Singapore cultures. A blend of Chinese and Malay cuisines, it can seem more Malay than Chinese thanks to its use of spices – except that pork is widely used.

Nyonya **popiah** (spring rolls) are very common: rather than being fried, the rolls are assembled by coating a steamed wrap with a sweet sauce made of palm sugar, then stuffed mainly with stir-fried *bangkwang*, a crunchy turnip-like vegetable. Another classic is **laksa**, noodles in a spicy soup with the distinctive *daun kesom* – a herb fittingly referred to in English as *laksa* leaf. Other well-known Nyonya dishes include **asam fish**, a spicy, sour fish stew featuring tamarind (the *asam* of the name), and **otak-otak**, fish mashed with coconut milk and chilli paste then put in a narrow banana-leaf envelope and steamed or barbecued.

SIX OF THE BEST

The dishes listed below are mostly easy to find, and many of these cut across ethnic boundaries as well, with each group modifying the recipe slightly to suit its cooking style.

Nasi lemak Rice fragrantly cooked in coconut milk and served with fried peanuts, tiny fried anchovies, cucumber, boiled egg and spicy *sambal*.

Roti canai Basically Indian paratha (indeed it's called *roti prata* in Singapore), a delicious griddle bread served with a curry sauce. It's ubiquitous, served up by Malay and Indian *kedai kopis* and stalls.

Nasi goreng Literally, fried rice, though not as in Chinese restaurants; Malay and Indian versions feature a little spice and chilli, along with the usual mix of vegetables plus shrimp, chicken and/or egg bits.

Char kuay teow A Hokkien Chinese dish of fried tagliatelle-style rice noodles, often darkly coated in soy sauce and garnished with egg, pork and prawns. The Singapore version is decidedly sweet. Malay *kuay teow goreng* is also available and tends to be spicier.

Satay A Malay dish of chicken, mutton or beef kebabs on bamboo sticks, marinated and barbecued. The meat is accompanied by cucumber, raw onion and *ketupat*, cubes of sticky rice steamed in a wrap of woven leaves. All are meant to be dipped in a spicy peanut sauce. Chinese pork satay also exists.

Laksa A spicy seafood noodle soup, Nyonya in origin. Singapore *laksa*, served with fishcake dumplings and beansprouts, is rich and a little sweet thanks to copious use of coconut milk, while Penang's *asam laksa* features flaked fish and a tamarind tang.

SPECIAL DIETS

Malay food is, unfortunately, a tough nut to crack for **vegetarians**, as meat and seafood are well blended into the cuisine. Among the standard savoury dishes, vegetarians can only really handle *sayur lodeh* (a rich mixed-veg curry made with coconut milk), *tauhu goreng* (deep-fried tofu with a peanut dressing similar to satay sauce) and *acar* (pickles). Chinese and Indian eating places are the best bets, thanks to the dietary influence of Buddhism and Hinduism. Chinese restaurants can always whip up veg stir-fries to order, and many places now feature **Chinese vegetarian** cuisine, using textured veg protein and gluten mock meats – often uncannily like the real thing, and delicious when done right.

Strict vegetarians will want to avoid **seafood derivatives** commonly used in cooking. This means eschewing dishes like *rojak* (containing fermented prawn paste) and the chilli dip called *sambal belacan* (containing *belacan*, the Malay answer to prawn paste). Oyster sauce, often used in Chinese stir-fries, can easily be substituted with soy sauce or just salt. Note also that the gravy served with **roti canai** often comes from a meat curry, though some places offer a lentil version, too.

If you need to **explain in Malay** that you're vegetarian, try *saya hanya makan sayuran* ("I only eat vegetables"). Even if the person taking your order speaks English, it can be useful to list the things you don't eat; in Malay you'd say, for example, *saya tak mahu ayam dan ikan dan udang* for "I don't want chicken or fish or prawn". Expect a few misunderstandings; the cook may leave out one thing on your proscribed list, only to put in another.

HALAL FOOD

Halal food doesn't just feature at Malay and *mamak* eating places. The catering at mid-range and top-tier Malaysian hotels is almost always halal (or at least "**pork-free**"), to the extent that you get turkey or beef "bacon" at breakfast. Of course, the pork-free billing doesn't equate to being halal, but many local Muslims are prepared to overlook this grey area.

In areas where the population is largely Muslim, such as **Kelantan** and **Terengganu**, halal or pork-free food is the norm, even at Chinese and Indian restaurants. In largely Chinese **Singapore**, most hawker centres have a row or two of Muslim stalls.

Indian food

The classic southern Indian dish is the *dosai* or *thosai*, a thin rice-flour pancake. It's usually served accompanied by *sambar*, a thin vegetable and lentil curry; *rasam*, a tamarind broth; and perhaps small helpings of other curries. Also very common are *roti* griddle breads, plus the more substantial *murtabak*, thicker than a *roti* and stuffed with egg, onion and minced meat, with sweet banana versions sometimes available. At lunchtime many South Indian cafés turn to serving *daun pisang* (literally, banana leaf) meals comprising rice heaped on a banana-leaf "platter" and small, replenishable heaps of various curries placed alongside. In some restaurants you'll find more substantial dishes such as the popular fish-head curry (don't be put off by the idea – the "cheeks" between the mouth and gills are packed with tasty flesh).

A notable aspect of the eating scene in Malaysia is the "**mamak**" *kedai kopis*, run by Muslims of South Indian descent (and easily distinguished from Hindu Tamil places by the framed Arabic inscriptions on the walls). *Mamak* establishments have become de facto meeting places for all creeds, being halal and open late, often round the clock.

Foodwise, they're similar to other South Indian places, though with more emphasis on meat.

The food served in **North Indian** restaurants (found only in big cities), is richer, less fiery and more reliant on mutton and chicken. You'll commonly come across **tandoori** dishes – named after the clay oven in which the food is cooked – and in particular tandoori chicken, marinated in yoghurt and spices and then baked. Breads such as *nan* also tend to feature rather than rice.

Borneo cuisine

The diet of the indigenous groups living in settled communities in **East Malaysia** can be not dissimilar to Malay and Chinese cooking. In remoter regions, however, or at festival times, you may have an opportunity to sample indigenous cuisine. Villagers in **Sabah**'s Klias Peninsula and in **Brunei** still produce *ambuyat*, a gluey, sago-starch porridge; then there's the Lun Bawang speciality of *jaruk* – raw wild boar, fermented in a bamboo tube and definitely an acquired taste. Sabah's most famous dishes include *hinava*, raw fish pickled in lime juice. In **Sarawak**, Iban and Kelabit communities sometimes serve wild boar cooked on a spit or stewed, and served with rice (perhaps *lemang* – glutinous rice cooked in bamboo) and jungle ferns. River fish is a longhouse basic; the most easily available, tilapia, is usually grilled with pepper and herbs, or steamed in bamboo cylinders.

Desserts

Given the steamy climate, stalls offer a range of desserts that often revolve around **ice** milled down to something resembling slush. More jarringly, desserts often include ingredients such as **pulses**, **sticky rice** or even **yam** and **sweet potato**, all of which can be turned into a sweet stew or porridge.

At their best, local desserts are certainly a lot more interesting than most ice-cream sundaes ever get. Easy to find and worth trying is **eis kacang** (also known as *air batu campur* – "mixed ice" – or ABC), comprising a small helping of aduki beans, sweetcorn and bits of jelly, covered with a snowy mound doused in colourful syrups. Even better, though high in cholesterol, is **cendol**, luscious coconut milk sweetened with *gula melaka* and mixed with green threads of mung-bean-flour jelly. You'll even find delicious red-bean ice cream on sale, its flavour dominated by coconut milk rather than the beans.

Drinks

While **tap water** is generally safe to drink, **bottled water** is widely and cheaply available. Among freshly squeezed **juices**, watermelon, orange and

---

TROPICAL FRUIT

Markets throughout the region feature a delightful range of locally grown **fruit**, though modern agricultural practices are leading to a decline in some varieties. Below are some of the more unusual fruits to watch out for.

Bananas (pisang) Look out for the delicious *pisang mas*, small, straight, thin-skinned and aromatically sweet; *pisang rastali*, slightly bigger, with dark blotches on the skin and not quite so sweet, and green- and even red-skinned varieties.

Cempedak This smaller version of the *nangka* (see jackfruit, below) is normally deep-fried, enabling the seed, not unlike a new potato, to be eaten too.

Ciku Looks like an apple; varies from yellow to pinkish brown when ripe, with a soft, pulpy flesh.

Durian One of Southeast Asia's most popular fruits, durians are also, for many visitors, the most repugnant thanks to their smell. In season (May–Aug & Nov–Feb), they're the size of soccer balls and have a thick green skin covered with sharp spikes. Inside, rows of large seeds are coated with squidgy yellow-white flesh, whose flavour has been likened to vomit-flavoured custard.

Jackfruit Like a giant grenade, the jackfruit (*nangka*) grows up to 40cm long and has a coarse greenish-yellow exterior, enclosing large seeds whose sweet flesh has a powerful odour like overripe pineapple. The unripe fruit, stir-fried, is a bit like bamboo shoots.

Langsat Together with its sister fruit, the *duku*, this looks like a small, round potato, with juicy, segmented white flesh containing small, bitter seeds.

Longan Not unlike the lychee, this stone fruit has sweet, juicy translucent flesh inside a thin brown skin.

Mangosteen Mangosteens have a segmented white flesh with a sweet, slightly tart flavour. Be warned: the thick purple rind can stain clothes indelibly.

Pomelo Much grown in Perak, this pale green citrus fruit is slightly smaller than a soccer ball and, at its best, is juicier and sweeter than grapefruit. Slice away the rind with a knife, then separate and peel the giant segments with your hands.

Rambutan The shape and size of hen's eggs, rambutans have a soft, spiny exterior that gives them their name – *rambut* means "hair" in Malay. To get at the sweet translucent flesh coating the stone inside, simply make a small tear in the peel with your nails and twist open.

Salak Teardrop-shaped, the *salak* has a skin rather like a snake's and a bitter taste.

Soursop Inside the bumpy, muddy-green skin is smooth white flesh that Margaret Brooke, wife of Sarawak's second rajah, Charles, described as "tasting like cotton wool dipped in vinegar and sugar".

Starfruit Also called carambola, this yellow-green fruit, star-shaped in cross section, is said to be good for high blood pressure – though it can be insipid to taste.

carrot are pretty common, as is the faintly sappy but invigorating sugar cane, extracted by pressing the canes through mangles. Lychee and *longan* drinks can also be good, made with diluted tinned juices and served with some of the fruit at the bottom. Sweetened soya milk in cartons or – much tastier – freshly made at stalls is another popular local choice, as is the refreshing, sweet *chin chow*, which looks like cola but is in fact made from a seaweed and comes with strands of seaweed jelly.

Tea (*teh*) and **coffee** (*kopi*) are as much national drinks as they are in the West, and locals adore them served **tarik**, literally "pulled" – which means frothing the drink by repeatedly pouring it between mugs in each hand. If ordered with milk, they'll come with a generous dollop of the sweetened condensed variety or sometimes evaporated milk (only large hotels and smarter Western-style cafés have regular milk). If you don't have a sweet tooth, either ask for your drink *kurang manis* ("lacking in sweetness"), in which case less condensed milk will be added, or have it black. Note that there can be even more intricacies involved when ordering drinks (see p.600).

Alcohol

Alcohol is not generally hard to find in **Malaysia**. Most big cities have a bar scene, though in Malaysian towns drinking is limited to non-Muslim eating places, food courts (drink stalls usually have beer and perhaps stout) and Chinese-run bars – sometimes little more than tarted-up *kedai kopis*, the walls plastered with posters of Hong Kong showbiz poppets. However, in strongly Muslim areas, particularly Kelantan and Terengganu, only a handful of establishments, usually Chinese, sell alcohol. **Brunei** is officially dry (see p.450), and different rules again apply for details of **Singapore** drinking (see p.543).

Anchor and Tiger **beer** (lager) are locally produced and easily available, and you can get Western and Thai beers as well as the Chinese Tsingtao and various **stouts**, including Guinness. More upmarket restaurants and bars serve beer on draught, cocktails and (generally pricey) imported **wine**. In the longhouses of Sabah and Sarawak, you will probably be invited to sample *tuak*, a rice wine that can be potent or weak and as sickly as sweet sherry.

At a food court or *kopitiam*, a 330ml can of Tiger, say, will cost up to RM8, a 640ml bottle up to RM15 – slightly above what they sell for at a supermarket or convenience store. Proper bars may charge up to fifty percent more, except during **happy hour** (which could last from opening time until 8pm), when prices are sharply lower. While some bars open from lunchtime, most tend to open from early evening until the small hours.

Health

No inoculations are required for visiting Malaysia, Singapore or Brunei, although the immigration authorities may require a yellow-fever vaccination certificate if you have transited an endemic area, normally Africa or South America, within the preceding six days.

Medical problems

Though levels of hygiene and medical care in Malaysia, Singapore and Brunei are higher than in much of Southeast Asia – with any luck, the most serious thing you'll go down with is an upset stomach – it's a wise precaution to visit your doctor no less than two months before you leave to check that you are up to date with your polio, typhoid, tetanus and hepatitis inoculations.

Heat problems

Travellers unused to tropical climates may suffer from sunburn and **dehydration**. The easiest way to avoid this is to restrict your exposure to the midday sun, use high-factor sun screens, wear sunglasses and a hat. You should also drink plenty of water and, if you do become dehydrated, keep up a regular intake of fluids. **Heat stroke** is more serious and can require hospitalization: its onset is indicated by a high temperature, dry red skin and a fast pulse.

Stomach problems

The most common complaint is a stomach problem, which can range from a mild dose of diarrhoea to full-blown dysentery. The majority of stomach bugs may be unpleasant, but are unthreatening; however, if you notice blood or mucus in your stools, then you may have amoebic or bacillary dysentery, in which case you should seek medical help.

Stomach bugs are usually transmitted by contaminated food and water, so steer clear of raw vegetables and shellfish, always wash unpeeled fruit, and stick to freshly cooked foods, avoiding anything reheated. However careful you are, food that's spicy or just different can sometimes upset your system, in which case, try to stick to relatively bland dishes and avoid fried food.

Tap water is drinkable throughout Malaysia, Singapore and Brunei, although in rural areas it's best to buy bottled water, which is widely available.

Dengue fever and malaria

The main mosquito-borne disease to be aware of – and the chief reason to take measures to avoid being bitten (see below) – is **dengue fever**. The disease is caused by a virus spread by the *Aedes aegypti* mosquito (with distinctive white markings on its legs) and breaks out periodically, even in major cities. Symptoms include severe headaches, pain in the bones (especially of the back), fever and often a fine, red rash over the body. There's no specific treatment, just plenty of rest, an adequate fluid intake and painkillers when required.

Although the risk of catching **malaria** is fairly low, consider taking antimalarial tablets if you think you might be staying in remote jungle areas of **Borneo** for some time. Bear in mind you have to start taking the tablets before you arrive in a malaria zone – ask your doctor for the latest advice.

Altitude sickness

Altitude sickness (or acute mountain sickness) can occur if you ascend above around 3500m. In Malaysia it's only likely to be relevant to those climbing **Mount Kinabalu** (4095m), and most people report only mild symptoms at this altitude. Those symptoms include dizziness, headache, shortness of breath and nausea; severe cases can be life-threatening. Painkillers and other over-the-counter drugs may bring symptomatic relief in mild cases, but you must descend to lower altitude if symptoms drag on after a day or two or are severe.

Cuts, bites and stings

Wearing protective clothing when swimming, snorkelling or diving can help avoid sunburn and protect against any sea stings. **Sea lice**, minute creatures that cause painful though harmless bites are the most common hazard; more dangerous are **jellyfish**, whose stings must be doused with vinegar to deactivate the poison before you seek medical help.

Coral can also cause nasty cuts and grazes; any wounds should be cleaned and kept as dry as possible until properly healed. The only way to avoid well-camouflaged sea urchins and stone fish is by not stepping on the seabed: even thick-soled shoes don't provide total protection against their sharp spines, which can be removed by softening the skin by holding it over a steaming pan of water.

As for **mosquitoes**, you can best avoid being bitten by covering up as much as is practical, and applying repellent to exposed flesh. Note that most repellents sold locally are based on **citronella**; if you want one containing **DEET**, which some say is more effective, it's best to buy it at home. Rural or beachside accommodation often features **mosquito nets**, and some places also provide slow-burning **mosquito coils** that generate a little smoke that can deter the insects.

For many people, the ubiquitous **leech** – whose bite is not actually harmful or painful – is the most irritating aspect to jungle trekking (see p.46). Venomous **snakes** are not that common, and any that you might encounter will usually slink away. If you are unlucky enough to be bitten then remain still and call for an ambulance or get someone else to summon help. If one of your limbs has been bitten, ideally a pressure bandage should also be applied to slow the spread of any venom.

Pharmacies, clinics and hospitals

Medical services in Malaysia, Singapore and Brunei are excellent; staff almost everywhere speak English and use up-to-date treatments. Details of pharmacies and hospitals are in the "Directory" sections of the Guide for cities and major towns.

Pharmacies stock a wide range of medicines and health-related items, from contraceptives to contact lens solution; opening hours are the same as for other shops. Only the largest pharmacies have **pharmacists**, though the sale of medicines is so poorly regulated in Malaysia at least that you may be able to buy antibiotics and other prescription drugs over the counter. The two big local chains are Watsons and Guardian, found in most towns.

Private **clinics** can be found even in small towns – your hotel or the local tourist office will be able to recommend a doctor. In Malaysia a consultation costs around RM30, not including the cost of any prescribed medication; keep the receipts for insurance-claim purposes. Finally, the emergency department of each town's general hospital will see foreigners for a small fee, though obviously costs rise rapidly if continued treatment or overnight stays are necessary.

The media

Both Malaysia and Singapore boast plenty of newspapers, TV channels and radio stations serving up lively reportage of events, sports and entertainment, though don't expect to come across hard-hitting or healthily sceptical coverage of domestic politics. The major media organizations in each country are at least partly owned by the establishment; in Singapore, most newspapers have actually been herded into a conglomerate in which the state has a major stake.

Furthermore, the media are kept on their toes by a legal requirement that they must periodically renew their licence to publish. Thus the *Sarawak Tribune* was suspended indefinitely in 2006 after it reproduced the controversial Danish cartoons of the Prophet Muhammad; only in 2010 did it resume publication as the *New Sarawak Tribune*.

Given these circumstances, it's no surprise that the **Press Freedom Index** issued annually by the pressure group Reporters Without Borders, regularly puts Malaysia and Singapore in the bottom third of the world's nations. Brunei, also languishing low down in the table, has a much less well-developed media sector, and its newspapers are packed with anodyne stories about the latest deeds of the sultan and other royals.

Foreign newspapers and magazines are sold in the main cities, and international TV channels are available via satellite and cable. That said, issues of foreign magazines containing pieces that displease the authorities have occasionally been banned, while Singapore's leaders have a long history of winning defamation suits against foreign publications in the island's courts.

If this all seems a bleak picture, it should be said that coverage of Malaysia's opposition parties has increased since they have become more of a force to contend with in recent elections. Added to that, the advent of **independent domestic news websites** and **blogs** has been a breath of fresh air in both Malaysia and Singapore. It's also possible to turn up **YouTube** clips of discussion forums and interviews with activists, offering an alternative take on local issues.

Newspapers, magazines and online news

Both Malaysia and Singapore have English, Malay, Chinese and Tamil newspapers, while Brunei's papers appear in English and Malay. Though Malaysia's national dailies are available in towns in East Malaysia, locally published English-language papers such as the *Borneo Post* in Sarawak (Ⓦtheborneopost.com) and the *Daily Express* in Sabah (Ⓦdailyexpress.com.my) are more popular there.

MALAYSIA

Aliran Monthly Ⓦ aliran.com. Campaigning magazine with an avowed pro-human-rights stance.

Free Malaysia Today Ⓦ freemalaysiatoday.com. Non-partisan coverage of Malaysian politics and society, with a dedicated East Malaysia section.

Malaysia Insider Ⓦ themalaysiainsider.com. Considered more moderate than some of its online counterparts, the *Insider* provides intelligent news and commentary in English and Malay.

Malaysiakini Ⓦ malaysiakini.com. Invigorating reportage and opinion with an anti-establishment slant.

New Straits Times Ⓦ nst.com.my. Closely linked to the UMNO party, this offshoot of Singapore's *Straits Times* was created after the island separated from the Federation. A tabloid, it offers a broad range of news, sports and arts coverage.

Sarawak Report Ⓦ sarawakreport.org. Not a Malaysian site – it's run out of London – but worth a look for its hard-hitting coverage of issues such as logging, native peoples' rights and the probity of Sarawak's government.

The Star Ⓦ thestar.com.my. Founded by the MCA party, *The Star* is Malaysia's best-selling English daily and has a separate Sarawak edition.

SINGAPORE

The Online Citizen Ⓦ theonlinecitizen.com. An alternative and rather less sanguine view of Singapore affairs than you find in the island's mainstream media.

Straits Times Ⓦ straitstimes.com. This venerable broadsheet was founded in 1845, though sadly its pedigree isn't matched by the candour of its journalism; not bad on foreign news, however.

Today Ⓦ todayonline.com. A free paper from the state-owned broadcaster Mediacorp, *Today* is generally less bland than the *Straits Times* and carries worthwhile arts reviews at the weekend.

TR Emeritus Ⓦ tremeritus.com. Formerly the Temasek Review, this website offers independent-minded reporting of the island's affairs.

BRUNEI

Brunei Times Ⓦ bt.com.bn. Pleasant enough but hardly the most challenging of reads.

Television and radio

TV and radio in Malaysia, Singapore and Brunei are dominated by the state-owned broadcasters **RTM**, **Mediacorp** and **RTB** respectively, putting out programmes in several languages. Terrestrial **television** features an unexceptional mix of news, documentaries and dramas made locally and abroad, cookery and talk shows, Islamic discussions and so forth; **radio** is even less original and tends to be dominated by pop music and talk shows. Various foreign TV channels, including CNN, BBC World, National Geographic, ESPN Sports and Al-Jazeera (which has its East Asian base in KL), are available on cable and satellite in Malaysia, and on cable in Singapore (where ownership of satellite dishes is banned). Note that Malaysian broadcasts are easily picked up in Singapore, and Singapore broadcasts in southern Johor.

MALAYSIA

Cats FM W catsfm.my. Kuching-based FM station offering music plus Sarawakian news; see the website for frequencies around the state.

RTM1 & RTM2 W www.rtm.gov.my. Malaysia's staple state-owned TV channels, with some programming in English, Chinese and Tamil. News in English is broadcast on RTM2 at 8pm daily.

Traxxfm W traxxfm.gov.my. Established RTM station with a mix of news and music in English, available on various frequencies around the Peninsula.

TV3 W tv3.com.my. English and Malay news, drama and documentaries, plus some Chinese programmes. It's part of the same conglomerate as the *New Straits Times*.

SINGAPORE

BBC World Service W bbcworldservice.com. 88.9FM, 24hr.

Channel News Asia W channelnewsasia.com. Mediacorp's CNN-like diet of rolling TV news, via cable.

Channel 5 W 5.mediacorptv.sg. The main terrestrial channel for English programming, with plenty of imported shows.

BRUNEI

Radio and Television Brunei (RTB) W www.rtb.gov.bn. Locally made dramas, religious programmes and news, interspersed with dramas and soaps from as far afield as Korea and Venezuela.

Festivals

With so many ethnic groups and religions represented in Malaysia, Singapore and Brunei, you'll be unlucky if your trip doesn't coincide with some sort of festival. Religious celebrations range from exuberant family-oriented pageants to blood-curdlingly gory displays of devotion. Chinese religious festivals are the best times to catch free performances of Chinese opera, or wayang, featuring crashing cymbals, clanging gongs and stylized singing. Secular events might comprise a parade with a cast of thousands, or just a local
market with a few cultural demonstrations laid on.

Bear in mind that the major festival periods may play havoc with even the best-planned travel itineraries, and that some festivals are also public holidays (see p.56).

A festival and events calendar

The dates of many festivals change annually according to the lunar calendar. The Islamic calendar in particular shifts forward relative to the Gregorian calendar by about ten days each year, so that, for example, a Muslim festival that happens in mid-April one year will be nearer the start of April the next. We've listed rough timings; actual dates can vary by a day or two in practice depending on the sighting of the new moon.

JANUARY & FEBRUARY

Ponggal (mid-Jan) A Tamil harvest and New Year festival held at the start of the Tamil month of Thai. Ponggal translates as "overflow", and the festival is celebrated by boiling sugar, rice and milk together in a new claypot over a wood fire till the mixture spills over, symbolizing plenty.

Thaipusam (late Jan/early Feb) Entranced Hindu penitents carry elaborate steel arches (*kavadi*), attached to their skin by hooks and skewers, to honour Lord Subramaniam. The biggest processions are at Kuala Lumpur's Batu Caves and from Singapore's Sri Srinivasa Perumal Temple to the Chettiar Hindu Temple.

Chinese New Year (late Jan/early to mid-Feb) At which Chinese communities settle debts, visit friends and relatives and give children red envelopes (*hong bao/ang pao*) containing money; Chinese operas and lion- and dragon-dance troupes perform in the streets, while markets sell sausages and waxed ducks, pussy willow, chrysanthemums and mandarin oranges. Singapore and the major towns of west coast Malaysia see Chingay parades, featuring stilt-walkers, lion dancers and floats.

Chap Goh Mei (Feb) The fifteenth and climactic night of the Chinese New Year period (known as Guan Hsiao Chieh in Sarawak), and a time for more feasting and firecrackers; women who throw an orange into the sea at this time are supposed to be granted a good husband.

Brunei National Day (Feb 23) The sultan and tens of thousands of Bruneians watch parades and fireworks at the Sultan Hassanal Bolkiah National Stadium, just outside Bandar Seri Begawan.

MARCH–MAY

Easter (March/April) Candlelit processions are held on Good Friday at churches such as St Peter's in Melaka and St Joseph's in Singapore.

Qing Ming (April) Ancestral graves are cleaned and restored, and offerings made by Chinese families at the beginning of the third lunar month, signifying the start of spring and a new farming year.

Vesak Day (May) Saffron-robed monks chant prayers at packed Buddhist temples, and devotees release caged birds to commemorate the Buddha's birth, enlightenment and attainment of Nirvana.

Sabah Fest (late May) A week of events in Kota Kinabalu, offering a chance to experience Sabah's food, handicrafts, dance and music; right at the end comes Rumah Terbuka Malaysia Tadau Kaamatan, a harvest festival in Kota Kinabalu.

JUNE–AUGUST

Yang di-Pertuan Agong's Birthday (June) Festivities in KL to celebrate the birthday of Malaysia's king, elected every five years by the country's nine sultans or rajahs from among their number.

Gawai Dayak (June) Sarawak's people, especially the Iban and Bidayuh, celebrate the end of rice harvesting with extravagant longhouse feasts. Aim to be in a longhouse on the Rejang or Batang Ai rivers, or around Bau.

Feast of St Peter (June 24) Melaka's Eurasian community decorate their boats to honour the patron saint of fishermen.

Dragon Boat Festival (June/July) Rowing boats, bearing a dragon's head and tail, race in Penang, Melaka, Singapore and Kota Kinabalu, to commemorate a Chinese scholar who drowned himself in protest against political corruption.

Georgetown Festival (June/July/Aug) One of the best arts festivals in Malaysia sees the historic streets and buildings of Penang given over to music recitals, art exhibitions and the like.

Sultan of Brunei's Birthday (July 15) Starting with a speech by the sultan on the padang, celebrations continue for two weeks with parades, lantern processions, traditional sports competitions and fireworks.

Sarawak Extravaganza (Aug) Kuching hosts a month of arts and crafts shows, street parades, food fairs and traditional games, all celebrating the culture of Sarawak.

Singapore National Day (Aug 9) Singapore celebrates its independence with a huge show featuring military parades and fireworks.

Festival of the Hungry Ghosts (late Aug) Held to appease the souls of the dead released from purgatory during the seventh lunar month.

Chinese street operas are staged, and joss sticks, red candles and paper money are burnt outside Chinese homes.

Ramadan (starts second week of July in 2013) Muslims spend the ninth month of the Islamic calendar fasting in the daytime, and breaking their fasts nightly with delicious Malay sweetmeats served at stalls outside mosques.

Hari Raya Puasa/Aidilfitri (falls in June or July) Muslims celebrate the end of Ramadan by feasting, and visiting family and friends; this is the only time the region's royal palaces are open to the public.

Malaysia National Day (Aug 31) Parades in KL's Merdeka Square and other cities mark the formation of the state of Malaysia.

SEPTEMBER–DECEMBER

Moon Cake Festival (Sept) Also known as the Mid-Autumn Festival, this is when Chinese people eat and exchange moon cakes, made from sesame and lotus seeds and sometimes stuffed with a duck egg. Essentially a harvest festival.

Hari Raya Haji/Aidiladha (Sept) Muslims gather at mosques to honour those who have completed the hajj, or pilgrimage to Mecca; goats are sacrificed and their meat given to the needy.

Navarathri (Sept–Oct) Hindu temples devote nine nights to classical dance and music in honour of the consorts of the Hindu gods, Shiva, Vishnu and Brahman.

Thimithi (Oct/Nov) Hindu firewalking ceremony in which devotees prove the strength of their faith by running across a pit of hot coals; best seen at the Sri Mariamman Temple in Singapore.

Deepavali (Oct/Nov) Also known as Diwali, this Hindu festival celebrates the victory of Light over Dark: oil lamps are lit outside homes to attract Lakshmi, the goddess of prosperity, and prayers are offered at all temples.

Christmas (Dec 25) Shopping centres in major cities compete to create the most spectacular Christmas decorations.

COMBATING LEECHES

Leeches are gruesome but pretty harmless creatures that almost all hikers will encounter – especially after rain, when you can rely upon them to come out. Slender, wormlike, muscular tubes with teeth at one end, they lie dormant in rainforest leaf litter until, activated by footfalls and body heat, they latch onto your boot, then climb until they find a way through socks and trousers and onto your skin. Their bites (about the size of a pinhead) are painless, but they bleed a lot and sometimes itch as they heal.

Keeping leeches off isn't easy; they can get through all but the closest-mesh fabrics. At the very least you should tuck your trousers into your socks and tie your bootlaces tight. The best anti-leech socks are made from calico and available in specialist stores. If you find the leeches are getting through, soak the outside of your socks and your boots in insect repellent. Tights also work (but get very hot). Some guides, however, recommend simply wearing open shoes and shorts, so that you can see them – an approach that requires an advanced jungle mentality.

The quickest way to **remove** a leech is to repeatedly flick its head end with your fingernail. Otherwise salt, tiger balm or tobacco juice, rubbed onto the leech, will cause them to let go rapidly.

Sports and outdoor activities

With some of the world's oldest tropical rainforest and countless beaches and islands, trekking, snorkelling and scuba diving are common pursuits in Malaysia. The more established resorts on the islands of Penang, Langkawi and Tioman also offer jet skiing and paragliding, while the exposed, windy bay at Cherating, the budget travellers' centre on the east coast, is a hot spot for windsurfers.

If you intend to take up any of the pursuits below, check that they are covered by your insurance policy.

Watersports

The crystal-clear waters and abundant tropical fish and coral of Malaysia make snorkelling and diving a must for any underwater enthusiast. This is particularly true of Sabah's **Sipidan Island Marine Reserve** and the Peninsula's east coast, with islands like the **Perhentians**, **Redang**, **Kapas** and **Tioman**.

Dive shops, for example in Sabah's Kota Kinabalu and Sarawak's Miri, offer all-inclusive, internationally recognized certification courses, ranging from a beginner's open-water course (around RM1300), right through to the dive-master certificate (RM2200). If you're already qualified, expect to pay RM180 per day for dive trips including gear rental.

Most beachside guesthouses rent snorkelling equipment for around RM20 per day. Some popular **snorkelling** areas mark out lanes for motorboats with buoy lines – stay on the correct side of the line to avoid a nasty accident. If you're not sure where it's safe to swim or snorkel, always seek local advice. Never touch or walk on coral as this will cause irreparable damage – besides which, you risk treading on the armour-piercing spines of sea urchins, or a painful encounter with fire coral.

CHECKLIST OF CAMPING AND TREKKING EQUIPMENT

As camping and trekking are not especially popular with Malaysians, you need to bring your own **gear** if possible – especially core items like tents and sleeping bags – or buy the locally made version available at markets and general stores. These might not look good or even last long, but at least won't cost a fortune. Hiking boots are especially hard to find, though one-piece rubber slip-on shoes (*kasut gatah*) costing just RM10 are sold everywhere (up to around size 40). Many national park guides use them as they dry out instantly and give good grip on forest floors, but they're not suitable for multiday trekking in difficult terrain.

There are small (and very expensive) "proper" outdoor gear stores in KL, Kota Bharu and elsewhere; you might also be able to rent some of what you'll need on site, especially at Taman Negara, or have it supplied as part of a hiking package.

ESSENTIALS

Backpack
Breathable shirts/T-shirts
Compass
First-aid kit (basic)
Fleece jacket
Hat, cotton, with brim
Insect repellent
Lightweight, quick-drying trousers
Lip balm
Mosquito net
Pocket knife
Rainproof coat or poncho

Sandals (for wading through streams)
Sewing kit
Sleeping bag
Socks, cotton and wool
Sun block
Sunglasses (UV protective)
Tent (if sleeping out)
Toilet paper
Toiletries
Torch (and/or head torch)
Trekking boots
Water bottle
Water purification tablets

OTHER USEFUL ITEMS

Binoculars
Bootlaces, spare
Emergency snack food
Heavy-duty refuse bag (to rainproof your

pack)
Insulation mat
Leech socks (see opposite)
Towel, small

Windsurfing has yet to take off in all but the most expensive resorts in Malaysia, with the notable exception of Cherating. Its large, open bay and shallow waters provide near-perfect conditions during the northeast monsoon season.

Whitewater rafting

Whitewater rafting has become a popular activity on Sabah's **Sungai Padas**, a grade 3 river which, at its northern end, runs through the spectacular Padas Gorge (see p.404). Opportunities for rafting in **Peninsular Malaysia** tend to be in out-of-the-way spots, with the exception of Gopeng (see p.121); it's best to go with an operator such as Nomad Adventure (W nomadadventure.com) or Khersonese Expedition (W thepaddlerz.com). Expect a day's rafting to cost around RM250, including equipment.

Trekking

The majority of **treks** in Malaysia require forethought and preparation. In addition to the fierce sun, the tropical climate can unleash torrential rain without warning, which rapidly affects the condition of trails or the height of a river – what started out as a ten-hour trip can end up taking twice as long. That said, the time of year is not a hugely significant factor when planning a trek. Although in the rainy season (Nov–Feb) trails can be slow going (or even closed for safety reasons), conditions are less humid then, and the parks and adventure tours are not oversubscribed.

Treks in national parks almost always require that you go in a group with a **guide**; solo travellers can usually join a group once there. Costs and conditions vary between parks; each park account in the Guide contains details, while tour operators in Kuala Lumpur, Kuching, Miri and Kota Kinabalu (listed throughout the relevant sections in the Guide) can also furnish information on conditions and options in the parks.

For inexperienced trekkers, **Taman Negara** is probably the best place to start, boasting the greatest range of walks, many of which can be done without a guide, while **Bako National Park** in southwest Sarawak offers fairly easy, day-long hikes. For more experienced walkers, other parks in Sarawak, especially **Gunung Mulu**, should offer sufficient challenges for most tastes, while Sabah's **Maliau Basin** is at the very demanding end of the scale. **Gunung Kinabalu** in Sabah is in a class of its own, the hike to the top of the mountain a demanding but highly rewarding combination of trekking and climbing.

Culture and etiquette

Despite their obvious openness to influences from around the globe, Malaysia, Singapore and Brunei remain fairly conservative and conformist. Behaviour that departs from established cultural and behavioural norms – basically, anything that draws attention to the individuals concerned – is avoided.

Allowances are made for foreigners, but until you acquire some familiarity with where the limits lie, it's best to err on the side of caution. Get the balance right and you'll find locals helpful and welcoming, while respectful of your need for some privacy.

Dress

For both men and women, exposing lots of bare flesh is generally a no-no, and the degree to which you should **cover up** can seem surprisingly prim. Islamic tradition suffuses the dress code for locals, Muslim or otherwise, and dictates that both men and women should keep torsos covered; shirt sleeves, if short, should come down to the elbow (for women, long-sleeved tops are preferable), while shorts or skirts should extend down to the knee (long trousers are ideal). Figure-hugging clothes are often frowned upon, particularly for women. All of this said, dress codes are more liberal in most cities, on the beach, and when pursuing sporting activities.

Note that in Muslim tradition, the soles of **shoes** are considered unclean, having been in contact with the dirt of the street. Thus before entering any home (Muslim or otherwise), it's almost universal practice to remove footwear at the threshold or before stepping on to any carpeted or matted area.

Body language

Two things to **avoid** are public shows of affection (holding hands is OK, kissing not) and drinking alcohol outside bars or clubs – even in resort areas frequented by foreigners. In a situation where you need to make a **complaint**, the most effective approach is not to raise your voice but to go out of your way to be reasonable while stating your case.

As for body language, note that **touching someone's head**, be they Muslim or otherwise, is to be avoided as the head is considered sacred. Handshakes are fairly commonplace

THE STATUS OF MALAY WOMEN

Malay women are among the most emancipated in the Islamic world. They often attain prominent roles in business, academia and other areas of public life and are very much the lynchpin of the family.

Although the more conservative tide running through the Islamic world has had relatively little impact on this situation, many Malay women now wear a *tudung* (headscarf). Sometimes this merely indicates an acceptance of the trappings of the religion – it's not unusual to see Malay women at a gig or club partying away in headscarf, T-shirt and jeans.

when meeting someone; Muslims often follow this by touching the palm of the right hand to their own chest. Some Muslims may be reluctant to shake hands with the opposite sex; however, in this case a smile, nod and that same right-hand-palm gesture will suffice. Muslims and Indians also avoid using their left hand for human contact or eating.

Visiting places of worship

It's common to see various temples and mosques happily existing side by side, each providing a social as well as a religious focal point for the corresponding community. Some shrines are among the oldest structures you're likely to see in the region and are worth a look around.

In theory all **mosques** are open to visitors outside prayer times, though in conservative areas they may not welcome tourists. Male visitors should wear long trousers and a shirt or top with sleeves coming down to the elbows (long sleeves are even better); women will also have to don a long cloak and headdress, which is provided by most mosques. You'll be required to remove your shoes before entering. Most Chinese and Hindu **temples** are open from early morning to early evening; devotees go in when they like, to make offerings or to pray. Hindu temples also expect visitors to remove shoes.

Even if there are no signs barring **photography**, staff at some temples don't take kindly to it; if in doubt, ask.

Women travellers

Women who respect local customs and exercise common sense should have few problems travelling alone or with other women.

Some Western women have been known to find the atmosphere in largely **Muslim areas**, such as Kelantan or Terengganu, off-putting. Arriving there from Thailand or from a more cosmopolitan part of Malaysia, some women still find themselves being stared at or subjected to wolf-whistles or lewd gestures, despite observing local dress codes. It's worth noting that the ground rules are different for locals; the Malay, Chinese and Indian communities, having lived together for generations, have an unspoken understanding as to how the respective communities can behave in public.

Shopping

Southeast Asia can offer bargain shopping, with electrical equipment, cameras and fabrics all selling at competitive prices. What's more, the region's ethnic diversity means you'll be spoiled for choice when it comes to souvenirs and handicrafts.

One point to be aware of is that a lot of the crafts on sale in Malaysia are in fact made elsewhere in the region, particularly in Indonesia. Worthwhile buys, especially domestically made ones, are highlighted throughout the Guide. Also be aware that prices in small outlets such as family-run shops tend to be negotiable, and **bargaining** is expected. Asking for the "best price" is always a good opening gambit; from there, it's a question of technique, though be realistic – shopkeepers will soon lose interest if you offer an unreasonably low price. If you buy any electrical goods, it can be worth ensuring you get an international guarantee, endorsed by the shop.

Fabrics

The art of producing **batik** cloth originated in Indonesia, but today batik is available across Southeast Asia and supports a thriving industry in Malaysia. It's made by applying hot wax to a piece of cloth with either a pen or a copper stamp; when the cloth is dyed, the wax resists the dye and a pattern appears, a process that can be repeated many times to build up colours. Note that some vendors try to pass off printed cloth as batik. Make sure the brightness of the pattern is equal on both sides – if it's obviously lighter on one side, it is likely the cloth is printed.

Batik is used to create shirts, skirts, bags and hats, as well as traditional **sarongs**. The exquisite gold-threaded brocade known as **songket**, used to make sarongs, headscarves and the like, is a big step up in price from batik; RM200 for a sarong-length of cloth is not uncommon, and prices soar for the finest pieces.

Unique to Sarawak is **pua kumbu** (in Iban, "blanket"), a textile whose complex designs are created using the *ikat* method of weaving (see p.321). The cloth is sold in longhouses as well as in some souvenir outlets.

Woodcarving

Woodcarving skills, once employed to decorate the palaces and public buildings of the early sultans, are today used to make less exotic articles such as mirror frames. However, it's still possible to see statues and masks created by the Orang Asli. As animists, Orang Asli artists draw upon the natural world – animals, trees, fish, as well as more abstract elements like fire and water – for their imagery. Of particular interest are the carvings of the Mah Meri of Selangor, which are improvisations on the theme of *moyang*, literally "ancestor", the generic name for all spirit images. In Borneo, look out for tribal face masks and rectangular shields adorned with intricate motifs. It's also possible to buy hardwood blowpipes, though these are drilled rather than carved.

Metalwork

Of the wealth of metalwork on offer, **silverware** from Kelantan is among the finest and most intricately designed; it's commonly used to make earrings, brooches and pendants, as well as more substantial pieces. Selangor is known for its **pewter** – a blend of tin, antimony and copper, which can be used to create elegant vases, tankards and ornaments.

Other souvenirs

Rattan, cane, **bamboo** and *mengkuang* (pandanus) are traditionally used to make baskets, bird cages, mats, hats and shoulder bags. The best items make surprisingly impressive accessories, and in Borneo it's possible to find baskets and bags bearing traditional motifs, too. Another unusual raw

---

DUTY-FREE GOODS

Malaysia has no duty on cameras, watches, cosmetics, perfumes or cigarettes. Labuan, Langkawi and Tioman are duty-free islands, which in practice means that goods there (including alcohol) can be a third cheaper than on the Malaysian mainland, though it's not as though a particularly impressive range of products is on sale. Duty-free products in Singapore include electronic and electrical goods, cosmetics, cameras, clocks, watches, jewellery, precious stones and metals.

---

material is **breadfruit bark**; in Sarawak it's pressed to produce a "cloth" that makes excellent hats and jackets, as well as a canvas for paintings.

Malay pastimes throw up some interesting purchases: leather *wayang kulit* (shadow play) **puppets**, portraying characters from Hindu legend, are attractive and light to carry; equally colourful but impractical if you have to carry them around are Malay **kites**, which can be a couple of metres long.

Pottery, though sometimes mass-produced, can be a worthwhile decorative acquisition. Examples include the Malay *labu*, a gourd-like slender-necked water jug (it's made in, among other places, Perak) and Sarawak pots and jars bearing tribal motifs. Finally, it's possible to buy some fine examples of **beadwork** – from pricey Peranakan beaded slippers to Kelabit jackets from the northern highlands of Sarawak.

Travel essentials

Climate

The climate in Malaysia, Singapore and Brunei remains remarkably consistent throughout the year (see box opposite), with typical daytime temperatures of around 30°C. However, the northeast monsoon brings torrential rains and heavy seas between September and February, concentrating its attentions on the west coast of the Peninsula in September and October, and on the east coast after that.

Costs

Anyone entering Malaysia from Thailand will find that costs are slightly higher – both food and accommodation are more expensive – whereas travellers arriving from Indonesia will find prices a little lower overall. Travelling in a group naturally helps keep costs down. The region affords some savings for senior citizens, and an ISIC student card (ⓦisic.org) might occasionally pay dividends.

Note that **bargaining** is routine throughout Malaysia and Singapore when buying stuff in markets or small shops, though you don't haggle for meals or accommodation.

Malaysia

In **Peninsular Malaysia** you can scrape by on £12/US$20/RM60 per day staying in dorms, eating at hawker stalls and getting around by bus. Double that and you'll be able to exist in relative comfort without thinking too hard about occasionally treating yourself. Over in **East Malaysia**, where accommodation and tours tend to cost a little more, the minimum daily outlay is more like £16/US$25/RM80.

Singapore and Brunei

Costs in **Singapore** are much steeper than in Malaysia, with a minimum budget of around £30/US$50/S$60 per day. Upgrading your lodgings to a private room in a guesthouse, eating one daily meal in a cheap restaurant, and having a beer or two could require £40/US$60/S$80 per day.

Costs in **Brunei** are on a par with Singapore if you manage to take advantage of the capital's limited budget accommodation, or stay in one of the cheaper mid-range hotels and don't do a lot of sightseeing. Otherwise, costs can spiral as you'll have to rely on taxis or package trips to reach outlying places of interest, notably Ulu Temburong National Park.

Crime and personal safety

If you lose something in Malaysia, Singapore or Brunei, you're more likely to have someone run after you with it than run away. Nevertheless,

AVERAGE DAILY TEMPERATURES AND RAINFALL

	Jan	Feb	Mar	Apr	May	Jun	Jul	Aug	Sep	Oct	Nov	Dec
CAMERON HIGHLANDS												
Max/min °C	21/14	22/14	23/14	23/15	23/15	23/15	22/14	22/15	22/15	22/15	22/15	21/15
Rain (mm)	120	111	198	277	273	137	165	172	241	334	305	202
KOTA BHARU												
Max/min °C	29/22	30/23	31/23	32/24	33/24	32/24	32/23	32/23	32/23	31/23	29/23	29/23
Rain (mm)	163	60	99	81	114	132	157	168	195	286	651	603
KOTA KINABALU												
Max/min °C	30/23	30/23	31/23	32/24	32/24	31/24	31/24	31/24	31/23	31/23	31/23	31/23
Rain (mm)	153	63	71	124	218	311	277	256	314	334	296	241
KUALA LUMPUR												
Max/min °C	32/22	33/22	33/23	33/23	33/23	32/23	32/23	32/23	32/23	32/23	31/23	31/23
Rain (mm)	159	154	223	276	182	119	120	133	173	258	263	223
KUCHING												
Max/min °C	30/23	30/23	31/23	32/23	33/23	33/23	32/23	33/23	32/23	32/23	31/23	31/23
Rain (mm)	683	522	339	286	253	199	199	211	271	326	343	465
PENANG												
Max/min °C	32/23	32/23	32/24	32/24	31/24	31/24	31/23	31/23	31/23	31/23	31/23	31/23
Rain (mm)	70	93	141	214	240	170	208	235	341	380	246	107
SINGAPORE												
Max/min °C	32/23	32/23	32/24	32/24	31/24	31/24	31/23	31/23	31/23	31/23	31/23	31/23
Rain (mm)	70	93	141	214	240	170	208	235	341	380	246	107

SALES TAXES AND SERVICE CHARGES

Top-end and many mid-range hotels and restaurants in Malaysia and Singapore levy two surcharges: a **service charge** (usually ten percent) and a **government tax** (six percent in Malaysia, 7.7 percent in Singapore). Always check if prices you are quoted include these charges (they are "nett" prices, in local parlance) or exclude them; the presence of "**++**" after a price indicates that you need to add them.

The government tax in Singapore is properly known as the goods and services tax (**GST**) and also applies to goods sold in shops. At the time of writing it appeared that Malaysia would be replacing its government tax with GST, and that it would be levied by all firms by the time you read this.

don't become complacent, as petty crime is an issue in Malaysia at least. Sensible **precautions** include carrying your passport and other valuables in a concealed money belt, and using the safety deposit box provided by many guesthouses and hotels. Take a photocopy of the relevant pages of your passport, too, in case it's lost or stolen. If you have to report a crime, be sure to get a copy of the police report for insurance purposes.

It's worth repeating here that on no account should you have anything to do with illegal drugs of any description in Malaysia, Singapore and Brunei (see p.54).

Malaysia

Pickpockets and **snatch-thieves** can be a problem in Malaysian cities, although violent crime is relatively rare; horrific incidents like the alcohol-fuelled murder of two British students in central Kuching in 2014 are quite out of the ordinary.

Restrictions on contact between people of the opposite sex (such as the offence of *khalwat*, or "close proximity") and eating in public during daylight hours in the Ramadan month apply to Muslims only.

EMERGENCY NUMBERS

MALAYSIA
Fire brigade ☏994
Police/Ambulance ☏999

SINGAPORE
Fire Brigade/Ambulance ☏995
Police ☏999

BRUNEI
Ambulance ☏991
Fire Brigade ☏995
Police ☏993

Singapore

Singapore is known locally as a "fine city". Substantial **fines** punish misdemeanours like littering, jaywalking – defined as crossing a main road within 50m of a designated pedestrian crossing – and so forth, though these penalties are seldom enforced as the populace has become compliant over the years. Bear in mind that **chewing gum** is not on sale in Singapore on the grounds that used gum can foul the streets, although you can bring in gum for your own consumption.

Electricity

Mains voltage in Malaysia, Singapore and Brunei is **230 volts**, so any equipment using 110 volts will need a converter. The plugs in all three countries have three square prongs like British ones.

Entry requirements

Nationals of the UK, Ireland, US, Canada, Australia, New Zealand and South Africa do not need **visas** in advance to stay in Malaysia, Singapore or Brunei, and it's easy to extend your permission to stay. That said, check with the relevant embassy or consulate, as the rules on visas are complex and subject to change. Ensure that your passport is valid for at least six months from the date of your trip, and has several blank pages for entry stamps.

Malaysia

Upon arrival in **Malaysia**, citizens of Australia, Canada, the UK, Ireland, US, New Zealand and South Africa receive a passport stamp entitling them to a ninety-day stay. Visitors who enter via **Sarawak**, however, receive a thirty-day stamp.

It's straightforward to **extend** your permit through the **Immigration Department**, who have offices (listed in the Guide) in Kuala Lumpur and major towns; you can also find details of visa requirements for various nationalities on their website, Ⓦwww.imi.gov.my. Visitors from the aforementioned countries can also cross into Singapore or Thailand and back to be granted a fresh Malaysia entry stamp.

Tourists travelling from the Peninsula to **East Malaysia** (Sarawak and Sabah) must be cleared again by immigration. Visitors to Sabah can remain as long as their original entry stamp is valid, but Sarawak maintains its own border controls – a condition of its joining the Federation in 1965 – which means you are always stamped in and given a thirty-day Sarawak visa even when arriving from other parts of Malaysia.

For more on Malaysia's embassies, see Ⓦkln .gov.my.

MALAYSIA EMBASSIES AND CONSULATES

Australia 7 Perth Ave, Yarralumla, Canberra (☎ 02 6120 0300, Ⓦmalaysia.org.au).
Brunei No. 61, Simpang 336, Jalan Kebangsaan BA 1211, Kg. Sungai Akar, PO Box 2826, Bandar Seri Begawan (☎ 02 381095, Ⓦkln.gov.my).
Canada 60 Boteler St, Ottawa, ON K1N 8Y7 (☎ 613 241 5182, Ⓦkln.gov.my).
Indonesia Jalan H.R. Rasuna Said, Kav. X/6, No. 1–3 Kuningan, Jakarta Selatan 12950 (☎ 021 522 4974, Ⓦkln.gov.my).
Ireland Shelbourne House, Level 3A–5A, Shelbourne Rd, Ballsbridge, Dublin 4 (☎ 01 667 7280, Ⓦkln.gov.my).
New Zealand 10 Washington Ave, Brooklyn, PO Box 9422, Wellington (☎ 04 385 2439, Ⓦkln.gov.my).
Singapore 301 Jervois Rd (☎ 6235 0111, Ⓦkln.gov.my).
South Africa 1007 Francis Baard St (formerly Schoeman St), Arcadia, Pretoria 0083 (☎ 012 342 5990, Ⓦkln.gov.my).
Thailand 33–35 South Sathorn Rd, Tungmahamek, Bangkok 10120 (☎ 02 629 6800, Ⓦkln.gov.my).
UK 45–46 Belgrave Square, London SW1X 8QT (☎ 020 7235 8033, Ⓦmalaysia.embassyhomepage.com).
US 3516 International Court, NW Washington, DC 20008 (☎ 202 572 9700, Ⓦkln.gov.my).

Singapore

Upon arrival in **Singapore**, citizens of the UK, Ireland and the US get a ninety-day stamp, while those of Canada, Australia, New Zealand and South Africa are given thirty days. To extend your stay beyond these limits, take a bus up to Johor Bahru just inside Malaysia, then return to Singapore, whereupon you will be given a new entry stamp.

For more about Singapore's embassies abroad, see Ⓦwww.mfa.gov.sg, and for visa requirements, Ⓦica.gov.sg.

SINGAPORE EMBASSIES AND CONSULATES

Australia 17 Forster Crescent, Yarralumla, Canberra, ACT 2600 (☎ 02 6271 2000, Ⓦwww.mfa.gov.sg/Canberra).
Indonesia Block X/4 Kav No. 2, Jalan H.R. Rasuna Said, Kuningan, Jakarta (☎ 021 2995 0400, Ⓦmfa.gov.sg/jkt).
Ireland 2 Ely Place Upper, Dublin 2 (☎ 01 669 1700, Ⓦwww.mfa .gov.sg/dublin).
Malaysia Level 15, West Wing, The Icon, 1 Jalan 1/68F, Jalan Tun Razak, Kuala Lumpur (☎ 03 2161 6277, Ⓦmfa.gov.sg/kualalumpur).
New Zealand 17 Kabul St, Khandallah, Wellington (☎ 04 470 0850, Ⓦwww.mfa.gov.sg/wellington).
South Africa 980–982 Francis Baard St (formerly Schoeman St), Arcadia, Pretoria 0083 (☎ 012 430 6035, Ⓦwww.mfa.gov.sg /pretoria).
Thailand 129 South Sathorn Rd, Bangkok 10120 (☎ 02 286 2111, Ⓦwww.mfa.gov.sg/bangkok).
UK 9 Wilton Crescent, Belgravia, London SW1X 8SP (☎ 020 7235 8315, Ⓦwww.mfa.gov.sg/london).
US 3501 International Place NW, Washington, DC 20008 (☎ 202 537 3100, Ⓦwww.mfa.gov.sg/washington).

Brunei

US nationals are allowed to stay in **Brunei** for up to ninety days on arrival; British, Australian and New Zealand passport holders are granted thirteen days; and Canadians get fourteen days. South African citizens need to apply for a visa in advance; the closest embassy is in Egypt but you can also apply in Singapore – the process takes around three working days. Once in Brunei, extending your permission to stay is usually a formality; apply at the Immigration Department in Bandar Seri Begawan. For details of Brunei's embassies, see Ⓦmofat.gov.bn.

BRUNEI EMBASSIES AND CONSULATES

Australia 10 Beale Crescent, Deakin, ACT 2600 Canberra (☎ 02 6285 4500, Ⓦbrunei.org.au).
Canada 395 Laurier Ave East, Ottawa, ON, KIN 6R4 (☎ 613 234 5656).
Indonesia Jalan Teuku Umar 51, Menteng, Jakarta 10350 (☎ 021 3190 6080).
Malaysia No. 19-01, 19th floor, Menara Tan & Tan, Jalan Tun Razak, Kuala Lumpur 50400 (☎ 03 2161 2800).
Singapore 325 Tanglin Rd (☎ 6733 9055).
South Africa see the embassy in Singapore, or contact the embassy in Egypt: 24 Hassan Assem St, Zamalek, Cairo (☎ 20 2341 6365).
Thailand 12 Ekamai soi 2, 63 Sukhumvit Rd, Prakhanong Nuea, Bangkok 10110 (☎ 02 714 7395).
UK 19–20 Belgrave Square, London SW1X 8PG (☎ 020 7581 0521, Ⓦbrunei.embassyhomepage.com).
US 3520 International Court NW, Washington, DC 20008 (☎ 202 237 1838, Ⓦbruneiembassy.org).

Customs allowances

Malaysia's duty-free allowances are 200 cigarettes or 225g of tobacco, and 1 litre of wine, spirits or liquor. There's no customs clearance for passengers travelling from Singapore or Peninsular Malaysia to East Malaysia, nor for people passing between Sabah and Sarawak.

Entering **Singapore** from anywhere other than Malaysia (with which there are no duty-free restrictions), you can bring in 1 litre each of spirits, wine and beer duty-free; duty is payable on all tobacco.

Visitors to **Brunei** may bring in 200 cigarettes, 50 cigars or 250g of tobacco, and 60ml of perfume; non-Muslims over 17 can also import two bottles of liquor and twelve cans of beer for personal consumption (any alcohol brought into the country must be declared upon arrival).

Gay and lesbian travellers

Though Malaysia's largest cities, plus Singapore, have long had a discreet gay scene, the public profile of gays and lesbians was until recently still summed up by the old "don't ask, don't tell" maxim. However, cyberspace has helped galvanize gay people in both countries, providing a virtual refuge within which to socialize and campaign. Hitherto strait-laced **Singapore** (see p.546) now permits exploration of gay themes in the arts, hosts a well-attended annual gay rally and for a time even played host to very successful outdoor gay rave parties. While the environment in **Malaysia** is always going to be more conservative, the Malaysian government has no obvious appetite, Islamically inspired or otherwise, to clamp down on the existing, limited gay nightlife.

For all the general loosening up over the years, it's very much a case of two steps forward and one step back, however. In 2007, following an extraordinary parliamentary debate, Singapore MPs finally agreed to repeal **colonial-era laws** criminalizing anal and oral sex, though they retained the injunction on such activity between men. The same colonial legislation remains on the statute book in Malaysia, and what gay-related campaigning exists tends to be channelled into the relatively uncontentious issue of HIV and AIDS. Meanwhile, Singapore has consistently declined to give official recognition to its **gay lobby** group, People Like Us (Ⓦplu.sg). Needless to say, all this makes legal recognition of gay partnerships a distant prospect in either country.

This mixed picture shouldn't deter gay visitors from getting to know and enjoy the local scene, such as it is. A small number of gay establishments

> ### DRUGS: A WARNING
>
> In Malaysia, Singapore and Brunei, the possession of **illegal drugs** – hard or soft – carries a hefty prison sentence or even the death penalty. If you are arrested for drugs offences you can expect no mercy from the authorities and little help from your consular representatives. The simple advice, therefore, is not to have anything whatsoever to do with drugs in any of these countries. Never agree to carry anything through customs for a third party.

are reviewed in this Guide, and more listings are available on the Bangkok-based Ⓦutopia-asia.com.

Insurance

A typical travel insurance policy usually provides cover for the loss of bags, tickets and – up to a certain limit – cash or cheques, as well as cancellation or curtailment of your journey. Some policy premiums include dangerous sports; in Malaysia, for example, this can mean scuba diving, whitewater rafting or trekking (notably in the Maliau Basin of Sabah). Always ascertain whether medical coverage will be paid out as treatment proceeds or only after return home, and whether there's a 24-hour medical emergency number. When securing baggage cover, make sure that the per-article limit will cover your most valuable possession. If you need to make a claim, you should keep receipts for medicines and medical treatment, and in the event you have anything stolen, you must obtain an official statement from the police.

Internet

The explosion in the use of mobile devices and wi-fi at accommodation and eating places has put paid to many Malaysian **internet** cafés. Those that still exist tend to be found in malls or in upstairs premises along central streets; they charge a few ringgit an hour for internet access, but now make most of their money as gaming parlours.

If you like being online constantly as you travel, it's probably worth buying a local **SIM card** and getting a data plan with it; Tune Talk (see p.58), for example, currently offers a useful phone time/data plan.

Details of internet access in Singapore are given in the relevant chapter of this Guide (see p.528).

ROUGH GUIDES TRAVEL INSURANCE

Rough Guides has teamed up with WorldNomads.com to offer great travel insurance deals. Policies are available to residents of over 150 countries, with cover for a wide range of adventure sports, 24hr emergency assistance, high levels of medical and evacuation cover and a stream of travel safety information. Roughguides.com users can take advantage of their policies online 24/7, from anywhere in the world – even if you're already travelling. And since plans often change when you're on the road, you can extend your policy and even claim online. Roughguides.com users who buy travel insurance with WorldNomads.com can also leave a positive footprint and donate to a community development project. For more information go to Ⓦroughguides.com/insurance.

Laundry

Most Malaysian towns have laundries (*dobi*) where you can have clothes washed cheaply and quickly, according to weight (typically RM3 a kilo), picking them up later in the day or early the next day. Some hostels and guesthouses have washing machines that guests can use for a small charge. Dry-cleaning services are less common, though any hotel of a decent standard will be able to oblige.

Living in Malaysia and Singapore

Opportunities for non-residents to find short-term **employment** in Malaysia and Singapore are few and far between. On an unofficial basis, helpers are often required in guesthouses; the wages for such tasks are low, but board and lodging are often included. On a more formal level, both Singapore and KL in particular hold large communities of skilled expats with work permits, secured by their employer. In Malaysia expats can still expect elevated salaries, but this perk is increasingly rare in Singapore, where living standards are high enough as it is.

English-language-teaching qualifications are in demand by language schools in both countries, while qualified **diving instructors** can also find work in Malaysia. There are also a few **volunteer schemes**, mainly focusing on nature conservation fieldwork, though they're seldom cheap to join.

STUDY AND WORK PROGRAMMES

AFS Intercultural Programs Ⓦafs.org. Community service schemes in Malaysia.

Ape Malaysia Ⓦapemalaysia.com. Opportunities to do wildlife conservation work, and not just with orang-utans – they have projects at the Sun Bear Conservation Centre near Sandakan, for example.

Earthwatch Institute Ⓦearthwatch.org. A range of nature-conservation projects; past projects include bat conservation and climate-change studies in Malaysia.

Fulbright Program Ⓦmacee.org.my. Regular opportunities for US citizens to spend several months teaching English in rural Malaysia, without requiring teaching experience.

Turtle Conservation Society Ⓦturtleconservationsociety.org .my. Lists organizations offering volunteer conservation work schemes in Peninsular Malaysia.

Mail

Malaysia has a well-organized postal service operated by Pos Malaysia (❶1300 300 300, Ⓦpos .com.my), whose website details postage rates, express mail and courier ("PosLaju") services and so forth. Expect airmail delivery to take one to two weeks depending on the destination.

In **Brunei**, post offices are open Monday to Thursday and Saturday between 8am and 4.30pm, while some may open part of Friday as well. Postal services in **Singapore** are detailed in the Singapore chapter of the Guide (see p.551).

Maps

The best commercially available **maps** of Malaysia are the city and regional maps published by the Johor Bahru-based *World Express Mapping*, sold in many local bookshops. Online mapping offered by the usual internet giants tends to be littered with inaccuracies, especially with regard to Malaysian road names. Most Malaysian tourist offices have their own free maps of the local area, though these are often of poor quality and offer little that the maps in this Guide don't already include. Whichever maps you use, be aware that the high rate of highway construction and road alterations in rural and urban areas alike means that inaccuracies plague many maps almost as soon as they appear. Singapore maps are covered in the Singapore chapter of this Guide (see p.526).

Money

Malaysia's currency is the **ringgit** (pronounced *ring-git* and abbreviated to "RM"), divided into 100 sen. Notes come in RM1, RM5, RM10, RM20, RM50 and RM100 denominations. Coins are currently minted in 5 sen, 10 sen, 20 sen and 50 sen denominations, with 1 sen coins still in circulation. You sometimes hear the word "dollar" used informally to refer to the ringgit.

At the time of writing, the **exchange rate** was around RM3.3 to US$1 and RM5.2 to £1. Rates are posted daily in banks and exchange kiosks, and published in the press.

Singapore's currency is the **Singapore dollar**, written simply as $ (or S$ in this book to distinguish it from other dollars) and divided into 100 cents. Notes are issued in denominations of S$2, S$5, S$10, S$20, S$50 and S$100, with a couple of larger notes, rarely seen; coins come in denominations of 1, 5, 10, 20 and 50 cents, and S$1. At the time of writing, the **exchange rate** was around S$1.3 to US$1, S$2 to £1.

Brunei's currency, the **Brunei dollar**, is divided into 100 cents; you'll see it written as B$, or simply as $. The Brunei dollar has parity with the Singapore dollar and both are accepted by banks and larger businesses in either country. Notes come in B$1, B$5, B$10, B$50, B$100, B$500 and B$1000 denominations; coins come in denominations of 1, 5, 10, 20 and 50 cents.

Banks

Major banks in **Malaysia** include Maybank, HSBC, Citibank, Standard Chartered, RHB and CIMB. Banks in all sizeable towns and most tourist areas have ATMs; details are given throughout the Guide.

Licensed **moneychangers'** kiosks, found in bigger towns all over the country, tend to open later than banks, until around 6pm; some open at weekends and until 9pm, too. Some hotels will exchange money at all hours. Exchange rates tend to be more generous at moneychangers, though anyone still depending on travellers' cheques should note that moneychangers don't generally exchange them.

You're only likely to be really stuck for accessing money in remote rural areas; if, for example, you're travelling upriver through the interior of Sabah or Sarawak, it's a wise idea to carry a fair amount of cash, in smallish denominations.

Singapore banks are detailed in the relevant chapter of the Guide (see p.551). Banks represented in **Brunei** include the International Bank of Brunei, Citibank, Standard Chartered Bank and the Overseas Union Bank.

Plastic

Credit and debit cards have limited uses in the region, except to pay for goods and services in upmarket locations – you won't, for example, be able to use your Visa card at a local *kedai kopis*, though a café chain in Kuala Lumpur or Singapore will probably accept it, as indeed might a guesthouse in either place.

Opening hours and public holidays

In **Malaysia**, shops are open daily from around 9.30am to 7pm, though outlets in shopping centres and malls are typically open daily from 10am to 10pm. Government offices tend to work Monday to Friday from 8am to 4.15pm or 9am to 5pm, with an hour off for lunch, except on Friday when the break lasts from 12.15 to 2.45pm to allow Muslims to attend prayers. Banking hours are generally Monday to Friday 9.30am to 4pm and Saturday 9.30 to 11.30am (closed on every first and third Sat of the month), except in the states where Friday is the day off: Kedah, Perlis, Kelantan, Terengganu and to a lesser extent Johor. In these states, the working week runs from Sunday to Thursday, with Friday and Saturday as days off.

In **Singapore**, offices generally work Monday to Friday 8.30am to 5pm and sometimes on Saturday mornings. Shopping hours may vary (see p.548).

Brunei **banking hours** are Monday to Friday 9am to 3pm and Saturday 9 to 11am.

Opening hours for temples and mosques are given in the text of the Guide where they keep to a formal schedule (often not the case).

Public and school holidays

The list of 2015 public holiday dates (see opposite) is a guide only – government websites issue new lists for each year a few months in advance. Note that Muslim holidays (marked with an asterisk) move earlier by ten or eleven days each year, and that precise dates depend on the sighting of the new moon, which determines when each month of the Muslim calendar begins. Note also that each Malaysian state has its own additional holidays, which could be to do with its sultan's birthday or an Islamic (in states with a largely Muslim population) or tribal event, such as the *gawai* in June in Sarawak. Some of the holidays below are marked by special festivities (see p.45).

It pays to be aware of not just public holidays but also local **school holidays**, as Malaysian accommodation can be hard to come by during these periods. In Malaysia, schools get a week off in mid-March and late August, and two weeks off at the start of June, with a long break from mid-November to the end of the year. Singapore school breaks are almost identical, except that the June holiday lasts the whole month, and kids get a week off in early September rather than late August.

MALAYSIAN PUBLIC HOLIDAYS

January 1 New Year's Day
January 3 Birthday of the Prophet Muhammad*
February 19 & 20 Chinese New Year
May 1 Labour Day
May 3 Vesak Day
June 6 Yang Dipertuan Agong's Birthday
July 17 & 18 Hari Raya Aidilfitri*
August 31 National Day
September 16 Malaysia Day
September 24 & 25 Hari Raya Haji*
October 14 Maal Hijrah (the Muslim New Year)*
November 10 Deepavali
December 24 Birthday of the Prophet Muhammad*
December 25 Christmas Day

SINGAPOREAN PUBLIC HOLIDAYS

Note that Singapore has designated dates for Islamic festivals and does not adjust them to fit sightings of the new moon.
January 1 New Year's Day
February 19 & 20 Chinese New Year
April 3 Good Friday
May 1 Labour Day
June 1 Vesak Day
July 17 Hari Raya Puasa*
August 9 National Day
September 24 Hari Raya Haji*
November 10 Deepavali
December 25 Christmas Day

BRUNEI PUBLIC HOLIDAYS

Brunei observes the same Muslim festivals as Malaysia, plus New Year, Chinese New Year, Christmas and the following:
February 23 National Day
May 15 Israk Mikraj (the night when the Prophet ascended to heaven)*
May 31 Armed Forces' Day
June 18 First day of Ramadan*
July 13 Anniversary of Revelation of the Koran*
July 15 Sultan's Birthday

Phones

Malaysia, Singapore and Brunei all have a comprehensive **mobile network**. There are many outlets selling mobiles (known locally as "hand phones"), even in the smallest of towns. If your own phone is unlocked and GSM compatible (likely unless you're from the US), you can buy a local SIM card from corner shops and 7–Eleven stores, which will of course give you a new number. You can top up at the same outlets; you either get a receipt with a pin number on it for you to dial and activate the recharge, or the shop staff will do this for you.

Malaysia

Local calls are very cheap at just 10 sen for three minutes, but for long-distance calls, it can be more convenient to buy a **phonecard**, from service stations, 7–Eleven outlets and newsagents. Your best bet is to use a card such as iTalk (Ⓦ tm.com.my; from RM10), which enables you to make discounted calls from the line in your hotel room as well as from payphones.

The two big players in the **mobile phone** market are Hotlink/Maxis (Ⓦ hotlink.com.my) and Celcom (Ⓦ celcom.com.my), with the smaller DiGi (Ⓦ digi .com.my) and Tune Talk (Ⓦ tunetalk.com/my/) bringing up the rear. On the Peninsula you'll usually get a signal on both coasts, along highways and major roads, and on touristy islands. In the forested

---

INTERNATIONAL CALLS

To make international calls to any of the countries below, dial your international access code (Ⓣ 00 in Malaysia and Brunei, usually Ⓣ 001 in Singapore) then the relevant country code from the list, then the number (including any area code, but excluding any initial zero). From Singapore, you can call Malaysia by dialling Ⓣ 020, then the area code (omitting the initial zero), then the number.

IDD COUNTRY CODES

Australia Ⓣ 61
Brunei Ⓣ 673
Ireland Ⓣ 353
Malaysia Ⓣ 60
New Zealand Ⓣ 64
Singapore Ⓣ 65
South Africa Ⓣ 27
UK Ⓣ 44
US & Canada Ⓣ 1

interior, as a rule your phone will work in any town large enough to be served by express trains (as well as at the Taman Negara headquarters). Sabah and Sarawak coverage is much patchier, focusing on cities and the populated river valleys, though even in the Kelabit Highlands mobile calls are possible.

Mobile tariffs can be complex, though you can expect calls made to other Malaysian numbers to cost no more than RM0.50 per minute. At the time of. writing, Tune Talk had a SIM card specifically aimed at travellers, offering not only a small amount of talk time but also 500 megabytes of data for around RM35.

Singapore

Two rival companies, Singtel (Ⓦ singtel.com) and Starhub (Ⓦ starhub.com) dominate the mobile phone market in Singapore (and also sell phonecards for payphones). Their **SIM cards** (from S$10) are available from post offices and *7–Eleven* stores, though note that your passport will be scanned as a form of registration of any SIM purchase.

Local calls cost 10¢ per minute from a mobile (10¢ for three minutes from a payphone). The island has no area codes – the only time you'll punch more than eight digits for a local number is if you're dialling a toll-free (Ⓣ 1800) or special-rate (eg Ⓣ 1900) number. For directory enquiries, call Ⓣ 100 (Ⓣ 104 for international enquiries).

Brunei

International calls can be made from cardphones. To call collect, substitute Ⓣ 01 for the usual Ⓣ 00 international code, then dial the number as

---

though making an ordinary international call; this brings the number up on the operator's system. **Phonecards** start at $10 and can be bought from post offices. **SIM cards** can be obtained from outlets of the mobile provider DST Communications (Ⓦ dst-group.com).

Time

For administrative convenience, Malaysia, Singapore and Brunei are all eight hours ahead of Universal Time (GMT), all year. This close to the equator, you can rely on dawn being around 6.30am in the Peninsula and Singapore, dusk at around 7.30pm; in Borneo both happen roughly an hour earlier. Not taking into account daylight saving time elsewhere, the three countries are two hours behind Sydney, thirteen hours ahead of US Eastern Standard Time and sixteen hours ahead of US Pacific Standard Time.

Tipping

Tipping is seldom necessary in Malaysia, Singapore and Brunei. That said, when eating out at a proper restaurant, it's customary to tip if a service charge isn't included, though you are never required to tip in *kedai kopis* or *kopitiams*. It's not necessary to tip taxi drivers either, unless they have gone out of their way to be helpful. Otherwise you might want to offer a modest tip to a hotel porter or hairdresser, or a tour guide who has been exceptional.

Tourist information

Most Malaysian state capitals have a tourist office run by the national agency **Tourism Malaysia** (Ⓦ tourism.gov.my) and may boast a second tourist office, sometimes called the **Tourism Information Centre**, run by the state government; details are given in the Guide. Where these state-level tourist offices exist, they can be better informed than the local Tourism Malaysia branch. Unfortunately some Malaysian states have allowed their tourism efforts to wither away or else subcontracted them to well-connected travel agencies that may try to sell tour packages on the back of dealing with queries.

Whichever tourist office you deal with, bear in mind that staff always have plenty of glossy brochures to hand out, but their practical knowledge is often patchy – reflecting the hopelessly incoherent way information circulates in Malaysia. To find out about out-of-the-way attractions, you may be better off contacting local

---

OPERATOR AND DIRECTORY SERVICES

MALAYSIA
Business number online searches
Ⓦ yellowpages.com.my
Local directory enquiries Ⓣ 103
Operator-assisted calls (including international collect/reverse charge) Ⓣ 101

SINGAPORE
Business number online searches
Ⓦ yellowpages.com.sg
Local directory enquiries Ⓣ 100
Operator-assisted international calls
Ⓣ 104

BRUNEI
Local directory enquiries Ⓣ 113

accommodation – calling is best, as emails often elicit slow responses.

Of the **online sources**, Ⓦ virtualmalaysia.com is the tourism/networking portal of Malaysia's Ministry of Tourism, with coverage of sights, tourism-related directories and assorted packages on sale, while Ⓦ malaysiasite.nl, run by an enthusiastic Dutchman, provides thumbnail sketches of popular destinations around Malaysia, including some out-of-the-way locations. The practical information can be wildly out of date, though.

Singapore is another proposition altogether. A huge amount of generally reliable information on everything from bus times to museum exhibitions is available in print and online. Tourist information is put out by the **Singapore Tourism Board**, which has a comprehensive website (Ⓦ yoursingapore .com) and app, and operates several downtown **Visitor Centres** (see p.528). Brunei's official tourism website is Ⓦ bruneitourism.travel.

Travellers with disabilities

Of the three countries covered in this guide, **Singapore** is the most accessible to travellers with disabilities; tax incentives are provided for developers who include disabled access features into new buildings. In contrast, Malaysia and Brunei make few provisions.

Across the region, life is made a lot easier if you can afford the more upmarket hotels, which usually have disabled provision, and to shell out for taxis and the odd domestic flight. Similarly, the more expensive international airlines tend to be better equipped to get you there in the first place: MAS, British Airways, KLM, Singapore and Qantas all carry aisle wheelchairs and have at least one toilet adapted for disabled passengers. However, few tour operators in the region accommodate the needs of those with disabilities.

Singapore is certainly making a concerted effort to improve disabled provision: the **MRT** metro system has lifts on most, if not all, of its stations, and

some ninety bus routes have wheelchair-accessible vehicles, though these operate only at certain times of day (see Ⓦ sbstransit.com.sg for details). Most major **taxi** companies have accessible vehicles available to book, too.

In Malaysia, wheelchair users will have a hard time negotiating the uneven pavements in most towns and cities, and find it difficult to board buses, trains, ferries and the LRT metro system in Kuala Lumpur, none of which has been adapted for wheelchairs. The situation is similar if not worse in East Malaysia and Brunei, with little provision for disabled travellers.

CONTACTS FOR TRAVELLERS WITH DISABILITIES

Caring Fleet Ⓦ caringfleet.com. Transport services in Singapore for people with disabilities.

Disabled People's Association Singapore ☎ 6791 1134, Ⓦ dpa.org.sg. Nonprofit organization whose website has information on accessible taxis and local buildings.

Handicaps Welfare Association Ⓦ hwa.org.sg. Transport services for people with disabilities in Singapore.

Malaysian Confederation of the Disabled ☎ 03 7931 9038, Ⓦ dpi.org. A member of Disabled Peoples International, working for equal opportunities for disabled people in Malaysia.

Silveray Transport Services Ⓦ silveray.com.sg. Transport services for people with disabilities in Singapore; also tours within the city.

Travelling with children

Malaysia, Singapore and Brunei are very child-friendly countries in which to travel. Disposable nappies and powdered milk are easy to find (fresh milk is sold in supermarkets), and bland Chinese soups and rice dishes, or bakery products, are ideal for systems unaccustomed to spicy food. Many restaurants and the slicker *kedai kopis* have high chairs, though only upmarket hotels provide baby cots or a baby-sitting service. However, rooms in the cheaper hotels can usually be booked with an extra bed for little extra cost. Children under 12 get into many attractions for half-price and enjoy discounts on buses and trains.

Kuala Lumpur and around

66 Colonial district

70 Chinatown

72 Jalan TAR

74 Golden Triangle

78 Lake Gardens and around

82 Brickfields and KL Sentral

83 Arrival and departure

85 Getting around

88 Information

88 Accommodation

92 Eating

98 Drinking

99 Nightlife

100 Arts and entertainment

101 Shopping

103 Directory

104 Around Kuala Lumpur

KL SKYLINE

1

Kuala Lumpur and around

Founded at the head of the Klang Valley in the mid-nineteenth century, Kuala Lumpur – widely known as KL – has never had a coherent style. The earliest grand buildings around Merdeka Square, dating from the 1890s, are eccentric fusings of influences from across the British Empire, now overshadowed by soaring modern landmarks (notably the Petronas Towers) that wouldn't be out of place in Hong Kong or New York. This melange extends to the people too; attractions aside, you could spend a visit simply soaking up KL's excitingly diverse Malay, Chinese and Indian cultures: the conversations heard on the street, the huge range of food, and the profusion of onion-domed mosques, incense-infused Buddhist temples and colourful Hindu shrines.

A stay of a few days is enough to appreciate the best of KL's **attractions**, including the colonial core around **Merdeka Square** and the adjacent enclaves of **Chinatown** and **Little India**, plus, to the east, the restaurants, shops and nightlife of the so-called **Golden Triangle**, the modern heart of downtown KL. It can be equally rewarding just to take in the street life, in particular the boisterous **markets**, ranging from fish and produce markets stuffed into alleyways, via clothes and accessories stalls, to stands selling cooked food of every shape and description. Indeed, the capital offers some of the most exciting **cuisine** in the country, not only in the street markets but also in a plethora of restaurants to suit all tastes and budgets.

KL's hinterland has a number of worthwhile sights, too, among them the rugged limestone **Batu Caves**, which contain the country's most sacred Hindu shrine; **FRIM**, or the **Forest Research Institute of Malaysia**, with a treetop canopy walkway for a quick taste of the rainforest; **Kuala Selangor** and its magical fireflies; and the hard-to-reach birding hotspot of **Fraser's Hill**.

Brief history

KL was founded in 1857 when the ruler of Selangor State, Rajah Abdullah, sent a party of Chinese to prospect for **tin** deposits around the junction of the Gombak and Klang rivers. The pioneers duly discovered rich deposits 6km from the confluence near **Ampang** (east of the present-day city centre), which grew into a staging post for Chinese mine labourers. Unusually, the settlement acquired the name Kuala Lumpur ("muddy confluence") rather than, as convention dictated, being named after the lesser of the two rivers – KL should, by rights, have been called "Kuala Gombak".

At first, KL was little more than a wooden shantytown; small steamers could approach within 30km along Sungai Klang (River Klang), but the rest of the trip was either by shallow boat or through the jungle. Yet settlers poured in, seeking to tap the wealth of this unexplored region: British investors, Malay farmers, Chinese *towkays*

Kuala Lumpur's Moorish Style p.66
Kuala Lumpur International Airport: in-town check-in p.84
Travel agents and tour operators p.85
Touch 'n Go cards p.86
Jalan Alor: KL'S outdoor food haven p.94

Gay KL p.99
The FRIM–Batu caves–Orang Asli Museum circuit p.105
Thaipusam at the Batu Caves p.106
Firefly trips p.109
Communists on the hill p.110

JALAN ALOR

Highlights

❶ Petronas Towers Come to gawp at these surprisingly serene twin structures, then browse in one of KL's best shopping malls, just beneath. **See p.74**

❷ Menara KL Forget the Petronas Towers' Skybridge – this is the place for bird's-eye views of KL in all its messy glory. **See p.78**

❸ Islamic Arts Museum One of the most sophisticated museums in the capital, documenting Muslim cultures through arts and crafts. **See p.80**

❹ Eating KL has excellent restaurants offering cuisine from around the world, but it's the street food, notably at Jalan Alor, that's often the most memorable. **See p.92**

❺ Clubbing KL is Malaysia's party capital, home to some exceptional clubs that draw big-name DJs. **See p.99**

❻ Shopping Whether you prefer the bright lights of the state-of-the-art malls or the bustle of the city's endless street markets and bazaars, KL is a city made for shopping. **See p.101**

❼ Batu Caves A blend of spiritual destination and theme park, these limestone caves on the edge of KL house a Hindu temple complex and offer adventure caving explorations. **See p.105**

HIGHLIGHTS ARE MARKED ON THE MAP ON P.64

(merchants) and labourers. The Chinese also formed two **secret societies**, the fierce rivalry between which restrained the township's growth until the influential former miner **Yap Ah Loy** was appointed as Kapitan Cina, or Chinese headman, in 1869. Ah Loy brought law and order to the frontier town by ruthlessly making an example of criminals, parading them through the streets on a first offence and executing them if they re offended twice. He led the rebuilding of KL after it was razed during the **Selangor Civil War** (1867–73) and personally bore much of the cost of a second rebuilding after a devastating fire in 1881.

The British Resident of Selangor State, **Frank Swettenham**, had most of KL's remaining wooden huts demolished in the 1880s and imported **British architects** from India to design solid, grand edifices suitable for a new capital. By 1887 the city had five hundred brick buildings, and eight times that number in the early 1900s, by which time KL had also become capital of the **Federated Malay States**.

The early twentieth century

Development continued steadily in the first quarter of the twentieth century, during which time Indians from Tamil Nadu swelled the population. Catastrophic floods in 1926 inspired a major engineering project that straightened the course of Sungai Klang, confining it within reinforced, raised banks. By the time the **Japanese invaded** the Peninsula in December 1941, the commercial zone around Chinatown had grown to eclipse the original colonial area, and the *towkays*, enriched by the rubber boom, were already installed in opulent townhouses along today's Jalan Tuanku Abdul Rahman and Jalan Ampang. While the city suffered little physical damage during World War II, the Japanese inflicted terrible brutality on their historic enemies, the Chinese (at least five thousand of whom were killed in the first few weeks of the occupation alone), and sent thousands of Indians to Burma to build the infamous railway, of whom very few survived. At the same time, the Japanese ingratiated themselves with certain Malays by suggesting that loyalty to the occupiers would be rewarded with independence after the war.

Following the **Japanese surrender** in September 1945, the British found that nationalist demands had replaced the Malays' former acceptance of the colonizers, while many Chinese felt alienated by talk that a future Malay government would deny them full citizenship. The ensuing Communist-inspired **Emergency** (see p.563) left KL relatively unscathed, but the atmosphere in the city was tense. These issues finally came to a head in KL's May 1969 **race riots**, in which at least two hundred people lost their lives, though things calmed down rapidly after the imposition of a state of emergency.

Recent times

In 1974 KL was plucked from the bosom of Selangor State and designated **Wilayah Persekutuan** (Federal Territory), an administrative zone in its own right; **Shah Alam**, west along the Klang Valley, replaced it as Selangor's capital. After a period of consolidation, KL and the rest of the Klang Valley, including KL's satellite new town of **Petaling Jaya**, became a thriving conurbation in the 1990s. That decade, and the early part of the new millennium, saw the realization of several huge infrastructural ventures that are part and parcel of local life today – KL's international **airport** and the **Formula One racetrack**, both at Sepang in the far south of Selangor; the **Petronas Towers** and the attendant **KLCC** shopping development; the various urban **rail systems** across the city; and **Putrajaya**, the government's administrative hub off to the south (though KL remains the legislative centre and seat of parliament). The transformation of swathes of KL and much of Selangor is less dramatic today, but still proceeds apace – not least in the ongoing construction of the **Klang Valley MRT rail network** – and concerns are being voiced over the potential strain on water resources and other environmental repercussions.

Today, while for visitors KL is a noticeably sociable and safe place, many Malaysians have mixed feelings about their capital. The city is second only to Singapore in regional economic clout, but it's undeniable that untrammelled development has bequeathed ess buildings, follies and terrible traffic snarl-ups, which some locals because KL offers them good money and experience before they retire l provincial village. Conversely, others feel that it has been their salvation, n the country where they can explore their artistic or spiritual identity.

Kuala Lumpur

Rather than a discernible city centre, Kuala Lumpur has several hubs of activity. Close to the rivers' original "muddy confluence", the former **colonial district** and its distinctive architecture surrounds **Merdeka Square** – don't miss the informative **Textile Museum** here – with the busy tourist hub of **Chinatown** just southeast. In between the two lie the attractive old **Jamek Mosque** and the craft cornucopia that is **Central Market**. Worthwhile forays can be made north to **Little India's** more locals-oriented shops and altogether grittier **Chow Kit Market**.

Some 2km east, the **Golden Triangle** presents the city's modern face, lively **Bukit Bintang** packed with upmarket hotels, restaurants and designer shopping malls. Overlooking it to the north is the tall, strikingly modernist **Petronas Towers**; visitors flock to the skybridge here, though in fact the westerly **Menara KL Tower**, poking out of wooded Bukit Nanas, has better views.

Southwest of the centre – and tricky to reach across one of KL's many pedestrian-unfriendly traffic flows – a clutch of worthwhile sights surround the green and airy **Lake Gardens**, notably **Masjid Negara**, one of the country's largest mosques, and the excellent **Islamic Arts Museum**. Below here, the **National Museum** is not as good as it could be, while **Brickfields** is another strongly Indian district, worth a peek for its day-to-day residential street life.

Colonial district

Pasar Seni or Masjid Jemak LRT; Kuala Lumpur KTM

The small **colonial district** that developed around the confluence of the Gombak and Klang rivers in the 1880s, is the area of KL that best retains its historic character. At its heart on the west bank of the Klang, the beautifully tended open padang (field) of **Merdeka Square** is where on August 31, 1957, Malaysia's first prime minister, Tuanku Abdul Rahman, hauled down the British flag and declared *merdeka*, or independence. The 95m-high **flagpole** to the south is supposedly the tallest in the world, and the tiled square below is a popular spot for people to gather in the evenings.

Royal Selangor Club

On the western side of Merdeka Square, the **Royal Selangor Club**, founded in 1884, was the British elite's favourite watering hole, popularly known as the "Spotted Dog"

KUALA LUMPUR'S MOORISH STYLE

KL's colonial "look" originated with **Charles Edwin Spooner**, the state engineer, and architect **Anthony Norman**, who in the 1890s fused a Neoclassical Renaissance style – then the standard for government buildings throughout the British Empire – with "Eastern" motifs, which were felt to be more appropriate for an Islamic country. This **Moorish style**, however, characterized by onion domes, cupolas, colonnades, arched windows and wedding-cake plasterwork, owed more to Indian Moghul architecture than wooden Malay structures. Buildings by Norman in this mould include the **Sultan Abdul Samad Building**, the old Post Office next door, and the Textile Museum further south. Norman was succeeded in 1903 by **A.B. Hubback**, who had actually lived in India and so smoothly continued the Moorish theme in the Jamek Mosque, old Kuala Lumpur train station and elsewhere.

after a former Dalmatian mascot. It was here on 30 November, 1938, that **Albert Gispert** and fellow drinkers at the club's *Hash House* bar organized a weekly cross-country run; thus the now international **Hash House Harriers** were born. The original KL group, respectfully regarded as the mother of all hashing groups, is still in existence (⊛motherhash.com). Closed to non-members, the club's history outweighs the appeal of its facade, an oversized 1970s mock-Tudor affair that replaced a 1910 structure built by A.B. Hubback after the original burned down.

To the north, the Anglican **St Mary's Cathedral** (1894), usually open in the daytime, welcomed the city's European inhabitants every Sunday before they repaired to the club.

National Textile Museum

26 Jalan Sultan Hishamuddin • Daily 9am–6pm • Free • ☎ 03 2694 3457, ⊛ muziumtekstilnegara.gov.my

Housed in an elegant Moghul-Islamic building dating back to 1905, KL's **National Textile Museum** traces the trends and development of textiles that have characterized and shaped the lifestyles of the people of Malaysia. With **four galleries** on two floors, it takes more than an hour to do the fairly dense collection justice – though the highlights can be skimmed over in far less time.

On the ground floor, the **Pohon Budi Gallery** focuses on the evolution of textiles from prehistory to modern times and the different weaving techniques adopted in Malaysia. Displays include fine double *ikat* textiles, a technique introduced from India in the eighteenth century, along with traditional equipment and paraphernalia for weaving, embroidery, batik making and beadwork. The adjacent **Pelangi Gallery** displays textiles from Malaysia's multiethnic communities, including Chinese and Baba Nyonya silk and brocades, the elaborate embroidered textiles of Sabah and handwoven *ikat* and *songket* of Sarawak. Look out for Sarawak's Iban *pua kumbu* blankets decorated with motifs of crocodiles and wild plants.

Upstairs, the **Teluk Beranti Gallery** is dedicated to Malay textiles, especially iridescent *songket* and *limar* cloth, which incorporates fine gold thread into its almost sarong-like patterns. There are several pieces of splendid *berayat*, or scripted cloths, with brocade woven into the design in Arabic. The final **Ratna Sari Gallery** departs into ceremonial metalwork for jewellery and personal adornments, including finely chased filigree tobacco boxes, golden anklets worn by Malay and Peranakan women in the early nineteenth century, and a small case of flame-bladed *kris* daggers and Iban head-hunting machetes from Sarawak.

Jamek Mosque (Masjid Jamek)

Entrance on Jalan Tun Perak • Sat–Thurs 8.30am–12.30pm & 2.30–4pm, Fri 3–4pm • Free

East of Merdeka Square, across the river, Lebuh Pasar Besar connects the colonial district with the more frenetic life of the old commercial district. Just north of the river bridge is the **Jamek Mosque**, on a promontory at the confluence of the Klang and Gombak rivers, pretty much where the first tin prospectors built their shacks in the 1850s. Part of the second great period of expansion in KL, the mosque was completed in 1909 by Hubback, its attractive pink brick walls and arched colonnades topped by oval cupolas and squat minarets. There's an intimacy here lacking at the modern, much larger Masjid Negara to the south, and the grounds, bordered by palms, are a pleasant place to sit and rest – though the best view of the mosque is from over the Klang at the base of the HSBC building on Jalan Benteng.

Central Market (Pasar Seni)

Jalan Hang Kasturi • Daily 10am–10pm • ☎ 1300 228688, ⊛ centralmarket.com.my

The Art Deco **Central Market** is housed in a blue and white brick hangar that was built in the 1920s as the capital's wet market. The butchers and fishmongers have long since left for places like Chow Kit and the back alleys of nearby Chinatown, however, and the market was converted in the mid-1980s into what's known as **Pasar**

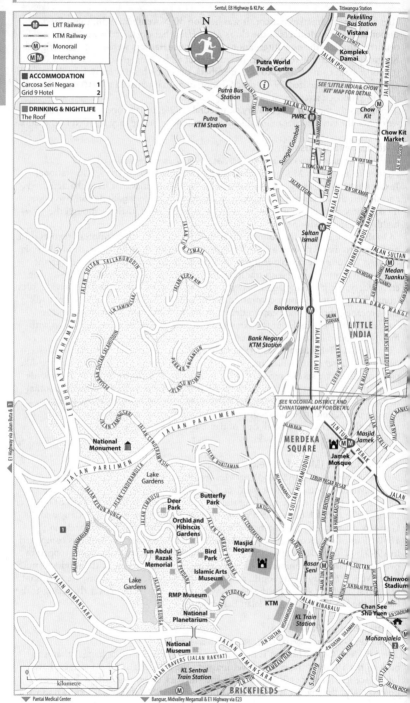

1

Sentul, E8 Highway & KLPac

Titiwangsa Station

Pekeliling
Bus Station

Vistana

Kompleks
Damai

Putra World
Trade Centre

Putra Bus
Station

The Mall

Chow
Kit

Putra
KTM Station

PWRC

Chow Kit
Market

SEE 'LITTLE INDIA & CHOW
KIT' MAP FOR DETAIL

Sultan
Ismail

Medan
Tuanku

Bandaraya

LITTLE
INDIA

Bank Negara
KTM Station

SEE 'COLONIAL DISTRICT AND
CHINATOWN' MAP FOR DETAIL

National
Monument

MERDEKA
SQUARE

Masjid
Jamek

Jamek
Mosque

Lake
Gardens

Deer
Park

Butterfly
Park

Orchid and
Hibiscus
Gardens

Masjid
Negara

Tun Abdul
Razak
Memorial

Bird
Park

Islamic Arts
Museum

Pasar
Seni

Chinwoo
Stadium

Chan See
Shu Yuen

Lake
Gardens

RMP Museum

KTM

National
Planetarium

KL Train
Station

Maharajalela

National
Museum

JALAN TRAVERS (JALAN RAKYAT)

KL Sentral
Train Station

BRICKFIELDS

- M — LRT Railway
- M — KTM Railway
- M — Monorail
- MM — Interchange

ACCOMMODATION

Carcosa Seri Negara	1
Grid 9 Hotel	2

DRINKING & NIGHTLIFE

The Roof	1

0 _____ 1
kilometre

Pantai Medical Center

Bangsar, Midvalley Megamall & E1 Highway via E23

E1 Highway via Jalan Buta & [1]

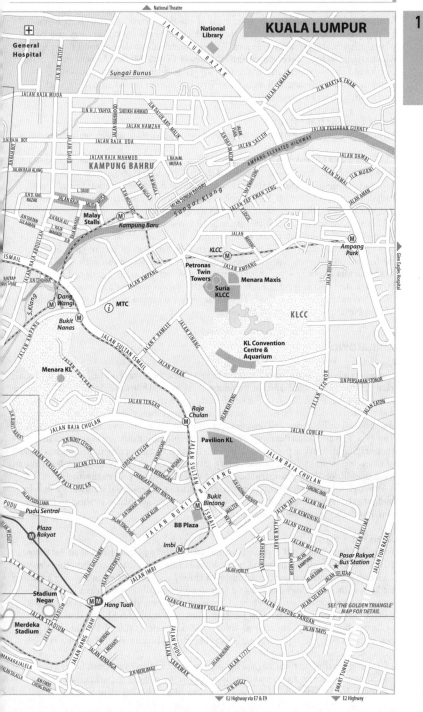

KUALA LUMPUR

1

Seni, meaning "art market". In fact, most of the shops now sell souvenirs: Royal Selangor pewter, specialist antique shops, Malay regional crafts, carvings and batiks, plus clothes, sarongs, silverware and T-shirts; there's also a decent food court upstairs. Most artists, in fact, have moved into the newer **Central Market Annexe** immediately north, and the pavement in between is clogged with their enthusiastic – if unmemorable – canvases. Blatantly touristy, the market is also enjoyable, with a lively atmosphere in the evenings.

Kuala Lumpur train station

Best reached south from Central Market along Jalan Tun Sambanthan, over the river and past the post office, then via the footbridge to the station

One of the city's best-known colonial buildings, **Kuala Lumpur train station** – now a stop on the KTM lines – was completed in 1911 by A.B. Hubback. As with his Jamek Mosque, its meshing spires, minarets and arches reflect his inspiration from North Indian Islamic architecture. Inside, the main platforms sit under an airy, light vault of fine ironwork, recalling those of Victorian stations in London.

Although the station is architecturally linked to similar-vintage buildings around Merdeka Square, feverish traffic makes it difficult to reach on foot from there. For the best view of the facade, you'll need to get across to the western side of Jalan Sultan Hishamuddin. Conveniently, a pedestrian subway links the station with the **KTM headquarters** opposite – yet another attractive Moorish structure designed by Hubback, finished around the same time as the station and actually more imposing than its counterpart. From the KTM headquarters it's a few minutes' walk to either Masjid Negara or the National Museum.

Chinatown

Pasar Seni LRT

Spreading out southeast from Central Market, **Chinatown** was KL's original commercial kernel, dating from the arrival of the first traders in the 1860s. Bordered by Jalan Sultan to the east, Jalan Tun Perak to the north and Jalan Maharajalela to the south, the area had reached its current extent by the late nineteenth century, with southern Chinese shophouses, coffee shops and temples springing up along narrow streets such as Jalan Tun H.S. Lee and **Jalan Petaling**. Though the shophouses today are fairly workaday, it is encouraging that many period buildings are being refurbished despite recurrent threats of redevelopment; in 2011, public outcry saved a row of old shophouses on **Jalan Sultan** from demolition during construction of the ongoing Klang Valley railway.

Although Chinatown scores more on atmosphere than essential sights, it's a hub for **budget accommodation**, and holds a wealth of inexpensive places to shop and eat, so you'll probably spend some time here.

Jalan Petaling

For locals and visitors alike, pedestrianized **Jalan Petaling** (still often called **Petaling Street**) is very much Chinatown's main draw. Home to brothels and gambling dens in KL's early years, these days it's a gauntlet of closely packed market stalls doing a roaring trade in selling clothing, watches and fake designer handbags to tourists from late morning until well into the evening. Check goods thoroughly for workmanship – stitching especially – and bargain hard; in truth, you might find better deals in ordinary shops nearby. The narrow lanes parallel and either side of Petaling host grittier **wet markets** too, and a popular early morning bric-a-brac market, selling everything from old clothes to mobile phones.

Crossing Petaling at right angles, the eastern end of **Jalan Hang Lekir** hosts a slew of good, inexpensive restaurants and stalls selling *ba kwa* (slices of pork, given a sweet marinade and grilled), local fruits and molasses-like herbal brews in tureens.

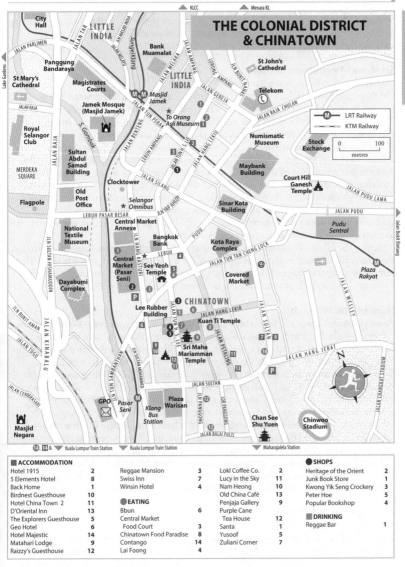

THE COLONIAL DISTRICT & CHINATOWN

1

ACCOMMODATION						
Hotel 1915	2	Reggae Mansion	3	Lokl Coffee Co.	2
5 Elements Hotel	8	Swiss Inn	7	Lucy in the Sky	11
Back Home	1	Winsin Hotel	4	Nam Heong	10
Birdnest Guesthouse	10			Old China Café	13
Hotel China Town 2	11	**EATING**		Penjaja Gallery	9
D'Oriental Inn	13	Bbun	6	Purple Cane	
The Explorers Guesthouse	5	Central Market		Tea House	12
Geo Hotel	6	Food Court	3	Santa	1
Hotel Majestic	14	Chinatown Food Paradise	8	Yusoof	5
Matahari Lodge	9	Contango	14	Zuliani Corner	7
Raizzy's Guesthouse	12	Lai Foong	4		

SHOPS	
Heritage of the Orient	2
Junk Book Store	1
Kwong Yik Seng Crockery	3
Peter Hoe	5
Popular Bookshop	4

DRINKING	
Reggae Bar	1

Chan See Shu Yuen

Southern end of Jalan Petaling • Daily 8.30am–5pm • Free

The largest of Chinatown's several Chinese shrines, **Chan See Shu Yuen** was founded at the turn of the twentieth century. It's not actually a temple (though it looks like one), but rather a clan hall for families with the very common name of Chan – also transliterated Chen and Tan. A classic of southern Chinese architecture, the eaves are decorated in a riot of three-dimensional ceramic friezes depicting events in Chinese history and mythology; inside the green walls are a series of courtyards and halls, with the inner shrine covered in scenes of lions, dragons and mythical creatures battling with warriors. Most engaging of all are the two gentleman figurines on the altar, representing ancestors of the clan or possibly their servants – and wearing Western top hats to indicate their link with the colonial past.

Sri Maha Mariamman Temple

Jalan Tun H.S. Lee • Daily 24hr • Free, small donation appreciated

Oddly perhaps, one of KL's main Hindu shrines, the **Sri Maha Mariamman Temple**, is located in the heart of Chinatown. The earliest shrine on the site was built in 1873 by Tamil immigrants and named after the Hindu deity, Mariamman, whose intercession was sought to provide protection against sickness and "unholy incidents". In the case of the Tamils, who had arrived to build the railways or work on the plantations, they needed all the solace they could find from the appalling rigours of their working life.

Significant rebuilding of the temple took place in the 1960s, when sculptors from India were commissioned to design idols to adorn the five tiers of the multicoloured, 22.9m-high gate tower – these now shine with gold embellishments, precious stones and exquisite Spanish and Italian tiles. Garland-makers sell their wares outside the entrance, while above it is a hectic profusion of Hindu gods, painted in realistic colours and frozen in dozens of scenes from the *Ramayana*.

During the Hindu **Thaipusam** festival, the temple's golden chariot is paraded through the streets on its route to the Batu Caves, on the city's northern edge (see p.105). The rest of the year, the chariot is kept in a large room in the temple; you might be able to persuade an attendant to unlock the door and let you have a peek.

Numismatic Museum

Maybank Building, where Jalan Tun Perak and Jalan Tun Tan Cheng Lock converge at the Puduraya intersection • Daily 10am–6pm • Free

Designed in the late 1980s by Hijjas Kasturi, the **Maybank Building**, on Chinatown's northeastern edge, is typical of the new KL, with a tall white facade designed with Islamic principles of purity in mind. On the lobby floor, the small, unusually interesting **Numismatic Museum** kicks off with tin ingots, gold dust and bars of silver and, for what the caption describes as "ordinary people", cowrie shells, rice and beads – all formerly used for transactions in the region. Coins were introduced with the arrival of the colonizing powers; early sixteenth-century Portuguese examples here are delicately engraved with miniatures of the Malay Peninsula and tiny kites billowing in the air. The first mass-produced coins, issued by the British East India Company, bore the company's coat of arms – a practice echoed later by timber and rubber companies, who until the late eighteenth century minted tokens to pay their expanding labour pool. During the Japanese invasion, the occupying administration produced its own banknotes which, after the Japanese surrender, the British diligently collected and stamped "not legal tender".

Court Hill Ganesh Temple

9 Jalan Pudu Lama • Daily 6am–8.30pm • Free

East of the Maybank Building and hidden up a small lane, **Court Hill Ganesh Temple** is KL's second most important Hindu shrine, dating to 1897 and reputedly founded by a gardener – which may explain why there's a **tree** growing beside the building. Being dedicated to the elephant-headed Lord Ganesh, who specializes in the removal of all obstacles to prosperity, peace and success, the temple was understandably popular with visitors on their way to KL's original law courts, which were once located nearby.

Jalan TAR

On foot from Chinatown, it takes around 1hr to reach Chow Kit via Little India along Jalan TAR; the LRT, Monorail and buses also traverse the area

Running north from Chinatown, **Jalan Tuanku Abdul Rahman** – universally abbreviated to **Jalan TAR** – brings you within reach of a series of small-scale, local neighbourhoods, somewhat unexpected in such a large city. First is **Little India**, a bustling commercial district renowned for fabrics, especially saris and *songket*s, as well as jewellery. The clothing theme persists immediately west, where Gulati's Silk House and the SOGO department store stock everything from saris to brand-name outdoor gear. There are also some fine 1920s Neoclassical and Art Deco buildings, including the dove-grey **Coliseum Cinema**, screening Indian releases, and the adjacent **Coliseum Bar** (at no. 98). Once a favourite watering hole with British rubber plantation owners, its interior can't have been decorated since Independence, and the clientele look of similar vintage. Drop in for the atmosphere and a cold beer rather than the food, which is very ordinary.

Beyond here, **Chow Kit Market** is somewhere to find bargain clothing and local produce, while **Kampung Bahru**, off to the east of Jalan TAR, is a low-key enclave of Malay housing. There are no major sights, but a visit adds depth to KL's character, and all three have excellent eating opportunities.

Little India

Masjid Jamek or Bandaraya LRT

East off the lower end of Jalan TAR, **Little India** is a commercial centre for KL's Indian community, though these days it is being eclipsed by Brickfields (see p.82). Only a few steps north from the Masjid Jamek LRT station, **Jalan Melayu** holds Indian stores, some selling excellent *burfi* and other sweet confections; its name derives from the former Malay community here. Approaching **Jalan Masjid India**, you encounter a popular covered market, smaller but otherwise similar to Chinatown's Jalan Petaling. Further up is **Masjid India** itself, an Indian-influenced affair dating from the 1960s and tiled in cream and brown.

A few minutes further along the street, you come to a little square, to the right (east) of which you'll find plenty of *kedai kopis* and, come evening, street vendors selling food; turn off to the left to reach Lorong Tuanku Abdul Rahman, whose northern end is dominated by a **night market**, busiest at weekends. Mainly Malay-run, the stalls sell both food and eclectic bits and pieces, from T-shirts to trinkets. Just past here, Madras and Semua are two huge haberdasheries, packed to their roofs with **Indian textiles**.

Chow Kit

Chow Kit Monorail; bus #16, #41, #43, #50 from Lebuh Pudu by Central Market, or almost any bus from Jalan Raja Laut, west of Little India

Chow Kit district, 1.5km north of Little India, is mostly known for the sprawling, busy **Chow Kit Market**, which fills the lanes east off Jalan TAR. It's one of KL's busiest, in-your-face produce markets, a tight, overcrowded grid of alleyways under low-slung awnings. Stalls sell everything fit to put in your mouth: bulk tropical fruits at bargain prices, live and dismembered fish and poultry, hunks and haunches of various animals, and piles of fresh or dried vegetables and fungi. Hawkers around the edge sell freshly cooked snacks too, many with a definite Indonesian slant.

Chow Kit is also a good place to buy **secondhand clothes** (sometimes called "*baju* bundle"). The best deals are west of Jalan TAR along Jalan Haji Taib, where you may chance upon items like Levi's 501s in reasonable condition and at prices that are almost too good to be true – starting from RM20 a pair. The market runs for much of the day and into the evening, but note that some locals prefer to give Chow Kit a wide berth after dark, as it's also something of a red-light area; even during the day the area can be pretty sketchy.

Kampung Bahru

Kampung Baru LRT

If you've time on your hands and enjoy a wander, head 1km east from Chow Kit (along either Jalan Raja Bot or Jalan Raja Alang) into **Kampung Bahru**, one of the Peninsula's several designated Malay reserve areas – land that only people whose ID defines them as ethnic Malays can own, and indeed with its own status in law, not under the direct control of the KL city council. Though the Petronas Towers are visible off to the south,

1

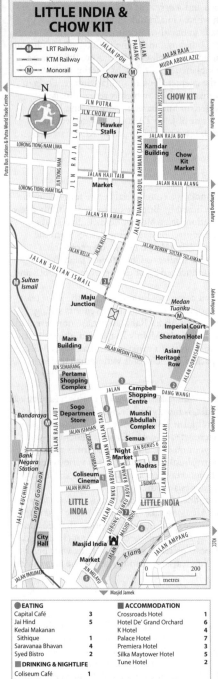

LITTLE INDIA & CHOW KIT

EATING
Capital Café	3
Jai Hind	5
Kedai Makanan Sithique	1
Saravanaa Bhavan	4
Syed Bistro	2

DRINKING & NIGHTLIFE
Coliseum Café	1

ACCOMMODATION
Crossroads Hotel	1
Hotel De' Grand Orchard	6
K Hotel	4
Palace Hotel	7
Premiera Hotel	3
Silka Maytower Hotel	5
Tune Hotel	2

Kampung Bahru's quiet lanes and painted wooden bungalows with gardens – not to mention chickens wandering the pavements – lend it a distinct village feel. Sadly, plans to "redevelop" the district may well involve wholesale demolitions.

Despite its proximity, you can't walk southeast to KLCC from here, owing to the riverside expressway.

Golden Triangle

The heart of modern KL, the **Golden Triangle** is a sprawling area bounded to its north by **Jalan Ampang**, and to the west by Chinatown and Sungai (River) Klang. Many visitors make a beeline for **KLCC** (Kuala Lumpur City Centre; ⊕klcc.com.my), a group of huge developments surrounding the bland KLCC Park, on a site once home to the Selangor Turf Club. The chief attractions here are the **Petronas Towers**, soaring above one of KL's best malls, **Suria KLCC**, and the city's glossy **aquarium**.

Further south, the Golden Triangle's other magnet is **Bukit Bintang** ("Star Hill"), home to upmarket and workaday malls, many of KL's best hotels and restaurants, and some engaging street life. East, **Kompleks Budaya Kraf** is the city's largest handicrafts gallery, while northwest lies **Bukit Nanas**, a forested hill where the **Menara KL** communications tower affords great views of the city.

Petronas Towers

Tues–Sun 9am–9pm, Fri closed 1–2.30pm • RM80; 1000 passes/day issued at the base of Tower 2 from 8.30am onwards, usually sold out by 11am; the easiest approach is to buy tickets online • ☎ 03 2331 8080, ⊕ petronastwintowers.com.my

Very much the symbol of modern Malaysia, the twin columns of the **Petronas Towers** rise 451.9m above KL's downtown, completely dwarfing the enormous **Suria KLCC mall** at their base. When they were completed in 1998, as the headquarters of the state-owned oil company Petronas, many questioned whether the US$1.6 billion price tag was an unwarranted drain on the Malaysian economy, but the tapering steel-clad structures (designed by the Argentinean architect Cesar Pelli) are a stunning piece of architecture. Despite a definite Art Deco feel, the unusual eight-pointed cross-sectional profile obviously draws on Islamic art, while the profusion of squares and circles on the interior walls symbolize harmony and strength. The project is also permeated by Chinese numerology in that the towers have 88 floors and the postcode 59088 – eight being a very auspicious number for the Chinese.

One tower was built by a Japanese team, the other by rivals from Korea; while the Japanese topped out first, the Koreans had the honour of engineering the **skybridge**, which joins the towers at both the 41st and 42nd floors. The **views** of KL's sprawl from the skybridge are pretty spectacular, thanks not least to the blue, glassy towers soaring either side of you – but they're not as good as from the **Observation Deck** on Level 86.

Aquarium

KLCC Complex, accessed by a long pedestrian underpass from Suria KLCC • Daily 10.30am–8pm, last tickets sold at 7pm; feeding times on website, book shark scuba dives via website • RM50 • ⓦ aquariaklcc.com

KL's **aquarium** is housed within the sizeable **KL Convention Centre**, which sits on the southern edge of KLCC. It's expensive, and labelling is occasionally lost in the muted lighting, but some sections are wonderful. Prime examples include the well-lit **Living Reef** tank, packed with multicoloured, multiform anemones and corals, which will help you make sense of the riches on view at the Perhentians and elsewhere, and the **Flooded Forest** tank, with its pair of hefty, 2m-long Amazonian arapaima freshwater fish. It also holds electric eels, otters and even piranhas, but the *pièce de résistance* is the vast **Living Ocean** tank, traversed on a moving walkway through a transparent tunnel, replete with sand tiger sharks, octopus and huge rays.

Bukit Bintang

Bukit Bintang Monorail

For tourists and locals alike, **Bukit Bintang** – the broad corridor either side of **Jalan Bukit Bintang** – is one of the best spots in town for a wander. There's a **mall** here to suit everyone: the gigantic, massively modern Pavilion KL and Berjaya Times Square, both packed with international chains and designer outlets; posh Starhill Gallery, with an exclusive, snazzy Art Deco feel; the more casually modest Lot 10 Mall and BB Plaza, and surprisingly bland Farenheit 88; and the glib, claustrophobic and slightly shifty Imbi Plaza. The southwestern end of Jalan Bukit Bintang is lined with royal palms and inexpensive clothing shops – and a few too many touts hissing "massage, woman, sexy massage" at passers-by – while the pavement around the Lot 10 Mall has evolved into **Bintang Walk**, home to a parade of smart cafés. By night the centre of attention, at least as regards dining, switches to nearby **Jalan Alor**, which boasts some great alfresco Chinese eating. Close by, Changkat Bukit Bintang and Tengkat Tong Shin hold more excellent restaurants, serving differing cuisines.

Kompleks Kraf

Sekseyen 63, Jalan Conlay, just south of KLCC • **Crafts centre and Museum** Daily 10am–6pm Museum Daily 9am–5pm • RM3 • ☎ 03 2162 7533, ⓦ kraftangan.gov.my

The sprawl of Malay-style buildings housing **Kompleks Kraf** offers a good opportunity to see excellent examples of Malaysia's crafts in one place – including carved wooden boxes, modern textiles and woven baskets – and to do some serious souvenir shopping. Their small, well-presented **museum** is also worth a quick browse to explore the intricacies of the weaving, tie-dyeing and batik processes, *keris* casting, and Malay kite construction.

Badan Warisan

2 Jalan Stonor • Mon–Sat 10am–5pm; guided house tours daily 11am & 3pm (45min) • Free; minimum donation for tours RM10 • ☎ 03 2144 9273, ⓦ badanwarisan.org.my

Badan Warisan, Malaysia's architecture conservation trust, campaigns to preserve the rich heritage of shophouses, temples and colonial buildings that developers and many

1

THE GOLDEN TRIANGLE

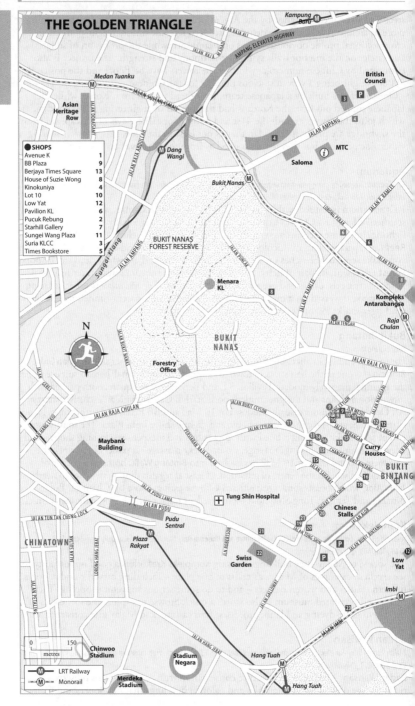

SHOPS	
Avenue K	1
BB Plaza	9
Berjaya Times Square	13
House of Suzie Wong	8
Kinokuniya	4
Lot 10	10
Low Yat	12
Pavilion KL	6
Pucuk Rebung	2
Starhill Gallery	7
Sungei Wang Plaza	11
Suria KLCC	3
Times Bookstore	5

Kampung Baru

British Council

Asian Heritage Row

Medan Tuanku

Dang Wangi

Bukit Nanas

MTC

Saloma

Kompleks Antarabangsa

Raja Chulan

BUKIT NANAS FOREST RESERVE

Menara KL

BUKIT NANAS

Forestry Office

Maybank Building

Curry Houses

BUKIT BINTANG

Tung Shin Hospital

Chinese Stalls

Pudu Sentral

CHINATOWN

Plaza Rakyat

Swiss Garden

Low Yat

Imbi

0 150
metres

Chinwoo Stadium

Stadium Negara

Merdeka Stadium

Hang Tuah

LRT Railway
Monorail

1

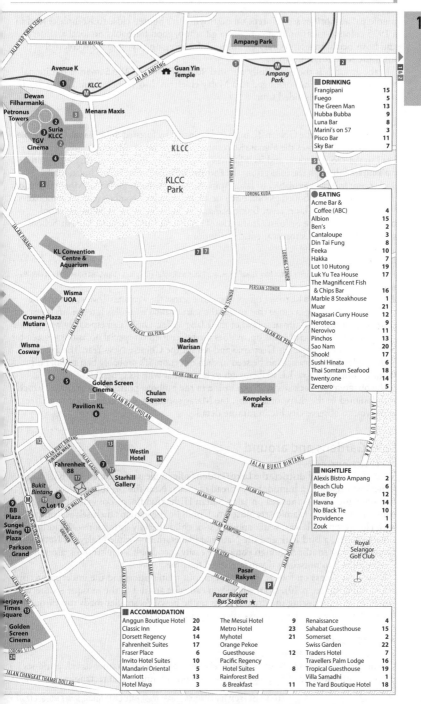

DRINKING

Frangipani	15
Fuego	5
The Green Man	13
Hubba Bubba	9
Luna Bar	8
Marini's on 57	3
Pisco Bar	11
Sky Bar	7

EATING

Acme Bar &	
Coffee (ABC)	4
Albion	15
Ben's	2
Cantaloupe	3
Din Tai Fung	8
Feeka	10
Hakka	7
Lot 10 Hutong	19
Luk Yu Tea House	17
The Magnificent Fish	
& Chips Bar	16
Marble 8 Steakhouse	1
Muar	21
Nagasari Curry House	12
Neroteca	9
Nerovivo	11
Pinchos	13
Sao Nam	20
Shook!	17
Sushi Hinata	6
Thai Somtam Seafood	18
twenty.one	14
Zenzero	5

NIGHTLIFE

Alexis Bistro Ampang	2
Beach Club	6
Blue Boy	12
Havana	14
No Black Tie	10
Providence	1
Zouk	4

ACCOMMODATION

Anggun Boutique Hotel	20	The Mesui Hotel	9	Renaissance	4
Classic Inn	24	Metro Hotel	23	Sahabat Guesthouse	15
Dorsett Regency	14	Myhotel	21	Somerset	2
Fahrenheit Suites	17	Orange Pekoe		Swiss Garden	22
Fraser Place	6	Guesthouse	12	Traders Hotel	7
Invito Hotel Suites	10	Pacific Regency		Travellers Palm Lodge	16
Mandarin Oriental	5	Hotel Suites	8	Tropical Guesthouse	19
Marriott	13	Rainforest Bed		Villa Samadhi	1
Hotel Maya	3	& Breakfast	11	The Yard Boutique Hotel	18

1

municipal authorities seem intent on destroying. It's housed close to Kompleks Kraf in a 1925 colonial mansion that contains a gift shop, good for books on local architecture, and hosts occasional temporary exhibitions, focusing on anything from colonial furniture to restoration work.

In the grounds is the beautifully restored **Rumah Penghulu Abu Seman**, a traditional timber house that once belonged to a Malay chieftain. Moved here from Kedah, it can only be visited on a guided tour.

Bukit Nanas

The western side of the Golden Triangle is dominated by forested **Bukit Nanas** ("**Pineapple Hill**"), above which rises the **Menara KL** communications tower. Although most people head straight for the tower and its brilliant views, you can also follow an easy forty-minute **walking trail** through the forest from the **Forestry Office** on Jalan Raja Chulan (daily 9am–6pm; free map available) to Jalan Ampang, close to the Bukit Nanas Monorail station; there are big trees, subdued gloom, bird's nest ferns, stands of bamboo and a few monkeys.

Just west of the hill, on Jalan Bukit Nanas, the fine collection of **colonial school buildings** include the St John's Institution (1904) and Bukit Nanas Convent School – still rated among KL's top academic institutions.

Menara KL

2 Jalan Puncak • Free shuttles every 15min from Jalan Puncak, or a 15min walk uphill • Daily 9am–10pm, last tickets 9.30pm • RM49 • ☎ 03 2020 5444, ⊛ menarakl.com.my

At 421m, the **Menara KL** tower offers vistas east across the Petronas Towers to the blue peaks of the Titiwangsa range that marks the start of the Peninsula's interior, and west along the unmitigated urban sprawl of the Klang Valley. Dusk is an especially worthwhile time to come, as the city lights up, as does the tower itself on special occasions – green for Muslim festivals, purple for Deepavali and red for the Chinese New Year. Though free audioguides describe what can be seen in each direction, it's probably best to hold off visiting until you know KL well enough to be familiar with its general layout.

The **observation deck** sits at 276m inside in the bulbous portion of the tower, which was designed in the shape of a *gasing*, the Malay spinning top. Fixed binoculars (free) allow you to observe city life in minute detail.

Lake Gardens and around

Kuala Lumpur train station KTM

West of the colonial district, the **Lake Gardens** offer a pleasant escape from KL's more frenetic streets amid a humid, hilly spread of green. Near the sizeable modern **Masjid Negara**, which fronts the area on Jalan Sultan Hishamuddin, a cool white building contains the superb **Islamic Arts Museum**. Uphill lie the gardens themselves, complete with close-cropped lawns, water and a host of child-friendly attractions – including a Butterfly Park, a Bird Park and the National Planetarium – while Malaysia's **National Museum** is just south. Although you could easily spend half a day strolling around, focus on the two museums if you're pushed for time.

The easiest **access** on foot is via Kuala Lumpur train station and the underpass to the KTM building (see p.70), from where you can edge around to the mosque – otherwise you have to risk crossing the usual furious traffic flows. As smaller roads run through the gardens, however, it's perhaps easiest to get here by taxi.

Masjid Negara

Jalan Sultan Hishamuddin • Sat–Wed 9am–6pm, Fri 2.45–6pm

Opened in 1965, **Masjid Negara** (**National Mosque**) is looking rather dated, but does impress with the scale of its paved courtyards and colonnades, all rectangles of white

1

marble bisected by pools of water. The prayer hall can hold up to ten thousand worshippers, though size gives way to decorative prowess in its finely detailed stone archways, the dome adorned with eighteen points signifying the five pillars of Islam and the thirteen states of Malaysia. To enter as a visitor (between prayers only), you must be properly dressed: robes can be borrowed (free) at the mosque entrance.

Islamic Arts Museum

Jalan Lembah Perdana • Daily 10am–6pm • RM12 • ☎ 03 2274 2020, ⊕ iamm.org.my

The ultramodern **Islamic Arts Museum** is housed in an elegant open-plan building with gleaming marble floors. This well-documented collection is a real standout; allow around ninety minutes to do it justice, and bear in mind that there's an excellent on-site Middle Eastern **restaurant** (open during museum hours, daily except Mon). If you're arriving by taxi, you may find that the driver will know only the museum's Malay name, Muzium Kesenian Islam – if that doesn't work, just ask for the Masjid Negara, just a short walk away.

Level 1 begins with a rather bland collection of dioramas of Muslim holy places, though that of the Great Mosque of Xi'an in central China draws attention to the neglected subject of Islam in the Far East, a theme continued elsewhere on this level. In the India gallery, devoted to the Moghuls, look for an intricately carved wooden locking mechanism, designed to cloister the harem away from the rest of the world; the China gallery features porcelain and scroll paintings bearing Arabic calligraphy. Best of all is an impressive 3m-high archway in the Malay gallery, once part of a house belonging to an Indonesian notable, with black, red and gold lacquering and a trelliswork of leaves as its main motif. An equally fine trunk below it was used as a travelling box by Terengganu royalty. Built of the much-prized *cengal* hardwood, it's decorated in red and gold and bears the names of Islam's revered first four caliphs.

Level 2

On **level 2**, richly embroidered textiles and marquetry back up unusual examples of Western European ceramic crockery, influenced by the Islamic world in their design – and sometimes produced for that market. Most interesting here is the terrace containing the museum's main **dome**, a blue-and-white affair with floral ornamentation. Built by Iranian craftsmen, it's the only one of several similar examples in the building that's intended to illustrate the exterior of a grand mosque. Finally, look out for the bizarre reversed dome ceiling, bulging downwards from above – it's the last thing you see as you make your way back to the foyer from the area containing the excellent **gift shop**.

RMP Museum

5 Jalan Perdana • Tues–Thurs, Sat & Sun 10am–6pm, Fri 10am–12.30pm & 3–6pm • Free • ☎ 03 2272 5689

The **RMP Museum** covers the vivid history of the **Royal Malaysian Police** force. Fascinating photographs include a shot of British officers and their local charges on patrol on buffaloes, around 1900. The museum also displays weapons confiscated from the Communists during the Emergency, including a vicious assortment of *parangs* and a curved, bladed implement known as a Sarawak or Iban axe. Once you've had a look around, you can, if you're feeling energetic, continue up Jalan Perdana into the Lake Gardens or head up the flight of steps opposite the museum to the hill where the National Planetarium is located (see opposite).

Lake Gardens (Taman Tasik Perdana)

KL's **Lake Gardens** were laid out in the 1890s by the British state treasurer to Malaya, Alfred Venning. Not quite parkland or gardens in the usual sense, they're probably best seen as a pleasant setting for various attractions, all connected by paths and sealed roads. If you're out this way in the afternoon, consider dropping into KL's most exclusive hotel, the **Carcosa Seri Negara** (see p.92), off to the west. Their oh-so-English **cream tea** is a fitting reward for a hot day's wander around the Lake Gardens – as long as you don't mind dressing smartly and paying RM80 a head for the privilege.

1

Butterfly Park

Lake Gardens • Daily 9am–6pm • RM20 • ☎ 03 2693 4799, ⓦ klbutterflypark.com

The beautiful **Butterfly Park** is an unexpected delight. Enclosed in invisibly fine netting, this garden of tropical vines, shrubs and ferns nurtures 120 species of gorgeous butterflies – some with 15cm wingspans – flitting about between the undergrowth and feed stations baited with pineapple and banana. There are also tranquil ponds full of giant koi carp, and a small but informative insect museum.

Bird Park

Lake Gardens • Daily 9am–6pm • RM48 • ☎ 03 2272 1010, ⓦ klbirdpark.com

Billed as the world's largest, KL's popular **Bird Park** features a well-designed network of ponds and streams underneath a huge mesh tent, all linked together by a looped walkway. There are free-flying egrets, storks, African starlings, nutmeg pigeons and parrots all over the place, a flock of flamingoes lives in one of the ponds, and cages of indigenous species that you might well encounter in Malaysia's wilder corners – hornbills, birds of prey such as the Brahminy kite, and the sizeable argus pheasant. Give yourself an hour to look around; the only real downside is the park's high cost, relative to any other attraction in town.

Orchid and Hibiscus Gardens

Lake Gardens • Daily 9am–6pm • Mon–Fri free, Sat & Sun RM1

If you're into tropical plants, you'll love the **Orchid and Hibiscus Gardens**. They claim to have more than eight hundred Malaysian orchids alone, all lining paved walkways in brightly coloured, formal arrangements. The hibiscus collection is laid out in terraces and includes Malaysia's national flower, the bright red *bunga raya*. There are also groves of South American **heliconias** in the gardens, looking a bit like a ginger plant but with brightly coloured, strikingly shaped flowers. The garden **shop** sells orchid cuttings in sterile gel, suitable to take home.

Tun Abdul Razak Memorial

Lake Gardens

The main road through the Lake Gardens weaves south past a field of deer to the **Tun Abdul Razak Memorial**, a house built for the second Malaysian prime minister. He's commemorated by assorted memorabilia inside, while his motorboat and golf trolley are ceremonially positioned outside. Behind here is the **lake** itself, which takes nearly an hour to walk around.

National Planetarium

Lake Gardens • Tues–Sun 9am–4.30pm • Free; planetarium shows RM12 • ☎ 03 2273 4301, ⓦ angkasa.gov.my/planetarium

Set on a forested hill east of the lake, the **National Planetarium** is reachable on foot using the steps opposite the RMP Museum (see opposite). Its blue dome and geometrically latticed walls make this an unlikely example of the city's Islamic-influenced architecture. The interior is, frankly, dull, albeit often full of happy, screaming children on school trips; there's a cutaway space capsule, a Viking rocket engine and spacesuits in glass cases, all lit by lavish blue lighting. The **Space Theatre** also shows an hourly film on various topics, not necessarily about space.

A **pedestrian bridge** runs south from the planetarium to the National Museum.

National Museum

Jalan Damansara • Daily 9am–6pm, 1hr free guided tours Mon–Sat 10am • RM5 • ☎ 03 2267 1111, ⓦ www.muziumnegara.gov.my •
KL train station; walking, use the underpass to the KTM building, as there are no other crossings on Jalan Sultan Hishamuddin

Built in 1963, the **National Museum** (Muzium Negara) has a sweeping roof characteristic of northern Malay architecture, and **four galleries** that focus perhaps too much on the Malay side of things, giving relatively little space to the Orang Asli, Indians, Chinese and Europeans who have also left their mark on the nation's history

1

and culture. Despite this, the museum is definitely worth an hour, especially if you've seen the Textile Museum's complementary exhibits.

On the first floor, **Gallery A** offers a dry stroll through prehistory, though human skeletal remains from Kelantan prove that settlers were present on the Peninsula around 6000 BC. **Gallery B** covers early Malay kingdoms, in particular the Melaka Sultanate, with a particularly good collection of finely chased *kris* daggers and items recovered from sunken Chinese trading vessels. The pace accelerates upstairs, where **Gallery C** covers the colonial era, from reconstructions of Melaka's Portuguese fortifications to a fine seventeenth-century German Bellarmine jug depicting a bearded face – characteristic of such jugs – on the neck of the vessel. There's also ungenerous coverage of the British "interference" in the Malay States, including a diorama of the signing of the Pangkor treaty (see p.559). Tin, the metal that opened up Malaysia to development, dominates the final part of the gallery; mining equipment sits alongside animal-shaped coinage – including a 30cm crocodile – once used in Selangor and Perak.

Gallery D parcels modern Malaysia into a triumphant photo parade of the nation's founding fathers, of various races, whose names you see on street signs in downtown – though there's only cursory coverage of broader history, such as the Emergency during the 1950s (see p.563). Finally, don't miss the open-air courtyard at the back, featuring an excellent run-down of the Peninsula's **indigenous groups**, alongside fantastic totem-pole-like objects and grotesque face masks such as the one-fanged *moyang melor*, which were used in rites of ancestor worship.

Brickfields and KL Sentral

KL Sentral LRT, KTM and Monorail

The laidback residential neighbourhood of **Brickfields**, 2km south of the city centre near **KL Sentral** station, was first settled by Tamils employed to build the railways, and

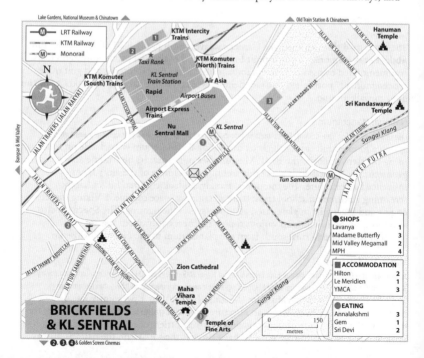

named after the brickworks that lined the rail tracks. Even today, the area retains a strong South Indian presence along **Jalan Tun Sambanthan** – the main thoroughfare – especially the western stretch beyond the huge pink fountain marking the intersection with Jalan Travers; the road has flowers painted on it, buildings are pastel-hued, and Indian pop tunes blare out of sari shops and grocers. This is one of the city's corners to visit for local ambience rather than monumental sights, though it does hold some good places to eat (see p.96).

Sri Kandaswamy Temple

3 Lorong Scott • Daily 5.30am–9.30pm • ☎ 03 2274 2987, ⓦ srikandaswamykovil.org

The Hindu **Sri Kandaswamy Temple** was founded by the Sri Lankan Tamil community in the 1900s, though the present structure was consecrated in 1997. Its facade, a riot of brightly coloured statues reminiscent of Chinatown's Sri Maha Mariamman Temple, is all the more appealing for being little visited by tourists; just don't expect to find anyone who can explain the layout, which includes, in the far right corner of the entrance wall, a collection of nine garlanded deities representing the planets.

ARRIVAL AND DEPARTURE   KUALA LUMPUR

BY PLANE

KL's three airports are some way out of the city, but linked to it by an efficient transit system. Between them they cover all major destinations and hubs across Malaysia, plus Singapore, Bandar Seri Begawan and many Southeast Asian and international airports.

KUALA LUMPUR INTERNATIONAL AIRPORT (KLIA)
The main airport, KLIA (☎ 03 8777 8888, ⓦ klia.com.my) is some 50km south of KL, and handles most domestic and international traffic.

Facilities The arrivals hall contains a Tourism Malaysia Visitor Centre (daily 8am–11pm; ☎ 03 8776 5647), a 24hr bureau de change, ATMs and other exchange facilities, and desks representing the main car rental outlets and KL's pricier hotels.

Trains Two fast, convenient rail links (ⓦ kliaekspres.com) connect the airport with downtown KL Sentral station: KLIA Transit (from KL Sentral 4.30am–midnight, from KLIA 5.30am–1am; every 30min; 35min; RM35), which stops three times along the way; and the nonstop KLIA Ekspres (from KL Sentral 5am–12.30am, from KLIA 5am–1am; every 15–30min; 28min; RM35).

Airport buses Buses between KLIA and KL are much cheaper, if slower, than the trains. Airport Coach (☎ 016 228 9070, ⓦ airportcoach.com.my) depart hourly round the clock for KL Sentral station (1hr; RM10); while Star Shuttle (☎ 017 373 1288, ⓦ starwira.com) runs hourly to Pudu Sentral bus station in Chinatown (from KLIA 5am–2.15am, from Pudu Sentral 3.15am–11.45pm; 1hr 15min; RM12). There are also buses to Ipoh with Star Shuttle, and some to Melaka and Seremban; if you want to bypass KL and catch a bus to another part of the Peninsula, go to TBS (see p.85).

Taxis The hour-long taxi drive to downtown KL costs around RM80–100. Buy a fixed-fare ticket from the counter near the arrivals exit.

KUALA LUMPUR INTERNATIONAL AIRPORT 2 (KLIA 2)

KLIA 2 (☎ 03 8778 5540, ⓦ klia2.info), just 2km north of KLIA, is used by budget airlines including AirAsia, Malindo Airways, Lion Air, Cebu Pacific and Tiger Airways, flying both domestic and international routes. Facilities include ATMs, a 24hr bureau de change and plenty of duty-free shops.

Trains The quickest way to get between the airport and KL Sentral station in downtown Kuala Lumpur is by using the Klia Ekspres (ⓦ kliaekspres.com) via KLIA airport (from KL Sentral 5am–12.30am, from KLIA2 4.55am–12.55am; every 15–30min; 33min). The KLIA Transit (ⓦ kliaekspres .com) from KL Sentral (from KL Sentral 4.33am–12.03am, from KLIA2 5.48am–12.59am) takes marginally longer (39min).

Airport buses Buses between KLIA2 and KL are cheaper, if slower, than the trains. Aerobus (☎ 010 292 3888, ⓦ aerobus.my) operates buses to KL Sentral (from KLIA2 4.30am–2am, from KL Sentral 2.45am–10.30pm; 1hr). Jetbus (☎ 017 583 8255, ⓦ jetbus.com.my) has services from Terminal Bersepadu Selatan (TBS) bus station (from KLIA2 4.30am–12.30am, from TBS 3am–11pm; 1hr 15min).

Taxis A taxi ride to KL will cost RM80–100, depending on type of vehicle; buy a ticket from the taxi counter.

SUBANG SKYPARK (SULTAN ABDUL AZIZ SHAH (SAAS) AIRPORT)

KL's small third airport, Subang Skypark (☎ 03 7842 2773, ⓦ subangskypark.com), 25km west of the city, hosts only Firefly and Berjaya airlines at present, covering a few domestic destinations plus Singapore and Koh Samui in Thailand.

Trains The quickest way into town is to catch a taxi from the airport to Kelana Jaya LRT train station (30min) and then the LRT to KL Sentral or Pasar Seni (35min).

1

KUALA LUMPUR INTERNATIONAL AIRPORT: IN-TOWN CHECK-IN

Passengers departing from KLIA with Malaysia Airlines, Royal Brunei, Cathay Pacific, Emirates and Etihad Airlines can check bags in up to 2hr before departure time at the KLIA Express ticket desks at KL Sentral station. It's a useful option if you have a late flight and don't want to lug your bags around all day after you check out of your accommodation.

Buses KL City Airport shuttle coaches (☎1300 888582, ⓦcityairport.com.my) connect the airport and Pudu Sentral (daily 6am–10.30pm; every 30min–1hr). Alternatively, RapidKL bus #U81 travels from the airport to Pasar Seni (Central Market) in Chinatown via KL Sentral (6am–midnight; every 30min; 40min; ⓦmyrapid.com .my); while bus #9 terminates at Klang bus station in Chinatown (every 30min; 40min).

Taxi A taxi from Subang Skypark to the city centre will set you back about RM50 (40min).

BY TRAIN

KL SENTRAL STATION

Located just southwest of downtown KL, this is the main hub for the Peninsula's intercity trains, and also for many of KL's local rail services. Inside, you'll find separate ticket counters for all train services, plus the various airport buses. By the north entrance near where the *Hilton* is located, there are also ATMs, left-luggage lockers (☎012 395 6969; 8am–10.30pm; RM5/day), and taxi ticket counters for the rank outside. Note that there's no pedestrian access to Jalan Travers north of the station, which rules out walking the 2km to Chinatown.

KTM Intercity trains arrive at KL Sentral from Singapore, Hat Yai in Thailand via Butterworth and the west coast towns, or from Tumpat via the "Jungle Railway" (see box, p.201) and Jerantut. For fares and timetables, see ⓦktmb.com.my.

Destinations Alor Star (1 daily; 9hr 30min); Butterworth (2 daily; 7hr 30min); Gemas (1 daily; 3hr); Hat Yai (Thailand; 1 daily; 12hr 30min); Ipoh (ETS: 10 daily; 2hr 30min; standard: 2 daily; 3hr 30min); Jerantut (1 daily; 7hr 45min); Johor Bahru (3 daily; 6hr 15min); Kuala Kangsar (2 daily; 5hr); Kuala Lipis (1 daily; 8hr 50min); Singapore (3 daily; 7hr); Wakaf Bharu (for Kota Bharu; 1 daily; 14hr 45min).

KTM Komuter Connects KL Sentral Port Klang (every 15–30min; 1hr 5min), where ferries from Indonesia (see p.29) dock at the Asa Niaga terminal near the station.

Getting into town Pasar Seni station in Chinatown is just one stop from KL Sentral on the Kelana Jaya–Gombak LRT line (ⓦmyrapid.com.my). For Bukit Bintang, you need the Monorail which, in a minor planning lapse, is 200m away on Jalan Tun Sambathan – descend to street level on the southeast side of KL Sentral and follow a signed walkway.

BY BUS

To buy tickets, you need to turn up and speak to the various bus companies directly. There are no central enquiry numbers for the bus stations, but a few of the larger companies can be contacted by phone.

PUDU SENTRAL (PUDURAYA) STATION

KL's largest long-distance bus station, Pudu Sentral Station, occupies a multistorey complex on Jalan Pudu, just east of Chinatown. It deals mainly with northbound traffic, with dozens of bus companies ensuring regular departures to most places. On the main passenger level are ATMs and food stalls, with a bank upstairs.

Arriving Exit the west side of the building for the short walk to Chinatown, or access to an alley leading east to Plaza Rakyat LRT station. A useful pedestrian bridge crosses Jalan Pudu from the north side, from where Bukit Bintang's hostels are a 15min walk. Alternatively, reach Bukit Bintang aboard RapidKL bus #U27, #U31, #U32, #U44, #U45, #U46, #U47 or #U48, which all head east along Jalan Pudu and Jalan Imbi, then north up Jalan Sultan Ismail to the Lot 10 Mall.

Departing In addition to seat number and departure time, your ticket will also be marked with the departure bay in the basement; each of the 23 bays is reached by a separate numbered staircase.

Destinations Alor Star (hourly; 7hr 30min); Butterworth (hourly; 5hr 30min); Cameron Highlands (hourly; 4hr 30min); Genting Highlands (every 30min; 1hr); Georgetown (hourly; 4hr); Hat Yai (2 daily; Thailand; 9hr); Ipoh (hourly; 3hr 30min); Kangar (8 daily; 8hr); Kuala Kangsar (6 daily; 3hr); Kuala Perlis (8 daily; 8hr); Lumut (every 1hr 30min; 3hr 30min); Penang (every 30min; 5hr); Taiping (5 daily; 4hr 30min).

PUTRA

Housed in a tunnel-like building 3km northwest of central KL, reached down an access ramp off a busy intersection, Putra bus station mostly handles traffic from the east coast, including Kuantan, Kuala Terengganu (via the Perhentian islands' jetty at Kuala Besut) and Kota Bharu (via Kuala Lipis and Gua Musang). Ticket offices are in a line down one side of the station, but there are no ATMs or much else on site. Putra KTM station is 200m from the bus station, while PWTC station and the LRT line are 500m away.

Destinations Gua Musang (every 2hr; 5hr); Kota Bharu (11 daily; 7hr 30min); Kuala Besut (for the Perhentians; 6 daily; 8hr); Kuala Terengganu (9 daily; 7hr); Kuantan (hourly; 3hr); Tasik Kenyir (2 daily; 8hr).

PEKELILING

Pekeliling bus station, 3km northwest of central KL on

Jalan Tun Razak, is used mainly by buses from the interior and Kuantan, along with some services to Genting Highlands and Terengganu state. The separate Titiwangsa stations on the Monorail and the LRT are just to the north.

Destinations Jerantut (for Taman Negara National Park; 5 daily; 3hr 30min); Kuala Lipis (5 daily; 4hr); Kuantan (3 daily; 3hr); Temerloh (hourly; 2hr 30min).

TERMINAL BERSEPADU SELATAN (TBS)

With services to points south and east especially, TBS (W tbsbts.com.my) is an important bus hub for KL, and the closest bus station to KLIA. It's 10km south of KL, next to Bandar Tasik Selatan station, and is served by some airport shuttles.

Destinations Alor Star (2 daily; 4hr 40min); Butterworth (3 daily; 3hr 40min); Johor (every 30min; 5hr); Kuala Perlis (1 daily; 5hr 30min); Ipoh (5 daily; 3hr 30min); Lumut (3 daily; 3hr 15min); Melaka (every 30min; 2hr 30min); Penang (5 daily; 4hr 30min); Singapore (every 30min; 6hr); Sungai Petani (1 daily; 4hr).

OTHER BUS STATIONS

KL train station Luxury buses from the old Kuala Lumpur train station serve destinations including Johor (every 30min; 5hr), Melaka (every 30min; 2hr 30min) and Singapore (every 30min; 6hr).

Klang bus station Located in Chinatown just below Pasar Seni train station, the Klang bus station serves Port Klang (every 15min; 1hr 30min), but it's far quicker to make this journey aboard the KTM Komuter train to Pelabuhan Klang station.

Jalan Imbi Transtar (W transtar.com.sg) luxury buses to and from Singapore (4 daily; 6hr) arrive and leave here. It's convenient, as it's practically in the heart of Bukit Bintang.

BY LONG-DISTANCE TAXI

Most long-distance taxis leave from Pudu Sentral bus station, with a handful from Putra station. Typical fares per vehicle: around RM300 to Cameron Highlands, RM410 to Kuala Tahan (the main Taman Negara entrance) and RM500 to Kota Bharu or Kuala Terengganu.

BY CAR

Leaving KL by car onto the Peninsula's main highways is hampered by confusing road signage, one-way systems and countless express bypasses.

E1 The North–South Expressway, northbound, is signed from Jalan Duta, which branches off Middle Ring Rd I west of the Lake Gardens.

E2 The North–South Expressway, southbound, starts at Sungai Besi 2km south of Chinatown, and is most quickly reached using the long underground SMART tunnel on the eastern section of Jalan Tun Razak.

E8 To reach the E8 (Karak Highway), which is linked to the East Coast Highway to Kuantan, and Route 8 into the interior, get onto Jalan Tun Razak (or Jalan Raja Laut if starting from Chinatown) and head northwest to Jalan Ipoh; proceed up this for a short distance, then turn right onto Jalan Sentul and follow signs for the highway.

BY FERRY

The only ferries from the vicinity of KL are those from Port Klang to Dumai (Sumatra; daily, 10.30am; 3hr 30min; RM110); check current schedules on ☎ 03 3167 7186. The port is on the KTM Komuter line to KL Sentral and Kuala Lumpur train stations.

GETTING AROUND

Downtown KL isn't that large, so it's tempting to do a lot of your exploring **on foot**, but many pedestrians soon find themselves wilting thanks to the combined effects of humidity and traffic fumes from the vehicle-choked roads. Thankfully, the light rail transit (**LRT**) lines and the **Monorail**, along with **KTM Komuter** train services and **taxis**, are efficient and inexpensive. However, having been created piecemeal, the services don't always coordinate

---

TRAVEL AGENTS AND TOUR OPERATORS

For advice on local tours, Perhentian trips, or packages to Taman Negara, either ask at your hotel or hostel, or visit **MaTiC** (see p.88). Specific **Taman Negara operators** include **NKS** (☎ 03 2072 0336, W taman-negara-nks.com) and **Han Travel** (☎ 03 2031 0899, W han-travel .com), who both charge upwards of RM300 per person for a three-day trip (see p.191). Kuala Lumpur Travel Tour (☎ 017 633 0062, W kualalumpurtraveltour.com), meanwhile, organizes plenty of private tours in and around the capital.

Recommended agents for domestic and international travel include:

Discovery Overland 66 Jalan Metro Pudu 2, Fraser Business Park, off Jalan Yew (near the Pudu LRT station) ☎ 03 9222 8113, W discovery overland.com.

Jet Asia 2-01-02, D'Alamanda, 2 Jalan Pudu Impian ☎ 03 9200 1911, W jetasiatravel.com.

MSL 66 Jalan Putra, Chow Kit ☎ 03 4042 4722, W msltravel.com.

1

well – ticketing isn't unified and interchanges may involve inconvenient walks. The main governing body is **RapidKL** (ⓦ myrapid.com.my), which runs the LRT and Monorail lines, plus many of the city's buses; its website includes network maps and details of monthly transport passes.

THE LRT

The Light Rail Transit (every 5–10min 6am–midnight; RM0.70–2.50; ⓦ myrapid.com.my) is a metro network comprising two, mostly elevated, lines, with a convenient central interchange at Masjid Jamek near Little India.

Kelana Jaya Line The more useful of the two LRT lines passes through KL Sentral, Chinatown and the old colonial district (Pasar Seni/Masjid Jamek stations) and KLCC.

Ampang and Sri Petaling The two branches of this LRT line join at Chan Sow Lin station and continue to Sentul Timur in the north of the city. For visitors, it's mainly of use for travel between Chinatown (Plaza Rakyat station) and Little India (Masjid Jamek or Bandaraya stations) and Chow Kit Market (Sultan Ismail station).

THE MONORAIL

Monorail Trains on this elevated rail system (every 5–10min 6am–midnight; RM1.20–2.50; ⓦ myrapid.com .my) have a noticeable tilt as they camber around bends. From its KL Sentral terminus (200m from the KL Sentral rail hub), the line at first heads east, through Brickfields and the southern edge of Chinatown, then swings north and west through Bukit Bintang and along Jalan Sultan Ismail, nearly reaching Jalan TAR before heading north through Chow Kit to terminate at Titiwangsa station on Jalan Tun Razak. There are interchanges with the LRT at Bukit Nanas (requiring a 5min walk to Dang Wangi station) and at Hang Tuah.

KTM KOMUTER TRAINS

KTM Komuter Trains Run by national rail operator KTM (ⓦ ktmkomuter.com.my), trains travel on two lines: one from Sungai Gadut, out past the airport, northwest to Tanjung Malim; the other from coastal Pelabuhan Klang, off to the southwest, up to the northern suburb of Batu Caves. Both connect downtown at four stations: Putra, near the Putra World Trade Centre; Bank Negara, near Little India; the Kuala Lumpur train station, in the colonial district; and KL Sentral. Trains run every 15–20min during the day, but only every 30min after 8pm. Tickets (RM1.50–9) can be purchased from the stations and automatic machines at the stops; return tickets cost double the one-way fare. Weekly and monthly passes for designated journeys are also available. Note that Komuter trains all have a central women-only carriage.

BUSES

KL has a comprehensive city bus network, with Metrobus and RapidKL as the two main operators, but the lack of clearly marked terminuses and bus stops can make it baffling for outsiders to use. Services start up around 6am and begin winding down from 10pm onwards. Given KL's frequent traffic snarl-ups, do allow plenty of time for your journey. The small grid of streets around Puduraya and Central Market is a hub of sorts; buildings with key stops close by, including the Sinarkota Building, the Kotaraya Building and the Bangkok Bank, appear on our Chinatown map (see p.71).

RapidKL Bus numbers on RapidKL (ⓦ myrapid.com.my) are prefixed B (downtown), E (express buses), T (local services) and U (for travel into and out of the centre). On RapidKL's unusual day-pass system, any ticket entitles you to make additional journeys on the same route the rest of the day; fares are RM2, RM5, RM1 and RM2 for B, E, T and U services respectively.

Metrobus Buses operated by Metrobus (ⓣ 03 5635 7897) have regular numbers, and use a zonal fare system, starting at under RM1 downtown and rising to RM2.50 for journeys to the city limits; you will need to pay the conductor.

TAXIS

KL taxis are cheap and convenient, though drivers are notorious for trying to negotiate an inflated price for journeys, rather than use the meter. There are two ways to deal with this: ask if they use the meter before getting in, failing which simply flag down another cab; or buy a prepaid coupon for your journey from booths attached to designated cab ranks. Some drivers don't speak much English, so you may want to have the address of your

---

TOUCH 'N GO CARDS

Though KL's dreams of a properly integrated transport system remain just that, the **Touch 'n Go card** (ⓦ touchngo.com.my) is a useful **stored-value card** that you simply brush across the sensors at KTM Kommuter, LRT and Monorail stations, and when you board RapidKL buses. You can also use it to pay Expressway tolls on the Peninsula, and in various car parks and fast-food joints around KL. Cards cost RM10 from many stations (look for the logo); ticket office staff at the same places can recharge them (RM10–500 at a time; cash only), as can 7–11 stores and highway toll stations. As the cards save time queuing, rather than money, they're of most use if you'll be in the city a good deal or plan to drive yourself around the Peninsula.

1

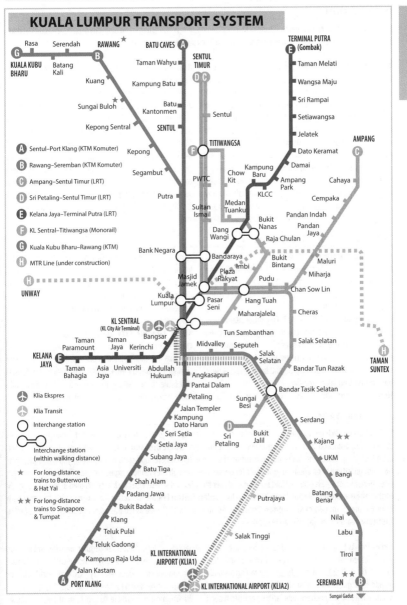

KUALA LUMPUR TRANSPORT SYSTEM

Rasa Serendah **RAWANG** ★ **BATU CAVES** **A**
G **KUALA KUBU** Batang Taman Wahyu
BHARU Kali **SENTUL**
Kuang **D C** **TIMUR**
Kampung Batu
Sungai Buloh ★ Batu
Kantonmen Sentul
Kepong Sentral **SENTUL**

A Sentul–Port Klang (KTM Komuter) Kepong **F** **TITIWANGSA**
B Rawang–Seremban (KTM Komuter) Segambut
C Ampang–Sentul Timur (LRT) Putra PWTC
D Sri Petaling–Sentul Timur (LRT) Sultan
E Kelana Jaya–Terminal Putra (LRT) Ismail
F KL Sentral–Titiwangsa (Monorail)
G Kuala Kubu Bharu–Rawang (KTM) Bank Negara
H MTR Line (under construction)

UNWAY

TERMINAL PUTRA
E (Gombak)
Taman Melati
Wangsa Maju
Sri Rampai
Setiawangsa
Jelatek
Dato Keramat **AMPANG**
Chow Kampung Damai
Kit Baru Ampang Cahaya
KLCC Park
Medan Cempaka
Tuanku Pandan Indah
Dang Bukit Pandan
Wangi Nanas Jaya
Raja Chulan
Bandaraya Bukit Maluri
Imbi Bintang
Masjid Plaza Pudu Miharja
Jamek Rakyat
Kuala Pasar Hang Tuah Chan Sow Lin
Lumpur Seni
Maharajalela Cheras
KL SENTRAL Tun Sambanthan **H**
(KL City Air Terminal) **F** Bangsar Midvalley Seputeh Salak Selatan **TAMAN**
Taman Taman Kerinchi Salak Bandar Tun Razak **SUNTEX**
Paramount Jaya Selatan
KELANA **E** Taman Asia Universiti Abdullah Angkasapuri Bandar Tasik Selatan
JAYA Bahagia Jaya Hukum Pantai Dalam
Petaling Sungai Serdang
Jalan Templer Besi Kajang ★★
Kampung
Dato Harun **D** UKM
Seri Setia Bukit Bangi
Setia Jaya Sri Jalil
Subang Jaya Petaling Batang
Batu Tiga Benar
Shah Alam Putrajaya Nilai
Padang Jawa Labu
Bukit Badak Tiroi
Klang Salak Tinggi ★★
Teluk Pulai **SEREMBAN**
Teluk Gadong Sungai Gadut
Kampung Raja Uda
Jalan Kastam **KL INTERNATIONAL** **KL INTERNATIONAL AIRPORT (KLIA2)** **B**
A **PORT KLANG** **AIRPORT (KLIA1)**

Klia Ekspres
Klia Transit
O Interchange station
Interchange station (within walking distance)
★ For long-distance trains to Butterworth & Hat Yai
★★ For long-distance trains to Singapore & Tumpat

---

destination written down in Malay, or mention a well-known landmark nearby.

Metered fares Generally low: in regular taxis the flagfall is RM3, and the tariff is 10 sen for every 150m travelled. This translates into just RM5–6 for a typical journey between Bukit Bintang and Chinatown, or RM7–8 for Bukit Bintang to KL Sentral or Chinatown to KLCC. Expect to pay a few ringgit more for downtown journeys in the smarter taxis; luggage in the boot is charged at RM1/bag.

Taxi ranks There are numerous taxi ranks around the city, usually close to bus stops and outside shopping malls.

Phone numbers To book a taxi, which costs an extra couple of ringgit, call: Sunlight Radio Taxis (☏ 03 9200 1166, ⓦ sunlighttaxi.com) or Supercab (☏ 03 2095 3399).

1

INFORMATION

Bear in mind that, given the chaotic nature of KL city planning, **maps** and listings tend to go out of date fairly quickly; don't be surprised if roads, venues and buildings have sprung into existence or ceased to be.

Tourism Malaysia The national tourist board has branches across the city (ⓦtourism.gov.my), handing out brochures and general advice. You can also book accommodation, local tours and packages to Taman Negara and the like through in-house travel agents. The main office is at MaTiC, 109 Jalan Ampang, not far from the Bukit Nanas Monorail stop (daily 8am–10pm; ☎03 9235 4900, ⓦmatic.gov.my); bus #B105 also runs here from Central Market in Chinatown. Other branches: Sultan Abdul Samad Building on Jalan Raja (daily 9am–6pm; ☎03 2602 2014, ⓦtourismmalaysia.gov .my); KL Sentral Station, Level 1 (daily 9am–6pm; ☎03 2272 5823); KLIA international arrivals hall (daily

8am–11pm; ☎03 8776 5647); KLIA 2 (daily 8am–11pm; ☎03 8778 7080).

Listings To keep an ear to the ground on happenings around town, check out the monthly *Time Out KL* (ⓦtimeoutkl.com). Also worth a look is ⓦvisionkl.com, a handy repository of sights, restaurants, clubs and events.

Maps *Road Map & Highway Guide of Kuala Lumpur* (RM10), published by World Express Mapping and available in most city bookstores, is a handy two-sided foldaway sheet covering the city and the surrounding Klang Valley, surprisingly detailed given the scale. Drivers might need *The Big Atlas of Klang Valley and Beyond* (RM37), a hefty street atlas for the same area.

TOURS AND SIGHTSEEING BUSES

Food Tour Malaysia ☎013 227 1505, ⓦfood tourmalaysia.com. Excellent "Off the Eaten Track" and KL walking tours both during the day and in the evenings – a great way to get acquainted with Malaysia's many cuisines. From RM110.

Go KL City Bus ☎1 800 887723. Free buses (daily every 5–15min, 6am–11pm) that stop off at major sights around the city; you can use the services as often as you please and hop on and hop off as many times as you fancy. Pick up a detailed map at the tourist office, and board the bus right outside MaTiC on Jalan Ampang.

Hop-on, hop-off bus ☎1 800 885546,

ⓦmyhoponhopoff.com. Hop-on, hop-off bus service, looping around a set circuit via a string of tourist sights (daily 9am–8pm; every 20–30min; unlimited use day ticket valid for 24hr RM45). Buses are open-top double-deckers, with running commentaries in a handful of languages.

Kuala Lumpur City Hall Tours ☎03 2698 0332, ⓔpelancongan@dbkl.gov.my, ⓦvisitkl.gov.my. Free Merdeka heritage guided tours (starting at the Kuala Lumpur City Gallery Mon, Wed & Sat at 9am; 2hr 45min) and Little India walking tours (starting at Vivekananda Ashram every Sat at 9am; 2hr 30min); register via email.

ACCOMMODATION

While **Chinatown** has traditionally been the favourite location for budget travellers, with its surfeit of inexpensive places to sleep, eat, drink and shop, it faces growing competition from **Bukit Bintang**, a 15min walk east. Here, close to the abundant fancy hotels and malls, not to mention the celebrated Chinese food stalls of Jalan Alor, you'll find plenty of excellent guesthouses on and around Tengkat Tong Shin. Even though they're more expensive than Chinatown, these are often better value – less cramped and noisy, with slicker facilities and self-service breakfasts included in the rate. Slightly further afield, more upscale hotels can be found along **Jalan Sultan Ismail** and **Jalan Ampang**, which, together with Bukit Bintang, form part of KL's **Golden Triangle**. All other parts of KL pale as regards accommodation, though **Little India** also features several mid-range options.

Rates Thanks to an over-supply of rooms for much of the year, rates remain competitive – a bed in a dorm can be had for as little as RM20, and it's seldom hard to find a simple double in a guesthouse with shared facilities for RM50/ night, or RM80 if you need en-suite facilities and a/c. A good mid-range hotel room costs around RM150, while anything above RM250/night will be pretty luxurious. Check online or ask when booking about promotional rates or weekday hotel discounts; the prices below refer to weekend rates.

Bookings Although it's almost inconceivable that you'd be unable to find somewhere to stay in your price range, it always make sense to book ahead, especially during busy

periods – July, August, November and December, plus school and public holidays. As well as individual accommodation websites, try ⓦhostelworld.com or ⓦhostelbookers.com for hostels and guesthouses.

Wi-fi Almost everywhere has wi-fi, or at least computer terminals, usually free for guests.

CHINATOWN AND AROUND

Chinatown's wealth of backpacker-oriented guesthouses are mostly concentrated either side of Jalan Petaling, alongside budget hotels offering simple rooms but with better facilities. Both are increasingly modern and efficiently run, though furnishings are minimal and the cheapest rooms are unlikely to have windows. Only upmarket options feature frills like in-house swimming pools, though there is an ageing public pool nearby at the Chinwoo Stadium (see p.104).

HOTELS

Hotel 1915 49 Jalan Leboh Ampang ☎03 2026 0042, ⓦhotel1915kl.com.my; map p.71. Just walking into the lobby of this hotel, located in a beautifully renovated building that dates back to 1915, is a welcome respite from the hubbub of Chinatown. The lobby features bare brick walls, black-and-white prints and Chinese stone sculptures and vases, while the contemporary rooms are equipped with modern amenities, en-suite facilities and in-room safes. RM236

5 Elements Hotel Lot 243 Jalan Sultan ☎03 2031 6888, ⓦthe5elementshotel.com.my; map p.71. Rooms are clean and comfortable at this fourteen-storey hotel with great views of Chinatown and beyond; the twelfth- to fourteenth-floor rooms will set you back RM30 extra. Some rooms are in better shape than others, so it's wise to take a look at a couple before settling in. RM220

Hotel China Town 2 70–72 Jalan Petaling ☎03 2072 9933, ⓦhotelchinatown2.com; map p.71. Located on bustling Jalan Petaling in the heart of Chinatown, this decent hotel offers clean rooms with private bath at affordable prices, including some singles (RM70). RM90

D'Oriental Inn 82 & 84 Jalan Petaling ☎03 2026 8181, ⓦdorientalinnchinatown.com; map p.71. A decent option nicely located in the thick of the market, featuring bland modern rooms that are kept clean; rooms are the same price with or without windows. RM90

Geo Hotel 7 Jalan Hang Kasturi ☎03 2032 2288, ⓦgeohotelkl.com; map p.71. Just steps from the Central Market, this great-value hotel offers well-kept a/c rooms with chocolate-coloured fittings and flat-screen TVs; the superior rooms (RM220) are just like the standards, although also include a fresh fruit basket. The premises are strictly non-smoking, except on the third floor, where all rooms are smoking. The friendly staff are an added bonus. RM203

★**Hotel Majestic** Jalan Sultan Hishamuddin ☎03 2785 8000, ⓦmajestickl.com; map p.71. Opposite the old Moorish-style railway station, this hotel, a wonderfully restored 1930s building houses exquisitely furnished suites with butler service; the contemporary fifteen-storey Tower Wing has deluxe rooms and suites, along with a swimming pool and gym. Other facilities include a bar, spa, barber's and screening room. RM660

Swiss Inn 62 Jalan Sultan ☎03 2072 3333, ⓦswissgarden.com; map p.71. A pleasant surprise in the heart of Chinatown, this clean, modern hotel has a range of inviting rooms spread out on seven colour-coded floors. Rooms have tasteful furnishings and crisp linen; the deluxe

options are brighter than the windowless superiors, at only RM20 more. The coffee house offers a good view of the Petaling Street market. Rates include breakfast. RM180

Winsin Hotel 1–3 Jalan Petaling ☎03 2031 5011, ⓦwinsinchinatownhotel.com.my; map p.71. This hotel is a bit dated but the small rooms are modern and in good nick, with en-suite facilities and a/c, and livened up with Chinese paintings. Well placed for Central Market. RM98

HOSTELS AND GUESTHOUSES

★**Back Home** 30 Jalan Tun H.S. Lee ☎03 2022 0788, ⓦbackhome.com.my; map p.71. This leafy hostel features hardwood floors, bare brick walls and comfortable modern rooms set around a courtyard with coffee tables where guests are invited to socialize. Staff are friendly and there's an excellent café next door under the same management. Dorms RM48, doubles RM116

Birdnest Guesthouse 64 Jalan Hang Kasturi ☎012 694 7366, ⓦbirdnestghouse.com; map p.71. Friendly place dotted with birdcages, some of which have been made into quirky lamps, that the owner has picked up from various flea markets; the furniture is all recycled, and there are even two pet iguanas. The little rooms, with fan or a/c units, feature polished hardwood floors, with most looking onto the interior courtyard; there are three-bed female and mixed dorms too. Singles just RM30. Dorms RM20, doubles RM40

The Explorers Guesthouse 128 & 130 Jalan Tun H.S. Lee ☎03 2022 2928, ⓦtheexplorersguesthouse.com; map p.71. An oasis of calm in the hubbub of Chinatown, this guesthouse features a pleasant communal area with a water feature, decorative fans, dangling dream-catchers and pebble tiles in the bathrooms. The neat and tidy rooms are on the smallish side but are kept immaculate, as are the bathrooms, and staff will happily advise on what to see and do in the area. Dorms RM33, doubles RM92

Matahari Lodge 58–1 Jalan Hang Kasturi ☎03 2070 5570, ⓦmataharilodge.com; map p.71. A popular backpacker choice, this place has a/c in the common areas; the cool air is sucked into the rooms – sparsely kitted out, with floral bed linen and the odd fancy lamp – by extractor fans in the walls. Singles are particularly austere, with just a bed and nothing else, although the premises are clean and there's a pleasant communal area and kitchenette where travellers can meet over a coffee or two. Dorms RM30, doubles RM73

Raizzy's Guesthouse 165g Jalan Tun H.S. Lee ☎03 2022 0873, ⓦraizzy.com; map p.71. Just a few steps from the Sri Maha Mariamman Temple, this friendly hostel offers small, darkish dorms (most are windowless or look onto the interior of the building), although the doubles are appealing enough and are a real bargain given the location. Guests are entitled to breakfast discounts at the *Lucy in the Sky* café next door. Dorms RM25, doubles RM78

1

★**Reggae Mansion** 53 Jalan Tun H.S Lee ☎03 2072 6877, ⓦreggaemansionkl.com; map p.71. Located in a three-storey colonial-era block, this is a flashpacker hostel at its best, although it is a bit of a tourist-trail factory. The spick-and-span premises are kitted out with mock-Louis XIV armchairs and prints that depict life in a British stately home. Each dorm bed is equipped with privacy curtain, reading lamp, socket and under-bed lockers. There's even an in-house cinema. Dorms RM40, doubles RM140

LITTLE INDIA AND CHOW KIT

Crossroads Hotel 1 Jalan Raja Muda Abdul Aziz ☎03 2698 7000, ⓦcrossroads-hotel.com; map p.74. A stone's throw away from Chow Kit market, this excellent budget hotel offers immaculate rooms kitted out with dark furnishings, in a pleasant interior with bare brick walls and funky orange chairs at reception. The area of Chow Kit, however, is known for prostitution and it's wise to watch your wallet at all times. Breakfast is an extra RM25. RM140

Hotel De' Grand Orchard 81–83 Medan Bunus ☎03 2691 2146, ⓦdegrandorchardhotel.com; map p.74. Not to be confused with their sister hotel *Grand Orchard*, this budget place, just off Jalan Masjid India, features welcoming rooms with chocolate-brown furnishings, faux wooden floors and smallish, albeit very clean, bathrooms. Rates increase by RM25 over the weekends. RM115

K Hotel 142–146 Jalan TAR ☎03 2693 4246, ⓦkhotel .com.my; map p.74. Make your way past a yogurt shop on the ground floor and up to the bright red lobby of this recently renovated hotel. The carpeted rooms with red and black undertones are smallish but are sparkling clean. It's worth asking for discounts. RM250

Palace Hotel 46–1 Jalan Masjid India ☎03 2698 6122, ⓦpalacehotel.com.my; map p.74. The simple rooms at this 1960s-style hotel are kitted out in olive green and are a bit drab and dated, though all have a/c and it's in a lively location. RM185

Premiera Hotel 232 Jalan Tuanku ☎03 2615 1000, ⓦpremiera.com.my; map p.74. In the heart of Little India and just a short walk from Chinatown, this is a great budget option offering spacious rooms with modern amenities, and wonderful views of the city from the higher floors. Note that 76 out of the hotel's 90 rooms are twins (RM275), so if you're after a double make sure you book ahead. RM390

Silka Maytower Hotel 7 Jalan Munshi Abdullah ☎03 2692 9298, ⓦsilkahotels.com/maytower; map p.74. This international-standard hotel, set over 32 floors, offers modern rooms or apartments with earthy tones, equipped with flat-screen TV and safe; the deluxes (RM460) are more spacious, with sofa and bathtub, and there are also two pools – one for adults, one for kids – on the eighth floor, along with a sauna and gym. Rooms RM350, apartments RM530

Tune Hotel 316 Jalan TAR ☎03 7962 5888, ⓦtunehotels.com; map p.74. AirAsia-supported no-frills hotel, very cheap if you book early. The en-suite rooms are small and functional, with fans; you pay extra for a/c, towels, TV, wi-fi and the like if you want them, which can add RM40 to the basic rate. Lobby facilities amount to a couple of fast-food outlets and a convenience store. This is a hotel best booked online; the rate quoted here is for walk-ins. RM104

THE GOLDEN TRIANGLE

Many of the Bukit Bintang guesthouses occupy nicely restored old shophouses, with small, comfortable rooms separated from each other by partitions. It's hard to go wrong with any of these, just as it's difficult to be badly disappointed with any of the Golden Triangle's upmarket hotels. The area also boasts excellent serviced apartments offering a lot more space than you'd get in a similarly priced hotel room.

HOTELS

★**Anggun Boutique Hotel** 7 & 9 Tengkat Tong Shin ☎03 2145 8003, ⓦanggunkl.com; map pp.76–77. This welcoming boutique hotel aims to recreate a Peranakan house from yesteryear, with rooms set around an airy central courtyard with a little fishpond and a lovely antique Chinese medicine cabinet. Some have four-poster beds, while the three suites have balconies overlooking the street; bathrooms feature beautiful Chinese sinks with lotus and fish motifs. RM350

Dorsett Regency 172 Jalan Imbi ☎03 2716 1000, ⓦdorsettregency.com; map pp.76–77. Within a rather unappealing salmon-pink tower block lies this great-value mid-range hotel with modern rooms, some with superb views of the Petronas Towers; facilities include a small pool. The central location is a real plus – it's just a couple of minutes' walk from Starhill Gallery and Pavilion mall, while the bars and clubs of Changkat Bukit Bintag are a 15min walk away. RM250

Fraser Place 10 Jalan Perak ☎03 2118 6288, ⓦkualalumpur.frasershospitality.com; map pp.76–77. Right by the Petronas Towers and KLCC, *Fraser Place* offers stylish, excellent-value rooms between the ninth and thirtieth floors of a retail and office complex. All rooms feature floor-to-ceiling windows boasting wonderful city views, and facilities include a well-equipped gym and eighteenth-floor infinity swimming pool. RM380

Invito Hotel Suites 1 Lorong Ceylon, Bukit Ceylon ☎02 2386 9288, ⓦinvitohotelsuites.com.my; map pp.76–77. The elegantly furnished rooms and suites feature modern designs and most boast terrific city views from the floor-to-ceiling windows. All rooms are equipped with kitchenette, and there's a particularly inviting pool, well-equipped gym and comfy TV lounge, too. RM550

Mandarin Oriental Kuala Lumpur City Centre ☎03 2380 8888, ⓦmandarinoriental.com; map pp.76–77.

Enormous hotel – it only looks small by virtue of being conveniently next to the Twin Towers – that's as sumptuous as they come, with its own luxury spa, swimming pools, tennis courts and tiptop restaurants. RM590

Marriott 183 Jalan Bukit Bintang ☎03 2715 9000, ⓦmarriott.com; map pp.76–77. In the heart of Bukit Bintang and with direct access to chic Starhill Gallery from the lobby, this branch offers well-appointed rooms with modern amenities, a huge pool and well-equipped gym. RM470

Hotel Maya 138 Jalan Ampang ☎03 2711 8866, ⓦhotelmaya.com.my; map pp.76–77. This stylish boutique hotel is sandwiched between two office blocks in the heart of KL's commercial district; the contemporary rooms with wooden floorboards feature modern amenities and floor-to-ceiling glass panels overlooking the city. There's an inviting hydrotherapy pool with massage jets, a welcome treat after a long day in the hustle and bustle of the capital, along with a gym and access to yoga classes. RM700

★ **The Mesui Hotel** 9 Jalan Mesui ☎03 2144 8188, ⓦthemesuihotel.com; map pp.76–77. Located in a unique building with a design that reflects the 70s – porthole windows and retro furnishings – this contemporary hotel offers tasteful rooms decorated with fun wall designs; "loft" rooms (RM208) are substantially larger than those in the "lush" category (RM168), but all are inviting and spick-and-span. RM168

Metro Hotel 208 Jalan Pudu ☎03 2143 7001, ⓦmetrohotel.com.my; map pp.76–77. This budget business hotel offers clean, carpeted rooms with crisp linen, just a few steps from Imbi monorail station and Berjaya Times Square. Breakfast is an extra RM20. RM170

Myhotel 120 Jalan Pudu ☎03 2143 5000, ⓦmyhotels .com.my; map pp.76–77. Budget business hotel, offering the usual value-conscious, low-frills rooms: trim modern furnishings, en-suite bathrooms and a/c, with little space for anything else. RM20 extra gets you a window. RM98

Renaissance Junction of Jalan Sultan Ismail and Jalan Ampang ☎03 2162 2233, ⓦmarriott.com; map pp.76–77. Part of the Marriott group, this sumptuous hotel overlooking the Twin Towers features two wings with well-appointed rooms, an Olympic-sized swimming pool, spa and fitness centre, along with a number of dining outlets. RM750

Swiss Garden 117 Jalan Pudu ☎03 2141 3333, ⓦswissgarden.com; map pp.76–77. This substantial modern hotel, which also features good-value serviced apartments, is conveniently located at the edge of Bukit Bintang and halfway to Chinatown. Facilities include satellite TV, a couple of restaurants plus a pool, gym and spa. Doubles RM270, serviced apartments RM300

Traders Hotel Kuala Lumpur City Centre ☎03 2332 9888, ⓦtradershotels.com; map pp.76–77. This excellent four-star hotel offers direct access to Suria KLCC mall – hotel buggies shuttle customers across the park to the mall. The well-appointed carpeted rooms feature modern amenities, and some have exceptional views of the Twin Towers. The real draw is the hotel's *Sky Bar*, on the 33rd floor, one of the city's most popular bars with 360° views of the capital. The hotel has four food outlets, including a steakhouse. RM510

★ **Villa Samadhi** 218 Jalan Ampang ☎03 2166 0601, ⓦsamadhiretreats.com; map pp.76–77. This luxurious villa has been converted to a sumptuous boutique hotel. Rooms, decorated with Asian furnishings, brim with individual character – the Sarang rooms feature their own private plunge pools, while the cosy Loft room, with its slanted ceiling, has its own shallow lap pool. Lower-ground floor rooms have direct access to the lagoon pool from their private balconies. RM660

The Yard Boutique Hotel 623 (51D) Jalan Tengkat Tong Shin ☎03 2141 1017, ⓦtheyard.com.my; map pp.76–77. Calling this place a boutique hotel may be a bit of an overstatement – it's more of a pleasant guesthouse, offering comfortable modern rooms set around a courtyard dripping with greenery and dotted with lanterns. The location, in the heart of Bukit Bintang, is a definite plus. RM180

GUESTHOUSES

Classic Inn 52 Jalan 1/77a, Changkat Thambi Dollah ☎03 2148 8648, ⓦclassicinn.com.my; map pp.76–77. Don't be put off by the anonymous backstreet location, nor the word "inn"; this pleasant guesthouse with wooden corridors and little piles of decorative pebbles has modern en-suite rooms with a/c and TV, and there's a peaceful café area with rustic wooden stools. A sister building a few doors down offers backpacker accommodation with travellers' notes plastered over the walls; the dorms are probably the tiniest you will ever come across. Dorms RM40, doubles RM128

★ **Orange Pekoe Guesthouse** 1-1 Jalan Angsoka, off Jalan Nagasari ☎03 2110 2000, ⓦorangepekoe .com.my; map pp.76–77. This cosy guesthouse, on a quiet road just a couple of streets back from Changkat's throng of activity, has clean and cosy rooms with wicker baskets as bedside tables. There are splashes of greenery throughout, and a communal area with cable TV and DVDs. RM109

Rainforest Bed & Breakfast 27 Jalan Mesui ☎03 2145 3525, ⓦrainforestbnbhotel.com; map pp.76–77. A welcoming place that creates a jungle lodge ambience with plenty of greenery complemented by tasteful wooden furniture. The clean and tidy rooms are all en suite, with TV, there are a couple of small dorms sleeping three. Really, it's more of a boutique hostel than a B&B, though breakfast is indeed included. Dorms RM39, doubles RM115

Sahabat Guesthouse 39 & 41 Jalan Sahabat, off Tengkat Tong Shin ☎03 2142 0689, ⓦsahabatguest house.com; map pp.76–77. The fourteen rooms at this bright blue guesthouse, just a few steps away from

1

Changkat's numerous bars, are named after spices. Each room is individually decorated with colourful wallpaper (stripes or rectangles) and has en-suite facilities. There's a little communal area where guests can socialize, and staff are always happy to help with suggestions on the area. RM109

Travellers Palm Lodge 10 Jalan Rembia ☎ 03 2145 4745, ⓦ travellerspalm-kl.com; map pp.76–77. This friendly little guesthouse with seven rooms is located down a lane off Tengkat Tong Shin and fronted by two travellers' palms in the tiny front garden. The colour-coded rooms are on the smallish side, although they are secure – only guests have a front gate key. The smiley owner makes guests feel right at home. Dorms RM30, doubles RM80

Tropical Guesthouse 2 Tengkat Tong Shin ☎ 03 2141 1168, ⓦ tropicalguesthousekl.com; map pp.76–77. A pleasant choice with leafy bamboo and pebble walkways leading to a myriad of cosy little rooms that are kept clean and tidy. Couples can opt for the two larger rooms that are interestingly named "sexy room" and "horny room" (RM120). RM80

SERVICED APARTMENTS

Fahrenheit Suites Floor 5, Fahrenheit 88 Mall, 179 Jalan Bukit Bintang ☎ 03 2148 2686, ⓦ fahrenheitsuites .com; map pp.76–77. Modern serviced apartments, including some sleeping six, with their own pleasant lounge, kitchenette, plus use of swimming pool. Parking available. Occasional excellent online rates. RM420

Pacific Regency Hotel Suites KH Tower, Jalan Punchak, off Jalan P. Ramlee ☎ 03 2332 7777, ⓦ pacific -regency.com; map pp.76–77. Luxury apartments with kitchenette, huge bathroom, satellite TV, free wi-fi and, on the roof, a swimming pool and the excellent *Luna* bar (see p.98). Ample parking too. Check the website for promotional rates. RM700

Somerset 8 Lorong Ceylon ☎ 03 2055 8887, ⓦ somerset.com; map pp.76–77. Popular with executive types, these immaculate studio, one-, two- and three-bed apartments in a modern tower block are equipped with swish furnishings, satellite TV/DVD systems and internet. Facilities include a rooftop infinity pool and jacuzzi, along with a fully equipped gym, café and restaurant. RM345

BRICKFIELDS AND KL SENTRAL

Hilton 3 Jalan Stesen Sentral ☎ 03 2264 2264, ⓦ kuala -lumpur.hilton.com; map p.82. Overlooking the National Museum and just a few steps from KL Sentral, this stylish hotel with a lavish lobby offers rooms as modern and comfortable as you'd expect from this reputable international chain. Facilities include ten dining outlets; the trendy *Zeta Bar* hosts international live bands and resident DJs. RM450

Le Meridien 2 Jalan Stesen Sentral ☎ 03 2263 7888, ⓦ lemeridienkualalumpur.com; map p.82. This 35-storey business hotel houses contemporary rooms, fully equipped with flat-screen TVs and DVD players; most of them boast panoramic views. Facilities include a freeform outdoor swimming pool with deckchairs partly immersed in water, a gym, spa and a handful of restaurants serving international cuisine. RM850

YMCA 95 Jalan Padang Belia ☎ 03 2274 1439, ⓦ ymcakl .com; map p.82. This institutional place has been here since 1931; rooms are stuffy and sterile, and could do with an upgrade, although there are plenty of facilities including a café, laundry and tennis courts (you'll need your own gear, though). Rates include breakfast. RM110

FURTHER OUT

Carcosa Seri Negara Taman Tasik Perdana ☎ 03 2295 0888, ⓦ shr.my; map pp.68–69. Set in 16 hectares of well-manicured grounds just west of the Lake Gardens, these two elegant, whitewashed colonial mansions, containing thirteen suites, date to 1904 – the management can truthfully boast "Queen Elizabeth slept here". If a night here is out of the question, consider donning smart-casual clothes and dropping in for their English cream tea (daily 3-6pm; RM75). RM1100

Grid 9 Hotel 9 Jalan Maharajalela ☎ 03 9226 2629, ⓦ grid9hotels.com; map pp.68–69. This excellent flashpacker hostel has a young and funky feel, with a welcoming lounge area dotted with colourful beanbags, communal computers, a pool table and flat-screen TV. The modern dorm rooms have reading lamps and individual sockets, while private doubles have a/c, TV and en-suite facilities. Guests enjoy complimentary access to *Zouk Club* (see p.99). Dorms RM45, doubles RM129

EATING

Without doubt a highlight of any visit to KL is the city's **food**. There are more opportunities to enjoy high-calibre cooking here, in assorted local and international styles, than anywhere else in the country, and whether you dine in a chic bistro-style restaurant or at a humble roadside stall, prices are almost always very reasonable. Despite plenty of scope for cosmopolitan, upmarket dining, eating for many locals is still fundamentally about Malay, Chinese and Indian **street food**. Stalls, whether on the street or collected into **food courts** (found in or close to major office blocks and shopping malls), are your best bets for inexpensive, satisfying meals, as are **kedai kopis**, though these are a little scarce in the Golden Triangle. The best-known food stalls are held in the same kind of reverence as a top-flight restaurant might be in a Western city, and people will travel across KL just to seek out a stall whose take on a particular dish is said to be better than anyone else's; if you find customers lining up to partake of some stall's spring rolls or *laksa*, it's a sure-fire indicator of quality. Ranging from small affairs in beautifully refurbished shophouses to banqueting halls in five-star hotels, KL's **restaurants** are an equally vital part of the food experience. Be aware, however, that price and decor are not a watertight indicator of consistency or quality, and that service can be hesitant even in big hotels.

CHINATOWN AND AROUND

Superb food stalls in Chinatown serve up everything from rich yet subtle *bak kut teh* (pork-rib consommé) to cooling sweet treats like *cendol*. Foreign visitors can find it hard to get to grips with the stalls, especially as some are signed only in Chinese or not at all. Still, for an excellent taster of how they operate, and of street food in general, try the *Tang City Food Court*. Otherwise, the area has plenty of *kedai kopis* and a few cheap or mid-priced restaurants, with some touristy places at the eastern end of Jalan Hang Lekir. You're not limited to Chinese food; since the fringes of Chinatown, especially north of Jalan Hang Lekir and around the Central Market, feature plenty of Indian and *mamak* places.

Bbun Lot 265 Jalan Hang Lekir ☎016 666 8704; map p.71. This great little stall stands out from the rest, with its sparkling shelves and nicely arrayed freshly baked buns (RM3) that come in five types: stuffed with chocolate, coffee, chocolate lava, blueberry and durian – the perfect snack as you explore Chinatown. They have home-made sorbet ice cream too, including mango and soursop (RM6.90). Daily 10am–10pm.

Central Market Food Court Jalan Hang Kasturi ☎03 2274 6542, ⊛centralmarket.com.my; map p.71. The Central Market has plenty of excellent outlets specializing in food from different corners of the Peninsula and beyond, from traditional Nyonya food to Japanese crêpes. Daily 10am–10pm.

Chinatown Food Paradise 65–67 Jalan Petaling; map p.71. Out of the various food stalls here the *Vegetarian Food* stall stands out; as the name suggests, it offers a tantalizing array of excellent vegetarian dishes including noodles, tofu, spring rolls and curried vegetables. Daily 8am–7pm.

Contango Majestic Hotel, Jalan Sultan Hishamuddin ☎03 2785 8000, ⊛majestickl.com; map p.71. Within the *Majestic Hotel*, this contemporary restaurant features a lively open kitchen with an incredible selection of cuisines on offer: Indian, Chinese, Japanese and Western, including Italian and grilled dishes. The buffet (breakfast RM58, lunch RM78, dinner RM98) includes a delectable selection of desserts, and can feature a free flow of wine (add RM45). Daily 6.30am–10.30am, noon–3pm & 6.30–10.30pm.

Lai Foong 138 Jalan Tun H.S. Lee ☎03 2072 8123; map p.71. The six stalls at this historic *kopitiam* rustle up all manner of local delicacies including noodle and rice dishes – try the Hainanese beef noodle, flavoured with herbs and served with not only beef slices but also tripe. Daily 6.30am–9pm.

Lokl Coffee Co. 30 Jalan Tun H.S. Lee ☎03 2072 1188, ⊛loklcoffee.com; map p.71. Small and welcoming café,

under the same management as the *Back Home* hostel, which is a great spot for a mid-morning snack or light lunch (set lunch of soup and main RM25.50) as you explore Chinatown and Little India. The interior is cosy with wooden tables and bare brick walls, and the menu offers a selection of pastries as well as Western dishes including burgers (RM20.90). Tues–Sun 8am–8pm.

Lucy in the Sky 167 Jalan Tun H.S. Lee ☎03 2022 1526, ⊜lucyintheskycafe@gmail.com; map p.71. Located in a former warehouse, this pleasant café with a minimalist interior, featuring bare brick walls and spotlights, offers Western dishes including pastas (RM15.90), burgers (RM20) and all-day breakfasts (RM20). There are plans to soon stay open for dinner, too. Tues–Sun 9am–7pm.

Nam Heong 56 Jalan Sultan ☎03 2078 5879, ⊛esquirekitchen.com; map p.71. Original Haiwanese chicken rice is rustled up in front of your very eyes as you enter this popular spick-and-span restaurant that attracts those in the know in Chinatown. A meal will set you back about RM10. Daily 10am–3pm.

★ **Old China Café** 11 Jalan Balai Polis ☎03 2072 5915, ⊛oldchina.com.my; map p.71. Wonderfully atmospheric café set in a pre-World War I shophouse with old-world charm; much of the decor, including the saloon-style swing doors at the entrance, is original and lovingly preserved. Must-trys include classic dishes such as *pie tee* (RM7.80), rice flour cones stuffed with minced chicken and vegetables, and *ikan asam* (RM20.90), mackerel cooked in tamarind. Daily 11.30am–11pm.

Penjaja Gallery Jalan Tun H.S. Lee & Jalan Petaling; map p.71. It's worth heading into the alleyway that connects Jalan Petaling with Jalan Tun H.S. Lee to get a feel for life in Chinatown – vendors here display all manner of meats, vegetables and other foods, and there are a handful of great stalls where you can sample local dishes such as curry *laksa* (RM4) as a morning snack. Tues–Sun 7am–noon.

Purple Cane Tea House Third floor, 6 Jalan Panggong ☎03 2072 1349; map p.71. This calm and peaceful retreat from Chinatown's hubbub serves a range of speciality Chinese teas. Customers are invited to remove their shoes before taking a seat at wooden benches or on cushions at low tables. Teas are ceremoniously served (RM5–20 depending on tea type), and the menu even features simmered black tea giant drumstick rice (RM10.90) as well as tea eggs (RM3), which, as the name suggests, have been boiled in tea. Daily 11am–7pm.

Santa 11 Jalan Tun H.S. Lee ☎019 269 9771; map p.71. This laidback restaurant hums with custom at lunchtime, when locals flock here for the freshly made *chapatti*

1

(RM1.50) and *kimma mutton* (RM3) that are undoubtedly among the best in town. Mon–Fri 6.30am–6.30pm, Sat 6.30am–3pm.

Yusoof 44 Jalan Hang Kasturi ☎03 2026 8685; map p.71. Clean and friendly Muslim-Indian Malay diner, offering tasty dishes including great *roti nan* with chicken tandoori (RM7) and *nasi biriyani* (RM7). Portions are generous and, inside, the piped Islamic music doesn't intrude as much as you'd think from the street. Daily 6am–11pm.

Zuliani Corner Corner Jalan Hang Lekir & Jalan Tun H.S. Lee ☎010 287 2216; map p.71. Just across the road from Popular Bookshop, this little stall churns out excellent Muslim Indian *rojak* (RM4) – fried dough fritters with potatoes, bean curd, egg and shredded cucumbers mixed with a sweet and spicy peanut sauce. Mon–Sat 9.30am–7pm.

THE GOLDEN TRIANGLE AND KAMPUNG BAHRU

Acme Bar & Coffee (ABC) Ground floor, the Troika, 19 Persiaran KLCC ☎03 2162 2288, ⓦacmebarcoffee.com; map pp.76–77. The interior of this stylish coffee house and restaurant is reminiscent of a converted warehouse, with floor-to-ceiling windows, low hanging light bulbs and exposed pipe work. It's a great spot for reliably good soups (RM25), salads (RM27), pastas (RM30) and other international favourites from salmon fillet to smoked duck breast, as well as all-day weekend brunches. There's a sister restaurant in Bangsar. Mon–Thurs 11am–midnight, Fri 11am–1am, Sat 9.30am–1am, Sun 9.30am–midnight.

Albion 31 Jalan Berangan ☎03 2141 9282, ⓦalbionkl .com; map pp.76–77. Superb Sunday roasts with Yorkshire pudding and all the trimmings (RM55) at this popular British restaurant that buzzes with expats. The modern British menu includes a succulent slow-roast pork belly with potato and leek bake (RM41), while the delicious apple crumble (RM19) is the perfect way to round off your meal. Tues–Sat noon–3pm & 5–11pm, Sun noon–10.30pm.

Ben's First floor, Suria KLCC mall ☎03 2163 1655, ⓦthebiggroup.co; map pp.76–77. One of KLCC's most

reputable restaurants, this is a reliably good choice serving international cuisine in a pleasant setting modelled after a Manhattan townhouse. The menu includes soups (RM15), salads (RM22), sandwiches (RM20) and meat pies (RM26), along with more substantial mains such as steak frites (RM65). Daily 10am–11pm.

Cantaloupe Level 23A, Tower B, the Troika, 19 Persiaran KLCC ☎03 2162 0886, ⓦtroikaskydining.com; map pp.76–77. This swanky French restaurant, on the top floor of KL's swish Norman Foster building, offers fine dining and a bird's-eye view of the city. The popular Sunday lunch (RM120) is a favourite among well-heeled Malays and expats alike, with dishes changing seasonally – expect the likes of smoked duck and caramelized onion bread, roast chicken and sage anchovy butter, and soursop *jalousies*. The six-course caviar-tasting menu is the ultimate decadence. Daily noon–2.30am & 6.30–10.30pm.

Din Tai Fung Level 6, Pavilion KL mall ☎03 2148 8292, ⓦdintaifung.com.my; map pp.76–77. This superb Michelin-starred Taiwanese light-meal chain specializes in Shanghainese *xiao long bao* – little pork dumplings served in a bamboo steamer, eaten dipped in ginger vinegar. You can watch the chefs at work at the open kitchen, painstakingly cutting out and stuffing each dumpling with minced pork and shrimp (RM15.80/six pieces). Mon–Sat 10.30am–10pm, Sun 10am–10pm.

Feeka 19 Jalan Mesui ☎03 2110 4599; map pp.76–77. Pleasant coffee house serving locally roasted beans and home-made pastries (RM6.50), as well as a smattering of light meals including omelettes (RM16) and French toast (RM16). It's a great spot to refuel the morning after a long night out. Daily 9am–midnight.

★**Hakka** 90 Jalan Raja Chulan ☎03 2143 1908; map pp.76–77. Excellent open-air Chinese restaurant with seating under twinkling fairy lights serving top-notch Hakka cuisine. The seafood is particularly good, although there are plenty of other dishes on offer including vegetables and even ostrich. Mains from RM15. Daily noon–3pm & 6–11.30pm.

Lot 10 Hutong Basement, Lot 10 Mall, Jalan Bukit Bintang; map pp.76–77. This gourmet heritage village

---

JALAN ALOR: KL'S OUTDOOR FOOD HAVEN

Along with numerous restaurants, the Golden Triangle also boasts one of KL's best alfresco experiences in **Jalan Alor**. The street actually has a double layer of food outlets: the open-fronted restaurants that line the street, and the food stalls arranged in front of them. Food is predominantly Chinese, with a strong seafood bias – and some of the city's tastiest Hokkien noodles, comprising egg noodles fried in lard, seasoned with dark soy sauce and garnished with prawn, pork and fishcake slices, and greens – but there are plenty of Thai and Malaysian options too, plus fresh fruit and drink vendors. It all fires up from 6pm, and the stalls stay open into the small hours. Some menus omit prices, so fix them when ordering to avoid nasty surprises when the bill arrives. Dishes cost RM5–25; you can usually order small, medium or large portions.

located in the basement of Lot 10 mall offers a plethora of authentic Malay items of food. With over 900 dishes on offer, there's plenty of choice, from *hokkian mee* noodles to freshly made *siew bao*. A dish will set you back about RM10–12. Daily 10am–10pm.

Luk Yu Tea House Basement, Starhill Gallery, 181 Jalan Bukit Bintang ☎03 2782 3850, ⓦstarhillgallery .com; map pp.76–77. Shaped like a teapot, this welcoming place is more of a restaurant than a teahouse as such, serving excellent Hong Kong-style pork-free dim sum (RM10) and other Chinese favourites; needless to say, there are plenty of fine teas on offer too, including silver needle jasmine and ginseng oolong. Mon–Sat noon–11pm, Sun 10am–11pm.

The Magnificent Fish & Chips Bar 28 Changkat Bukit Bintang ☎03 2142 7021; map pp.76–77. This funky restaurant with British-referenced decor (take a look at the first floor, with Minis "crashed" into the wall) truly lives up to its name, with excellent battered fish and chips (RM30) served in newspaper wrapping – there are four types of fish to choose from, including Icelandic cod and barramundi. The menu, scribbled in chalk on blackboards, includes plenty of other British staples such as Guinness and steak pie (RM34) and kedgeree with smoked haddock (RM20); full all-day English breakfasts (RM28), too. Daily 9am–3am.

Marble 8 Steakhouse 163 Jalan Binjai ☎03 2386 6030, ⓦmarble-8.com; map pp.76–77. Exceptional upmarket steakhouse serving fine cuts of Wagyu (RM268) and wet-aged Angus (RM148) beef, with unparalleled views of the Twin Towers. The stylish *M8* bar, with its dark glittering decor, is a great spot for a pre-or post-prandial cocktail, while the *Privé* lounge offers a fine collection of whiskies and cigars. Sun–Fri noon–2.30pm & 7–11pm, Sat 7–11pm.

Muar 6G Tengkat Tong Shin ☎03 2144 2072; map pp.76–77. This great restaurant in the heart of bustling Bukit Bintang offers a chance to try specialities from Muar, a little town that is renowned for its tasty variations of Chinese and Malay dishes. The menu includes tasty dishes such as butter *kalian* (RM10), deep-fried vegetables with butter and evaporated milk, and crispy fried egg (RM5). Tues–Sun 11am–3pm & 6–10pm.

Nagasari Curry House 17-1 Jalan Angsoka; map pp.76–77. This no-frills curry house buzzes with custom and dishes out some of the best curry you'll find in the city; it offers a range of tasty North and South Indian dishes including tandoori chicken (RM9), chicken tikka (RM14.50) and vegetable banana-leaf curries (RM7.50). Daily 24hr.

Neroteca Unit G-1, Seri Bukit Ceylon, 8 Lorong Ceylon ☎03 2070 0530, ⓦneroteca.com; map pp.76–77. This stylish Italian restaurant has floor-to-ceiling shelves lined with wine bottles, and a deli counter displaying meats and cheese. There's a wide selection of cold cuts and platters of antipasti, and it's a great spot for Sunday brunch, too.

At RM98 (RM148 with unlimited – selected – wines and Prosecco) it doesn't come cheap, but won't be leaving hungry. Mon–Fri 11.30am–3pm & 6–11.30pm, Sat 6–11.30pm, Sun noon–3pm & 6–11.30pm.

Nerovivo 3a Jalan Ceylon ☎03 2070 3120, ⓦnerovivo .com; map pp.76–77. Among the best Italian places in KL, with upmarket, chic modern decor and an extensive menu including plenty of excellent meat and seafood options. Busy rather than intimate ambience, and not cheap –pasta dishes start at RM36, while main courses cost RM55 and up. Booking essential. Mon–Fri noon–3pm & 6–11.30pm, Sat 6–11.30pm.

★**Pinchos** 18 Changkat Bukit Bintang ☎03 2145 8482, ⓦpinchos.com.my; map pp.76–77. Authentic tapas and pinchos (RM11–26) are served at this bustling Spanish tapas bar that gets packed in the evenings. The atmosphere is warm and cosy, with seating at the bar or at wooden tables, and service is friendly and efficient. Tues–Sun 5pm–3am.

Sao Nam 21 Tengkat Tong Shin ☎03 2144 1225, ⓦsaonam.com.my; map pp.76–77. This welcoming Vietnamese restaurant continues to attract plenty of custom mainly thanks to the plethora of awards it has won in the past. The dishes are still very good, with the likes of deep-fried chicken spring rolls (RM20) and house speciality mangosteen and prawn salad (RM36), all served beneath wall posters extolling the collectivist life. Tues–Fri 12.30–2.30pm & 7.30–10.30pm.

Shook! Basement, Starhill Gallery 181 Jalan Bukit Bintang ☎03 2719 8535, ⓦstarhillgallery.com; map pp.76–77. Attracting celebrities and moneyed Malaysians and expats, this interactive restaurant with four show kitchens offers Japanese, Chinese, Italian and Western grill dishes. There's an extensive wine list (the walk-in cellar holds more than three thousand bottles), and the daily live jazz adds a nice touch to the restaurant's already appealing ambience. The crunchy snow-white dancing prawns starter (lightly wok-fried prawns coated in a hot mayonnaise and honey-glazed walnut sauce; RM58) is an absolute must. Daily 6am–11pm.

Sushi Hinata A-01, St Mary Residence, 1 Jalan Tengah ☎03 2022 1349, ⓦshin-hinata.com; map pp.76–77. Touted as one of the capital's best Japanese restaurants, this superb place specializes in sushi and fine cuts of sashimi. Ingredients are flown in from Japan, and dishes are expertly prepared by the experienced Japanese chef at the open counter. Mon–Sat noon–3pm & 6-11pm.

Thai Somtam Seafood 88 Changkat Bukit Bintang ☎014 637 6583; map pp.76–77. Climb up a flight of little steps to reach this unassuming Thai place that rustles up some pretty tasty grub, including an exceptionally spicy papaya salad (RM10) and other Thai specials such as green chicken curry (RM18). Daily 11am–11.30pm.

twenty.one 20–1 Changkat Bukit Bintang ☎03 2142 0021, ⓦdrbar.asia; map pp.76–77. This trendy place is a

1

restaurant, bar and club venue all in one. The modern European cuisine with a touch of Asian is top-notch, with dishes of the likes of crispy-skin salmon (RM38) and lamb shank (RM46). Cocktails (RM26) are enjoyed on the modish first-floor balcony that overlooks the hustle and bustle of Changkat Bukit Bintang. Daily noon–2am.

Zenzero A-09 Ground Floor, St Mary Place, 1 Jalan Tengah ☎ 03 2022 3883, ⓦ zenzero.com.my; map pp.76–77. With an understated casual-chic interior, this relatively new addition to the KL dining scene has undoubtedly found its place as one of the capital's best restaurants. The refined Italian cuisine is prepared by the experienced Italian chef; the menu changes seasonally, and the wine list includes an excellent selection from Italy and beyond. Mains from RM42. Sun–Fri noon–2.30pm & 6–11pm, Sat 6–11pm.

LITTLE INDIA, CHOW KIT AND BEYOND

Little India is a good area for both Indian and Malay food – inexpensive Indian restaurants and sweetmeat shops are ranged along Jalan Melayu, while in and around Lorong TAR's *pasar malam* are quite a few Malay food stalls and Indian *kedai kopis*, and a useful food court opposite the *Palace Hotel* stays open late. A few truly venerable *kedai kopis*, some housed in equally venerable shophouses, can be found along hectic Jalan TAR, while there are more stalls, Malay and even Indonesian, around Chow Kit Market.

★**Capital Café** 213 Jalan TAR ☎ 03 2698 2884; map p.74. Locals flock to this endearing family-run *kedai kopis* which first opened its doors in 1956 for morning *nasi lemak* (RM4) or toast with *kaya* (coconut jam; RM2.50); plenty of other dishes are offered at lunch, including beef *rendang* (RM4) and fried noodles (RM4), while the sizzling satay, said to be one of the best in town (ten sticks RM9) is available from 5pm. Mon–Fri 7am–8pm, Sat 10am–8pm.

Jai Hind 13 Jalan Melayu ☎ 03 2692 0041; map p.74. Friendly *kedai kopis* which, besides an impressively wide-ranging spread of curries and stir-fries, also has an extensive menu of North Indian savouries and sweets, as good as you'll get in smarter restaurants but at half the price. RM15 should see you full. Daily 8am–9pm.

Kedai Makanan Sithique 237 Jalan Tuanku Abdul Rahman; map p.74. One of a handful of popular *kedai kopis* specializing in *nasi kandar* with chicken (RM6) or fish (RM4–5); fluffy *roti canai* and *thosai* are made on the spot, along with pretty tasty *mee goreng* (RM4). Daily 7am–7.30pm.

Saravanaa Bhavan 1007 Selangor Mansion, Jalan Masjid India ☎ 03 2698 3293, ⓦ saravanabhavan.com; map p.74. One of a slightly eccentric Madras-based chain of vegetarian restaurants that's spread its tentacles as far afield as London and New York. Concentrate on the South Indian dishes – *dosai, idli, uthapam*, and so forth – and be warned that spicing can be incendiary. Inexpensive, with main courses under RM10. Daily 8am–11pm.

Syed Bistro 57 Jalan Dang Wangi ⓦ syedbistro.com; map p.74. This laidback place proudly boasts they have "the one and only *biriyani*" and in all fairness it's pretty tasty – there's chicken (RM13), mutton (RM16) and lamb (RM25), as well as a selection of fiery curries and freshly baked *roti canai* to choose from. Daily 24hr.

BRICKFIELDS

★**Annalakshmi** Temple of Fine Arts, 116 Jalan Berhala ☎ 03 2272 3799, ⓦ annalakshmi.com.sg; map p.82. This community-run South Indian vegetarian restaurant, with a warm and welcoming ethnic interior, offers a stupendous eat-all-you-want lunchtime buffet for RM16; in the evenings it's à la carte only, and the profits go to support various projects. There's a small informal canteen at the car park beneath the building, where you pay what you feel the meal is worth to you. Smart-casual dress; no shorts, sports clothes or open shoes. Tues–Sun 11.30am–3pm & 6.30–11pm.

Gem 124 Jalan Tun Sambanthan ☎ 03 2260 1373; map p.82. Reliable, moderately smart restaurant serving South Indian chicken, mutton and seafood curries. The vegetarian thali costs around RM14. Conveniently close to the Monorail station. Daily 11.30am–10.30pm.

Sri Devi Jalan Travers 9 ☎ 03 2260 1553; map p.82. Widely reckoned to sell some of Brickfields' best Indian food, this little place does excellent banana-leaf curries from noon onwards and wonderful *dosai* (RM6) all day. Daily 6am–11pm.

BANGSAR

The small grid of streets known as Bangsar Baru, 4km southwest of Chinatown, is one of several satellite suburbs known for smart restaurants and bars, here catering to expats as well as well-heeled professionals. Bus #U87 travels to Bangsar from the Sultan Mohamed terminal in Chinatown, via KL Sentral. Bangsar LRT station isn't convenient for Bangsar Baru, being some way downhill with busy highways to cross in between. A taxi from Chinatown shouldn't cost more than RM10.

Alexis Bistro 29 Jalan Telawi 3 ☎ 03 2284 2880, ⓦ alexis .com.my; map opposite. This sleek café, bistro and wine-bar is worth visiting for its delectable cakes alone (RM13), although the menu includes Asian and Western dishes, along with hearty breakfasts (RM32); it's popular among expats and well-heeled Malaysians. Daily 9am–2am.

La Bodega 16 Jalan Telawi 2 ☎ 03 2287 8318, ⓦ bodega.com.my; map opposite. This well-liked tapas chain attracts a loyal expat following for its tapas (from RM14) and paella (RM35); this branch is augmented by a lounge and deli that serves imported Spanish produce. Daily 10am–2am.

Mercat 51g Jalan Telawi 3 ☎ 03 2201 5288, ⓦ mercat .my; map opposite. Catalan gastro-bar with walls embellished with sketches of Barcelona's landmarks. Exceptional tapas include *patatas bravas* (creamy potato nuggets; RM22) and Catalan *fuet* (succulent pork salami; RM19), as well as more substantial mains including iberico meatballs of minced pork and beef served with cuttlefish and peas (RM39). Tues–Fri 4–11pm, Sat & Sun noon–11pm.

Rendez-vous 100 Lorong Maarof ☎03 2202 0206, ⓦrendez-vous.com.my; map below. An expat favourite, this restaurant serves authentic French food at very reasonable prices. The menu includes the classics with an emphasis on seafood, which is flown in from France. The appetizing seafood platter includes oysters, langoustine, whelks, prawns, cockles, clams and winkles (RM119). Tues–Sun noon–3pm & 6pm–1am.

Sri Nirwana Maju 43 Jalan Telawi 3 ☎03 2287 8445; map below. This hugely popular banana-leaf curry house with canteen decor stands out in the swanky

expat area that is Bangsar, and attracts crowds for its excellent dishes (RM8.50) Be prepared to queue. Daily 10am–2am.

WTF 98 Lorong Maarof ☎019 261 7070, ⓦwtfrestaurants.com.my; map below. It actually stands for What Tasty Food, and so it is – this place serves excellent Indian vegetarian dishes, although there are also other cuisines to choose from including Chinese, Mexican and Italian. Mon–Thurs 11.30am–10pm, Fri–Sun 11.30am–11pm.

Yeast 24g Jalan Telawi 2 ☎03 2282 0118, ⓦyeastbistronomy.com; map below. A boulangerie, bistro and bar all in one, this is a great spot for a morning coffee and croissant (RM4) or for more substantial mains. The experienced French chef rustles up exceptional dishes including *boeuf bourguignon* (RM76) and confit of lamb shoulder (RM68). Tues–Thurs & Sun 8am–10pm, Fri & Sat 8am–10.30pm.

1

DRINKING

KL's most fashionable **bars** and clubs are concentrated in the Golden Triangle, while Bangsar (see p.96) also plays host to a few slick bars. Only during Ramadan are both the bars (and clubs) distinctly quiet. Beer in KL costs around RM12 a pint (when available on draught; bottles and cans are more common), a couple of ringgit less during the **happy hours** that most places offer.

CHINATOWN AND AROUND

Reggae Bar 158 Jalan Tun H.S. Lee, Chinatown ☎ 03 2041 8163; map p.71. No-frills bar that's very popular with backpackers, though a few locals drop by too. The walls are plastered with Bob Marley memorabilia, though the DJs do recognize that other reggae artistes are available. Daily noon–2am.

LITTLE INDIA, CHOW KIT AND BEYOND

Coliseum Café 98–100 & 102 Jalan TAR ☎ 03 2692 6270, ⓦ coliseum1921.com; map p.74. Endearingly antiquated – or creakingly ancient – the bar here has a rich history (it was established in 1921) and relaxed atmosphere; some of the furnishings date back to the 1920s, although the original tables and stools didn't make it to the present day. Sip a Gunner A (the bar's signature cocktail of ginger beer, ginger ale and angostura bitters; RM10.50) and imagine the planters and colonial administrators of yesteryear gathering to quench their thirst. Daily 10am–10pm.

THE GOLDEN TRIANGLE AND KAMPUNG BAHRU

Frangipani 25 Changkat Bukit Bintang, ☎ 03 2144 3001, ⓦ frangipani.com.my; map pp.76–77. Behind the impressive Art Deco-style facade lies a bar with sleek minimalist decor, excellent cocktails (RM30), pumping house sounds and a beautiful straight and gay clientele, almost as pretty as the downstairs restaurant's pricey nouvelle cuisine (mains RM60), served 7.30–10.30pm only. Tues–Sun 6pm–midnight, Fri & Sat 6pm–3am.

Fuego Level 23A, Tower B, the Troika, 19 Persiaran KLCC ☎ 03 2162 0886, ⓦ troikaskydining.com; map pp.76–77. As you'd expect from a 23rd-floor location, this tapas bar with open-air seating boasts stunning views of the cityscape; it's a great spot for a sundowner as you watch the sun set over the Twin Towers – the views don't get much better than this. Daily 6.30pm–1am.

The Green Man 40 Changkat Bukit Bintang ☎ 03 2141 9924, ⓦ greenman.com.my; map pp.76–77. This small, likeable pub serves good traditional pub grub, including pork pies and bangers and mash, washed down with a refreshing pint (RM23) or jug (RM46) of lager. It gets particularly busy when there's football or rugby on TV. Mon–Fri 10am–1am, Sat & Sun 9am–2am.

Hubba Hubba Ground Floor Invito Hotel Suites, 1 Lorong Ceylon ☎ 017 786 7611; map pp.76–77. This large restaurant and bar, with high ceilings and a warehouse-style feel, serves great Western and Asian dishes including Japanese, Malay and Indian, plus early breakfasts, and rustles up some great cocktails (RM25). On Thurs, Fri and Sat nights at 10pm DJs spin house, commercial and R&B tracks. Sun–Wed 6am–1am, Thurs–Sat 6am–3am.

Luna Bar Level 34, Pacific Regency Hotel Suites, KH Tower, Jalan Punchak, off Jalan P. Ramlee ☎ 03 2332 7777, ⓦ luna.my; map pp.76–77. If you've only time to take in one bar while in KL, you could do far worse than head for this gorgeous rooftop poolside venue, with loungey sounds and breathtaking views of KL's skyline. Cocktails from RM20. Sun–Thurs 10am–1am, Fri & Sat 10am–3am.

Marini's on 57 Level 57, Menara 3 Petronas ☎ 03 2161 2880, ⓦ marinis57.com; map pp.76–77. As you'd expect, the capital's highest rooftop bar boasts spectacular views of the city. Here, too, award-winning mixologists shake up classic and signature cocktails such as the White Dame (RM38), with bourbon, cointreau, grapefruit juice, lemon, honey and egg white. Smart attire only, or you will be refused entry. Sun–Thurs 5pm–1.30am, Fri & Sat 5pm–3am.

Pisco Bar 29 Jalan Mesui ☎ 03 2142 2900, ⓦ piscobarkl.com; map pp.76–77. A range of excellent Peruvian/Spanish tapas (RM20) are to be had at this trendy nightlife spot where pisco sours (RM28) are the drink of choice. Walls are adorned with blown-up photographs of pop icons and other celebs, while upturned buckets serve as bar lamps. Tues–Sun 5pm–1am, Fri & Sat 5pm–3am.

Sky Bar Floor 33, Traders Hotel, KLCC ☎ 03 2332 9888, ⓦ skybar.com.my; map pp.76–77. One of the capital's most renowned bars offers the chance to sip cocktails (RM35) at the poolside while taking in exceptional views of the city from the 33rd floor. The bar hosts themed events nights (check the website) and guest DJs on Saturday nights spin an eclectic mix, from EDM to R&B. Sun–Thurs 10am–1am, Fri & Sat 10am–3am.

BANGSAR

Ronnie Q's 32 Jalan Telawi 2, Bangsar ☎ 03 2282 0722, ⓦ ronnieqpub.com; map p.97. The focus at this watering hole with four TVs and a projector is very much on sport – not just soccer but also cricket and rugby. Plenty of drinks including Guinness (RM27.75/pint) and Tiger beer (RM22.05/pint). Mon–Thurs 4pm–1am, Fri–Sun noon–1am.

NIGHTLIFE

If the drinking scene seems to tick over healthily enough, KL's **clubbing** scene appears surprisingly buoyant for its size (although as with the bars, things are quiet during Ramadan). KL's clubland largely focuses around the junction of Jalan Sultan Ismail and Jalan P. Ramlee in the Golden Triangle, although venues are also springing up around Asian Heritage Row on Jalan Doraisamy, near Medan Tuanku Monorail station. The music policy at each venue tends to change with alarming frequency, but as a rule weekends feature more serious dance sounds, while during the week retro hits and fairly accessible R&B take over. To keep up with happenings, including which big-name DJs might be in town, check out the Friday **club listings** in the *Star* newspaper, *Juice* magazine (ⓦ juiceonline.com) or the clubs' own websites. Most clubs open Wednesday to Sunday 10pm to 3am or so; the typical cover charge of RM20–40 rises if well-known DJs are playing. Unfortunately, **live music** in KL isn't much to write home about. With Malaysia a centre for music piracy, most international bands choose not to play here, and it doesn't help that religious conservatives have kicked up a huge stink when the likes of Avril Lavigne and Gwen Stefani have performed. Consequently most concerts are safe big-name pop, soul or country artists, plus occasional indie bands. That said, KL has a few small venues where local English-language singer-songwriters and bands get to strut their stuff, and shows by Malay pop stars and old-school rockers are occasionally publicized in the press.

CLUBS

Beach Club 924 Jalan P. Ramlee, Golden Triangle ☎ 03 2170 6666, ⓦ beachclubcafe.com; map pp.76–77. Established venue with a somewhat clichéd thatched-tropical-hut theme, with towering coconut trees and an aquarium. The mix of commercial chart and house sounds does pull in the punters most nights of the week, although it is a bit of a meat market. Daily noon–3am.

Blue Boy 50 Jalan Sultan Ismail (actually in a small lane off the main drag), Golden Triangle ☎ 03 2142 1067; map pp.76–77. Kuala Lumpur's chief gay venue is a bit of a dive but still attracts a large local and foreign crowd to its bar and dance area, though beware the odd hustler. Daily 8pm–3am.

Havana Changkat Bukit Bintang, Golden Triangle ☎ 03 2142 7170, ⓦ havanakl.com; map pp.76–77. Located just above the bustling steak-and-grill restaurant of the same name, this place has been attracting punters for two decades. At weekends locals and expats alike hang out over beers and stomp about to old school and retro hits. There's also a lounge and rooftop terrace bar for those who want to natter away over a few drinks. Fri & Sat 10am–2am.

Providence The Intermark, 182 Jalan Tun Razak, Golden Triangle ☎ 017 291 2396; map pp.76–77. One of the capital's hottest clubs is also one of its most exclusive, attracting well-heeled Malays who come here to see and be seen. With its plush velvet sofas and backlit menus, the club hosts big-name international DJs. Wed–Sat 10pm–3am.

The Roof 1 First Ave, Bandar Utama, Petaling Jaya ☎ 012 691 0628, ⓦ theroof.com.my; map pp.76–77. This large entertainment hub in Petaling Jaya to the west of

the centre hosts five nightlife outlets including a bar on a grassed helipad, a gastro-lounge with great cocktails and a super-club (Wed–Sat 10pm–3am) hosting DJs and live gigs. Daily noon–2am.

Zouk 113 Jalan Ampang, Golden Triangle ☎ 03 2171 1997, ⓦ zoukclub.com.my; map pp.76–77. Set inside a distinctive, organically curvy building, this offshoot of one of Singapore's top clubs has become a mainstay of the KL scene. The half-dozen venues here – *Zouk*, *Barsonic*, *Phuture*, *Velvet Underground*, *Aristo* and the *Relish* terrace bar – spin an eclectic range of music, including a smidgeon of indie. Cover charge varies according to the night (RM18–38). Tues–Sat 10pm.

LIVE MUSIC VENUES

Alexis Bistro Ampang Lot 10 & 11, Great Eastern Mall, 303 Jalan Ampang, Golden Triangle ☎ 03 4260 2288, ⓦ alexis.com.my; map pp.76–77. Under the same management as *Alexis Bistro* in Bangsar, this pleasant bistro and wine bar hosts excellent local and international jazz acts on Friday and Saturday nights at 10pm. Mon–Thurs 11am–midnight, Fri & Sat 11am–2am, Sun 10am–midnight.

No Black Tie 17 Jalan Mesui, Golden Triangle ☎ 03 2142 3737, ⓦ noblacktie.com.my; map pp.76–77. The venue of choice for discerning music lovers, this great jazz and gastro-bar hosts regular jazz, classical blues and folk sets, as well as international poetry readings. Pricey Japanese food (set menu RM98) and cocktails (RM25) can be enjoyed in the performance/dining area while you watch the show. Mon–Sat 7pm–1am.

GAY KL

KL's gay community is fairly discreet, though the smart cafés of fashionable **Changkat Bukit Bintang** attract a noticeably gay clientele at weekends. Friday is gay night at *Frangipani* (see opposite), and if you see other clubs advertising "boys' nights", gay men will know they can head there too. There's also *Blue Boy* (see above). For more on gay venues and social events in the city, try ⓦ utopia-asia.com or ⓦ gaygetter.com.

1

ARTS AND ENTERTAINMENT

The modest local **performing arts** scene is split between KL and its satellite town Petaling Jaya, which, with its complex system of numbered roads that even residents don't understand, is best accessed by taxi. **Theatre** is probably the strongest suit, with concerts, musicals and so forth throughout the year, by local as well as international performers and troupes. There's also a dedicated community of people working in the **visual arts**. For **listings**, check the national press and also the monthly magazine *Time Out* (Ⓦ timeoutkl.com). Ⓦ kakiseni.com is also worth consulting, not only for listings but also for an intelligent look at how the performing arts can find a balance with the multicultural Asian and Muslim values that hold sway in Malaysia.

THEATRE AND CLASSICAL MUSIC

Aside from the Actors Studio, other drama companies worth making time for include the Five Arts Centre (Ⓦ fiveartscentre .org) and the satirical Instant Café (Ⓦ instantcafetheatre .com). There are two home-grown orchestras, namely the Malaysian Philharmonic Orchestra (Ⓦ mpo.com.my) and the Dama Orchestra (Ⓦ damaorchestra.com), the latter specializing in Chinese classical music and musicals. Watch the press for news of international recitals. Besides the venues listed here, there are occasional concerts at the KL Convention Centre and also at out-of-town resorts such as Genting Highlands; check the press for details.

Actors Studio ☏ 03 2142 2009, Ⓦ theactorsstudio .com.my. The most prominent of KL's theatre companies, the studio mounts several productions each year, ranging from Malaysianized versions of foreign classics to work by local playwrights, and has been instrumental in the creation and running of one of the city's more impressive independent arts centres, KLPac (see below). At the time of research the studio was relocating, although the company continues to stage productions at KLPac.

Dewan Filharmonik Level 2, Tower 2, Petronas Twin Towers, Golden Triangle box office ☏ 03 2051 7007, Ⓦ mpo.com.my; map pp.76–77. The home of the Malaysian Philharmonic, it also hosts concerts by other performers, not just in the classical domain. The box office is on the ground floor, Tower 2. Box office Tues–Sat 10.30am–6.30pm.

Istana Budaya (National Theatre) Jalan Tun Razak, east of the junction with Jalan Pahang and south of Titiwangsa Gardens, Titiwangsa ☏ 03 4026 5555, Ⓦ istanabudaya.gov.my; map pp.76–77. Besides providing a spacious modern home for the National Theatre Company and the National Symphony Orchestra, this venue sees performances by visiting international orchestras as well as staging pop concerts, plays and ballets. Just over 1km from Titiwangsa (LRT/Monorail) or Chow Kit (Monorail) stations.

KLPac Jalan Strachan, off Jalan Ipoh, Sentul ☏ 03 4047 9000, Ⓦ klpac.org; map pp.76–77. A joint project of the stalwart Actors Studio company and the construction conglomerate that's redeveloping the area, the KL Performing Arts Centre is housed in a former rail depot revamped to look like a Frank Lloyd Wright doodle. It hosts jazz, indie and dance events plus, of course, plays by various companies. The location couldn't be more awkward, in the depths of the old Sentul Raya Golf Club and cut off from the

nearby Sentul Komuter station by the rail line, which you can't cross safely without a big detour. Get here by taxi; just pray that the driver is a culture vulture or remembers the golf course. As for heading back, be prepared for a trudge out to Jalan Ipoh, where you can pick up a taxi.

Panggung Bandaraya Sultan Abdul Samad Building, Jalan Tuanku Abdul Rahman, Colonial District ☏ 03 2602 3335, Ⓦ dbkl.gov.my; map p.71. Occasional performances of Malay drama (*bangsawan*) take place in this historic theatre with a Moorish facade.

CULTURAL SHOWS

Traditional dance can be seen at the cultural shows put on by the Malaysian Tourism Centre and by a couple of restaurant theatres, though what's on offer is inevitably touristy. Indian dance is better catered for, thanks to the Temple of Fine Arts.

Malaysia Tourism Centre (MaTiC) 109 Jalan Ampang, Golden Triangle ☏ 03 2164 3929, Ⓦ matic gov.my. Forty-five minute dance shows, featuring performers from Borneo as well as the Peninsula, are held Mon–Thurs at 3pm and on Sat at 8.30pm (RM5).

Saloma Next to MaTiC, Jalan Ampang, Golden Triangle ☏ 03 2161 0122, Ⓦ saloma.com.my. This place offers "tiffin set lunch" (RM38/person, minimum two), and an evening buffet (RM100) with a performance of traditional dance (daily 8.30–9.30pm), supposedly focusing on different states of the Federation each night. Daily 10am–10pm.

Temple of Fine Arts 116 Jalan Berhala, Brickfields ☏ 03 2274 3709, Ⓦ tfa.org.my. Community-run cultural centre set up to preserve Tamil culture by promoting dance, theatre, folk, classical music and craft-making. Probably the best place in KL to see traditional Indian dance.

CINEMA

Coliseum Cinema Jalan TAR, Little India. As a total contrast to the main chains, this cinema is worth a trip for its 1930s Art Deco character, even if Bollywood and Chinese kung fu films aren't your thing.

Golden Screen Cinemas Ⓦ gsc.com.my. Branches in Pavilion KL and Berjaya Times Square in Bukit Bintang; their Mid Valley Megamall screen is your best bet for occasional foreign art-house films. RM12–50.

TGV Suria KLCC mall, Golden Triangle Ⓦ tgv.com.my. A conveniently located multiplex. RM12–50, depending on the time and film.

SHOPPING

There's no city in Malaysia where consumerism is as widespread and in-your-face as KL. The malls of the Golden Triangle are big haunts for youths and yuppies alike, while **street markets** remain a draw for everyone, offering a gregarious atmosphere and goods of all sorts. Jalan Petaling in Chinatown (see p.70) is where to find fake watches and leather goods; some of these have started to creep into the covered market on Jalan Masjid India and the nearby Lorong Tuanku Abdul Rahman *pasar malam* (see p.73), but their mainstays remain clothes and fabrics, plus a few eccentricities such as herbal tonics and various charms alleged to improve male vigour. Chow Kit Market (see p.73) has some clothing bargains but little else of interest. A great just-out-of-town market for knick-knacks and general bric-a-brac happens every weekend inside the **Amcorp Mall** in Petaling Jaya, close to Taman Jaya station on the LRT.

ANTIQUES

Antiques are extremely expensive in Southeast Asia, and often fake; dealers listed below are sound but even experts can be fooled, so don't fork out unless you know what you're doing. The biggest market is for Chinese and Peranakan (Nyonya) porcelain, woodcarvings and artefacts, though there are also some Malaysian and Asian specialists in town.
Heritage of the Orient Ground Floor, Central Market, Chinatown ☎03 2274 6443, ⓦheritageoftheorient.com; map p.71. Select range of genuine antiques from Tibet, China and Central Asia, plus a few pieces from Sarawak. Pricey. Daily 10am–8pm.
House of Suzie Wong 4th floor, Lot 10 Mall, Bukit Bintang, Golden Triangle ☎03 2143 3220; map pp.76–77. Interesting, eclectic range of antiques and collectibles from mainland China and Tibet, including furniture and carpets; high quality but reasonable prices. Daily 10am–10pm.
Madame Butterfly Floor 2, Mid Valley Megamall, Mid Valley City ☎03 2282 8088; map p.82. Antiques and antique-style arts and crafts; best for Burmese jade jewellery and Nyonya porcelain. Daily 10am–10pm.
Pucuk Rebung Level 3, Ampang Mall, Suria KLCC mall, Golden Triangle ☎03 2382 0769; map pp.76–77. Excellent range of Malaysian modern art and museum-quality antiques, from Chinese shipwreck porcelain to Malay betel-nut scissors and tobacco boxes. The manager is a mine of information about the history of Chinese culture in Malaysia. Daily 10am–10pm.
Tomlinson Collection 30 Jalan Telawi 5, Bangsar ☎03 2283 2196, ⓦtomlinson-collection.com; map p.97. One of Asia's leading antique specialists showcasing a fine selection of classic Ming style Chinese furniture in prized woods, as well as Khmer sculptures, fine porcelain, Chinese robes and textiles and terracotta Han, Tung and Ming figurines. Daily 11am–7pm.

BOOKS AND MUSIC

The larger KL bookshops are pretty impressive, split into Chinese-, English- and Malay-language sections, and carrying a good range of publications. They tend to be strong in literature about Malaysia and the rest of Southeast Asia – everything from historical monographs and classics-in-translation, to Manga, cookbooks and coffee-table tomes on architecture and garden design. Unfortunately, in this country of rampant piracy, music shops are nothing to write home about.
Junk Book Store 78 Jalan T.S. Lee, Chinatown ☎017 292 0855, ⓦjunkbookstore.com; map p.71. Ancient establishment, jammed to its dusty rafters with secondhand books, most in English, covering every conceivable topic from pulp fiction to gardening. Mon–Fri 8.30am–5pm, Sat 8.30am–2pm.
Kinokuniya Level 4, Suria KLCC mall, Golden Triangle ☎03 2164 8133, ⓦkinokuniya.com; map pp.76–77. Huge and efficient Japanese chain, with the broadest selection of books in KL. Daily 10am–10pm.
MPH Lower ground floor, Mid Valley Megamall, Mid Valley City ☎03 2938 3800, ⓦmphonline.com; map p.82. This veteran survivor of the local book trade is resting on its laurels somewhat, though it still carries a decent mix of novels and nonfiction titles. They also have smaller outlets at KL Sentral and at the Bangsar Village mall. Daily 10am–10pm.
Popular Bookshop Lee Rubber Building, Jalan T.S. Lee, Chinatown ☎03 2078 1953, ⓦpopular.com.my; map p.71. Stationer-style bookshop, worth checking for maps, paperbacks and cookbooks before heading further afield. Daily 10am–8.30pm.
Rock Corner First floor, Bangsar Village mall, Bangsar ☎03 2202 1139; map p.97. Bravely independent music retailer, good for hard-to-find rock and indie CDs. Daily 10am–10pm.
Times Bookstore Level 6, Pavilion KL mall, Golden Triangle ☎03 2148 8813, ⓦtimesbookstores.com.my; map pp.76–77. Large, well-organized member of the Singapore-based chain. Daily 10am–10pm.

HANDICRAFTS

KL is a good place to stock up on handicrafts, though they tend to be available a little more cheaply in the provincial areas where they originate, and some here might even have been imported from overseas. For a broad range – everything from Royal Selangor pewter models of the Petronas Towers to bright batik, tribal textiles and original paintings or sculptures – visit Chinatown's Central Market (see p.67) and Kompleks Kraf (see p.75).

1

Kwong Yik Seng Crockery 144 Jalan Tun H.S. Lee, Chinatown ☎03 2078 3620; map p.71. Hand-carved wooden Chinese cake moulds, Nyonya *pie tee* moulds, and stacks of modern pink-and-green Nyonya porcelain (at almost antique prices, however). They'll generally bargain a little. Mon–Sat 9am–5pm.

Lavanya Temple of Fine Arts, 114–116 Jalan Berhala, Brickfields ☎03 2272 1330, ⓦlavanya.org.my; map p.82. This pleasant shop in the Temple of Fine Arts sells Indian artefacts made from clay, wood, stone, metal and fabric. Part of the proceeds go to a hospital clinic nearby. Tues–Sat 10am–9.30pm, Sun 10am–3pm.

Peter Hoe Second floor, 145 Lee Rubber Building, corner of Jalan Tun H.S. Lee, Chinatown ☎03 2026 0711; map p.71. Reached by the side entrance of the Lee Rubber Building, this large shop sells a range of arty-crafty soft furnishings, knick-knacks, textile bags and so forth, with a Southeast Asian flavour. A smaller outlet at 2 Jalan Hang Lekir specializes in batik, made in Indonesia to their own designs and in less garish colours than usual. There's also a pleasant café within the shop. Daily 10am–7pm.

Royal Selangor Pewter Factory 4 Jalan Usahawan 6, Setapak Jaya ☎03 4145 6000, ⓦroyalselangor.com. Pewter – an alloy of tin – is something of a souvenir cliché in Malaysia, though platters, mugs and other objects can be elegant. This factory, 5km northeast of Chow Kit, is most easily reached by taxi from the Wangsa Maju LRT stop, 2km east, and offers free guided tours as well as the opportunity to buy their products. They also have stores in Bangsar and Suria KLCC malls. Daily 9am–5pm.

MALLS

Locals and visitors alike come to KL's shopping malls to seek refuge from the heat as much as to shop; for local young people, the malls are also important places to socialize. Mostly located outside the old centre, particularly in the Golden Triangle, the malls divide into two categories – gargantuan affairs in the manner of Western malls, featuring international chains and designer names, and smaller, denser Southeast Asian-style complexes, basically indoor bazaars with row upon row of tiny independent retailers. The simpler malls tend to be much more popular than their more sophisticated, pricier counterparts, and can be atmospheric places to wander. Many malls, of whatever type, house a supermarket or department store of one sort or another.

BUKIT BINTANG

BB Plaza Jalan Bukit Bintang, just west of Jalan Sultan Ismail; map pp.76–77. Teeming local-style mall with good deals on cameras and electronic equipment. Daily 10am–10pm.

Berjaya Times Square Jalan Imbi, opposite the Monorail's Imbi stop ⓦtimessquarekl.com; map pp.76–77. Enormous mall with indoor theme park rides,

though not as buzzing as it really ought to be considering its size, and living somewhat in the shadow of Pavilion KL and Suria KLCC. Daily 10am–10pm.

Lot 10 Bintang Walk ⓦlot10.com.my; map pp.76–77. Specializes in designer clothes and accessories. Daily 10am–10pm.

Low Yat Off Jalan Bukit Bintang ⓦplazalowyat.com; map pp.76–77. The best place in KL for electronic and digital purchases, from laptops to cameras. Daily 10am–10pm.

Pavilion KL Between Jalan Bukit Bintang and Jalan Raja Chulan ⓦpavilion-kl.com; map pp.76–77. One of the very largest malls in the city – and that's saying something – with a parade of big-name designer outlets on Jalan Bukit Bintang and branches of Singapore's Tangs department store and Malaysia's Parkson chain, present here in an especially upmarket version. There's also a Times bookshop, GSC cinema and a plethora of eating and nightlife outlets. Daily 10am–10pm.

Starhill Gallery Next to the Marriott, Bintang Walk ⓦstarhillgallery.com; map pp.76–77. More designer names than is healthy, orbiting a suitably grand atrium. Just as noteworthy is the maze of top-notch restaurants at the base of the building. Daily 10am–10pm.

Sungei Wang Plaza Jalan Sultan Ismail ⓦsungeiwang.com; map pp.76–77. Joined onto BB Plaza and just as popular as its neighbour, KL's first mall offers everything from clothes to consumer electronics. Generally keenly priced. Daily 10am–10pm.

KLCC

Avenue K 156 Jalan Ampang ⓦavenuek.com.my; map pp.76–77. Worth a look if you're into designer outlets, but a bit staid. Daily 10am–10pm.

Suria KLCC At the base of the Petronas Twin Towers ⓦsuriaklcc.com.my; map pp.76–77. A mall so large it's subdivided into sub-malls for ease of reference, Suria KLCC's oval atriums are home to UK department store Marks & Spencer, Isetan and Cold Storage supermarkets, plus numerous restaurants and a TGV multiplex cinema. Daily 10am–10pm.

BANGSAR AND MID VALLEY CITY

Bangsar Shopping Centre 285 Jalan Maarof, Bangsar ⓦbsc.com.my; map p.97. Upmarket affair, a good place to have a suit made, buy gifts or just find some food from home that you miss. Plenty of restaurants and coffee shops to boot. Daily 10am–10pm.

Bangsar Village and Village II Bangsar Baru ⓦbangsarvillage.com; map p.97. The boutiques tend to play second fiddle to the restaurants in these two malls, joined by a bridge above street level. Shopping highlights include an MPH bookshop and the Country Farm Organics supermarket, selling organic produce and even

1

eco-friendly detergent – the likes of which you'll hardly see on sale anywhere else in the country. Daily 10am–10pm.

Mid Valley Megamall/Gardens Mall Off Jalan Syed Putra, 2km south of Brickfields @midvalley.com.my; map p.82. The sprawling Mid Valley Megamall certainly gives Suria KLCC a run for its money; come here for the Carrefour hypermarket, the Jusco and Metrojaya department stores, the MPH bookshop, the GSC cinema and the usual plethora of outlets selling everything from cosmetics to computers. The newer, adjacent Gardens Mall has sprung up alongside, joined by a bridge from Level 2, home to designer labels and the Singapore-based department store Robinsons. Both malls are easy to reach, as the KTM Mid Valley Komuter station is close by. Daily 10am–10pm.

OUTDOOR GEAR

Lafuma 16 Jalan Telawi, Bangsar Baru ☎03 2287 1118, @lafuma.com.my; map p.97. Also known as Yellow Stone, this small but serious outdoor shop features hiking boots, waterproofs, sleeping bags, water purifiers, camping stoves, packs, water bottles, tents, trekking clothing and accessories. They can also organize trekking guides in Peninsular Malaysia, Mount Kinabalu and beyond. Daily 11am–9pm.

Ufl Outdoors 26 Jalan Telawi 5, Bangsar Baru ☎03 2282 5721, @ufl.com.my; map p.97. Good for small, low-tech essentials – seam sealer, plastic water bottles, small nylon bags – plus sleeping bags and even basic tents. Some decent snorkelling gear, too. Daily 10am–8.30pm.

DIRECTORY

Banks and exchange Banks with ATMs are located throughout KL; Maybank is usually your best bet for foreign exchange. You may get better rates from official moneychangers, which can be found in shopping malls and in and around transport hubs.

Casino KL has long had a casino at Genting Highlands (@rwgenting.com), which also attracts vacationing locals, as it features several fairly pricey resorts, a theme park, shopping malls and so forth. It's 30km out of town, best reached via the Karak Highway (E8); express buses head there from Puduraya and Pekeliling bus stations, and there are also share taxis from Pudu Station.

Cultural centres Alliance Française, 15 Lorong Gurney (☎03 2694 7880, @alliancefrancaise.org.my); British Council, West Block, Wisma Selangor Dredging, Jalan Ampangm next to the *Maya* hotel (☎03 2723 7900, @britishcouncil.org/malaysia.htm); Goethe-Institut, sixth floor, 374 Jalan Tun Razak (☎03 2164 2011, @goethe.de).

Embassies and consulates Australia, 6 Jalan Yap Kwan Seng (☎03 2146 5555, @malaysia.embassy.gov.au); Brunei, 19-01 Tingkat 19, Menara Tan & Tan, Jalan Tun Razak (☎03 2161 2800, @mofat.gov.bn); Cambodia, 46 Jalan U Thant (☎03 4257 1150, @embassyofcambodia-malaysia.org); Canada, Menara Tan & Tan, 207 Jalan Tun Razak (☎03 2718 3333, @canadainternational.gc.ca); China, Plaza OSK, 25 Jalan Ampang (☎03 2164 5250, @my.china-embassy.org); India, 2 Jalan Taman Duta (☎03 2093 3510, @indianhighcommission.com.my); Indonesia, 233 Jalan Tun Razak (☎03 2116 4016, @kbrikualalumpur.org); Ireland, The Amp Walk, 218 Jalan Ampang (☎03 2161 2963, @embassyofireland.my); Japan, 11 Persiaran Stonor (☎03 2177 2600, @my.emb-japan.go.jp); Laos, 12 A Persiaran Madge (☎03 4251 1118); Netherlands, The Amp Walk, 218 Jalan Ampang (☎03 2168 6200, @malaysia.nlembassy.org); New Zealand, Level 21, Menara IMC, 8 Jalan Sultan Ismail (☎03 2078 2533, @nzembassy.com/malaysia); Philippines, 1 Changkat Kia Peng (☎03 2148 9989, @philembassykl.org.my); Singapore, Level 15, West Wing, The Icon, 1 Jalan 1/68f, Jalan Tun Razak (☎03 2161 6277, @mfa.gov.sg/kualalumpur); South Africa, 3 Jalan Kia Peng (☎03 2170 2400, @sahighcomkl.com.my); South Korea, 9 & 11 Jalan Nipah, off Jalan Ampang (☎03 4251 2336, @mys.mofa.go.kr); Thailand, 206 Jalan Ampang (☎03 2145 8004, @thaiembassy.org/kualalumpur); UK, Level 27 Menara Binjai, 2 Jalan Binjai (☎03 2170 2200, @gov.uk /government/world/malaysia); US, 376 Jalan Tun Razak (☎03 2168 5000, @malaysia.usembassy.gov); Vietnam, 4 Persiaran Stonor (☎03 2148 4858, @mofa.gov.vn).

Emergencies Police and ambulance ☎999, fire and rescue ☎994.

Hospitals and clinics General Hospital, Jalan Pahang (☎03 2615 5555, @hkl.gov.my); Gleneagles Hospital, Jalan Ampang (☎03 4257 1300, @gleneagleskl.com.my); Pantai Medical Centre, 8 Jalan Bukit Pantai (☎03 2296 0888, @pantai.com.my); Tung Shin Hospital, 102 Jalan Pudu (☎03 2037 2300, @tungshin.com.my).

Left luggage Luggage can be stored for a few ringgit/day at KL Sentral station and Pudu Sentral bus station (look out for a couple of counters at the back of the passenger level). At KLIA, the service costs RM10–30/day depending on the size of the bags.

Police KL has its own Tourist Police station, where you can report stolen property for insurance claims, within the same complex as MATIC tourist office at MTC, 109 Jalan Ampang (☎03 2163 4422).

Post office The General Post Office is just south of the Dayabumi Complex (Mon–Fri 8am–4pm, Sat 8am–2pm); poste restante/general delivery mail comes here. A post office with extended hours can be found at Suria KLCC (daily 10am–6pm).

Rock climbing Guide Pro (☎03 4011 1939, @theguideproshop.com) runs excursions for novices or experienced climbers to sites around Batu Caves. Trips cost RM150–300/person, guides and all equipment supplied; hotel pick-ups upon request at extra cost.

1

Sports facilities Public sports facilities in downtown KL are limited. The most convenient pool is at Chinwoo Stadium, uphill south off Jalan Hang Jabat in Chinatown (Mon–Fri 2–8pm, Sat & Sun 9am–8pm; RM4). The pool is well maintained but the showers and changing faciltiies are basic, and baggy swimwear is not allowed (they'll sell men appropriate swimming trunks if required). Private health clubs, with gyms and other facilities, include Fitness First (ⓦfitnessfirst.com.my), with central locations at Avenue K mall, Jalan Ampang, next to the KLCC LRT station, and at 22 Jalan Ismail, near the Raja Chulan Monorail station. The KL Golf and Country Club is at Bukit Kiara, 8km west of the centre (ⓣ03 2011 9188, ⓦwww.klgcc.com).

Visa extensions The Immigration Office is at Kompleks Kementerian, Dalam Negeri, 69 Jalan Sri Hartamas 1 (Mon–Fri 7.30am–5pm, counter closes at 4pm; ⓣ03 6205 7400, ⓦimi.gov.my).

Around Kuala Lumpur

With the reckless urbanization of the Klang Valley proceeding apace, worthwhile excursions from KL are becoming increasingly rare. The most obvious attraction is 13km north, where limestone peaks rise up from the forest at the Hindu shrine of **Batu Caves**, one of Malaysia's main tourist attractions. Nearby, the **Forest Research Institute of Malaysia** (FRIM) encompasses a small but surprisingly thick portion of primary rainforest, where you can see birds and a few animals within an hour of downtown KL.

Further northwest of KL, the quiet town of **Kuala Selangor** offers the chance to observe the nightly dance of **fireflies**, while northeast, **Fraser's Hill** is one of Malaysia's many hill stations, set up in colonial times to allow government officials an escape from lowland heat. The most surreal day-trip you can make from KL is to the very Chinese fishing village on **Pulau Ketam**, off the coast near southwesterly Pelabuhan Klang, which hardly feels like Malaysia at all.

Batu Caves and Pulau Ketam are easy to reach on **public transport**, but you'll need a car or taxi to reach FRIM. About the only package trip widely offered by KL's accommodation and tour agents goes to see the fireflies; you can do this on public transport, but it's a bit of a slog and requires an overnight stay at Kuala Selangor.

Forest Research Institute of Malaysia

16km northwest of KL • Daily 5am–7.30pm, canopy walk Tues–Thurs, Sat & Sun 9.30am–2.30pm (last registration at 1.30pm) • RM5, canopy walk RM10 • ⓣ03 6279 7592, ⓦfrim.gov.my • KMT Komuter train to Kepong station (20min), then taxi final 5km (10min)

The **Forest Research Institute of Malaysia** (**FRIM**) sits amid a fifteen-square-kilometre reserve of rainforest and parkland, threaded with sealed roads and walking trails. A popular spot for weekend picnics, appealing to birdwatchers, joggers and anyone after some greenery and fresh air, it has the added attraction of a short **canopy walk** between the treetops, providing views of KL's skyline. It also makes a good warm-up for wilder affairs at Taman Negara (see p.185). A couple of hours here is plenty of time for a walk around; for a full day out you could always continue to the Batu Caves and Orang Asli Museum (see opposite).

Taxis deliver to the gates; pick up a **map** and follow the main road 1km into the park, past open woodland and lawns, to the **One Stop Centre**, where you can book the canopy walk and seek general advice. A small **museum** nearby, strongly biased towards the timber industry, gives thumbnail sketches of the different types of tropical forests and the commercial uses of various woods.

For a good walk, follow the clear "Rover" walking track past the mosque and uphill into the forest; there are some huge trees, birds and butterflies here, and a rougher side-track to the canopy walk, a single-plank suspension bridge across a deep gully. You may see monkeys too, and can join up with a couple of other tracks that bring you back to the One Stop Centre in about ninety minutes.

Batu Caves

13km north of KL on Jalan Batu Caves, roughly midway between the junctions with Jalan Ipoh and the E8 • Free • KTM Komuter train from KL Sentral to Batu Caves (every 15–30min; 30min)

The **Batu Caves** sit right on the northern edge of Greater KL, where forested limestone thumbs poke out of a ridge of hills in the suburb of Gombak. In 1891, ten years after the caves were noticed by American explorer William Hornaby, local Indian dignitaries convinced the British administration that the caves were ideal places in which to worship (probably because their geography was reminiscent of the sacred Himalayas). Soon ever-increasing numbers of devotees were visiting the caves to pray at the shrine established here to Lord Murugan, also known as **Lord Subramaniam**; later the temple complex was expanded to include a shrine to the elephant-headed deity **Ganesh**. Although the caves are always packed with visitors, to be honest they're a little underwhelming – unless, of course, you join the thousands upon thousands of devotees who descend during the annual three-day **Thaipusam festival** in late January or early February.

Arriving at the site, you're immediately struck by the immense staircase leading up into the limestone crags, with a gigantic golden statue of **Lord Murugan**, the Hindu god of war, to one side; it's claimed to be the tallest such statue in the world. A number of minor temples stand at ground level, but most visitors head straight up the 272 steps to the caves, pausing only to catch their breath or take photos of the marauding macaques who make their presence all too obvious.

Dark Caves

Batu Caves • Tues–Sun 9.30am–5pm • **Educational tour** Tues–Fri 10am–5pm, Sat & Sun 10.30am–5.30pm; 45min • RM35 **Adventure tour** Weekends only; 3–4hr; in group of ten or more only (age 12 and above) • RM80 • Book at least a week ahead on ✆ info@cave -management.com • ⊕ darkcavemalaysia.com

Three-quarters of the way up the steps to the Batu Caves – at step 204, to be precise – a turning on the left leads to a vast side cavern known as the **Dark Caves**, which can only be visited on a guided tour. Here a 2km-long passageway opens into five chambers populated by a large range of insects and at least three types of **bats**, which can be distinguished by their faces and calls. The caves also house interesting limestone formations, including several towering **flow stones**, so called because a continuous sheet of water runs down them.

Subramaniam Swamy Temple

Batu Caves • Daily 8am–7pm

At the top of the main staircase in the Batu Caves, there's a clear view through to the **Subramaniam Swamy Temple**, devoted to Lord Subramaniam and another deity, Rama. It's set deep in a cave around 100m high and 80m long, the walls of which are lined with idols representing the six lives of Lord Subramaniam. Illuminated via the huge void in the cave ceiling beyond another set of steps far inside the caves, the temple has an entrance guarded by two statues, their index fingers pointing upwards towards the light. A dome inside is densely sculpted with more scenes from the scriptures. In a chamber at the back, a statue of Rama, adorned with silver jewellery and a silk sarong, watches over the wellbeing of all immigrants. If you want to look closely at this inner

---

THE FRIM–BATU CAVES–ORANG ASLI MUSEUM CIRCUIT

The proximity of FRIM, the Orang Asli Museum and the Batu Caves to Middle Ring Road II (also known as Jalan Batu Caves) makes it feasible for drivers to visit all three in a circuit. From KL, either take the E8 highway, which intersects Jalan Batu Caves, or use Jalan Ipoh, which starts at Chow Kit and meets Jalan Batu Caves 4km west of the E8. FRIM is west of Jalan Ipoh, the Orang Asli Museum close to the E8, and the caves are in between the two.

Unfortunately, no buses connect the three, but you could use taxis to reach FRIM and the Orang Asli Museum from Batu Caves.

1

THAIPUSAM AT THE BATU CAVES

The most important festival in the Malaysian Hindu calendar (along with Deepavali), **Thaipusam** honours the Hindu deity Lord Subramaniam. It's held during full moon in the month of "Thai" (which in the Gregorian calendar always falls between mid-Jan and mid-Feb), when huge crowds arrive at the Batu Caves. Originally intended to be a day of penance for past sins, it has now become a major tourist attraction, attracting Malaysians and foreigners alike each year.

The start of Thaipusam is marked by the departure at dawn, from KL's Sri Maha Mariamman Temple, of a golden chariot bearing a statue of Subramaniam. Thousands of devotees follow on foot as it makes its seven-hour procession to the caves. As part of their penance – and in a trance-like state – devotees carry numerous types of **kavadi** ("burdens" in Tamil), the most popular being milk jugs decorated with peacock feathers placed on top of the head, which are connected to the penitents' flesh by hooks. Others wear wooden frames with sharp protruding spikes, which are carried on the back and hooked into the skin; trident-shaped skewers are placed through some devotees' tongues and cheeks. This rather grisly procession has its origins in India, where most of Lord Subramaniam's temples were sited on high ridges that pilgrims would walk up, carrying heavy pitchers or pots. At Batu Caves, the 272-step climb up to the main chamber expresses the idea that you cannot reach God without expending effort.

Once at the caves, the Subramaniam statue is placed in a tent before being carried up to the temple cave, where devotees participate in ceremonies and rituals to Subramaniam and Ganesh. Things climax with a celebration for Rama, when milk from the *kavadi* vessel can be spilt as an offering; incense and camphor are burned as the bearers unload their devotional burdens.

Extra buses run to the caves during Thaipusam. Get there early (say 7am) for a good view. Numerous vendors sell food and drink, but it's a good idea to take water and snacks with you, as the size of the crowd is horrendous.

sanctum, the temple staff will mark a small red dot on your forehead, giving you a spiritual right to enter.

Orang Asli Museum

20km north of KL • Sat–Thurs 9am–5pm • Free • ☏ 03 7189 2122, ⊛ jaoak.gov.my • Bus #174 (signed "Gombak Batu 12") from Lebuh Ampang in Chinatown (ask where to get out, as it's not obvious) – leaving the bus, cross to the east side of the road and head 50m further up, where a steep side road leads to the museum; driving, turn east off E8 onto Jalan Batu Caves and after reaching Jalan Gombak (after 1km), turn left (north) and continue another 2km to reach the site

Run by the government's Department for Orang Asli Affairs, the **Orang Asli Museum** aims to present a portrait of the various groups of Orang Asli, former nomadic hunter-gatherers in the jungle who are now largely resident in rural settlements. A large map of the Peninsula in the foyer makes it clear that the Orang Asli can be found, in varying numbers, in just about every state. That surprises some visitors, who see little sign of them during their travels. Besides collections of the fishing nets, guns and blowpipes the Orang Asli use to eke out their traditional existence, the museum also has photographs of Orang Asli press-ganged by the Malay and British military to fight Communist guerrillas in the 1950s (see p.563). Other displays describe the changes forced more recently on the Orang Asli – some positive, like the development of health and school networks, others less encouraging, like the erosion of the family system as young men drift off to look for seasonal work.

Head carvings

Hidden in an annexe to the rear of the building, examples of traditional handicrafts include the **head carvings** made by the Mah Meri tribe from the swampy region on the borders of Selangor and Negeri Sembilan, and the Jah Hut from the slopes of Gunung Benom in central Pehang. Around 50cm high, the carvings show stylized, fierce facial expressions, and are fashioned from a strong, heavy hardwood. They still have religious significance – the most common image used, the *moyang*, represents the spirit of the ancestors.

OPPOSITE GOLDEN STATUE OF LORD MURUGAN, BATU CAVES >

1

Kuala Selangor

Coastal **KUALA SELANGOR** lies 70km northwest of KL, close to the junction of routes 5 and 54 on the banks of Sungai Selangor (Selangor River). A former royal town, today it's a small, sleepy affair; the chief reason visitors continue to come here is to see the river's **fireflies**, which glow spectacularly in the early evening. This natural spectacle appeared at one stage to be in terminal decline: the fireflies' mangrove habitat was rapidly being cleared, and the river becoming polluted. Government intervention seems to have stabilized things, and you stand a reasonable chance of enjoying a decent light show, **weather** permitting – the flies don't perform in rain. It's easiest to see Selangor's highlights on an evening firefly **package tour** from KL, though you can visit independently if you're prepared to stay overnight.

Fort Altingsburg

Daily 9am–4.30pm • Free

All that remains of Kuala Selangor's glorious past are the remnants of two forts overlooking the town. The largest, **Fort Altingsburg**, recalls an era when this part of the country changed hands, bloodily, on several occasions. Originally called Fort Melawati, Altingsberg was built by local people during the reign of Sultan Ibrahim of Selangor in the eighteenth century, and later captured by the Dutch (who renamed it) as part of an attempt to wrestle the tin trade from the sultans. The fortress was partly destroyed during local skirmishes in the Selangor Civil War (1867–73). Within its grounds is a cannon, reputed to be from the Dutch era, and a rock used for executions. **Bukit Melawati**, the hill on which the fort is based, also holds a **lighthouse** and a British colonial resthouse.

Kuala Selangor Nature Park

Directly below Fort Altingsburg • Daily 9am–6pm • RM4 • ☎ 03 3289 2294 • The park is a 500m walk from Bukit Melawati (follow signs for "Taman Alam"); you can also get here on the buses that run up Route 5 from Klang – ask to be let off at the park, and you'll be dropped at a petrol station, from where the park is 200m up Jalan Klinik

The **Kuala Selangor Nature Park**, which encompasses mud flats, mangroves and a small patch of forest, is host to around 150 species of birds, with thirty more migratory species passing through, as well as silverleaf monkeys, which live in the forest, and crabs and fish in the mangroves. Clearly marked trails take between 30min and 1hr 30min to walk.

ARRIVAL AND DEPARTURE
KUALA SELANGOR

By bus Selangor Omnibus buses to Kuala Selangor leave from KL's Pudu Sentral station (every 30min; 2hr; the last bus back leaves at 7.45pm).

ACCOMMODATION AND EATING

Your best bet for **eating** in the Kuala Selangor area is the row of waterside restaurants, serving mainly Chinese seafood, in Pasir Penambang, on the north bank of the Selangor River 5km from town. Make your way across the river bridge, turn left and it's signed down a turning on the left; it's a very romantic spot at night.

Firefly Park Resort Jalan Haji Omar, Kampung Bukit Belimbing ☎ 03 3260 1208, ⌨ fireflypark.com. Slick accommodation with simple, modern, a/c en-suite chalets for four. There's a BBQ area and Chinese seafood restaurant, with breakfast upon request (weekends only; RM50). Rates drop by RM50 Mon–Thurs. RM180

Firefly Villa 1 Jalan SGG5/4 Sungai Gulang-Gulang, Tanjong Karang ⌨ fireflyvilla.com. Located about 12km north of town, this is a pleasant option offering four en-suite rooms set around a quiet pool area amid palm and banana trees. The friendly owners are keen to share their knowledge of the area, and each morning rustle up hearty breakfasts. RM289

Nature Park Chalets Kuala Selangor Nature Park ☎ 03 3289 2294, ✉ ksnaturepark@gmail.com. A mix of basic chalet and hostel accommodation. Book in advance, as school groups can fill the place up. There's nowhere to eat nearby, so bring all provisions. Dorms RM25, chalets RM45

FIREFLY TRIPS

Kuala Selangor's **fireflies**, known as *kelip-kelip* in Malay, are actually 6mm-long beetles of a kind found between India and Papua New Guinea. During the day, the fireflies rest on blades of grass or in palm trees behind the river's mangrove swamps. After sunset they move to the mangroves themselves, the males attracting mates with **synchronized flashes** of light at a rate of three/second. Females flash back at males to indicate interest and initiate mating. The most successful males are apparently those that flash brightest and fly fastest.

Boats leave on 30min firefly-spotting trips from two locations several kilometres from town: **Bukit Belimbing**, fibreglass boats run by *Firefly Park Resort*, on the north bank across the river bridge (daily 7.40–10.30pm; RM15/person); and **Kampung Kuantan**, on the south bank (manually steered wooden boats; daily 7.30–11.30pm; RM50/four-person boat). There are no buses to either of the jetties, so taxis from Kuala Selangor get away with pretty steep prices – expect the ride to cost at least RM20. It's important to remain quiet when watching the firefly display and not to take flash photographs, as such behaviour scares the insects away.

It's also possible to take firefly tours all the way **from KL** with Han Travel (RM190/person including return transport, all fees and seafood dinner; ⓦhan-travel.com).

Pulau Ketam

The moment you set foot aboard ferries to **PULAU KETAM** (Crab Island) you're in a kind of parallel universe: this is Chinese day-tripper land, with videos of Chinese karaoke clips or soap operas blaring from the on-board screens. Ketam's five thousand inhabitants are Teochew and Hokkien Chinese, who traditionally live almost entirely by fishing from their low, flat, mangrove-encrusted island. Every house is built on pilings above the sand, and practically every street is a concrete walkway or boardwalk raised in the same fashion. Aside from the chance to eat tasty, inexpensive seafood, you'd visit mainly for a slightly surreal break from KL's pace, with a couple of places to stay if you like the quiet.

From the jetty, walk past the mosque and into the village main street, lined with grocers, general stores, and stalls and **restaurants** selling seafood – including, of course, crab. Beyond a shop selling Buddhist paraphernalia is a sort of central square where you'll find the **Hock Leng Temple**, as well as a small grotto containing a representation of Kwan Yin, the Goddess of Mercy, looking decidedly Madonna-like with a halo of red electric lights. Beyond here, you come to a residential area of concrete and wooden houses, nearly all with their front doors left wide open. There's plenty of refuse littering the mud flats beneath, unfortunately, but more appealingly you'll also see shrines outside many homes and occasional collections of pans made of netting containing seafood products being left out to dry.

ARRIVAL AND INFORMATION   PULAU KETAM

By train and ferry Take the KTM Komuter train 25km southwest of KL to Pelabuhan Klang (Klang Port; every 15–20min; 1hr 20min); the ferry terminal is opposite the train station. Ferries depart daily 8.45am–6.30pm; at the weekends the last ferry is at 7.10pm, with the last

ferry back at 6pm (every 45min; 45min; RM7).
Tours Not far from the jetty, Greenway (ⓦgreenway2u .com) offers walking tours and boat rides to a floating fish farm (RM60 for four people).

ACCOMMODATION AND EATING

Hotel Sea Lion S3 Jalan Merdeka ☏03 3110 4121, ⓦsealion.com.my. Near the jetty, in a distinctive yellow and white building, this simple establishment has a nice deck overlooking the water; cheapest rooms are windowless with a fan, while others have a/c and a bit of space. You can book good-value packages here, including accommodation, food and a fishing trip. <u>RM38</u>

Restoran Seng Huat On the main street. Typical of many similar friendly places to eat nearby, but just a bit livelier; excellent seafood omelettes, prawns, crab, noodles soups and generic stir-fries. RM15 should leave you stuffed. Daily 8am–8pm.

1

Fraser's Hill (Bukit Fraser)

Set 1500m up in the forested Titiwangsa mountains, 98km northeast of KL, the collection of colonial bungalows comprising **FRASER'S HILL** was established after World War I as one of Malaysia's earliest **hill stations**, a retreat for administrators seeking relief from the torrid lowland climate. Though less visited than the much larger Cameron Highlands to the north, Fraser's Hill boasts excellent **nature trails** and superb **birdwatching**; some 250 species have been recorded here, and the **Fraser's Hill International Bird Race** each June (⊛pkbf.org.my) sees teams competing to clock up as many as possible within a day. Even if you don't have the slightest interest in twitching, the hill remains a good getaway from the heat and hubbub of KL, and at weekends (when accommodation prices shoot up) it draws families from as far away as Singapore. Bear in mind that **no public transport** comes all the way up here.

Hill station

Sprawling amid a handful of wooded slopes, the **hill station** focuses on a T-intersection at the south end of a **golf course**. *Puncak Inn* is located here, along with a distinctive **clock tower**, post office and bank, while roads and trails head off in all directions to clusters of hidden bungalows and cabins.

The easiest targets for a **stroll** are **Allan's Water**, a small lake less than 1km from the clock tower, and **Jeriau Waterfall**, 4km north via *Ye Olde Smokehouse*, where the convincing English country decor and **cream teas** (daily 3–6pm) are a strong inducement to pause for a breather. Another good walk involves taking Jalan Lady Guillemard east to the loop road, Jalan Girdle; this leads to the most remote section of the hill station, bordering **Ulu Tramin Forest Reserve**, though completing the entire circle only takes around ninety minutes.

Trails

Most of the **longer trails** can be covered in less than two hours; indeed it would only take a couple of days to cover them all. Signage, however, can be spotty – don't be paranoid about losing your way, but talk to the tourist office about your route before you set out, and consider hiring a guide. The trails can get slippery in wet weather, so be sure to wear proper footgear; leeches can sometimes be a problem.

The **Abu Suradi trail** begins on Jalan Genting close to the mosque, and takes about twenty minutes to reach its southern end, also on Jalan Genting, near the clinic. Also starting near the mosque, the **Hemmant trail** snakes along the edge of the golf course just within the jungle. At its far end, you can turn left and either walk on to Jalan Lady Maxwell, or continue as far as the Bishop's House, where you can pick up the **Bishop's trail**. After about 45 minutes, this route joins the **Maxwell trail**, at which point you can either leave the trail by turning right up the hill and returning to town via Jalan Lady Maxwell, or continue another hour on the Maxwell trail until it reaches Jalan Quarry. Here there's a course for **woodball** – a hybrid of croquet and golf, played with long mallets – with equipment to rent.

COMMUNISTS ON THE HILL

During the Emergency in the 1950s (see p.563), the mountainous jungle at Fraser's Hill provided perfect cover for some of the Communist guerrillas' secret camps, from where they launched strikes on British-owned plantations and neighbouring towns.

If you approach Fraser's Hill via Kuala Kubu Bharu, due north of KL, roughly halfway up you'll see a sign, "Emergency Historical Site", marking the spot where **Sir Henry Gurney**, the British High Commissioner for Malaya at the height of the communist insurgency in 1951, was ambushed and killed. The guerrillas hadn't known how important their quarry was: their aim had been only to steal guns, ammunition and food, but when Gurney strode towards them demanding that they put down their weapons, they opened fire.

ARRIVAL AND DEPARTURE

By car Fraser's Hill is reached by a single-lane road that branches off Route 55, which connects Kuala Kubu Bharu (KKB, on Route 1) and Raub (Route 8) at a spot called the Gap. In theory, this road takes summit-bound traffic only, while downhill traffic uses a road that joins the KKB–Raub road 1km northeast. When either is closed by landslips, however, traffic alternates hourly in each direction on the other. The entire journey to or from KL typically takes 2hr or so. There is no fuel station at Fraser's Hill.

By public transport Catch a Komuter train (blue Seremban line north) from KL to Kuala Kubu Bharu, commonly referred to as KKB (1hr 15min); note that not all trains stop off at KKB so make sure you ask before boarding. From KKB, you have to catch a taxi to Fraser's Hill (45min; RM80–100).

INFORMATION

Tourist office In the colonial building alongside the vine-covered clock tower at the centre of the hill station (daily 8am–11pm; ☎09 362 2007, ⓦpkbf.org.my); they can provide maps, advise on current trail conditions and put you in touch with local guides.

Useful website ⓦ fraserhill.info.
Banks There is a small branch of Maybank at the *Shahzan Inn* (see below) where you can change money (Mon–Thurs 9.15am–4.30pm, Fri 9.15am–4pm); there is also an ATM, although it only accepts local cards.

ACCOMMODATION

Accommodation in Fraser's Hill is mostly motel-like and geared to families and groups, though some **bungalows** – here either detached single-storey houses or small apartment blocks – are also available. Always book in advance, and expect rates quoted here to rise by fifty percent at weekends and during holidays.

★**Puncak Inn** Jalan Genting ☎09 362 2007, ⓦpkbf .org.my. The block of this tourist-office-run hotel is not the most inspiring in town, but this is one of the best options in Fraser's Hill, featuring neat and tidy rooms with flowery curtains, heating and en-suite facilities. There is free wi-fi at reception, but not in the rooms. **RM110**

Shahzan Inn Jalan Lady Guillemard ☎09 362 2300, ✉shahzan7@yahoo.com. Located in a large white concrete block, this bland hotel consists of tiers of rooms ascending a terraced hillside. Rooms are a bit dated and don't have much personality, although they are spacious and pretty comfortable, and either look onto the garden or the town's golf course. **RM184**

★**Ye Olde Smokehouse** Jalan Jeriau ☎09 362 2226, ⓦthesmokehouse.my. Founded in 1924 as a resort for British servicemen who fought in World War I, this stereotypical English country inn offers fireside chairs and spacious rooms with four-poster beds, guaranteed to make the cool nights pass all the more blissfully. There's a good restaurant, too (see below). Rates (it doesn't hurt to ask about discounts) include a full English breakfast. **RM308**

EATING AND DRINKING

Fraser's Hill doesn't offer much choice for eating: aside from the two restaurants reviewed here, there's a central **food court** offering a mix of Malay, Indian and Chinese staples for about RM5 a dish.

Scott Restaurant 2 Jalan Genting ☎09 362 2118. Under the same management as *Ye Olde Smokehouse*, this pleasant restaurant is reminiscent of a British country pub, with a cosy fireplace, wooden tables and chintzy sofas. Food can also be enjoyed on the little patio-cum-garden at the front of the building. The menu offers British classics including fish and chips (RM17), and there are some Asian dishes too, such as Thai green curry with chicken (RM18). Thurs–Tues noon–10pm.

Ye Olde Smokehouse Jalan Jeriau ☎09 362 2226, ⓦthesmokehouse.my. This quaint hill resort (see above) is the epitome of British country living, with its charming conservatory and log fire lit on colder days. English afternoon tea (daily 3–6pm) is served in the garden, and includes freshly baked scones and home-made strawberry jam. The restaurant menu features traditional British staples such as roast beef and Yorkshire pudding (RM65) and chicken and mushroom pie (RM48). Things are fairly informal during the day, but it's best not to turn up in a T-shirt and shorts in the evening. Daily noon–2.30pm & 6.30–9.30pm.

The west coast

114 Perak

134 Penang

158 Kedah and Perlis

171 Cameron Highlands

PULAU LANGKAWI

The west coast

It was on the west coast that the British got their first toehold in the Malay Peninsula, and long exposure to colonial influence has made it in many ways the most historical, multicultural and well-developed part of Malaysia today. Nowhere epitomizes this better than the island of Penang, whose capital, Georgetown, is arguably the most endearing city in the country, a fascinating conglomeration of temples, museums and shophouses. Penang aside, the west coast's major attraction is another island, Langkawi, best known for its pricey resort hotels although it also has plenty of budget places to stay along its southern beaches. The only other significant island off this coast, Pangkor, pales in comparison but offers a more down-to-earth seaside experience.

Over on the mainland, the largest city is **Ipoh**, an excellent base for visiting the **Cameron Highlands** (also easily reached from Kuala Lumpur), once a British hill station and still a popular refuge from the stifling heat of the plains. Ipoh's hinterland encompasses a number of attractions, including opportunities to take in Malay royal architecture or indulge in a spot of **whitewater rafting**. Points of interest thin out inland, but it is possible to see the rainforest at the **Ulu Muda Eco Park** and the **Royal Belum State Park**, both bordering Thailand, and explore Malaysia's newest World Heritage Site, the archeologically important **Lenggong Valley** – though all are tricky to reach.

GETTING AROUND   THE WEST COAST

By plane Penang has frequent flights to and from many other Malaysian and Southeast Asian cities, notably Singapore. Flights from KL, Singapore and Kuching, among others, serve Langkawi.

By road The west coast's major artery is the North–South Expressway (also referred to as "NSE", and north of KL, as the E1). Access to the east coast is mainly via Route 76, which links up with Route 4 (the East–West Highway) to Kelantan state in the northeast.

By bus Frequent express buses link the west coast with KL, the south and Singapore, but there are only a handful of services to the east coast.

By train The belated modernization of Malaysia's rail network (see p.31) is being pioneered on the west coast, with new stations next to existing ones and daily express services between KL and Ipoh every couple of hours. Trains between the Thai border and KL and between Butterworth and Singapore remain infrequent and slow.

By boat Langkawi is linked with southern Thailand by ferry, and there are also daily boat services between Langkawi and Penang.

Perak

Lacking in top-drawer sights, **Perak** is an unsung part of the country, seen as merely a pleasant corridor between the capital and the delights of Penang and Langkawi. The state's topography is surprisingly diverse – monotonous coastal plains of mangrove and oil palm

Pangkor watersports p.124
Georgetown's CAT shuttle p.136
UNESCO and Georgetown p.141
Georgetown's street art p.142
The Penang riots p.144
Penang room taxes p.147

Penang's cultural resurgence p.151
Langkawi tours and activities p.166
Tea plantations p.173
Walking in the Cameron Highlands p.178

PULAU PANGKOR

Highlights

❶ Ipoh Fast-gentrifying mining city of old, surrounded by intriguing attractions including cave temples and the bizarre Kellie's Castle. **See p.117**

❷ Gopeng This whitewater rafting destination is easily accessible. **See p.121**

❸ Pulau Pangkor Laidback tropical island with some of the best beaches on the west coast. **See p.122**

❹ Taiping Traditional town with tranquil gardens and a mini hill station; Malaysia's largest mangrove reserve lies nearby. **See p.128**

❺ Royal Belum State Park Bordering Thailand, this unexpectedly fine nature reserve is a great place to spot *Rafflesia* flowers. **See p.134**

❻ Georgetown Rows of old shophouses and elaborate temples and clan houses characterize Penang's capital. **See p.136**

❼ Langkawi Upmarket resort island on the Thai border, featuring white-sand beaches and a cable car over the forested interior. **See p.163**

❽ Cameron Highlands Cool down amid the tea plantations and jungle trails of this former colonial hill station. **See p.171**

HIGHLIGHTS ARE MARKED ON THE MAP ON P.116

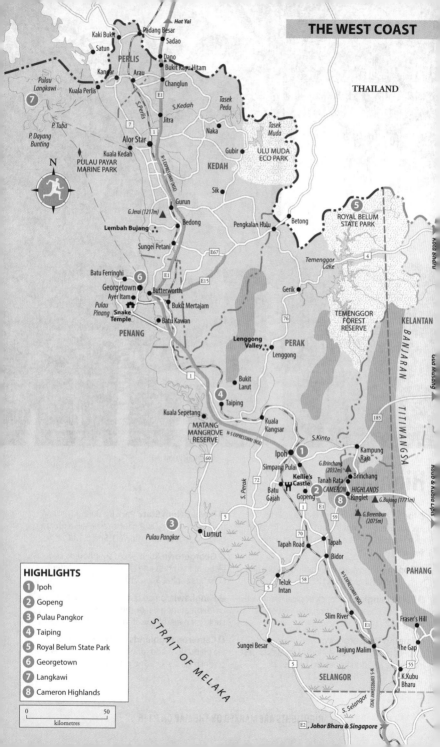

giving way inland to jagged limestone hills and the Titiwangsa mountain range – and so, in fact, are its attractions, not least its history. This was where the British began branching out from the Straits Settlements to open up the rest of the Peninsula, and consequently Perak's towns have relatively deep roots and more than a veneer of prosperity. Much of that wealth was founded on **tin** – a little ironic given that *perak* is Malay for "silver". Malaysia was the world's biggest tin producer as recently as the 1970s, but a collapse in prices in the mid-1980s led to the country turning away from the metal. The old mining centres now offer inducements to visit that are anything but obviously linked to mining: grand Malay buildings at **Kuala Kangsar**, lush gardens and hill hiking at **Taiping**, and **whitewater rafting** at **Gopeng**. One hub for all these is the state capital, **Ipoh**, a likeable city with solid colonial architecture, though few specific sights. In contrast are the laidback resort island of **Pangkor**, Perak's most mainstream draw, and the **Royal Belum State Park** in the interior, an excellent place to spot stinky *Rafflesia* blooms. The most overlooked attraction is the UNESCO World Heritage Site at **Lenggong Valley**, also in the interior, where important ancient human remains have been found in a series of caves. Sadly, it languishes due to lack of public transport and any proper tourist infrastructure.

Ipoh and around

IPOH was founded on the back of the great tin rush that kicked off in the 1880s, when major deposits were found in the area. The new settlement was sited at the highest navigable point on the **Kinta River**, a tributary of the Perak River – the Peninsula's second longest river – so was well placed for the ores to be collected for export. In common with the rest of the state, the city has seen a mini-exodus with the decline in mining, but in recent years people have been returning to invest in their hometown. Some half a million live here, making Ipoh the third largest city in the country, its centre an architectural snapshot of how the tin boom helped create the diverse Malaysia of today, with the bonus of nearby sights such as the outlying Chinese cave temple of **Perak Tong**, set in dramatic surroundings, and the eccentric, anachronistic ruin of **Kellie's Castle**. With excellent places to stay and eat, Ipoh is also a good springboard for the rest of Perak and the Cameron Highlands.

Old town

Ipoh began on the west bank of the Kinta, an area still known as the **old town**. The padang and the colonial core lie in the northwest, the centrepiece being the grand **train station**, another Anglo-Moorish effort by A.B. Hubback (see p.66), completed in 1917. A plaque marks out a specimen of an innocuous-looking tree at the front of the station – the upas, or *pokok ipoh* in Malay, which gave the city its name; once common in the area, it produces a toxic sap that the Orang Asli used on blowpipe darts. Opposite the station and nearly as handsome is the old **City Hall** (another Hubback creation), restored but used only for receptions and functions. Just east, the elegant **Birch Memorial Clock Tower**, commemorating the first British Resident of Perak (see p.559), takes some of the sting out of the jarringly ugly 1960s **Masjid Negeri** nearby on Jalan Sultan Iskandar.

Chinatown

South of the colonial area is what might be deemed Ipoh's historic **Chinatown**, a tight grid of streets lined with pastel-coloured shophouses that are starting to gentrify as new cafés and restaurants spring up. Amid the still mainly Chinese shops selling dried goods and textiles, look out for narrow **Panglima Lane**, nicknamed Concubine Lane as this back alley was where wealthy merchants kept their mistresses; and for dying trades – Lau Hooi Kee, for example, is a maker of **bamboo blinds** on a lane just north of Jalan Sultan Iskandar. There's the occasional touch of grandeur too, such as at **Han Chin Pet Soo**, an Art Deco former mining tycoon's club on Jalan Bijeh Timah; now refurbished, it may be open as a mini local history museum by the time you read this.

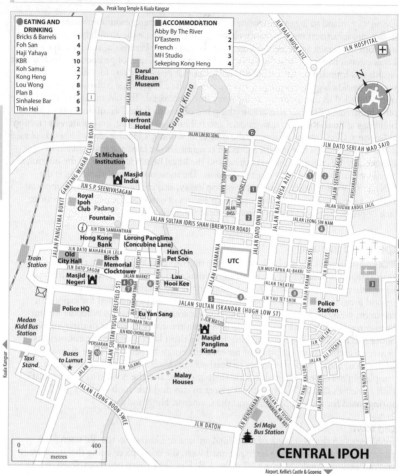

Perak Tong Temple & Kuala Kangsar

● EATING AND DRINKING

Bricks & Barrels	1
Foh San	4
Haji Yahaya	9
KBR	10
Koh Samui	2
Kong Heng	7
Lou Wong	8
Plan B	5
Sinhalese Bar	6
Thin Hei	3

■ ACCOMMODATION

Abby By The River	5
D'Eastern	2
French	1
MH Studio	3
Sekeping Kong Heng	4

CENTRAL IPOH

Airport, Kellie's Castle & Gopeng

New town

The tin boom had been under way for barely a decade when the cramped, wooden old town was devastated by fire in 1892. It underlined the pressing need for Ipoh to expand across the river, where hundreds of new shophouses were built on land once devoted to pig farms. But the tin price had slumped by the time this **new town** was completed in 1909, and the buildings remained vacant for some time – only to pick up when, in a smart move, the old town's brothels were moved here.

Today there's little sense of a transition upon crossing the Kinta, except that the new town has some modern high-rises, almost totally absent in the old town. The only sight here is the pretty blue-and-white **Panglima Kinta mosque**, close to the river and named after a prominent line of local Malay chieftains.

Perak Tong Temple

On the Kuala Kangsar Rd 6km north of Ipoh • Daily roughly 9am–6pm • Free • Perak Transit bus #35 from the Medan Kidd bus station (20min)

Ipoh's sprawling suburbs and noisy outer roads are overlooked by craggy limestone peaks, some riddled with caves where Chinese workers established popular **shrines** that are now especially busy during Chinese New Year. The best of these, **Perak Tong Temple**, doubles as a centre for Chinese art. Its gaudy exterior – bright red-and-yellow pavilions flanked by feathery willows and lotus ponds – gives no hint of the eerie atmosphere inside, where darkened caverns honeycomb up into the rock formation. The huge first chamber is dominated by a 15m-high golden statue of the Buddha flanked by two startled-looking companions dancing and playing instruments. In the next chamber, the walls are decorated with complex calligraphy and delicate flower paintings. Towards the back, a steep flight of 385 crudely fashioned steps climbs up and out of the cave to a sort of balcony, with views of great limestone outcrops and ugly factory buildings.

2

Kellie's Castle

Kinta Kelas Rubber Estate, 12km south of Ipoh • Taxi from Ipoh about RM50 return including a wait while you look around; alternatively, take any bus from Medan Kidd to Batu Gajah (for example Perak Transit #47 or #471; 30min), from where you can either walk the remaining 4km on the clearly signposted A8 road or take a taxi (around RM7)

Kellie's Castle symbolizes the prosperity achieved by many enterprising foreigners in the rubber and tin industries in the early 1900s. One of these was **William Kellie Smith**, a Scot who celebrated his success – and the birth of a long-desired son – by designing this extraordinary mansion. A flu epidemic in 1920 killed many of the Tamil workers; when work resumed, Smith embarked on a trip to Britain but fell ill and died in Portugal, and the building was never completed.

Far from being a ruin, however, the mansion is a sort of tropical palace in apricot-coloured bricks, with a rectangular, off-centre tower. It incorporates a lift (the first in the Peninsula), underground tunnels only rediscovered in 2003, and rows of arched colonnades in Moorish style. Heavily influenced by Indian culture, Smith imported many of the bricks from Madras and even constructed an adjacent **Hindu temple** in thanks for the birth of his son. Amid the rooftop deities you can see a figure dressed in a white suit and pith helmet, presumably Smith himself.

ARRIVAL AND DEPARTURE　　　　　　　　　　　　　　　　　　　　　　　　**IPOH**

Ipoh's compact **centre** has two major thoroughfares: Jalan Sultan Idris Shah, taking eastbound traffic, and westbound Jalan Sultan Iskandar. The **suburbs** are anything but compact, however, which could pose a problem if you arrive by express bus, as the main bus station and most drop-off points lie in outlying residential areas. **Taxis** can be useful; they park opposite the Medan Kidd bus station and outside major hotels. A trip from any central hotel to the train station, say, should cost no more than RM8. To book a taxi, call ☎ 05 254 0251.

BY PLANE
Sultan Azlan Shah airport The airport, 5km southeast of the centre (☎ 05 318 8202, ⊚ ipoh.airport-authority .com), has services to Johor Bahru (1–2 daily; 1hr 20min) and Singapore, with Firefly (2 daily; 1hr 30min). A taxi into the centre costs around RM20.

BY TRAIN
Ipoh is the first beneficiary of the gradual conversion of the west coast railway line from a single set of tracks to two, which has allowed KTM to run fast, frequent ETS trains to and from KL.

Train station The train station is on Jalan Panglima Bukit Gantang Wahab, at the western end of the centre (☎ 05 254 7987).

Destinations Alor Star (1 daily; 7hr); Butterworth (2 daily; 3hr 15min); Hat Yai (Thailand; 1 daily; 9hr); Johor Bahru (1 daily; 10hr 15min); Kuala Kangsar (2 daily; 1hr); Kuala Lumpur (ETS:

10 daily 5am–9pm; 2hr 30min; standard: 2 daily; 3hr 30min); Seremban (1 daily; 4hr 30min); Singapore (1 daily; 11hr); Sungai Petani (1 daily; 6hr 15min); Taiping (2 daily; 1hr 30min).

BY BUS
A multitude of firms provide bus services within Perak, most of them operated by Perak Transit (⊚ peraktransit .com.my). Few local buses run after sunset.

Local bus station Buses out to the suburbs and other Perak towns, as well as express buses to the Cameron Highlands, use the Medan Kidd bus station, a 10min walk south of the train station.

Destinations Cameron Highlands (4 daily; 2hr 30min); Gerik (5 daily; 3hr); Gopeng (#66; every 90min; 45min); Kuala Kangsar (#35; every 20–30min; 1hr 15min); Lenggong (5 daily; 2hr 30min); Taiping (every 45min; 1hr 45min).

Lumut buses Perak Roadways buses head to Lumut, the port for Pulau Pangkor (see p.122), from a depot next to the

2

Shell Garage on Jalan Leong Boon Swee (every 90min–2hr; 2hr). There are also a few express services to Lumut from Amanjaya (see below).

Express bus stations Ipoh's main bus station has been moved twice in recent years, ending up at Amanjaya, nearly 10km north of the centre in an isolated Malay township. From here Perak Transit bus #116 runs to Medan Kidd and east through the new town to the Ipoh Parade mall. Only the Sri Maju bus company (ⓦ srimaju.com) now serves the city centre from its own depot at Jalan Bendahara. Star Shuttle (ⓦ starwira.com), which has

useful services to and from KLIA, serves both Amanjaya and the busy suburb of Bercham 8km northeast of the centre, where its office is located.

Destinations Alor Star (8 daily; 3hr 30min); Butterworth (at least 8 daily; 2hr 30min); Johor Bahru (4 daily; 8hr); Kangar (4 daily; 4hr); KLIA (9 daily; 3hr 30min); Kota Bharu (2 daily; 8hr); Kuala Lumpur (hourly; 3hr 30min); Kuala Perlis (3 daily; 3hr 45min); Kuantan (3 daily; 8hr); Lumut (3 daily; 1hr 15min); Melaka (at least 6 daily; 5hr); Penang (several daily; 2hr 30min); Seremban (4 daily; 4hr); Singapore (4 daily; 9hr 30min); Sungai Petani (4 daily; 3hr).

INFORMATION

Tourist office Ipoh City Council runs an information centre at Jalan Tun Sambanthan, by the padang (Mon–Thurs 8am–1pm & 2–5pm, Fri 8am–12.15am &

2.45–5pm; ⓣ 05 208 3155). Although staff dispense brochures liberally, their practical knowledge is variable and they may not keep to their opening hours.

ACCOMMODATION

Abby By The River 55 & 57 Jalan Sultan Iskandar ⓣ 05 251 4500, ⓦ abbyhotel.my. The closest thing Ipoh has to a guesthouse, the *Abby* is a new budget hotel that has dorms (one en suite, one not) as well as unadorned, overpriced rooms. Rates rise ten percent at weekends. Dorms RM30, doubles RM90

★**D'Eastern** 118 Jalan Sultan Idris Shah ⓣ 05 254 3936. Recently refurbished and given a name tweak, but still widely called the *Eastern*, this hotel has spacious rooms with equally spacious bathrooms at ridiculously good rates – perhaps because its limited parking puts off Malaysian would-be guests. No breakfast. RM100

★**French** 60 & 62 Jalan Dato Onn Jaafar ⓣ 05 241 3030, ⓦ frenchhotel.com.my. The best value in town, the *French* is a marvellous halfway house between bland modern comforts and a full-on boutique hotel. Rooms boast tasteful contemporary styling and even the

breakfasts, cooked to order and included in the rate, are nicely presented. RM135

MH Studio Off Jalan Sultan Idris Shah ⓣ 05 242 1000, ⓦ mhstudio.com.my. A new tower (if coming by taxi, make sure the driver doesn't confuse it with the *MH Hotel* in the suburbs) holding a collection of plush, snazzy rooms, each with its own sitting area, safe, microwave and fridge. Every floor is individually themed – choose from quasi-oriental or Balinese, among others. Breakfast included. RM200

Sekeping Kong Heng 75 Jalan Panglima ⓣ 05 227 2745, ⓦ sekeping.com/kongheng. Once a hostel for travelling troupes of Chinese opera performers, *Sekeping Kong Heng* seeded the old town's gentrification when it was artfully restored. Now it's an offbeat, informally run hotel in shabby-chic style. Modern doubles plus two overpriced elevated glass-walled quarters, reached by ladders in the huge loft. No breakfast. RM220

EATING AND DRINKING

Although most of Ipoh's incredible range of restaurants and bars are in the burgeoning **suburbs**, there's a reasonable choice in the low-key centre as well. The numerous *kopitiam* joints of the **old town** are pretty foolproof for decent, cheap meals, but few are open at night. As hardly any of the smarter new cafés and bars here have so far proved up to much, in the evening you're generally better off in the **new town**.

★**Bricks & Barrels** 28–30 Jalan Lau Ek Ching ⓣ 05 253 8558. The city centre's most appealing and busiest bar, the decor themed around, erm, brick walls and beer barrels, where a wide range of draught beers and bench seating ensure everyone can have a convivial chinwag. Live music most nights from 10pm. Sun–Thurs 4pm–1am, Fri & Sat 4pm–2am.

★**Foh San** 51 Jalan Leong Sin Nam ⓣ 05 254 0308, ⓦ fohsan.com.my. On two open-sided floors, this palatial restaurant is a fun place to come for a dim sum breakfast – order from counters packed with dumplings, *pow*, steamed sticky rice, custard tarts and other morsels. Some dishes

cooked to order, especially from noon when the lunch menu kicks in. Breakfast RM20. Wed–Mon 6.30am–2.30pm.

Haji Yahaya Jalan Dato Onn Jaafar, a 2min walk south of the UTC market complex. Marvellous Malay joint serving fried chicken and fish, curries, stews, noodles and rice all day – choose from *nasi kunyit* (bright yellow with turmeric) or even the purplish Kelantan-style *nasi kerabu*. Daily roughly 7.30am–8pm.

KBR 8 Jalan Lahat ⓣ 012 510 8880. In Ipoh's "Little India", just south of Chinatown, *KBR* is a cheap vegetarian place serving up the usual *vadai*, *thosai* and thalis, plus noodles and sweets. Daily 8am–8pm.

Koh Samui 83 & 85 Jalan Raja Ekram ☎ 05 255 6608. Sedate by local standards, but with fumbling service, this blandly decorated restaurant does a wide range of Chinese-accented Thai dishes, with a general tilt toward seafood. Try the rich green curries or unusual steamed fish with lime. Around RM35 excluding drinks. Daily 11.30am–3pm & 6.30–10.30pm.

Kong Heng Jalan Bandar Timah. Popular old town, old-school *kopitiam* where the stalls excel at any number of things: *rojak, laksa, chee cheong fun* (Cantonese noodle rolls in a savoury sauce, with optional pork filling)... You may have to line up for a table at lunchtime. Thurs–Tues roughly 7.30am–4pm.

Lou Wong 49 Jalan Yau Tet Shin ☎ 05 254 4199. Ipoh natives wax lyrical over – of all things – local bean sprouts, supposedly plumper, crunchier and sweeter than any in the country. The favoured way to have them is stir-fried, with a separate plate of steamed sliced chicken and a bowl of noodles – and *Lou Wong* is the most popular of a cluster of restaurants serving it (around RM10). Daily 10.30am–11pm.

★**Plan B** 75 Jalan Panglima ☎ 05 249 8286, ⊛ thebiggroup.co/planb. Part of *Sekeping Kong*

Heng, this glossy restaurant/café revels in high ceilings and glass panelling. It's especially busy at weekends, when people come for brunch (around RM30), but just as worthwhile are the fusion-inspired mains, excellent pastries and cakes – try their appley twist on the local speciality *sugee* cake, made with semolina – and even Malaysian dishes like *nasi lemak*, unusually served with prawns. Fair selection of beers, ciders and wines too. Sun–Thurs 9am–10pm, Fri & Sat 9am–midnight.

★**Sinhalese Bar** 2 Jalan Bijeh Timah ☎ 05 241 2235. There's no better place in the old town for a drink than this boxy institution, opened in the 1930s, with saloon-style doors, lace curtains and what look like bathroom tiles on the walls. Come for cheap, cold beer to a backdrop of Tamil pop music and the whirring of fans overhead. Daily noon–10pm.

Thin Hei 22 Jalan Dass ☎ 05 253 7388. Best bet for vegetarians, serving up Chinese stir-fries and lots of fake soy/gluten "meats", including an excellent spicy mock mutton. Around RM25, minus drinks. Daily 11am–2.30pm & 6–9.30pm.

DIRECTORY

Banks There are several banks on Jalan Sultan Idris Shah.
Hospital Jalan Hospital (☎ 05 208 5000, ⊛ hrpb.moh .gov.my).
Police Jalan Panglima Bukit Gantang Wahab, south of the train station (☎ 05 245 1562).
Shopping Recently given a facelift, Ipoh Parade at the eastern end of Jalan Sultan Idris Shah is the one downtown

mall worth browsing; there are pharmacies here and a branch of Popular Bookstore. Look out also for the nightly *pasar malam* on Jalan Dato Tahwil Azar, close to the *Lou Wong* restaurant, and the Sunday morning Memory Lane flea market on Jalan Horley.
Visa extensions The Immigration Department is at the UTC market complex on Jalan Laxamana (☎ 05 241 3524).

Gopeng

On Route 1 some 20km southeast of Ipoh, **GOPENG** was one of the first of the Kinta Valley boom towns and also spawned an international chain of Chinese pharmacies, **Eu Yan Sang**, which began in 1879 as a shop catering to miners (in Ipoh, you can visit their outlet on Jalan Bandar Timah in the old town). Gopeng holds a minor assortment of old temples and shophouses, but draws a steady stream of visitors mainly because it is a centre for **whitewater rafting** down the **Kampar River** (rated Grade I–III depending on how rainy it's been) with a cluster of accommodation close by. Although it's possible to come here on a day-trip, many stay at least a night, combining rafting with a jungle hike or a visit to nearby caves.

ARRIVAL AND DEPARTURE   GOPENG

Gopeng is 7km from the river valley and its places to stay, reached by an informally signed country road via **Kampung Sungai Itek**. Driving, note that this road becomes very narrow as it passes through woods en route.

By bus Bus #66 from Ipoh's Medan Kidd bus station (every 90min; 45min) drops you on Jalan Pasar in the heart of the old town. Although you could attempt to trudge to the river from here, far better to pay a little extra for your accommodation or rafting operator to collect you.
Day-trips Most visitors come on combined

accommodation/activity deals, but for day-trippers a reliable bet is the veteran Sabah-based operator Riverbug (☎ 012 313 1006, ⊛ riverbug.asia), now established in Perak. Rafting will cost around RM150; a full-day package (from RM200) adds a second activity such as a visit to the Tempurong caves or abseiling down a little waterfall.

2

ACCOMMODATION

★**Adeline's** Kampung Geruntum ☎05 359 2833, ⓦadelinevilla.com. Superbly run by a sociable hairdresser-turned-hotelier, *Adeline's* offers slick timber-and-glass solar-powered "villas", with a/c and en-suite rooms and dorms, alongside a "resthouse" complex of dorms in bamboo and rattan buildings, sharing facilities. Everyone eats together in the restaurant, with basic meals and fancier ones, including buffets. Add on rafting and other activities as you like, or go for a package. One night full board per person: villa rooms RM275, resthouse RM105

Rainforest Resort Kampung Geruntum ☎012 510 7555, ⓦgopengrainforest.com. Likeable assortment of rustic houses in Malay and Indonesian styles, where you sleep several people to a room on mattresses on the floor. Packages include rafting, plus hikes through the woods to Orang Asli villages and caving. One night full board per person RM110

Pangkor and Lumut

The laidback island of **Pangkor**, barely 10km long, is known to every student of Malaysian history as the place where the **Pangkor Treaty** was signed, leading to the creation of the Resident system by which the British gradually brought every sultanate in the Peninsula under their wing (see p.559). Now it's a popular, affordable weekend beach retreat for families, taking advantage of the ease of getting here from cities like KL and Ipoh: there are frequent ferries from **LUMUT**, a small port and naval base 80km southwest of Ipoh.

Visitors mostly stay on the beaches of the island's west coast, at **Pasir Bogak** or **Teluk Nipah**. The islanders are concentrated in a town and villages on the east coast, and the interior is hilly and forested. Things are pretty quiet except during holidays and the annual Hindu festival of **Thaipusam**, centred on the Sri Pathirakaliaman Temple in the east coast village of **Sungai Pinang Kecil**. There's also a community-run **arts festival** with outdoor film screenings and concerts (Sept; ⓦpangkorislandfestival.com).

Pangkor Town and around

Ferries from Lumut dock at **PANGKOR TOWN**, the island's principal settlement. The town has a few shops, banks and places to stay, but most people get straight on a minibus taxi to one of the beaches.

Just a couple of minutes' walk east of the jetty, **Galeri Pangkor** (daily 9am–5pm; free) is a small museum with nineteenth-century photos of the Pangkor Treaty signatories, a few fish traps and pieces of Chinese porcelain. From the terrace, you can survey the boats docked at wooden wharves in **Kampung Sungai Pinang Besar**, then descend to the mainly Malay village itself and take a signed road 1km inland to **Foo Lin Kong**. This Taoist complex is a riot of red and gold decorations and bright sculptures of animals – real and imaginary. There's a semi-wild garden behind, with a fishpond inhabited by enormous arapaima, and a miniature version of the Great Wall of China snaking up the hillside above.

Kampung Teluk Gedong and around

The wooden stilt houses at **KAMPUNG TELUK GEDONG** stand 1.5km south of town along the coastal road. Set back from the road is **Kota Belanda**, or Dutch fort, founded in 1670 to store tin supplies from Perak and keep a check on piracy in the Straits. Destroyed twenty years later, it was rebuilt in 1743 but abandoned again in 1748; the half-built structure you see today is a recent reconstruction. About 100m south, **Batu Bersurat** is a huge granite boulder under a canopy. Look here for carvings of the Dutch East India Company logo, an intertwined "VOC", and a **tiger** – a warning after a Dutch child was carted off by one while playing nearby in 1743.

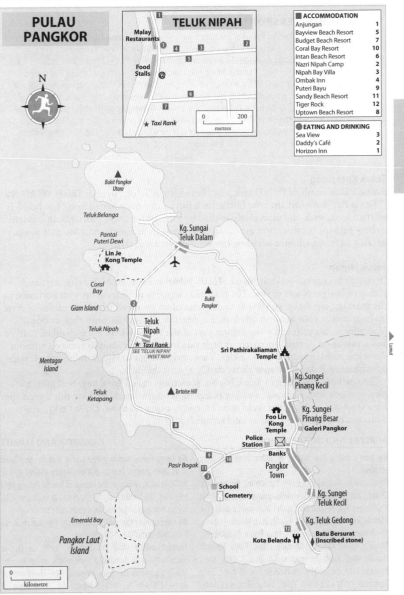

PULAU PANGKOR

TELUK NIPAH

Malay Restaurants

Food Stalls

@

★ Taxi Rank

0   200
metres

ACCOMMODATION	
Anjungan	1
Bayview Beach Resort	5
Budget Beach Resort	7
Coral Bay Resort	10
Intan Beach Resort	6
Nazri Nipah Camp	2
Nipah Bay Villa	3
Ombak Inn	4
Puteri Bayu	9
Sandy Beach Resort	11
Tiger Rock	12
Uptown Beach Resort	8

EATING AND DRINKING	
Sea View	3
Daddy's Café	2
Horizon Inn	1

2

N

Bukit Pangkor Utara

Teluk Belanga

Pantai Puteri Dewi

Lin Je Kong Temple

Kg. Sungai Teluk Dalam

Coral Bay

Giam Island

Bukit Pangkor

Teluk Nipah

Teluk Nipah
★ Taxi Rank
SEE 'TELUK NIPAH' INSET MAP

Mentagor Island

Sri Pathirakaliaman Temple

Lumut

Teluk Ketapang

Tortoise Hill

Kg. Sungei Pinang Kecil

Kg. Sungei Pinang Besar

Foo Lin Kong Temple

Galeri Pangkor

Police Station

Banks

Pasir Bogak

School

Cemetery

Pangkor Town

Kg. Sungei Teluk Kecil

Emerald Bay

Kg. Teluk Gedong

Pangkor Laut Island

Kota Belanda

Batu Bersurat (inscribed stone)

0   1
kilometre

Pasir Bogak

It's just 2km from Pangkor Town to the west coast and the southern end of **PASIR BOGAK**, one of the island's two main tourist beaches. This initial stretch is as busy as Pangkor gets, clustered with mid-range resorts popular with Malaysian Chinese. The beach itself is a lovely 2km arc of sand, looking out over a placid bay to the much smaller, privately owned **Pangkor Laut island**, and largely tranquil even though there is accommodation scattered across its length.

2

PANGKOR WATERSPORTS

Malaysian holidaymakers at Pangkor are particularly keen on **banana boat** rides, with four people being towed around one of the bays astride an elongated float, culminating in an obligatory dunking at the end (RM15). Rides on other bizarrely shaped floats are available too, as is **jetskiing** (RM60 for two; 15min). Much more worthwhile than any of these is a 45min **island-hopping tour** (RM150 for a group of up to ten), taking you out to Mentagor, Pangkor Laut and other islets for views of odd rock formations, after which you can swim and snorkel (no time limit – just arrange to be collected). For serious **fishing** or snorkelling you'll need to charter a boat out to the Sembilan Islands, well west of Pangkor, costing at least RM1000.

On Pasir Bogak, one well-established operator is Happy Island (☎012 414 1749), benefiting from its location close to the resorts at the south end of the bay.

Teluk Ketapang

Around 2km north of Pasir Bogak and 1km south of Teluk Nipah is **TELUK KETAPANG** ("Turtle Bay"), named after the leatherback turtles that once nested here. The beach is worth a look, wide and attractively backed by forested hills, and quieter than it ought to be – perhaps because there are no facilities apart from a jetty and a lookout tower, or because a certain amount of debris can wash up on a bad day.

Teluk Nipah

In complete contrast to Pasir Bogak, **TELUK NIPAH** has a more Malay character and plenty of budget places to stay. The place also happens to be teeming with **hornbills**; in the morning especially, you'll spot them perched on overhead telephone cables or even on balconies at your accommodation. The beach is slightly narrower than at Bogak, especially at its north end – the busiest part of the strip – where the embanked road and a profusion of stalls encroach; at high tide there's barely sand to stroll on without the water rushing around your ankles. Views over the bay are beautiful at sunset, with hunchbacked **Pulau Mentagor** rising darkly against the dusk.

The northern extension of Teluk Nipah, sometimes called **Coral Bay**, is a quieter, pleasant cove with a couple of eating places right on the beach, making this a great spot for a sundowner. Amid the rocks at its far end is a bizarre shrine, **Lin Je Kong**, replete with concrete toadstools and animal statues.

ARRIVAL AND INFORMATION
PANGKOR AND LUMUT

By bus Lumut's bus station is 100m from the ferry terminal.

Destinations Alor Setar (1 daily; 3hr 30min); Butterworth (7 daily; 2hr 30min); Ipoh (Perak Roadways buses to Medan Kidd: every 90min–2hr; 2hr); Ipoh (Amanjaya; 3 daily; 1hr 15min); Johor Bahru (at least 4 daily; 9hr); Melaka (3 daily; 5hr 30min); KLIA (5 daily; 5hr); Kota Bharu (3 daily; 9hr 30min); Kuala Lumpur (2 daily; 2hr); Kuala Lumpur (hourly; 4hr); Kuala Terengganu (at least 3 daily; 6hr); Kuantan (at least 2 daily; 9hr); Seremban (2 daily; 5hr); Singapore (at least 3 daily; 10hr); Sungai Petani (3 daily; 3hr); Taiping (4 daily; 1hr 10min).

By ferry Ferries run between Lumut and Pangkor Town daily from around 7am to 8.30pm (every 45min; 35min; RM10 return), calling at the village of Sungai Pinang Kecil en route. The Lumut ferry terminal has at least one ATM, with a moneychanger and food court close by.

By taxi Lumut's taxi rank is outside the bus station. A cab from Ipoh costs RM150 (1hr 30min).

Tourist office None on Pangkor itself; in Lumut, Tourism Malaysia occupies a traditionally styled wooden building close to the ferry terminal (Sat–Thurs roughly 9am–12.30pm & 1.30–5.30pm, Fri 9am–noon & 3–5.30pm; ☎05 683 4057).

GETTING AROUND

An 18km coast road, steep in places, loops around Pangkor, cutting inland only between Pangkor Town and Pasir Bogak. There are no buses.

By minibus taxi Lilac-and-yellow minibus taxis park outside Pangkor's ferry terminal and at the southern end of both Pasir Bogak and Teluk Nipah. A sign at the ferry terminal displays fares, for up to four passengers: from RM10 to Pasir

Bogak (2km) to RM70 for a 2hr, round-island circuit. For journeys between points that aren't specified on the display, or with a group of more than four, expect to haggle a little.

By bicycle/motorbike Renting a motorbike in Pangkor Town or via your hotel costs RM30–40/day; some guesthouses have bikes to rent at RM10–15/day.

ACCOMMODATION

Pangkor has plenty of accommodation, all rather hit-and-miss. Most budget places are at **Teluk Nipah**, which has a bustling neighbourhood feel and is cluttered with cheap eating places and shops. Mid-range hotels, meanwhile are concentrated at **Pasir Bogak**, which is more upmarket and more dispersed, with few shops and restaurants outside the resorts (it can be worth taking a full-board package). The rates we quote below are typical outside holidays and weekends, when prices can rise by ten to fifty percent depending on the establishment.

PASIR BOGAK

Coral Bay Resort Pasir Bogak ✆05 685 5111, ⓦpangkorcoralbay.com.my. More like a city-centre hotel, a monolithic slab of rooms and apartments alongside restaurants, jacuzzi, gym and a pool with a waterslide. Devoid of character, but popular with Malaysian families. Breakfast included. Doubles RM170, apartments RM260

Puteri Bayu Pasir Bogak ✆05 685 1929, ⓦputeribayu .com. Pleasant complex of not bad rooms and some quite attractive chalets. Breakfast included. Doubles RM120, chalets RM200

Sandy Beach Resort Pasir Bogak ✆05 685 3027, ⓦpangkorsandybeach.com. Low-key buildings curling around a snazzy freeform pool. Rooms boast all the customary conveniences, including fridge and safe, but are a little plain for the rate, which includes breakfast. RM195

Uptown Beach Resort North end of Pasir Bogak ✆05 685 4510. A jumble of dull concrete and more appealing tall wooden buildings containing plain rooms, with tiny bathrooms at the lower end of the price range. If you don't mind climbing flights of steps, ask to stay in the buildings up the hillside at the back, which have good views and don't necessarily cost more. Breakfast included. RM120

TELUK NIPAH

Anjungan Northern end of Teluk Nipah ✆05 685 1500, ⓦanjunganresortpangkor.com. The only mid-range resort here, comprising four-storey buildings surrounding a boat-shaped pool, with a popular restaurant. The rooms are comfortable enough, if rather plain; still, the overall tone is relaxed and the place competently run. Rate excludes breakfast. RM160

Bayview Beach Resort Teluk Nipah ✆05 685 3540, ⓦpangkorbayview.com. No views of the bay at all, but this large, family-friendly chalet resort does feature a pool and a restaurant. All rooms have a/c, and full-board packages for groups are available. RM115

Budget Beach Resort Teluk Nipah ✆05 685 3529, ⓦbudgetbeachresort.com. The densely packed chalets aren't anything special at first sight, but they are in above-average condition, each with balcony and bathroom, and helpful staff keep the whole place shipshape. A sound choice. RM75

Intan Beach Resort Teluk Nipah ✆013 454 3823, ⓦpangkorintantravel.com.my. Choose from unusually spacious A-frames or so-called chalet rooms in long low buildings, simply furnished and with newish tiled bathrooms. Kitchen and laundry facilities available. A-frames RM75, chalets RM85

Nazri Nipah Camp Teluk Nipah ✆05 685 2014 or ✆012 585 4511. Laidback to a fault, with slightly frayed chalets and poky A-frames, some with bathroom, around a pleasant communal garden area. Some a/c chalets available too. Dorms RM20, A-frames RM40, chalets RM50, a/c chalets RM80

Nipah Bay Villa Teluk Nipah ✆05 685 2198, ⓦpulaupangkornipahbayvilla.blogspot.com. Behind the shaded restaurant at the front is a tall, institutional block of rooms as well as rather better chalets, all with a/c, TV and bathroom. Doubles RM90, chalets RM130

Ombak Inn Teluk Nipah ✆05 685 5223, ⓦombakinnchalet.com. Like a little kampung in the woods, this is a homely collection of chalets in grounds overgrown with bougainvillea. Rooms have a/c, TV and slightly cramped bathrooms. RM100

ELSEWHERE

Tiger Rock Inland of Kota Belanda ⓦtigerrock.info. *Tiger Rock* is almost a mini country estate, but set in the tropics. There's a huge, wooden main house and various other buildings, all recent constructions but in colonial-era styles, containing a total of eight tasteful rooms and with a beautiful pool and tennis court. Full-board double plus round-island trip RM1400

EATING AND DRINKING

There are plenty of places to eat at **Teluk Nipah**, including simple Malay restaurants and stalls on the main road selling snacks like barbecued sweetcorn and *lempeng pisang* (a banana and coconut pancake grilled inside a banana-leaf wrapping). At **Pasir Bogak**, a few stalls cluster on the road to the *Sea View* hotel, but most visitors eat at their resort.

PASIR BOGAK

★**Sea View** Sea View Hotel, Pasir Bogak ☎ 05 685 1605. With tables on a beachside veranda, this perennially popular restaurant has an all-round menu of Chinese food (RM12–30) – try standbys like tangy chicken in lemon sauce or the curry fish with *asam* (tamarind) – plus Western mains and snacks including black pepper steak (RM40). Daily 7am–11pm.

TELUK NIPAH

★**Daddy's Café** A 5min walk up the road from Teluk Nipah. This beachside restaurant-bar has tables on the sand overlooking the bay, a nice setting for a candlelit dinner. The menu covers a range of Western dishes, including steak and fish and chips, but the jumbo grilled prawns are spectacular (the priciest thing on the menu, around RM70). Beer is frosty-cold. Mains from RM30. Daily 11am–11pm.

Horizon Inn Teluk Nipah ☎ 05 685 3398. At the hotel of the same name, this simple Chinese restaurant offers the best value on Teluk Nipah. Choose from an extensive menu of stir-fries (meat/chicken from RM15, seafood from RM25) plus a few simple Western dishes such as omelettes and fish and chips (RM10–15). Great freshly squeezed juices, too. Daily roughly 12.30–10pm.

Kuala Kangsar

A bustling country town, **KUALA KANGSAR** is Perak's **royal seat**, playing a similar role opposite Ipoh as Pekan on the east coast (see p.225) does for Kuantan, Pahang's capital. For Malaysians, Kuala Kangsar is best known as a centre for the production of **labu** – water pitchers with a pumpkin-shaped base (*labu* means "gourd" in Malay), excellent as souvenirs – and as the home of the **Malay College**. Founded in 1905 as a British-style boarding school, it began educating the most promising or well-connected Malay boys, thus bringing the community least involved in the colonial project into the Western intellectual fold; many of its students have gone on to achieve greatness in Malaysian public life, notably the opposition leader Anwar Ibrahim. For visitors, the town is worthwhile for its royal and Islamic buildings, although note that the most interesting of these, the Perak Royal Museum, was closed for long-term repairs at the time of writing. The range of hotels is lousy, though – best come on a **day-trip** from Ipoh or Taiping.

Royal quarter

What passes for the town's **royal quarter** is **Bukit Chandan**, the hilly area south of the little Kangsar River, spanned by a road bridge as well as by wobbly suspension footbridges close to the golden-topped clock tower in the town centre. The most prominent sight is the hilltop **Sultan Azlan Shah Gallery**, a colonially styled former

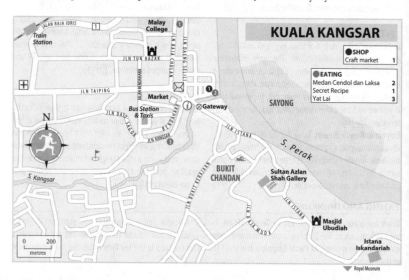

palace containing daft regalia and ephemera pertaining to the Perak royals (Sat–Thurs 10am–5pm, Fri 10am–12.15pm & 2.45–5pm; RM4; ☎05 777 5362). Some 500m beyond, **Masjid Ubudiah** sports a splendid array of golden onion domes amid a thicket of striped minarets.

Royal Museum of Perak

Around 1km beyond Masjid Ubudiah, past the marble 1930s **Istana Iskandariah**, the sultan's palace, is the former palace, the **Istana Kenangan**. Now the **Royal Museum of Perak**, it was built in the 1920s as a modest temporary residence while the present palace was being finished, and is of interest not for its exhibits but as a beautiful example of a traditional Malay mansion. Fashioned from wood without a single nail being used, the house is adorned with friezes and geometric-patterned panels. Sadly, it was closed for long-term repairs at the time of writing; local tourist offices should know if it has reopened.

Sayong

Head east from the clock tower and you come almost immediately to the **estuary** of the **Kangsar** and the wide **Perak River** that the town is named for. Visible on the east bank of the latter is the village of **Sayong**, where the production and sale of *labu* is a major cottage industry. Boats shuttle across the river sporadically for a nominal sum; once across you can ask around for the location of *labu* makers, no more than a fifteen-minute walk away.

ARRIVAL AND INFORMATION   KUALA KANGSAR

The town centre is on the north bank of the Kangsar River. Although Route 1 runs through town, skirting the train station, the historic main street is Jalan Kangsar.

By train The train station (☎05 776 1094) is on the northwestern outskirts of town, a 20min walk from the central clock tower.
Destinations Alor Star (1 daily; 5hr 30min); Butterworth (2 daily; 2hr 15min–3hr); Hat Yai (Thailand; 1 daily; 8hr 30min); Ipoh (2 daily; 1hr); Johor Bahru (1 daily; 11hr); Kuala Lumpur (2 daily; 3hr 45min–4hr 45min); Seremban (1 daily; 5hr 15min); Singapore (1 daily; 11hr 45min); Sungai Petani (1 daily; 4hr 30min); Taiping (2 daily; 40min).
By bus On Jalan Bendahara, a few minutes' walk from

Jalan Kangsar, the bus station is used mainly by local services, although some express buses call here too.
Destinations Butterworth (at least 4 daily; 1hr 30min); Ipoh (#35; every 20–30min; 1hr 15min); Kota Bharu (2 daily; 7hr); Kuala Lumpur (several daily; 3hr 30min); Lenggong (#99; every 90min; 75min); Lumut (2 daily; 2hr); Sungai Petani (2 daily; 2hr 45min); Taiping (every 45min; 1hr).
Tourist office By the clock tower, the tourist office has plenty of leaflets (Tues–Thurs & Sat 9am–1pm & 2–6pm, Fri 9am–12.30pm & 3–6pm, Sun 9am–1pm; ☎05 777 7717).

EATING

If you're in town at the weekend, consider checking out the wide range of sweet and savoury snacks available at the **pasar malam** around the main market off Jalan Kangsar (Fri 4.30–8pm), and at the **pasar tani** close to the jetty (Sat & Sun 7.30am–noon).

Medan Cendol dan Laksa By the jetty. A food court where every stall does the same two dishes: spicy *laksa* and the deliciously unhealthy coconut-milk dessert *cendol*. A few stalls have additional offerings to pull focus from competitors. Daily roughly 7.30am–10pm.
Secret Recipe 4c Jalan Raja Chulan ☎05 776 1017. With its lack of options, Kuala Kangsar is one town where it's worth shelling out to eat at a middling café chain like this – good for spaghetti, steak and chips, overpriced

renditions of local dishes and a wide range of cakes. Daily 11am–11pm.
Yat Lai Jalan Kangsar. Also signed *Yut Loy*, this is a gloriously antiquated, Chinese-owned, Malay-run *kedai kopis* – look out for the ancient notice from the days when Malay was still written in Arabic script, imploring people not to spit or beg. It serves simple rice and noodle dishes plus attempts at steak and scrambled egg, all cooked to order, sometimes glacially slowly. Hardly anything over RM10. Mon–Sat 9am–6pm.

SHOPPING

Craft market Close to the jetty. Kuala Kangsar isn't a bad place to buy crafts and souvenirs. Here you'll find a good range of basketry, wickerwork (including bags), some textiles and of course the obligatory *labu* – a 20cm-tall specimen will set you back just RM20.

Taiping

Set against the mist-laden Bintang Hills, **TAIPING** is one of few big towns in Malaysia with a Chinese name – one that could mean "great peace", though the latter would be an irony given the **clan wars** here between rival Cantonese and Hakka factions during the town's early days. Relaxed and mostly low-rise, it doesn't look like it was once one of the most important towns in the Peninsula. Yet the great **tin** boom in the second half of the nineteenth century, to which Taiping owes its existence, meant that by the 1890s it was in a race with Kuala Lumpur to be chosen as capital of the newly constituted Federated Malay States. Taiping evidently lost. Within a few years it suffered a second ignominy as Ipoh outgrew it, usurping even its role as state capital in 1937.

Today's Taiping is a discreetly prosperous affair, regarded as a desirable place to retire. Few foreign visitors come, which is a pity as it's one of the nicest provincial towns to relax in for a day or two. As you'd expect from its Chinese heritage, much of **central Taiping** comprises old shophouses, some being restored, centred on an unusual old

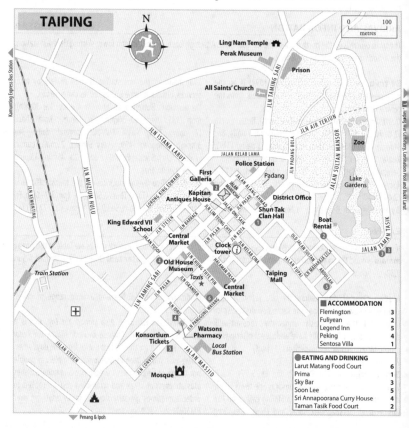

TAIPING

0   100
metres

Ling Nam Temple
Perak Museum
Prison
All Saints' Church
Zoo
Lake Gardens
Police Station
First Galleria
Padang
Kapitan Antiques House
District Office
Shun Tak Clan Hall
King Edward VII School
Boat Rental
Central Market
Clock tower
Old House Museum
Taxis
Taiping Mall
Central Market
Watsons Pharmacy
Konsortium Tickets
Local Bus Station
Mosque
Train Station
Kamunting Express Bus Station

■ ACCOMMODATION	
Flemington	3
Fuliyean	2
Legend Inn	5
Peking	4
Sentosa Villa	1

● EATING AND DRINKING	
Larut Matang Food Court	6
Prima	1
Sky Bar	3
Soon Lee	5
Sri Annapoorana Curry House	4
Taman Tasik Food Court	2

Penang & Ipoh

market housed inside two huge, century-old wooden hangars. In addition to its **museums** there's a fourth heritage sight on the way: the 1896 **Shun Tak clan hall** at 36 Jalan Kota, due to be completed by late 2015. The green **Lake Gardens** on its eastern edge and the former hill retreat of **Bukit Larut** and **Matang mangrove reserve** are also worth exploring.

First Galleria

Jalan Stesen • Mon–Thurs & Sat 9.30am–5.30pm, Fri 9.30am–12.30pm, Sun 12.30–5.30pm • RM10 • ☎ 05 805 2136

Inside an Anglo-Malay hybrid building that once served as the colonial surveyor's headquarters, **First Galleria** is a museum of Taiping's early years. The artefacts are unmemorable although period photos add some depth, proving just how rapidly the town burgeoned. On the mandatory half-hour **guided tour** you will hear about the building itself and be filled in on some of the town's many firsts: for example, the first railway in the Peninsula was built here (to facilitate the shipment of tin, naturally) in the 1880s.

Old House Museum

2a Medan Pasar • Daily roughly 10am–6pm • RM5

The **Old House Museum** nicely evokes how a well-to-do Taiping family might have lived decades ago. Beautifully carved screens and altars figure prominently downstairs at this late nineteenth-century timber shophouse, where there's also a rustic kitchen at the back with a heavy granite pestle and mortar of the sort once used to pound chillies and spices. Upstairs, accessed by stairs that could be sealed off for privacy using a large trapdoor, are bedrooms graced by Chinese-style four-poster beds and archaic kerosene-driven table fans.

All Saints' Church

Jalan Taming Sari

Founded in 1887, **All Saints' Church** is the oldest Anglican church in what would become the Federated Malay States. It's built in a lightweight English Gothic style – though the roof is tiled in very Malaysian wooden shingles – and is also noteworthy for having one of the very few pipe organs in the country. The tiny churchyard contains the graves of some of the earliest British and Australian settlers.

Perak Museum

Jalan Taming Sari • Daily 9am–6pm • RM5 • ☎ 05 807 2057

Housed in a purpose-built colonial building, the state-run **Perak Museum** is another Taiping "first" – it's the oldest museum in the Malay Peninsula, opened in 1883 at the instigation of the Resident Hugh Low. There are three collections, portraying Malaysia's anthropology, zoology and local history with displays of stuffed local fauna, as well as an extensive collection of ancient weapons and Orang Asli implements and ornaments. Incidentally, the grim grey wall opposite the museum is the outside of Taiping's **prison**, built in 1879 and used by the Japanese during World War II.

Lake Gardens (Taman Tasik)

Pedal boats From the south side of the gardens: Mon–Thurs 10am–7.30pm, Fri–Sun 9am–7.30pm • From RM12 for 15min

Taiping's extensive **Lake Gardens**, at the eastern edge of the centre, were created in 1880 when Hugh Low decided that the mess left by two tin mines should be landscaped and turned into a park. Today it's an inviting expanse of lawns, clumps of bamboo and mature trees covered in moss and ferns. The view from the town side is particularly impressive on a bright evening when the gardens seem to merge with the sunlit forested hills to the east, though the goofy duck-shaped **pedal boats** can mar the most meticulously composed photos.

Taiping zoo and night safari

Daily: zoo 8.30am–6pm, night safari 8–11pm (Sat until midnight) • Zoo RM16, night safari RM20 • ☎ 05 808 6577, ⓦ zootaiping.gov.my

A big magnet for Malaysian visitors, the **zoo** on the Lake Gardens' far side houses plenty of local fauna, including *siamang* (a type of gibbon), civets, elephants and bearded pig. It also boasts a **night safari** – a modest copy of Singapore's – showcasing nocturnal animals.

Taiping War Cemetery

On the Bukit Larut Rd, 1.2km from the start of the Lake Gardens • ⓦ cwgc.org

A serene memorial to the casualties of World War II, the Taiping **War Cemetery** contains the graves of 866 men, more than five hundred of whom are unidentified. Split in two by the road, it's divided between Hindu and Muslim Indians on one side and Christian British and Australians on the other.

ARRIVAL AND INFORMATION   TAIPING

Although Taiping is built on a grid layout, it's easy to lose your bearings thanks to patchy street signage (note that many of the north–south streets change their name across Jalan Kota). **Jalan Taming Sari** is the main street, busy by day but dead at night.

By train The station is on Jalan Stesen, just north of the centre (☎ 05 807 2591).
Destinations Alor Star (1 daily; 5hr); Butterworth (2 daily; 1hr 45min–2hr 45min); Hat Yai (Thailand; 1 daily; 7hr 30min); Ipoh (2 daily; 1hr 30min); Johor Bahru (1 daily; 11hr 30min); Kuala Kangsar (2 daily; 35min); Kuala Lumpur (2 daily; 4hr 30min); Seremban (1 daily; 5hr 45min); Singapore (1 daily; 12hr 15min); Sungai Petani (1 daily; 4hr).
By local bus The local station is off Jalan Masjid.
Destinations Ipoh (every 45min; 1hr 45min); Kamunting (#8; every 40min; 30min); (Kuala Kangsar (every 45min; 1hr); Kuala Sepetang (#77; every 80min; 30min).
By express bus The nearest express bus station is 7km north in the industrial town of Kamunting; confusingly, some bus firms advertise services for Taiping when they mean this station. Local bus #8 between Taiping and Parit Buntar runs via the station; a taxi costs RM10. You can buy tickets for one bus company, Konsortium, in Taiping at its office on Jalan Panggung Wayang across from the bus station.
Destinations Butterworth (hourly; 1hr 15min); Johor Bahru (several daily; 8hr 30min); Kota Bharu (at least 1 daily; 6hr); Kuala Lumpur (hourly; 3hr 30min); Penang (several daily; 1hr 30min); Singapore (3 daily; 9hr 30min).
Tourist office Run by volunteers, inside the old clock tower on Jalan Kota (Mon–Sat 10am–5pm; ☎ 05 805 3245).

ACCOMMODATION

Taiping has a good range of hotels for its size, although for top-end comforts your only real option is the *Novotel*, part of the Taiping Mall development; it should be open by the time you read this.

★ **Flemington** Jalan Samanea Saman ☎ 05 820 7777, ⓦ flemingtonhotel.com.my. A recently modernized hotel, with a rooftop pool offering great views out over the Lake Gardens and east to the mountains (pricier rooms also have good vistas). That said, the rooms could be a little more distinctive for the price, although breakfast is thrown in. RM140

Fuliyean 14 Jalan Barrack ☎ 05 806 8648. One of several established cheapies in the centre with neat en-suite rooms, although it suffers from street noise, despite a/c. RM60

Legend Inn 2 Jalan Long Jaafar ☎ 05 806 0000, ⓦ legendinn.com. The best of the mid-range hotels in the centre, convenient for local buses. An extra RM10 or so per head pays for the buffet breakfast in the coffee house. RM110

Peking 2 Jalan Idris ☎ 05 807 2975, ⓦ hotelfurama .com.my. In an old detached house that the Japanese turned into a police station during the war, the *Peking* appears to be going to seed but is actually quite sound. The rooms have a/c and bathroom, and the building itself is a pleasing mishmash of colonial and Chinese features. RM60

Sentosa Villa In the Taman Sentosa residential estate off the Bukit Larut Rd, 2km from the Lake Gardens ☎ 05 805 1000, ⓦ sentosavilla.com. The reward for staying this far from town is to be in a sort of back-to-nature motel, the buildings styled like jumbo treehouses in a leafy compound with a stream-fed pool to swim in and ducks and geese waddling around. There's a café, although rates don't include breakfast. RM130

EATING AND DRINKING

Larut Matang Food Court Jalan Panggung Wayang. Split into halal (basically Malay) and non-halal (Chinese) halves; the Malay section opens and shuts later, and is a good place to sample *popiah* and *pasembur* – the latter similar to the Indian *rojak* you get in Singapore or KL, except that everything is served in one bowl with spicy gravy instead of a dip. Daily 7am–10pm.

Prima Jalan Kota, opposite Jalan Maneksha. Two *kopitiam*-type places on opposite street corners, with tables out on the street come evening, *Prima* runs the gamut of Malaysian hawker food: *laksa, rojak, nasi lemak* and more, plus some Western options too. Daily 8am–11pm.

Sky Bar Top of the Flemington Hotel. The only bar worth the name in the centre, a good place for a sundowner as the light changes over the mountains and the Lake Gardens. Daily 8am–midnight.

Soon Lee 11–15 Jalan Lim Swee Aun ☎ 05 807 6624. Taiping's grandest Chinese restaurant, with a chandeliered

main dining room and an emphasis on seafood, although there's also a separate vegetarian section. Go for steamed grouper, butter mantis prawns, braised pigs' trotters and other specialities, some not on the menu. RM35/head, minus drinks. Daily 11am–2.30pm & 5.30–10.30pm.

Sri Annapoorana Curry House Corner of Jalan Taming Sari and Jalan Yusof. The friendliest eating place in Taiping's Indian quarter, with *roti* and *thosai* made to order, noodles, more substantial meals with or without meat, plus starchy South Indian breakfasts like *pongal* – almost a lightly spiced risotto. Mon–Sat 7.30am–8pm, Sun 7.30am–3pm.

Taman Tasik Food Court Western side of the Lake Gardens. Excellent, inexpensive Chinese food, including seafood noodles, rice with chicken *rendang* and, more unusually, century-egg porridge (rice gruel with gelatinous pickled eggs). Locals rate the stalls on the outside edge, facing the gardens, as the best. Busiest in the evening. Daily 24hr.

DIRECTORY

Bike rental The pedal-boat rental outlet at the Lake Gardens also has bicycles (RM15 for 4hr) – useful given how scattered some of the town's sights are.

Pharmacy Several around the town centre, including a Watsons on Jalan Idris and a Guardian on Jalan Kota opposite the clock tower.

Shopping Run by the people behind the Old House Museum, Kapitan Antiques House at 61 Jalan Taming

Sari (daily 10am–7pm) has porcelain tea sets, tiffin carriers and some bric-a-brac. For general shopping, head to the brand new Taiping Mall – another first for the town, dwarfing everything around it – on Jalan Panggung Wayang.

Swimming The Coronation Pool, off the Bukit Larut Rd 200m beyond the war cemetery (daily 7.30am–6pm; RM3) is fed by hill streams and is occasionally chilly.

Bukit Larut (Maxwell Hill)

Summit Rd begins 1.5km beyond the Lake Gardens (turn right at the Coronation Pool for Ranger Station) • **Land Rovers** Hourly 8am–3pm; 35min; RM7 return • ☎ 05 807 7241

Still widely known by its colonial-era name, Maxwell Hill, **BUKIT LARUT** is Malaysia's smallest and oldest hill station, its summit a mere 6km east of Taiping as the crow flies. The climate is wonderfully cool; when it isn't raining – this is one of the wettest places in the country – you can be treated to good views down to the coast. Local visitors prefer to ride the Land Rovers up and down, but the long, often steep hike up offers the chance to do some **birdwatching** or spot unusual **pig-tailed macaques** (the name makes complete sense when you come across one) which live in the forests lower down. Most of the accommodation options at the top have been languishing for years, so it's best to treat the hill as a day-trip from Taiping.

Walking to the summit

The **summit road** (10km to the top) twists and turns round some 72 terrifying bends; walking, allow at least three hours up, two hours down if you only take short breathers. About halfway up, the Tea Garden House, once part of an extensive tea estate but now little more than a shelter, makes an ideal rest stop, with a view of Taiping and the mirror-like waters of the gardens visible below. The main **hill station area** (1036m) has a few minor trails and circuits in the vicinity. Ambitious walkers continue a further 3km through groves of evergreens to the 1250m-high summit of **Gunung Hijau**, although it's as well to seek advice from the rangers if you want to attempt this.

Matang Mangrove Forest Reserve

16km west of Taiping, 2km before Kuala Sepetang (Port Weld) • Daily 9am–5pm • Free • ☎ 05 858 1762 • Bus #77 from Taiping bus station (every 80min) to Kuala Sepetang

More than a century old, the **Matang Mangrove Forest Reserve** is Peninsular Malaysia's largest surviving spread of mangrove, most of which has been extensively cleared for development or for **charcoal production** (still practised, sustainably, in the nearby town of **Kuala Sepetang**). Since the 2004 Indian Ocean tsunami, there's been renewed local interest in the mangroves; the trees' mesh of aerial support roots can absorb some of the force of tsunamis and thus protect coastlines. They're also breeding grounds for small marine creatures from fiddler crabs to mudskippers and archer fish. Extensive **boardwalks** at the reserve lead through a forest of tall, thin trunks and mangrove ferns; keep your eyes peeled for dusky-leaf monkeys.

A knowledgeable local guide, John Chan, can arrange **tours** that cover Matang, charcoal-making and a trip to nearby **Kampung Dew**, with a decent chance of seeing **fireflies** (☎ 016 356 9169, ✉ greenjohnchan@gmail.com).

Lenggong Valley

Among the *dramatis personae* of ancient human remains, **Perak Man**, found in 1991, has a mere bit part. Yet this 10,000-year-old skeleton, thought to be the oldest in Southeast Asia, played a useful role in ensuring that the **Lenggong Valley** was declared a UNESCO World Heritage Site in 2012. Some 30km north of Kuala Kangsar, nestling close to the Titiwangsa range, the valley also contains two groups of **caves** that have yielded important evidence of Paleolithic toolmaking.

For visitors, however, there's precious little to see. At the time of writing the caves were mostly sealed off to secure them in the wake of the UNESCO listing. There is a so-so **museum** where the skeleton takes pride of place, but it's marooned in an area of oil palm, tricky to reach unless you happen to be driving Route 76 to or from the Royal Belum State Park or Kota Bharu.

Archeological Gallery of the Lenggong Valley

Signed off Route 76, 6km south of Lenggong town near the village of Kota Tampan • Sat–Thurs 9am–5pm, Fri 9am–noon & 3–5pm • Free • ☎ 05 767 9700, �🌐 lenggong.heritage.gov.my • Lenggong's bus station is by the central market; to visit the museum by bus, ask the driver for "Muzium Arkeologi Lenggong" or Kota Tampan and hope to be let off at the right spot on the main road (still about 2km away); alternatively, try to find an unofficial taxi in Lenggong – generally not easy, and be prepared to bargain – or charter a taxi in Kuala Kangsar (although you might have to pay RM100 for the return trip)

The most interesting sections of the **Archeological Gallery of the Lenggong Valley** cover Perak Man, whose bones appear jumbled and inscrutable to the untrained eye, although it has deformities that indicate he had a congenital disease. He was buried together with shells and tools, making him one of few known examples of ancient people with disabilities given a ceremonial burial, indicating they were respected by their community.

The museum can arrange a guided tour to the caves if you apply in advance.

ACCOMMODATION AND EATING   LENGGONG

Permaculture Perak On a remote hill south of Lenggong, only reachable by 4WD �🌐 permacultureperak.com. A one-of-a-kind off-grid farm built by a dreadlocked Czech named Ladia, who collects guests from Lenggong by arrangement. It's rustic but not overly so: the guests' farmhouse has proper bedrooms and cold showers, and there's solar power and even wi-fi. You share the compound with various goats; diversions include swimming in a stream full of tiny fish, and wooded trails further uphill. Full board per person RM130

★ **Restoran Tasik Raban** Route 76, 8km south of Lenggong ☎ 019 521 5657. Superb Malay place with one of the best *nasi campur* spreads in the country: innumerable curries, barbecued fish, *ulam* – the Malay salad, often with exotic leaves – and *tempoyak*, the surprisingly palatable durian sauce which actually tastes like cheese. Self-service; you pay after eating (a staff member will check your plate early on to see what you've had). Daily 11am–4pm.

FROM TOP STREET FOOD STALL, GEORGETOWN (P.136); CHEONG FATT TZE MANSION (P.144) >

Royal Belum State Park

Perak's last outpost before Kelantan is the underrated **Royal Belum State Park**, a pocket of rainforest and lakeland snuggled up against a Thai national park across the border. The lake in question, **Temenggor**, was created in the 1970s as a hydropower project, although locals say it was also intended to frustrate infiltration by Communist insurgents from the Emergency days, who had taken refuge in Thailand. Whatever the truth of that, the park itself and the adjoining Temenggor forest reserve to the south offer an excellent taste of Malaysian nature: the area is home to all ten of the country's indigenous **hornbill** species, plus elephants, gaur and other wildlife, and **Rafflesia** flowers bloom year-round too. Unfortunately, park bureaucracy is such that visitors need to apply for **permits** in advance – which in practice means that it's best to come on a pricey package.

ARRIVAL AND DEPARTURE · ROYAL BELUM STATE PARK

Visitors reach the park via the **Banding jetty** on the western edge, just off Route 4. Some 25km away on Route 76 is the nearest town, **Gerik** (or Grik), which is 65km east of Butterworth and 95km north of Ipoh as the crow flies.

By bus and taxi Local buses from Ipoh head to Gerik via Lenggong (5 daily; 3hr), from where a taxi to the jetty costs RM55. Express buses travelling between Penang (or other west coast cities) and Kota Bharu should call at Gerik and may be able to drop you at the access road for the jetty.

By car From Penang, take the E15/Route 67 to just before Kupang, where you turn right on to a minor road that eventually links up with Route 4 near Gerik. From points south, join Route 76 at the Kuala Kangsar exit on the North–South Expressway.

ACCOMMODATION

Privately run lodges and houseboats are outside the park in the **Temenggor** reserve. Book a week in advance so they can sort out your park permits.

Belum Eco Resort Temenggor forest reserve ☎ 05 281 0834, 🔾 belumecoresort.com.my. Affordable, well-run place with simple chalets that have a shower built in, although toilets are shared. There's also a Malay-style houseboat that sleeps up to six people. Packages include boat rides, kayaking, trekking to salt licks and a visit to an Orang Asli community. Three days full board including activities and permits, per person RM750,

similar deal entirely within Temenggor RM680
Belum Rainforest Resort Temenggor forest reserve ☎ 05 791 6800, 🔾 belumresort.com. The slickest accommodation in the area, offering big-city creature comforts and style in a range of spacious rooms and chalets. They price activities separately: a day's worth of boat rides and trekking can cost more than a night's stay. Breakfast included. RM350

Penang

In the far northwest of Peninsular Malaysia, **PENANG** is the most ambiguously named part of the country: depending on context, the moniker may refer to the **island** (**Pulau Pinang** in Malay, *pinang* being what Malays call the betel-nut palm), or the state (the island plus a blob of mainland opposite, around the town of Butterworth), or even just the state capital – properly **Georgetown**. This was where the British established their first Malay port in the late eighteenth century, laying the foundations for the Georgetown of today, a fascinating blend of colonial, Indian, Malay and – especially – Chinese and Peranakan heritage (Penang is the one Peninsular state where the Chinese are probably still the largest ethnic group, though only just). The city has seen a renaissance since its central old quarter, along with that of Melaka, were jointly made a UNESCO World Heritage Site in 2008, and makes a wonderful base to see all of Penang. Elsewhere on the 285-square-kilometre island are a coastal national park where you might see **nesting turtles**, a couple of unusual temples and a rather overdeveloped beach at **Batu Ferringhi**.

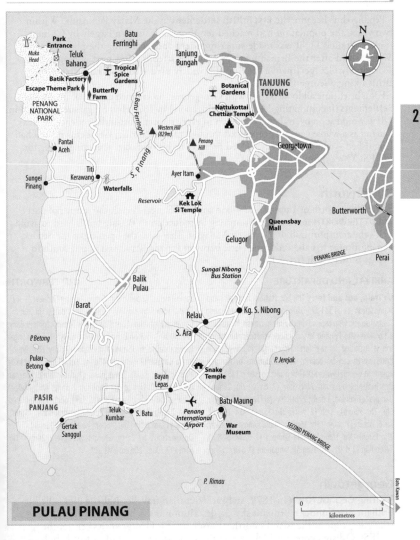

PULAU PINANG

Map labels:
N

Park Entrance
Muka Head
Teluk Bahang
Batu Ferringhi
Tanjung Bungah
Tropical Spice Gardens
Batik Factory
Escape Theme Park
Butterfly Farm
PENANG NATIONAL PARK
Botanical Gardens
TANJUNG TOKONG
Nattukottai Chettiar Temple
S. Batu Ferringhi
S. Pinang
Western Hill (829m)
Penang Hill
Georgetown
Pantai Aceh
Titi Kerawang
Ayer Itam
Waterfalls
Sungei Pinang
Reservoir
Kek Lok Si Temple
Butterworth
Queensbay Mall
Gelugor
PENANG BRIDGE
Perai
Sungai Nibong Bus Station
Balik Pulau
Barat
Relau
Kg. S. Nibong
S. Ara
P. Betong
Pulau Betong
Bayan Lepas
Snake Temple
P. Jerejak
PASIR PANJANG
Teluk Kumbar
S. Batu
Penang International Airport
Batu Maung
War Museum
Gertak Sanggul
SECOND PENANG BRIDGE
P. Rimau
Batu Kawan

0   4
kilometres

Brief history

Pulau Pinang was ruled by the **sultans of Kedah** until the late eighteenth century. But increasing harassment by Thai and Burmese raiding parties encouraged the sultan to seek help from **Francis Light**, a plausible British adventurer searching for a regional trading base to counter the Dutch presence in Sumatra. A deal was struck: Light would provide military aid through the **British East India Company** and the sultan would receive 30,000 Spanish dollars a year. There was one snag – the East India Company's Governor-General, **Charles Cornwallis**, refused to get involved. Concealing the full facts from both the sultan and Cornwallis, Light went ahead anyway and took **possession** of Penang on August 11, 1786, then spent five years assuring the sultan that the matter was being referred to London. The sultan finally caught on but failed to evict the British, ending up with a modest annuity and no role in the island's government.

2

Penang thus became the **first British settlement** in the Malay Peninsula. Within two years, the population had reached ten thousand, swollen largely by Chinese traders. Francis Light was made superintendent and, renaming the place Prince of Wales Island after the British heir apparent, declared it a **free port**. Georgetown – originally George Town, a spelling still widely used – took its name from the British king, George III.

For a brief time all looked rosy, with Georgetown proclaimed capital of the **Straits Settlements** (incorporating Melaka and Singapore) in 1826. But Singapore, founded in 1819, would soon overtake Georgetown in every respect. Post-independence, even as Penang as a whole generally prospered through manufacturing, Georgetown itself had languished – which, ironically, helped preserve its historic core, rendering it ripe for UNESCO recognition (see p.141).

Butterworth

Some 70km north of Taiping and 40km south of Sungai Petani, the industrial port of **BUTTERWORTH** makes an unpromising introduction to Penang but is hard to avoid, as it's the transport hub of northwest Malaysia. That said, the opening of the Second Penang Bridge has allowed some buses between Penang island and points south to bypass Butterworth (see p.146).

ARRIVAL AND DEPARTURE BUTTERWORTH

By train, bus and ferry The bus station, ferry pier and train station (☏ 04 331 2796) are in a cluster, called Penang Sentral, so you won't spend much time in transit. If catching a taxi across to Penang island, check whether the bridge toll is included in the fare. Tickets for journeys from Butterworth can be bought at the stations or through agents at Georgetown's KOMTAR building (see p.145). Destinations by train Alor Star (2 daily; 2hr 15min); Bangkok (Thailand; 1 daily; 22hr); Hat Yai (Thailand; 2 daily; 6hr–7hr 30min); Ipoh (2 daily; 3hr 15min–4hr 15min); Johor Bahru (1 daily; 13hr 15min); Kuala Kangsar (2 daily; 2hr 15min–3hr 15min); Kuala Lumpur (2 daily; 6–8hr); Seremban (1 daily; 7hr 30min); Singapore (1 daily; 14hr).

Sungai Petani (2 daily; 1hr 15min); Taiping (2 daily; 2–3hr). Destinations by bus Alor Star (several daily; 1hr 30min); Cameron Highlands (2 or 3 daily; 4hr 30min); Ipoh (9 daily; 2hr 30min); Johor Bahru (several daily; 10hr); Kangar (several daily; 2hr 15min); Kota Bharu (2 daily; 6hr 30min); Kuala Kangsar (2 daily; 2hr 45min); Kuala Lumpur (at least hourly; 5hr); Kuala Terengganu (1 daily; 8hr); Kuantan (4 daily; 9hr); Lumut (for Pangkor; 2 daily; 4hr); Melaka (several daily; 8hr); Seremban (6 daily; 6hr); Singapore (at least 2 daily; 11hr); Sungai Petani (several daily; 45min); Taiping (Kamunting bus station; hourly; 1hr 15min). Destinations by ferry Georgetown (every 20min–1hr; 6am–12.30am; 20min; RM1.20).

Georgetown

Visiting **GEORGETOWN** in 1879, stalwart Victorian traveller **Isabella Bird** called it "a brilliant place under a brilliant sky", a description that's hard to improve. Filling a triangular cape at the island's northeastern corner is Georgetown's centre, the UNESCO-listed core of which is essentially the area south and east of Lebuh Farquhar, Lebuh Cinta (Love Lane) and Lebuh Melayu. It's a surprisingly harmonious maze of lanes lined with **shophouses** in various states of repair and liberally sprinkled with religious buildings, impressive **clan associations** or

GEORGETOWN'S CAT SHUTTLE

Georgetown's centre is served by the **CAT shuttle bus** (also signed as #5; daily 6am–11.40pm; every 15–30min; free), which can be useful especially if you're flagging in the heat. Operated by Rapid Penang, it sets off from the Pengkalan Weld terminal, heading north to Little India and the colonial district, then Lebuh Muntri. It then turns southwest along Jalan Penang to the KOMTAR building, meandering in the vicinity before returning east via Lebuh Carnavon, Jalan Masjid Kapitan Kling and the colonial district to the bus terminal.

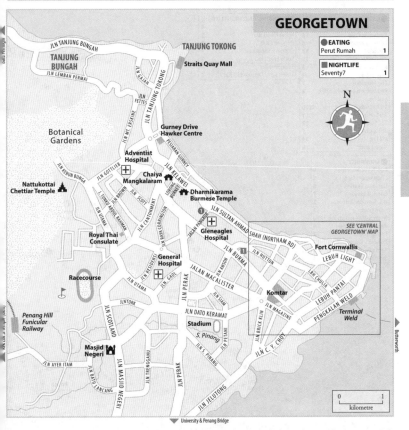

kongsi – a blend of Chinese welfare organization, social club and temple (see p.575) and other monuments. The obvious comparison is with Singapore, but it's as if the same ingredients have created an altogether mellower dish, without the slickness, crowds and incessant din of its former Straits Settlements cohort. If time is short, make a point of seeing the **Khoo Kongsi** and the **Cheong Fatt Tze mansion**; otherwise simply enjoy the relaxed pace and stroll at will.

The main arteries are **Jalan Penang**, **Jalan Masjid Kapitan Kling** and **Lebuh Pantai**, which run roughly west–east, along with traffic-clogged **Lebuh Chulia**, which runs northwest–southeast. Note that parts of Lebuh Chulia and Jalan Penang are distinctly seedy at night. Georgetown's northern fringes and the rugged, forested hills of the island's centre are home to a few interesting **temples** and the attractive **Botanic Gardens**.

Colonial district

Clustered around historic **Fort Cornwallis** are a motley collection of colonial buildings, including the former Town and City halls, St George's Church and some of Georgetown's oldest and most prestigious schools. A useful landmark, at the eastern end of Lebuh Pantai and close to the tourist offices, is the graceful Moorish-style **clock tower**, with onion-dome roof and scalloped Arabesque windows. Presented in 1897 to mark Queen Victoria's Diamond Jubilee, it's 60ft (20m) high, a foot for each year of her reign.

2

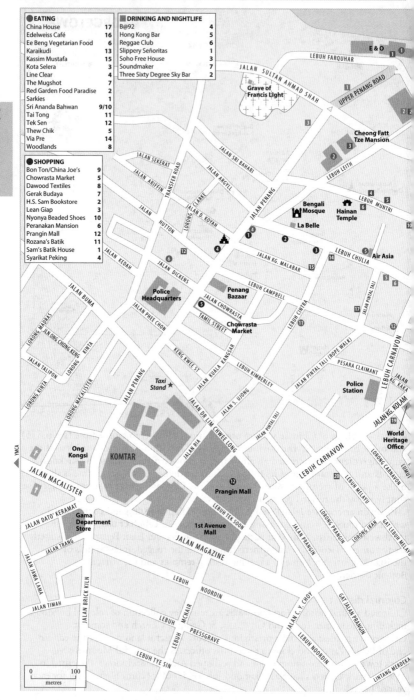

● EATING

China House	17
Edelweiss Café	16
Ee Beng Vegetarian Food	6
Karaikudi	13
Kassim Mustafa	15
Kota Selera	3
Line Clear	4
The Mugshot	7
Red Garden Food Paradise	2
Sarkies	1
Sri Ananda Bahwan	9/10
Tai Tong	11
Tek Sen	12
Thew Chik	5
Via Pre	14
Woodlands	8

■ DRINKING AND NIGHTLIFE

B@92	4
Hong Kong Bar	5
Reggae Club	6
Slippery Señoritas	1
Soho Free House	3
Soundmaker	7
Three Sixty Degree Sky Bar	2

● SHOPPING

Bon Ton/China Joe's	9
Chowrasta Market	5
Dawood Textiles	8
Gerak Budaya	7
H.S. Sam Bookstore	2
Lean Giap	3
Nyonya Beaded Shoes	10
Peranakan Mansion	6
Prangin Mall	12
Rozana's Batik	11
Sam's Batik House	1
Syarikat Peking	4

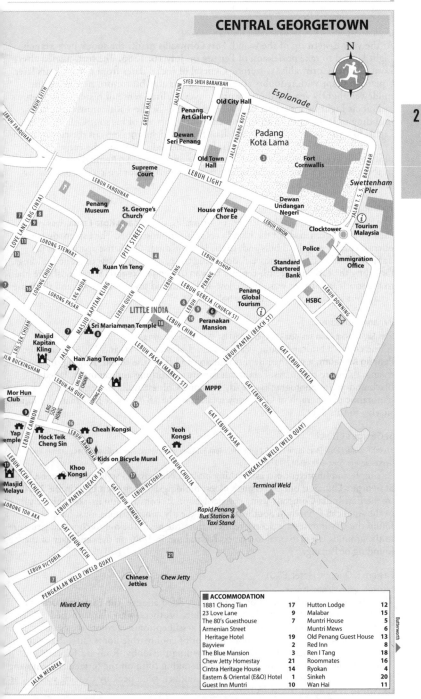

CENTRAL GEORGETOWN

N

Esplanade

SYED SHEH BARAKBAH
Old City Hall
Penang Art Gallery
Dewan Seri Penang
Old Town Hall
Padang Kota Lama **3**
Fort Cornwallis
Swettenham Pier

JALAN TUN
GREEN HALL
LEBUH LEITH
LEBUH FARQUHAR

Supreme Court
LEBUH FARQUHAR
LEBUH LIGHT
JALAN PADANG KOTA
Dewan Undangan Negeri

JALAN S.S. BARAKBAH

Penang Museum
St. George's Church
House of Yeap Chor Ee
LEBUH UNION
Clocktower
Tourism Malaysia

LOVE LANE (LRG CINTA)
LORONG STEWART
(PITT STREET)
Kuan Yin Teng
LEBUH BISHOP
Penang Global Tourism
Police
Immigration Office

LORONG CHULIA
LORONG PASAR
LRG MUDA
MASJID KAPITAN KLING
LEBUH QUEEN
LEBUH KING
LEBUH GEREJA (CHURCH ST)
LEBUH PENANG
Standard Chartered Bank
LEBUH DOWNING
HSBC

LRG SEK CHUAN
LITTLE INDIA
Sri Mariamman Temple
LEBUH CHINA
Peranakan Mansion
LEBUH PANTAI (BEACH ST)
GAT LEBUH GEREJA

Masjid Kapitan Kling
JLN BUCKINGHAM
Han Jiang Temple
HS SEK CHUAN
LORONG PITT
LEBUH PASAR (MARKET ST)
GAT LEBUH CHINA

Mor Hun Club
LEBUH AH QUEE
LRG 500 HONG
MPPP
GAT LEBUH PASAR

Yap Temple
LEBUH CANNON
LEBUH ARMENIAN
Hock Teik Cheng Sin
Cheah Kongsi
Yeoh Kongsi
PENGKALAN WELD (WELD QUAY)

Khoo Kongsi
Kids on Bicycle Mural
GAT LEBUH ARMENIAN
GAT LEBUH CHULIA
Terminal Weld

Masjid Melayu
LEBUH ACEH (ACHEEN ST)
LORONG TOH AKA
LEBUH PANTAI (BEACH ST)
LEBUH VICTORIA
Rapid Penang Bus Station & Taxi Stand

LEBUH VICTORIA
GAT LEBUH ACEH
21
PENGKALAN WELD (WELD QUAY)
Chinese Jetties
Chew Jetty

Mixed Jetty
JALAN MERDEKA

Butterworth

ACCOMMODATION			
1881 Chong Tian	**17**	Hutton Lodge	**12**
23 Love Lane	**9**	Malabar	**15**
The 80's Guesthouse	**7**	Muntri House	**5**
Armenian Street		Muntri Mews	**6**
Heritage Hotel	**19**	Old Penang Guest House	**13**
Bayview	**2**	Red Inn	**8**
The Blue Mansion	**3**	Ren I Tang	**18**
Chew Jetty Homestay	**21**	Roommates	**16**
Cintra Heritage House	**14**	Ryokan	**4**
Eastern & Oriental (E&O) Hotel	**1**	Sinkeh	**20**
Guest Inn Muntri	**10**	Wan Hai	**11**

2

Fort Cornwallis

Entrance in the northwest of the site, via the Padang • Daily 9am–7pm • RM2

At the very eastern tip of the island, **Fort Cornwallis** marks the spot where Francis Light landed to take possession of Penang on July 16, 1786. The fort, named after Lord Charles Cornwallis, Governor-General of India, dates from twenty years later. Square in shape with redoubts at each corner, it's all a bit forlorn nowadays, the mildewed, lightly vegetated brickwork conveying little sense of history. The **statue** of Francis Light by the entrance was cast in 1936 for the 150th anniversary of the founding of Penang, his features copied from a portrait of his son, Colonel William Light, founder of Adelaide in Australia. (Francis Light's **grave** is in the cemetery on Jalan Sultan Ahmad Shah, 1km west). Inside the walls, look for the early nineteenth-century chapel, powder magazine and bronze **Sri Rambai cannon**, sited in the northwest corner – local belief was that infertile women could conceive by laying flowers in its barrel.

Padang Kota Lama

The expanse of green that borders Fort Cornwallis, the **Padang Kota Lama**, was once the favourite promenade of the island's colonial administrators. The **Esplanade** here offers a vista of mainland hills and, to the left, the distant high-rise apartments of Tanjung Tokong in the northwest. Bordering the padang are a slew of grand buildings, including the early nineteenth-century **Dewan Undangan Negeri** (State Legislative Hall) to the south and, to the west, the yellow-and-white old **town hall** (1879) and the more ornate but less attractive former **city hall** (1903).

Penang Museum

Lebuh Farquhar • Sat–Thurs 9am–5pm • RM1 • ☎ 04 226 1461, ⓦ penangmuseum.gov.my

A fine colonial building, built as a free school between 1896 and 1906, houses the **Penang Museum**, a worthwhile introduction to life on the island. Among the memorabilia are rickshaws, Peranakan furniture, clothing and ceramics, faded black-and-white photographs of early Penang's Chinese millionaires, and a panoramic photograph of Georgetown taken in the 1870s (note how many buildings survive to this day).

St George's Church

1 Lebuh Farquhar • Mon–Thurs 10am–noon & 2–4pm, Fri 2–4pm, Sat 10am–noon; visitors may be allowed in at other times if no services are in progress • Free • ☎ 04 261 2739

As simple and unpretentious as anything built in Neoclassical style in Asia can be, **St George's Church** is one of Penang's oldest buildings, having been built in the 1810s by the East India Company using convict labour. Its construction marked the arrival of the Anglican Church in Southeast Asia, and early congregations must have found the airy interior a welcome reprieve from the heat. The round cupolaed structure in the grounds is a memorial to Francis Light, built in 1886 on the centenary of the founding of Penang.

Eastern & Oriental Hotel (E&O)

10 Lebuh Farquhar • ⓦ eohotels.com

Though a little overshadowed by its recently added annexe, the **Eastern & Oriental Hotel** – built in 1885 by the Armenian Sarkies brothers, who also launched Singapore's even more famous *Raffles Hotel* – still epitomizes colonial elegance. Behind the Neoclassical facade is an interior of cool marble floors, airy, dark timber and plasterwork, with a domed ceiling crowning the lobby; Rudyard Kipling and Somerset Maugham were among the guests, taking tiffin on the terrace and enjoying the sea breeze. If the rates are beyond your budget, get a peek by treating yourself at its *Sarkies* restaurant (see p.150).

UNESCO AND GEORGETOWN

It might be hard to believe today, but Georgetown was in a bad way as the new millennium arrived. This was a classic case of inner-city decay: the centre, its shophouses shabby and unloved, was a place to make a hasty exit from once the day's work was done.

Then came the idea of putting Georgetown forward for consideration as a **UNESCO World Heritage Site**. So it would become, though not in the form Penangites envisaged. Georgetown was perhaps too Chinese a city in the context of the country's politics, and Malaysia wound up lobbying for an odd joint ticket comprising Georgetown and Melaka – less well preserved but with historical Malay roots. It was this two-headed entity that was honoured as a single World Heritage Site in 2008. Watershed elections that same year saw, among other surprises, Penang captured by the opposition. Suddenly the state was being run along pragmatic, less racially focused lines, and had a UNESCO listing to boot. The scene was set for the city's regeneration.

The results are obvious for anyone to see. Properties all over the centre are being restored, some as boutique hotels and slick restaurants; young people are back in Georgetown, lounging in wannabe hipster cafés or cycling around checking out street art (see p.142); and the city has a real sense of its own heritage and creativity, celebrated in a slew of festivals and cultural events (see p.151).

However, as gentrification compels old businesses and community organizations to relocate, conservation groups are worried that Georgetown is losing its **intangible heritage** – a key ingredient in the UNESCO listing. Rapid social change is also an important factor, of course, and it may be that even with principled management, in twenty years central Georgetown could become like Singapore's Chinatown: immaculate, thriving, but with little sense of deep-rooted neighbourhoods and traditions.

House of Yeap Chor Ee

4 Lebuh Penang • Mon–Fri 10am–6pm • RM12 including audioguide • ☎ 04 261 0190, ⓦ houseyce.com

The **House of Yeap Chor Ee** nestles within Georgetown's historical **business district**, dominated by the banks of Lebuh Pantai; look for it next to the bright yellow former Chinese Chamber of Commerce building. Slicker than most of the country's state-owned museums, it's a privately run concern highlighting Malaya's El Dorado-like allure for immigrants, a few of whom went on to make a fortune. One such was Yeap Chor Ee, who arrived from southern China in 1885. Initially he cut hair and plaited pigtails, saving enough to become, eventually, a sugar magnate and banker. The shophouse on Lebuh Penang, now handsomely refurbished, was one of his earlier homes, but the grand cast-iron spiral staircase, antique inlaid furniture and many of the artefacts – fancy kitchenware and memorabilia including old photos showing Yeap and his descendants gradually adopting Western ways – are transplants from the vast mansion he later acquired on Jalan Sultan Ahmad Shah.

Peranakan Mansion

29 Lebuh Gereja • Daily 9.30am–5pm • RM20 • ☎ 04 264 2929, ⓦ pinangperanakanmansion.com.my

A sprinkling of Peranakan restaurants aside, Georgetown's one nod to Baba-Nyonya culture (see p.575) is a museum, the **Peranakan Mansion**. Painted pastel green, the house was built in the 1890s for Kapitan Cina Chung Keng Kwee, a Penang personality and secret-society leader. Chinese wooden doors, gorgeous inlaid furniture and carved screens are everywhere, alongside more European touches including florid glass light fittings. The **display cases** are full of trinkets and heirlooms: green-and-pink Chinese-made porcelain painted with phoenixes and peonies, snuffboxes, embroideries and shoes. Upstairs, a **bedroom** with a four-poster bed has been left pretty much intact. There's also a section devoted to traditional **jewellery**, an adjoining shrine holding ancestral tablets, and a small **gift shop** selling Peranakan-themed souvenirs (see p.152).

2

Jalan Masjid Kapitan Kling (Pitt Street)

For many locals, **Jalan Masjid Kapitan Kling** will always be **Pitt Street**, named after William Pitt the Younger, British prime minister when Francis Light founded Penang. It's also nicknamed the Street of Harmony because – if you include the compound of St George's Church at its eastern end – there are places of worship representing all of Malaysia's major faiths along its length.

Kuan Yin Teng

Jalan Masjid Kapitan Kling, close to the start of Lebuh China • Daily 7am–7pm • Free

The oldest and liveliest of Georgetown's Chinese temples, **Kuan Yin Teng** (Kuan Yin Pavilion) is a down-to-earth granite hall dating to 1801, whose dragon-carved pillars and wooden roof beams are blackened by incense smoke. Kuan Yin being the goddess of mercy, the temple is perpetually jammed with devotees, mostly beggars down on their luck and women praying for children, grandchildren and safe childbirth. The huge bronze bell in the first hall is rung by those who have made a donation; the flagstoned forecourt may feature performances of **Chinese opera** during festivals.

Sri Mahamariamman Temple

Lebuh Queen, with a second entrance on Jalan Masjid Kapitan Kling • Daily 8am–noon & 4–9pm • Free

The **Sri Mahamariamman Temple**, founded in 1833, is the chief sight in Georgetown's small but characterful **Little India**, centred on Lebuh Pasar. Its pale green and red entrance tower is a riot of sculpted deities, among which four **swans** represent incarnations of the goddess Mariamman.

Masjid Kapitan Kling

Western end of Jalan Masjid Kapitan Kling • Sat–Mon 1–5pm, Fri 3–5pm • Free

The oldest and largest mosque in Penang, **Masjid Kapitan Kling** dates back to 1801, when Indian Muslim migrants built a mosque here on land granted them by the East India Company. *Kling* is an old term, nowadays regarded as derogatory, for Indians, and Kapitan Kling was one Cauder Mohudeen, a successful businessman appointed by the East India Company to speak for the community. The present mosque was refashioned in Anglo-Moorish style at the start of the last century, and its dark onion domes, arched portico and minaret are especially attractive at night, when the whole place is subtly lit.

GEORGETOWN'S STREET ART

Street art is a recent phenomenon in Georgetown but has already become a big draw for local visitors, who wander around the centre tracking down the murals and cartoons executed in steel wire on shophouse walls. The **wire pieces** – some fifty of them – were commissioned from KL studio **Sculpture at Work** as a whimsical way of marking out the UNESCO-listed parts of the city. They caricature and celebrate all aspects of local life, from the stereotypical dodgy backpacker hostel to the spot, at the corner of Leith and Muntri streets, where famed shoe designer **Jimmy Choo** first learnt his trade.

There are around twenty **murals**, all rather kitsch. The best-known ones are by Lithuanian artist **Ernest Zaharevic**, invariably described as "Malaysia's Banksy": he lives in Penang, and examples of his work can now be spotted in quite a few Malaysian cities. Zaharevic was responsible for the single most popular piece of Georgetown art, *Kids on Bicycle*, depicting two children astride a real bike propped up against the wall; the spot on Lebuh Armenian draws a procession of admirers and selfie-snappers throughout the day.

All the artworks are catalogued on the handy *Marking Georgetown* **map**, available from tourist offices and at ⓦ mypenang.gov.my.

Lebuh Armenian

Short and curved at one end, **Lebuh Armenian** offers good value for visitors, packing in a number of minor sights along its now clearly gentrifying length, including at its southern end the popular *Kids on Bicycle* street art (see opposite). The narrow house at the street's northern end is the **Syed Alatas mansion**, named after a merchant and arms dealer from Aceh, in northern Sumatra, who lived here in the 1870s. Now somewhat dilapidated after being restored briefly as an Islamic museum, it's easy to identify from the pediment decorated with a blue crescent moon and star.

Mor Hun Club

122 Lebuh Armenian • Museum Tues–Sun 10am–5pm • RM10

The **Mor Hun Club** is one of Georgetown's surviving traditional social clubs, its entrance distinguished by colourful tilework and gorgeously carved gilt doors; walk past at night and you may hear the clacking of a game of mahjong from the upstairs windows. Downstairs is a small **museum** with displays on Chinese opera and puppetry, not worth the price of admission; better to attend one of their sporadic **puppet shows** (1hr with some English explanations; around RM25 including museum entry).

Yap Kongsi

Corner of Lebuh Armenian and Lebuh Cannon • Daily 8am–6pm • Free • ☎ 04 261 0679

It's hard to imagine two more contrasting shrines than the pair that make up the most obvious sight on Lebuh Armenian, the **Yap Kongsi**. On the left is the conventionally styled **Ciji Temple** (also called **Choo Chee Keong**), its roof photogenically bedecked with dragons; next door, built in the 1920s on land furnished by the tycoon Yeap Chor Ee, the green-and-white **Yap Temple** looks like a European-style villa and holds the clan's ancestral tablets.

Hock Teik Cheng Sin Temple

57 Lebuh Armenian • No fixed times • Free

Just south of the corner with Lebuh Cannon, a passageway beneath a Chinese facade gives access to the gaudy, two-storey **Hock Teik Cheng Sin Temple**, with altars on both levels. It's dedicated to **Tua Peh Kong**, sometimes described as the god of prosperity and one of the most popular Chinese deities in Malaysia – many cities have at least one Tua Peh Kong shrine. In the mid-nineteenth century the temple and surrounding area was a stronghold of the Kean Teik secret society, one of the parties embroiled in the Penang Riots (see box, p.144), and a bricked-up passageway can still be seen that once allowed a surreptitious escape to the street or to the Khoo Kongsi compound.

Khoo Kongsi

18 Cannon Square • Daily 9am–5pm • RM10 • ☎ 04 261 4609, ⓦ khookongsi.com.my

Khoo Kongsi is the best known of Penang's clan associations, and no wonder: this is practically a gated community in its own right, reached by an alleyway off Lebuh Cannon. It brings you into an overpoweringly gaudy complex that includes shrines, opera stage, ancestral hall and residences. The *kongsi* represents Khoos from a particular village in southern China; one such was Khoo Thean Teik, the ringleader of the Kean Teik secret society during the Penang Riots (see box, p.144), although he later rehabilitated himself and became a very wealthy pillar of local society.

The two-storey **main building** looks ready to collapse under the weight of the multicoloured ceramic sculptures, woodcarvings and shining gold leaf adorning its roof. Finished in 1906, this is a lesser version of an even more extravagant original that had just burned down – some say destroyed by jealous deities, angered by its ostentation.

Every inch of the main hall's portico is superbly carved, featuring the obligatory dragon pillars alongside scenes of Confucian moral tales. The interior sports more of

2

THE PENANG RIOTS

Chinese immigrants to Penang brought their traditions with them, including **secret societies**, which provided mutual aid and protection for the community – bolstered in Georgetown by alliances with similar Malay groups.

As the societies grew in wealth and power, gang warfare and extortion rackets became commonplace. Matters came to a head in the **Penang Riots** of 1867: for nine days Georgetown was shaken by fighting between the Kean Teik or Tua Peh Kong society, supported by the Malay Red Flag, and the Ghee Hin, allied with the Malay White Flag. Police intervention resulted in a truce, but on August 1, the Kean Teik headman falsely charged the Ghee Hin and White Flag societies with stealing cloth belonging to Kean Teik dyers. All hell broke loose, and fighting raged around Armenian, Church and Chulia streets, where the groups were holed up.

The unrest was eventually quelled by **sepoys**, Indian troops brought in from Singapore, but by then hundreds had been killed and scores of houses burned. The secret societies had to pay a heavy fine, with some of the money later used to finance the building of four police stations to deal with any future trouble. It's said that the shophouses in the vicinity of the riots are even now scarred by the odd bullethole.

---

the same, plus plain murals of Taoist guardian figures astride mostly mythical beasts. Not all the ornamentation is traditional: the two statues of turbaned guards outside the main hall reflect, a little stereotypically, the work some Sikhs did in Malaya.

The building opposite was the **opera stage**, beside which is the slightly incongruous administration building, a colonially styled affair which houses some ancestral tablets. A former kitchen next to the main building is now a little **museum** explaining the evolution of the complex. Note the wall-filling display here showing forty illuminated Chinese characters, each used as a kind of shared middle name across a generation of Khoos – the point of the display being that few clans can match this one's grasp of its genealogy.

Clan jetties
Pengkalan Weld

They're not as atmospheric as the water villages at Pulau Ketam near Kuala Lumpur or in the capital of Brunei, but the seven **clan jetties** of Georgetown still make for a good wander. Communities of stilt houses built over the water, they were set up by Chinese immigrants before Georgetown properly got going, and are so named because six of them are inhabited by individual clans whose roots are in specific villages in Fujian province, southeast China. The houses are connected by wooden boardwalks and dotted with temples. The **Chew jetty**, smack in the middle, is the largest and, as the target of most tourists, drowning in tacky souvenir shops; best to try one of the other jetties, though bear in mind that this cramped residential environment is not a great place for loud conversation and incessant photography.

Cheong Fatt Tze Mansion
14 Lebuh Leith · Compulsory tours: daily 11am, 2pm & 3.30pm; 1hr · RM16 · ☎ 04 262 0006, ⓦ cheongfatttzemansion.com

Leith Street was once lined by a gaggle of villas belonging to Hakka Chinese tycoons, one such being the **Cheong Fatt Tze Mansion**, a splendid example of Penang's eclectic late nineteenth-century house design. Cheong (1840–1907) had already made his money through shipping and tin mining, among many business interests, by the time he moved to Penang from the Dutch East Indies in the 1890s, and fairly soon set about commissioning his new home. Now trading mainly as a hotel, the *Blue Mansion* (see p.148), it's broadly southern Chinese in form, with projecting fire-baffle eaves, good-luck motifs and complex decorative mouldings along the tiled roof, though its **arches** and **shutters** are definitely European touches, as are the Art Nouveau stained glass and the sweeping interior staircase, even if the delicate iron tracery and balconies might owe a nod to wooden Malay verandas. The interiors are again furnished with a pleasant cross-cultural mix of screens, dining tables and stone-flagged light wells decorated with potted plants.

KOMTAR

Georgetown's most prominent landmark, the **Kompleks Tun Abdul Razak** (**KOMTAR**) is a 65-storey cylindrical tower at the western end of the city centre. Its main purpose is to house local government offices, but it's of more interest to visitors as a transport hub (see p.147) and shopping precinct, with malls clustered beneath and around it. There's also a **viewing deck** near the top, with spectacular vistas; by the time you read this it should be open again after a major refit, though check with one of the tourist offices to be sure.

Wat Chaiya Mangkalaram

Lorong Burma, in the Pulau Tikus area on the northern edge of Georgetown • Daily 7am–5.30pm • Free • Bus #101, #103 or #304; get off on Jalan Kelawei

Wat Chaiya Mangkalaram is a Thai Buddhist temple dating to the 1900s, very different in design from Chinese equivalents elsewhere in Penang with its bright colours, flame-edged eaves and huge gilded pagoda, all soft curves, to one side. The main hall's entrance is flanked by nagas – fierce snake-like creatures painted gold and bright green – and guarded by two hefty demons holding swords. The aircraft-hangar-like interior is a stark contrast, filled by a 33m-long **reclining Buddha** statue, draped in a gold sarong and with his aura flaming about him.

Dharmikarama Temple

Lorong Burma, Pulau Tikus • Daily 8am–5pm • Free • ☎ 04 226 9575 • Bus #101, #103 or #304; get off on Jalan Kelawei

Although the Burmese **Dharmikarama Temple** is similar to the Wat Chaiya Mangkalaram opposite, its guardians are two snarling white and gold lions, with scales, claws and fiery trim. The Buddha here is standing, smiling mysteriously into the gloom and with oversized white hands, one pointing upwards and one down. The grounds are a bit nicer than those over the road, with more greenery and less concrete, and a few naturalistically painted statues.

Nattukottai Chettiar Temple

Jalan Kebun Bunga • Daily 7am–noon & 4–9pm • Free • ☎ 04 227 1322 • Bus #10 from Pengkalan Weld

The **Nattukottai Chettiar Temple** (more formally the **Arulmigu Thandayuthapani Temple**) is the focus of the riotous three-day Hindu **Thaipusam** festival, in honour of Lord Subramanian (Jan or Feb). One of the crowning moments is the arrival of a silver chariot and statue of Lord Murugan, which have been carried from the sister temple in Georgetown. The temple itself has an unusual wooden colonnaded walkway with exquisite pictorial tiles, leading up to the inner sanctum, where a life-sized solid-silver peacock bows its head to the deity, Lord Subramanian.

Botanical Gardens

Jalan Kebun Bunga, 6km west of central Georgetown • Daily 5am–8pm • Free • ☎ 04 227 0428, ⓦ botanicalgardens.penang.gov.my • Bus #10 (every 45min; 45min)

Dating to 1884, Georgetown's **Botanical Gardens** boast extensive lawns, a stream and little jungly waterfall, and several (rather paltry) plant houses. Weekend mornings it's packed with groups of exercising Chinese, who storm around the circuit trail in about thirty minutes.

You can **walk to Penang Hill** (see p.154) from here using the so-called jeep track, but it's a tough uphill hike (3hr) – better to head down this way. A much easier hike just outside the gardens begins at the circular Chinese **moon gate arch** easily spotted on the main road; from here a wooded trail leads uphill, with views back over Georgetown. Most people head back down once they've reached the signed "Station 3" (allow thirty minutes to get here).

ARRIVAL AND DEPARTURE   GEORGETOWN

Unless on a plane or ferry, you'll reach or leave Penang island by one of two mammoth bridges linking it with the mainland part of the state: the 14km **Penang Bridge** (from Seberang Prai, just south of Butterworth) and the 24km **Second Penang Bridge** (from Batu Kawan, 15km south of Butterworth). Leaving, you don't have to buy tickets from the relevant terminal: there are bus company kiosks on the ground floor of the Prangin Mall close to the KOMTAR building, and informal travel agents on Lebuh Chulia plus some hostels sell train, bus and Langkawi ferry tickets.

BY PLANE

Penang International Airport One of the busiest in the country, the airport (ⓦ penangairport.com), 16km south of Georgetown at Bayan Lepas, has two tourist information counters (daily: Tourism Malaysia 8am–10pm; Penang Global Tourism 9am–5pm), a few ATMs and car rental kiosks. Buses #401 and #401E (both every 30min) run from outside the building to the terminal at Pengkalan Weld (1hr) via the KOMTAR building in the west of the city centre (see p.145); bus #102 (hourly) also serves KOMTAR and then heads out to the beach at Batu Ferringhi. A taxi into the city costs RM38 (RM50 in the small hours) – buy a coupon from inside the airport building.

Airlines AirAsia, 332 Lebuh Chulia (☎ 04 250 0020); Firefly, ground floor, KOMTAR building, Jalan Penang (☎ 04 250 2000); Malaysia Airlines, airport (☎ 04 619 0107); Malindo Air, 73 Lebuh Penang (☎ 04 262 9858); Silk Air, 12th floor, Plaza MWE, 8 Lebuh Farquhar (☎ 04 263 3201). **Destinations** Johor Bahru (2 daily; 1hr 10min); Kota Bharu (1–2 daily; 1hr); Kota Kinabalu (daily; 2hr); Kuala Lumpur (KLIA: every 1–2hr; Subang: at least 5 daily; 45min); Kuantan (3 weekly; 1hr 15min); Kuching (2 daily; 2hr); Langkawi (2–3 daily; 35min); Miri (4 weekly; 2hr 30min); Singapore (at least 8 daily; 1hr 20min).

BY TRAIN

Train station Penang's train station is in Butterworth (see p.136). From here, you can either catch a cab to Georgetown (20min; RM20) or follow the signed footbridge to the ferry. There is also a ticket office at Georgetown's ferry terminal (Sat–Thurs 10am–2pm & 3–5pm, Fri 10am–1pm & 3–5pm).

BY BUS

Express bus station At Sungai Nibong, 8km southwest of Georgetown on Jalan Sultan Azlan Shah, the express bus station is served by several local buses, including #102 (for the airport, the KOMTAR building and Batu Ferringhi; hourly), plus #307 and #401 (both serve KOMTAR and the

Pengkalan Weld terminal; every 30–45min). A taxi into the town costs about RM25. Departures from the bus station often head first to Butterworth, although a few southbound buses bypass it. In general, though, Butterworth still has more frequent services and a wider range of destinations, so it may pay to catch the ferry to the mainland and pick up a bus there.

Backpacker minibuses Run by tour agencies, minivan shuttles serving the east coast, Cameron Highlands and southern Thailand, among other destinations, pick up and drop passengers at hostels and the Prangin Mall, with tickets sold at both of these. The journey across the border to Hat Yai, for example, costs around RM35.

BY FERRY

Butterworth Ferries shuttle between Butterworth and Pengkalan Weld (every 20min–1hr, 5.40am–12.30am; 20min; RM1.20 to Georgetown, free to Butterworth), docking at a terminal close to the local bus station.

Langkawi Langkawi ferries use the Swettenham Pier, just east of Fort Cornwallis, with tickets available from a cluster of agencies just outside, by the clock tower. There are daily departures at 8.15am and 8.30am (2hr 45min; RM67 including port fees); the earlier of these calls also at the Pulau Payar Marine Park, making it possible to do (expensive) day-trips there with dive operators like East Marine (see p.166). At the time of writing a third departure at 2.30pm had been launched; check the latest schedules and prices at ⓦ langkawi-ferry.com and buy tickets at least a day in advance.

BY CAR

Driving to Georgetown Whichever bridge you use, tolls are payable only on the journey over from the mainland (Penang Bridge RM7, Second Penang Bridge RM8.50). Arriving on the island, bear right (north) up the coast for Georgetown. There's a reasonably central car park in the KOMTAR building on Jalan Penang.

GETTING AROUND

As befits one of the most populous parts of Malaysia, Penang has a **bus service** that puts much of the rest of the country to shame.

By bus Rapid Penang (W rapidpg.com.my) operates buses across Penang state. Many island routes originate at their station on Pengkalan Weld, with a station beneath the KOMTAR building serving as a secondary hub. The website gives a breakdown of routes, operating times (daily roughly 6am–9.30pm, although some services wind down much earlier or later) and frequencies (every 15min–1hr depending on the route). Fares climb with distance from RM1.40 (any trip within Georgetown) to RM4 in four steps; the airport to Georgetown, say, is RM2.70. A seven-day pass, Rapid Passport, offers unlimited travel for RM30 and is available at the bus station, KOMTAR and the Penang Global Tourism tourist office (see below). Note a few hassles about the buses: drivers don't give change; some bus stops, poles with a faded pink logo, are easily missed; and the one-way system around Georgetown makes some routes convoluted and means the stops for outward and return journeys may be on different roads.

By taxi There are ranks on Pengkalan Weld, on Penang Rd near the *Cititel* hotel, and on Jalan Dr Lim Chwee Long, around the Prangin Mall. Drivers don't use their meters, so agree the fare in advance – a trip to across town will be around RM12, out to Penang Hill or Batu Ferringhi about RM30. To book a taxi in advance, use MyTeksi (see p.35) or call ☎ 04 262 5721.

By trishaw The humble *beca* or trishaw clings on in Georgetown, mainly for the benefit of tourists. You'll find trishaws parked up on Lebuh Penang at the corner with Lebuh Muntri, and on Lebuh Armenian close to the Yap Kongsi, among other places. An hour's pedal around the old town starts at RM35; for other journeys you'll have to bargain.

By bike Cycling around the centre has caught on with visitors. Outlets scattered around the centre, including La Belle (see below), along with some guesthouses, rent bicycles out for around RM10 for half a day. An official Penang bike rental system is being set up too, which could launch in 2015 or 2016.

By motorcycle The odd hostel, La Belle (see below) plus the H.S. Sam bookshop (see p.152) have motorbikes available for rent, starting at around RM35/day.

Car rental Hawk, at the airport (☎ 04 227 9440); Hertz, 38 Lebuh Farquhar (☎ 04 263 5914); La Belle, 48 Lebuh Leith (☎ 04 264 2717, W labelle.net.my); Mayflower, at the airport (☎ 04 641 1191).

INFORMATION AND TOURS

Penang Global Tourism Ground floor of the Whiteaways Arcade, Lebuh Pantai ☎ 04 263 1166, W mypenang.gov.my. Penang state's tourist office can provide maps and leaflets on various aspects of local history and culture, some of which can be downloaded from their website, and an app that repackages much of the website for use on the go. Mon–Fri 9am–5pm, Sat 9am–3pm, Sun 9am–1pm.

Tourism Malaysia 10 Jalan Tun Syed Shah Barakbah ☎ 04 262 2093. Close to Fort Cornwallis, this is one of the more knowledgeable Tourism Malaysia offices. Mon–Fri 8am–5pm.

Tourist guides If you have a special interest in, for example, architecture or history, or want to get off the beaten track, it can be worth engaging a professional guide at the Penang Tourist Guides Association (7 Lebuh Cannon; Tues–Sun; ☎ 04 261 4461). There's also the Penang Nature Tourist Guide Association (booth opposite entrance to Penang National Park; ☎ 04 881 4788); its members can lead you on unusual hikes through forested areas – for example, a whole-day trek from the Penang National Park to Penang Hill.

ACCOMMODATION

There's such a vast choice of hotels and guesthouses in **central Georgetown** – mainly on the fringes of the UNESCO zone, where new places to stay are springing up in refurbished shophouses on Love Lane and Lebuh Muntri in particular – that there's little reason to base yourself further afield. That said, it's feasible to stay at the Batu Ferringhi beach and see Georgetown on day-trips (see p.155).

HOSTELS AND GUESTHOUSES

The 80's Guesthouse 46 Love Lane ☎ 04 263 8806, W the80sguesthouse.com; map pp.138–139. It's hard to discern anything Eighties-related at this niftily modernized building, one of the more upmarket places of its kind. There's a range of a/c rooms and dorms – including some containing double beds, meant for couples. Dorms RM35,

double beds in dorms RM60, doubles RM85

Chew Jetty Homestay 59a Chew Jetty ☎ 013 438 1217, W mychewjetty.com; map pp.138–139. One of the families at the old clan jetties offers a/c rooms in their house, with shared facilities; it's a good opportunity to mingle with the community and wake to the sight of the sun rising over the mainland. Breakfast included. RM138

PENANG ROOM TAXES

Note that in addition to the usual Malaysian **taxes** (see p.52) Penang state levies a nominal **accommodation tax** of RM3 per room per night.

2

Guest Inn Muntri 17 Lebuh Muntri ☎04 263 3228, ⓦguestinn.com.my; map pp.138–139. Newish, fairly slick place with a relaxing lounge boasting a pool table and its own bar. Some single rooms. Dorms RM28, doubles RM60

★**Hutton Lodge** 17 Jalan Hutton ☎04 263 6003, ⓦhuttonlodge.com; map pp.138–139. It calls itself a budget hotel, but operates more like an informal guesthouse with a dorm and a wide range of plainly furnished rooms, singles and doubles, some en suite. What gives it a proper homely feel is that it occupies a detached two-storey former mansion that's perhaps 100 years old, although what you see now was largely rebuilt after a major fire in 2003. Breakfast included; good value. Dorms RM30, doubles RM75

Malabar 26 & 28 Lebuh Chulia ☎012 485 5670; map pp.138–139. Reasonably well kept but nondescript, except that it boasts one of the tiniest en-suite singles you'll ever see. A good choice for a low-key stay. No breakfast. En-suite rooms cost at least RM10 more. Doubles RM60

Muntri House 48 Lebuh Muntri ☎04 261 3067, ⓔmuntrihouse.gmail.com; map pp.138–139. One of the more impressive new hostels, in a refurbished shophouse boasting cane furniture and courtyard greenery around a plasticky water feature. Dorms and rooms are much plainer than the communal areas; all have a/c but none is en suite. Dorms RM25, doubles RM65

★**Old Penang Guest House** 53 Lorong Cinta ☎04 263 8805, ⓦoldpenang.com; map pp.138–139. One of the better restored shophouses, with a range of a/c rooms and two dorms. The sheets are crisp and clean, there's a relaxing airy lounge with plasma TV, and staff are helpful. Light breakfast included. Dorms RM25, doubles RM80

Red Inn 55 Lorong Cinta ☎04 261 3931, ⓦredinnpenang.com; map pp.138–139. A nicely converted shophouse with polished wooden floors, although the dorms are basic and unremarkable. They also have branches in the vicinity with double rooms as well as dorms. Perhaps the best feature is the generous breakfast – they go out to buy noodles and *roti canai*. RM28

Roommates 17b Lorong Chulia ☎04 261 1567, ⓦroommatespenang.com; map pp.138–139. This tiny hostel has just two eight-bed dorms and feels all the homelier for it. They're cosy too, with privacy curtains for each bunk bed and lights built in. RM30

Ryokan 62 Lebuh Muntri ☎04 250 0287, ⓦmyryokan.com; map pp.138–139. Despite naming itself after a certain class of traditional inns in Japan, there's little Japanese about *Ryokan* other than perhaps a fascination with slickness and modernity. Popular with budget-conscious locals, the place certainly goes all out for the flashpacker vote, with individual power points, lights and lockers for every dorm bed, and breakfasts that stretch to sausage and egg. They have en-suite rooms, too, and a bar. Dorms RM30, doubles RM140

Wan Hai 35 Love Lane ☎04 261 3470, ⓔwanhai_pg @yahoo.com; map pp.138–139. This rambling, slightly run-down place is a glimpse of how many Malaysian budget hotels looked a generation ago – although in pricing it belongs with today's guesthouses. There's neither a/c nor en-suite options, and no dorms; everything is (more than tolerably) basic, and there's a leafy shared balcony that's pleasant in the evening. RM25

HOTELS

1881 Chong Tian 38–42 Jalan Pintal Tali, ☎04 263 1881, ⓦ1881chongtian.com; map pp.138–139. This recently opened boutique hotel harks back to its original nineteenth-century incarnation as a place where rich businessmen stayed. Think retro Chinese chic: antique sideboards and screens; a central courtyard set off by dark wood window shutters, potted bamboo and red drapes; and narrow swing doors giving access to spacious rooms on several levels. RM380

★**23 Love Lane** 23 Love Lane ☎04 262 1323, ⓦ23lovelane.com; map pp.138–139. Step through the square gateway hung with lanterns and it immediately feels like you've arrived at a private villa. Set around a lush garden of frangipani trees are ten spacious rooms, eclectically done out in snazzy hues. Besides doubles, there's also a two-level family unit and a glorious three-bedroom shophouse. Breakfast and afternoon tea included. RM500

Armenian Street Heritage Hotel 139 Jalan Masjid Kapitan Kling ☎04 262 3888, ⓦarmenianthe heritagehotel.com; map pp.138–139. Despite the obligatory heritage tag, this is a fairly slick, modern affair, all wood flooring and unfussy decor. Keen rates, especially given the central location. RM170

Bayview 25a Lebuh Farquhar ☎04 263 3161, ⓦbayviewhotels.com/georgetown; map pp.138–139. Modern, characterless high-rise close to the sea, with its own pool and gym, and good views from the revolving rooftop restaurant and bar. RM220

The Blue Mansion 14 Lebuh Leith ☎04 262 0006, ⓦcheongfatttzemansion.com; map pp.138–139. There are few more characterful places to stay in Penang, although you pay through the nose to do so. Cheong Fatt Tze's former villa (see p.144) now offers eighteen stylish suites plus a swimming pool, spa, reading room and its own restaurant and bar. Noise from the adjacent *Red Garden* food court can be a little annoying at night, though. Breakfast included. RM600

Cintra Heritage House 1–7 Lebuh Cintra ☎04 262 8232, ⓦcintrahouse.com; map pp.138–139. Behind the restored facades of four shophouses lurks this new hotel with a small leafy courtyard and thirteen rooms, all kitted out with retro furniture and with an emphasis on quiet, TV-free, snugness rather than ostentation. Breakfast included. RM220

★ **Eastern & Oriental (E&O) Hotel** 10 Lebuh Farquhar ☎ 04 222 2000, W eohotels.com; map pp.138–139. Penang's historic hotel (see p.140) has finally outgrown its colonial trappings by sprouting a new fifteen-storey wing to meet demand for rooms. But you'll pay hardly any more to stay in the original buildings, when you can immerse yourself in what feels like a period mansion right on the seafront. The new wing has an infinity pool; the original wing a pool within a couple of metres of the sea. Breakfast included. RM780

★ **Muntri Mews** 77 Lebuh Muntri ☎ 04 263 5125, W muntrimews.com; map pp.138–139. This long, narrow two-storey building really was a set of stables once, serving the mansions that dominated the neighbourhood. Now it's an artfully decorated collection of nine suites, the pricier upstairs ones boasting four-poster beds and wood flooring, downstairs units featuring mattresses tucked into an alcove and marble floors; both come with their own

lounge area. There's also a marvellous café where you can enjoy breakfast, covered by the surprisingly affordable rates. RM350

★ **Ren I Tang** 82a Lebuh Penang (entrance on Lebuh China) ☎ 04 250 8383, W renitang.com; map pp.138–139. This imposing three-storey colonial building originally housed a Chinese apothecary, its name now given to the mid-range hotel that has emerged following a splendid conversion – although they've deliberately retained a herbalist's shop downstairs. There's a vast range of rooms, including a family unit, a self-contained apartment and assorted doubles, some with distressed paintwork for that aged look. Note that there's no lift, but they can winch your luggage to the top floor, on request. Breakfast included. RM200

Sinkeh 105 Lebuh Melayu ☎ 04 261 3966, W sinkeh .com; map pp.138–139. An example of a recent trend for turning old shophouses into boutique hotels with designer mod cons, but run on a shoestring, meaning they won't suit everyone. One point in *Sinkeh*'s favour is that it has its own performance space and staff are drawn from the arts community, so you may be treated to sparky conversation and the occasional show. RM230

EATING

Despite lacking the glitz of KL's eating scene, Penang has been attracting the notice of international food writers and celebrity chefs. They come to relish the authentic **street food**, including specialities such as **asam laksa**, a rendition of *laksa* with the tang of tamarind; and **nasi kandar**, Indian Muslim curries served with rice. The latter is ubiquitous in Malaysia now, of course, but originated, so the story goes, with Penang street vendors who carried their dishes in pots hanging from a shoulder pole (*kandar*). For cheap eats, central Georgetown has several good food courts, although some close once the office workers have gone home. After 5pm, your best bets are the Chinese **hawker stalls** on streets such as Lebuh Chulia and Lebuh Kimberley, or the two food courts (see below).

FOOD COURTS

Kota Selera Padang Kota Lama; map pp.138–139. A range of Malay food, including a novel *mee sotong* (fried or stewed yellow noodles with squid) and unhealthy but deliciously rich coconut shakes. Daily 11am–10pm.

Red Garden Food Paradise 20 Lebuh Leith W redgarden-food.com; map pp.138–139. Touristy and thus regarded as a bit suspect by locals, although it offers an excellent range of hawker dishes, even stretching to Japanese and Filipino cuisine. If you're feeling flush, order some spicy fish, prawn or crab dishes from the East Coast Grill Seafood outlet, which prices by weight. Mon–Fri 5pm–midnight, later at weekends.

RESTAURANTS AND CAFÉS

★ **China House** 153 & 155 Lebuh Pantai, with another entrance at 183b Lebuh Victoria ☎ 04 263 7299, W chinahouse.com.my; map pp.138–139. The hippest place in town, this café-restaurant-gallery led the charge of Western-style venues setting up shop in

Georgetown a few years ago. It's famed for its enormous range of luscious cakes – more than two dozen at any time, including their signature tiramisu – though it also serves great light meals (pies, pasta, etc) and breakfasts. Reckon on RM12 for cake, RM20 for breakfast, RM35 for a main course, not including drinks. Mon–Thurs 9am–midnight, Fri–Sun 9am–1am.

Edelweiss Café 38 Lebuh Armenian ☎ 04 261 8935, W edelweisscafe.com; map pp.138–139. Swiss restaurant inside a quirkily restored shophouse. A B-52 – a large pork sausage, salad and rösti or chips – and fondue are the most traditional dishes; pork ribs are good too. Mains RM30 and up. Tues–Fri noon–3pm & 6.30–10pm, Sat noon–10pm, Sun noon–6pm.

★ **Ee Beng Vegetarian Food** Lebuh Dickens; map pp.138–139. Likeable, often-busy Chinese vegetarian place with the obligatory spread of stir-fry toppings for rice, as well as meatless, fishless renditions of hawker standards such as *nasi lemak*. A good spot for a local breakfast, even if you're a meat eater. It's hard to spend more than RM10. Mon–Sat 7am–8pm.

2

Karaikudi 20 Lebuh Pasar ☎04 263 1345; map pp.138–139. Behind coloured glass doors is this haven in Little India with good-value lunchtime thalis. Their North Indian dishes, including an excellent butter chicken masala and fragrant *nan* bread, stand out, but the South Indian offerings are ordinary. RM20 excluding drinks. Daily 11am–11pm.

Kassim Mustafa 12 Lebuh Chulia (at the corner with Lebuh Penang); map pp.138–139. Filling half a block with green and yellow frontage, *Kassim's* is a pretty standard *mamak* joint, probably the slickest place in town for *nasi kandar*. Daily 24hr.

Line Clear In an alleyway by 177 Jalan Penang; map pp.138–139. The origins of the name are lost, although it may have been a cry related to cleaning drains or settling the bill. What isn't in doubt is the decades-long popularity of the *nasi kandar* in this unprepossessing joint. Daily 24hr.

★**The Mugshot** 302 Lebuh Chulia; map pp.138–139. This little café does excellent sesame bagels, baked in their own wood-fired oven. Choose from fillings such as corned beef and rocket (RM10) or simple cream cheese (RM5), and wash it down with their excellent coffee or freshly squeezed juice. There's also home-made yoghurt in exotic flavours such as jackfruit and *gula melaka* (palm molasses). The artisan bakery next door is run by the same people, offering focaccia, poppy seed bloomers and the like. Daily 8am–midnight.

Perut Rumah 17 Jalan Kelawei ☎04 227 9917; map p.137. There are adequate Nyonya restaurants in the city centre, but it's worth trekking out here to make believe you're in an opulent Peranakan household of the past, kitted out with marble tables and colourful tiled floors. Extended families flock for favourites such as *inche kabin* (seasoned fried chicken, a Penang speciality), duck with pickled vegetables and *pai tee*, pastry cups with a spring-roll-type filling. For an unusual accompaniment, there's tangy nutmeg juice. Around RM40/head. Bus #101 from Pengkalan Weld or #103 from KOMTAR to the second stop after the Gleneagles Hospital (15min). Returning, it's easiest to head to the same stop and catch the #103, which soon doubles back into the centre. Daily 11am–3pm & 6–10pm.

Sarkies E&O Hotel, 10 Lebuh Farquhar ☎04 222 2000; map pp.138–139. Not to be confused with the hotel's *Sarkies Corner* café, *Sarkies* is known for its indulgent buffet meals. Evening menus may be themed – call for the latest details – and are extra expensive at over RM100; most

people come for brunch (RM85) featuring a wide range of local and international treats (including fish-head curry on Sun). Daily 6.30–10.30am, noon–2.30pm & 7–10.30pm.

Sri Ananda Bahwan 53 & 55 Lebuh Penang ☎04 264 4204; map pp.138–139. Popular Indian cheapie with two outlets churning out the usual range of starchy, spicy breakfasts, *thosai* and curries; the one on the corner with Lebuh China serves meat, the other doesn't. Daily 7am–11pm.

★**Tai Tong** 45 Lebuh Cintra ☎04 263 6625; map pp.138–139. An evergreen dim sum restaurant with plastic chairs, wall fans and utilitarian metal trolleys groaning with food. The dim sum – until 11.30am and all evening – is excellent, including standards such as yam puffs, prawn dumplings and custard tarts; at lunchtime and at night the kitchen does à la carte orders, with dishes such as victory chicken (crisply roasted) and veg stir-fries. RM30 without drinks. Daily 7am–2.30pm & 7–10.30pm.

Tek Sen 18 & 20 Lebuh Carnarvon ☎012 981 5117; map pp.138–139. Occupying two blandly refurbished shophouses, *Teksen* thrives on being a jack-of-all-trades rather than specializing in one Chinese cooking style. Trademark dishes including *char siew*, the Cantonese red roast pork, here unusually stir-fried with fiery bird's eye chillies, and trotters in black rice vinegar. RM35 excluding drinks. Mon & Wed–Sun noon–2.30pm & 6–9pm.

Thew Chik 338a/b Lebuh Chulia ☎04 261 8650; map pp.138–139. Rapid-turnover Chinese joint full of lunchtime crowds clamouring for their renowned Hainanese chicken rice. May close early if they sell out. RM5. Daily 11am–5pm.

★**Via Pre** 5 Pengkalan Weld ☎04 262 0560, ⓦviaforever.com; map pp.138–139. This authentically Italian restaurant boasts a vast menu of thin-crust pizzas (from RM25), pasta dishes (including their popular wild boar ragout and mushroom spaghetti; from RM20), and oodles of cured meats and specialist tipples (grappa, limoncello and so forth). Some lunch specials available, and breakfast too. Daily 10am–10pm.

Woodlands 60 Lebuh Penang ☎04 263 9764; map pp.138–139. Run by two brothers, this a/c place is a tad smarter than the other Indian veg places in the area, and the cooking is a cut above, too. Come here for the usual banana-leaf meals, *thosai* and South Indian snacks, plus North Indian dishes like *malai kofta* (cheesy potato dumplings in a creamy sauce). RM15, excluding drinks. Daily 8.30am–10pm.

DRINKING AND NIGHTLIFE

Whereas Georgetown's restaurants punch above their weight, its **bars and clubs** are a little underwhelming, despite a constant trickle of new arrivals. As ever most of the venues are on the fringes of the conservation zone, notably on the pedestrianized eastern end of **Jalan Penang** (sometimes called Upper Penang Rd) and to a lesser extent on Lebuh Chulia, although heritage buildings south of Lebuh Pantai aren't immune from infiltration nowadays. Besides the venues

PENANG'S CULTURAL RESURGENCE

For its size, Penang hosts an impressive number of cultural events, the jewel in the crown being the annual **Georgetown Festival** (June, July or August; ⓦgeorgetownfestival.com). Spread over four weeks, it's packed with local and international art, music, drama, film and dance. KL gets bigger names, but there's nothing as focused as this in the capital. The state has even made a virtue of its lack of purpose-built arts venues: during the festival, many historic sites and businesses are briefly transformed into galleries or concert halls – so expect music in *kopitiams*, films at Khoo Kongsi, pop-up craft stalls on Lebuh Armenian and so on.

Other cultural fixtures, again with international figures in attendance, include the **Penang Island Jazz Festival**, presenting a wide range of jazz styles supported by workshops and exhibitions (Batu Ferringhi; December; ⓦpenangjazz.com) and the **Georgetown Literary Festival** (late November or early December; ⓦgtlfestival.com). Also look out for events on the **last Sunday** of the month in Georgetown: free Chinese opera or dance performances at Khoo Kongsi, music at the Botanic Gardens and so on.

2

mentioned here, for **live music** it's also worth heading to *China House* (see p.149), which hosts jazz/acoustic acts at the Lebuh Victoria end of the building (Fri–Sun from 9.30pm).

BARS

B@92 92 Lebuh Gereja ⓣ04 263 7144; map pp.138–139. Small bar in a former shophouse with original tiled floor and shutters, long mirrors and dark wooden furniture. Bit of a barfly hangout and best for beer and conversation, plus pub staples – sandwiches and pasta – at around RM15. Daily noon–midnight.

Hong Kong Bar 371 Lebuh Chulia ⓣ04 261 9796; map pp.138–139. You can't miss this Chinese-run dive, adorned with military insignia – a haven for the over-40s compared with other venues on Chulia. Daily 2pm–midnight.

Reggae Club 361 Lebuh Chulia; map pp.138–139. The archetypal backpacker ghetto, with cheap beer, vintage reggae sounds and occasional covers bands. Daily 6pm–3am.

Seventy7 34 Jalan Nagor, off Jalan Burma; map p.137. A 10min walk from KOMTAR, Penang's main gay venue is a friendly affair in a chic refurbished shophouse, drawing a crowd of 20- and 30-somethings. Mon–Thurs & Sun 6.30pm–1am, Fri & Sat 6.30pm–3am.

Soho Free House 50a Jalan Penang ⓣ04 263 3331; map pp.138–139. Pub-style place with a lurid purple exterior, sports on a big-screen TV upstairs, a pool table and a menu including the likes of shepherd's pie. Daily noon–late.

Three Sixty Degree Sky Bar Bayview Hotel, 25a Lebuh Farquhar ⓣ04 261 3540; map pp.138–139. Rooftop bars often work brilliantly in KL and Singapore, far less well amid Georgetown's modest cityscape. Still, this open space around the *Bayview* revolving restaurant is a good spot for cocktails, Nyonya snacks and a bird's-eye view of the *E&O Hotel*, St George's Church and the dimly lit expanses of shophouses, dwarfed by the cylindrical KOMTAR building and more modest towers beyond the conservation zone. Daily 4pm–1am.

CLUBS

Slippery Señoritas 2 Jalan Penang ⓣ04 263 6868; map pp.138–139. Georgetown's liveliest disco is a vaguely latin-themed joint with different sounds on different nights and live music from 9.30pm. Cover charge of around RM30 Wed, Fri & Sat includes first drink; happy hour Mon–Fri until 9pm. Daily 5pm–3am.

Soundmaker Second floor, 62 Pengkalan Weld; map pp.138–139. One of a rare breed in Malaysia, *Soundmaker* is a countercultural rock venue specializing in indie, punk, metal and so forth, with the occasional shot of hip-hop for good measure. Live bands Fri 10pm–midnight and sporadically on other nights, when admission is charged. Thurs–Sun 5pm–1am.

SHOPPING

Out-of-town **malls** rule the retail roost in Penang. Georgetown has a mixture of old shops selling traditional goods, cheap-and-cheerful touristy outlets, and several pricier galleries and souvenir shops, generally rather chichi.

MARKETS

Chowrasta Market Jalan Chowrasta; map pp.138–139. One of the city's oldest markets, Chowrasta mainly sells produce although there are some secondhand book stalls upstairs. Proceedings spill over colourfully into Jalan Kuala Kangsar behind (note too the traditional spring-roll-wrap maker on Jalan Chowrasta). Daily 7.30am–noon.

2

Little Penang Street Market Pedestrianized section of Jalan Penang ⓦ littlepenang.com.my; map pp.138–139. This community-run affair is a great place to pick up knick-knacks and accessories as well as take in street art events. Last Sun of the month 10am–5pm.

Occupy Beach Street Lebuh Pantai; map pp.138–139. Not a market as such, but there are craft and other stalls amid the general weekly merrymaking when the street becomes pedestrianized for buskers, dancers and other groups. Sun 7am–1pm.

MALLS

Prangin Mall Jalan Dr Lim Chwee Leong ⓦ prangin-mall.com; map pp.138–139. The most popular of the malls around KOMTAR, Prangin proves yet again that in Malaysia upmarket isn't usually best. There's something for everyone – a Parkson department store, a supermarket, bargain clothes shops, electronics and phone shops (fourth floor) and a food court (fifth floor). Daily 10am–10pm.

BOOKSHOPS

Gerak Budaya 78 Jalan Masjid Kapitan Kling ☎ 04 261 0282; map pp.138–139. The best bookshop in town is a radical upstart with hard-to-find titles on Malaysian society and politics, as well as more general locally published titles. Daily 11am–8pm.

H.S. Sam Bookstore 473 Lebuh Chulia ☎ 04 262 2705; map pp.138–139. The "most organized used bookshop in town" is a small-time affair with some new maps and books, although it survives partly by diversifying into bike rental and backpacker travel services. Daily 9.30am–9.30pm.

CLOTHES, TEXTILES AND SHOES

Dawood Textiles 50 Lebuh Queen ☎ 04 262 5263; map pp.138–139. Traditional sarong seller offering muted checked fabrics of the kind popular with older Malay men. Mon–Sat 9am–8.30pm, Sun 9am–1pm.

Nyonya Beaded Shoes 4 Lebuh Armenian ☎ 016 454 3075; map pp.138–139. The name says it all. Peranakan beadwork embroidery is a vanishing, painstaking art, so don't be surprised that the results don't come cheap: slippers/clogs with just the straps beaded cost around RM250, fully beaded shoes RM900. Mon–Sat 9.30am–6pm.

Rozana's Batik 81b & c Lebuh Aceh ☎ 014 247 5347; map pp.138–139. Small, family-run store specializing in hand-painted textiles on cotton or silk, with some clothing available to buy and walk-in batik classes (2hr; RM50). Daily 11.30am–6pm

Sam's Batik House 183 & 185 Jalan Penang ⓦ samsbatikhouse.com; map pp.138–139. Mounds of slightly garish batik and silk, including tops and dresses galore; there's more of this a few doors south at the Penang Bazaar. Daily 10am–6pm.

SOUVENIRS, CURIOS AND GIFTS

Bon Ton/China Joe's 86 Lebuh Armenian ☎ 04 262 7299; map pp.138–139. Asian-inspired knick-knacks and decorative items for the home, along with batiks, porcelain and art books. Daily 10am–7pm.

Lean Giap 443 & 449 Lebuh Chulia ☎ 04 262 0520; map pp.138–139. Old-style crockery, old fob watches, tobacco tins, amulets and so forth. Mon–Sat 10.30am–6pm.

Peranakan Mansion 29 Lebuh Gereja; map pp.138–139. Besides trinkets and Nyonya *kebaya* clothing, the small gift shop here stocks some antique porcelain. Daily 9.30am–5pm.

Syarikat Peking 230 Jalan Penang ☎ 04 263 4334; map pp.138–139. A hotchpotch of Chinese and Southeast Asian gear, including porcelain and shadow puppets, though there's not a lot that's Malaysian. Mon–Sat 10.30am–6pm.

DIRECTORY

Banks and exchange The major banks are on Lebuh Pantai, with ATMs also located on Jalan Penang and at the KOMTAR development; moneychangers are easily found on Jalan Masjid Kapitan Kling and elsewhere.

Consulates Australia, YMCA, 211 Jalan Macalister (☎ 04 226 7285); Indonesia, 467 Jalan Burma (☎ 04 227 4686); Thailand, 1 Jalan Tuanku Abdul Rahman (☎ 04 226 8029); UK, Suite 9-04, Menara Zurich, 170 Jalan Argyll (☎ 04 227 5336).

Hospitals General Hospital, Jalan Residensi (☎ 04 222 5333); Gleneagles, 1 Jalan Pangkor (☎ 04 222 9111).

Internet access The island's Wireless@Penang service offers free wi-fi at malls, the KOMTAR building, the ferry terminal and even a few sights, including the top of Penang Hill. When connecting for the first time, you'll need to register: just type in an arbitrary twelve-digit number in response to the question about your ID card/MyKad – you won't need it again.

Left luggage MPPP Building, Lebuh Pantai (daily 9am–6pm; ⓦ storeyourluggage.com).

Pharmacies Guardian and Watsons both have branches at KOMTAR and the Prangin Mall (both daily 10am–10pm).

Police The police headquarters is on Jalan Penang; emergencies ☎ 999.

Post office The General Post Office is on Lebuh Downing, with a branch at KOMTAR (both Mon–Fri 8.30am–5pm, Sat 8.30am–1pm).

Visa extensions Pejabat Imigresen, corner Lebuh Pantai and Lebuh Light (Mon–Thurs 7.30am–1pm & 2–5.30pm, Fri 7.30am–12.15am & 2.45–5.30pm; ☎ 04 250 3410).

OPPOSITE FUNICULAR RAILWAY, PENANG HILL (P.154) >

Ayer Itam (Air Hitam)

6km west of Georgetown • Bus #201, 203, 204 or #502 (45min)

The town of **AYER ITAM** amounts to little more than a 100m-long bottleneck, with the traffic squeezed between shops and the canvas awnings of a busy wet market. There are three reasons to visit: **Kek Lok Si**, a ludicrously overbuilt hilltop Buddhist complex; the colonial-era retreat of **Penang Hill** to the north; and the best-known *laksa* stall on the island. You could easily do all three, arriving at lunchtime for *laksa*, then spending a couple of hours at Kek Lok Si before heading up Penang Hill for views of the island lighting up at dusk.

Kek Lok Si

A 5min walk west from Jalan Pasar • Daily roughly 8.30am–6pm • Free; climbing the steps to the top or use of the Sky Lift (shuts at 5.30pm) costs RM2 • ☏ 04 828 3317

Supposedly the largest Buddhist temple in Malaysia, **Kek Lok Si** was founded by the abbot of Georgetown's Kuan Yin Teng in the 1890s, when the initial bout of construction was bankrolled by Cheong Fatt Tze and other local tycoons. Today the hill sprouts all sorts of fantastic shrines and pagodas, linked by multiple flights of steps, and bedecked with flags, lanterns and statues. To reach the complex from the market bus stop on Jalan Pasar, follow the road towards the temple and look out for a passageway on the left lined with trinket stalls. From here steps ascend to the temple forecourt past a pond full of terrapins, which represent eternity.

The two most prominent features are the white, seven-tier wedding-cake assemblage that is the **Ten Thousand Buddhas Pagoda**, capped by a golden Burmese stupa; and a 30m-high bronze statue of the goddess of mercy, **Kuan Yin**, sheltered from the elements by an open-sided pavilion, its pillars wreathed in carved dragons. Both can be reached either on foot (193 steps) or using the **Sky Lift**, a sort of glass-sided funicular compartment that glides up and down the 45-degree slope.

Penang Hill (Bukit Bendera)

Jalan Stesen Bukit Bendera, a 20min walk from Air Hitam, 25min from Kek Lok Si; turn left at the roundabout signed "Bukit Bendera" • **Funicular** 2 hourly from 6.30am: Mon–Fri last service down at 10pm, Sat & Sun at 11pm • RM17 one way, RM30 return • ☏ 04 828 8880, ⓦ penanghill.gov.my • Bus #204 (last bus back to Georgetown at around 10.40pm)

Once called Flagstaff Hill, when it was a retreat for British administrators, **Penang Hill** is now a mixed bag of gardens, woodland, shrines and colonial houses in various states of repair. Most visitors literally chill out at the summit, over 700m above sea level, although there are also hiking trails to explore.

The bus drops you at the foot of the hill close to the lower funicular station, where signs point the way to the **Bats Cave Temple**, worth a quick look for its colony of bats in a cave shrine at the back; they're regarded as auspicious because part of the Chinese term for "bat" sounds like the word for "luck". The **funicular** itself, a modern version of the original, built in 1923, can whisk you to the summit in just over five minutes. From here there's a great vista of the cape of Georgetown and across the straits to Butterworth. Both Penang bridges are also on view, although the second, much longer bridge can be hard to make out as it's far away to the south.

Scattered around the hilltop park are a multicoloured Hindu temple, a mosque, an utterly pointless museum of owl figurines and artwork, some places to eat and a forgettable hotel. For a decent couple of hours' **walk**, follow the main summit road round counterclockwise, heading towards the start of the path to Tiger Hill, then veer left on to Moniot Road. From here you can eventually join Viaduct Road, from where there are various routes back up to the summit. The sketch map on the leaflet given out with funicular tickets shows the options.

Bellevue Hotel Summit of Penang Hill ☎ 04 227 4006 or ☎ 04 829 9500. Despite its name, the *Bellevue* is no colonial haven but in fact a dreary 1960s building. Its saving grace is the terrace restaurant, which has good views, cream teas and highly regarded – though undeniably pricey – steamboat (RM66 for two people). Daily 7am–9pm.

David Brown's Restaurant and Tea Terraces On its own mound 100m from the upper funicular station, Penang Hill ☎ 04 828 8337, ⊕ penanghillco.com.my. A very English menu of cream teas, pies and steaks, plus a roast of the day and an excellent wine list, all in a smart country-pub-like setting – or as close to it as a house perched on a tropical hilltop can get. A few tables are set out on the immaculate lawn, and there's a separate *Sky Terrace* section for drinks and snacks. Tea and scones costs RM28, and beef wellington will set you back RM90 – when it's available. Daily: restaurant 11am–9pm; Sky Terrace 9am–9pm.

★**Pasar Air Itam Laksa** Jalan Pasar, Ayer Itam, where the bus sets down. Look for a small stall with a big red sign behind, with the name written in Malay and Chinese characters, and you'll find what many rate as the best *asam laksa* in Penang, costing just RM3. The sauce is salty, sour and thick with *heh koh* prawn paste, all topped off with rice noodles, shredded vegetables, pounded fish and a handful of fresh herbs. Daily morning until mid-afternoon.

Northwest Penang

An 18km-long road runs along Penang's northern coast, squeezed for much of the way between the sea and forests inland. The main settlement here, the dull beach resort of **Batu Ferringhi**, remains moderately popular as an alternative base to Georgetown and has a frequent bus service to the city, but frankly you're not missing much if you simply shoot through to the **Tropical Spice Garden** or the coastal jungle of **Penang National Park** at **Teluk Bahang**, in the island's northwest corner. There is also a small clutch of minor sights along the road south of Teluk Bahang, en route to Balik Pulau.

Batu Ferringhi

Bus #101 from Pengkalan Weld/KOMTAR (every 20–30min) or #102 from the airport/KOMTAR (hourly)

To look at it now, you wouldn't think that **BATU FERRINGHI** was the standard-bearer for Penang tourism during the long years when Georgetown was in the doldrums. These days it distinctly plays second fiddle, thanks as much to ugly overdevelopment as Georgetown's successes.

Its centrepiece is some 2km of **beach**, not too narrow but with sand that, disappointingly, is the colour of milky tea. The whole beach is publicly accessible: either stride through the hotel compounds to reach it or, in the unlikely event staff are obstructive, use the path lined by beach-gear stalls that begins roughly opposite the McDonald's at the start of the strip. All that said, the beach still makes for a nice contrast with Georgetown and is decent enough for **water sports**, with multiple firms competing for custom. For a general look, turn up in the late afternoon when the beach starts to get busy, and perhaps linger for an evening meal when the road comes alive with stalls selling batik, T-shirts and fake designer watches.

BATU FERRINGHI

0 ___ 250
metres

● EATING AND DRINKING		■ ACCOMMODATION	
Bora Bora By Sunset	5	Ali's	2
Ferringhi Garden	2	Bayview Beach Resort	1
Happy Garden	1	Lazyboys Travelodge	4
Khaleel Nasi Kandar	6	Lone Pine	5
Lebanon	4	Rasa Sayang	6
Living Room Café	3	Roomies	3

JALAN BATU FERRINGHI

JALAN SUNGAI

JALAN BATU FERRINGHI
Ferringhi Plaza

Eden Parade
Shopping Mall

2

Tropical Spice Garden

Lone Crag Villa, Jalan Teluk Bahang • Daily 9am–6pm • RM26 with audioguide, RM35 on guided tour (4 daily) • ☎ 04 881 1210,
Ⓦ tropicalspicegarden.com • Bus #101 or #102

Between Batu Ferringhi and Teluk Bahang, the delightful **Tropical Spice Garden** has
turned an abandoned rubber plantation into a cornucopia of herbs, spices and
decorative flora, all set in a stylishly landscaped gully and shaded by former plantation
trees. Three easy circuit trails loop between waterfalls and streams and introduce you to
the plants and their commercial, culinary and traditional uses. There are **cookery
classes** too, daily except Monday.

Balik Pulau Road

Bus #101 or #102 both make a short detour here

Once the coast road reaches the small town of **Teluk Bahang**, it veers south and inland,
passing two minor sights within the first kilometre before continuing to Balik Pulau.
The first is the overpriced **Escape** theme park, a series of obstacle-course-type challenges
including zip lines and climbing ropes (Tues–Sun 9am–6pm; RM60; ☎ 04 881 1106,
Ⓦ escape.my). A few hundred metres on is the **Butterfly Farm** (daily 9am–6pm; RM27;
☎ 04 885 1253, Ⓦ butterfly-insect.com), also home to all manner of frogs, snakes, stick
insects and scorpions.

Penang National Park (Taman Negara Pulau Pinang)

At the end of a small coastal road 1.5km beyond the centre of Teluk Bahang • **Park office** Mon–Fri 8am–5pm, Sat & Sun 8am–6pm
Canopy walkway Sat–Wed 10am–4pm • Free • ☎ 04 881 3530, Ⓦ wildlife.gov.my • Bus #101 calls at the park (1hr from Georgetown)
before doubling back to terminate at Teluk Bahang; bus #102 terminates at Teluk Bahang

PENANG NATIONAL PARK tends to fly under visitors' radar, but it's likeable all the same,
a hilly chunk of old-growth forest, pandanus and mangroves. The trails lead to a
handful of secluded, undeveloped **beaches**, where marine **turtles** nest throughout the
year; the park also has some resident dusty-leaf monkeys in addition to the predictable
long-tailed macaques.

Besides the obligatory **canopy walkway**, there are two main trails, generally easy to
follow though steep and eroded in places. At the end of the initial 500m boardwalk,
turn right for the 4.7km route to the **Muka Head Lighthouse**, where you might see sea
eagles, passing **Monkey Beach** (3.4km), a good spot for a swim. Turn left for **Kerachut
Beach** (3.4km), a cove with a turtle hatchery at the far end, and **Teluk Kampi** (4.9km),
yet another secluded beach.

If you're short on time, talk to the various boat operators opposite the park entrance;
they offer surprisingly cheap rides to the beaches (RM40–50 per boat one way to
Monkey Beach, RM80 to Kerachut). Another booth here is staffed by **nature guides**
(☎ 04 881 4788; RM250 for a half-day guided trek for up to five people) and sells
useful gear, such as waterproof ponchos.

ACCOMMODATION   **NORTHWEST PENANG**

BATU FERRINGHI

Ali's 53 & 54b Jalan Batu Ferringhi ☎ 04 881 1316.
Friendly Malay-run beachfront guesthouse with bland,
old-fashioned a/c rooms, some en suite, in a two-storey
brick building surrounding a courtyard packed with pot
plants. RM100

Bayview Beach Resort Western end of Batu Ferringhi
☎ 04 881 2123, Ⓦ bayviewhotels.com/beach. Rooms
are arrayed around the impressive pyramid atrium at this
reasonably priced hotel, with tennis courts and two
swimming pools. Booking weeks in advance might bring
discounts. RM330

Lazyboys Travelodge 392 Jalan Batu Ferringhi,
behind Happy Mart and diagonally across
from the Ship restaurant ☎ 04 881 1252, Ⓔ lazyboys
travelodge@gmail.com. The one guesthouse that isn't by
the beach compensates by being the most hospitable –
you can believe you're in a Malay home here. There's a huge
choice of rooms: fan singles, doubles with or without a/c
and bathroom, a six-bed a/c dorm and a family room
sleeping four. Dorms RM25, doubles RM50

Lone Pine 97 Jalan Batu Ferringhi ☎ 04 886 8686,
Ⓦ lonepinehotel.com. Now run by Georgetown's
Eastern & Oriental, this boutique hotel was founded as a

humble lodge in 1948. Completely renovated and extended since, it now comprises what might as well be a swanky apartment building behind the original, low-rise block with shuttered windows next to a well-tended sea-facing garden. The rooms are bright and contemporary, complemented by a spa, pool and several restaurants. RM600

★**Rasa Sayang** Batu Ferringhi ☎04 888 8888, ⓦshangri-la.com. One of the very first resorts at Batu Ferringhi is still recommendable today, a lush, sprawling complex topped by Malay-style roofs and with an excellent freeform pool. There's a garden wing for the hoi polloi and, for a premium of at least twenty percent, a boutique "Rasa" wing with its own pool plus free cocktails and afternoon tea. RM820

Roomies Fourth floor of the block opposite the Parkroyal Hotel, Jalan Batu Ferringhi ☎04 881 1344, ⓦroomiespenang.com. The slickest guesthouse on the strip, with flashpacker capsule-style bunk beds plus two overpriced rooms, one sleeping three, the other a double with its own bathroom. Dorms RM40, three-bed room RM150, en-suite double RM180

PENANG NATIONAL PARK
Campsites Penang National Park ☎04 881 3530, ⓦwildlife.gov.my. There are campsites at Monkey and Kerachut beaches, though bear in mind that either is a 75min trek from the entrance. Kerachut has bathrooms and a kitchen, but wherever you stay, bring your own tent and kitchenware. Free.

EATING AND DRINKING

BATU FERRINGHI
Eating in Batu Ferringhi is dominated by slightly overpriced restaurants, including an assortment of Middle Eastern places catering to the steady stream of Saudi and Gulf tourists.

Bora Bora By Sunset 415 Jalan Batu Ferringhi ☎04 885 1313. Fairly standard beach bar and restaurant with tables out on the sand and within the bar area under an *atap* roof. Food ranges from pizza through to Malaysian staples, typically costing RM10–15; it's not haute cuisine but the sunset compensates. Sun–Thurs noon–1am, Fri & Sat noon–3am.

Ferringhi Garden 34A, b & c & 43d Jalan Batu Ferringhi ☎04 881 1193. The most elegant of the strip's restaurants, the outdoor tables drowning in potted orchids, ferns and pitcher plants, with plenty of stylish wood panelling and screens inside. There are two parts to the place: the *Coffee Garden*, serving light meals and snacks by day, and the main restaurant, with a more ambitious menu of Western/fusion dishes. Mains from RM30. Daily: Coffee Garden 8am–6pm; restaurant 4pm–midnight.

Happy Garden Western end of Batu Ferringhi ☎016 490 3543. This looks more like a residential bungalow, in a lovely garden planted with bougainvillea, than a Hainanese restaurant. There's plenty of seafood on the menu, plus predictable Western-inspired dishes like chicken chop. Breakfasts include oats, pancakes or sausage and egg. Daily 9am–2.30pm & 6–10.30pm.

Khaleel Nasi Kandar Ground floor, towards the rear of the Eden Parade Shopping Centre. A fine place to escape inflated prices and get your daily curry, *roti* and *teh tarik* fix – the food is genuinely above par, too. Daily 24hr.

Lebanon 190a Jalan Batu Ferringhi ☎04 881 3228. Middling among the Arabic restaurants in terms of price and quality. The mainstays are, unsurprisingly, kebabs (RM30) and meze (RM10), with curries and pizza for conservative local palates. Daily 7am–11pm.

Living Room Café 43c Batu Ferringhi ☎017 477 2148. This informal place majors on Nyonya and other local cuisines, offering a limited number of dishes and doing them right. Locals go for the beef *rendang*, although you can also take your pick from Western mains such as burgers and barbecued ribs. Around RM45, excluding drinks. Thurs–Tues 10am–3pm & 6–10pm.

Snake Temple

Jalan Sultan Azlan Shah, close to the airport • Daily 6am–7pm • Free • ☎04 643 7273 • Bus #102 from KOMTAR or #401 or #401E from Georgetown's Pengkalan Weld

Visible from the airport road, Penang's **Snake Temple** is a bright Buddhist affair, its forecourt guarded by two stone lions. Inside, the front altar – along with strategically placed shrubs in other halls – is draped in poisonous **green pit vipers** which, legend has it, mysteriously appeared upon completion of the temple in 1850. Pit vipers are naturally lethargic, but even so it's hard to account for quite how dozy the temple's specimens are – though you'd best not poke them to see if they're real.

Penang War Museum

Batu Maung • Daily 9am–6pm • RM35 • ☎ 04 626 5142 • Bus #302

The **Penang War Museum** stands on the site of a 1930s British military fortress. You climb the hill to an area of bunkers, forts, underground tunnels and an observation tower, all sensibly designed to defend the position from a naval attack; unfortunately for the British, the Japanese stormed it from inland. The fort became a prison, abandoned after the war partly because it was believed to be haunted by those tortured to death here. It was recovered from the undergrowth and opened as a private museum during the 1980s.

2

Balik Pulau

BALIK PULAU (literally "back of the island") is set on a plain between Penang's west coast and the steep hills of the centre. The 250m-long main street is lined in old buildings, though only **Fong Silversmith**, on the corner near the roundabout, is especially compelling; its charming owner has been turning out simple, attractive jewellery for decades. At the other end of town there's a nineteenth-century convent and the **Sacred Heart Church**, a pale grey and cream tin-sided structure dating to 1854.

ARRIVAL AND DEPARTURE   BALIK PULAU

By bus Bus #401, #401E or #502 runs to Balik Pulau from Georgetown (#502 via Ayer Itam is the most direct service).

It's also possible to catch the #501 from Teluk Bahang.

EATING

Nan Guang 67 Jalan Balik Pulau. The pineapple-tinged *asam laksa* and Thai curried *laksa* (RM3) at this down-at-heel, main-street *kopitiam* have people lining up some

time before they start serving to make sure they get a bowl. Thurs–Tues 11am–late afternoon.

Kedah and Perlis

The far northwest of Peninsular Malaysia is taken up by the states of Kedah and Perlis, which, in common with the northeast, were historically part of the Siamese sphere of influence. British rule this far north, in marked contrast to Penang and Perak, was relatively brief, kicking off in 1909 when the region was ceded to them by the Thais, who briefly reclaimed it during World War II courtesy of another treaty, this time with the invading Japanese.

Kedah has long been billed as the Peninsula's *jelapang padi*, or rice bowl, and its landscape remains largely a mosaic of lustrous paddy fields. By far the best-known part of the state is the popular resort island of **Langkawi**, with good air links as well as ferry connections with Penang and southern Thailand. The mainland is easily bypassed, then, and the rewards for passing through are low-key, chiefly the **Ulu Muda Eco Reserve** and the odd **archeological remains** near the town of **Sungai Petani**, which is busier and more likeable than the capital, **Alor Setar**. **Perlis**, Malaysia's smallest state (at just 800 square km, it's just ten percent larger than Singapore), holds practically nothing of interest.

Sungai Petani and around

On the north bank of the Petani River, **SUNGAI PETANI** is the most populous town in Kedah, with bustling suburbs and industrial areas that thrive on its location in Penang's hinterland (Butterworth is just 35km away). There's nothing to see in the old town centre other than the Art Deco King George V **clock tower** on the main street, but the town is the jumping-off point for anyone travelling to the **Bujang Valley** archeological site by public transport.

Bujang Valley (Merbok Museum/Lembah Bujang)

2km from Merbok's main street along a signed lane • Daily 9am–5pm • Free • ☎ 04 457 2005 • Merbok bus from Sungai Petani's local bus station (hourly; 45min), or charter a taxi (around RM50 return, with a 1hr wait)

A 15km drive northwest of Sungai Petani, outside the town of **Merbok**, the **Bujang Valley** site commemorates a significant Hindu-Buddhist kingdom that flourished here for hundreds of years, possibly from as early as the second century. That said, there's not that much to see; a 90min stay would be ample. First impressions are that you've arrived at the most surreal attraction in Malaysia, where a team of bricklayers has run riot on a landscaped hillside. What you see are actually the low, stepped remains of *candi* (temples) from various locations nearby, reassembled here in an unnaturally tight cluster.

The centrepiece **Candi Bukit Batu Pahat** is a 27m-long granite structure that was not moved but restored *in situ*; the other *candi* are much smaller, some made of what look like worn, crimson-tinged brick, others suspiciously pristine. The on-site **museum** explains, somewhat incoherently, what little is known about the Bujang Valley kingdom, and how prewar excavations brought its existence back to light. There are also some interesting finds from the various *candi*, including pots, gems and stone carvings of deities.

2

ARRIVAL AND INFORMATION

SUNGAI PETANI

By bus and train Sungai Petani lies on Route 1, which doubles up as the main street. A couple of blocks south of the clock tower, a bridge up and over the railway line leads east to the train station (☎ 04 421 2604) and, opposite it, the long-distance bus station. A further block south of the clock tower is Jalan Petri, which runs west past the local bus station, taxi stand and some budget hotels.

Destinations by bus Alor Star (local bus #2; every 45min–1hr; 1hr 30min); Butterworth (several local buses daily; 45min); Ipoh (7 daily; 3hr); Kota Bharu (2 daily; 6hr); Kuala Lumpur (hourly; 5hr); Kuala Terengganu (1 daily; 5hr 30min); and Sik (en route to Ulu Muda; 2hr); Lumut (for

Pangkor; 3 daily; 4hr 30min); Melaka (4 daily; 6hr 30min); Seremban (3 daily; 5hr 30min).

Destinations by train Alor Star (2 daily; 1hr 10min); Bangkok (Thailand; 1 daily; 21hr); Butterworth (2 daily; 1hr–1hr 30min); Hat Yai (Thailand; 2 daily; 4–5hr); Ipoh (1 daily; 5hr 30min); Kuala Kangsar (1 daily; 4hr 30min); Kuala Lumpur (1 daily; 9hr 15min); Taiping (1 daily; 4hr).

Accommodation and eating There's no reason to stay in Sungai Petani, but the old town centre has a few inexpensive hotels as well as Malay and Chinese stalls in food courts just north of Jalan Petri.

Alor Star (Alor Setar)

A largely Malay town, conservative in feel, **ALOR STAR**, Kedah's transport hub, is remarkably somnolent for a state capital, especially at night. Clustered around the padang are several historic buildings, including a prominent mosque and former **sultan's palace**, providing enough architectural and cultural interest that you might want to pause here for half a day en route to or from Langkawi, the Thai border or Ulu Muda Eco Park. **Orientation** is simple: the padang forms the heart of town, with the commercial centre to the east and what passes for Chinatown to the west across Route 1.

Padang

Alor Star's **padang** and the open space on its north side are dotted with a mishmash of buildings, some associated with Kedah's ruling house. Within the padang itself, the long white-stucco **Balai Seni Negeri** is a courthouse-turned-gallery showcasing local artists (daily 9am–5pm; free). The curious octagonal tower topped by a yellow onion dome, on the western side of the open space, is the **Balai Nobat**, housing sacred instruments played only during royal ceremonies. At the north end is the low, Neoclassical facade of the former **High Court**, now the **Galeri Sultan Abdul Halim**, showcasing assorted royal regalia (Sun–Thurs 10am–5pm; RM2). The most refined building here, though, is the **Masjid Zahir** just across Jalan Pekan Melayu, which succeeds admirably despite being a mishmash of Moorish arches, a Turkish pencil minaret and weighty black bulbous domes.

2

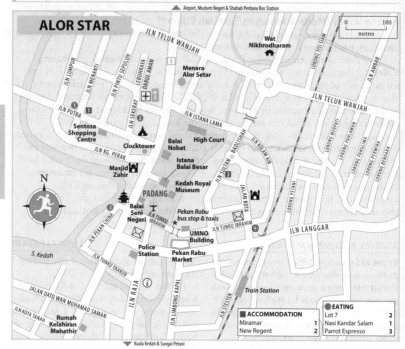

Istana Balai Besar

The history of the padang's most important building, the elegant **Istana Balai Besar** (Royal Audience Hall), mirrors that of the town. Founded in 1735, it was badly damaged in 1770 by the Bugis (seafaring raiders from Sulawesi in Indonesia), and later by Thai armies in 1821. The present, late nineteenth-century version has a Malay multilayered shingle roof, supported by colonial-style iron columns and eave decorations, alongside a very European-influenced flowing staircase. One of its first functions was to host the **marriages** of Sultan Abdul Hamid's five eldest children in 1904: the celebrations lasted three months, and the cost bankrupted Kedah – forty buffaloes had to be slaughtered to feed the crowds each day.

Kedah Royal Museum (Muzium Diraja)

Behind the Balai Besar, northeast of the padang • Sat–Mon 9am–5pm, Fri 9am–12.30pm & 2.30–5pm • Free

Guarded by a motley collection of bronze cannon (some stamped with the "VOC" of the Dutch East India Company), the **Kedah Royal Museum** was once the royal palace. Squat and compact, dating to 1930, it must have made a fairly modest palace, and though the cases of ceremonial *keris* daggers, silver dinner services, gold anklets and brass betel sets hint at wealth, there's no feeling of splendid indulgence – indeed, many exhibits (including a pair of binoculars used by one sultan on safari in Africa) are decidedly mundane.

Menara Alor Setar

Route 1 north of the padang • Daily 10am–10pm • RM12

A mini-version of KL's similar Menara Tower, **Menara Alor Setar** is a 165m-tall communications tower with an observation platform halfway up. Come here for views of pancake-flat paddy fields pierced by distant limestone outcrops, and the mostly low-rise, unprepossessing town below.

Muzium Negeri

Jalan Lebuhraya Darulaman (Route 1), 2km north of the centre • Sat–Thurs 9am–5pm, Fri 9am–12.30pm & 2.30–5pm • Free • Any bus from Pekan Rabu bound for Shahab Perdana

The **Muzium Negeri** (State Museum) fills you in on Kedah's traditions and history, including background to the archeological finds at the Bujang Valley (see p.159). One noteworthy exhibit is the *bunga mas dan perak* ("the gold and silver flowers"), a pair of 1m-tall "trees", one in gold, one in silver – in the past, the Malay rulers would have despatched such items in tribute to their Thai overlords.

Pekan Rabu

Jalan Tunku Ibrahim

Pekan Rabu is the town's main market, three concrete floors of preserved, fresh and cooked food, clothes, handicrafts and household necessities, plus local farm produce. Look for stalls selling **dodol durian** (a sort of black, gooey jam made from the fruit) and "durian cake" a plain mix of pulp and palm sugar.

Rumah Kelahiran Mahathir

18 Lorong Kilang Ais, southwest of the padang • Tues–Thurs 10am–5.30pm, Fri 10am–noon & 3–5.30pm • Free

The life of the local doctor who became the most powerful Malaysian prime minister of modern times, Mahathir Mohamad, is documented at his birthplace and family home, **Rumah Kelahiran Mahathir**, now a museum. Even if you're not interested in the brash former premier, it's worth dropping by to get an idea of what a traditional middle-class Malay home looked like in the middle of the last century.

ARRIVAL AND DEPARTURE

ALOR STAR

By plane The Sultan Abdul Halim Airport is 11km north of town, accessible by the hourly Kepala Batas bus from the express bus station, or by taxi (around RM25).

Destinations Kuala Lumpur (KLIA; 4–5 daily; 1hr); Kuala Lumpur (Subang; 8 daily; 1hr).

By train The station is centrally located, just southeast of the centre on Jalan Stesyen (☎04 731 4045).

Destinations Arau (2 daily; 40min); Bangkok (Thailand; 1 daily; 20hr); Butterworth (2 daily; 2hr–2 30min); Hat Yai (Thailand; 2 daily; 3–4hr); Ipoh (1 daily; 6hr); Kuala Kangsar (1 daily; 5hr); Kuala Lumpur (1 daily; 9hr 30min); Sungai Petani (2 daily; 1hr 10min); Taiping (1 daily; 4hr 15min).

By local bus A small number of firms, including HBR, MARA and Cityliner, run local buses to most parts of the state (daily 6am–8pm). They all use a central bus stop – with no ticket office or timetables – on the north side of Jalan Tunku Ibrahim, opposite the Pekan Rabu market. Some long-distance buses also call here en route to/from Shahab Perdana.

Destinations Kangar (hourly; 1hr 15min); Kuala Kedah (1–2 hourly; 20min); Naka (for the Ulu Muda Eco Park; hourly; 2hr); Sungai Petani (#2; every 45min–1hr; 1hr 30min).

By long-distance bus Long-distance buses use the Shahab Perdana station, annoyingly far away at 5km northwest of the centre, connected to town by local buses and taxis (RM10). Some express buses pass through town first, setting passengers down at Pekan Rabu; some northbound local buses pass through Shahab Perdana en route to their destination.

Destinations Butterworth (8 daily; 2hr); Ipoh (10 daily; 4hr); Johor Bahru (4 daily; 12hr); Kota Bharu (2 daily; 5hr); Kuala Kedah (15min); Kuala Lumpur (6hr); Kuala Terengganu (2 daily; 8hr 30min); Kuantan (2 daily; 9hr); Melaka (3 daily; 7hr); Seremban (at least 2 daily; 6hr); Singapore (3 daily; 13hr).

By ferry Langkawi ferries (🌐 langkawi-ferry.com) dock at Kuala Kedah, 12km west of town. Local buses drop off and pick up on the main road outside the ferry terminal; a taxi costs around RM20.

Destinations Langkawi (Kuah; 11 daily, 7am–7pm; 1hr 45min; RM23).

By taxi Taxis can be found around Pekan Rabu. A ride to the main Thai border crossing at Bukit Kayu Hitam costs RM55 (45min).

INFORMATION

Tourist office Tourism Malaysia occupies a yellow building behind the 1930s former courthouse on Jalan Raja

(Sat–Wed 8am–5pm, Thurs 8am–3.30pm; ☎04 730 1322).

2

ACCOMMODATION

With mainland Kedah seeing few visitors, Alor Setar's selection of hotels is as dreary as much of the town itself.

Miramar 46 Jalan Putra ☎04 733 8144. One of the better cheapies, the *Miramar* is a low-rise concrete block with dull but more than adequate a/c en-suite rooms, nicely located for the eating places elsewhere on the street. RM65

★**New Regent** 1536 Jalan Sultan Badlishah ☎04 731 5000, ⓦnewregent.my. It's rare to see a modest facelift successfully transform an ageing hotel, giving the atrium a light, airy feel and imbuing the rooms with touches of contemporary style. Nothing lavish but cosy and good value. Breakfast is sometimes free. RM170

EATING

The best part of the town centre for eating is **Chinatown**, especially at night when the food courts around Jalan Putra are buzzing even as the rest of the centre shuts down. *Kedai kopis* places are oddly thin on the ground more centrally, although Jalan Langgar and Jalan Tunku Ibrahim hold a handful that are good for daytime *nasi lemak* and noodles.

Lot 7 Jalan Sekerat. One of several popular evening food courts in the area serving a huge range of dishes: pork rice, oyster omelette, seafood, even Western-style lamb chops with fries, to name just a few. Daily 5pm till late; some stalls may open at other times.

Nasi Kandar Salam Jalan Putra, close to Jalan Menanti. Friendly joint with a lunchtime *biriyani* offering in addition to the usual *nasi kandar* curries, plus *roti canai* and tandoori chicken. Daily 24hr.

Parrot Espresso 95 Pekan Cina ☎04 731 0232. This tiny shophouse place, with just a couple of tables and sofas, is proof that the zeal of 20-something Malaysians for launching Western-style cafés isn't confined to Georgetown. The coffee is more than tolerable, as are the cream cakes, including an interesting *pandan* layer cake, flavoured with the much-used screwpine leaf. Bottled beers and ciders available too. Daily noon–midnight.

Ulu Muda Eco Park

Tucked up against the Thai border and enclosing three hydro lakes, **Ulu Muda Eco Park** has similarities to Perak's Royal Belum. However, this isn't a state-level park, but a mere forest reserve which, in the context of Malaysia, confers little protection – indeed, logging remains an issue in an area that remains rich in wildlife. Due to its remoteness, the only practical way to see the park is on a pricey **package trip**, but the rewards can be substantial. Thick with salt licks that lure animals, the park offers a reasonable chance of encountering **elephants** and **wild boar**, as well as reptiles and birds, including the rare **plain-pouched hornbill**.

The park is accessed by boat from **Gubir**, not much more than a jetty 75km east of Alor Star; a two-hour sampan ride from here lands you at the only accommodation, **Earth Lodge**. Hiking tracks link the lodge to limestone caves, hot springs (which many animals visit early in the morning or at night, when the temperatures drop) and wildlife hides.

ARRIVAL AND DEPARTURE ULU MUDA ECO PARK

By bus and taxi The closest you can get to Gubir by public bus is either Sik, 30km southwest (buses from Sungai Petani), or Naka, 25km northwest (buses from Alor Star). From either of these, you'll need to find a taxi (most likely, just a local with a car); expect to pay RM50.

By car From Alor Star, take Route 175/K8 through Langgar and on up the K11 to Kuala Nerang, where you turn southeast for Gubir. From Butterworth take the North–South Expressway and exit at Gurun, taking route K10 to Sik, where you turn on to Route K8 to Gubir.

ACCOMMODATION

Earth Lodge Kuala Labua, inside the park ☎04 899 7926 or ☎019 442 8926, ⓦearthlodgemalaysia.com. Newly renovated cabins, managed by two committed conservationists. Book at least two weeks in advance. Three days, including meals, boat rides and park permits, per person: dorms RM630, doubles RM900

Langkawi

Situated 30km off the coast, just south of the Thai border, **LANGKAWI** is, at 500 square kilometres, the largest of an archipelago of mostly uninhabited islands. Once a haven for pirates, the island is now home to some of the priciest resorts in the country, taking advantage of **beaches** that are among the best on the west coast. Thankfully there's relatively little high-density development, and there is a sprinkling of budget and mid-range accommodation at two beaches, **Pantai Tengah** and **Pantai Cenang**. The island is also popular with international yachties for its **marinas**, which are relatively cheap – and Langkawi's **duty/GST-free status** means beer is ridiculously cheap. Many diversions are on offer beyond lazing around on the sand, including taking a **mangrove cruise** after sea eagles, snorkelling or scuba diving at the **Pulau Payar Marine Park** to the south, and riding the terrific **Langkawi Cable Car** over the interior forests to the top of **Gunung Machinchang**.

Langkawi is sufficiently far north that, as at Phuket and other west coast Thai resorts, the **southwest monsoon** can have some bite. From May to August, rainy days can be more frequent here than elsewhere in Malaysia, with a dampening effect on the crowds and room rates.

2

Kuah

If you fly in, chances are that you'll never glimpse Langkawi's forgettable main town, **KUAH**, in the southeast of the island; indeed visitors off the ferries stay barely long enough to use the ATMs at the boat terminal and find a taxi to their accommodation. Just north of the ferry terminal, a separate section of the waterfront is home to **Dataran Lang** or Eagle Square, graced by the town's only landmark: an enormous sculpture of a sea eagle (*lang* being a contraction of *helang*, Malay for "eagle").

Pantai Cenang

Around 18km west from Kuah, **Pantai Cenang** is Langkawi at its most built-up, a 2km stretch that has seen an orgy of seemingly unrestrained get-rich-quick development in recent years, packing in numerous cheap places to stay and eat as well as duty-free shopping malls. Whatever you think of the strip, you'll almost certainly warm to the **beach**, Langkawi's most popular, a long, broad strip of fine white sand. There may be **jellyfish** in the water, so take local advice about swimming.

Underwater World

On the headland at the southern end of Pantai Cenang • Daily 10am–6pm (public and school holidays 9.30am–6.30pm) • RM40 • ☏ 04 955 6100, ⊕ underwaterworld.com.my

Although their Coco Valley duty-free emporium seems to be a significant reason for the enterprise, **Underwater World** is actually a substantial aquarium, with more than a hundred tanks housing thousands of marine and freshwater fish. The highlight is the obligatory walk-through tunnel where sharks, turtles and hundreds of other sea creatures swim around and above you. There are also penguin and seal sections, with daily feeding sessions.

Pantai Tengah

In marked contrast to Cenang, **Pantai Tengah** still has something of a rural feel, and although one or two new hotels are sprouting, at least development here has always been focused on low-density, mid-range places. The beach is slightly shorter than Cenang and not quite as nice, with coarser sand and occasionally **rough surf**. All this means, of course, that there are fewer people about, which can be a bonus.

Pantai Kok and around

North up the coast from Pantai Cenang, beyond the **airport**, is **Pantai Kok**, another of Langkawi's well-known beaches, with a handful of resorts scattered on

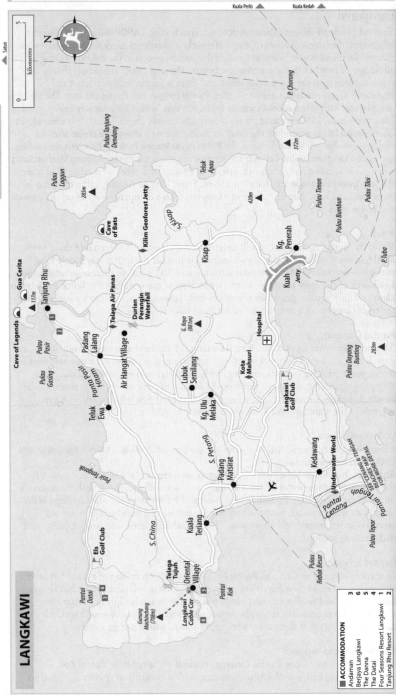

Kuala Perlis ▲   Kuala Kedah ▲

N

0 ——— 5
kilometres

Satun ▲

LANGKAWI

P. Charong

Pulau Tanjung
Dendang

Pulau
Loggun
285m ▲

372m ▲

Teluk
Apau

Pulau Tilol

Cave
of Bats

Kilim Geoforest Jetty

S. Kisap

420m ▲

Pulau Timon

Pulau Bumbun

Gua Cerita

Cave of Legends

117m ▲ Tanjung Rhu

Telaga Air Panas

Durian
Perangin
Waterfall

Kisap

Kg.
Penerah

P. Tuba

Kuah
Jetty

Padang
Lalang

Pulau
Pasir

Air Hangat Village

G. Raya
(881m) ▲

Hospital ✚

283m ▲

Pulau
Gasing

Pulau
Hitam

pantai pasir

Teluk
Ewa

Lubuk
Semilang

Kota
Mahsuri

Kg. Ulu
Melaka

Langkawi
Golf Club

Pulau Dayang
Bunting

Pasir Tengkorak

S. Perang

Padang
Matsirat

Kedawang

Underwater World

SEE 'CENANG & TENGAH
BEACHES MAP' FOR
MORE DETAIL

Els
Golf Club

S. China

Kuala
Teriang

✈

Pantai
Cenang

pantai Tengah

Pulau Tepor

Pantai
Datai

Telaga Tujuh

Oriental
Village

Gunung
Machinchang
(708m) ▲

Langkawi
Cable Car

Pantai
Kok

Pulau
Rebak Besar

■ ACCOMMODATION

Andaman   3
Bejaya Langkawi   6
The Danna   5
The Datai   4
Four Seasons Resort Langkawi   1
Tanjung Rhu Resort   2

or near it. Just inland are two major sights: the **Langkawi Cable Car**, the only one of the island's man-made attractions that ranks as essential, and the cascades at **Telaga Tujuh**.

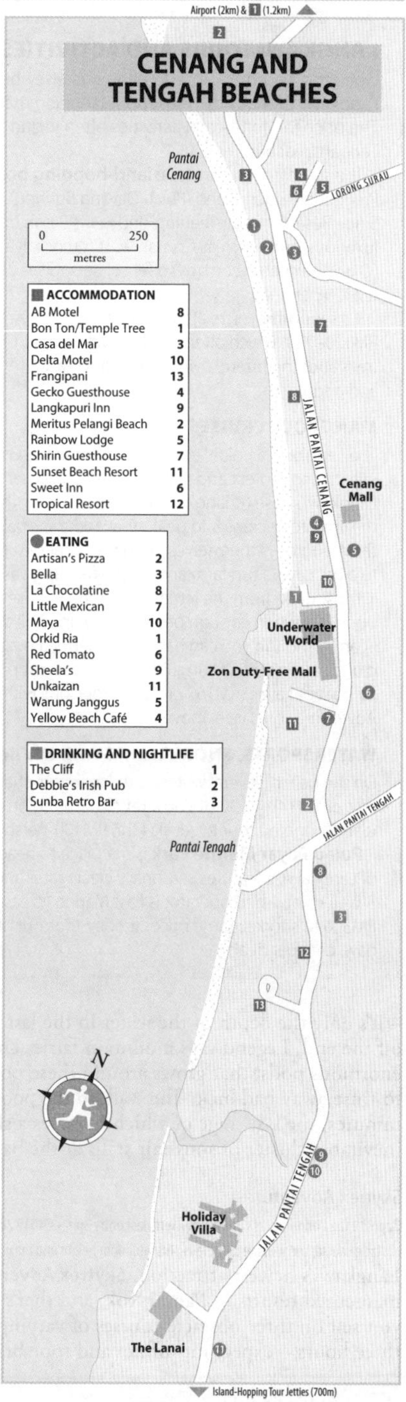
Airport (2km) & 1 (1.2km)
CENANG AND TENGAH BEACHES
Pantai Cenang
LORONG SURAU
0 250 metres
ACCOMMODATION
AB Motel 8
Bon Ton/Temple Tree 1
Casa del Mar 3
Delta Motel 10
Frangipani 13
Gecko Guesthouse 4
Langkapuri Inn 9
Meritus Pelangi Beach 2
Rainbow Lodge 5
Shirin Guesthouse 7
Sunset Beach Resort 11
Sweet Inn 6
Tropical Resort 12
EATING
Artisan's Pizza 2
Bella 3
La Chocolatine 8
Little Mexican 7
Maya 10
Orkid Ria 1
Red Tomato 6
Sheela's 9
Unkaizan 11
Warung Janggus 5
Yellow Beach Café 4
DRINKING AND NIGHTLIFE
The Cliff 1
Debbie's Irish Pub 2
Sunba Retro Bar 3
JALAN PANTAI CENANG
Cenang Mall
Underwater World
Zon Duty-Free Mall
JALAN PANTAI TENGAH
Pantai Tengah
N
Holiday Villa
JALAN PANTAI TENGAH
The Lanai
Island-Hopping Tour Jetties (700m)

Langkawi Cable Car

Oriental Village Shopping Complex • Mon, Tues & Thurs 10am–7pm, Wed noon–7pm, Fri–Sun 9.30am–7.30pm • RM30 return • ☎ 04 959 4225, Ⓦ panoramalangkawi.com

Much of Langkawi's northwest is untouched rainforest atop low peaks of mixed sandstone and shale, one of which is **Gunung Machinchang** (710m). At its foot, the tourist-trap Oriental Village Shopping Complex offers quad biking and other diversions, but its most important role by far is as the lower terminus of the magnificent **Langkawi Cable Car** up the mountain. With a 42-degree incline, the ride is not only the steepest of its kind, but also boasts the longest free span for a mono-cable car: a thrilling 950m long, great for eagle-spotting.

At the top, a 125m-long **SkyBridge** spans a deep valley – it's really not for acrophobics – and gives a spectacular view over the Andaman Sea. At the time of writing, however, it had been closed for more than two years for major repairs; although it should be open again by the time you read this, ask locally to be sure. Incidentally, do *not* follow tracks down the mountain from the cable car's upper station; they are not looked after and people have disappeared attempting them.

Telaga Tujuh

About 1.5km beyond the Langkawi Cable Car turning, the main road terminates at the entrance to **Telaga Tujuh** (literally, "Seven Wells"), where a cascading freshwater stream has eroded the rock to form several pools down a slope. During the rainy season, the slipperiness of the moss covering the rock in between the pools helps you slide from one pool to another, before the fast-flowing water disappears over the cliff to form the 90m-high **waterfall** visible from below

2

LANGKAWI TOURS AND ACTIVITIES

Operators based at Pantai Cenang and elsewhere offer a wide range of activities around Langkawi, perhaps the most popular being mangrove cruises and island-hopping trips. The price for non-beach activities often includes free pick-up from Cenang or Tengah beaches.

The standard itinerary for **island-hopping boat trips** (4hr; RM30/person) takes in forested Pregnant Maiden Island (Pulau Dayang Bunting), whose crater lake is good for swimming, Singa Besar for eagle feeding, and Beras Basah for beach and clear water. For something more luxurious, firms such as Crystal Yacht (ⓦ crystalyacht.com) and Tropical Charter (ⓦ tropicalcharter.com.my) offer sunset cruises with drinks and a barbecue dinner for around RM320 per head.

If it's **wildlife** you're after, your best bet is Dev's Adventure Tours (ⓦ langkawi-nature.com; RM120–220) which offers guided cycling trips, birding, mangrove tours and evening jungle treks after the bizarre flying lemur (also called the colugo), like a cross between a fruitbat and a squirrel.

MANGROVE CRUISES

The Langkawi archipelago is a member of the Global Geoparks Network, a UNESCO-endorsed initiative to protect and promote "geological heritage of international significance". In Langkawi's case (ⓦ langkawigeopark.com.my), that geology includes **karst** landscapes, and it's the limestone crags and peaks that add a special flavour to local **mangrove cruises**. In fact the mangroves themselves often play a mere supporting role, as these trips also involve a visit to a bat cave, a fish farm and **eagle-feeding** sessions.

Trips set off from the jetties at Tanjung Rhu (see opposite) and the Kilim Geoforest Park (see opposite) when enough people show up to fill them (RM90 for 4hr); ideally turn up at 9 or 10am, although you can haggle to charter a boat privately (RM350 for eight people). These cruises are essentially unguided as the fee just pays for the ride; for a professionally guided trip by boat or kayak (RM160 or RM220/person), with a restaurant meal along the way, try Dev's Adventure Tours (see above).

WATERSPORTS, SNORKELLING AND DIVING

On the beach, several watersports operators charge about RM90 for **parasailing** around their bay, or RM140 for 30min on a **jet ski**, among other activities. It's even possible to do an island-hopping tour by jet ski (3hr; RM400/person).

Pulau Payar Marine Park is the place to head for **snorkelling and scuba diving**; south of Langkawi, it features seasonally clear water and colourful fish life including giant potato cod. A well-established operator is East Marine (ⓦ eastmarine.com.my; diving day-trips RM400, or RM300 to snorkel; same prices for day-trips out of Penang), though agents in Pantai Cenang have cheaper deals.

– it's only the depth of the water in the last pool that prevents you from shooting off the end. Legend says mountain fairies created the *sintuk*, a climbing plant with enormous pods, that grows around these pools; the locals use it as a hair wash, said to rinse away bad luck. The walk to the pools from the car park takes about 45 minutes, the last stage of which involves a steep 200m-high climb up from the inevitable cluster of souvenir stalls at the base of the hill.

Skytrex Adventure

Opposite the Danna resort • Daily 9am–5pm, last entry 3pm • ☎ 019 280 5679, ⓦ skytrex-adventure.com • RM35–55 depending on the obstacle course; see website for details plus minimum height and maximum weight restrictions

Langkawi's newest attraction, **Skytrex Adventure** sounds a discordant note amid the manicured resorts of Pantai Kok, and that's no bad thing. Here you can challenge yourself on three obstacle courses of varying levels of toughness, each taking two to three hours – expect lots of net and rope bridges and the odd spot of abseiling.

Pantai Pasir Hitam

Around halfway along Langkawi's north coast, **Pantai Pasir Hitam** (Black Sand Beach) is actually pale grey – said to have been caused by ash, after locals torched their rice fields during a war with the Thais in the eighteenth century. It's a pleasant place to pull up, with little craft hauled up on the gently sloping shoreline.

Tanjung Rhu

Langkawi's northernmost road runs to the tip of **Tanjung Rhu**, a 4km-long promontory fringed in casuarina trees, where you can join a **mangrove** cruise from the jetty. There's a good **beach**, sheltered and overlooking several islets – one of which, **Pulau Chabang**, can be reached on foot at low tide (be sure to check tide times to avoid being stranded or swimming 500m back to shore).

Kilim Geoforest Park

Taking up the northeastern part of the island, **Kilim Geoforest Park** showcases contorted limestone formations, some forested, others starkly beautiful, interspersed with valleys where mangroves thrive. There are no trails, however; most visitors make a beeline for the **jetty** to sign up for a **mangrove boat** trip or **kayaking**. If you don't fancy either, you can simply survey the mangroves from a boardwalk, which ends at a cave populated by bats.

Gunung Raya

Summit lookout tower daily 9am–6.30pm • RM10

Reached off a road through the centre of the island, **Gunung Raya** (881m) is Langkawi's highest point. It also happens to be driveable, although if you plan to head up in a rental vehicle, check with the agent that it can cope with the steep, twisting 7km access road. Once at the top, you're rewarded with views down over jungle to the coast that can rival those from the cable car. This is also one promising place on the island to spot **hornbills**.

ARRIVAL AND DEPARTURE   **LANGKAWI**

Langkawi's excellent travel links with other parts of Malaysia, plus Singapore and southern Thailand, mean you don't have to return the way you arrived. Various **agents** at Cenang and Tengah beaches can assist with onward travel, including combined boat-and-van transfers to Thailand.

By plane Langkawi Airport is on the west coast at Padang Matsirat, 20km by road from Kuah and only 5km from Pantai Cenang. There's a tourist information point and a taxi counter where you buy a coupon for your destination; the fare to Pantai Tengah, say, is around RM22.
Destinations Kuala Lumpur (KLIA: at least 9 daily; 1hr; Subang: 3–5 daily; 1hr); Kuching (4 weekly; 2hr 10min); (Penang (3–4 daily; 35min); Singapore (1–2 daily; 1hr 30min).
By ferry At the southeastern edge of Kuah, Langkawi's ferry terminal feels like a shopping mall with piers out the back. There are ATMs inside the building, while at

the front is a separate building housing a tourist office and booths selling ferry tickets (schedules for most routes at ⓦlangkawi-ferry.com). This is also the departure point for taxis, with fares of around RM30 to Cenang or Tengah beaches, RM40 to Tanjung Rhu and RM45 to Pantai Kok.
Destinations Koh Lipe (Thailand; 1 daily; 1hr 20min); Kuala Kedah (11 daily; 1hr 45min; RM23); Kuala Perlis (11 daily; 1hr 15min; RM18); Penang (2–3 daily; 2hr 45min; RM67); Satun (Thailand; 3 daily; 1hr 15min; RM30). It's worth booking Penang tickets a day in advance.

GETTING AROUND

Langkawi has a reasonable network of country roads, with a veritable expressway between Kuah and Pantai Cenang, for example. Unfortunately there are no buses, so you'll be using taxis at some point or renting a vehicle. As the island is barely 25km across at its widest point, even a comprehensive tour is unlikely to cover more than 100km.

By taxi Taxis follow set fares from the airport, ferry terminal and taxi stands, which can be found at the northern end of Pantai Cenang and at the *Tropical Resort* on Pantai Tengah, among other places. If you think you're being overcharged, ask to see the official tariff sheet or check with tourist offices. For journeys that start elsewhere, you may need to haggle.

Vehicle rental Some car rental agents at Cenang soundly beat the usual chains on price: a basic Malaysian-built Perodua will set you back RM70/day, for example. Scooters, motorbikes or bicycles all cost around RM20/day. Note that rates can rise by fifty percent or even double over busy holiday periods, at which time the chains may not be such a bad deal.

INFORMATION

Tourism Malaysia Both the counters at the airport (daily 9am–10pm; ☏ 04 955 7155) and at the back of the small building fronting the ferry terminal (daily 9am–5pm; ☏ 04 966 0494) have leaflets covering tours and activities and

can help with practical advice on taxi fares and sightseeing. **LADA** The authority that manages Langkawi runs a centralized tourist information website of varying usefulness (ⓦ naturallylangkawi.my).

ACCOMMODATION

Practically all the worthwhile cheap places to stay are at Cenang beach, all of the upmarket resorts are elsewhere, and you'll find a few mid-range options at **Tengah** and **Cenang**. If it's a toss-up between the last two, choose Cenang for buzz, cheap food and ready access to shops; Tengah if you'd prefer to pay a bit more for food and lodging in leafier surroundings. As ever, book a few days ahead over holiday periods, when rates can rise by 10–50 percent above those listed below.

PANTAI CENANG

AB Motel Jalan Pantai Cenang ☏ 04 955 1300, ⓦ abmotel.weebly.com. This beachside motel isn't much to look at, but it's well established and popular. All rooms are a/c and en suite, some in the main block, others in single-storey rows. RM100

★**Bon Ton/Temple Tree** Coast road 2km north of Pantai Cenang ☏ 04 955 1688, ⓦ bontonresort.com.my or ⓦ templetree.com.my. Adjacent resorts run by the same team and both comprising vintage timber houses from all over the country that have been dismantled and rebuilt here using a harmonious mixture of period and contemporary fittings. *Bon Ton* is a collection of fine Malay kampung houses; *Temple Tree* features some quite substantial buildings from towns or plantations. Both have their own restaurants and pools, and *Bon Ton* overlooks a lagoon rich in birdlife. Breakfast included. Every house is priced differently depending on how many they sleep. Bon Ton RM750, Temple Tree RM800

Casa del Mar Northern end of Jalan Pantai Cenang ☏ 04 955 2388, ⓦ casadelmar-langkawi.com. With buildings in a terracotta hue, creating a faintly Moroccan feel, this boutique resort succeeds in screening out the general hubbub of the strip. It's slightly overpriced, but does boast spacious rooms and suites, a spa, beachside pool and two restaurants. RM800

★**Delta Motel** Southern end of Pantai Cenang ☏ 04 955 1307. Set around a pleasant garden, this is an excellent little collection of en-suite, a/c A-frame chalets plus motel-style rooms. They're all rather plainly furnished but also sedate for Cenang, and the compound is right on the beach. Breakfast included. A-frames RM100, doubles RM160

Gecko Guesthouse Off Jalan Pantai Cenang ☏ 019 428 3801. Properly rustic accommodation in kampung-style chalets as well as a boring concrete block, all set in a gorgeous, shady garden teeming with cats and the odd goat. Paying a little extra will get you en suite, even a/c. Dorms RM20, doubles RM40

Langkapuri Inn Jalan Pantai Cenang ☏ 04 955 1202. Another motel-like collection of slightly faded rooms with tiled interiors, tiny balconies and satellite TV, comfortable enough but in need of a refresh. Breakfast included. RM170

Meritus Pelangi Beach Jalan Pantai Cenang ☏ 04 952 8888, ⓦ meritushotels.com. Top-notch resort with two-storey chalets, echoing traditional Malay architecture, in expansive gardens. There's a pool, spa, tennis and squash courts, and several restaurants. RM750

★**Rainbow Lodge** Lorong Surau, off Jalan Pantai Cenang ☏ 04 955 8103, ⓦ rainbowlangkawi.com. Resortdom, backpacker-style, this is practically an estate in its own right, with fifty rooms plus more than a dozen self-contained bungalows, some in kampung style, including one built over a pond. It also has a simple restaurant. Dorms RM20, fan doubles RM45, a/c doubles RM80, bungalows RM180

Shirin Guesthouse Just off Jalan Pantai Cenang ☏ 04 955 5991, ✉ shiringh@yahoo.com. Run by a friendly Iranian/japanese couple, this humble but likeable assortment of multicoloured chalets is set around a path lined with spider lilies. Women's dorm RM20, a/c doubles RM55

Sweet Inn Pantai Cenang ☏ 04 955 8864, ⓦ sweetinns .net. Rather institutional but good value, with a variety of well-kept en-suite rooms featuring tiled floors, TV and a/c, run by a helpful Malay family. Breakfast – toast, fruit and either noodles or rice – is better than you might expect for the price. RM90

PANTAI TENGAH

Frangipani Jalan Teluk Baru ☎04 952 0000, ⓦfrangipanilangkawi.com. A sprawling complex of buildings with roofs shaped like those of traditional Malay houses. There are rooms in two-storey buildings and a selection of so-called beach villas, really bungalow accommodation, plus two pools (one saltwater – odd when the beach is just a minute away), spa, gym and jacuzzi. Doubles RM600, villas RM650

★**Sunset Beach Resort** Southern end of Jalan Pantai Cenang ☎04 955 1751, ⓦsungroup-langkawi.com. Surprisingly slick affair for the price, its star feature being the gorgeous compound planted with frangipani trees, palms and ferns. Rooms don't quite live up to the grounds, but feature some unusual touches including decorative wall screens and corner sofas. No breakfast. RM220

Tropical Resort Jalan Teluk Baru ☎04 955 4075, ⓦtropicalresortlangkawi.com. A series of bungalows, each containing modern, blandly furnished rooms facing in different directions, and just a 2min walk from the beach along a leafy path. A good deal; breakfast included. RM150

NORTHWEST

Andaman Teluk Datai ☎04 959 1088, ⓦtheandaman .com. Pretty chic rooms at this substantial place, set in rainforest above one of Langkawi's best beaches, where hornbills are often seen. The unusual feature here is the coral nursery, set up following the discovery of a nearby reef damaged by the 2004 Indian Ocean tsunami. Now the resort rehabilitates coral in its own pool, where guests can take part in guided snorkelling sessions. RM800

Berjaya Langkawi Pantai Kok ☎04 959 1888, ⓦberjayahotel.com/langkawi. The resort for the hoi polloi, better value than much of the competition, with some newly refurbished chalets set in woods or out over the sea. Facilities include watersports, tennis and the obligatory pool and spa. Breakfast included. RM700

The Danna Pantai Kok ☎04 959 3288, ⓦthedanna .com. Generically grand, with a glut of marble and high ceilings, but scores with its conceit of an infinity pool, Olympic-sized and right by the beach, and large, slick rooms overlooking the leafy courtyard, the marina or the sea. Breakfast included. RM1000

The Datai Teluk Datai ☎04 950 0500, ⓦthedatai.com /langkawi. On the gloriously secluded Datai beach, this is the quintessential luxury retreat, with self-contained mini-villas embedded in the woods or out on the beach, some with their own paddling pool or jacuzzi, as well as less extortionately priced rooms in the main building. Facilities include two pools, a Malay-style spa, watersports and use of the adjacent golf course. RM1800

TANJUNG RHU

Four Seasons Resort Langkawi Tanjung Rhu ☎04 950 8888, ⓦfourseasons.com/langkawi. Close to the karst formations of Langkawi's northeast, this phenomenally expensive retreat doesn't so much have rooms as mini-apartments taking up a whole floor of their two-storey pavilions, as well as self-contained villas, all with outdoor showers in addition to their bathroom. RM2500

Tanjung Rhu Resort Tanjung Rhu ☎04 959 1033, ⓦtanjungrhu.com.my. Well-designed rooms, all billed as suites, set this resort apart, featuring wooden floors, teak furnishings and balconies. They have two pools, tennis courts and a spa, and run their own short mangrove trips. RM1100

EATING

The eating scene on Langkawi is predictably **cosmopolitan** and, away from the resorts, tends to focus on mid-range restaurants, although there are stalls and snack places to be found, especially at Cenang beach.

PANTAI CENANG

Artisan's Pizza Pantai Cenang ☎04 955 1232. A roadside outlet with just a few tables, as they concentrate on takeaway (or free local delivery). Aside from 11″ pizzas (RM30), they also turn out pasta, burgers and fish and chips. Daily 9am–2am.

Bella Jalan Pantai Cenang. Humble, zinc-roofed place for a good *roti canai* breakfast and *laksa* or chicken-rice meals at lunchtime, all for just a few ringgit. Wed–Mon 7.30am–4.30pm.

★**Orkid Ria** Pantai Cenang ☎04 955 4128. Popular alfresco Chinese place specializing in fresh seafood, grilled, steamed, fried or however you want it. Huge

tiger prawns, lobster and whole crab, all sold by weight (be careful not to over-order and risk a large bill), are some of the best you'll find in town. Around RM40 without drinks, more if you go for lots of seafood. Daily 11am–3pm & 6–11pm.

Red Tomato Jalan Pantai Cenang, across from Underwater World ☎04 955 40 55, ⓦredtomato.com .my. Middle-of-the-road, touristy restaurant easily spotted by virtue of the fuchsia VW Beetle usually parked outside (but don't confuse it with the *Red Sky* restaurant close by). Come here for Western cooked breakfasts (RM12) and a largely Italian menu of pizza and pasta meals (RM22). Daily 9am–10.30pm.

2

2

★**Warung Janggus** Jalan Pantai Cenang. There's no better place on Cenang for a tasty, filling *nasi campur* lunch, the trays groaning with at least two dozen Malay stir-fries, stews and curries. Less interesting by night, when it's a choice between *ikan bakar* (barbecued fish) or going à la carte. Mon & Wed–Sun 10am–11pm.

Yellow Beach Café Jalan Pantai Cenang ☎012 459 3190. Fronting the beach, good for a sundowner, with a smarter restaurant section serving "surf and turf" mains such as Australian beef burgers (RM40). Mon & Wed–Sun noon–1am.

PANTAI TENGAH

La Chocolatine North end of Pantai Tengah ☎04 955 8891. Tiny French-owned café with pastries – croissants, *millefeuilles*, etc – crêpes, quiche and sandwiches, complemented (or not) by Edith Piaf over the speakers. It's all acceptable rather than exceptional, but still a welcome change from *roti canai*. Coffee and cake will set you back around RM25. Daily 9am–6pm.

Little Mexican Jalan Pantai Cenang, where Cenang shades into Tengah ☎017 429 3100. This friendly Lebanese-owned place is the better of two local joints to satisfy any craving for *quesadillas*, *burritos* or similar – although their mealy *taco* shells need more work. All

fillings are available in three grades of heat ("spicy" is scorching). Covers bands play some nights. Daily 9am–6pm.

Maya Jalan Pantai Tengah ☎017 551 9873. Endearingly down-to-earth restaurant housed in a simple pavilion, and serving Malay and Thai-style dishes – everything from seafood *tom yam* to the spicy noodle soup *mee bandung*. The incongruous chicken nuggets and garlic *nan* somehow just add to the fun. Bring your own alcohol. Most dishes cost RM10 or so, although a whole fish (steamed, fried or grilled) hovers around RM35. Daily 12.30–11pm.

Sheela's Jalan Pantai Tengah ☎04 955 2308. With tables arrayed in a luxuriant garden setting, *Sheela's* serves mainly Western meals – steak (RM40), pasta (RM20) or more unusual mains such as Moroccan-style lamb, as well as a few unexpected Asian starters. Tues–Sun 6–11pm.

Unkaizan Far southern end of Pantai Tengah ☎04 955 4118, ⓦunkaizan.com. Up a jungly slope is this hidden gem of a Japanese restaurant where you can dine out on the terrace or indoors. The range of sushi and sashimi offerings is impressive (around RM60), although the set meals – chicken cutlet or tempura with rice, soup and pickles, say – are better value at around RM45. Japanese ice cream, too. Daily 6–11pm; closed every other Wed.

DRINKING AND NIGHTLIFE

Langkawi has a more pragmatic attitude to **alcohol** than anywhere else in the four overwhelmingly Malay states of the north: many restaurants are licensed, and then of course there are the duty-free outlets where you buy cheap spirits and beer – a can of Tiger is only RM2 (see below).

★**The Cliff** Built out over the water at the south end of Cenang beach ☎04 953 3228, ⓦtheclifflangkawi .com. One of the priciest standalone restaurants in Cenang, the *Cliff* majors on fusion cooking (mostly spicy seafood, with mains around RM50), but it's the little bar that stands out. Get here around 6pm, park yourself at one of the few beachside seats, and be amazed as the parasailing winds down against a scarlet sky, darkening to crimson. Daily noon–11pm.

Debbie's Irish Pub Jalan Pantai Cenang, practically where Tengah beach begins ☎012 595 3413.

Mundane-looking but lively little bolt hole, with Guinness, Gaymers cider and soccer matches on TV. They also serve Irish stew except in low season. Tues–Sun 7pm–late.

Sunba Retro Bar Pantai Tengah ☎04 953 1801. Part of a modern complex but decked out in wood to simulate an old kampung house, this is a relaxed bar with pretensions of being a proper club. There's a live band most nights from 11pm; otherwise DJs spin mainly mainstream oldies and some dance sounds. Fri–Wed 8pm–4am.

DIRECTORY

Banks and exchange There are ATMs at Cenang Mall, the Zon duty-free mall, Underwater World (all at Cenang beach), the airport and the ferry terminal. Cenang Mall also has a Maybank foreign-exchange counter.

Hospital Midway between Kuah and Pantai Cenang on Jalan Padang Matsirat, the main road linking the two (☎04 966 3333).

Internet Wi-Fi@Langkawi is a free service available in certain spots on Pantai Cenang's main street, at the ferry terminal and elsewhere, though not necessarily reliable.

Pharmacies Guardian has an outlet at Cenang Mall.

Shopping Langkawi's duty-free status can suck in even those not normally obsessed with cheap booze and fags, and at some point you may find yourself among the hordes at the malls around Underwater World, grabbing armfuls of beer, imported chocolates and the like. The Cenang Mall, also on the main drag, is a more orthodox and underwhelming shopping complex, best for branches of Western fast-food and coffee chains.

Kangar and around

If you're spending more than a couple of hours in **Perlis**, chances are something gone amiss with a transport connection: there's little to see, and the fastest road from Thailand passes through Kedah rather than here. The few travellers who up here are either bent on using **Kuala Perlis** to access Langkawi, or else doing a visa run to Penang via a slightly unorthodox route from Thailand.

Unremarkable **KANGAR**, Perlis's capital, sits immediately north of little **Sungai Perlis**. About 10km east, **ARAU** is the least interesting of all Malaysia's royal towns; from the main road you can peek at the istana, looking like a small European stately home except that it sports two golden domes.

ARRIVAL AND DEPARTURE

KANGAR AND AROUND

Train station In Arau (☏ 04 986 1225).
Destinations Alor Star (2 daily; 40min); Bangkok (1 daily; 19hr); Butterworth (2hr 30min–3hr); Hat Yai (Thailand; 2 daily; 3hr); Ipoh (daily; 7hr 30min); Kuala Kangsar (1 daily; 6hr 30min); Kuala Lumpur (1 daily; 11hr 15min); Sungai Petani (2 daily; 2hr); Taiping (daily; 6hr).

By bus Express services use the long-distance bus station on Jalan Bukit Lagi in Kangar, just south of the river. The local bus station is at the shopping complex housing the Store department store on Jalan Penjara, where you'll also find share taxis; it's on the north side of the river, a 10min zigzagging walk northeast of Kangar's express bus station. Local and express buses call at Kuala Perlis (see above) on their way out of Kangar.

Destinations from long-distance bus station Alor Star (several daily; 45min); Butterworth (at least 3 daily; 2hr 30min); Ipoh (3 daily; 4hr); Johor Bahru (2 daily; 12–13hr); Kota Bharu (2 daily; 6hr 30min); Kuala Lumpur (at least 6 daily; 7hr); Kuala Terengganu (2 daily; 8hr); Kuantan (1 daily; 10hr); Melaka (3 daily; 11hr).

Destinations from local bus station Alor Star (hourly; 1hr 15min); Kuala Perlis (30min); Padang Besar (2hr).

By ferry Langkawi ferries (🌐 langkawi-ferry.com) dock at

Kuala Perlis, 15km west of Kangar. Turn left out of the jetty, then right once you come to what's obviously a main street, to reach the bus station, a 5min walk.
Destinations Langkawi (11 daily; 1hr 15min; RM18).

TO THAILAND

The border crossings (daily 6am–10pm) are at Padang Besar, 30km north of Kangar, where the rail line enters Thailand, and at Bukit Kayu Hitam in Kedah, 30km northeast of Kangar as the crow flies. The latter is overwhelmingly more popular as it's on the North–South Expressway.

By train Thai Railways runs between Butterworth and Bangkok once a day, while KTM has another daily service between KL and Hat Yai. At Padang Besar, a very long platform connects the Malaysian rail network with its Thai counterpart; you must disembark, clear immigration and then get back on the train to resume the journey.

By bus There are no buses to Thailand, although tour-agency minivans service the Hat Yai route (you can book a place on ☏ 016 673 8082). It's also possible to charter a taxi to Padang Besar (RM50), where you have to get off before the border and cover the 2km to the Thai border post on foot or by motorbike taxi.

ACCOMMODATION

Sanctuary Garden Opposite Arau's train station ☏ 014 246 5999, 🌐 sancgarden.com. Family-run, pleasant new budget hotel with well-kept if plain rooms and a gaudy café, a modern re-imagining of the family's original

kopitiam, serving breakfast (for a small surcharge) and Hainanese meals. There's also an impressive atrium topped with a pyramid glass roof for natural light. **RM80**

Cameron Highlands

On the western fringes of Pahang state, the **CAMERON HIGHLANDS** take their name from William Cameron, a colonial surveyor who stumbled across the area in 1885, though not until forty years later did civil servant Sir George Maxwell propose it be turned into what would become the Peninsula's largest hill station. Indian planters, Chinese vegetable farmers and wealthy landowners in search of a weekend retreat flocked in, establishing **tea plantations** and leaving a swathe of what can only be called mock-mock-Tudor buildings in their wake.

The Camerons remain one of the most publicized attractions in Malaysia, although very much trading on past glories. Don't come expecting the pastoral idyll of the

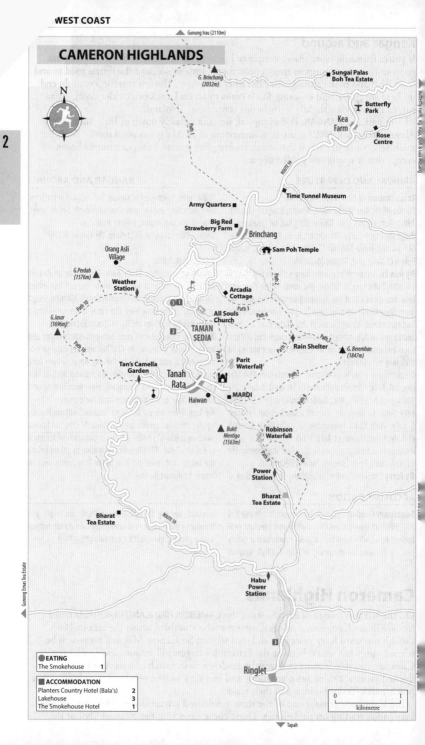

CAMERON HIGHLANDS

Gunung Irau (2110m)

G. Brinchang (2032m)

Sungai Palas Boh Tea Estate

Butterfly Park

Kea Farm

Rose Centre

Path 1

ROUTE 59

Time Tunnel Museum

Army Quarters

Big Red Strawberry Farm

Brinchang

Sam Poh Temple

Orang Asli Village

G.Perdah (1576m)

Path 2

Weather Station

Arcadia Cottage

Path 3

All Souls Church

Path 6

G.Jasar (1696m)

TAMAN SEDIA

Path 5

Rain Shelter

Path 3

Path 10

G. Beremban (1847m)

Path 4

Tan's Camella Garden

Parit Waterfall

Path 7

Tanah Rata

Path 8

Haiwan

MARDI

Bukit Mentiga (1563m)

Robinson Waterfall

Path 9

Path 9

Power Station

Bharat Tea Estate

Bharat Tea Estate

ROUTE 59

Habu Power Station

Gunung Emas Tea Estate

3

Ringlet

Tapah

EATING
The Smokehouse   1

ACCOMMODATION
Planters Country Hotel (Bala's)   2
Lakehouse   3
The Smokehouse Hotel   1

0   1
kilometre

TEA PLANTATIONS

The countless cups of *teh tarik* served up daily in Malaysia are likely to be made with home-grown **tea**, which is – no pun intended – a bit of a mixed bag. Some people think local tea simply doesn't taste very good, although the stuff served up at food courts and *kedai kopis* is usually so swamped with condensed milk that it's impossible to tell what the underlying taste is. Even if it doesn't float your boat, tea is such a feature of the Cameron Highlands that it would be perverse not to visit a plantation during your stay: all have **teahouses** with views over the terraces, and two offer brief, free **tours** that give a glimpse of the production process. Despite the romantic imagery used on packaging, the **handpicking** of tea leaves is giving way to mechanical pruning, often by migrant workers. At the factory, the leaves are withered and partly dried by alternate blasts of hot and cold air, then rolled by machine to release more moisture for the all-important process of **fermentation**. The soggy mass is eventually heated to 90°C to halt the process; finally, the leaves are graded by shaking them through meshes of different grades.

PLANTATIONS

Bharat 4.5km south of Tanah Rata (☎ 05 491 1133, ⓦ bharattea.com.my). Two teahouses, though no tours. Daily 8.30am–6pm.

Boh Near Habu, 6km southeast of Tanah Rata, and several kilometres off the main road (☎ 05 493 1324, ⓦ boh.com.my). Tours Tues–Sun 9am–4.45pm.

Sungai Palas 6km north of Brinchang (☎ 05 496 1363, ⓦ boh.com.my). Boh's northern branch offers not just the usual cursory tour but also a worthwhile tea-tasting tour (45min; RM35), on which you get a proper introduction to tea production, with a chance to taste various brews at the end along with scones. There are sessions at 9am, 11am and 1pm; the middle one is best as this is when the tea tends to arrive for processing. Call in advance as tours may be cancelled during periods of low harvest. Daily 8.30am–4.30pm.

brochures. This is a major agroindustrial area, producing not only tea but also flowers, vegetables and fruit that are exotic for Malaysia (notably **strawberries**), much of it under unsightly plastic. What's more, it gets packed out during holidays and school breaks, when there can be long tailbacks on the main road, and then there's the din of building work wherever hotels and holiday apartments are springing up. Many from the Camerons bemoan the commercialization, but as ever in Malaysia, the real problem is the haphazard and unsustainable way in which it happens. If you want to know more about the **environmental challenges** facing the area, contact the local campaigning group REACH (ⓦ reach.org.my). That said, many visitors have a perfectly pleasant time here. Lying more than 1000m above sea level, the area offers **cool relief** from the sultriness of just about everywhere else in the country, which is the main reason locals visit. Throw in forest hikes and tea plantations, and you have promising ingredients for a short break.

The Camerons' 700 square kilometres are threaded by the twisty **Route 59**, linking all the main towns and officially called Jalan Besar (or just "main road") where it becomes a town's main street. The towns themselves are mundane concrete affairs, although plenty of buildings sport a webbing of dark lines in homage to that ersatz half-timbered look. A three-night stay suits many, allowing two full days for treks and seeing a tea plantation and other minor sights. Although it never really gets cold, have a warm sweater to hand for nights. Hikers should also have waterproofs for the frequent showers or storms (local general stores sell plastic ponchos for just a few ringgit) and footwear that can cope with slippery, muddy conditions.

Tanah Rata

Some 1400m above sea level, **TANAH RATA** is both the Camerons' biggest town and the least spoiled. With plenty of places to stay and eat along or just off the 500m-long

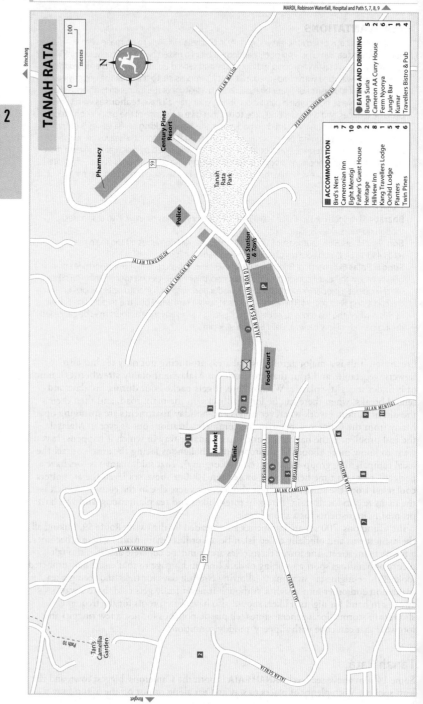

MARDI, Robinson Waterfall, Hospital and Path 5, 7, 8, 9

Brinchang

TANAH RATA

0 ———— 100
metres

N

Century Pines Resort

Pharmacy

Police

JALAN MASJID

PERSIARAN DAYANG ENDAH

Tanah Rata Park

JALAN TENGKOLOK

JALAN LANGGAK MERCU

Bus Station & Taxis

JALAN BESAR (MAIN ROAD)

P

Food Court

Market

Clinic

PERSIARAN CAMELLIA 3

PERSIARAN CAMELLIA 4

JALAN CAMELLIA

JALAN MENTIGI

JALAN MENTIGI

JALAN CANATIONV

JALAN GEREJA

JALAN GEREJA

Tan's Camellia Garden

Path 10

Ringlet

59

59

■ ACCOMMODATION

Bird's Nest	3
Cameronian Inn	7
Eight Mentigi	10
Father's Guest House	9
Heritage	2
Hillview Inn	8
Kang Travellers Lodge	1
Orchid Lodge	5
Planters	4
Twin Pines	6

● EATING AND DRINKING

Bunga Suria	5
Cameron AA Curry House	2
Fern Nyonya	6
Jungle Bar	1
Kumar	3
Travellers Bistro & Pub	4

main road (officially **Jalan Besar**), it's the ideal base for visitors, although there are no sights except perhaps the delightfully wild **Tan's Camellia Garden**, brimming with lilies, agapanthus and pitcher plants. It's just a five-minute walk west from the defunct tourist office and despite appearances, operates as a nursery.

Brinchang

BRINCHANG is a scruffy town some 5km from Tanah Rata via the main road, although walkers can use a shortcut around the golf course (see p.176). With something resembling a town square, it's denser and more built up than Tanah Rata, but in its favour it has a **market** just uphill from the centre – the first of several on the road north – which morphs in the afternoon as

one set of stalls is replaced by another, forming a *pasar malam*. Aside from the ubiquitous strawberry-themed souvenirs, the markets sell snacks and produce, including **sea coconuts**, which look like purple cannonballs.

Time Tunnel

A 15min walk northeast of Brinchang's centre on Route 59 • Daily 8.30am–6pm • RM5 • ☎ 05 491 4481

On the edge of town, the quirky **Time Tunnel** is part of one of the area's many "self-plucking" strawberry farms. It serves as a museum of Malaysian ephemera, worth a quick look to see just how much the country has changed over the past few decades. The best section is the evocation of a simple 1950s domestic interior, although for no obvious reason it has a colonial poster of the time announcing the creation of a Home Guard to combat the "bandits", as the British were wont to refer to the Communists during the Emergency. Elsewhere, you can gaze at vintage photos of a once-bucolic Camerons and weep.

North of Brinchang

The area **north of Brinchang** is the Cameron Highlands at its most intensively farmed; head up on a bus from Ipoh or Penang and you'll see the plastic tunnels off the Simpang Pulai Road even before it joins Route 59 at Kampung Raja. The Camerons' two highest peaks, Irau and Brinchang (see box, p.178), are here too, as is the Sungai Palas tea estate and a couple of minor attractions locals make a beeline for. Three kilometres from Brinchang, **Kea Farm** is known for hosting a **butterfly farm**, home to other insects and snakes too (daily 8am–6pm; RM5; ⓦcameronbutterflyfarm.com.my), and, slightly further on, a **rose centre** (daily 8am–6pm; RM5; ☎05 496 2988), a garden and nursery featuring a kitsch nursery-rhyme shoe house. Even more popular – cars double-park on the road close by, causing tedious jams – is the new **Lavender Garden**, some 9km from Brinchang just beyond **Tringkap** (Mon–Thurs 9am–6pm, Fri–Sun 9am–6pm; RM5; ☎05 496 1208, ⓦcameronlavender.com). It's another sizeable nursery, for lavender and other plants, with lavender-scented gifts and lavender-themed food.

ARRIVAL AND DEPARTURE — CAMERON HIGHLANDS

By bus The Highlands' main bus station is at the east end of Tanah Rata, and is used by both local and express buses. Some buses arriving from KL may head on to Brinchang. Backpacker minivans also operate to and

from the Highlands and other popular destinations.
Destinations Butterworth (2 or 3 daily; 4hr); Ipoh (4 daily; 2hr); Kuala Lumpur (at least 9 daily; 3hr 30min); Melaka (2 daily; 5hr 30min); Penang (2 daily; 5hr); Raub (3 daily; 3hr 30min); Singapore (1 daily; 10hr); Taman Negara (Kuala Tembeling; 1 daily; 4hr 30min).
By car The Camerons can be easily reached off the E1, the North–South Expressway; use the exits at Tapah (if arriving from the south) or Simpang Pulai near Ipoh (from the north). The Simpang Pulai Rd meets Route 59 at Kampung Raja before continuing to Gua Musang and Route 8 to Kota Bharu. A minor road links up with Route 8 in the heart of the Pahang interior, connecting Ringlet on Route 59 with Raub and Kuala Lipis.

GETTING AROUND

If the infrequent bus service irks you, note that you can easily **walk** directly between Tanah Rata and Brinchang (40min) via **Taman Sedia**, the Malay village in the little depression in between. Signs on Route 59 outside both towns point the way to the village, the walk taking you past the Anglican All Souls' Church and skirting the golf course.

By bus Local services from Tanah Rata's bus station run north to Kampung Raja via Brinchang (hourly 6.30am–7.30pm) and south to Tapah via Ringlet (4 daily).

By taxi Taxis park next to Tanah Rata's bus station (☏ 05 491 2355) and on the main road in Brinchang. A taxi between Tanah Rata and Brinchang costs around RM8; to charter a taxi for excursions, expect to pay RM25/hr.

INFORMATION AND TOURS

Pahang Tourism used to run a tourist office at the western end of Tanah Rata, now occupied by a tour agency that still advertises itself as an information point – as does just about every other tour agency in town. The only reason to deal with an agency is if you want to arrange a guided trek or a taste-of-everything day tour (from RM70). The standard ingredients for the latter include a drive up Gunung (Mount) Brinchang to see the mossy forest, visits to a tea plantation and an Orang Asli settlement (although the latter might be modern and charmless), and a foray to find *Rafflesia* flowers if in bloom.

TOUR AGENTS
Cameron Secrets Father's Guesthouse, Tanah Rata (see below) ⓦ cameronsecrets.com.
CS Travel & Tours 47 Jalan Besar, Tanah Rata
☏ 05 491 1200, ⓦ cstravel.com.my.
Titiwangsa Tours & Travel 36 Jalan Besar, Brinchang
☏ 05 491 1452, ⓦ titiwangsatours.com.

ACCOMMODATION

Both Tanah Rata and Brinchang have a fair amount of mid-range **accommodation**, although the former's hotels tend to be better run. Tanah Rata is also where you find most of the Camerons' budget **guesthouses**, the best of which are in converted houses rather than the chunky concrete blocks typical of the mid-range places; all have hot water. Some places also have **apartments** to rent, listed on their websites. The rates given below rise by ten to fifty percent at weekends and can double at during school breaks and public holidays, when it's best to book ahead.

TANAH RATA
Bird's Nest 1 Lorong Perdah ☏ 05 491 4375, ⓦ birdsnesthotel.com. The mundane grey exterior of this five-storey block is unpromising, but inside is a modern hotel with slick rooms as well as a Sarawakian Orang Ulu-style mural in the lobby. Terrific value midweek, but to be avoided during school-break weekends, when rates almost treble. RM75
Cameronian Inn 16 Jalan Mentigi ☏ 05 491 1327, ⓦ thecameronianinn.com. Guesthouse with plain but airy dorms and doubles (some en suite) in a spotless bungalow, surrounded by a bougainvillea trellis and small garden. Dorms RM20, doubles RM55
Eight Mentigi 8a Jalan Mentigi ☏ 05 491 5988, ⓦ eightmentigi.com. It looks like a plain family home from the outside, but this guesthouse is rather fancier

inside, packed out with well-kept rooms and a couple of dorms. Some doubles have their own bath, but otherwise toilets and showers are shared. A good deal. Dorms RM20, doubles RM60
★**Father's Guest House** 4 Jalan Mentigi ☏ 016 566 1111, ⓦ fathersguesthouse.net. No longer linked with the Catholic Church, *Father's* is the best-run budget guesthouse in the Camerons and the best informed on trekking. Occupying a modern house with a small garden, they offer a range of pleasant rooms and a dorm; if they're full they can put you up at their branch, *Gerard's Place*, a few minutes' walk away. Dorms RM20, doubles RM70, en-suite doubles RM90
Heritage Jalan Gereja ☏ 05 491 3888, ⓦ heritage .com.my. A 10min uphill walk from town, this hotel is the closest Tanah Rata has to a resort-style complex,

with "heritage" dating all the way back to the 1990s. Besides tidy, unexceptional rooms, it has a choice of restaurants plus indoor recreational facilities, such as snooker, for those inevitable wet spells. Breakfast included. RM220

Hillview Inn 17 Jalan Mentigi ☎05 491 2915, ⓦhillview-inn.com. Run by a friendly Indian family, this simple hotel is decked out in predictable half-timbered style and appealingly surrounded by pines. Rooms are a little worn but come with nicely tiled bathrooms and balconies. No breakfast. RM80

Kang Travellers Lodge (Daniel's Lodge) 9 Lorong Perdah ☎05 491 5823, ⓦkangholiday.com. Not the friendliest place but certainly laidback, *Kang's* guesthouse is a worthy standby with a relaxing patio plus its own little bar right at the back. Choose between the large upstairs dorm and institutional rooms, some with attached bathroom. Dorms RM15, doubles RM50, en-suite doubles RM80

Orchid Lodge 82d Persiaran Camellia 4 ☎010 395 1247, ⓦorchidlodge.cameronhighlands.com. Accessed from the lane just south of the main road, this top-floor guesthouse is run by a friendly Bangladeshi ex-gardener, which helps explain why it's festooned with orchids. Rooms are simple but spacious and en suite. Self-service breakfast included. The owner also manages a new lodge nearby, with dorms as well as rooms. RM90

Planters 44a Jalan Besar ☎05 490 1001, ⓦplantershotel.com.my. Eccentrically decorated hotel, the corridors randomly kitted out with mirrors and fittings like something from a very bad fake Greek temple. Modern, decent and bland rooms. RM90

Twin Pines 2 Jalan Mentigi ☎05 491 2169, ⓦtwinpines.cameronhighlands.com. It can be noisy due to the thin-walled rooms, although it partly compensates with the most attractive garden of any guesthouse in Tanah Rata. Some singles. Doubles RM30, doubles with shower RM50

BETWEEN TANAH RATA AND BRINCHANG

Planters Country Hotel Route 59, about 1km north of Tanah Rata ☎05 491 1660, ⓦbalaschalet .com. Also known by its old name, *Bala's*, this former colonial school still oozes old-world charm, doing a passable impression of English cottages with the lushest gardens imaginable, complete with country-pub-style

dining room and a lounge with chintzy sofas. It's a bargain if you can cope with the slightly wayward management. Free lifts to and from town, although breakfast costs extra. RM140

★**The Smokehouse Hotel** Route 59, midway between Tanah Rata and Brinchang ☎05 491 1215, ⓦthesmokehouse.com.my. If ever a 1930s building could capture that mythical English country look, it's this one. Long the classiest place to stay in the Camerons, it boasts fifteen individually decorated suites, some with four-poster beds, others more modern in feel, plus more affordable rooms. Throw in the leaded windows, roast-beef meals (see p.178) and private garden with immaculate lawns, and well, you could pretend it's Surrey. Full English breakfast included. RM440

BRINCHANG

★**Parkland** 45 Jalan Besar ☎05 491 1299. Newly refurbished and given a more contemporary look, the friendly *Parkland* has uncluttered rooms that are good value midweek. The snag is that there's no lift, although you can pay fifteen percent more to stay at their more upmarket *Express* branch next door. RM110

Pop Ash 24 Jalan Besar ☎05 490 1188, ⓔhotelbutik .ks@gmail.com. A newish hotel with correspondingly smart rooms for the price. The cheapest are windowless, but then the townscape doesn't exactly tempt you to pay fifty percent extra for one with a view. RM60

Ria Cameron Jalan Angsana 3 ☎05 490 1777, ⓦriacameronhotel.com.my. In a block that's ugly even by Brinchang standards, but well looked after and not a bad option for no-frills accommodation. RM60

Rosa Passadena 1 Bandar Baru Brinchang ☎05 491 2288, ⓦcameronpremierhotels.com.my/rosa. Gargantuan hotel packing in more than a hundred rooms which, though slightly tatty, are quite comfortable and bigger than average – plus two restaurants. Breakfast included. RM150

RINGLET

Lakehouse Ringlet, 15km south of Tanah Rata ☎05 495 6152, ⓦlakehouse-cameron.com. With your own transport, it's worth staying at this retro boutique hotel in Ringlet. Stone fireplaces and old-fashioned furniture meet plasma-screen TVs in the rooms; there's a suitably pub-like restaurant and bar, and a reading lounge, too. RM500

EATING AND DRINKING

Two things sum up Cameron Highlands cuisine – **steamboat** and **scones**. The former are highly popular with locals, with RM20 per head as the going rate; many restaurants up here still heat the stock using old-fashioned charcoal vessels with a central chimney. Plenty of hotels and even curry houses bake fine scones as part of their take on English cream teas – if only they weren't marred by the artificially pink local strawberry jam and "cream" with the colour and consistency of toothpaste.

2

2

WALKING IN THE CAMERON HIGHLANDS

A network of **walking trails** makes it possible to take in the Cameron Highlands' forests, packed with ferns, pitcher plants, orchids, thick moss and even *Rafflesia*. But despite the presence of mammals such as honey bears, you're unlikely to see interesting fauna other than insects and the odd wild pig.

Unfortunately, the trails are often poorly marked and maintained, and seem to have little immunity from being bulldozed to make way for development. The account below should be treated as a snapshot and is certainly not meant to provide turn-by-turn directions. *Father's Guest House* in Tanah Rata (see p.176) is a good place to get current trail information, and produces maps that mention lots of useful landmarks as well as wrong turns to avoid on each trail. It is also one of several tour operators offering guided treks – again, a good option given the state of the trails.

If **hiking independently**, tell staff at your accommodation where you intend to go and when you expect to be back. On longer hikes, take warm clothing and ample water. If you do get lost and can get a cellular signal, call your accommodation for them to alert the authorities.

TRAILS

The paths below are numbered according to local convention. Timings are one way, for people going at an average pace.

Path 1 (2hr 30min) The ascent of **Gunung Brinchang** (2000m) is a tiring proposition, but there happens to be a road up – the highest road in Peninsular Malaysia – so you can cheat by taking a taxi up from Brinchang (RM15) and walking down. The road begins close to Kea Farm, passing a turning for the Sungai Palas Tea Estate, whereas the trail starts just north of Brinchang's street market – look for a track opposite the police headquarters. There's a terrific view from the summit, plus a boardwalk through the ethereal **Mossy Forest**, where the trees are covered in a spongy, soft coat of green.

Path 2 (1hr 30min) Starting just before the Sam Poh Temple below Brinchang, it's not clearly marked and is often a bit of a scramble. The route undulates severely and eventually joins Path 3.

TANAH RATA

★**Bunga Suria** Persiaran Camellia 3 ☎05 491 4666. Cheap and cheerful South Indian establishment, good for *thosai*, self-service *nasi campur*, great samosas and banana *lassi*, and local breakfasts like half-boiled eggs and *kaya* toast. Daily 24hr.

Cameron AA Curry House Corner Jalan Besar and Lorong Perdah ☎05 491 4409. A bright, convivial restaurant that snares a lot of tourist trade and which, despite the name, majors in Western food – the curries are clearly overpriced. The pizzas are decent (medium ones will feed two; from RM20), and steaks, omelettes and pasta bakes are also popular. Breakfasts too. Daily 7am–midnight.

Ferm Nyonya 78a–d Persiaran Camellia 4 ☎05 491 5891. Nyonya and Chinese home cooking, including *kerabu* (spicy salad of shredded vegetables with lime juice and chillies), fish with tamarind and, of course, steamboat. Mains from RM10. Daily noon–10pm.

Jungle Bar Kang Travellers Lodge (Daniel's Lodge), 9 Lorong Perdah ☎05 491 5823, ⓦkangholiday.com. With a pool table and fireplace, this backpacker's watering hole is a great hangout when busy, although it can be dead some nights – perhaps because it's so discreetly tucked away at the back of the guesthouse. Daily roughly 7pm–midnight.

Kumar 26 Jalan Besar ☎05 491 2624. Brighter and brasher than the copycat place next door, and popular with backpackers especially for reasonably priced banana-leaf meals and *nasi campur*, along with tandoori chicken, fresh *nan* bread and even Chinese claypot dishes. Around RM12. Daily 7am–10pm.

Travellers Bistro & Pub 68a Persiaran Camellia 3 ☎05 491 3666. Tanah Rata's sole attempt to emulate a city bar doesn't exactly nail it, but at least it's there for a tipple in vaguely shiny surroundings. Iffy acoustic cover sessions most evenings. Daily 6pm–midnight.

BETWEEN TANAH RATA AND BRINCHANG

The Smokehouse Route 59, between Tanah Rata and Brinchang ☎05 491 1215. If you feel a visit to the Camerons isn't complete without pukka English food, head here for roasts (beef Wellington RM95; duck and lamb are available too) or cream teas (with quality jam and cream; 11am–6pm; RM30). They also do a full breakfast (until 11am; RM55) – and this is one of very few pricey hotels left in Malaysia that still serves pork

2

Path 3 (2hr 30min) Starts at Arcadia Cottage southeast of the golf course, crossing streams and climbing quite steeply to reach the peak of Gunung Beremban (1841m). Once at the top, you can retrace your steps, or head down via paths 5, 7 or 8.

Path 4 (20min) Paved in stretches, this walk starts south of the golf course and goes past Parit Waterfall, then on to the Forestry Office (Pejabat Hutan), where a sealed path leads back to the main road.

Path 5 (1hr) Branches off from Path 3 at the rain shelter – a little gazebo – and ends up at the Malaysian Agriculture Research and Development Institute (MARDI). From here the road, Persiaran Dayang Indah, takes you into Tanah Rata just north of the bus station.

Path 6 (2hr) From the Forestry Office on Path 4, this branches away to the rain shelter.

Path 7 (2hr) Starts near MARDI and climbs steeply to Gunung Beremban; an arduous and overgrown hike better done as a descent from Path 3.

Path 8 (2hr 30min) Another route to Gunung Beremban. From Tanah Rata, head up Persiaran Dayang Indah, ignore the MARDI turning on the left, and then turn right up a paved path for Robinson Waterfall. Just before the waterfall, turn left and you're on Path 8. Even more taxing than Path 7.

Path 9 As Path 8 initially, except that you head all the way to Robinson Waterfall (20min). You then descend to the access road to the Boh tea plantation, although there's a choice of routes. **Path 9B** (45min) is the direct, steep option via the hydropower station, where you may have to ask staff to let you through to the Boh road. **Path 9A** (1hr) curls away from it and descends more gently, though note that the last part is overgrown, so many people turn right here on to an easier trail to a vegetable farm, after which the track joins the path down to the Boh Road.

Path 10 (3hr) Beginning at the back of Tan's Camellia Garden in Tanah Rata (see p.175), this involves a fairly strenuous climb to Gunung Jasar (1696m), descending northeast to an electricity substation, where a small road leads back to Route 59.

Gunung Irau (sometimes called **Path 14**; 3hr) The ascent of Irau, the Highlands' highest peak (2110m), commences at the end of Gunung Brinchang's Mossy Forest walkway (take a taxi up rather than attempting this as an extension of Path 1). You return the way you came. The most demanding trail of all, it's best not done alone, and an early start is advisable as people often get lost when the light fades in the late afternoon.

bacon and sausages. There's an atmospheric pub section (from 6.30pm). Daily 7.30am–11pm.

BRINCHANG

Cameron Organic Jalan Angsana 📞05 491 4807. Down-to-earth eating place popular for its steamboats which, unusually, come with either chicken or vegetable stock and really do use organic local produce. Daily 11am–9pm.

DIRECTORY

TANAH RATA

Banks It's easy to find banks with ATMs on and just off the main road in both Tanah Rata and Brinchang.

Hospital Persiaran Dayang Indah (📞05 491 1966). Dr Ayob also runs a clinic on the main road (📞05 491 1654).

Fu Guang Jalan Angsana. A tiny Chinese vegetarian place serving ridiculously cheap one-plate rice and noodle dishes, including a spicy prawn noodle soup that will blow your head off. Daily 8am–3pm & 5–8pm.

OK Tuck 26 Jalan Besar 📞05 491 2380. Busy Chinese place with an extensive menu, including excellent black vinegar sparerib and fried prawns. Mains around RM10. Daily 11am–9pm.

Pharmacy There's a branch of Watsons just a 5min walk from the centre of Tanah Rata, beyond the *Century Pines Resort*.

Police station Jalan Besar (📞05 491 1222).

The interior

185 Taman Negara: Kuala Tahan

200 Kenong Rimba State Park

203 Kuala Lipis

205 Merapoh (Sungai Relau)

206 Gua Musang

207 Kuala Koh

208 Stong State Park (Jelawang Jungle)

CANOPY WALKWAY, TAMAN NEGARA

The interior

Peninsular Malaysia's interior comprises a vast swathe of territory, stretching northeast of Kuala Lumpur all the way up to Kota Bharu on the east coast. Until recent times this was a remote region of steep, limestone peaks with knife-edge ridges and luxuriant valleys inhabited by Orang Asli groups. Colonial administrator Hugh Clifford described the terrain in the 1880s as "smothered in deep, damp forest, threaded across a network of streams and rivers". Indeed, rivers were the sole means of transportation until prospectors and planters opened the interior up through the twentieth century; companies built the earliest roads and a railway arrived in the 1920s, helping to establish the towns of Temerloh, Gua Musang and Kuala Lipis.

Much of the interior has now been logged, settled and tamed, though Clifford's deep, damp forests survive in the dense chunk of undeveloped jungle that is **Taman Negara** (literally "National Park"). Gazetted as Malaysia's **first national park** in 1925 and covering 4343 square kilometres, Taman Negara forms the largest tract of rainforest in Peninsular Malaysia; it contains some of the **oldest rainforest** in the world, which has evolved over 130 million years as a home for a fabulous array of wildlife. Some of the Peninsula's fifteen hundred **Batek** Orang Asli live here too, many as hunter-gatherers; the park authorities generally turn a blind eye to their hunting game.

Reached via the transport nexus of **Jerantut**, Taman Negara's main entry point, the riverside town of **Kuala Tahan** is the trailhead for jungle hikes lasting from anywhere from a few minutes to two weeks. With so much to see here, it's easy to overlook the rest of the region, but outside the park you can ride the Jungle Railway north through the interior, touching on lesser known sections of wilds – caves and waterfalls at **Kenong Rimba State Park**; remoter areas of Taman Negara at **Merapoh** and **Kuala Koh**; and more forest, waterfalls and views at **Stong State Park**.

GETTING AROUND

THE INTERIOR

By bus Buses along Route 8 and the East Coast Highway can get you within range of all the main sights, but remoter corners require the help of your own vehicle, taxis or local tour operators.

By car Route 8, the interior's main artery, runs for 500km from Bentong near KL to Kota Bharu. It's a relatively old road, not a multilane highway, so expect to be periodically slowed behind ponderous lorries. The quickest way to reach Route 8 from KL is the E8 (the Karak Highway), a roller coaster of a road that careers northeast from KL through the foothills of the Genting Highlands. Expect a few thrilling, cambered descents – and be warned that there are often nasty accidents, too.

The Orang Asli p.185
Planning a visit to Taman Negara p.187
The Kuala Gandah elephant sanctuary p.189
Taman Negara packages p.191
Kuala Tahan activities p.192
Hiking at Kuala Tahan p.195
Kuala Tahan hides (blinds) p.195
The Jungle Railway p.201

SUNGAI TAHAN

Highlights

❶ Taman Negara via Kuala Tahan The Peninsula's largest and oldest nature reserve offers river trips, hikes and wildlife spotting amid a swathe of ancient rainforest, best visited via the park headquarters at Kuala Tahan. **See p.185**

❷ Kenong Rimba State Park A barely developed reserve adjoining Taman Negara, offering its own trekking and animal spotting opportunities. **See p.200**

❸ The Jungle Railway Ride the train across the interior past country villages, oil-palm plantations, and – between Kuala Lipis and Gua Musang – patches of rainforest. **See p.201**

❹ Taman Negara via Kuala Koh Though isolated, Kuala Koh is worth the effort of reaching: this is Kuala Tahan in miniature, rewarding visitors with trails, river excursions and a canopy walkway. **See p.207**

❺ Stong State Park In the interior of Kelantan state, Stong boasts a picturesque waterfall, good mountain trekking and a marvellous jungle camp. **See p.208**

HIGHLIGHTS ARE MARKED ON THE MAP ON P.184

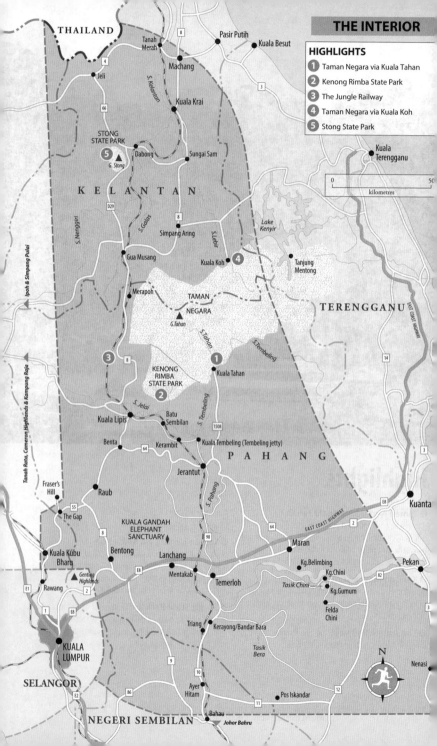

THE ORANG ASLI

The twentieth-century spread of the timber, rubber and palm oil industries through the interior had a huge impact upon the region's **Orang Asli**, who were traditionally nomadic peoples living by hunting and slash-and-burn agriculture. These days many have been forced to settle down, existing at the fringes of the cash economy. The mountain-dwelling **Temiar**, for instance, trade in forest products such as herbal medicines and, increasingly, **timber** (though their logging activities are minimal compared with those of the State Forestry Department). Some **Batek** do still live fairly traditional lives at Taman Negara, where you might meet shy groups walking in single file along trails, or come across their temporary vine-and-forest-brush shelters in jungle clearings.

However, three-quarters of Orang Asli peoples (including many local Batek, **Senoi** and **Semang**) live below the poverty line, compared to less than a tenth of the population as a whole. That fact makes it all the harder for them to confront the many forces, from planning agencies to Christian and Muslim groups, who seek to influence their destiny. The issue of **land rights** is among their gravest problems, for while the country's Aboriginal People's Act has led to the creation of Orang Asli reserves, at the same time many Asli traditional areas have been gazetted as state land, rendering the inhabitants there, at best, tolerated guests of the government.

3

Taman Negara: Kuala Tahan

The main gateway to Taman Negara, the town of **Kuala Tahan**, 250km northeast of KL, is where you'll find the **national park headquarters** and the pick of its visitor facilities. It's also where to get your bearings and seek advice before crossing the Sungai Tembeling and heading into the forest: well-marked **trails** include an easy boardwalk stroll to a popular **canopy walkway**; tougher day-treks out to waterfalls and hides overlooking salt licks in the jungle; or the seven-day return ascent of **Gunung Tahan**, Peninsular Malaysia's highest peak, involving steep climbs and river crossings. If you've never been inside tropical rainforest before, just listening to the bird, insect and animal sounds, marvelling at the sheer size of the trees and peering into the tangled understorey of flowering lianas, luminous fungi and giant bamboo is a memorable experience. You don't have to go far to encounter **wildlife** either; monkeys, elephant, tapir, seladang (wild oxen) and a host of smaller creatures can be found – with a dash of luck – within minutes of Kuala Tahan's park headquarters. And if you're not a hard-core hiker or wildlife spotter, you can take advantage of opportunities for a river swim, low-key rafting or angling.

Kuala Tahan is reached via the service town of **Jerantut**, or – increasingly – directly on minibuses from the Cameron Highlands or the Pulau Perhentian jetty at Kuala Besut. It's also possible to enter Taman Negara further north at **Merapoh** (see p.205) and **Kuala Koh** (see p.207) – or even to hike to either from Kuala Tahan in a week-long traverse of the park. Both require more effort to reach and have fewer facilities, but they're also less crowded than Kuala Tahan – though not necessarily easier places to see wildlife.

Jerantut

In bustling **JERANTUT**, 70km south of Kuala Tahan, road, rail and river converge on a small grid of streets. Activity revolves around the central, open-air **bus station**, set among market stalls, with the **train station** 500m west and **Tembeling Jetty**, for traffic upriver to Kuala Tahan, a short taxi ride north. And that's about it; the town is just somewhere to find last-minute supplies and top up with **cash**, as there are no banks at Kuala Tahan.

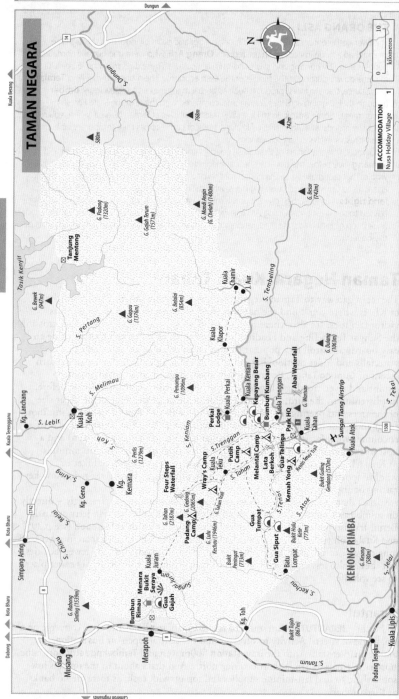

TAMAN NEGARA

ACCOMMODATION
Nusa Holiday Village 1

PLANNING A VISIT TO TAMAN NEGARA

Given that tropical rainforest is always sodden, the **driest** time of year is between February and mid-October, with the **peak tourist season** roughly from May to August – make sure you book ahead. Mid-November to mid-January is extremely **wet**, and movement within the park can be restricted as paths are submerged and rivers flood. Usually, however, most of the park's **trails** require no more than an average level of fitness, though of course longer trails require some stamina. Some essential **camping and trekking gear** (see p.47) is available to buy at Jerantut, or to rent at Kuala Tahan, but take your own if possible.

Campsites are scattered through the park; they have absolutely no facilities at all, though most are close to rivers where you can wash. There's a small fee for hides and campsites (see below), payable at the national park office, where you can also reserve bunks in hides.

To **budget** for your trip, remember that for any trek involving overnighting in the forest (other than in a hide close to a park office, or accessible by boat), you must hire a guide. It's generally more cost-effective to arrange guides through outside operators than through the park headquarters, although the latter may be preferable if you would like a guide with a particular area of expertise. The fees for guides and boat excursions are the only substantial outlays you'll face, as inexpensive accommodation, eating and transport options are easy to find.

FEES AND CHARGES

The following fees apply to all sections of Taman Negara:

Park entry	RM1/person
Camping permit	RM1/person/night
Camera licence	RM5/camera
Fishing licence	RM10/rod
Use of hides or fishing lodges	RM5–8/person
Guide hire	Around RM180/day, plus RM100 for overnighting

GETTING AROUND THE PARK

If you simply need to **cross the river** from Kuala Tahan, you can take one of the small wooden boats (daily dawn–11pm; RM1) that cross on demand from Kuala Tahan's floating restaurants to the jetty below the resort and national park headquarters. Put your fare in the tin by the ferryman.

Aside from trekking, **wooden longboats** seating four to ten people are the only way to get around Taman Negara from Kuala Tahan; you can use them like a taxi service to reach distant trekking trails, or speed your return journey after a long hike. Boats might wait for you or, more likely, return at an agreed time; don't expect them to hang around indefinitely if you are late. Book through the national park office; prices are the same for single or return trips.

Destination	Cost	Destination	Cost
Blau/Yong hides	RM80	Kuala Trenggan	RM120
Canopy walkway	RM60	Lata Berkoh	RM160
Gua Telinga	RM60	Lubok Lesong	RM100
Kuala Keniam	RM300		
Kuala Keniam Kecil	RM650	Nusa Camp	RM90
Kuala Perkai (for Perkai Lodge)	RM480	Tabing/Cegar Anjing hides	RM60

ARRIVAL AND DEPARTURE

JERANTUT

From Jerantut, you can reach Kuala Tahan by bus (1hr 45min) or by boat (2hr 30min).

By train Jerantut is on the Jungle Railway (see p.201); there is one circuitous, midnight service a day to KL and an overnight one from Singapore, but it's faster and more convenient to take the bus.

Destinations Dabong (2 daily; 4hr 20min); Gua Musang (2 daily; 3hr); Johor Bahru (1 daily; 8hr); Kuala Lipis (2 daily; 1hr); Kuala Lumpur (1 daily; 7hr 45min); Singapore (1 daily; 10hr); Wakaf Bharu (for Kota Bharu; 2 daily; 7hr).

By bus There are two separate bus bays – helpful staff will quickly point you to the right one. An hourly service for Kuala Tahan (7am–7pm) was planned at the time of research. For Tembeling Jetty, take a bus towards Kuala Lipis and ask to be let off near the jetty.

Destinations Kota Bharu (1 daily; 8hr); Kuala Lipis (3 daily;

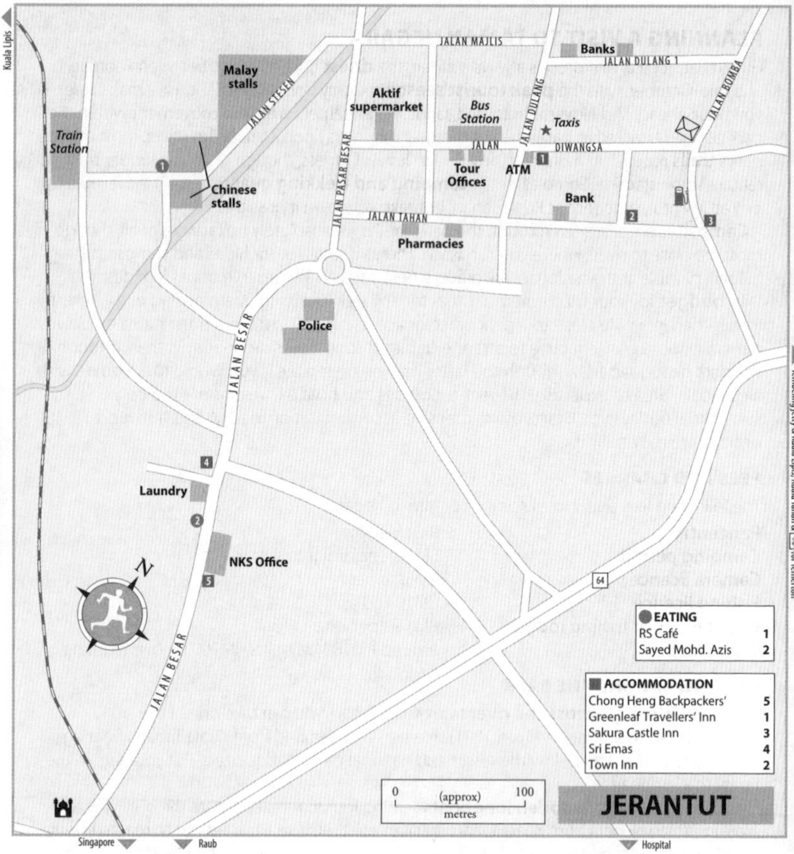
Kuala Lipis
JALAN MAJLIS
Banks
JALAN DULANG 1
JALAN BOMBA
Malay stalls
JALAN STESEN
Aktif supermarket
Bus Station
JALAN DULANG
Taxis
Train Station
JALAN PASAR BESAR
JALAN DIWANGSA
Tour Offices
ATM
Chinese stalls
Bank
JALAN TAHAN
Pharmacies
Police
JALAN BESAR
Laundry
NKS Office
N
64
EATING
RS Café 1
Sayed Mohd. Azis 2
ACCOMMODATION
Chong Heng Backpackers' 5
Greenleaf Travellers' Inn 1
Sakura Castle Inn 3
Sri Emas 4
Town Inn 2
0 (approx) 100 metres
JERANTUT
Singapore
Raub
Hospital

1hr 30min); Kuala Lumpur (hourly 7am–8pm; 3hr 30min); Kuala Tahan (8am & 1.30pm; 1hr 45min); Kuantan (3 daily; 3hr); Tembeling Jetty (3 daily; 40min).

By taxi Taxis from the bus station run to Tembeling Jetty (RM26), Kuala Tahan (RM70) and various east coast destinations; it's RM200 to Kuantan, or RM440 to Kota Bharu.

By boat Boating up to Kuala Tahan on the muddy Sungai Tembeling takes in age-old rainforest lining both banks and the ride, in motorized ten-seater sampans, is an essential part of the Taman Negara experience – though you may prefer to take the faster return trip downstream. Boats to Kuala Tahan (Mon–Thurs, Sat & Sun 9am & 2pm, Fri 9am & 2.30pm; 2hr 30min; RM35 one way) depart from Tembeling Jetty, 17km north of Jerantut; catch a local bus (RM2) or taxi (RM30). Tickets can be purchased at NKS in Jerantut or the NKS and Han Travel desks at the jetty.

ACCOMMODATION

★**Chong Heng Backpackers'** Jalan Besar ☎09 266 3693 or ☎013 963 6019. A 1930s shophouse converted to a simple hostel, with tidy partitioned rooms and shared facilities. The kindly owner, Tan, is a great source of information on the area, and runs a café and fishing supplies shop downstairs. No wi-fi. Fan doubles RM20

Greenleaf Travellers' Inn Jalan Diwangsa ☎09 267 2131, greenleaf-tamannegara.com. A homely backpackers' place, with dorm beds and a variety of unexciting rooms with a/c and shared bathrooms. They also run package tours into the park and non-guests can shower and get online for RM3/person. Dorms RM10, doubles RM25

Sakura Castle Inn Jalan Tahan ☎09 266 6200. A decent mid-range option not far from the bus station. The en-suite rooms with a/c are spacious and clean, if occasionally smoky – it's popular with local business travellers. RM55

Sri Emas 21–22 Jalan Besar ☎09 260 1779, taman-negara-nks.com. Part of the NKS empire (see p.191), shipping backpackers to and from Taman Negara every day as though on a conveyor belt. Besides dorms, there are rooms with fan or a/c, some en suite and with TV. Everything's well run, if a little shabby, with laundry service and fast internet. Dorms RM8, en-suite a/c doubles RM48

Town Inn Jalan Tahan ☎09 266 6811, ⓦtowninn-hotel.com. A friendly mid-range hotel in a big block of a building. The comfortable, boxy rooms come with a/c, bathroom and TV. RM55

EATING

During the day, open-air **food courts** either side of the train station access road serve inexpensive pan-Asian dishes.

RS Café Jalan Stesen ☎09 266 1230. This cool little Chinese-run café serves up the standard range of noodle and rice dishes (RM5–8), with icy desserts and a range of beers on tap (from RM9). Daily 2pm–1am.

Sayed Mohd. Aziz Jalan Besar. Good *roti canai*, decent curries and *nasi lemak*, all for under RM10. Daily breakfast & dinner.

DIRECTORY

Banks There are banks with ATMs along Jalan Tahan and Jalan Dulang 1.
Camping and hiking gear Numerous stores opposite the bus station on Jalan Diwangsa sell day packs, rubber shoes, canvas track shoes and flashlights; check the quality

before buying, especially stitching and straps on packs.
Laundry 200m southwest of centre on Jalan Besar.
Pharmacy Jalan Tahan holds two well-stocked pharmacies.
Supermarkets Aktif supermarket, west of the bus bays, is the place to stock up for the park.

3

Kuala Tahan

Around 70km north of Jerantut, **KUALA TAHAN** is a knot of guesthouses and floating restaurants facing a solid green wall of jungle across the turbid, 50m-wide **Sungai Tembeling**. As a base, it has many virtues: reasonable transport connections, plenty of accommodation, a few stores selling (and renting) basics, and even mobile coverage, though there are **no banks** or ATMs. Most importantly, the **national park headquarters** – where you can pick up information, register and pay park fees (see p.190) – is a quick ferry ride over the river at the start of the park's **hiking trails**. Take a torch when wandering around the village after dark, as **electricity** can be flaky.

In December 2014 Kuala Tahan was hit by record **floods**, which saw many riverside restaurants and several of the smaller guesthouses destroyed. At the time of going to print it was unclear which businesses would reopen; call ahead to check.

ARRIVAL AND DEPARTURE

KUALA TAHAN

By bus Buses drop at a roadside shelter on the edge of Kuala Tahan, a 5min walk from the river. Hourly buses to Jerantut

were planned at the time of research, which would replace the twice-daily existing service (10am & 3pm; 1hr 45min).

THE KUALA GANDAH ELEPHANT SANCTUARY

One attraction in the southern part of the interior worth making a diversion for is the **Kuala Gandah Elephant Conservation Centre** (Mon–Fri 8am–4.30pm, Sat & Sun 9am–4.30pm; donations appreciated; ☎013 908 8207, ⓦwildlife.gov.my). Here staff from the Wildlife Department care for elephants being relocated to reserves from areas of habitat destruction, or which had to be sedated while *mengamuk* – a Malay term that would be untranslatable were it not the origin of the English word "amok". The best time to turn up is 2pm (2.45pm on Friday), when for a couple of hours visitors have the chance to get hands-on with the elephants, feeding or bathing them. Numbers are limited for bathing, though it's possible to book your spot (RM30 guide fee/group, plus RM10/participant) up to three days in advance. The centre gets very crowded on weekends and holidays – visit midweek if possible.

Driving Route E8 east from KL, turn north at **Lanchang**, about 70km along, for the twenty-minute drive to the sanctuary. **Day-trips** are offered **from Kuala Lumpur** by NKS (ⓦtaman-negara-nks.com) and Han Travel (ⓦtaman-negara.com); and **from Jerantut** through Greenleaf Holidays (ⓦgreenleaf-tamannegara.com; RM160/person).

By minibus Several tour operators run minibuses between Kuala Tahan and regional tourist destinations. Prices vary little between operators, usually with a single morning departure.

Destinations Jerantut (1hr 30min; RM25); Kota Bharu (8hr; RM100); Kuala Besut (for Perhentian islands; 7hr; RM90); Kuala Lumpur (5hr; RM70); Tanah Rata (for Cameron Highlands; 6hr; RM85).

By boat Arriving boats deposit passengers at the park jetty, where steps lead up to the sprawling *Mutiara Taman Negara Resort* and park headquarters, or among the floating restaurants on the shingle beach opposite, with Kuala Tahan village on the bank above. Tickets downstream to Tembeling (Sat–Thurs 9am & 2pm, Fri 9am & 2.30pm; RM35) can be purchased the day before your journey at the Han Travel (*Mama Chop Restaurant*) or NKS (*Wan Café*) jetties. In low season, afternoon departures may be curtailed; to avoid any nasty surprises, double-check with the boat operator the day before. Once at the Tembeling jetty, catch a bus, minibus (RM5) or taxi (RM30) to Jerantut.

By car The road to Kuala Tahan, Route 1508, branches north off Route 64 10km east of Jerantut. From KL, leave the East Coast Highway at Temerloh, heading up Route 98 for Jerantut, then pick up Route 64 eastwards for the Kuala Tahan Rd. From Kuantan, pick up Route 64 at Maran.

INFORMATION

National Park Headquarters An essential first port of call to pay the nominal entry fee, pick up a map and check the latest trail conditions (Sat–Thurs 8am–6pm, Fri 8am–noon & 3–6pm; ☎ 09 266 1122, ⊛ wildlife.gov .my). You can also book hides (see p.195) and activity packages, charter boats and hire guides. Make sure you check the whiteboard, where sightings of interesting creatures are listed; for the record, there are about fifty tigers in Taman Negara, with some three or four sightings per year, usually deep in the forest (many national park staff have never seen one).

Guides If you have a specialist interest, call the headquarters a week in advance to see if a guide with matching knowledge can be arranged. Being trained by the Wildlife Department, the guides are generally better on fauna than flora, though many are experts on neither. As the most important component of their training is knowledge of the trails, they may fall short when it comes to more general skills, such as offering support in the event of a mishap.

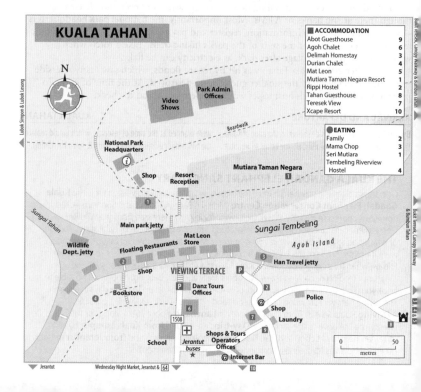

KUALA TAHAN

N

■ ACCOMMODATION	
Abot Guesthouse	9
Agoh Chalet	6
Delimah Homestay	3
Durian Chalet	4
Mat Leon	5
Mutiara Taman Negara Resort	1
Rippi Hostel	2
Tahan Guesthouse	8
Teresek View	7
Xcape Resort	10

● EATING	
Family	2
Mama Chop	3
Seri Mutiara	1
Tembeling Riverview Hostel	4

Video Shows

Park Admin Offices

Boardwalk

National Park Headquarters

Shop   Resort Reception

Mutiara Taman Negara

Main park jetty

Sungai Tahan

Wildlife Dept. jetty

Floating Restaurants

Mat Leon Store

Sungai Tembeling

Agoh Island

Han Travel jetty

Shop   VIEWING TERRACE

Bookstore

Danz Tours Offices

Police

Shop

Laundry

1508

Jerantut buses

School

Shops & Tours Operators Offices

@ Internet Bar

0   50
metres

Lubok Simpon & Lubok Lesong

Bukit Teresek, Canopy Walkway & Gunung Tahan

Boat Teresek, Canopy Walkway & Bumbun Tahan

TAMAN NEGARA PACKAGES

Though it's easy enough to travel to Kuala Tahan and explore Taman Negara independently – the most inexpensive and flexible way to arrange things – many visitors book themselves on a convenient **package trip**. These typically comprise two or three nights at Kuala Tahan with a range of accommodation and meal options, and possibly activities such as walks and boat excursions as well; expect to pay upwards of RM350/person.

The most established operators, **NKS** (W taman-negara-nks.com) and **Han Travel** (W taman-negara.com), have offices in KL and at the Tembeling jetty. Both have dedicated restaurants in Kuala Tahan, and NKS also runs the *Sri Emas Hotel* in Jerantut. Jerantut-based agents include **Danz Travel** (W tamannegara-danz.com) and **Greenleaf Holidays** (W greenleaf-tamannegara.com).

If you're using one of the expensive but convenient minibus **transfers** to Kuala Tahan, your journey will typically feature a stop at the tour company offices. Despite what you may be told, there's no need to book park accommodation or day-trips through the same company; simply shop around once you've arrived or call ahead.

3

ACCOMMODATION

Almost all accommodation is in the village of Kuala Tahan itself, with the exception of the *Mutiara* resort on the opposite bank, and a couple of places upriver. Book in advance, especially during the peak season (May–August). Several guesthouses have facilities for camping, and at the time of research there was a **campsite** (☏ 017 924 4202) on mid-river Agoh Island, though the island's size and usage vary from one year to the next, thanks to the monsoon floods. Should you wish to **overnight in the forest**, the best option is to use one of **five hides** (see p.195); these sleep up to twelve people in bare wooden bunks (bring your own bedding), and some have tank water and toilets.

Abot Guesthouse At the top of the hill from the bus stop ☏ 017 916 9616. New, low-set house with ten sparklingly clean en-suite rooms in two blocks, all with a/c. Light sleepers should avoid rooms facing the road from the bus stop. RM90

Agoh Chalet Up the river road from the bus stop ☏ 09 266 9570, W agoh.com.my. Initially unpromising, with a shaded lawn ringed by concrete chalets textured to look like wood, but the good-value rooms are clean and come with a/c and attached shower. The friendly staff are slowly redecorating and the rooms they've finished are nicest. RM60

★**Delimah Homestay** A 5min walk past Teresek View, just below the mosque ☏ 019 996 5263. A cosy bungalow with just three en-suite rooms, presided over by the cheery Delimah. The spotless double rooms have hot water, a/c and mosquito nets; breakfast and complimentary hot drinks are included. RM90

★**Durian Chalet** A 10min walk past Teresek View, down a steep hill and through a small stand of rubber trees ☏ 014 212 7151. Brightly painted double rooms and chalets with mosquito nets and shack-like bathrooms, clustered around a pretty hillside garden with a teeming fishpond – a great place to get away from it all. Breakfast available but not included. Doubles RM40, chalets RM60

Mat Leon Reception at their floating store in Kuala Tahan; accommodation in a forest clearing above the river, 2km upstream past Tahan Guesthouse ☏ 013 998 9517, W matleon.com. Metal-roofed bamboo chalets with simple furnishings, cell-like bathrooms and breakfast,

plus a few newer a/c chalets and a small canteen. It's nice out here, but a bit isolated when occupancy is low. Dorms RM15, fan chalets RM60, a/c chalets RM180

★**Mutiara Taman Negara Resort** In front of the national park headquarters, across the river from Kuala Tahan ☏ 09 266 3500, W mutiarahotels.com. Busy three-star resort occupying a strip of land between the river and forest, mostly comprising a/c chalets with spacious bathrooms, woven bamboo walls, cane furniture and jungle or river views. There's also an expensive, institutional dorm with bunk beds. Boat transfers to and from Tembeling can be arranged for a fee. Buffet breakfast included. Dorm RM80, chalets RM490

Nusa Holiday Village Around 15min upstream by boat ☏ 09 266 2369, W tamannegara-nusaholiday .com.my. Accommodation at this SPKG-run riverside resort ranges from fan-cooled dorms with shared facilities to en-suite "Malay-style" houses, with cane furniture, netted windows and a/c. Their tours receive good reports and there's a decent restaurant, though you'll need to budget a few ringgit extra/day to shuttle to and from the park HQ. Dorms RM20, doubles RM160

Rippi Hostel On the river road ☏ 012 901 2793. A popular backpackers' hostel run by trekking guides, offering a collection of down-at-heel dorms with shared facilities and no frills. Overlooking the floating restaurants, the hostel balcony is a popular evening hangout, and they run their own budget treks and tours. Dorms RM10

Tahan Guesthouse Walk uphill from the bus stop, turn left at the top and right 50m further on, and it's

2min along on the right ☎ 017 970 2025. Well-kept two-storey affair, brightly painted with wildlife murals. Accommodation comprises en-suite twins and doubles, all fan-cooled with mosquito nets and squat toilets; the double rooms have small balconies. The only downside is the proximity of the mosque at 5.30am. RM50

Teresek View Motel Up the hill from the bus stop, on the left ☎ 09 266 9744, ✉ teresekviewmotel@gmail .com. A large pale pink motel-like place with lurid but comfy en-suite rooms (some with a/c) on two floors. It's well run, too; you won't envy staff trying to keep the place free of muddy footprints. Fan doubles RM70, a/c doubles RM90

Xcape Resort Just south of Kuala Tahan ☎ 09 266 1111, ⊛ xcape.com.my. One of a handful of incongruous developments in this area, with regimented rows of chalets. The rooms are characterless but do pack in the creature comforts – a/c, TV, fridge and modern bathroom. The indigo-tiled swimming pool is probably the best feature. Rates include breakfast. RM160

EATING

Most visitors gravitate towards the row of ten or so floating, glorified **kedai kopis** moored beside the shingle beach. Opening around 8am and not closing until well into the evening, the restaurants offer the usual rice and noodle dishes, plus Western travellers' favourites including pancakes, sandwiches and milk shakes. The establishments we review are the most popular, but other places often serve similar food at lower cost. If you're in town on a Wednesday, head to the **night market** (6–8pm), 3km back towards Jerantut, for some variety; stallholders cook up *murtabak* and *apam balik* (crispy peanut pancakes) among other treats. If you're in need of a drink, you could try the bar in the *Xcape Resort* car park; alcohol is also served at the *Seri Mutiara*.

Family On the river. With its clear view of the river, bamboo roll-up blinds and potted orchids, it's easy to see why this place is constantly packed with Western visitors. They don't like solo diners, however, and in the evening, and staff can be quite abrupt. Mains RM10. Daily 8am–2pm & 6–9pm.

KUALA TAHAN ACTIVITIES

Most people who are in the park for just a few days sign up for various **activity packages** offered through Kuala Tahan guesthouses and tour operators. Many operators work together – you might book onto one company's trip, only to find yourself tagging along with another (often larger) group – if in doubt, clarify before you book.

SHORT TRIPS

Night jungle walks (1hr 30min; RM25; bring your own torch) are easy and, despite being crowded and held along the park's most heavily used paths, can turn up everything from tapirs to scorpions; the sharp-eyed guides invariably spot camouflaged creatures you'd otherwise miss.
Night safaris (2hr; RM40) actually take place outside the park; you're driven around a plantation in a 4WD, and may get to see leopard cats, wild pigs, civets and the occasional snake.
Orang Asli village visit (2hr; RM45) shows you how to use a blowpipe and fire-making using sticks at a semi-permanent Batek encampment; very touristy, but interesting too.

RIVER TRIPS AND FISHING

Rapids shooting trips (2hr; RM40), taking place a few kilometres upstream, are fairly tame, designed to appeal to families rather than hard-core rafters; you'll ride this stretch anyway if you catch a boat back from Kuala Trenggan (see p.196).
Night river safaris (2hr; RM45) uses a tamer stretch of water, where you often see larger animals along the riverside.
Fishing The most popular area is the Sungai Keniam, northeast of Kuala Tahan, where you can hope to catch catfish or snakehead; all fish must be returned. The very basic *Perkai Fishing Lodge*, around 2hr upstream from Kuala Tahan, is a popular base; a boat there costs RM480.

LONGER TRIPS

Guided forest walks The best have you staying overnight at a hide – Bumbun Kumbang is a favourite (see p.196) or cave; you usually make your way down to the river on the second day and catch a boat back to Kuala Tahan. This far into the forest you really might see anything – or nothing at all. Prices depend on numbers, duration and destination, but expect to pay at least RM200/person for an all-inclusive two-day, one-night trip.

Mama Chop On the river. Housing the Han Travel headquarters means that *Mama Chop* has a captive audience of visitors waiting to begin tours, enabling them to charge high prices for average food and lacklustre service. Though it's open all day, it can be hard to get served outside main meal times. Mains around RM10. Daily 8am–9pm or later.

★ **Seri Mutiara** Beside the Mutiara resort ☎ 09 266 2200, ⊚ mutiarahotels.com. This smart, open-sided dining room in the jungle is well worth a splurge if you've been out in the wilds for a few days. The menu is geared to Taman Negara's better-heeled Malay and Western guests – pizza, *nasi lemak*, prawn *sambal*, T-bone steak, *rendang* – and the relatively steep prices reflect this, though a coffee and slice of black forest gateau will only set you back RM20 or so. Around RM85 for a full meal. Daily 8am–2pm & 6–9pm.

Tembeling Riverview Hostel From the bus stop, take the road to the river, turn left and it's just downhill ☎ 09 266 6766. The attached guesthouse may not be great, but the restaurant is well located and popular with trekking guides – perhaps because it's the only place in town that serves *roti canai* (RM3). Daily 8am–11pm.

DIRECTORY

Books There's a small secondhand bookstore on your right as you enter the grounds of *Tembeling Riverview Hostel*.

Camping and trekking gear Mat Leon's floating store rents out well-worn sleeping bags and mats, canvas jungle boots, tents, mosquito nets, backpacks, flashlights and gas stoves, as does the bookstore in the *Tembeling Riverview Hostel*, the daily charge being slightly lower at the latter (RM5/day for a sleeping bag), though you'll need to leave a deposit. Minimarts around town sell torches, batteries, rubber ankle boots and day packs; a few places near the bus stop sell dry bags.

Internet Wi-fi is available at most of the mid-range guesthouses in Kuala Tahan, but if you can't get online at your accommodation, try the netbar opposite *Teresek View* or Junglewalla's offices (both RM6/hr).

Supplies Kuala Tahan's minimarts (roughly 8am–10pm), sell water, biscuits and snacks, tinned sardines, soft drinks, ice cream, insect repellent and toothpaste. Across the river the only store is a pricey one attached to the *Mutiara Taman Negara Resort*.

Day treks

Cross the river and turn right at the national park headquarters, and you're at the start of most of the **hiking trails** that spread into the park. Popular and easy places to visit close to the park headquarters include **Bukit Teresek**; the **canopy walkway**, where you can observe treetop jungle life close up; and the waterfall at **Lata Berkoh** (following the first part of the trail there is a good way to kill a couple of spare hours). You could feasibly tackle two, perhaps three, of these in a day.

Bukit Teresek

2.5km one way from the park headquarters; 1hr

Although it's the most heavily used trail in the park, the route to the summit of **Bukit Teresek** (342m) is an excellent starter trek, taking about an hour in each direction along a boardwalk. Heading northeast away from the river, the trail passes an impressive stand of **giant bamboo** before ascending Bukit Teresek itself via a steep series of fibreglass **steps**; if you haven't already noticed the sauna-like conditions, you will now. The clanking of your shoes against the fibreglass is enough to scare off most wildlife, so content yourself with the promise of views – though the clearing at the top is partially screened by trees. Continue along the hilltop for another fifteen minutes to reach the so-called **second view**, where on clear days you can get marvellous vistas north over the valley to 2187m-high **Gunung Tahan** (see p.198) and smaller Gunung Gedong. Return the way you came and the canopy walkway will be just 300m to the south along a clearly marked path, or make the more challenging descent from the second view to the side of Sungai Tahan, from where you can loop back to the park headquarters (3km; 90min).

Canopy walkway

Sat–Thurs 9.30am–3.30pm, Fri 9am–noon; closed during rain or if lightning is likely; numbers are limited, so waits possible • RM5

About thirty minutes' walk from the national park office along the boardwalk, the **canopy walkway** is one of Taman Negara's highlights – though it's better for views down over the canopy to the Sungai Tembeling than wildlife spotting. You climb a

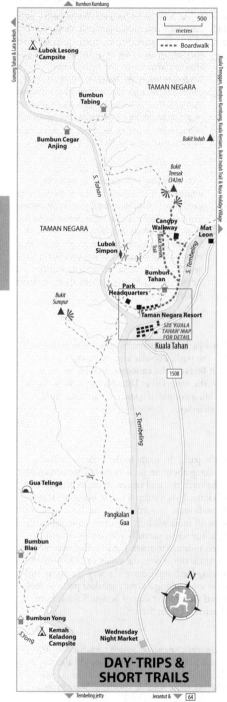

sturdy wooden tower and step out, 30m above the forest floor, onto a 500m-long swaying aluminium bridge, anchored to some suitably placed, 250-year-old *tualang* trees. Animals you may well see include the grey-banded leaf monkey, with a call that sounds like a rattling tin can, and the white-eyed dusky leaf monkey, with its deep, nasal "ha-haw" cry; both lope about in groups of six to eight. At the end, you return to terra firma by another wooden stairwell.

Bukit Indah

3.5km from the park headquarters; 2hr

The route to **Bukit Indah** follows the boardwalk as far as the canopy walkway, before continuing along a rougher trail that tracks the river upstream towards Kuala Trenggan and Bumbun Kumbang. After about 3km you'll see a signposted path leading to a 500m scramble. Use the fixed ropes to haul yourself up to the top of Bukit Indah, and enjoy views over Sungai Tembeling. Despite its proximity to Kuala Tahan, early in the day you're likely to see monkeys, plenty of birdlife, squirrels, a multitude of insects and – with some luck – perhaps tapir or seladang (wild ox).

Kemah Keladong

5km from the park headquarters; 3hr

In the quiet **Kemah Keladong** area, 5km downriver from Kuala Tahan on the far side of Sungai Tembeling, trails link the Blau and Yong **hides** with a **campsite** at Kemah Keladong. You can tackle this either by catching a boat to drop-off points for the hides (15–20min); or by crossing by sampan to a trailhead just up the Sungai Tahan from Kuala Tahan (ask national park staff about this) and hiking – in which case, allow a full day for the return trip. A major attraction of this route used to be **Gua Telinga**, but the cave – home to thousands of tiny **roundleaf bats** – has been off-limits since a roof collapse in 2013.

From the turn-off to Gua Telinga the trail continues for another 2km

HIKING AT KUALA TAHAN

The shortest hiking trails from Kuala Tahan are clearly signposted and easy to follow, but go any distance and trails deteriorate into slippery tangles of roots and leaf litter; you'll be relying on small, reflective **markers** attached to convenient trees, and the photocopied **trail maps** handed out by the national park headquarters. On treks ranging more than about 5km from base, it's strongly recommended that you **hire a guide** – you'll pass rather forbidding signs to that effect at the trailheads. The Kumbang hide (see p.196) is the furthest you're meant to go without one, and they're absolutely essential for any of the longer trails. If you're moderately fit, the hiking **time estimates** given out by the park authorities (and in the text of this Guide) are pretty reliable; expect to average 2km/hour.

Except on the very simplest day hikes, you should **inform** park staff of your plans so they know where to look if you get into difficulty. You won't be able to phone for help, as the mobile phone signal dies out just a little way from Kuala Tahan. Perhaps the most important advice is to **know your limitations** and not run out of time. Slipping and sliding along in the dark is no fun and can be dangerous – it's easy to fall and impossible to spot snakes or other forest-floor creatures that might be on the path. If you do get **lost** and night is about to close in, it's best to make your way down to Sungai Tahan or Sungai Tembeling (assuming you're near either river); there is boat traffic on both into the evening, and if you are unlucky enough not to be spotted, you may be able to find a dry section of bank where you can spend the night.

Don't be paranoid about encountering large **wildlife** on the trails – in fact, you could count yourself lucky if you do, as most animals don't hang around after they hear you coming. Unfortunately there's almost no way you can avoid getting bitten by a few **leeches**, whose numbers increase dramatically after rain; there are a few general guidelines, however, on keeping them at bay (see p.46).

through beautiful tall forest, past the **Yong** and **Blau hides**, to where the trail divides. North is the track to Kemah Rentis (see p.200), while southeast it's just 500m to the tranquil **Kemah Keladong campsite** on the terraced bank of Sungai Yong. With an early start, it's possible to reach this point, have a swim in the river and get back before dusk.

Lata Berkoh

8.5km; 4hr from the park headquarters; ask about river levels before setting out • Return boat trip RM160

Most visitors catch a boat (at least in one direction) to the "roaring rapids" of **Lata Berkoh**, around 8.5km up the Sungai Tahan; the return trip is a long way to walk in a day, and if water levels are high you may face a swim across the river near the end.

The trail from the park HQ leads gently downhill. About fifteen minutes on is an excellent swimming spot, **Lubok Simpon**, a deep pool in the Sungai Tahan next to a pebbled beach. After another 2km you pass the turning for **Bumbun Tabing** and then, 5km from the park HQ, the **Lubok Lesong** campsite. The route to the waterfall veers west from the main trail, crossing gullies and steep ridges before reaching the river, which must be forded. The final part of the trail runs up the west side of the Sungai Tahan, passing the simple **Berkoh Lodge**, a small shelter in a clearing and a **campsite** before reaching the falls.

KUALA TAHAN HIDES (BLINDS)

Spending a night in one of the park's **hides** (known as **bumbuns**) doesn't guarantee sightings of large mammals, especially in the dry season when the **salt licks** – where plant-eating animals come to supplement their mineral intake – are often so waterless that there's little reason for deer, tapir, elephant, leopard or seladang to visit, but it's an experience you're unlikely to forget. It's best to go in a group and take turns keeping watch, listening hard and occasionally shining a **torch** at the salt lick – if an animal is present its eyes will reflect brightly in the beam.

Kuala Tahan's five hides are covered in the hiking trail accounts within this Guide. We have also listed details of costs and time-saving boat rides to/from the hides (see p.187).

The **waterfall** itself drops into a deep pool with surprisingly clear water for swimming (tread carefully around the large rocks on the river bed). You can picnic here, too, overlooking the swirling water. Keep eyes peeled for kingfishers with their yellow-and-red wings and white beaks; large grey-and-green fish eagles; and, on the rocks, camouflaged monitor lizards.

Overnight trips

There are a number of possible **overnight trips**. The 28km-long, two- to three-day trail northeast of Kuala Tahan to **Kuala Perkai** involves overnighting in the jungle, either at **Bumbun Kumbang** or one of several **caves**, with the chance of seeing large animals, after which you could organize a **boat** back to base, rather than having to retrace your steps. If you're pushed for time or simply not so dedicated, hiking as far as Bumbun Kumbang (12km), staying the night there, then taking the alternative return trail – or again, catching a boat – is an excellent compromise. Note that you need to arrange any **boat transfers** before you head out, and that **guides** are recommended beyond the hide.

Trails to Bumbun Kumbang
10–12km from the park headquarters; 5–7hr hike, depending on route • Boat to Kuala Tahan (45min) RM120

Both the **two trails** to **Bumbun Kumbang** are fairly damp and muddy. The longer, flatter, easier route initially follows the Lata Berkoh trail (see p.195), then arcs northeast to the narrow **Sungai Trenggan** – which has to be waded across, and may be impassable after heavy rain – beyond which you're just 1km from the hide.

The tougher, more direct route follows the Sungai Tembeling upstream past the Bukit Indah turn-off (see p.194), crossing numerous **creeks**, each involving a steep, slippery descent and clamber up the far side. Eventually things settle down, and you might see signs of **Batek** people – abandoned shacks and camps – before crossing the small Sungai Trenggan **bridge**. The path seems to peter out on the far side, but keep going and you soon come to a definite junction. Turn left and Bumbun Kumbang is a thirty-minute walk; right, and it's 1km to **Kuala Trenggan**, where some broken-down wooden cabins overlook the confluence of the Tembeling and Trenggan rivers.

Bumbun Kumbang
Book bunks through the park headquarters

Raised high off the ground on concrete posts, the **Bumbun Kumbang** hide sits at the edge of a clearing, about 200m from a natural **salt lick** that attracts animals at wetter times of the year. As always, seeing anything is down to luck, though scan the muddy trails nearby and you'll often find three-toed tapir prints. Given the distance between the hide and the salt lick, however, you'll need binoculars and a powerful torch if you're hoping for more than a glimpse of vague grey shapes.

Bumbun Kumbang to Kuala Keniam
13km one way, 7hr

The superb hike between Bumbun Kumbang and Kuala Keniam forms the basis of most tour operators' shortest overnight treks, and combines the real possibility of seeing **elephants** with visits to three **caves**, one of which is big enough for an army to camp in. The trail is slow going, even in drier conditions, with innumerable streams to wade through, hills to circumvent and trees blocking the path. Most groups take two days, typically hiking this route in reverse and overnighting at **Kempayang Besar**.

Limestone caves

From Bumbun Kumbang, it takes around three hours on a boggy trail before you enter limestone-cave country, first reaching **Kepayang Kecil**. A line of fig trees here drops a curtain

FROM TOP THE JUNGLE RAILWAY (P.201); KUALA LIPIS (P.203) >

of roots down the rock, behind which lies a small chamber, with a slightly larger one to the right, containing stalactites and stalagmites. A short way on is much larger **Kepayang Besar**, where the huge chamber at the eastern side of the outcrop makes an excellent place to spend the night, especially as you can dispense with tents. Despite its popularity with trekkers (on public holidays, the cave can see upwards of a hundred people overnighting here), civets and leopard cats are often seen after dark. Fifteen minutes north – keep an eye on the indistinct path – are **Gua Luas** and more impressive **Gua Daun Menari** ("Cave of the Dancing Leaves"), a breezy chamber inhabited by thousands of roundleaf bats.

Kuala Keniam

Once beyond the limestone band, the rest of the route to **Kuala Keniam** passes through *meranti* forest of tall, straight trees with distinctive reddish-brown bark, much prized as timber. Finally, you reach the river at **Kuala Keniam**, where there's a **campsite** and **jetty** for boats back to Kuala Tahan (RM300).

3   Kuala Keniam to Kuala Perkai

3km; 2hr • Book Perkai Lodge through the park headquarters

From Kuala Keniam, you can hike northwest beside the Sungai Keniam to **Kuala Perkai**, where the grandly named **Perkai Lodge** – actually a basic shelter with beds but no mattresses – is a popular base for fishing groups, who cruise up directly from Kuala Tahan (there's a **campsite** too). This far from civilization, the region is rich in **wildlife**, including banded and dusky leaf monkeys, long-tailed macaques and white-handed gibbons, all of which are relatively easy to spot, especially with binoculars. As for big mammals, elephants certainly roam in these parts; smaller animals such as tapirs, civets and deer are most easily seen at night or early in the morning.

Longer trails

For the two major **long-distance hiking trails** at Taman Negara, you'll need to hire guides and bring full camping and trekking gear, including food, cooking equipment and water-purifying tablets. The four-day **Gunung Tahan trail**, undoubtedly the toughest in the park, culminates in the ascent of one of Malaysia's highest peaks, after which you have to hike out again, perhaps via the alternative, shorter trail to Merapoh (see p.205); you'll definitely need sleeping bags for a couple of nights spent at altitude. The other option is the three- to four-day **Tenor trail**, a lasso-shaped trek leading west from Kuala Tahan to Gua Telinga, then northwest to the campsite on the Sungai Tenor. Either way, expect to see plenty of jungle, and to get soaked during river crossings and rain; allow a day extra either side of the trek to sort out arrangements.

Gunung Tahan trail

55km one way, seven-day return from Kuala Tahan • Book one month in advance

To the Batek Orang Asli, **Gunung Tahan** – Peninsular Malaysia's highest peak at 2187m – is the Forbidden Mountain, its summit the home of a vast monkey, who stands guard over magic stones. Though the Batek rarely venture beyond the foothills, ascending Gunung Tahan is the highlight of any adventurous visitor's stay in Taman Negara. Although hundreds complete the trail every year, the sense of individual achievement after tackling the innumerable river crossings, steep hills and nights camping in the jungle – let alone the arduous ascent – is supreme.

Day 1–2

The **first day** involves an easy six-hour walk from Kuala Tahan to **Melantai**, the campsite on the east bank of Sungai Tahan, not far from Lata Berkoh. On the **second day** more ground is covered, the route taking eight hours and crossing 27 hills, including a long trudge up Bukit Malang ("Unlucky Hill"). This section culminates at

Gunung Rajah (576m), before descending to Sungai Puteh, a tiny tributary of the Tahan. Before the campsite at **Kuala Teku** you'll ford the Tahan half a dozen times – if the river's high, extra time and energy is spent following paths along the edge of the river, crossing at shallower spots.

If you're really enjoying the hike, consider a two-day detour from Kuala Teku to **Four-Steps Waterfall**, east of Gunung Tahan. The trail up to it follows the course of the Sungai Tahan for eight hours, right to the foot of the 30m-high falls; it's a gorgeous forest setting, and flat stones by the path are a good point to rest, listen to the sound of the water and look out for birds and monkeys.

Day 3

The **third day** on the trail to Gunung Tahan sees you climb from 168m to 1100m in seven hours of steady, unrelenting legwork, leaving you on a ridge. Prominent among the large trees here is *seraya*, with a reddish-brown trunk, though as the ridge runs west these are replaced by montane oak forest, where **elephant tracks** are common – though less dense than lower down, the forest is still rich enough in foliage to provide the elephants with food. The night is spent at the Gunung Tahan base camp, **Wray's Camp**, named after the leader of the first team to climb the mountain in 1905.

Day 4: to the summit

Day four involves six hours of hard climbing along steep gullies, ending up at **Padang Camp**, on the Tangga Lima Belas Ridge, sited on a plateau sheltered by tall trees. The summit is now only two and a half hours away, through open, hilly ground with knee-high plants, exposed rocks and peaty streams, which support thick shrubs and small trees – look for pitcher plants and orchids. The trail follows a ridge and soon reaches **Gunung Tahan's summit**; provided it's clear, there's a stupendous view of around 50km in all directions. Weather conditions up here can't be relied upon, however: the **moss forest**, which dominates above 1500m, is often shrouded in cloud.

On from the summit

Most hikers make a straight return trip, spending the **fifth night** back at the padang, the **sixth** at Sungai Puteh, and reaching Kuala Tahan late on **day seven**.

If you don't fancy retracing your steps, it's also possible to continue westwards from the mountain for a further two days, completing a **traverse** of the park and exiting Taman Negara at **Merapoh**. For more information about this route, contact a Merapoh-based tour operator (see p.206).

Tenor trail

30km circuit from Kuala Tahan; 3–4 days

Shorter and not as tough as the hike to Gunung Tahan, the mostly low-lying **Tenor trail** is more likely to be flooded out during extra-wet conditions, but is otherwise an extremely satisfying trek, with a few easy ascents to viewpoints along the way. Note that few guides are familiar with this trail, and you may need to ask around before you find someone who can lead the trek.

Day 1

On **day one**, initially the **Tenor trail** follows the track southwest from Kuala Tahan to Gua Telinga and the Yong hide (see p.194), before bearing northwest along the small **Sungai Yong** and reaching the campsite at **Kemah Yong**, around 10km from the start.

A side trail from here ascends **Bukit Guling Gendang** (570m), a steep ninety-minute climb best undertaken in the morning, after a good night's rest. Towards the summit the terrain changes from lowland tropical to montane forest, where tall conifer trees allow light to penetrate to the forest floor and **squirrels** predominate, with the black giant and cream giant the main species. Both are as big as a domestic cat, their call varying from a grunt to a machine-gun burst of small squeaks. From the top, views reach north to Gunung Tahan, west to Gua Siput and beyond that to Bukit Peningat (713m), the highest limestone outcrop in Peninsular Malaysia.

Day 2

From Kemah Yong campsite, the main trail continues on **day two** into the upper catchment of Sungai Yong, then over a low saddle into the catchment of **Sungai Rentis**. The path narrows through thick forest alongside the river, crossing it several times, until it joins **Sungai Tenor** three hours later, marked by a remote and beautiful riverside clearing, **Kemah Rentis**, where you camp, roughly at the halfway point.

Day 3

You can make it back to Kuala Tahan in one day from Kemah Rentis, though many people take it easy and rest up in one of the campsites along the way. Following the river downstream through undulating terrain on **day three** brings you first to rapids at **Lata Keitiah**, beyond which there's a campsite at **Kemah Lameh**. You're now in lowland open forest where walking is fairly easy; after four hours the trail leads to **Bumbun Cegar Anjing** (another possible overnight stop) from where it's a final 3km to Kuala Tahan.

North through the interior

North of Jerantut, Route 8 and the parallel **Jungle Railway** run around 350km to Kota Bharu, up on the east coast. Head this way if you want to spend time among the region's abundant forests and limestone hills at **Kenong Rimba State Park**, reach the alternative entrances to Taman Negara at **Merapoh** and **Kuala Koh**, or trek along forested waterfall trails at **Gunung Stong State Park**. Settlements along the way – including relatively substantial **Gua Musang** and **Kuala Lipis** – are more jumping-off points for nearby sections of wilds, rather than destinations in their own right.

ESSENTIALS NORTH THROUGH THE INTERIOR

Banks The only regional banks are at Kuala Lipis and Gua Musang, though there is an ATM in Dabong, near Gunung Stong.

Climate Conditions are damp throughout the year, though driest from April to September; you'll need to check in advance about access if heading here during the wet season (November–January).

Kenong Rimba State Park

Covering 128 square kilometres and backing onto the remote southwestern corner of Taman Negara, **Kenong Rimba State Park** offers jungle trails, riverside camping, mammal-spotting and excellent birdwatching, plus the likelihood of crossing paths with the nomadic **Batek** people. You can see the main sights in **five days**, on a 50km-long **loop** through the park past a series of caves, the seven-step **Lata Kenong waterfall** and limestone outcrops with **rock-climbing** potential. If you've only time for a brief visit, explore the **caves** strung out along the main trail, stop overnight at the Gunung Kesong campsite or *Kenong Lodge* (see p.203) and retrace your steps the following day. The park is far less developed than the area around Kuala Tahan, and trails quickly get overgrown – arranging a **tour** from Kuala Lipis (see p.203), or at least a guide, is strongly recommended. There is some accommodation at the park, otherwise bring everything you'll need with you.

ARRIVAL AND INFORMATION KENONG RIMBA STATE PARK

Kenong Rimba lies about 20km east of Kuala Lipis; the nearest village is **Kuala Kenong**, from where you can get a boat to the trailhead at **Tanjung Kiara**. The Jungle Railway (see box, p.201) in theory stops nearby at

THE JUNGLE RAILWAY

It took indentured Tamil labourers eight years to build the 500km-long **Jungle Railway** from **Gemas**, southeast of KL, to **Tumpat**, on the northeast coast near Kota Bharu. The first section from Gemas to Kuala Lipis opened in 1920, with the full extent of the line following in 1931. Initially it was used exclusively for freight – tin and rubber, and later oil palm – until a passenger service, originally known as the "Golden Blowpipe", opened in 1938. Today the route – officially the less romantic "Sektor Timur & Selatan" (East and South Route), managed by KTM – is mostly served by trains from **Singapore**, with just one daily service from KL.

By dint of its very existence, the line doesn't pass through virgin jungle; instead much of the route **south of Gua Musang** is flanked by regrowth forest and belukar-type woodland, and the line often dips through cuttings below ferny embankments, or skirts the backs of kampung gardens. On the final section, the mountainous, river-gashed terrain is replaced by plantations of rubber, pepper and oil palm, which – given their sprawl of uninterrupted vegetation – actually look more jungly than the real forest. None of this is to detract from the fact that as a way to encounter **rural life**, a ride on the jungle train can't be beaten, giving you the chance to take in backwater scenery in the company of cheroot-smoking old men in sarongs, and fast-talking women hauling kids, poultry and vegetables to and from the nearest market. For the unadulterated Jungle Railway experience, you need to be on one of the slow **local trains**, which call at just about every obscure hamlet on the route, some with Orang Asli names.

Rolling stock is worn and fairly ordinary, dating to the 1980s, with several classes of sleeper and seat available on all routes. Buy **tickets** at the station if possible (you shouldn't need to book in advance except on express services during school holidays), though you can also pay the conductor on board – indeed, you often have to, as rural station offices keep erratic hours. It's also possible to book through KTM's website (ⓦ ktmb.com.my).

You should check the website, too, for the latest **timetables** – though these are to be taken with a pinch of salt, as delays aren't uncommon. Trains may even show up early; be at the station fifteen minutes ahead of the scheduled departure. Even if everything appears to be going to schedule, note that there's only one set of tracks on long stretches of the route: delays elsewhere may mean your train being held at a siding or even reversing for an extended period to let another train pass.

Note that any delays may be compounded by the fact that the railway is currently undergoing **long-term maintenance** work, scheduled to last until 2016. Daytime services between Gua Musang and Gemas have been suspended for the duration, though overnight express trains to KL Sentral and Singapore are running, as are two "shuttle" stopping services between Tumpat and Gua Musang.

Batu Sembilan, but services are suspended until at least 2016 due to long-term maintenance. Check ⓦ ktmb.com .my for the latest information.

By 4WD The *Kenong Lodge* (see p.203) runs an on-demand transfer service from Kuala Lipis bus station to Kuala Kenong (prices vary with group size, starting from RM100/ person each way, minimum two people).
By boat All boats are by arrangement only, through an agent (see below). Kuala Kenong to the Tanjung Kiara jetty costs RM10/person.
Entry fee RM50.
Contact details ☏ 019 965 7388, ⓦ my-greenpark .blogspot.com.

TOURS

Though it's possible to explore Kenong Rimba independently, it's much easier to visit on a **tour from Kuala Lipis**; guides, transport, meals and accommodation (in cabins or tents) are all part of the deal.

Appu Appu's Guesthouse, 63 Jalan Besar, Kuala Lipis ☏ 017 947 1520, ✉ jungleappu@yahoo.com. Appu has been exploring Kenong Rimba since the 1990s, and organizes budget hiking and camping trips in the park. Die-hards can make a five-day circuit with him, on which the trekking can be quite tough, despite short daily distances. Expect to pay RM80/person/day (minimum four people) including food, plus RM150 return/group to cover transport, not including the park entry fee.
Green Park Travel Kenong Lodge ☏ 012 688 8314,

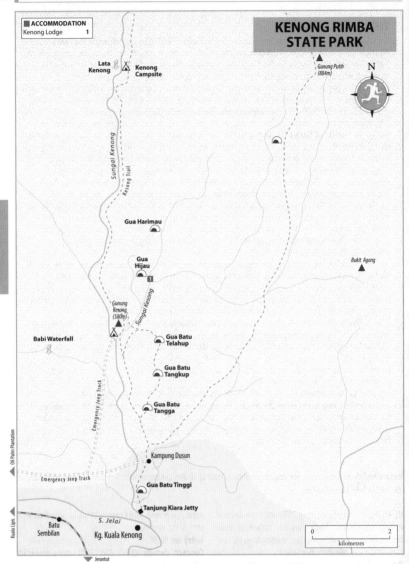

3

@my-greenpark.blogspot.com. Currently managing the park on behalf of the Forestry Department, Green Park runs the *Kenong Lodge* and can arrange 4WD transfers to Kuala Kenong and boats to Tanjung Kiara, as well as a range of tours.

Kiara Holidays Level 4, Centrepoint Complex, Kuala Lipis ☎09 312 2777, @centrepointhotel.com.my /pkiaraholidays.html. Don't be put off by their threadbare office or the shabby building; the friendly staff can arrange packages from RM300/person including transfers, meals and accommodation in chalets, dorms or tents. Rock climbing and rafting also available.

ACCOMMODATION AND EATING

To **camp** in the park costs RM5 per person per night; the most established campsite is at Gunung Kesong, about 2hr in from the entrance, with the popular Kenong campsite another 5hr north of here at Lata Kenong waterfall.

Kenong Lodge 30min from the Gunung Kesong campsite, 5km from Tanjung Kiara ☎ 019 965 7388, ⓦ kenong-lodge.blogspot.com. A handful of private rooms in the jungle; this is the only alternative to camping in the park. Meals available by arrangement (RM8–15). **RM50**

Kuala Lipis

It's hard to believe that **KUALA LIPIS**, 50km northwest of Jerantut, was the state capital of **Pahang** from 1898 to 1955. Today, it's a sleepy, inconsequential place, situated at the confluence of Sungai Lipis and Sungai Jelai, and surrounded by rolling hills and plantations. There are a few mementoes from colonial days – many associated with the veteran administrator, **Sir Hugh Clifford** (the Pahang Resident 1896–1905), plus plenty of shops and places to eat, but Kuala Lipis' biggest draw is access to the relatively unvisited rainforest trails at nearby **Kenong Rimba State Park**.

Old town

Kuala Lipis started life as a **trading centre** for *gaharu* (a fragrant aloe wood used to make joss sticks) and other jungle products, collected by the Semiar and traded with Chinese *towkays*. The remnants of these origins survive in the **old town**, a busy grid of pastel-coloured **shophouses** squeezed between the railway and the Sungai Jelai, where the jetty and steps still stand, though goods no longer arrive and depart by river. Overlooking the river to the west, the small, tin-roofed **Masjid Negeri**, dating from 1888, was reputedly founded by a trader from Yemen.

Pahang Club

Jalan Pahang Club

Incongruously hidden behind the huge new **hospital**, the old **Pahang Club** dates to 1907. It's an archetypal tropical colonial building, a sprawling structure of whitewashed timber with black trim and wraparound veranda, raised slightly off the ground on stumps as protection against damp and termites – which, given the lean on the building, clearly hasn't been entirely successful and the club has fallen into disuse.

Lipis District Office

Kuala Lipis was chosen as a headquarters for the colonial government despite the town's relative isolation – the trip upriver from Singapore took more than two weeks, and there was no road out until the 1890s – though minor **tin deposits** brought short-lived prosperity. These boom days led to the construction of the surprisingly large **Lipis District Office**, which overlooks Kuala Lipis from a hilltop 1km southeast of town; a solid crimson-and-white Edwardian edifice, it now serves as local government offices.

Clifford School

Below the District Office, at the back of green playing fields, **Clifford School** was built in 1913 and part-funded by Hugh Clifford; the original buildings are at the far end of the compound, visible from Jalan Pahang Club. The school is still one of a select group where the country's leaders and royalty are educated – though these days it's equally well known for being the alma mater of Malaysia's biggest-selling female pop star, Siti Nurhaliza.

Bukit Residen

A small rise just south of town is crowned by **Bukit Residen**, a graceful two-storey house built in the 1890s as Hugh Clifford's residence. Clifford arrived in Malaysia in 1883, aged 17, and worked his way up through the colonial administration, serving in Malaysia, Sri Lanka and West Africa before ending his career as the Malaya High Commissioner in 1930. The house's associations are more interesting than the building itself – it's now the *Government Rest House* – though it does enjoy great views out over the surrounding hills.

3

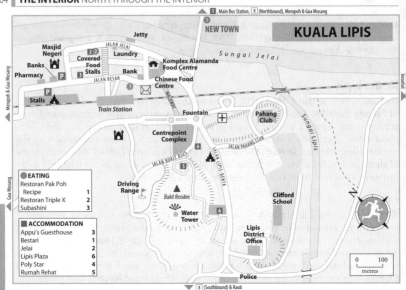

ARRIVAL AND DEPARTURE

KUALA LIPIS

By train Kuala Lipis' 1926 train station is right in the old town (ticket office daily 9.30am–2.30pm & 3.30–4.30pm; ☏09 312 1341), on the Jungle Railway line. Note that services to Batu Sembilan (for Kenong Rimba) are suspended until at least 2016. Check ⒲ktmb .com.my for the latest.

Destinations Dabong (2 daily; 3hr); Gua Musang (2 daily; 2hr); Jerantut (2 daily; 1hr 30min); Kuala Lumpur (1 daily; 9hr); Merapoh (1 daily; 1hr 20min);

Singapore (1 daily; 9hr); Wakaf Bharu (for Kota Bharu; 1 daily; 6hr).

By bus The main bus station, Terminal Anggerik, sits 1km north of the centre; cross the river, head up the hill and turn right into the small cluster of shops, where you'll see the open-sided barn of a station.

Destinations Gua Musang (daily; 2hr); Jerantut (3 daily; 1hr 30min); Kuala Lumpur (10 daily; 4hr); Kuantan (2 daily; 6hr); Merapoh (daily; 1hr 30min).

ACCOMMODATION

Appu's Guesthouse 63 Jalan Besar ☏09 312 3142, ⒺJungleappu@yahoo.com. A bedrock, no-frills hostel geared to foreign backpackers; a range of basic rooms share facilities. Owner Appu has been leading trips to Kenong Rimba State Park for decades (see p.200), the guesthouse operating on "self-service" lines when he's away. No wi-fi. Dorms **RM10**, a/c doubles **RM35**

Bestari 42–43 Lorong BBKL, just north of town ☏09 312 6626. A 5min walk from the bus station on the opposite side of the main road, this modern, motel-like affair, owned by the Hotel Jelai group, is popular with travelling business folk; they take credit cards and the spacious en-suite rooms all have cable TV and a/c. **RM83**

★**Jelai** 44 Jalan Jelai ☏09 312 1192, ⒲hoteljelai .com. First impressions here are of receptionists barricaded behind glass like bank tellers, and bare, tiled corridors. However, it's well run, secure and spotless; rooms have a/c, bathroom and TV, and some overlook

the river. Book ahead; they're often full. **RM55**

Lipis Plaza Komplex Taipan, Jalan Benta-Lipis ☏09 312 5521, ⒲lipisplaza.com. Spacious but rather plain rooms in a modern complex at the base of Bukit Residen. Rates include breakfast. **RM100**

Poly Star 5 Jalan Bukit Bius ☏09 312 3225. Your best bet if the *Jelai* is full. Rooms here are newer and of a similar standard – tiled, with basic furnishings, attached bathrooms and a/c – but much smaller. No wi-fi. **RM53**

Rumah Rehat (Government Rest House) Bukit Residen ☏09 312 2784. Clifford's former home has been converted to a rather odd guesthouse, with an abandoned museum on the ground floor and fifteen vast but shabby en-suite rooms, all with a/c and TV. The VIP suite will set you back RM150 and there's a café on site (lunch and dinner only). A taxi from town will cost around RM6. No wi-fi. **RM40**

EATING AND DRINKING

The area around the taxi stand holds a few despondent Malay stalls, but there's more atmosphere to be had in the bustling **kedai kopis** that line the covered arcade between Jalan Besar and Jalan Jelai. There's also a **night market** with plenty of food from 3pm every Friday in the purpose-built Kompleks Melati next to the bus station, a 15min walk from the old town.

Restoran Pak Boh Recipe Overlooking town from the north bank of the river, near the Bestari Hotel ☎ 09 312 6082. Great setting, and nice "jungle" theme with rattan decor, potted palms and water misters. The food – from staples like noodle soup and chicken chop'n'chips, through to beef stew with medicinal herbs – is adequate but rather overpriced. Mains RM10–25. Daily 11.30am–11.30pm.
★ **Restoran Triple X** 44 Jalan Jelai, below the Jelai hotel. A bright, bustling, barely furnished room opening onto the street, serving the tastiest Chinese food in town.

Try the boneless "Thai-style" chicken, served in a hot and sour sauce (RM25 for a large portion). Daily 10am–3pm & 6–10pm.
Subashini 94 Jalan Besar ☎ 09 312 2422. A terrific, friendly Tamil curry house with the usual spread of fiery food for around RM10, as well as *roti canai, nasi lemak* and *mee goreng* at breakfast; go for lunch over dinner, as they've often run out of the tastiest curries come evening. Daily 6.30am–8pm.

DIRECTORY

Bank There's a Maybank with ATM on Jalan Besar.
Laundry A same-day service is available at a laundry on Jalan Jelai; make sure you fix the price in advance, as the manageress likes to charge foreigners extra.
Supplies If you can't find what you need along Jalan Besar

in the old town, head south of the tracks to the Aktif supermarket on the ground floor of the Centrepoint Complex – intended to be a grand shopping development, but in reality a shoddy, graffiti-covered block awaiting redevelopment.

Merapoh (Sungai Relau)

The small market town of **MERAPOH**, served by road and rail 80km north of Kuala Lipis, marks a 7km-long access road east to **Taman Negara's western entrance**, officially known as **Sungai Relau**. This is the only part of Taman Negara where a proper vehicle road runs deep into the park, providing access to the trails – most famously, that to **Gunung Tahan** (see p.198). There's not much point in turning up here with your own car, however, as the 14km-long park road is closed to private vehicles. What might make it worth stumping up for guide fees and official transportation is the above-average chance of seeing elephants and even tigers (though don't get your hopes up – sightings are extremely rare), plus leopard cats, civets, otters, and packs of dog-like **dhole**.

Into the park

RM1, RM5 camera fee • ☎ 09 915 0214, ⓦ wildlife.gov.my

Beyond the park office and picnic ground, you cross the little Sungai Relau via a small **bridge** and find yourself on the narrow surfaced road that undulates through the jungle. Several trails lead off the initial few kilometres, including the **Rentis Gajah** ("elephant trail"), leading south off the road to Gua Gajah ("elephant cave"); allow four hours for the return hike from the gate, plus an hour exploring. A few kilometres further, a short trail north off the road leads down to the park's **hide**, Bumbun Rimau (where you can stay overnight in the hides' wooden bunks), close to a salt lick. Drive another few kilometres on to reach the red Menara Bukit Seraya, an **observation tower** with views of forested ridges and valleys to the north, and, on a clear day, east to Gunung Tahan. Some 2km beyond Bukit Seraya is Air Terjun Kelam, a pretty **waterfall** in a secluded woodland setting.

The road ends at **Kuala Juram**, a picturesque spot where trees overhang the limpid Sungai Juram, a stretch of which teems with *kelah* (mahseer), and where it's possible to kayak and fish. The suspension bridge over the river here is the gateway to the Gunung Tahan mountain trail.

3

ARRIVAL AND DEPARTURE   MERAPOH

Merapoh is tiny, with the train station to the west of Route 8, and a few shops clustered around the entrance of the road to the park office.

By bus There's no bus station, but the daily bus between Kuala Lipis and Gua Musang can drop you off; local tour operators (see below) can also deliver/collect from Gua Musang, just 30min north (RM40).

By train There is no local transport between Merapoh train station and the park; it takes 2hr to walk the rolling 7km through oil palm-plantations if you can't get a ride.

Destinations Dabong (daily; 1hr 40min); Gua Musang (daily; 30min); Kuala Lipis (daily; 1hr 30min); Singapore (daily; 10hr 30min); Wakaf Bharu (for Kota Bharu; daily; 4hr).

TOURS AND GUIDES

Guides from either of the agencies below cost RM180/day, with RM80/night for overnight stays; there are no guides available from the park office. The four-day trek from Merapoh up Gunung Tahan (see p.198) and back costs RM960; a week-long traverse of the park between Merapoh and Kuala Tahan costs RM1740.

Relau Agency Merapoh ☏017 915 3034. The most established operator in Merapoh, organizing tours and local transport, and working extensively with the park authorities. Fees include RM10/person for the ride between Merapoh and the park gates; and RM65 for a night safari (minimum four people). Their drivers tend to speak little English, but park staff should be able to smooth communication once you've arrived.

SGI Outdoor 200m towards the park from Merapoh down the access road ☏09 912 1443 or ☏017 907 4241, ⓦnatureguidemerapoh.webs.com. Accommodation in Merapoh, plus tours and transport into the park; they also run caving trips in the surrounding area. Tents (RM10) and sleeping bags (RM5) are available to rent from their welcoming offices; there's also a decent range of gear (including boots and waterproofs) for sale.

ACCOMMODATION AND EATING

Food and accommodation options are very limited in this part of Taman Negara. The park office has a minimarket (8am–5pm) that sells crisps and drinks, but their canteen only opens during busy periods; at other times you'll need to bring all your own food and cooking gear, or use the clutch of *kedai kopis* 7km away in Merapoh.

Park Headquarters ☏012 983 2651, ⓔtnsgrelau @wildlife.gov.my. The accommodation at the park was closed for renovation at the time of research, and was expected to reopen in 2016. For the time being, you'll need to put up at the campsite, which is equipped with toilets and showers, or at the hide. Camping <u>RM1</u>, hide <u>RM5</u>

Speleo Inn Merapoh, not far from Route 8 ☏09 912 1443. Simple bunk-bed dorms run by SGI Outdoor, housed in a well-maintained block. Book ahead, especially during school holidays, as it's often used by student groups. Dorms <u>RM25</u>

Gua Musang

GUA MUSANG (Civet Cave), 30km from Merapoh, is a former logging town strung thinly along a stretch of Route 8. A 100m-wide knot of scruffy buildings and shops surrounds the old **train station**, while a **new satellite town** coalesces 3km south. This being Kelantan, the Malay accent here displays a distinctive Kelantanese twang, and alcohol is practically unavailable.

Gua Musang is fairly close to **Taman Negara entrances** at Merapoh (see p.205) and Kuala Koh (see opposite). Time spent between connections can be filled exploring the **caves** that riddle a mass of limestone that looms over the train tracks – that said, it's a tricky path, steep, crumbling and very overgrown, and particularly difficult after rain – best attempted with a local guide (RM10).

ARRIVAL AND INFORMATION   GUA MUSANG

By train The new train station sits astride the Jungle Railway's tracks 400m south of its predecessor, just off Route 8, between the old and new parts of town. A taxi to the old town or bus station costs RM10.

Destinations Dabong (4 daily; 1hr 40min); Jerantut (2 daily; 3hr 15min); Kuala Lipis (2 daily; 2hr); Kuala Lumpur (1 daily; 11hr); Merapoh (daily; 30min); Singapore (daily; 11hr); Wakaf Bharu (for Kota Bharu; 4 daily; 4hr).

By bus Gua Musang's main bus station is 2.5km south of the train station in the new town. Some services set down or collect at a stop just south of the old town.

Destinations Kota Bharu (3 daily; 3hr); Kuala Lipis (daily; 2hr); Kuala Lumpur (2 daily; 5hr).

Banks There are several banks with ATMs on Route 8 near the train station.

Supplies Stores along Jalan Besar sell everything from food to batteries and umbrellas.

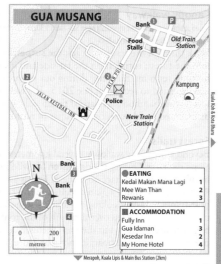

GUA MUSANG

EATING
Kedai Makan Mana Lagi   1
Mee Wan Than   2
Rewanis   3

ACCOMMODATION
Fully Inn   1
Gua Idaman   3
Kesedar Inn   2
My Home Hotel   4

Merapoh, Kuala Lipis & Main Bus Station (2km)

ACCOMMODATION

Fully Inn 75 Jalan Pekan Lama ☎ 09 912 3311. Once smart, scuffed Chinese-run hotel with faded carpets and wallpaper starting to peel. The large, comfortable rooms have satellite TV, a/c and bathrooms. Rates include breakfast, and there are cheaper single rooms (RM80). RM110

Gua Idaman 400m west of the station ☎ 09 912 0081. The nearest accommodation to the train station, with largely windowless and slightly musty rooms, each with TV and a tiny bathroom. Little English spoken. RM60

Kesedar Inn About 1km from the station ☎ 09 912 1229, Malay-only site ⊛ kesedarinn.com.my. Modern motel complex with mildewed twin rooms, nicer doubles and self-contained chalets, at the end of a 400m-long kampung lane lined with wooden stilt houses and fruit trees. Twins RM60, doubles RM140, chalets RM170

My Home Hotel Jalan Persiaran Raya ☎ 09 912 3191, ⊛ myhomehotel.com.my. Part of a nationwide chain, with dismissive staff and clean but poky rooms, the cheapest sharing bathrooms, all with a/c. Shared bathrooms RM40, en suite RM60

EATING

Kedai Makan Mana Lagi Jalan Besar. Open-air Malay food court that's festooned with coloured lights in the evening. Food has a Thai twist, as is often the case in Kelantan; even the humble fried *kangkung* with squid has a lemongrass kick to it. A good range of *tom yam* and *kerabu*-style dishes for around RM10, plus seafood, including house speciality *ikan tiga rasa* – though none of the staff can explain what the three flavours of the name derive from. Daily 5pm–late.

Mee Wan Than Jalan Pulai. Chinese *kedai kopis* not far from the station, serving noodles (try their wonton noodles, RM5) in the morning and evening, with *nasi campur* available at lunchtime. Daily 7am–11am, noon–2pm & 6.30–10pm.

Rewanis Jalan Pulai. One of the best of a series of restaurants along this flyblown strip, with a selection of rice and noodle dishes, and a few Western offerings, such as fish and chips (RM10). Daily 1.30pm–midnight.

Kuala Koh

At first glance, **Kuala Koh**, Taman Negara's northern entrance, 85km east of Gua Musang, offers similar facilities to Kuala Tahan, with marked trails, boat trips and a canopy walkway. On the ground, however, the experience is dramatically different; the trails are shorter but wilder, with elephant footprints outnumbering their human counterparts, and it's nowhere near as crowded. **Wildlife** isn't obviously more abundant, though it certainly includes wild boar (whose wallows you see everywhere), tapir, mouse deer and elephants. Get here at the right time of year – park staff advise February – and you might strike lucky and encounter the bizarre stinky blooms of **Rafflesia** (see p.586). It's also possible to **trek** right through to other park entrances at Kuala Tahan (p.185) or Merapoh (p.205) – these routes are seldom used and require advance preparation. There's good-value **accommodation and food** at Kuala Koh, but transport here can be expensive, and guides are recommended for most treks.

Canopy walkway

Closed at time of research but previously open Sat–Thurs 9.30am–12.30pm & 2.30–4.30pm, Fri 9.30am–noon & 3.30–4.30pm; closed during rain or if lightning is likely • RM5

Walk through the resort to reach the **suspension bridge** that leads over the Sungai Lebir into the forest; turn left on the far side and it's 100m to the **canopy walkway**. Closed for long-term maintenance during our research, this narrow, swaying aerial pathway was expected to reopen in late 2015. The walkway is 20m up, over partially cleared forest with bamboo and barbed rattan palms below; from the top you can expect to see birds, insects and occasional troupes of monkeys.

Forest trails

Beyond the canopy walkway, several kilometres of **trails** weave through the forest and along the river. During the day, **listen** for wildlife – the zithering of cicadas, whooshing of hornbill wings, and staccato rustle of lizards amid the leaf litter. Pick of the routes are the **Rentis Ara** (Fig Trail), a 3km circuit, and the 1.5km-long **Rentis Bumbun**, ending at a pole-frame **hide** overlooking a salt lick – somewhere to sit still for an hour and see what turns up, or even sleep overnight. All of the routes are marked with coloured circles of plastic nailed to trees, but the trails themselves are occasionally obscured by the activities of elephants and wild boar; it's not a bad idea to take a guide with you.

On the river

A pleasant **river trip** heads up the Lebir for half an hour to **Kuala Pertang**, passing a few sandy banks where you can camp, swim or fish; the river is home to *ikan kelah* and other freshwater denizens. The ride takes you under the overhanging boughs of leaning neram trees, some hung with the leafy tresses of **tiger orchids**, among the world's largest orchid species. You can also go **tubing** along the river, being carried downstream on an inflated rubber ring, or arrange a trip to a semipermanent **Batek camp** 2hr upstream.

ARRIVAL AND INFORMATION   KUALA KOH

By car Driving, turn off Route 8 at Simpang Aring (40km north of Gua Musang) and follow signs along a sealed but bumpy road through the Felda Aring oil-palm plantation, looking out for plantation vehicles, before turning off onto a roller coaster of an access road for the last 15km. The road passes an Orang Asli village just before entering the park, with the headquarters a short drive further on above the confluence of the Lebir and Koh rivers.

By taxi Taxis from Gua Musang charge a negotiable RM150 each way; alternatively, the management at *Taman*

Negara Kuala Koh Resort (see below) might be able to give you a ride to Gua Musang for RM70.

Park office ☎ 017 900 9522, ✉ tnkelantan@wildlife .gov.my, ⍾ wildlife.gov.my. Staff can give you a photocopied schematic map of Kuala Koh, and accept payment of the nominal entry (RM1) and photography (RM5) fees. Book guides, hides and all river activities here too: tubing on the river costs RM25 each (minimum of four people), while an hour-long guided night walk, when you might see slow loris and civets, is RM40.

ACCOMMODATION AND EATING

Bumbun Book the hide through the park office and take food, water, sleeping bag and a strong flashlight to watch for animals using the accompanying salt lick. Be warned, there's no toilet and you'll need gallons of insect repellent. **RM5**

Taman Negara Kuala Koh Resort Park entrance ☎ 012 965 4788, ⍾ taman-negara-koh.blogspot.com. The reception is at the restaurant, next to the park office desk, with cabins and a bunkhouse hostel on the lawn behind; you

can also camp. The elderly cabins are spacious and come with a/c and en-suite bathrooms; dorms have fans and shared bathrooms. Book in advance; given the lack of transport, you're stuck if they don't have any room. The restaurant serves decent *kedai kopis* food, including fried rice, *tom yam*, grilled fish, *char kway teow* and cold drinks, at only slightly inflated prices – around RM6 a dish. Restaurant daily 8am–10pm. Camping **RM5**, dorms **RM15**, cabins **RM50**

Stong State Park (Jelawang Jungle)

Around 70km north of Gua Musang, **Stong State Park** is an off-the-beaten-track gem based around 1420m-high **Gunung Stong**, a prominent, forested granite mountain 7km outside the small rail township of **DABONG**. Current train schedules make it a great day stop, with a short but tough hike up through lush forest to a series of **waterfalls** and plunge pools, where you can have a swim and catch a late afternoon train out. That said, it's also worth staying **overnight** on the mountainside for the magical sunrise views.

Air Terjun Jelawang

The access road from Dabong ends at the foot of the mountain, where you buy your entry ticket. From here, follow a path that crosses a rickety suspension bridge into the forest, where the paving quickly gives way to a muddy path, tangled with tree roots but perfectly clear. This is extremely steep, with ropes and chains to help you up the worst bits – fortunately the gritty mud gives a decent grip. After about 1km, you'll reach a ramshackle pavilion where a side trail leads sharply down 300m to a pretty spot near the foot of the largest cascade.

As you continue along the main trail, *Baha's Camp* (see below) sits a sweaty 1.5km further up the hillside on the river bank between the first and second tiers of **Air Terjun Jelawang**, also known as Lata Jelawang, Peninsular Malaysia's **highest waterfall**, which cascades a total of 540m down a bald granite rock face in seven steps. There's a pool that's great for swimming and a wonderful viewpoint – if you stay overnight, this is where you'll want to be at dawn to watch the **sunrise** over a sea of cotton-wool clouds blanketing the plains. Do take care, though; the rocks are slick and a Singaporean student slipped to his death here in 2013.

Mountain trails

Baha's Camp is the trailhead for the **Elephant trek**, which follows the main path up the mountain for two hours to the top of Gunung Stong, before winding along the ridge and crossing over onto neighbouring **Gunung Ayam** (1500m). Although it's possible to return to *Baha's* the same day, it's recommended to camp for the night on top of Gunung Ayam – you'll need warm clothing and a sleeping bag. Elephants are sometimes seen here, and there's a chance of encountering **tapir** and **deer** in the early morning or early evening.

ARRIVAL AND DEPARTURE   STONG STATE PARK

By train It's feasible to come on a day-trip, visit the falls and have a swim, arriving at Dabong on an early train from either direction, and leaving the same evening (timetables on ⓦ ktmb.com.my). Ask at Dabong station for a lift to the park (RM30 return).
Destinations Gua Musang (4 daily; 1hr 15min); Jerantut (2 daily; 4hr 20min); Kuala Lipis (2 daily; 3hr); Kuala Lumpur (daily; 11hr); Merapoh (daily; 1hr 40min);

Singapore (daily; 12hr); Wakaf Bharu (for Kota Bharu; 4 daily; 2hr 45min).
By car Dabong is just off Route 66, 70km north of Gua Musang; from Route 8, it's 40km west of Sungai Sam. From the Dabong turning, cross the river and drive north for 7km, before taking the signed road to the mountain that ends at the park gates.
Admission fee RM2.

ACCOMMODATION AND EATING

Simple meals are available from the restaurant at the **park gates** (daily 8am–7pm), with *nasi campur* (RM6) set up at lunchtime. Meals at *Baha's Camp* are by arrangement only. There are several *kedai kopis* around Dabong train station, but the closest place to buy supplies is Gua Musang.

Baha's Camp Inside the forest, 1hr 30min from the park gates, by the waterfall ☎ 012 968 1554. A superb – if extremely basic – place to stay, with tents scattered around a jungle clearing. There's no electricity or running water, unless you count the nearby waterfall, and you might find yourself sharing the tent with some of the smaller forest creatures. If you can't contact the camp in advance (they're sometimes out of range), bring all your own food – and a tent, just in case their own are full – and they should be able

to cook it for you. The camp can organize knowledgeable guides and treks throughout the park, and food is available if you call ahead. Four-person tent **RM20**
★**Rose House** Close to the road bridge across the railway, Dabong ☎ 013 960 6789. With six rooms in two rose-pink blocks, this homely guesthouse is a great place to recuperate after a trip into the mountains. Squeaky-clean rooms have fans, a/c and private bathrooms, and the friendly owner, Abe Din, may throw in *nasi kerabu* for breakfast. **RM60**

The east coast

215 Kota Bharu

224 From Kota Bharu to Kuala Terengganu

227 Pulau Perhentian

235 Pulau Redang

236 Pulau Lang Tengah

237 Kuala Terengganu

243 Tasik Kenyir

244 Marang

245 Pulau Kapas

247 Southern Terengganu

249 Cherating

253 Kuantan

257 Gua Charas

257 Sungai Lembing

257 Pekan

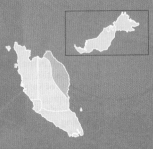

KITE MAKER NEAR KOTA BHARU

The east coast

The 400km-long stretch from the northeastern corner of the Peninsula to Kuantan, roughly halfway down the east coast, draws visitors for two major reasons: the beaches and islands, and traditional Malay culture. Islands such as Pulau Perhentian, Pulau Redang and Pulau Kapas offer great opportunities for diving and snorkelling; further south, the backpackers' coastal enclave of Cherating is a deservedly popular place simply to kick back for a few days. Among the cities, vibrant Kota Bharu, close to the Thai border, stands out for its opportunities to access Malay crafts and performing arts.

The east coast displays a different cultural legacy to the more populous, commercial western seaboard, from which it is separated by the mountainous, jungled interior. For hundreds of years, the Malay rulers of the northern states of **Kelantan** and **Terengganu** were vassals of the Thai kingdom of **Ayutthaya**, suffering repeated invasions as well as the unruly squabbles of their own princes. Nevertheless, the Malays enjoyed a great deal of autonomy, and both states remained free of British control until 1909. Only in 1931 did the railway arrive in Kelantan; previously, the journey from KL involved thirteen river crossings. In 1941 Kelantan saw the landing of the first Japanese troops, facilitated by the Thai government – who were rewarded by being given control over Kelantan once more from 1943 until 1945.

While immigrants poured into the tin and rubber towns of the west during the twentieth century, the east remained rural. As a result, Kelantan and Terengganu remain very much **Malay heartland** states. There's a rustic feel to the area, the economy being largely based on agriculture and fishing, with the obvious exception of Terengganu's petroleum industry.

The country's religious opposition party, **PAS**, which was born in Kelantan in the middle of the last century, has governed its home state since 1990. For foreign visitors, the political backdrop distils down to the simple truth that the **social climate** of Kelantan and Terengganu is more obviously **conservative** than elsewhere in Malaysia: **alcohol** is harder to obtain than in other states; most restaurants, whatever cuisine they serve, are **halal**; and **dress** – for both men and women – needs to be circumspect, except at well-touristed beaches. You will also find that **English** is less understood in Kelantan and Terengganu than in most other parts of the Peninsula.

GETTING AROUND

While **flights** to Kota Bharu or Kuala Terengganu can be useful time-savers, road access to the east coast has really opened up with the development of the East Coast Expressway (E8). The expressway arrives on the coast just north of Kuantan, reducing the drive from KL to a 3hr whizz, then runs north as far as Kuala Terengganu; the road is planned to reach Kota Bharu by 2020.

The east coast in the off-season p.215
Islam in Kelantan p.217
The markets of Kota Bharu p.218
The performing arts in Kelantan p.219
Perhentians dos and don'ts p.229
Snorkelling and diving around the Perhentians p.230

The kris p.239
Boat-building on Pulau Duyong p.240
Snorkelling and diving around Pulau Kapas p.246
Activities in Cherating p.250
Marine turtles p.252

GREEN TURTLE OFF PULAU PERHENTIAN

Highlights

❶ **Kota Bharu** One of the Peninsula's most appealing cities, home to Malay crafts, traditional art forms and a popular night food market, with Buddhist temples within easy reach. **See p.215**

❷ **Pulau Perhentian** Two of the most enticing islands the Peninsula has to offer, with excellent snorkelling and accommodation ranging from backpacker chalets to slick resorts. **See p.227**

❸ **Pulau Kapas** A delightful little island with decent sands and opportunities for snorkelling

and kayaking – perfect for a couple of days' relaxation. **See p.245**

❹ **Cherating** Chill by the beach, watch fireflies or just enjoy the amiable, low-key nightlife in this long-established travellers' hangout. **See p.249**

❺ **Pekan** An appealingly quiet royal town, with a scattering of palaces, impeccable kampung houses and a newly renovated museum housed in a colonial building. **See p.257**

HIGHLIGHTS ARE MARKED ON THE MAP ON P.214

By bus The express buses that ply the east coast's main roads are convenient for trips between the major towns, but if you're heading anywhere else often the only option is to take one of the slower, local buses that serve the smaller stops.

By car In addition to the E8, the region's old backbone roads remain intact: the coast road (called Route 3 between Kuala Terengganu and Kuantan) and its shadow 10–20km inland (Route 14 south of Kuala Terengganu, Route 3 to the north). Unsurprisingly, the coast road, connecting a string of laidback towns and fishing kampungs, is the most interesting.

By train The only rail service is the atmospheric "Jungle Railway" through the interior (see p.201) to Tumpat, near Kota Bharu.

THE EAST COAST

HIGHLIGHTS

1. Kota Bharu
2. Pulau Perhentian
3. Pulau Kapas
4. Cherating
5. Pekan

0 ———— 25 kilometres

THE EAST COAST IN THE OFF-SEASON

Many visitors give the east coast a wide berth during the **northeast monsoon**, which sets in during late October and continues until February. It's true that heavy rains and sea swells put paid to most boat services to the islands at this time, and most beach accommodation, whether on the mainland or offshore, is shut anyway. The rains will, however, usually be interspersed with good sunny spells, just as the so-called dry season can bring its share of torrential downpours. With luck, and a flexible schedule, you will find boats heading sporadically to and from the islands during the monsoon; some island accommodation opens year-round, although you should contact places to be sure. While diving and snorkelling aren't great at this time of year, due to reduced visibility, the east coast comes into its own for **surfing** and **windsurfing**, with Cherating the prime destination. Away from the beaches, there's always reasonable sightseeing in Kota Bharu and Kuala Terengganu – just be prepared to take lengthy refuge in cafés or malls when yet another thunderstorm breaks.

Kota Bharu

The capital of Kelantan, **KOTA BHARU**, sits at the very northeastern corner of the Peninsula, on the east bank of the broad, muddy Sungai Kelantan. Many visitors arrive across the nearby Thai border, and for most the city is simply a half-decent place to rest and get their Malaysian bearings. To breeze through Kota Bharu and the rest of Kelantan, however, would be to gloss over one of the country's most culturally fascinating states.

Kelantan has historically been a crucible for **Malay culture**, fostering art forms that drew on influences from around Southeast Asia and as far away as India. Kota Bharu is the ideal place to witness the region's distinctive heritage, on show at its **Cultural Centre** and in the various **cottage industries** that thrive in its hinterland – among them kite-making, batik printing and woodcarving. The city also boasts its share of historical buildings, now largely **museums**, plus some excellent **markets** and numerous **Buddhist temples** in the surrounding countryside.

The city centre is compact, with most of the **markets**, many of the **banks** and the biggest stores between Jalan Hospital and Jalan Pintu Pong, a few blocks north.

Around Padang Merdeka

West of the main markets, close to the river, the quiet oasis of **Padang Merdeka** marks Kota Bharu's historical centre. It was here that the British displayed the body of the defeated Tok Janggut (Father Beard), a peasant spiritual leader who spearheaded a revolt against colonial land taxes and tenancy regulations in 1915. Today the main attractions are a handful of historic buildings, several of which have been converted into **museums**.

One of the most obvious landmarks is the **Sultan Ismail Petra Arch**, beyond which is the **Istana Balai Besar** – a mid-nineteenth-century palace, closed to the public but still used for ceremonial functions – and the squat former **State Treasury**.

Istana Jahar

North of Sultan Ismail Petra Arch, Jalan Sultan • Sat–Wed 8.30am–4.45pm, Thurs 8.30am–3.30pm • RM3 • ☎ 09 748 2266

The well-preserved **Istana Jahar** was built in 1887 with a timber portico and pillars painted a regal shade of yellow. In 1911 Sultan Muhammad IV added an Italian marble floor and two wrought-iron spiral staircases. The palace now houses an exhibition on **royal ceremonies**, which can be seen in an hour (although you may want to linger on the breezy first-floor veranda). Rites illustrated include *istiadat pijak tanah*, a ceremony that marked the point when young royals – aged between 5 and 7 years – were allowed to set foot on soil for the first time.

The **weapons gallery**, in a separate building just behind the palace, features an exhibit devoted to the *kris*, a dagger that has important symbolic value to Malays (see box, p.239).

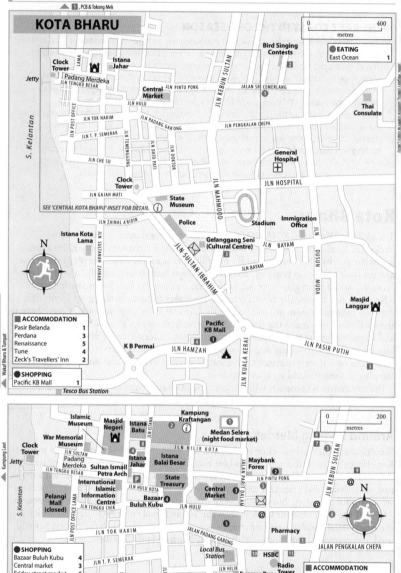

ISLAM IN KELANTAN

Unlike elsewhere in the country, Kelantan's legal system traditionally operated according to **Islamic law** – an important source of national pride under Thai overlordship. This wholehearted embrace of Islam was encouraged by trading contacts with the Arab world, enabling a free flow of new ideas from as early as the 1600s. One of Kota Bharu's most famous sons is **To' Kenali**, a religious teacher who, after years of study in Cairo, returned at the start of the twentieth century to establish *sekolah pondok* – religious schools housed in simple huts.

Kelantan retains its distinctive identity today, to the extent that it's even difficult for anyone from outside the state to buy property here. It's also the scene for an intense political rivalry that has, for example, seen the national government blocking the state government's ongoing attempts to introduce *hudud* (punishments including flogging, amputation, stoning and execution, meted out for specific types of crime).

This rivalry is producing dramatic changes in Kota Bharu. After years of stagnation under PAS and a refusal by UMNO to release funds from federal coffers, both parties have decided that development is the avenue to political glory. As a result, the city now boasts a major shopping mall – the Pacific KB Mall – and a sprinkling of fancy developments – all of which would have been unthinkable until recently. While some foreign visitors find Kelantan's conservatism tangible, especially if they've arrived from Thailand, by and large Kota Bharu comes across as a bustling, pragmatic sort of place.

Istana Batu

North of Istana Jahar, Jalan Istana • Sat–Wed 8.30am–4.45pm, Thurs 8.30am–3.30pm • RM3 • ☎ 09 748 2266

An incongruous 1930s villa, **Istana Batu** was built as a wedding present for Muhammad IV's grandson. One of the first concrete constructions in the state (its name means "stone palace"), today it functions as the **Kelantan Royal Museum**.

Several rooms remain as they were when the royal family moved out, and a brief wander through is worthwhile if only to survey the tat that royals the world over seem to accumulate. Here it includes – among other treasures – tigerskin rugs, a glass revolver and piles of imported crockery.

Kampung Kraftangan

Opposite Istana Batu, Jalan Hilir Kota • Sat–Thurs 8.30am–4.45pm • Free

In the **Kampung Kraftangan** (Handicraft Village), gift shops sell everything from tacky souvenirs to silverware, rattan baskets and other local products. You can try your hand at batik at Zecsman Design (classes from RM50; ☎ 012 929 2822), and the complex is home to two branches of the excellent *Cikgu* restaurant (see p.223).

Handicraft Museum

Sat–Thurs 8.30am–4.45pm • RM3 • ☎ 09 744 3949

The small **Handicraft Museum** upstairs in Kampung Kraftangan is worth a few minutes of your time; it displays traditional craft items including silverware, woven *pandan*, bamboo and rattan objects, woodcarving and *songket* (textiles woven with gold thread).

Masjid Negeri

Jalan Sultan • Permission required from International Islamic Information Centre on Jalan Sultanah Zainab (Sat–Thurs 10am–6pm; ☎ 09 747 7824) • Free

The white **Masjid Negeri**, on the northern side of the padang, was completed in the late 1920s. Once you have permission and are inside the mosque – each gender sticking to their respective prayer halls – male visitors should keep an eye out for the enormous drum (*bedok*) that once summoned the faithful to prayer. The small and rather dull **Islamic Museum** is housed in a mint-green villa immediately west of the mosque.

THE MARKETS OF KOTA BHARU

Kota Bharu has a fine array of **markets**, reflecting its role as state capital and as a centre for Malay culture and handicrafts. There is also an excellent nightly **food market** (see p.223).

Bazaar Buluh Kubu West of the central market. Though lacking in atmosphere, this market does have a good range of batik, *songket* and other crafts on sale. Daily 9am–6pm.

Central market East of the historical centre. Kota Bharu's humming central market, Pasar Besar Siti Khadijah, is one of the city's focal points. The main building, an octagonal hall, has a perspex roof casting a soft light over the patchwork of the main trading floor – a mass of fruit, vegetables and textiles. The whole scene is worth contemplating at length from the upper levels. Trading continues east of here in an extension to the original market; some brilliant first-floor food stalls make it a great place to sample Kelantanese flavours. Daily 8am–6pm.

Friday street market Jalan Ismail, south of Jalan Hulu Pasar. A visit to the informal, morning-only Friday market is recommended as a way to witness the rustic heart of Kelantan laid bare, as traders and shoppers pour in from the surrounding kampungs on their weekend day out in the city. Fri 8am–noon.

War Memorial Museum

Jalan Sultan • Sat–Wed 8.30am–4.45pm, Thurs 8.30am–3.30pm • RM3 • ☎ 09 748 2266

In a solid yellow building that once housed the Mercantile Bank of India, the **War Memorial Museum** commemorates the fact that Japanese troops first set foot in Malaya on Kelantan's beaches. They captured the entire state in December 1941, and Singapore fell just two months later. During the occupation, the bank was the local base for the Japanese secret police.

While the war artefacts are desultory (fragments of ordnance, ration pouches and the like), the accompanying text gives insight into the swiftness of the Japanese advance – aided by their use of bicycles – and the British collapse. The exhibition downstairs also covers the years leading up to independence, while upstairs there's an exhibit on Kelantan's peacetime history, the walls covered with fading photographs of colonial administrators.

State Museum

Jalan Hospital • Sat–Wed 9am–4.45pm, Thurs 8.30am–3.30pm • RM3

Much of the ground floor of Kelantan's **State Museum** is used for temporary exhibits, although it also includes a "time tunnel", where old photographs of locations in the city are paired with contemporary images taken of the same spots. It's fascinating to see what has – and hasn't – changed. The upper floor focuses on traditional local pastimes, with displays of kites, spinning tops, *wayang kulit* puppets and various musical instruments.

Cultural Centre

Jalan Mahmood • Feb–Oct Mon 3.30pm, Wed 3.30pm & 9pm, Sat 3.30pm & 9pm; closed during Ramadan • Free

A high point of any visit to Kota Bharu, the excellent **Cultural Centre** (Gelanggang Seni) holds demonstrations of Kelantan's cultural and recreational activities. Each day's session is different; check with the state tourist office if you have a particular interest. Performances might include a combination of *gasing* (spinning tops), *pencak silat* (martial arts), *rebana ubi* (giant drums), *kertok* (smaller drums formed from coconuts) and *congkak* (a game involving the strategic movement of seeds around the holes on a wooden board). Best of all, Wednesday evenings see **wayang kulit** (shadow puppetry) performances from 9–11pm.

Craft workshops

Most of Kota Bharu's **craft workshops** lie on the road to **PCB**, the uninspiring beach 11km north of the city. As they are quite spread out, the best way to see a variety of

THE PERFORMING ARTS IN KELANTAN

Kelantan has a rich artistic tradition, boasting two costumed dance/drama forms, **mak yong** and the Thai-influenced **menora**. Even more striking is **wayang kulit**, shadow puppetry, traditionally staged on a dais screened from the audience by a large sheet and illuminated from behind. The cast consists of a set of stencils made of hide and cut into silhouettes of the various characters; these are manipulated against the screen by a sole puppeteer, who also improvises all the dialogue. Reflecting India's historic influence in the region, the tales are taken from the Hindu epic, the *Ramayana*. In the past, *wayang kulit* functioned as a sort of kampung soap opera, serializing *Ramayana* instalments nightly during the months after the rice harvest. Performances are gripping affairs, with a hypnotic soundtrack provided by an ensemble of drums, gongs and the oboe-like *serunai*, whose players are seated behind the puppeteer.

Sadly, all three of the above traditional arts have been **banned** in Kelantan since the 1990s by the PAS-led state government. PAS has cited issues of public morality, which could mean they object to the fact that both *mak yong* and *menora* can involve an element of cross-dressing. PAS also objects to the non-Islamic nature of these performances, since they involve folk tales or Hindu mythology. Finally, the party also has a problem with the **spiritualism** permeating these arts. A *wayang kulit* performance begins with a *buka panggung* ceremony, in which the puppeteer readies the stage by reciting mantras and making offerings of food to the spirits, while *mak yong* can be staged for an individual as part of a folk-healing tradition called *main puteri*, in which the performers enter a trance to remove a spirit believed to be affecting that person.

Whatever the reasons for the ban, it has effectively deprived a generation of Kelantanese of their own traditions. A mere handful of *wayang kulit* troupes survive, performing outside Kelantan or, thanks to one **concession** from PAS, for the benefit of the largely tourist audience at Kota Bharu's Cultural Centre. On a brighter note, all three forms mentioned here are being passed on to a new generation outside their home state, at the National Academy of Arts, Culture and Heritage in KL (ⓦaswara.edu.my, Malay-only site), which occasionally stages performances.

4

workshops (including kite-making, batik and more) is on a tour, arranged either via your accommodation or through the state tourist office. Half-day tours cost RM60–90 per person, and often require a minimum of two people. The workshops listed here are not on the way to PCB, and are easier to visit independently.

K.B. Permai (silverware)

Jalan Sultanah Zainab, near Jalan Hamzah intersection · Sat–Thurs 9am–6pm · ☎ 09 748 5661

Kelantanese **silverware** is well known throughout the Peninsula. At the **K.B. Permai** workshop, you can watch artisans shaping silver wire into fine filigree, and producing items such as embossed gongs and jewellery. You can buy pieces here, or at their retail outlet in Kampung Kraftangan (see p.217), at much keener prices than in Kuala Lumpur.

Pak Yusoff (puppets)

Kampung Laut · Boat (RM1) from the jetty close to the Ridel Hotel · ☎ 012 340 6498

A *wayang kulit* **puppeteer** who also makes the tools of his trade, Pak Yusoff can be visited in **Kampung Laut** on the west bank of the Sungai Kelantan. His workshop, to the right of the pier as you get off the boat, holds examples of his distinctive translucent puppets. Call ahead, as he is not always around.

Buddhist temples

The area **north of Kota Bharu** is dotted with **Buddhist temples**, many decorated with a striking combination of Thai and Chinese motifs. The temples can be visited using buses bound for the Thai border at **Pengkalan Kubor**. It's a slow process, getting from

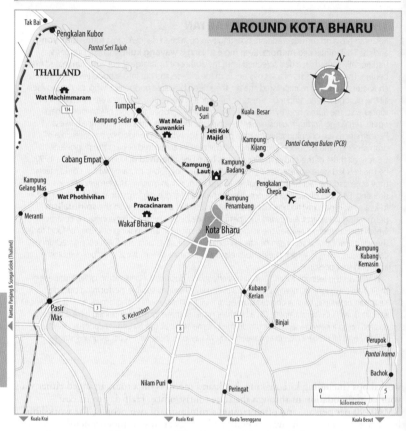

one to the next on public transport; if you're pushed for time it's best to take a tour from the state tourist office or your guesthouse. The temples are especially worth visiting during **Wesak**, the festival (usually in May) celebrating the Buddha's birthday.

Wat Pracacinaram

Kampung Kulim, just outside Wakaf Bharu, on the road to Cabang Empat • Bus #19 or #27

The highly conspicuous main building of **Wat Pracacinaram** has an elaborate triple-layered roof decorated in gold, sapphire and red. The temple offers a herbal **steam bath** – with separate facilities for men and women – for RM5.

Wat Phothivihan

Kampung Jambu • Bus #19 or #27; get off at Cabang Empat then walk 3.5km or take a taxi

The 40m-long reclining Buddha at **Wat Phothivihan** is the largest in Malaysia. The rather bland plaster statue was made by the monks themselves and contains ashes of the deceased who have been laid to rest here. Refreshments are available from *kopi kedais* inside the temple grounds.

Wat Machimmaram

Kampung Jubakar, 7km north of Cabang Empat • Bus #27

Topped by a 30m-high bronze-tiled seated Buddha, **Wat Machimmaram** contains bas-reliefs that depict the graphic punishments of hell – the corrupt are, for example, doomed to have molten tin poured into their mouths, while meat eaters are shown reincarnated as pigs on the carving block. Thai **massages** (RM40, ☎011 1931 5752) are available in a separate block.

Wat Mai Suwankiri

Around 4.5km southeast of Tumpat • Bus #43

The most striking construction at **Wat Mai Suwankiri** is a shrine built in the shape of a dragon boat, surrounded by a narrow moat to give the impression that it is afloat. The main temple hall is crowned by an elongated standing Buddha, its gorgeous interior decorated with hundreds of golden plaques.

Pulau Suri

Taxi to Kuala Besar (20–30min; RM25) then boat (15–20min; RM2); alternatively #43 bus to Jeti Kok Majid (1hr) then boat (40min; RM10/person, or RM50/boat)

One of many small riverine islands north of Kota Bharu, **Pulau Suri** is home to around five hundred people. Getting there is half the fun, requiring a trip down the tea-coloured Kelantan River in a motorized sampan, and the island itself has some pleasant paths for walking and a well-developed **homestay** programme (see p.223).

There are two ways to reach Pulau Suri from Kota Bharu. The most common route goes via **Kuala Besar** (not to be confused with Kuala Besut in Terengganu). While the second route, via **Jeti Kok Majid**, an hour's bus ride from the city centre, is considerably more scenic, it's also more time-consuming. If you're staying on the island, contact the homestay organizer in advance to arrange transport.

Arriving at Pulau Suri, you'll spot a boatyard next to the jetty where they mend traditional wooden craft. There's also a simple **café** or two for refreshments. From here you can head inland along a path lined with coconut trees.

ARRIVAL AND DEPARTURE · KOTA BHARU

BY PLANE

Sultan Ismail Petra Airport The airport lies 9km northeast of the centre. The #9 bus runs between town and airport until 7pm. Official airport taxis cost RM25 to get into town and RM78 to the Perhentians jetty at Kuala Besut. MAS (☎09 771 4700) and AirAsia (☎09 774 1421) have flights between Kota Bharu and KL; Firefly (☎09 774 1377) flies to KL's Subang Airport, Johor Bharu and Penang.

BY TRAIN

Train station The nearest station is 7km away in Wakaf Bharu (☎09 719 6986), a 20min ride on bus #19 (daytime only) from the local bus station – watch for the late-afternoon rush hour – or a RM20 taxi journey. Trains depart early each evening for KL, with the Singapore-bound express several hours later. Check the latest schedules at ⓦwww.ktmb.com.my.

Destinations Dabong (4 daily; 2hr 45min); Gua Musang (4 daily; 4hr); Jerantut (2 daily; 7hr); Johor Bahru (daily; 14hr 40min); Kuala Lipis (2 daily; 6hr); Kuala Lumpur (daily; 15hr); Merapoh (1 daily; 4hr); Singapore (daily; 15hr).

BY BUS

Express bus station (aka Tesco Bus Station) Close to the eponymous supermarket, near the Kelantan river bridge on the southern edge of town; a RM15 taxi ride from the centre. Express bus tickets can be purchased from a row of cabins just south of the local bus station.

Destinations Alor Star (2 daily; 7hr); Butterworth (2 daily; 7hr); Gua Musang (3 daily; 3hr); Ipoh (2 daily; 7hr); Johor Bahru (2 daily; 12hr); Kuala Kangsar (2 daily; 6hr); Kuala Lumpur (12 daily; 9hr); Kuala Terengganu (12 daily; 3hr); Kuantan (10 daily; 7hr); Melaka (1 daily; 10hr); Mersing (1 daily; 12hr); Pekan (1 daily; 7hr); Penang (2 daily; 8hr); Seremban (2 daily; 10hr); Singapore (1 daily; 13hr).

Local bus station Off Jalan Doktor in the town centre. Used by Cityliner buses running to places within or just outside Kelantan – notably Wakaf Bharu (#19 or #27, for trains), the Thai border crossings at Rantau Panjang (#29) and Pengkalan Kubor (#27 and #43) and Kuala Besut (#639, for the Perhentians; 4 daily; 2hr).

BY TAXI OR MINIVAN

Long-distance taxis Taxis depart from a yard on Jalan Doktor, south of the local bus station. A taxi to Kuala Besut will set you back RM48. Call ☎09 748 1386 to book.

Minivans Guesthouses can arrange transfers to popular destinations including the Cameron Highlands (5hr 30min;

RM70), Taman Negara (8hr; RM75) and Kuala Besut (1hr; RM10).

TO THAILAND

There are two road crossings into Thailand – and none by rail – on the east coast. The closest large Thai town to either is Narathiwat, served by buses to other parts of southern Thailand and flights to Bangkok. Although the security situation in southern Thailand has improved in recent years, it's worth checking on the current situation. Visas for Thailand can be obtained from the consulate in Kota Bharu (see p.224) if required. Note that Thailand is one hour behind Malaysia.

Rantau Panjang The recommended crossing is at Rantau Panjang (daily 8am–9pm), 45km southwest of Kota Bharu; get there by local bus #29 (hourly, 6.45am–6.30pm; 45min) or taxi (RM40). From Sungai Kolok, a short walk across the border on the Thai side, trains run to Bangkok, via Hat Yai and Surat Thani (11.30am & 2.20pm; 20–22hr; ⓦ railway.co.th), and frequent buses head to Hat Yai (4hr).

Pengkalan Kubor The other crossing – slower to get through and with worse transport links – is at Pengkalan Kubor (daily around 8am–7pm), 25km northwest of Kota Bharu; take local bus #19, #27 or #43 (30min), or a taxi (RM30) then a car ferry. The small town of Tak Bai stands on the Thai side.

GETTING AROUND

By bus SKMK's red Cityliner buses serve most parts of the city and its environs in daylight hours. Useful routes include #10, which runs to PCB from Kampung Kraftangan.

By taxi Local taxis wait in the same yard as long-distance taxis. Drivers don't use meters, so agree the price before you leave. Journeys within the centre typically cost RM10.

By trishaw A few trishaws can be found around the central market; agree fares, usually RM5–10, in advance.

Car rental Hawk (ⓣ 09 773 3824, ⓦ hawkrentacar.com .my) and J&W (ⓣ 09 773 7312, ⓦ jwcarental.com) have offices at the airport.

INFORMATION AND TOURS

Tourist information The state tourist office (Sun–Wed 8am–5pm, Thurs 8am–3.30pm, Fri 8am–12.30pm & 2–3.30pm; ⓣ 09 748 5534, ⓦ tic.kelantan.gov.my) on Jalan Sultan Ibrahim can tell you about festivals and give you a timetable of events at the Cultural Centre. The Tourism Malaysia office (Sun–Wed 8am–5pm, Thurs 8am–3.30pm; ⓣ 09 747 7554) is at Kampung Kraftangan, northwest of the central market.

Tours Ping Anchorage, Jalan Padang Garong (ⓣ 09 774 2020, ⓦ pinganchorage.com.my), Doremi Travel & Tours (ⓣ 09 774 7458), or any of the town's backpacker hostels can arrange city and craft tours. Roselan Hanafiah, based at the state tourist office, can also put together craft workshop tours. Suzilan Mohammed Salleh (ⓣ 019 942 4033, ⓔ keltga@yahoo.com) runs regular hiking, rafting and climbing trips to Stong State Park and beyond.

Internet access There are a few internet cafés on the lanes between Jalan Pintu Pong and Jalan Padang Garong, usually upstairs. Wi-fi is available at the 24hr *McDonald's* on Jalan Parit Dalam and in most accommodation options.

ACCOMMODATION

Kota Bharu has an excellent range of accommodation. Budget travellers will appreciate the good-value if occasionally scruffy **guesthouses**, many of which can arrange tickets for onward travel and offer packages to Taman Negara via Kuala Koh (see p.207) and Stong State Park (see p.208).

HOTELS

Crown Garden 302 & 303 Jalan Kebun Sultan ⓣ 09 743 2228, ⓦ crowngardenhotel.com. At the upper end of the city's accommodation options, this 88-room hotel has marble floors and striking modern decor plus a seventh-floor bar. The cheapest rooms are cramped but still nicely appointed, with good discounts for walk-in guests. Breakfast included. **RM220**

Crystal Lodge 124 Jalan Che Su ⓣ 09 747 0888, ⓦ crystallodge.my. Sleek mid-range hotel, with a café-restaurant, parking and satellite TV. The compact single rooms (RM89) and superior (RM159) rooms are good value, though the standard doubles and windowless twins are a bit disappointing. Breakfast included. **RM129**

Habib Lot 1159–1162, Jalan Maju ⓣ 09 747 4788, ⓦ habibhotel.com.my. Solid mid-range choice, though the squeaky clean rooms with flat-screen TVs are scuffed in places. Deluxe rooms (RM180) are more spacious but otherwise identical to their cheaper counterparts. Breakfast included. **RM160**

Perdana Jalan Mahmood ⓣ 09 745 8888, ⓦ hotel perdanakotabharu.com. This Malaysian-owned five-star hotel is divided into two wings, "classic" and "executive", with slightly higher prices in the latter; both have the same comfortable rooms and psychedelic carpets. The multiple food outlets are alcohol-free. Breakfast included. **RM300**

Renaissance Jalan Sultan Yahya Petra ⓣ 09 746 2233, ⓦ marriott.com. Some of the 298 rooms in Kota Bharu's first five-star hotel enjoy great views over the city. Facilities include two restaurants, a gorgeous semi-outdoor pool, spa and a 24-hour gym. No alcohol is served, but you can bring your own; they charge for wi-fi. RM385

Royal Guesthouse Jalan Hilir Kota ☎09 743 0008, ✉royalgh@streamyx.com. Despite its far-from-regal exterior, this conveniently central 45-room hotel is comparatively stylish inside. It also offers a multicuisine restaurant plus room service, though the proximity to the mosque (which occasionally broadcasts day-long sermons) may not suit light sleepers. Breakfast included. RM119

Tune Jalan Hamzah ☎03 7962 5888, ⓦtunehotels .com. This out-of-town hotel, beside KB Pacific Mall, is part of the low-cost AirAsia group. Book well in advance for the best prices (walk-in rates start at RM134), and expect charges for all extras – even a/c and towels. RM60

GUESTHOUSES

Ideal Travellers' House 3954 f & g Jalan Kebun Sultan ☎09 744 2246. The oldest guesthouse in town, somewhat worn but great value; most rooms have a fan and shared bathroom, but the three a/c rooms have private bathrooms, hot water and balconies. Friendly owner Kang offers temple tours (3hr; RM90) and sells Perhentian boat tickets. Fan doubles RM30, a/c doubles RM50

KB Backpackers Lodge First floor, 1872d Jalan Padang Garong ☎09 748 8841, ✉backpackerslodge2 @yahoo.co.uk. Friendly travellers' haunt with private rooms, a bare-bones dorm and a dusty gym and small library. Knowledgeable staff can arrange transfers, excursions and city tours (RM80). Not to be confused with the run-down *KB Backpacker Inn* across the road. Dorms RM15, doubles RM35, en-suite a/c doubles RM65

★**My Place Guesthouse** 4340 Jalan Kebun Sultan ☎013 901 1463, ✉myplacekb@yahoo.com. Good backpacker option with appealing common areas, free tea and toast, and a movie room. The seven partitioned

bedrooms are small but decent, all with shared bathrooms; there are plans to add more. Owner Zaidi arranges city tours (RM60) and trips to Taman Negara. Doubles RM35, a/c doubles RM49

★**Pasir Belanda** Jalan PCB, Banggol district, 5km north of the city ☎09 747 7046, ⓦpasirbelanda.com. This rural Dutch-run establishment consists of seven traditionally styled chalets, set in an immaculate garden with a swimming pool overlooking a creek. Activities include batik (RM35) and Malay cookery lessons (RM60), and they offer kayak and bike rental. Catch #10 bus to Banggol mosque, then follow signs 1.5km east, or take a RM20 taxi. Two-night minimum stay. RM160

Zeck's Travellers' Inn Off Jalan Sri Cemerlang ☎09 743 1613, ✉zecktravellers@yahoo.com. Friendly Malay guesthouse in a quiet residential area, with dorms and simple rooms with fan or a/c, some with private bathrooms. Tours and ticket booking are available, and bird-singing contests are held nearby on Friday and Saturday mornings. Dorms RM10, doubles RM25, a/c en-suite doubles RM60

HOMESTAYS

KB homestay programme Various locations. Roselan Hanafiah, at the state tourist office, can arrange for visitors to stay with a local family whose members are expert in a particular craft. The price given here is per night, based on a standard two-night package for two people including all meals and craft materials. RM490

Pantai Suri homestay programme Pulau Suri ☎013 900 8820, ⓦhomestaypantaisuri.blogspot.com. Contact Fadhila Hanim, the programme coordinator, or book through the state tourist office to stay in one of the participating homes; conditions can be fairly basic. You can pay per night (including all meals) or for a two-night package that may include fishing, crab catching and *kuih sepit* (wafer snack) making. RM160, package per night for two people RM300

EATING AND DRINKING

Kota Bharu has plenty of **restaurants** dotted around the centre, plus some excellent food options at the main market and the nightly **Medan Selera** (night food market). The Chinese places on Jalan Kebun Sultan are among the few restaurants that aren't halal, and are your best bet for **alcohol**, along with the odd bar such as *Golden City* on Jalan Padang Garong (Sun–Fri 4pm–midnight).

★**Cikgu** Kampung Kraftangan ☎019 940 6066. Busy self-service lunch place, offering the classic Malay meal *nasi ulam*. Dishes like fried chicken, vegetable curry and *asam pedas ikan patin* (catfish in spicy sauce) are laid out alongside rice and *ulam*, a salad of blanched vegetables and herbs – some of them incredibly bitter. If you're feeling brave, take the dip made of *tempoyak* (fermented durian) and *budu* (fermented fish sauce). Cheap (around RM8 for a filling meal) and best enjoyed with a group. Daily except Fri 11.30am–4.30pm.

East Ocean Jalan Sri Cemerlang ☎09 748 9361. This busy, brightly lit Chinese restaurant stands out like a beacon in this quiet neighbourhood. The non-halal menu includes reliable winners such as steamed fish in soy sauce and oyster pancake, as well as classic dishes including *mapo tofu*, from RM10/dish. Daily 11.30am–2.30pm & 6–10pm.

★**Medan Selera (night food market)** Off Jalan Pintu Pong. The few dozen stalls here offer a great range of *murtabak* (savoury stuffed pancakes) as well as

Kelantanese specialities such as *nasi kerabu* (rice tinted blue, traditionally using flower petals, and typically served with fish curry). Wash your meal down with *sup ekor* (oxtail soup) or *sup tulang* (made from beef bones), and round it off by sampling the colourful *kuih* (sweets). Daily 6pm–midnight.

Muhibah Jalan Pintu Pong ☎ 09 744 3668. Excellent, inexpensive vegetarian establishment. Downstairs a bakery café serves pastries and ice-blended shakes; the upstairs restaurant puts on a great veggie *nasi campur* spread (RM5), as well as à la carte dishes including "chicken" *rendang* (RM15) and other usually meat-based Malay favourites. Daily: restaurant 10am–9.30pm; bakery 8.30am–10pm.

Sri Devi Jalan Kebun Sultan ☎ 09 746 2980. Top-notch South Indian *kedai kopi*, popular with locals but often with a scattering of foreigners, serving excellent banana-leaf curries (from RM5) and tasty mango *lassi*. Daily 7.30am–8.30pm.

UP 2 U Jalan Sultanah Zainab ☎ 012 938 1160. Small

candy-striped dessert station that's a refreshing stop on a hot day, with a wide range of shakes, floats and shaved ice treats; some savoury snacks available. Mon–Sat 4–11.30pm.

Warisan Nasi Kukus Jalan Kebun Sultan. In a small row of Malay stalls, this humble pushcart operation is renowned for fresh *sambal* fish, okra curry, *ikan bakar* (grilled fish) and the like for around RM4 a helping. Your preferred toppings will be poured over steamed rice (*nasi kukus*), on a banana leaf that's folded into a cone and wrapped for you to take away. Daily 6pm–late.

White House Jalan Sultanah Zainab ☎ 09 748 4119. No grand mansion, but a ramshackle bungalow housing a *kedai kopis* that's a city institution. The trademark dish is humble *telur setengah masak* – soft-boiled eggs cracked into a saucer, seasoned with soy sauce and white pepper (RM2.60), and delicious scooped up with *roti bakar* (buttered toast). Washed down with *teh* or *kopi tarik*, it's great for breakfast or a late snack. Daily 8am–1pm & 9pm–1am.

SHOPPING

In addition to its **markets** Kota Bharu is also a good place to buy Malay **handicrafts**, with most of the workshops located outside town (see p.218).

Mydin Jalan Pintu Pong. Useful supermarket selling essentials. Daily 9am–10pm.

Pacific KB Mall Jalan Hamzah ☎ 09 747 6622, ⓦ mallofmalaysia.com.my. For general shopping, this mall is useful, housing the huge Pacific supermarket, a branch of Popular Books and a handful of smaller

bookshops, a branch of the Guardian pharmacy and plenty more besides. Daily 10am–10.30pm.

Parkson Jalan Parit Dalam. A department store that includes a branch of the Giant supermarket. Daily 10am–10pm.

DIRECTORY

Banks and exchange There are several banks around the rectangle bounded by Jalan Pintu Pong, Jalan Padang Garong and Jalan Kebun Sultan. Change money outside banking hours at Azam (Sat–Thurs 9.30am–9.30pm), next to *KB Backpackers Lodge* on Jalan Padang Garong.

Hospital Jalan Hospital ☎ 09 745 2000.

Left luggage At the local bus station (daily 8am–8pm, Fri closed 12.30–2pm; RM2/day).

Pharmacies Central pharmacies include Guardian on Jalan Padang Garong and in the Pacific KB Mall.

Police Jalan Sultan Ibrahim (☎ 09 748 5522).

Post office GPO on Jalan Sultan Ibrahim; there's a

convenient branch post office on Jalan Parit Dalam, just south of Jalan Pintu Pong.

Thai visas Many nationalities can get a visa at the border. Otherwise, visas can be obtained in advance from the Thai Consulate, 4426 Jalan Pengkalan Chepa (Sun–Thurs 9am–noon & 2–3.30pm; ☎ 09 743 0640); they have been known to refuse entry to people in shorts, so dress smartly.

Visa extensions At the Pejabat Imigresen (Immigration Department), Wisma Persekutuan, Jalan Bayam (Sun–Thurs 8am–4pm; ☎ 09 748 2120). Take bus #11 or #639; a taxi will cost RM10.

From Kota Bharu to Kuala Terengganu

Though there are a few good resorts by the shore, plus some interesting villages and wildlife in the **Setiu Wetlands**, few travellers linger on the coast south of Kota Bharu; most are simply waiting for a boat from **Kuala Besut** (for Pulau Perhentian) or **Merang** (to Pulau Redang or Pulau Lang Tengah; not to be confused with Marang further south). Whether you're staying or passing through, get money before you set out; there are **no ATMs** on any of the islands, or near the jetty in Kuala Besut, though some hotels accept cards, and you might be able to get a cash advance (at punitive rates).

Kuala Besut

The only reason to visit the mainland town of **KUALA BESUT** is to catch a boat to Pulau Perhentian. Kuala Besut comprises a few lanes lined with **hotel offices** and **travel agencies** selling Perhentians packages and boat tickets at similar prices, with most of the action concentrated between the peach-coloured **boat terminal** complex and the **bus and taxi station**.

ARRIVAL AND DEPARTURE   KUALA BESUT

By bus There are express buses from KL and Penang directly to Kuala Besut, but for other destinations you'll need to take a taxi (RM20) to the closest transport hub, Jerteh. From Kota Bharu, take Cityliner bus #639 from the local bus station. S.P. Bumi runs a slow, sweaty bus service between Kuala Besut and Kuala Terengganu via Merang.

Destinations Kota Bharu (4 daily; 2hr); Kuala Lumpur (8 daily; 8hr); Kuala Terengganu (4 daily; 3hr); Penang (daily; 8hr).

By taxi The taxi stand is next to the bus station, but drivers will also swoop on new arrivals from the islands.

Destinations Jerteh (RM20); Kota Bharu (RM65; RM75 to airport); Kuala Terengganu (RM120).

By minibus Several travel agents arrange minibuses to a handful of major destinations, including the Cameron Highlands (RM60), Penang (RM70) and Taman Negara (RM80); most services depart mid-morning.

By boat Boats sail from Kuala Besut to the Perhentians several times a day, leaving when full (40min; RM35 one way). Operators usually sell open-return tickets (RM70), with boats returning to Kuala Besut at 8am, noon and, if there's demand, 4pm. Boat service is regular from March to October; at other times sailings are much reduced.

ACCOMMODATION

Nan Hotel Down a lane opposite the boat terminal ☏09 697 4892. Among Kuala Besut's cheaper rooms, all in decent condition. A couple of rooms have a/c and TV, while the most expensive (RM130) even has hot water. No wi-fi. Fan <u>RM49</u>, a/c <u>RM79</u>

Samudera Jalan Pantai ☏09 697 9326, ⓦkekal -samudera.com. The 28 candy-coloured a/c rooms here are spacious, comfortable and reasonably good value, and it's handy for the bus station. <u>RM112</u>

EATING AND DRINKING

Restoran Seafood Lucky Beside the bus station ☏013 997 9354. This place opens extra early for breakfast, offering dishes such as *nasi ayam* (RM6) and noodles throughout the day, but it's the fresh seafood served later on that attracts most people. Daily 5am–10pm.

T'Cafe Near the bus ticket offices ☏09 697 8777. Popular *kopi kedai* dishing up *roti canai* and *nasi dagang* (RM4) for breakfast, with variations on the rice-and-noodle theme and *kerabu* salads (RM6) to keep you going for the rest of the day. Daily 7am–10pm.

Setiu Wetlands

As a breeding ground for the painted terrapin and green turtle, the **Setiu wetlands**, between Kuala Besut and Merang, have been a focus for WWF projects since the early 1990s, but even now they attract only a trickle of tourists. Both the main settlements hereabouts, namely **Penarik**, on the T1 coastal road, and **Mangkok**, 4km to the north, are small villages with poor transport connections, so the easiest way to explore is on a tour organized by an operator in Kuala Terengganu (see p.241).

Pewanis

Pink House, Kampung Mangkok • Sun–Thurs 8.30am–5pm • ☏013 997 1195

The **Pewanis** community project improves the financial position of local women, while working with the WWF on environmental projects. With advance notice, visitors can learn how to make banana chip snacks, help plant mangrove trees or take part in kite-making sessions. Staff can arrange bicycle rental and organize trips to the nearby turtle hatchery.

ARRIVAL AND DEPARTURE
SETIU WETLANDS

By taxi Public transport is limited, so if you don't come on a tour it's best to rent a car or take a taxi (RM80 from Kuala Terengganu).

By bus Buses between Kuala Besut and Kuala Terengganu (4 daily) can drop you at the turning for Mangkok, and you can walk the 3km from there.

Tours By far the best option is to come on an organized tour. Ping Anchorage (see p.241), for example, can arrange a trip including a visit to Pewanis, a turtle hatchery and a man raising *ayam serama* (chickens bred for competition, which sell for up to a staggering RM8000 each).

ACCOMMODATION AND EATING

The women of Pewanis plan to start a homestay scheme, but in the meantime the area has a couple of places to stay (with more in the pipeline), including a stunning **resort**. There are few notable places to **eat** other than at accommodation or roadside *kedai kopis* – look out for local speciality *ikan celup tebung* (battered fish).

Pandan Laut 4km south of Penarik on Pantai Rhu Sepuluh ☎013 681 2495, ⚲pandanlaut.com. Set in a leafy site, the fifteen aged but tidy rooms range from a decent A-frame through wooden chalets to a vast family suite. You'll need to take your meals elsewhere, but turtle watching is free – the WWF staff stay here – and they can arrange island day-trips (RM150/person). A-frame **RM50**, chalet **RM160**

★Terrapuri Heritage Village Kampung Mangkok ☎09 624 5020, ⚲terrapuri.com. A labour of love for the owner of Ping Anchorage travel agency (see p.241), this site, sandwiched between wetlands and beach, features traditional wooden buildings that have been saved from neglect elsewhere in Terengganu and carefully reconstructed. Staff can arrange day-trips or you can lounge by the pool; there's also a spa. Breakfast included. **RM599**

Merang

Most travellers who make it to **MERANG**, on the coastal road just south of the Sungai Merang creek, only glimpse the back of the village on their way to the jetty. The **beach**, accessible along a couple of side roads, is not exceptional, but if you have time to kill there's reasonable swimming and memorable views of the islands offshore – from left to right, the Perhentians, Lang Tengah, Redang and finally Bidung Laut, now uninhabited but once the site of a refugee camp for Vietnamese boat people.

ARRIVAL AND DEPARTURE
MERANG

By bus S.P. Bumi's daily buses between Kuala Besut and Kuala Terengganu (4 daily) stop close to Merang's school.

By taxi A taxi to Merang costs around RM70 from Kuala Besut, RM60 from Kuala Terengganu.

By boat Jetties for the resorts on Redang and Lang Tengah line the riverside, 500m walk from the bus stop (walk

towards and past the traffic lights). Most packages include boat transfers, but tickets are also available from the boatmen. In peak season Nurul Boat Services (☎019 929 9587) runs three daily return trips to Pulau Redang (9am–3pm; RM50) and one to Pulau Lang Tengah (timing varies; RM80).

ACCOMMODATION AND EATING

This quiet stretch of coast has a limited amount of beachfront accommodation, with one or two peeling resorts 4km south of the jetty, near Kampung Rhu Tapai. Merang's **dining scene** is limited to a handful of stalls near the jetty, and a few *kedai kopis* on the road to Kuala Terengganu.

Kembara Resort 474 Pantai Peranginan ☎09 653 1770, ⚲kembararesort.tripod.com. A little run-down but the only budget accommodation in Merang, set in a large well-shaded garden; follow signs down a side road from the bus stop then turn right. The rooms, a mix of cabins and two single-sex dorms, some with a/c, are popular with groups – call ahead before lugging your bags

out here. Dorms **RM15**, cabins **RM50**

Merang Suria Kampung Rhu Tapai ☎09 653 1600, ⚲suriaresorts.com/merang. The seventy gently dilapidated and occasionally downright grubby rooms at this mid-range beach resort fill up at weekends; there are attractive promotional rates for advance bookings. Breakfast included. **RM159**

Pulau Perhentian

The name **Pulau Perhentian** actually covers two islands, **Perhentian Besar** and **Perhentian Kecil** (which mean large and small stopping places, respectively; Big Island and Small Island are sometimes used instead). Both are textbook tropical paradises, which retain considerable appeal despite having been developed for tourism. The essentials of any idyllic island holiday – fantastic sandy beaches, great **snorkelling** and **diving** – are all in place. Both islands have jungly hills in their interior, with paths for **walking** and opportunities to spot flying foxes, monkeys and monitor lizards. All this is capped by a refreshingly laidback atmosphere that can make it difficult to tear yourself away.

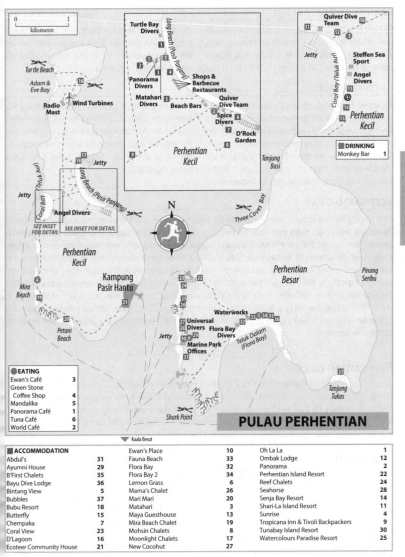

4

● EATING	
Ewan's Café	3
Green Stone Coffee Shop	4
Mandalika	5
Panorama Café	1
Tuna Café	6
World Café	2

■ DRINKING	
Monkey Bar	1

■ ACCOMMODATION					
Abdul's	31	Ewan's Place	10	Oh La La	1
Ayumni House	29	Fauna Beach	33	Ombak Lodge	12
B'First Chalets	35	Flora Bay	32	Panorama	2
Bayu Dive Lodge	36	Flora Bay 2	34	Perhentian Island Resort	22
Bintang View	5	Lemon Grass	6	Reef Chalets	24
Bubbles	37	Mama's Chalet	26	Seahorse	28
Bubu Resort	18	Mari Mari	20	Senja Bay Resort	14
Butterfly	15	Matahari	3	Shari-La Island Resort	11
Chempaka	7	Maya Guesthouse	13	Sunrise	4
Coral View	23	Mira Beach Chalet	19	Tropicana Inn & Tivoli Backpackers	9
D'Lagoon	16	Mohsin Chalets	8	Tunabay Island Resort	30
Ecoteer Community House	21	Moonlight Chalets	17	Watercolours Paradise Resort	25
		New Cocohut	27		

For many years, large-scale development on the Perhentians was kept to a minimum. This was just as well, given that both islands have several **turtle nesting** sites, active from April to early August – the only organized viewing is through the *Bubbles* resort (see p.234) – and that the impact of the existing resorts on the environment is far from negligible. Shortages of **water**, for example, can be a hassle during peak season. The state government's attitude towards development has loosened in recent years, however, and a few larger resorts have been completed, with more in the works – particularly on Perhentian Kecil. **Alcohol** is sold openly at a handful of restaurants and bars, although it seems that it is not strictly legal: the police periodically confiscate booze but it isn't long before things are back in full swing.

ARRIVAL AND DEPARTURE   PULAU PERHENTIAN

By boat All access to the Perhentians is from the mainland town of Kuala Besut (see p.225); boats depart several times a day, regularly from March to October, with reduced sailings at other times. All will drop you at the bay of your choice, though at beaches without a jetty you may have to transfer to a smaller boat (RM2) or wade ashore. The day before your departure, staff at your accommodation will arrange for you to be picked up.

GETTING AROUND

By water-taxi Small speedboats operate a so-called water-taxi service around the Perhentians. Fares start at a few ringgit per person for a journey between adjacent bays – rocky obstructions often preclude walking – rising to RM25 to travel from one side of Besar to the other, or one island to the other. Prices are clearly displayed in front of each water-taxi stand, with little room for bargaining, and it's usually possible to rustle up a boatman within a few minutes. The exception to this is after dark, when water-taxis can become scarce and you may have to pay double the usual fare. If you simply need to get to the next beach, you may be able to use a footpath instead (after dark a torch is essential).

ACCOMMODATION

Until recently Perhentian Kecil catered largely to the backpacker scene, much of its accommodation in low-priced chalets and resorts, and many with restricted electricity supply. The construction of several **mid-range resorts**, however, has brought the same families, package tourists and better-heeled independent travellers that have traditionally gravitated to Perhentian Besar. Book in advance for the **peak season** – roughly June until the end of August – and at weekends, or you may have trouble getting a room. Many mid-range places offer full-board packages, typically for three days and two nights, and include boat transfers and some snorkelling or diving. B&B deals are also available, and unless you're on one of the more remote beaches, there's no shortage of places to eat. Outside peak season rates fall by at least a quarter. Many resorts begin closing in late October, sometimes earlier, and don't open again until February or March, but for a truly isolated island experience a few places stay open during the northeast monsoon.

Perhentian Kecil

The small island of **Perhentian Kecil** has something to please most people. If you're looking for a laidback backpacker scene with the odd beach party, you've come to the right place, but several mid-range resorts cater for those who need a comfortable bed after a day snorkelling. The most popular beaches, **Coral Bay** and **Long Beach**, are only ten minutes' walk apart, along a woodland footpath.

Long Beach

For many visitors, east-facing **Long Beach**, boasting a wide stretch of glistening-white, deep, soft sand, is the prime attraction of Perhentian Kecil. The pretty beach is busy, far from litter free, and lacks a view of the sunset, but somehow that really doesn't matter: the light gently fades away, leaving the illumination from the beach restaurants (and their Bob Marley or dance music playlists) to dominate the senses. Come nightfall there's a genuinely infectious buzz; in peak season, pop-up bars host fairly frequent **beach parties**.

PERHENTIANS DOS AND DON'TS

• Do bring more than enough **cash** – there are no banks or ATMs. Only mid-range places accept plastic for accommodation and food, often with a small surcharge. Several places offer cash advances for a significant fee.

• Do bring mosquito repellent.

• Don't leave **valuables**, even clothes, on the beach – whether crowded or deserted – while you swim or snorkel. Thieves can appear seemingly from nowhere on snatch-and-grab raids, a particular problem on Perhentian Kecil.

• Do **swim with care**: look out for boat lanes, marked by strings of buoys, and stay on the correct side to avoid being wiped out by a speedboat. Note also that Long Beach can have a significant **undertow** from February to April and in October; a few people get swept out every year and have to be rescued.

• Do be mindful of volleyball nets and sharp-pronged boat **anchors** sticking out of the sand as you walk along the beach at night – particularly if you're looking up at the stars.

• As always, don't touch the **coral** or disturb **marine life** when you snorkel or dive.

Coral Bay and the west coast

While west-facing **Coral Bay** has become significantly more developed since the building of its huge and ugly jetty, it remains quieter than Long Beach. It also has sheltered waters, which make it a better bet than its eastern rival during the northeast monsoon, plus good snorkelling and sunset views, if you can ignore the jetty.

A couple of quieter and more secluded beaches lie south of Coral Bay, with accommodation in rustic campsites or guesthouses reached along a shady coastal footpath. **Mira Beach** has just one backpacker hangout, while **Petani Beach** was in an uncertain state at the time of research, with two resorts (one closed, one under construction) awkwardly jammed into its eastern end, and two smaller guesthouses enjoying the remaining stretch of beach.

ACCOMMODATION   PERHENTIAN KECIL

Room rates on Perhentian Kecil – particularly on **Long Beach** – are rather fluid, varying from day to day with demand. The prices quoted here are at the higher end of the range for each property; ask about discounts if you visit midweek or either side of the July–August peak.

LONG BEACH

★**Bintang View** A short walk uphill from the beach ☎09 691 1249. Run by a friendly Malay-Irish couple. Not the fanciest of chalets, but well kept and very homely. Some of the fan-cooled chalets have en-suite bathrooms, while cheaper cabins lack power sockets and share facilities in a separate block. No wi-fi. Shared RM50, en suite RM80

Bubu Resort Long Beach ☎09 697 8888, ⓦbuburesort.com.my. With a motel-like complex of en-suite a/c rooms at one end of Long Beach, and a clutch of deluxe villas at the other, plus two spas and three restaurants, *Bubu* dominates the upper end of Perhentian Kecil's accommodation. The rooms and villas are perfectly nice, but it jars a little here. Doubles RM465, villas RM550

Chempaka End of the beach ☎013 946 6791. This tucked-away place has a mishmash of run-down A-frames, and better en-suite chalets in a longhouse-type block around a pleasant garden. Electricity 7pm–7am; no wi-fi. A-frames RM50, chalets RM80

Lemon Grass Long Beach ☎019 938 3893. Splintery but sound chalets with fans, hammocks and mosquito nets; bathrooms in a separate shack. Three sea-view rooms were under construction at the time of research. There's sporadic electricity and a two-night minimum stay in peak season; prices drop to RM50 at other times. No wi-fi. RM80

Matahari Set back from Long Beach ☎019 914 2883, ⓦmataharichalet.com. A hotel of two halves, with a collection of wooden chalets (fan and newer a/c ones) and A-frames, to which an incongruous two-storey modern block is being added. The largely en-suite chalets are a little rough around the edges, but pretty good value and popular; it remains to be seen what the new wing is like. Both are accessed down a footpath that runs over a smelly creek. Electricity 6.30pm–2pm; no wi-fi. Fan RM90, a/c RM160

Mohsin Chalets On a hillside behind Long Beach ☎09 691 1363. Four tiers of longhouse-style wooden buildings ranked on the hill. The decent-sized rooms are en suite and many have a/c, while a peeling mixed-sex a/c dorm sleeps 24. The restaurant has great views, free wi-fi and occasional

4

4

SNORKELLING AND DIVING AROUND THE PERHENTIANS

Outside the monsoon, the waters around the Perhentians are superb with gentle currents and visibility up to 20m (although sea lice can sometimes be an irritant, inflicting unpleasant but harmless stings). A **snorkelling** foray around the rocks at the ends of most bays turns up an astonishing array of brightly coloured fish, including blacktip reef sharks, and an occasional turtle. The seas around the islands belong to a national park and the coral is protected, although as elsewhere in the region it suffered bleaching due to high sea temperatures in 2010. It remains to be seen whether this was an isolated incident.

If you just want to explore around the main beaches, then snorkels and masks can be rented from accommodation, dive shops or shacks on the main beaches – most places can also arrange **snorkelling trips** to undeveloped coves for around RM35 per person. Many travellers recommend the trips operated by *Maya Guesthouse* (☎ 019 222 9257) on Coral Beach; like most operators, though, they often take very large groups. Typical itineraries include Turtle Point (between the islands), Shark Point, Romantic Beach and the lighthouse; lunch, normally in the village on Perhentian Kecil, costs extra.

Some very good **dive sites** lie a short boat ride offshore, including the Pinnacle (or Temple of the Sea), T3 and Sugar Wreck (a boat that sank while carrying a cargo of sugar). Several of the islands' numerous dive shops organize night dives on the "Vietnamese" Wreck (actually a 1976 US landing craft, Advanced Open Water qualification required). In addition to fun dives (RM70–80), the shops also offer **courses**, including Open Water (around RM1000), Advanced Open Water (around RM900) and the introductory Discover Scuba Diving (around RM200); a handful also offer specialist facilities such as Nitrox. Most places teach **PADI courses**, although Alu Alu (Perhentian Besar; ☎ 09 691 1650, ⊕ alualudivers.com) offers both PADI and SSI.

RECOMMENDED DIVE SHOPS

Bubbles Dive Resort Tanjung Tukas ☎ 012 983 8038, ⊕ bubblesdc.com.

Flora Bay Divers Flora Bay ☎ 09 691 9266, ⊕ florabaydivers.com.

Quiver Dive Team Long Beach and Coral Bay ☎ 012 213 8885, ⊕ quiver-perhentian.com.

Turtle Bay Divers Long Beach and Perhentian Besar Main Beach ☎ 019 669 0028.

movie or karaoke nights. Dorms RM40, fan doubles RM130, a/c doubles RM160

Moonlight Chalets Near the jetty at the northern end of Long Beach ☎ 09 691 1777. A wide range of rooms with 24-hour electricity, including a fan-cooled, seven-bed dorm, cheap A-frames and a/c chalets. No wi-fi and no reservations taken. Dorms RM30, fan doubles RM80, a/c doubles RM120

Oh La La Long Beach, ☎ 019 331 9624, ⊕ ohlalaperhentian.com. Ten simple, good-value rooms with shared bathrooms. Above one bar and beside another, so it's quite noisy at night. There's a pleasant communal balcony with hammocks and RM35 massages are available downstairs (noon–9pm). No electricity 9am–noon; no reservations. RM60

Panorama Set back from Long Beach ☎ 09 691 1590, ⊕ panoramaperhentianisland.com. Overpriced chalets with fans and a/c, plus better-value dorms all set around a messy hillside garden. There's a popular restaurant plus a dive shop; they offer all-inclusive diving packages. High-season rates often include one free meal. Electricity 11am–4.30pm & 6.30pm–8am; no wi-fi. Dorms RM40, fan chalets RM120, a/c chalets RM180

Sunrise Long Beach ☎ 017 930 9053. In the thick of things on the top floor of a two-storey block. Dorms and fan-cooled rooms are decent and understandably popular with those on a tight budget; the two five-bed rooms (RM150) are good value if you're travelling in numbers. No wi-fi. Dorms RM25, doubles RM80

Tropicana Inn & Tivoli Backpackers Midway between Long Beach and Coral Bay ☎ 09 691 8888. A compact development with 120 rooms in neat whitewashed bungalows, with budget and full-price sections that share a reception. The good-value fan rooms and dorms are the stars here, being bright and far cleaner than their equivalents on Long Beach. Dorms RM20, fan doubles RM40, a/c doubles RM120

CORAL BAY

Butterfly At the end of Coral Bay ☎ 013 956 3082. The tucked away, budget chalets here are run-down but charming, popular with long-term guests including dive masters. The further you get from reception, the better the sea views become. Electricity 7pm–7am; no wi-fi. RM50

Ewan's Place Just behind Coral Bay ☎ 014 817 8303. A great choice if you don't mind being a couple of minutes from the beach, with clean and tidy rooms set around a scrubby clearing. The en-suite chalets are nicely maintained, with mosquito nets and *almost* 24hr electricity. Friendly owner Ewan also runs the on-site café. RM80

Maya Guesthouse Coral Bay ☎09 691 1037, ✉mayaguesthouse@yahoo.com.my. En-suite fan chalets around a garden compound, with electricity 7pm–7am and a premium for sea-view rooms (RM120). They allow camping in the garden and can rent you a tent for RM10/day, as well as organizing popular snorkelling trips. No wi-fi. Camping RM10, chalets RM80

Ombak Lodge Coral Bay ☎09 691 1002, ⒲ombak.my. A modern multistorey complex, *Ombak* has 29 fan and a/c rooms awkwardly shoehorned behind their popular seafront restaurant and dive shop. All have en-suite bathrooms, some with balconies too. Fan doubles RM100, a/c doubles RM180

Senja Bay Resort Coral Bay ☎09 691 1799, ⒲senjabay.com. This complex of en-suite chalets, built on a hillside and connected by decking, contains quite spacious and well-maintained rooms. There's also a restaurant and dive shop; snorkelling and diving packages are available. Breakfast included, and there's 24-hour electricity. Fan doubles RM100, a/c doubles RM150

Shari-La Island Resort Northern end of Coral Bay ☎09 691 1500, ⒲shari-la.com. Dozens of chalets, under the same management as *Coral View* on Perhentian Besar. The rooms are slightly overpriced and over-furnished but comfortable nonetheless. Note that the "budget" rooms are for walk-in guests only. Budget doubles RM150, a/c doubles RM230

THE REST OF THE ISLAND

★**D'Lagoon** Teluk Kerma ☎019 985 7089, ⒲dlagoon .my. Nestling in a secluded cove at the island's northeastern tip, this friendly, family-run place makes for a great escape. Accommodation includes two dorms, fan-cooled, en-suite cabins, and a treehouse (RM100). It's a long walk to the cove, but a water-taxi costs just RM10/person from Long Beach. Dive shop on site; no wi-fi. Dorms RM20, cabins RM60

Ecoteer Community House Kampung Pasir Hantu ⒲ecoteerresponsibletravel.com. Staying in the islands' sole village gives a very different island experience, helping with turtle conservation and other projects while getting to know the community. Accommodation is in mixed dorms near the community house, with the weekly price dropping the longer you stay. Prices include boat transfers, meals and a snorkel tour; there's no wi-fi. Per week RM1089

★**Mari Mari** Petani Beach ☎017 998 5462. The three rooms at this quirky guesthouse have been lovingly constructed from flotsam and jetsam, making it a great spot to live out your desert island dreams. Two rooms share bathroom facilities, while one has its own open-air bathroom (RM130). No wi-fi. Open year-round, with substantial monsoon season discounts. RM60

Mira Beach Chalet Mira Beach ☎016 647 6406. A range of rustic chalets clustered in an isolated cove, a 20min walk south of Coral Bay. Despite a recent hike in prices and slightly chaotic management, it's still a backpacker favourite. Most of the nine rooms share bathroom facilities. Snorkelling trips RM40–55, and there's a small restaurant. Electricity noon–3pm & 7pm–7am. Doubles with shared bathroom RM90, en-suite doubles RM200

EATING AND DRINKING

Many places to **eat** are connected to accommodation; they're fine but rarely very exciting. Evening beach **barbecues** – such as at the restaurants around Long Beach's Lazy Buoy shop – are popular and often tasty, but the novelty can wear thin after a few days. Coral Bay's only real bar is the pricey *Ombak Café*; beers sold from coolers on the beach can be taken into most restaurants.

LONG BEACH

Monkey Bar Long Beach. As the only permanent bar on Long Beach, this place is consistently busy; sit by the bar or lounge around in the two-storey wooden building. Beers go for RM9 while a small bottle of "monkey juice" (20 percent alcohol) costs RM20. Live music every night. Daily 6pm–around 2am.

Panorama Café Long Beach ☎09 691 1590, ⒲panoramaperhentianisland.com. Very popular for its early-evening movie screenings, after which most people decamp to the *Monkey Bar* nearby. It's worth trying the food, though; the pizzas (RM26) are particularly recommended. Daily lunch until late.

World Café Long Beach ☎09 697 8888, ⒲buburesort.com.my. This good-looking beach

restaurant serves tasty but pricey Western food, from sandwiches (RM30) to grilled lobster (RM75), with a buffet breakfast (RM33) each morning. Daily 7.30–10.30am & 12.30–10.30pm.

CORAL BAY

Ewan's Café Between Coral Bay and Long Beach. Superfriendly owner Ewan ("Ee-wan") serves great Malay dishes. Pick a main ingredient – chicken (RM12), veg (RM7.50) or prawn (RM18) – then select a cooking style and/or sauce. Daily 7.30am–10pm.

Green Stone Coffee Shop Between Coral Bay and Mira Beach ☎017 931 0263. On a quiet bay a 5min walk north of Mira Beach, *Green Stone* serves hot drinks, juices and simple snacks in a Robinson Crusoe-esque environment, the floor covered with coral, the walls hung with fishing nets, making it a great place to break the coastal walk. There's a campsite attached, handy if you can't bring yourself to leave. Daily 9am–9pm.

Perhentian Besar

The larger of the two islands, **Perhentian Besar**, has a more grown-up atmosphere. Although it holds a few relatively cheap options in addition to the mid-range resorts, it doesn't have the backpacker scene or nightlife of its neighbour. On the other hand, the beaches remain relaxed, despite some nearly continuous strings of development.

Western shore

The chain of attractive beaches on the **western shore** facing Perhentian Kecil are separated by rocks. At high tide most **beaches** can be accessed along concrete walkways, with the notable exception of the path between *Mama's* and *Cozy Chalet*, which is essentially a fifteen-minute jungle trek – a boat taxi may be preferable, especially if you're carrying luggage. Most beaches are lined with resorts, but in a pleasingly organic way; the main beach has a good vibe after dark when the restaurants get busy. At the northern end of the main strip, the *Perhentian Island Resort* sits alone on one of the best stretches of sand, Teluk Pauh.

Teluk Dalam and the south coast

Also known as Flora Bay, **Teluk Dalam** is less cramped than the western shore but also tends to feel slightly institutional, and holds several of the larger resorts. The beach isn't the best on the island, especially when the tide is out. Further east, the *Bubbles* resort sits on its own beach, only accessible by boat.

From the western shore, a steep **trail** (1km; 30min) to Flora Bay begins just past the second jetty south of *Abdul's*, behind the Teluk Keke beach restaurant. Another, prettier trail links Teluk Dalam with the *Perhentian Island Resort* (1.5km; 40min), starting behind the island's waterworks in Flora Bay.

Three Coves Bay

For the finest beaches on Besar, take a water-taxi to **Three Coves Bay** (Teluk Tiga Ruang) on the north of the island, a stunning chain of three beaches separated from the western shore by rocky outcrops. This area also provides a secluded haven for green and hawksbill **turtles** to lay their eggs and as such may be off-limits during nesting season.

ACCOMMODATION

PERHENTIAN BESAR

WESTERN SHORE

Abdul's Southern main beach ☎019 912 7303, ⓦabdulchalet.com. Sturdy en-suite chalets in semidetached pairs, all with a/c. Most of the better and roomier ones, fronting the beach, are significantly more expensive than the garden-facing options, although a couple of "standard seaview" chalets cost RM180. RM160

Ayumni House Southern main beach ☎09 691 1680 or ☎019 436 4463, ⓦd-ayumnihouse.blogspot.com. Set back from the beach, this well-run place has single-sex a/c dorms and adequate semidetached chalets (fan and a/c), as well as a computer and kitchen for guests' use, all set around a small, sandy lot. Breakfast included; electricity 6pm–8am. Dorms RM55, fan chalets RM120, a/c chalets RM240

Coral View Northern main beach ☎09 691 1700, ⓦcoralviewislandresort.com. A range of wood-panelled rooms, mainly in steep-roofed chalets with small attached bathrooms. They're connected by walkways through a pleasant garden, and the standard rooms in particular are good value. There's a restaurant, dive shop, minimart, batik shop, library and foreign currency exchange. Fan doubles RM140, a/c doubles RM190

Mama's Chalet Northern main beach ☎013 984 0232 or ☎019 985 3359, ⓦmamaschalet .com.my. Prim, very decent chalets along a narrow stretch of beach, including a few sea-facing ones with multicoloured fanlights. All rooms have private facilities, and there's a popular restaurant.

OPPOSITE BEACH CHALETS, PULAU PERHENTIAN KECIL (P.229) >

Wi-fi available for a fee (RM5/2hr). Fan doubles RM70, a/c doubles RM160

New Cocohut Southern main beach ☎ 09 691 1811 or ☎ 697 4982, ⊛ perhentianislandcocohut.com. Friendly Chinese-run establishment with reasonable en-suite chalets; the same management also runs *Cozy Chalet* resort, with spacious but scuffed chalets ranged over a nearby hillside. All chalets have a/c, TV and fridge; the more expensive ones have sea views, and there's a popular restaurant. Rates include breakfast and are discounted by a quarter either side of peak season. RM250

Perhentian Island Resort Teluk Pauh ☎ 09 691 1112 or ☎ 03 2144 8532, ⊛ perhentianislandresort.net. Set on a very appealing stretch of beach, this resort – known as *PIR* – has a veritable campus of bungalows and chalets, all spacious and boasting modern furnishings and verandas. There's even a swimming pool, although whether there any need for it here is debatable. RM380

★ **Reef Chalets** Northern main beach ☎ 09 691 1762 or ☎ 013 981 6762. A semicircle of a/c chalets with hints of traditional Malay architecture in the design and spotless bathrooms. The interiors are simple, most rooms with mosquito nets and pleasant verandas, and the garden setting is very attractive. Fan doubles RM120, a/c doubles RM180

Seahorse Southern main beach ☎ 019 984 1881. Connected to a dive shop, offering six acceptable budget rooms with lino floors, wooden walls and firm beds; some lack windows rendering them stuffy and airless. No wi-fi. Fan doubles RM80, a/c doubles RM120

★ **Tunabay Island Resort** Southern main beach ☎ 09 690 2902, ⊛ tunabay.com.my. This slickly managed collection of chalets gets it just right, combining the comforts of a mid-range city hotel (including beach towels for guests) with a cool informality that's perfect for a laidback beach holiday. The bar and restaurant are deservedly popular. Breakfast included. RM280

Watercolours Paradise Resort Northern main beach ☎ 09 691 1850, ⊛ watercoloursworld.com. This resort offers en-suite chalet rooms with fans and small verandas; those with a sea view and a/c are brighter and boast more interesting furnishings, while fan rooms have no power sockets. There's a well-run dive shop and a busy restaurant (7.30am–10pm). Note that an RM20 surcharge is levied on school and public holidays. Fan doubles RM100, a/c doubles RM120

TELUK DALAM AND THE SOUTH COAST

B'First Chalets Teluk Dalam ☎ 019 915 9871. This row of six concrete buildings is nothing special, but the fan rooms are good value. There's a typical beach café at the front, and all-day electricity, but no wi-fi. Fan doubles RM60, a/c doubles RM120

★ **Bayu Dive Lodge** Teluk Dalam ☎ 09 691 1650, ⊛ bayudivelodge.com. You don't have to be a diver to stay in the friendly guesthouse, linked to the Alu-Alu dive shop. There's a large range of rooms arranged compactly in a lush garden, including sea-view cottages, chalets and terraced fan rooms. Cottages are designed along traditional Malaysian lines, while other room categories are more standard. Fan rooms RM80, cottages RM200

★ **Bubbles** Tanjung Tukas ☎ 012 983 8038, ⊛ bubblesdsc.com. A RM10 boat ride from Teluk Dalam, this family-friendly resort has a beach to itself, and combines isolation with good facilities including a dive shop and in-house zoologist who looks after the resort's turtle hatchery. Rooms cost RM60 extra on Friday and Saturday nights. 24hr electricity. RM240

Fauna Beach Teluk Dalam ☎ 09 691 1607. Some of these 35 pleasant, unremarkable chalets are fan-cooled, and a couple of them enjoy Perhentian Besar's cheapest sea views (RM80). The remainder have a/c, but are shabby and overpriced. Fan doubles RM65, a/c doubles RM155

Flora Bay & Flora Bay 2 Teluk Dalam ☎ 09 691 1666, ⊛ florabayresort.com. En-suite accommodation ranging from inexpensive fan rooms to beachfront chalets, including some overpriced a/c units. *Flora Bay*, with its garden of frangipanis and oleanders, is marginally preferable; its counterpart (where the fan rooms are located) features utilitarian two-storey blocks. There's a good dive shop attached. Fan doubles RM70, a/c doubles RM150

EATING AND DRINKING

Almost all Besar's places to eat are affiliated with resorts. Most of the best options are on the **western shore**: you can't go far wrong at *New Cocohut* for Chinese food, *Mama's Chalet* for Malay or *Watercolours* for pizza. The food on **Flora Bay** is generally less interesting, with a few open-air restaurants serving Western and Asian standards plus the odd barbecue. As for drinking, it's largely a matter of choosing one of the few **resort bars** that serves beer.

Mandalika Teluk Dalam ☎ 019 983 7690. With an extensive menu that ranges from *roti canai* (RM2) to fish and chips (RM15) and a nightly barbecue, this cool beach shack is a good way to escape expensive resort food. Owner Halim's sister runs *Nia Cafe* (south of the Marine Park Offices on Main Beach) along the same lines. No alcohol. Daily 7am–11pm.

Tuna Café Tunabay Island Resort, southern main beach ☎ 09 690 2902, ⊛ tunabay.com.my. One of the most adventurous kitchens on either island, serving pasta, salads and seafood, plus evening barbecues (RM28–50) and wine by the bottle. Daily 7.15–10am & 11.30am–9.45pm.

Pulau Redang

The beautiful island of **Pulau Redang** is geared primarily toward visitors on resort-based package trips. Don't expect a quiet island getaway; at weekends and school holidays, bars along the main beach have music or karaoke until midnight.

A **kampung** has been built inland for the two-thousand-strong fishing community who formerly lived in a traditional floating village here, which was removed in 2001 to make way for a jetty and other tourist developments. The highlight of the social calendar, April's **candat sotong** festival, celebrates a pastime popular all along the east coast of the Peninsula, catching squid using small hand-held lures with hooks on one end.

Snorkelling and diving

For most visitors, the chief attraction of Redang is the abundant marine life. The **reefs** have endured a lot over recent decades, including a mid-1970s attack by the crown-of-thorns starfish, and silt deposition caused by development. More recently the coral has suffered from bleaching due to high water temperatures. Thankfully, coral reefs have remarkable properties of self-renewal, and Redang's marine environment appears to have stabilized in a reasonable state.

Conservation has certainly been helped by the designation of the Redang archipelago as one of Malaysia's **marine parks**, and by the regulation of activities such as spear-fishing, trawling and watersports. The best **snorkelling** is off the southern coast around the islets of Pulau Pinang and Pulau Ekor Tibu; the larger resorts take endless boats stuffed with tourists – and bags of fish food – to the main sites, so find a smaller group if you can. **Diving** is also excellent, with most sites off Redang's eastern shore – almost every resort has its own dive shop.

4

ARRIVAL AND DEPARTURE	PULAU REDANG

Regular transport to Redang only runs between **March and October**, when the resorts are open. A conservation fee of RM5 covers three days' stay.

By plane Berjaya Air (☏03 7845 1338, ⊕berjaya-air
.com) flies to Redang's airstrip from KL's Subang Airport
(5 weekly) and Singapore (3 weekly). Transfers from the
airstrip to the resorts are typically included.
By boat Most packages include a boat ticket to Redang.

Departures are from Merang (see p.226), except for boats to
the *Coral Redang* and *Redang Beach* resorts, which use Kuala
Terengganu's Shahbandar jetty; if in doubt, check with your
accommodation. If you're on a room-only deal, expect to pay
RM100 for the return trip from Merang or Kuala Terengganu.

ACCOMMODATION

Most of Redang's accommodation is on the island's **eastern shore**, on Pasir Panjang (Long Beach), the adjacent Shark Bay or, just to the south, Teluk Kalong. Pasir Panjang has a particularly gorgeous stretch of fine white sand; Teluk Kalong's beach is narrower and pebbly in places, but inviting nonetheless. Unless otherwise noted, the resorts have en-suite, a/c rooms and their own restaurants. Many also have dive shops and offer diving-specific packages.

Rates Given that packages tend to be the cheapest way to
visit, reviews here include the price per night of a basic
two-night full-board package for two people, which
typically includes meals, snorkelling (but not equipment
rental) and transfers. Rates shown do not include typical
weekend surcharges of RM30–70/person, and apply to the
high season (July and Aug); look for discounts at the start
or end of the season.

PASIR PANJANG/SHARK BAY
Coral Redang Pasir Panjang ☏09 630 7110,

⊕coralredang.com.my. Recently renovated, with much
more character than most others on Redang, located at the
quieter end of the beach. Rooms are arranged in quaint
two-storey buildings, and there's a small swimming pool
with a poolside bar. The food isn't great, so you may prefer
the B&B option over full board. B&B RM295, full board
RM585
Laguna Redang Shark Bay ☏09 630 7888,
⊕lagunaredang.com.my. Huge, luxurious establishment,
with more than two hundred rooms and a large free-form
pool, famous within Asia as the location of the Hong Kong

comedy movie *Summer Holiday* (1999). A wide range of packages and rooms, all very comfortable and well equipped. Activities include snorkelling, canoe rental, archery and massage. Wi-fi only available for a fee, in the lobby. RM628

Redang Beach Resort Shark Bay ☎ 09 623 8188, Ⓦ redang.com.my. This is a sizeable collection of two-storey units with comfortable rooms, some of which have been recently remodelled. There's a tiny swimming pool and nightly entertainment, should you need either. RM469

Redang Lagoon Chalet Pasir Panjang ☎ 09 666 5020, Ⓦ redanglagoon.com. While the wooden chalets – arranged in two long rows – are nothing special, this is still good value, and is particularly popular with Malay families. RM300

Redang Pelangi Pasir Panjang ☎ 09 624 2158, Ⓦ redangpelangi.com. Standard rooms, plus chalets that are marginally better and more expensive. All are pretty functional; it's cheap for Redang, but you'd pay a fraction of the rate on the Perhentians. There's also a popular (and noisy) bar. RM400

Redang Reef Shark Bay ☎ 09 630 2181, Ⓦ redangreefresort.com.my. Perched on the headland at the southern end of Shark Bay, reached by a long wooden walkway, this good-value resort is less luxurious than its neighbours, with simply furnished rooms and a bar overlooking the sea. RM338

TELUK KALONG

Redang Kalong Teluk Kalong ☎ 03 7960 7163 (KL), Ⓦ redangkalong.com. While this peaceful beach isn't quite as nice as Pasir Panjang, its only resort is popular nonetheless. Many of the 39 basic and rather sparsely furnished rooms offer sea views, and the five-star IDC "Divers' Den" dive centre gets rave reviews. RM420

TELUK DALAM

The Taaras Beach & Spa Resort Teluk Dalam ☎ 09 221 3997, Ⓦ thetaaras.com. Formerly known as the *Berjaya*, this luxury resort is a cut above the rest in terms of service, facilities and prices, with golf buggies to help you get between the well-appointed rooms, spa, restaurants, dive shop, swimming pools and tennis courts. RM960

Pulau Lang Tengah

Although **Pulau Lang Tengah** is largely a package destination, it holds just a handful of spread-out places to stay and therefore offers a lower-key experience than its near-neighbour Pulau Redang. As well as attractive and quiet beaches, there's some good **snorkelling**, including a patch of blue coral (*Heliopora coerulea*) offshore from the *Sari Pacifica*. All the resorts, with the exception of *Lang Sari*, have **dive shops**.

Turtles lay their eggs on certain beaches; staff at *D'Coconut Lagoon* (see below) wake guests if any are spotted during the night on the nearby Turtle Beach.

ARRIVAL AND DEPARTURE

By boat Most people visit on packages, which usually include boat transfers (and the RM5 per visitor conservation charge) from Merang. Otherwise *Lang Sari* charges RM80 return, and other resorts a little more. Most boats leave early in the morning, but afternoon charters are possible (contact resorts for details).

ACCOMMODATION

Lang Tengah holds just four resorts, all of which are popular with Malaysian and Singaporean tourists and as such can get very busy at weekends and public holidays (when prices rise). The **full-board prices** listed below are per night, based on two people sharing on a two-night package (which includes boat transfers but not snorkelling).

D'Coconut Lagoon Pulau Lang Tengah ☎ 03 4252 6686, Ⓦ dcoconutlagoon.com. Split into two wings a couple of minutes' walk apart. All rooms have a/c and hot showers; those in the nicer west wing are more expensive than those in the east wing, quoted here. The resort gives out a very handy sketch map of the island. B&B RM395, full board RM460

Lang Sari Resort Pulau Lang Tengah ☎ 03 2181 8370, Ⓦ langsari.com. This down-to-earth – and rather down-at-heel – resort has some sea-view rooms pretty much on the beach. Full board RM410

Sari Pacifica Pulau Lang Tengah ☎ 09 690 0300, Ⓦ saripacifica.com. The bling decor may be getting shabby, but a jacuzzi in each bathroom goes some way in compensation. B&B RM374, full board RM468

Summer Bay Resort Pulau Lang Tengah ☎ 09 623 9911, Ⓦ summerbayresort.com.my. Packages at this resort, with simple, wood-panelled, en-suite rooms in two-storey blocks, include meals as well as snorkelling and jungle trekking. The resort also has the only minimart on the island. Full board RM688

Kuala Terengganu

After a long spell as an important port trading with the Chinese, **KUALA TERENGGANU** (the capital of Terengganu state) had by the late nineteenth century been eclipsed by the rise of Singapore and other new ports in the Melaka Straits. Following the transfer of Terengganu from Siamese to British control in the early twentieth century, the state became the last in the Peninsula to take a British Adviser, in 1919. It continued to languish as a rural state with, unusually, most of its settlements at river mouths rather than on the lower reaches of rivers, as elsewhere in Peninsular Malaysia.

The discovery of oil in the 1980s transformed its fortunes; modern Kuala Terengganu is even more of a hotchpotch than most Malaysian cities, the remnants of its constituent kampungs sprinkled with oil-funded showpieces and construction sites. There is, nevertheless, a certain **austerity** about Terengganu state that's noticeable in Kuala Terengganu. It lacks the commercial buzz of Kuantan or even Kota Bharu, partly because oil revenues have barely trickled down to ordinary people but also because in some respects the state is more conservative and inward-looking than neighbouring Kelantan.

Many visitors use the city simply as a transit point for Terengganu's best-known attractions – the pleasant **beaches** that line most of the coastline, and glorious **islands** including the Perhentians, Pulau Redang, Pulau Lang Tengah and Pulau Kapas. Using the city as a base, you can also venture inland to the lake of **Tasik Kenyir**. Even in itself Kuala Terengganu holds enough to reward a day or two's sightseeing, in particular the **old town** with its lively **Central Market** and the adjacent historic **Chinatown**; the **State Museum**, among the best of such complexes in Malaysia; and **Pulau Duyong**, where the city's maritime heritage just about survives.

Old town

Kuala Terengganu's compact centre is built on a semicircular parcel of land that bulges north into the mouth of the Terengganu River, which flows past the western half of the city, where the **old town** is located. The eastern half of the city is flanked by the South China Sea, with ongoing land reclamation rapidly altering the shoreline.

Bukit Puteri

Daily 9am–5pm, closed Fri noon–3pm • RM1 • ☎ 09 622 1444

A lovely little park with mature trees and chirruping cicadas, the steep hillock of **Bukit Puteri** ("Princess Hill") is crowned by a white tower that still serves as a lighthouse. You can access the hill via the escalators at the Bazaar Warisan (Heritage Bazaar) on Jalan Sultan Zainal Abidin.

Wide-ranging views take in the Sungai Terengganu and the bell-shaped roofs of the blindingly white **Masjid Zainal Abidin** just to the south. Relics of the hill's time as an early nineteenth-century stronghold include a fort, its bricks once bound with honey (although it's now concrete), and several cannons imported from Spain and Portugal.

Central Market

Daily 6am to mid-afternoon

Close to the lacklustre Bazaar Warisan with its assorted batik shops and jewellers, the ground floor of the much more rewarding **Central Market** (Pasar Payang) is occupied by a thriving wet market. Look out for stalls selling *keropok* (dried fish paste) and Malay confections in just about every conceivable hue. The upper floors comprise a maze of food stalls and outlets selling batik, *songket* and brassware.

4

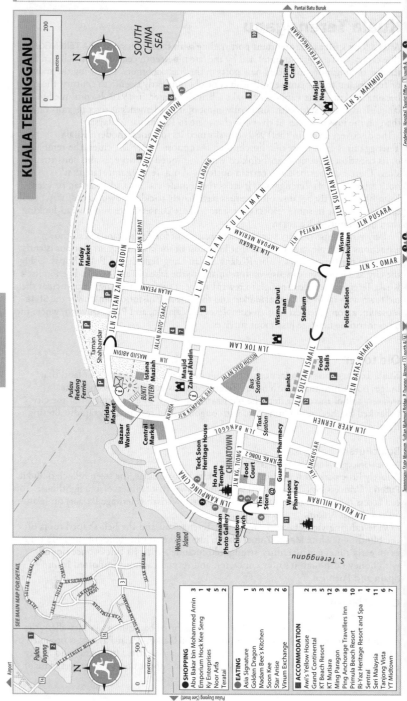

KUALA TERENGGANU

▲ Pantai Batu Buruk

SOUTH CHINA SEA

N

0   200
metres

Wanisma Craft

Masjid Negeri

JLN S. MAHMUD

JLN S. MAHMUD

JLN PERSINGGAHAN

JLN SULTAN ZAINAL ABIDIN

JLN LADANG

JLN SULTAN ISMAIL

JLN PUSARA

Wisma Persekutuan

JLN S. OMAR

JLN PEJABAT

JLN TENGKU MAHMUD

AMPANG MERIAM

JLN SULTAN SULAIMAN

Wisma Darul Iman

Stadium

Police Station

JLN SULTAN ISMAIL

Food Stalls

JLN BATAS BHARU

JLN AYER JERNEH

Friday Market

JLN SULTAN ZAINAL ABIDIN

JLN NESAN EMPAT

JALAN PETANI

JALAN DATO' ISAACS

JALAN DATO' ISAACS

Taman Shahbandar

Pulau Redang Ferries

Bazaar Warisan

Friday Market

Central Market

BUKIT PUTERI

JLN KOTA

JLN KAMPUNG DALAM

Masjid Abidin

Istana Maziah

Masjid Zainal Abidin

JALAN SYED HUSSIN

JLN TOK LAM

Bus Station

Banks

JLN SULTAN ISMAIL

Taxi Station

Teck Soon Heritage House

JLN KAMPUNG CINA

Ho Ann Temple

CHINATOWN

JLN KG. TIONG 1

Food Court

The Store @

Guardian Pharmacy

JLN KG. TIONG 2

JLN BANGGOL

JLN ENGKUSAR

Watsons Pharmacy

Peranakan Photo Gallery

Chinatown Arch

JLN KUALA HILIRAN

Warisan Island

S. Terengganu

Cenderan Hospital Tourist Office ▶ ▶ ▶ ▶ ▶
Terengganu State Museum Sultan Mahmud Bridge ▶ Duyong Airport (13) north & TM

SEE MAIN MAP FOR DETAIL

JLN SULTAN ZAINAL ABIDIN
JLN SULTAN OMAR
JLN TERENG LANJUT
JLN KEMBAGA
JLN SH IBRAHIM

Pulau Duyong

Airport ▲

JALAN TENGKU MIZAN

0   500
metres

N

▶ Pulau Duyong (See Inset)

● SHOPPING	
Abu Bakar bin Mohammed Amin	3
Emporium Hock Kee Seng	1
Ky Enterprises	4
Noor Arfa	5
Teratai	2

● EATING	
Asia Signature	1
Golden Dragon	5
Madam Bee's Kitchen	3
Soon Kee	4
Star Anise	2
Vinum Exchange	6

■ ACCOMMODATION	
Awi's Yellow House	2
Grand Continental	3
KT Beach Resort	5
KT Mutiara	12
Ming Paragon	9
Ping Anchorage Travellers Inn	8
Primula Beach Resort	10
Ri-Yaz Heritage Resort and Spa	1
Sentral	4
Seri Malaysia	11
Tanjong Vista	6
YT Midtown	7

Chinatown

Reached via Jalan Kampung Cina, south of the central market, Kuala Terengganu's **Chinatown** was established in the eighteenth century, when the trading links between Terengganu and China drew in early Chinese settlers. The main street is lined with pastel-coloured **shophouses**, one of the finest examples of which, the sky-blue **Teck Soon Heritage House**, is occasionally open to the public as a museum. Further south, the **Peranakan Photo Gallery** displays black-and-white photographs showing the town's development (daily 9am–5pm; free). Nearby, the photogenic **Ho Ann Temple** (daily 7.30am–7.30pm; free) is dedicated to Mazu, the Goddess of the Sea. The current complex was reconstructed in 2010 after its predecessor burned down, but the temple has occupied the same spot since the late eighteenth century. A useful leaflet, *Chinatown Heritage Trail*, is available from the state tourist office.

Terengganu State Museum

Bukit Losong, 6km west of town centre • Daily 9am–5pm, closed Fri noon–3pm • RM15 • ☎ 09 632 1200, ⓦ museum.terengganu.gov.my • Bas bandar service (see p.240) from city centre (C-02; 45min) or RM20 taxi ride (one way)

Arriving at the **Terengganu State Museum**, you might think you've strayed into *Gulliver's Travels*. Visitors are confronted by a series of buildings modelled on the archetypal Terengganu village house, but absolutely Brobdingnagian in scale. Along with being Malaysia's biggest state museum, the buildings also house one of the country's best collections.

The ground floor of the **main building** holds exquisite **fabrics** from around Southeast Asia, while the next floor up displays various **crafts**. The top floor details the **history** of Terengganu. The **Petronas Oil Gallery**, in the building to the left, is sporadically interesting but predictably skewed. Behind it, the old-fashioned **Islamic Gallery** displays fine examples of Koranic calligraphy.

Allow time to see the rest of the site. Beside the river are two examples of the **sailing boats** for which Kuala Terengganu is famed – unique blends of European ships and Chinese junks. The small **Seafaring Gallery** and larger **Fisheries and Marine Park Gallery** are close by, as is a collection of smaller, beautifully decorated fishing boats. Five old timber buildings have been disassembled and reconstructed within the grounds. Among them, the **Istana Tengku Long** was originally built in 1888 entirely without nails, which to Malays signify death because of their use in coffins.

4

THE KRIS

The **kris** (or *keris*) occupies a treasured position in Malay culture, a symbol of manhood and honour believed to harbour protective spirits. Traditionally, all young men crossing the barrier of puberty receive one that remains with them for the rest of their lives, tucked into the folds of a sarong; for an enemy to relieve someone of a *kris* is tantamount to stripping him of his virility. In the past some weapons were reputed to have magical powers, able to fly from their owners' hand to seek out and kill an enemy.

The *kris* itself is intended to deliver a horizontal thrust rather than the more usual downward stab. When a sultan executed a treacherous subject, he did so by sliding a long *kris* through his windpipe, just above the collarbone, thereby inflicting a swift – though bloody – death. The distinguishing feature of the dagger is the hilt, shaped like the butt of a gun to facilitate a sure grip. The hilt can also be used to inflict a damaging blow to the head in combat, especially if there isn't time to unsheathe the weapon.

The daggers can be highly decorative: the iron blade is often embellished with fingerprint patterns or the body of a snake, while the hilt can be made from ivory, wood or metal. Hilt designs usually take the form of birds' heads.

BOAT-BUILDING ON PULAU DUYONG

Historically, the boatyards of Pulau Duyong produced **schooners** that ranged from humble fishing craft to the hulking *perahu besar*, up to 30m in length. These days however, motorized, modern alternatives to the old-fashioned wooden boats, the increasing cost of timber, and the lure of other careers have all contributed to a steep decline in this traditional industry. Salvation for the handful of boatyards that remain has come from overseas, as clients from around the world place orders for all manner of bespoke craft.

The shipwrights of Pulau Duyong work mostly from memory rather than set plans. For hulls, their preferred material is **cengal**, a wood whose toughness and imperviousness to termite attack make it prized not only for boats but also the best kampung houses. After the hull planking is fastened with strong hardwood pegs, a special sealant – derived from swampland trees, and resistant to rot – is applied. Unusually, the frame is fitted afterwards, giving the whole structure strength and flexibility. As construction takes place in **dry docks**, the finished boats have to be manoeuvred on rollers into the water, an effort that often requires local villagers to pitch in.

Pulau Duyong

Sporadic water-taxis from moorings north of the Central Market; better to take the C-03 bas bandar service (see below) or taxi (RM20)

The proud home of a venerable **boat-building** tradition, **Pulau Duyong** ("Mermaid Island") was once two islets in the Terengganu River; they were joined by reclamation to form what you see today. Although the northern end of Duyong was levelled to build a resort (see p.242) and a prestigious **yacht club** for the annual Monsoon Cup race (ⓦmonsooncup.com.my), the southeastern side of the island is essentially still a rustic kampung that's great for an hour's stroll.

If you want to visit one of the handful of surviving **boatyards**, ask around for directions or enquire at long-standing backpacker favourite *Awi's Yellow House* (see opposite). One boatyard is owned by Awi, while several others are close to the Sultan Mahmud bridge on the island's eastern shore.

ARRIVAL AND DEPARTURE
KUALA TERENGGANU

By plane The airport is 14km north of the city; a taxi into the centre costs RM30. MAS (ⓣ09 662 6600, ⓦmalaysiaairlines.com) and AirAsia (ⓣ09 667 1017, ⓦairasia.com), both with offices at the airport, fly to KLIA, and Firefly (ⓣ09 667 5377, ⓦfireflyz.com.my) operates daily flights to the capital's Subang airport.

By bus The spacious, modern bus station, smack in the centre on Jalan Masjid Abidin, is used by intercity and local buses.

Destinations Alor Star (daily; 9hr 30min); Batu Pahat (2 daily; 8hr); Butterworth (daily; 12hr); Cherating (6 daily; 3hr 30min); Dungun (8 daily; 2hr); Johor Bahru (11 daily; 9hr); Kangar (daily; 10hr 30min); Kemaman/Chukai (7 daily; 3hr); Kota Bharu (12 daily; 3hr); Kuala Besut (4 daily;

3hr); Kuala Lumpur (13 daily; 7hr); Kuantan (10 daily; 4–5hr); Marang (several daily; 30min); Melaka (2 daily; 9hr); Merang (4 daily; 1hr); Mersing (7 daily; 7hr); Muar (2 daily; 8hr); Pekan (5 daily; 5hr 30min); Rantau Abang (8 daily; 1hr 30min); Segamat (2 daily; 7hr); Seremban (2 daily, 7hr); Singapore (3 daily; 10hr); Sungai Petani (daily; 8hr).

By taxi Long-distance taxis depart for destinations across the Peninsula from outside an office (ⓣ06 626 5150) just south of the bus station. The fare to Kota Bharu is around RM140, and it's RM120 to Kuantan.

By boat The Shahbandar jetty on the seafront is used by a few resort boats to Pulau Redang.

GETTING AROUND

Bas bandar Besides the city's standard bus services, an hourly "heritage bus" (*bas bandar*) service runs a hop-on, hop-off route to the main attractions. There are three different routes, each starting at the Taman Shahbandar park and stopping at the main bus station before going on to destinations including the State Museum (C-02), Pulau Duyong (C-03) and

Noor Arfa (C-01). Enquire at tourist offices for schedules and fares.

By taxi Taxis are easily found near the bus station or around the Central Market; you'd be lucky to flag one down in the street.

By trishaw Trishaws can be found near the Central Market, charging around RM30/hr.

By car Car rental is available through Ping Anchorage (see below) for around RM189/day; there are also booths in the airport arrivals hall (from RM110/day).

INFORMATION

Tourist information The state tourist office is next to the GPO on Jalan Sultan Zainal Abidin (Sat–Thurs 8.30am–4.30pm; ☎09 622 1553, ⓦtourism.terengganu .gov.my). The Tourism Malaysia office is a little way south on Jalan Kampung Daik (Sun–Wed 8am–5pm, Thurs 8am–3.30pm; ☎09 630 9433). Ask at either about homestays in the city and its surroundings.

Travel agents Ping Anchorage Travel and Tours, 77a Jalan Sultan Sulaiman (daily 8am–5pm; ☎09 626 2020, ⓦpinganchorage.com.my), is efficient and well organized, offering packages throughout the east coast and the interior. They also run the *Ping Anchorage Travellers Inn* (see below) and the brilliant *Terrapuri Heritage Village* north of the city (see p.226).

ACCOMMODATION

Kuala Terengganu has a reasonable range of places to stay, including a few hotels overlooking the South China Sea east of the centre. On **Pulau Duyong**, the contrast between the huge (but often half-empty) resort development and the basic village homestays and friendly backpacker hangout could not be greater. With your own transport, and a taste for pricey, traditionally styled accommodation, you could base yourself at *Terrapuri Heritage Village* in Penarik (see p.226).

CITY CENTRE AND BEACH

Grand Continental Jalan Sultan Zainal Abidin ☎09 625 1888, ⓦghihotels.com. The fanciest place in town when it opened in 1997, this chain hotel is showing its age despite recent renovations. However, the spacious rooms have marbled bathrooms and satellite TV, and there's a pool and coffee shop. Breakfast included. RM238

KT Beach Resort 548e Jalan Sultan Zainal Abidin ☎09 631 5555, ⓦktbeachresort.wordpress.com. This old-school hotel no longer enjoys a beachside position, thanks to recent land reclamation. Fan and a/c rooms are squeaky clean if unexciting, and they also manage some surprisingly appealing, fully furnished apartments in the residential block across from the *Tian Kee* restaurant. Fan doubles RM95, apartments RM200

KT Mutiara 67 Jalan Sultan Ismail ☎09 622 2655. While some fittings look worn and dated, these are comfortable rooms for a decent price. Some have no windows, though at least they're quieter. Discounts available midweek. RM85

Ming Paragon 219e Jalan Sultan Zainal Abidin ☎09 631 9966, ⓦmingstarhotel.com. A newer sister hotel to the nearby *Ming Star*. The executive room (RM220) has a computer and complimentary minibar (no alcohol), but even the cheapest standard rooms have flat-screen TV, hairdryer, iron and kettle – all they're missing is windows, for which you have to pay extra (RM167). Breakfast included, and there's a spa (2–10.30pm). RM146

Ping Anchorage Travellers Inn 77a Jalan Sultan Sulaiman ☎09 626 2020, ⓦpinganchorage.com.my. The cheapest place in town, above a helpful travel agency. Rooms are basic and sparsely furnished, mostly with fans, cement floors and shared facilities, though some have en-suite bathrooms and a/c. You'll need to check in during the travel agency's office hours (8am–5pm) otherwise they'll lock up and go home. No wi-fi. Fan doubles RM25, a/c doubles RM65

Primula Beach Resort Jalan Persinggahan ☎09 622 2100, ⓦprimulahotels.com. Behind the ugly facade is a decent 246-room hotel complete with pool, spa, gym and two restaurants. While the public areas are getting a little ragged, the a/c rooms are spacious and well kept. "Superior" rooms on the ground floor of an older block have patio doors leading to the beach. Ample parking, and free shuttle into the centre. Breakfast included. RM195

Sentral 28 Jalan Tok Lam ☎09 622 0318, ✉travel @redang.com.my. Part of the *Redang Beach Resort* group, this centrally located hotel has a range of bright, attractive, en-suite rooms at equally attractive prices. All fifty have a/c, though some lack windows. RM79

Seri Malaysia Jalan Hiliran ☎09 623 6454, ⓦserimalaysia.com.my. Standard but sound chain hotel with views of Pulau Duyong from some rooms, including certain standard rooms (ask when you book). Rates include breakfast in the riverside dining room. RM158

Tanjong Vista 132d Jalan Sultan Zainal Abidin ☎09 631 9988, ⓦhoteltanjongvista.com.my. The logo and uniforms may be bright pink but the rooms in this business hotel are tastefully furnished and good value. The small semi-outdoor swimming pool on the fourth floor has views of the beach and sea; there's also a small gym. Breakfast included. RM172

★YT Midtown 30 Jalan Tok Lam ☎09 622 3088, ⓦhotelytmidtown.com.my. While this convenient central hotel is neither fancy nor flashy, it does stand out for its comfortable beds and reasonable prices. All rooms have TV, a/c and en-suite bathroom, breakfast is included and there's a car park lot. RM108

PULAU DUYONG

★Awi's Yellow House Pulau Duyong ☎017 984 0337. You'll need to ask for directions to reach this delightful no-frills timber complex, which sits on stilts over the water.

4

Accommodation is in dorms and thatched-roof huts with mosquito nets; some have private bathrooms. There's also a kitchen and kayaks (RM10/day) available to rent; Awi's small boatyard is nearby. No wi-fi. Dorms RM15, huts RM35

Ri-Yaz Heritage Resort and Spa Pulau Duyong ☎ 09 627 7888, ⒲ ri-yazheritage.com. It isn't clear where

"heritage" comes into this sprawling development, but the wooden chalets are comfortable and well outfitted. The pool is a bonus, as is the restaurant with a terrace overlooking the river. The resort can arrange transfers by taxi (RM20) given notice. Look out for promotional rates. RM440

EATING AND DRINKING

Terengganu's signature dish, **nasi dagang**, consists of slightly sticky rice, steamed with a little coconut milk and chopped shallots, and often served with fish curry for breakfast. Other key dishes include **laksam** (rolled rice noodles in a thick fish and coconut milk gravy) and **keropok** – dried fish paste, served *lekor* (long and chewy), *losong* (steamed) or *keping* (crispy). There are a few decent **Malay restaurants**, and the Malay stalls at the Central Market, as well as just south of the junction of Jalan Sultan Ismail and Jalan Tok Lam, are worth trying. Chinatown is the obvious focus for **Chinese food** – especially after dark, when many other areas are quiet – with a hawker centre along Jalan Kampung Tiong 1 and several excellent restaurants on the main street. Chinatown is also your best bet for finding **alcohol** in this largely dry city.

Asia Signature Jalan Sultan Zainal Abidin ☎ 09 620 5421. This bright, airy café is handy if you find yourself east of the town centre. The menu ranges from chicken *rendang* to *keropok* and dim sum (the salted egg bun, RM5.90, comes recommended) and they also offer vegetarian versions of a few Malay classics, including a tasty *nasi lemak* (RM4.90). Daily noon–3pm & 6–9.30pm.

Golden Dragon Jalan Kampung Cina ☎ 09 622 3034. One of the most established and popular restaurants in Chinatown, with a great *nasi campur* at lunchtime (around RM8), and reliable seafood (try the steamed fish) and other stir-fried dishes in the evening. Daily noon–3pm & 6–9.30pm.

Madam Bee's Kitchen 177 Jalan Kampung Cina ☎ 012 988 7495. Specializing in Terengganu Peranakan dishes, this is the place to come to try local Malay and Chinese dishes, including *nasi kerabu* (RM7.50) and Terengganu *loh mee* (egg noodles in thick gravy with chicken and crab;

RM6.50). Thurs–Tues 9.30am–5.30pm.

Soon Kee Jalan Kampung Cina. This Chinatown staple has been serving superlative *bah kut teh* for decades. If you don't like herbal pork broth then look elsewhere, as it's the only thing on the menu. Daily 7–10am & 6–9pm.

Star Anise 82 Jalan Kampung Cina ☎ 017 664 2368. Head to this funky café for excellent coffee, locally grown tea (from RM5), and a slice of cake. Outdoor seating on a quiet side street and plenty of decorative touches make this one of the nicest spots to take a break in Chinatown. Daily 10.30am–12.30am.

Vinum Exchange 221 Jalan Kampung Cina ☎ 011 1697 1433. With one wall covered by racks of spirits, pork chop (RM19) on the menu and tinted glass in the windows, this bar feels downright subversive in straight-laced KT. Lavazza coffee (espresso RM4) and pastries are served in the daytime, but crowds congregate in the evening for beer and wine (from RM8) – spirits are takeaway only. Daily 11am–11pm.

SHOPPING

Emporium Hock Kee Seng Jalan Sultan Zainal Abidin. Small shopping complex good for everyday purchases. Like the Store in Chinatown, this is more of a general emporium and supermarket. 10am–10pm daily.

Noor Arfa Cendering Industrial Area, 7km south of the city. ☎ 09 617 9700, ⒲ noor-arfa.com.my. Large showroom with a more extensive choice of batik than the

shops on Jalan Sultan Zainal Abidin, and occasional demonstrations. Take the *bas bandar* service to Cendering. Sat–Thurs 9am–7pm.

Teratai 151 Jalan Kampung Cina ☎ 09 625 2157. The most established of several boutiques and souvenir shops taking root on Jalan Kampung Cina, housed in a well-preserved shophouse. Sat–Thurs 10am–5pm.

ARTS AND CRAFTS WORKSHOPS

Like neighbouring Kelantan, Terengganu is renowned for its **handicrafts**. At several places in and around the city, visitors can watch craftspeople at work and buy their products.

Abu Bakar bin Mohammed Amin 500m west of Jalan Panji Alam, 1406 Lorong Saga in Pasir Panjang ☎ 09 622 7968. Watch the making of the *kris*, a two-edged dagger (see box, p.239), and its decorated wooden sheath. On S.P. Bumi local bus route; get off at Sekolah Kebangsaan Pasir Panjang. By appointment only.

Ky Enterprises Jalan Panji Alam, Kampung Gong Pak Maseh, 3km south of centre ☎ 09 622 1063. Specializes in *mengkuang* (pandanus weaving), fashioning the long, slender leaves into delicate but functional items including bags and floor mats. Catch S.P. Bumi local bus towards Pasir Panjang; get off on Jalan Panji Alam. Sat–Thurs 9am–4.30pm.

Wanisma Craft Near junction of Jalan Sultan Zainal Abidin and Kampung Ladang Sekolah ☎019 983 7910, ⓦwanisma.com. Local artisans have long been known for their brassware, working in a "white brass" alloy unique to the state. Containing at least forty percent zinc, with added nickel to make it less yellow, white brass is used for decorative items such as candlesticks. At Wanisma Craft it was once possible to watch craftsmen using the traditional "lost wax" technique to make brass objects, but construction nearby has forced them into a temporary facility. They hope to relocate soon, but for now it's only possible to buy metalware and batik in their small shop. Sun–Thurs 10am–6pm.

DIRECTORY

Banks and exchange All the major banks have offices on Jalan Sultan Ismail, west of the junction with Jalan Tok Lam; the Maybank is your best bet for changing money. There's also an ATM at the bus station.

Hospitals and clinics The Hospital Sultanah Nur Zahirah is 1km southeast of the centre on Jalan Sultan Mahmud (☎09 621 2121). There are plenty of privately run walk-in clinics and the odd dentist's surgery along Jalan Tok Lam, some staying open well into the evening.

Left luggage At the bus station (daily 8am–10pm;

☎019 920 9679).

Pharmacy There are branches of Watsons and Guardian on Jalan Sultan Ismail.

Police The main police station is on Jalan Sultan Ismail (☎09 624 6222).

Post office The GPO (Sun–Thurs 8am–6pm) is on Jalan Sultan Zainal Abidin.

Visa extensions The Immigration Department is in Wisma Persekutuan on Jalan Sultan Ismail (Sun–Wed 7.30am–5pm, Thurs 7.30am–4pm; ☎09 622 1424).

Tasik Kenyir

More than three hundred square kilometres in area, **Tasik Kenyir** (Lake Kenyir) was created in the 1980s by the building of the Kenyir hydroelectric dam across Sungai Terengganu. Much touted locally as a back-to-nature experience, the lake offers scope for **fishing**, waterborne excursions and wildlife-spotting – **elephants** are even glimpsed on the shore from time to time, thanks to the Department of Wildlife's policy of transporting wild elephants here from elsewhere in the country. It's possible to swim in **waterfalls** on the periphery, while at the lake's southern end you can visit the limestone **Bewah and Taat caves**. The lake is also Terengganu's gateway to Taman Negara, thanks to the park entrance at **Tanjung Mentong** – though this is so little used as to be practically moribund.

Sadly, due to poor transport connections and the fact that the attractions are so scattered, Tasik Kenyir remains something of a half-baked proposition. The government is in the process of jollying the lake up, creating – among other things – a **duty-free island**, several botanical gardens and an aviary. What impact these will have remains to be seen, but for now, a lack of accommodation adds to the difficulty of visiting. Unless you plan to stay at the upmarket, easily accessible *Lake Kenyir Resort*, your best bet is to book through a travel agent in Kuala Terengganu (see p.241). If you do arrive independently you can book trips on a per-person basis from the resort, while the packages from the main jetty are aimed at groups, so – for example – a trip to **Kelah fish sanctuary** costs RM450 for the whole boat, plus an RM15 per person entry fee.

ARRIVAL AND DEPARTURE   TASIK KENYIR

The jetty in the northeast of the lake, **Pangkalan Gawi** (also known as Gawi), can be reached by road and serves as the focal point for arrivals; a handful of tour operators have desks at the jetty and can arrange day-trips.

By bus No buses run to the lake from Kuala Terengganu, even though there's a service all the way from KL: the Tasik Kenyir Express (☎09 822 2176) leaves from Putra bus station (daily 9am & 9pm; 8hr).

By taxi A taxi to the jetty costs around RM80 from Kuala Terengganu or RM100 from the airport.

By car Take Route 3 towards Kota Bharu, turning off onto the T11 after 30km and following signs; alternatively, head south on Route 14, turning off after 30km at Ajil and taking Route 106 west to Kuala Berang, then northwest on the T11. It is also possible to reach the jetty from the interior, by turning off Route 8 at Simpang Aring onto Route 1742, which serves the

4

Taman Negara entrance at Kuala Koh; stay on the main road and you will eventually skirt around the northern edge of the lake. The drive from Gua Musang to the jetty will take around two hours, and it's a rough road in places.

INFORMATION

Tourist office At the Gawi jetty (daily 8am–5pm; ☎09 626 7788). Staff can hand out leaflets and advice, but cannot book you onto any tours – for that, speak to the companies with desks at the jetty or go to *Lake Kenyir Resort*.

Tours Packages are available from companies including Ping Anchorage (see p.241) or Kenyir Naturally Holidays (☎011 1996 6276). Gawi-based local guide Kamarul (☎019 984 6012) can also help if you want something tailor-made.

ACCOMMODATION

A few chalets and rafthouses around the lake offer modest comforts at modest rates. However, they're presently only accessible by boat from the Gawi jetty – and chartering a standard six-seater vessel can cost several hundred ringgit a day. A **houseboat** sleeping 12–18 people costs RM1000–1500 for two days.

Lake Kenyir Resort 1.5km from Gawi Jetty ☎09 666 8888, ⚲lakekenyir.com. This elegant collection of buildings, with Terengganu-style pitched roofs, is the swankiest accommodation at Tasik Kenyir. It's also the easiest to arrange and the most expensive, although you should be able to get discounts (such as the price indicated here) on the published rate. Numerous tours and activities are available. ATM on site. **RM295**

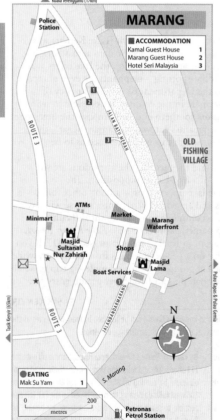

Marang

The coastal village of **MARANG**, 17km south of Kuala Terengganu and not to be confused with Merang further north, is only visited by tourists as the departure point for the delightful **Pulau Kapas** and **Pulau Gemia**, just 6km offshore. The islands have no banks or ATMs, so this is your last chance to withdraw money – there are a couple of ATMs around 400m from the jetty.

ARRIVAL AND DEPARTURE   MARANG

By bus Local buses run between Kuala Terengganu and Marang roughly every two hours in daytime. It's also possible to reach Marang on the long-distance Kuantan–Kuala Terengganu buses that travel the coast road. To move on from Marang you can flag down a local bus, although southbound services go no further than Dungun or Kemaman (see p.248). To catch an express bus further afield you'll need to make arrangements in Kuala Terengganu.

By taxi Chartering a taxi between Kuala Terengganu and Marang costs around RM30.

By boat The two main boat operators for the trip to Pulau Kapas and Pulau Gemia, MGH (☎09 618 1976) and Suria Link (☎09 618 3754), have their offices side by side at Marang's jetty. Both offer the same deal – RM20 one way or RM40 return – and can book accommodation. Boats usually run from 9.30am–4.30pm, though services peter out during the northeast monsoon. Check whether your boat will stop at your desired beach; you may have to choose between wading ashore close to your resort, or getting off at the sole jetty then walking a short distance.

ACCOMMODATION

Kamal Guest House B283 Kampung Paya ☏ 09 618 2181. The seven rooms at this colourful motel-style place, just downhill from *Marang Guest House*, are pricier than their neighbours, but they're also more comfortable and spacious. Not all rooms have hot water. Fan doubles RM50, a/c doubles RM80

Marang Guest House Bukit Batu Merah, 1367 & 1368 Kampung Paya ☏ 09 618 1976. At the top of the hill, the rooms here are careworn but a good choice if you're on a tight budget. Also known as the *Travellers' Checkpoint*. Fan doubles RM40, a/c doubles RM60

Hotel Seri Malaysia 3964 Kampung Paya ☏ 09 618 2889, ✉ hotelserimalaysiamarang@gmail.com. This modern block up a switchback driveway is Marang's most upmarket accommodation, with neat, if bland, rooms and a tiny swimming pool. The higher floors have views across to Pulau Kapas. Breakfast included. RM85

EATING AND DRINKING

Marang's best **waterside dining** is at the *Marang Waterfront*, a basic food court opposite the main market, where a handful of stalls do a roaring trade in *roti canai* and *nasi goreng* until well into the evening.

Mak Su Yam Marang. Convenient for the jetty, at the top of a short flight of steps, this is a simple place with an inexpensive *nasi campur* spread. Fine if you just want to fill up while waiting for transport. Sat–Thurs 7am–6pm.

Pulau Kapas

4

Diminutive **Pulau Kapas**, less than half an hour from Marang by speedboat, boasts arcs of sandy beach the colour of pale brown sugar, and aquamarine waters that visibly teem with fish. It's a very appealing little island with a laidback charm, emphasized by the friendly approach of the best of the resorts. Just offshore, the even smaller **Pulau Gemia** is the site of just one resort. In theory it's possible to visit Kapas as a day-trip, by catching an early boat out and returning late in the afternoon, but this means dealing with the midday heat – and besides, it's really worth staying for at least a night or two.

The only **season** when things are not quite so idyllic is from June to August, particularly at the weekends, when the island can get pretty busy. The rest of the time it's a great place to do very little for a few days; the one notable highlight in the slim social calendar is the annual Kapas–Marang **swimathon** in April. During the northeast monsoon almost all the resorts close down.

A couple of marked trails make it possible to **hike** to the undeveloped

ACCOMMODATION
Captain's Longhouse	7
Gem Island Resort and Spa	1
Harmony Campsite	2
Kapas Beach Chalet	4
Kapas Island Resort	6
Kapas Turtle Valley	8
Pak Ya Sea View Chalet	5
Qimi Chalet	3

EATING
Koko	1

PULAU KAPAS

SNORKELLING AND DIVING AROUND PULAU KAPAS

Snorkelling is of course a draw on Kapas; most places to stay can rent out gear (from RM15), or arrange a boat trip out to a choice site (from RM35). Visibility is best between May and August, but jellyfish can be a nuisance in June and July. Some of the most popular snorkelling spots are around rocky **Pulau Gemia**. If you're just renting equipment then try the rocks at the edges of the beaches beyond *Qimi Chalet* and the campsite.

    Diving isn't generally considered to be as good as on the Perhentians or Redang, but there are opportunities, particularly on the eastern side of the island. Popular sites include Berakit Reef, Octopus Reef and Coral Garden. Blacktip reef sharks are sometimes seen, and you can find turtles at Coral Garden and near *Kapas Turtle Valley*. There's only one **dive shop**, Aqua-Sport (☎019 983 5879, ⓦaquasportdiver.com.my), which offers PADI courses as well as regular dives (RM120).

---

eastern side of Kapas, ending up at the pebbly (and sadly far from litter-free) **Berakit Beach**, where you can take a dip. The longer but more interesting route (1.5km) starts close to *Kapas Turtle Valley*, the shorter (1km) from behind *Kapas Island Resort*, running alongside a stream for most of the way. You can combine them to take a circular route; both include steep sections close to Berakit. Bring plenty of water and use insect repellent, and avoid being in the forest after 5pm when the mosquitoes come out in force. The paths can be very slippery after rain.

ARRIVAL AND INFORMATION   PULAU KAPAS

By boat Boats to Pulau Kapas leave from Marang (see p.244).
Conservation fee As Kapas is a designated marine park, a conservation fee of RM5 applies for a stay of up to three days, though there isn't always an official present to collect it.

ACCOMMODATION AND EATING

For such a tiny island, Kapas has a surprising range of accommodation. Some mid-range places levy surcharges of twenty percent or more at weekends and during holidays, and most close down from November to February. Each guesthouse has its own **restaurant**, but it's worth seeking out *Koko*, the only standalone restaurant of note.

PULAU KAPAS

Captain's Longhouse Southwestern shore ☎012 377 0214. This rustic elevated longhouse of dark timber has eight decent fan rooms and a large, rather bohemian open dorm. All beds have mosquito nets and shared facilities. The driftwood beach-hut bar gives the impression that someone was shipwrecked here but made the best of it. No wi-fi. Dorm RM30, doubles RM70

Harmony Campsite Western shore. This campsite is used mainly by locals and (despite the name) can be noisy. It's aimed at large groups and when none are in residence you are unlikely to find any staff. Tent rental RM15. Camping per person RM10

★**Kapas Beach Chalet (KBC)** Western shore ☎012 288 2008. This Malay/Dutch-run establishment has decent A-frame chalets plus small dorms and more basic rooms in a long bungalow; all are en suite. The restaurant is good and the *Lazy Islander Lounge* is, along with the *Captain's Longhouse*, the best backpacker hangout on Kapas. Snorkelling equipment is free for guests. No wi-fi. Dorms RM20, doubles RM40, chalets RM65

Kapas Island Resort Western shore ☎019 912 4557, ⓦkapasislandresort.com. Neat Malay-style a/c bungalows, all en suite and with more character than most, set in an unkempt garden near the jetty. Western and Malay food is served in an airy restaurant; squid catching and snorkelling can be arranged. Breakfast included. RM120

Koko Western shore, Pulau Kapas. For a change from resort dining, head to this restaurant, which serves up great local food in a breezy beachfront dining room. Daily 9am–4pm & 7–10pm.

★**Kapas Turtle Valley** Southwestern shore ☎013 354 3650, ⓦkapasturtlevalley.com. Marvellously low-key resort, run by a Dutch couple and set on a secluded cove a short but steep walk from the western shore – boats from Marang can drop you off here. It has just eight chalets, including two for families, featuring four-poster beds and swish bathrooms; the menu in the restaurant is sophisticated if pricey. There's a two-night minimum stay, and booking is essential. Breakfast included. RM185

Pak Ya Sea View Chalet Western shore ☎ 019 960 3130. A collection of seven tidy A-frames behind a low protective wall on the beach, all with double beds, fans, lino floors and small but clean bathrooms. The beach café serves the usual gamut of Malay rice dishes. No wi-fi. RM70

Qimi Chalet Western shore ☎ 019 648 1714. Comfortable chalets ranged across a slope, the most expensive (RM350) with sea-facing balcony and open-air bathroom; the cheaper ones are nicely decorated but much more basic. It can take a while for the food to arrive in the beachfront restaurant, but it's worth the wait. Open all year, with discounts during the monsoon and for stays of three nights or more. RM80

PULAU GEMIA

Gem Island Resort and Spa Southeastern tip ☎ 09 612 5110, ⍉ gemisland.com.my. This quiet spot is the only resort on Pulau Gemia, with chalets on stilts; the cheapest are in a long block, with better views away from the restaurant. Turtles land to lay eggs and the resort is involved in their conservation; facilities include a spa (under renovation at the time of research), small swimming pool and restaurant. Two-night half-board package for two per night RM565

Southern Terengganu

The stretch of **southern Terengganu** between Marang and the Pahang border offers fairly slim pickings for travellers. Pleasant **beaches** are the main draw, any of which make a good break during a drive along the coast road, though facilities at most amount to a mere straggle of food stalls.

Rantau Abang

Little more than a handful of guesthouses strung out along a dusty road 40km south of Marang, **RANTAU ABANG** used to reap a rich reward as one of a handful of places in the world where the giant **leatherback turtle** came to lay its eggs. No longer, thanks to overfishing, pollution and poaching – at the time of writing, the last leatherback nesting was in 2010. In the meantime Rantau Abang has drifted into relative obscurity. It's still a pleasant enough way station though, offering a beach with fine sand and, being on a straight stretch of coast, superb 180-degree views of blue-green sea.

Turtle Conservation and Information Centre

Rantau Abang • Sun–Thurs 8am–5pm • Free • ☎ 09 844 4169

The small **Turtle Conservation and Information Centre**, or *Hentian Penyu*, holds informative, if dry, displays on turtle biology and conservation, plus a paddling pool full of hatchlings. If you want to spot nesting turtles, your best bets are elsewhere in Malaysia (see p.252).

(see p.252)

ARRIVAL AND DEPARTURE   RANTAU ABANG

By bus Buses stop on the main road close to the Turtle Conservation and Information Centre. Local services from Kuala Terengganu and Marang, and Dungun pass through Rantau Abang every two hours in the daytime.

By taxi Ask at your accommodation about long-distance taxis to Kuala Terengganu (RM40) or Dungun (RM25).

ACCOMMODATION AND EATING

The decline in tourism means that most places are now geared up for student groups and team-building sessions. The exception is the luxurious *Tanjong Jara Resort*, just south of Rantau Abang. Few accommodation options in Rantau Abang serve **food** other than for groups, but a handful of simple places to eat lie within walking distance.

Awang's 100m south of information centre ☎ 019 911 7500. Friendly and long-established resort, on a stretch of golden sand. Simple en-suite rooms, with a few nice touches such as tinted glass and batik sheets. Food is only served to groups, so you'll have to eat elsewhere. No wi-fi. Fan doubles RM60, a/c doubles RM120

Dahimah's Guesthouse 1km south of information centre ☎ 09 845 2843, ✉ dahimahs@hotmail.com. Run by Dahimah – originally from the UK – and her Malay husband. Accommodation ranges from simple fan doubles to huge family rooms with TV, a/c and hot water. Fan doubles RM40, a/c doubles RM70, family rooms RM140

Tanjong Jara Resort 4km south of Rantau Abang ☎ 09 845 1100, ⓦ tanjongjararesort.com. One of the priciest east coast resorts, a complex of timber pavilions and houses almost fit for a sultan. Traditional treatments are on offer in the spa, and there's a diving and watersports centre. Activities range from waterfall treks to cooking classes. **RM730**

Dungun to the Pahang border

Driving south from **Dungun to the Pahang border** takes you through the heartland of Terengganu's oil industry, with refineries lining both side of Route 3 around the town of **Paka**. Most of the towns have little to detain tourists, but there are a few upmarket resorts along the coast.

Dungun

The backwater town of **DUNGUN** straggles for 9km along the coast south of Tanjong Jara. The bus station lies towards the northern end of town in a largely Chinese neighbourhood, with a handful of shophouses and a night market each Thursday. The only reason to stop here is because it's a **transport hub**; there's a taxi stand next to the bus station.

Pulau Tenggol

Further from the mainland than the popular islands further north, **Pulau Tenggol** (reached by boat from Dungun) is correspondingly less developed. While the few visitors who stay out here have to make do with rather run-down accommodation, there's beautiful, unspoiled scenery and arguably the best **diving** and snorkelling on the east coast. It's possible to arrange a diving trip from the mainland through *Tanjong Jara* resort (see above).

Ma'Daerah Turtle Sanctuary
Kerteh, 12km south of Paka and 30km north of Chukai

Near the town of **Kertih**, on the road south of Paka, is the **Ma'Daerah Turtle Sanctuary**, with a hatchery on a quiet beach where green turtles lay their eggs. Contact the Rantau Abang Turtle Information Centre (see p.247) about volunteering.

Kemaman/Chukai

The southernmost settlement of significance in Terengganu is the fusion of **Kemaman** and neighbouring **Chukai**. The town, home of a major port, holds little attraction for visitors, but its two bus stations (Geliga Bus Station for express buses, and the local bus station in town) are useful, and it has the closest **banks** and ATMs to Cherating.

ARRIVAL AND DEPARTURE	DUNGUN TO THE PAHANG BORDER
By plane Firefly has services between Kuala Lumpur and Kerteh (2 daily; 1hr).	**By boat** Speedboats run from Dungun to Pulau Tenggol (45min); transfers are normally included in accommodation packages.
By bus You may need to change at Dungun or Kemaman/ Chukai if you are using local buses to travel the coast.	

ACCOMMODATION

The **resorts** along the coast are largely aimed at business travellers, so look for weekend discounts. Those on Tenggol are only open from February to November, and only when there are guests, so it is essential to book ahead.

DUNGUN
Sri Gate K201 Jalan Sura Gate ☎ 09 848 1648. A taxi ride south of the bus station, this three-storey Chinese hotel is above a hair salon, with clean rooms that are fine for a night. Avoid the lowest floor; people tend to hang out around reception watching TV. No wi-fi, but all rooms have a/c. **RM65**

PULAU TENGGOL
Tenggol Coral Beach Resort Pulau Tenggol ☎ 012 784

7357, Ⓦtenggol.com.my. Pleasant, spacious rooms are linked by sandy paths facing Teluk Air Tawar ("Freshwater Bay") in the largest of Tenggol's three resorts. Rates given here are per night on the basis of two people sharing a two-night all-inclusive snorkelling package; the diving equivalent, including five dives, costs around fifty percent extra. **RM768**

Cherating

At first it can be hard to discern the enduring appeal of **CHERATING**, a laidback village 45km north of Kuantan. Its heyday as a tourist destination is clearly over; for proof you only need to see the former tourist office – now a karaoke lounge – at one end of **Cherating Lama** (the old town), and the closed cultural centre at the other end. Many locals have long since moved out, to the new settlement of **Cherating Baru**, 4km to the south. What's more, the **beach** is pleasant but hardly the best on the coast – it's best suited to windsurfing and kitesurfing (March–September), and **surfing** during the northeastern monsoon (October–December).

Nevertheless, at its best, Cherating Lama is still an appealing little travellers' community, chilled out yet warm-spirited, a place to share quality time with old companions and – chances are – to end up with a whole bunch of new acquaintances

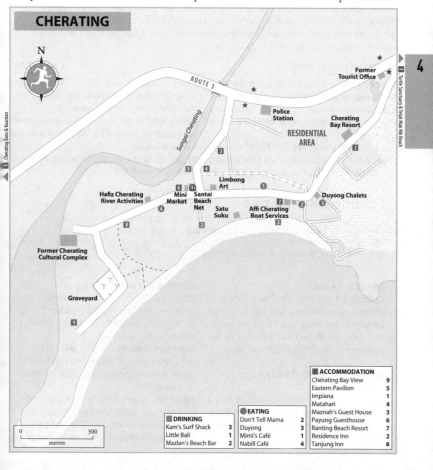

CHERATING

N

ROUTE 3

Sungai Cherating

Former Tourist Office

Police Station

Cherating Bay Resort

RESIDENTIAL AREA

Limbong Art

Hafiz Cherating River Activities

Mini Market

Santai Beach Net

Satu Suku

Affi Cherating Boat Services

Duyong Chalets

Former Cherating Cultural Complex

Graveyard

4 Turtle Sanctuary & Teluk Mak Mik Beach

Cherating Baru & Kuantan

0 — 300 metres

ACCOMMODATION	
Cherating Bay View	9
Eastern Pavilion	5
Impiana	1
Matahari	4
Maznah's Guest House	3
Payung Guesthouse	6
Ranting Beach Resort	7
Residence Inn	2
Tanjung Inn	8

● EATING	
Don't Tell Mama	2
Duyong	3
Mimi's Café	1
Nabill Café	4

■ DRINKING	
Kam's Surf Shack	3
Little Bali	1
Mazlan's Beach Bar	2

too. Local entrepreneurs have devised an array of **activities** to keep tourists coming, and it's well worth giving it a few days. Along the coast are a series of mid-range resorts that draw in families looking for a comfortable seaside break.

Cherating beach

No trip to Cherating would be complete without time spent on the **beach**. While the shelter of the bay ensures calm waters, jellyfish and currents are occasionally a problem, and it's best to avoid swimming at low tide, when the sea recedes 100m or more. The headland obliterates any sunrise views, but in good weather it's still worth taking a dawn stroll on the beach, when only a few fishing boats disturb the stillness.

Turtle sanctuary

2km east of Cherating village • Information centre daily 9am–5pm • Free • ☎ 09 581 9078

Around the rocky headland at the eastern end of the bay sits Cherating's **turtle sanctuary** (signed from Route 3 as Santuari Penyu). Once a handy place to watch turtles nesting on the beach, the development at *Club Med* nearby has caused the turtles to nest further north at Kemaman's Teluk Mak Nik beach. Today the information centre has displays about the creatures, plus a few holding tanks at the back where you can see hatchlings in season.

4

ARRIVAL AND DEPARTURE   **CHERATING**

By express bus Express buses on the coast road between Kuala Terengganu and Kuantan drop passengers on request at both Cherating Lama and Cherating Baru. However, they won't stop to pick up passengers, so reserve ahead when you want to leave.

Destinations Ipoh (2 daily; 7hr); Johor Bahru (2 daily; 6hr 30min); Kota Bharu (4 daily; 6hr); Kuala Besut (4 daily); Kuala Lumpur (7 daily; 4hr); Kuala Terengganu (4 daily; 5hr 30min); Kuantan (4 daily; 1hr–1hr 30min); Marang (4 daily; 2hr 30min); Melaka (2 daily; 5hr); Mersing (2 daily; 4hr); Rantau Abang (4 daily; 1hr 30min).

By local bus If you don't have a reservation on an express bus, you can wait for one of the sporadic local services to Kuantan or Dungun.

By taxi It's possible to catch a taxi from Kuantan to Cherating (45 min; RM80).

ACTIVITIES IN CHERATING

During the northeast monsoon – and especially mid-October to early January, when the waves are good and the rain not too bad – **surfing** is the big attraction in Cherating. **Windsurfing** and kitesurfing are possible throughout the year, weather allowing, while there's also a range of **activities** and organized tours (see opposite).

CRAFTS CLASSES

Limbong Art Cherating Lama ☎ 017 950 1281, ✉ umilimbong@gmail.com. Batik classes, in which you get your own designs onto T-shirts and sarongs. Classes take around two hours, depending on your project, and cost from RM30. Daily 10am–10pm.

SURFING, WINDSURFING AND KITESURFING

Equipment rental and lessons are available from a range of operators. If your board needs repairing, drop in to see Affi, who runs a shaping workshop next to *Travel Post*.

Cherating Point ☎ 012 933 7590, ⓦ cheratingpoint.com. Surfboard rental (RM70/day) and lessons (90min plus 2hr board rental; from RM120), plus beginners' packages; they don't have a fixed office in Cherating. Nov–June daily.

Kam's Surf Shack On the beach ☎ 017 362 4839. Surfing lessons in season; windsurfing and kitesurfing lessons, and equipment rental are available year-round. Daily 10am–9pm.

Satu Suku Pok Lan's Beach Bar ☎ 012 949 3404, ⓦ satusuku.com. Surfing lessons plus equipment rental and sales. They can also advise on the best surf spots, and run a Billabong boutique. Oct–March daily 7am–7pm.

TOUR OPERATORS AND GUIDES

Agencies along the main drag can book bus tickets and other travel arrangements, such as transfers to Taman Negara or islands off the east coast. All agencies and most guesthouses offer a range of **tours**, the selection and prices being similar wherever you go; night-time turtle-watching (RM60 including transport), firefly-watching (RM25–30) and snorkelling trips to Snake Island (RM60) being the most popular options.

Blissful Walk Cherating Lama ☏014 719 8824. Working out of a small roadside shack (daily 8am–11pm), the friendly folk at Blissful Walk are relative newcomers to Cherating, arranging local tours, bus tickets for a RM5 fee (including transport to the bus stop) and bike and kayak rental (RM5/hr). They also arrange traditional activities, including *gasing* (top spinning), kite-flying and handicraft demonstrations.

Hafiz Cherating River Activities Lot 1156, Cherating Lama ☏017 978 9256, ⓦcheratingbeachinfo.com.my. A self-taught expert on fireflies, Hafiz has developed a

method of attracting the insects. The effect, as seen on evening excursions, is magical, although the trips have become very busy; many other agencies book guests onto his trips. Snorkelling, fishing and kayak rental also available.

Pak Su Cherating Lama ☏013 906 4828. Licensed nature guide, Pak Su, specializes in taking people to see turtles nesting on Teluk Mak Nik Beach. He works extensively with the Fisheries Department, buying turtle eggs from locals to prevent them ending up in the market.

ACCOMMODATION

Prices drop by up to twenty percent on weekdays (weekend prices shown below), with further **discounts** available during the northeast monsoon.

CHERATING LAMA

Cherating Bay View Cherating Lama ☏09 581 9248, ⓦcheratingbayviewresort.com. At the quieter end of the bay, this complex has a range of a/c chalets, the cheapest of them around a greenish swimming pool. While the standard seafront chalets lack the modern fixtures and fittings of the deluxe options, they actually have better sea views. Poolside chalets RM135, seafront chalets RM150

Matahari Cherating Lama ☏019 935 9420. A mishmash of units, from spartan A-frames to larger chalets, all arranged around a pleasant grassy area. Toilets and showers are in a separate block; while a few rooms have private bathrooms, none have a/c. There's a communal kitchen. No wi-fi. Fan doubles RM30, en-suite doubles RM50

Maznah's Guest House Cherating Lama ☏09 581 9307, ⓦmaznahguesthouse.blogspot.com. The basic A-frames share facilities, but you can hardly complain for the price. The spotless en-suite chalets are also good value, but the sole a/c chalet is overpriced. Including breakfast. A-frames RM30, en-suite chalets RM50, a/c chalet RM150

Payung Guesthouse Cherating Lama ☏019 917 1934, ⓦpayung-guesthouse.com. A deservedly popular collection of ten no-frills chalets set in a small, very tidy garden. All are en suite, with fan and mosquito net; most have double beds. The one drawback (as with its neighbours) is night-time noise from the nearby bars. RM60

Ranting Beach Resort Cherating Lama ☏09 581 9068. Spacious, well-kept garden rooms, plus pricier beach chalets; good views compensate for the generally

uninspiring decor – some have breezy verandas. All options are en suite, some with a/c and TV. No wi-fi. Doubles RM140, chalets RM200

Residence Inn Cherating Lama ☏09 581 9333 ⓦric .my. If you prefer resort-style accommodation but want to stay in Cherating Lama, then this complex of 73 tidy en-suite rooms is the place to come. They have a couple of small swimming pools and can arrange snorkelling, fishing and other activities. Breakfast included. RM270

★**Tanjung Inn (aka Villa de Fedelia)** Cherating Lama ☏09 581 9081, ⓦtanjunginn.com. Timber-built en-suite accommodation, ranging from simple fan chalets to brilliant traditionally styled kampung houses boasting a/c, four-poster beds and slate-tiled bathrooms with hot water. All are set around two large ponds in a peaceful, pretty garden. Plans are afoot to add more chalets and a pool sometime in 2015. Fan chalets RM70, a/c kampung house RM170

NORTH OF CHERATING LAMA

Impiana 3.5km north of Cherating Lama ☏09 581 9000, ⓦimpianacherating.com. One of the classier resorts north of Cherating, with tastefully decorated rooms that make appealing use of dark wood. All rooms have sea views – although some have more of a sea-glimpse – but it's worth plumping for the more spacious "superior deluxe" rooms if your budget allows. The resort is complete with swimming pool, tennis courts and outdoor jacuzzi. Deluxe RM278, superior deluxe RM420

CHERATING BARU

Eastern Pavilion Cherating Baru ☏09 581 9500,

4

MARINE TURTLES

While four types of marine turtle lay their eggs on Malaysia's east coast, for years the sight of the largest – the giant, critically endangered **leatherback turtle** – was the star attraction, drawing visitors to Rantau Abang in Terengganu. In fact all other kinds of marine turtle – **green** (Malaysian nesting sites include the Perhentians, Pulau Redang, Cherating, Penarik and the Turtle Islands National Park in Sabah), **hawksbill** (Pulau Redang, Turtle Islands National Park, Pulau Tioman and Padang Kemunting near Melaka), **olive ridley** (rarely seen), and **Kemp's ridley** and **loggerhead** (neither of which nest in Malaysia) – are also at risk.

Harmful fishing methods, such as the use of **trawl nets**, kill thousands of marine turtles each year, and help explain the dramatic reduction in leatherbacks nesting on the Terengganu coast. In 1956, more than ten thousand were recorded; in 2000, just three; in 2002, there were no sightings of leatherbacks in Rantau Abang for the first time since records began; by 2005, leatherback, hawksbill and olive ridley statistics in Terengganu were all at zero, and green turtle figures were significantly down. On the rare occasions when a leatherback turns up – there was a lone turtle in 2010 – their eggs often fail to hatch. This is probably because of the increasing rarity of male–female turtle encounters.

With a very meagre survival rate among hatchlings under ordinary conditions, any human pressure on turtle populations has drastic consequences for their survival. For the Chinese in Malaysia and Singapore, turtle soup is a classic delicacy, and while Malays eschew turtle meat, they do consume **turtle eggs**, which look like ping-pong balls and are sold at markets throughout the east coast. Their collection is licensed at certain sites, but there's no guarantee that anything on sale was collected legally. There appears to be no political will to outlaw this traditional food, a sad irony given Malaysia's general turtle conservation efforts: in many places, hatcheries pay licensed collectors for eggs rather than see them go to markets. At least the deliberate slaughter of turtles for their shells, once fashioned into bowls and earrings, has been banned since 1992.

TURTLE SPOTTING AND CONSERVATION

Nowadays, humans are excluded from various designated **sanctuaries** for nesting turtles. At these sites the eggs are dug up immediately after the turtle has laid them and reburied in sealed-off **hatcheries** on the beach. Burying the eggs in sand of the correct temperature is crucial as warm sand produces more females, while cooler sand favours males. When the hatchlings emerge, they are released at the top of the beach and their scurry to the sea is supervised to ensure their safe progress.

There are several officially sanctioned opportunities to watch nesting turtles on the east coast beaches and islands, including at Cherating, Pulau Perhentian Besar and Pulau Tioman (at Juara Beach). It is also possible to volunteer at the turtle sites (see p.248).

W easternpavilion.com. Twelve luxurious villas in traditional kampung houses from different Malaysian states. All have one or two beautifully appointed bedrooms, lounge and private outdoor jacuzzis; there's also a spa. Published rates are significantly higher than the typical promotional rate given here. **RM660**

EATING AND DRINKING

Cherating Lama has a string of inexpensive **restaurants**, many emphasizing seafood including the *lala* – a sort of clam, which turns up in various sauces – but a couple of places also offer decent Western food. *Kedai kopis* across from the *Payung Guesthouse* serve reasonable Malay cuisine, with *roti canai* in the morning and *nasi campur* later in the day.

★**Don't Tell Mama** Cherating Lama ✆ 019 996 1723. Open year-round, *Don't Tell Mama* is a great place to chill out with a beer (RM10) and one of their giant cheeseburgers (RM20), enjoying the relaxed playlist or playing pool. Wed–Mon 6pm–1am; food served until 10pm.

Duyong Cherating Lama ✆ 09 581 9578. An old faithful, this large place overlooking the eastern end of the beach offers excellent Chinese and Thai dishes, plus a few Western standbys such as lamb chop (RM16) and steak (RM23). Veggie dishes can be cooked to order. Daily 11am–11pm.

Kam's Surf Shack Cherating Lama ✆ 017 362 4839. Owned by a pair of local brothers, this beach bar serves up cold beer (RM10), reggae and surfing lessons; there's talk of offering food in the near future. Daily 10am–9pm.

Little Bali Cherating Lama ☎019 983 6536. It's hard to see how resort guests can get much sleep; this bar pulls in visiting businessmen with the promise of beer (from RM13), karaoke and pounding dance music. Daily 6pm–4am; music from 10.30pm.

Mazlan's Beach Bar Cherating Lama ☎010 439 6486. In a great spot in the middle of the beach, this simple bar – owned by the eponymous Mazlan and his Mexican wife – serves up cold beer and simple snacks. Daily noon–late.

Mimi's Café Cherating Lama ☎017 908 8421. Popular hangout, serving Western breakfasts, including French toast (RM5), throughout the day; Malaysian rice dishes, including a great *nasi goreng kampung* (RM5) are also available. Tues–Sun 9am–5pm.

Nabill Café Cherating Lama ☎019 985 3302. Locals come here for their great *ikan bakar* (prices vary by weight), but if they've run out of fish you can choose from a range of Chinese-style dishes (from RM5), and long list of rice- and noodle-based standards. Daily 6pm–1am.

Kuantan

The state capital of **Pahang** since 1955, **KUANTAN** is an undistinguished agglomeration of concrete buildings around an older core of shophouses close to Sungai Kuantan. While there's very little by way of historical or cultural interest in the city itself, Kuantan can be a breath of fresh air after a sojourn in Kelantan or Terengganu – it's closer in feel to the west coast cities than to Kuala Terengganu or Kota Bharu. If you're arriving from elsewhere in the country, however, Kuantan can seem mundane. With the creation of the **East Coast Highway** to Pelabuhan Kuantan, the port 40km north of the city, it's easy to bypass Kuantan altogether if you're travelling between KL and the east coast.

If Kuantan has a focus of sorts, it's the **padang**. The city's oldest streets, between there and the river, hold quite a few hotels and restaurants. The best reason to hang around for a night or two, though, is to take a day-trip to the cave temple of **Gua Charas** or the royal town of **Pekan**.

Masjid Negeri

Northeastern edge of the padang • Sat–Thurs 10am–noon, 3–4pm & 5.30–6pm • Free

The town's one real sight, the **Masjid Negeri**, was built in 1991, with a pastel exterior – green for Islam, blue for peace and white for purity. It's distinctly Turkish in appearance, thanks to the pencil minarets at all four corners of the sturdy square prayer hall, topped with a looming central dome. Non-Muslims can visit outside of prayer times: men should wear long trousers, while women are advised to cover their hair and dress modestly.

Promenade

Boat trips depart Thurs–Tues 11am, 1pm, 3pm & 6pm, 8pm night cruises by advance booking only • RM38 • ☎011 2575 8033

Down by the river, starting at the *Megaview Hotel*, a **promenade** clings to the banks of Sungai Kuantan. Early evening is a good time to take a stroll, to see fishing boats returning with the day's catch and perhaps the occasional red eagle swooping on its prey. A small **night market** sets up here each evening (6–10pm) and boat trips depart from the jetty at the southwest end of the promenade.

Teluk Chempedak

5km east of centre following Jalan Besar, which becomes Jalan Teluk Sisek then Jalan Teluk Chempedak • Bus #200 from local bus station (daily 6am–11pm; 30min); taxis RM25

Around the corner from a wooded headland, on an east-facing stretch of coast, **Teluk Chempedak** has long been a popular evening and weekend hangout for

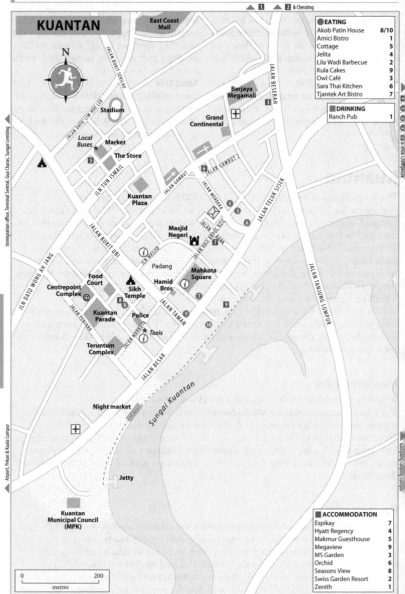

KUANTAN

N

East Coast Mall

EATING

Akob Patin House	8/10
Amici Bistro	1
Cottage	5
Jelita	4
Lila Wadi Barbecue	2
Kula Cakes	9
Owl Café	3
Sara Thai Kitchen	6
Tjantek Art Bistro	7

DRINKING

Ranch Pub	1

Berjaya Megamall

Grand Continental

Stadium

Local Buses

Market

The Store

Kuantan Plaza

Masjid Negeri

Padang

Mahkota Square

Food Court

Centrepoint Complex

Sikh Temple

Hamid Bros

Kuantan Parade

Police

Teruntum Complex

Taxis

Night market

Jetty

Kuantan Municipal Council (MPK)

JALAN BUKIT SEKILAU

JALAN DATO' LIM HOE LEK

JLN TUN ISMAIL

JALAN BUKIT UBI

JLN DATO' WONG AH JANG

JALAN ZENHRA

JLN MASJID

JALAN TAMAN

JLN MAKOTA

JALAN BESAR

JALAN GAMBUT

JALAN MERDEKA

JALAN GAMBUT 2

JALAN BESERAH

JALAN TELUK SISEK

JALAN TANJUNG LUMPUR

JALAN HAJI ABDUL AZIZ

Sungai Kuantan

Immigration office, Terminal Sentral, Gua Charas, Sungai Lembing

Airport, Pekan & Kuala Lumpur

Kampung Tanjung Lumpur

& Cherating

Pekan

0   200
metres

ACCOMMODATION

Espikay	7
Hyatt Regency	4
Makmur Guesthouse	5
Megaview	9
MS Garden	3
Orchid	6
Seasons View	8
Swiss Garden Resort	2
Zenith	1

families and young people. The sands of the bay are encouragingly white, although undertows can render the sea off-limits (watch out for red flags). There is an appealing liveliness about the place, quite at variance from the langourous mood on the otherwise better sands of rural Terengganu. Bars and restaurants line the main road as you arrive, before you reach the *Hyatt*, and there are more places to eat on the promenade.

ARRIVAL AND DEPARTURE

KUANTAN

By plane Sultan Ahmad Shah airport is 15km west of town, 20min (RM35) by taxi. KL flights (3 daily; 45min) are operated by MAS (☎09 538 5430), while Penang (3 weekly; 1hr 30min) and Singapore (daily; 1hr) flights are with Firefly (☎09 538 2911).

By express bus Express buses depart from the lower level of Kuantan's modern Terminal Sentral bus station, 7.5km northwest of downtown Kuantan. It's a RM20 taxi ride, or you can take the #303 bus.

Destinations Alor Star (3 daily; 10hr); Butterworth (3 daily; 9hr); Dungun via Cherating (4 daily; 3hr); Ipoh (3 daily; 6hr); Jerantut (3 daily; 3hr); Johor Bahru (10 daily; 5hr 30min); Kota Bharu (10 daily; 7hr); Kuala Lipis (2 daily; 6hr); Kuala Lumpur (hourly; 3hr); Kuala Terengganu (10 daily; 4–5hr); Marang (daily; 3hr 30min); Melaka (8 daily; 4hr); Mersing (4 daily; 3hr); Seremban (7 daily; 7hr); Singapore (4 daily; 6hr 30min).

By local bus The local bus station is on Jalan Stadium, with regular buses to the Terminal Sentral bus station (every 30min), Pekan, Sungai Lembing and Teluk Chempedak.

By taxi Local taxis can be found near the mosque; long-distance taxis arrive and depart from Terminal Sentral. Call ☎09 572 9892 to book.

Car rental Avis (☎09 539 8768, ⊛avis.com), Hertz (☎09 538 4848, ⊛simedarbycarrental.com) and Mayflower (☎09 538 4490, ⊛mayflowercarrental.com.my) are all at the airport.

INFORMATION

Tourist offices Tourism Malaysia has an office at street level in the Mahkota Square business complex, south of the padang (Mon–Thurs 8am–1pm & 2–5pm, Fri 8am–noon & 2.45–5pm; ☎09 517 7111). Pahang Tourism, the state tourism office (Mon–Thurs 9am–1pm & 2–5pm, Fri 9am–1pm & 2.45pm–5pm; ☎09 516 1007, ⊛pahangtourism.com.my), runs two information centres in the town, on Jalan Mahkota and near the mosque.

ACCOMMODATION

There's no shortage of places to stay in Kuantan, and you can also stay out of town at **Teluk Chempedak** or the pleasant **Balok Beach**. For details of **homestays**, pick up the well-produced *Homestay Pahang* booklet from the state tourist office or visit ⊛go2homestay.com.

CENTRAL KUANTAN

Espikay Jalan Mahkota ☎09 513 0655, ✉espikayhotel_shah@yahoo.com. A decent option right next to the main mosque, *Espikay* has modern rooms all with a/c, flat-screen TVs and hot showers. Solo travellers can stay in the cheapish singles (RM70), although they're tiny and windowless. RM100

Makmur Guesthouse Jalan Pasar Baru ☎09 514 1363. The best of the cheapies close to the bus station, although that isn't saying a lot; fan rooms with shared facilities as well as a/c en-suite rooms, all simple and fairly shabby. No wi-fi. Fan doubles RM35, a/c en-suite doubles RM75

Megaview Jalan Besar ☎09 517 1888, ⊛megaviewhotel.com. Business-oriented, efficient high-rise hotel on the river, with coffee house, bar and spa, with comfortable and recently renovated rooms. Regular promotions make it good value. Breakfast included. RM135

MS Garden Lorong Gambut, off Jalan Beserah ☎09 511 8888, ⊛msgarden.com.my. From its palatial lobby on up, this slick central hotel offers spacious rooms, several food outlets, a fitness centre and a pool complete with waterfall. Breakfast included. RM310

Orchid Jalan Merdeka ☎09 515 5570. Despite the unpromising steps up to reception, the rooms in this quirky backstreet Chinese hotel – while in need of a lick of paint – are decent for the price. No wi-fi. Doubles with shared bathroom RM45, en-suite doubles RM55

Seasons View A22 Lorong Haji Abdul Rahman 1 ☎09 516 2828, ⊛seasonsview-kuantan.com. A self-proclaimed "oasis of gracious hospitality", the rooms here are not exactly luxurious but they're immaculate and easy to recommend for the price. Breakfast included. RM98

Zenith Jalan Putra Square 6 ☎09 565 9595, ⊛thezenithhotel.com. It's hard to miss the hulking twin buildings close to the East Coast Mall, one of which holds this 519-room business hotel. Rooms are a decent size and finished to a high standard; add in the pool and spa, and there's a lot to like – assuming the grand scale doesn't put you off. RM319

TELUK CHEMPEDAK

Hyatt Regency ☎09 518 1234, ⊛kuantan.regency .hyatt.com. A long-established beach retreat for well-heeled folk from KL and Singapore, with two swimming pools, a gym, tennis and squash courts, childcare facilities, multiple restaurants and a bar in a converted ship. Breakfast included; in-room internet costs an extortionate RM45/day but wi-fi is free in the restaurants. RM405

BALOK BEACH

Some 15km north of Kuantan, Balok Beach can be reached by taxi (around RM30) or on the #600 bus from the local bus station (45min).

4

Swiss Garden Resort ☎ 09 544 7333, ⓦ swissgardenkuantan.com. Balconied rooms overlooking a landscaped garden or the South China Sea, plus a free-form swimming pool, a spa and several restaurants. A large range of activities are available for adults and children. Breakfast included. **RM316**

EATING AND DRINKING

Laidback **kedai kopis** dot the streets west and south of the padang, while the area around **Berjaya Megamall** is packed with cafés and *mamak* joints. For inexpensive **Malay** food, try the places on and around the northern end of Jalan Haji Abdul Aziz or the area around the Central Market. **Teluk Chempedak** also holds plenty of eating choices, including many on the seafront, some open until as late as 2am. The **nightlife** in Teluk Chempedak is more lively than that in town, revolving around a handful of bars on the main road just before the beach.

CENTRAL KUANTAN

★**Akob Patin House** By the river near Megaview hotel ☎ 019 987 4463. The signature ingredient at this humble place under a tented canopy is *patin* (silver catfish), served at lunchtime as *ikan patin tempoyak* (RM15) – with chilli, tamarind and fermented durian – it's surprisingly tasty. Breakfast includes *mee rebus* (noodles in curry-like gravy), while you'll need to order *patin* in advance if you want it in the evening. There's another branch on Lorong Tun Ismail. Mon–Sat 8am–5pm.

Cottage 63 Jalan Haji Abdul Aziz ☎ 012 928 2128. More adventurous than most local Chinese restaurants, serving dishes such as fish-head curry (RM28) and *nasi petai* (RM6), fried rice with *sambal* and strong-smelling *petai* beans; if you prefer noodles then order *petai bee hoon*. Beer is served. Mon–Sat 11am–2.30pm & 5pm–12.30am, Sun 6pm–12.30am.

Jelita Jalan Haji Abdul Aziz. Essentially a posh-looking metal hangar housing several food outlets, the star attraction among which is a branch of *Satay Zul*, Kuantan's best-loved satay house, offering beef, chicken, *kambing* (goat), *rusa* (venison) and even *perut* (stomach) at around 80 sen a stick. Stalls elsewhere offer rice, noodles and doner kebabs. Mon–Sat 7.30am–midnight.

Lila Wadi Barbecue Jalan Teluk Sisek ☎ 012 664 4054, ⓦ lilawadi.com.my. This great spot serves barbecue that's cooked at your table; you choose a main ingredient – beef, chicken or seafood – and receive a "set" (minimum two people; RM40) that includes side dishes. Leave space for a slice of their excellent cheesecake, which is so popular that *Lila Wadi* has opened a spin-off cake shop, *Kula Cakes*, on Jalan Taman. Tues–Thurs 12.30–3pm & 5–11.30pm, Fri–Sun 4pm–midnight.

Owl Café 236 Jalan Teluk Sisek ☎ 019 944 9433. Formerly *O's Corner*, this large, airy bar and diner offers a welcome combination of Malay and Western dishes such as fish and chips (RM6 and up), plus draught and bottled beers (from RM10). Live music nightly from 8pm. Mon–Sat 2pm–1.30am.

Sara Thai Kitchen Jalan Gambut ☎ 012 946 5591. Thai food seems to be particularly popular in Kuantan, and this busy restaurant – part of a small chain with another branch on Jalan Besar – is one of several places specializing in dishes like green curry, *tom yam* (RM5 for a small bowl) and mango salad. Daily 1–11pm.

★**Tjantek Art Bistro** 46 Jalan Besar ☎ 09 516 4144, ⓦ tjantek.blogspot.com. With soft lighting and vintage artwork plastering the walls, this is one of Kuantan's most atmospheric dining spots. The pasta dishes (from RM12) are great; steak, sandwiches and salads also feature on the simple menu. There's no alcohol, but locals head here for their fresh juices and punches. Mon–Sat 8pm–late.

TELUK CHEMPEDAK

Amici Bistro 41–43 Teluk Chempedak ☎ 09 560 5717. A cut above most places hereabouts, with Western dishes that attract expats and foreign tourists as well as locals, and imported beers. Food isn't cheap though: a steak goes for RM46 and medium pizza for RM22. Mon & Wed–Fri 4pm–midnight, Sat & Sun noon–midnight.

Ranch Pub 41 Teluk Chempedak ☎ 09 560 5717. If you're a fan of English football you'll certainly find a talking point here – it's been owned by a string of Liverpool supporters. More of a straightforward pub than some of its neighbours, with a free pool table, sport on TV and no karaoke. Daily 5pm–1am.

DIRECTORY

Banks Standard Chartered Bank and HSBC are situated around the intersection of the aptly named Jalan Bank and Jalan Besar; Hamid Bros can change money outside banking hours.

Cinemas Two Golden Screen Cinemas (Berjaya Megamall and East Coast Mall; ⓦ gsc.com.my) show some English-language films, as does Lotus Five-Star cinema in the Teruntum Complex (☎ 09 515 6881).

Hospital Hospital Tengku Ampuan Afzan (☎ 09 513 3333) is on Jalan Besar; the private Kuantan Medical Centre is next to the Berjaya Megamall (☎ 09 514 2828).

Post The GPO is on Jalan Haji Abdul Aziz.

Shops Popular malls include the Berjaya Megamall on Jalan Tun Ismail, Kuantan Parade on Jalan Penjara, and the East Coast Mall. Hamid Bros (9am–9pm Mon–Sat, 10am–3pm Sun) on Jalan Haji Abdul Aziz has a limited range of English-language books, plus maps of Malaysia; a better selection is available at the Berjaya Megamall branch of Popular Bookstore (daily 10am–10pm).

Visa extensions The immigration office is out near the express bus station at Kompleks KDN, Bandar Indera Mahkota (Mon–Fri 7.30am–1pm & 2–5.30pm; ☎ 09 573 2200); take bus #302 from the local bus station.

Gua Charas

25km northwest of Kuantan on Route C4 • RM2 donation • Local bus #500 to Pekan Panching (30min) then 4km walk, or taxi from Kuantan

One of the great limestone outcrops close to Kuantan is home to **Gua Charas**, a **cave temple** that can be visited as a leisurely day-trip: if you charter a taxi from Kuantan (RM100 return including waiting) then you can also visit the nearby Sungai Pandan **waterfall**, where you can splash around in various pools. If you're taking the bus then you start at **Panching** village, where a sign to the cave points down a track through oil palm plantations. It's a long, hot walk, so take plenty of water with you; you may be able to hitch a lift for a few ringgit.

Once you've reached the outcrop and paid your donation, you're faced with a steep climb to the cave temple itself. Halfway up, a flight of metal steps leads to the entrance of the main cave. It isn't for the faint-hearted, even though the damp mud path is dimly lit by fluorescent tubes. Inside the echoing cavern, illuminated shrines gleam from gloomy corners, guiding you past a phallic shrine dedicated to the Hindu god **Shiva** and to the oldest shrine deep in the cave. Here a 9m-long reclining **Buddha** is almost dwarfed by its giant surroundings. Back through the cave, steps lead to another, lighter hollow where the rear wall opens out to give a great view of the surrounding countryside.

4

Sungai Lembing

42km northwest of Kuantan on Route C4 • Local bus #500 (50min)

15km northwest of Panching, the small town of **SUNGAI LEMBING** retains an old-fangled, unhurried feel that's fading from the likes of Kuala Lipis and Pekan. Once the richest tin mining town in Pahang, the now sleepy town sits in a lush valley with steep forested hills on both sides, its main road planted with banyans and lined with 1920s **shophouses**. At the end of the main street is a **padang**, flanked by a dark timber building, once the **staff clubhouse** of the Pahang Consolidated Company Limited (PCCL), which ran the nearby mines from 1905 until tin prices collapsed in the mid-1980s.

The history of the town and the PCCL are explored in the **Muzium Sungai Lembing** (daily 9am–6pm; RM60; ⓦsungailembingmines.com.my) crowning the hill beyond the padang, formerly accommodation for PCCL's top managers. The steep ticket price includes an hour-long tour of one of the mining tunnels, as well as entry to less exciting displays of old mining equipment. Beyond the museum are several excellent **hikes** around the valley, the most popular of which is the hour-long walk up **Panorama Hill**, signposted from the town. Sungai Lembing is popular with domestic tourists, who flock here on weekends for a hit of nostalgia; it's better to come on a weekday, when you'll find plentiful accommodation and few other visitors.

Pekan

Nearly 50km south of Kuantan lies the royal town of **PEKAN**, whose name literally means "small town". State capital of Pahang until 1898, Pekan still retains a measure of its charm and tranquillity, although this has been challenged in recent years with the

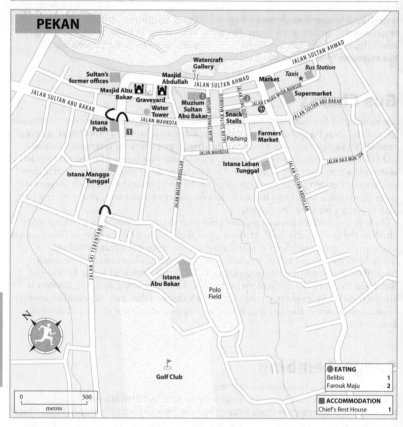

growth of its modern centre. This is thanks in no small part – so locals say – to the fact that the town's MP is none other than prime minister Najib Tun Razak. Still, the town is definitely a worthwhile day-trip from Kuantan: you'll find unusually spruce **kampung houses** with pretty gardens, a couple of **museums** and a few wooden former **royal residences**.

Muzium Sultan Abu Bakar

Jalan Sultan Ahmad • Museum Tues–Sun 9.30am–5pm, closed Fri 12.15–2.45pm • ☎ 09 422 1371 • RM15 Watercraft Gallery Tues–Sun 9.30am–5pm, closed Fri 12.15–2.45pm • Free

At the edge of the commercial area, Jalan Sultan Ahmad faces the languid riverfront and holds the **Muzium Sultan Abu Bakar** – the State Museum of Pahang. It's housed in a well-proportioned Straits colonial building that has variously served as the sultan's istana, the centre of British administration, and the headquarters of the Japanese army during the occupation.

You'll need to take your shoes off to pad around the galleries, which cover a wide range of topics, from Sultan Abu Bakar's predilection for polo to the Orang Asli. Displays are nicely designed but poorly lit, and content is thin in places – the most informative gallery is dedicated to Pahang's traditional arts and crafts. The open-air **Watercraft Gallery**, part of the state museum but just across the river, houses a good selection of decorative boats that once plied Pahang's rivers and coast, the centrepiece being a boxy white houseboat built for Sultan Abu Bakar in the 1950s.

The palaces

At the intersection of Jalan Sultan Abu Bakar and Jalan Sri Terentang, an archway built to resemble elephants' tusks marks the way to the royal quarter of the town. The white timber building on the corner, once the **Istana Putih**, is now a centre for Koranic recitation. A few minutes' walk south, the squat **Istana Mangga Tunggal** is painted a dark blue. Continue and turn left at the archway to reach the expansive walled grounds of the **Istana Abu Bakar** – the gate flanked by a pair of fighter jets – current home of the royal family and closed to the public. The other side of the road holds some attractively colourful kampung houses. Follow the walls, and after nearly ten minutes you'll come to a vast **polo field**, home to a polo club founded in 1926.

South of the padang sits **Istana Leban Tunggal**, an unusual wooden porticoed building with two octagonal towers crowned with yellow cupolas. Sadly, the 1935 palace, once the only one of Pekan's istanas open to the public, is now locked up, its gardens slowly returning to the jungle.

ARRIVAL AND INFORMATION   PEKAN

By bus Cream-coloured rapid Kuantan bus #400 departs every 20min from Kuantan's local bus station for the hour-long journey to Pekan. If your main interest is the palaces, ask to be let off at the "Daulat Tuanku" arch on Jalan Sultan Abu Bakar, before the UFO-like water tower. Pekan's own bus station is in the modern centre, east of the padang.

Destinations Destinations Kota Bharu via Kuala Terengganu (4 daily; 7hr); Kuala Lumpur (8 daily; 5hr);

Kuantan (frequent; 50min); Singapore via Mersing and Johor Bharu (7 daily; 7hr); Tasik Chini (4 daily; 2hr 30min).
By taxi Taxis (☎ 09 422 2211) depart from close to the bus station, with fixed fares to Kuantan (RM60), Tasik Chini (RM70) and other destinations.
Banks Bank Rakyat and various ATMs are concentrated on the block between the padang and the river.
Internet Get online at Internet Station (daily 9.30am–11pm; RM2/hr) on Jalan Sultan Abu Bakar.

ACCOMMODATION AND EATING

The streets around the padang hold several places to **eat**, including a small row of stalls selling juice and snacks, with parasols providing a welcome break from the sun.

Belibis Jalan Sultan Ahmad ☎ 013 345 5054. You don't need to visit the Muzium Sultan Abu Bakar to use its stylish café, decorated with carved birds (a *belibis* is a kind of grouse); Malaysian dishes – *nasi lemak* and the like – are served all day with a few simple Western dishes available after noon. Mon–Fri 8am–5.30pm, Sat 10am–6pm.
Chief's Rest House Jalan Istana Permai ☎ 09 422 6941. Occupying a spacious timber bungalow not unlike

some of the istanas, this resthouse has nine high-ceilinged rooms, some with four-poster beds and bamboo blinds, with a/c and TV. Booking is essential; it's a popular place, in a town with few alternatives. No wi-fi. RM55
Farouk Maju 1 Jalan Engku Muda Mansor. This typical *mamak* restaurant serves tasty and cheap *biriyani* (RM7), curries and cold drinks to a constant stream of locals. Daily 7am–10pm.

The south

262 Negeri Sembilan

268 Melaka

281 Around Melaka

284 From Melaka to Johor Bahru

285 Johor Bahru

290 The east coast

292 Pulau Tioman

302 Seribuat Archipelago: the other islands

304 Endau Rompin National Park

MELAKA

5

The south

The south of the Malay Peninsula, below Kuala Lumpur and Kuantan, holds some of the country's most historically and culturally significant towns. Foremost among these is the west coast city of Melaka, founded in the fifteenth century and ushering in a Malay "golden age" under the Melaka Sultanate. For all its enduring influence, though, the sultanate was short-lived and its fall to the Portuguese early in the sixteenth century marked the start of centuries of colonial involvement in Malaysia. Today Melaka fascinates visitors with its historical buildings and cultural blend, including the Peranakan community (also called Baba-Nyonya), which grew from the intermarriage of early Chinese immigrant traders and Malay women.

Melaka is not, however, the only place in the region with historical resonance. Between KL and Melaka, what's now the state of Negeri Sembilan is where the intrepid **Minangkabau** tribes from Sumatra settled, making their mark with architecture that can still be seen in **Seremban** and **Sri Menanti**. Both lie just over an hour south of the capital by road. Continuing down the west coast on the train line or the North–South Expressway (NSE), travellers soon reach the tip of the Peninsula and the thriving border city of **Johor Bahru** (JB) which dates back only to 1855. Beyond it lies Singapore.

Visitors tend to avoid the mountainous interior, where the road network is poor, but Route 3 on the east coast is a good deal more varied than the NSE, and winds for 300km through oil-palm country and past pleasant beaches. The biggest attractions along the east coast are **Pulau Tioman** and the other islands of the **Seribuat Archipelago**; they are havens for divers, snorkellers and anyone else in search of white sandy beaches, clear water and a tranquil atmosphere. Back on the Peninsula, and accessible from either east or west coast, the **Endau Rompin National Park** is a more rugged and less visited alternative to Taman Negara.

Negeri Sembilan

During the fifteenth century, the **Minangkabau** tribes from Sumatra established themselves in what is now the Malay state of **Negeri Sembilan**. While the modern-day capital is **Seremban**, 67km south of Kuala Lumpur, the cultural heart of the state lies 30km east in the royal town of **Sri Menanti**. Both towns showcase traditional Minangkabau architecture, with its distinctive, saddle-shaped roofs.

Brief history

The modern state of Negeri Sembilan is based on an old confederacy of nine districts (hence its name – *sembilan* is Malay for "nine"). By the middle of the nineteenth century, the thriving **tin trade** and British control over the area were well established, with colonial authority administered from Sungai Ujong (today's Seremban). Rival

The Minangkabau p.267
Getting from Johor Bahru to Singapore p.288
Snorkelling and diving around Pulau Tioman p.294
Sandflies p.303

PULAU TIOMAN

Highlights

❶ Minangkabau architecture The spectacular and distinctive architecture of this ancient Sumatran tribe survives in Sri Menanti and Seremban. **See p.267**

❷ Melaka The UNESCO World Heritage Site of Melaka has Portuguese, Dutch and British colonial buildings as well as unique Peranakan ancestral homes and some of Malaysia's best food. **See p.268**

❸ Johor Bahru It may still be gritty by Malaysian standards, but this border city is smartening itself up with a combination of

major public projects and small-scale entrepreneurship. **See p.285**

❹ Pulau Tioman Palm-fringed, scenic and with great diving, this island is understandably popular but retains a laidback feel. **See p.292**

❺ Seribuat Archipelago Tioman attracts all the attention, but the other islands of the Seribuat Archipelago offer even better beaches. **See p.302**

❻ Endau Rompin National Park A little-visited lush tropical rainforest, rich with rare species of flora and fauna. **See p.304**

HIGHLIGHTS ARE MARKED ON THE MAP ON P.264

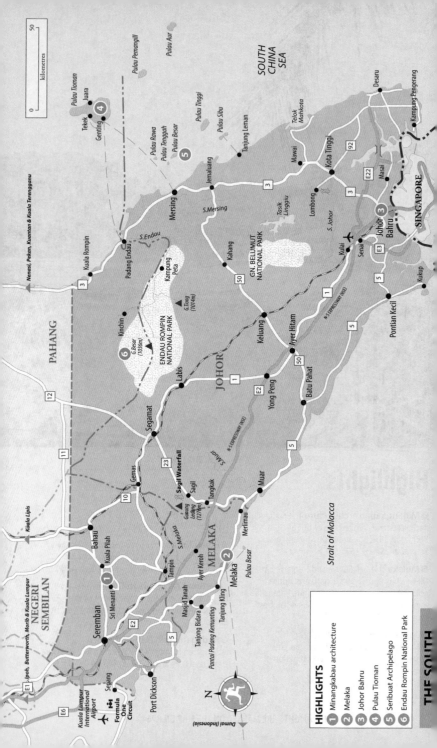

HIGHLIGHTS

1 Minangkabau architecture
2 Melaka
3 Johor Bahru
4 Pulau Tioman
5 Seribuat Archipelago
6 Endau Rompin National Park

THE SOUTH

Malay and Minangkabau groups fought several wars for control over the mining and transport of tin, with Chinese secret societies (triads) manipulating the situation to gain local influence, before a treaty was eventually signed in 1895.

Seremban

An hour south of the capital and just twenty minutes from KL International Airport, the bustling town of **SEREMBAN** is often overlooked by passing tourists. It is, however, the access point for **Sri Menanti** and has good examples of Minangkabau architecture at the **Taman Seni Budaya Negeri** museum complex.

Lake Garden and around

The area around the **Lake Garden** – more lake than garden – holds the most appeal. Heading north alongside it you pass the **Craft Complex** (Kompleks Kraf; daily 9am–6pm), a good place to view and buy handmade ceramics and textiles. Nearby is the white-stuccoed Neoclassical former **State Library** – built as the centre of colonial administration – with its graceful columns and portico. Beyond the black-and-gilt wrought-iron gates of the Istana (closed to the public), just north, a left turn leads to the **State Secretariat**, whose architecture (such as the layered, buffalo-horn roof) reflects the Minangkabau tradition.

Taman Seni Budaya Negeri

Near North–South Expressway, 3km northwest of the centre • Daily 10am–6pm • Free • ☎ 06 763 1149 • Bus from Terminal 1 (every 30min; 10–15min); taxi from the centre RM7

Although the small museum at the centre of the **Taman Seni Budaya Negeri** (State Arts and Culture Park) is unlikely to hold your attention for long, two reconstructed buildings in the grounds provide a good introduction to the principles of Minangkabau architecture. The **Istana Ampang Tinggi** was built as a royal residence in the mid-nineteenth century. The interior of the veranda, where male guests were entertained, displays a wealth of exuberant and intricate leaf carvings, with a pair of unusual heavy timber doors. The other building was used for formal state events and also bears elaborate carving on the exterior.

ARRIVAL AND INFORMATION   SEREMBAN

By train Seremban's train station, just south of the centre, has regular connections with Kuala Lumpur; take the Komuter train from KL Sentral or the old Kuala Lumpur station.
Destinations Butterworth (1 daily; 8hr); Gemas (4 daily; 1hr 15min); Ipoh (1 daily; 5hr); Johor Bahru (3 daily; 5hr); Kuala Lumpur (every 30min; 1hr 30min); Singapore (3 daily; 5hr 30min).

By bus The bus station is just across the river west of the town centre on Jalan Sungai Ujong, connected to a handy shopping mall (daily 10am–10pm) that houses a myriad of shops as well as a Golden Screen Cinema.
Destinations Alor Star (2 daily; 8hr); Butterworth

(2 daily; 6hr); Gua Musang (2 daily; 8hr); Hat Yai (Thailand; 2 daily; 10hr) Ipoh (1 daily; 5hr); Johor Bahru (every 1.5hr; 4hr); KLIA & KLIA2 (hourly; 1hr); Kota Bharu (2 daily; 8hr); Kuala Lumpur (every 15min; 1hr); Kuala Pilah (hourly; 45min); Kuala Terengganu (2 daily; 8hr); Kuantan (1 daily; 4hr); Melaka (hourly; 1hr 15min); Mersing (1 daily; 6hr); Singapore (4 daily, 5hr).

By taxi A taxi from KL Sentral's taxi station costs around RM100.

Information Tourism Malaysia, Seremban Plaza, Jalan Dato' Muda Linggi (Mon–Fri 8am–5pm; ☎ 06 763 5388) about 3km east of the centre.

ACCOMMODATION

★**The Dusun** Kampung Kolam Air, Mukim Pantai ⓦ thedusun.com.my. This wonderful orchard retreat, 15km northeast of Seremban, offers accommodation in six classic kampung-style units dotted amid mangosteen, mango, durian and orange trees in twelve acres of land.

Most units are open-fronted with unobstructed views of the rainforest, and each is equipped with kitchenette and BBQ sets. Note that meals are only available upon request, well in advance, so you should bring your own food. Facilities include two inviting saltwater pools and a deer

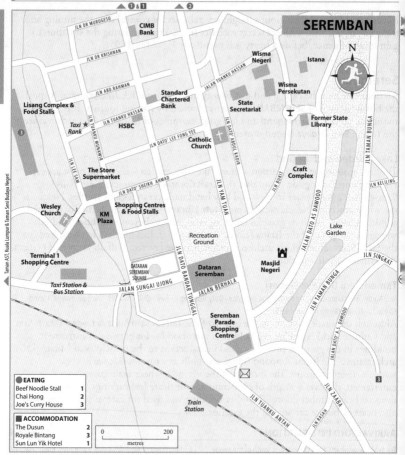

SEREMBAN

● EATING
Beef Noodle Stall	1
Chai Hong	2
Joe's Curry House	3

■ ACCOMMODATION
The Dusun	2
Royale Bintang	3
Sun Lun Yik Hotel	1

0   200
metres

park; staff organize jungle treks and bird walks. Rates include breakfast. Online bookings only. **RM500**

Royale Bintang Jalan Dato' A.S. Dawood ☎ 06 766 6666, ⓦ royalebintang-seremban.com. This large establishment is Seremban's most upmarket option; rooms are spacious and comfortable, if a bit dated. Good facilities, including a large swimming pool, gym and tennis court. **RM300**

Sun Lun Yik Hotel 19 Jalan Tun Dr Ismail ☎ 06 7635 572, ⓦ www.sunlunyik.com. This lovely heritage style hotel is one of Seremban's best options, offering nine spick-and-span rooms giving onto a hallway lined with colourful local art (all paintings are for sale). There's an airy lounge area with marble tables and wooden stools, too. Dorms **RM34**, doubles **RM89**

EATING, DRINKING AND NIGHTLIFE

There's no shortage of **places to eat** in the town centre; Seremban is known for its *pao* (Chinese steamed buns) and crab dishes. **Nightlife** focuses on the Taman AST area west of the centre, particularly in the new **Era Square** development, connected to the bus station.

Beef Noodle Stall Stall 742, upper floor of Pasar Besar (main market). It's a little out of the way, but the fantastic (and cheap) noodles here, and those at the nearby stall 648, are a local favourite – make sure you get here early. Wed–Mon 9am–1.30pm.

Chai Hong 50 Jalan Kapitan Tam Yeong ☎ 06 762 4357. Ask any local and they'll tell you this place makes the best chicken rice they have ever tasted, although they will also tell you it's the most expensive they have ever had at RM18. Customers can opt for an "economy set" (RM6) too. Service

is lethargic, but it's well worth the wait. Wed–Mon 10am–6pm.
Joe's Curry House Jalan Lisang Complex. Within a bustling food court lined with laidback eating houses, this great Indian joint rustles up tasty fish, chicken, mutton and vegetable dishes. A meal will set you back about RM6. Mon–Sat 11am–3pm.

Sri Menanti

The former royal capital of Negeri Sembilan, **SRI MENANTI**, is set in a lush, mountainous landscape 30km east of Seremban. The only reason to visit is to see a jewel of Minangkabau architecture, the **Istana Lama**. As you look for it, don't be misled by the sign for the **Istana Besar**, the current royal palace, which is topped by a startling blue roof.

Istana Lama
Daily 10am–6pm • Free

A timber palace set in geometric gardens, the splendid **Istana Lama** was the seat of the Minangkabau rulers (see box below). The sacking of Sri Menanti during the Sungai Ujong tin wars destroyed the original palace; today's four-storey version was designed and built in 1902 by two Malay master craftsmen, using no nails or screws. Until 1931, the building was used as a royal residence. Its tower, which once held the treasury and royal archives, offers a lovely view and can be reached by ladder from the sultan's private rooms. At its apex is a forked projection of a type known as "open scissors", now very rarely seen.

The whole rectangular building is raised nearly 2m off the ground by 99 pillars, 26 of which have been carved in low relief with complex foliated designs. Though the main doors and windows are plain, a long external veranda is covered with a design of

---

THE MINANGKABAU

The **Minangkabau people**, whose cultural heartland is in the mountainous region of western Sumatra (Indonesia), established a community in Malaysia in the early fifteenth century. As they had no written language until the arrival of Islam, knowledge of their origins is somewhat sketchy; their own oral accounts trace their ancestry to Alexander the Great, while the *Sejarah Melayu*, or Malay Annals, talks of a mysterious leader, Nila Pahlawan, who was pronounced king of the Palembang natives by a man who was magically transformed from the spittle of an ox.

In early times the Minangkabau were ruled in Sumatra by their own overlords or rajahs, though political centralization never really rivalled the role of the strongly autonomous *nagari* (Sumatran for village). Each *nagari* consisted of numerous **matrilineal clans** (*suku*), each of which took the name of the mother and lived in the ancestral home. The household was also in control of ancestral property, which was passed down the maternal line. The *sumando* (husband) stayed in his wife's house at night but was a constituent member of his mother's house, where most of his day was spent. Although the house and clan name belonged to the woman, and women dominated the domestic sphere, political and ceremonial power was in the hands of men; it was the *mamak* (mother's brother) who took responsibility for the continued prosperity of the lineage.

When and why the Minangkabau initially emigrated to what is now **Negeri Sembilan** in Malaysia is uncertain. Their subsequent history is closely bound up with that of Melaka and Johor, with the Minangkabau frequently called upon to supplement the armies of ambitious Malay princes and sultans. Evidence of intermarriage with the region's predominant tribal group, the Sakai, suggests some acceptance by the Malays of the matrilineal system. What is certain is that the Minangkabau were a political force to be reckoned with, aided by their reputation for supernatural powers. Today, the Minangkabau are very much integrated with the Malays, and their dialect is almost indistinguishable from standard Bahasa Melayu.

5

leaves and branches known as *awan larat*, or "driving clouds". Above the front porch is the most elaborate decoration, a pair of Chinese-style creatures with lions' heads, horses' legs and long feathery tails.

ARRIVAL AND DEPARTURE

SRI MENANTI

By bus From Seremban, take a United bus for the 45min journey to Kuala Pilah, then either wait for an infrequent local bus to Sri Menanti, or take a taxi (10 min; RM14).
By taxi A cab from Seremban costs RM70 (45min).

ACCOMMODATION

Sri Menanti Resort Next to the Istana Lama ☎ 06 497 0049. Reaasonable double rooms and chalets in Sri Menanti's only accommodation option. There's also a pleasant pool where you can cool off. It doesn't hurt to ask about discounts. Doubles RM159, chalets RM212

Melaka

When Penang was known only for its oysters and Singapore was just a fishing village, the influence of **MELAKA** (also spelled "Malacca") already extended beyond the Peninsula. Political and cultural life flourished in this trading centre under the auspices of the **Melaka Sultanate**, founded early in the fifteenth century, and helped to define what it means to be Malay.

The city subsequently suffered neglect from colonial rulers and fared little better after Independence, but in some respects this added to its faded charm. Recent years, though, have seen such developments as a land reclamation project that created the Taman Melaka Raya district and, in 2008, the gaining of UNESCO World Heritage Site status jointly with Penang. The latter has helped to encourage the development of a new wave of guesthouses and restoration projects, but has also brought some less welcome tourism schemes. Melaka remains, nevertheless, an undoubted highlight of any Malaysian itinerary.

Brief history

Melaka has its roots in the fourteenth-century struggles between Java and the Thai kingdom of Ayuthaya for control of the Malay Peninsula. The *Sejarah Melayu* (Malay Annals) records that when the Sumatran prince **Paramesvara** could no longer tolerate subservience to Java, he fled to the island of Temasek (later renamed Singapore), where he set himself up as ruler. The Javanese subsequently forced him to flee north to Bertam, where he was welcomed by the local community. While his son, Iskandar Shah, was out hunting near modern-day Melaka Hill, a mouse deer turned on the pursuing hunting dogs, driving them into the sea. Taking this courageous act to be a good omen, Shah asked his father to build a new settlement there and named it after the *melaka* tree under which he had been sitting.

A trading centre

Melaka under its sultans rapidly became a wealthy and cosmopolitan market town, trading spices and textiles with Indonesia and India. This meteoric rise was initially assisted by its powerful neighbours Ayuthaya and Java, who made good use of its trading facilities, but they soon found that they had a serious rival as Melaka started a campaign of **territorial expansion**.

By the reign of its last ruler, Sultan Mahmud Shah (1488–1530), Melaka's territory included the west coast of the Peninsula as far as Perak, the whole of Pahang, Singapore and most of east coast Sumatra. Culturally, too, Melaka was supreme – its sophisticated language, literature, hierarchical court structure and dances were all benchmarks in the Malay world.

5

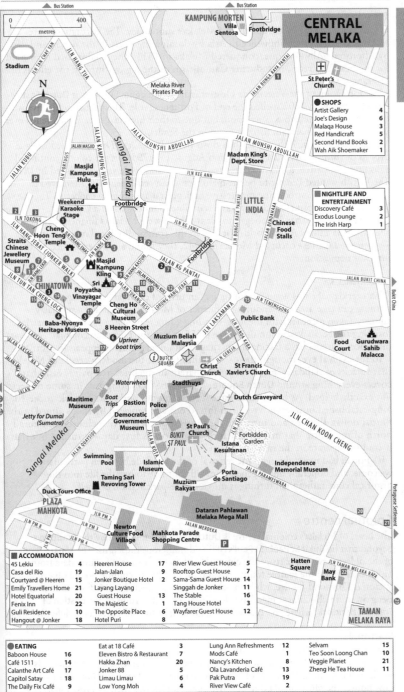

Bus Station

Bus Station

KAMPUNG MORTEN
Villa
Sentosa   Footbridge

**CENTRAL
MELAKA**

0   400
metres

Stadium

N

JLN TAN CHAY YAN

JLN HANG TUA

Melaka River
Pirates Park

JALAN BUNGA RAYA PANTAI

St Peter's
Church

● **SHOPS**
Artist Gallery	4
Joe's Design	6
Malaqa House	3
Red Handicraft	5
Second Hand Books	2
Wah Aik Shoemaker	1

JALAN MASJID

JALAN KUBU

JALAN KAMPUNG HULU

JLN PORTUGIS

Sungai Melaka

JALAN MUNSHI ABDULLAH

JALAN MUNSHI ABDULLAH

Madam King's
Dept. Store

P

Masjid
Kampung
Hulu

JLN KEE ANN

LITTLE
INDIA

Weekend
Karaoke
Stage

Footbridge

JLN BUNGA RAYA PANTAI

JLN BANDAHARA

Chinese
Food
Stalls

■ **NIGHTLIFE AND
ENTERTAINMENT**
Discovery Café	3
Exodus Lounge	2
The Irish Harp	1

JLN TOKONG

Cheng
Hoon Teng
Temple

JLN HANG JEBAT (JONKER WALK)

JLN TUKANG EMAS

JLN HANG LEKIU

JLN KG JAWA

Footbridge

Straits
Chinese
Jewellery
Museum

Masjid
Kampung
Kling

JALAN KAMPUNG KLIN

JALAN KG PANTAI

CHINATOWN

Sri
Poyyatha
Vinayagar
Temple

JLN TUKANG BESI

LORONG HANG JEBAT

JALAN BUKIT CHINA

JLN TUN TAN CHENG LOCK

Cheng Ho
Cultural
Museum

JLN TEMENGGONG

Bukit China

Baba-Nyonya
Heritage Museum

8 Heeren Street

Public Bank

JALAN LAKSAMANA

JLN BANDA KABA

JALAN LAKSAMANA 3

Upriver
boat trips

Muzium Beliah
Malaysia

Food
Court

Gurudwara
Sahib
Malacca

JALAN LAKSAMANA 2

JALAN KOTA LAKSAMANA 1

DUTCH
SQUARE

JLN GEREJA

Christ
Church

St Francis
Xavier's Church

Waterwheel

Stadthuys

Maritime
Museum

Boat
Trips

Bastion   Police

Dutch Graveyard

JLN CHAN KOON CHENG

Jetty for Dumai
(Sumatra)

Democratic
Government
Museum

JLN ISTANA

St Paul's
Church

BUKIT
ST PAUL

Forbidden
Garden

Istana
Kesultanan

Portuguese Settlement

Sungai Melaka

JALAN QUAYSIDE

JALAN KOTA

Swimming
Pool

Islamic
Museum

Taming Sari
Revolving Tower

Muzium
Rakyat

Porta
de Santiago

JALAN PARAMESWARA

Independence
Memorial Museum

Duck Tours Office

PLAZA
MAHKOTA

JLN PM 2

Newton
Culture Food
Village

Mahkota Parade
Shopping Centre

Dataran Pahlawan
Melaka Mega Mall

JALAN MERDEKA

P

Hatten
Square

JLN TAMAN MELAKA RAYA

JLN PM 3

JLN PM 8

JLN PM 4

May
Bank

TAMAN
MELAKA RAYA

■ **ACCOMMODATION**
45 Lekiu	4	Heeren House	17	River View Guest House	5
Casa del Rio	19	Jalan-Jalan	9	Rooftop Guest House	7
Courtyard @ Heeren	15	Jonker Boutique Hotel	2	Sama-Sama Guest House	14
Emily Travellers Home	21	Layang Layang		Singgah de Jonker	11
Hotel Equatorial	20	Guest House	13	The Stable	16
Fenix Inn	22	The Majestic	1	Tang House Hotel	3
Guli Residence	10	The Opposite Place	6	Wayfarer Guest House	12
Hangout @ Jonker	18	Hotel Puri	8		

● **EATING**
Baboon House	16	Eat at 18 Café	3	Lung Ann Refreshments	12	Selvam	15
Café 1511	14	Eleven Bistro & Restaurant	7	Mods Café	1	Teo Soon Loong Chan	10
Calanthe Art Café	17	Hakka Zhan	20	Nancy's Kitchen	8	Veggie Planet	21
Capitol Satay	18	Jonker 88	5	Ola Lavanderia Café	13	Zheng He Tea House	11
The Daily Fix Café	9	Limau Limau	6	Pak Putra	19		
		Low Yong Moh	4	River View Café	2		

5

The colonial era

It took a sea change in Europe to end Melaka's supremacy. The Portuguese were seeking to extend their influence in Asia by dominating ports in the region and, led by Alfonso de Albuquerque, conquered Melaka in 1511. They maintained their hold for the next 130 years, introducing Catholicism to the region through the efforts of St Francis Xavier.

The formation of the Vereenigde Oostindische Compagnie (VOC), or **Dutch East India Company**, in 1602 spelled the end of Portuguese rule. The primary objective was trade rather than religious conversion, but due to their high taxes the Dutch relied ever more on force to maintain their position in the Straits.

Weakened by French threats to their posts in the Indies, the Dutch handed Melaka over to the **British East India Company** on August 15, 1795. Yet the colony continued a decline that hastened when the free-trade port of Singapore was established in 1819. The British wanted Penang to be the main west coast settlement but attempted to revitalize Melaka, introducing progressive agricultural and mining concerns. They invested in new hospitals, schools and a train line, but only when a Chinese entrepreneur, Tan Chay Yan, began to plant **rubber** were Melaka's financial problems alleviated for a time. After World War I, even this commodity faced mixed fortunes – when the **Japanese occupied** Melaka in 1942, they found a town exhausted by the interwar depression.

Modern Melaka

Whatever damage was wrought during its centuries of colonial mismanagement, nothing can take away the enduring influence of Melaka's contribution to Malay culture. Taken together with the long-standing Chinese presence – with intermarriage fostering the Peranakan community (see p.575) – and the European colonial influences, Melaka has a fascinating heritage that understandably appeals to tourists.

To the cynical eye, though, there's something about the modern centre of Melaka that smacks of slapdash "preservation", apparent in the brick-red paint wash that covers everything around **Dutch Square**. The UNESCO listing has, in some respects, not exactly helped. As landowners have scented money and rents have skyrocketed, long-established businesses have been forced out and replaced by shops aimed at the tourist dollar. Ill-fated and incongruous tourism projects have included a monorail north of the centre that memorably broke down on its first day – it turned out that it couldn't operate in the rain.

It's not all bad news, though. The renewal of the riverside has been particularly welcome, and hopefully any regeneration will continue to breathe life into the historical core, rather than turning it into a theme-park version of itself.

Colonial centre

The heart of Melaka's colonial centre is **Dutch Square**, dominated by the **Stadthuys**; beyond that lie **Bukit St Paul (St Paul's Hill)** and numerous museums. The square is one of the oldest surviving parts of the city, although two of its main features date from much later times: the marble fountain was built in 1904 to commemorate Queen Victoria's Diamond Jubilee, while the clock tower was erected in 1886 in honour of Tan Beng Swee, a rich Chinese merchant. Rather older are the ruins of the **Bastion of Fredrick Hendrick**, where you can see the alignment of the old Portuguese defensive wall.

Stadthuys

Dutch Square • Daily 9am–5.30pm • RM5 • ⓦ perzim.gov.my

The sturdy red **Stadthuys**, presiding over the entire south side of Dutch Square, is not a single building but a collection of structures dating from between 1660 and 1700; one now houses the **Museum of Ethnography**. The complex was used as a town hall throughout the Dutch and British administrations and the wide, monumental interior staircases, together with the high windows, are typical of seventeenth-century Dutch municipal buildings.

It's worth visiting mostly for the buildings themselves: the Museum of Ethnography displays an array of Malay and Chinese ceramics, weaponry, musical instruments and the like, plus a few dioramas and countless paintings depicting Melakan history. Several other **smaller museums** lurk behind the main buildings although, covering topics such as the Malaysian education system, they are aimed mostly at domestic visitors.

Christ Church

Mon–Sat 9am–4.30pm; services Sun 8.30am (English), 10.30am (Mandarin) & 4.30pm (Malay) • Free

Christ Church was built in 1753 to commemorate the centenary of the Dutch occupation of Melaka. Its simple design, with neither aisles nor chancel, is typically Dutch; the porch and vestry were nineteenth-century afterthoughts. The cool, whitewashed interior has decorative fanlights high up on the walls and elaborate, 200-year-old hand-carved pews, while the roof features heavy timber beams each cut from a single tree. The plaques on the walls tell a sorry tale of early deaths in epidemics.

Dutch Graveyard

East of Christ Church, along Jalan Kota

Although the overgrown **Dutch Graveyard** was first used in the late seventeenth century, when the VOC was still in control (hence the name), British graves easily outnumber those of their predecessors. The tall column towards the centre of the tiny cemetery is a memorial to two of the many officers killed in the Naning War in 1831, a costly attempt to incorporate the nearby Naning region into Melaka's territory.

Istana Kesultanan

Daily 9am–5.30pm • RM2 • ☎ 06 282 7464, ⓦ perzim.gov.my

The **Istana Kesultanan** (Sultan's Palace) has played a central role in Malaysian history, although the current dark-timber palace is a contemporary reconstruction of the original fifteenth-century building. In the best Malay architectural tradition, its multilayered, sharply sloping roofs contain no nails. It was here that the administrative duties of the state were carried out, and also where the sultan resided when in the city (he mostly lived further upriver at Bertam, safe from attacks on Melaka). Remove your shoes to ascend the wide staircase to the ground floor, where you'll find a cultural museum housing dioramas of scenes from Malay court life.

Porta de Santiago

At the time they conquered Melaka, the Portuguese used the forced labour of fifteen hundred slaves to construct the mighty **A Famosa** fort. The Dutch East India Company later used the fort as its headquarters, but the British demolished it at the start of the nineteenth century when they relocated to Penang. All that's left today is a single gate, the crumbling **Porta de Santiago**, which was only saved thanks to last-minute intervention from Sir Stamford Raffles, the founder of Singapore.

St Paul's Church

St Paul's Hill • Reached by climbing the steps behind the Porta de Santiago • Free

On the summit of St Paul's Hill (**Bukit St Paul**), and now no more than a roofless shell, **St Paul's Church** was constructed in 1521 by the Portuguese as Our Lady of the Mount. The Jesuit missionary **St Francis Xavier** visited the church between 1545 and 1552, and his body was brought here for burial after his death in 1553, before being exhumed and transferred to its final resting place in Goa (India) the following year. The Dutch Calvinists changed the denomination of the church when they took over in 1641, renaming it St Paul's Church, and it remained in use until the construction of Christ

5

Church at the foot of the hill. The British found St Paul's more useful for military than for religious purposes, storing their gunpowder here during successive wars.

Muzium Rakyat

Jalan Kota • Sat–Thurs 9am–5.30pm, Fri 9am–12.15pm & 2.45–5.30pm • RM3 • ⦿ perzim.gov.my

The **Muzium Rakyat** (People's Museum) is the most interesting of the museums that you pass as you skirt west around the base of St Paul's Hill from Porta de Santiago. Its ground and first floors house exhibits on such topics as the construction and competitive use of spinning tops. The third floor contains the much more interesting – and at times gruesome – **Museum of Enduring Beauty**. Taking "endure" in the sense of "to suffer", the exhibits show how people around the world have sought to alter their appearance: head deformation, dental mutilations, tattooing, scarification, corsetry and foot-binding and the like. The fourth floor is home to the Kite Museum, which speaks for itself.

Maritime Museum

Quayside • Daily 9am–5.30pm • RM3 • ⦿ perzim.gov.my

The main part of the **Maritime Museum** (Muzeum Samudera) is housed in a towering replica of a Portuguese cargo ship, the *Flor de la Mar*, which sank in 1511 carrying treasure plundered from Melaka. Inside its hull, model ships, information boards and paintings chart the settlement's maritime history from the time of the Malay Sultanate to the arrival of the British in the eighteenth century.

It feels a little disjointed, rather than telling a single story, but there are some interesting facts in there. The same cannot be said of the drab displays across the road in the other section of the museum; the Royal Malaysian Navy patrol craft in the gardens is, however, popular with kids.

Taming Sari Revolving Tower

Jalan Merdaka • Daily 10am–11pm • RM20

You can't miss the 80m-tall **Taming Sari Revolving Tower**, which offers a great (if relatively expensive) 360-degree view of the city and the sea. Its construction so close to the colonial district in 2008 was controversial, but it has nevertheless proved to be a popular attraction, with big queues at the weekend. Duck Tour tickets are sold next door (see p.276).

Chinatown

Melaka owed a great deal of its nineteenth-century economic recovery to its Chinese community: it was one Tan Chay Yan who first planted rubber here, and a Chinese immigrant called Tan Kim Seng established what became the great Straits Steam Ship Company. Most of these entrepreneurs settled in what became known as **Chinatown**, across Sungai Melaka from the colonial district. For many visitors, it's the most interesting part of town.

Jalan Hang Jebat

Night market Fri–Sun 7pm–midnight

Chinatown's main street, **Jalan Hang Jebat** – previously named Jonker Street, or Jonker Walk – runs parallel to Jalan Tun Tan Cheng Lock. It was formerly known for its antiques, but these days most shops sell souvenirs and cheap handicrafts. Still, its bars and restaurants continue to make it a centre of tourist activity.

The street is closed to traffic on weekend evenings, for the **Jonker Walk Night Market** when shops stay open late and the street is lined with vendors. Although very popular and often considered a must-do by visitors, it's nothing special by Malaysian street market standards – in particular, anyone looking for good street food is likely to come away disappointed.

Cheng Ho Cultural Museum

51 Lorong Hang Jebat • Daily 9am–6pm • RM10 • ☎ 06 283 1135, ⓦ chengho.org/museum

5

Dedicated to the life of Chinese Admiral **Cheng Ho** (also spelled Zheng He), who visited Melaka several times on his epic travels across Asia, the Middle East and Africa, the **Cheng Ho Cultural Museum** provides an insight into early fifteenth-century Melaka, as well as trading and seafaring during the Ming Dynasty. Exhibits include a model of Cheng Ho's treasure ship and various navigational instruments; there's also a teahouse on the premises.

Jalan Tun Tan Cheng Lock

The elegant townhouses that line **Jalan Tun Tan Cheng Lock**, formerly Heeren Street, are the ancestral homes of the Baba-Nyonya community (see p.575). The wealthiest and most successful of these merchants built long, narrow-fronted houses, minimizing the "window tax" by incorporating internal courtyards designed for ventilation and the collection of rainwater.

Several of the houses are now open to the public as shops, hotels and restaurants. You can't enter the **Chee Ancestral House** at no. 117, but it's worth checking out the exterior: an imperious Dutch building of pale green stucco topped by a gold dome, it's home to one of Melaka's wealthiest families.

8 Heeren Street

8 Jalan Tun Tan Cheng Lock • Daily 11am–4pm • Free (donations welcome) • ⓦ badanwarisan.org.my

Make time for a visit to the model conservation project at **8 Heeren Street**, where you can see how the building (dating from the 1790s) has been used and modified over the years. Printed information gives background on topics such as building materials and techniques, while the knowledgeable staff are happy to answer questions. Some commercial restoration projects in Melaka introduce inauthentic elements in the name of "heritage", but here the history of the building is laid bare.

Baba-Nyonya Heritage Museum

48 & 50 Jalan Tun Tan Cheng Lock • Daily 10am–1pm & 2–4.30pm • RM15 • ☎ 06 283 1273, ⓦ babanyonyamuseum.com

An amalgam of three adjacent houses belonging to a single family, the **Baba-Nyonya Heritage Museum** is an excellent example of the Chinese Palladian style (which blends Chinese and European influences). Connected by a common covered footway, decorated with hand-painted tiles, each front entrance has an outer swing door of elaborately carved teak, while a heavier internal door provides extra security at night. Two red lanterns, one bearing the household name, the other messages of good luck, hang either side of the doorway, framed by heavy Greco-Roman columns.

The upper level of the building is the most eye-catching: a canopy of Chinese tiles over the porch frames the shuttered windows, almost Venetian in character with their glass protected by intricate wrought-iron grilles. The eaves and fascias are covered in painted floral designs. Inside, the homes are filled with gold-leaf fittings, blackwood furniture inlaid with mother-of-pearl, delicately carved lacquer screens and Victorian chandeliers. The guided tours, included in the entry price, add a great deal to the experience, revealing much about the Baba-Nyonyas themselves.

Straits Chinese Jewellery Museum

108 Jalan Tan Tun Cheng Lock • Daily 10am–5pm • RM15 • ☎ 06 281 9763

The **Straits Chinese Jewellery Museum** displays a beautiful collection of Peranakan jewellery with Chinese, Malay and Indo-European designs and motifs. Nyonya traditionally kept their hair very long, tied up during the day in a tightly coiled bun known as *sanggul*, held in place by three gold, silver or diamond hairpins; examples of these are on display. Look out too for the gold anklets, Indian in inspiration, worn by younger women before the turn of the twentieth century. The museum also

5

showcases elaborate tobacco boxes, traditionally made for decorative or ceremonial purposes and often festooned with implements made of precious metals such as silver and gold.

Jalan Tukang Emas

Jalan Tukang Emas, continuing on from Jalan Tokong, is sometimes known as "Harmony Street" in reference to its buildings from different religions. A short way east from Jalan Hang Jebat, **Cheng Hoon Teng temple** – dedicated to the goddess of mercy – is reputed to be the oldest Chinese temple in the country. A little further along, the 1748 **Masjid Kampung Kling** displays an unusual blend of styles: the minaret looks like a pagoda, there are English and Portuguese glazed tiles, and a Victorian chandelier hangs over a pulpit carved with Hindu and Chinese designs. Next door, the Hindu **Sri Poyyatha Vinayagar Temple** also has a minaret, decorated with red cows, and dates back to the 1780s.

Masjid Kampung Hulu

Jalan Kampung Hulu • Daily 5am–10pm

Thought to be the oldest mosque in Malaysia that remains in its original location, **Masjid Kampung Hulu** was constructed around 1728 in typical Melakan style. It's a solid-looking structure, surmounted by a bell-shaped roof with red Chinese tiles, and has more than a hint of pagoda in its minaret. Such architecture has its origins in Sumatra, perhaps brought over by the Minangkabau (see p.267) who settled in nearby Negeri Sembilan.

Northeast of the centre

From Christ Church, Jalan Laksamana leads north past **St Francis Xavier's Church**, a twin-towered, nineteenth-century, Neo-Gothic structure. Further up from here on Jalan Bendahara you pass through the centre of Melaka's tumbledown **Little India**, a rather desultory line of incense and saree shops interspersed with a few eating houses.

Riverside walk

Melaka River Pirates Park Daily 5pm–midnight • Entry free; RM5/ride • ☎ 06 288 1100

The redevelopment of Melaka's **riverside** has been a recent success story, encouraging the opening of guesthouses and cafés where once there were dilapidated buildings. It's a pleasant 1.5km walk from Dutch Square to Kampung Morten (see below), and almost the whole stretch is illuminated at night. On the western side you'll find the **Melaka River Pirates Park**; not exactly in keeping with Melaka's heritage feel, this entertainment park – which includes a ferris wheel and a pirate ship – should keep children occupied for an hour or two, but closes on rainy days.

St Peter's Church

Just north of the Jalan Bendahara and Jalan Munshi Abdullah crossroads • Daily 7.30am–1pm • Free • ⓦ stpetersmelaka.org

The oldest Roman Catholic church in Malaysia, **St Peter's Church** was built by a Dutch convert in 1710 as a gift to the Portuguese Catholics, and has an unusual barrel-vaulted ceiling. The church really comes into its own at Easter as the centre of the Catholic community's celebrations.

Kampung Morten

The village of **Kampung Morten**, named after the British district officer who donated RM10,000 to buy the land, is a surprising find so close to the heart of Melaka. The wooden **stilt houses** here are distinctively Melakan, with their long, rectangular living rooms and kitchens, and narrow verandas approached by ornamental steps. It's easiest to explore on foot, and the riverside walk to get here is part of the experience.

Villa Sentosa
Daily 9.30am–6pm • Donation expected • ☎ 06 282 3988

The **Villa Sentosa**, with its miniature kampung house and mini-lighthouse, is a 70-year-old family home that now functions as a museum. The owner will gladly show you their artefacts and heirlooms.

Bukit China

East of the colonial heart of Melaka, **Bukit China** is the ancestral burial ground of the town's Chinese community – it's said to be the oldest and largest such graveyard outside China. Although Chinese contacts with the Malay Peninsula probably began in the first century BC, formal commercial relations were only established when the Ming Emperor Yung-Lo sent his envoy Admiral Cheng Ho here in 1409. Today, Bukit China is more an inner-city park than burial ground, where you're likely to encounter locals jogging, practising martial arts or simply admiring the view.

Sam Poh Kong temple
At the foot of Bukit China, at the eastern end of Jalan Temenggong

The **Sam Poh Kong temple** is a working temple dedicated to Admiral Cheng Ho. Accounts are vague when it comes to the arrival of the first Chinese settlers, though it's said that on the marriage of Sultan Mansur Shah (1458–77) to the daughter of the emperor, Princess Hang Liu, the five hundred nobles who accompanied her stayed to set up home on Bukit China. It was supposedly these early Chinese settlers who dug the **Sultan's Well** behind the temple.

Portuguese settlement
Bus #17 from Dutch Square or Jalan Merdeka (every 30min; 15min); taxi RM20

The road east of Jalan Taman Melaka Raya leads, after about 3km, to Melaka's **Portuguese settlement**; turn right into Jalan Albuquerque, clearly signposted off the main road, and you enter its heart. Today you're likely to recognize the descendants of the original Portuguese settlers only by hearing their language, **Kristao**, a blend of Malay and old Portuguese. Note too the many Portuguese street names, including Fernandez, Rodriguez and Dominguez.

Medan Portugis

You could almost be forgiven for thinking that the whitewashed **Medan Portugis** (Portuguese Square), at the end of the road into the Portuguese settlement, is a remnant from colonial times. In fact it dates only from 1985, but the local restaurateurs make an effort to conjure up a Portuguese atmosphere even if the food is Malay in character. A three-day **fiesta** – the feast of St Pedro – starts on June 29 every year, with traditional Portuguese food, live music and dancing. Just beyond the square is a row of waterfront seafood restaurants.

ARRIVAL AND DEPARTURE   **MELAKA**

By plane Melaka's airport is 10km north of the city centre. At the time of research Rayani Air (Melaka airport ☎ 06 319 1588, main office ☎ 03 5518 5786; ⊛ rayaniair.com) were due to launch services to Kota Bharu, Kuching, Kota Kinabalu, Penang and Langkawi. Irregular buses connect the airport to Malaka Sentral (every 40min; 40min), from

where you'll have to change and catch #17 bus to the historical centre (every 30min; 20–30min). A taxi from the airport to the city centre is about RM30.

By train Tampin train station, 38km north of Melaka (☎ 06 441 1034), is connected by irregular buses to Melaka Sentral, although the journey can take up to 1hr 30min as

5

the bus stops frequently; it's much more convenient to catch a taxi (40min; RM70). Note that it's quicker to take a bus to Singapore than the train.

Destinations Butterworth, via Ipoh (1 daily; 8hr 40min); Jerantut (1 daily; 6hr); Kuala Lipis (1 daily; 7hr); Kuala Lumpur (4 daily; 2hr); Wakaf Bharu (daily; 12hr 45min); Woodlands, Singapore, via JB Sentral (3 daily; 5–6hr).

By bus Melaka's bus station, Melaka Sentral, is just under 4km north of the centre, at the corner of Jalan Panglima Awang and Jalan Tun Razak, close to a large Tesco supermarket. The #17 bus (every 30min; 20–30min) from the domestic part of the station stops off at the Clock House as well as at Jalan Kabu at the western end of Jalan Hang Jebat; a taxi will cost RM20 (15min). Transnasional (ⓦtransnasional.com.my) operates buses from Melaka Sentral (11 daily; 3hr) to KLIA and KLIA 2, with four daily services also departing from Mahkota Medical Centre, close to the Mahkota Parade Shopping Centre.

Destinations Alor Star (4 daily; 7hr); Butterworth (5 daily; 6hr); Ipoh (3 daily; 4hr); Johor Bahru (hourly 8am–8pm; 3hr); Kluang (11 daily; 2hr); Kota Bharu (2 daily; 10hr); KLIA/KLIA 2 (11 daily; 3hr); Kuala Lumpur (hourly 5am–10pm; 2hr 30min); Kuala Terengganu (daily; 8hr); Kuantan (daily; 5hr); Mersing (3 daily; 4hr); Singapore (hourly 7.30am–7pm; 4hr).

By ferry From the jetty on Jalan Quayside, ferries head to Dumai in Sumatra (daily, 10am; 2hr 30min; RM110 one way or RM170 return plus RM20 port tax). For information and tickets, best bought a day in advance, contact Tunas Rupat Follow Me Express at G29, Jalan PM10, Plaza Mahkota (ⓣ06 283 2506, ⓦtunasrupat.com).

By car Melaka's streets are very narrow and the one-way system is awkward, so drivers should park at the first opportunity and get around the city by foot, bus, trishaw or taxi. You'll have to display a coupon (1 day/RM5), which can be bought from the booth by the Taming Sari Tower. One local car rental operator is Hawk, 34 Jalan Laksamana (Mon–Fri 8am–5.30pm; ⓣ06 283 7878, ⓦhawkrentacar.com.my).

GETTING AROUND

By bus There are several useful routes for visitors, departing from Melaka Sentral: #17 runs through the historical centre to Taman Melaka Raya and stops off at the entrance of the Portuguese Settlement.

By taxi or trishaw For longer journeys, taxis or the colourful disco trishaws are the best bet. Both cost roughly the same, and you can book trishaws for tours (see below). You should be able to get a trishaw around the Dutch

Square or in front of the Tming Sari Revolving Tower; there's a taxi rank by the Mahkota Parade. Note that a commission system operates between Melaka's taxi drivers and some guesthouses; if you know where you want to go, don't necessarily believe a driver who tells you that the place is full.

On foot Most places of interest lie within the compact historical centre, and so are best visited on foot.

INFORMATION AND TOURS

Tourist information The helpful Tourism Malaysia office is on the ground floor of Bangunan Surau Warisan Dunia on Dutch Square (daily 9am–6pm; ⓣ06 283 6220; ⓦtourismmalaysia.gov.my). There is a state tourist office at Melaka Sentral bus station (daily 9am–5.30pm; ⓣ06 288 1340).

Internet access The tourist office has three computers with internet access (daily 9am–5.30pm; free for 15min) and the *River View Café*, 82 Jalan Kampong Pantai (see p.279) has a computer terminal (15min free for customers, or RM1 for 30min). Virtually every hotel, café and restaurant has wi-fi.

Duck Tours The Duck Tour uses an amphibious vehicle to

explore Melaka on land and water. The main ticket office is by the Taming Sari Revolving Tower (daily 9am–6pm; 1hr; RM45; ⓣ06 292 2595, ⓦmelakaducktours.com).

Trishaw tours A sightseeing tour by trishaw, covering the major sights, should cost RM40/hr for two people.

Boat trips Boat trips up the river set off from the jetty behind the Maritime Museum (daily every 30min 9am–11pm, Fri no trips 12.15–2.15pm; return [45min] RM15; hop-on, hop-off, valid all day RM30; ⓣ06 286 1531). Offering a good way to see the restored riverside area, the boat stops at seven points along the river, taking you past the old Dutch quarter of red-roofed godowns as far as Kampung Morten.

ACCOMMODATION

Melaka has a huge selection of **hotels** and guesthouses, including many that are good value and well kept, and a scattering of lovely boutique properties; there are even a couple of highly recommended **apartments**. Book ahead for Friday and Saturday nights, as Melaka is a popular weekend break destination – rates rise by as much as RM100.

HOTELS AND GUESTHOUSES

Casa del Rio 88 Jalan Kota Laksamana ⓣ06 292 1113, ⓦcasadelrio-melaka.com. This resort-style riverfront complex offers spacious well-appointed rooms with

balconies, some with river views. The excellent restaurant (open to non-guests) serves traditional sweet and savoury Nyonya dishes at high tea (noon–4pm; RM48), served in pretty tiffin boxes. RM550

★ **Courtyard @ Heeren** 91 Jalan Tun Tan Cheng Lock ☎ 06 281 0088, ⓦ courtyardatheeren.com. The lobby of this boutique hotel sets the tone, with a soothing water feature, original marble floors, and the owner's collection of antique wooden furniture. The welcoming rooms offer a delightful mix of old and new, with intricately carved bedsteads and flat-screen TVs, while the deluxe rooms feature heritage design with four-poster wooden beds and replica period tiles. Prices increase by RM60–70 over the weekends. **RM212**

★ **Emily Travellers Home** 71 Jalan Parameswara ☎ 06 281 6648 or ☎ 016 925 8902 (no reservations). A real backpacker gem near Taman Melaka Raya, which feels a world apart from the bustling streets of Melaka. Step over the threshold into an oasis of greenery, where cats, a friendly pet rabbit and even a duck roam free. Rooms are simple but welcoming with shared bath – those on the first floor are in better nick. There are also a couple of cottages with private bathroom. Doubles **RM50**, cottages **RM70**

Hotel Equatorial Bandar Hilir ☎ 06 282 8333, ⓦ equatorial.com. With 496 well-appointed rooms and suites set over 22 floors, this is one of Melaka's largest hotels. Facilities include a tennis court, fitness centre, four interconnected swimming pools, two restaurants and four cafés. **RM270**

Fenix Inn 156 Jalan Merdaka, Taman Melaka Raya ☎ 06 281 5511, ⓦ fenixinn.com. A decent budget choice with comfortable, practical, good-value rooms. It's a short walk to the historical centre, and there are plenty of shopping malls just close by. Rates rise by RM30 over the weekends. **RM102**

Guli Residence 3 Jalan Kuli ☎ 016 764 0588, ⓔ guliresidence@yahoo.com. Above the *Zheng He Tea House*, this guesthouse features four spacious rooms, most with parquet floors and some with wicker lamps, including a duplex family room sleeping six (RM450). There's no breakfast, but guests can enjoy complimentary all-day tea from the teahouse. **RM260**

Hangout @ Jonker 19 & 21 Lorong Hang Jebat ☎ 06 282 8318, ⓦ hangouthotels.com. This spotless flashpackers' place with a sister hotel in Singapore features modern rooms with cable TV, a/c and private bath set over four floors in the heart of town. There's a kitchen and lounge area with communal computers. **RM150**

Heeren House 1 Jalan Tun Tan Cheng Lock ☎ 06 281 4241, ⓦ heerenhouse.com. Formerly a warehouse, a coffee shop, a family home and eventually a guesthouse, this is a pleasant choice right in the historical centre, offering spacious rooms with colonial and Peranakan furniture – some could do with a splash of paint here and there. Weekend surcharge RM20. **RM130**

Jalan-Jalan 8 Jalan Tukang Emas ☎ 06 283 3937. This excellent backpacker hangout is so popular that it now occupies two non-connected buildings. The main building

has the reception and the more lively common area, while the other has a/c. There's a large ten-bed dorm, as well as a six-bed and a female-only dorm sleeping four. Free wi-fi, coffee and tea, and bike rental at RM5/day. Dorms **RM16**, fan doubles **RM40**, a/c en-suite doubles **RM70**

★ **Jonker Boutique Hotel** 82–86a & b Jalan Tokong ☎ 06 282 5151, ⓦ jonkerboutiquehotel.com. Housed in a three-storey Art Deco building, the spacious rooms at this welcoming boutique hotel feature beautiful teak flooring and high ceilings. The central location, just a stone's throw away from Jonker Walk, is a plus. Rates rise by RM50 at the weekend. **RM198**

Layang Layang Guest House 24–26 Jalan Tukang Besi ☎ 06 292 2722, ⓔ layanglayang26@gmail.com. A lovely guesthouse with clean, welcoming rooms with parquet floors, set around a peaceful courtyard with a fishpond. The communal area is dotted with trinkets, including a guitar, the odd lantern and wooden giraffes; there are board games, too. **RM72**

★ **The Majestic** 188 Jalan Bunga Raya ☎ 06 289 8000, ⓦ www.majesticmalacca.com. Located in a beautiful 1920s colonial mansion, the inviting rooms at this luxurious hotel feature polished timber floors, teakwood fittings and indulgent roll-top baths. The excellent spa offers therapies based on the healing heritage of the Peranakans, descendants of Chinese immigrants who intermarried with Malays; the restaurant offers traditional Nyonya cuisine, which combines Chinese cooking methods with Malay ingredients and spices. **RM500**

★ **The Opposite Place** 18 Jalan Hang Lekiu ☎ 016 274 9686, ⓦ opposite-place.com. In a beautifully refurbished pre-World War II building, this boutique guesthouse features two sleek, individually designed suites – Opposite West has a living area with antique wooden furniture and a voyeuristic bathroom, while Opposite East has open-brick walls, hardwood floors and mock period armchairs. *Eat at 18 Café* downstairs (see p.279) serves excellent breakfasts. **RM599**

Hotel Puri 118 Jalan Tun Tan Cheng Lock ☎ 06 282 5588, ⓦ hotelpuri.com. Set in a beautifully restored Peranakan shophouse with a large foyer with polished marble floors, the rooms here are contemporary, though they could do with a little touching up. The *Galeri Café*, open to non-guests, serves Peranakan and Western dishes to the soothing sound of the courtyard fountain. **RM162**

★ **River View Guest House** 94 & 96 Jalan Kampong Pantai ☎ 012 327 7746 or ☎ 012 380 7211, ⓔ riverviewguesthouse@yahoo.com. This guesthouse, with a three-bed mixed-sex dorm and doubles (all with fan and a/c) with shared bath is full of character; the owners even bake cakes and pies for guests in the afternoons. The leafy terrace, with wonderful views over the river, makes a perfect spot to unwind at sunset. Dorms **RM20**, doubles **RM58**

5

Rooftop Guest House 39 Jalan Kampong Pantai ☎012 380 7211 or ☎012 327 7746, ❺rooftopguest house@yahoo.com. Opened by the owners of the *River View*, this well-run guesthouse has a small four-bed dorm with lockers and doubles with shared and private bath. The common area has a couple of sofas and there's book exchange, too. Families and large groups should consider the *River View House*, a self-catered apartment owned by the same friendly couple, with two doubles and a master room with king-sized bed (RM450). Dorm RM25, doubles with shared bath RM58, en-suite doubles RM88

Sama-Sama Guest House 4 Jalan Tukang Besi ☎06 281 5216. A popular budget choice with a pleasant living area featuring pretty floor tiles, wicker chairs and sofas and a few curios including a vintage suitcase. The family room sleeps four (RM85), while the doubles come with fan or a/c; singles are RM55. Breakfast is an extra RM10. Fan RM55, a/c RM70

Singgah de Jonker 112 Lorong Hang Jebat ☎012 200 8544. This B&B features clean, freshly painted a/c rooms with sturdy wooden beds and crisp linen in a historical building (note the original wall calligraphy) with some rooms overlooking the river, interior courtyard or the street. All have shared bath, and there's also a large attic dorm sleeping eight (groups only; RM180). Breakfast is served by the river and there's a small terrace with lovely views that's a pleasant spot to soak up the atmosphere at all times of day. RM110

Tang House Hotel 78 Jalan Tokong ☎06 283 3969, ⓦtanghouse.com.my. This welcoming family-run guesthouse features very simple rooms with mattresses on the floor, as well as newly built a/c rooms that are a steal; great rates for single travellers (RM35), too. The Jonker Walk karaoke stage means it can get noisy on weekend evenings. Basic doubles RM55, a/c doubles RM120

Wayfarer Guest House 104 Lorong Hang Jebat ☎012 723 0875, ⓦwayfarermelaka.com. Formerly a rubber trading house, this airy guesthouse offers spacious well-appointed a/c rooms with hardwood floors; room 6 (RM160) has lovely views over the river and the Church of St Francis, while the large duplex room (RM240) features a double bed and two twins on the mezzanine. Prices increase by RM20–50 over the weekends. RM130

APARTMENTS

★**45 Lekiu** 45 Jalan Lekiu ☎012 698 4917, ⓦ45lekiu .com. This wonderfully restored Art Deco building is today a stylish two-floor apartment featuring bare-brick walls and sleek dark furnishings. There's an inviting pool and a terrace with panoramic views over the city's rooftops. RM1299

★**The Stable** D Jalan Hang Kasturi ☎012 623 4459, ⓦthestablemalacca.com. Formerly a stable, dating back to the sixteenth-century Dutch occupation, this trendy little apartment features original wooden beams, exposed brick walls and beautiful Peranakan tiles. The bedroom, on the first floor, dons stylish black furnishings, while the ground-floor living area is decorated with paintings depicting city life of yesteryear. RM450

EATING

Melaka offers excellent dining, especially in **Chinatown**, where new and established restaurants, bars and cafés compete for the hungry tourists and locals. **Taman Melaka Raya** is fast catching up; it's also worth trying the area aound **Jalan Kota Laksamana** southwest of Chinatown. For seafood, you could try the row of near-identical restaurants on the waterfront just beyond the Medan Portugis in the **Portuguese settlement**, where you can choose from the day's catch from around 7pm. Don't miss the chance to sample **Nyonya cuisine**; the emphasis is on spicy dishes, using sour ingredients like tamarind, tempered by sweeter, creamy coconut milk. One particularly unusual ingredient is *buah keluak*, a nut that contains hydrogen cyanide (prussic acid) but which is harmless once cooked.

★**Baboon House** 89 Jalan Tun Tan Cheng Lock. Artist and owner Roger displays his artworks and funky installations at this lovely art-café (he even made the tables) with a courtyard dripping with greenery. The menu features seven types of burgers, made with chicken, lamb, beef or pork and served on home-made buns. Don't forget to check out the pretty gardens at the back. Mon–Thurs 10am–5pm, Fri–Sun 10am–7pm.

Café 1511 52 Jalan Tun Tan Cheng Lock ☎06 286 0150. This pleasant little café was formerly the servants' quarter of what is now the Baba-Nyonya Heritage Museum (see p.273) next door. The marble tables and wooden stools lend the place historical character and add to the building's charm. The cuisine is mainly Nyonya and Malay, with dishes such as *otak-otak* fish cakes (RM5), a range of curries

(RM16) and a sprinkling of Western dishes. Fri–Wed 9am–5pm.

Calanthe Art Café 11 Jalan Hang Kasturi ☎06 292 2960. Jam-packed with odds and ends from vinyl discs to recycled coffee can drinks and condensed milk tins, this laidback café and restaurant is a great spot for a morning coffee (there are thirteen types, one from each Malaysian state) or a bite for lunch; the Baba chef rustles up a mean *laksa* (RM10.45) and *ponteh chicken* (drumstick cooked with palm sugar and potatoes; RM9.25). The water feature, wicker chairs and soothing background tunes add to the place's easy-going atmosphere. Fri–Wed noon–11pm.

★**Capitol Satay** Lorong Bukit China. Experience the Melaka version of hotpot – satay *celup* – at this lively café, where you take your pick of assorted fish, meat and vegetables skewered on sticks and cook them in a spicy peanut sauce before eating. It's cheap – RM0.90 per stick – and delicious, so there are often queues; a sign out front warns customers to beware of similarly named imitators. Tues–Sun 5pm–midnight.

The Daily Fix Café 55 Jalan Hang Jebat ☎ 06 283 4858. Not too obvious to spot, as it's located at the back of a shop, this relaxed café offers excellent home-made goodies including pancakes with maple syrup or honey (RM9.90), and plenty of home-baked cakes including cheesecake (RM11.90) and brownies (RM9.90). Wash them down with a refreshing lemongrass drink (RM5). Wed–Mon 10am–5.30pm.

★ **Eat at 18 Café** 18 Jalan Hang Lekiu ☎ 06 281 4679, ⊚ eat18.com. Healthy, wholesome dishes are lovingly prepared at this little gem of a café, featuring open brick walls, books, chandeliers and artworks. Delicious home-made organic bread accompanies most dishes, from grilled salmon with salad (RM29.90) to fresh roast chicken leg (RM28.90). Breakfasts are excellent, too, and there are sweet treats throughout the day such as home-made cheesecake (RM12.90) and meringues with Häagen-Dazs ice cream and strawberry jam (RM12.90). Thurs–Mon 8.30am–6.30pm.

Eleven Bistro & Restaurant 9, 11 & 13 Jalan Hang Lekir ☎ 06 282 0011, ⊚ elevenbistro.com.my. This pleasant bistro serves a great mix of Portuguese and Malay dishes such as salted egg crab (RM40) and Portuguese *sambal* prawns cooked with spicy chilli paste (RM25). It's also a good spot to grab a cocktail – in the evenings it morphs into a bar, with a house DJ after 10pm. Mon–Thurs 10am–2am, Fri–Sun 10am–3am.

Hakka Zhan 76 Jalan Laksamana 5 ☎ 017 225 8373. Genuine Hakka cuisine is served at this Chinese place just a short walk south of the historical centre, with a scarlet a/c interior featuring dangling Chinese lamps. Among the best sellers are *hakka* mutton (RM25) and *hakka yong tau foo* (RM12), vegetables stuffed with pork paste. Tues–Sun 11am–2pm & 5.30–9pm.

Jonker 88 88 Jalan Hang Jebat ☎ 019 669 5959, ⊚ jonker88.com. This well-established restaurant is renowned for its tasty *laksa* (RM7), which comes in three main varieties: sour-spicy, coconut spicy or a mix of the two. The *baba cendol* (RM4), a popular Malaysian dessert made with coconut milk, jelly noodles, palm sugar and shaved ice, is a sweet tooth's delight. Sun–Thurs 9.30am–5pm, Fri & Sat 9.30am–8pm.

Limau Limau 9 Jalan Hang Lekiu ☎ 012 698 4917. This itsy-bitsy café, playing mellow background tunes and with wooden stools lining the bar, serves great freshly squeezed juices (try the pineapple and passion fruit; RM12) and light lunches including toasted focaccia sandwiches (RM11.90) and lasagne (RM19.90). There's also a cosy room upstairs featuring mismatched furniture and a motley range of lamps. Thurs–Mon 9am–6pm.

Low Yong Moh 32 Jalan Tukang Emas. This excellent little place just opposite the mosque rustles up outstanding prawn, pork and fish dim sum (from RM2.20) steamed in front of your very eyes; the buns stuffed with pork (RM1.40) are also a real winner. Wed–Mon 5.30am–1pm.

Lung Ann Refreshments 91 Lorong Hang Jebat. This buzzing café and restaurant functions as a popular noodle stall in the morning, a hugely popular chicken satay hangout in the afternoons and a café throughout the day. The delicious *kaya* toast (with coconut jam) is worth trying for breakfast (RM1.50), the duck noodles (RM5) and fish ball noodles (RM6) are a real hit, and the crowds are drawn in the afternoons for the sizzling charcoal satay (RM0.80/stick) traditionally dipped in a peanut and pineapple sauce. Fri–Wed 8am–5pm.

Mods Café 14 Jalan Tokong ☎ 012 756 4441. The decor of this unique little café takes its inspiration from 1960s British mod culture; the emphasis is on coffees, roasted and brewed on the premises, served from a bright orange VW camper van. It's a cool place to hang out over a coffee (RM7) and cake (RM10). Daily except Wed 10am–6pm.

Nancy's Kitchen 7 Jalan Hang Lekir ☎ 06 283 6099. One of the best places to try Nyonya food, including the signature chicken candlenut (chicken served with a creamy candlenut sauce; RM12) or the prawn or fish fillet with coconut milk (RM18). There's also a little store at the back when you can buy Nyonya ingredients. Wed–Mon 11.30am–5.30pm.

Ola Lavanderia Café 25 Jalan Tukang Besi ☎ 012 612 6665, ⊚ olalavanderiacafe.com. This cosy little café with a minimalist design doubles as a laundry. It's a great spot to grab a morning coffee (RM5) and a freshly baked croissant (RM6) as you wait for your washing (RM4.80/kg); there's wi-fi, too. Light Western meals are served, including chicken and mushroom pies (RM5.90), Caesar salads (RM9.80) and all-day breakfast (RM9.80). Mon–Sat 9am–5pm.

★ **Pak Putra** 56 & 58 Jalan Kota Laksamana ☎ 5012 601 5876. Staggeringly good tandoori chicken (RM8) is the main draw here, although all the dishes are exceptional, from the mutton *rogan josh* (RM10) to the chicken curries (RM9), accompanied by fluffy *nan* (RM2.50) that is prepared in front of you. It gets very busy around 7–9pm on weekend evenings – make sure you arrive early. Daily 5.30pm–1am, closed every other Mon.

River View Café 82 Jalan Kampong Pantai ☎ 012 327 7746. Under the same management as the nearby *River View Guesthouse*, this laidback café mainly catering to backpackers offers great *nasi lemak kukus* with beef *rendang* (rice steamed in coconut cream served with chilli paste, boiled egg, fried anchovies, ground nuts and Nyonya pickles; RM12.50), as well as good old comfort food like fish and chips (RM12.50), club sandwiches (RM14) and all-day breakfasts (8am–3pm; RM8). There's a computer terminal, too (see p.276). Daily 8am–10pm.

Selvam 3 Jalan Temenggong. Consistently good Indian restaurant serving set meal banana leaf curries (RM4) with

5

rice, three types of vegetables and *papadams*, and your choice of chicken, lamb, fish or seafood (RM5) at very reasonable prices. Daily 7am–10pm.

Teo Soon Loong Chan 55 Jalan Hang Kasturi ☏ 06 282 2353. This bustling Chinese restaurant is one of the best in town, serving traditional Teochew cuisine from southern China; the oyster noodles (RM13) and yam pudding (made with yam paste and sugar; RM9) both sell like hot cakes. Tues–Sun 12.30–2.30pm & 6–9.30pm.

★**Veggie Planet** 41 Jalan Melaka Raya 8, Taman Melaka Raya ☏ 06 292 2819, ⓦ veggieplanet.com.my. Excellent, child-friendly, vegetarian café serving healthy organic dishes in a peaceful leafy interior. The Nyonya curry (RM13.90), made with cashew nuts instead of coconut cream, is a must, as is the *hoi lok feng* (RM13.90), a beautifully presented dish of brown rice with cabbage, beans, radish, ground nuts and other greens, accompanied by a healthy basil soup. Daily 9am–10pm.

★**Zheng He Tea House** 3 Jalan Kuli ☏ 016 764 0588. Experience a traditional Chinese kung fu tea ceremony at this welcoming teahouse where the friendly staff explain the properties behind different types of tea as they pour the warm beverage in little ceramic cups; you will leave feeling calm and rejuvenated. There's home-cooked local Chinese food, too, including minced pork rice (RM8). Ms Pak, the friendly manager, is also a great source of information about Melaka. Daily 11am–8pm.

DRINKING AND NIGHTLIFE

Melaka's **nightlife** is no great shakes; most places tend to shut at around 1am. Cafés and bars spill into Jalan Hang Lekir, the liveliest street in **Chinatown**; more places are also opening up along the revitalized riverfront, and **Taman Melaka Raya** also holds some lively places for a drink, along with numerous seedy karaoke bars.

Discovery Café 3 Jalan Bunga Raya ☏ 06 292 5606. This riverside café hosts local live bands daily at 9pm – expect old school music with some recent pop songs thrown in. Beers RM10.90, local dishes RM12. They also organize evening bike tours (RM50; 3hr). Daily 9am–midnight.

Exodus Lounge 4 Jalan Hang Lekir. It's debatable whether Melaka really needed a reggae bar, but this place has blazed the trail as the first in town. As the evening progresses, though, the music generally turns to more commercial R&B, with some old school and dance thrown in. Happy hour 6–9pm. Mon–Thurs 6.30pm–3am, Fri–Sun 6pm–3.30am.

The Irish Harp 3 Jalan Hang Lekir. Under the same management as the *Exodus Lounge*, this pub features the latest sports fixtures on the big screen and hosts live bands from Indonesia; Thurs–Sun 9pm–midnight. Wed–Mon 4pm–3am.

SHOPPING

Melaka's Chinatown was once famed for its **antiques**, but these days you'll find few bargains. If the item you're thinking of buying is a genuine antique rather than a modern reproduction, check that it can be exported legally and fill in an official clearance form; the dealer should provide you with this. For general shopping there are plenty of options along Jalan Bunga Raya and Jalan Munshi Abdullah; the **malls** – including Dataran Pahlawan, Mahkota Parade and Hatten Square – are concentrated in the south of the centre.

Artist Gallery 49 Jalan Tun Tan Cheng Lock ☏ 06 281 2112, ⓦ thamsiewinn.com. This family-run gallery offers arts and crafts, including limited-edition prints, hand-crafted Chinese "chops" (seals for documents), watercolours and pencil sketches. Daily 10am–6pm, sometimes closed Wed.

Joe's Design 6 Jalan Tun Tan Cheng Lock ☏ 06 281 2960, ⓦ joedesignjewellery.blogspot.com. Handmade artisan jewellery with one-of-a-kind designs, more interesting than most of Melaka's mass-produced handicrafts. Daily 9am–7pm.

Malaqa House 70 Jalan Tun Tan Cheng Lock ☏ 06 281 4770. It describes itself as a museum, but really it's a shop where much of what is on sale – mostly furniture – happens to be exquisite. Well worth a wander even if you aren't planning to buy. Daily 10am–6pm.

Red Handicraft 30c Jalan Hang Kasturi ☏ 019 374 1668. This little shop keeps alive the old Chinese tradition of paper cutting; you can even try your hand at it for RM5. Paper cuts start at RM5 (and can go well beyond RM100) – look out for the beautiful Chinese postcards featuring nineteenth-century photographs. Daily 11am–6pm.

Second Hand Books 45 Jalan Kampung Pantai ☏ 017 616 5884. Although there are chain bookshops in the malls, this place is worth a look if you're after a bargain. Books are mostly in English, German or French, including a few guidebooks; prices range from RM3–25. They buy books, too. Daily noon–6pm.

Wah Aik Shoemaker 56 Jalan Tokong ☏ 06 284 9726, ⓦ wahaikshoemakermelaka.webs.com. This store has long been renowned for making silk shoes for bound feet. With foot binding no longer practised, the shoes are now lined up in the window as slightly macabre souvenirs at RM95/pair. At the time of research the shop was due to relocate elsewhere – ask around for its new location. Daily 9am–5.30pm.

DIRECTORY

Banks In addition to ATMs in the shopping malls, banks include Maybank at 227 Jalan Melaka Raya 6, Public Bank at 60 Jalan Laksamana and HSBC, north of the centre at 777 Jalan Hang Tuah.

Cinema The Golden Screen Cinema on the top floor of Dataran Pahlawan Melaka Megamall shows English-language films.

Hospital The Hospital Besar Melaka (General Hospital) is in the north of town on Jalan Mufti Haji Khalil (☎ 06 282 2344, ⓦ hmelaka.moh.gov.my). The well-equipped Mahkota Medical Centre is at 3 Mahkota Melaka, Jalan Merdeka (☎ 06 281 3333, ⓦ mahkotamedical.com).

Police At the time of research a new tourist police station was being built on Lorong Hang Jebat.

Post office There is a post office branch on Jalan Laksamana just a few steps from Christ Church, while the GPO is inconveniently situated on the way to Ayer Keroh on Jalan Bukit Baru (both Mon–Fri 8.30am–5.30pm, Sat 8.30am–1pm).

Sport There's a public swimming pool (☎ 06 223 8796, ⓦ mbmb.gov.my) on Jalan Kota.

Visa extensions The immigration office is out in Ayer Keroh, on floors 1–3 of Blok Pentadbiran, Kompleks Kementerian Dalam Negeri, Jalan Seri Negeri (Mon–Fri 7.30am–4pm; ☎ 06 232 2662).

Around Melaka

While there's more than enough to keep you occupied in Melaka, there are also a few popular getaways within day-trip distance. These include several opportunities to see animals: the tranquil coastal village of **Padang Kemunting** is a hatching site for hawksbill turtles, while **Ayer Keroh** has several wildlife parks and cultural attractions. Alternatively, the nearby island **Pulau Besar** provides an opportunity to feel some sand between your toes, even if the sea is fairly polluted.

Padang Kemunting Turtle Sanctuary

24km up the coast northwest of Melaka • Tues–Sat 8am–4pm • Free • ☎ 06 384 6754 • Drive north towards Klebang Besar and proceed to Sungai Udang and then on to Masjid Tanah; from here take the junction to Padang Kemunting, commonly also referred to as Pengkalan Balak; or take a Panorama bus from Melaka Sentral to Masjid Tanah (every 30min; 1hr 30min), then taxi 8km (RM10–20); or taxi from Melaka Sentral (RM70)

Padang Kemunting is one of the last nesting areas of the hawksbill turtle and the painted terrapin in south Malaysia. Although open all year, it's only worth visiting the **turtle sanctuary** during hatchling season (March–Sept). It's a friendly place with lots of information, including an introductory video about the turtle population of Melaka.

ACCOMMODATION AND EATING   PADANG KEMUNTING

There are a handful of places to stay near the sanctuary, plus several Malay **seafood restaurants** along the shore and a couple of convenience stores.

Ismah Beach Resort Next door to Padang Kemunting Turtle Sanctuary ☎ 06 384 8141, ⓦ ismahresort.com. This resort has a restaurant and swimming pool; if the turtles appear at night, the sanctuary can let you know, by prior arrangement. RM138

Ayer Keroh

Despite its position adjacent to the North–South Expressway, 14km north of Melaka, **AYER KEROH** is a leafy recreational area with numerous attractions and a handful of places to stay. Although it's much cheaper to visit by bus, the attractions are quite spread out across both sides of the expressway so if you plan to visit several then it's better to rent a car or charter a taxi for the duration of the trip.

In addition to the attractions listed separately below, there are several others; many are detailed on the *Melaka Street Map* (see p.282). They include the **Botanical Gardens** (daily 24hr; free), an area of woodland set aside for walking and picnicking; the **Melaka**

5

Zoo (Mon–Fri 9am–6pm, Sat, Sun and eve of holidays 9am–6pm & 8–11pm; RM22), Malaysia's oldest and second largest; the **Taman Rama-Rama & Reptilia** (Butterfly and Reptile Sanctuary; daily 9am–7pm; RM15), and the **Taman Buaya** (Mon–Fri 9am–6pm, Sat & Sun 9am–7pm; Mon–Fri RM10, Sat & Sun RM15), which has a crocodile show on weekends at 11.30am and 2.30pm.

Taman Mini Malaysia & ASEAN

Ayer Keroh • Daily 9am–5pm, cultural shows Mon–Fri 11am & 2.30pm, Fri & Sat 11am & 4pm (30min) • RM22.50 • ☎ 06 234 9988, ⓦ minimalysiaasean.com • Bus #19 from Melaka Sentral (hourly; 45min) drops you off at the Melaka Zoo, from where it's a short walk; taxi from Melaka RM30–40 (20–30min)

Ayer Keroh's most interesting attraction, **Taman Mini Malaysia & ASEAN**, holds full-sized reconstructions of typical houses from all thirteen Malay states and the other members of the Association of Southeast Asian Nations. Some buildings have displays inside and sell food, drink and souvenirs; cultural shows are also staged at the park's open-air arena.

Melaka Wonderland

Lebuh Ayer Keroh, Hang Tuah Jaya • Tues–Fri 11am–7pm, Sat & Sun 9am–7pm • Tues–Fri RM31.50, children RM24.75, Sat & Sun RM36/ RM30.40 • ☎ 06 231 3333, ⓦ melakawonderland.com.my

The **Melaka Wonderland** water park can provide a welcome break on a hot day. Attractions include the Tornado Chaser (where you start in a giant bowl before passing through a darkened tunnel and into a pool) and a wide range of twisting and straight slides, as well as more sedate swimming pools. The place is quiet on weekdays outside school holidays.

ARRIVAL AND INFORMATION   AYER KEROH

By bus Town bus #19 (hourly; 45min) from Melaka Sentral.
By taxi A taxi from Melaka costs RM30–40.
Maps The *Melaka Street Map* (RM5), sold at the shop in

Melaka's Taming Sari Tower (see p.272) includes a map of Ayer Keroh.

ACCOMMODATION AND EATING

INB Resort Lot 3169 Sempang Padang Keladi, Lebuh Ayer Keroh ☎ 06 553 3022, ⓦ inbresort.hotels.net.my. An affordable option, 15–20min on foot from Taman Mini Malaysia & ASEAN. It's popular with local families, with comfortable rooms in pink concrete buildings arrayed around a pool. Breakfast is only served at the weekend, but there's a small place to eat outside. **RM120**

Philea 2940 Jalan Ayer Keroh, off Jalan Plaza Tol ☎ 06 233 3399, ⓦ phileahotel.com. The stylish cabins at this site, built from Russian pine logs and with stone in the bathrooms, make great use of natural materials – although this does mean that ground-floor rooms can be a bit noisy. There's a spa, sauna and gym; the two Royal Villas have their own swimming pools. Doubles **RM675**, Royal Villas **RM6500**

Pulau Besar

If you're looking for a beach getaway and don't have time to go much further afield, then **PULAU BESAR** ("Big Island", though in reality it covers just 16 square kilometres) may fit the bill. The island's beaches and hilly scenery are pleasant, although the waters are fairly polluted. Located 5km off the coast of Melaka, Pulau Besar was known as the burial ground of passing Muslim traders and missionaries; as a result locals – particularly Indian Muslims – see the island as a holy place and visitors are asked to behave accordingly.

ARRIVAL AND DEPARTURE   PULAU BESAR

By ferry Two jetties southeast of Melaka have boats to the island; neither is on bus routes, and a taxi to either should cost RM30. The Anjung Batu jetty sees regular ferries

(6 daily, starting 8am, last boat back 7pm; RM14 return), while the Pengkalan Pernu jetty in Umbai has boats only on request (RM100 one way for up to five people).

OPPOSITE WATERFALL NEAR KOTA TINGGI >

5

ACCOMMODATION AND EATING

D'Puteri Pulau Besar ☎06 295 5899, ⓦdputeriresortPulaubesar.blogspot.com. You won't want to spend much time in your room, but luckily the island's only resort – simple cabins with cold water and either fan or a/c – is right on the beach. They also have a campsite (you'll need your own tent). Camping per tent RM30, fan doubles RM120, a/c doubles RM140

From Melaka to Johor Bahru

The journey from Melaka southeast along **Route 5** to Johor Bahru covers just over 200km. The first 45km, as far as the town of **Muar**, passes through verdant countryside dotted with neatly kept timber stilt houses in some of Malaysia's prettiest kampungs. Further south, the towns of Batu Pahat and Pontian Kecil hold scant interest (the former, slightly inland, has a reputation as a red-light resort for Singaporeans). If you want to stop anywhere else before Johor Bahru and Singapore, aim instead for **Kukup**, right at the southern end of the west coast and terrific for seafood.

To get to Johor Bahru in a hurry, skip scenic Route 5 and use the **North–South Expressway** instead. From Melaka, you can head north to the expressway via Ayer Keroh; it's also straightforward to join the expressway from Muar (take the Bukit Pasir road for about 20km).

Muar

Also known as Bandar Maharani, the old port town of **MUAR** is a calm and elegant place that attracts few tourists but should reward a day's exploration. Legend has it that Paramesvara, the fifteenth-century founder of Melaka, fled here from Singapore to establish his kingdom on the southern bank of Sungai Muar, before being persuaded to choose Melaka. The town later became an important port in the Johor empire (see p.286), as well as a centre for the sentimental Malay folk-pop called **ghazal music**, and its **dialect** is considered the purest Bahasa Malaysia in the Peninsula.

Today, Muar's commercial centre looks like any other, with Chinese shophouses and *kedai kopis* lining its streets. Turn right out of the **bus station**, however, following the river as the road turns into Jalan Peteri, and you'll find Muar's **Neoclassical colonial buildings**. The Custom House and Government Offices (Bangunan Sultan Abu Bakar) are on your right, and the District Police Office and Courthouse on your left; they still have an air of confidence and prosperity dating back to the town's days as a British administrative centre. Completed in 1930, the graceful **Masjid Jamek Sultan Ibrahim** successfully combines Western and Moorish styles of architecture. Further along Jalan Petri you'll pass a jetty on your right, from where irregular **river cruises** depart.

ARRIVAL AND DEPARTURE MUAR

By bus Muar's bus station, on Jalan Maharani, is served by regular buses from Melaka's Sentral station (every 30min; 1hr 30min).
By taxi A taxi from Melaka costs RM70–80 one way (1hr).

ACCOMMODATION

Hotel Leewa Jalan Ali ☎06 952 1605. The rooms at this concrete block are basic, but do the trick if you're in town for just one night. Staff are friendly; there is another branch with slightly nicer rooms and slightly higher prices at 75 Jalan Arab. RM50

Streetview Hotel 11 & 13 Jalan Ali ☎06 953 7088, ⓦstreetviewhotel.com.my. One of the town's best options, this hotel, in a beautiful colonial building, features clean and comfortable a/c rooms, some of which look onto the pretty row of shophouses just opposite. RM120

EATING

Muar has a good reputation for its **coffee** and its **food**, particularly *otak-otak* (fish dumplings) and *mee bandung* (see opposite). Another local speciality is satay (particularly satay *perut*, made from intestines) for breakfast.

Bentayan Hawker Centre Jalan Bentayan. The stalls here – some of which have been operating for decades – serve up a range of dishes (RM5) including Muar's famous colourful steamed rice cakes, dim sum, *otak-otak* and more. Daily 5.30am–midnight.

Wah San 69a Jalan Abdullah. Up to 30kg of noodles are churned out at this popular place every day; the speciality is *mee bandung* (noodles, beansprouts, egg, beef and tofu served in a sauce made from prawn, chillies and beef soup; RM4.50), which has been selling like hotcakes since 1961, and is regarded as the best in town. Daily 7am–5pm; closed alternate Thursdays.

Kukup

The small fishing community of **KUKUP**, 60km southwest of Johor Bahru and 20km south of Pontian Kecil along Route 5, is a regular stop for the Singapore package-tour trade. Busloads of tourists arrive to see the old stilt houses built over the murky river and to sample Kukup's real attraction, the **seafood**: the town's single tumbledown street is packed with restaurants.

ARRIVAL AND DEPARTURE   KUKUP

By bus and taxi In the absence of direct buses from Johor Bahru, you have to catch a bus to Pontian Kecil (every 15min; 1hr) then take a taxi (RM25).

By ferry The jetty at Kukup is a little-known exit point from Malaysia to Indonesia. Ferries operated by Penaga Timur (☎07 696 9098) run to Tanjung Balai on Karimun island (hourly; 1hr; RM60).

ACCOMMODATION

Kukup is a small and compact town, and most travellers only stay for a few hours. If you do choose to overnight, you will easily find a bed; virtually all the **houses** double as basic guesthouses and restaurants. Accommodation is normally for groups of eight or more, but with a bit of bargaining you may well be able to persuade them otherwise – most people would rather their rooms didn't go empty. Expect to pay about RM80 including meals.

Tanjung Piai Resort 1km north of Kukup towards Pontian Kecil ☎012 767 0699, ⌨tanjungpiairesort .com.my. This string of large wooden buildings stands on concrete stilts at the edge of the mangrove swamps. The resort commands a dramatic vista of the ships coming to and from Singapore, and has a decent seafood restaurant, but is generally in need of repair. Prices rise by about fifty percent at weekends. **RM140**

EATING

New Kukup Restaurant 1 Kukup Laut ☎07 696 0216. This large waterfront restaurant with hanging lanterns serves good Chinese-style seafood dishes – crayfish, prawn, crab, baby squid and cuttlefish are accompanied by stir-fried vegetables including pak choi, bean sprouts and green tea shoots. A meal will set you back about RM25. Daily 10am–9pm.

Restoran Zaiton Hussin 631 Kukup Laut. Laidback establishment offering tasty Malay seafood a stone's throw from the ferry terminal, served with *nasi goreng* (RM4). Dishes from RM8. Wed–Mon 6am–6pm.

Johor Bahru

The southernmost Malaysian city of any size, **JOHOR BAHRU** – or simply **JB** – is the main gateway into **Singapore**, linked to the city-state by a **causeway** carrying a road, a railway, and the pipes through which Singapore imports its fresh water. More than fifty thousand vehicles each day travel across the causeway (the newer **second crossing** from Geylang Patah, 20km west of JB, is much less used because of its higher tolls), and the ensuing traffic, noise and smog affects most of downtown.

The city has been moulded by its proximity to Singapore, for better or for worse – it has the air of both a border town and a boom town. The vast majority of visitors are **day-trippers**, many drawn by the cheap shopping. JB's environs are also being transformed by **Iskandar Malaysia**, a vast Singapore-backed project to create

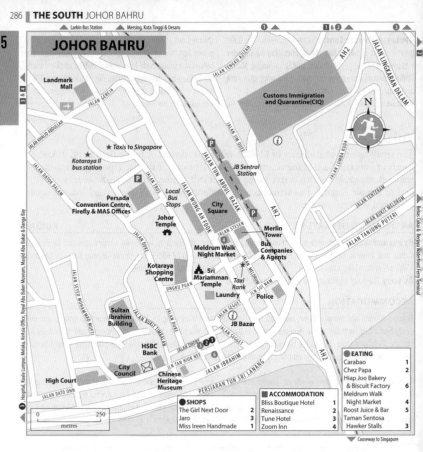

5

JOHOR BAHRU

Landmark Mall

★ Taxis to Singapore

Kotaraya II bus station

Persada Convention Centre, Firefly & MAS Offices

Local Bus Stops

JB Sentral Station

Customs Immigration and Quarantine (CIQ)

City Square

Johor Temple

Merlin Tower

Meldrum Walk Night Market

Bus Companies & Agents

Kotaraya Shopping Centre

Sri Mariamman Temple

Taxi Rank

Laundry

Police

Sultan Ibrahim Building

JB Bazar

HSBC Bank

City Council

Chinese Heritage Museum

High Court

0 ——— 250 metres

N

● EATING

Carabao	1
Chez Papa	2
Hiap Joo Bakery & Biscuit Factory	6
Meldrum Walk Night Market	4
Roost Juice & Bar	5
Taman Sentosa Hawker Stalls	3

● SHOPS

The Girl Next Door	2
Jaro	3
Miss Ireen Handmade	1

█ ACCOMMODATION

Bliss Boutique Hotel	1
Renaissance	2
Tune Hotel	3
Zoom Inn	4

▼ Causeway to Singapore

essentially a new city west of the existing one. It boasts industrial zones, universities, leisure facilities (notably Legoland Malaysia), and a glut of expensive property developments.

Brief history

JB stands with Melaka as one of the country's most historic sites. Chased from its seat of power by the Portuguese in 1511, the Melakan court decamped to the Riau Archipelago, south of modern Singapore, before upping sticks again in the 1530s and shifting to the upper reaches of the Johor River. There they endured a century of offensives by both the Portuguese and the Acehnese of northern Sumatra.

Stability was finally achieved by courting the friendship of the Dutch in the 1640s, and the kingdom of Johor blossomed into a thriving trading entrepôt. By the end of the century, though, the rule of the tyrannical **Sultan Mahmud** had halted Johor's pre-eminence among the Malay kingdoms, and piracy was causing a decline in trade. In 1699, Sultan Mahmud was killed by his own nobles. With the Melaka-Johor dynasty finally over, successive power struggles crippled the kingdom.

Immigration of the Bugis peoples to Johor eventually eclipsed the power of the sultans (see p.557), and though the Bugis were finally chased out by the Dutch in 1784, the kingdom was a shadow of its former self. The Johor-Riau empire – and the

Malay world – was split in two, with the Melaka Straits forming the dividing line following the Anglo-Dutch Treaty of 1824. As links with the court in Riau faded, Sultan Ibrahim assumed power, amassing a fortune based upon hefty profits culled from plantations. He established his administrative headquarters in the fishing village of Tanjung Puteri, which his son Abu Bakar – widely regarded as the father of modern Johor – later renamed Johor Bahru ("New Johor").

Downtown

JB is a sprawling city, and many of the administrative offices have been moved out of the centre to **Kota Iskandar** in the west. Most places of interest to visitors, though, are still **downtown** or close to the **waterfront** near the Singapore causeway. The downtown area blends the scruffy with the modern: the claustrophobic alleys of the sprawling market are within a few paces of thoroughly contemporary shopping malls such as **City Square**. Close by, the huge **CIQ** (Customs, Immigration and Quarantine) complex – built to streamline travel between JB and Singapore – includes **JB Sentral** station, combining bus and train terminals.

Arguably the most interesting part of the area, though, is on and around **Jalan Tan Hiok Nee** and **Jalan Dhoby**. Formerly quite seedy, these streets have been tidied up and are now at the centre of a vibrant shopping and dining scene.

Sri Mariamman Temple

Jalan Ungku Puan, south of City Square

The **Sri Mariamman Temple** lends a welcome splash of colour to JB's cityscape. Underneath its *gopuram*, and beyond the two gatekeepers on horseback who guard the temple, stand vividly depicted figures from the Hindu pantheon. Shops outside the temple sell Bollywood movies and garlands of flowers used in worship, while on the street you can have your fortune told using cowrie shells.

Around the seafront

The views across to Singapore from the **seafront**, just a short walk from Sri Mariamman Temple, are doubly impressive after the cramped streets of the city centre. Several interesting attractions lie on or around Jalan Ibrahim, while just north of here is the fortress-like **Sultan Ibrahim Building**; formerly the home of the state government, which has been moved west to Kota Iskandar, the building is eventually scheduled to become a museum.

Chinese Heritage Museum

42 Jalan Ibrahim • Tues–Sun 9am–5pm • RM5

As the name suggests, the **Chinese Heritage Museum** focuses on the Chinese contribution to the founding and development of Johor Bahru, and specifically on the production of gambier (a tropical shrub traditionally used in leather tanning and textile dyeing) and pepper, both of which were the economic lifeline of the Chinese community in the nineteenth century.

Royal Abu Bakar Museum

Jalan Tun Dr Ismail, the western continuation of Jalan Ibrahim • Daily except Fri 9am–5pm • US$7 (converted to ringgit) • ☎ 07 223 0222

Heading west along the waterfront you soon reach the Istana Besar, the former residence of Johor's royal family, which now functions as the **Royal Abu Bakar Museum**. Ornate golden lamps line the path to the Istana, a magnificent building with chalk-white walls and a low, blue roof, set on a hillock overlooking the Johor Straits. At the time of research the museum was being renovated, due to reopen in 2015 with the promise of interactive exhibits covering the local royalty.

5

Masjid Abu Bakar

5min walk west of Royal Abu Bakar Museum • Daily 8am–5pm, closes Fri noon–3pm for prayers

The four rounded towers of the **Masjid Abu Bakar** make it the most elegant building in town. Completed in 1900 under the orders of Sultan Abu Bakar, the mosque is largely based on colonial Victorian architecture, although also incorporates Moorish and Malay elements. The grand mosque can accommodate up to two thousand worshippers.

Danga Bay

5km west of centre • ⓦ dangabay.com • Taxi RM15

A key component of the Iskandar Malaysia development project, the waterfront **Danga Bay** complex includes several restaurants, stalls offering outdoor dining, a stage for live performances and even a beach bar (on an unappealing scrap of sand). Very quiet on weekdays, it's a popular spot in the evenings and at the weekend.

ARRIVAL AND DEPARTURE
JOHOR BAHRU

By plane Senai Airport (ⓞ 07 599 4500, ⓦ senaiairport .com) is 28km north of the city. Taxis to the city centre cost RM40; bus #333 travels to Larkin bus station (45min), while the white Causeway Link airport shuttle bus (ⓦ causewaylink.com.my) serves JB Sentral (45min). SkyBus offers a bus service (ⓦ skybus.com.my) to major hotels including *Tune Hotel*.
Destinations Ipoh (daily; 1hr 20min); Kota Kinabalu (2 daily; 2hr 20min); Kuala Lumpur (5–6 daily; 45min); Kuching (2 daily; 1hr 25min); Miri (3–4 weekly; 2hr); Penang (2 daily; 1hr); Sibu (3–4 weekly; 1hr 40min); Subang (KL; 2 daily; 45min).

By train JB Sentral train station is part of the JB Sentral terminal on Jalan Tun Abdul Razak, just across the road from CIQ.

Destinations Butterworth (1 daily; 13hr 15min); Gemas (5 daily; 4hr 25min); Ipoh (1 daily; 10hr 40min); Kuala Lipis (1 daily; 10hr 30min); Kuala Lumpur (3 daily; 7hr 15min); Segamat (4 daily; 3hr 50min); Seremban (3 daily; 5hr); Singapore (5 daily; 40min); Tumpat (1 daily; 17hr 30min).

By long-distance bus Larkin bus station, on Jalan Geruda, 5km north of the centre (RM10–15 by taxi), is used by most long-distance services. If you don't want to go there for a ticket, try the row of bus company offices running along the side of the Merlin Tower building in the city centre.
Destinations Alor Star (3 daily; 10hr); Batu Pahat (every 15min; 2hr); Butterworth (7 daily; 12hr); Dungun (2 daily; 9hr); Hap Chai (Thailand; daily; 12hr); Ipoh (8 daily; 7hr);

GETTING FROM JOHOR BAHRU TO SINGAPORE

There are several ways to head into Singapore from Johor Bahru.

BY TRAIN

The most obvious but least sensible route would be to use the **train** from JB Sentral – the problem is that Singapore's station is only just across the causeway, at Woodlands.

BY BUS

It is far easier to get to downtown Singapore by bus. Starting from **Larkin bus station**, north of town, you can catch SBS #170X or #170 (daily 5.20am–midnight), or the faster yellow Causeway Link #CW1 and #CW2 services. All buses then proceed to the **CIQ** (Customs, Immigration and Quarantine) complex; at this point you need to get off the bus and clear customs, before getting on another to complete the journey to Singapore (take your luggage off the bus, keep your ticket and get on the same type of bus on the other side). If you're already in downtown Johor Bahru, simply board the bus at **JB Sentral**, which is part of the CIQ complex, and complete immigration formalities before you buy your ticket.

Once through customs, the Causeway Link buses run nonstop to Kranji MRT (#CW1) or Queen Street (#CW2); the SBS services go to Kranji MRT, with the #170 continuing to Little India and terminating at Queen Street, near Bugis MRT. There are also Transtar buses to Changi Airport from Larkin (hourly; 1hr 15min).

BY TAXI

It is also possible to reach downtown Singapore by **taxi** – which costs RM15 per person or RM60 for the whole vehicle – from outside JB Sentral station.

Klang (4 daily; 4hr 30min); Kota Bharu (3 daily; 8hr 30min); Kuala Lumpur (every 30min; 4hr 30min); Kuala Perlis (2 daily; 12hr); Kuala Terengganu (4 daily; 8hr); Kuantan (3 daily; 6hr); Melaka (every 30min; 3hr); Mersing (10 daily; 2hr 30min); Muar (every 30min; 2hr 30min); Segamat (hourly; 3hr); Seremban (hourly; 3hr 30min); Singapore (every 10min; 1hr).

By local bus Buses heading east start from the JB Sentral combined bus and train terminal; local buses heading west run from around City Square.

By ferry Ferries from Tanjung Pinang (3 daily; 2hr 30min; RM86) and Pulau Batam (hourly 7.15am–5.45pm; 2hr; RM69) in Indonesia arrive at Berjaya Waterfront Ferry Terminal, 4km east of central JB; book tickets on ⓦ zonferry .com.my.

By taxi Taxis are available at JB Sentral station. Share taxis to Singapore charge RM60/vehicle (45min).

Car rental Avis, 15 Jalan Dato Abdullah Tahir (☎ 07 331 7644, ⓦ avis.com); Hertz is based in Menara Ansar at 65 Jalan Trus (☎ 07 223 7520, ⓦ hertz.com).

INFORMATION

Banks and exchange The main shopping centres hold ATMs and moneychangers. There's also an HSBC on Jalan Bukit Timbalan; in JB Sentral there's a 24hr moneychanger at the main entrance.

Tourist information JOTIC (Johor Tourist Information Centre) is at 50c, Tingkat 2, Bangunan KPMNJ, Jalan Segget (Sun–Thurs 8am–1pm & 2–5pm; ☎ 07 222 3590, ⓦ tourism.gov.my), with branches at Senai Airport, JB Sentral and CIQ.

ACCOMMODATION

JB's manufacturing boom means the city attracts more business travellers than tourists, so **hotel** prices tend to be on the high side. The city's budget and mid-range hotels are mostly just outside the city centre; some of the cheapest (not listed here) double as brothels.

Bliss Boutique Hotel 50 Jalan Jaya, Taman Maju Jaya ☎ 07 332 7188, ⓦ blissboutiquehotel.com. Boutique hotel may be a slight overstatement – the decor is pretty kitsch, with cheesy love statements decorating the bedroom walls, but it is great value and just a few steps away from *Chez Papa*, one of JB's best international restaurants. <u>RM132</u>

Renaissance 2 Jalan Permas 11, Bandar Baru Permas Jaya ☎ 07 381 3333, ⓦ marriott.co.uk/hotels/travel /jhbbr-renaissance-johor-bahru-hotel. Located just ten minutes from the Singapore–Malaysia border, this five-star hotel offers modern, tastefully furnished rooms and state of the art facilities, including an outdoor swimming pool, spa, fitness centre and business centre. <u>RM380</u>

Tune Hotel Danga Bay, Jalan Skudai ☎ 07 962 5888, ⓦ tunehotels.com. This popular chain of budget hotels offers modern, clean and practical rooms, with add-ons such as wi-fi, TV and a/c. There's also a good-value restaurant, computers for guests' use and a shuttle bus from Senai airport (RM8) that drops you off at the hotel door. <u>RM88</u>

Zoom Inn Unit 7, 8 & 9, Block 7, Danga Bay, Jalan Skudai ☎ 07 237 9323, ⓦ zoominn.com.my. Don't be fooled by the slightly drab exterior – this hotel in Danga Bay is a pleasant surprise. Rooms are warm and welcoming with quirky colourful wall drawings and modern bathrooms; there's also a small convenience store on the ground floor. <u>RM119</u>

EATING

There are scores of **restaurants** in JB, and some good street food on offer. The most interesting little cafés and restaurants are to the west of Jalan Segget, which also has its own **night market**.

FOOD MARKETS AND MALLS

Meldrum Walk Night Market Meldrum Walk. Colourful and vibrant night market with a mouthwatering array. Try the local speciality *mee rebus* – noodles in a thick sauce garnished with bean curd, sliced egg, green chillies and shallots. Daily 6pm–midnight.

Taman Sentosa Hawker Stalls Jalan Sutera. A popular night food market where Chinese stalls line one side of the street and Malay places sit side by side on the other. Plenty of dishes on offer including prawn *mee* and *bak kut teh* (about RM6). Tues–Sun 5pm–midnight.

RESTAURANTS AND CAFÉS

Carabao 16 Jalan Dato Abdullah Tahir ☎ 07 335 9333, ⓦ carabaorestaurant.com. The setting of JB's only Thai restaurant is particularly pleasant, with seating in an airy open-fronted area featuring natural materials and decorated with hanging lanterns, draped scarves and shell wind chimes singing in the breeze. The extensive menu includes a range of fish dishes (fried, steamed or curried; RM15), as well as seafood (RM16), chicken (RM16) and sweet and sour beef (RM17). Daily noon–3pm & 6pm–1am.

★**Chez Papa** 38 & 40 Jalan Jaya, Taman Maju Jaya

5

☎ 07 333 4988, ⓦ chezpapa.com.my. This French bistro and wine bar offers traditional home cooking in a particularly welcoming interior that bursts with character; customers can sit at the bar lined with dangling wine bottle lamps, or at rustic wooden tables. There's a particular emphasis on hearty stews, and the menu includes French classics such as *escargots de Bourgogne* (RM32), *foie gras* (RM68) and chicken cordon bleu (RM48). Good selection of wines from France and beyond. Mon–Sat 6pm–midnight.

Hiap Joo Bakery & Biscuit Factory 13 Jln Tan Hiok Nee ☎ 07 223 1703. Opened in 1919, this historic bakery is one of the very few in the country that bakes in a wood-fired oven. The coconut buns (RM3.50) and the banana cake (RM9) are the real winners. Mon–Sat 7am–5.30pm.

Roost Juice & Bar 9 Jalan Dhoby ⓦ roostjuicebar .blogspot.sg. This quirky little café and restaurant in the heart of JB features mismatched vintage furniture and exudes a shabby-chic feel. The international menu includes Western dishes such as fish and chips (RM14.90) and Malay favourites like *nasi lemak* (RM8.90), nicely washed down with a freshly made juice (RM7.90). Mon–Sat noon–4pm & 6pm–midnight, Sun 6pm–midnight.

SHOPPING

Although JB has plenty of shopping malls, it's much more enjoyable to explore the **boutiques** around Jalan Tan Hiok Nee and Jalan Dhoby.

The Girl Next Door Above Roost Juice & Bar, 9 Jalan Dhoby ☎ 07 222 4178. Typical of the boutiques in this area, with a young and enthusiastic owner selling mostly vintage clothes and shoes but also other bits and pieces which take her fancy; there's also a hairdressing section. Mon–Sat 1pm–midnight.

Jaro 2125 Jalan Sungei Chat ☎ 07 224 5632, ⓦ jaro .org.my. The Johor Area Rehabilitation Ogranisation (JARO) shop features handicrafts and artworks made by the physically or mentally impaired. Among the products on display are rattan baskets, picture frames and handmade cane furniture. Buying products here endures the workers continue to have source of employment, while also preserving traditional craft making skills that have been passed down for generations. Sun–Thurs 8am–5pm.

Miss Ireen Handmade Above Roost Juice & Bar, 9 Jalan Dhoby ☎ 016 782 9215, ⓦ missireen .blogspot.com. A tiny, very cute shop, where Ireen Tan sells her vintage-style handmade jewellery plus assorted items such as plush toys. Mon–Sat 1pm–midnight.

The east coast

Without the patronage of neighbouring Singapore, the area around Johor Bahru would have quietly nodded off into a peaceful slumber. Most people heading to the **east coast** beat a hasty path along Route 3 to **Mersing**, a dusty little town that is the departure point for boats to **Pulau Tioman**.

Mersing

The industrious little fishing port of **MERSING**, 130km north of Johor Bahru, lies on the languid Sungai Mersing. It serves as the main gateway to **Pulau Tioman** and most of the smaller islands of the **Seribuat Archipelago**.

ARRIVAL AND DEPARTURE   MERSING

By boat Mersing is the main departure point for Pulau Tioman (see p.292) and most of the other islands of the Seribuat Archipelago, although boats to Pulau Sibu leave from Tanjung Leman (see p.303). At the jetty there's a secure car park (RM7–10/day), while there and in the R&R Plaza nearby, assorted booths and offices represent various islands, boats and resorts.

By bus Buses normally stop at the bus station on the western edge of town, and also at the R&R Plaza beside the jetty; if you're leaving Mersing, for most destinations there is no need to walk to the bus station; buy tickets from SS International (ⓦ ssinternational.com.my) based inside Pure Value Travel & Tours (see opposite) by the jetty. They will make sure the bus picks you up at the plaza. Leaving by bus in peak season can be problematic; many are full. Buy express bus tickets in advance, at the station or from a resort or travel agency.

Destinations Alor Star (1 daily; 12hr); Butterworth (1 daily; 9hr); Cherating (4 daily; 4hr 30min); Endau (hourly 45min); Ipoh (1 daily; 7hr); Johor Bahru (9 daily; 2hr)

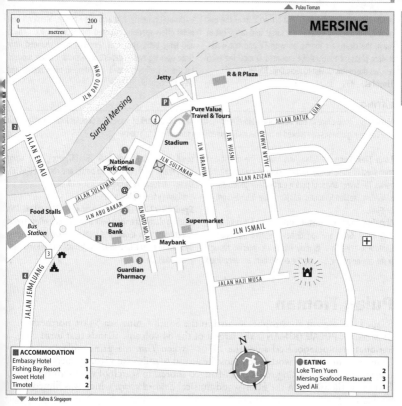

30min); Kluang (5 daily; 1hr 30min); Kota Bahru (2 daily; 10hr); Kota Tinggi (hourly; 2hr 30min), Kuala Lumpur (5 daily; 6hr); Kuala Perlis (1 daily; 12hr); Kuala Terengganu (5 daily, 8hr); Kuantan (5 daily; 3hr); Melaka (3 daily; 4hr 30min); Muar (3 daily; 4hr); Pengkalan Kubor (1 daily; 11hr); Singapore (5 daily; 4hr).

By taxi Taxis can be picked up either at the main bus station or at the jetty.

INFORMATION

Tourist information Mersing's tourist office at Jalan Abu Bakar was under renovation at the time of research (METIC; Mon–Fri 8am–5pm; ☎07 798 1979).

Travel agents Numerous agents, operators and resort offices in and around the jetty complex deal primarily with Tioman and the Seribuat Archipelago. Pure Value Travel & Tours, 7 Jalan Abu Bakar (☎019 753 4250, ⓦ purevalue.com.my), also organize full-day tailor-made island-hopping trips (from RM150/person; minimum six people), and trips to Endau Rompin National Park (see p.304).

Internet access Blue Skynet, 11 Jalan Abu Bakar (daily 10am–midnight; RM2/hr); wi-fi is available in all the accommodation options we review.

ACCOMMODATION

Embassy Hotel 2 Jalan Ismail ☎07 799 3545. A rather soulless three-storey hotel in the centre of town, featuring a selection of ageing rooms that will do the trick for the night if you're on a tight budget. The wi-fi reaches the first two floors. **RM50**

Fishing Bay Resort 15km north of Mersing ☎07 799 6753, ⓔ fishingbbr@yahoo.com.sg. This good-value place has bungalows and rooms set around a beachside garden and small pool, and a restaurant serving excellent local and Thai food. Kayaks are available for a trip to Pulau Batu Gajah just offshore. A taxi costs RM30–40 one way, or ask about transfers. Weekend rates rise by almost fifty percent. **RM168**

Sweet Hotel 5a Jalan Jemaluang ☎07 799 2228,

5

ⓦ sweethotelmersing.com. A short walk from the bus station, this friendly hotel is the safest mid-range bet in town; the clean, a/c rooms, all with TV and hot water, feature pleasant touches like mounted fabrics. The wi-fi reaches the rooms closest to reception. RM90

Timotel 839 Jalan Endau ☎ 07 799 5888,

ⓦ timotel.com.my. Just across the bridge, Mersing's best hotel offers spacious carpeted rooms with wicker chairs and large beds. The hotel seems to have changed little since opening two decades ago, although a few modern touches have been added, including in-room kettles and wi-fi throughout. RM180

EATING

Mersing is a good place to **eat** out, with seafood topping the menu. The **market** serves the popular local breakfast dish *nasi dagang*: glutinous rice cooked in coconut milk, served with *sambal* and fish curry.

Loke Tien Yuen 55 Jalan Abu Bakar. The oldest and friendliest Chinese restaurant in town with a small, reliable menu. The sweet and sour pork is particularly good. Around RM6/dish; seafood around RM30. Daily 12.30–3pm & 6–9pm.

Mersing Seafood Restaurant 56 Jalan Ismail ☎ 07 799 2550. Great seafood dishes prepared Szechuan or Cantonese style in a slightly kitsch a/c interior, though some can be pricey; among the best sellers are deep-fried

squid with salted egg yolk (RM14/piece), BBQ squid (RM14) and fried prawns with butter and coconut (RM16). Daily 11.30am–2.30pm & 5.30–10.30pm; closes on Wed every fortnight.

Syed Ali 7273 Jalan Sulaiman ☎ 07 799 6336. This bustling place just a short walk from the jetty offers a good selection of tasty Indian and local grub that is considered by most to be the best in town. A meal will set you back about RM8. Daily 24hr.

Pulau Tioman

Shaped like a giant apostrophe, located in the South China Sea 54km northeast of Mersing, **PULAU TIOMAN** is the largest of the 64 volcanic islands that form the **Seribuat Archipelago**. Ever since the 1970s – when *Time* magazine ranked Tioman as one of the world's ten most beautiful islands – sun worshippers and divers have been flocking to its palm-fringed shores, in search of the mythical Bali H'ai (the island in the Hollywood musical *South Pacific*, which was filmed on Tioman).

It could be argued that this popularity, and its **duty-free** status, have dented the romantic isolation that once made the island so desirable. Pulau Tioman does, however, display a remarkable resilience – and in part due to the lack of a decent road network, the greater part of the island retains something of its intimate, village atmosphere. Anyone in search of unspoiled beaches is likely to be disappointed, though superb exceptions do exist; divers and snorkellers will find plenty to enjoy, and there are also opportunities to take jungle hikes in the largely untouched interior.

Accommodation possibilities range from international-standard resorts to simple beachfront A-frames; it takes time and/or money to get from one beach to another, so choose your destination carefully. During the **monsoon**, from November to February/March, the whole island winds down dramatically; many places close until at least mid-January. July and August are the busiest months, when prices increase and accommodation is best booked in advance; visibility for divers is also at its lowest during these months.

ARRIVAL AND DEPARTURE

PULAU TIOMAN

By boat Blue Water Express (☎ 07 799 4811) has services from Mersing (2hr; RM35) to the island, with boats stopping off at Genting, Paya, Tekek, ABC and Sabang (in that order); note that when leaving the island, once the boats fills up, they travel directly to the mainland without picking up passengers at the

remaining stops (although they always stop at Tekek, the main port). There are other ferries from Tanjung Gemok ferry terminal (1 daily; 2hr; RM35), about 40km north of Mersing. Allow extra time if you need to catch a flight from the mainland, as the boat services are not entirely reliable. Boats are also often full, especially in

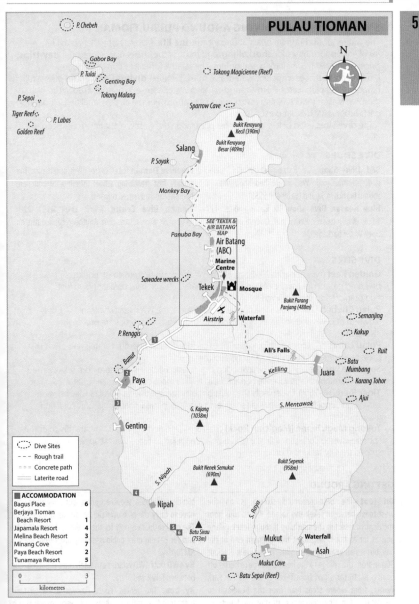

PULAU TIOMAN

P. Chebeh

Gabor Bay

P. Tulai

Genting Bay

Tokong Malang

Tokong Magicienne (Reef)

P. Sepoi

Tiger Reef

P. Labas

Golden Reef

Sparrow Cave

Bukit Kerayung
Kecil (390m)

Bukit Kerayung
Besar (409m)

Salang

P. Soyak

Monkey Bay

SEE 'TEKEK &
AIR BATANG'
MAP

Panuba Bay

Air Batang
(ABC)

Marine
Centre

Sawadee wrecks

Tekek

Mosque

Bukit Parang
Panjang (488m)

Semanjing

Kukup

Airstrip

Waterfall

Ruit

P. Renggis

Ali's Falls

Batu
Mumbang

Bukit

Juara

Karang Tohor

S. Keliling

Paya

Ajui

S. Mentawak

Genting

G. Kajang
(1038m)

S. Roya

Dive Sites

Rough trail

Concrete path

Laterite road

S. Nipah

Bukit Nenek Semukut
(690m)

Bukit Seperok
(958m)

ACCOMMODATION

Bagus Place	6
Berjaya Tioman	
Beach Resort	1
Japamala Resort	4
Melina Beach Resort	3
Minang Cove	7
Paya Beach Resort	2
Tunamaya Resort	5

Nipah

Batu Sirau
(753m)

Mukut

Waterfall

Asah

0   3

kilometres

Mukut Cove

Batu Sepoi (Reef)

high season, when ferries get booked up days or even weeks in advance. Tickets can be booked online with Tioman Ferry (w tiomanferry.com) for a small fee; check the website for the latest schedules. Note that there is also an infrastructure fee of RM25, payable when arriving at the island.

By plane At the time of research Berjaya Air (t 03 7847 1338, w berjaya-air.com) had suspended their flights to the island. The flights may resume in due course from KL – check the website for the latest details. *Tunamaya Resort* has recently launched a private eight-seater service from JB's Senai airport (1hr) and KL's Subang Airport; the flights can be booked over the phone or via email (t 07 798 8108, w tunamayaresort.com).

5

SNORKELLING AND DIVING AROUND PULAU TIOMAN

The waters around Tioman boast abundant **marine life**. Many nearby islets provide excellent opportunities for **snorkelling**, and most of the chalet operations offer **day-trips**; prices start at RM75, including equipment. The relatively healthy coral and huge biodiversity in these temperate waters also make for great **diving**. Dive centres offer a full range of PADI certificates, from a four-day Open Water course (around RM1000), through to the Dive Master (RM3200) and instructor qualifications. For the already qualified, a boat dive costs around RM105 per person.

The **dive sites** listed below are the most popular on the west coast, where most people dive.

DIVE SHOPS

B&J Dive Shop Air Batang ☎09 419 1218, ⓦdivetioman.com. Well-established shop with a second branch in Salang (☎09 419 5555).

Blue Heaven Dive Shop Air Batang ☎09 419 1413, ⓦblueheavendivers.com. Offers a good-value Open Water package.

Freedive Tioman Tekek ⓦfreedivetioman.com. The island's first freediving school, offering introduction, beginner and advanced courses.

Tioman Dive Centre Tekek ☎09 4191 228, ⓦtioman-dive-centre.com. Another reliable outfit, on Tekek.

DIVE SITES

Golden Reef (typical depth 10–20m). 15min off the northwestern coast; boulders provide a breeding ground for marine life, and produce many soft and hard corals. Known for nudibranchs and other macro life.

Pulau Chebeh (15–30m). In the northwestern waters, this is a massive volcanic labyrinth of caves and channels. Napoleon fish, triggerfish and turtles are present in abundance.

Pulau Labas (5–20m). South of Pulau Tulai, this island has numerous tunnels and caves that provide a home for pufferfish, stingrays and moray eels.

Sawadee wrecks (25–30m). Two wooden Thai fishing boats just offshore from Tekek airport attract scorpionfish and juvenile barracuda, as well as more common marine life.

Tiger Reef (10–25m). Deservedly the most popular site, southwest of Pulau Tulai between Labas and Sepoi islands. Yellow-tail snappers, trevally and tuna, spectacular soft coral and gorgonian fans.

Tokong Magicienne (Magician Rock) (10–25m). Due north of Pulau Tioman, this colourful, sponge-layered coral pinnacle is a feeding station for larger fish – silver snappers, golden-striped trevally, jacks and groupers.

GETTING AROUND

On foot The best-connected stretch is on the west coast, between Tekek and Salang. A road runs from the *Berjaya* resort in the south, up through Tekek village and as far as the headland at the northern end of the bay, but it's an exposed and uninteresting walk – about 30min from the village to the headland. You're better off paying RM16 for a taxi from Tekek to the Marine Park Centre, from where steps lead over the headland to Air Batang. A narrow concrete path runs the length of the beach to the point where a jungle trail sets off to Penuba Bay, Monkey Beach and Salang. Other coastal trails include one that connects Genting with Paya, while you can walk across the island from Tekek to Juara (see p.301).

By bicycle Since so much of the west coast is paved,

bicycle rental is a sensible option, but remember you'll have to carry the bike over the headlands at some point. The road to Juara is only for the resilient. Outlets in Tekek and Air Batang offer dubious-quality bikes from RM5/hr, RM20/day.

By 4WD Only 4WD vehicles can safely drive the steep route between Tekek and Juara.

By boat The rented boats (known as water-taxis) that travel along the shore are very expensive by Malaysian standards, ranging from RM25 for the hop between ABC and Tekek up to RM150 between ABC and Juara. To save money you can join the Mersing ferry as it makes its scheduled stops, if there's room, although they will still charge you a fair bit (RM20–35/person).

INFORMATION

Banks and exchange Change money in Mersing before you head out to Pulau Tioman, where the exchange rates are lousy; the only ATM on Tioman is in Tekek, opposite the airport.

Tourist information There is no official information office on Tioman, despite the fact that many agencies tout themselves as tourist information points – your best bet is to ask your hotel or guesthouse for information.

Wi-fi Wi-fi is available at most mid-range resorts, and certainly at the pricier ones, usually in the communal areas. Cheaper accommodation options may have a connection, although don't bank on it being very strong; there are a handful of internet cafés around the island although they aren't cheap at about RM8/hr.

Tekek

The main settlement on Tioman, **TEKEK**, doesn't make a great first impression. The area around the airport, marina and public jetty has been unappealingly developed, while coming from Air Batang you first pass a long stretch of deserted waterfront promenade. South of the marina, though, things start to get much better. Not only are there a handful of good resorts, but the beach is also attractive and has a dive shop as well as one of the island's best bars. Further south still is the high-end *Berjaya* resort.

Marine Park Centre

North of the main jetty, at the very end of the bay • Sat–Thurs 8am–1pm & 2–5pm, Fri 8am–12.15pm & 2.45–5pm • Free

The hefty concrete jetty and dazzlingly blue roofs of the government-sponsored **Marine Park Centre** make it hard to miss. Set up to protect the island's coral and marine life, and to patrol the fishing in its waters, the centre also contains an aquarium and displays about marine conservation.

ARRIVAL AND INFORMATION   TEKEK

By plane and boat Whether you fly or come by boat, you're close enough to walk to most of the resorts within Tekek, although the *Berjaya* is too far and offers a transfer. Services in and around the terminal complex next to the airstrip include an ATM, moneychangers, duty-free shops and an internet café.

Internet access Casa Rock, about 200m south of the airstrip (daily 9am–11pm; RM8/hr; ☎016 794 5380). Many of the accommodation options have wi-fi, although as a rule the cheaper ones don't – this may well change, however.

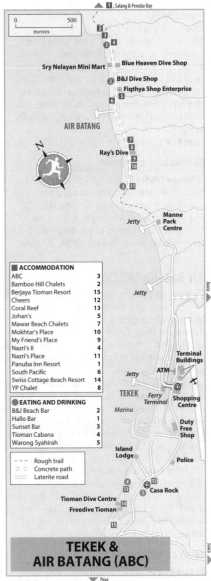

ACCOMMODATION

ABC	3
Bamboo Hill Chalets	2
Berjaya Tioman Resort	15
Cheers	12
Coral Reef	13
Johan's	5
Mawar Beach Chalets	7
Mokhtar's Place	10
My Friend's Place	9
Nazri's II	4
Nazri's Place	11
Panuba Inn Resort	1
South Pacific	6
Swiss Cottage Beach Resort	14
YP Chalet	8

EATING AND DRINKING

B&J Beach Bar	2
Hallo Bar	1
Sunset Bar	3
Tioman Cabana	4
Warong Syahirah	5

– – – Rough trail
= = Concrete path
—— Laterite road

TEKEK & AIR BATANG (ABC)

5

ACCOMMODATION

Berjaya Tioman Resort Just south of Tekek ☎ 09 419 1000, ⓦ berjayahotel.com. The standard doubles are not as nice as you'd expect at this village-sized complex at the end of Tekek beach – the rooms are somewhat dated and the bathrooms could do with a revamp; things get better as the price increases. Two pools, tennis courts, watersports and jungle trekking. RM500

Cheers Tekek ☎ 09 419 1425 or ☎ 013 931 1425, ⓔ cheersteo@yahoo.com. Just a few hundred metres inland, this decent budget choice offers simple fan doubles aimed at backpackers, plus a/c rooms with hot showers giving onto a pleasant leafy garden with potted plants. Fish, lamb, squid or chicken barbecues can be rustled up upon request (RM35/person; minimum six people). Bike (RM5/hr) and motorbike (RM15/hr) rental, too. Fan RM60, a/c RM120

Coral Reef Tekek ☎ 09 419 1868 or ☎ 013 357 8326, ⓔ info@coralreeftioman.com. The crumbling fan rooms you walk past if coming from the main road are definitely worth a miss (overpriced and rather grotty), but the deluxe beachside rooms are a big step up, with decorative stone work on the walls, kettles, hot showers and hammocks slung between the trees just outside the rooms. Garden doubles RM100, deluxe doubles RM200

★Swiss Cottage Beach Resort Tekek ⓦ swiss-cottage-tioman.com. Tekek's best all-round choice is a real winner – the clean and welcoming rooms feature tasteful individual furnishings, from pretty chests to sturdy wooden wardrobes. Fan-cooled rooms are in a shady beachside spot ensuring they don't get too warm, and the resort is located on a wonderful stretch of beach. The friendly, helpful owners can organize snorkelling trips, hikes to waterfalls and jungle tours. Fan RM110, a/c RM145

EATING AND DRINKING

★Tioman Cabana Tekek beach. This quirky beach bar bursts with character, with its worn-out stools, mismatched wicker chairs, flags from the world over and a rusty anchor. It's a great spot to unwind over a drink or two, and the food's good too – including burgers (RM16) and local dishes including chicken fried rice (RM10) and curries (RM18). Daily 1.30pm–midnight.

Warong Syahirah Tekek village. The cook at this friendly and popular roadside place fires up the barbecue at around 6pm, after which you'll find chicken, crab, squid, stingray and barracuda all on the menu. Daily 4.30–10.30pm.

Air Batang (ABC)

Despite its ever-increasing popularity, **AIR BATANG**, 2km north of Tekek from jetty to jetty, retains a sleepy charm and rivals Juara (which admittedly has a better beach) in its appeal for budget travellers. Larger than Salang or Juara, less developed than Tekek and well connected by boat services, Air Batang (or **ABC** as it's often called), is a happy medium as far as many visitors are concerned. What development there is tends to be relatively low-key and there's still a definite sense of community.

A jetty divides the bay roughly in half; the **beach** is better at the southern end of the bay, where there are fewer rocks, though the shallow northern end is safer for children. The cement path that runs the length of the beach is interrupted by little wooden bridges over streams and overhung with greenery; stretches are unlit at night. Between the guesthouses, a few small shops sell essentials such as shorts, T-shirts, sun cream and toiletries. Like the guesthouses they also arrange snorkelling trips and boat taxis.

A fifteen-minute **trail** leads over the headland to the north. After an initial scramble, it flattens out into an easy walk and ends up at **Panuba Bay**, a secluded cove that holds just one resort and a quiet little beach, and offers some of the best snorkelling on the island. From Panuba Bay, it's an hour's walk to **Monkey Beach** and then a further 45 minutes to Salang. Heading south instead from ABC, steps lead over the headland to Tekek.

ARRIVAL AND DEPARTURE

AIR BATANG (ABC)

By boat Ferries from the mainland stop off at Air Batang along with other major stops including Genting and Tekek. There are also private taxi boats that connect the island's main beaches.

ACCOMMODATION

As you get off the boat, a helpful signpost indicates the numerous **places to stay** in the bay. All but the most basic A-frames have fans and their own bathrooms, and mosquito nets are usually provided. The pricier options should have hot showers. Some places charge significantly more at peak times, such as during school holidays. **Internet** facilities are available at several guesthouses (and in some of the small general stores), and a handful of places offer wi-fi. Many guesthouses also rent out **bikes**.

ABC At the far northern end of the bay ☎ 013 922 0263. A little quieter than most, due to its location, this is one of ABC's best options, with pretty chalets set in a well-tended garden. The cheapest are fair for the price, while the a/c doubles have great views, kettles and hot showers. Fan RM50, a/c RM150

★**Bamboo Hill Chalets** On the northern headland of Air Batang ☎ 09 419 1339 or ☎ 019 952 4392, ⓦ bamboohillchalets.com. Six beautiful wooden chalets perch on the headland, all with wonderful sea views. All rooms are fan only, although the location means there's a nice breeze anyway. The cosy reception area has book exchange and free wi-fi. RM90

Johan's Just north of the jetty ☎ 013 349 0953, ⓦ johanchalet7.blogspot.com. A pleasant spot with chalets dotted around a leafy slope offering fan and larger a/c doubles, plus a four-bed fan dorm nestled at the top of the hillside. They arrange snorkelling trips (RM85), as well as trips round the island (RM150). Dorm RM20, fan doubles RM60, a/c doubles RM100

Mawar Beach Chalets Just south of the jetty ☎ 013 9315 5695. Simple chalets with smallish rooms and verandas; the cheapest use fans. The service is very friendly and the restaurant serves local dishes that are among the best on ABC. Fan doubles RM60, a/c doubles RM150

Mokhtar's Place South of the jetty ☎ 019 724 5336. The rust-coloured chalets are clean and airy with little porches, although they face inwards, rather than out to sea. Staff can book buses on the mainland, snorkelling and fishing trips and water-taxis. RM60

My Friend's Place South of the jetty ☎ 019 789 4813. A series of uninspiring basic rooms lining a straggly grassy area; the rooms for RM15 more are in better shape, and there's a pretty stretch of beach just a stone's throw away. Fan doubles RM60, a/c doubles RM130

Nazri's II Northern end of Air Batang ☎ 019 767 7496, ⓔ info@nazrisplace.com. Owned by the same family as *Nazri's Place*, this outfit boasts cottages dotted around a pleasant garden area with swings and shaded by palm trees. Fan cottages RM80, a/c cottages RM150

Nazri's Place Southern end of the bay ☎ 016 362 3120 or ☎ 013 980 6072, ⓦ nazrisplace.com.my. Clean a/c rooms in a series of red blocks that look onto a large courtyard. The rooms are some of the best on the beach, and often get booked up in advance. RM150

Panuba Inn Resort Panuba Bay ☎ 09 419 1424, ⓦ panubainn.com. Set on stilts, these chalets enjoy fantastic views out to sea. This is the only accommodation at Panuba Bay, so unless you scramble over the unlit headland you have to eat in the run-of-the-mill restaurant every night. They have a dive shop and internet café. A water-taxi from ABC to the resort costs RM8 during the day. RM55

South Pacific Close to the jetty ☎ 09 419 1176. Clean chalets with attached bathrooms and mozzie nets; those right on the beach are good value. There are also a few modern spacious chalets with hot showers and a/c; the beach just opposite is very rocky, though, so you're best off walking further south if you want to have a swim. Standard chalets RM50, a/c chalets RM130

YP Chalet South of the jetty (no phone). The most basic place on this part of the island, with simple fan rooms that are very worn around the edges. It's best to scope out some of the other places first, but if you're on a very tight budget *YP* may be the answer. RM50

EATING, DRINKING AND NIGHTLIFE

Most chalets have their own, generally unadventurous, **restaurants**, open to non-residents. Menus tend to reflect Western tastes and feature a lot of fish. Air Batang is the only place on the island with significant **nightlife**; there are a handful of laidback beach bars open until the early hours. Most have a **happy hour**, usually from around 5–7pm.

B&J Beach Bar Opposite B&J dive shop. A real diver hangout, which generally kicks off at about 7pm when divers have returned to shore, ready to share their underwater tales. A nice little spot to socialize over a beer (RM5) and meet other travellers. Daily 6pm–midnight.

Hallo Bar Northern end of Air Batang. Lively beach bar where you can enjoy drinks in one of the breezy *cabañas* on stilts that stretch out into the sea. Three beers cost RM12 during happy hour. Daily 6pm–late.

★**Sunset Bar** Southern end of the beach. The most popular bar on the beach, this laidback place is a great spot for a sundowner. They shake up excellent mojitos (RM10) and offer tasty pizzas (RM22), too. Daily 6pm–2am.

5

Salang and around

Just over 4km north of Air Batang, **SALANG** is a smaller bay with a pretty stretch of beach at its southern end by the jetty. The bay has seen a lot of development, but it still retains its own charm. The southern end of the beach is the more scenic; swimming can be an ordeal at the northern end due to the sharp rocks and coral. Just off the southern headland a small island, **Pulau Soyak**, has a pretty reef for snorkelling. There are also several dive shops.

A rough trail takes you over the headland to the south for the 45-minute scramble to **Monkey Bay**. There are few monkeys around these days, but the well-hidden cove is more than adequate compensation. Walkers can carry on to **Panuba Bay** (which will take about 1hr) and Air Batang.

ARRIVAL AND DEPARTURE   SALANG

By boat Ferries from the mainland stop off at Salang, along with other major stops including Genting and Tekek, and is also served by served by private taxi boats (as is Monkey Bay).

ACCOMMODATION

Ella's Place Northern end of the bay ☎ 09 419 5004. This place brims with character and oozes a mellow vibe, with its chaos of potted plants, dangling buoys, little fishpond and hammocks slung between palm trees. The little restaurant serves a handful of dishes for breakfast, including omelettes and pancakes (both RM3). Fan rooms are pretty simple, while the larger a/c rooms all sleep three. Fan doubles RM80, a/c triples RM90

Puteri Salang Inn Set back at the southern end of the beach ☎ 013 707 0320 or ☎ 013 931 2953. Seventeen pretty chalets, mostly A-frames, are set around a carefully landscaped garden with hammocks – the most peaceful spot in Salang. The cheaper rooms are pretty simple, but the friendly staff make up for it, and there's all-day tea and coffee, book exchange and wi-fi for an additional RM10. Fan doubles RM50, a/c doubles RM110

Salang Beach Resort ☎ 07 799 2337, ⊕ tiomansalang .com. This Chinese-run place has a popular restaurant serving Chinese dishes, albeit with no pork. Accommodation is in pleasant wooden chalets, and ranges from simple fan doubles to a/c doubles that are kept pretty clean. Fan doubles RM80, a/c doubles RM110

Salang Indah Towards the centre of the bay ☎ 09 419

5015, ⊕ salangindah@yahoo.com. The largest outfit in Salang, popular with groups and tending to fill at weekends. They offer a range of options, from run-of-the-mill boxy rooms with fans to larger a/c chalets with hot shower. Prices increase substantially over the weekends. Fan doubles RM60, a/c chalets RM120

Salang Pusaka Resort ☎ 09 419 5034, ⊕ salangpusaka@yahoo.com. Set back from the beach, most of the chalets here give onto a spacious verdant garden. All rooms have a/c, and the basic rooms are pretty good value overall – some are in better shape than others, so it's wise to look at a few before settling in. Basic a/c doubles RM80, standard a/c doubles RM130

Salang Sayang Resort Southern end of the beach ☎ 013 746 5118, ⊕ salangsayangresorts.webs.com. At the southern end of the beach, this place offers a range of accommodation, from garden and seafront fan rooms to larger a/c hillside chalets on "banana hill", from where there are lovely views over the bay. The attached restaurant serves a range of Malay dishes, and a nightly BBQ kicks off at 7pm. There are deckchairs for guests' use, too (RM10 for non-guests). Fan doubles RM80, a/c doubles RM130

EATING AND DRINKING

Mini White House Café ☎ 019 729 9563. Sizzling prawns and squid form the basis of the nightly seafood BBQ (RM70 for two) at this laidback restaurant – you'll probably smell the grilled seafood as you make your way up the beach. Their *tom yam* soup (RM10) is also a bestseller. Daily 7–10.30pm.

Salang Dreams Close to the jetty ☎ 019 790 0655. The first place you see as you walk down the jetty, this laidback restaurant serves a range of Malay and Western dishes that are considered to be among the best on Salang, from Malay curries (RM7) to burgers and fries (RM15). Sat–Thurs 9am–5pm & 7–11pm, Fri 9am–noon & 3–11pm.

Paya

Just 5km south of Tekek, the pristine stretch of beach in **PAYA**, only accessible by private boat transfer from Genting, has been developed but still seems peaceful when compared to Genting a little further south. **Jungle walks** are worth exploring here, where the island's greenery is at its most lush. The thirty-minute trail north to Bunut ends up at a fantastic deserted beach. From here it's a hot 45-minute walk through the golf course to the *Berjaya Tioman Beach Resort* and a further half-hour to Tekek.

ACCOMMODATION   PAYA

Melina Beach Resort Between Paya and Genting ☎ 09 419 7080, ⊛ melinabeachresort.com. Very appealing resort on its own beach, but accessible on foot from both Paya and Genting, which gives you more eating options – if you can tear yourself away. There's a good range of accommodation, from the cheapest garden-view rooms with bunks (and sleeping four) to suites overlooking the forest canopy. Wi-fi available at the bar and reception area. Garden-view rooms RM290

Paya Beach Resort Northern end of Paya Bay ☎ 07 799 1432, ⊛ payabeach.com. Paya's best accommodation, with comfortable chalets plus a restaurant, dive shop, swimming pool and spa. There's good snorkelling just in front of the resort, and staff can arrange excursions further afield. Rates include breakfast. Wi-fi available throughout. RM250

Genting

Usually the first stop for boats from the mainland, **GENTING** has been very heavily developed, especially around the jetty. Its beach is not as appealing as its neighbours', and as a result doesn't attract as many travellers – sadly it's often littered especially by the jetty, although there's a nice stretch to the north by *Dumba Bay Resort*, and towards the southern end too. On the plus side, there are several dive shops and the beach is usually very quiet during the week.

ARRIVAL AND DEPARTURE   GENTING

By boat Genting is the first port of call for ferries from Mersing; from here, private water-taxis take passengers to other beaches around the island.

ACCOMMODATION AND EATING

Dumba Bay Resort ☎ 09 419 7008 or ☎ 019 764 2792, ⊛ dumbabayresort.com. This laidback place offers basic sea-facing chalets, although they are just on the main pathway, which means they can get quite noisy at night as mopeds scoot past. The draw is the pleasant stretch of beach with picnic tables and the odd hammock. Nightly fish and seafood BBQs, too. RM120

★**Impiana Inn** ☎ 07 434 9373, ⊛ impianinn .com. Popular with divers, and for good reason: the rooms are the best in Genting and the common areas are well kept. The deluxe rooms with TV are worth the extra RM20 – they are attractively furnished with sturdy wooden beds and the bathrooms are spick-and-span. A couple of attractive wooden garden pavilions make a pleasant spot to unwind and read a book; there's wi-fi at reception. Rates include breakfast. RM160

Sun Beach Resort ☎ 09 419 7069, ⊛ sunbeachresort .com.my. A large enterprise with Genting's widest range of rooms. The deluxe rooms with TV are mostly on the hillside, while the cheaper rooms are on the beach. Overall they are relatively clean, although you should take a look at a couple before deciding. Wi-fi around reception. Fan-cooled budget rooms RM58, standard rooms RM98, deluxe rooms RM158

DRINKING

Bar Rumah Northern end of the beach. A surprisingly good little beach bar, serving beer and cocktails from a shack on the main path. There are chairs, hammocks and even a table (with attached chairs) suspended from a palm tree. Daily 6pm–midnight or later.

5

South of Genting

The area **south of Genting** is home to a number of upmarket resorts on private stretches of beach, which tend to be busiest at the weekend and on holidays and are reachable only by private boat transfer from Genting. The exception is **Nipah**, which has a couple of laidback places and is accessible by water-taxi from Genting.

Nipah

There's no jetty, so access is by water-taxi from Genting (RM25)

Located on the southwest coast, **NIPAH** is the closest you'll get to an idyllic yet affordable backpacker beach hideaway on the island. There is good **snorkelling** around a nearby islet, and although there's no dive shop, the local accommodation options can make arrangements (expect to pay around RM150 for two dives, plus RM85 for equipment rental). They also offer kayak rental and jungle trekking. Don't turn up at Nipah without having first made a booking.

Mukut

Private taxi boats take passengers to Mukut from different points around Pulau Tioman

Lying in the shadow of granite outcrops, the ramshackle little fishing village of **MUKUT** is shrouded by dense forest. It's a peaceful and friendly spot to unwind, with a fine beach, though note that locals are unused to Western sunbathing habits and frown upon the open intake of alcohol.

One good reason to stay here is to hike up **Bukit Nenet Semukut**, whose twin peaks are known as the Dragons' Horns; guides can be arranged at *Tanjung Inn Adventure* (RM80/person).

ACCOMMODATION   SOUTH OF GENTING

NIPAH AND AROUND

★**Bagus Place** South of Nipah ☎03 4270 1502, ⓦbagusplace.com. This peaceful resort offers accommodation in unique chalets – the *Tree House* features an airy living space built around a sturdy tree trunk, while the *Boat House* offers accommodation in a mock boat with a sun deck. Popular with couples and honeymooners. Full board for two **RM990**

Bersatu Nipah Nipah ☎07 797 0091, ⓔbersatunipah _tioman@yahoo.com. All nine rooms in this friendly place are on the beach, in a single long building. Discounts for long-term stays, and during the monsoon. Fan doubles **RM60**, a/c doubles **RM90**

★**Japamala Resort & Spa** On its own beach just north of Nipah ☎07 419 6001, ⓦjapamalaresorts.com. This first-class eco-luxe resort offers thirteen Malay village-style villas and chalets tucked away amid lush tropical rainforest. No trees were felled in building the resort – the villas were built with reclaimed timber around their natural landscape. **RM750**

Nipah Nema Nipah ☎010 781 1036, ⓦnipahnema .com. Welcoming, eco-friendly place offering five huts made from wood, nipah and bamboo in a lush tropical setting a short walk from the beach; rooms are en suite and all have balconies with hammocks. There's a small restaurant and bar serving great international cuisine, as well as nightly riverside BBQs and beach campfires. **RM100**

Tunamaya Resort On its own stretch of beach south of Nipah ☎07 798 8108, ⓦtunamayaresort.com. This pleasant upmarket resort with wonderful views of the Twin Peaks features more than fifty villas set on both sides of a small leafy stream that is atmospherically lit up in the evenings. The well-appointed rooms feature modern amenities and there's an inviting swimming pool and spa. The restaurant serves great Asian dishes, with weekend seafood BBQs. At the time of research the resort had just launched a private plane service from Johor Bahru and KL (see p.293). **RM830**

MUKUT AND AROUND

Minang Cove Standing alone on the southern end of the island, west of Mukut ☎07 799 7372, ⓦminangcove.com.my. The rooms at this delightful resort are not the classiest around, but the location and service raise it well above the average. Excellent snorkelling, and they also arrange round-island trips. Half-board for two **RM500**

Tanjung Inn Adventure At the far western end of Mukut cove ☎013 293 1619. Overlooking a small patch of beach, this place feels semi-abandoned unless a group of hikers is staying – but once you find manager Uncle Sam, you'll receive a warm welcome. Rooms are simple, with cold showers. **RM60**

Juara

With Tioman's western shore now extensively developed, those eager for a hideaway often head for **JUARA**. The only east coast settlement, it's a quiet and peaceful kampung with two excellent beaches – **Juara Beach**, aka **Barok Beach**, where you arrive from Tekek, and Mentawak Beach just south. The sand is cleaner and less crowded than on the other side of the island, and Juara is altogether more laidback even than Air Batang.

The beaches here do, however, have a reputation for harbouring **sandflies** (see box, p.303), so take what precautions you can. The bay, facing out to the open sea, is also susceptible to bad weather. The constant sea breeze keeps the water choppy; it attracts **surfers** from November to March, with 3m-plus waves in February. The beach break is good for beginners, while more experienced surfers favour the point at the southern end of Mentawak.

A popular, clearly marked 45-minute walk leads from the south beach to a small **waterfall** with a big freshwater pond that's good for swimming. Someone from the *Beach Shack* will take you for RM15 per person.

Juara Turtle Project

Mentawak Beach • Tours (15– 30min) daily 10am–5pm • Minimum donation RM10 • ☎ 09 419 3244 or ☎ 017 704 8911, ⓦ juaraturtleproject.com

The southern beach is home to the **Juara Turtle Project**, whose work takes several forms. They collect eggs from the eastern beaches, then hatch and release turtles, and also campaign for greater protection, with a small Visitor Centre to raise awareness. Volunteers are welcome to get involved for a payment of RM120 per day for a minimum of four days, which includes accommodation, breakfast and lunch.

ARRIVAL AND INFORMATION
JUARA

By road A road starting just before the *Berjaya Tioman Beach, Golf & Spa Resort* (see p.296) has given 4WD vehicles easy access to Juara, costing RM140/car or RM35/person for four people for the 30min journey (you may need to bargain hard). If you've booked a place to stay, they will probably be able to organize transport for you from Tekek, which is likely to work out cheaper than sorting it yourself. Regular cars will struggle with the steep roads, but it's theoretically possible by motorbike or mountain bike (don't undertake either lightly). Several guesthouses in Juara can arrange transport back to Tekek.

On foot You can also reach Juara on foot through the jungle. The steep trek from Tekek takes about 2hr 30min, not counting rest stops, and is definitely not recommended if you have luggage. Don't walk the less appealing vehicle road, and carry plenty of water. Starting as a concrete path a 5min walk away from the airstrip, the trail soon becomes rocky, running uphill with intermittent sections of concrete steps. After an hour or so you reach the highest point, and the route then tapers off into a smooth, downhill path, eventually joining the main road. There's a waterfall just off the main road that's a good spot for a refreshing dip; it's easy to miss – keep your eyes peeled for the little wooden hut on your right. Look carefully and you will see the words "waterfall" lightly inscribed on the side of the hut. It's just a couple of minutes' walk from there.

Information desk An unofficial information desk

(daily 9am–6pm) by the jetty rents out motorbikes (RM30/ day) and snorkelling equipment (RM10/day for mask and snorkel, RM7 for fins), and arranges full-day boat tours from RM100.

ACCOMMODATION

★**1511 Coconut Grove** Mentawak Beach ☎010 766 4089, ⓦ 1511asia.com. This pleasant resort offers inviting chalets just a short walk from the beach; at the time of research a couple of viewing towers were being converted to duplex rooms along the seafront (RM700).

South Bay, Juara Turtle Project, 7 & 8

JUARA

Cafés & Mini-Mart

Jetty

Mini Market

N

Scuba Amigo

● EATING AND DRINKING
Tobak's Place — 1

■ ACCOMMODATION
1511 Coconut Grove — 8
Beach Shack — 7
Bushman's — 6
Juara Beach — 2
Mutiara — 4
Rainbow Chalets — 5
Riverview — 1
Santai Bistro & Chalet — 3

Tekek

0   200
metres

5

Rates include breakfast and, unusually for the island, there's wi-fi throughout. **RM350**

★ **Beach Shack** Mentawak Beach ☎012 696 1093, ✉izanhussain2@yahoo.com. Ozzie/Malay-run place with a relaxed backpacker vibe, offering accommodation in simple colourful A-frame chalets along the beach; there's also an a/c deluxe room, made of recycled timber, with great sea views. There's a café with internet access and book exchange, and there are rumours the owner will soon feature Ozzie kangaroo steak on the menu. Open year-round. A-frame chalets **RM45**, a/c sea-view room **RM140**

Bushman's End of the northern bay ☎09 419 3109 or ☎013 781 0005, ✉matbushman@hotmail.com. This friendly and easy-going option offers a handful of simple but welcoming chalets at the northern end of the beach; all are clean, with hot water. There are a couple of a/c rooms, and meals can be cooked upon request. Open all year. Fan doubles **RM60**, a/c doubles **RM80**

Juara Beach Close to the jetty ☎09 419 3188 or ☎013 771 1137. This Chinese-run place is a good choice if you're looking for a/c and hot showers, and there's also an excellent Chinese restaurant. Spacious rooms, set around a verdant garden, all feature TV and fridge, and include breakfast. Wi-fi at the restaurant. Standard doubles **RM140**, deluxe doubles **RM160**

Mutiara Near the jetty ☎09 419 3161, ✇juaramutiararesort.com. Some of the rooms here are set on the beach, while others look onto a well-kept garden

with palm trees and benches outside each room. There's a mini-market and they can arrange fishing trips. Open all year. Fan doubles **RM80**, a/c doubles **RM130**

Rainbow Chalets South of the jetty ☎012 989 8572 or ☎09 419 3140, ✉rainbow.chalets@ymail.com. These brightly painted chalets on a pleasant stretch of beach, with their own bathrooms and mosquito nets; there are basic fan rooms as well as more spacious a/c doubles with hot showers. They can organize a taxi service from Tekek from RM25/person (RM35 after 6pm). Fan doubles **RM60**, a/c doubles **RM100**

Riverview North end of the bay ☎09 419 3168, ✇tioman-riverview.com. Run by a friendly English woman, Julie, this place offers three types of rooms; the breezy and well-kept Indonesian kampung-style huts facing the river are a great choice, as are the sea-view chalets. The basic huts, the same price as the river views, are a bit dated and run-down. All rooms have fan and cold water only; there's a billiards table and wi-fi in the communal area. Kayak rental RM30/day. Huts **RM120**, chalets **RM150**

Santai Bistro & Chalet Near the jetty ☎017 777 7200. The first place you see when arriving by car from Tekek, this very decent option offers clean and pleasant rooms (all with a/c and hot water) decorated with more care than usual for Tioman, and named after different types of fish and seafood. Some face the beach, while others give onto a garden area, and there's a good restaurant, with wi-fi, serving Malay dishes. **RM150**

EATING AND DRINKING

Tobak's Place North of the jetty. Sometimes referred to as *Coconuts Café*, this laidback beach bar in a shambolic wooden structure is a good place to relax and watch the sand and surf. There are also chairs and tables on the beach.

It's possible to pre-book for a BBQ – just let the staff know a day or two in advance and they'll rustle one up for you. Otherwise, it's drinks only. Daily 7pm–2am or later.

Seribuat Archipelago: the other islands

Pulau Tioman may be the best known and most visited of the 64 volcanic islands in the **SERIBUAT ARCHIPELAGO**, but a handful of other accessible islands hold beaches and opportunities for seclusion that outstrip those of their larger rival. For archetypal azure waters and table-salt sand, three in particular stand out: **Pulau Sibu**, **Pulau Besar** and **Pulau Rawa**. There are, however, a few resorts on other islands; Pulau Aur, for example, is popular among Singapore-based scuba divers. The tourist office in Mersing (see p.291) can advise on the various options.

Pulau Sibu

Closest to the mainland, accessible from the village of Tanjung Leman, 30km south of Mersing, **PULAU SIBU** is actually a cluster of four islands that are collectively the most popular after Tioman. Most resorts are on **Pulau Sibu Besar**, which, although not as scenically interesting as some of its neighbours, does have butterflies and huge monitor lizards. The sand here is yellower and the current more turbulent than at some others; most of the coves have good offshore coral.

5

SANDFLIES

Sandflies can be a real problem throught the Seribuat Archipelago, including on Pulau Tioman. These little pests, looking like tiny fruit flies with black bodies and white wings, suck blood and cause an extremely itchy lump, which may become a nasty blister if scratched. The effectiveness of various treatments and deterrents is much debated; the general feeling is that short of dousing yourself all over with insect repellent, covering up completely or hiding out in the sea all day long, there's not much you can do. You may find that Tiger Balm, available at any pharmacy, can reduce the maddening itch and help you sleep. If you are able to take them, antihistamines also provide some relief.

Pulau Besar

Long, narrow **PULAU BESAR**, about 13km from the mainland, measures 4km by 1km. It holds several resorts and sets of chalets, but you're likely to have the place pretty much to yourself outside weekends and public holidays.

Pulau Rawa

The tiny island of **PULAU RAWA**, just 16km (a thirty-minute boat ride) from Mersing, holds a glorious stretch of fine, sugary-sanded beach. The only sure way to get there is by resort-owned speedboat, booked in advance, but if you're lucky then the Tioman-bound ferry might make a stop (on request).

Pulau Tengah

Approximately 16km from Mersing, **PULAU TENGAH** has a 3km circumference with eight powdery white sand beaches. Between 1998 and 2010 the island was the setting for Swedish reality TV show *Expedition Robinson*, the predecessor to the world-famous *Survivor* series. The private island is today home to only one resort.

ARRIVAL AND DEPARTURE

Day-trips from Mersing Pure Value Travel and Tours, 7 Jalan Abu Bakar (☎ 019 753 4250, 🌐 purevalue.com.my) organize full-day tailor-made island-hopping trips from RM150/person (minimum six people).

SERIBUAT ARCHIPELAGO: THE OTHER ISLANDS

By resort transfer People staying on the islands take a resort boat from Mersing. Note that Pulau Sibu is reached by resort boats from Tanjung Leman, a tiny coastal village 30km south of Mersing.

ACCOMMODATION AND EATING

Except where noted, resorts operate on package deals, and the prices given in the reviews below are for two people for one night; subsequent nights may be cheaper. All resorts offer watersports facilities, and most have dive shops, too.

PULAU SIBU

Rimba Beach Resort ☎ 0127 106855. Friendly resort offering rustic, welcoming rooms on a lovely stretch of beach dotted with palm trees. There's an unspoilt reef just by the shore, which means you'll spot plenty of fish as you snorkel or dive. The tasty food is all home-made, and staff (mostly Western) couldn't be friendlier. Call ahead to book transfers from Singapore (RM160 return). Free (if slow) wi-fi available. **RM580**

Sea Gypsy Village Resort East coast ☎ 019 753 4250, 🌐 siburesort.com. Set in well-manicured grounds in a 5-acre jungle clearing, this family-friendly resort offers accommodation in traditional Malay-style wooden chalets;

all are sea facing and feature private verandas. There are complimentary kids' clubs (6–10pm) and buckets of kids' activities throughout the day (extra charge), as well as plenty of activities from sailing to subwing. Wi-fi is free for the first 15min, and then a steep RM1/min thereafter. **RM180**

PULAU BESAR

Aseania Island Resort Middle of the bay, west-facing beach ☎ 07 797 0057, 🌐 saripacifica.com. Set on an appealing stretch of sand, with decent chalets, a swimming pool and good service – a great place to relax. Full board per couple **RM540**

★**Mirage Island Resort** Just south of the jetty, west-facing beach ☏019 789 6355, ⓦmirageislandresort.com.my. This is a great choice for its friendly service, well-appointed chalets and reasonable prices. Cheaper rooms are A-frames, but still clean and comfortable. Rates include breakfast; all-inclusive packages are also available. Half-board per couple RM460

PULAU RAWA
Rawa Island Resort West-facing beach ☏07 799 1204, ⓦrawaislandresort.com. Dated wooden chalets equipped with a/c and hot showers, and there's kayaking,

snorkelling and scuba diving. Rates include boat transfers, and decrease after the first night. Full board per couple RM1500

PULAU TENGAH
Batu Batu ☏017 755 2813, ⓦbatubatu.com.my. This luxurious private island resort, built in the style of a kampung village, comprises 22 villas sprinkled around lush grounds. Being the only resort means that guests have all the island's beaches to themselves – it's a wonderful spot to relax, and the resort welcomes families with young children. Full board per couple RM1285

Endau Rompin National Park

One of the few remaining areas of lowland tropical rainforest left in Peninsular Malaysia, the **ENDAU ROMPIN NATIONAL PARK** covers 870 square kilometres. Despite its rich **flora and fauna**, prized by conservationists, the area has only been adequately protected from logging since 1989. There's plenty on offer for nature lovers, from gentle **trekking** to more strenuous **mountain climbing** and **rafting**; for the moment, its trails remain refreshingly untrampled.

Surrounding the headwaters of the lengthy Sungai Endau, and sitting astride the Johor–Pahang state border, the region was shaped by volcanic eruptions more than 150 million years ago. The force of the explosions sent up huge clouds of ash, creating the quartz crystal ignimbrite that's still very much in evidence along the park's trails and rivers, its glassy shards glinting in the light. Endau Rompin's steeply sloped mountains level out into sandstone plateaus, and the park is watered by three **river systems** based around the main tributaries of Sungai Marong, Sungai Jasin and Sungai Endau, reaching out to the south and east.

Visiting the park
As it can be hard to arrange transport, most people come on one- or two-night **tours**, although day-trips can be organized from Mersing. The **best time** to visit is between March and October, while the paths are dry and the rivers calm. Take loose-fitting, lightweight cotton clothing that dries quickly – even in the dry season you're bound to get wet from crossing rivers – and helps to protect you from scratches and bites. Waterproofs will come in handy, and you'll need tons of insect repellent.

ARRIVAL AND DEPARTURE   **ENDAU ROMPIN NATIONAL PARK**

ENTRY POINTS
The park has three entry points: one from the west at Selai via Bekok (Johor), and two from the east, at Kuala Kinchin via Kuala Rompin (Pahang) and Kampung Peta via Kahang (Johor). The best is Kampung Peta, where more activities are available; the least interesting, Kuala Kinchin, is often used for one-night tours, but is not recommended as they don't give enough time to get into the jungle.

ON TOURS
While it is possible, if tricky, to visit under your own steam, most visitors come on tours that include transport. Mersing (see p.291) is the best place to approach from the east; ask

agents in KL for the western Selai entry. Pure Value Travel & Tours in Mersing charges RM230 per person per day, which includes all fees, transport to and from Mersing and accommodation.

ARRIVING INDEPENDENTLY
Kampung Peta Approaching from the south on the North–South Expressway, take the Ayer Hitam exit and continue straight through Kluang to Kahang town (1hr from Mersing); the park's administrative office is located here, at 11 Tingkat Bawah, Jalan Bawal 1 (☏07 788 2812), where you'll need to register and pay the RM20 entrance fee – given notice, they can help organize 4WD transport into the park. From here continue 5km east, turn north at

the park sign and follow logging tracks for 48km (2hr; 4WD is strongly advised) until you reach the Visitor's Complex at Kampung Peta (daily 8am–5pm, registration ends 3pm; ☎ 07 788 2812). There are fan dorms (RM20) and chalets (RM80) here. A licensed guide will cost RM250/day. You can also catch a boat (return trip RM140/boat, or RM25/person – minimum five) to Kuala Jasin, where there are basic A-frame chalets.

Kuala Kinchin From Kuala Rompin in Pahang, a road runs through paddy fields 20km to Selandang; continue another 15km to Kuala Kinchin (gate open 9am–5pm), on the park boundary. Although a 4WD is not required, there's no public transport; a taxi to the park entrance from Kuala Rompin costs RM140. Contact the Forestry Department in Kuala Rompin (☎ 09 414 5204).

Selai Catch a train to Bekok from KL Sentral, then rent a 4WD to get to the park entrance. By road from the west, exit the North–South Expressway at Yong Peng and head for Chaah, Segamat (20min). After Chaah, follow signs for Bekok (15min) then Sungai Bantang (another 7km). Go past the Sungai Bantang turn-off and carry on for 20km, through an oil-palm estate and past several resettled Orang Asli villages. There is a Visitor Centre at Selai (daily 8am–5pm; ☎ 07 922 2875).

Sarawak

315 Southwestern Sarawak

341 Central Sarawak

355 The northern coast

364 The northern interior

PROBOSCIS MONKEY, BAKO NATIONAL PARK

Sarawak

With its beguiling tribal cultures and jungled highlands, Sarawak would seem to epitomize what Borneo is all about. By far the largest state in Malaysia, it packs in a host of national parks that showcase everything from coastal swamp forest to vast cave systems, and help preserve some of the world's richest and most diverse ecosystems. There are numerous opportunities for short or extended treks both inside and outside these protected areas, and it's also possible to visit remote longhouse communities, some of which can only be reached by venturing far upriver.

For all its attractions, however, Sarawak is not quite the paradise it might seem on paper. The state encapsulates the bitter dichotomy between development and conservation more clearly than anywhere else in Malaysia. Many of its forests have been degraded by **logging** or cleared for oil palm, putting wildlife and the traditional lifestyles of tribal communities under severe pressure. The state government has repeatedly won electoral mandates for its policies, but critics complain it has opened up Sarawak's resources to corporate exploitation in a way that's at best not transparent and at worst mired in corruption. While much of this may have little practical impact on visitors as they travel through, it's good to be aware that the changes you will see throughout the state have a subtext in the ongoing struggle for Sarawak's soul (see p.313).

The lie of the land is complex on many levels, not least **demographically**. Malays and Chinese each make up almost a quarter of Sarawak's almost two and a half million people, but indigenous tribal peoples account for nearly half that figure. They're sometimes subdivided under three broad headings, though it's nowadays much more common to refer to the tribes by name. The largest tribe by far, the **Iban**, constitute nearly thirty percent of Sarawak's population. They, along with the Muslim **Melanau** and other tribes, comprise the so-called **Sea Dyaks**, a slightly odd name given that these groups historically lived along river valleys. Then there are the **Land Dyaks**, who live up in the hills; chief among them are the **Bidayuh** of southwestern Sarawak, representing almost a tenth of the population. Finally, the **Orang Ulu** include disparate groups of the northern interior such as the **Berawan**, **Kenyah**, **Kelabit**, **Kayan** and the traditionally nomadic **Penan**. They're grouped together in that they live in the "ulu" or upriver regions of this part of the state.

While this cultural mosaic is a huge highlight of Sarawak, social and economic change, along with widespread conversion to **Christianity**, mean that the old ways are fast dying out. Classic multidoored **longhouses** do survive and can be superb places to

Sarawak place names p.312
Sarawak's ceramic jars p.319
Iban tattoos p.328
Spotting Santubong wildlife p.330
The Rainforest Music Festival p.332
Visiting Sarawak's national parks p.333
The Iban p.339
Longhouse architecture p.340
Longhouses near Sibu p.344
Rejang boats p.346
The Kayan and Kenyah p.349

The Bakun Dam p.351
Bintulu to Belaga by road p.353
Twin Otters p.366
Adventure caving p.368
The Headhunters' Trail p.370
Highlands treks p.375
The Bario to Pa' Lungan trek p.378
Gunung Murud p.379
The Baram Dam p.380
The Penan p.381

Highlights

❶ **Kuching** One of Malaysia's most endearingly chilled-out cities, with a pretty waterfront, reasonable museums and great food. **See p.315**

❷ **Santubong Peninsula** Lovely beaches hosting resort hotels and an impressive folk museum, all beneath the slopes of Gunung Santubong. **See p.330**

❸ **Bako National Park** This beautiful reserve has good trekking and sublime sea views and is home to proboscis monkeys. **See p.332**

❹ **Iban longhouses at Batang Ai** Traditional communities dot the rivers near the Kalimantan border in southwestern Sarawak. **See p.338**

❺ **Niah National Park** The superb caves here are not only a natural wonder, easily explored on foot, but also a workplace for men collecting edible swiftlet nests. **See p.361**

❻ **Gunung Mulu National Park** Sarawak's top attraction, with astonishing caves and a popular three-day trek to see the shard-like Pinnacles. **See p.366**

❼ **Kelabit Highlands** Trek to remote communities dotted around this cool upland backwater. **See p.373**

HIGHLIGHTS ARE MARKED ON THE MAP ON P.310

visit, and some peoples do still subsist semi-nomadically in the forest, but you'd be hard-pushed to find any Orang Ulu aged under 50 still sporting, say, the once-prized distended earlobes that previous generations developed by wearing heavy earrings. Meanwhile, there's no shortage of indigenous people pursuing careers in Sarawak's cities, and the future of indigenous languages appears under threat as Malay and English dominate the majority of state-run education.

HIGHLIGHTS

1. Kuching
2. Santubong Peninsula
3. Bako National Park
4. Iban longhouses at Batang Ai
5. Niah National Park
6. Gunung Mulu National Park
7. Kelabit Highlands

For visitors, the most popular attractions are concentrated at either end of the state. In the southwest, **Kuching**, the understated, attractive capital, makes a perfect base to explore the superb **Bako National Park**, with its wild shoreline of mangrove swamp and hinterland of *kerangas* bush teeming with proboscis monkeys. The Kuching area also packs in lesser national parks, an **orang-utan** sanctuary and substantial **caves**. Although Sarawak is not noted for its **beaches**, there are beautiful ones in Bako and decent

6

SARAWAK PLACE NAMES

As you travel through Sarawak, you'll notice certain terms cropping up repeatedly in the names of places, longhouses and other features. You'll seldom encounter them elsewhere in Malaysia, so it pays to know what they mean:

Ulu From the Malay *hulu*, meaning "upriver"; when used before the name of a river, it indicates the region surrounding the headwaters of that river – for example, the Ulu Ai is the upriver part of the Ai River and its tributaries there.

Batang "Trunk" or "strip"; used before a river name, it denotes that the river is the central member of a system of rivers.

Long "Confluence"; used in town names in the same way as the Malay "Kuala".

Nanga "Longhouse" in Iban; many longhouses are named "Nanga" followed by the name of the river they are next to.

Pa or **Pa'** In the Kelabit Highlands – denotes a village.

Rumah "House" in Malay; some longhouses are named "Rumah" followed by the name of the headman (if there's a change of headman, the longhouse name follows suit).

options nearer Kuching at the family-friendly resorts of Santubong. A handful of **longhouses** are also worth visiting, notably east of Kuching at **Batang Ai**.

In terms of pulling power, Bako is exceeded only by **Gunung Mulu National Park** ("Mulu" to locals) in the far northeast. Most tourists fly in, either making the short hop from nearby **Miri**, Sarawak's second city, or direct from Kuching, to trek to the park's limestone Pinnacles and see its extraordinary caves. Miri itself, though a bland affair that thrives on the proceeds of Sarawak's oil and gas industry, has good accommodation and is the hub for Twin Otter flights (see p.366) to interior settlements, most notably **Bario** and **Ba'Kelalan** in the **Kelabit Highlands**. Here, close to the Indonesian border, you can undertake extended treks through jungled and mountainous terrain, overnighting in Kelabit villages. Other Twin Otter flights head to settlements in the upper reaches of the **Baram** river system, from where it's possible to reach isolated **Penan villages** offering homestays and yet more treks. Another major draw, visitable on a day-trip from Miri, is **Niah National Park**, its extensive caves a site of major archeological significance as well as a centre for the harvesting of swiftlet nests and bat guano.

Visitors who overland between Kuching and Miri tend to breeze through central Sarawak, but the region is worth considering for the state's most accessible river journey – the popular route along the **Batang Rejang**. The boat ride, beginning at the city of **Sibu**, is its own reward for making it up to nondescript Rejang towns such as **Kapit** and **Belaga**, though it's possible to arrange longhouse trips from either. Also noteworthy in this region is **Bintulu**, a coastal oil town like Miri that's conveniently placed for the beachside forests of **Similajau National Park**.

Brief history

Cave-dwelling **hunter-gatherers** were living in Sarawak forty thousand years ago. Their isolation ended when the first trading boats arrived from Sumatra and Java around 3000 BC, exchanging cloth and pottery for jungle produce. By the thirteenth century Chinese merchants were dominant, bartering beads and porcelain with the coastal Melanau people for bezoar stones (from the gall bladders of monkeys) and birds' nests, both considered aphrodisiacs. In time, the traders were forced to deal with the rising power of the Malay sultans including the Sultan of Brunei. Meanwhile, Sarawak was attracting interest from Europe; the Dutch and English established short-lived trading posts near Kuching in the seventeenth century, to obtain pepper and other spices.

With the decline of the Brunei sultanate, civil war erupted early in the eighteenth century. Local rulers feuded, while piracy threatened to destroy what was left of the trade in spices, animals and minerals. In addition, the indigenous groups' predilection for **head-hunting** had led to a number of deaths among the traders and the sultan's officials, and violent territorial confrontations between powerful tribes were increasing.

The White Rajahs

Just when matters were at their most explosive, the Englishman **James Brooke** took an interest in the area. A former soldier, he helped the Sultan of Brunei quell a rebellion by miners and, as a reward, demanded sovereignty over the area around Kuching. The weakened sultan had little choice but to relinquish control of the awkward territory and in 1841 James Brooke was installed as the first White Rajah of Sarawak. He had essentially created a new kingdom, not formally part of the British Empire.

Brooke built a network of small **forts** – many are now museums – to repel pirates or tribal warring parties. He also sent officials into the malarial swamps and mountainous interior to make contact with the Orang Ulu. But his administration was not without its troubles. In one incident his men killed dozens of marauding tribesmen, while in 1857 Hakka Chinese **gold-miners**, based in Bau near Kuching, retaliated against his attempts to eliminate their trade in opium and suppress their secret societies. When they attacked Kuching, Brooke got away by the skin of his teeth. His nephew, **Charles Brooke**, assembled a massive force of warrior tribesmen and followed the miners; in the ensuing battle over a thousand Chinese were killed.

In 1863 Charles Brooke took over and continued to acquire territory from the Sultan of Brunei. River valleys were bought for a few thousand pounds, the local tribes either persuaded to enter into deals or crushed if they resisted. The sultan's territory had shrunk so much it was now surrounded on all three sides by Brooke's Sarawak, establishing the geographical boundaries that still define Brunei today.

Charles was succeeded by his son, **Vyner Brooke**, who consolidated his father's gains. However, the **Japanese occupation** of World War II effectively put an end to his control. Vyner escaped, but most of his officials were interned and some executed. Upon his return in 1946, he was compelled to cede Sarawak to the British government. The Brooke dynasty was effectively at an end, and a last link with its past was severed in 2011 when Vyner's nephew **Anthony Brooke**, his designated successor who had briefly run Sarawak before World War II while Vyner was in the UK, died.

To the present

With Malaysian independence in 1957, attempts were made to include Sarawak, Sabah and Brunei, but Brunei declined at the last minute to join the present-day **Federation of Malaysia**, inaugurated in 1963. Sarawak's inclusion was opposed by Indonesia, and the **Konfrontasi** broke out, with Indonesia arming communist guerrillas inside Sarawak. The insurgency continued for three years until Malaysian troops, aided by the British, put it down. To this day, many inhabitants of the interior remain displaced.

Since then, Sarawak has developed apace with the rest of Malaysia, though at considerable cost to the **environment**, with up to ninety percent of its forests having been logged. Politically, the state today is closely identified with the policies of **Taib Mahmud**, a Melanau, who was chief minister from 1981 to 2014, and who to an extent oversaw a time of infrastructural and economic growth, yet also passed laws that gave him control of the logging industry during that time. The support of his PBB party and allied parties has helped prop up the ruling coalition in general elections, and the PBB is often viewed as a proxy for UMNO. Sarawak is the only state where Malaysia's main Malay party has no presence.

There are signs of a backlash, however, brought on perhaps by the rising cost of living, economic disparity, and allegations from international environmental groups as well as Taib's opponents and the Malaysian media, that Sarawak's administration is tainted by **corruption** – the list of allegations is far too long to include here, but an internet search will return dozens of examples including damning leaked US embassy cables published by Wikileaks in 2011.

6

The 2011 local elections saw an unprecedented swing to the opposition in the cities, though the PBB and allies still won comfortably – ironically enough, given what is happening with the state's natural resources, with the help of rural voters. In 2014, Taib resigned as chief minister (a role taken over by Adenan Satem, his former brother-in-law) to become **Governor of Sarawak**.

The latest Taib-conceived project to cause a ruckus is the **Baram Dam** (see p.380), the fourth of twelve dams to be constructed in Sarawak, and the site of a long-term protest by local tribal peoples whose land will be flooded.

ARRIVAL AND DEPARTURE   SARAWAK

By plane It's easy enough to fly into Kuching, Miri, Bintulu or Sibu from the Peninsula, and there are also decent connections with Sabah, Brunei and Singapore; Malaysia Airlines, AirAsia, Firefly, MASwings and SilkAir provide a comprehensive service between them. There are also flights from Pontianak in Indonesian Kalimantan to Kuching, operated by MASwings. Note that Sarawak has its own immigration controls (see p.53), so you will be stamped in and out even if flying between here and the other states of Malaysia.

By boat There's a boat from Labuan island, off the Sabah coast, to Lawas.

By bus A handful of buses connect Bandar Seri Begawan and Miri, and Kota Kinabalu and Miri via Lawas. The only official border crossing between Kalimantan and Sarawak is at Entikong/Tebedu (daily, roughly 6am–6pm), 100km south of Kuching by road; it's used by frequent buses plying between Pontianak and Kuching and all the way to Miri.

GETTING AROUND

Sarawak covers pretty much the same area as England or the state of Mississippi, but with much of the state wild and thinly populated, there's not that much ground to cover unless you wish to visit remote communities or the interior's national parks, such as Mulu. As ever, it's essential to book **public transport** at least a week in advance if you want to travel around the time of a major festival, notably the two-day *gawai* harvest festival at the start of June, when huge numbers of indigenous people return to their original longhouses.

By plane Flying is a useful timesaver between Kuching and Miri, and to reach Mulu from either Kuching or Miri. However, the most memorable flights are on the tiny Twin Otter planes (see p.366), connecting the interior with Bario and Ba Ke Lalan.

By bus Numerous buses ply the trunk road between Kuching and Miri, though thanks to slow-moving trucks journeys take a little longer than distances might suggest. Buses operated by MTC (w mtcmiri.com), Biaramas/Bus Asia (no relation of AirAsia; w ba.my) and Asia Star (Biaramas's luxury brand; w www.asiastar.my) are a cut above the rest in terms of comfort. Fares are reasonable – Kuching to Sibu, for example, costs RM50 one way (7hr). Local bus services also radiate from the main cities, in daylight hours only.

By boat The only scheduled boat services you're likely to catch are those between Kuching and Sibu, and express boats along the Rejang River.

By taxi On some routes, buses are supplemented by *kereta sapu* (see p.32); any "taxis" mentioned in small towns here will usually be of this type. Useful in rural areas, such share taxi services are generally reliable though, of course, their operators are neither licensed nor insured. Prices are comparable to bus fares, unless you're in a 4WD (see below).

By car Sarawak's road network is simplicity itself. Given that signage is adequate and drivers' behaviour a little less manic than in the Peninsula, renting a car is worth considering. The state's one and only trunk road, part of the so-called Pan-Borneo Highway, runs between Kuching and Miri, via Sibu and Bintulu, and on into Brunei. It's a dual carriageway only as far east as the turning for Sri Aman, a 3hr drive from Kuching; beyond that it becomes little more than a two-lane country road. The coastal highway between Bintulu and Miri is also mostly a two-lane affair. Unlike its counterpart, it holds few facilities or settlements; if you intend to use it, fill up beforehand and set off in plenty of time to arrive before nightfall.

By longboat or 4WD Finally, in remote areas, you might need to charter a longboat for a river trip or a 4WD to gain access to the network of rough logging roads that have begun to supplant boat travel. As always in Malaysia, getting off the beaten track isn't cheap unless you're travelling in a small group – ideally of three to four people. Chartering a longboat for a 2hr trip might cost RM200–250 for three passengers, assuming you can get hold of a boatman at all, while four passengers might pay the driver up to RM200 to go 100km in a 4WD. Details are given in the text where relevant, but unless you're on a budget it's often more worthwhile to pay a tour operator to arrange things.

Hitchhiking Although we don't recommend it in general, for male travellers and couples, hitching can significantly reduce your travel costs and help you meet Sarawak people. It's possible to hitch along logging tracks, for example.

Southwestern Sarawak

Visitors flying in from Peninsular Malaysia or Singapore are treated to a spellbinding view of muddy rivers snaking their way through the jungle beneath lush peaks. It not only just about sums up Borneo, but also sets the tone for what the southwest of Sarawak has in store. The area is home to several of Sarawak's national parks, notably **Bako**, with its proboscis monkeys and excellent trekking. It's also a good place to get a grounding in Borneo's tribal cultures, which you can do at the museums in the likeable state capital **Kuching**. Among other top draws are the orang-utans of the **Semenggoh Wildlife Rehabilitation Centre** and the **Sarawak Cultural Village**, a brilliant collection of tribal houses near the beaches of Damai. You can also see a proper longhouse at Ana Rais, or head east to the edges of **Batang Ai National Park**, home to many Iban communities.

Kuching

KUCHING, the state's oldest, largest city, is the perfect gateway to Sarawak. This is one of Malaysia's most charming and laidback cities, revelling in a picturesque setting on the Sarawak River, with Gunung Santubong looming on the western horizon. Despite central high-rises, much of the recent development has been confined to the bland but burgeoning suburbs, and the historical core remains appealingly sleepy and human in scale, its colonial architecture redolent of a bygone era. Kuching's blend of contradictions – of commerce alongside a sedate pace of life, of fashionable cafés rubbing shoulders with old-fangled *kedai kopis* – makes it an appealing place to chill out for several days while exploring sights such as the **Sarawak Museum**, showcasing the state's ethnological heritage, and making excursions to the numerous national parks and other sights in the vicinity.

Most of Kuching lies on the south bank of the river, its core an easily walkable warren of crowded lanes. The area sandwiched between Jalan Courthouse to the west, Jalan Wayang to the east and Reservoir Park to the south, usually referred to as **old Kuching**, includes several colonial churches and administrative buildings. **Chinatown** occupies the same general area, incorporating what were once the main shopping streets of Main Bazaar, facing the river, and Carpenter Street, and Chinese businesses and restaurants also dominate Jalan Padungan to the east. The traditional **Malay district** is dominated by the domes of the **Masjid Negeri**, with several Malay kampungs north of the river too. The Chinese and Malays together make up nearly two-thirds of Kuching's population of just over 700,000, though there are also substantial communities of Bidayuh and Iban.

Brief history

When **James Brooke** came up the river in 1841, he arrived at a village known as Sarawak, on a small stream called Sungai Mata Kuching ("Cat's Eye"), adjoining the main river; he probably shortened the stream's name, which came to refer to the fast-expanding settlement. However, a much-repeated tale has it that the first rajah pointed to the village and asked its name. The Malay locals, thinking Brooke was pointing to a cat, replied – reasonably enough – "kuching" ("cat"). Either way, in 1872 Charles Brooke officially changed the settlement's name from Sarawak to Kuching.

Until the 1920s, the capital was largely confined to the south bank of the Sarawak River, stretching only from the Chinese heartland around Jalan Temple, east of today's centre, to the Malay kampung around the mosque to the west. On the north bank, activity revolved around the fort and a few dozen houses reserved for British officials. The prewar **rubber boom** financed the town's expansion, with tree-lined Jalan Padungan, running east from Chinatown, becoming one of its smartest streets. Kuching escaped relatively lightly during World War II, since Japanese bombing raids largely focused on destroying the oil wells in northern Sarawak.

6

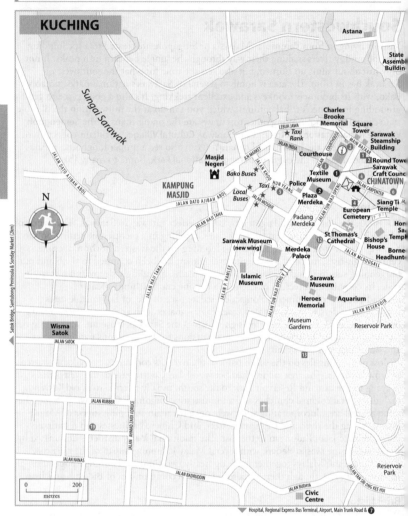

In recent decades the city sprawled south and port facilities and warehouses in the centre closed as new shipping terminals and industrial estates were created downriver, to the northeast. Robbed of waterborne traffic, downtown's **riverside** was reinvented in the 1990s with partial success as a leafy, pedestrianized recreation area, its quaint panoramas spoiled only by the bizarre oversized hulk of the State Assembly building, completed in 2009 on the north bank.

Kuching waterfront

Beginning along Jalan Gambier and continuing for just over 1km until it peters out close to the *Grand Margherita* hotel, Kuching's central **waterfront** is where most visitors begin exploring the city – almost everything of interest is within 500m of this esplanade. Sporting the odd fountain and several dull food kiosks, it has a somewhat sanitized feel, but a sprinkling of whitewashed colonial buildings, tranquil river views and the shophouses of Main Bazaar and Jalan Gambier make for a worthwhile wander.

6

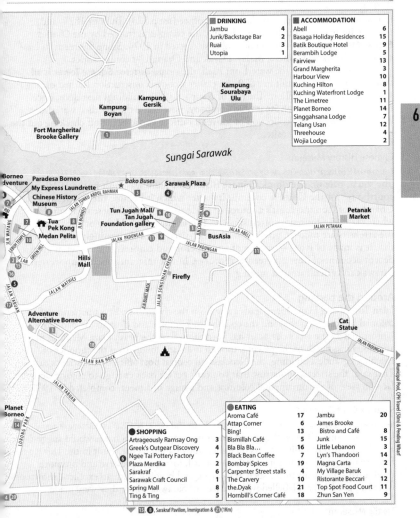

DRINKING	
Jambu	4
Junk/Backstage Bar	2
Ruai	3
Utopia	1

ACCOMMODATION	
Abell	6
Basaga Holiday Residences	15
Batik Boutique Hotel	9
Berambih Lodge	5
Fairview	13
Grand Margherita	3
Harbour View	10
Kuching Hilton	8
Kuching Waterfront Lodge	1
The Limetree	11
Planet Borneo	14
Singgahsana Lodge	7
Telang Usan	12
Threehouse	4
Wojia Lodge	2

SHOPPING	
Artrageously Ramsay Ong	3
Greek's Outgear Discovery	4
Ngee Tai Pottery Factory	7
Plaza Merdika	2
Sarakraf	6
Sarawak Craft Council	1
Spring Mall	8
Ting & Ting	5

EATING			
Aroma Café	17	Jambu	20
Attap Corner	6	James Brooke	
Bing!	13	Bistro and Café	8
Bismillah Café	5	Junk	15
Bla Bla Bla…	16	Little Lebanon	3
Black Bean Coffee	7	Lyn's Thandoori	14
Bombay Spices	19	Magna Carta	2
Carpenter Street stalls	4	My Village Baruk	1
The Carvery	10	Ristorante Beccari	12
the.Dyak	21	Top Spot Food Court	11
Hornbill's Corner Café	18	Zhun San Yen	9

For views alone, the best time to turn up is around 6pm on a fine day, when you'll be treated within an hour to a fiery **sunset** behind Gunung Serapi (one of the peaks of Kubah National Park), casting an orange glow over city and river. To get an aerial view, head up to the cinema on the top floor of the nearby Medan Pelita building on Lebuh Temple, where a large balcony offers a fine vista over old Kuching. It's possible to do an expensive sunset river trip, marketed as the **Sarawak River Cruise** (daily 5.30pm, from the jetty near the Sarawak Steamship Company building; 1hr 30min; RM60, children up to 12 RM30), but the views are little better than those from dry land.

Along Main Bazaar

The fast-gentrifying **Main Bazaar** is home to a couple of guesthouses and tour agencies, several souvenir shops and galleries, the odd attempt at a posh café, and a handful of more traditional shops. At its junction with Jalan Tun Haji Openg, the renovated **Old Courthouse** complex is the natural place to begin a wander, as it houses the helpful tourist office and a national parks booking office (see p.323). Built in 1874, and sporting impressive Romanesque columns, the complex is fronted by the **Charles Brooke Memorial**, a 6m-high granite obelisk erected in 1924. Stone figures at its base represent the state's Chinese, Malay, Dayak and Orang Ulu communities.

Diagonally across, on the waterfront itself, the single-turreted **Square Tower** is all that's left of a fortress built in 1879. An earlier wooden construction burned during the 1857 gold-miners' rebellion. The trio of compact 1930s buildings next door, once belonging to the **Sarawak Steamship Company**, now house the so-called waterfront bazaar, a disappointing collection of souvenir outlets; you're better off checking out the touristy shophouses opposite.

Chinese History Museum

Eastern end of Main Bazaar • Mon–Fri 9am–4.30pm, Sat & Sun 10am–4pm • Free; no photography allowed • ☎ 082 231520

The squat, pale orangey-pink **Chinese History Museum** was built in the 1910s as a courthouse for the Chinese community, after which it became the Chinese Chamber of Commerce. It's a source of pride to the local Chinese in a country where state-run museums often snub traditions that aren't Malay or tribal. While the artefacts are modest, apart from the half-sized – but depressingly large, given that it is made of ivory – carving of an emperor and empress, the museum gives a decent account of how nineteenth-century Chinese migrants opened up western Sarawak to agriculture and mining.

Around the padang

Jalan Tun Abang Haji Openg leads away from the riverfront past a smattering of colonial buildings just beyond the courthouse complex and close to the **padang**. Unfortunately the area's character has been diluted by the brash Plaza Merdeka mall and hotel just north of the padang, though it doesn't totally steal the thunder of Kuching's grandest building, the Neoclassical central **post office** on the street's east side. That said, the street is so narrow that you can't get far back enough to enjoy a decent face-on view of the ornamental columns and a huge pediment, completed in 1931.

Sarawak Craft Council

Next to the Old Courthouse complex • Mon–Fri 8.30am–1pm & 2–4.30pm • Free • ☎ 082 245652, ⓦ sarawakhandicraft.com.my

Unlike the Square Tower, the **Round Tower** is not the shape its name would suggest – it actually has two roundish towers on either side of a flat facade. Built in the 1880s as a fort, it's now used by the **Sarawak Craft Council**, formed to preserve and promote traditional skills in art forms such as weaving and beading, with an excellent showroom where all products are labelled with the part of Sarawak where they were made.

Textile Museum

Beside the Round Tower, Jalan Tun Haji Openg • Daily 9am–4.30pm • Free • ⓦ museum.sarawak.gov.my

"A piece of New Orleans transplanted to Kuching" is how the tourist office describes the ornate building with shuttered windows beside the Round Tower. They advisedly didn't say "literally", for it was originally built here in the early twentieth century as a hospital. The handsome restored structure certainly catches the eye, unlike the low-key signs announcing its present-day role as the city's **Textile Museum**, presenting Borneo costumes and artefacts across the centuries – headdresses, belts, traditional woven fabrics known as *pua kumbu*, alongside models of traditional Iban and Malay weddings. Worthwhile though the collection is, it's less well presented than the Iban weaving at the gallery of the Tun Jugah Foundation (see p.321).

St Thomas's Cathedral and the Bishop's House

On a hillock off the east side of Jalan Tun Haji Openg, the Anglican **St Thomas's Cathedral** is a tidy, plain 1950s edifice, one of a cluster of colonial churches and mission schools hereabouts. Only the vaguely mock-Tudor **Bishop's House**, built in 1849, which is still the Anglican bishop's residence and the oldest surviving building in the city, is worth a look, though the inside is not usually open to the public; reach it by turning left off Jalan McDougall and walking uphill for a couple of minutes.

Chinatown

East of the Old Courthouse complex, a gaudy Chinese archway marks the entrance to Kuching's historic **Chinatown** via **Carpenter Street** (the name is still used rather than the Malay "Jalan Carpenter"), which becomes Jalan Ewe Hai at its eastern end. Truth be told, the district's Chinese flavour is somewhat diluted these days, but a few old-fashioned *kopitiams*, herbalists and snack shops still dot the shophouses of Carpenter Street and the tiny lanes running off it, and a handful of well-maintained temples merit a peek, the largest being **Tua Pek Kong** on Jalan Temple, at the district's eastern end. Tua Pek Kong, one explanation has it, is a sort of patron saint of Chinese communities in Southeast Asia; temples throughout Malaysia and Singapore bear his name. Raised behind a gaudy retaining wall, Kuching's version was built in the mid-eighteenth century, though a rather plastic restoration has left it slightly charmless; you may find the Siang Ti (Northern Deity) temple on Carpenter Street and the Hong San (Phoenix Hill) temple on Jalan Ewe Hai more atmospheric. Any of these temples may play host to theatrical or musical performances during **festivals**, especially Chinese New Year. There is a high concentration of **backpacker hostels** in this area.

Sarawak Museum

Jalan Tun Abang Haji Openg, a little way southeast of the padang • Mon–Fri 9am–4.30pm, Sat & Sun 10am–4pm, closed on the first day of public holidays; 1hr guided tour Fri 9.30am • Free • ☎ 082 244232, ⊕ museum.sarawak.gov.my

Borneo's oldest museum and housed in a lovely nineteenth-century faux Normandy townhouse set in lush grounds, the **Sarawak Museum** used to be regarded locally as one of the country's finest museums, thanks largely to its former curator, **Tom Harrisson** (1911–76). Best remembered for discovering a 39,000-year-old skull at Niah in 1957, which led to a reappraisal of the origins of early man in Southeast Asia, he also frequently visited tribal peoples to collect the artefacts that comprise the museum's biggest attraction. Sadly the museum has been resting on its laurels for too long, and funding for various ideas to rid it of its fusty, static feel has yet to materialize; the unexciting new wing southwest of the padang, linked to the original building by a long footbridge over Jalan Tun Abang Haji Openg, has not helped either. Still, it certainly rewards at least an hour of exploration.

SARAWAK'S CERAMIC JARS

The status and wealth of members of Sarawak's indigenous tribes depended on how many **ceramic jars** they possessed, and you can still see impressive models in longhouses as well as in the Sarawak Museum. Ranging from tiny, elegantly detailed bowls to much larger vessels, more than 1m in height, the jars were used for such purposes as storage, brewing rice wine and making payments – dowries and fines for adultery and divorce settlements. The most valuable jars were only used for ceremonies like the Gawai Kenyalang (the rite of passage for a mature man of means, involving the recitation of stories by the longhouse bard), or for funerary purposes. When a member of the Kelabit people died, the corpse was packed into a jar in a foetal position to await rebirth from the jar, its "womb". The Berawan did the same, and as decomposition took place, the liquid from the body was drained through a bamboo pipe, leaving the individual's bones or clothing to be placed in a canister and hoisted onto an ossuary above the river bank. It's said that the jars can also be used to foretell the future, and can summon spirits through the sounds they emit when struck.

The old wing

Charles Brooke conceived the idea of a museum in Kuching, prompted by the nineteenth-century naturalist Alfred Russel Wallace, who spent two years in Sarawak in the 1850s. Wallace's specimens now dominate the fairly pedestrian displays on the ground floor of the old wing, which also houses even duller displays on Sarawak's oil industry, but the English Baroque building itself remains impressive: the largest colonial edifice in Kuching, it was built in the 1890s.

Most visitors linger in the **ethnographic** section upstairs, containing a huge model of a wooden Iban longhouse. You can climb up into the rafters of the *sadau* (loft), traditionally used to store bamboo fish baskets, ironwork and sleeping mats. There's also a Penan hut of bamboo and rattan, containing blowpipes and *parang*s (machetes), animal hides and coconut husks used as drinking vessels. Other exhibits include intricately glazed, sturdy Chinese ceramic jars, fearsome Iban war totems, and woodcarvings from the Kayan and Kenyah ethnic groups who live in the headwaters of the Rejang, Baram and Balui rivers. Wall cabinets showcase **musical instruments** used by various tribes, such as the Bidayuh's heavy gongs and the Kayan *sape*, a lute-like instrument.

The Dewan Tun Abdul Razak Building (new wing)

The Sarawak Museum's **new wing** packs in a miscellany that ranges from unexciting Neolithic shards to the Brunei sultanate and World War II. The best exhibition shows how Chinese ceramics arrived through trade and wormed their way into the culture of the local Malays and tribal peoples, and includes some fine *celadon* jars. The building is slated for demolition to make way for a new museum extension.

Islamic Museum

Mon–Fri 9am–4.45pm, Sat & Sun 10am–4pm • Free • ☎ 082 244232, ⓦ museum.sarawak.gov.my

Just southwest of the Sarawak Museum's new wing, a former Malay college and religious school houses the **Islamic Museum**. Seven galleries in its cool, tiled interior hold unexpectedly fine examples of Islamic art and displays on architecture, coinage and textiles, which are all set around a pleasant central courtyard garden.

West of the centre

The pocket of town immediately west of the padang has a noticeably Islamic feel, with the golden-domed **Kuching Mosque** (Masjid Negeri; daily except Fri 9am–3pm, closed at prayer-times) atop a hillock at its heart and nearby streets packed with Malay and Indian Muslim *kedai kopis*. The most colourful approach to the area is via pedestrianized **Jalan India**, named for the Indian coolies who arrived in the early twentieth century to work at Kuching's port; today it's packed with market stalls selling cheap shoes, clothing and household items. The mosque aside, the only specific sight is a popular **weekend market**, further southwest.

Sunday market

Just north of the Tun Abdul Rahman Bridge at Medan Niaga Satok • Sat mid-afternoon until late, Sun early morning until noon • City Public Link buses #K5 and #K7 leave every 30min or so from Jalan Masjid bus park, or 3km walk from the tourist office – head to Kuching Mosque, then down Jalan Haji Taha and under the flyover at Jalan Kulas, turning right into Jalan Satok at the second flyover, then follow Jalan Satok until it crosses the bridge

Variously known as the **Sunday market** or night market, the weekend market on Medan Niaga Satok is not quite the spectacle it used to be when it was in the street – but for once, that's no bad thing. The bush meat trade of years gone by has been halted by better environmental enforcement; these days the most exotic thing you might see on sale are edible sago grubs, which live on thorny sago palms in the jungle. However, the market is certainly colourful and frenetic, selling a good range of snacks as well as tribal souvenirs, jungle products including wild honey and local vegetables such as the ubiquitous fern tops.

East of the centre

Downtown Kuching's commercial district, east of Chinatown, is home to most of the city's modern hotels, a handful of ordinary shopping malls and several banks. The easiest way to get there is to follow Jalan Tuanku Abdul Rahman, the continuation of Main Bazaar, east until it swings away from the river at the *Grand Margherita* hotel to join the area's other main thoroughfare, **Jalan Padungan**, which feels like a natural extension of Chinatown, its shophouses still home to several largely Chinese restaurants and *kopitiams*, though Western-style cafés and bars have made their presence felt too.

The archway by the major gyratory further east on Jalan Padungan has a certain notoriety as the site of Kuching's original **cat statue**, a tacky 1.5m-high white-plaster effigy, paw raised in welcome. Though the location isn't at all prepossessing, the statue was regarded as a city icon for many years, so much so that more cat statues have since appeared elsewhere on Jalan Padungan and in other parts of town.

Tun Jugah Foundation gallery

Level 4, Tun Jugah mall, 18 Jalan Tuanku Abdul Rahman • Mon–Fri 9am–noon & 1–4.30pm • ☎ 082 239672, ⓦ tunjugahfoundation.org.my

The excellent modern **Tun Jugah Foundation gallery**, the showcase for a charity set up to honour a long-serving Iban politician who died in 1981, showcases fine Iban weaving – three dozen examples of **pua kumbu** cloth, wall-mounted or framed in sliding panels. The geometrical patterns are fascinating but bafflingly abstract to the untrained eye, though once you read the labelling you might be able to make out the animal and other motifs. Most are in shades of reddish brown and black, the colour applied through *ikat* (tie-dyeing) with a base brown pigment traditionally made from the bark of the *engkudu* tree (*Morinda citrifolia*); vegetable indigos are added on top, yielding black in areas already dyed brown. The depth of colour depends on the type of yarn and the number of times it's dipped in the dyes.

In a large **teaching room**, the arts of weaving are passed on to a new generation of local women, not just Iban; you may be able to sit in on some classes or talk to the instructors or participants. An additional side gallery is devoted to **beads**, as used in the jewellery of the Iban and other tribes, and featuring examples in semiprecious stone and snazzy multicoloured glass.

The north bank

The leafy far side of the Sarawak River, views of which are the major part of the waterfront's appeal, is underwhelming once you get there – one of the two important colonial buildings here, the **Astana**, is largely closed to the public, and the shoreline is dominated by the outlandish **State Assembly Building** (also called the DUN Building), a sort of giant espresso maker crossed with a spaceship that locals disdain as a waste of taxpayers' money. Still, it is worth crossing the water to look back at downtown Kuching and perhaps to wander through the Malay kampungs. **Sampans** shuttle across the river all day and into the evening, leaving when full from four small jetties along the waterfront (RM0.50 before 10pm, RM1 after 10pm); ideally you should depart from the jetty more or less opposite where you want to go.

Fort Margherita/Brooke Gallery and around

600m east of the Astana • Orchid Garden Tues–Sun 10am–6pm • Free • ⓦ brooketrust.org

Dwarfed by the State Assembly Building, **Fort Margherita** is one of the best examples of the Brookes' system of fortifications, and named after James's wife Margaret – she must have been quite a woman, as one of Oscar Wilde's fairy tales, *The Young King*, is also dedicated to her. It's a fine sturdy building, well preserved, too, since it never saw any action. The interior should soon be open to the public in the form of the **Brooke Gallery**, explaining his life and works – remember to bring your ID, as it's within the police training barracks. The nearby **orchid garden** is home to around one hundred orchid species.

Malay kampungs

Quite a few **Malay kampungs** are visible on the north bank from downtown Kuching; the cluster of three east of Fort Margherita are the most visited. The obvious target is **Kampung Boyan**, marked out by its waterside food court with its twin-humped roof, though the mixture of traditional clapboard dwellings and more modern houses is not particularly atmospheric. Look out for the local cottage industry, the manufacture of multicoloured *kek lapis* (layer cake); street traders all along Main Bazaar hawk examples. If you come in the evening, consider dining at *My Village Baruk* (see p.326), a fine Malay restaurant.

ARRIVAL AND DEPARTURE   KUCHING

BY PLANE

KUCHING INTERNATIONAL AIRPORT

The airport (☎082 457373) is 12km south of the city. AirAsia, Malaysia Airlines, Malindo Air and MASwings all have ticket offices in the departure terminal.

Facilities There's a small Tourism Malaysia desk (generally daily 9am–10pm) in the baggage hall, though the tourist office in the courthouse complex is much better. The arrivals hall also holds car rental agencies, ATMs and a foreign exchange counter, while at least one booth sells coupons for the taxi ride into town (RM26, RM39 11pm–6am).

Getting into town If you walk to the main road beyond the car park (about 2km), you can cross at the lights where there is a bus stop heading north, and you can flag down any local bus (6am–8pm; 25min), all of which end up at one of the stops in the Kuching mosque area – ask here for which buses head out to the airport too.

Destinations Bintulu (4–6 daily; 55min); Johor Bahru (3–5 daily; 1hr 25min); Kota Kinabalu (3–5 daily; 1hr 25min); Kuala Lumpur (frequent; 1hr 40min); Miri (6–7 daily; 1hr); Mukah (3 daily; 1hr); Mulu (1 daily; 1hr 30min); Pontianak (1 daily; 45min); Sibu (8–9 daily; 40min); Singapore (2–3 daily; 1hr 20min).

BY BUS

If you're leaving by bus, and want to avoid trekking out to the new bus station to buy a ticket in advance – advisable around the time of a festival – it's useful to travel with Biaramas/BusAsia, which has a ticket office just off Jalan Padungan.

KUCHING SENTRAL REGIONAL EXPRESS BUS TERMINAL

All the bus companies arrive and depart from Kuching's long-distance bus station, 6.5km south of the centre on Jalan Tun Ahmad Zaidi Adruce.

Getting into town Taxi drivers may attempt to charge RM26 to take you to the city centre, and are unlikely to be bargained below RM20 – those figures double between midnight and 6am. Alternatively, cross the main road and flag down any bus for RM1 – all will take you to the centre, most likely one of the stops in the Kuching mosque area.

Destinations Bintulu (every 20min–1hr; 11hr); Miri (every 20min–1hr; 15hr); Mukah (3 daily; 9hr); Pontianak (Indonesia; 6 daily, last at 1pm; 8hr); Sarikei (7 hourly; 5hr 30min–6hr); Sibu (7 hourly; 8hr); Sri Aman (20 daily; 3hr).

BY BOAT

Ferries Express Bahagia (☎082 410076 or ☎016 896 6235) operates passenger ferries to and from Sibu (daily 8.30am; 4hr 30min; RM45), via Sarikei on the coast, using the Pending terminal 6km east of the centre. A taxi to the terminal from town costs RM26.

GETTING AROUND

By city bus and minivan You're unlikely to use Kuching's city buses in the easily walkable downtown area, where bus stops offer practically no information or labelling. Also, while some services run two or three times per hour, many only go a few times a day, and local buses have in any case been in flux for years; ask at the Visitors' Information Centre (see opposite) for the latest schedules. All buses operate between dawn and dusk only, and most start out from the area just east of the Kuching mosque, where cramped minivans shadow many bus routes. Minivans leave when full – avoid if you value comfort.

By local bus Most bus services that start and end inside Kuching are run by Rapid Kuching (red vehicles) or City Public Link (largely green vehicles). Both firms, along with the Sarawak Transport Company (green and cream buses) and some minor operators, also provide handy services out into Kuching's hinterland; details are given in the relevant accounts.

By motorbike A couple of guesthouses along Jalan Carpenter rent motorbikes, but the best deals are to be had from Ah Hui Motor (☎082 240508), who rent 110cc bikes from RM30/day or RM175/week.

By taxi There are taxi ranks near the mosque and in front of hotels along Jalan Tuanku Abdul Rahman; alternatively, try Kuching Taxi (☎082 480000) or T&T (☎082 343343). Downtown journeys should cost RM15–20; double that between midnight and 6am.

By bike Planet Borneo (see opposite) rents bikes (RM20/

day), as does the more central Paredesa Borneo (RM25/day). The latter also organizes bike tours of Kuching and the surrounding kampungs (see below).
By car Kuching Holidays (☎016 882 8222, ⓦkuchingholidays.com) at the airport and the Old Courthouse; Flexi (☎082 452200, ⓦflexicarrental.com) at the airport and Jalan Sekama; Hornbill (☎082 613369, ⓔhbcrsb@streamyx.com) at the airport and Jalan Mendu; Hertz at the airport (☎082 450740). Prices start at around RM100/day.

INFORMATION

Visitors' Information Centre Excellent service operated by the state's tourism authority, in the Old Courthouse complex at the western edge of the waterfront (Mon–Fri 8am–5pm; ☎082 410944, ⓦsarawaktourism.com).
Sarawak Forestry Corporation Next door to the information centre in the courthouse complex; it takes bookings for accommodation at many national parks, though not Mulu (Mon–Fri 8am–5pm; ☎082 248088, ⓦsarawakforestry.com). They can also tell you where *Rafflesia* flowers (see p.586) are blooming.
Newspapers English-language newspapers such as the *Borneo Post, New Sarawak Tribune* and *The Star* (which has a separate Sarawak edition) detail cultural and other happenings in town and around the state.
Guides Kuching is the ideal place to engage the services of a licensed guide through the Sarawak Tourist Guides Association (☎082 415027, ⓔsktgasecretary@gmail.com). Guides are experienced, speak good English and have expert knowledge. Although they cannot by law arrange a package (you'll have to book everything yourself), they can help arrange visits – sometimes more cheaply than a tour agency – to longhouses, parks or other points of interest that are otherwise hard to reach or have few amenities. You will need to give them at least one week's notice.

6

TOUR OPERATORS

Sarawak's tour operators come into their own for **longhouse stays**, typically around the Batang Ai area, and other trips off the beaten track – which could mean the less touristy national parks or a foray into an *ulu* area where local contacts are needed to ensure transport and accommodation. That said, if you're an experienced traveller, many of these destinations are perfectly easy to visit by organizing yourself using this Guide – and considerably cheaper, especially if you travel with companions.

Adventure Alternative Borneo Lot 37, Jalan Tabuan ☎082 248000, ⓦaaborneo.com. Interesting off-the-beaten track tours at reasonable prices.
Borneo Adventure 55 Main Bazaar ☎082 245175, ⓦborneoadventure.com. Award-winning, pioneering operation, particularly good on longhouse stays. Its jungle lodge along the Batang Ai at Nanga Sumpa (see p.340), is a fine example of best practice when it comes to Malaysian ecotourism; prices for three days/two nights start at RM1588. They also have a lodge at Mulu.
CPH Travel 70 Jalan Padungan ☎082 243708, ⓦcphtravel.com.my. Especially good on boat trips, for example to the mouth of the Santubong River (RM160) to spot Irrawaddy dolphins (see p.330), though they also do longhouse tours on the Lemanak River from RM480 (two days, one night).
Kuching Caving ☎012 886 2347, ⓦkuchingcaving.com. Knowledgeable day tours (RM260–400) to little-visited limestone cave systems near Serian, southeast of Kuching. All you need is a reasonable level of fitness; gloves, helmets and helmet-mounted lamps are provided, while boots and other gear can be rented if they're not included. Two-day trips may feature accommodation in Bidayuh villages.
Paredesa Borneo 1 Jalan Wayang ☎082 238801, ⓦparadesaborneo.com. A great one-day bike tour of Kuching (RM98), as well as one- and two-day kayaking, biking and trekking tours – or a combination of all three – out in the wild.
Planet Borneo 10 Lorang Park ☎082 241300, ⓦplanetborneotours.com. The Kuching branch of this established Miri adventure travel/diving specialist offers the usual longhouse stays at Batang Ai (from RM1082 for three days/two nights) and further afield, plus Mulu packages (two days/one night RM380) and a couple of off-the-beaten-track options in the north of Sarawak, as well as tours in Sabah and Brunei.
Rainforest Kayaking ☎082 240571, ⓦrainforestkayaking.com. Superb kayaking day-trips down a tributary of the Sarawak River, taking in a couple of Bidayuh villages and bizarrely shaped limestone hills. Packages start at RM188 including a riverside picnic, photo CD, and transfers; pricier trips include side visits to the Annah Rais longhouse or Semenggoh Wildlife Rehabilitation Centre.

ACCOMMODATION

There's plenty of choice when it comes to places to stay. **Guesthouses** are clustered in and south of Chinatown (especially Carpenter St); they all have pretty similar rooms and prices, and include a "simple breakfast" which invariably turns out to be toast and jam. Most **hotels** are in the commercial district to the east. To stay at or near the **beach**, consider the

Santubong Peninsula, a 30min bus ride west (see p.330). As ever, you should book ahead to stay during a major **festival** – a month ahead if you plan to be here over the weekend of June's Rainforest Music Festival (see p.332).

GUESTHOUSES AND B&BS

Berambih Lodge 26 Carpenter St ☎082 248852, ⊛berambihlodge.com. Pretty typical for the budget guesthouses along here, with small a/c rooms and dorms; its "longhouse style" lobby makes a nice place to hang out. Dorms RM20, doubles RM50

Fairview 6 Jalan Taman Budaya ☎082 240017, ⊛thefairview.com.my. This family-run guesthouse – a rare thing in Kuching – has assorted a/c, en-suite rooms. It's fraying slightly at the edges, but it's hospitable and set amid the lushest of gardens. On the downside, traffic can be noisy and Jalan Reservoir, the shortest route to Chinatown, is badly lit and eerie at night. Rates drop by a third Sept–May. RM90

Kuching Waterfront Lodge 15 Main Bazaar ☎082 231111, ⊛kuchingwaterfrontlodge.com. Atmospheric and cosy lodge housed in a refurbished shophouse done out like a Chinese mansion with floor tiles, wooden beams and a chandelier in the foyer. Rooms are less slick and occasionally a bit tatty, but all are en suite, with a/c and TV, and some even have four-poster beds. RM115

Planet Borneo Lodge 10 Lorong Park ☎082 412100, ⊛planetborneolodge.com. A 1960s luxury home, now a high-end lodge run by the eponymous tour operator. Three a/c dorms of various sizes plus two a/c en-suite family rooms, though no doubles. The best feature is the pleasant courtyard area with loungers and a paddling pool – a converted fishpond. Bike rental (RM20/day) available, worthwhile as it's a 20min walk from Chinatown. Dorms RM50, 3-bed room RM120

★**Singgahsana Lodge** 3 Lorong Temple ☎082 429277, ⊛singgahsana.com. Behind the unprepossessing orange and yellow facade is a warren of rooms, all in bright colours, with a spacious central lounge featuring rattan lamps. Impeccably run and deservedly popular. Single or mixed ten-person dorms, en-suite twins and doubles, and shared family rooms and triples. Dorms RM31, doubles RM112

Threehouse 51 Lebuh China ☎082 423499, ⊛threehousebnb.com. Run by noted Iban tattoo artist Ernesto Kalum and his Swedish partner, *Threehouse* impresses with well-maintained, cosy six-bed fan dorms and a/c doubles, decorated in bright colours in a kind of 70s-tribal fusion. Dorms RM20, doubles RM60

★**Wojia Lodge** 17 Main Bazaar ☎082 251776, ⊛wojialodge.com. The name means "my house" in Mandarin and the place does try to be homely, its spacious lounge featuring floor matting and a large sofa, and although nothing is terribly fancy (even the river view), it's very comfortable. There's an a/c dorm, plus singles and doubles, some of which are a/c. Dorms RM20, non-a/c doubles RM48, a/c doubles RM52

HOTELS

Abell 22 Jalan Tuanku Abdul Rahman ☎082 239449, ⊛abellhotel.com. Every floor is themed around a different colour at this business-oriented, modern hotel – and that would be its most exciting aspect, except that it's non-smoking throughout and they have a popular, meaty, restaurant (see p.326). Most rooms are doubles of various kinds, though there are a handful of singles. You'll pay extra for a view. RM200

Basaga Holiday Residences Jalan Tabuan, nearly 2km south of the centre ☎082 417069, ⊛basaga.com. Take one disused school built around a colonial mansion, apply a large dose of design expertise, and the result is this charming complex where you can only just tell the sleek rooms were once classrooms and dorms. Choose from rooms in the old house, or facing the swimming pool or the back garden (the latter have outdoor showers). The distance from town is a drag, but they have a convivial restaurant and bar with a central open-air dining area shaded by a great old tree. Rates include breakfast, and airport pick-up if you book directly. RM186

★**Batik Boutique Hotel** 38 Jalan Padungan ☎082 422845, ⊛batikboutiquehotel.com. Kuching's only true boutique hotel has some of the classiest and cosiest rooms in town. Though not eye-poppingly stunning, all the funkily decorated rooms boast silk bedding, an iPod dock and a terrazzo bath or overhead rain shower, and there's also a decent Western restaurant, a small lobby bar and a courtyard. Rates include breakfast, and are heavily discounted online. RM280

Grand Margherita Jalan Tuanku Abdul Rahman ☎082 423111, ⊛grandmargherita.com. Swanky top-end affair, with Cantonese restaurant, river-facing pool, spa, and shuttle services to many local attractions and the airport. It's also pretty child-friendly, with a children's pool, playground and babysitting service. Rates on Fri & Sat can fall by RM50 or so. RM215

Harbour View Lebuh Temple ☎082 274666, ⊛harbourview.com.my. Popular with locals for its location and decent rates. The recently refurbished rooms, although often smallish, are good value; the views and the wi-fi are free. Not much in the way of other facilities though. RM155

Kuching Hilton Jalan Tuanku Abdul Rahman ☎082 223888, ⊛kuching.hilton.com. As well organized as you'd expect a *Hilton* to be, with many large, newly refurbished rooms, boasting comfortable beds; those on upper floors have great views. There is also a pool (with bar), mini-gym and five restaurants, but you have to pay for in-room internet access. RM330

The Limetree Jalan Abell ☎082 414600,

@ limetreehotel.com.my. Occupying what was a failed office development, the *Limetree* boasts modern rooms with slightly minimalist decor, including some jumbo-sized executive suites, and a pleasant rooftop bar. As befits a hotel whose owners made a pile from citrus agriculture, it also features lime-based toiletries and lime-green fittings. Non-smoking throughout. Rates include breakfast. **RM178**

Telang Usan Off Jalan Ban Hock ☎082 415588, @ telangusan.com. Now in its fourth decade, this pioneering hotel is Kayan-owned, hence the swirly Orang Ulu motifs in its decor. The rooms are recently renovated and comfortable enough; on the downside, reaching the waterfront requires you to head south to Jalan Ban Hock and double back. Rates include breakfast. **RM130**

EATING AND DRINKING

Kuching's lively and dynamic **eating** scene offers opportunities to sample indigenous dishes as well as international cuisine. Popular **local dishes** include *manok pansoh* (or *ayam pansoh*), a Bidayuh/Iban dish of chicken and tapioca leaves stewed in bamboo tubes; *umai*, Sarawak's answer to sashimi, raw fish or prawn shreds mixed with chilli and lime juice; *ambal*, delicious rubbery little clams, usually curried; and, as greens, the ubiquitous fern tops *paku* and *midin*. And of course Sarawak has its own variants of common Malaysian dishes, notably *laksa* – the Sarawakian variety uses rice vermicelli and is usually served in the morning – and *kuay teow*, often prepared in a tangy tomato gravy (outside the state people add a little vinegar to get the same sourness). Many top-end restaurants close for several days over the **gawai festival**, when staff return to their "hometown" longhouses or jungle villages.

HAWKERS, FOOD COURTS AND KEDAI KOPIS

Bismillah Café Jalan Khoo Hung Yeang ☎082 415803. This little Malay place does a good range of rice and noodle dishes, plus *roti* and curries, at mostly RM4–5 – just the place to fill up before catching a bus. Daily 7am–4pm.

Carpenter Street stalls Opposite Siang Ti temple. A tiny, venerable clutch of stalls selling Sarawak *laksa* (from RM6) plus other popular favourites such as chicken rice and *kuey chap* (pork and pig offal in broth). As ever stalls keep their own time; don't expect to find *laksa* in the afternoon. Open early until late – one is 24hr.

★**Top Spot Food Court** Jalan Padungan. Forget the unpromising location – atop a blue multistorey car park topped with a giant plastic prawn – this is a great place, featuring a dozen large stalls focusing on seafood. Sit near a stall you like the look of, and they'll present you with their menu; try *ambal*, or crab and prawns done with garlic or chilli, or *oh jian* – the Sarawak version of this oyster omelette is like an enormous bowl-shaped crêpe. No pork served. Not super-pricey – one seafood dish plus veg and other things to share should cost RM30/head, excluding alcohol. Generally 5–11pm.

CAFÉS

Bing! 84 Jalan Padungan ☎082 421880, @ bingcoffee .com. Kuching's plushest, slickest independent café chain, with a stylish a/c interior and prices to match – you'll pay at least RM16 for coffee and, say, a brownie. Serves Illy coffee, has a smoking room, and free wi-fi. Mon–Thurs 10am–midnight & Fri–Sun 10am–1am.

Black Bean Coffee 87 Carpenter St ☎082 420290. This tiny café and shop serves locally grown coffee from the Bau area and parts of Indonesia, made using *robusta* and the little-known *liberica* beans – certainly worth a try, though some people find it sourish or even "burnt". A takeaway cappuccino blended from both types of bean costs around RM5. Daily except Sun 9am–6pm.

Magna Carta Old Courthouse complex. It's a little touristy, the service can be lackadaisical and the food and drink merely so-so – but the airiness of the building, the antique fittings, the location and faintly colonial ambience largely compensate. Quench your thirst with coffees and teas (from RM7), smoothies (RM12), plus a limited range of alcoholic drinks, including *tuak*. Also light meals such as pasta and burgers (around RM15–20). Free wi-fi. Tues–Sun 7am–11pm.

RESTAURANTS

★**Aroma Café** Jalan Tabuan ☎082 417163. This simple Bidayuh-run restaurant, on the ground floor of a dreary commercial block, is a fine place to sample tribal dishes such as *umai*, *ayam pansoh* and *midin* with garlic. Best value is the popular lunchtime *campur*-style spread (Mon–Fri 11.30am–1.30pm; RM5–7), but going à la carte is unlikely to cost more than RM15/person with soft drinks. Daily 7am–11pm.

Attap Corner 21 Carpenter St ☎016 893 0044. Smack in the middle of Chinatown, this homely restaurant serves Malay, Chinese, Thai and Western food to a mixed clientele of backpackers and locals, who can dine overlooking the street. Most dishes, such as *mee mamak* with curry are RM6–10, though Western options, say fish'n'chips, can cost as much as RM15. Daily 8am–3.30pm.

Bla Bla Bla... 27 Jalan Tabuan ☎082 233944. Designer touches such as oriental water features set the tone at this fusion restaurant where you can savour Chinese-style renditions of un-Chinese ingredients such as salmon and lamb, and round off your meal with cheesecake (RM10). Their speciality is a tangy *midin* salad (RM18), but many main courses will set you back double that. Daily except Tues 6–11.30pm.

★**Bombay Spices** Lot 62, Lorang 4, Jalan Nanas ☎016

6

856 3142. One of the best curry houses in town, serving excellent and authentic North Indian food. It's a little difficult to find unless you take a taxi – it's about 2km out from the centre just off Jalan Tun Ahmad Zaidi Adruce. The tandoori items are the speciality (including a fine chicken *tikka masala*), with great *nan* bread, and you can sit inside the a/c interior or outside if you want to smoke. Veg mains RM6–15, non-veg RM10–16. Daily 10am–10pm.

The Carvery Abell Hotel, 22 Jalan Tuanku Abdul Rahman ☎082 239449, ⊛abellhotel.com. Much of the hotel's ground floor is taken up by this busy Brazilian-style *churrasco* restaurant. Indulge in a protein-heavy buffet of nine (lunch; RM48) or fourteen (dinner; RM75) grilled meats and steaks, plus salads and desserts, or simply order a steak – it'll be much cheaper and they'll cook it how you like it (the buffet is mostly medium to well done). Daily 11.30am–2pm & 6.30–10.30pm.

★**the.Dyak** GF, Panovel Commercial Complex, Jalan Simpang Tiga, almost 3km south of the centre ☎082 234068. Tribal food (and decor) meets haute cuisine at this popular high-class Dayak restaurant that serves jungle foods such as *jani tunu* (chargrilled pork longhouse style) – they also cater for vegetarians and vegans with the tasty *ubi randau* (a type of fern) among others. Dishes are impeccably presented and you can eat either in the stylish a/c interior or outside. Vegetable mains are RM10–14, meat dishes RM20–25. They also serve Tuak Laki Stambak Ulu (RM80/bottle), the best *tuak* you're likely to encounter, which compares well with quality European-style wines, and made to a traditional family recipe. Daily noon–8.30pm.

Hornbill's Corner Café Close to the Telang Usan hotel, off Jalan Ban Hock, ☎016 856 5495. Among the best-known places in town for steamboat – for RM18/head you get unlimited helpings from their spread of seafood, meat and other morsels, to be cooked by yourself at the outdoor tables. Daily 5–11.30pm.

★**Jambu** 32 Jalan Crookshank ☎082 235292, ⊛jamburestaurant.com. Housed in a sumptuously refurbished colonial house, a 30min walk from the centre, *Jambu* combines Western and Malaysian and much else into "modern Borneo cuisine". Quite expensive – main courses come in at RM24–40, though cheaper tapas, pasta and sizzling meat plates are available, along with to-die-for desserts like Moroccan date tart. Tues–Sun 6–11pm.

James Brooke Bistro and Café Waterfront, near the Hilton. It's very touristy, but this open-sided, greenery-surrounded building offers nice views, even if the food – a mixture of Western and local standards such as Sarawak *laksa* (RM10) – is nothing special and the prices on the high side (mains from RM20). Unusually for this class of

restaurant, they don't take plastic. Daily 10.30am–11pm.

Junk 80 Jalan Wayang ☎082 259450. Part of the labyrinthine *Backstage Bar* (see opposite) this place has the same higgledy-piggeldy junk-store look, serving hearty and good-quality plates of Western cuisine, such as lamb shank, steak, fish'n'chips and other standards. Mains RM30–68. Daily except Tues 6–11pm.

Little Lebanon Under the arches at the Old Courthouse complex (Jalan India end) ☎082 233523. The food can be ersatz, just like their Tutankhamun face-mask replica, but they do offer a good range of Levantine dishes, such as falafel sandwiches (RM12), hummus (RM7.50), and chicken or lamb kebabs (RM16). There are also lots of shisha tobaccos to savour (RM14.50), and you can eat in an a/c dining room or (like the local youths) lounge on divans outdoors. Mon–Fri 4pm–midnight, Sat & Sun 9am–midnight.

Lyn's Thandoori Jalan Song Thian Cheok ☎082 234934. This fairly central restaurant offers largely North Indian food with a few South Indian items thrown in for good measure. Tandoori chicken is the speciality (RM17). Otherwise, there's a wide choice of curries (RM10–20) and *biriyanis* (from RM8) and, in the morning, *roti* and noodles. Daily 10am–10pm.

★**My Village Baruk** Kampung Boyan, down the lane from the jetty and then to the right ☎082 448970. Here's that rare thing, an excellent Malay restaurant in interesting surroundings – a two-storey wooden building decorated with drapes and lanterns and meant to recall a *baruk*, or Bidayuh roundhouse. *Nasi ayam penyet* – chicken tenderized by pummelling and then grilled – is the speciality, but they also grill mussels and fish, plus (off-menu) *ayam pansoh*, emptied gloopily from bamboo tubes, and *nasi goreng dabai*, rice fried with the locally grown olive-like *dabai* fruit, when available. Most dishes around RM10. Service can be slow at busy times. Daily 4.30pm–midnight or so.

Ristorante Beccari Merdeka Palace Hotel, Jalan Tun Abang Haji Openg ☎082 258000, ⊛merdekapalace .com. Smart and convivial, and one of the few places in east Malaysia where you can get a decent thin-crust pizza straight from the wood oven, as well as excellent risotto and pasta – though don't imagine you'll pay anything less than RM40 for a meal here. There's a lunchtime salad bar, too. Daily noon–10.30pm.

Zhun San Yen Jalan Chan Chin Ann, ☎016 898 8367. The best of a handful of Chinese vegetarian places in the area, a cafeteria-like place where you can choose from a spread of two dozen stir-fries and soups (noodles dominate at breakfast). A meal with soft drinks seldom comes to more than RM10. Mon–Fri 8am–6pm, Sat 9am–3pm.

DRINKING AND ENTERTAINMENT

Kuching's **drinking** scene is pretty good in a low-key kind of way. Venues are intimate for the most part, and the locals are very approachable. For a city with a sizeable middle class, the **entertainment** on offer is surprisingly meagre, however.

The Rainforest Music Festival is the highlight of the cultural year (see box, p.332), but otherwise a lack of performance venues means there's not that much on apart from the occasional *wayang* (Chinese opera) on or close to Carpenter St during Chinese festivals, and some free events involving local performers on a riverside stage by the Square Tower, again at festival time.

BARS

Jambu 32 Jalan Crookshank ☎082 235292, ⓦjamburestaurant.com. If you don't come here to dine, it's worth making the trek out from the centre to enjoy the lovely garden bar and terrace. There's a good house red wine plus Strongbow cider, *tuak* and even a *tuak mojito* – and fabulous tapas to go with them. Tues–Sun 6pm–late.

Junk/Backstage Bar 80 Jalan Wayang. The tiny *Junk* bar feels like an extension of the restaurant (see opposite), whereas *Backstage* has its own look, festooned with Chinese lanterns. Both draw in a suave clientele. There's draught Heineken and Hoegaarden, among other beers. Sun–Fri 6pm–midnight, Sat 6pm–2am.

★**Ruai** Off Jalan Ban Hock. A simple but excellent Iban- and Pakistani-run community chill-out joint featuring tribal decor, with occasional Iban, Bidayuh and Orang Ulu sounds

(with a couple of live music sessions a month at weekends) and home-made *tuak* – not just regular rice wine (RM25/ bottle) but also varieties they've concocted from fruits such as apple or dragon fruit (RM5 more). For the adventurous, there's also *langkan*, a surprisingly smooth yet potent scorpion liquor. A couple of BBQ stalls out back cater to the hungry. Happy hour 4–10pm. Daily 4pm–2am.

Utopia Around the corner from the Abell Hotel, Tuanku Abdul Rahman ☎082 410588. The best of Kuching's two dance-bars (and less likely to host violent fights), this fun place plays loud dance music throughout the night, occasionally interrupted by the entertaining house band, who do 30min sets of standards. It's a good, friendly crowd and one of the few LGTB-friendly bars in town – you can even play spot-the-ladyboy-waitresses if you so wish. Daily 4pm–midnight (or at least 2am at weekends).

SHOPPING

Although Kuching offers the best **shopping** in Sarawak, that's not always obvious from a stroll around downtown, which remains refreshingly devoid of huge modern malls. There are certainly more souvenir shops than anywhere else in Sarawak; outlets along Main Bazaar sell tribal textiles, pottery, rattan mats, locally grown pepper and so forth. As ever, however, their handicrafts may well have been made abroad – especially in Indonesian Kalimantan. The listings here concentrate on places selling domestically made items; the Sarawak Craft Council is the obvious place to start. If you're heading out to longhouses, you may prefer to defer buying crafts until you get there, though what you'll be offered will probably vary considerably in quality.

ARTS AND CRAFTS

Artrageously Ramsay Ong 94 Main Bazaar ☎082 244346. This unusual shop sells paintings by two artists – Ramsey Ong himself, whose work tends to be abstract, and more naturalist art by Narong Duan. Also their craftwork – necklaces, cat statuettes, even phenomenally expensive beaded dresses. Mon–Sat 9.30am–6.30pm, Sun 9.30am–5.30pm.

Ngee Tai Pottery Factory 5th mile, Jalan Penrissen (the airport road) ☎082 576020. Kuching has a cottage industry producing Chinese ceramics with tribal influences, and this is probably the best of the potteries. Watch the potters in action at the wheel and firing kilns, and buy wares ranging from huge pots to coffee mugs or vases. Take Rapid Kuching bus #3a or #6, or STC bus #K3 or #K6. Daily 8am–6pm.

Sarakraf 78 Jalan Tabuan ☎082 232771. Locally produced high-quality (and pricey) crafts, near Sarawak Plaza, with a decent stock of baskets, woodcarvings, ceramics and other items, some made to their own designs. Mon–Sat 8am–5pm.

Sarawak Craft Council Round Tower, Jalan Tun Abang Haji Openg. The Craft Council's (see p.318) shop showcases

some of the best crafts made in the state, labelled by area of origin. Here you'll find beaded necklaces, hats made from breadfruit-tree bark and bags woven from *bemban* reeds, all costing several tens of ringgit, and the sun hats of the Orang Ulu, shaped like giant mushroom caps and sold for several hundred ringgit. Mon–Fri 8.30am–1pm & 2–4.30pm.

CAMPING GEAR

Greek's Outgear Discovery Second floor, Sarawak Plaza, Jalan Tuanku Abdul Rahman ☎082 235205. This oddly named store sells a range of high-end rucksacks, waterproofs, tents and so forth. Daily 10.30am–9pm.

MALLS AND SUPERMARKETS

Plaza Merdika 88 Jalan Tun Haji Openg ⓦplazamerdeka.com. The biggest and best of the downtown malls, with a good range of foreign and domestic shops and food outlets, including a Parkson, a decent supermarket, and pharmacies. Daily 10am–10pm.

Spring Mall 3km south of the centre, Jalan Simpang Tiga ⓦthespring.com.my. Kuching's biggest, busiest mall holds a Parkson department store, a supermarket and

6

6

IBAN TATTOOS

For the Iban, **tattooing** is not just a form of ornamentation, but also an indication of personal wealth and other achievements. Many designs are used, from a simple circular outline for the shoulder, chest or outer side of the wrists, to more elaborate motifs (highly stylized dogs, scorpions or crabs) for the inner and outer thigh. The two most important places for tattoos are the hand and the throat. The tattooing process starts with a carved design on a block of wood that's smeared with ink and pressed to the skin; the resulting outline is then punctured with needles dipped in dark ink, made from sugar-cane juice, water and soot. For the actual tattooing a hammer-like instrument with two or three needles protruding from its head is used. These are dipped in ink and the hammer is then placed against the skin and tapped repeatedly with a wooden block.

Kuching has become a magnet for people wanting to have a Bornean tattoo, and guesthouses may be able to introduce you to practitioners. The leading light of the scene, however, is the Iban artist and musician Ernesto Kalum, whose studio, **Borneo Headhunter**, is upstairs at 47 Jalan Wayang (best to make appointments two weeks in advance; ☎082 237062, ⓦborneoheadhunter.com). He offers traditional motifs done either the traditional way or by machine (as in any Western tattoo parlour), and can also do modern designs (always by machine). Prices depend on size and complexity.

---

outlets selling electronic gadgets, clothes, household items and so forth. Buses #K8 and #K11 come here from the centre. Daily 10am–10pm.

DIRECTORY

Banks and exchange There are numerous banks with ATMs downtown, especially in the commercial area east of Chinatown, and you'll also find moneychangers in a few malls, such as Mohamad Yahia & Sons, the bookshop in the basement of the Sarawak Plaza.

Consulates Australia, 5th Floor, Wisma Bukit Mata Kuching, Jalan Tuanku Abdul Rahman (☎082 233350); Indonesia, 21 Lot 16557, Block 11, Jalan Sutong (☎082 241734); UK, The English Language Centre, Fortune Land Business Centre, 2½ Miles, Jalan Rock Rd (☎082 250950).

Cookery classes At the Bumbu cookery class, 57 Carpenter St (9am–1pm & 2.30–6.30pm; ☎019 879 1050, ⓔbumbucookingclass@hotmail.com), you'll learn how to cook a four-course indigenous meal of local dishes – meat, veg, dessert and cut fruit– and you get to eat the results afterwards (minimum class size is two; RM120, RM150 if you add a market tour-cum-shopping trip; book at least 24hr ahead).

Hospitals The main state-run hospital is the Sarawak General Hospital, 2km south of the centre off Jalan Tun Abang Haji Openg (☎082 276666). You can also try the

Ting & Ting Jalan Tabuan. This well-established supermarket is a convenient place to buy cheese and pork products. Mon–Sat 9am–9pm.

private clinics at the Timberland Medical Centre at the southern end of Jalan Rock (☎082 234466, ⓦtimberlandmedical.com).

Internet All guesthouses and many cafés offer free wi-fi; there are no downtown internet cafés.

Laundry My Express, at the eastern end of Carpenter St at 11 Jalan Wayang (wash RM5–7, dry RM5; 24hr).

Massage The Batu Lintang Blind Centre behind the wedding shop on Jalan Batu Lintang offers excellent massage from blind people at very reasonable prices (RM25 for 1hr; 10am–7pm).

Pharmacy All of the shopping centres have either a Watsons, a Guardian, or both.

Police Jalan Khoo Hun Yeang, opposite the Padang Merdeka (☎082 241222).

Post office The main post office is on Jalan Tun Haji Openg (Mon–Sat 8am–6pm, Sun 10am–1pm).

Visa extensions Immigration Office, first floor, Bangunan Sultan Iskandar, Jalan Simpang Tiga (Mon–Fri 8am–noon & 2–4.30pm; ☎082 245661). Get there by 3pm to have your application processed on the day.

Around Kuching

One joy of visiting Kuching is the sheer number of potential excursions within the vicinity, including several worthy of an overnight stay. Within an hour's bus ride north are the beaches and resorts of the **Santubong Peninsula**, also known as **Damai** after the beach area at its tip. Nearby is the **Sarawak Cultural Village**, a showpiece community where model

OPPOSITE BAKO NATIONAL PARK (P.332) >

longhouses are staffed by guides from each ethnic group. **Bako** is the essential national park to visit nearby, but there's also decent trekking at **Kubah National Park**.

South of Kuching, the main attractions are the orang-utans at the **Semenggoh Wildlife Rehabilitation Centre** and the Bidayuh longhouse at **Annah Rais**. Sarawak's remote western edge draws a trickle of visitors who mainly head to the **Gunung Gading National Park** to see *Rafflesia* blooms, though the beaches at **Sematan** and near **Lundu**, and the stunning **Tanjung Datu National Park**, further west, are also worthwhile.

Unless otherwise stated, all **buses** mentioned below are local services leaving from the area east of Kuching mosque.

Santubong Peninsula

Cut off from Kuching by the Santubong River to the south, the **Santubong Peninsula** has been inhabited since prehistoric times. Excavation in the 1960s and 1970s found tens of thousands of artefacts, including digging implements, across six neighbouring sites; they dated back to 3000 BC, when the Indian/Javanese Empire extended here, though little of any ancient civilization can be seen today.

Dominated by the 810m **Gunung Santubong**, the area is dotted with oddly shaped geological formations amid patches of thick forest. The mountain is actually a **national park** (though there are no facilities and no entrance fee to pay) and makes for a moderately taxing trek. It takes around four hours to reach the summit, with rope ladders to help where things get steep; one trail up is clearly signed next to the *Green Paradise Café* on the main road. However, most visitors prefer to venture out to the **beaches** of **Damai**, 35km from Kuching at the Peninsula's northwest tip, or the excellent if pricey folk museum nearby, the **Sarawak Cultural Village**. Since the 1980s, stretches of the river and coastline have been developed as retreats for tourists and city-weary locals, though thankfully the resorts have left the tranquil, almost lonesome, nature of the area largely undisturbed. There are also two low-key villages, **Buntal** and **Kampung Santubong**.

Buntal

Around 25km from Kuching, you come to the narrow strip of land that connects Santubong Peninsula to the mainland and the low-key village of **BUNTAL**. A quiet riverside kampung, it's rated by locals for its **seafood**; there are several inexpensive, ramshackle seafood restaurants on the seafront just east of the bus stop.

Sarawak Cultural Village

33km north of Kuching • Daily 9am–5pm (cultural shows 11.30am & 4pm) • RM60, day-tours from Kuching around RM110 • ☎ 082 846411, ⓦ scv.com.my

After crossing onto the peninsula from Buntal, the main road continues west and then north past several resorts, ending at the modern leisure development of Damai Central.

SPOTTING SANTUBONG WILDLIFE

The mouth of the Santubong River is a promising spot to see the rare **Irrawaddy dolphin**. With a rounded snout rather than a beak, these marine mammals live in brackish coastal waters and river deltas, as well as in fresh water further upriver – for example, along the Mekong in Indochina, where the population is dwindling. In fact the dolphin is considered vulnerable in many habitats due to human activity – they may get snared in nets or see their range whittled away by barrages, for example.

Several tour operators can take you on dolphin-spotting cruises, though the specialist is **CPH Travel** (see p.323), which has its own launch; their trips leave in the late afternoon, taking you along the Santubong River in search of proboscis monkeys and fireflies as well as dolphins (3hr 30min; RM160). The odds of spotting dolphins aren't great during the rainy season if seas are rough; the rest of the time you have a fair chance of seeing them though not necessarily close up.

Not far from the end, the **Sarawak Cultural Village** features seven authentically styled, if rather too perfect, tribal dwellings of timber and thatch, close to a central lake, with the jungle escarpment of Gunung Santubong looming dramatically behind. As folk museums go, it's worth the steep price of admission and doesn't feel forced; in fact, many of the staff you see kitted out in traditional finery live on site, and the place has become a community in itself.

Arguably the most impressive dwelling is the massive **Orang Ulu longhouse**, raised almost impossibly high off the ground, though the Melanau "tall house" also grabs the eye, with windows on two levels. You'll also see Iban and Bidayuh longhouses, a refreshingly simple Penan lean-to shelter, and – mundane by comparison – a Chinese kampung house and a formal Malay house in a style that only someone of status could have afforded to build.

Despite being out of context, the twice-daily 45-minute cultural shows are worth catching, striking the right balance between entertainment and education, and demonstrations of activities such as weaving, sago-processing and blowpipe-making are staged throughout the day.

Damai beach

While the pleasant stretches of beige sand at Damai have individual names, such as Teluk Bandung and Teluk Penyuk, most people simply refer to the area as **Damai beach**. The beaches don't belong to the resorts, though resort staff may levy a small fee if you try to access them via their compounds. One way to avoid this is to head to **Damai Central**, the new shopping development opposite the Cultural Village, from where a path leads down to the beach. It's also possible to arrange activities in the area, such as trekking in the nearby **Kuching Wetland National Park** (which also has a birdwatching tower) or kayaking along the coast – you can arrange these at the *Permai Rainforest Resort* (see below) or the Damai Central Recreation Centre (☏012894 6436); the latter also rents bikes (RM15/hr) and has a **campsite** (RM15/person).

ARRIVAL AND DEPARTURE   SANTUBONG PENINSULA

Transport from Kuching Private shuttles leave from the *Grand Margherita* hotel for Damai and the Cultural Village (every 1–2hr; RM50 return), and some Kuching guesthouses can arrange transport for the same price.

Otherwise, unreliable minibuses (RM10) leave when full from opposite the food stalls near the Mosque bus station, while a taxi should cost RM100 one way.

ACCOMMODATION

★ Damai Beach Resort Teluk Bandung beach, Damai, 1km north of Damai Central ☏082 846200, ⓦdamaibeachresort.com. The rooms are mostly modern and not all that special, but the lovely freeform pool set back from the beach sets the tone beautifully at this huge complex, all the more homely for being one of the area's oldest resorts. Rooms near the reception and in the blocks stacked up on the lush hillside behind are cheaper, though you might feel like splashing out on a *baruk* suite, built to look like a Bidayuh roundhouse with a conical roof. There's also a spa plus a couple of restaurants and a bar, and staff can organize guided jungle walks (RM5) and other activities. Rates include breakfast. Rooms RM277, suites RM572

Damai Puri Resort Teluk Penyuk beach, Damai ☏082 846900, ⓦdamaipuriresort-kuching.com. Secluded at the end of the road, this newish place has a nice beach, along with a pool, gym and tennis courts, but can be

overpriced unless you're there off-season (below half price) or find a good deal online. Rates include breakfast. RM791

Nanga Damai 2km from Santubong village, right of the road as you head north ☏019 887 1017, ⓦnangadamai.com. Not a longhouse, as *nanga* might suggest, but a swish six-room B&B in a substantial, beautifully decorated modern house. Good value, with rates including breakfast. Note that they have a two-night stay minimum and no under-14s. RM110

Permai Rainforest Resort Cross the car park by the Damai Puri Resort's front gate (at Teluk Penyuk beach, Damai), then follow a boardwalk into the forest ☏082 846487, ⓦpermairainforest.com. You could come to this slightly hard-to-find place to laze by the beach, but the emphasis is on being active – they offer kayaking, Santubong climbs and even an obstacle course. Guests stay in individual en-suite timber units, mostly sleeping up to six and good value if you're in a group of three or more, and

6

they also have a small campsite. Only the two-person treehouse and some of the so-called cabins have a/c. Rates include breakfast but activities cost extra. Rates drop slightly midweek. Cabins RM340, treehouses RM330, camping per person RM10

★ **The Village House** Kampung Santubong, 30m down the track to the beach from Santubong crossroads ☎ 082 846166, ⓦvillagehouse.com.my. Owned by the same people as as Kuching's *Singgahsana Lodge* (see p.324), this gorgeous timber-built development features en-suite rooms set around a long, narrow swimming pool. Many have four-poster beds, but otherwise the decor is elegant without being over the top. They also have two of the slickest six-bed dorms you'll ever see, each with its own bathroom. The restaurant serves Western, local and fusion food. No under-12s. Rates include breakfast. Dorms RM88, doubles RM278

EATING AND NIGHTLIFE

If you don't want to eat where you're staying, your best bet is one of Buntal's celebrated, rustic **seafood restaurants**; your accommodation may be able to arrange transport. Stalls at Damai Central's food court are nothing out of the ordinary.

Escobar Bar and Grill Damai Central ☎ 082 846039. This place by the beach offers Western bar food such as burgers and meat/fish with chips, (not so good) pasta, and a few Indian and Malay dishes. Mains from RM20. It's a great place to watch the sunset, especially with a glass of their *tuak*. Daily 11am–11pm.

Bako National Park

East of the Santubong Peninsula, and no further away from Kuching, a second peninsula is occupied by the fabulous **BAKO NATIONAL PARK**, named for its location at the mouth of the Bako River. Sarawak's oldest national park (once a timber reserve, it attained its current, fully protected status in 1957), it's also among its most memorable. Its steep coastal cliffs, offering huge vistas over the South China Sea, are thrillingly different from the rest of the predominantly flat and muddy Sarawak coastline, and there are opportunities to spot proboscis monkeys, swim in jungle streams or at isolated sandy coves, and hike through terrain that takes in rainforest, mangrove and *kerangas* (see opposite), with pitcher plants easily visible on some trails.

Bako is such a gem that trying to pack it all into one day is not ideal, though you can make a go of it if you set out early from Kuching and pay a boatman at the park to take you out to a remote beach, then walk back to the park headquarters; this gives you a good taste of the park without having to do a trek in both directions. A stay of at least one night is still preferable, though, and there's a range of accommodation to choose from.

Note that the entire eastern side of the park (east of the Tajor Waterfall) is **closed for path renovation** until at least 2016.

Inside the park

First impressions of Bako, the coastal forest and craggy outcrops you see as you head here by boat, don't begin to do justice to its riches. The park boasts a multitude of different types of **vegetation**, including peat bog, scrub and mangrove; most trails run through a mixture of primary dipterocarp forest and *kerangas*, an Iban term referring to soil too poor to support rice, and now used to mean a type of woodland on poor soil characterized by fairly sparse, small trees and scrub, plus insect-eating plants such as pitcher plants. The *kerangas* stems from the unusual, largely infertile **sandstone** geology of the peninsula, eroded down to produce striking honeycomb weathering on some trails, and contorted rock arches rising from the sea. As for fauna, **proboscis monkeys** (see p.451) are top of most visitors' lists; there's a good chance of seeing them not far from the park headquarters itself, though silverleaf monkeys tend to be harder to spot. Less exotically, monitor lizards and assorted snakes are sometimes seen, along with bearded pigs (a group have even made themselves at home close to the park cafeteria) and the usual assortment of creepy-crawlies, best spotted on a guided night walk.

No special equipment is needed, but pay particular attention to **sun protection** – it's amazing how you can be walking through a jungle glade one minute and in baking hot *kerangas* the next.

The trails

A free map from the park headquarters shows the **trails**, colour-coded and waymarked with splashes of paint on trees and rocks. Park staff can advise on what you can expect to complete in the time you have available, or whether to take a boat ride as a short cut (see p.335).

Most trails start from a spot north of the park headquarters, back towards the jetty and reached by a series of boardwalks through mangrove. You then ascend through steepish jungle, with the option of branching off left early on to **Teluk Paku**, a small, not particularly attractive cove where proboscis monkeys are often seen. Most people carry on, to reach the **Padang** about 45 minutes from the start – here not a grassy colonial town square, but a rocky plateau of *kerangas* that's another hangout for proboscis monkeys.

At the Padang you're on the park's most popular trail, the looping **Lintang** trail that leads alternately through jungled slopes and *kerangas* via occasional stretches of boardwalk, and returns to the park headquarters from the south. Taking around four hours to complete if you don't pause frequently to rest or take photos, it can get monotonous after a while.

You may find it more interesting to branch off the Lintang trail at a clearly marked point only a few minutes' walk along the Padang. This two-hour side trail heads east to the **Tajor Waterfall**; a couple of low cascades in a jungled stream, the waterfall itself is no great shakes, but the pool just down from it is good for a swim. From here you can

---

VISITING SARAWAK'S NATIONAL PARKS

Sarawak's two dozen or so **national parks** vary enormously, not just in terms of terrain and habitats – some boast accommodation for various budgets, well-marked trails and other amenities, while many others have nothing more than a ranger post and require a minor expedition to reach. All are managed by the state-owned **Sarawak Forestry Corporation** (W sarawakforestry.com) with the notable exception of Mulu, where tourist facilities have been privatized. You can pick up information about park conditions and accommodation at Sarawak Forestry's downtown offices in Kuching (see p.323) and Miri (see p.358). Informal accommodation bookings can be made by calling the park concerned, while the Kuching office can confirm reservations – with payment up front. Almost all have well-organized **campsites** (RM5/person), usually covered, with bathrooms and cooking facilities, as well as a basic canteen nearby.

Guides can be engaged at just a few parks for around RM80–100/day, though they may well not speak good English. Many, but not all, know about the local wildlife. Knowledgeable, licensed guides for parks in the Kuching area can be contacted through the Tourist Guide Association (see p.323).

6

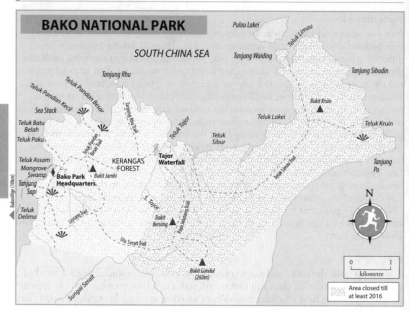

BAKO NATIONAL PARK

SOUTH CHINA SEA

Pulau Lakei

Teluk Limau

Tanjung Waiding

Tanjung Sibudin

Tanjung Rhu

Teluk Pandan Besar

Teluk Pandan Kecil

Bukit Kruin

Sea Stack

Teluk Batu Belah

Teluk Lakei

Teluk Kruin

Teluk Paku

Teluk Tajor

Teluk Sibur

Teluk Assam

Mangrove Swamp

KERANGAS FOREST

Tajor Waterfall

Tanjung Po

Bako Park Headquarters

Bukit Jambi

Tanjung Sapi

Teluk Delima

Lintang Trail

Bukit Keruing

Paya Jelutong Trail

Teluk Limau Trail

S. Tajor

Ulu Serait trail

Bukit Gondol (260m)

Sungai Serait

Bakoville (10km)

Tanjung Rhu Trail

Teluk Padan Rock Trail

N

0   1
kilometre

Area closed till at least 2016

return to the headquarters the way you came, or continue east and south along a much bigger loop, the **Ulu Serait trail**, and returning along the southern part of the Lintang trail; allow at least six hours to do this.

Even more worthwhile may be to branch off the Tajor trail at another signed side trail, less than a quarter of the way towards the falls, which leads north towards two beautiful **beaches**, Teluk Pandan Kecil and Teluk Pandan Besar. Curiously, semi-dry stream beds seem to serve as the trail in some sections, eventually bringing you to viewpoints with superb views of the beaches and the South China Sea. The Pandan Kecil viewpoint also features bizarre hexagonal sandstone formations in the ground, where iron-rich rock has eroded less than the surrounding material. The steep descent to Pandan Kecil (15min) is rewarded with a swim at a secluded cove with whitish sand; unfortunately no path leads down to Pandan Besar.

Other possible treks include heading to the remote Teluk Limau or Teluk Kruin beaches at the park's eastern end, taking at least eight hours (you'll probably want to travel one way by boat), or hikes off the main trails up to hills such as Bukit Gondol (260m) for great views.

ARRIVAL AND DEPARTURE

BAKO NATIONAL PARK

By bus Reaching the park from Kuching is straightforward: Rapid Kuching's red bus #1 heads east to Bako village roughly hourly from Jalan Khoo Hun Yeang, close to the Kuching mosque (1hr). It stops en route at the Old Courthouse complex and along Jalan Tuanku Abdul Rahman, though given the lack of signage at bus stops, be sure to ask other commuters if the

bus will call where you hope to flag it down. The bus stops at the Bako boat terminal for onward travel to the park.

By boat At the Bako boat terminal you can buy your park permit (see opposite), register, and board a park-bound boat (25min; RM20). They leave when full, from early morning until dark.

INFORMATION

Park HQ Just a few minutes' walk from the jetty, where you can pick up a simple park map, hire a green-jacketed official guide (RM80/day for up to eight people) or book to go on a

guided night walk (at 8pm; 1hr 30min; RM20), which takes you south along the Lintang trail to spot insects, spiders and, with luck, nocturnal mammals and birds.

Information Centre Close to the Park HQ, the excellent information centre holds displays on the park's geology and history, and plenty of photographs to help you get a handle on the plants and animals you may see on the trails.

Admission Park permits, which you buy from the Bako boat terminal, cost RM20; a day-tour from Kuching (including admission) costs around RM260.

Contact details ☎ 017 807 0150, ⓦ sarawakforestry.com.

GETTING AROUND

By boat Saving time by using a boat to reach one of Bako's beaches is well worth considering; park staff can give an idea of the going rate, though you'll still have to negotiate with the boatmen at the jetty once you've signed in at the headquarters. The longest journey possible, out to Teluk Kruin (closed until 2016), costs around RM250 one way for a group of five, but you're more likely to make the short hop to a popular beach such as Teluk Paku (around RM20) or Teluk Pandan Kecil (around RM40); prices are per person and boats leave when full.

ACCOMMODATION AND EATING

Bako National Park accommodation ☎ 082 478011, ⓦ sarawakforestry.com. The park's accommodations include a campsite; a slightly scruffy hostel with four-bed dorms; forest lodges, also a little worn, where the three-bedded rooms share facilities; and en-suite doubles. Best are the gleaming new chalets, with two bedrooms that sleep up to seven. Camping RM5, dorms RM16, lodge rooms RM106, en-suite doubles RM53, chalets RM238

Park cafeteria Near the park HQ. This self-service cafeteria is the only place to eat in the park; it's much cheaper to buy provisions in town before you arrive. It does *nasi campur* and a limited range of other dishes and breakfasts at inflated prices (RM15–20 for a main meal), plus bottled water and snacks. The outdoor tables are targeted by intrepid macaques, who snatch food and drink at lightning speed. Daily 7.30am–10pm.

Kubah National Park

Some 20km west of Kuching, **KUBAH NATIONAL PARK** is a rainforest reserve considered one of the world's richest sites for **palm** species: of the 95 types found, including coconut, sago and many rattans, eighteen are endemic to the region.

Three modest peaks, **Selang**, **Sendok** and **Serapi**, emerge out of the lush forest; they're crisscrossed by trails, waterfalls and streams. Marked hikes include the three-hour **Ulu Raya Trail**, a good walk to catch sight of the palms, and the **Waterfall Trail**, a ninety-minute uphill hike to impressive, split-level falls. Kubah's best views, however, come on the three-hour **Gunung Serapi (Summit) Trail** – from the top of the peak, you can take in Kuching and much of southwestern Sarawak.

ARRIVAL AND INFORMATION   KUBAH NATIONAL PARK

By bus City Public Link bus #21 runs to Kubah from Kuching (every 3hr – check timetable with the tourist office; 30min).

Contact details ☎ 082 845033, ⓦ sarawakforestry.com.

ACCOMMODATION AND EATING

Kubah National Park accommodation ☎ 082 845033 (often doesn't work due to the cable being stolen), ⓦ sarawakforestry.com. The park offers accommodation in either a hostel or a two-bedroom lodge. There's no canteen, or anywhere to eat nearby, but guests cook their own supplies. Dorms RM15, standard lodge RM150, en-suite lodge RM225

Semenggoh Wildlife Rehabilitation Centre

Off Sarawak's main trunk road, 25km south of Kuching • Feeding times daily 9am & 3pm • RM3; a day-tour from Kuching costs around RM70 • ☎ 082 442180 • City Public Link bus #K6 and Sarawak Transport Company bus #6 (6 daily combined; 45min) will drop you close by on the main road, a 1.5km walk from the centre along an undulating access road

The first forest reserve in the state, the **Semenggoh Wildlife Rehabilitation Centre** was set aside by Vyner Brooke in 1920. Today it's a sort of open zoo in a surviving pocket of forest, where tourists flock to watch orang-utans being fed fruit by rangers, who have names for all of them. How many you're likely to see will depend on the time of year – when wild fruits are in season, fewer orang-utans emerge from the forest to seek out the rangers.

Most of the action takes place at a clearing, with seating close by, reached by a short jungle trail from the car park. Don't be surprised if you see the critters roaming around the car park itself – and give them a wide berth if you do. Look out also for orang-utan nests,

6

which they build in the treetops using clumps of leaves and branches, for sleeping. The morning feeding is usually better, and arriving by 8.30am will give you a decent seat.

Annah Rais

Near the mountains that straddle the border with Kalimantan, 55km south of Kuching, the Bidayuh longhouse settlement of **ANNAH RAIS**, while occasionally touristy, makes a decent day-trip from Kuching, particularly if you don't have time to see longhouses elsewhere in Sarawak. It's easy to combine a visit with a trip to Semenggoh if you're driving, and not too hard by bus, though confirm bus times with the tourist office.

The settlement of around 1300 feels like a hybrid of **longhouse** and **village** – assorted differently styled wooden "houses" are joined together in two long parallel rows and raised off the ground, with platforms of bamboo slats on planks serving as "streets". This higgledy-piggledy style is in part due to the fact that it is one of the oldest remaining wooden longhouses in Sarawak, with a written history of more than 175 years, and an oral tradition that goes back 500. Behind the facades, individual family quarters open off vast corridors, just as in a regular longhouse, and as ever there's a **river** nearby for bathing (a bridge brings you to a third longhouse). You'll probably be offered a small glass of *tuak* (or Borneo brandy) upon arrival, while depending on the season, you may see the rice harvest or longhouse-made latex sheets being dried. Be sure to pop into the **panggah**, or skull house, where skulls hark back to a martial tradition that only ceased a few generations ago – the villagers claim that they were actually used as part of a ceremony to bring peace.

ARRIVAL AND INFORMATION   ANNAH RAIS

By bus City Public Link bus #K6 and Sarawak Transport Company bus #6, which also serve Semenggoh, head from Kuching to the small town of Kota Padawan (8 daily; 30min) from whose market you can catch a minivan (1hr; RM6) to Annah Rais.

Admission fee RM8, payable at the information booth in front of the longhouse.

ACCOMMODATION

★**Annah Rais Homestay Programmes** ☎ +65 090 049762, ⊛ longhouseadventure.com Several longhouse homes host homestay programmes, which are for the most part very basic but clean. Two- to four-day packages are available; these include activities such as jungle-trekking, hunting with blow-pipes and rafting, as well as cooking, basket-weaving and traditional dancing and music. Full board/person RM100, packages RM298

Bau and around

Nineteenth-century prospectors were drawn to **BAU**, half an hour's drive southwest of Kuching, by the gold that veined the surrounding countryside, but the modern-day market town is mundane in the extreme, though it does have a picturesque mining lake, **Blue Lake**, on its southwestern edge. Pretty though the lake is, it contains arsenic and is unsafe to swim in; the main reason to come to Bau is to visit the two nearby **caves**, around 4km apart to the west.

Bau caves

Daily 8.30am–5pm • Each cave RM5 • Sarawak Transport Company bus #2 goes from Kuching to Bau (3 daily), from where the Bau Transport Company #3 bus (6 daily) runs to the caves (catch the 11.40am service if you want to return to Kuching by bus; the last service back to Kuching is at 4.30pm) – each cave has its own bus stop on the main road, at least 15min walk from its entrance; there are also taxis from Bau (RM20 each way for Fairy Cave, RM14 for Wind Cave) – get the driver's number for the return

If you have to pick one of the two **Bau caves** – which you may well have to do if relying on public transport – choose the larger, **Fairy Cave**. Steps inside enable you to wander through the gloom towards a gaping maw at one end of the system, which lets in refreshing breezes and enough light for the cave floor to be blanketed in ferns and moss. The smaller **Wind Cave** is less impressive, and is currently closed due to a rock fall.

★ **Lan e Tuyang** 14km short of Bau and 23km from Kuching on the Batu Kawa Rd, parallel to and north of the main Bau Rd ☎013 820 3365, ✉mathew _ngau@yahoo.com. This excellent homestay is run by the Kenyah *sape* exponent and artist Mathew Ngau Jau, a mainstay of the Rainforest Music Festival (see box, p.332), who has created a sort of mini-longhouse decorated with Orang Ulu motifs and *sapes* built in his workshop below. He can teach you the rudiments of the lute-like instrument and how to build one, or you can try your hand at woodcarving. Five simple guest rooms have fans and mosquito nets, with toilets and showers in a separate block; take meals (RM20) in the house or at simple restaurants in the Chinese hamlet of Tondong a few minutes' walk away. Arrange ahead for pick-up from Bau town, Kuching or the airport. **RM50**

6

Gunung Gading National Park

The main claim to fame of **GUNUNG GADING NATIONAL PARK**, 75km by road west of Kuching, is that it's home to the parasitic **Rafflesia** plant (see p.586), with its stinky blooms. However, when the buds are maturing the park can go for months without a single *Rafflesia* in flower; if you're coming specifically to see the plants (as the vast majority of visitors are), check with the park in advance.

The park can be visited as a day-trip from Kuching. With an early start, you can tackle the **Waterfall Trail**, on which it takes ninety minutes to reach the end at waterfall 7 – it really is the seventh waterfall en route – where you can have a good, refreshing swim. With more time, you can also climb Gading, one of the park's two hills. It's a full-on hike and a six-hour round trip, though it's a well-marked trail and a guide is not needed.

ARRIVAL AND INFORMATION GUNUNG GADING NATIONAL PARK

By bus There are eight daily buses from Kuching's regional express bus terminal to the town of Lundu (1hr 30min), from where you can either walk 3km north along the main road, or catch a minivan or taxi (RM5) – Raymond Leman (☎013 841 0882) is a decent English-speaking driver in Lundu (and also works behind the Sarawak Transport Company ticket counter at the bus station).
Admission fee RM10.
Contact details ☎082 735144.

ACCOMMODATION

Gunung Gading National Park accommodation ☎082 735144. Gunung Gading has a campsite, a hostel where four rooms offer dorm beds (or can be let as four-bed rooms) and a lodge holding six-bed chalets. There's no canteen, but you can cook at the park's kitchens. Camping **RM5**, dorms **RM15**, rooms **RM40**, chalets **RM150**

Pandan and Siar beaches

Considered by many locals to be the best in the area, **Pandan Beach**, 11km north of Lundu (see above) – from where you can catch a taxi (RM30, or a few ringgit if you can find a share one) – is a 0.5km-long stretch of white sand near a beachfront kampung, where's there's not much apart from one small café overlooking the sand. Two kilometres before Pandan, the smaller **Siar Beach** is another pleasing spot with a good place to stay, though fairly busy at weekends.

ACCOMMODATION AND EATING SIAR

Siar Beach Resort Jalan Siar ☎082 412898, ⊕www.siarbeachresort. Not a bad little basic resort with clean, plain rooms and family bungalows holding two, three or four rooms. There's also a campsite and they provide tents. There's not much as far as food is concerned, but the small, basic canteen is open till 9pm and will stop you from starving. Weekend prices are about a third more. Camping for two **RM35**, rooms **RM150**, two-room bungalows **RM280**

Tanjung Datu National Park and around

Some 40km west of **Lundu** town, and at the end of the road from Kuching, the seaside town of **SEMATAN** has a long, picturesque beach and reasonably clean almost-yellow sands. However, most foreign visitors are here to visit **TANJUNG DATU NATIONAL PARK** (⊕sarawakforestry.com), whose beaches are far superior to the wide flat beach here.

6

At the very western tip of Sarawak, this tiny park covers a mountainous region around a coastal spur close to the Kalimantan border. Although it offers splendid rainforest, swift, clean rivers and isolated bays, the main draws are its dazzling **beaches**, with shallow, unspoilt **coral reefs** perfect for snorkelling only a short distance from the shore, and often frequented by dolphins.

The park is also among the few destinations in Sarawak where green **turtles** come to lay eggs. It holds four marked **trails**, too; the longest, the Belian trail, takes just two hours, leading to the summit of Gunung Melano (542m). Visits are not advised in the **rainy season** (Nov–Feb) because of rough seas; boats seldom go in those months.

ARRIVAL AND INFORMATION   TANJUNG DATU NATIONAL PARK

By boat The only independent access to the park is by boat from Sematan (40min; RM550 for up to eight people, RM600 overnight; contact Nazit, ☏ 014 880 9696). You could also wait by the Sematan jetty for a boat taking locals back to the village of Telok Melano (RM40), a 90min walk from the park HQ and location of the park's only accommodation. Getting to Sematan itself is fairly straightforward, with four daily express buses leaving from Kuching's regional express bus terminal, two of them via Lundu.

Package tours You can also come to the park on a package tour from Kuching, such as from CPH Travel (see p.323), or locally from *Telok Melano Homestay* (see below).

Admission fee RM10, payable at the Park HQ.

ACCOMMODATION

Sematan Hotel About 100m out from the bus station, Sematan (no phone). The only option in Sematan itself, and although the rooms are a bit shabby and badly maintained and the manageress usually absent (if you can't find her by yelling upstairs, ask at the cafés opposite the bus station), it's at least fairly inexpensive and clean, and has a/c and en-suite bathrooms. __RM50__

Telok Melano Homestay Tanjang Datu ☏ 082 711101, ⓦ rightsarawak.com/Homestay/Telok_Melano. Telok Melano, a tiny Malay fishing village around 90min walk from Park HQ, operates a local homestay programme. It is used by tour operators (who charge around RM1500/person for a two-night package from Kuching), but they also organize their own one- or two-night packages (one to five people), which include food, lodging and transfer from Sematan. You can stay on an independent, nightly basis too. Full board per person __RM100__, packages __RM1150__

Batang Ai – the Iban longhouses

The **Iban longhouses** of the Ai headwaters, both 150km due east of Kuching beyond the lake of the Batang Ai hydroelectric dam, and also to the north along the **Lemanak** river system, are the best excuse for anyone travelling between western and central Sarawak not to catch the fast Kuching–Sibu ferry. Despite being on the tourist trail, the longhouses continue to offer a glimpse of a semi-traditional lifestyle in a remote corner of the state, much of which is protected as a **national park** and wildlife sanctuary.

Batang Ai dam and lake

Around three and a half hours' drive from Kuching, a couple of kilometres beyond the village of **Jelukong**, a signed 38km turning branches southeast off the main trunk road, passing a few modernish longhouses en route to the small border town of **Lubok Antu**. Some 12km short of that, another small road branches east (left) towards the **Batang Ai dam**, a way station en route to the upper Ai. Built in the 1980s as Sarawak's first hydroelectric venture, the Ai dam created a lake covering 90 square kilometres. Though now dwarfed in scale, generating capacity and controversy by the Bakun dam (see p.351), it's an impressive sight nonetheless and the road up gives good views of the narrow valley downriver.

No parts of the dam are open to tourists, though, and once you get there you'll head to one of the jetties to continue east by boat to an Ai longhouse or the *Hilton Batang Ai*.

6

THE IBAN

Easily the most numerous of Sarawak's indigenous peoples, the **Iban** make up nearly thirty percent of the state's population. Their language is from the same family as Malay, and any Malay speakers will notice considerable overlap in vocabulary as well as predictable changes in word endings – *datang* (come) and *makan* (eat) in Malay, for example, become *datai* and *makai* in Iban.

ORIGINS AND CONFLICTS

Having outgrown their original home in the Kapuas river basin of west Kalimantan, the Iban migrated to the Lupar River in southwest Sarawak in the sixteenth century, and came into conflict with the Melanau and Malays. With the Brunei sultanate at its height, the Malays pushed the Iban back inland up rivers such as the Rejang, into interior areas dominated by the Kayan. Great battles were waged between the two groups; one source recorded seeing "a mass of boats drifting along the stream, [the combatants] spearing and stabbing each other; decapitated trunks and heads without bodies, scattered about in ghastly profusion". Although such inter-ethnic conflict stopped as migration itself slowed, the Iban were still taking heads as recently as the 1960s during the Konfrontasi, when the Indonesian army came up against Iban who had thrown their lot in with Malaysia.

SOCIETY

The Iban figure prominently in the minds of visitors, thanks to their traditional communal dwelling, the **longhouse** (see p.340). Each has its own *tuai* (headman), who leads more by consensus than by barking orders. Traditionally, young men left the longhouse to go on **bejalai**, the act of joining a warring party – essentially a rite of passage for a youth to establish his independence and social position before marriage. Nowadays, to the extent that *bejalai* has meaning, it may translate into going to university or earning a good wage on offshore oil rigs or in a hotel or factory in Singapore.

Further complicating the *bejalai* tradition is the fact that **women** are now much more socially mobile, and can pursue education and their own careers. Traditionally, however, women had distinct duties, which is cited as a reason why a woman is not permitted to be *tuai*. They never went hunting, but were great weavers – an Iban woman's weaving prowess would once have determined her status in the community. The women are most renowned for their **pua kumbu** (blanket or coverlet) work, a cloth of intricate design and colour. The *pua kumbu* once played an integral part in Iban rituals, hung up prominently during harvest festivals and weddings, or used to cover structures containing charms and offerings to the gods.

DEVELOPMENT AND URBANIZATION

More than half of Sarawak's Iban have moved permanently to the cities and towns in the west of the state, or may spend the working week there and weekends back in their longhouse. Most rural Iban no longer live purely off the land but also undertake seasonal work in the rubber and oil industries. By no small irony, logging – the business that most devastated their traditional lands – also long supplied plentiful and lucrative work; these days oil-palm cultivation and production provide more employment.

Batang Ai National Park

Only accessible with an official guide, who can be hired in Lubok Antu; if you're on a tour, you have to pay a tour operator for a day-trip to be added onto a longhouse package • RM10 • ⓦ sarawakforestry.com

East of the lakeshore, an hour by boat from the dam, the little-visited **BATANG AI NATIONAL PARK** preserves an important area of rainforest that merges with the Lanjak Entimau Wildlife Sanctuary (LEWS; off-limits to visitors), which itself merges with another protected area across the border in Kalimantan. **Orang-utans** are occasionally spotted on various trails in the national park; it holds no residential or other facilities, and all visitors must be accompanied by a guide.

Ai River

An hour east from the Batang Ai dam, longhouse-bound boats leave the lake and head up the **Ai River**. As is clear from the tall trees that come right to the water's edge, the initial stretch is still a drowned portion of the river. Further up you'll observe a transition

6

> ## LONGHOUSE ARCHITECTURE
>
> **Longhouses** can be thought of as indoor villages, housing entire communities under one roof. Although several indigenous peoples build dwellings that are sometimes called longhouses, the definitive article is the **Iban** longhouse. This has a long veranda or *tanju* at the front where rice, rubber and other produce can be laid out to dry; it's accessed by steps or sometimes a log into which notches are cut. Behind the front wall, running the entire length of the building, a corridor or *ruai* serves as a sort of main street where the community can socialize. Multiple doors (*pintu*) open on to the *ruai*, behind which lie each family's quarters (*bilik*); locals describe a longhouse not in terms of its length or the number of inhabitants, but by how many *bilik* or *pintu* it has. Above the living quarters, a loft space (*sadau*) is used for storage.
>
> Traditionally longhouses were built of hardwood timber and bamboo, perhaps with ironwood shingles on the roof. Even though most longhouses now feature plenty of unsightly concrete, they still retain their characteristic *ruai* inside, and most continue to be sited close to rivers or streams, where people enjoy bathing even when piped water supplies exist.

to the true river banks, the vegetation more open and compact. Also visible sporadically to either side are the odd school and clinic in simple metal-roofed timber buildings, and areas of hillslope cleared for traditional rice cultivation. The Iban leave paddies to the jungle once the soil is exhausted and move on to clear new areas. As the river narrows, you also begin to see the occasional **longhouse** lurking in the vegetation. Among those that take tourists are **Nanga Delok** (also called Rumah Ipang, on the Delok, a tributary of the Ai) and the more distant **Nanga Sumpa** (the Sumpa being a tributary of the Delok). Wherever you stay, you will be offered opportunities for additional longboat trips to areas where you can make short treks or local beauty spots such as waterfalls.

Lemanak River

The **Lemanak River** is, like the Batang Ai dam, reached by the Lubok Antu Road, though you turn off earlier to head to the jetties. Several longhouses here regularly host travellers, notably **Ngemah Ulu**, where guests are put up in the longhouse itself, which has been adopted by Diethelm Travel in Kuching (ⓦ diethelmtravel.com). Independent travel here is not easy. Coming on a two-night package offers the option of a great local trek.

ARRIVAL AND DEPARTURE — BATANG AI

Package tours Most visitors book with a Kuching or Miri tour operator, which usually includes the road transfers, the journey in and out by longboat, plus all meals.

Travelling independently Roads have reached some longhouses north of the Ai, but since many longhouses aren't signposted, having your own car is little advantage unless you have local friends or hire a guide in Lubok Antu. That said, you can visit by public transport. If you get dropped at Jelukong Junction on the main road by any bus to or from Miri, then it's 39km to Lubok Antu (RM50 taxi, often possible to share) where there is accommodation and you can ask around to find a guide (around RM100–150/day). When leaving, there's no need to backtrack all the way to Kuching; to head on to Sibu and beyond, flag down a bus on the main road. There are at least a couple of buses per hour and tickets can be bought on board.

ACCOMMODATION

Hilton Batang Ai Southeastern shore of Batang Ai lake, 40min from the dam ☎ 082 584388, ⓦ hilton.com. A *Hilton* is definitely a misfit in this isolated area, but then, so is the dam – so you might as well just enjoy the lake vistas from the hotel terrace. Each block is a timber building with rooms on one side of a long corridor, just as in a longhouse; built in the 1990s, the rooms now look a tad dated. Either drive up and be collected at the dam, or pay extra for shuttle transport from the *Kuching Hilton*, who can also tell you about packages and add-on longhouse visits. __RM250__

Nanga Sumpa Ai River, a 90min boat ride from the dam; only bookable as part of a package. This longhouse deserves special mention as the site of an excellent purpose-built tourist lodge, sited at a discreet distance from the longhouse itself across a creek. Rooms have wooden platforms that hold a simple mattress and a mosquito net, but little else, though there's a pleasant open sitting/dining area and modern shared bathrooms. Prices vary; only bookable through tour operators.

Central Sarawak

For travellers, central Sarawak offers rather slim pickings compared to Kuching's hinterland and the north of the state. Those visitors who venture here tend to be drawn by the prospect of travelling into the interior along the **Rejang** (also spelled **Rajang**), Malaysia's longest river. All such trips start from the bustling city of **Sibu**, some 50km inland near where another major river, the **Igan**, splits away from the Rejang. Express boats depart daily to zip up the Rejang to **Kapit**, beyond which, through the **Pelagus Rapids** and on to the sleepy town of **Belaga**, eight hours from Sibu, the Rejang becomes wild and unpredictable and the scenery spectacular. There's not much to do in either Kapit or Belaga, and while there are longhouse communities near both, almost all are made from concrete – the last easily accessible traditional wooden longhouse is east of Kapit along the Balui River. Public transport is thin on the ground, so it's best to regard the Rejang journey as an end in itself or else fork out for (pricey) local guides to arrange trips for you.

With Sibu being so far from the sea, and the coast here dominated by mangrove swamp, the main trunk road runs deep inland until it finally hits the coast again at Bintulu. Halfway along, a side road leads off through a chink in the vegetation to the coastal town of **Mukah**, which has an appealing museum-cum-guesthouse nearby. **Bintulu** itself is a nondescript but (thanks to oil and gas) prosperous town, whose main attraction is as a base for **Similajau National Park**, easily reached yet appealingly quiet.

6

Sibu

From its humble 1850s origins as a tiny Melanau encampment, **SIBU** has grown into Sarawak's third largest city and its biggest port. Nearly half its quarter-million population are ethnic Chinese. Unusually for Malaysia, many are Foochow, descended from migrants from what's now Fuzhou in southeast China. Their diligence is often credited with helping the city become the commercial centre it is today. Its Foochow flavour aside, Sibu is also identified with Sarawak's controversial **logging** industry, which helped the city recover from the Japanese occupation, when many Chinese were forced into slave labour. Sibu subsequently became, for a time, the centre for timber processing in Sarawak and investors, many drawn from long-established Chinese families, made large fortunes as a result.

Having experienced devastating fires in 1889 and 1928, plus serious damage during World War II, Sibu is characterized more by energy than visual appeal. However, boasting a huge **market** and a lively **waterfront**, it has enough sights to keep you occupied for half a day – just as well, as most travellers en route to or from the upper Rejang spend at least a night here.

Waterfront

If you arrive on the boat from Kuching, you'll find yourself on the **waterfront** on the Rejang's right bank, facing rows of dull modern shophouses and commercial buildings. Efforts have been made to landscape and beautify the **Rejang Esplanade** – the tiny riverside recreation area by the ferry terminal – but it's still a fairly humdrum spot. Look out, however, for a riverside marker indicating the Rejang's level during historic floods. Sibu's commercial lifeline is also a scourge; every few years the river overtops this area and inundates the city centre. Efforts are ongoing to tame the Rejang by dredging away sediment, some of which no doubt results from forest clearance.

Tua Pek Kong temple

Eastern end of Jalan Temple • Daily 6.30am–8pm • Free • ☎ 082 312005

A small wooden temple stood on the site of Sibu's **Tua Pek Kong temple**, at the northern end of the riverfront, as early as 1870. Soon afterwards it was rebuilt on a much grander scale, with a tiled roof, stone block floor and decorative fixtures imported from China.

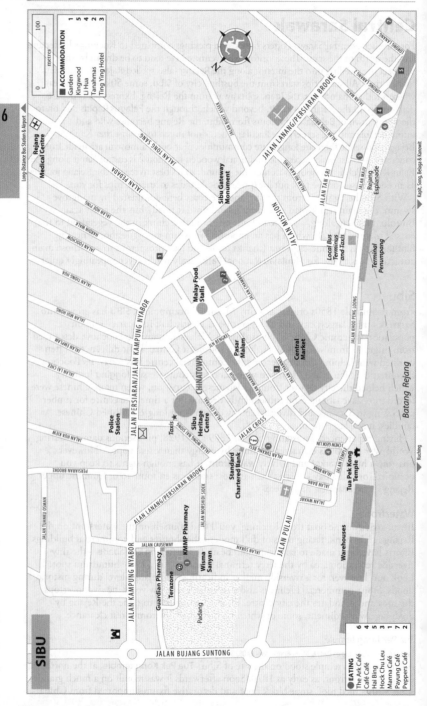

SIBU

ACCOMMODATION
Garden	1
Kingwood	5
Li Hua	4
Tanahmas	2
Ting Ying Hotel	3

EATING
The Ark Café	6
Café Café	4
Hai Bing	5
Hock Chu Leu	3
Manna Café	1
Payung Café	7
Peppers Café	2

Long-Distance Bus Station & Airport

Rejang Medical Centre

JALAN BUKIT ASSEK

JALAN LONG SANG

JALAN PEDADA

JALAN HOE PING

HARDIN WALK

JALAN TOOCHOW

JALAN TIONG HUA

JALAN MUI HONG

JALAN EMPLAM

JALAN LAI CHEE

JALAN HUA KIEW

PERSIARAN BROOKE

JALAN TUANKU OSMAN

JALAN PERSIARAN/JALAN KAMPUNG NYABOR

JALAN KAMPUNG NYABOR

JALAN CAUSEWAY

Guardian Pharmacy

Terazone

KMMP Pharmacy

Wisma Sanyan

Padang

JALAN SUKAN

JALAN MORSHIDI SIDEK

ALAN LANANG/PERSIARAN BROOKE

Police Station

Taxis

Sibu Heritage Centre

CHINATOWN

JALAN CENTRAL

JALAN WONG NAI SIONG

Standard Chartered Bank

JALAN CROSS

JALAN PULAU

JALAN WHARF

JALAN BANK

JALAN TUKANG BESI

JALAN TEMPLE

Tua Pek Kong Temple

LORONG GEOK LIN

Warehouses

JALAN BUJANG SUNTONG

Sibu Gateway Monument

JALAN LANANG/PERSIARAN BROOKE

JALAN MISSION

JALAN HII KAI TING

JALAN TAN SRI

JALAN MAJU

JALAN CHAMBERS

Malay Food Stalls

JLN BENGKEL

Pasar Malam

HIGH ST

JLN MARKET

JALAN CENTRAL

Central Market

JALAN KHOO PENG LOONG

Local Bus Terminus and Taxis

Terminal Penumpang

Rejang Esplanade

LORONG LANANG 2

LORONG LANANG 4

JALAN MAJU

Batang Rejang

Kuching

Kapit, Song, Belaga & Kanowit

metres 0 100

Two large concrete lions guard the entrance. The **statue** of Tua Pek Kong, the temple's most important image, survived both the fire of 1928 and Japanese bombardment.

Central Market

Northern end of the riverside Jalan Khoo Peng Loong • Daily dawn–dusk, hawker stalls upstairs stay open into the evening

Sibu's modern and entertaining **Central Market** is housed in a long, curved-roofed building. It's best to turn up on a Saturday, when it's at its busiest and the entire ground floor is taken up with vendors selling items such as bamboo tubes for stewing *ayam pansoh*, live roosters tied up in newspaper, slabs of what look like mummified bats but are in fact smoked fish, and, in the run-up to tribal festivals, gongs – which prospective buyers have no qualms about trying out. Stalls at the edge offer a tasty Sibu speciality, *kongbian*, sometimes called Chinese bagels but more like dainty versions of the sesame-seed breads sold in Turkey and Lebanon. An upstairs **food court** offers a few vantage points overlooking the colourful goings-on below.

Sibu Heritage Centre

Jalan Central • Tues–Sun 9am–5pm • Free • ☎ 084 331315

The **Sibu Heritage Centre** is a fine museum highlighting the city's history and cultural diversity. There's a good discussion of how Chinese pioneers, with the support of Brooke officials, founded the settlement and got it off the ground with crops such as rubber – logging didn't arrive until the 1930s – and of Foochow immigration, which only began in earnest at the start of the twentieth century. Among the basketware, beadwork and so forth you can see a striking nineteenth-century Kayan burial hut or *salong* atop a 1m-high totem pole.

ARRIVAL AND DEPARTURE   SIBU

By plane Sibu's airport (☎ 084 307770) is 25km east of the centre. While you could walk 10min to the nearest major road junction and flag down a passing bus or yellow-topped van into town (roughly hourly; RM3), it's a lot easier to pay for a taxi (RM32). Heading out to the airport, any bus from the local bus station bound for Sibujaya or Kanowit can drop you at the same junction. MAS, AirAsia, and Malindo all have offices at the airport.

Destinations Bintulu (2 daily; 35min); Johor Bahru (1 daily; 1hr 35min); Kota Kinabalu (2 daily; 1hr 35min); Kuala Lumpur (6–10 daily; 1hr 55min); Kuching (8–9 daily; 40min); Miri (3–4 daily; 55min).

By boat Sibu's express-boat terminal on the esplanade, Terminal Penumpang, is used by Bahagia fast boats between here and Kuching via Sarikei downriver; it's advised to take the more expensive upper-deck seats,

which have better views and a/c (1 daily, 11.30am; 4–5hr; RM45/55; ☎ 084 319228). There are also more frequent boats upriver to Kanowit (3 daily, last at 8.30am; 30min; RM10); Kapit (18 daily, last 2.30pm; 3hr; RM20/25/30); and Belaga (1 daily at 5.45am; 8hr; RM55).

By long-distance bus All express buses use the long-distance bus station, 5km northeast of the centre off Jalan Pahlawan. Hourly Lanang Bus Company services #20 and #21 go to the local bus station, which is in front of the express-boat terminal close to the centre. A taxi to the centre costs around RM15.

Destinations Bintulu (every 20–30min; 4hr); Kuching (every 20–30min; 7hr); Miri (every 20–30min; 8hr); Mukah (around 5 daily, last at 4.30pm; 3hr 30min); Pontianak (Indonesia; at least 2 daily; 18hr).

INFORMATION AND TOURS

Tourist information Knowledgeable and helpful staff at Sibu's central Visitors' Information Centre, 16 Jalan Tukang Besi (Mon–Fri 8am–5pm; ☎ 084 340980, ✉ vic-sibu @sarawaktourism.com) also cover the Rejang River towns plus Bintulu and Mukah, which don't have tourist offices. They produce a very good guide with several maps included.

TOUR OPERATORS

Great Holiday ☎ 084 348196, ☜ ghtborneo.com. This agency does a one-day Sibu tour (RM160/person),

which includes a visit to the Bawang Assan longhouses (see box, p.344).

Greatown Travel ☎ 084 211243, ☜ greatown.com. Unusual one-day trips downriver to Sarikei (RM220), where you can do some trekking, see pepper being cultivated and visit a wooden Iban longhouse where you can also add on a homestay (RM100). Even more unusually, they can take you north down the Igan River to Mukah (three days/two nights full board RM900), which includes a visit to Lamin Dana (see p.351). Book a few days in advance.

6

ACCOMMODATION

Sibu has a couple of decent inexpensive **hotels**, plus loads of choice once you get to mid-range and above. The cheapest guesthouses are around Chinatown, though this area also hosts a couple of loud bars and is also frequented by prostitutes.

Garden Jalan Hoe Ping ⓣ084 317888, ⓦgardenhotelsibu.com.my. A decent fallback if the *Li Hua* is full – rooms cost quite a bit more, but you get a breakfast buffet. Executive rooms on the upper floors cost around RM30 extra. **RM108**

Kingwood 12 Lorong Lanang ⓣ084 335888, ⓔkingwood.sibu@yahoo.com.my. Incredibly, this huge hotel, with a gleaming new extension back from the river, has never seen fit to have a website despite boasting a pool, gym, sauna and other amenities. Rooms in the old wing are unexceptional; the new wing costs RM30 or so extra, and features unfussy, more contemporary decor. Prices can be slashed when things are quiet, making the place an absolute steal. Rates include breakfast, though you can save yourself RM69 if you get a rate without. **RM185**

★**Li Hua** By the river at the junction of Lorong Lanang 2 and Jalan Maju ⓣ084 324000. It's not the place to come for little refinements, and the sound of guests' chatter can echo around the small lobby, but this is a terrific budget hotel, efficiently run, with dated and plain but well-kept en-suite rooms and free wi-fi on quite a few floors. Reserve ahead. **RM65**

★**Tanahmas** Off the eastern end of Jalan Chambers ⓣ084 333188, ⓦtanahmas.com.my. This slick mid-range hotel boasts some of the nicest rooms in its class, fairly spacious with elegant modern furnishings, a swimming pool and a popular Chinese restaurant on the second floor. **RM220**

Ting Ying Hotel Jalan Channel (directly opposite the market) ⓣ016 885 6602. By far the best (non-sleazy) budget option, it has small but clean rooms with good bathrooms, and is fairly quiet at night – the market is noisy in the morning, but if you're getting a boat you'll need to be up early anyway. No wi-fi. **RM42**

EATING AND DRINKING

Other than a few moderately upmarket restaurants scattered downtown, the eating scene is dominated by the usual *kopitiams* – particularly in the streets back from the Esplanade and in Chinatown – and food courts, such as at the Central Market. Local specialities include **Foochow noodles** – steamed and then served in a soy and oyster sauce with spring onions, chilli, garlic and dried fish; and *kang puan mee*, which literally translates as "dry-plate noodles" though it is in fact *mee* fried in lard and garnished with pork slices. Good **bars** are thin on the ground, but not for lack of trying; a few venues, such as along Jalan Tukang Besi, are beautifully done out but lack finesse and descend into karaoke at the slightest opportunity – there is also quite a lot of prostitution.

The Ark Café Rejang Esplanade ⓣ084 313445. It may look like a designer home, but *The Ark* is actually a Thai restaurant and bar that also serves a few Western and Malaysian dishes. The food, at best, is not bad (try the crispy fish fillet with salted egg), but the contemporary decor compensates, and prices are reasonable (around

LONGHOUSES NEAR SIBU

There are very few traditional wooden **longhouses** left along the Rejang, but there are a couple of semi-traditional ones within easy striking distance of Sibu.

Bawang Assan Sibu Longhouse Homestay Program 14km southwest of Sibu ⓣ014 582 8105, ⓦrantaukemiding.blogspot.com. Just 40min by road from Sibu (RM50–70 by charter taxi, or RM2 by infrequent minivan from the Central Market), there are eight colourful longhouses here where Iban families (all with English-speaking members) take guests. The longhouses are a mix of traditional and modern, and prices include food, board and a range of activities such as padi planting and fishing. The tourist office in Sibu (see p.343) can help you make the arrangements. **RM110**

Rumah Benjamin Angki Rantau Kemiding, 4km southwest of Kanowit, which is a boat stop or a 40min bus ride upriver from Sibu ⓣ013 882 3076, ⓦrantaukemiding.blogspot.com. Painted bright yellow, this venerable longhouse with more than 53 doors and a correspondingly vast *ruai* dates back to 1936. Being set in an agricultural area just uphill from the Kanowit River, it isn't a full-on outback experience, and is great for families with young children. Guests can stay in a purpose-built modern block with two a/c rooms, or in the longhouse itself, where some of the Iban speak good English. Call Benjamin in advance to discuss prices and some kind of programme as well as to arrange a pick-up from Kanowit; potential activities, all costing extra, include guided walks through the woods, fishing trips and so forth. Per person, full board in modern block **RM65**, longhouse without meals **RM75**

RM25 without alcohol; set lunch RM10). Several outdoor tables, set around a courtyard that's nicely lit at night, have river views by day. Daily 11am–11pm.

Café Café 8 Jalan Chew Geok Lin ☎084 328101. While not as swish as *Le Ark*, *Café Café* is for many middle-class locals the place for a smart night out. The food is mostly a mix of Chinese, Malay and Thai dishes (the Thai chicken salad is very popular), served in different portion sizes with rice. Mains RM18–38. Tues–Sun noon–4pm & 6–11pm.

Hai Bing 31 Jalan Maju ☎084 321491. Well-established and often busy Chinese restaurant known for its seafood, such as ginger crab (RM60/kg). If you stick with the rice and noodle dishes you can eat for under RM10. Daily 11.30am–1.30pm & 5.30–11.30pm.

Hock Chu Leu Upstairs at 28 Jalan Tukang Besi ☎084 330254. *Kopitiams* aside, you'd expect Sibu to have a more formal downtown place offering Foochow cuisine – and this is it, and though it's a little fusty it's certainly Chinese-looking. Come here for classics such as Foochow noodles and *ang chow kai*, chicken that's red from being cooked with the sediment from a certain type of Chinese wine. Around RM20, excluding drinks. Daily 11am–1.30pm & 5–8pm; sometimes closed Tues.

Manna Café Fifth floor, Wisma Sanyan mall ☎084 344308. Sharing its premises with a bookshop, this Chinese-run place has good views over the padang and a variety of surprisingly tasty and authentic Korean dishes such as *bibimbab* (rice), *kimchi chiggae* (stew) and *bulgogi* (fried beef). They even make their own *kimchi*. Around RM17–20 with a soft drink. Daily 11am–9pm.

★**Payung Café** Jalan Lanang. This simple restaurant, smartened up with tribal artefacts and a thatched awning, is one of the quirkiest in Sarawak, with a fusion menu that reflects enthusiasm rather than fancy culinary training. Their cooking often uses local herbs and could feature anything from Indochinese pomelo salad to prawns with starfruit and spaghetti. You can wash down your meal with, say, roselle tea – better known as the Egyptian hibiscus drink *karkaday* – or their brilliant home-made pineapple ginger soda, or even fresh durian milk shake, if the pongy fruits are in season. Around RM30 with soft drinks. Daily 11am–3pm & 6–11pm.

Peppers Café Tanahmas Hotel, off eastern end of Jalan Chambers ☎084 333188, ⓦtanahmas.com.my. The usual hotel restaurant menu ranging from Western staples – including lamb chop and rump steak – to Chinese noodles, in plush surroundings and at somewhat elevated prices (most mains RM17–21.50). It's the best Western grub in town, and not a bad option for a slap-up buffet breakfast (RM29). Daily 6am–1.30am.

DIRECTORY

Banks There are quite a few banks downtown, including a convenient branch of Standard Chartered just up the road from the tourist office where Jalan Tukang Besi splits off from Jalan Cross.

Hospitals and clinics The Sibu Hospital is a taxi ride away at 5 1/2 mile on Jalan Ulu Oya (☎084 343333); alternatively, try the Rejang Medical Centre, 29 Jalan Pedada (☎084 330733).

Internet access Forever Link, Wisma Sanyan (10am–10pm; RM4/hr).

Pharmacies Guardian is just outside Wisma Sanyan mall, and KKMP is just inside the mall (both daily 9.30am–10pm).

Police Jalan Kampung Nyabor (☎084 336144).

Post office Jalan Kampung Nyabor (Mon–Fri 8am–5pm, every other Sat 9am–noon).

Up the Batang Rejang

Even though much of the traditional culture and architecture of the region has been lost, a journey to the **upper reaches of the Rejang** should still engender a little frisson of excitement. This area was, after all, once synonymous with remoteness and with mysterious warring tribes. Even a century ago, conflict persisted between the Iban and the Orang Ulu, particularly the Kayan. Things had been much worse before the arrival of the Brookes, who wanted to develop – and therefore subjugate – the interior. To that end, James Brooke bought a section of the Rejang from the Sultan of Brunei in 1853, while his successor, Charles, asserted his authority over the Iban and Kayan tribes and encouraged the Chinese to open up the interior to agriculture and trade.

Thus began the gradual pacification of the Rejang. Even today, despite development and modern communications, it's possible to glimpse something of that pioneer spirit in these upriver towns, while forts at **Kanowit** and **Kapit** hint at the lengths taken by the Brookes to get the region under their thumb. The furthest boats go upriver is the nondescript town of **Belaga**, reached by a thrilling ride through the **Pelagus Rapids**. There is, however, another exciting route into or out of Belaga – by **4WD**, the road connecting up with the main trunk road near Bintulu (see p.353).

6

REJANG BOATS

One explanation for the nickname "flying coffins" – formerly attached jokingly to the **Rejang express boats** – is that they are long and narrow, and feature aircraft-like seating. Otherwise they are serviceable, if not massively comfortable or user-friendly: boarding entails stepping off the jetty onto the boat's rim or gunwale and walking around until you reach the entrance hatch. You may also have to fling your luggage on the roof yourself, although sometimes staff are on hand to help load and unload.

Several companies operate the boats, but look out for people selling **Bahagia** and **Husqvarna** tickets at the boat terminal; both companies stand out for having more comfortable boats that are also more likely to leave on time and to have windows through which you can see clearly – though the jungle views may get monotonous after a while. Otherwise you'll have to be entertained by the onboard DVDs of Hong Kong soaps or gory Hollywood action flicks – one of the advantages of going first class are that they often leave the volume down.

SCHEDULES AND FARES

Boats **depart** Sibu at least twice an hour from 6.15am until 11am, then every 45 minutes until 3pm. All go to Kapit (around 3hr), just a couple to Kanowit (45min) and many more serve Song, the stop before Kapit. Downriver boats from Kapit operate to a similar schedule. Only one a day, leaving Sibu at 5.45 am, sails all the way to Belaga, with a half-hour stop at Kapit at 8.30am. The Belaga leg takes around five hours, with frequent stops. Note that during the dry season, if the river level is low, Belaga boats are cancelled – ask at the jetty or tourist office in Sibu (see p.343) for the latest.

The **fare** from Sibu to Kapit is RM20 (RM5/10 extra for second/first class, which when available offers a bit more legroom and slightly better air conditioning). A Sibu–Belaga ticket costs RM55, Kapit–Belaga RM25. You should try and arrive thirty minutes before departure time, and at busy times, say during the run-up to a festival, buy tickets a day or two before.

Unfortunately **visits to traditional wooden longhouses** can be difficult to pull off. The vast majority are now made of concrete – notable exceptions are Bawang Assan near Sibu, the Rumah Benjamin Angki Longhouse near Kanowit (see box, p.344), the Rumha Jandok longhouse near Kapit, and a few up the tributaries near Belega or Kapit – though the transportation and guides required for the last option will involve considerable expense.

Kapit

KAPIT is the main commercial centre upriver from Sibu, and it looks it too, trapped in an architectural no-man's-land between the modern town it could become and the rustic backwater it was a generation ago – the place feels like an utter jumble, despite a certain appealing energy. If you do end up here, you may well stay the night – either because you can't face the journey to Belaga in one go or because this is as far as you intend to get – and fortunately it has some good accommodation options. Although there are a couple of **museums** (plus several banks and a couple of internet cafés), there's not much else to do beyond wandering the river bank or having a look around the market.

Fort Sylvia

Tues–Sun 10am–noon & 2–5pm (you may need to wait for the caretaker to show up with the keys) • Free • ☎ 082 239672

Fort Sylvia, the white, low-slung building a couple of minutes' walk upriver from the boat terminal, makes quite a grand first impression. Built in 1880 of tough *belian* (ironwood) timber, it was an attempt to prevent the marauding Iban attacking smaller and more peaceable tribes, and to limit Iban migration along the nearby Sungai Baleh, confining them to the Rejang below Kapit; note the diamond-shaped gun holes all along the facade.

CLOCKWISE FROM TOP LEFT TREKKING AND BOAT RIDES IN GUNUNG MULU (P.366); LONGHOUSE, SARAWAK CULTURAL VILLAGE (P.330) >

6

The fort is now a small **museum** and conference venue, managed by the people behind Kuching's Tun Jugah Gallery (see p.321). Evocative photographs depict great moments in the history of the Ulu Rejang, including the 1924 peace-making ceremony in Kapit between Brooke officials and the warring Iban and Kayan tribal representatives. In addition, ceramic jars, *pua kumba* textiles and small cannon are on display.

Civic Centre and Museum

Jalan Hospital • Tues–Sun 8am–5pm • ☎ 084 796003 • Free

Also known by its Malay name, **Dewan Suarah**, Kapit's **Civic Centre and Museum** holds interesting exhibits on the tribes in the Rejang region, including a well-constructed longhouse and a mural painted by local Iban. Sketches and watercolours of Kapit, Belaga and Song portray a life that is slowly disappearing. The museum also describes the lives of the Hokkien traders who helped put towns like Kapit on the map.

Rumah Jandok Longhouse

Sungai Yong • Entry, photo permit and community donation for 1–6 people RM65, skull room RM40 extra • Contact Cikgu (teacher) Jega Keling on ☎ 014 881 2906 or ☎ 084 796903 • You can visit using a guide from Kapit, though it's not that difficult to organize yourself; a minivan from Kapit's market square should cost around RM120–130 return

Some 15km southwest from Kapit, the weather-worn **Rumah Jandok Longhouse** is one of the last remaining traditional wooden longhouses in the region, and one of the few anywhere which still keep the skulls hanging outside the skull room. It's also possible to **stay** here (RM100/person), and although you'll have to bring your own food, they'll help you to cook it.

ARRIVAL, INFORMATION AND TOURS   KAPIT

By boat Kapit's large boat terminal is used by all boats except Belaga services, which use a pier just a couple of minutes' walk downriver.

Destinations Belaga (1 daily; 5hr); Kanowit (1–2 daily; 2hr); Sibu (18 daily; 2hr 30min).

Alice and Christina Chua ☎ 013 846 6133, ✉ arisjohn_yek@yahoo.com. This mother-and-daughter team of licensed guides, based near Kapit, arrange trips to Rumah Jandok Longhouse. Prices vary depending on the size of the group and your requirements, but a one-night stay at Rumah Jandok Longhouse might cost around

RM550 for two people, including land transport, meals and guide. Day-trips, longer stays, and trips further afield are possible; call (several days in advance) to discuss your needs and negotiate.

Local guides You can ask at your hotel about other local guides, who are much cheaper – the *Dragon Inn*, for example, can organize a day-trip to Rumah Jandok (RM250 for two, RM50 for each extra person) and they speak good English. Make sure all the terms are clearly agreed before you set out.

ACCOMMODATION

Kapit has a few reasonable budget hotels (if the ones listed here are full, you'll easily stumble upon a handful more around town) and two mid-range options, though accommodation tends to be slightly overpriced. There is also the option of staying at the **Rumah Jandok Longhouse** nearby.

Ark Hill Inn Jalan Penghulu Gerinang ☎ 084 796168, ✉ arkhill168@gmail.com. Good-value budget place with spartan but quite serviceable and clean en-suite doubles, twins, triples and a couple of "single" rooms that hold a bed large enough for two. Wi-fi in lobby only. Singles RM55, doubles RM90

Dragon Inn Lot 46, Jalan Teo Chow Beng ☎ 084 796105, ✉ kingsingwong@yahoo.com. It's the first hotel you come to walking up from the jetty, and it has the most economical rooms. Most are a/c, and bare but

clean. The fan rooms on the top floor are more worn, with shared bathrooms, but they're the cheapest in town. Wi-fi in lower floor rooms only. Fan doubles RM40, a/c doubles RM60

★**Greenland Inn** Jalan Teo Chow Beng ☎ 084 796388. Snug, clean and carpeted en-suite rooms, all with a/c, TV, comfy beds and the best bathrooms in town. It can be noisy at reception, so try to get a room on an upper floor. No breakfast. Wi-fi throughout. RM120

EATING

Eating in Kapit is largely a matter of picking from the numerous **kedai kopis** and ordering from a fairly predictable range of dishes. If you want to stick your neck out, ask if they can cook fish or even wild boar (*babi hutan*) to order – though of course don't try ordering the latter in a Muslim establishment. All eating places – apart from the *Taman Selera Empurau*, the *KFC*, and the *Sugarbuns* – close by 6.30pm.

Ah Mu Café Across from the Orchard Inn on Jalan Yong Mun Chai ☎013 801 8682. This unremarkable-looking *kopitiam* is one of the livelier examples of its kind in town, serving *nasi campur* by day plus the usual noodle options and the odd dessert. Best of all, they can also whip up stir-fries and other Chinese dishes to order using ingredients to hand – anything from a whole steamed fish to fried chicken. Daily 6.30am–6.30pm.

Taman Selera Empurau One block back from Jalan Teo Cheow Beng, behind the Methodist church. The only decent option after dark, this open-air food market serves inexpensive and delicious Malay food at plastic tables – noodles, fried rice, excellent satay sticks and of course *nasi goreng*. It would be hard to spend more than RM10. Daily 5pm–1am.

Belaga

Belaga-bound boats make frequent stops upriver from Kapit, and some passengers decamp to the roof for views of longhouses as the Rejang narrows. Forty minutes from Kapit, the **Pelagus Rapids** is an 800m-long, deceptively shallow stretch of the river where large, submerged stones make the through passage treacherous. Further upriver, the population shifts from being largely Iban to featuring a mix of other tribes, including the Kayan and Kenyah.

Five hours beyond Kapit, the boat finally reaches tiny **BELAGA**, 40km west of the confluence of the Rejang and the Balui. The town started life as a small bazaar, and by 1900 pioneering Chinese *towkays* were supplying the tribespeople – both the Kayan and the then-nomadic Punan and Penan – with kerosene, cooking oil and cartridges, in exchange for beadwork and mats, beeswax, ebony and tree gums. The British presence in this region was nominal; Belaga has no crumbling fort to serve as a museum, as no fort was built this far upriver.

THE KAYAN AND KENYAH

The **Kayan** and the **Kenyah** are the most populous and powerful of the Orang Ulu groups who have lived for centuries in the upper Rejang and, in the northern interior, along the Batang Baram. The Kayan are more numerous, at around forty thousand, while the Kenyah population is around ten thousand (with substantially more Kenyah over the mountains in Kalimantan). Both groups migrated from East Kalimantan into Sarawak roughly six hundred years ago; they were pushed back to the lands they occupy today during the nineteenth century, when Iban migration led to clashes between the groups,

The Kayan and the Kenyah have a fair amount in common: their language, though of the same family as the other Bornean tongues and Malay, has a singsong quality that sounds like Chinese, and they have a well-defined social hierarchy, unlike the Iban or Penan. Traditionally, the **social order** was topped by the **tuai rumah** (chief) of the longhouse, followed by a group of three or four lesser aristocrats or **payin**, lay families and slaves (slavery no longer exists). Both groups take pride in their **longhouses**, which can be massive.

KAYAN ART

Artistic expression plays an important role in longhouse culture. The Kayan especially maintain a wide range of **musical traditions** including the lute-like **sape**, used to accompany long voice epics. **Textiles** are woven by traditional techniques in the upriver longhouses, and Kayan and Kenyah **woodcarvings**, among the most spectacular in Southeast Asia, are produced both for sale and for ceremonial uses. One artist, Tusau Padan, originally from Kalimantan, became much revered. He used mixed media of vibrant colours to create the flowing motifs he applied to painting and textiles – adorning burial poles, longboats and the walls of many Ulu Sarawak chiefs' homes. Some Kayan still drink potent **rice wine**, although now that nearly all the communities have converted to Christianity, alcohol is harder to come by.

6

The town square and around

The first sight that confronts new arrivals climbing the steps from the river bank is Belaga's slightly shabby tennis and basketball court. Next door a small garden serves as the **town square**, with a hornbill statue atop a traditional-style round pillar bearing tribal motifs. There are just six streets and alleys in the centre, and while quite a few shops sell provisions, there's no market, though Orang Ulu traders may arrive at weekends to sell jungle produce in the streets. In the morning, picturesque mists settle on the Rejang.

Walks around Belaga

Having made it all the way here, the best thing you can do is luxuriate in Belaga's tranquillity, a welcome contrast from Kapit. Short walks lead through the **Malay kampung** just downriver (which includes the shanty town by the river for children from outlying villages attending the school here) or cross the river (boat RM5) and walk two hours through the jungle to the **Sihan** (a semi-nomadic people) village – there are only a handful of inhabitants now.

ARRIVAL AND DEPARTURE   BELAGA

By bus The one daily boat to Kapit, and on to Sibu, leaves around 7am. Boats terminate at a large sandbank below the town.

By 4WD Most days at least a couple of 4WD vehicles leave for Bintulu from the town square, usually in the early morning (3hr 30min; RM60/person). It costs RM50 to reach the main trunk road, where you can flag down a long-distance bus. Contact Daniel Levoh (see below) for a booking. Alternatively, it's possible for men and groups to hitch the route (just stand by the bridge in Belaga or at the junction on the main road) – you may be asked to pay RM20–60, so clarify whether you're expected to pay before you get in.

INFORMATION AND TOURS

Banks The town has a Bank Simpanan National, with ATM, three streets back from the river.

Tours and longhouse trips About the only person seriously organizing tours in Belaga is Daniel Levoh (see below), who runs trips to the small waterfall 20min away up a tributary (RM80 for one to four people), as well as an all-day tour to the Bakum Dam using 4WD and boat, which stops in various old and new longhouses on the way (RM600; one to three people) – this tour could drop you on the Bintalu–Miri highway. Although his guesthouse is very good value, the tours are pricey. However, if you bargain, prices may come down considerably.

ACCOMMODATION AND EATING

The town's Malay *kedai kopis* cluster on the main street, while there are a couple of Chinese places, which serve beer, a few doors down from the *Daniel Levoh Guesthouse*. None of them are bad, but none particularly good, and all close shortly after dark. This is when you can get the best food at the small **night food stalls** just north of the centre, which dish up inexpensive Malay foods including outstanding grilled meats and satay.

Belaga Main St ☎ 086 461244. The oldest of the main street's three all-but-identical hotels (all the same price) and it looks it too, with dated fittings. The simple en-suite rooms have a/c, and – this gives it the edge – there's a café below with wi-fi. **RM35**

★ **Daniel Levoh Guesthouse** Two blocks behind Main St ☎ 013 848 6351. More like a homestay, with two double rooms and a dorm that open up on to a nice and homely communal area where there is also a small kitchen. Daniel, an ex-history teacher, is a good host, and can tell you stories in the evening about the local area over a glass of *tuak*. Dorm **RM15**, doubles **RM40**

Sing Soon Huat At the end of a lane, just back from the Sing Soon Hing ☎ 086 461346. Sharing management with the nearby *Sing Soon Hing*, these are probably the best rooms in town; bigger and a little quieter than those on the main street, with a/c, TV and better en-suite bathrooms. **RM50**

The coast from Sibu to Bintulu

The drive from Sibu to Bintulu is mundane, the roadscape lacking the grandeur of southwest Sarawak's mountains, though there are occasional glimpses of (usually modern) longhouses by the highway. The chief point of interest on this coastal stretch is **Similajau National Park**, a strip of forest with isolated beaches thirty minutes' drive beyond the industrial town of **Bintulu**. With plenty of time, you could also get a dose of the culture of the largely Muslim Melanau people by diverting off the trunk road to the small coastal market town of **Mukah**. While not of huge interest in itself, it's a potential base for the Melanau water village of **Kampung Tellian**, which has a heritage centre, **Lamin Dana**, that you can also stay at.

Kampung Tellian and around

The Melanau water village of **KAMPUNG TELLIAN**, 3km east of **MUKAH**, is a veritable spaghetti junction of ramshackle wooden houses connected by precarious crisscrossing boardwalks and bridges. It's an immensely atmospheric and peaceful spot, the kind of place where you might wish you were born so that you could always go back there. Some of the Melanau residents of its many stilt houses still process sago the traditional way – by pulverizing the pith in large troughs and squeezing the pulp through a sieve, then leaving it to dry.

Lamin Dana

Daily 9am–5pm for non-residents; closed public hols • RM3 • ☎ 019 849 5962, ✉ genistarose@gmail.com

Aside from its picturesque appeal, Tellian's main attraction is its beautiful heritage centre and guesthouse, **Lamin Dana**, built in 1999 in the style of a traditional Melanau tall house, though not quite on the scale of the one at the Sarawak Cultural Village in Santubong (see p.330). Exhibits include a collection of betel-nut jars, once used to store heirlooms, finely woven textiles for ceremonial occasions, musical instruments – including the obligatory gongs – and handicrafts such as hand-woven rattan baskets for which the Melanau are well known. A short walk along the plankway to the front of the tall house reveals a Melanau burial ground, or *bakut*, amid a clump of bare, ancient trees.

ARRIVAL AND DEPARTURE	KAMPUNG TELLIAN AND AROUND

By plane No buses run between Mukah's airport, 4km northwest of town, and the town itself; a taxi costs around RM15.

Destinations Kuching (3 daily; 1hr); Miri (1 daily; 1hr 10min) – both on MASwings.

By bus The bus station in Mukah lies off Jalan Sedia Raja,

THE BAKUN DAM

The massive **Bakun hydroelectric dam** (ⓦ sarawak-hidro.com), 37km east of Belaga on the Balui tributary of the Rejang, has been dogged by controversy since the project got the go-ahead in the 1990s. The 200m-high dam was designed to generate 2400 megawatts – much more power than Sarawak could use – but construction would flood an area of rainforest the size of Singapore, displacing ten thousand Orang Ulu and destroying many thriving longhouses.

Furious environmentalists and human-rights campaigners asked what was the point, and for years their concerns seemed vindicated as the dam was beset by delays. First, the Asian economic crisis of 1997 put the project on hold, but even so the government continued to resettle local communities to Asap, two hours' drive along the logging road connecting Belaga with the coast. When construction resumed it lumbered on until, in mid-2011, the dam finally began operating. However, it still doesn't run at anything near capacity, since there is no obvious market for the surplus power (one idea, to lay a submarine cable to Peninsular Malaysia, would be technically challenging and prohibitively expensive). Despite this, yet another dam is being built just upriver on the Rejang at Long Murum, with another proposed at Baram (see p.380) – the latter two have seen massive protests and blockades by local people.

Attempts have already begun to create tourist facilities at the Bakun Dam lake, as has been tried with limited success at Batang Ai and Tasik Kenyir in Terengganu, though these have yet to bear fruit and the hotel there is mostly used to house dam workers. Sibu's tourist office (see p.343) and Daniel Levoh (see opposite) in Belaga (whose family live there) have details of the enormous and quite swanky Kenyah **longhouses** at Asap that accept guests (RM30/person), and whose inhabitants have a fishing lodge on the lake itself.

6

on the southern edge of the old town.
Destinations Bintulu (3 daily; 3hr); Miri (1–2 daily; 7hr); Sibu (3 daily; 3hr 30min).

By taxi Taxis from Mukah's bus terminus can take you to Kampung Tellian for RM6–10. Note that all taxi-drivers finish work at around 4 or 5pm.

ACCOMMODATION AND EATING

Lamin Dana Kampung Tellian ☎019 849 5962, ⊕ lamindana.blogspot.com. This recreated tall house is an atmospheric place to stay, with ten variously sized, airy doubles and a couple of family rooms. Bathrooms are shared and there's no a/c. If you come on a package, you'll be taken on a boat trip through the mangroves, do a guided village walk, and see a sago-processing demonstration; contact proprietor Diana Rose for details and to customize an itinerary. Doubles

with breakfast RM80, three-day, two-night full-board package including pick-up from Mukah for two RM400

Sri Umpang Hotel 29 Jalan Lintang, Mukah ☎084 872415. Mukah's best choice is a 20min walk from the bus station in the old town, with a bright and appealing foyer and clean, a/c rooms with sizeable bathrooms. Best to book ahead as it's often full; the similar, though slightly more expensive, *Weiming Hotel* is just a few doors down. RM40

Bintulu

Forty years ago, **BINTULU** was little more than a resting point en route between Sibu (220km to the southwest) and Miri (210km northeast). Since large **natural gas** reserves were discovered offshore in the 1960s, however, speedy expansion has seen Bintulu follow in Miri's footsteps as a primary resources boom town. Today some quite prosperous neighbourhoods can be seen on the outskirts, though the old centre remains as unassuming as ever. There are only two reasons why you might want to stop over: to use Bintulu as a base for the excellent **Similajau National Park** or, if you're heading south from Miri, as a springboard for **Belaga** and the Batang Rejang (see p.349). You can also reach **Niah National Park** (see p.361) from here (though it's easier to go on a trip with one of the Miri backpacker lodges), while any express bus to Miri can drop you at **Lambir Hills National Park** (see p.361).

The old centre

You could spend a couple of hours strolling around Bintulu's **old centre**, a grid of streets squashed between the defunct airfield to the east and the wide Kemena River to the west. This is why the town feels so low-key: the centre simply hasn't been able to grow. It looks as though developers and road builders may soon finally be allowed to chip away at the unaccountably abandoned airfield, however, so the heart of Bintulu may soon look very different.

The obvious place to start is on Main Bazaar in front of **Tian En Ting**, a grand Chinese temple that's really in too good a state of repair to impress. Recent beautification of the **riverfront** has created the open square here, as well as an esplanade and parkland area

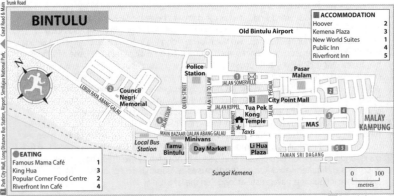

BINTULU TO BELAGA BY ROAD

When the water level in the Batang Rejang is too low for boats to reach Belaga, the one sure way to get there – and an interesting drive through remote terrain – is by **4WD** from Bintulu. The 4hr journey involves turning south off the main trunk road, 50km out of Bintulu, on to the road for the Bakun dam (see p.351), 125km southeast.

After 80km, another right turn puts you on a logging road which, while not a classic bone-shaker, is roughish much of the way. The road undulates at first through jungled areas, then climbs steadily, snaking past isolated communities and through areas either already under oil palm or being cleared for it. Eventually there are gorgeous views of lushly forested peaks in the distance; the highest, **Bukit Lumut** at nearly 1000m, is 25km west of Belaga. If you do the return leg in the morning you'll probably see whole valleys blanketed in mist, too. Just as bumping along begins to pall, the road descends quite steeply, and you pull into Belaga.

One or two 4WDs leave Bintulu daily at around 1.30pm for Belaga, with pick-up from hotels or other central locations by arrangement; a seat costs RM60. You can book the service with Daniel Levoh in Belaga (see p.350).

6

leading north towards the South China Sea – only 3km away, concealed beyond the Kemena's final bend.

Just downriver are the modern **day market** (*pasar utama*) and the more informal **Tamu Bintulu**, where locals still bring in goods and lay them on rough tables to sell. The jetties behind are a good place to observe life on the river: fishing boats bring their catch in every morning, barges laden with timber or building materials lumber past, while the opposite bank is dotted with rustic kampung houses.

ARRIVAL AND DEPARTURE

BINTULU

By plane Bintulu's airport, 5km southwest of town (☎086 331073), holds an AirAsia and a MAS ticket office. It can only be reached by a circuitous road route, detouring east and then south of town. A taxi into the centre costs RM37 (25min).

Destinations Kota Kinabalu (1–2 daily; 1hr 15min); Kuala Lumpur (4 daily; 2hr 10min); Kuching (5–6 daily; 55min); Miri (2–3 daily; 35min); Sibu (10 daily; 35min).

By bus Bintulu's long-distance bus station is 5km northeast of town in the lively suburb of Medan Jaya. You might be able to find an hourly local bus into the centre, but otherwise you'll have to pay around RM15 for a taxi.

Destinations Kuching (every 20min–hourly; 11hr); Miri (every 20–30min; 4hr); Mukah (3 daily; 3hr); Pontianak (Indonesia; at least 3 daily; 19hr); Sibu (every 20–30min; 4hr).

By minivan Minivans (which leave when full) ply the highway up to Miri and down to Sibu; the depot is in front of Tamu Bintulu. One route north passes the turning to Similajau National Park (RM5).

By taxi The main taxi rank (☎086 332009) is next to the Tian En Ting temple.

ACCOMMODATION

Central Bintulu holds a number of unexciting **budget hotels**, all with a/c, en-suite rooms. The cheapest are in the red-light district east of Li Hua Plaza, but are a bit unsavoury. Several business-oriented hotels, including some north of the centre towards the seafront, cater to visiting oil-industry executives.

Hoover 92 Jalan Keppel ☎086 337166, ✉hoover hotelbtu@gmail.com. Brightly lit at night, this concrete block has slightly more comfortable rooms than others in its class (with carpet, thick curtains and clean bathrooms). Also has a comfortable lobby with wi-fi. **RM81**

Kemena Plaza Jalan Abang Galau ☎086 335111, ✉kemanaplazahotel@yahoo.com. A business-oriented hotel with an opulent lobby, rooftop swimming pool, bar, restaurant and café – though the atmosphere can be sterile. The unusually keen rates include breakfast. **RM150**

Public Inn 47 Jalan Abang Galau (Main Bazaar) ☎019 815 5510. Very clean, safe, quiet and respectable guesthouse with good-value rooms that have comfortable beds, TV, a/c and wi-fi, as well as friendly, helpful staff. There's a food court right next door. **RM60**

★ **Riverfront Inn** 256 Taman Sri Dagang ☎086 333111, ✉riverfrontinn@hotmail.com. Both smart (for Bintulu) and homely, and thus deservedly popular even though it lacks the facilities of the *Kemena Plaza*. Rooms are comfortable and done out in muted colours, and the busy restaurant is open all hours (see p.354) and does room service. Doubles vary in size, but discounts for single occupancy are trifling. **RM110**

EATING

Buoyed by oil and gas money and a small expat population, Bintulu boasts several decent restaurants, though many – along with a handful of bars – are in the suburbs. Still, quite a few **central eating places** are worth trying, and for evening snacks you can always try the *pasar malam* in the open space close to the airfield.

★**Famous Mama Café** Jalan Somerville ☎086 336541. The closest thing you'll find to a West Malaysian *mamak*-style joint, this excellent Indian *kedai kopis* draws in people of all colours and faiths to socialize and stuff their faces from the great *nasi campur* spread (eaten with plain or *biriyani* rice) or various *roti* plates – around RM5–10. Daily 7.30am–11pm.

★**King Hua** Between Jalan Keppel and Jalan Masjid ☎086 337255. The most popular venue on a lane turned over to open-air restaurants, the *King Hua* packs them in with its yummy fresh seafood – black pepper crab, steamed pomfret, even prawns cooked in Guinness – plus more usual Chinese dishes such as lemon chicken and vegetable stir-fries. While not in any way salubrious, it's hugely atmospheric. The menu is devoid of prices, partly because seafood is sold by weight; reckon on RM25/person for fresh, excluding drinks, or RM10–20 if

you choose a regular rice or noodle dish. Daily 8am–midnight.

Popular Corner Food Centre Lebuhraya Abang Galau. The size of four or five *kedai kopis* put together, this brilliant food court could hold its own in downtown KL. An endless range of stalls sell the likes of duck noodles, *yong tau foo* and dim sum, and there's a pastry stall doing custard tarts and local savouries including sweet potato or yam fritters. You can easily eat for RM4–10. Daily 7am–10pm.

Riverfront Inn Café Riverfront Inn, 256 Taman Sri Dagang ☎086 333111. A mere hotel coffee house it may be, but in Bintulu's centre it counts as posh. Come for the slap-up "Borneo breakfast" (sausage, beans and eggs, plus toast and coffee or tea for RM10) or a late meal if you arrive at an ungodly hour. Western choices include fish and chips and spaghetti. Daily 24hr.

DIRECTORY

Hospital Bintulu Jalan Nyabau (☎086 255899, ⊛hbtu .moh.gov.my) is 13km from downtown (a 15min taxi ride at least).

Pharmacies The Park City Mall has branches of Guardian and Watsons.

Police Jalan Somerville ☎086 332004.

Post office There's a branch post office on the unnamed road behind Jalan Somervile.

Visa extensions Immigration Department, 3km north of the centre on Jalan Tun Razak (☎086 331441).

Similajau National Park

With its sandy beaches broken only by rocky headlands and freshwater streams, the seventy-square-kilometre **SIMILAJAU NATIONAL PARK**, 28km northeast of Bintulu by road, has something of the appeal of the highly popular Bako, near Kuching. Enjoyable trekking makes for a great day-trip, and there's even good accommodation. Though wildlife is not a major highlight, the park is well known for its population of saltwater **crocodiles** (signs along the creeks pointedly warn against swimming), with a few dolphins also sighted each year off the coast outside the rainy season. Birdlife includes black hornbills and, in the mangroves, kingfishers.

The main trail

The first stretch of the 10km **main trail** – which runs northeast, mostly just inland, from the park office – has you crossing a bridge over the mouth of the Likau, more of a large brown creek than a river, and heading into the jungle. Around 1km in, a short side branch leads west to a **viewpoint** – a wooden pavilion perched over a rocky beach, from where you can just spot Bintulu's oil and gas installations at Tanjung Kidurong, 15km north of town. Return to the trail and you come eventually to **Turtle Beach I** (6km along; allow 3hr to reach it), then **Turtle Beach II** (total 7.5km along) and finally **Golden Beach** (10km; 4hr). You can overnight at any of them in the hope of spotting **turtles**, who nest here from March to September, though there are no facilities and you should inform park staff of your intentions. Sadly, **swimming** at these beaches is not advised, because the sea is deep even close to shore and there's a strong undertow, though other smaller stretches of sand en route are okay for a dip.

Minor trails

A few short trails branch inland off the main trail within its first kilometre. The best leads to **Batu Anchau**, a curious flat rock formation in a stream bed, close to a small waterfall. It's a good site for a picnic and for spotting pitcher plants; allow ninety minutes to reach it from the park headquarters. You don't need to return the way you came – continue north along the trail, and you soon rejoin the main trail near the 3km marker.

ARRIVAL AND INFORMATION   SIMILAJAU NATIONAL PARK   6

By minibus The park lies 9km down an access road off the coastal road to Miri; minibuses heading along the coast road from Bintulu can drop you at the junction from where you can walk or hitch.

By taxi Taxis from Bintulu cost at least RM50 one way, and the driver can collect you for the same price.

Park HQ The friendly and helpful staff at the Park HQ (☎ 086 327284, ☎ 019 861998, ☎ sarawakforestry.com), where you pay the admission fee (RM20), can provide a schematic trail map; find you a guide (RM30/hr); book you on a night walk on which you just might see pangolins or wild boar (RM40/person, minimum five people); and arrange boat trips.

GETTING AROUND

By boat Boats are a useful timesaver – instead of trekking in two directions, you can pay RM220 (RM280 return) for a boat for up to five passengers to head out to Golden Beach, or RM180 (RM230 return) to either of the Turtle beaches, then trek back. You can also use boats to reach Batu Mandi

("bath rock" in Malay), a rock formation out at sea with large depressions that regularly fill with sea water (RM150), or do a so-called night cruise along the Likau to spot kingfishers and those notorious crocodiles (RM150, up to six people).

ACCOMMODATION AND EATING

Similajau National Park accommodation ☎ 086 391284. The park's generally under-utilized accommodation makes it a relaxing place to spend a night or two. There's quite a range on offer, from two hostels that have rooms rather than dorms, each with one bunk

bed and some with a bathroom too, to quite fancy new a/c accommodation; check for the latest pricing. A simple canteen serves the usual rice and noodle dishes for RM5–12. Camping RM5, hostel rooms RM42, a/c lodge rooms RM159

The northern coast

North of Bintulu, the scenery along the main trunk road is increasingly dominated by oil-palm estates; if you're driving, the quiet coastal highway is a more scenic option for the 210km drive to **Miri**, Sarawak's second largest city. Though boasting no important sights, Miri is nearly as important a gateway to Sarawak as Kuching, thanks to good flight connections and its location amid the riches of northern Sarawak, mostly deep inland and requiring days to explore properly. A couple of national parks lie close to the coast south of Miri: **Niah** is noted for its formidable **limestone caves**, while **Lambir Hills** offers more predictable jungle trekking.

Sarawak's northern coastal strip is also home to **Lawas**, near the Sabah state boundary. It has an air connection to Ba Kelalan that's useful if you want to see the Kelabit Highlands immediately after or before visiting Sabah.

Miri

Before oil was discovered in 1882, **MIRI** was a tiny, unimportant settlement. While production has now shifted offshore, the petroleum industry largely accounts for the thriving city of today, with a population of 300,000. Some of Miri's earliest inhabitants were pioneering **Chinese** merchants who set up shops to trade with the Kayan longhouses southeast along the Batang Baram, and the city retains a strong Chinese flavour, though the Iban and Malays are also well represented, along with a significant number of Orang Ulu.

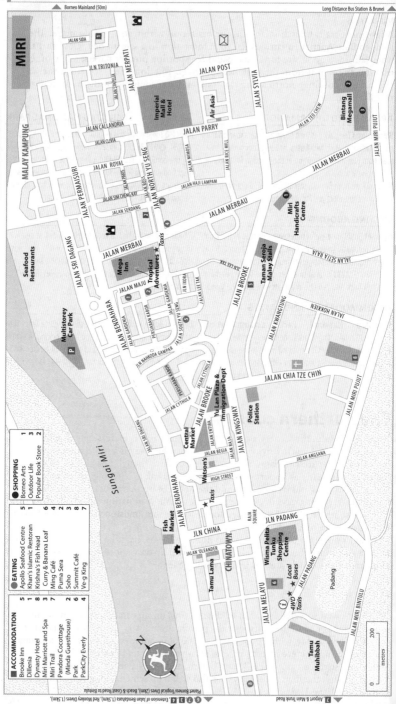

MIRI

Borneo Mainland (50m)

Long Distance Bus Station & Brunei

JALAN SIDA
JLN TRITONIA
JALAN MERPATI
JALAN STAPELIA
JALAN POST
JALAN SYLVIA
JALAN CALLANDRIA
JALAN CLIVIA
Imperial Mall & Hotel
Air Asia
JALAN PARRY
JALAN TEO CHEW
Bintang Megamall
JALAN MIRI PUJUT
MALAY KAMPUNG
JALAN ROYAL
JALAN PERMAISURI
JALAN SRI DAGANG
JALAN PARIS
JALAN SIM CHENG KAY
JALAN ROSS
JALAN NORTH YU SENG
JALAN MIMOSA
JALAN RICE MILL
JALAN HAJI LAMPAM
JALAN SERDANG
JALAN MERBAU
JALAN MERBAU
Seafood Restaurants
Miri Handicrafts Centre
Multistorey Car Park
P
JALAN MERBAU
Mega Inn
Tropical Adventures ★
Taxis
JAN LEE TAK
Taman Seroja Malay Stalls
JALAN BENDAHARA
JALAN MAJU
JALAN GARDENIA
JALAN GARDENIA
PERSIARAN KABOR
JALAN GARDENIA
JALAN SOUTH YU SENG
JLN IXORA
JALAN LEE TAK
JALAN BROOKE
JALAN SETIA RAJA
JALAN KWANGTUNG
JLN NAHKODA GAMPAR
PERSIARAN KABOR
JALAN CYTHULA
JALAN HOKKIEN
JALAN CHIA TZE CHIN
JALAN MIRI PUJUT
JALAN SRI DAGANG
JALAN CYTHULA
JALAN CYTHULA
Yu Lan Plaza & Immigration Dept
Police Station
Central Market
JALAN BROOKE
JALAN ERITEA
JALAN KINGSWAY
JALAN BEGIA
JALAN RAJA
Watson's
HIGH STREET
JALAN ANGSANA
Fish Market
Taxis
JALAN BENDAHARA
RAJA SQUARE
JLN CHINA
JLN PADANG
Wisma Pelita Tunku Shopping Centre
CHINATOWN
JALAN 'OLEANDER
Tamu Lama
JALAN MELAYU
Local Buses ★
4WD Taxis
JALAN PADANG
Padang
JALAN MIRI BINTULU
Tamu Muhibbah

Sungai Miri

N

0   200   metres

Planet Borneo/Tropical Dives (2km), Red Monkey Divers (1.5km),
Extension of Jalan Bendahara (1.5km), Beach & Coast Road to Bintulu
Airport & Main Trunk Road

■ ACCOMMODATION	
Brooke Inn	5
Dillenia	1
Dynasty Hotel	8
Krishna's Fish Head	3
Miri Trail	7
Pandora Cocottage (Minda Guesthouse)	2
Park	6
ParkCity Everly	4

● EATING	
Apollo Seafood Centre	5
Khan's Islamic Restoran	1
Krishna's Fish Head	8
Curry & Banana Leaf	6
Ming Café	4
Puma Sera	2
Soho	3
Summit Café	6
Ve-g King	7

● SHOPPING	
Borneo Arts	1
Outdoor Life	3
Popular Book Store	2

6

   Now blandly modern for the most part, Miri makes a surprisingly pleasant base from which to see northern Sarawak; visitors generally wind up staying longer than expected, sometimes in several stints interspersed with trips into the interior. The town is unusually placed within a hairpin bend of the Miri River, with its centre on the east bank close to the river mouth; beyond the west "bank", a mere sliver of land seldom more than 500m wide, lies the South China Sea. In terms of sights, it holds one museum focusing on – guess – the oil industry, plus a few **markets** and a not bad stretch of beach. Where Miri shines is in its great restaurants, accommodation and **air connections**. The hub for MASwings' services to the tiny settlements of the interior (see p.366), Miri also has flights to Kuching, KK, KL and Singapore.

6

Markets
Mostly open daily during daylight hours

Though eminently walkable and easy to navigate, the centre lacks any obvious focus. It makes sense to start exploring at the clutch of **markets** close to Jalan China and the padang. The most interesting, the **Tamu Muhibbah** on Jalan Padang, is across from the tourist office. Nothing very unusual is sold in its main building, but the little building at the back is used by indigenous traders selling produce such as *akar bakawali*, spiny twigs boiled up as a high blood pressure cure, and "Bario rice" in various colours (it may in fact be varieties from Bario and grown elsewhere, rather than the genuine article for which the Kelabit Highlands are known). Less positively, you may also spot items that it's no longer legal to sell, such as porcupine quills and other animal-derived products.

   A few minutes' walk north, in the **Tamu Lama** (also signed **Tamu Kedayan**) on Jalan Oleander, Malay traders sell foodstuffs and dried-leaf strips woven into square parcels for cooking *ketupat*, the rice cakes eaten with satay. Just beyond on Jalan Bendahara, next to the Chinese temple, is a lively **fish market**. Most prominent but least interesting of all is the large **Central Market** a couple of minutes' walk east on Jalan Brooke, known to Malays as the *pasar babi* or "pig market", as it's where Chinese meat traders operate. If you're around at the weekend, look out for more jungle produce being sold at a **Sunday market** in the streets to the south of the Tamu Lama (until around 1pm).

Petroleum Museum
Canada Hill (aka Bukit Tenaga); turn off Jalan Miri Pujut opposite Jalan Setia Raja • Tues–Sun 9am–4.30pm, closed some public hols • Free • Taxis up cost at least RM18, or it's a stiff 20min climb

From certain points in downtown Miri, for example along Jalan Kingsway, you can catch glimpses of what appears to be a tapering tower on the wooded ridge east of the centre. The tower is the **Grand Old Lady**, Miri's first oil well, drilled in 1910 and now marking Miri's one purpose-built sight, the **Petroleum Museum**. Unfortunately the displays are – pardon the pun – boring, concentrating on the technical aspects of drilling and refining, with some historical context but no tales of the human impact the nascent industry must surely have had.

The beach
Just over 3km southwest of the padang • Buses #13 and #15 (RM2) head out here from the local bus station; taxi around RM18

The coast road out of town (the extension of Jalan Kubu) holds a stretch of public beach around 500m long. The sands are fairly narrow, but it's a relaxed enough spot and a fine place to watch the sun go down. The beach's proper name is **Tanjung Lobang**, though many locals (and bus timetables) call it **Taman Selera** as Malay stalls sell seafood at a simple evenings-only food court. Buses stop around 6pm, so hanging around for the sunset means either trudging back into town or hoping that a taxi is available at the *ParkCity Everly* hotel, 800m in towards the centre.

ARRIVAL AND DEPARTURE   MIRI

By plane Miri Airport is 10km south of town   (☎085 417315, ⌨miriairport.com); AirAsia and MAS/

MASwings have ticket offices in the departure lounge. To get a taxi into town, buy a RM25 voucher from the taxi counter. Destinations Ba Kelalan (4 weekly, 3 of them via Lawas; 55min–1hr 30min); Bario (2 daily, plus one via Marudi; 50min–1hr 15min); Bintulu (2–3 daily; 35min); Johor Bahru (1 daily; 1hr 55min); Kota Kinabalu (3–5 daily; 50min); Kuala Lumpur (8–10 daily; 2hr 10min); Kuching (6–7daily; 1hr); Labuan (5 daily; 40min); Lawas (4–5 daily; 45min); Limbang (3 daily; 35min); Long Akah (2 weekly, via Marudi; 40min–1hr); Long Banga (1 weekly via Marudi; 1hr 20min); Long Lellang (2 weekly, 1 via Marudi; 45min–1hr 15min); Long Seridan (2 weekly, 1 via Marudi; 40min–1hr); Marudi (3–5 daily; 20min); Mukah (1 daily; 1hr); Mulu (2 daily; 30min); Sibu (3 daily; 55min); Singapore (4 weekly; 2hr).

By bus The long-distance bus station is at Pujut Corner, 4km northeast of the centre off Jalan Miri Pujut. Services to Bandar Seri Begawan in Brunei, via Kuala Belait and Seria, are run by PHLS (☎085 407175; daily 8.15am & 3.45pm; 4hr); it's seldom necessary to book tickets in advance, but you must show up 30min before departure, as the conductor gathers passport details for the border crossing. Borneo Express runs a bus to Kota Kinabalu (☎085 430420;

daily 8am; 11hr), which passes through Brunei but does not call at the capital. Heading all the way to KK is laborious and entails four border crossings and thus eight new stamps in your passport, so many people choose to fly via Mulu or Bario. To get into town, you can either wait around for the infrequent #20 bus (every 60–90min) or take a taxi (RM18) or, better still, a *kereta sapu* (RM10). Destinations Bintulu (every 20–30min; 4hr); Kota Kinabalu (1 daily; 11hr); Kuching (every 20min–hourly; 15hr); Lawas (3 daily; 6hr 30min); Limbang (2–3 daily; 5hr); Mukah (1–2 daily; 7hr); Pontianak (Indonesia; at least 3 daily; 24hr); Sibu (every 20–30min; 8hr).

By kereta sapu Miri is one part of Sarawak where you might want to make use of informal taxis to head into the northern interior – most places can be reached by logging roads, although it will be a long and expensive slog. Some vehicles leave regularly from the streets close to the tourist office; others will need to be arranged in advance through you accommodation in Miri or Barrio.

Car rental Transworld, second floor, Wisma Pelita Tunku (☎085 422227, ⓦtwtmiri.com.my); Kong Teck, at the airport (☎085 617767, ⓦ kongteck.com.my).

GETTING AROUND

By local bus As Miri's centre is easily walkable, you're only likely to catch a bus from the tiny local bus station, across the padang next to the tourist office, to get to the beach, airport (#22 and #28; hourly at best), or long-distance bus terminal (#20; hourly).

By bicycle If you need to putter around town or head to

the beach, rent bicycles (RM10/week) from Hock Sen Hin (☎085 412255) on Jalan Rice Mill.

By taxi Miri Taxi Association (☎085 432277) and Koperasi Teksi Miri (☎085 431000) are both 24hr. Meters are not used, so agree the price beforehand; the minimum fare is RM18.

INFORMATION

Tourist office Miri's excellent Visitors' Information Centre, on Jalan Padang at the southern end of downtown (Mon–Fri 8am–5pm, Sat & Sun 9am–3pm; ☎085 434181, ⓔvic-miri@sarawaktourism.com),

covers all of northern Sarawak as well as Bintulu, and has good maps and leaflets. A Sarawak Forestry desk here (Mon–Fri) has up-to-date information on nearby national parks.

TOUR OPERATORS

A small number of tour operators offer Mulu and Kelabit Highlands packages, as well as, more usefully, genuinely imaginative trips to help you get off the beaten track in the upriver Baram and other parts of the interior. A couple of firms offer **dive trips** at the reefs off Miri's coast, which offer a few wreck dives; practically all sites are within an hour's boat ride.

Borneo Mainland Lot 1081 Jalan Merpati ☎085 433511, ⓦ borneomainland.com. One- to three-day birdwatching trips to little-visited Loagan Bunut National Park, as well as packages to the usual Sarawak and Sabah destinations.

Planet Borneo/Tropical Dives Brighton Centre, Jalan Temenggong Datuk Oyong Lawai, on road out to the beach ☎085 415582, ⓦplanetborneotours.com. A veteran company with a range of trips throughout Borneo and especially northern Sarawak. Offerings include several day-trips around Miri, Mulu overland starting from Miri, plus trips to the Kelabit Highlands and the Batang Ai. They also have a dive operation.

Red Monkey Divers Off Jalan Dato Abang Indeh, a few minutes' walk south of the Visitors' Information Centre ☎014 699 8296, ⓦredmonkeydivers.com. PADI courses plus guided and unguided dives, and other courses up to and including dive master.

Tropical Adventure Across the road from Puma Sera restaurant on Jalan Maju ☎085 419337, ⓦborneo tropicaladventure.com. Well-thought-through packages from this excellent outfit include trips to Mulu, the Kelabit Highlands – some taking the route from Bario to Ba Kelalan, and other much longer trips of up to fourteen days. They're also good for excursions on the Headhunters' Trail (see p.370).

ACCOMMODATION

Miri's accommodation is mostly used by **business travellers**, or tourists just passing through. It's not cheap, and although there are quite a few budget hotels (under RM40) in the backstreets around *Mega Hotel* they are pretty bad, with tiny airless rooms, and the area is a bit of a red-light district.

GUESTHOUSES

Brooke Inn 14 Brooke Inn ☎085 412881, ✉brookeinn @hotmail.com. One of the oldest (and strangely atmospheric) hotels in town, and a bit of a museum piece, too – the rooms are plain and worn, and don't seem to have been altered much in almost fifty years. Still, they are spotless, with a/c and TV, and rates are low. RM55

★**Dillenia** Jalan Sida ☎085 434204, ⓦsites.google .com/site/dilleniaguesthouse. Named after a shrub found all over Malaysia, this guesthouse has a cosy lounge painted green, plus dorms and rooms on two floors, including a family room that sleeps four. It's very relaxed, but what really sets it apart is that it's impeccably managed by the super-efficient Mrs Lee, who can organize transport to the two nearby national parks and other local destinations (service available to non-guests). Dorms RM30, doubles RM80, family room RM110

★**Dynasty** Jalan Miri Pujut ☎085 421111, ⓦdynasty hotelmiri.com.my. The good impression given by this hotel's sizeable marbled lobby is reinforced by the spacious, comfortable rooms; some have bathtubs and sea views, too. Facilities include a mini-gym and sauna, though no pool; it's among the best-value places in its class. Rates include breakfast, unless you get their weekend RM60 discount. RM191

Miri Marriott and Spa Jalan Temenggong Datuk Oyong Lawai, nearly 2km south of the padang ☎085 421121, ⓦmarriotthotels.com/myymc. One of Miri's two seaside hotels, this has had to smother its beach with boulders after the new marina nearby raised the risk of flooding; if you stay, it will be for the five-star amenities, Sarawak's largest freeform swimming pool and the spa

offering Balinese massage. Packages offering spa discounts usually available. RM335

Miri Trail Across the road from the airport, behind the MASWings office ☎017 850 3666, ⓦmiritrail.weebly .com. This useful guesthouse saves air passengers the taxi fare into town, but also means you miss out on Miri's restaurants and shops. Both rooms and dorms are clean and comfortable, if a little spartan. Discounts if you stay just a few hours. Dorms RM25, doubles RM55

Pandora Cocottage (previously Minda Guesthouse) F1, 637 North Yu Seng Rd ☎085 411422, ✉pandora cocottage@gmail.com. With new management (they're having trouble getting everyone to note their name change), this guesthouse is still somewhat haphazardly run, though it partly makes amends through its informality and sociabilty, and the rooms are clean and comfortable enough. It's on a busy stretch for bars and restaurants and so the rooms by the street (which includes both dorms) can be noisy till late. It's also big, with a rooftop area from where you can take in the nightlife below. Dorms RM20, doubles RM50

Park Jalan Raja, by the tourist office ☎085 414555. This large 1970s hotel, one of the oldest in town, could do with a little refurbishment, though rooms aren't a bad size. Good value, with parking, wi-fi, and some decent views from the upper floors – rates include breakfast. RM87

ParkCity Everly Jalan Temenggong Datuk Oyong Lawai, 2.5km southwest of padang ☎085 440288, ⓦvhhotels.com. Unlike the *Marriott*, this seaside hotel has kept its beach and boasts reasonable rates, too. Some of the luxurious, spacious rooms have great views over the lush garden with its pool, and the sands just beyond; sea views cost RM25 extra. RM148

EATING, DRINKING AND ENTERTAINMENT

Miri's eating scene rivals Kuching's for quality, if not variety – it's a treat to taste genuinely delicious and interesting food after days spent hiking in the northern interior. **North and South Yu Seng roads** hold a particular concentration of restaurants, while along the riverfront you'll find a bunch of not-bad seafood places (no sea views, but occasional sightings of crocodiles in the Miri River). For inexpensive **stalls**, try the Chinese options at the Central Market (also good for cheap beer) or the Malay outlets on Jalan North Yu Seng and at Taman Seroja, up the road from the *Brooke Inn*. Unfortunately the **bars** aren't up to much. Apart from a couple of so-so establishments near the *Dillenia* guesthouse, not geared towards backpackers, venues opposite the *Minda* guesthouse on Jalan North Yu Seng are your best bet for a drink in generally karaoke-free surroundings. Miri does have one annual cultural event of note – the **Borneo Jazz Festival**, held in May at various locations (ⓦjazzborneo.com).

Apollo Seafood Centre 4 Jalan South Yu Seng ☎085 420813. Not much to look at, this old-fashioned Chinese place serves well-regarded standards such as fish-head curry. Around RM25 without drinks, though much more if eating fresh seafood. Daily 10.30am–11pm.

Khan's Islamic Restoran 233 Jalan Maju ☎085 418440. Though a little dreary, this is a well-established *kedai kopis* where the cheap-and-cheerful description really does apply (most dishes RM4–5). Offerings are predictable: *nasi campur*, a range of *biriyani* dishes, vindaloo curries (veg and non-veg) and tandoori chicken, plus various *roti* and *murtabak* options. Daily 6am–9pm or so.

★**Krishna's Fish Head Curry & Banana Leaf** Centrepoint 2, Jalan Kubu ☎ 085 430095. A modern, airy open-air restaurant serving enormous portions of "South Indian" food: order a plain or *biriyani* set plate and you'll be presented with a mound of rice, four curries, four dhal curries and soups, and poppadoms – enough to feed two. Around RM12–15 with a soft drink; there are also less expensive *dosas* and *roti*. Daily 7am–10pm.

Ming Café Corner of Jalan North Yu Seng and Jalan Merbau ☎ 085 422797. One of the most popular restaurants with foreigners, with an a/c indoor section and a prominent, more bar-like, section outside with powerful ceiling fans. Separate menus feature Chinese stir-fries (under RM10), Indian curries (RM5–10) and some Western offerings (RM11–28) such as fish and chips, all OK if a little overpriced. Still, it's not a bad place for a drink – they offer Corona and Paulaner bottled beers, among other imported brands. Daily 10am–11pm; later on Fri & Sat.

★**Puma Sera** Corner of Jalan Maju and Persiaran Kabor ☎ 085 413468. A tiptop Malay/Indonesian *kedai kopis* with a fantastic *nasi campur* spread that might feature *ikan patin* (catfish) curry or *umai* or chilli-fried aubergine. It's also a good place to try the Indonesian dish that's become a fad in Miri, *lalapan*: *lapan* means "eight" in Malay, so chicken *lalapan*, for example, is a plate of fried chicken, rice, Malay *ulam* (herbal salad) and condiments – eight items in all. Reckon on RM10–15 with a soft drink. Daily 24hr.

★**Soho** Jalan North Yu Seng ☎ 085 413388. Only one page of the menu at this so-called tapas bar features the stuff, followed by vast lists of pizzas, pasta dishes and sandwiches. The good news is that everything is pretty tasty – the pizzas especially – and the venue itself features an outdoor bar under a thatched roof, a pool table and chilled-out R&B/jazzy sounds. Reckon on RM25 with a soft drink. As a bar, it's one of Miri's busiest nightspots; happy hour until 9pm. Daily 4pm–1am.

★**Summit Café** Off Jalan Melayu; head up the lane with Maybank on the corner and you'll see it on the left. One of Sarawak's most interesting restaurants: run by a friendly Kenyah woman whose husband is Kelabit, it serves Kelabit food of a sort you may struggle to turn up in Bario. Specialities include *labo senutuk*, smoked shredded pork or wild boar, and *kasam*, a sour/salty fermented combination of wild boar and rice. The latter is sold in plastic tubs, but you order most dishes from a *nasi campur* spread to be eaten with rice or *nuba laya*, made by pounding cooked rice till smooth and then steaming it wrapped in leaves – around RM10. Mon–Sat 7am–4pm (or when the food runs out); closed two weeks at Christmas/New Year.

Ve-g King A few doors down from Krishna's on Jalan Kubu ☎ 085 432005. Slicker than most Chinese vegetarian places and, unusually, not vegan – they do use egg. There's a popular lunchtime-only *nasi campur* spread and, the rest of the day, a good range of rice and noodle options plus dishes such as vegetarian satay. Around RM20 with soft drinks if you order à la carte. Daily 7.30am–3pm & 5–9pm.

SHOPPING

Miri's shopping isn't especially distinguished and it's disappointing when it comes to handicrafts, though the malls are lively. The best downtown mall is the **Bintang Megamall** (ⓦ bintangmegamall.com) at the corner of Jalan Miri Pujut and Jalan Merbau. With two wings – the newer extension is at the back – it houses a branch of the Parkson department store, a Giant supermarket and outlets of several Western fast-food chains. Numerous small shops sell phone chargers, memory cards and the like, while Chinese discount shops here and in the Imperial Mall stock endless camping paraphernalia. Rubber shoes are sold in the small shops of Chinatown, and some may also sell mosquito nets, though you'll need to ask around.

Borneo Arts Miri Handicraft Centre, corner of Jalan Brooke and Jalan Merbau ☎ 085 422373. The best of the shops in the handicraft centre is worth a look, with some woodcarving and Kenyah shields on show – the other shops here are a little desultory, and many of their wares are from Kalimantan. Daily 8am–6pm.

Outdoor Life 2nd floor, new wing, Bintang Megamall ☎ 085 425303. Expensive torches, sleeping bags, tents and so forth. Daily 10am–9.30pm.

Popular Book Store 2nd floor, Bintang Megamall ☎ 085 439052. As good a bookshop as Miri can muster. A couple of newsagents in the same mall stock small selections of English-language books and magazines. Daily 10am–10pm.

DIRECTORY

Banks and exchange As well as banks all over downtown, there's a moneychanger on the ground floor of the Imperial Mall on Jalan North Yu Seng.

Hospital Miri General Hospital, Jalan Lopeng (☎ 085 420033).

Laundry Two excellent laundries stand practically side by side a couple of doors along from the *Cocottage Guesthouse* (daily 7am–6pm; RM5/Kg).

Pharmacy Guardian and Watsons are both at Bintang Megamall.

Police HQ Jalan Kingsway (☎ 085 433677).
Post office Jalan Post (Mon–Fri 8.30am–4.30pm, Sat 8am–12.30pm).

Visa extensions First floor of the Yu Lan Plaza, the tallest building in town, unmissable on Jalan Kingsway (Mon–Fri 8am–5pm; ☎ 085 442112).

Lambir Hills National Park

Popular with weekend day-trippers, **LAMBIR HILLS NATIONAL PARK**, 35km out of Miri and the closest national park to the city, holds some pleasant trails – though leeches can be annoying – and good accommodation. Mixed dipterocarp forest makes up more than half the park, with giant hardwood trees such as *meranti*, *kapur* and *keruing* creating deep shadows on the forest floor; there's also *kerangas* forest, with its peat soils and scrubby vegetation.

Trails

The park's most popular trail, the short **Latak trail**, passes three **waterfalls**. The furthest – Latak itself, 1.5km (or 30min) from the park office – is the nicest, its 25m cascade feeding an alluring pool, but is inevitably busy at the weekends. The **Inoue trail** from the park office joins the **Lepoh–Ridan trail** half an hour along, which leads after about an hour to three more falls, **Dinding**, **Tengkorong** and **Pancur**; swimming isn't allowed at the last two as their pools are deep. The end of the Lepoh–Ridan trail marks the start of the trek to the top of **Bukit Lambir** (2hr 30min one way from here; set off by 10am from the park office to be back by sunset). It's a tough, hot, but rewarding climb with a wonderful view across the park.

ARRIVAL AND INFORMATION   LAMBIR HILLS NATIONAL PARK

By bus The park lies beside the main trunk road to Bintulu; any long-distance bus en route between Miri and Bintulu can drop you here.
By taxi A taxi from Miri will cost RM70 and can collect you

for the same price.
Admission fee RM20.
Contact details ☎ 085 471630, ⊚ sarawakforestry.com.

ACCOMMODATION AND EATING

Lambir Hills National Park accommodation ☎ 085 471630, ⊚ sarawakforestry.com. Though accommodation in the park is limited, more rooms have recently been built, and as few people stay you shouldn't have trouble overnighting. Choose either a two-bedroom lodge, or take a room within a lodge, sharing facilities. There's also a campsite, and a canteen serving simple Malay

and Chinese dishes, that will usually close at 5pm unless there are guests overnighting. Camping RM5, fan lodge rooms RM40, a/c chalet rooms RM100, six-person a/c lodges RM150

Sungai Tangap longhouse Patrick Libau village ☎ 013 834 2461. Good homestay inside the park itself. Full board two people RM80

Niah National Park

NIAH NATIONAL PARK, 110km south of Miri and 130km from Bintulu, is practically a compulsory visit even if you're already caved out from visiting Mulu. Yes, its main attractions are massive **limestone caves**, but there any similarity with Mulu ends. Whereas almost all excursions at Mulu are regimented and chaperoned, visitors at Niah simply wander the caves at will, in places stumbling along tunnels – lightless but for your own torch – like questers from *The Lord of the Rings*. Elsewhere the caves are alive, with not just bats but people, who harvest bat guano and swiftlet nests for much of the year. This potent combination of vast caverns, communities at work, the rainforest and Niah's archeological significance – it's famous for prehistoric cave paintings and early human settlement – makes even a day-trip to Niah a wonderful experience. It is indeed possible to see much of Niah in a day: allow two to three hours to get from the park offices to the most distant caves, with breaks along the way.

Niah Archaeological Museum

Tues–Sun 9.30am–4.30pm • Free; no photography

Before becoming a national park in 1974, Niah was made a National Historic Monument in 1958, after Tom Harrisson discovered that early man had been using it as a cemetery. Fragments of human skull, nearly 40,000 years old, were the earliest examples of *homo sapiens* found in Southeast Asia. For a sense of the park's history and archeological importance, spend half an hour at the simple but worthwhile **Niah Archeological Museum** across the stream beyond the park headquarters. Fascinating photos, from a mere half-century ago, but seeming much older, show Harrisson at work, and Iban and other indigenous people engaged in traditional dances or sporting activities.

Caves

Trader's Cave, the nearest cave to the museum, is nearly 3km along a concrete path that soon becomes a jungle boardwalk. En route, you may stumble upon monkeys (including silverleafs and even gibbons), butterflies, snakes, skinks and odd scarlet millipedes. Twenty minutes' walk from the museum, a few traders sell refreshments and souvenirs at the start of a clearly marked path on the left that leads in ten minutes to a small, not all that enthralling, village, **Rumah Patrick Ribau** (often still signed Rumah Chang) where they have a homestay programme at the Sungai Tangap longhouse.

Trader's Cave

A 45-minute walk from the museum, a great metal grille crosses the entire boardwalk, with a small gate below marking the entrance to the cave area. Within a few minutes you reach the **Trader's Cave**, not so much a cave as a long, wedge-shaped gash in the rock, open to the jungle along the entire right-hand side. The wooden platforms here were used as shelters by nest-gatherers, who until the 1970s used to barter their harvests here for goods brought by the townsfolk.

Great Cave and Gan Kira (Moon Cave)

Labelled "Niah Cave" on some maps, the huge, 250m-wide west mouth of the **Great Cave** is not far beyond Trader's Cave. A fenced-off stretch to the left marks the site of Tom Harrisson's groundbreaking archeological **digs** in 1957. The dark, gradually ascending area of cave floor beyond is known thanks to its breadth and flatness as the **Padang**; bear left to begin a path that leads down into the depths of the cave, where you will certainly need your torch. The earthy smell of bat **guano** is pervasive; people you may see wandering off-path with sacks on their backs are harvesting it to sell as fertilizer. Between September and March you'll also see **bird's-nest collectors**, who work in groups of three, shinning up bamboo poles and hanging from ropes dangling from the ceiling in search of the edible swiftlet nests so prized by the Chinese. At around 6 or 7pm, visitors can see the swiftlets fly in and vast numbers of bats stream out for the night, and from much closer up than at Mulu – arrange this with a boatman (see opposite) and remember it takes at least forty minutes to walk back to the river.

The path curls round and then branches, the right-hand track taking you back up and out towards the padang. Head more or less straight on, past several cave mouths with jungle views on the left, to reach the pitch-black, stuffy tunnel out to Gan Kira at the southern end of the Great Cave system. It takes ten minutes to traverse, though it feels like years.

At the mouth of **Gan Kira**, a delightful spot nearly 4km from the park offices, the boardwalk ends at a shelter bathed in fabulous breezes. A blessed relief after the stuffiness of the preceding tunnel, it offers views of lushly forested hillside beyond.

Painted Cave

A ten-minute walk through the jungle from Gan Kira, and then up some steep stairs, brings you to the mouth of the **Painted Cave**. Early Sarawak communities buried their

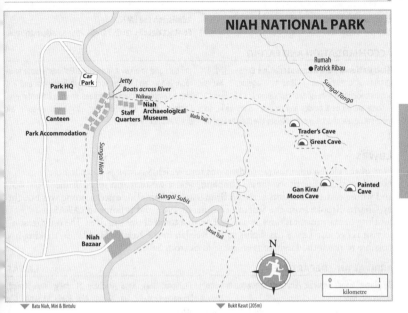

NIAH NATIONAL PARK

Rumah
● Patrick Ribau

Sungai Tanga

Park HQ — Car Park — Jetty — Boats across River — Walkway

Niah Archaeological Museum

Staff Quarters

Madu Trail

Canteen

Park Accommodation

Sungai Niah

Trader's Cave
Great Cave

Gan Kira/
Moon Cave

Painted
Cave

Sungai Subis

Kasut Trail

Niah
Bazaar

N

0   1
kilometre

▼ Batu Niah, Miri & Bintulu   ▼ Bukit Kasut (205m)

6

dead in **boat-shaped coffins**, or "death ships", perched around the cave walls. When Harrisson first entered, the cave had partially collapsed, and the contents were spilled all around. Subsequent dating proved that the caves had been used as a cemetery for tens of thousands of years.

Although the reason visitors plod here is to view the cave's **wall paintings**, they're fenced off and so faded as to be almost impossible to make out – quite at odds with park photos showing bright red boats on a journey, ridden by figures that look to be jumping or dancing.

Trails

It would be tough to squeeze in the park's two trails plus the caves on a day-trip. Splitting off very near the start of the walkway to the caves, the **Jalan Madu** trail cuts south, across a peat swamp forest, where you see sword-leaved pandanus plants. It crosses the Subis River to end after an hour at the start of the **Bukit Kasut trail**. It's nearly another hour's walk to the hilltop, which has a fine view of both of the forest canopy and the plains beyond. Park staff may advise against the Bukit Kasut trail if it has recently rained, as it can be slippery when wet.

ARRIVAL AND INFORMATION   **NIAH NATIONAL PARK**

By road The park is accessible from both the main trunk road and the coastal highway. All Miri guesthouses organize trips (RM60), or catch any express bus between Miri and Bintulu and get off at the Batu Niah junction from Miri, slightly more from Bintulu), where buses use the food court as a rest stop. Catch a *kereta sapu* for the 15km drive to the park entrance (RM25–30/car one way); park staff can summon a vehicle for the return trip. Driving, following signs from either the main road for Batu Niah, Niah Bazaar or the park; after a few minutes take a signed turning east for Niah Bazaar, and then another turning north (left) for the park itself.

Ferry crossings To cross the stream just beyond the park headquarters to the museum and trails, you have to take a RM1 ferry ride (RM1.50 after 5.30pm). To see the bats flying out at the Great Cave, tell the boatman on your way out that you'll be back at 7.30pm – he finishes work then, but won't leave before you come back if he knows to expect you. It's best to leave the cave by 6.45pm at the very latest – a RM5 gratuity may be appropriate if you're a bit late. You will need a torch to get back to the jetty at that time and if you get stuck in the park, you can stay the night at the Rumah Patrick Ribau village.

Equipment A reliable torch (flashlight) with fresh batteries is essential.

ACCOMMODATION AND EATING

Niah National Park accommodation ☎ 085 737454, ⓦ sarawakforestry.com. Though ageing, Niah's accommodation is in reasonable condition as it's little used – there are no park guides and thus no night walks, so there's little reason to stay except to see the dusk exodus of

Admission fee RM20.
Contact details ☎ 085 737454, ⓦ sarawakforestry.com.

the bats and to enjoy a little quiet. Options include four-room lodges and fancier rooms with bathroom and a/c, plus a campsite. A simple canteen serves a limited menu. Camping RM5, lodge doubles RM42.40, en-suite a/c doubles RM159

Lawas

One of the eleven administrative **divisions** into which Sarawak is parcelled is a horseshoe-shaped territory named **Limbang**, whose western arm splits Brunei into two and whose eastern arm slots between Brunei and Sabah. This eastern prong was bought by Charles Brooke from the Sultan of Brunei in 1905 and is home to **LAWAS**, a bustling bazaar town on the Lawas River, with a **tamu** above the river. The only reason to visit is because Lawas has flights to Ba' Kelalan in the Kelabit Highlands, making it possible to reach the Highlands en route to or from Sabah.

ARRIVAL AND DEPARTURE   LAWAS

By plane Lawas's airport is 2km south of town; a taxi into town costs RM8.
Destinations Ba' Kelalan (3 weekly; 35min); Kota Kinabalu (2 weekly; 45min); Miri (at least 2 daily; 45min).
By bus The bus station is on Jalan Liaw Siew Ann, about 200m from the main junction and just behind the indoor market. Virtually all buses leave in the morning.
Destinations Bandar Seri Begawan, Brunei (daily

12.30pm; 3hr); Kota Kinabalu (4 daily; 4hr 30min); Limbang (2 daily; 1hr 30min); Miri (daily 11.30am; 6hr 30min).
By boat Boats leave from the Customs Wharf beside the old mosque, 300m east of town.
Destinations Labuan (daily, 7.30am; 2hr 30min; RM30); Limbang (daily, 9am; 2hr; RM25); Serasa Ferry Terminal in Muara, Brunei (daily, noon; 2hr; RM25).

ACCOMMODATION

Mandarin Lot 466, Jalan Trusan ☎ 085 283222. Centrally located on the main street, and next to the excellent *Leeya Café*, this place isn't exciting, but the rooms are fairly large, clean, and have nice bathrooms – some even have windows. There's wi-fi throughout. RM75
Seri Malaysia Jalan Gaya ☎ 085 283200,

ⓦ serimalaysia.com.my. This enormous modern hotel, just over the bridge as you enter town from the airport, is the plushest place to stay – which isn't saying much. Its few amenities are little more than a coffee house and a pool and there's no wi-fi beyond the lobby. Rates include breakfast. RM149

The northern interior

For visitors who take the time and trouble to explore it, Sarawak's **northern interior** often ends up being the most memorable part of their stay. Some of the wildest, most untouched parts of Sarawak are interspersed, sometimes in close proximity, with badly degraded patches, thus putting everything you may have read about the state's environmental problems into sharp relief. The timber industry has been systematically logging here since the 1960s, with tracts of land already under oil palm or being cleared to grow it, yet the rugged terrain still offers fabulous **trekking** – something most visitors only experience at **Gunung Mulu National Park**, with its limestone Pinnacles and extensive caves.

As central Sarawak has the Rejang, so the north has its major river system, the **Batang Baram**. There the resemblance ends, for only the lowest part of the Baram – from **Marudi**, 50km southeast of Miri, to the river mouth at **Kuala Baram** near the Brunei border – has anything like a proper boat service, and that stretch is any case devoid of sights. Further

6

TWIN OTTERS

One entertaining aspect of travel in the northern interior is the chance to fly on **Twin Otters**, nineteen-seater propeller planes. More formally known as the de Havilland DHC-6, the Twin Otter can turn on the proverbial dime and take off from a standing start in around ten seconds, making it ideally suited to the tiny airfields hereabouts. As such, the plane forms the backbone of the Rural Air Services operated by Malaysia Airlines subsidiary **MASwings**, mostly out of Miri (though it's not used for Mulu, where the airport can take larger aircraft).

As the Twin Otter isn't pressurized – you can see daylight around the door rim – it doesn't fly above 3000m, and affords great views of the north's mountain ranges. That MASwings' Twin Otters are 30 years old and slightly shabby (though perfectly serviceable) only adds to the experience; the cabin will be fan-cooled and the cockpit door may well be open, letting you see what the pilots are up to.

On a practical note, passengers sit where they like, and luggage is limited to 10kg per person (you may well have to weigh yourself at check-in so staff know the laden weight of the plane). Prices are lower if booked well ahead, rising one week before and three days before travel; the most expensive tickets can be bought at the airport on the day. At some airfields, departing passengers are slapped with a "service fee" of RM10–15 atop the taxes included in ticket prices. Levied by the small private concerns that run the airfields, these fees appear to be condoned by the authorities. Note that the planes get booked solid during public and school holidays and over Christmas and New Year, when you may have to reserve weeks in advance. Flights are seldom cancelled except in very gusty or stormy weather.

upriver, the days of being able to just turn up and find a longboat and someone who can pilot it have long since gone. Much travel is therefore by small **aircraft** (see above) or **4WD**, using the spider's web of logging roads, which adds to the outback feel. Anyone wanting to get off the beaten track will most likely have to talk to the Miri tour operators (see p.358), who have contacts with boatmen and drivers and can arrange accommodation in towns with hardly any formal places to stay. That said, it is possible to visit remote **Penan settlements** in the upper Baram using a homestay programme called **Picnic with the Penan**.

Mulu aside, the highlight is the lush **Kelabit Highlands**, accessible by air and an upgraded logging road, where the pleasant climate is ideal for long treks in the rainforest. Of much less significance unless you're an avid birdwatcher is **Loagan Bunut National Park**, some distance off the Miri–Bintulu road and difficult to visit independently.

Gunung Mulu National Park

GUNUNG MULU NATIONAL PARK, Sarawak's premier national park and a UNESCO World Heritage Site, is named after the 2376m mountain at its heart. Modern explorers have been coming here since Spenser St John in the 1850s, who didn't reach the summit but wrote inspiringly about the region in *Life in the Forests of the Far East*. A more successful bid in 1932 saw Edward Shackleton, son of the Antarctic explorer, get to the top during a research trip organized by Tom Harrisson.

The park's best-known features, however, are the mind-bogglingly big **Deer Cave** and, atop another mountain, Gunung Api, the dozens of 50m-high razor-sharp limestone spikes known as the **Pinnacles**. Visitors stream into Mulu (as the park is generally known) year-round to catch sight of them – a three-day trek, there and back, from the park offices – and also to see the park's incredible network of **caves**. Mulu contains the largest limestone cave system in the world, formed when surface water eroded vast amounts of material, dividing the limestone belt that runs southwest–northeast across the middle of the park into separate mountains as well as carving cave passages within. Most people see some or all four of the dramatic **show caves**, though other caves are accessible on adventure packages and yet more are still being explored (see ⓦmulucaves.org).

Mulu is unique in Sarawak for having been **privatized**. While the Sarawak Forestry Corporation remains in overall charge, most things to do with tourism, including the accommodation, is now run by Borsarmulu, the firm that presently owns the *Royal Mulu Resort* a few kilometres away. This means that Mulu feels more like Singapore than Sarawak: **tours** are timetabled and formatted, and you can explore few parts of the park unaccompanied. The tours are well run, the guides are better communicators than at any other Sarawak park, and close supervision has helped prevent the poaching of valuable plants – but if it were possible to make the jungle somehow corporate, this is it. The only way to avoid taking the tours is by having your own registered guide, which enables you to book boat charter and accommodation on the trails separately, though this only makes sense if you are in a group.

The caves

The show caves – **Clearwater**, **Wind**, **Lang's** and **Deer** – are a must, though interest can begin to wane if you see all four. If you're doing a Pinnacles trek, the cost will usually include a tour of the Clearwater and Wind caves. If not, and you don't want to spend ages underground, opt for the Lang's and Deer caves – the last is the most impressive of the lot – then hang around for the incredible "**changing of the guard**", when the bats leave Deer Cave at sunset. Tours of these caves fill up quickly, so book as soon as your plans are fixed. It's also possible to do tours of **Lagang Cave**, where obscure cave-dwelling fauna is the highlight, plus more challenging caving trips.

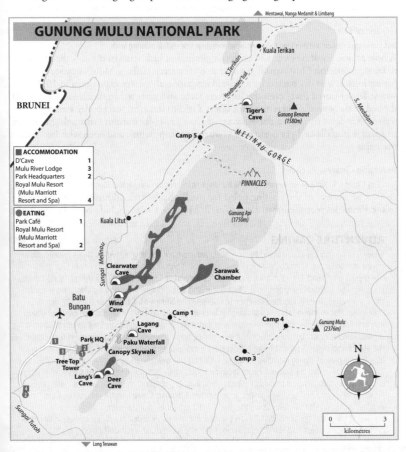

GUNUNG MULU NATIONAL PARK

Mentawai, Nanga Medamit & Limbang

Kuala Terikan

S. Terikan

Headhunters Trail

BRUNEI

Tiger's Cave

Gunung Benarat (1580m)

Camp 5

MELINAU GORGE

PINNACLES

ACCOMMODATION
D'Cave — 1
Mulu River Lodge — 3
Park Headquarters — 2
Royal Mulu Resort (Mulu Marriott Resort and Spa) — 4

EATING
Park Café — 1
Royal Mulu Resort (Mulu Marriott Resort and Spa) — 2

Kuala Litut

Gunung Api (1750m)

Sungai Melinau

Clearwater Cave

Sarawak Chamber

Batu Bungan

Wind Cave

Camp 1

Camp 4

Gunung Mulu (2376m)

Lagang Cave

Park HQ

Paku Waterfall

Canopy Skywalk

Camp 3

Tree Top Tower

Lang's Cave

Deer Cave

N

S. Medalam

Sungai Tutoh

Long Terawan

0 — 3
kilometres

Lang's and Deer caves

3km from the park office • Tours leave park office daily 2pm & 2.30pm • RM25

Lang's Cave, an hour's walk from the park office, is the smallest of the show caves. It makes an unremarkable appetizer for the splendid Deer Cave, though your guide will point out unusual rock formations, most interestingly the curtain stalactites and coral-like growths – helictites – gripping the curved walls.

Deer Cave, a few minutes' walk futher, was once inhabited by deer that sheltered in its cavernous reaches. Dim artificial lighting helps you appreciate one of the world's largest cave passages, more than 2km long and up to 174m high, though what's really striking is how scenic it can be: silvery curtains of water plummet from the cave ceiling, while there's at least one chimney-like structure, formed by erosion of a weaker section of limestone, where rainwater jets down as though from a tap. Elsewhere, your guide will point out the cave's Abraham Lincoln-in-profile rock formation and the entrance to the Garden of Eden (see below).

Once the tour is over, walk back to the park offices unaccompanied or linger with the guide at a viewpoint – the so-called Bat Observatory, with snacks on sale and toilets – near the caves. As it approaches 6pm, swiflets fly into the caves for the night, which isn't necessarily easy to make out, but what you can't fail to notice is the **bats**. They emerge from various holes in the roof – there's about three million of them – at first in little cloud-like bursts, then in continuous streams that can last for minutes at a time.

Garden of Eden

Tour, including Lang's Cave and Deer Cave, daily 9am; minimum three people • RM130 including lunch

A hole at one point in Deer Cave offers a glimpse of lush ferns in the so-called **Garden of Eden**, a veritable "lost world" penned in by the steep cliffs of Mulu's limestone formations. It was discovered by a Royal Geographical Society expedition in 1976 whose leader noted that "even the fish were tame and gathered in shoals around a hand dipped in the water". Today the park offers a trip to the area, reached by wading along a river that flows through a dark passage at Deer Cave. It continues through the jungle to small waterfalls and yet more pools (where you can swim), and ends with lunch in the wilds.

Wind and Clearwater caves

Tours daily 8.45am & 9.15am from the park offices • RM50 including boat transport and a stop at Batu Bungan

As they lie upriver of the starting point for the Pinnacles trek, almost everyone heading to the Pinnacles sees these two caves as well. Most park trips include boat transport and

---

ADVENTURE CAVING

Several of Mulu's caves are open for so-called **adventure caving** activities, though only a few count as hard-core, with caving experience compulsory; all require a group of at least three for the trip to go ahead. One advanced trip, the **Clearwater Connection** (RM185/person), takes you through a chamber linking the Clearwater and Wind caves, wading or swimming through the Clearwater River en route. Another, the visit to the **Sarawak Chamber** (RM250), at 9.5 million cubic metres the world's largest known cave chamber – starts at the crack of dawn and lasts an entire day, but there's no descent into the chamber itself, and it's so big that regular torches can't actually reach the walls or ceiling, so all you can experience is turning off the lights and being in the "biggest darkness" – note, they'll need proof of fitness to do this trip, which means doing another adventure caving trip beforehand.

If you just want to try something that isn't a regular trek or cave walk, **Racer Cave** (RM120) is probably best; you spend two hours ascending and descending through tunnels, with guide ropes to help you pull yourself along. More simply, **Lagang Cave** can be visited on a trip in which you search for wildlife, as on the standard "Fast Lane" tour (see opposite), but in a separate, "off-piste" section (RM120), an escapade that's suitable for families. For details of other caving opportunities and what equipment to bring, speak to the park office (see p.371).

a not-very-interesting stop en route at the Penan settlement of Batu Bungan (see below) where you can buy tribal knick-knacks.

Wind Cave feels rather closed in compared to its much larger siblings, and is home to a great array of golden, contorted rock shapes and pillars, best seen from extended metal stairways. It's five minutes on to the base of **Clearwater Cave**, either by boat along the Melinau River or using a cliffside walkway that passes some "mini-Pinnacles", waist-high limestone shards embedded in the cliff face. Two hundred steps lead up to the cave mouth itself, adorned with curious glossy one-leafed plants unique to Mulu. Inside, the cave certainly impresses with its size – the entire system, probing 150km through Mulu's substratum, is thought to be the longest in Southeast Asia – though it's not all that visually interesting other than for its subterranean river, which joins the Melinau, and for its **notch**, a great horizontal groove in the cave wall running alongside the river. Thirty minutes are set aside for a dip in the chilly Melinau after the tour (there are changing facilities).

Lagang Cave

Lagang "Fast Lane" tours leave daily 1.30pm from the park office; bring a torch • RM60 including boat rides

Animals rather than geology are the highlight in the **Lagang Cave**. The tour proceeds at a relaxed pace, the guide encouraging people to use their torches to spot the different beasties lurking in the darkness; the blue racer snakes who feed on the bats, the reflective eyes of cave spiders, and the blind white crabs in shallow pools. Of course there are no problems locating the many bats sleeping in little round holes in the ceiling along with mossy-nest swiflet nests (made of a mixture of moss and saliva). Later, as the cave widens out, you'll also see some well-lit and interesting rock formations.

Batu Bungan

A stop on boat tours to Wind/Clearwater caves, or a signed 30min walk from the airport in the opposite direction from the park

Just outside the park boundary, a couple of kilometres northwest of the park entrance, is a somewhat desultory collection of concrete houses called **Batu Bungan** which, a worthwhile information display notes, is "probably the most-visited Penan settlement in Sarawak". Tourists indeed visit every morning en route to the caves, and the locals sell souvenirs, but the whole experience is rather artificial. The Penan here perhaps quite haven't got the hang of the whole living-in-houses thing, and the present concrete longhouses are there because previous two wooden ones burned down within ten years.

Canopy skywalk and Tree Top Tower

Six skywalk tours daily; 2hr • RM40, Tree Top Tower free (get key from the park office; RM50 deposit; no guide needed)

Mulu's **canopy skywalk**, 480m long and 20m up in the air, is reached by a side trail off the Deer Cave trail. The skywalk laces around six broad hardwood *kasai*, *betang*, *meranti*, *peran* and *segera* trees and takes around half an hour to complete. Though it's not that different to the canopy walkways at Taman Negara or at Temburong in Brunei, the tours are often full, so book promptly or try spotting birdlife from the elevated hide called the **Tree Top Tower**, just fifteen minutes from the park office.

Paku waterfall

3km from the park office • Free, but notify the Sarawak Forestry office (close to the park office)

As somewhere you can walk to on your own, the **Paku waterfall** is useful for whiling away a spare half-day. The signed track to the falls (actually the start of the multiday 24km trek to Gunung Mulu) branches off the Deer Cave path 1.5km from the park headquarters, eventually arriving at a stream where a couple of minor cascades empty out of low gashes in the limestone cliff face. It's a pleasant, shady spot for a swim, though there are no facilities.

6

The Pinnacles

The park charges RM350 for the trek, including accommodation but no food; tour operators offer similar packages, as well as to the Headhunters' Trail north of the Pinnacles (see below)

Five million years ago, the splatter of raindrops gradually dissolved Gunung Api's limestone and carved out the **Pinnacles** – 50m-high shards, as sharp as samurai swords – from a solid block of rock. Erosion is still continuing, and the entire region is pockmarked with deep shafts penetrating far into the heart of the mountain: one third of Gunung Api has already been washed away, and in another ten million years it might all be gone.

The chance to view the Pinnacles draws many visitors to Mulu, and the trek offers exactly that, by heading not to the Pinnacles but to a **ridge** across the way from where you can take everything in. It's a three-day, two-night hike, but only the ascent of the steep final ridge and the awkward descent are genuinely demanding. That said, if you're reasonably fit and suitably equipped, you should cope, and the guides put safety first and make allowances as appropriate for the slower members of their group. With whomever you arrange the trek, book or make enquiries at least a week in advance; base camp, **Camp 5**, sleeps fifty people, so there's a firm ceiling on the number of climbers per day. Considering the tough journey, some people are a little disappointed when they arrive at the Pinnacles, but as with many things in life, the journey is everything.

The hike

The itinerary is simple. **Day 1** usually sees trekkers visiting the Wind and Clearwater caves after which the boat takes them down the Melinau to **Kuala Litut**, the start of the 8km trek to Camp 5. Following a rough track of coarse stones embedded in the ground, it's mostly flat and perfectly straightforward, and you can expect to arrive well before sunset.

Camp 5 itself is spruce and homely; all accommodation is dorm-style, and there's a large, reasonably well-equipped kitchen and communal eating area. If you book through the park office, you'll have to bring your own provisions (see p.372). It's close to the **Melinau Gorge**, across which nearby **Gunung Api** (1750m) and **Gunung Benarat** (1580m) cast long shadows in the fading afternoon light. A bridge straddles the river here, with a path disappearing into the jungle on the far side – the first stage of the Headhunters' Trail. It's possible to explore the gorge instead of tackling the Pinnacles; ask at the park office for details.

THE HEADHUNTERS' TRAIL

A wonderful way to start or end a Pinnacles trek, the **Headhunters' Trail** adds just one day to the total duration, but when you consider the itinerary it's clearly all but impossible to make the necessary arrangements independently. The 11km trail – which corresponds to a route once taken by Kenyah and Kayan warring parties – leads north from Camp 5 to **Kuala Terikan**, at the confluence of the Terikan and Medalam rivers on the park's northern boundary. From here it's necessary to find a longboat down the Terikan to reach **Mentawai**, also on the park's edge, where you sign out of the park at a **ranger post** (or sign in if doing the route in reverse). The boat then continues to a longhouse near **Nanga Medamit** where tour operators put visitors up for the night. From here you can drive to the coastal town of **Limbang**, in between the two lumps of Brunei, and pick up a flight to Miri or bus to Kota Kinabalu, Bandar Seri Begawan or Miri.

As a trek, the trail is similar to the path from Kuala Litut to Camp 5, but less well maintained and 3km longer. Some say it's therefore better for exiting the park than entering it, as there's a lot of ground to cover to reach Camp 5 from Nanga Medalan before dark. In practice, people continue to trek in both directions.

To tackle the route, contact a tour operator in Miri or Kuching (the park itself is not currently offering this service). As an example, Tropical Adventure (see p.358) has a five-day excursion from RM1710/person, covering the flight from Miri to Mulu, a night's accommodation at their own lodge near the park, meals, the Pinnacles trek (including the two show caves), and the exit to Limbang via Nanga Medamit.

Day 2 is the only time you are accompanied by a guide, setting off around 7.30am for the ascent. Departure may be delayed in heavy rain; if the weather fails to let up, and the climb has to be called off, you'll get half your money back if you booked through the park office. After two hours, a striking vista opens up: the rainforest stretches below as far as the eye can see, and wispy clouds drift along your line of vision. Eventually the trail reaches **moss forest**, where pitcher plants feed on insects, and ants and squirrels dart in and out among the roots of trees. The last thirty minutes of the climb is especially steep, with ladders and ropes to assist.

Parties usually arrive at the top of the **ridge** that overlooks the Pinnacles in late morning. The ridge is itself a pinnacle, sited across a ravine from the main cluster, and if you tap the rocks around you, they reverberate because of the large holes in the limestone underneath. After an hour it's time for the return slog, which can be more awkward on the legs and nerves, and takes longer, especially when the route is slippery. You'll probably arrive back at Camp 5 around 4pm.

On **day 3** trekkers retrace their steps to Kuala Litut for the boat ride back to the park office, usually arriving in plenty of time to catch an afternoon flight out.

Gunung Mulu

Expect to pay around RM475/person, including accommodation and a guide, though you'll have to bring provisions and sleeping bags; a porter costs around RM100/day extra

The route to the summit of **Gunung Mulu** (2376m) was first discovered in the 1920s by Tama Nilong, a Berawan rhinoceros-hunter. Earlier explorers had failed to find a way around the huge surrounding cliffs, but Nilong followed rhinoceros tracks along the southwest ridge trail, and thus enabled Lord Shackleton to become the first mountaineer to reach the summit in 1932. It's still an arduous climb, a 48km round trip that usually takes four days. Few visitors attempt it, but with enough notice, the park office can usually arrange it for groups of three or more.

Day 1, for most groups, is usually spent heading to **Camp 3** roughly midway along the route, passing Camp 1 en route (there is no Camp 2). The trek takes you from the limestone belt that most tourists associate with Mulu into sandstone terrain that dominates the southeast of the park. On **day 2** you spend the night 1800m up at **Camp 4**. Most climbers set off well before dawn on **day 3** for the hard ninety-minute trek to the **summit**, if possible arriving there at sunrise. Big clumps of pitcher plants dot the final stretch, though it's easy to miss them as by this point you are hauling yourself up by ropes onto the cold, windswept, craggy peak. From here, the view is exhilarating, looking down on Gunung Api and, on a clear day, far across the forest to Brunei Bay. Once again you spend the night at Camp 4. **Day 4** is a very full day as the aim is to get right back to the park HQ by nightfall.

ARRIVAL AND DEPARTURE	GUNUNG MULU NATIONAL PARK

By plane MASwings flies from Mulu's airport, 1500m from the park entrance, to Kota Kinabalu (1 daily, sometimes via Miri; 50min–2hr), Kuching (1 daily; 1hr 30min) and Miri (2 daily; 40min). They're not Twin Otter services, but demand is high, so book a week or two in advance.

GETTING AROUND

By private taxi For transport around the Mulu area – for example, to eat somewhere other than where you are staying – contact Edward at the *Sweetwater Café* (see p.372), who drives people around for a few ringgit per trip.

By bicycle Bikes are a useful way of getting to and from the park if you're staying outside. The *Royal Mulu Resort* (see p.372) rents bikes for RM15/day, to non-guests as well.

INFORMATION

Park office The office stocks good listings of treks, cave tours and activities, as well as browsable reference books on the park and Borneo.

Discovery Centre The informative displays on cave formation and Mulu's topography and ecology in the excellent Discovery Centre, a small free museum alongside the park office, are worth at least half an hour of your time. The gift shop offers internet access at RM10/day, or you could just ask another tourist for the password.

Entrance fee RM30 for five days.

Contact details ☎085 792300, ⌨mulupark.com; ⌨mulucaves.org is also a useful resource.

Equipment Unless you are climbing Gunung Mulu itself or doing advanced caving, you will need the same gear that you would bring to other national parks. As people tend to do longer treks here than at most parks, however, items that may seem optional elsewhere become necessities. A poncho (or umbrella) is essential for extended downpours, while rubber shoes come into their own when paths and

trails are flooded or waterlogged; carry bandages to deal with any blisters. If you are using regular shoes, they must have a good grip. Ponchos, rubber shoes and food you can cook on multiday treks are sold at the park gift shop, but it's much cheaper to buy these before you arrive.

Money Bring a reasonable amount of cash – there are no ATMs – though this is the one park where you can pay for rooms and tours with plastic, and it's occasionally possible to take cash out on your credit card at the park office.

Leeches Leeches are not a problem on trails near the park headquarters, though you might want to take precautions on the Pinnacles climb.

ACCOMMODATION

Accommodation within the park is limited to a hostel – basically a twenty-bed dorm – and 43 much more expensive private rooms and chalets; the dorm fills up, so enquire at least a week in advance to use it. Other places to stay **nearby** range from hostel-type places and homestays to the *Royal Mulu Resort*.

★**D'Cave** 700m from the airport, at the turning to the park entrance. ☎010 771 4098, ✉beckhamjunior40 @yahoo.com. By far the best of the homestays, with a basic ten-person fan dorm and a couple of double rooms – they're building a new block where there will be more. The friendly family is absolutely lovely, and the rate includes an astonishingly good breakfast served at a long table – they just don't stop bringing out food. Dorm RM25, doubles RM35

Mulu River Lodge Outside the park entrance ☎012 852 7471. Friendly guesthouse in a large timber building backing onto the Melinau River, containing a 22-bed dorm and clean bathrooms. When things are quiet they may give you a private room at the back of the *Sweetwater Café* next door, which they also run, at no extra cost. With advance warning they may be able to provide an independent guide for Mulu. The good-value rates include a simple cooked breakfast. Dorm RM35

Park Headquarters ☎085 792300, ⌨mulupark .com. Clustered around the park office are various chalets, some recently built and all with a/c and bathroom, plus its hostel. All rates include breakfast. Dorms RM41, doubles RM180

Royal Mulu Resort (Mulu Marriott Resort and Spa) 2km from the park entrance ☎085 792388, ⌨royalmuluresort.com. The only upmarket place to stay at Mulu, the *Resort* is well known for its swimming pool, which sticks out amid the jungle when viewed from the air, and its sprawling collection of longhouse-like blocks, raised on stilts. Rooms are spacious, and there's a vaguely smart bar and restaurant – although, unless you're having the buffet, it's quite overpriced (mains around RM35), so many guests go to the small restaurant just across the river. By 2015 it will have been rebranded as a five-star *Marriott*, so rates may alter. RM475

EATING

Most people simply **eat** where they're staying, but it can be worth moving around a bit for variety. For the Pinnacles and other long treks, the park gift shop sells sachets of instant pasta, canned beans and curries, biscuits, chocolate and so forth. If you want to save a few ringgit, use the shop for the locals on the way from the park to the *Royal Mulu Resort*.

Park Café Next to park office. An airy modern affair, overlooking the Melinau River and serving pretty decent international food. Their highly spicy and creamy Sarawak *laksa* is their strongest suit (RM12), and they also do a tasty Indian platter (RM12), a limited range of stir-fries to be eaten with rice (including a good Indonesian beef *rendang* for RM17), and the odd dessert such as chocolate cake. At breakfast they offer Western and Asian options and fruit. Beer and wine available too. Around RM15 with a soft drink. Daily 7.30am–9pm.

Royal Mulu Resort (Mulu Marriott Resort and Spa) 2km from park entrance ☎085 792388, ⌨royalmulu resort.com. The hotel restaurant's buffet dinner – a grand spread of rice and pasta, salads and stir-fries, and *kuih* for dessert, plus a half-hour tribal dance show at 8pm – will set you back RM78. *Tuak* is available at a shocking RM50 a bottle. There's also a bar, which serves reasonably priced light bites at night. Daily 7am–9.30pm; bar late afternoon till 11pm.

Loagan Bunut National Park

Some 80km south of Miri as the crow flies, **LOAGAN BUNUT NATIONAL PARK**, best visited on an overnight trip, is a good spot for dedicated birdwatchers, boasting stork-billed kingfishers and hornbills among many other species. Many live around the park's lake, **Tasik Bunut**, tucked away on the upper reaches of the **Teru River**, a tributary of the Tinjar, which in turn flows into the Baram. During prolonged dry spells, when the lake level drops drastically, a peculiar form of fishing, which the local **Berawan** people call *selambau*, is carried out. Just before the lake dries out, fishermen use giant spoon-shaped wooden frames to scoop up any fish that haven't escaped down the lake's two watercourses.

For birds, these dry times are a perfect time to feed too, and in May and June the surrounding peat-swamp forest supports breeding colonies of such species as darters, egrets and bitterns. Initially the lake can appear huge, its edges hard to detect as the sunlight is often hazy; however, it's only around 500m wide and 1km long. Small cabins built on rafts house Berawan fishermen, while around them lies an intricate network of fishing plots, with underwater nets and lines tied to stakes pushed into the lake bed. The best times to drift by boat across the lake are early morning and dusk, when the birds are at their most active.

6

ARRIVAL AND DEPARTURE — LOAGAN BUNUT NATIONAL PARK

By 4WD There's no public transport to the park, but *kereta sapu* 4WDs may head here in the morning from near Miri's tourist office; ask staff there where to wait (3hr; RM50/person if you can fill the car). When you want to head back, park staff can usually arrange a vehicle.

Tours Miri tour operators such as Borneo Mainland (see p.358) offer one- to three-day trips to the park.
Admission fee RM20.
Contact details ☎ 085 775119, ⓦ sarawakforestry.com.

ACCOMMODATION AND EATING

If you're here on a trip with Borneo Mainland you have the option to stay at a nearby farm with which the company has links. Note that there are some **water** issues at the park accommodation and you should phone ahead to ascertain the situation.

Loagan Bunut National Park accommodation ☎ 085 775119, ⓦ sarawakforestry.com. Located near the lake, the in-park accommodation is limited to a hostel and a so-called VIP chalet with two bedrooms, a/c and its own bathroom; a small canteen serves basic meals (RM10) and snacks. Dorms RM15, chalet RM225

Kelabit Highlands

Right up against the Kalimantan border, 100km southeast of Gunung Mulu, the long, high plateau of the **Kelabit Highlands** has been home to the Kelabit people for hundreds of years. Western explorers had no idea this self-sufficient mountain community existed until the early twentieth century, and the Highlands were literally not put on the map until World War II, when British and Australian commandos, led by Major Tom Harrisson, used Kelabit settlements as bases during a guerrilla war against the occupying Japanese. Before Harrisson's men built an airstrip at Bario, trekking over inhospitable terrain was the only way to get here – it took two weeks from the nearest large town, Marudi, on the opposite side of Mulu. When missionaries arrived and converted the animist Kelabit to Christianity after the war, many traditions, like burial rituals and wild parties called *iraus* (where Chinese jars full of rice wine were consumed) disappeared. Many of the magnificent Kelabit **megaliths** associated with these traditions have been swallowed up by the jungle, but some dolmens, urns, rock carvings and ossuaries used in funeral processes can still be found, so the region draws archeologists and anthropologists from far and wide.

Nowadays the Kelabit (well certainly the males) seem to be the good ol' boys of Asia; cowboy hats are much in evidence and they are very keen on pick-up trucks, country music, hunting, and their dogs. The Kelabit are not the only inhabitants of this part of the state, however; there are also populations of **Penan** and **Lun Bawang** (formerly called the Murut).

6

Despite logging in the Bario area, the Highlands remain generally unspoiled, with occasional wildlife sightings and a refreshing climate – temperatures are only a few degrees lower than in Miri by day, but in winter at night they can drop to an untropical 15°C (60°F). As such the region is a great target for **walkers**, and it is easily accessible by air, with three villages served by MASwings.

Most visitors head to **Bario** (much to the bemusement of locals) as it has the main airport and well-established formal accommodation, but the real point of being here is to get out into the countryside, doing day-walks or longer treks through the jungle, on which you can be hosted in little settlements or longhouses en route such as at **Pa' Lungan** and **Pa' Dalih**. It's also possible to do more challenging treks up to the peaks of the **Pulong Tau National Park** (which has no facilities and no one to collect the entrance fee), notably **Gunung Murud**. Another option is the Picnic with the Penan scheme, further south along the Upper Baram region, which enables you to really get off the beaten track and explore the jungle with the Penan people.

There are **no banks** in the Kelabit Highlands, so bring enough cash to cover board and lodging plus guiding/trekking fees. Although the soon-to-be-opened immigration centre in Bario promises to have an ATM and post office, this would need to be confirmed.

Bario and around

The short flight from Miri makes a thrilling introduction to this corner of Sarawak, the Twin Otter giving passengers amazing **views** (sit on the left on the way in, on the right on the way back) of serried ranks of blue limestone ridges at Gunung Mulu National Park and then of the double-humped **Batu Lawi** (see p.379) before landing at **BARIO**. From the air, it's a sprawling jumble of little paths and houses, as well as fields planted with the **rice** for which the village is well known. There is a centre of sorts, a grassy space 2km northwest of the airfield, ringed by a few modern buildings housing a few shops, including one selling Penan baskets, and uninteresting *kedai kopis*, but much of the village is scattered around the fields 2km further northwest, along the main road and a couple of minor tracks off or parallel to it.

HIGHLANDS TREKS

Guesthouse owners can either find **guides** for longer treks or say in which villages guides can be found. Guides can be in short supply, during the June–August peak season, and you can't arrange one weeks in advance, so make enquiries a couple of days before you plan to set out. Guides estimate the **fitness** of the group and set the pace accordingly. Trips may involve gathering wild vegetables, catching fish and cooking, Kelabit-style, on the campfire, as well as locating dolmens and visiting longhouses.

The usual **rate** to hire a guide in the Bario area or Ba Kelalan is RM100/day, or RM120 if overnighting, slightly less in Pa' Dalih. There is a guide association in Bario (contact Florence on ☎019 885 1385), though they're not very active, and since Pa' Dalih and Pa' Lungan are at the start of the more interesting trails (and easily walkable solo from Bario), it makes sense to get guides in those places. For a challenging mountain trek, you may be charged an extra RM20/day; a **porter** costs around RM100/day. These fees generally do not include provisions, which cost around RM15/person/day. Where you overnight in villages, expect to pay RM70–80/person for board and lodging and remember that if you don't return to where you started your trek, you'll have to pay your guide per day for their return journey.

As regards **equipment**, travel light bearing in mind the strict baggage limits on Twin Otters, and slogging through the jungle with more than 10kg is a real drag. On top of what you'd normally bring for a day-trek at a national park, it makes sense to have a thin sleeping bag and poncho, plus warmish clothing if you want to overnight outdoors or do any mountain trekking. A tent can be useful, though it obviously weighs down luggage; guides will usually stop overnight in villages or at shelters, though may have canvas sheets that will suffice for shelter at a pinch. For jungle trekking the best footwear is by far Wellington (rubber) boots as they not only make walking through mud and rivers less hassle but also help keep the leeches off (as does wearing thick, long trousers or anti-leech socks) – all are available in Miri or Lawas.

Leeches are quite common in this region, and although mostly harmless, they are not pleasant to have on you, or worse, biting you. There are a number of ways to discourage them, but they're not fail-safe (see p.46). Certainly forget trying to use a lighter/cigarette to remove them, a technique that only works in movies. If all else fails simply do as the locals do and use the sharp pinch and pull technique to get them off, and at least carry some salt, which dissolves them.

Situated on a plateau, with very little shade thanks to agriculture, Bario is visually dull in places but scenic in others, with vistas of rice fields and water buffalo against the lush mountains of the **Tama Abu Range** to the north and west. Although there are a few half-day walking opportunities, and a couple of things to look at in the village itself, it is only a taster of what you can experience elsewhere in the region.

Bario Asal

While not the sole longhouse in the vicinity, **Bario Asal** is the oldest and the only one in the village proper, close to the northern end of the main street. The unassuming timber building is unusual for effectively having two *ruais* – the second one, at the back, houses a communal kitchen with a long row of individual fireplaces for cooking. As a social venue, it's as important as the main *ruai* at the front. The longhouse also has a special area where travellers can stay (see p.377), and sells Kelabit beadwork, jackets and hats.

Tom Harrisson memorial

Beyond the Bario Asal longhouse the road soon curls round to the left, passing a hillock atop which stands a **memorial to Tom Harrisson** in the shape of a *sape*, the Orang Ulu lute. Celebrating the enormous contribution Harrisson made to our understanding of Sarawak's history, as curator of the Sarawak Museum in Kuching and as a roving anthropologist and archeologist (notably at Niah), the memorial has an inscription that, besides paying tribute to the military work of Harrisson and his British and Australian comrades, also cites the "sacrifice of the tribal warriors of the Baram and Rejang basins" in helping liberate Sarawak from Japanese occupation.

6

Millennium Gap

If you want to experience the rainforest and don't have time for the more remote treks, try this jungle walk from Bario, a four-hour round trip to the (rapidly disappearing) hilltop gap in the forest northwest of the village. Local custom dictates that trees can be felled to create a visible dent in the jungle to celebrate major events, so it's not hard to guess when this example, the **Millennium Gap**, was created.

To reach it, head out of the village using the track parallel to the main road, which passes the secondary school and the far end of the Bario Asal longhouse. It soon takes a left turn around paddy fields and then swings to the right, bringing you after ten minutes to a hamlet called **Arul Daran**, with a few longhouse-style buildings. Beyond, through another rice field or two and then over a stile, is a slightly scruffy **Penan settlement** with a few wooden houses; the inhabitants only arrived a decade ago. After this the track simply heads uphill into the jungle, eventually reaching the gap – although since the jungle has grown back at the top, there's actually little to see once you get there.

Prayer Hill

The best views of Bario are a short hike away up **Prayer Hill**, which will give you a great panorama across the village and to the mountains in the middle distance including Gunung Murud. Coming from the village, turn right at Bario Asal and follow the stony path for ten minutes until you reach the end. Here there is a small house up the hill and you should follow the smaller path to the right of it. The path then climbs steeply (with ropes to help haul yourself up) for another twenty minutes until you reach a small wooden church, where services are occasionally held. The summit is another ten minutes up from here, where you'll find a small cross and magnificent views.

ARRIVAL AND DEPARTURE BARIO

By land Perhaps the best way to enter the Kelabit Highlands is by car, which gives you a real sense of how remote it is, affords some great views along the way (despite the logging) and offers the chance to stop off at villages such as Pa' Dalih. It's 400km from Miri to Bario via the Lapok Junction (on the Miri–Bintulu highway, and from which you can hitch), from where a decent logging road heads inland through Kiloten, Long Supit (where there are food stalls), Long Kerong, and Pa' Dalih (see opposite), finally arriving in Bario some 10–20hr later. Every few kilometres there's a muddy bit where you really need a 4WD, and rain will slow you down considerably.

By plane Passengers arriving by plane are met by Bario's guesthouse owners every morning, so you should be collected if you've booked to stay, and be able to arrange a room if not.

Destinations Marudi (2 weekly; 40min); Miri (3 daily, one via Marudi; 50min–1hr 15min).

INFORMATION

Maps Stephen at *Junglebluesdream* (see opposite) produces beautifully drawn and useful maps of the area, including several of Bario's limited treks, which you can photograph and use on your phone or camera. Most guesthouse owners can provide less-good sketch maps of Bario's trekking options and talk you through them.

Internet Although the Telecentre next to the *kedai kopis* is never open, it does provide free wi-fi that you can pick up from the restaurants next door. Alternatively, villagers (as well as travellers) have been popping into Bario's airfield to get on the staff wi-fi network, which sits atop a satellite internet connection – neither require a password.

ACCOMMODATION AND EATING

There are several simple places to **stay** in and around Bario, and although some have 24hr electricity, many only have some solar-powered lighting at night. Furthermore, very few have wi-fi, and hot water is a bit of a luxury. You may have trouble finding a place to stay over Christmas and New Year – when guesthouses may shut for lack of incoming tourists – and during the annual **Bario Food Festival** in July (⊕nukenen.com), when the village centre is transformed into a mini-fair. Rates all include meals, so people usually eat where they stay. Not spicy by Malaysian standards, **Bario cuisine** features ingredients such as wild boar and locally farmed fish such as carp, though guesthouses may not serve traditional staples unless you request them. If you're out for the day, you can request a packed lunch. The Y2K shop on the main road, nearly 10min walk north of the centre, sells drinks and snacks at steepish prices.

★**Bario Asal (Sonarang Homestay)** 4km northwest of the airport ☎019 825 9505. The longhouse has a nice guest area with four homely bedrooms with double beds, one reasonable bathroom (with hot water and washing machine), a huge lounge area (with wi-fi and 24hr electricity) plus a little balcony where you can take coffee and watch the longhouse's semi-tame hornbill flap around hoping for scraps. Sonarang and her family are excellent hosts, and occasionally host cultural shows. RM70

De Plateau Lodge 3km east of Bario centre, towards Pa Umor ☎019 855 9458, ✉deplateau@gmail.com. Douglas Munney Bala's tranquil and well-equipped compound comprises seven comfortable rooms, and a sitting and dining area, as well as 24hr electricity. Bala specializes in birdwatching trips (though no expert), and is a fount of knowledge on Kelabit culture. RM80

★**Junglebluesdream** Ulung Palang Longhouse, 3km from centre, reached by a signed path northeast off main road ☎019 884 9892, ⊚junglebluesdream .weebly.com. Local artist Stephen and his Danish partner Tine offer nice accommodation, with four simple, cosy rooms in their section of a longhouse. Stephen's artwork decorates a lot of the building and his cooking is a treat; everyone eats together on a spacious terrace. RM80

Libal Paradise A 10min walk east of the airport ☎019 807 1640, ✉roachas@hotmail.com. By far the most modern and comfortable rooms in Bario, and the only ones which have any privacy, this Canadian-Kelablit-run place has two lovely little chalets which were made by the owner Stu, who also runs kayaking trips from Pa' Lungan back to Bario. Rose will keep you fed and watered, and often uses the pineapples that grow in the garden. RM80

Pa' Dalih and around

Around 25km south of Bario, and strung out along the banks of the Kelapang River, the village of **PA' DALIH** consists of a couple of longhouses, a smattering of houses, a church, a school and little else. There's a **homestay** programme here at the longhouses, and a guesthouse run by the headman Andreas, but the few outsiders who visit here are mostly archeologists, botanists and anthropologists. Planet Borneo (see p.323) have put the village at the centre of their pricey Highlands Cultural and Heritage Trail, because as well as having access to some great bits of primary rainforest, it's central to a great many ancient Kelabit cultural sites. While not incredibly impressive-looking in themselves, these are an atmospheric reminder of the region's long history, and destinations for some interesting journeys.

Treks from Pa' Dalih

Offering swimming and fishing in the river, Pa' Dalih is also a springboard for several half-day highland jungle adventure trips. Among destinations are the huge **stone drums** that were once used as caskets, a couple of hours northeast at Pa' Di'it, and the megalith at Pa' Bangar an equal distance north. Further afield there's the lovely 30m-high **Pa' Di'it Waterfall**, deep within the virgin primary rainforest and a five-hour trek east, which is a great place to swim and has an overnight shelter. All of these treks require guides (RM80–100/day) which you can arrange though the English-speaking headman Andreas, or Petros (see below).

Much closer to the village is a rock niche called **Batuh Liban**, about 100m south along the road, where you can see the less-impressive broken remains of funerary jars.

ARRIVAL AND DEPARTURE   PA' DALIH

By 4WD Since the main logging road between Bario and the coast has been upgraded, the long-used Harrisson Trail has become overgrown and is rarely used, leaving 4WD (or walking along the road) the only option; a charter costs around RM300 (up to five people) from Bario, around RM70–100 if there's one passing, or nothing if you hitchhike.

ACCOMMODATION AND EATING

If headman Andreas is out of town, you can also contact **Petros** (☎013 813 7242) who can arrange the longhouse stay and is also an experienced and knowledgeable guide – he is often to be found in the **canteen** (a green-roofed building at the entrance to the village) which is somewhat of a social centre that also serves very simple meals and sub-standard Dutch beer.

Andreas House ☎013 569 6809. The headman of Pa' Dalih runs a sort of guesthouse with basic but clean rooms at his neat house on a pretty spot by the river about 200m opposite the church. He can also arrange a homestay at one of the two longhouses. Full board per person, guesthouse or longhouse RM80

6

THE BARIO TO PA' LUNGAN TREK

The five-hour **hike from Bario to Pa' Lungan** is fairly easy for the most part, although it becomes trickier if it's been raining. Otherwise the trail is pretty clear and a guide is not needed, though you will be getting your feet wet at some point. The first stretch involves heading past the airport and northeast out of town along the main road. About 3km from the centre the road forks; take the left-hand branch to reach, 1km on, the settlement of **Pa' Ukat** – don't follow the obvious path here, but take a right at the church. From here, the path passes through a very swampy part, after which it rises into mainly secondary jungle – the really swampy sections are crossed on maintained log or bamboo "bridges" of up to 60m long. Using a stick to stabilize yourself while shuffling forward will make these crossings much easier. Along the way you may come across monkeys and other arboreal mammals, as well as **carvings** on a rock called Batu Narit, an hour out of Pa' Ukat, which shows a masked man and a hornbill, along with more than three hundred notches at the bottom which are thought to represent heads taken. Three or four hours on, you finally arrive at Pa' Lungan.

To save time, some trekkers opt to be taken part of the way to Pa' Lungan (or back) by **boat** (1–2hr; RM250 for four passengers), which Bario guesthouses can usually arrange. The boatman takes you to a point on the river called **Long Palungan**, and can point out the trail to follow uphill from the bank; from the right spot on the hilltop, a clear wide trail takes you on to Pa' Lungan (1hr). At this point you can also arrange kayaking to get back to Bario.

Pa' Lungan

The lovely, tranquil village of **PA' LUNGAN**, around a four- to five-hour trek north from Bario (see box above), is made up of a group of detached houses on stilts built around a large rectangular field for buffalo. While for many it's just an overnight stay on the way somewhere else, it actually makes a great trekking base as well as being a peaceful place to hang out for a few days. There are several **trails** from here; day-treks into dense forest, with the possibility of camping overnight at Long Rapung (6hr), as well much more challenging treks to Ba Kelalan (two days) or the remote villages over the border in Kalimantan (8hr) where there are many homestays (RM30–50/person). It is advised that you use a guide; the village, although only having a population of around a hundred, has a selection of guides available. Supang (see below) is probably the best person to ask for a recommendation.

Shorter walks that don't need guides include to the two megaliths within a few minutes' walk of the village. One is leaning drunkenly, thanks to some sloppy archeology by Tom Harrisson, and the other collapsed, damaged by villagers looking for foundation stones. There's also a hill to the north of the village, topped with a tin cross and offering fabulous views – it's a steep forty-minute hike through some nice jungle, but be warned there's little cover at the top.

ACCOMMODATION AND EATING   PA' LUNGAN

★**Batu Ritung Lodge** ☎019 805 2119. The best-known homestay is run by the hospitable and welcoming Supang and her husband Master Chew, both of whom are retired. The house is fairly large and well equipped, with clean, basic rooms and shared bathrooms, and Supang puts out a fine spread at mealtimes using mostly jungle-sourced ingredients – Master Chew can take you out on a 3–4hr tour of the "jungle supermarket" to collect some if you wish. If Supang has no room, she can point you to several decent alternatives. She'll also advise on the best guides in the village and rent you trekking equipment. **RM80**

Pa' Lungan to Ba' Kelalan

It's possible to walk from **Pa' Lungan to Ba' Kelalan**, either via Indonesia (two days one way) or Gunung Murud, which takes five days (see box, p.379). From **Pa' Lungan**, the first day is not too arduous, with just one tough 45-minute climb; it takes around six hours to arrive at **Long Rapung**, just across a fairly big stream which you must cross on a fallen tree (which will be submerged after rain). Here you spend the night in a jungle shelter before a much tougher second day that has many

GUNUNG MURUD

Barring the way between Bario to the south and Ba'Kelalan to the northeast, **Gunung Murud** is the highest peak in Sarawak at 2423m, and is part of the Pulong Tau National Park. It presents a challenging but rewarding trek, with spectacular views across the Highlands to Batu Lawi and even Mulu. From Ba'Kelalan, it takes six days there and back; from Bario, allow one day extra.

Leaving Ba'Kelalan, trekkers generally head to Base Camp 1 at Lepo Bunga (8hr) on the first night, traversing some steep hills. If you need (or want) to save a day, you can take 4WD on this leg (RM50/person). On day 2 the target is **Church Camp** (4–5hr) – a wooden shelter built by local Lun Bawang evangelical groups for a three-day Christian meeting held once a year, and otherwise deserted. The next morning sees the haul up to the summit (3hr) via the **Rock Garden**, an exposed area of stunted trees and sharpish boulders. After another night back at Church Camp, you retrace your steps back to Ba'Kelalan.

If you're starting from Bario, the first day is spent reaching **Pa'Lungan**, where you stay the night. The next day brings a trek to a simple wooden shelter at **Long Rapung** (7hr), with about half an hour's worth of climbing en route. On day 3 some guides head to Church Camp (7hr), others to the slightly nearer Camp 2 at **Long Belaban**, with hammocks to sleep in (5–6hr), though you have to ford a few streams en route and climb for a couple of hours at the end of the day. If you start from Camp 2, day 4 is gruelling, the climb up to the summit beginning at dawn (5–6hr); the descent usually means heading to the Rock Garden and Church Camp (4hr). On day 5 you head back to Camp 2 for the night; it's then possible, with some effort, to get all the way back to Pa'Lungan on day 6.

more climbs and involves fording more than eight streams, until you reach **Pa Rupai** (4–5hr). You're now in Kalimantan, though it's hard to tell as there's no border post – there is, however, a small quarry and road that will lead you down and across some paddy-fields to the village of **Long Medang** (45min), where there's an Indonesian border post at the top a steep hill. If you're just trekking through, they'll note down your passport details and no visa is required. Further down the hill you repeat the process at the Malaysian checkpoint; a couple of hours later you should be safely in Ba' Kelalan.

Batu Lawi

The most challenging local trek, apart from the one to Murud (see box above), is the climb up **Batu Lawi** (2044m), the strange double-horned peak that you may have seen on the flight out. The trek is an attractive prospect as it's less arduous and time-consuming than tackling Gunung Murud, though as ever logging roads blight the landscape here and there, making it look as though the forest has been gnawed by rats.

The first night out from Bario is spent camping at **Bila Bigan**, reached via Pa' Ukat. On the second day you scramble to the lower and much blunter of the peak's two "horns" for an amazing view of the other, looking like a huge upright stone pillar, though ruder interpretations are possible. The descent has trekkers camping at the base of the mountain, from where it should be possible to head back to Bario on the third day. It's also possible to do the trek from Ba' Kelalan; contact Mr Gukang in Ba' Kelalan (see below), your guesthouse or the guide association in Bario (see p.375) for details.

Ba' Kelalan

Apart from a few fruit orchards, **Ba' Kelalan** amounts to a mere smattering of houses in five settlements along the valley floor, a handful of coffee shops and places selling basic provisions, and an airfield. The chief reason to come here is to trek – as at Pa' Lungan, you can head to Bario or Gunung Murud and Batu Lawi, or less ambitiously do short walks, say, into Kalimantan and then back within a day, or a four-hour round trip up to the **viewpoint** at Budukteudal.

By plane The airfield, right next to the village, has flights to Miri (3 weekly; 1hr 35min; RM101) via Lawas (3 weekly; 35min; RM89).

By 4WD A logging road from Ba'Kelalan to Lawas makes it possible to take a 4WD (6hr; RM70/person), which you can arrange through Mr Gukang (see below).

Guides Guides, along with 4WDs and information, can be arranged via Mr Gukang (☎017 855 5048), who speaks good English and can arrange trips to Gunung Murud, Bario, Batu Lawi, or Kalimantan (guide RM120/day, plus return trip), as well as the viewpoint at Budukteudal (RM60–80).

ACCOMMODATION AND EATING

Green Valley Just across the landing strip from the airport "terminal" ☎085 422595. This surprisingly large and well-maintained place has a total of twenty single and double rooms, some of them en suite (RM10 extra).

Breakfast is RM8 per person, and lunch and dinner RM12 each, and the food is very good. In the (unlikely) event that it's full, there are a couple of other options. **RM60**

Ulu Baram

The Baram River system so dominates northern Sarawak that you could consider virtually all the interior here, excepting Limbang division, to be the **Ulu Baram** – practically every river, including the Melinau and Tutoh at Mulu, the Tinjar at Loagan Bunut and the Dapur and Kelapang at Bario, ends up flowing into the Baram. The Batang Baram itself, however, wends its way more or less constantly southwest from the town of **Marudi**, 80km from Miri, occasionally passing little confluence towns such as **Long Lama** and **Long San**, before approaching the border with Kalimantan. Here it swings east to peter out beyond **Lio Matoh**, 200km southeast of Miri.

This Ulu Baram, due south of Mulu and southwest of the Kelabit Highlands, is definitely outback territory, rugged and lushly forested, with no specific sights; the reason you might venture here is to **trek** through virgin rainforest and stay in remote settlements as part of a **homestay** programme. The usual **caveats** about Malaysia homestays apply here (see p.36). One key point is that villagers take turns to put up guests, so quite how adept your hosts will be is a matter of luck. You may have your own room or space, or sleep alongside everyone and their screaming babies; meals are mostly rice and veggies and there may be little to drink other than tepid, weak and sickly sweet coffee. Communication is another problem, as few villagers speak good English.

THE BARAM DAM

Ulu Baram has not been spared the attention of the logging companies, whose roads penetrate even here. The proposed **Baram Dam** site, the latest in Sarawak's twelve dams project, is facing a long-term blockade by Kenyah, Kayan and Penan people as they try and prevent an area of their land the size of Athens being flooded and around 20,000 of them being displaced.

The state government argues that Sarawak's twelve dams will develop the region's economy and infrastructure, as well as guarantee power for the state, and allow profitable electricity exports to West Malaysia, Sabah, Brunei and Indonesia, until 2030 (🔾sarawakenergy.com.my). However, Sarawak already has over-production of electricity (none of the present dam turbines are working to capacity) and no solid plans or talks have yet been made to export it.

Opponents not only challenge the government's energy-demand projections, but point out the massive environmental and social costs of these projects, and also allege widespread corruption, with kickbacks and contracts going to politicians and their companies (🔾sarawakreport.org/baram). There are also question marks over the resettlement schemes and compensation on the previous dam projects, as well as the fact that promised economic and infrastructure benefits have not materialized.

Time will tell which side will win, though one current Sarawak government minister told us, "these projects are going ahead whether they like it or not. They [the Baram Dam protesters] are wasting their time. You can't stop progress."

Ulu Baram trekking

It can be difficult to get to Ulu Baram, but when you finally arrive the rewards can be considerable. There are ample chances to **trek** through dense, unspoiled jungle, using "trails" hacked out by your guide with a machete, spending the night perhaps in a simple hut of the type the Penan erect near their fields, or in a makeshift shelter that your guide might build using branches and leaves. From the Selungo River it's also possible to climb **Gunung Murud Kecil** ("Little Murud"; 2112m), at the opposite end of the Tama Abu Range from its larger and more famous sibling, and there are many other intesting trips to hidden and little-visited caves and waterfalls.

6

Ulu Baram villages

Village life can itself be a highlight in Ulu Baram. Local people can teach crafts such as basket-making, and then there's the simple pleasure of bathing in the river with the villagers, or the spectacle of being at the simple village church on Sunday (many Penan belong to the evangelical Sidang Injil Borneo or SIB movement, which has churches throughout Sarawak); it's great to witness hymns sung in Penan with the village youths showing off their self-taught skills on guitar, keyboards and drums. After the rice is planted (June) or harvested (February), you can even accompany the men as they **hunt** wild pig, aided by dogs, blowpipes and the odd antique rifle.

ARRIVAL AND INFORMATION

ULU BARAM

Picnic with the Penan Though feasibly it's possible to visit the area independently, the best way to visit Penan settlements near Lio Matoh, such as Long Kerong and Ajeng close to the Selungo River, and Long Lamai on the Balong, is as part of a scheme calling itself Picnic with the Penan (ⓦpicnicwiththepenan.org). The experience is similar to visiting tiny villages in the Kelabit Highlands (see p.373), but much more cut off from the wider world. Unfortunately, it doesn't come cheap. As this area has, to an

extent, resisted the blandishments of the logging industry, logging roads and bridges are fewer and further between, and expensive boat charter is required to reach the villages. Furthermore, while MASwings flies to Long Banga near Lio Matoh, until (and if) the logging roads there are repaired, you will have to fly into Long Akah or Long Lellang, 50km away, and then head in by 4WD – another major expense. Travelling in a group of three is ideal, as that is the maximum that the longboats can carry with luggage.

THE PENAN

For some travellers, the **Penan** have a mystique beyond that of any of Sarawak's many Orang Ulu groups, as a kind of poster child for the ongoing struggle for native peoples' rights. That status is largely thanks to the high-profile campaign waged on their behalf by the Swiss activist **Bruno Manser** in the 1980s and 1990s. Manser lived with the Penan for many years and became a thorn in the side of the Sarawak government, successfully drawing the world's attention to the destruction of their traditional forest habitat, though his PR successes had little impact on the juggernaut that is Sarawak's logging industry. The Penan lost their champion when Manser suspiciously disappeared in 2000, having trekked alone from Bario to meet the Penan in the jungle; he was never seen again, but the campaign he founded soldiers on (ⓦbmf.ch).

Most of Sarawak's twelve thousand Penan live in the upper reaches of the Baram, Tutoh and Belaga rivers, with only two or three hundred still following their nomadic lifestyle. Their language is of the same family as Iban and Malay. Traditionally they were nomadic hunter-gatherers, but these days the vast majority live in tiny villages – thanks not only to habitat loss but also to the inescapable embrace of the outside world and the cash economy. Their old staple of sago has often been supplanted by rice, which the Penan grow like the Iban, in jungle clearings using shifting cultivation. Many Penan still struggle to make ends meet, both in towns where they may be in poorly paid work, and in their villages, where food is in reasonable supply but cash hard to come by. Another perennial problem is the lack of formal identity documents, without which many Penan cannot access services, education and jobs.

Sabah

388 Kota Kinabalu

398 Around KK

401 The interior

404 Southwest of KK

407 Labuan

410 North of KK

414 Kinabalu National Park

420 Around Gunung Kinabalu

422 East Sabah

431 Sungai Kinabatangan

434 From Lahad Datu to the Maliau Basin

443 Maliau Basin

KINABATANGAN SUNGAI

Sabah

Until European powers gained a foothold at the northern tip of Borneo in the nineteenth century, the tribal peoples of Sabah had only minimal contact with the outside world. Since then – and particularly since joining the Malaysian Federation in 1963 – these groups have largely exchanged traditional ways for a collective Malaysian identity. As Sabah's cultural landscape has changed, so has its environment: the logging industry has been allowed to exploit huge swathes of the rainforests, with cleared regions used to plant oil palm – a monoculture that makes a poor habitat for wildlife. On the other hand, many locals would argue, this agro-industry provides work for thousands, and generates much-needed income into the state coffers.

7

While arguments rage between campaigners, corporations and politicians, tourists continue to enjoy the remaining natural riches of "the land below the wind" (so called because Sabah's 72,500 square kilometres lie just south of the typhoon belt). The **terrain** ranges from wild, swampy, mangrove-tangled coastal areas, through the dazzling greens of paddy fields and pristine rainforests, to the dizzy heights of the Crocker mountain range – home to the highest peak between the Himalayas and New Guinea, Gunung Kinabalu (Mount Kinabalu). Although habitats for Sabah's indigenous animals have shrunk dramatically with the majority of the eastern half of the state now palms as far as the eye can see, the remaining forests still offer some of the best **wildlife-watching** opportunities in Malaysia. Offshore, damaging fishing practices have, as elsewhere in the region, taken their toll, but marine parks protect areas of magnificent coral – most famously around **Sipadan** – and the attendant sea life.

Sabah's **urban centres** are not especially attractive or historically rich, thanks to World War II bombs and hurried urban redevelopment. While places like **KK** (**Kota Kinabalu**) and **Sandakan** lack notable buildings, however, they abound in atmosphere and energy, plus good places to eat and sleep. That said, Sabah's remarkable natural attractions are the major draw for most visitors.

The **Klias Peninsula** south of KK offers activity-based day-trips such as whitewater rafting or firefly cruises, while with more time you could visit the island of **Pulau Tiga**; you may also need to transit through the duty-free island of **Labuan** on the way to Brunei. North of KK lie the beaches and coconut groves of the **Kudat Peninsula**, where it's possible to visit longhouses belonging to the Rungus tribe; the northernmost point, the **Tip of Borneo**, features windy shorelines and splendid isolation.

As you head east from KK, things get truly exciting. Dominating the landscape are the huge granite shelves of the awesome **Gunung Kinabalu**, a major part of the attraction of which is that getting up and down involves spending just one night on the

Security in eastern Sabah p.387
The people of Sabah p.390
KK's waterfront markets p.391
Exploring the interior p.401
The Murut heartland p.403
Crossing into Sarawak p.405
Diving around Pulau Tiga p.406
Kota Belud market p.411

The Rungus p.412
Kinabalu flora and fauna p.416
Mountain Torq p.418
Orang-utans at Sepilok p.428
Lower Kinabatangan Wildlife Sanctuary p.431
The sea gypsies p.437

Highlights

❶ Pulau Tiga With the TV crews long gone, "Survivor Island" remains largely undeveloped with attractive beaches, jungle walks and a natural mud bath for good measure. **See p.406**

❷ Gunung Kinabalu The arduous climb to see dawn over the South China Sea is well worth the effort. **See p.414**

❸ Sepilok Orang-utan Rehabilitation Centre Orphaned and injured orang-utans are nursed back to health in this popular rainforest reserve; visitors can observe feeding sessions. **See p.427**

❹ Labuk Bay Proboscis Monkey Sanctuary With their distinctive noses and round bellies, proboscis monkeys are among Borneo's most

sought-after endemic species. **See p.429**

❺ Kinabatangan River Home to a great diversity of bird and animal life including orang-utans, proboscis monkeys and the occasional pygmy elephant herd. **See p.431**

❻ Tabin Wildlife Reserve More animal-spotting possibilities in a well-run jungle camp. **See p.435**

❼ Danum Valley Stunning stretches of untouched rainforest with treks and wildlife galore. **See p.436**

❽ Sipadan and Mabul Spectacular marine life makes these two islands a must for scuba divers; reefs off other nearby islands are also worth exploring. **See p.438**

HIGHLIGHTS ARE MARKED ON THE MAP ON P.386

SABAH

HIGHLIGHTS

1. Pulau Tiga
2. Gunung Kinabalu
3. Sepilok Orang-utan Rehabilitation Centre
4. Labuk Bay Proboscis Monkey Sanctuary
5. Kinabatangan River
6. Tabin Wildlife Reserve
7. Danum Valley
8. Sipadan and Mabul

▲ Zamboanga (Philippines)

SULAWESI SEA

CELEBES SEA

KALIMANTAN

BRUNEI

SARAWAK

Murara (Brunei) & Limbang (Sarawak)

Pulau Layang Layang

Pulau Mantanani

Pulau Mantanani Kecil

Pulau Lobuan

Pulau Penyu

Pulau Balambangan

Pulau Banggi

Cagayan Sulu (Philippines)

Pulau Lankayan

Sibutu (Philippines)

Pulau Maataking

Pulau Pom Pom

Pulau Mabul

Pulau Kapalai

Karakit

Kudat

Teluk Marudu

Sikuati

Kampung Bavanggazo

Matungong

Kota Marudu

Pitas

Kanibongan

Tip of Borneo

Penambawan

Tuaran

Kota Belud

Kinabalu Park HQ

KOTA KINABALU

Papar

Kuala Penyu

PULAU TIGA

TUNKU ABDUL RAHMAN PARK

Klias Peninsula

Menumbok

Sitipang

Sindumin

Merapok

Lawas

Bangar

Padas Gorge

Membakut

Beaufort

Tenom

Kinarut

KINABALU NATIONAL PARK

Gunung Kinabalu (4095m) ▲

Kundasang

Poring

Ranau

ROAD UNDER CONSTRUCTION

CROCKER RANGE

Gunung Trus Madi (2642m) ▲

Tambunan

Kampung Patau

Keningau

Kg. Sook

Kampung Dalit

Kampung Tulid

Tatalvan

Sapulut

Pensiangan

Batu Punggul

MALIAU BASIN CONSERVATION AREA

☒ **Park Entrance**

S. Padas

Telupid

S. Sugut

Kanibongan

TURTLE ISLANDS NATIONAL PARK

Sandakan

Sepilok ③

Labuk Bay Proboscis Monkey Sanctuary ④

Gomantong Caves

Batu Putih

Abai

Bilit

Sukau

⑤ LOWER KINABATANGAN WILDLIFE SANCTUARY

S. Segama

Lahad Datu

Kunak

Reserve Entrance ☒

SAPAGAYA FOREST RESERVE

DANUM VALLEY CONSERVATION AREA ⑦

Sungai Kinabatangan

TAWAU HILLS STATE PARK

⑥ TABIN WILDLIFE RESERVE

Tungku

Bandar Sahabat

TUN SAKARAN MARINE PARK

Semporna ⑧

Tawau

0   50
km

N

SECURITY IN EASTERN SABAH

During 2013 and 2014, there were several **fatal attacks** and kidnapping cases in **eastern Sabah** at Semporna, Mabul, and near Lahad Datu, all of which were carried out by armed Filipino (so-called) Islamic groups who have been fighting the Philippine government on the island of Mindanao and in the Sulu archipelago since 1970. Obviously, security has been stepped up in the region but it's unlikely that attacks will stop soon, so be sure to check the local situation before heading to the eastern coastal region.

mountain. Further east is Sandakan, a rapidly modernizing town with offshore attractions including the **Turtle Islands National Park**. Back on the mainland, at the nearby **Sepilok Orang-utan Rehabilitation Centre** and **Labuk Bay Proboscis Monkey Sanctuary**, you can get a ringside view of animals at feeding times.

Deeper into the oil-palm plantations of east Sabah lies the protected **Sungai Kinabatangan**, where visitors can take boat trips to see wild proboscis monkeys, elephants and orang-utans. Further south, the **Danum Valley Conservation Area** offers a spectacular canopy walkway, with the choice of staying at a luxury lodge or a humbler research centre. Alternatively, try the more affordable **Tabin Wildlife Reserve**, with a mud volcano and an elephant colony. In the deep south, accessible via the boom town of Tawau, nestles the untouched forest sector of the **Maliau Basin**, open for challenging trekking.

For divers, the offshore islands near the southern town of **Semporna** are the jewel in Sabah's crown. **Sipadan** offers world-class diving off coral walls, while its neighbour **Mabul** is known for its fabulous macro marine life. These two are simply the best known, and the area can keep divers and snorkellers enchanted for days.

Brief history

Little is known of Sabah's **early history**, though archeological finds in limestone caves indicate that the northern tip of Borneo has been inhabited for well over ten thousand years. **Chinese merchants** were trading with local settlements by 700 AD, and by the fourteenth century the area was under the sway of the sultans of **Brunei** and **Sulu**.

Colonialism

Europe's superpowers first arrived in 1521, when the ships of **Portuguese** navigator Ferdinand Magellan stopped off at Brunei before sailing northwards. Almost 250 years later, in 1763, colonial settlement began when one Captain Cowley established a short-lived trading post on Pulau Balambangan, an island north of Kudat, on behalf of the **British East India Company**. Further colonial involvement came in 1846, when Pulau Labuan (at the mouth of Brunei Bay) was ceded to the British by the Sultan of Brunei. By 1881 the **British North Borneo Chartered Company** had full sovereignty over northern Borneo.

First steps were then taken towards making the territory pay its way: rubber, tobacco and, after 1885, timber were commercially harvested. By 1905 a **rail line** linked the coastal town of **Jesselton** (later Kota Kinabalu) with the resource-rich interior. When the company introduced taxes, the locals were understandably displeased and some resisted; **Mat Salleh**, the son of a Bajau chief, and his followers sacked the company's settlement on Pulau Gaya in 1897. Another uprising, in **Rundum** in 1915, resulted in the slaughter of hundreds of Murut tribespeople by British forces.

World War II and independence

On New Year's Day 1942, Japanese imperial forces invaded Pulau Labuan; Sandakan fell less than three weeks later. By the time the Japanese surrendered on September 9, 1945, almost nothing of Jesselton and Sandakan remained standing (although the worst structural damage was inflicted by Allied bombing). Even worse were the hardships endured by civilians and captured Allied troops, the most notorious of which were the Death Marches of 1945 (see p.423).

Unable to finance the postwar rebuilding of North Borneo, the Chartered Company sold the territory to the British Crown in 1946, and Jesselton was declared the new capital of the **Crown Colony of North Borneo**. Within fifteen years, however, plans had been laid for an independent federation consisting of Malaya, Singapore, Sarawak, North Borneo and (it was intended) Brunei. The **Federation** was proclaimed at midnight on September 15, 1963, with North Borneo renamed Sabah.

Modern politics

Relations with federal Kuala Lumpur have seldom been smooth, but differences had seemed to narrow until, in 1985, the opposition **Parti Bersatu Sabah** (PBS), led by the Christian Joseph Pairin Kitingan, was returned to office in the state elections. This was the first time a non-Muslim had attained power in a Malaysian state. Anti-federal feelings were worsened by much of the profits from Sabah's flourishing **crude oil** exports being siphoned off to KL. This political state of affairs persisted until 1994 when the PBS joined the country's ruling BN coalition, since when the central government has been following a policy of patching up long-running, cross-state disunity to realize a vision of a multiethnic – but Muslim-dominated – nation.

ARRIVAL AND DEPARTURE   SABAH

By plane Kota Kinabalu airport, the major international gateway, is also served by domestic airlines AirAsia, Firefly, Malaysian Airlines and MASwings. Domestic airports in Labuan, Lahad Datu, Sandakan and Tawau are served by flights from the Peninsula as well as within Borneo.

Overland The only overland route into Sabah is from Lawas in Sarawak, which is a short bus ride from the border at Merapok, close to Sipitang (see p.405). Express buses follow this route all the way to KK from Bandar Seri Begawan in Brunei and also from Miri in Sarawak.

By boat Ferries run from Sarawak and Brunei to Labuan, and from there to Sipitang Menumbok or KK. Ferries also sail from Kalimantan (Indonesian Borneo) to Tawau, and from the Philippines to Sandakan.

GETTING AROUND

By plane Internal flights are inexpensive and can save a lot of time. Thus flying from KK to Lahad Datu – for onward travel to Semporna and Sipadan – costs as little as RM89–204 (with MASwings, depending on how far ahead you book) and takes just 50min, compared to around 8hr by bus.

By bus and minivan Travel in the morning if at all possible: minivans leave throughout the day once full, but other passengers can be in short supply by the afternoon, while buses are usually more frequent in the mornings. For travel on rough upcountry roads, say for the Tawau–Keningau loop (see p.403), you may have to charter or take a seat in a 4WD.

Kota Kinabalu

While first impressions of **KOTA KINABALU**, which everyone calls KK, may be of a rather utilitarian concrete sprawl, many visitors end up charmed by its lively buzz and the friendliness of its citizens. As well as good places to eat, it also has excellent transport links and is the headquarters of most of the main tour operators. The best of the city's few sights are its **markets**, the **Sabah Museum** and the **Mari Mari Cultural Village**. A further highlight lies offshore in the **Tuanku Abdul Rahman Park**, whose popular islands are just a short trip away by boat.

Brief history

Modern-day KK can trace its history back to 1882, when the British North Borneo Chartered Company established an outpost on nearby **Pulau Gaya**. After followers of the Bajau rebel, Mat Salleh, burned that down in 1897, the Company chose a mainland site – a fishing village called **Api-Api** – to develop as a new town. Renamed **Jesselton** after Sir Charles Jessel, the vice-chairman of the Chartered

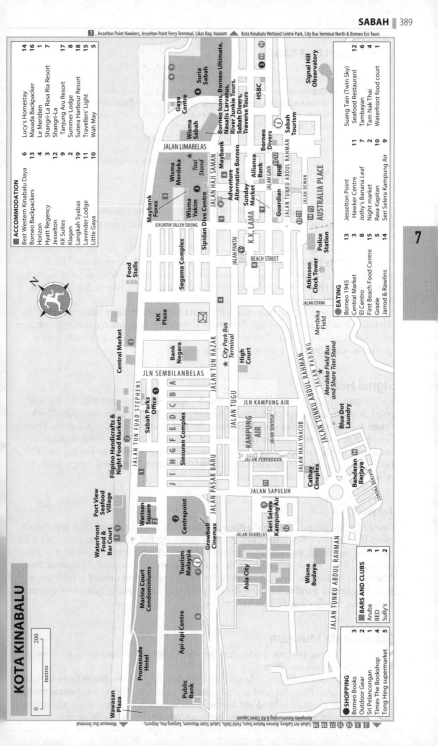

KOTA KINABALU

■ ACCOMMODATION			
Best Western Kinabalu Daya	6	Lucy's Homestay	14
Borneo Backpackers	13	Masada Backpacker	16
Horizon	4	Le Meridien	1
Hyatt Regency	3	Shangri-La Rasa Ria Resort	7
Jesselton	12	Shangri-La	
KK Suites	9	Tanjung Aru Resort	17
Klagan	2	Summer Lodge	8
Langkah Syabas	19	Sutera Harbour Resort	18
Lavender Lodge	11	Travellers' Light	15
Little Gaya	10	Wah May	5

● EATING			
Borneo 1945	13	Suang Tain (Twin Sky)	12
Central Market	3	Seafood Restaurant	6
El Centro	8	Tambayan	7
First Beach Food Centre	15	Tam Nak Thai	4
Grazie	5	Waterfront food court	1
Jarrod & Rawlins	14		
Jesselton Point			
Hawker Centre	11		
Jothy's Banana Leaf	7		
Night market	8		
Rasa Kapitan	10		
Seri Selera Kampung Air	9		

● SHOPPING	
Borneo Books	3
Outdoor Gear	2
Sri Pelancongan	4
Times The Bookshop	1
Tong Hing supermarket	5

■ BARS AND CLUBS	
Aruba	3
BED	1
Sully's	2

0 ─── 200 metres

7

THE PEOPLE OF SABAH

Although many traditions have died out, Sabah's three-million-plus population includes more than a dozen recognized ethnic groups, and numerous dialects are still in use. The peoples of the **Kadazan/Dusun** tribes constitute the largest indigenous group; then there are the **Murut** of the southwest, and Sabah's so-called "sea gypsies", the **Bajau**. In recent years, Sabah has also seen an influx of **Filipino** and **Indonesian** immigrants, particularly on its east coast.

Town and village **tamus** (markets), usually held weekly, are a wonderful opportunity for visitors to take in the colourful mixture of cultures. Large **tamus** include those held on Sundays in the state capital **Kota Kinabalu** (KK) and in the small town of **Kota Belud**, two hours north by bus. The biggest annual **festival** is the **Pesta Kaamatan**, a harvest festival celebrated in May by the Kadazan/Dusun.

Company, the town prospered. By 1905 the Trans-Borneo Railway reached from Jesselton to Beaufort, allowing rubber to be transported efficiently from the interior to the coast.

The Japanese invasion of North Borneo in 1942 marked the start of three and a half years of **military occupation**. Little of old Jesselton survived the resultant Allied bombing, but you can find a few remnants of the past in the east of the city – among them **Merdeka Field**, where Sabah declared independence leading to the formation of modern Malaysia, but left no permanent mark.

In 1968 the town's name was changed to **Kota Kinabalu** and city planners began the expansion outwards into the sea. Progress was startling, with interconnecting concrete buildings constructed on reclaimed land; today, with a population of more than a quarter of a million, KK is a hive of activity once again.

Signal Hill

KK's **historical centre** lies between the South China Sea and **Signal Hill**, the highest point in town. In the lower reaches of the hill, the robust wooden **Atkinson's Clock Tower** was built in 1903 to commemorate the first district official of Jesselton, Francis George Atkinson, who died of malaria at 28. The city's oldest surviving structure, it occupies a lovely vantage point overlooking the padang. Further up the hill on Jalan Bukit Bandera, the more modern **Signal Hill Observatory Platform** is best visited at sunset when the views are particularly dramatic.

Jalan Gaya

One block northwest of **Australia Place**, so named because the Australian army made camp here in 1945, lies **Jalan Gaya**. Known under the British as Bond Street, it's KK's most elegant stretch and includes the city's oldest and most attractive hotel, the *Jesselton* (built in 1954). A few metres away, the wood-boarded, belian-tiled old **General Post Office** now houses the Sarawak Tourism Board. A lively **street market** is held along Jalan Gaya every Sunday morning (6am–1pm), with stalls selling items as disparate as herbal teas, handicrafts, orchids and rabbits.

Sabah State Museum

Jalan Muzium, 3km southeast of the centre • Daily 9am–5pm • RM15 • ☏ 088 253199, ⓦ museum.sabah.gov.my • Bus #13 from Shangrila Hotel (6.30am–8pm), or taxi (RM20)

Styled after Murut and Rungus longhouses, the buildings of the **Sabah State Museum** are set in grounds that also hold several splendid steam engines. The **botanical garden** in front of the museum is bordered by finely crafted traditional houses, representing all Sabah's major tribes and known as the **Heritage Village** (Kampung Warisan).

KK'S WATERFRONT MARKETS

In addition to Jalan Gaya's excellent street market (see opposite), a huddle of **markets** on the waterfront are open daily, and together form one of the city's highlights. Approaching from the northeast, you first reach the labyrinthine **Central Market** (daily 6am–6pm), which includes a **fish market** (from 5am) that's at its best very early in the morning. Next comes the **Handicraft Market** (daily 7am–8pm), also known as the Filipino Market thanks to the ethnicity of many of its stallholders. Around sundown, the area west of here becomes a gargantuan **night food market** (daily 5–11pm); further west still is the waterfront parade of bars and restaurants.

The other highlight of the complex, the **ethnographic collection** in the main building, includes human skulls dating from Sabah's head-hunting days, and a *sininggazanak*, a totemic wooden figurine placed in the field of a Kadazan man who died without heirs. Photographs in the **history gallery** depict the city when Jalan Gaya still constituted the waterfront, lined with lean-tos thatched with nipah palm leaves.

Sabah Art Gallery

Jalan Penampan, off Jalan Muzium, 3km southeast of the centre • Daily 9am–5pm • RM5 • ☎ 088 268748, ⓦ sabah.gov.my • Bus #13 from Shangrila Hotel (6.30am–8pm), or taxi (RM20)

If you want a taste of modern Sabah culture, head to the **Sabah Art Gallery**, just 50m down the road from the State Museum. The basket-shaped building, decorated with indigenous cultural motif panels, houses a collection of more than three thousand works by **contemporary artists**. Brightly coloured paintings, woodcarvings, sculptures, and installations mostly stick to natural themes and depictions of rural life, to reflect Sabah's diverse nature (and possibly to be more attractive to tourists, as many of the paintings are for sale). This is the first official "green building" in Borneo, and one of its many green technologies is that the paintings are lit by motion-activated lights, so you will have to keep moving if you want to keep them on for more than thirty seconds.

Kota Kinabalu Wetland Centre Park

3km north of the city centre in Likas Bay • Tues–Sun 8am–6pm • RM10 • ☎ 088 247955, ⓔ likaswetlands@hotmail.com • Bus #1A from the Hotel Shangrila – ask the driver to drop you at the junction and walk for 5–10min; taxis RM20

The 24 hectares of mangrove forest at **Kota Kinabalu Wetland Centre Park** is the only remaining patch of an extensive system that once covered the coastline. Designated as a bird sanctuary in 1996, it's an important refuge and feeding ground for many species. From marked trails on **boardwalks**, you may catch sight of herons, egrets, sandpipers, pigeons and doves; come early in the morning or late in the afternoon for optimum viewing conditions. Other mangrove wildlife includes fiddler crabs, mudskippers, monitor lizards, weaver ants, water snakes and mud lobsters.

ARRIVAL AND DEPARTURE   KOTA KINABALU

BY PLANE

KK International Airport (KKIA) The two terminals are 5km from each other, so check which you need before setting out. Terminal 1, 7km south of the centre in the Kepayan district, covers international destinations and many domestic flights; the older Terminal 2, 5km from the centre in Tanjung Aru, is used by AirAsia and Cebu Pacific. An airport shuttle bus (hourly; daily 7.30am–7pm; RM5) runs from the terminals to a stop outside the *Marina Court Hotel* in the centre and Merdeka Field, or you can take a coupon taxi (RM30 from T2, RM35 from T1; RM45/52 at

night). For domestic flights, MASwings (book through ⓦ maswings.com.my, or at any travel agent) are the cheapest, while for international flights it's AirAsia (☎ 088 447049), which has offices at Terminal 2 and in town on the ground floor of the Wisma Sabah mall.

Destinations Bandar Seri Bagawan (1–2 daily; 40min); Bintulu (1–2 daily; 1hr 15min); Hong Kong (4–5 daily; 3hr); Johor Bahru (2–3 daily; 2hr 15min); Kuala Lumpur (18–21 daily; 2hr 30min); Kuching (3–4 daily; 1hr 25min); Kudat (2 weekly; 40min); Labuan (6 daily; 30min); Lahad Datu (5 daily; 55min); Manila (1–2 daily; 2hr);

Miri (3–5 daily; 55min); Mulu (2–3 daily; 55min); Penang (1–2 daily; 1hr 40min); Perth (2 weekly; 5hr 30min); Sandakan (8–10 daily; 40min); Seoul (1–2 daily; 5hr); Sibu (2 daily; 1hr 35min); Singapore (2 daily; 2hr 10min); Tawau (7 daily; 55min); Tokyo (3 weekly; 5hr 40min).

BY TRAIN

Tanjung Aru Sabah State Railway (☎ 088 254 611) provides a limited service from Tanjung Aru station, 5km southwest of central KK (bus #18 from the Marina Court bus stop, taxi RM15). Trains stop at Kinarut and Papar before terminating in Beaufort (daily; 2hr 15min), where you can change for Tenom (daily; 1hr).

BY BUS

City Bus Terminal North (CBTN) Better known as Inanam, after the suburb where it's located, 11km east of the centre, this is used by buses to Sandakan and other places north or east of KK. Bus #4 (6am–8pm; every 30–40min; 30min) runs between Inanam and the Merdeka Fields in the city centre. Arriving at Inanam outside these hours requires a taxi (RM25–30, though they might start at RM50) from directly outside the terminal.

Destinations Lahad Datu (4 daily, 7–9am & 7–8pm only; 8hr); Sandakan (17 daily, most before 2pm; 6hr); Semporna (3 daily; 9hr); Tawau (7 daily; 10hr).

Merdeka Field This more central bus stand on Jalan Tuanku Abdul Rahman is served mostly by buses and minivans from northern and southern Sabah.

Destinations Beaufort (5 daily; 2hr); Keningau (5 daily; 2hr 30min); Kota Belud (hourly 7am–5pm; 1hr); Kudat (hourly 7am–4pm; 3hr); Ranau (hourly 7am–5pm; 2hr);

Tambunan (hourly 7am–5pm; 1hr 30min); Tenom (3 daily; 3hr); Tuaran (hourly 7am–5pm; 30min).

KK City Park Bus Terminal A few useful buses depart from in front of the City Hall, including services to Sarawak and Brunei.

Destinations Brunei (daily, 8am; 7hr); Lawas (2–3 daily; 4hr); Menumbok (3 daily; 2hr 30min); Miri (3 weekly; 11hr).

BY FERRY

Jesselton Point Ferry Terminal On Jalan Haji Saman. Services to Labuan are operated by Double Power (☎ 088 236834; 3hr 30min; daily 8am & 1.30pm; RM26.60–44.60); Labuan has connections to Muara in Brunei (take the 8am ferry from KK; combined ticket RM46.60–63.60). Book at least a day ahead for weekend or holiday travel.

BY TAXI

Merdeka Field Share taxis are available at Merdeka Field for Gunung Kinabalu, Ranau, Poring, Beuafort and Tenom, with bays indicated for different destinations. Many are served both by ordinary taxis (seating four passengers) and by larger Toyota Unsers (seating seven). For Kota Belud, the CBTN and Tuoan, the stop is about 300m further west. Unser prices can be a little cheaper but vehicles take longer to fill up, and chartering the whole vehicle is more costly.

Destinations Beaufort (RM15); Gunung Kinabalu (RM20); Keningau (RM30); Kuala Penyu (for Pulau Tiga; RM30); Kudat (RM35); Menumbok (RM30); Papar (RM10); Ranau (RM20); Sipitang (RM25); Tenom (RM25).

GETTING AROUND

On foot The city centre is compact enough to cover on foot inside an hour.

By taxi Drivers rarely turn the meter on, but taxis are inexpensive – it costs no more than RM12 to travel across the city centre. There are ranks outside the *Hyatt* hotel, at the post office on Jalan Tun Razak, along Jalan Perpaduan in Kampung Air and at Centre Point Mall.

By bus or minivan Local buses and minivans leave from the Wawasan bus terminal, 600m southwest of

the Waterfront complex along Jalan Tun Fuad Stephens.

Car rental Companies include Across Borneo, GF, Block D, Riverside, Kingfisher Plaza, Kuala Inanam (☎ 088 733227, ⊕ hawkrentacar.com.my); Hertz, Arrival Level, Terminal 1, KK International Airport (☎ 088 413326, ⊕ hertz.com); Kinabalu Rent-A-Car, Ground floor, Wisma Sabah (☎ 088 232602, ⊕ kinabalurac.com.my). Rent a 4WD if you plan to get far off the beaten track.

INFORMATION

Sabah Tourism Board In the old GPO at 51 Jalan Gaya (Mon–Fri 8am–5pm, Sat & Sun 9am–4pm; ☎ 088 212121, ⊕ sabahtourism.com). The friendly and well-organized staff can help with just about anything. Be sure to pick up the excellent free tourist map of KK.

Tourism Malaysia 107 Api-Api Centre, Jalan Pasar Barul (Mon–Thurs 8am–5pm, Fri 8–11.30am & 2–5pm; ☎ 088 248698, ⊕ tourism.gov.my). They also stock leaflets on Sabah but are better at answering questions about

Peninsular Malaysia or Sarawak.

National parks For information about the environment and ecology of Sabah's national parks, visit the Sabah Parks office, 45 & 46, Block H, KK Times Square (Mon–Fri 8am–5pm; ☎ 088 523500, ⊕ sabahparks.org.my).

Internet Most accommodation has wi-fi, while many hostels also have computers with internet access.

Magazines The monthly *Sabah Malaysian Borneo* magazine lists upcoming events.

TOURS

KK has plenty of handy **tour operators**, many based in the Wisma Sabah building, offering trekking, rafting, diving and wildlife-watching packages, for example to see proboscis monkeys on the Garama River near Beaufort. Most of these things can be arranged independently, including trips on the **Kinabatangan River**, but going through a tour operator can save time and effort. The companies are also useful for arranging day-trips from KK such as wildlife cruises or firefly-watching on the **Klias Peninsula**. Check too the list of operators in Sandakan (see p.425).

★**Adventure Alternative Borneo** 32 Jalan Haji Saman ☏019 802 0549, ⓦaaborneo.com. Specializes in off-the-beaten-track destinations across Borneo at very reasonable prices, and constantly opening up new, untouched places. Current destinations include Sapulot near the Maliau Basin, the Deramakot Forest Reserve and various remote Sarawak longhouses. Don't expect luxury.

Borneo Divers 9th floor, Menara Jubili, 53 Jalan Gaya ☏088 222226, ⓦborneodivers.info. Diving specialists with many years' experience in Sabah and with a resort on Mabul. They can also arrange dives off the Tuanku Abdul Rahman islands.

★**Borneo Eco Tours** Lot 1, Pusat Perindustrian, Kolombong Jaya, Jalan Kolombong, Mile 5.5 ☏088 438300, ⓦborneoecotours.com. Ecotourism pioneer running *Borneo Backpacks* in town (see below) and the superb *Sukau Rainforest Lodge* on the Kinabatangan River, as well as offering a wide array of tours including the Maliau Basin.

Borneo Icons Ground floor, Wismah Sabah ☏088 255513, ⓦborneoicons.com. This outfit arranges tours ranging from Klias river cruises to trips to the Tip of Borneo.

Borneo Nature Tours Ground floor, Lot 10, Sadong Jaya Complex ☏088 267637, ⓦborneonaturetours.com. BNT runs the luxurious *Borneo Rainforest Lodge* in Danum Valley (see p.436); it's also one of the operators with a licence to take groups into the inaccessible Maliau Basin, Sabah's "lost world".

Borneo Ultimate Ground floor, Wisma Sabah ☏088 225188, ⓦborneoultimate.com.my. Adventurous options including kayaking on the river/sea (RM250/300), mountain biking (from RM300) and whitewater rafting (RM170–200).

Field Skills Second floor, Block C, City Mall, Jalan Lintas ☏088 484734, ⓦfieldskills.com.my. This unusual outfit offers rock-climbing and mountain biking, as well as survival and first-aid courses.

Nasalis Larvatus Second floor, Wisma Sabah ☏088 230534, ⓦnasalislarvatustours.com. Named after the scientific name for proboscis monkeys, this operator runs *Nature Lodge Kinabatangan* in Bilit plus a full range of nature tours.

River Junkie Tours Ground floor, Wisma Sabah ☏019 601 2145, ⓦriver-junkie.com. Part of Semporna-based Scuba Junkie (see p.438), offering whitewater rafting on the Padas and a proboscis monkey river cruise.

Sabah Divers Ground floor, Wisma Sabah ☏088 256483, ⓦsabahdivers.com. Diving outfit offering both PADI and SSI courses, plus fun dives around Semporna and off the Tuanku Abdul Rahman islands.

Sipadan Dive Centre 11th floor, A1103, Wisma Merdeka ☏088 240584, ⓦsipadandivers.com. Offers diving trips around Semporna and also runs the *Pulau Tiga Resort* (see p.406).

Traverse Tours Second floor, Wisma Sabah ☏088 260501, ⓦtraversetours.com. Provides the full range of tours, including trips to Pulan Mantanani, and operates Mari-Mari Cultural Village. Their whitewater rafting arm is known as Riverbug.

ACCOMMODATION

KK is king when it comes to **accommodation** in east Malaysia, with good deals to be had in all price ranges. Note that most hostels are set above shopfronts, while for the **resorts**, you need to head out of the city. All accommodation has wi-fi unless otherwise stated, and all hostels provide a "simple breakfast", usually toast and coffee.

HOSTELS

Borneo Backpackers 24 Lorong Dewan ☏088 234009, ⓦborneobackpackers.com. An excellent hostel above *Borneo 1945* café in Australia Place. As well as four double rooms and a number of a/c four- to ten-bed dorms, there's a communal area with TV and a nice rooftop area for smoking. Shared bathrooms only. Dorms RM25, fan doubles RM60, a/c doubles RM70

Lavender Lodge 6 Jalan Laiman Diki, Kampung Air ☏088 217119, ⓦlavenderlodge.com.my. Immaculate private rooms and single-sex a/c dorms, plus a helpful manager, make this a great backpacker choice. You can pay a little extra for an en-suite room or dorm. The communal areas have a TV and internet terminals. Dorms RM35, doubles RM75

★**Lucy's Homestay (aka Backpacker Lodge)** Lot 25, Lorong Dewan, Australia Place ☏088 261495, ⓦwelcome.to/backpackerkk. This homely, cluttered place with small four- and six-bed dorms, TV, library, balcony and washing facilities, is a KK institution. As is the knowledgeable and indomitable owner Lucy, who is a fantastic host so long as you follow her house-rules – no noise after 10pm, and there's a midnight curfew. Fan dorms RM28, fan doubles RM68

★**Masada Backpacker** No. 9, 1st Floor, Jalan Masjid Lama ☎088 238494, ⒲masadabackpacker.com. Winning rave reviews from travellers, this was the hostel to beat at the time of research. Rooms are clean and comfortable, breakfasts are better than average, staff go the extra mile to help and it's an oasis of calm. A/c throughout, and free use of their computer. Dorms RM35, doubles RM80

Summer Lodge 120 Jalan Gaya ☎088 244499, ⒲summerlodge.com. This hostel has prime position above the Beach St action. A magnet for young travellers, it has small, functional doubles (a window will cost RM10 extra) and compact dorms – all have a/c. Dorms RM25, doubles RM60

Travellers' Light 19 Lorong Dewan, Australia Place ☎088 250141, ⒲travellerslight.com. A small and very quiet place tucked up against the KK hill, with simple, clean, cosy doubles and decent six-bed dorms. There's a small terrace at the back where you can talk, smoke or just relax. Dorms RM30, doubles RM70

HOTELS

Best Western Kinabalu Daya Lot 3 & 4, 9, Jalan Pantai ☎088 240000, ⒲kkdayahotel.com. Very good mid-range establishment, perfectly placed in the busy northern section of town opposite Wisma Merdeka. Rooms are snug and en suite, and there's a ground-floor café and an alfresco bar which makes a nice place for a cocktail at sunset. RM162

Horizon Jalan Tun Razak ☎088 518000, ⒲horizonhotelsabah.com. It's hard to miss this bold place thanks to its size and prominent location, and the chic contemporary rooms and interior make it one of the plushest downtown options. Amenities include a gym, sky-spa and pool, several high-class cafés and restaurants and a babysitting service. RM410

★**Hyatt Regency** Jalan Dutuk Salleh Sulong ☎088 221234, ⒲kinabalu.regency.hyatt.com. The elegant, four-star *Hyatt* ranks among Southeast Asia's best city-centre hotels. From its sprawling dining area to the wonderful swimming pool and the perfectly appointed rooms with sea views, the *Hyatt* ticks all the boxes. RM520

Jesselton 69 Jalan Gaya ☎088 223333, ⒲jesseltonhotel.com. Lady Mountbatten and Muhammad Ali are just two of this KK's institution's most famous guests. A combination of central location and colonial-era charm, with a grand piano in the marble lobby, make this hard to beat. As elsewhere in KK, promotional prices are often on offer. RM255

Klagan Warisan Square, Jalan Tun Fuad Stephens ☎088 488908, ⒲theklagan.com. The rooms in this

mid-range hotel have more character than most, with furnishings such as big red designer chairs. Super-deluxe rooms have sea views and bathrooms with huge windows (and blinds) so you can watch the sun set. There's also a rooftop restaurant. Free internet access. RM249

Le Meridien Jalan Tun Fuad Stephens ☎088 322222, ⒲lemeridienkotakinabalu.com. A convenient location and sumptuous facilities, including high-spec rooms, two bars, three restaurants, pool, spa and a 24hr gym. Although many guests will be more interested in higher-end dining, it's right opposite the lively Filipino night market. Check website for discounts. RM490

★**Little Gaya** F1, Lot 52, Jalan Gaya ☎088 261838, ⒲littlegayahotel.com. A tiny boutique hotel at the quiet eastern end of Jalan Gaya. Rooms are cosy (and many don't have windows) but for the price the beds are extraordinarily comfortable and the bathrooms modern, stylish and clean. RM150

KK Suites 98 Jalan Gaya ☎088 233750, ⒲sarangnova.com. An understandably popular choice – rooms are good value (including single rooms for RM25 less online), the location is central and the staff are helpful. The funky lobby has a stylish café. RM130

Wah May 36 Jalan Haji Saman ☎088 266118, ⒲wahmayhotel.com. This friendly, central place has well-maintained rooms and neat bathrooms. Most rooms face the front; the standard ones are rather cramped, but the deluxe twins at the back are larger and quieter. RM83

RESORTS

Langkah Syabas Kampung Kinarut Laut, Kinarut, 20km south of KK ☎088 752000, ⒲langkahsyabas.com.my. Appealing, small-scale beachfront resort, managed by an Australian/Malaysian couple and attracting plenty of Antipodean guests. The older chalets are set in a garden and encircle a small swimming pool, while the newer ones facing the sea cost almost double. The surprisingly good Kinarut Beach Cheese is made on the premises. RM260

Shangri-La Rasa Ria Resort Pantai Dalit, Tuaran, 30km north of KK ☎088 792888, ⒲shangri-la.com. This massive yet laidback resort is set on a gorgeous bay. The grounds include a large forest nature reserve where monkeys can be spotted and there are even a few resident orang-utans. Good-value promotional rates are often available. RM990

Shangri-La Tanjung Aru Resort Tanjung Aru Beach, 4km southwest of central KK ☎088 327888, ⒲shangri-la.com. Set in rolling, landscaped grounds, this luxury resort boasts two pools, watersports and fitness centres, plus several high-class food outlets and bars. Shuttle buses run to their sister *Shangri-La Rasa Ria Resort* and the airport. They also run a golf club nearby. RM1370

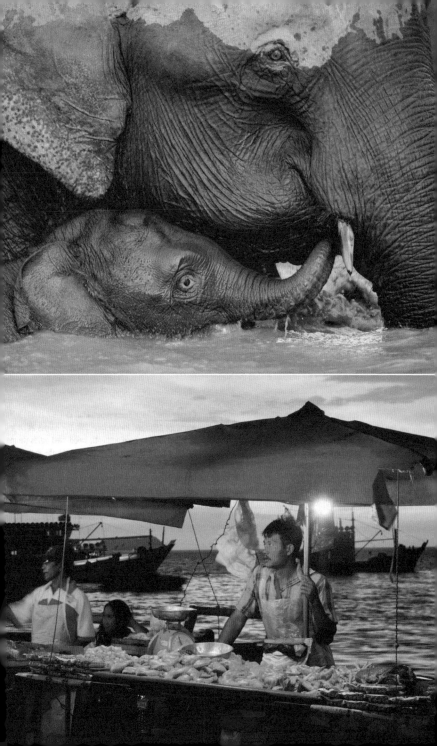

Sutera Harbour Resort 1 Sutera Harbour Blvd, Sutera Harbour, 1.5km south of central KK ☎088 318888, ⓦsuteraharbour.com. This spectacular shoreside development is divided into two hotels: *Pacifica* is designed with business needs to the fore, whereas *Magellan* goes for luxury. From the marina, squeezed between the two, boats run to the islands of the Tuanku Abdul Rahman Park; there's also a massive golf course. RM750

EATING

In recent years KK has become one of Malaysia's best cities for **dining**; the only real disappointment is that Sabahan food is poorly represented compared to Malay, Chinese and international cuisines. There are plenty of restaurants and food courts within the centre, but if you're after seafood then join the locals at the beach in **Tanjung Aru** (bus #16 from Wawasan Plaza).

HAWKER STALLS AND FOOD COURTS

Central Market Jalan Tun Fuad Stephens. The *nasi campur* stalls on the upper floor of the market provide filling, good-value meals. Daily 7am–5pm.

First Beach Food Centre Tanjung Aru First Beach. This popular collection of around sixty stalls, at the north end of the promenade, unsurprisingly specializes in seafood, but you can also get other Malay favourites such as satay. There's a great atmosphere in the evening – particularly at weekends – when families arrive to dine and socialize. Daily 11am–11pm.

Jesselton Point Hawker Centre Jesselton Point, Jalan Haji Saman. These stalls roar to life in the evenings selling satay, fried fish and other popular dishes. There's even an Aussie steakhouse and the seating is pleasantly alfresco, looking out over the harbour toward the islands. Daily 8am–11pm.

★**Night market** Jalan Tun Fuad Stephens. West of the Central Market, the narrow stretch between the road and the South China Sea is transformed at sunset by dozens of stalls selling vegetables, fruit, juices and fresh fish as well as spicy barbecued meats, noodles and rice. Locals complain that tourists have driven up the price of seafood here. Daily 5–10pm.

Seri Selera Kampung Air Jalan Sepuluh. Cavernous indoor food court, still widely known as Sedco Square. It holds half a dozen seafood outlets as well as more than twenty other food stalls – serving satay, chicken rice, noodles and more – and hundreds of tables. Considered a little expensive, it's nevertheless popular with local families and tour groups. Daily 3pm–2am.

★**Waterfront** Jalan Tun Fuad Stephens. A boardwalk in the western corner of the city where more than a dozen restaurants, bars and cafés compete for business, including the *Cock and Bull Bistro* (Western), *The Aussie* (barbecue), *Kohinoor* (Indian) and *Oregano Café* (Asian and Mediterranean). One cheap option is satay and *ketupat* (small parcels of rice) at *Aesha Corner*. Opening times vary, most 6pm–late.

CAFÉS AND RESTAURANTS

Borneo 1945 24 Lorong Dewan, Australia Place ☎088 252891, ⓦborneo1945museumkopitiam.com. This welcoming British-run coffee shop doubles as a tiny World War II museum, serving excellent coffee as well as dishes such as *kaya* (coconut jam; RM1.20) toast for breakfast, *pandan* chicken rice (RM9.50) and a spicy *sup kambing* (lamb soup; RM9.90). It's something of an international and domestic budget-traveller hangout at night and serves cheap beer. Mon–Sat 7.30am–midnight.

★**El Centro** 32 Jalan Haji Saman ☎019 893 5499, ⓦelcentro.my. Fairly new British-run hangout, which has quickly become an institution for foreign tourists and expats alike. With a pleasant interior, comfortable seating and art on the walls, it's especially popular in the evenings for dinner or drinks – they have a good selection of well-priced beers, wine and cocktails. Portions of the mainly Western and fusion food can be pretty large – the tacos (RM14–18), for example, are too big for one person. They also have a good range of vegetarian options. Daily 10am–midnight.

Grazie Third floor, Suria Sabah Mall ☎019 821 6936. If you want Asianized Italian food, join the hordes at *Little Italy*, but for very good authentic wood-fired pizzas (from RM28), pasta and other dishes (RM20–30), this is the top place in KK. Also has a good range of Italian wines and liqueurs. Daily 10am–11pm.

★**Jarrod & Rawlins** KK Times Square ☎088 231860, ⓦjarrod-rawlins.com. What sets this pub apart is the attached pricey deli, which stocks many of the things that Western visitors may be missing from home, including sausages, cheese, serrano ham and steaks. You can buy to take away, but they'll also whip up dishes such as sausage and mash to eat on the premises for around RM18. Daily 10am–1am.

★**Jothy's Banana Leaf** 1/G9, Api-Api Centre ☎088 261595. Excellent South Indian establishment serving satisfying *dosai* after lunchtime and a variety of delicious curries. Foreign diners rate the "chicken 65" (small, boneless fried pieces; RM18), while the locals' favourite is the fish-head curry (RM35) – significantly tastier than it may sound. Daily 11am–10pm.

Rasa Kapitan 50 Jalan Gaya ☎016 860 9601. A/c restaurant serving very good versions of *Nyonya* (fusion Chinese and Malay) cuisine. Specialities include *ayam limanu purut* (chicken cooked with lime leaves in coconut milk; RM14) and oxtail *asam pedas* (in a spicy and sour broth; RM24). Free wi-fi. Mon–Fri 11.30am–2.15pm & 6–9.45pm, Sat & Sun 6–9.45pm.

Suang Tain (Twin Sky) Seafood Restaurant No 12, Block A, Seri Selera Kampung Air ☎ 088 223080. Tucked away behind the Seri Selera Kampung Air food court, this has been a local favourite since 1983. It's known particularly for its crab dishes, as well as its keen prices – rice or noodle dishes are around RM10, and a plate of big prawns RM35. Daily 2pm–12.30am.

Tambayan Block 3/G8, Api-Api Centre ☎ 016 818 2008. Standing out due to the kitsch bamboo and palm-hut decor, this is a favourite for KK's sizeable Filipino population.

Classic dishes include chicken *adobo* (cooked with soy sauce and vinegar), *sinigang baboy* (pork and vegetables in a sour tamarind broth) and breakfasts such as *longsilog* (sweet sausage with rice and egg) – most RM10–12. They have cheap Filipino San Miguel (RM7.50) and you can even try *balut* – fertilized duck egg. Daily 24hr.

Tam Nak Thai Third floor, Suria Sabah Mall ☎ 088 258328. Fine Thai cuisine and a pleasing ambience (and some tables with a view) make this place popular: it's best to book, especially if you intend to eat after 8pm. The green curry (RM18) is good, as is the pineapple rice (RM12). Mon–Sat 11.30am–2.30pm & 6–10.15pm, Sun 6–10.15pm.

DRINKING AND NIGHTLIFE

Although there are a few good **bars**, KK is not generally noted for its **nightlife**. Within the centre there's a backpacker scene on Beach St but the bars are nothing special and the karaoke may not appeal; the **Waterfront** complex is generally a better place to hang out, though *El Centro* and *Borneo1945* are the current popular choices with travellers for a quiet drink. One up-and-coming area is **Times Square KK**, 1km southwest of the centre, although it only really gets going around 11pm.

Aruba Aru Drive, Tanjung Aru First Beach ☎ 017 819 0688. The main draw at this large open-fronted bar, which serves drinks and Malay meals, is its prime beachfront position for KK's famous sunset. Arrive a while before the sun goes down if you can to grab a table on the beach itself. Daily 11am–9pm.

BED Waterfront. The name stands for Best Entertainment Destination, apparently, and it does indeed host some of the liveliest nights out in the city, with Philippine bands

playing popular standards most nights and DJs on Fri and Sat – best to go with a few drinks inside you to fully appreciate the entertainment. Daily 9pm–2am.

Sully's Lot 12, Block B, KK Times Square ⊛ sullys.com .my. Opened by English expats, this bar is trying to do something a little different to the KK norm: it has a resident jazz and blues band, plus an emphasis on cocktails, wines and single malt whisky designed to appeal to the 30-plus crowd. Daily 5pm–2am.

SHOPPING

The newest and shiniest shopping mall in the centre is **Suria Sabah**, built on reclaimed land and with plenty of big-brand stores plus good sea views from many of the quality restaurants on the third floor. Older shopping centres include **Wisma Merdeka** and **Centre Point Mall**, both of which have mostly small local stores rather than international brands. The biggest mall is **1Borneo**, 7km north of the centre – about RM30 by taxi.

Borneo Books Basement, Wisma Merdeka ☎ 088 241050, ⊛ borneobooks.com. Books on Southeast Asia, plus a few secondhand novels. Daily 10am–10pm.

Outdoor Gear Asia City Complex ☎ 088 448806, ⊛ outdoorgear.mariniaga.com. A range of affordable clothing and accessories, including backpacks, footwear and torches. There's a smaller branch at Centrepoint in town. Daily 11.30am–10pm.

Sri Pelancongan Ground floor, Lot 4, Block L, Sinsuran Complex ☎ 088 232121. Tourist board subsidiary for a small but high-quality selection of baskets, artwork and textiles. Mon–Fri 8.30am–5pm, Sat 9am–4pm.

Times The Bookshop Second floor, 1Borneo and GF, Suria Sabah ☎ 088 487118 or ☎ 088 485018, ⊛ timesbookstores.com.my. A wide range of English-language books from this national chain, including Rough Guides to other Asian countries. Daily 10.30am–10pm.

Tong Hing supermarket 55 Jalan Gaya ☎ 088 230300. Specializing in imported food such as wines, cheeses and pork products, Tong Hing also stocks a range of international newspapers and magazines plus imported wines, spirits, cigars and rolling tobacco (along with papers). Added bonus: there's a very good bakery, too. Daily 8am–10.30pm.

DIRECTORY

Banks and exchange Banks include HSBC, Alliance and RHB on Jalan Gaya and Maybank on Jalan Haji Saman. There's a Maybank foreign exchange booth on the ground

floor of Wisma Merdeka, along with several other independent moneychangers.

Cinemas Places showing some films in English include

7

Cathay Cineplex (☎88 313777) on Jalan Haji Yaacob, or more centrally the Growball Cinemax (☎088 256836, ⓦgrowball.com) in Centrepoint Mall and Golden Screen Cinemas (☎037 806 8888, ⓦgsc.com.my) at Suria Sabah and 1Borneo.

Consulates The Indonesian Consulate General Jalan Kemajuan (☎088 218600), issues visas for Kalimantan. There is also one in Tawau.

Hospital Queen Elizabeth Hospital is beyond the Sabah State Museum, on Jalan Penampang (☎088 517555).

Laundry Blue Dot Laundry Services is centrally located near the hostels at 68 Jalan Bandaran Berjaya (daily 8.30am–6pm; ☎088 221914).

Pharmacies In addition to the pharmacies in many malls, there's a handy branch of Guardian on Jalan Gaya.

Police The main police station, Balai Polis KK (☎088 247111), is below Atkinson's Clock Tower on Jalan Padang.

Post office The GPO (Mon–Sat 8am–5pm, Sun 10am–1pm) lies between the Sinsuran and Segama complexes, on Jalan Tun Razak.

Visa extensions Immigration Department, Block B, Federal Administration Complex, Jalan Sulaman (Mon–Thurs 7.30am–1pm & 2–5.30pm; ☎088 488700). Bus #5A from Wawasan.

7 Around KK

There are a number of attractions and activities available around KK, including **Mari Mari Cultural Village** and **Monsopiad Cultural Village** for anyone interested in local culture, or taking a ride south on the **North Borneo Railway** for a taste of colonial Sabah. Most popular of all, however, are the beaches of **Tuanku Abdul Rahman Park** just offshore.

Tuanku Abdul Rahman Park

Named after Malaysia's first prime minister, and just a short boat trip away from KK, the five islands of **Tuanku Abdul Rahman Park** (TAR Park) represent the most westerly ripples of the Crocker mountain range. The islands' forests, beaches and coral reefs lie within 8km of the city, with park territory as close as 3km off the mainland. The three most often visited are **Manukan**, **Mamutik** and **Sapi**, and it's easy to book a day's island hopping. Try to avoid weekends and public holidays, when facilities are often overstretched; don't expect desert island solitude at any time.

Snorkelling is popular around the islands. Although careless tourists have damaged much of the coral, there's enough marine life around to make it worthwhile. **Scuba divers** will find the best conditions from January to March, although visibility is still typically just 5m.

Pulau Gaya

The site of the British North Borneo Chartered Company's first outpost in the region, **Pulau Gaya** is the closest of the islands to KK and also the largest. It doesn't feature on standard island-hopping routes, so is much quieter than the other islands; tourists can simply take any boat to Sapi and ask to be dropped off across the channel.

If you do make it over, you'll find idyllic stretches of sand such as **Polis Beach** as well as lovely hiking **trails** through the jungle where you might see proboscis moneys and hornbills – it takes around a day to walk all the way around.

Pulau Sapi

Though far smaller than its neighbour Gaya, **Pulau Sapi** also has trails and is home to monitor lizards, macaques and hornbills. With the best **beaches** of any of the islands, it is perhaps too popular with swimmers, snorkellers and picnickers – head to the beaches away from the jetty for a little more space. Sapi has simple facilities including toilets, a small café (daily 8am–4pm) and changing rooms. There is also a line of dive-outfits charging a steep RM250 per dive, and beachside vendors rent snorkels and flippers for RM10 per day.

Pulau Manukan

The park office is situated on crescent-shaped **Pulau Manukan**, site of a former stone quarry and now the most developed island. Indeed Manukan has become something of a victim of its own success, drawing hundreds of visitors on a busy day. That said, the beach is attractive, watersports are good and there's a pricey café, and a restaurant at the *Manukan Island Resort*. To escape the crowds, take the thirty-minute walk to Sunset Point. Manukan is at its best at night, as the crowds depart by 5pm, so it's worth considering a stay here.

Pulau Mamutik

Across a narrow channel from Manukan, tiny **Pulau Mamutik** is a snorkeller's delight. The island is surrounded by coral gardens, with the best stretch off the beach at the southwest, towards the back of where the boat drops you, but to reach it it's necessary either to clamber over rocks or to swim right round.

Borneo Divers (☎088 222 226, ⓦborneodivers.info) has a small dive shop on the island, offering better walk-in prices than you'll get by booking ahead. Head out on the first boats of the day if that's your plan; it's much more cost-effective to do two or three dives than just one.

Pulau Sulug

The last island of the group, **Pulau Sulug**, is the most remote and consequently the quietest, though its lovely coral makes it popular with divers. It has no facilities, and few boats visit.

ARRIVAL AND DEPARTURE — TUANKU ABDUL RAHMAN PARK

By boat Frequent boats to Manukan, Mamutik and Sapi leave from the Jesselton Point Ferry Terminal (departures from around 8.30am, last boat back leaves around 5pm). Boat company desks at the terminal compete for business; prices vary slightly but are officially RM23 for one island, RM33 for two or RM43 for all three. If you find an operator that includes Sulug, the official price for four islands is RM53. The operator should give you a timetable and explain the arrangements for moving from one island to another. There's also an RM10 park fee and RM7.20 terminal fee. The same companies also arrange activities such as parasailing, jet skiing and wakeboarding. Rent your snorkelling gear (RM15) at the terminal if you plan to go to more than one island. You could also charter a whole boat (up to twelve people) for around RM200/island.

ACCOMMODATION

In addition to the resorts listed here, all owned by the same company, it's possible to **camp** on the three main islands through the park offices (for just RM5; tents can be rented for RM30, but don't rely too much on availability).

Bunga Raya Resort Pulau Gaya ☎088 380390, ⓦbunga rayaresort.com. A delightful luxury resort with villas hidden away within the forest and access to a secluded white-sand beach. Free transfers to sister property *Gayana Eco Resort* if you want a change of scene or to try the excellent seafood restaurant. Prices can be half the quoted rate online. RM1700
Gayana Eco Resort Pulau Gaya, office at Jesselton Point ticketing office ☎088 380390, ⓦgayana-eco -resort.com. This resort has attractive chalets on either side of a boardwalk jutting out from the beach over the sea, plus two fantastic restaurants in the same rustic complex.

At one end of the plankway, a marine conservation centre holds various tanks containing eels, lobsters and strange-looking flora and fauna. Online discounts of around 25 percent are possible. RM1250
Manukan Island Resort Pulau Manukan ☎088 308914, ⓦsuterasanctuarylodges.com.my. The only accommodation on Manukan, with around twenty well-appointed units; if you're splashing out anyway, it's worth paying the extra RM300 or so for a more luxurious hillside villa. Prices include boat transfers, park entrance and breakfast. RM1200

Monsopiad Cultural Village

Penampang, 13km south of KK • Daily 9am–5pm; guided tours 10am, noon, 3pm & 5pm; cultural show 11am, 2pm & 4pm • RM75 •
☎088 774337, ⓦmonsopiad.com • Bus #13 (or minivan) towards Penampang to Donggongon; from there take the "Teriawi" bus and ask to be dropped off; private taxi from KK (20 min; RM40)

Based around the tale of a legendary head-hunter, **Monsopiad Cultural Village** provides an introduction to the history and traditions of the Kadazan/Dusun people. Tours are led by knowledgeable guides who take visitors to a hut where Monsopiad's grisly harvest of 42 skulls is displayed, and then explain traditions such as the rituals practised by the *bobohizan* (priestess). Next comes the chance to taste *lihing* (rice wine) and test your accuracy with a blowpipe and sling. Finally there's a dance show with scope for a little audience participation.

Although the exhibits and activities are interesting, the entrance price is high and the slightly dated approach has stiff competition from the newer Mari Mari Cultural Village. That said, it has an advantage in that it deals with people from a single tribe – and in the place where they lived – rather than taking a scattergun approach to tribal culture.

Mari Mari Cultural Village

Near Inanam, 18km east of KK • Tours daily 10am–noon, 2–4pm, 6–8pm; 2hr • RM160, including lunch and transport from KK; RM80 without transport (in which case a taxi will cost RM60 each way) • Operated by Traverse Tours, Lot 227–229, 2nd Floor, Wisma Sabah ☎ 088 260 501, ⓦ riverbug.asia

Mari Mari Cultural Village is a newer and more inclusive alternative to the similar Monsopiad Cultural Village (see above), with rather more of a theme park feel but also more interaction right from the start: groups have to assign a leader who will introduce them to the costumed "tribal leader" at the village entrance. Inside, visitors are taken on a whistle-stop tour through the longhouses and customs of all of Sabah's various tribes.

Activities and demonstrations include rice wine tasting, beekeeping for honey and glue production, starting a fire using bamboo, bouncing on a trampoline, making sweets and using a blowpipe. Towards the end there's a dance show, followed by a buffet meal. It may all feel a little phoney but, taken in the right spirit, it is also great fun and you come away both entertained and educated.

Lok Kawi Wildlife Park

South of Penampang, 25km from KK • Daily 9.30am–5.30pm (last ticket 4.30pm); animal show daily (except Fri) 11.15–11.45am & 3.15–3.45pm; public tiger feedings daily (except Fri) 10.20am & 2–2.30pm • RM20 • ☎ 088 765793, ⓦ lokkawiwildlifepark.com • #19B bus from the Hotel Shangri-La bus stop; taxi RM20 (one way)

If you don't like zoos, the rather old-fashioned **Lok Kawi Wildlife Park** – covering 280 acres on the old road between Penampang and Papar – is unlikely to change your mind. While its enclosures generally seem pretty good, in a few cases the animals look quite miserable. The star exhibits are indigenous species such as orang-utans, sun bears, pygmy elephants and tigers, but other attractions include ankole (African cattle with huge horns), as well as a botanical garden and *Rafflesia* trail.

North Borneo Railway

Departures Wed & Sat 9.30am; 4hr • Return RM290; prices include breakfast and lunch, advance booking essential • ☎ 088 308500, ⓦ suteraharbour.com

You don't have to be a railway buff to appreciate the romance of taking a steam train along the 36km of the colonial-era **North Borneo Railway** from Tanjung Aru station (see p.392) to the small town of Papar. The locomotive is a wood-burning British Vulcan, while the five carriages were built to a 1900s-style design in the 1970s – in truth they're the most attractive thing about the trip, as the scenery isn't much to write home about.

The interior

The highway southeast out of KK claws its way up onto the ridges of the **Crocker mountain range**, passing Gunung Alab (1964m). The mountains separate the state's west coast and the swampy Klias Peninsula from the area christened the **interior** in the days of the Chartered Company. The former isolation of this sparsely populated region ended at the start of the twentieth century, when a rail line was built between Jesselton (modern-day KK) and Tenom to transport the raw materials being produced by the region's thriving **rubber** industry. Today, **oil-palm** cultivation takes precedence, though the Kadazan/Dusun and Murut peoples still cultivate rice, maize and cocoa.

Tambunan and around

The drive into the interior from KK starts with teasing glimpses of valleys until, far beyond the **Tambunan Rafflesia Reserve**, a kink in the road reveals the paddy fields of **Tambunan Plain** below. **Gunung Trus Madi**, Sabah's second highest mountain (2642m), towers above the plain's eastern flank; climbing it is an exciting – if rather less easily arranged – alternative to ascending Gunung Kinabalu.

After such a riveting approach, bustling little **TAMBUNAN**, centred on an ugly square of modern shophouses, is bound to disappoint. The best thing about the town itself is its lively *tamu*, held on Thursday in town and Saturday mornings nearby in Kampung Toboh.

Tambunan Rafflesia Reserve

On the main highway, 61km southeast of KK and 20km north of Tambunan • Daily 8am–3pm • RM5, guide RM100 (for up to six people) • ☏ 088 899589

If you feel you really must see a *Rafflesia* (see p.586) in flower while you are in Sabah, then the prospects at the **Tambunan Rafflesia Reserve**, often visited as a day-trip from KK, are good. As each bloom lasts for only a few days, however, it's essential to check ahead. Assuming that one is flowering, expect a walk of up to two hours in total.

Gunung Trus Madi

4WD from Tambunan to Taman Kitangan (1hr)

Rarely climbed, **Gunung Trus Madi**, the second tallest mountain in Sabah, is renowned as a good place to catch sight of rare insectivorous pitcher plants, including one endemic species (*Nepenthes x trusmadiensis*). Climbing it can be arranged through tour operators in KK, but it's essential to plan ahead; getting a permit from the forestry office in KK (☏088 899589) takes around a month, and you'll also need a guide and transport which you may be able to organize with them.

EXPLORING THE INTERIOR

Travelling by bus or car, it's possible to circumnavigate the interior from KK, starting with a drive southeast over the mountains to the Kadazan/Dusun town of **Tambunan**, which sits on a plain chequered with paddy fields. From Tambunan, the road continues further south to **Keningau** and **Tenom**, which marks the start of Murut territory stretching down to the Brunei–Kalimantan **border**. Although this is one route to the **Maliau Basin** – only negotiable by 4WD vehicles at present – most trekkers arrive from the other direction, via Tawau in eastern Sabah (see p.441).

From Tenom, the road west makes for **Beaufort**, once a favourite outpost for colonial officials, arriving back at the coast at **Kuala Penyu**, from where boats travel to the tiny **Pulau Tiga National Park**.

By bus and minivan Buses and vans to and from KK (2hr), Ranau (last bus 11.30am), and Keningau (1hr) stop in Tambunan's main square, surrounded by unremarkable cafés.

ACCOMMODATION

Borneo Heritage Village (aka Tambunan Village Resort Centre or TVRC) 2km north of Tambunan ☎087 774076. Although there's accommodation in Tambunan, this lodge just north of town is a bit more rural. A large site with a holiday camp feel, it's set around a lake and has a riverside café. Accommodation ranges from backpacker rooms – reached via 127 steps – to family chalets with kitchens. Staff can organize activities such as boating on their lake or hiking in the nearby jungle. Transport from KK should be able to drop you at the turning (or even take you to the door if you're in a taxi or van). Doubles <u>RM118</u>, chalets <u>RM248</u>

Keningau

A 50km journey south from Tambunan brings you to the town of **KENINGAU**. A hectic, noisy place, it holds some decent hotels. If you're here on a Thursday morning, check out the *tamu* a short walk up the main Keningau–Tambunan road; on Sundays there's another *tamu* in the town centre. Keningau's single attraction is its **Chinese temple**, right beside the bus terminus. The brightly painted murals that cover its walls and ceilings are more reminiscent of those in a Hindu temple, while the altars are packed with figurines.

By road Minivans run roughly hourly to Keningau from Tambunan (90min; RM9), Tenom (1hr; RM6) and KK (2hr 30min; RM18). Most terminate around the central square (close to the *Juta* hotel) or near BSN Bank (near *Honey Sweet* restaurant), though the town has around a dozen different stops. Ask at the station by the Juta if you need a 4WD to Tawau (RM100–150 depending on number of passengers); you'll need to turn up early (around 6.30–7.30am) and have a little luck, as some days there aren't enough passengers to make the trip viable – you may have to wait several hours to collect some. Prices to Tataluan (see box opposite) are the same as for Tawau, which is still cheaper than arranging transport there.

Internet access Central internet cafés include BJ Nethouse, Lot 1, Block A3, Juta Commercial Centre (Mon–Fri 8.30am–8.30pm, Sat 8.30am–7pm, Sun 10.30am–8.30pm; RM2.50/hr).

ACCOMMODATION

Juta Jalan Milimewa Lama ☎087 337888, ⊛sabah .com.my/juta. The classiest accommodation in town, close to the padang, with stylish rooms with crisp white bed linen and (in the larger, more expensive rooms) art on the walls. The building has a business centre and gym, plus you can arrange a massage. There's also a good restaurant and a non-smoking floor. <u>RM143</u>

Kristal Above Hiap Lee Shopping Centre ☎087 338888. The best budget option, with no-frills a/c rooms that are clean and reasonably priced. There's no restaurant, but plenty of restaurants close by as well a supermarket in the same building. <u>RM50</u>

EATING AND DRINKING

For the most economical food, try the cluster of **food stalls** in the main square, close to the *Juta* hotel (daily 4–11pm). Keep an eye open for yellow dragonfruit, a Keningau speciality.

Honey Sweet Café First floor, Pengalan Shopping Centre ☎087 331078. One of the few places in town serving Western dishes such as fish 'n' chips and steak (RM18–20) they also serve other more local rice and noodle dishes for around RM8–10 – the speciality is chicken rice (RM5.50) with the meat either fried or steamed. There's a/c seating inside and a balcony, and it's a popular bar after dark. Daily 10am–1am.

Tenom

Named after Ontoros Antanom, a Murut warrior, and once the bustling headquarters of the Interior District of British North Borneo, **TENOM**, 42km southwest of Keningau,

THE MURUT HEARTLAND

Rather than moving on from Keningau to either Tenom or Tambunan, a more exciting alternative is to head 122km southeast by 4WD to the remote square of clapper-board shacks that is **Tataluan Village** to explore Sabah's Murut heartland; a boat trip (RM60 for the boat, RM40 for the guide; 90min) from Tataluan will take you to the 130m-high limestone outcrop of **Batu Punggul**, which has magnificent views. After that you can either backtrack by 4WD to Keningau (charter RM200) or strike east along the roads that connect the interior with Tawau (charter RM500), southern Sabah's largest town, through the ancient jungle of the Meliau Basin. You'll save money if you can arrange transport beforehand in Keningau or Tawau.

is now a peaceful backwater with simple hotels and good cafés. Lying within a mantle of forested hills, the town also boasts tasteful wooden shophouses and a blue-domed mosque.

The surroundings are extremely fertile, supporting maize, cocoa and soybean – predominantly cultivated by the indigenous Murut people. Within Malaysia, though, Tenom is best known for **coffee**; there are opportunities to taste the local product or to stay in a small plantation. The town's *tamu* takes place on Sunday (6am–12.30pm).

Sabah Agricultural Park

15km northeast of Tenom • Tues–Sun 8am–5.30pm • RM25 • ☎ 087 737952, ⓦ sabah.net.my/agripark • Taxi (RM15 each way) or minivan (leave when full; RM2–3) from Tenom (ask to be dropped at Lagud Seberang, then walk 1km)

The **Sabah Agricultural Park** (Taman Pertanian), where the state's Agricultural Department carries out studies on a wide range of crops, is a pleasant enough spot to spend an hour or two. The research station is renowned for its **Orchid Centre**, which has four hundred species, and there's a **Living Crop Museum** with groves of exotic fruit trees and tropical plants. Other attractions include the **Bee Centre**, planned gardens, a mini zoo and a couple of lakes. Stay overnight if you want to explore the park's three well-marked trekking routes.

ARRIVAL AND DEPARTURE   TENOM

By train The train station is on the eastern side of the padang.

Destinations Beaufort (2 daily; 2hr 45min), where you can change for Papar, Kinarut or Tanjung Aru (for KK).

By bus Buses stop by the train station at the padang – there are Nai Lok Express (☎ 087 735325) and Tung Ma (☎ 087 735325) ticket offices across from the train station.

Destinations Beaufort (hourly; 50min); Keningau (hourly; 1hr); KK (hourly; 1hr 30min).

By minivan Minivans congregate on Tenom's main street, Jalan Padas, which runs along the north side of the padang; minivans north to Keningau (RM6) circle around Tenom all day, looking for passengers.

By taxi Share taxis wait at the southern edge of the padang.

Destinations Beaufort (2hr 30min; RM35); Keningau (30min; RM10/person); Sipitang (2hr; RM28).

ACCOMMODATION

Sabah Agriculture Park 15km northeast of Tenom ☎ 087 737952. The park has simple accommodation, with dorm rooms and also camping spaces. Staying the night is a requirement if you want to go jungle trekking (for which it's best to contact them in advance). Camping RM10, dorms RM25

Sri Perdana Jalan Tun Mustapha ☎ 087 734001. A reliable choice, just west of the padang across the main road; although a bit grubby in places, the floors and bedding are clean enough. Only one room has a

queen-sized bed; the rest are all twin or larger. RM36

Teak Wood Cabin Fatt Choi coffee plantation ☎ 087 735230, ⓦ fccoffee.com. The four- or six-person cabins at this site, in the hills just behind Tenom, come with fan and hot water. No meals are provided, although you can bring your own food to barbecue. Ask about transfers from the owner's café (see p.404), and about activities such as an early-morning t'ai chi lesson or a hike to see a *Rafflesia*. RM80

EATING

Places to eat are plentiful, with a clutch of coffee shops and restaurants along the main street, as well as a great **night market** in front of the station where dozens of stalls sell local snacks and fried things.

Borneo Coffee Tiam Across from the train station (no phone). This hip joint makes a great place to stop and get your bearings. Many varied and good coffees (RM1.50–1.70), as well as some decent food – the fried-rice dishes (RM5–7) are excellent. Daily 10am–9pm.

Tenom Fatt Choi Coffee Jalan Tun Mustapha, just beyond the fire station ☎087 735230,

⊛fccoffee.com. There may be no such thing as a free meal, but here you can partake of a free coffee. An outlet for one of Tenom's (and Sabah's) best-known coffee brands, it sells beans, ground coffee and instant powders and also provides free tasters – with no pressure to buy. Mon–Sat 8am–5pm.

Southwest of KK

Following the coast southwest of KK, the highway passes through Kinarut and Papar before reaching **Beaufort**, the main access point for the **Klias Peninsula**. This is prime country for **day-trips** organized by tour operators in KK, whether for whitewater rafting, proboscis monkey watching or firefly tours. Offshore is **Pulau Tiga**, the setting for the first series of the TV show *Survivor*.

Beaufort

Named after Leicester P. Beaufort, an early governor of British North Borneo, **BEAUFORT** is a quiet, uneventful town whose commercial significance has declined since the sealed road from KK into the interior lessened the importance of its rail link with Tenom. The town's position on the banks of the Padas leaves it prone to flooding, which explains why its shophouses are raised on steps.

It's also the river that attracts most of the tourists who visit the town – Beaufort is the starting point for many **whitewater rafting** trips. Once you've poked around in the market, inspected angular **St Paul's Church** at the top of town and taken a walk past the stilt houses on the river bank, you've exhausted its sights.

ARRIVAL AND DEPARTURE   BEAUFORT

By train Beaufort is the main hub on the railway line. Trains run in one direction to Tenom (2 daily; 2hr 45min), and in the other to Papar, Kinarut and Tanjung Aru (for KK).

By bus and minibus Buses for KK and Sipitang stop outside the train station, although there is another bus station just opposite the big mosque which is used by most

of the KK buses, as well as minibuses to Tenom, Kuala Penyu and Menumbok. If you're heading for Lawas in Sarawak, the sole daily bus from KK arrives around 3pm (1hr 45min; RM13).

Destinations KK (4 daily; 90min); Kuala Penyu (several daily; 1hr); Menumbok (several; 1hr); Sipitang (1 daily, 3pm; 1hr 30min).

ACCOMMODATION

Rainbow Hotel In the bus station by the big mosque ☎087 212632, ✉meldehotel.bfort2007@hotmail .com. Nothing special, but the small, en-suite rooms are

clean, with a/c, cable TV and hot water. There are several eating options nearby including *Kim Wah*, which serves decent, if pricey, Chinese food. **RM69**

Sipitang

Reached by road southwest of Beaufort, the seafront town of **SIPITANG** is notable only as a departure point for **boats to Labuan**. As you approach from the north, a bridge marks the start of town – look out for the pretty stilt houses to your left as you cross. The jetty is just beyond the bridge, behind the Shell petrol station.

> ### CROSSING INTO SARAWAK
>
> **Buses** from KK to Lawas – or continuing on to Brunei – stop in Sipitang, but if you're already in town it's easier to get a seat in a taxi. Heading west from Sipitang, buses stop at Merapok, where your passport is stamped by the Sabah control, and then passed to the next desk to be processed by the Sarawak side entitling you to remain in Sarawak for thirty days.
>
> Official **taxis** from Sipitang cannot cross into Sarawak, so you'll need to pay RM10 to the border then take another RM10 taxi on the other side. The other option is to take an unlicensed share taxi all the way from Sipitang to Lawas for RM10 per person.

ARRIVAL AND DEPARTURE SIPITANG

By bus Sipitang Express (☎ 0168 265722, ⌨ sipitang express.com.my) runs two daily buses each way between KK and Bandar in Brunei (via Lawas in Sarawak) that stop in the town centre, with another six services travelling only between here and KK. Sairah Express (☎ 089 757357) runs two daily buses to Tawau at 11.30am and 3pm (13hr).

By boat Speedboats run by Kaka Express leave the jetty twice daily for Labuan (11am & 4pm; RM30).

By taxi From the share taxi stand, next to the bus stop, you can join a vehicle to Beaufort (RM6) or Tenom (RM10).

ACCOMMODATION AND EATING

By far the best **places to eat** are the satay and fried-chicken stalls on the waterfront; some open at lunchtime but most start operating around dusk.

Azmia Curry House Lot 16, Sabaran Lega, at the southern end of the Esplanade opposite the street market ☎ 050 585 8388. The most inviting of a row of similar Indian restaurants, serving rice and noodle dishes plus an impressive *nasi campur* buffet for under RM10. The *roti canai* (RM1) are excellent too. Daily 6.30am–11.30pm.

Dhiya Esplanad Upper floors, Bangunan TBB ☎ 016 811 6442. The first hotel you come to as you head along the main road from the jetty, with simple but clean rooms. Some of the more spacious deluxe rooms have sea views. <u>RM60</u>

Klias Peninsula

Thirty kilometres west of Beaufort, and served by regular minivans from the centre of town, the **Klias Peninsula** is an area of flat marshland that's popular with KK-based tour operators for proboscis monkey or firefly tours (see p.393).

Menumbok

The most westerly settlement on the Klias Peninsula, tiny **MENUMBOK** has no accommodation. It's notable only for the jetty that links it to Labuan; a couple of cafés here may be useful when waiting for a boat.

Kuala Penyu

Around an hour northeast of Beaufort, or 45 minutes from Menumbok, at the northern point of the peninsula, **KUALA PENYU** is the departure point for **Pulau Tiga National Park**. It's a simple grid of streets with little more than a few stores, filled with basic supplies, and a couple of *kedai kopis*.

ARRIVAL AND DEPARTURE KLIAS PENINSULA

MENUMBOK

By bus and share taxi Buses are scheduled to take arriving ferry passengers to KK, and share taxis to KK (2hr 30min; RM35) wait for the speedboats. You may have to wait for a share taxi to smaller destinations, such as Beaufort (1hr; RM10) or Kuala Penyu (45min; RM10). Another way to Kuala Penyu is to take a KK-bound vehicle to Kayul, where there are of onward minibuses or share taxis (RM10).

By boat Regular speedboats and two larger ferries travel daily between Menumbok and Labuan (see p.407).

KUALA PENYU

By minivan Leaving Kuala Penyu, it takes just over 2hr to travel by minivan to KK's Merdeka Field bus stand (RM40), or you can get a minivan to Beaufort (RM5). These vehicles leave from one block back from the jetty.

By boat Boats run to the *Pulau Tiga Resort* (see p.406) twice daily, usually at 10am and 3pm (RM100).

ACCOMMODATION

★**Tempurung Seaside Lodge** 13km west of Kuala Penyu ☎088 773066, ⓦborneotempurung.com. Charming wooden chalets connected by wooden walkways on a hillside overlooking the South China Sea. The lodge has a beautiful private beach, though sandflies can be a problem. You can go jungle-trekking, they have mountain bikes for rent (RM15/hr), and you can arrange a day-trip to Pulau Tiga for RM185/person (minimum of four people). Full board **RM300**

Pulau Tiga National Park

Nestled in the South China Sea 12km north of Kuala Penyu, **Pulau Tiga National Park** is a beautiful and peaceful island that acquired a degree of fame in 2001 as the paradise location of the first series of the American reality TV show *Survivor*. It used to consist of three islands, one of which has since been reduced to a mere sand bar by wave erosion. Of the remaining two – **Tiga** and **Kalampunian Damit** – only the former holds any accommodation. The latter is normally visited as part of a morning snorkelling trip from *Pulau Tiga Resort*.

Most visitors content themselves with relaxing on the sandy beaches and **snorkelling** or **diving** in the azure sea. It's possible to hike right around the jungle-cloaked island in six hours, but the paths are poorly maintained, so check at the park office which ones are passable. The best is the easy twenty-minute walk to the centre of Pulau Tiga, which leads to a couple of (cool) **mud volcanoes** – although one wonders how clean they are by now. There's a much cleaner, though much smaller one (more like a mud bowl), on the east of the island off the path to the *Borneo Survivor Resort*, where the mud is wonderfully nourishing and smoothing for the skin.

ARRIVAL AND DEPARTURE   PULAU TIGA NATIONAL PARK

By boat No public boats run to Pulau Tiga; most visitors come on tour packages that include transport. If you're staying at the Sabah Parks accommodation, check if you can hitch a lift if they're doing a supply-run that day, or whether there's room on a resort boat – expect to pay RM100 each way (departures around 10am & 3pm daily; 30min). Otherwise you may be able to charter a boat (30min; RM700 return), which can hold twelve people; talk to the Sabah Parks office at the Kuala Penyu jetty, and if that doesn't help try the *Pulau Tiga Resort* office. Boats back to Kuala Penyu leave the island at 9am and 2pm. All visitors must pay a RM10 conservation fee to visit the park.

ACCOMMODATION AND EATING

At the time of research only two **accommodation** options were open on Pulau Tiga, although the *Borneo Survivor Resort* was expected to reopen at some point (most likely with a new name).

Pulau Tiga Resort ☎088 240584, ⓦpulautiga.com .my. This well-run beach resort has dozens of twin-bed chalets, with triples shared slightly cheaper as small dorms. Activities include kayaking and snorkelling, plus there's a dive shop, restaurant, bar and karaoke room. Full board including ferry from Kuala Penyu **RM300**, extra nights **RM210**

Sabah Parks accommodations ☎087 884695, ⓦsabahparks.org.my/eng/pulau_tiga_park. The park authorities offer two simple (and very hot) dormitories and a chalet with two twin-bed rooms; you can also camp (with your own tent). There is no restaurant but you can use the kitchens or go to *Pulau Tiga Resort*. Camping **RM5**, dorms **RM30**, chalet **RM240**

DIVING AROUND PULAU TIGA

Pulau Tiga's prime dive site is probably **Asmara Point**, close to the Sabah Parks jetty. With a maximum depth of 10m it's a nice easy dive, albeit sometimes with a slight current, with good coral attracting lionfish, Moorish idols and groupers, plus sometimes sea turtles. Other good sites include Phukat Point (where they very occasionally see white-tip sharks), Larai Point (notable for its excellent coral) and Dunlop Point.

Expect to pay RM180 for two dives (minimum two people), plus RM150/day for equipment rental. Discover Scuba Diving classes (RM150) get non-divers underwater straight away.

Labuan

A short distance west of the Klias Peninsula, **LABUAN** is not part of Sabah; it was part of the Straits Settlements, and is now Federal Territory governed directly from KL. Labuan town holds few tourist attractions, but its centre has decent eating, good mid-range accommodation and a lively nightlife. Some worthwhile sights lie beyond the town, and scuba divers are attracted by the chance to dive four **wrecks**. You might also want to take advantage of the island's **duty-free** prices while passing through.

Labuan Town and around

The centre of Labuan, previously known as Victoria but now simply **LABUAN TOWN**, lies on the island's southeastern side. Along with the international airport, the gleaming ferry terminal on Jalan Merdeka attests to the island's prosperity and geographic importance. Apart from the stretch where the road up from Labuan Town hits the beach road at Layang Layangan, where families come at weekends and there are a couple of food stalls, the lovely **beaches** outside town, from Batu Manikar Beach to Sungai Miri Beach (an area known as UN Beach), are mostly devoid of development and facilities.

7

General Market

Western end of Labuan Town • **Market** Daily 6am–6pm **Bazaar** Mon–Sat 7am–5pm, Sun 7am–1pm

The upper floor of the busy *gerai* (**General Market**) affords good views of Kampung Patau Patau – the modest **water village** northwest of town. To reach the *gerai* itself you pass through **Labuan Bazar**, which sells clothes, handicrafts and souvenirs.

Labuan Museum

Behind the padang on Jalan Dewan • Daily 8.30am–5pm • Free • ☎ 087 414135, ⓦ jmm.gov.my

Housed in a yellow concrete building, the small **Labuan Museum** contains a maze of rooms where photo- and caption-led exhibits document the island's history. Most notable were the dramatic events of World War II, as it was through Labuan that the Japanese forces penetrated British North Borneo.

Marine Museum

Labuan International Sea Sports Complex (Kompleks Sukan Laut), Jalan Tanjun Purun, 1km east of Labuan Museum • Daily 8.30am–5pm; fish feeding Sat 10am • Free • ☎ 087 425927 • RM10 by taxi

Set within a complex that also houses a food court and businesses including Borneo Star Dive (see p.409), the **Marine Museum** mostly features conventional tanks with fish and other sea creatures, but starts with a pool of small black-tip sharks that guests are allowed to touch.

World War II Cemetery

3km northeast of town centre, Jalan Tanjung Batu • #1 bus or taxi (RM10–15)

In Malaysia's largest **World War II Cemetery**, more than 3900 war graves are neatly laid out on perfectly manicured lawns. It's a serene, reflective spot, with a memorial at one side where the soldiers' names are listed.

Labuan Bird Park

North of the island, Jalan Tanjung Kubong • Daily 10am–4.30pm, Fri 2–4.30pm • RM5 • ☎ 087 463544 • From Labuan Town bus #6 (30min); taxi RM36

Arranged around three aviaries in geodesic domes, the **Labuan Bird Park** holds tropical birds from throughout the region, such as hornbills, kingfishers, sharmas, herons, ostriches and peacocks. Perhaps the biggest hits are the mynah birds that say "hello" as you approach; there are printed lists of words to which they will respond.

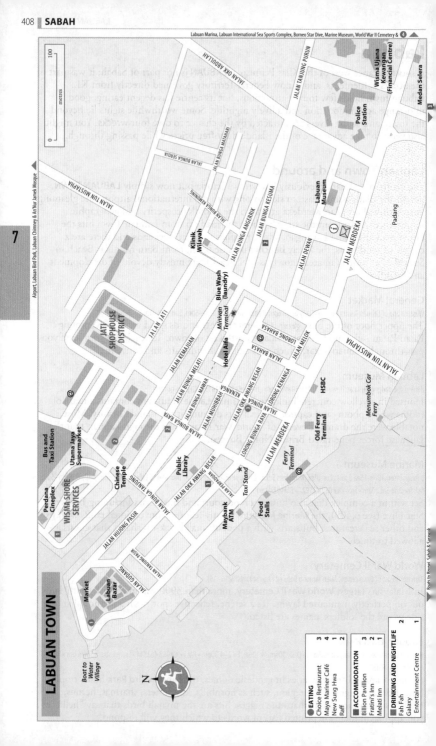

LABUAN TOWN

Labuan Marina, Labuan International Sea Sports Complex, Borneo Star Dive, Marine Museum, World War II Cemetery &

Airport, Labuan Bird Park, Labuan Chimney & Air Nur Jamek Mosque

JALAN OKK ABDULLAH

JALAN TANJUNG PURUN

Wisma Ujana Kewangan (Financial Centre)

Medan Selera

Police Station

JALAN BUNGA MATAHARI

JALAN BUNGA SEROJA

JALAN TUN MUSTAPHA

JALAN BUNGA KEMUNING

JALAN BUNGA KESUMA

Labuan Museum

Klinik Wilayah

JALAN BUNGA ANGGERIK

JALAN DEWAN

JALAN MERDEKA

Padang

JALAN JATI

JATI SHOPHOUSE DISTRICT

Blue Wash (laundry)

Miriwan Terminal

JALAN KEMAJUAN

Hotel Aifa

LORONG BAHASA

JALAN MELUR

JALAN TUN MUSTAPHA

JALAN BUNGA MELATI

JALAN BAHASA

JALAN BUNGA MAWAR

KENANGA

JALAN BUNGA RAYA

JALAN MUHIBBAH

JALAN OKK AWANG BESAR

LORONG KENANGA

Menumbok Car Ferry

HSBC

JALAN BUNGA RAYA

LORONG BUNGA RAYA

Old Ferry Terminal

Bus and Taxi Station

Utama Jaya Supermarket

Perdana Cineplex

WISMA SHORE SERVICES

Chinese Temple

Public Library

JALAN BUNGA TANJUNG

JALAN OKK AWANG BESAR

JALAN MERDEKA

Ferry Terminal

Maybank ATM

Taxi Stand

JALAN MUHIBBAH

Food Stalls

Market

Labuan Bazar

JALAN GUDANG

JALAN TANJUNG PASIR

JALAN HUJUNG PASIR

Boat to Water Village

Boat to Rimai, Sabah & Sarawak

N

● EATING	
Choice Restaurant	3
Maya Mariner Café	4
New Sung Hwa	1
Raff	2

■ ACCOMMODATION	
Billion Pavillion	3
Fratini's Inn	2
Melati Inn	1

■ DRINKING AND NIGHTLIFE	
Fah Fah	2
Galaxy Entertainment Centre	1

0   meters   100

ARRIVAL AND DEPARTURE

By plane From Labuan Town's airport, 5km north of town, the only way into the centre is by taxi (RM15).
Destinations KK (6 daily; 30min); Kuala Lumpur (3–5 daily; 2hr 20min); Miri (5 daily; 40min).

By boat Most ferries dock at Labuan Town's international ferry terminal on Jalan Merdeka (ticket office ☎087 581006; daily 7.10am–5.30pm). Passenger ferries to Menumbok leave from the main terminal, while vehicle ferries use a separate jetty close by. They connect on the mainland to bus services for KK (see p.405); buy bus tickets

from the booth in Labuan's international ferry terminal. In addition, smaller speedboats run hourly to Menumbok (45min; RM15).
Destinations KK (2 daily; 3hr 15min); Lawas (daily 10am; 2hr 15min); Limbang (2 daily at 2pm; 2hr); Menumbok (car ferry 2–3 daily; 50min); Muara, Brunei (4 daily; 1hr 15min).

Vehicle rental and taxis There are car rental counters at the ferry terminal and you can charter a taxi for RM45/hr.

INFORMATION AND ACTIVITIES

Tourist information centre Jalan Merdeka, close to the Labuan Museum in Labuan Town (Mon–Sat 9am–5pm; ☎087 423445). Helpful, with plenty of material, including very good maps; ask about the island's highly recommended homestay programme.

Internet There's an internet café in the ferry terminal (daily 8am–midnight; RM4/hr).

Diving The only company arranging diving on Labuan's wrecks is Borneo Star Dive, based at Labuan International Sea Sports Complex (☎087 429278, ✉stardivers2005@yahoo

.com); a day's diving starts at RM408 (minimum four people).

Island hopping For island-hopping trips in the nearby marine park, enquire at the tourist office or try Seri Ganti (☎016 840006) in the old ferry terminal (just next to the new one) who usually ferry oil workers but can take tourists just as easily – prices are much lower if there are five or more of you. They can take you either on the 45min trip to the remote Kuraman or on a 5min ride to the more popular Papan, though there are no shops at either island so you'll need to take your own water, food and snorkelling equipment.

7

ACCOMMODATION

As a business centre, Labuan Town holds plenty of **hotels**, almost all of them mid-range or higher. All of the few budget hotels that exist, except *Melati*, are really quite awful – if you're on a budget you're far better using the excellent **homestay** programme. Whatever you're looking for, it pays to book ahead. There are chalets on the islands of **Kuraman and Papan** (and a campsite on Papan), which are often full at weekends – contact the Labuan Corporation (☎013 850 7144).

LABUAN TOWN

Billion Pavilion Jalan Wawasan ☎087 418111, ⦿billion pavilion.com. Stylish foyer, perfectly appointed rooms and prompt service. All rooms at this three-star are basically the same; prices vary according to location and view. Facilities include a pool, fitness centre, restaurant and – perhaps best of all – the poolside bar where they also have Saturday night buffets (RM55). Rates drop by RM110 at weekends. RM358
Fratini's Inn Jalan Bunga Kesuma ☎087 424545, ✉fratinilabuan@gmail.com. Upstairs from *Fratini's Restaurant* (which serves fairly good Italian food), this place goes some way towards living up to its billing of "boutique hotel" with small, well-furnished modern rooms and suites. RM130

★ **Labuan Homestay Programme** Contact tourist information centre (☎087 423445) or Ministry of Tourism and Culture office at the Sea Sports Complex (☎087 422622). The participants in this well-organized scheme include homes in a water village as well as on land, and hosts can arrange affordable activities such as night fishing or traditional cooking. Meals RM5–10. RM65
Melati Inn Tingkat 1 & 2, Jalan Perpandua, just behind the taxi stand ☎087 416307. Labuan's only decent budget choice, this first-floor guesthouse has reasonable, clean, a/c rooms, which even have carpets on the floor. Friendly staff and a central location. En suites cost RM10 more. RM60

EATING

Labuan Town is particularly known for its seafood; to try something distinctively Brunei-Malay, look out for *ambuyat* – a gluey white substance made from sago and water, it's almost flavourless and served instead of rice. In addition to the places listed here, Jalan Merdeka and Jalan OKK Awang Besar hold lots of adequate, no-frills, Chinese and Indian **restaurants**. If you're stuck late at night then seek out the Malay, Thai and even vegetarian dishes at the 24hr outdoor **food court** (Medan Selera) close to the *Grand Dorsett*.

★ **Choice Restaurant** Jalan Okk Awang Besar. Spacious a/c café with a long à la carte menu, as well as a

lunch and dinnertime *nasi campur* buffet (RM8–12) with a wide range of meat and fish curries. The *roti* and *dosai* are excellent – try the *ghee masala dosa* for breakfast (RM3.80). Daily 8am–10.30pm.

Maya Mariner Café Labuan Marina, Jalan Wawasan ☎ 016 839 6479. This small café at the back of the main marina building serves up very good authentic Punjabi cuisine including chicken *biriyani* on Saturdays (RM15). More unusual dishes include deer meat curry (RM14), while for breakfast they serve *aloo paratha* bread. Mon & Wed–Sat 9.30am–9pm, Sun 9.30am–2pm.

New Sung Hwa Ujong Pasir, PCK Building ☎ 087 411 008. It may not look especially promising from outside, but

this Chinese seafood restaurant on the edge of the market is incredibly popular, especially for their crispy calamari (RM10). Book ahead if possible, particularly at the weekend. Fresh fish costs around RM33/kg. Daily 10am–2pm & 6–10.30pm.

Raff 240c Jalan Kemajuan ☎ 087 421902. This restaurant specializes in home-style Malay cooking, such as a popular *nasi ayam penyek* (chicken rice; RM5.80) and has the best *nasi campur* (RM5–10) in town. They also do a good *laksa (RM5)*, based on a Kuching recipe. Daily 7.45am–3.30pm.

DRINKING AND NIGHTLIFE

Labuan Town is somewhat notorious when it comes to **nightlife**. You're unlikely to see anything particularly sleazy out in the open, but single men may be approached in the karaoke bars. The main bar districts are the Jati Shophouses, the area north of Jalan Bunga Angerrik, and the Shore Services Centre (behind the Utama Jaya supermarket).

Fah Fah Jalan Bunga Mawar ☎ 087 425 5863. With most of its seating outdoors on a street corner, this café serves *bak kut teh* and a few other dishes, but mostly it's popular with both expats and locals as a place to enjoy a few beers. In fact, the drinking starts pretty early in the afternoon. Daily 7am–1am.

Galaxy Entertainment Centre Shore Services Centre ✉ galaxy_labuan@yahoo.com. Unapologetically loud, this place has live music (usually the house band playing covers) on a small stage inside the shiny modern interior. There are also DJs and even a small dancefloor. Daily 7.30pm–2.30am.

DIRECTORY

Banks and exchange The bureau de change (8.45am–3.30pm) at the ferry terminal has a 24hr ATM; there's also an HSBC next door.

Laundry Blue Wash on Jalan Kemajuan (7am–10pm) has coin-operated machines, a rarity in Malaysia, as well as offering service washes, plus wi-fi.

Medical clinic Klinik Wiliyah, 391 Jalan Bunga Rampai (Mon–Thurs & Sat 8am–9pm, Fri 8am–noon & 2–9pm,

Sun 8am–1pm & 6–9pm; ☎ 087 413140).

Shopping All the shops are duty-free, including places selling alcohol in the ferry terminal; there are lots more outlets on Jalan Merdeka and Jalan Tun Mustapha. For general shopping, try the mall at Ujama Kewangan (Financial Park), which has a Parkson department store, food court, internet café and CIMB Bank.

North of KK

Sabah's trunk highway hurries through the northern suburbs of KK to the more pastoral environs of **Tuaran**, where the main road forks, with the eastern branch heading towards Gunung Kinabalu National Park and Ranau, then onwards to Sandakan.

Continuing north instead, the main road arrives at bustling **Kota Belud**, where a weekly *tamu* attracts tribespeople from all over the region. Beyond, the landscape becomes more colourful: jewel-bright paddy fields and stilted wooden houses line the road for much of the way up to the **Kudat Peninsula**, with Gunung Kinabalu dominating the far distance.

On the way to **Kudat**, the first administrative capital of the East India Company, it's possible to stay at a Rungus longhouse in **Kampung Bavanggazo**. North of town the area known as the **Tip of Borneo** has quiet beaches and a few guesthouses. Remote islands reached from the peninsula include **Pulau Banggi** and **Pulau Mantanani**.

Pulau Mantanani

Popular with KK tour operators as a day-trip destination, **Pulau Mantanani** is actually a collection of three tiny islands 40km off the coast from Kota Belud (from where you

---

KOTA BELUD MARKET

For six days of the week, **Kota Belud**, 75km northeast of KK, is a busy but undistinguished town; arriving tourists usually head straight to the jetty for **Pulau Mantanani**. Early on Sunday, however, the town springs to life as hordes of villagers congregate at Sabah's largest weekly **tamu**. Fulfilling a social as well as commercial role, the market draws Rungus, Kadazan/Dusun and Bajau indigenous groups.

Though the market's popularity among KK's tour operators means there are always a few tourists, you won't see many souvenirs for sale: instead you're far more likely to come across dried fish, chains of yeast beads (used to make rice wine), buffalo, betel nut and *tudung saji* (colourful food covers used to keep flies at bay). Arrive early – if you're coming from KK, set off by 8am at the latest. Buses, minivans and tour boats make the trip.

Kota Belud's annual **tamu besar**, or "big market", usually held in October, sees cultural performances, traditional horseback games and handicraft demonstrations in addition to the more typical stalls.

7

can take a boat) that also holds a few resorts. It's a lot of travel for a single day, but a lovely place to stay for a night or two; snorkelling, kayaking and scuba diving are available by arrangement, though independent travel is not possible and you'll have to book a tour or stay at one of the resorts.

ACCOMMODATION   **PULAU MANTANANI**

Mari Mari Mantanani Backpacker Lodge Pulau Mantanani, c/o Traverse Tours ☎088 260501, ⓦmantananiisland.com. A collection of simple *sulaps* (huts) on stilts, with a hammock and chairs under each one, plus more expensive chalets that are en suite but otherwise very similar. There are also dorms in one of the two sister resorts on the island. Rates include transfers from KK and breakfast. Per person: huts RM290, each additional night RM100, dorms RM245, each additional night RM65

Kampung Bavanggazo

Although the shift to modern housing means that few traditional **Rungus longhouses** survive, a couple have been constructed in **KAMPUNG BAVANGGAZO**, 98km north of KK, to give tourists a chance to spend the night. In addition to room-only prices, it's possible to book a package (RM75) including dinner, breakfast and a **tribal dance** performance – call a couple of days ahead, to make sure that a performance is scheduled. You can also organize a trip to the tribal dances independently (RM150). Other activities include an early-morning jungle trek (2–3hr; RM50/group), local Inavol weaving and jewellery-making (both RM25/person).

ARRIVAL AND DEPARTURE   **KAMPUNG BAVANGGAZO**

By bus or taxi Kampung Bavanggazo is 41km south of Kudat, 2.5km off the main highway. Public transport will only go as far as the junction on the highway; alternatively, you can take a share taxi from Kudat (RM8/person) or KK (RM18/person).

ACCOMMODATION

Maranjak Longhouse Lodge Kampung Bavangazzo ☎088 622524, ✉maranjaklonghouse@gmail.com. Made from traditional materials, the two longhouses offer mattresses, each with their own mosquito net, on low sleeping platforms in one of 21 rooms. You can also camp – they provide the tent. Mattress RM45, camping for two people RM60

Kudat

Overlooking Marudu Bay, **KUDAT** is a friendly but scruffy town centred on the intersection of Jalan Ibrahim Arshad and Jalan Lo Thien Chock. The latter, the main

---

THE RUNGUS

The Kudat Peninsula is home to the **Rungus people**, members of the wider Kadazan/Dusun ethnic group. Just two generations ago some Rungus wore coils of brass and copper on their bodies, but like most, they have gradually modernized. Many still hold their traditions dear, however, and older people in the kampungs still dress in black.

The architectural style of the traditional longhouse is distinctive, built with outward leaning walls and decorated with motifs and imagery from farming and nature. Today, though, most dwellings are made from sheets of corrugated zinc, whose durability makes it preferable to the traditional materials like timber, tree bark, rattan and nipah leaves.

---

street, holds some of Sabah's oldest wooden shophouses and a Standard Chartered Bank. During a visit, leave time to peek at the central, orange-hued **Chinese temple** close to the *Ria Hotel*, plus the **stilt village** and the **harbour**, now significantly quieter than in the days when Kudat had an active fishing industry.

ARRIVAL AND DEPARTURE — KUDAT

By plane Kudat's airport, which meets twice weekly MASwings flights from KK (40min) and Sandakan (50min), is 9km northwest of town (minivan RM2; taxi RM10).

By boat Ferries to Pulau Banggi (daily 9am & 2.30pm; 1hr; RM15) leave from the jetty at the southern end of Jalan Lo Thien Chock.

By taxi Share taxis to and from Kota Belud and KK stop around the corner from the *Hotel Sunrise*. Ask there or around the market for a taxi to the Tip of Borneo (20–30min); an entire car costs around RM45–50 each.

ACCOMMODATION

Hotel Kinabalu Jalan Kecil, Block C, Sedco Building ☎088 613 8888. Typical of the hotels in the Sedco Building area, east of the *Upper Deck Hotel*, but better value than some of its neighbours. Rooms are en suite and have a/c. It's also near some good restaurants and the market. **RM70**

Kudat Golf & Marina Resort 4km north of town ☎088 611211, ⌨kudatgolfmarinaresort.com. Airy, pleasant rooms, many overlooking the large pool and the sea with the 18-hole golf course close by; check online for discounts, and about golf packages or promotions. **RM270**

Ria Hotel 3 Jalan Marudu ☎088 622794, ⌨riahotel.blogspot.com. The nicest place to stay in Kudat. Beyond the scrupulously clean foyer lie 24 small and neat en-suite rooms. The cheapest (superior) rooms have twin beds, while they are king size in the deluxe rooms. **RM128**

EATING

For a choice of places to eat, head to the **Esplanade** seafront area east of the Sedco Building complex; at the nearest end there's a small food court, while further along you'll find a series of "floating" restaurants on stilts. The Sedco Building area itself is also reasonably lively in the evening, and there's a **night market** on the other side where you can also buy inexpensive food.

Sungai Wang Lot 7 & 8, Block F, Sedco Building ☎088 612312. While it looks a bit grubby, this restaurant has some of the best food in town, with dishes such as butter tiger prawn (RM120/kg) and steamed fish (RM30/kg) though they also do individual dishes for RM15 upwards. Daily 10am–2pm & 6pm–midnight.

Terminal Tom Yam Block D, Sedco Building ☎088 613080. A popular place serving Thai food, with most of the seating outdoors and walls painted with underwater scenes. *Tom yam* costs RM4–9, while the excellent sizzling noodles are RM6–7. Evening showings of Malay movies pull a crowd. Tues–Sun 11am–11pm.

Tip of Borneo

The thin promontory known as the **Tip of Borneo** (Tanjung Simpang Mengayau) has seen limited development but retains a great deal of charm. It's easy to see what keeps visitors coming: cliffs drop away to steep, forested hills and waves crash onto the golden sandy beaches. While it's well worth a visit – or, better, a night or two – if you're in the vicinity, whether it's worth a special journey all the way from KK is more debatable. Tourism is developing, though, and as well as surfing and kayaking on the main beach (note that swimming is hazardous here), there are dive shops, mountain-biking opportunities and several coastal and jungle walks – though many beaches (though not the main one) are blighted by plastics and rubbish.

At the tip itself, Sabah Tourism has built a car park where steps lead down to a viewing area and a monumental globe. It's busiest at the weekend, when local families visit; no buses or minivans come this way, so you'll need to use your own transport, or a taxi.

ACCOMMODATION   TIP OF BORNEO

As well as the places listed here, there are several mid-range places on the main beach, and three pricey resorts on the tip itself.

Community Turtle Homestay Bavang Jamal Village, 4km from the Tip ☎019 852 0163, ✉rolandagasai @yahoo.com. Run by a member of the local turtle conservation society, this friendly homestay has four basic rooms in a Rungus-style longhouse, and is just a few minutes' walk from Jamal (Turtle) Beach. They can also arrange jungle-trekking and fishing trips. Full board per person **RM60**

Tampat Do Aman ☎013 880 8395, ⊛tampatdoaman .com. A masterclass in how to set up a backpackers' camp, this Rungus/British-run place offers simple rooms in a Rungus-style longhouse, private huts and a couple of upmarket fan chalets. They arrange trekking, mountain

biking, surfing and other activities, as well as having a tiny museum of Rungus culture and a small nature reserve across the road. They run a shuttle service between the camp and their excellent restaurant *Tip Top* on the Tip of Borneo beach. Longhouse or huts per person **RM40**, chalet **RM120**

Tip of Borneo Resort On the approach to the tip from Kudat ☎013 811 2315, ⊛tipofborneoresort.com. The last accommodation option on the seafront road, also known as *Tommy's Place*, is before you reach the car park and the tip itself. There are clean rooms either by the (so-so) restaurant or, a bit quieter, behind the main building, each with a veranda. They have a laundry, too, and there's a dive shop next door. Rates include breakfast. **RM160**

Pulau Banggi and around

The island of **Pulau Banggi**, 40km north of Kudat and accessible by daily ferry, is the largest in Sabah. It's quite rugged, hardly touched by tourism, and with not a great deal to see: one fairly hard-to-get-to **beach** on the northeast coast a couple of hours from the main settlement, **Karakit**, and the volcano-shaped 529m **Gunung Sinambung**, on the north of the island, whose jungled slopes also hide the 70m-high **Sinambung Waterfall**. Getting to any of these will involve renting a taxi for a day (around RM150). Few people speak English; to dive the reefs, for example, you'd need to make arrangements with a tour company in KK.

It might actually be easier to visit two nearby islands, which are also accessible by boat and have pristine beaches, good snorkelling and accommodation possibilities. **Pulau Moliangin Pasar**, the island you pass as you approach Karakit on the ferry, has a beautiful stretch of sand and is very tranquil. **Pulau Panukaren** around 4km to the northeast, is bigger and quite populated, but also has nice beaches.

ARRIVAL AND DEPARTURE   PULAU BANGGI AND AROUND

By ferry The Kudat Express ferry leaves Kudat at 9am and 3pm, and departs from Karakit at 7.45am and 1.30pm (1hr; RM15). Make sure you arrive a little early, as the ticketing system is quite inefficient – give your passport at the counter and then wait for your name to be read.
To Pulau Moliangin Pasar or Pulau Panukaren It's

quite hard organizing a boat to Pulau Moliangin Pasar or Pulau Panukaren as few captains speak English. Contact Ganjir (☎017 820 6308), who runs the secondhand clothes stall near the fish market in Karakit and speaks good English. He can take two passengers in his boat (Pulau Moliangin Pasar RM150; Pulau Panukaren RM300) or help arrange a bigger boat.

ACCOMMODATION

It's possible to camp for free on **Pulau Moliangin Pasar** beach, with your own supplies – though you should probably ask one of the five families who live here beforehand. On **Pulau Panukaren** there's a homestay programme (RM30), but again you'll need to bring your own supplies.

Banggi Resort Karakit, Pulau Banggi ☎ 088 671495. Optimistically calling itself a resort, this no-frills place offers fan or a/c accommodation in a long wooden building. There are cooking facilities for guests to use, or you can use the food court next to the nearby mosque. It's just behind the school, next to the water village. Fan chalets RM40, a/c doubles RM55

Kinabalu National Park

Sabah holds no more impressive sight than **Gunung Kinabalu** (Mount Kinabalu), 85km northeast of KK and plainly visible from the west coast. Revered as "aki nabalu" (home of the spirits of the dead) by the Kadazan/Dusun, it's 4095m high and dominates the 750 square kilometres of **KINABALU NATIONAL PARK**, a World Heritage Site renowned for its ecology, flora and geology. Although there are other hikes within the park, the prospect of reaching the summit fires the imagination of Malaysian and foreign tourists alike. Because the hike usually (but not always) takes two days, most people are obliged to **stay** on the mountain, which entails booking an expensive three-day/two-night package (see p.417).

Gunung Kinabalu

Conquering **Gunung Kinabalu** today is easier than it was in 1858, when Spenser St John, British consul-general to the native states of Borneo, found his progress blocked by Kadazan "shaking their spears and giving us other hostile signs". Hugh Low, then British colonial secretary on Labuan, had made the first recorded ascent of the mountain seven years earlier, though he baulked at climbing its highest peak, considering it "inaccessible to any but winged animals". The peak – subsequently named after Low – was finally conquered in 1888 by John Whitehead.

Climbing the mountain has since become a must-do on Borneo itineraries. For the thousands of people who come here annually to haul themselves up, the process is made easier by a well-defined, 8.5km-long path that weaves up through jungle on the southern side to the bare granite of the summit. Despite its popularity, however, it's a very **tough trek** and not to be undertaken lightly. Even given perfect weather conditions, there's a remorseless, freezing, final **pre-dawn ascent** to contend with and it's quite possible to suffer from altitude sickness and not get to the top. Bad weather can also scupper an ascent, or at least make it a pretty miserable experience.

Don't undertake the challenge unless you are fully prepared, with **suitable clothing** and in **good general health**. If you suffer from **vertigo** then you shouldn't have a problem on the route up to Laban Rata (where there's foliage to hide any drops), or even for the summit ascent (since it's in the dark), but the way down from the summit may cause you problems. From time to time they do repairs and maintenance on the trail, so check the website for the summit closure dates.

Gunung Kinabalu: the climb

For the vast majority of visitors, ascending and descending Gunung Kinabalu takes **two days**. The **Timpohon trail** is the main route and used by the majority of climbers, though the longer and quieter **Mesilau trail**, which starts 17km east of the park HQ, offers a greater chance of spotting wildlife. The standard route begins at the park HQ, two hours from KK and 1588m up. It's possible to arrive on the morning of the climb, but spending the previous night in the area is a good idea; it gives time to acclimatize and means you can make an **earlier start** in the morning. Climbers then have to spend a night two-thirds of the way up the mountain in huts at Laban Rata, allowing for a final **dawn ascent**.

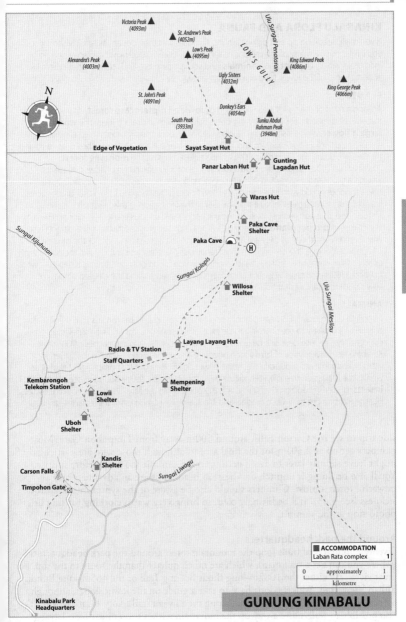

GUNUNG KINABALU

Timpohon trail

The main route begins with an optional but time-saving minibus ride (25min; RM16.50) to the start of the **Timpohon trail**. The day's climb to the mountain huts at **Laban Rata** takes between five and seven hours, depending on your fitness and trail conditions. There are regular rest shelters with toilets along the path and also a small

KINABALU FLORA AND FAUNA

If you dash headlong up and down Gunung Kinabalu and then depart, as many visitors do, you'll miss out on many of the national park's riches. Its diverse terrains have spawned an incredible variety of **plants** and **animals**, and you are far more likely to appreciate them by walking some of the lower trails at a leisurely pace.

PLANTS

Around a third of the park's area is covered by **lowland dipterocarp forest**, characterized by massive, buttressed trees and allowing only sparse growth at ground level. The **world's largest flower**, the parasitic – and elusive – *Rafflesia*, occasionally blooms in the lowland forest (see p.586). Between 900m and 1800m, you'll come across the oaks, chestnuts, ferns and mosses (including the *Dawsonia* – the world's tallest moss) of the **montane forest**.

Higher up (1800–2600m), the **cloud forest** supports a huge range of flowering plants: around a thousand orchids and 26 varieties of rhododendron have been identified, including Low's rhododendron with its enormous yellow flowers. The hanging lichen that drapes across branches of stunted trees lends a magical feel to the landscape at this height. It's at this altitude, too, that you're most likely to see the park's most famous plants – its nine species of insectivorous **pitcher plants** (*Nepenthes*) whose cups secrete a nectar that first attracts insects and then drowns them, as they are unable to escape up the slippery sides of the pitcher.

Higher still, above 2600m, only the most tenacious plantlife can survive – like the agonizingly gnarled sayat-sayat tree, and the heath rhododendron found only on Gunung Kinabalu – while beyond 3300m, soil gives way to granite. Here, grasses, sedges and the elegant blooms of Low's buttercup are all that flourish.

ANIMALS

Although orang-utans, Bornean gibbons and tarsiers are among **mammals** that dwell in the park, you're unlikely to see anything more exotic than squirrels, rats and tree shrews, or conceivably a mouse deer or a bearded pig if you're lucky. The higher reaches of Gunung Kinabalu boast two types of **birds** seen nowhere else in the world – the Kinabalu friendly warbler and Kinabalu mountain blackbird. Lower down, look out for hornbills and eagles, as well as the Malaysian tree pie, identifiable by its foot-long tail. You're bound to see plenty of **insects**: butterflies and moths flit through the trees, while the forest floor is home to creatures like the trilobite beetle, whose orange-and-black armour-plating lends it a fearsome aspect.

---

side trip to see the Carson Falls, around 500m away from Timpohon Gate. Most climbers get up at 2.30am for the final ascent, although those who are particularly fit might leave slightly later to avoid getting to the summit too long before sunrise. You'll also be doing it in pitch darkness, so headlamps are an advantage and a powerful torch a must. Climbers should also be aware of the symptoms of altitude sickness (see p.43). It'll be bitingly cold, so bring very warm clothing for that brief photo stop at the summit.

Around the park headquarters

Twenty kilometres of **trails** loop the mountain forest around the **park headquarters** (where you can get a trail map), which are much quieter than the route to the top. For great views, try either the 1082m-long Bukit Burung Trail or the 465m-long Bundu Tuhan View Trail. Walkers don't have to take a guide on the lower slopes, although there is a daily guided two-hour walk along the Liwagu trail (daily 11am; RM3). It's also possible to walk quite a way up the mountain without too much cost; Layang Layang (2702m) is the last checkpoint you can get to without paying the mountain fees (apart from the RM10 fee at the Timpohon gate).

ARRIVAL AND INFORMATION   KINABALU NATIONAL PARK

By bus, minivan or taxi Get to the park HQ as early as possible: the last group usually sets off by 10.30am, but ideally you should be here by 9am, in order to reach Laban Rata before the hot water runs out in the showers. Hourly buses

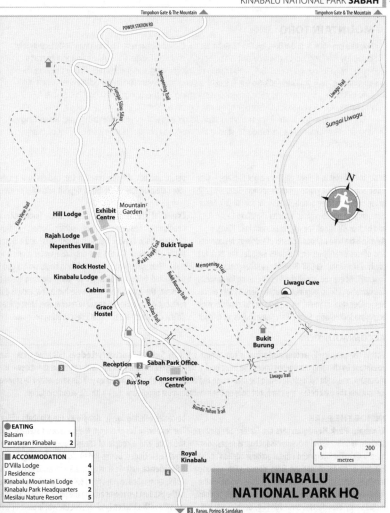

EATING
Balsam	1
Panataran Kinabalu	2

ACCOMMODATION
D'Villa Lodge	4
J Residence	3
Kinabalu Mountain Lodge	1
Kinabalu Park Headquarters	2
Mesilau Nature Resort	5

**KINABALU
NATIONAL PARK HQ**

(RM15) leave KK's Inanam bus terminal from 7am onwards for Sandakan and Ranau, taking 2hr to reach the park entrance. A better option is to catch a Ranau minivan (roughly hourly; RM20), or split a share taxi (RM15–18/person); both leave from the Merdeka Field bus stand from 7am.

Booking packages All the accommodation on the mountain is controlled by *Sutera Sanctuary Lodges* (see p.418) and the number of visitors that can climb each day is determined by how many beds they have. Unless you can do the climb in one day, you must book a three-day/two-night package. Tours get booked up long in advance (up to three months in the summer), though you can call direct closer to the time in the hope of a cancellation, and tour operators in KK may be able to offer a package at short notice for an additional fee. Avoid booking packages with overseas tour operators, which can work out a lot more expensive.

One-day climbs Five one-day spaces are allowed on the mountain, granted only to the fittest of climbers. Undertaking a one-day climb substantially cuts costs but it is an exceptionally long and tiring day on the mountain, the view from the top will almost certainly be obscured by clouds by the time you get there, and unless you're super-fit, you will need several days to recover. If undeterred, either enquire with tour operators based in KK (see box, p.85) or turn up on spec at around 7am.

Fees Besides the conservation fee (RM15), climbing permit (RM100) and insurance (RM7) – the latter two are included

7

MOUNTAIN TORQ

Mountain Torq office: 3–36, 3rd Floor, Asia City, KK ☎ 088 268126, ⓦ mountaintorq.com • Via ferrata from RM450 (activity only)
If merely walking up to the summit isn't enough of a challenge, then Asia's first **via ferrata** – pathways of rungs, ropes, rails and planks running along sheer cliffsides – may provide the adrenaline rush you are looking for. It's exhilarating stuff with some incredible views, yet it's safe because you're always clipped onto something. Of the two routes, one is suitable for anyone over 10 years old, the other has a minimum age of 17.

Located close to Laban Rata, the Mountain Torq centre also runs **climbing** and **abseiling** courses. Participants can arrange to stay at the no-frills *Pendant Hut* as part of their package instead of at Laban Rata.

in the overall cost of a three-day/two-night package – you must also pay for a guide (from Timpohon Gate, RM128/group of one to three people; RM150 for four to six). Some climbers also opt to pay for a porter (RM80 to Laban Rata and back or RM102 all the way; maximum load 10kg).

Administrative offices A cluster of lodgings, restaurants and offices directly inside the gates includes the park HQ (daily 7am–7pm; ☎ 088 889888, ✉ sabahparks@sabah.gov.my), where you pay all the fees (including for guides). You can also pick up information at the Sabah Parks office. Remember, too, if you're on a package, to confirm your accommodation with *Sutera Sanctuary Lodges* next door

before you pay the conservation fee. Lockers and a safe room are available at the HQ to deposit valuables or even your pack.

Essential items You will need a torch (preferably a headlamp), headache tablets, suntan lotion, energy boosters (such as nuts, fruit and muesli bars) and a water bottle (there's unfiltered but drinkable water along the trail). Wear waterproof shoes or hiking boots with a good tread, and bring a few layers of warm clothing for the summit; the Laban Rata resthouse has a few jackets for rent, but you need to call ahead to reserve one. Most guides do not carry first-aid kits, so it's best to bring your own.

ACCOMMODATION

Within the park itself, **accommodation** is run almost solely by **Sutera Sanctuary Lodges** (SSL), who take full advantage by charging outrageous prices. You must book a three-day/two-night package, with one night spent down the mountain, one night up. If you're taking the main route and doing the climb in one day, then you can save money by staying just outside the park before the climb, but once on the mountain most people are stuck with SSL accommodation.

INSIDE THE PARK

Kinabalu Park Headquarters C/o Sutera Sanctuary Lodges ☎ 088 243629, ⓦ suterasanctuarylodges.com; map p.417. The overpriced official accommodation at the HQ has a range of options from dorms with cooking facilities, through more comfortable private rooms, to the full-board *Rajah Lodge* which sleeps six (other options include only breakfast). Dorms RM160, doubles RM506, *Rajah Lodge* RM8480

Mesilau Nature Resort 17km east of park HQ, c/o Sutera Sanctuary Lodges ☎ 088 871519, ⓦ sutera sanctuarylodges.com; map p.417. Reached by minivan shuttle from park HQ (RM85), this resort has a special atmosphere with a gushing river running through it and abundant birdlife; accommodation consists of simple dorms as well as spacious chalets and lodges. Dorms RM180, doubles RM450

OUTSIDE THE PARK

D'Villa Lodge 10min walk east from the park entrance ☎ 088 889 282, ⓦ dvillalodge.com.my; map p.417. A twelve-bed dorm, plus pricey standard rooms with

balconies offering lovely views over the Kinabalu valley. The restaurant benefits from the same great scenery, and there are also a couple of cheap places to eat opposite. Breakfast included. Dorms RM30, doubles RM120

J Residence Just west of the park entrance ☎ 012 869 6969, ⓦ jresidence.com; map p.417. A great choice close to the HQ. Just ten rooms among the pines, including three in a villa with a kitchen (you can rent the whole place or just one room). The design and furnishings are much more modern than most places around here, though there are no views. Book ahead as it fills up; prices rise by more than half at the weekend. RM88

★ **Kinabalu Mountain Lodge** 1km from a turn-off from the main road about 1km west of the park entrance ☎ 016 208 4909; map p.417. One of the only lodges off the main road, this peaceful wooden building nestles on a spur of the mountain, has a lovely view from the terrace, and also attracts dozens of different moth species from the jungle at night. The rooms are fairly basic, the dorms have squeaky bunks, and it's all shared bathrooms. They also make very good vegetarian dinners for RM8. Dorm RM30, doubles RM90

ON THE MOUNTAIN

Laban Rata complex Gunung Kinabalu, c/o Sutera Sanctuary Lodges ☎ 017 833 5611, ⓦ suterasanctuary lodges.com; map p.415. A complex of several separate guesthouses, some of them unheated, at an altitude of 3000m. Prices are calculated per person, including three buffet meals, and can hardly be regarded as good value for money, but there's no choice unless you qualify to stay at the *Pendant Hut* (see p.418). Can only be booked as part of a three-day/two-night package with the other night at one of the two hotels at the park entrance. With *Kinabalu Park*: dorms RM798, doubles RM1884; with *Mesilau Nature Resort* dorms RM767, doubles RM1734

EATING

Balsam Within the park HQ; map p.417. A restaurant offering predictably expensive, but wholesome, buffets with Chinese, Malay, Indian and Western dishes for RM65. Most people eat here at the end of their hike, as part of the package. Mon–Fri 7am–10pm, Sat & Sun 7am–11pm.

Panataran Kinabalu At the turning for the park HQ ☎ 088 889117; map p.417. Considerably cheaper than the caterers inside the park, this Chinese place actually serves pretty good food too, and the views from the car park are certainly impressive. Mostly rice and noodle dishes (RM4.50–8), with a few Western snacks and breakfasts. They also do a packed lunch for RM15, which may be useful if you're hiking around the HQ. Daily 6.30am–8pm.

Around Gunung Kinabalu

The most popular attraction near the national park entrance is the **Poring Hot Springs**, where you can also stay at a jungle camp, but World War II buffs may also want to visit the memorial at **Kundasang**. The town of **Ranau** is mostly just a transport hub, but a nearby **tea plantation** serves as a relaxing place to hang out.

Poring Hot Springs

43km from park HQ, on the southeastern side of Kinabalu National Park • Daily 6.30am–6.30pm • RM15, including use of outdoor tubs; RM15/hr for indoor sulphur bath tubs; canopy walkway RM5

The **Poring Hot Springs** were developed during World War II by the Japanese, who installed wooden tubs that have been replaced by tiled versions. Don't come expecting natural pools, luxury or solitude, but it can be a good place to relax aching muscles after descending from Gunung Kinabalu. The best time to visit (when there aren't hordes of tourists) is early morning or after 4pm.

There are also a few other attractions within the site, including an orchid garden, a butterfly farm, a **canopy walkway** and a few walking trails. Outside the gates you'll see signs advertising places to see **Rafflesia flowers** for RM30, but these are best avoided: the plants have often been dug up and brought to Poring from more remote areas.

ARRIVAL AND DEPARTURE   PORING HOT SPRINGS

By bus or minivan Official shuttle buses run from park HQ (1hr; RM18) and *Mesilau Nature Resort* (1hr 30min; RM60), although it's cheaper to flag down a share taxi (RM40–60). From Poring it's impossible to get direct public transport to Sandakan or back to KK; instead take a minivan (RM10) from outside the park gates to Ranau, where buses stop on trips across the state.

ACCOMMODATION

The official **accommodation** within the hot springs area is run by *Sutera Sanctuary Lodges* and is very expensive. Luckily a handful of more affordable (if unexceptional) lodges lie just outside the entrance, with a great option in the jungle nearby.

Ernah Lodge On the main road ☎ 014 855 5543, ⓔ ernahlodge@yahoo.com. The lino-covered floors are pretty uneven, but the eight rooms are clean enough (a/c RM35 extra) and there's a common area where you can watch TV. They also do laundry (8am–5pm; RM7/kg) and run a taxi service. RM60

★**Lupa Masa** 20min walk from the park entrance ☎ 019 581 3863 or ☎ 019 802 0549,

@ lupamasaborneo@gmail.com. Set in a glorious patch of jungle, this place (whose name means "forget time") has everything you could want in a jungle lodge – so long as your wish list doesn't include creature comforts. Food (included in the price) and accommodation are both very basic, but the experience earns plaudits from visitors. Call ahead to be guided into the camp. RM85

Sutera Sanctuary Lodges Within the park @ 088 243629, @ suterasanctuarylodges.com. The official accommodation includes everything from camping to a dorm – nice enough but beyond the budget of most backpackers – to rooms that are just upgraded hostel rooms, to the very expensive *Palm Villa* which sleeps six. Camping per person RM58, Dorms RM178, doubles RM345, *Palm Villa* RM4500

EATING

Rainforest Restaurant Just inside the park @ 088 877215. The surroundings are pleasant, and the location near the springs is convenient, but the prices are hard to stomach. The buffets have plenty of choice, but at RM30 (lunch) or RM40 (dinner) they don't feel like good value; à la carte dishes include hot and sour mackerel (RM40) and spaghetti (RM40–

45). Quality is variable, too. Daily 7am–8pm.

Round Inn On the main road close to the entrance. This place stands out among the options on the main road, not least for its circular entrance and large drum that customers are allowed to beat. Decent Chinese meals will set you back around RM10–15. Daily 7am–10pm.

Kundasang War Memorial

Just off the Poring–Ranau rd, Kundasang • Daily 8.30am–5.30pm • RM10 • Buses and minivans stop close to the main junction on the highway, though when returning you may need to flag them down

Ten kilometres along the road from Poring to Ranau, **Kundasang** is little more than a junction where simple stalls sell fruit and vegetables. It is, however, worth a stop for anyone interested in the World War II history of Borneo. The **Kundasang war memorial** commemorates the victims of the Sandakan Death Marches of 1945, when Japanese troops force-marched POWs from Sandakan to Ranau (see p.423). The site has been extensively renovated, and now includes an information centre that shows an Australian documentary about the death marches, plus three peaceful and well-tended memorial gardens (Australian, British and Bornean). No soldiers are buried here.

ACCOMMODATION   KUNDASANG

Cottage Hotel @ 088 888882, @ thecottagehotel .com.my. The rooms here are small but clean with crisp white linen; the views of hills and vegetable farms are

appealing. A Chinese restaurant on the ground floor specializes in steamboat (hot pot). Weekday RM115, weekend RM135

Ranau

While there's little reason to spend time in the undistinguished town of **RANAU**, it's the main hub for travelling between Kinabalu National Park and eastern Sabah. The first day of each month sees a large and lively *tamu* (market), 1km out of town towards Sandakan; there's also a smaller *tamu* every Saturday.

Sabah Tea Garden

Kampung Nalapak, 18km east of Ranau • @ 088 440882, @ sabahtea.com.my • Take a bus in the direction of Sandakan from KK, or taxi from Ranau

The **Sabah Tea Garden** is a well-run organic tea plantation that makes a great place to stay for a night or two, but may also be worth a daytime visit if you're passing through. Contact them in advance to arrange **hikes** and **factory tours**, as it's very popular with groups and gets busy. Ask also about getting a **fish massage** at nearby Kampong Luanti, where surprisingly large river fish nibble at customers' dead skin.

ARRIVAL AND DEPARTURE   RANAU

By bus or minivan Long-distance buses stop on the trunk road beside the turning into town, while minivans

arrive at the eastern edge of town.

ACCOMMODATION AND EATING

Sabah Baru/Sabah Baru View Block D, Jalan Persiaran ☎088 876188. A decent option with simple rooms with a/c or fan. The cheapest are not en suite, but the shared bathrooms are fine. Its sister hotel, *Sabah Baru View*, is a block away and has more modern fan rooms for RM20 more, and a/c rooms for RM30 less – there's also a very good 24hr food court, *Anjung Selera*, between the two. Fan RM58, a/c RM108

★**Sabah Tea Garden** Kampung Nalapak, 17km from Ranau on the road to Sandakan ☎088 440882, ⓦsabahtea.com.my. This plantation has a campsite and longhouses popular with student groups, as well as cosy cottages equipped with flat-screen TVs. The food in the restaurant is excellent. Call about transfers from Ranau. Camping (own tent) RM11, camping (their tent) RM33, longhouse rooms RM132, cottages RM264

East Sabah

While the west may have majestic Gunung Kinabalu, East Sabah is the destination of choice for animal encounters. Around former capital **Sandakan** alone, visitors can see orang-utans in **Sepilok**, proboscis monkeys at **Labuk Bay** – and there are no prizes for guessing the attraction at the **Turtle Islands National Park**.

Next stop on the itinerary is the **Kinabatangan River**, where lodges arrange longboat journeys to see pygmy elephants, orang-utans and more in the wild. Further into the interior, there is the option of visiting **Danum Valley**, a primary rainforest area with a majestic canopy walkway, or the equally appealing **Tabin Wildlife Reserve**. Back on the coast, divers especially are pulled to **Semporna**, the jumping-off point for the myriad flora and fauna hidden in the waters surrounding **Pulau Sipadan**, **Pulau Mabul** and numerous other islands. Serious trekkers keen to explore the **Maliau Basin**, referred to by some as "Sabah's Lost World", set off by 4WD from the frontier boom town **Tawau**.

Mention must be made of the recent **security issues** in East Sabah (see p.387) – before making any travel plans it's vital to keep track of the current safety advice.

Sandakan

Situated at the neck of Sandakan Bay, facing the Sulu Sea and towards the Philippines, the commandingly positioned town of **SANDAKAN** was all but destroyed during World War II. Postwar reconstruction on reclaimed land, worked around an unimaginative grid system of indistinguishable concrete blocks but without the sense of space you find in KK. Today, though, there's a bracing sense of regeneration focused on the **waterfront**.

Sandakan's main visitor attractions, beyond its excellent accommodation and eating options, are away from the centre. The **Sandakan Memorial Park**, commemorating the horrors of the Sandakan POW camp, is west of town, whereas Sandakan's **colonial heritage** is mostly concentrated immediately north of the centre on Trig Hill.

Brief history

Although eighteenth-century accounts mention a trading outpost called Sandakan within the Sultanate of Sulu, whose centre was in what's now the Philippines, the town's modern history began in the late 1870s. The area of northeast Borneo between Brunei Bay and the Kinabatangan River had been leased by the Sultan of Brunei to the American Trading Company in 1865 but its attempt to establish a settlement here failed, and in 1879 an Anglo-American partnership took up the lease, naming Englishman **William Pryer** as the first Resident of the east coast. By 1884 Sandakan was the **capital** of British North Borneo, its natural harbour and proximity to sources of timber, beeswax, rattan and edible birds' nests transforming it into a thriving commercial centre.

In 1942 the Japanese army took control, establishing the POW camp from which the **death marches to Ranau** commenced (see opposite). What little of the town was left standing after intensive Allied bombing was burned down by the Japanese, and the end of the war saw Sabah's administration shift to KK. Nevertheless, by the 1950s a rebuilt Sandakan profited from the **timber** boom and by the 1970s had generated such wealth that the town was reputed to have the world's greatest concentration of millionaires.

Once the region's decent timber had been exhausted in the early 1980s, Sandakan looked to **oil palm** and cocoa, crops that now dominate the surrounding landscape.

The waterfront

Sandakan's central grid of streets is hemmed in by Bukit Berenda (Trig Hill) to the north and Sandakan Bay to the south. The massive three-storey **Central Market** (daily 6am–8pm) dominates the eastern end of the waterfront, while the esplanade known as **Sandakan Harbour Square** lies to the southwest of it. The streets around the esplanade form a major tourist district, with cafés, hostels and hotels including the *Four Points by Sheraton* and attached Harbour Mall.

Around Padang Bandaran Sandakan

Close to **Padang Bandaran Sandakan**, now rarely used, are a couple of the oldest buildings in Sandakan. On the northern side, the Taoist **Sam Sing Kung Temple** (daily 7am–4pm), completed in 1887, is dedicated to three deities – Lui Bei, Guan Gong and Zhang Fei – who were the heroes of the fourteenth-century *Romance of the Three Kingdoms*. Northwest of the padang, **St Michael's and All Angels Church** (daily 9.30am–4.30pm, English service Sun 7.15am; RM10, except for service) is a quintessentially English stone building dating back to 1893.

Trig Hill

Most of the colonial relics of Sandakan can be found in the hills north of the centre. The easiest way up is to use the so-called **hundred steps** (there are rather more) leading up from the tourist office, which bring you out on **Jalan Istana**. From here head left to the **Agnes Keith House** or right to the huge **town cemetery**, with horseshoe-shaped Chinese graves arranged for good feng shui on the hillside.

Agnes Keith House

Jalan Istana • Daily 9am–5pm • RM15 • ☎ 089 221140

The **Agnes Keith House** is a museum based on the life and achievements of the American writer whose works (see p.587) introduced many in the West to the history and culture of Borneo. Downstairs, reproductions of colonial furniture and period photographs decorate the rooms, while the staircase landing is adorned with artefacts including Murut blowpipes; upstairs the highlight is a small cinema showing a documentary called *Sandakan 1950*, a vivid home-movie testimony to the era.

Sandakan Memorial Park

Mile 7, 10km west of Sandakan • Daily 9am–5pm • Free • Minibus #7 from Jalan Pryer bus station (every 30min; 30min; RM1); RM30 taxi from central Sandakan

Sandakan Memorial Park marks the site of the World War II POW camp where the infamous **death marches** began. In 1942, around 2700 British and Australian soldiers were transported from Singapore to Sandakan and set to work building an airstrip. They were kept in appalling conditions and around three hundred had already died by early 1945, when the decision was made to relocate them to Ranau (260km away through mud and jungle). Around five hundred prisoners died on three forced marches, while many more either perished after they arrived in Ranau or – if ill or injured – were left behind to die in Sandakan. In the end only six soldiers, all Australian, survived.

SANDAKAN

ACCOMMODATION	
Ibis Styles	4
May Fair	3
Sabah	1
Sandakan Backpackers	5
Seaview Sandakan Budget Hotel	2

N

Long-Distance Bus Station & Karamunting Jetty

7

St Michael's & All Angels

Recreation Club

Sam Sing Kung Temple

JALAN SINGAPORA

JALAN PADANG

JALAN SINGAPORA

St Mary Catholic Church

JALAN PUNCAK

JALAN SEKOLAH

LORONG SEKOLAH

JALAN CHENG MING

JALAN LEILA

JALAN LEILA

JALAN ELOPURA

Sandakan Regional Library

Night Food Market

Tun Abdul Razak Memorial Park

Sandakan Community Hall

Hokkien Association

Halal Food Court

JALAN COASTAL 1

JALAN COASTAL 1

SULU SEA

0   200
metres

Signboards explain the few scattered remnants of the camp, while a small but informative and moving museum covers the harsh conditions in the camp and the actual marches. If you are interested in walking or cycling part of the death march route, contact **TYK Adventure Tours** (☎088 232821, ⊛tykadventuretours.com).

ARRIVAL AND DEPARTURE   SANDAKAN

By plane Sandakan's airport, 11km north of town, welcomes daily flights on AirAsia, MAS and MASwings from KL (8–9 daily; 2hr 45min) and KK (8–9 daily; 45min); MASwings also flies from Tawau (2 daily; 30min) and Kudat (2 weekly; 50min). For buses into town walk to the main road; otherwise catch a minivan from arrivals (RM1.20), or a RM30 taxi. MAS has its office at the airport (☎089 674813).

By bus The long-distance bus station is currently 5km northwest of town; local buses and minivans pass along the main road in front, as do taxis (RM20 to the centre), which also congregate in the station. The new station will be outside town on the main road at 2 1/2 Mile, not far from the current site.

Destinations Gunung Kinabalu park (around hourly, but

none 2–8pm; 4hr 30min); KK (around hourly, but none 2–8pm; 6hr); Lahad Datu (7.30am, 8am & 2pm; 3hr); Ranau (around hourly, but none 2–8pm; 4hr); Semporna (7.30am, 8am & 2pm; 5hr 30min); Tawau (5 daily; 5hr 30min).

By minivan Minivans, which cost just a little more than the buses, head from the long-distance bus station to destinations including Lahad Datu, Semporna and Sukau (for the Kinabatangan River).

By ferry Aleson Lines (⊛aleson-shipping.com), whose agent is Timarine (☎089 212063), runs ferries from the Karamunting Jetty, 4km west of town via Pasir Putih bus, minivan or taxi (RM15).

Destinations Zamboanga in the Philippines (Tues; 20hr; RM283 economy, RM303 a/c, RM323 cabin).

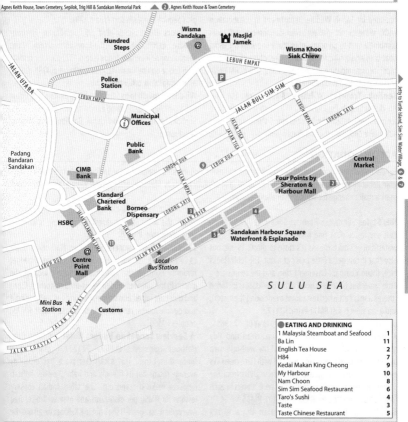

Agnes Keith House, Town Cemetery, Sepilok, Trig Hill & Sandakan Memorial Park   ▲ ② , Agnes Keith House & Town Cemetery

● EATING AND DRINKING	
1 Malaysia Steamboat and Seafood	1
Ba Lin	11
English Tea House	2
H84	7
Kedai Makan King Cheong	9
My Harbour	10
Nam Choon	8
Sim Sim Seafood Restaurant	6
Taro's Sushi	4
Taste	3
Taste Chinese Restaurant	5

GETTING AROUND

By bus Local buses vie for space on Jalan Pryer, although only the blue-and-white ones marked "Batu 14" or higher (for Sepilok Junction) are likely to be of use. Getting to Sepilok, including the Orang-utan Rehabilitation Centre, is straightforward by bus/minibus (see p.429).

By taxi It's not hard to find a taxi on the main streets or outside large hotels; the minimum charge is RM10.

By car Cars can be rented from Borneo Express (☎016 886 0789, ⒲borneocar.com), Lot 8, Ground Level, at the airport terminal.

INFORMATION

Tourist information There are municipal offices across the square from the police station on Lebuh Empat; the English-speaking tourism department on the second floor has copies of the self-guided *Sandakan Heritage Trail* leaflet.

Addresses Sandakan addresses rely on numbers rather than street names – Jalan Tiga, for example, literally means "Road Three". Similarly, addresses outside the centre are described according to the distance from downtown: "Mile 4" (also called "Batu 4") is the entertainment district four miles (6.5km) out of town.

Internet access Cyberjazz.net & Komputer Jazz, second floor, Centre Point Mall (daily 9am–8pm); Sandakan Cybercafé, second floor, room 219, Wisma Sandakan (daily 9am–5pm). Both RM4/hr.

TOURS

Pulau Sipadan Resort and Tours Block C, ground floor, Lot 38 & 39, Mile 6, Bandar Tyng ☎089 673999, ⒲dive-malaysia.com. For Sepilok Nature Resort and accommodation at *Lankayan Island Dive Resort*.

Red Ape Encounters ☎088 413293, ⒲redape encounters.com. A community-based ecotourism project operated by Sabah Wildlife Department in collaboration with villagers in Sukau. Four-day/three-night tours combine a visit to an orang-utan study site with the usual boat trips and a hike to an oxbow lake, plus optional side trips; accommodation is in homestays (from RM1990/person, minimum two people).

Sepilok Tropical Wildlife Adventure Lot 3a, Block 13, Lebuh Tiga ☎089 271077, ☎stwadventure .com. Well-established operator that runs *Bilit Adventure Lodge* on the Kinabatangan River (see p.432),

plus *Sepilok Jungle Resort* (see p.429).

SI Tours Block HS-5, Lot 59, Sandakan Harbour Square ☎089 213502, ☎sitoursborneo.com. Runs *Kinabatangan Riverside Lodge* (see p.432) plus the remote *Abai Lodge* on the Kinabatangan River (see p.433), as well as offering many other tours.

Wildlife Expeditions 9th floor, Wisma Khoo Siak Chew ☎089 219616, ☎wildlife-expeditions.com. For Sukau, Sepilok, Turtle Islands and Labuk Bay Proboscis Monkey Sanctuary.

ACCOMMODATION

Sandakan holds a wide range of accommodation, but many visitors head straight for the **lodges** close to Sepilok Orang-utan Rehabilitation Centre, 20km west. The opening of the *Four Points by Sheraton*, after several years in the making, will mark a major change for visitors with a large budget.

Ibis Styles Sandakan Harbour Square ☎089 240888, ☎ibisstyles.com. A fine mid-range choice right on the waterfront – which means it's close to places to eat, but also that it can get a little noisy at night. The lobby looks nice, though bargain-basement chic, and the rooms are a little small but have very good beds. Breakfast is included (there's a small attached restaurant overlooking the water), and a sea view is just RM11 extra. RM172

★**May Fair** First floor, 24 Jalan Pryer ☎089 219855. A great find: a well-located, well-run, clean and tidy guesthouse that's the pride and joy of the well-informed owner Mr Lum. All rooms are equipped with flat-screen TVs and DVD players, and guests can borrow DVDs from the owner's massive collection. Individual wi-fi routers in each room, plus computers available (RM4/hr). RM55

Sabah 1km north of town on Jalan Utara ☎089 213299, ☎sabahhotel.com.my. Sandakan's finest atmospheric five-star, with a restful lobby, two swish restaurants, business centre, swimming pool and sports facilities all set within its pretty grounds. The place has two

wings; the older (and cheaper) Borneo wing is in many ways preferable. RM170

Sandakan Backpackers Sandakan Harbour Square ☎089 221104, ☎sandakanbackpackers.com. A budget favourite right on the waterfront – take a look at the graffiti in the stairwell, added by satisfied customers. Clean and quiet a/c mixed and single-sex dorms as well as single and double rooms; rates include breakfast. Dorms RM25, doubles RM60

★**Seaview Sandakan Budget Hotel** 126 Jalan Dua, Harbour Square ☎089 221221, ☎sandakan budgethotel.com. This backpacker place has distinctly average rooms but its friendly and helpful owner Nafisah helps to make it stand out. She offers Indian cookery lessons for RM50 per dish (2hr) and may well offer free Ayurvedic massages – if she's not in KK. Rates for all but the fan-cooled dorm include breakfast, which is either *roti* with curry, or pancakes. They also have a couple of mopeds for rent (RM60/day). Fan dorms RM18, a/c dorms RM27, fan doubles RM60, a/c doubles RM84

EATING, DRINKING AND NIGHTLIFE

Sandakan may not be able to match KK's range of **restaurants**, but it has enough choice to suit most people, with Malay, Chinese, Indian and Western food all well represented. The cafés in Sandakan Harbour Square are a good starting point, while many of the best **seafood** places are outside the centre. You're best off taking a taxi, for example, to reach **Sim Sim water village**. For **hawker stalls**, head for the Central Market (especially for breakfast) or the small night market on Jalan Leila. Beer is widely available in Chinese restaurants and coffee shops but the centre holds few dedicated **bars**. There's significantly more **nightlife**, as well as numerous restaurants, in the **Mile 4** district (aka Bandar Indah) west of town. A taxi should cost RM20 each way.

1 Malaysia Steamboat and Seafood Trig Hill ☎089 238878. The first and most popular of several similar places on the hill. Either take your pick of the seafood – a kilo of crab costs RM28 – or help yourself to the steamboat (hotpot buffet) at RM38. Just don't take more than you can eat, as there's a fine for wastage. Daily 6–10.30pm.

★**Ba Lin** Nak Hotel, Jalan Pelahuban ☎089 272988,

☎balin-sandakan.com. A real surprise: a seriously stylish rooftop bar and restaurant which, while not cheap, is a great place to hang out and serves actually very good Western food. The menu, designed to look like a newspaper, includes pizza (starting at RM25.50), pasta (from RM21) and the signature dish of sticky New Zealand lamb with greens and mash (RM40.60). They also do a great brunch. Daily 7am–1am.

★**English Tea House** Jalan Istana ☎089 222544, ⓦenglishteahouse.org. A genteel hillside spot close to Agnes Keith House, with a colonial theme including a small croquet lawn. Waitresses dressed in black and white serve English favourites including shepherd's pie (RM36), as well as local dishes. You can also get afternoon tea (RM25) with scones, jam and cream. Daily 10am–9pm.

H84 House H84 between bridges 7 and 8, Sim Sim water village. Simply known by its address, *H84* is a family home that serves fish balls and wonton, as well as dishes such as *wan tan hor* (rice noodles with seafood) and a mean fried prawn toast – everything is under RM10. You may have to ask several times to find it, as it has no sign. Daily 6am–3pm.

Kedai Makan King Cheong Block 19, Lot 6, Jalan Dua ☎089 216812. Central, good-value Chinese joint serving the usual rice and noodle dishes (RM5.50–6.50), but notable for its excellent and inexpensive dim sum served in the mornings (around RM10 per person for a good selection). Daily 6.30am–5pm.

My Harbour Lot 94–96, Block HS-10, Sandakan Harbour Square ☎016 367 6499. One of a few good cafés on the waterfront strip, serving set meals (main, rice, soup and water) for RM6.50 as well as an à la carte menu at RM5.30–15 with very good sweet and sour chicken. Daily 9am–9pm.

★**Nam Choon** Block A, Lot 2a, Old Slipway. You could easily walk past this local favourite without realizing that it's special. It only serves four dishes: *nasi ayam* (chicken rice, RM4), *nasi paha-paha atas* (the same, with chicken on the bone RM4.50), *nasi* fish ball (RM4) and *nasi ikan* (fried fish, RM4–10). Each dish is brilliant, and you get free hot or cold Chinese tea. You may have to share a table at busy times. Mon–Sat 6am–3pm.

★**Sim Sim Seafood Restaurant** Bridge 8, Sim Sim Water Village ☎012 816 3633. The most highly regarded of the various restaurants in the Sim Sim water village, known for having the freshest, tastiest and best-value seafood. It's out on stilts over the water, on the left-hand side of the bridge. A meal here is a great local experience, though if there are fewer than five of you you'll be shunted next door to its sister restaurant *Sim Sim 88*, where they serve similar food in smaller quantities. Daily except Wed 8am–10pm.

MILE 4

Taro's Sushi Lot 1, Block 4, Jalan Bandar Indah, Mile 4 ☎089 275008. A decent Japanese restaurant – unfortunately, the sign reads Tard's Sushi – serving sushi (RM6–10), sashimi (RM28–37), and noodle dishes such as salmon *shahan* (RM18). The menu also includes set meals for RM16–30. Daily 11.30am–9.30pm.

Taste Lot 2–3, Block 9, Bandar Indah, Mile 4 ☎012 818 1819. Much better as a place to drink than to eat, this bar-steakhouse has a wide range of foreign and domestic booze, and serves various Western-style meat dishes (RM15–28). The decor has a pleasing, fairly European feel, it's not sleazy, and the mainly Chinese clientele is friendly. Daily 4.30pm–2.30am.

Taste Chinese Restaurant 8 Jalan Utara, Mile 4 ☎089 214625. Specializing in Hakka cuisine, with a particular emphasis on pig-based dishes such as herbal pork leg or pineapple with pork intestine (both RM14). Portions are big enough to share, although they also do set meals (main, rice, veg and drink) for RM10.50. Tues–Sun 8.30am–10pm.

7

DIRECTORY

Banks There are several banks at the intersection of Jalan Pelabuhan and Lebuh Tiga, including HSBC, Standard Chartered and CIMB. There's a Public Bank nearby on Lebuh Tiga.

Hospital Duchess of Kent, Jalan Utara, 2km north of the centre (☎089 212111).

Pharmacy Several branches of Borneo Dispensary including one at 11b Jalan Dua, as well as the usual Guardian and Watsons.

Police The main police station is on Jalan Utara, 1.5 km from town (☎089 211222) with a smaller one near the municipal offices.

Post office Sandakan's GPO is 5min walk west of town, off Jalan Leila.

Visa extensions Immigration Office, Mile 7, Ranau Rd (☎089 668308).

Sepilok

The town of **SEPILOK**, 25km west of Sandakan, has a trio of excellent attractions: the famous **Orang-utan Rehabilitation Centre**, the **Rainforest Discovery Centre** with its canopy walkway, and the new **Bornean Sun Bear Conservation Centre**, devoted to the protection of the world's smallest bear species.

Sepilok Orang-utan Rehabilitation Centre

3km south of Sepilok Junction, a turning at Mile 14 on the highway to KK, 23km west of Sandakan • Daily 9–11am & 2–3.30pm, feeding times 10am & 3pm • RM30, photo pass RM10 • ☎089 531180, ⓦorangutan-appeal.org.uk

---

ORANG-UTANS AT SEPILOK

Orang-utans – tail-less, red-haired apes (their name means "man of the forest" in Malay) – can reach a height of around 1.65m, and can live to over 30 years old. Solitary but not aggressively territorial, these primates live a largely arboreal existence, eating fruit, leaves, bark and the occasional insect.

Most of the orang-utans at the Sepilok centre are victims of forest clearance; many have been orphaned, injured and traumatized in the process. Some have also been kept as pets, something now prohibited by law, which means that their survival instincts remain undeveloped. Orang-utans are trained at Sepilok to fend for themselves in the wild. Although not always successful, the training process has seen many animals reintroduced to their natural habitat.

7

Set up in 1964 and occupying a 43-square-kilometre patch of lowland rainforest, the **Sepilok Orang-utan Rehabilitation Centre** is one of only a few such sanctuaries. It's also among Sabah's most popular tourist sites, with more than two hundred people crowding onto the viewing platform during feeding hours on most days. In general it's best to go for the afternoon session, as most tour buses come in the morning.

Leave valuables in the free lockers (the orang-utans will try and steal anything hanging off you), along with food, drink and insect repellent (which can be harmful to the orang-utans if they ingest it). There's little shade on the viewing platform, so bring a hat. You'll find a café near the information centre.

The **feeding station** is a ten-minute walk from the entrance, so arrive in plenty of time. There are usually at least a couple of orang-utans waiting for their meal, often the very young ones, and they immediately cluster round the warden as he sets out the fruit. Others may soon come along, swinging, shimmying and strolling towards their breakfast or lunch, jealously watched by gangs of more aggressive pig-tailed macaques that loiter around for scraps.

If you go to the morning feeding and have time afterwards, take the **trail** that leads from feeding station two through the forest; you'll need to register at reception and the trail closes at 2pm. Besides the pleasure of the walk, there's a chance you may see one or more orang-utans.

Bornean Sun Bear Conservation Centre

Opposite the Sepilok Orang-utan Rehabilitation Centre • Daily 9am–3.30pm, feeding times 10am & 3pm • RM30, photo pass RM10 • ☎ 089 534491, ⦿ bsbcc.org.my

The Bornean sun bear is the smallest and least understood of all bears and, resembling a teddy bear, it looks as cute as a button. However, this has meant they have become desirable pets, with super-cute baby sun bears being taken from the wild and the mother usually killed. This is where the **Bornean Sun Bear Conservation Centre** comes to the rescue. Dozens of these orphaned bears are kept in eight jungle enclosures, with the aim of rehabilitating them and releasing them in the wild – viewing platforms means they are easy to spot. Be warned though: cute as they look, sun bears are vicious animals if they get spooked, and if one escapes the centre will be evacuated.

Rainforest Discovery Centre

2km north of the Sepilok Orang-utan Rehabilitation Centre, turn off Jalan Sepilok at the Sabah Forest Research Centre • Daily 8am–5pm • RM15 • ☎ 089 533780, ⦿ forest.sabah.gov.my/rdc

For most visitors (vertigo sufferers aside) the highlight of the **Rainforest Discovery Centre** is the 150m-long series of walkways through the forest canopy. Other attractions include boating on the lake at the weekend; forest trails that take in more than 250 species of orchid and cross a suspension bridge; and an exhibition hall with displays on Borneo's flora and fauna.

ARRIVAL AND DEPARTURE

SEPILOK

By bus or minibus To reach Sepilok from Sandakan, the best choice is the Sepilok Batu #14 bus from beside the Milimewa Supermarket at Centre Point Mall (4 daily; 40min); the last bus back is at 4pm. Otherwise find a bus or minibus (around hourly; they leave when full) from the chaotic bus stand nearby – keep asking and you'll get there in the end. In addition, all long-distance buses go past Sepilok Junction, from where unlicensed taxis head to accommodation (from RM3) or the Orang-utan Rehabilitation Centre (RM10) – though it's only a 3–4km walk.

By taxi A taxi between Sepilok and Sandakan should be around RM50.

ACCOMMODATION

Many visitors stay in Sepilok rather than Sandakan, for its high-standard, good-value **accommodation**, and handy location for onward bus travel to Lahud Datu or Semporna. All options have **wi-fi**, but this is generally restricted to their restaurants and nearby rooms and public areas.

★**Paganakan Dii Tropical Retreat** 2km northwest of Sepilok Junction ☎089 532005, ✉info @paganakandii.com. The furthest lodge from the orang-utan centre, in the opposite direction from all the rest. Jungle views and relaxed atmosphere, plus neat little touches that would normally be found in more expensive accommodation. The fourteen chalets have particularly good rainforest views, and also have one wall open to the jungle. There's also a basic but wi-fi-equipped restaurant where they serve meals for RM18, though breakfast is included in the price – along with shuttles to the sanctuary and Rainforest Discovery Centre. Dorms RM30, doubles RM85, cabins RM140

Sepilok B&B Jalan Arboretum ☎089 534050, ✉sepilokbednbreakfast.com. This friendly place, close to the Rainforest Discovery Centre, has small, pleasant rooms and above-average fan dorms. You can also camp here with your own tent. Rates include breakfast at their pleasant little restaurant, which serves local and Western food. Camping per person RM18, dorms RM31, fan doubles RM68, a/c doubles RM108

★**Sepilok Forest Edge Resort and Labuk B&B** Jalan Rambutan, 1km from orang-utan centre ☎089 533190, ✉sepilokforestedge.com. This charming place has a "longhouse" with small dorms and simple rooms plus a series of appealing chalets, all dotted around a multilevel landscaped garden with a plunge pool. Dorms RM30, doubles RM70, chalets RM180

Sepilok Jungle Resort Jalan Rambutan, close to the orang-utan centre ☎089 533031, ✉sepilokjungleresort.com. A large complex with dorms and private rooms; the latter have interesting touches such as labels for the different types of wood used. You can also camp with your own tent. There's a pool, although even guests have to pay RM5 to use it (RM35 for non-guests). Dorms RM28, fan doubles RM69, a/c doubles RM105

Sepilok Nature Resort Jalan Sepilok, close to the orang-utan centre ☎089 673999, ✉sepilok.com. Twenty-three plush, spacious and eco-aware chalets nestling in lush jungle; the in-house restaurant serves the best food in Sepilok, although like the accommodation it's quite pricey (around RM25 for a main course, or buffet for RM37/47/58), though it does have wi-fi. RM250

Uncle Tan's B&B Jalan Sepilok, 300m south of Sepilok Junction ☎016 824 4749, ✉uncletan.com. A Sabah institution, enormously popular with backpackers. Prices include all meals, making it quite a bargain even if the dorms and a/c rooms are nothing fancy. They also offer packages at *Uncle Tan's Wildlife Camp* on the Kinabatangan River. Free shuttle to the orang-utan sanctuary. Dorms RM48, doubles RM100

7

Labuk Bay Proboscis Monkey Sanctuary

Near Kampung Samawang; turn north 23km from Sandakan, from where it's signposted and another 15km • Daily 9am–5.30pm; feeding times: platform A 9.30am & 2.30pm, platform B 11.30am & 4.30pm • RM60, RM10 camera permit • ☎089 674133, ✉proboscis.cc • Shuttle minibus (RM20 one way) leaves Sandakan 9.30am, Sepilok 10.30am, returning at 3pm; taxis RM300 return from Sandakan, RM160–200 from Sepilok

Set amid mangrove forest and reached via a track through an oil-palm plantation, **Labuk Bay Proboscis Monkey Sanctuary** functions as a companion to the more famous orang-utan sanctuary at Sepilok. Most visitors come on a **day-trip** from Sandakan or Sepilok, which is significantly closer, but it's also possible to stay **overnight**.

Two large observation platforms, each open at two different feeding times, offer perfect vantage points from which to view the long-nosed monkeys (see p.451); at the same time you can also see silverleaf monkeys scavenge fruit left behind, and there's some fantastic birdlife including hornbills. On a day-trip you could see all four feedings if you like, or even leave after just one, but it's more usual to see one from each platform. Unless you have your own transport, it is advised that you use the shuttle bus, as the park is quite spread out, and the shuttle will take you to two feedings and the café in between at lunchtime – otherwise it's a hot trek through the oil-palm plantation.

Other activities

If you're staying at the lodge, and you make arrangements in advance, then it's possible to combine watching the monkey feeding with other **activities**. These include a short jungle trek or a birdwatching walk (each 1hr; RM30) or a boat trip (2hr; RM250/boat) to a fishing village. If you're staying the night then you can also sign up for a firefly walk (45min; RM20) and a morning birdwatching walk (1hr; RM30).

ACCOMMODATION AND EATING   LABUK BAY

★ **Nipah Lodge** Labuk Bay ☎ 089 230708, �🌐 labukbay .com.my. As well as a large communal area and café, Labuk Bay's only accommodation offers eight lovely double-room chalets – and two three-bedroom family units – amid the mangroves, and a couple of longer

buildings with small dorms. The latter have mosquito screens but no nets; insect spray is available. Rates include breakfast at the café, where you can eat for around RM25–28. Dorms **RM35**, doubles **RM180**, family chalet **RM550**

Pulau Lankayan

Ninety minutes' boat ride north of Sandakan in the Sulu Sea lies the **Sugud Islands Marine Conservation Area**, managed by a nonprofit organization called Reef Guardian (�🌐 reef-guardian.com), and consisting of three islands: Lankayan, Billiean and Tegaipil. Only **PULAU LANKAYAN** is open, with a single resort. Although the island itself is beautiful and has an active turtle-hatching programme, **diving** and **snorkelling** is the real pull, thanks to a marine environment protected by a ban on fishing. The island is surrounded by hard and soft corals that are in very good condition, and the macro life in particular is excellent. Divers may see whale sharks in April and May.

ACCOMMODATION   PULAU LANKAYAN

Lankayan Island Dive Resort C/o Pulau Sipadan Resort and Tours, ground floor, Block C, Lot 38 & 39, Mile 6, Bandar Tyng, Sandakan ☎ 089 673999, �🌐 lankayan-island.com. A delightful resort with large, comfortable chalets and helpful staff. The dive shop is also

excellent, well equipped and with good guides. It's normal to book multiday packages including transport. Three-day/ two-night package for two people: non-diving **RM3620**, diving **RM4450**

Turtle Islands National Park

Peeping out of the Sulu Sea 40km north of Sandakan, three tiny islands comprise the **TURTLE ISLANDS NATIONAL PARK** (⌐ turtleislandborneo.com). They are favoured egg-laying sites of green and hawksbill turtles, which haul themselves laboriously above the high-tide mark to bury their clutches of eggs almost every night of the year. Although all three islands – Pulau Selingan, Pulau Bakungan Kecil and Pulau Gulisan – hold **hatcheries**, tourists can only visit **Selingan**, as part of an overnight tour that includes transfer and accommodation. Book with a travel agent or, cheaper, direct with Crystal Quest (☎ 089 212711, ✉ cquest1996@gmail.com).

All the action is at night. As well as seeing a mother turtle laying her eggs, you can watch as the park wardens release newly hatched turtles that waddle, Chaplin-like, into the sea to face an uncertain future – October is the best time to see this. Before dark there's plenty of time – arguably too much time, given the lack of facilities – for **swimming**, **snorkelling** (equipment rental RM25) and **sunbathing**. Sandflies can be voracious, especially when it rains.

Sungai Kinabatangan

Southeast of Sandakan Bay, Sabah's longest river – the 560km **Sungai Kinabatangan** – ends its journey to the Sulu Sea. Whereas logging has had an adverse impact on the river's ecology upstream, the creation of the **Lower Kinabatangan Wildlife Sanctuary** has kept its lower reaches largely free of development. This is the largest forested flood plain in Malaysia, laden with oxbow lakes, mangrove and grass swamps, and distinctive vegetation including massive fig trees overhanging the water's edge.

The sanctuary offers some of Sabah's best opportunities for seeing wildlife. Although some tour operators offer day-trips from Sandakan, it's much better to stay overnight given the travel time; the ideal is a two-night stay. Although there are a few exceptions, most lodges are located either in or around the villages of **Sukau** or **Bilit**. Note that from November to April, the rainy season can lead to flooding at some lodges – at its worst in January – and even force their closure.

Sukau and Bilit

The first tourist lodges on the Sungai Kinabatangan opened around the kampung of **SUKAU**, 134km from Sandakan by road or 87km by boat. Still the easiest place to reach, it's particularly popular with independent travellers as it's possible to stay in the village itself on a B&B basis and then charter boats as needed. Most of the all-inclusive lodges are on the river banks close to the village. Many would argue, however, that Sukau is a victim of **overdevelopment**. In July and August in particular, dozens of boats converge along the same narrow tributaries at the same times and shatter any sense of peace. Although many boats now use quieter electric motors when the current allows, some still do not.

Once tourism became established in Sukau, a few operators opened lodges further upriver around the kampung of **BILIT**. Although not the undeveloped spot it once was, Bilit remains quieter than Sukau partly because there's no public transport to the village – it's upstream of Sukau and reached via a lower-quality road.

LOWER KINABATANGAN WILDLIFE SANCTUARY

Despite Sabah's rather haphazard approach to making the most of its superb natural resources, the designation of the Lower Kinabatangan as a **wildlife sanctuary** in 2005 was a commendable move. That said, sanctuary status is one level below that of a national park, so villages and agricultural development have been allowed to crisscross the protected sections. Furthermore, only the area immediately alongside the river is protected; as animals have lost their habitats when the surrounding areas have been converted into palm-oil plantations, they have effectively been pushed into the narrow protected corridor.

This means that it is highly likely that, over a number of boat rides and short treks, you will see elephants (if they are in the area), orang-utans, proboscis monkeys, macaques and gibbons. The resident **birdlife** is equally impressive. With luck, visitors get glimpses of hornbills, brahminy kites, crested serpent eagles, egrets, exquisite blue-banded and stork-billed kingfishers, and oriental darters, which dive underwater to find food and then sit on the shore, their wings stretched out to dry. The river itself holds freshwater sharks, crocodiles and rays, and a great variety of fish species.

ARRIVAL AND DEPARTURE

SUKAU AND BILIT

Although tour operators arrange transport to their lodges and camps – if you have the choice go by **boat** (2hr 30min to Sukau; not possible to Bilit), as it's a great journey – it's relatively easy to get all the way to **Sukau** by public transport. There are two reasons to do this: if you're staying on a B&B basis, or if you want to arrange a discount on a tour package by removing transfers from the equation. No public transport goes to **Bilit**; arrange a pick-up with your accommodation from Sukau Junction.

By bus From Sandakan, take any southbound bus 89km to Sukau Junction (3hr), then wait for a Sukau minivan to depart when full (45min; RM15–20). From KK, catch a bus bound for Tawau or Lahad Datu, and get off at Sukau Junction; from Lahad Datu take any northbound vehicle.

ACCOMMODATION

Most people visit the Lower Kinabatangan Wildlife Sanctuary on a **tour**, typically including all meals plus boat trips. While tour operators normally quote prices for two-day/one-night itineraries, as indicated below, it's far preferable (and more common) to stay for at least two nights. A single night may only allow time for one boat trip, whereas two-night itineraries generally include three, plus a short jungle hike and optional night walk. Furthermore, the second and subsequent nights are usually significantly cheaper (about 40 percent) than the first. New lodges open regularly; get the latest information from Sandakan tour operators. Although booking a package is often a good idea, **independent** travellers can save money by staying at a B&B, then paying for any boat trips. If you really are pushed for time consider a **day-trip** from Sandakan, possible by bus or taxi if you leave very early. Unless otherwise stated, all room and package prices below are for two people sharing.

KAMPUNG SUKAU

Balai Kito Homestay Various locations ☎013 869 9026, ⓦsukauhomestay.com, ✉ahbamabulani @yahoo.com. This homestay programme arranges B&B accommodation in one of sixteen houses, to which you can add other meals (RM15 each) and boat trips (RM50). It's a great experience, inexpensive, though pot luck as to whether anyone in the host family will speak English well. B&B __RM60__

Barefoot Lodge Eastern side of Kampung Sukau ☎089 235525. Owned by prominent local nature photographer Cede Prudente (ⓦcedeprudente.com), who sometimes runs specialist tours. A two-night package (RM525/person) includes four cruises, and food; transport from Sandakan is RM100 each way. Otherwise breakfast is free, while lunch and dinner cost RM20 each, and cruises are RM50. Look out for promotions March–June. Dorms __RM35__, doubles __RM85__

★ **Sukau B&B** Eastern side of Kampung Sukau at the end of the road ☎013 553 2619 or ☎019 583 5580, ✉sukaubnb@yahoo.com. The best bet for independent travellers, this homely place at the edge of the village is right next to the jungle, and animals can sometimes be seen wandering around the grounds. The thirteen rooms – either twin or triple, with fans and shared bathrooms – are nothing special but breakfast is included, other meals are RM10, and boat trips cost RM45. __RM50__

AROUND SUKAU

★ **Borneo Nature Lodge** ☎089 210718, ⓦborneonaturelodge.com.my. A more interesting site than most, with comfortable cabins linked by wooden walkways to the only a/c restaurant in Sukau. The owners have taken steps to make the place environmentally friendly, using excess heat from the a/c to heat water in the showers. Two-day/one-night package __RM1508__

Kinabatangan Riverside Lodge Run by S.I. Tours ☎089 213503, ⓦwww.sitoursborneo.com. A large site with good accommodation and a room for massage and reflexology. The same company also runs the *Abai Lodge*, an hour away, and can organize trips combining the two. The package includes a trip to Sepilok for an orang-utan feeding, all food, accommodation, and mostly boat transfers from Sandakan. Three-day/two-night package __US$1082__

Osman Homestay ☎019 841 5259. The only place offering B&B accommodation on the river around Sukau, rather than in the village itself. It's a very friendly, family-run affair, popular with backpackers – reports describe them being a little overstretched at times. They charge RM50/person for each cruise (maximum 8 people), with the morning cruise including a jungle trek. If they're full, you may end up sleeping at a relative's house on the floor. Full board per person __RM200__

AROUND BILIT

Bilit Adventure Lodge ☎089 271077. The first lodge to open in Bilit, and currently extending its restaurant. Associated with the *Sepilok Jungle Resort* (see p.429), it's a deservedly popular place with appealing a/c and fan rooms. Someone has a sense of humour: if you get bitten by a leech, you'll be awarded a blood donor certificate. Two-day/one-night package: fan doubles __RM750__, a/c doubles __RM900__

Bilit Homestay Programme Various locations ☎013 891 3078, ⓦbilithomestay.wordpress.com. Twelve houses in the village, offering two-night packages that include food, transport from Sandakan (Sukau Junction or Sepilok), accommodation, three boat trips and a jungle walk – other trips are also available for extra cost. Two-day/one-night package RM780, three-day/two-night package RM840

★**Bilit Kinabatangan Heritage B&B** ☎016 552 5709, ⓦkinabatangansunshines.com. The nearest thing to a budget option in the Bilit area, with two no-frills private rooms and a ten-bed dorm. The latter is handy for solo travellers, as most other places charge a single supplement. Packages include return transport from Sandakan. Two-day/one-night package: dorms RM310, doubles RM740; three-day/two-night package: dorms RM360, doubles RM840

★**Kinabatangan Jungle Camp (KJC)** ☎013 540 5333 or ☎019 804 7756, ⓦkinabatangan-jungle-camp .com. While the rooms are simpler than most along this stretch, what draws visitors is the wealth of experience of no-nonsense owner Robert Chong. He tailors trips to meet the needs of guests, making it popular with birdwatchers, photographers and naturalists; the listed price is therefore for comparison only. Groups are kept small and smaller engines are used; for birdwatching the staff use paddles to keep it quiet. Two-day/one-night package including transport RM700

★**Last Frontier** ☎016 676 5922, ⓦthelastfrontier resort.com. A "boutique" resort located up a jungled hill, and only accessible via 538 steps (ask about porters if you need help with your luggage); the reward for the effort is a wonderfully isolated lodge with just four guest rooms and great food. Packages include river trips. Two-day/one-night package RM1000

OTHER LOCATIONS

Abai Homestay Kampung Abai ☎013 550 5349. This community-run homestay project offers simple accommodation in a quiet village with just one tourist lodge. The basic package includes a guided village walk (you can try out various local activities), jungle walk, boat

trip, night boat trip, boat from Sandakan plus all food and board. Three-day/two-night package per person RM870

Abai Jungle Lodge Kampung Abai run by S.I. Tours ☎089 213503, ⓦsitoursborneo.com. A spacious base, 47km from Sandakan, with easy access to quiet tributaries – there are no other lodges in the area, only a homestay programme. The lodge has 24 en-suite singles, doubles, twins and triples and is run along environmentally friendly lines. In addition to boat trips, it's possible to walk short trails. Two-day/one-night package per person US$368

★**Miso Walai Homestay/Tungog Rainforest Eco Camp** Kampung Mengaris ☎089 551064, ⓦmisowalaihomestay.com. Also known as *Mescot*, the name of the overall community initiative, this very well-organized scheme places tourists in village homes as well as having a modern but quite basic rainforest camp. Boat tours and trips to burial caves at the Batu Putih limestone outcrop can be arranged, and they run volunteer projects. Public transport can stop at the office, under the bridge where the Sandakan–Lahad Datu highway crosses the Kinabatangan. Per person rates including meals RM70, rainforest camp RM95

Nature Lodge Kinabatangan Downstream from Sukau ☎013 863 6263, ⓦnaturelodgekinabatangan .com. This budget option, located on its own stretch of river bank, has the added advantage of trails in the surrounding forest. Unusually, one-night itineraries include both an afternoon and a morning boat trip; transfers from Sandakan or Sepilok cost RM40. Two-day/one-night package: dorms RM330, doubles RM630; three-day/two-night package: dorms RM380, doubles RM900

Uncle Tan's Wildlife Camp Next to the Lokan River, a tributary of the Kinabatangan ☎089 535784 or ☎016 824 4749, ⓦuncletan.com. Relocated upriver from Bilit, this long-standing budget favourite continues to attract backpackers. As their printed information points out "the camp is not exactly the *Hilton*", but intrepid travellers consistently come away recommending the place. Twinned with *Uncle Tan's B&B* in Sepilok (see p.429). Dorm with meals RM48, double with meals RM100, two-day/one-night package per person RM320

Gomantong Caves

4.7km south of a turning between Kampung Sukau (22km) and Sukau Junction (19km) • Daily 8am–1pm & 2–5pm • RM30, RM30 camera permit • ☎019 882 0759 • Best visited as a tour from Sungai Kinabatangan lodges; or take a Sukau-bound minivan from Sandakan and get off at the Gomantong junction; from Lahad Datu, get off at the turning for Sukau and catch a minivan or motorbike taxi (either RM10) to the Gomantong junction; either way you'll probably need to walk the last 4.7km

The **Gomantong Caves** are vast limestone cavities inhabited by swiftlets whose nests are harvested twice a year (normally Feb–April and July–Sept) for the bird's-nest-soup trade. The caves are also home to a huge number of **bats**, which emerge at dusk in long sinewy streams – many people watch this phenomenon from the car park.

There are two main caves. Tourists usually only visit **Simud Hitam**, the "black cave", just a ten-minute walk from the ticket office. Though it's the smaller of the two, it is still fairly big, impressive if you haven't been to any of Sarawak's huge caves, and mostly contains black nests, a combination of twigs and bird saliva. The experience isn't entirely pleasant, however, due to the fact that the guano (which has an acrid stink) attracts a huge number of cockroaches that crunch underfoot or crawl on your feet.

The bigger **White Cave** is rarely visited by tourists (in fact the path there is completely overgrown), but nest collectors go there for the more valuable white nests, made from pure saliva, and it is possible to use their paths to get to one opening. If you time it just right to arrive at dusk, you'll be met with the astounding vision of hundreds of thousands of bats streaming out just 30m away. To get there, take the steep, rugged path to the left of the Black Cave mouth, and clamber up a couple of hundred metres till you get to the nest-collectors' shacks. If you ask, they can point or lead you up to the opening in the top of White Cave. Take good care not to go near the edge or enter the cave itself, as there are no safety measures, and try and get down before it gets too dark.

There's nowhere to stay or eat in and around Gomantong, so plan to leave the caves well before night-time if you are not on a tour.

From Lahad Datu to the Maliau Basin

Sabah's main trunk road continues southeast from Sandakan and the Sungai Kinabatangan to **Lahad Datu**. This unenthralling town offers access to two excellent rainforest areas: **Danum Valley Conservation Area** and **Tabin Wildlife Reserve**, as well as the less spectacular and much less expensive **Sapagaya Forest Reserve**. Further south, **Semporna** draws scuba divers headed for the world-renowned **Pulau Sipadan**. It's possible to stay in town or in an island resort; the latter range from backpacker shacks to luxurious retreats.

The main road around Sabah stops at the busy, noisy town of **Tawau**, from which ferries depart for Indonesian Kalimantan. Also from Tawau, 4WDs head daily for Keningau along rough routes that complete a **ring road** of sorts. This is also the way to the **Maliau Basin**, a magnet for trekkers although only accessible within expensive tour packages.

Lahad Datu

LAHAD DATU, 175km south of Sandakan, has something of a frontier feel. Once a centre for cocoa production, it could not compete with South American rivals and turned to palm oil instead. During its 1990s boom, it became a magnet for immigrants, mostly Indonesian and Filipino, many of whom have found gainful (if often illegal) employment on the plantations and in the construction industry.

Most visitors use Lahad Datu as a jumping-off point for the outstanding natural attractions of **Danum Valley Conservation Area** and **Tabin Wildlife Reserve**, though can see the jungle more cheaply (along with great views) at the **Sapagaya Forest Reserve**. Within the town, almost everything of interest is on or just off the main road, Jalan Teratai.

ARRIVAL AND DEPARTURE   LAHAD DATU

By plane The airport north of town sees daily MASwings flights to KK (5 daily; 55min). It's just a short taxi ride (RM7) from the centre; no buses serve the route.

By bus Buses from Sandakan, Semporna and Tawau stop at the bus terminus on Jalan Bunga Raya, a couple of minutes' walk east of Jalan Teratai near *Hotel Asia*, the tallest building in town.

ACCOMMODATION

Hotel De Leon Block L, Lot 1–6, Darvel Bay Commercial Centre ☎ 089 881222, ⌨ hoteldeleon.com.my. Set back from Jalan Teratai, this business hotel has rather mixed decor – the lobby has a Zen-like water feature *and* a tacky glittering dolphin sculpture, while the rooms have a little pizzazz, with 1970s wallpaper and sunken baths. Breakfast included. **RM148**

Borneo Home Lot 2, Jalan Mawar ☎ 089 881818. If *Tabin Lodge* isn't to your taste, and nowhere else will do a decent discount, this place next to the night market (you can see its sign from the bus stand) is probably your best

budget bet. The a/c rooms are clean but spartan, and staff are friendly and speak English. They do have the best-value singles for just RM40. Wi-fi is only available in the lobby. **RM52**

Tabin Lodge Jalan Urusetia Kecil ☎ 017 892 0158, ⌨ yan.hock@hotmail.com. One of the few budget options in town, conveniently located opposite the bus and minivan terminus. The rooms are just about OK, and there are plans for renovation. The owner is also planning a budget hostel by a river on the northern edge of the Tabin Wildlife Reserve. Fan **RM37**, a/c **RM52**

EATING AND DRINKING

★ **Ka Tini** Jalan AMDLD, Bandar Wilayah ☎ 016 995 1774. A cut above the average *kedai kopi*, this open-sided Malay place serves really good food, with a great *nasi*

campur spread for RM5–10, several local fish delicacies, including *ikan bilis* (crispy fried anchovies), and regular rice and noodle dishes for RM5–7. Daily 24hr.

Sapagaya Forest Reserve

10 km south of Lahad Datu Junction • Daily 8am–5pm • RM10, RM5 camera permit • ☎ 089 242500 • Take any bus from Lahad Datu heading towards Semporna and get off at the turning to Danum Valley

The **Sapagaya Forest Reserve** is one of the easier of the reserves to visit in the vicinity of Lahad Datu. The main attraction here is the **Tower of Heaven** (Menara Kayangan), a 33m tower set 620m up the 844m Mount Silam, the tallest peak in the area. Views from the top are phenomenal; you can see Lahad Duta to the north, the many islands in Darvel Bay out to sea, and the jungle towards Danum Valley.

From the entrance on the main road, a 10km road snakes its way up the mountain; you can walk it in a couple of hours. As well as the viewing tower, there is also a small hostel from where six well-marked **trails** of between 300m to 6km wend their way through the jungle – you may see samba deer, Bornean gibbons, pig-tailed macaques, the arboreal (cute and shy) loris, two types of pitcher plants, and, if you're very lucky the small and orange-red **silam crab**, unique to this mountain. You can hire a guide at the entrance for RM100 per day.

ACCOMMODATION   SAPAGAYA FOREST RESERVE

Sapagaya Forest Reserve Lodge Atop Mount Silam ☎ 089 880207. The reserve's new accommodation includes dorm rooms, a campsite and comfortable chalets.

Best book ahead at weekends. No wi-fi. Camping **RM5**, dorms **RM20**, chalets **RM80**

Tabin Wildlife Reserve

44km northeast of Lahad Datu airport, where the reserve office is based • The resort runs a daily minivan (leaves 8am, returns 1.30pm; 1hr 30min) from the office by the airport; the last 25km is unsurfaced

Tabin Wildlife Reserve, a government-owned tract of land twice the size of Singapore, holds a single resort managed by a private company that is only open to visitors as part of an overnight package. Although just eleven percent primary dipterocarp forest, its combination of primary forest, secondary forest and plantation (which is rich in fruit for animals to eat) offers excellent opportunities to see wildlife.

Hiking and **night drives** (included in the price of the package) offer opportunities to come across pygmy elephants, macaques or wild boar as they cross the tracks from the forest to the plantations in search of food; orang-utans can also be spotted, and even the rare clouded leopard. Birdwatchers can look out for more than three hundred kinds

endemic species such as the Bornean bristlehead, blue-headed pitta and
species of hornbills.

bin will typically include a walk to a **mud volcano**, used by animals
ck; a nearby tower (if repaired) allows guests to observe the scene,
even sleep there by arrangement. Serious trekkers can explore the
virgin primary rainforest 23km away in the Core Area, although this is not part
of the normal schedule (ask at the Lahad Datu airport office) and involves
considerable cost.

ACCOMMODATION   TABIN WILDLIFE RESERVE

Some **budget accommodation** may well be available soon in the northeast of the park – contact the *Tabin Lodge* in
Lahad Datu (see p.435).

★ **Tabin Wildlife Resort** ☎ 088 267266,
ⓦ tabinwildlife.com.my. Chalets beside the river and ten
more on a hillside; all are comfortable and spacious with
nice balconies. The food is excellent, with buffets including
a wide range of Western, Malaysian and Asian dishes.
Packages include transfers from Lahad Datu. Per person:
two-day/one-night full-board package RM1313, three-
day/two-night package RM1835

Danum Valley Conservation Area

65km west of Lahad Datu • Owned by nonprofit Sabah Foundation ☎ 089 841101, ⓦ ysnet.org.my

Spanning 438 square kilometres, more than ninety percent of it primary dipterocarp
rainforest, the **Danum Valley Conservation Area** (DVCA) is contained within a
sprawling logging concession, only open to visits as part of a package. **Wildlife** includes
bearded pigs, orang-utans, proboscis monkeys, clouded leopards and elephants, as well
as reptiles, fish, insects and more than 320 bird species. Short hiking **trails** are limited
to the eastern side, where the tourist accommodation is located. The remainder is
pristine forest, out of bounds to all but researchers.

Activities

Your experience of Danum Valley will depend greatly on which accommodation option
you choose. The more expensive, the **Borneo Rainforest Lodge** offers highly skilled
guides to take you on walks. The standard itinerary includes a walk on a 27m-high
canopy walkway, night safaris and a visit to a burial hill with a coffin belonging to a
tribal chief.

Staying at the much cheaper **Danum Valley Field Centre**, your options are more
limited. The centre is primarily set up for researchers, so although rangers will
accompany you on the well-marked trails (RM20/hr), they're not employed to spot
wildlife on your behalf or speak English. If you're a nature enthusiast and know
what you're looking for, that may suit you; otherwise you may come away
disappointed.

ACCOMMODATION   DANUM VALLEY

Borneo Rainforest Lodge On a bend on the Danum
River, 1hr by 4WD into the conservation area; c/o
Borneo Nature Tours office: Lot 20, Block 3, Fajar
Lorong 9, Fajar Centre, Lahad Datu ☎ 089 880207,
ⓦ borneonaturetours.com. A luxurious network of
hardwood chalets, each with an outdoor deck. It's all very
stylish considering that it's within the primary forest; rates
include permit, excellent buffet meals, transfer and a range
of activities. A single night would be too much of a rush.
Three-day/two-night package for two RM5440
Danum Valley Field Centre On the eastern edge of
the conservation area; office: Block 3, Fajar Lorong 9,
Fajar Centre, Lahad Datu ☎ 089 841101, ⓔ cemdinfo
@icsb-sabah.com.my. Mainly for researchers, and not set
up for tourism, but considerably cheaper than the *Borneo
Rainforest Lodge* and considerably more basic. You'll need
to organize a permit (RM50) with the office, ideally at least
a week before; transport (leaves Lahad Datu at 3.30pm,
returns at 8am; RM65 one way) runs Mon, Wed and Fri. The
simple accommodation is mostly in 48-bed dorms; there's a
café (three meals RM111). Camping RM78, dorms RM91,
doubles RM286

Semporna

Travellers usually only visit the chaotic, traffic-clogged town of **SEMPORNA** because they plan to **scuba dive** and **snorkel** off nearby islands such as **Sipadan**, **Mabul** and **Kapalai**. While some divers base themselves on the islands, particularly Mabul, a **backpacker** scene has developed in Semporna, which also gives access to the more northerly islands, not usually visited from Mabul.

Semporna broadly consists of three sections: **downtown**, the commercial centre where buses and minivans stop; **Semporna Seafront**, home to dive operators (there are yet more out in the resorts themselves) and most tourist accommodation; and the jetty-lined **Jalan Kastam**, which holds more dive kiosks, a few cafés and the business-oriented *Seafest Hotel*.

Mention must be made of the **crime and terrorist incidents** that have occurred on and around the islands in recent times (see p.387). Security has been beefed up on all the islands and security personnel are accompanying tourist boats on trips. Check the current situation before you book.

ARRIVAL AND INFORMATION   SEMPORNA

By plane Tawau airport is located between Semporna and Tawau (see p.441), with buses and minibuses running direct to Semporna so you don't need to go into Tawau at all. A taxi costs RM90.

By bus The main bus terminal is on the same road as the mosque, northwest of the Seafront. Dyana Express buses (☎089 784494) leave further back from the sea in the downtown area. Note that almost all buses leave before 9am or after 7pm.

Destinations KK (4 daily; 10hr); Lahad Datu (4 daily; 2hr); Sandakan (4–5 daily; 5hr); Tawau (5 daily; 1hr 30min).

By minivan Most minivans leave from just beside the main bus terminal, though Tawau services set off from close to *KFC*, downtown.

Destinations Lahad Datu (daily 7am–5pm; RM29); Tawau (RM15; RM20 to airport).

Bank There's a Maybank ATM downtown, near the mosque.

ACTIVITIES

★ Scuba Junkie Block B, Lot 36, Semporna Seafront ☎089 785372, ⏸scuba-junkie.com. This highly regarded outfit runs courses all the way from Discover Scuba Diving to Instructor. They use their excellent Mabul resort as a base for Sipadan trips, while from Semporna you can visit the more northerly islands. Dedicated to environmental protection, the company is staffed by enthusiastic instructors and divemasters. Open Water

course RM975, three fun dives RM300, snorkelling trip RM120.

Sipidan Scuba Lot B7–B8, Semporna Seafront ☎089 919128, ⏸sipadanscuba.com. This well-established and popular dive shop has many dive trips to the smaller, less-visited islands, and is marginally cheaper than Scuba Junkie – a trip to an island with three dives is RM210–260, and the Open Water course is RM870.

ACCOMMODATION

Borneo Global Sipadan Backpackers Jalan Causeway, close to the Seafest Hotel ☎089 785088, ⏸bgbackpackers.com. A no-nonsense (but none too exciting) backpacker place, 10min walk from the main

Seafront area, with private triple rooms (the cheapest of which have a bunk bed) and eight-bed dorms. They also arrange scuba diving and snorkelling. Wi-fi in lobby. Dorms <u>RM25</u>, triples <u>RM90</u>

THE SEA GYPSIES

Generations of Muslim Bajau and Suluk peoples have farmed the Celebes and Sulu seas for fish, sea cucumbers, shells and other marine products. Often dubbed **sea gypsies**, these people were originally nomads who lived aboard intricately carved wooden boats called *lepa-lepa*. Most are now settled in Semporna or on the islands around it, but their love of (and dependence upon) the sea remains strong, and the traditional red and yellow sails of the Bajau boats can sometimes still be seen billowing in the breeze. Every April, the Regatta Lepa Semporna (☎089 781518, ⏸sabahtourism.com) sees the boats converge on the town for two days. Amid traditional singing and dancing, as well as sea sports and competitions, awards are given for the best *lepa-lepa*.

Scuba Junkie 36 Semporna Seafront ☎089 785372, ⓦscuba-junkie.com. This hectic, super-friendly place is a focal point for budget travellers, with a recommended dive shop next door. The rooms are overpriced at the standard rate, but prices are halved for divers, who get great value. They also do room and board deals. Wi-fi in lobby. Dorms RM50, doubles RM140

Seafest Hotel Jalan Kastam ☎089 782333, ⓦseafesthotel.com. This imposing painted concrete block, 10min walk from the main tourist area, is the smartest hotel in town. It's also the only one with a pool; other facilities include a gym and sauna, plus (unreliable) in-room wi-fi. RM125

EATING

Anjung Lepa Jalan Kastam ☎089 782333, ⓦseafesthotel.com. The outdoor restaurant attached to the Seafest Hotel may be a short walk from the main Seafront area, but it's worth seeking out. Take a table on the waterfront terrace, strung with coloured lights, and pick from an admittedly limited menu of fried rice and noodle dishes (and some reasonably priced seafood) while boats drift past. Mains around RM8–9. Daily 4pm–midnight.

Mabul Café and Seafood Restaurant Semporna Seafront ☎089 781785, ⓦmabulcafe.com. Popular with foreign visitors partly for its first-floor location, where you can watch the world go by, and partly because the food

is decent enough, and portions large; a plate of tasty butter prawns (RM10) is enough for two with rice. However, service, however friendly, can be erratic. Daily 10am–10pm.

★ **Scuba Junkie** 36 Semporna Seafront ☎089 785372, ⓦscuba-junkie.com. Benefiting from the skills of Kiwi chef Rory, this bar-restaurant is the number-one social hub in town, serving reasonable pizzas (RM22–28), better burgers (RM16–26), sandwiches (RM10–12) and salads (RM6–14). In keeping with the company's emphasis on conservation, the restaurant does not serve fish since local fishing practices are not sustainable. Daily 7am–late.

Islands around Semporna

Visitors come to Semporna not to hang out in town, but to explore the magnificent **islands** offshore. The prime destination for experienced divers is **Pulau Sipadan**, but nearby **Pulau Mabul** and **Pulau Kapalai** are also renowned for marine life, and the latter in particular offers great snorkelling. These well-known islands are, however, just the beginning. **Sibuan**, on the edge of the chain and just over 45 minutes by boat from Semporna, has a breathtaking beach and shallow coral reefs, while on **Mantubuan** there's amazing pristine coral and very good visibility – a popular dive is to a section of very rare black coral (actually white), where you swim through a forest of what resemble underwater Christmas trees.

Pulau Sipadan

Acclaimed by Jacques Cousteau as "an untouched piece of art", **Pulau Sipadan** offers a cornucopia of marine life, its waters teeming with turtles, moray eels, sharks, barracuda, vast schools of colourful tropical fish and a diversity of coral comparable to that at Australia's Great Barrier Reef.

Only **experienced divers** are allowed to dive here, so you'll need an Advanced Open Water certificate or an Open Water certificate with a minimum of twenty log dives. There is no accommodation, and thanks to Sipadan's popularity, a **permit system** limits the number of divers each day. As a result, dive shops and resorts will typically require you to dive with them at other islands for three or four days before you get a day at Sipadan; you should also book **well in advance**. You can also use the same permit to **snorkel** in Sipadan, but it's hard to justify the huge premium over snorkelling trips to the other islands.

Dive sites

Most of the dozen-plus commonly visited **dive sites** around Sipadan offer the chance to see abundant turtles and white-tip sharks. The most popular, **Barracuda Point**, is a drift dive where divers hold onto rocks while shoals of barracuda pass by. Another great site is the **Drop-off**, close to the jetty, where you often find large schools of barracuda, bump-head parrot fish and Napoleon wrasse. Close to here is the entrance to **Turtle Cave**, a watery grave for the skeletal remains of turtles that have strayed in and become lost; fatal accidents have occurred when divers have gone in without proper guidance.

Pulau Mabul

Pulau Mabul, the chain's largest island, holds the lion's share of **accommodation**. Although there's a beach on the eastern side, development means that this is not a very picturesque island and non-divers are not likely to find much to do (other than, perhaps, laze around the more upmarket resorts). Litter is also a major problem on the western side.

Visibility in the water can be 20m or more but it's much less reliable than at Sipadan, particularly from July to September. Actually, though, the **muck diving** – seeking out creatures in the sediment – is famous here. Divemasters tend to prefer Mabul to Sipadan: while the latter has the big-ticket attractions, Mabul rewards patience. Among the marine life close to the island are many turtles of all sizes, seahorses – including the rare pygmy seahorse – frog fish, cuttlefish, mimic octopus, lion fish, stone fish, ribbon eels, mandarin fish and crocodile fish. Beware of the trigger fish, however.

Pulau Kapalai

Little more than a sand bar, tiny **Pulau Kapalai** is exquisite and otherworldly. It has room only for one, expensive, resort, although its reef is enjoyed by many visitors who are staying on Mabul. Again, the main attractions are the macro life: divers go looking for pygmy seahorses, harlequin ghost pipefish, frog fish and mandarin fish.

Pulau Pom Pom

The diving at lovely **Pulau Pom Pom** itself is not the best in the area, but this is a real desert-island escape that even has a relatively affordable resort. You also have access to plenty of other islands if diving is your passion.

Pulau Mataking

Beautiful, teardrop-shaped little **Pulau Mataking** is renowned for its crystal-clear waters and fine white sand, and is home to just two swish resorts. Dive boats do come here sometimes, though, to see the turtles, magnificent rays and interesting hammerhead nudibranchs.

ACCOMMODATION	ISLANDS AROUND SEMPORNA

Whether at a posh resort or cheap guesthouse, most accommodation on the islands is on a **package** basis including transport to the island and all meals. Pricing is often quoted per person; other than for dorms the prices listed here are for **two people for one night**, unless otherwise noted, but single supplements mean that solo travellers pay more than half that price. In many resorts, the nightly price drops significantly after the first night as it includes the boat transfer from Semporna (at least RM50 each way). Very short stays do not, therefore, make financial sense. Almost all accommodation offers **diving for an extra fee**, though less reputable places employ uncertified "dive masters"; ask for proof of qualifications.

PULAU MABUL

Accommodation on Pulau Mabul is evenly split between posh resorts and affordable guesthouses; many of the latter are on the western side of the island, also home to a lively stilt-village inhabited by Bajau fisherfolk.

RESORTS

Borneo Divers Mabul Pulau Mabul ☎ 088 222226, ⓦ borneodivers.net. A very good mid-range choice: fifteen lovely two-room chalets, a small pool, a good wi-fi-equipped restaurant and a fine stretch of beach. *Borneo Divers* is also a very well-established dive operator; you have to stay for four nights to receive a Sipadan permit. Diving package RM1530

★ **Mabul Beach Resort** Pulau Mabul ☎ 089 785372, ⓦ scuba-junkie.com. Run by Scuba Junkie in Semporna, this is a perfect middle ground between the resorts and the village guesthouses, with its own stretch of public beach but without the price tags of its neighbours. There are private rooms (a/c and fan) and dorms, fine buffet food and a bar for post-dive socializing. Twenty percent discounts are available for divers. Dorms RM175, fan doubles RM410 a/c doubles RM520

Mabul Water Bungalows Pulau Mabul ☎088 486389, ⓦmabulwaterbungalows.com. Now infamous as the site of a murder and a kidnapping in 2014, the posh sibling of the *Sipidan-Mabul Resort*, with chalets perched on stilts over the sea, is still one of the island's best resorts. The spa is open to the sea, while VIP rooms have their own jacuzzis plus glass-floored living rooms. Check when booking that your balcony faces the sea, not the restaurant. Non-divers US$1212, divers US$2032

Seaventure Just off the coast of Pulau Mabul ☎088 261669, ⓦseaventuresdive.com. It may be painted in bright colours, but that doesn't disguise the fact that it's an oil rig and a bit of an eyesore. It is, nevertheless, popular with divers and the rooms are comfortable enough. Prices are for the minimum four-day/three-night package. Non-divers RM2185, divers RM2730

Sipadan Water Village Pulau Mabul ☎089 752996, ⓦswvresort.com. While marginally less plush than the rival *Mabul Water Bungalows*, it's a good deal cheaper and is still a lovely kampung-style resort. Chalets are built to Bajau design, and the big verandas are particularly good. Massage is available (2–10pm; RM120/hr). Non-divers US$1030, divers US$1260

Sipadan-Mabul Resort (aka SMART) Pulau Mabul ☎088 486389, ⓦsipadan-mabul.com.my. This well-run resort boasts more than forty wooden en-suite chalets, a swimming pool and a very good restaurant. They have a good dive shop with some unusual offerings such as photography tuition and trips into Turtle Cave. Non-divers US$802, divers US$998

GUESTHOUSES

Arung Hayat Resort Kampung Bajau, Pulau Mabul ☎089 78246, ⓦsipadanadventures.com. This longhouse on stilts has 39 compact, neat rooms and a dive shop that offers a wide variety of diving packages. There are small discounts on the accommodation for divers. Full board: fan doubles RM240, a/c doubles RM300

★**Summerfriends Mabul Homestay** Kampung Bajau, Pulau Mabul ☎089 781671 or ☎013 557 1668 ⓦsummerfriendshomestay.com. A basic, very friendly, homely homestay near *Uncle Chang's*. The bedrooms aren't anything special, but it's clean and comfortable and the food is tasty – they can also help arrange diving, and there's a great sundeck with hammocks. Doubles RM100, full board RM180

Uncle Chang's Backpacker Lodge Kampung Bajau, Pulau Mabul ☎017 895 0002, ⓦucsipadan.com.

Always-busy backpacker favourite, perched on stilts over the sea, with shabby dorms (the shared bathrooms are not so clean either) and basic private rooms (the more expensive ones have a/c). The diving is cheap (three dives RM300), but there are varying reports as to the quality of the rental equipment and of the experience overall. Divers pay RM100 less. Full board: dorm package RM175, doubles RM380, a/c doubles RM420

PULAU KAPALAI

Sipadan-Kapalai Resort Pulau Kapalai; run by Pulau Sipadan Resort and Tours, 484 Bandar Sabindo, Tawau ☎089 765200, ⓦsipadan-kapalai.com. Spectacular chalets built on stilts, and shallow azure water that's perfect for snorkelling. Boats take divers to nearby Sipadan and Mabul, although there is also good diving on the artificial house reef. Three-day/two-night packages: non-divers RM3520, divers RM4400,

PULAU POM POM

★**Celebes Beach Resort** Pulau Pom Pom ☎089 782828, ⓦcelebescuba.com. This down-to-earth (and relatively affordable) resort was the second to open on Pom Pom. The ten a/c chalets are simple white concrete boxes, but surprisingly well furnished (a sea view costs RM50 extra), with slightly cheaper rooms in the garden longhouse. Dive packages include unlimited shore dives as well as three boat dives/day (equipment RM70/day). Longhouse: non-diving package RM1120, diving package RM1360; chalet: non-diving package RM1210, diving package RM1460

Pom Pom Island Resort Pulau Pom Pom; Office: Block B, Seafest Fishery Complex, Jalan Causeway ☎089 781918, ⓦpompomisland.com. Arriving at the jetty here on a sunny day – with clear blue sea to both sides, pale sands ahead and chalets both on stilts and on the beach – is a truly memorable experience. It's a delightful resort, with some environmental credentials. There's also a spa and a dive shop (under RM125/dive plus RM100 equipment rental/day). Three-day/two-night package RM4800

PULAU MATAKING

Reef Dive Resort Pulau Mataking ☎089 770022, ⓦmataking.com. Attractive and spacious luxury development, with appealing rooms, friendly staff and facilities including a spa and jacuzzi. The dive shop is consistently praised by guests and the snorkelling is great. It's much cheaper to arrange diving in advance rather than once you arrive. Dive packages include unlimited shore dives as well as three boat dives/day. Non-diving package RM2470, diving package RM2830

Tawau

The only town of any size in southeast Sabah, **TAWAU** is growing quickly and losing its previous Chinese character. While most travellers don't even give the town a nod, as they head straight from the airport to Semporna, as the only gateway into **Kalimantan** from Sabah it does see a steady trickle of foreign visitors. Central Tawau is a heady mixture of polluting vehicles and sprawling, chaotic **markets**; of these the most interesting are the clothes and trinket stalls beside the *Soon Yee Hotel* and the markets around the wharf.

Tawau Hills Park

Almost 30km north of Tawau • Daily 7am–6pm • RM45, botanical garden RM5 • ☎ 089 925719 • No bus; taxi RM35 one way; vehicles back to Tawau can be scarce, so ask for a return price including waiting, or get their mobile number

The hard-to-reach 270-square-kilometre **Tawau Hills Park**, a stretch of lowland rainforest with the Tawau River cutting through its centre, is the only attraction worth visiting near Tawau. The thirty-minute **Bombalai** trail leads up a hill from park HQ, but the main trail is a three-hour hike up **Gelas Hill** to a hot spring and waterfall that's perfect for swimming. Though it is open close to the start, as the lower reaches of the park have been logged, the trail continues through thick, damp, mossy forest. There are shelters, toilets and changing rooms at the waterfall, plus a small museum of the local area and a botanical garden by the park HQ.

ARRIVAL AND DEPARTURE
TAWAU

By plane MAS and AirAsia fly from Tawau's airport, 30km northeast of the centre. AirAsia has an office on the first floor. Small buses run from the airport to Tawau's local bus station (daily, hourly 7am–8pm; 30min); taxis cost RM45, and buses and minivans also run east to Semporna.

Destinations Johor Bahru (4 weekly; 2hr 35min); KK (9 daily; 50min); Kuala Lumpur (5 daily; 2hr 45min); Sandakan (2 daily; 40min); Tarakan, Indonesia (1 daily; 40min).

By long-distance bus Most long-distance buses use the bus station in a square at the eastern end of Tawau's main street, Jalan Dunlop, while KK buses depart from the ticket offices on Jalan Chen Fook nearby. Most buses to KK leave between 7–8am and 7–8pm, and there are very few buses anywhere in the afternoon.

Destinations KK (7 daily; 9hr); Lahad Datu (9 daily; 2hr); Sandakan (6 daily; 5hr 30min); Semporna (6 daily; 1hr 30min).

By minivan or local bus Minivans to Semporna run from

the long-distance bus station; local buses stop at the Apas bus station on Jalan Belian. The airport buses also run from here.

By ferry Two companies have ferry services to and from Indonesia; these run from Customs Wharf, Jalan Pelabuhan, 150m south of Jalan Dunlop's Shell petrol station. Tawindo Express (☎ 019 831 3182) runs to Nunakan, while Indomay Express (☎ 013 861 3330) handles services to Tarakan; arrive at least 1hr before departure.

Destinations Nunakan (daily 10am & 3pm Tues & Sun; 3hr); Tarakan (Tues, Thurs & Sat 11am; 3hr).

By 4WD While uncomfortable and not cheap, the 344km route from Tawau to Keningau by 4WD (departure by arrangement; 8hr; RM100) is quite an experience. The main reason to venture this way is to visit the Maliau Basin (5hr) or Batu Punggul (6hr). Talk to the 4WD drivers who hang out by the long-distance bus station from around 6.30am to noon (though check first that a bus service hasn't started up if they've finished the road).

ACCOMMODATION

Belmont Marco Polo Jalan Stephen Tan ☎ 089 777988, ✉ reservation@marcopolohotel-tawau.com .my. Classy address, with large and well-furnished a/c rooms, a friendly bar and a coffee shop. The more expensive rooms are higher up, to take advantage of the views and they arrange tours to Tawau Hills Park. **RM175**

Prince 208 Jalan Bunga ☎ 089 778989. A good mid-range choice in a central location for the higher-end restaurants, with a travel agent and convenience store in the lobby. Bedrooms have mood lighting and bold wallpaper, and there's a spa. **RM88**

Soon Yee 1362 Jalan Stephan Tan ☎ 089 772447. The

best budget spot; most rooms share bathrooms but a few are en suite (RM5 extra). It might be a bit rough around the edges but owner Joseph makes up for it by being happy to impart advice and information. **RM30**

Tawau Hills Resort Park HQ, Tawau Hills Park ☎ 089 768719, ✆ etawau.com. There are two lodges with comfortable four-bed rooms and shared bathrooms, as well as a (large) campsite and a swankier two-bedroom family chalet. An on-site canteen serves up simple dishes – included in room rates, but not for those camping. Camping **RM5**, beds **RM40**, chalet **RM200**

7

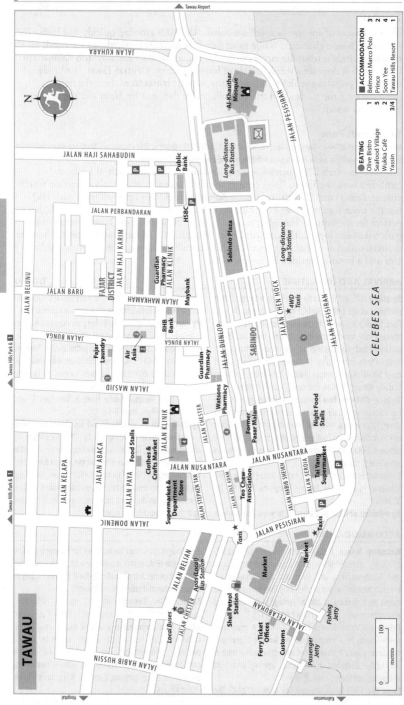

TAWAU

▲ Tawau Airport

JALAN KUHARA

N

Al-Khauthar Mosque

JALAN PESISIRAN

JALAN HAJI SAHABUDIN

Public Bank

Long-distance Bus Station

JALAN PERBANDARAN

HSBC

Sabindo Plaza

Long-distance Bus Station

JALAN BELUNU

JALAN BARU

FAJAR DISTRICT

JALAN HAJI KARIM

Guardian Pharmacy
JALAN KLINIK

Maybank

JALAN MAHKAMAH

JALAN BUNGA

Fajar Laundry

Air Asia

RHB Bank

JALAN BUNGA

Guardian Pharmacy

JALAN DUNLOP

JALAN CHEN HOCK

★ 4WD Taxis

SABINDO

JALAN PESISIRAN

CELEBES SEA

JALAN MASJID

Watsons Pharmacy

JALAN CHESTER

Former Pasar Malam

Night Food Stalls

JALAN KELAPA

JALAN ABACA

Food Stalls

Clothes & Crafts Market

JALAN KLINIK

JALAN NUSANTARA

JALAN NUSANTARA

JALAN PAYA

Supermarket & Department Store

JALAN STEPHEN TAN

JALAN COLE ADAM

Teo Chew Association

JALAN HABIB SHEIKH

JALAN SEROJA

Tai Yang Supermarket

JALAN DOMENIC

★ Taxis

JALAN PESISIRAN

★ Taxis

Market

JALAN BELIAN

Apas (Local) Bus Station

JALAN CHESTER

Local Buses

Shell Petrol Station

Market

Ferry Ticket Offices

Customs

Passenger Jetty

Fishing Jetty

JALAN PELABUHAN

JALAN HABIB HUSSIN

◄ Hospital

◄ Kalimantan

◄ Tawau Hills Park & 1

◄ Tawau Hills Park & 1

0	100
metres	

● **EATING**

Olive Bistro	1
Seafood Village	5
Wukka Café	2
Yassin	3/4

■ **ACCOMMODATION**

Belmont Marco Polo	3
Prince	2
Soon Yee	4
Tawau Hills Resort	1

EATING

Olive Bistro Jalan Masjid ☎089 770093. Appealing restaurant, with a quiet jazz soundtrack and Western dishes including Asian-style pizzas and much better pastas and salads, plus twists on local food such as garlic chicken rice. The *kerabu mango* (a mango salad with peanuts and Thai sauce) makes for a tasty, if sour, starter. From RM15 upwards. Daily 11.30am–2pm & 6–10pm.

Seafood Village Jalan Chen Fook. Considered a little pricey by locals, this food court is still very popular. The stalls on the main road are Chinese, and therefore serve alcohol, while the Malay places such as *Restoran 101* are closer to the sea. Daily 4.30–11pm.

★**Wukka Café** 8 Bangunan MAA, Fajar Complex. Cute little café with stylish decor and a focus on high-quality cakes, a small range of ice cream, and other delicious sweet things. The menu also includes some interesting pasta (the one with squid ink is good) and other Western food, as well as a couple of less good Malay dishes. Mains around RM12. Daily noon–10pm.

Yassin Branches on Jalan Dunlop and Jalan Chester. Indian café with curries, *rotis* and *murtabak*. The Jalan Chester branch has the more extensive menu, but most popular in both is the *nasi biriyani (RM7)*, rice served with chicken, beef or mutton. The fish-head curry (RM15) is another speciality. Daily 6.30am–10pm.

Maliau Basin

Sabah's last true wilderness, and one of the world's oldest rainforests, the otherworldly **MALIAU BASIN CONSERVATION AREA** (ⓦborneoforestheritage.org.my) remains barely explored; most visitors are scientists or researchers. Featuring various types of forest including lower montane, heath and dipterocarp, the basin is home to an impressive range of large mammals, notably the Borneo pygmy elephant, clouded leopard, Malayan sun bear and banteng (wild cattle), while birds include rare species found otherwise only at Gunung Kinabalu and Gunung Trus Madi.

To visit you must, in theory, be on a **tour**. It might just about be feasible to turn up and ask to do the two-hour trek near the entrance on the Tawau–Keningau road, but it's not a sure thing and very unofficial (and you'd have to pay RM100 for a guide). A standard five-day itinerary starts at Tawau, a five-hour drive from the park, and includes long and strenuous hikes suitable only for the fit. You'll need a doctor's certificate to prove this, plus insurance that covers helicopter evacuation. Less expensive options in similar jungle nearby include Batu Punggul (see p.403) and Sapulut, which can be visited with a package from more adventurous KK tour operators.

ACCOMMODATION   MALIAU BASIN CONSERVATION AREA

Borneo Nature Tours ☎088 267637, ⓦborneo naturetours.com. The best-known operators, with a circular itinerary, spending the first and last night in dorms at the spartan *Agathis Camp* close to the park entrance, and the rest at the similarly basic *Nepenthes* (aka *Camel Trophy*) *Camp*, a 6hr walk deeper in to the forest. Also included are night drives and a side trip to the Maliau Falls. Five-day tours: per person RM4575; in larger groups RM3969

Brunei

451 Bandar Seri Begawan

461 Muara district

463 Temburong district

464 Belait district

OMAR ALI SAIFUDDIEN MOSQUE

Brunei

A tiny oil-rich monarchy that seems, superficially, more Middle Eastern than Southeast Asian, the enigmatic country of Brunei intrigues visitors. Its official title is Negara Brunei Darussalam, Darussalam meaning "Abode of Peace" – and tranquil it certainly is, with little crime and a sense of calm, bordering on ennui, thanks to the income generated by massive offshore oil and gas deposits. The 400,000 inhabitants – two-thirds Malay, a tenth Chinese, nearly a fifth expatriates and foreign workers, and just a few percent indigenous peoples – enjoy a cosseted existence. While the genuinely wealthy elite form a select few, there's a large middle class; education and healthcare are free; and houses, cars and even pilgrimages to Mecca are subsidized.

Brunei's sultan, **Hassanal Bolkiah** (see p.449), is famously one of the world's richest men. Ruling as an absolute monarch, he is prime minister, defence minister and finance minister rolled into one, and his extended family, the Bolkiahs, control virtually all government departments and the vast majority of the nation's wealth; it's said that nothing of any real importance is decided without the thumbs-up from a family member.

This is, however, no glitzy Gulf sheikhdom. Brunei is basically low-rise and low-key, feeling not unlike Malaysia's oil-rich state of Terengganu, only more torpid and with more discernible signs of wealth. Primary and secondary tropical forest still cover seventy percent of the land area; indeed the country's boundaries are easily discerned from the air, as Sarawak's logging roads and oil-palm plantations halt as if by magic at the border. Most of Brunei is less than 150m above sea level, its rainforest, peat swamp and heath forest running down to sandy beaches and mangrove swamps. The country is divided into four districts: **Muara**, which contains the capital, **Bandar Seri Begawan**; agricultural **Tutong**; oil-rich **Belait**; and **Temburong**, a sparsely populated enclave severed from the rest of Brunei by Sarawak's Limbang district.

For most travellers, Brunei is simply a transit zone on the long bus ride between Miri and Kota Kinabalu. Those who stay seldom do so for more than two or three nights, long enough to glimpse the main sights and the way of life without the cost of living – much higher than in Malaysia – creating too much of a dent in their bank account. Conveniently, the capital is home to many of the key attractions, notably the fascinating **Kampung Ayer**, a rambling collection of houses built over the wide Brunei River, and offers one of the best chances to see **proboscis monkeys** in all of Borneo. The other big attraction is the pristine rainforest in **Ulu Temburong National Park** in Temburong, though this is a much more sanitized experience than any Malaysian national park, with few trails to explore. Otherwise, the sultanate holds some interesting Islamic architecture; a clutch of moderately interesting museums, beaches, small nature parks and modern longhouses; and one solitary nod to Dubai-style excess – a hotel/country club, the *Empire*, that's worth seeing for its ludicrous grandiosity.

Brief history

The Brunei of today is just the rump of a vast, powerful sultanate that was gradually gobbled up by the Brookes' regime in Sarawak in the nineteenth century. Trade was the

The Sultan of Brunei p.449

Proboscis monkeys p.457

Kampung Ayer p.453

Brunei River trips p.456

ULU TEMBURONG NATIONAL PARK

Highlights

❶ Proboscis monkeys Just minutes from downtown by boat, a group of these curious-looking creatures can usually be seen foraging by the Brunei River. **See p.451**

❷ Kampung Ayer This scenic collection of wooden houses, built out over the Brunei River, offers a glimpse of traditional life. **See p.453**

❸ The Royal Regalia Building One of Brunei's most entertaining museums, housing

processional chariots, ceremonial paraphernalia and offbeat official gifts. **See p.454**

❹ The Empire Hotel Come to witness how a royal folly with a cavernous marble atrium now functions as a successful hotel, then hang around for a bite. **See p.463**

❺ Ulu Temburong National Park Brunei's premier nature reserve holds a heart-stopping canopy walkway and opportunities for river rafting and tubing. **See p.464**

HIGHLIGHTS ARE MARKED ON THE MAP ON P.448

THE SULTAN OF BRUNEI

Brunei's head of state, **Sultan Hassanal Bolkiah** (whose full title is 31 words long), is the 29th in a line stretching back six hundred years. Educated in Malaysia and Britain, he has been sultan since 1967, following the voluntary abdication of his father, Omar.

Hassanal Bolkiah was once deemed the world's richest man, though today a conservative estimate of his net worth, at a mere US$20 billion, would put him only in the top thirty of *Forbes*' list of billionaires, behind the king of Thailand. Tales of his extravagance are legion – of private jets festooned with gold bathroom fittings, for example. However, the sultan takes pains to live down that persona by cultivating an image of accessibility. Brunei's highly compliant press is full of stories of his majesty's presence at community events – the launching of a new school, say – and for two days a year, at Hari Raya Aidilfitri, the sultan throws open the Istana Nurul Iman to the public, with tens of thousands standing in line for hours to meet him and other members of the royal family. Despite the pious nature of the regime, there have been many accusations of corruption and debauchery within the palace, though these tend to be settled out of court.

The sultan defined the philosophy underlying his rule when, in the 1990s, he introduced an ideology called Melayu Islam Beraja, essentially that the monarchy is founded on the twin pillars of Islam and Malayness. There are few signs of participatory democracy, however. In 2004 the sultan reconvened Brunei's **legislative assembly**, two decades after it was suspended, with sixteen appointed members. They voted to enlarge the assembly to include up to fifteen elected members, but no elections have so far taken place. In 2006 the sultan amended Brunei's constitution to make himself infallible under Bruneian law, and in 2014 he took the controversial step of introducing harsh traditional punishments under Islamic law.

8

powerhouse behind its growth. Tang and Sung dynasty coins and ceramics, found a few kilometres from Bandar Seri Begawan, suggest that China was trading with Brunei as early as the seventh century. Brunei subsequently benefited from its strategic position on the **trade route** between India, Melaka and China, and exercised a lucrative control over merchant traffic in the South China Sea. As well as being a staging post, where traders could stock up on supplies and off-load cargo, Brunei was by the fourteenth century commercially active in its own right; the *nakhoda*, or Bruneian sea traders, traded local produce such as camphor, rattan and brassware for ceramics, spices, wood and fabrics.

The Brunei Sultanate

Islam had begun to make inroads into Bruneian society by the mid-fifteenth century, a process accelerated when wealthy Muslim merchant families decamped to Brunei after Melaka fell to the Portuguese in 1511. Brunei was certainly an Islamic sultanate by the time its first **European visitors** arrived from Spain in 1521. Commonly acknowledged as the sultanate's golden age, this period saw its territory and influence stretch as far as the modern-day Philippines.

However, things turned sour towards the close of the sixteenth century. Following a sea battle in 1578, Spain took the capital, only to relinquish it days later due to a cholera epidemic. The threat of piracy caused more problems, scaring off passing trade. Worse still, factional struggles loosened the sultan's control at home. With the arrival of **James Brooke** (see p.560) in 1839, the sultanate was to shrink steadily as he siphoned off its territory to neighbouring Sarawak. This trend culminated when Charles Brooke's capture of the Limbang region split Brunei in two. By 1888, the British had declared Brunei a **protected state**, meaning responsibility for its foreign affairs lay with London.

The twentieth century and beyond

The start of the twentieth century was marked by the **discovery of oil**, which drove the British to set up a Residency in 1906. By 1931 the **Seria oil field** was on stream, but the Japanese invasion of 1941 temporarily halted Brunei's path to prosperity. As in Sabah, Allied bombing during the occupation that followed left much rebuilding to be done.

While Sabah, Sarawak and Labuan became Crown Colonies in the early postwar years, Brunei remained a British protectorate. The British Residency was finally withdrawn in 1959, and a new constitution established, with provisions for a democratically elected legislative council. At the same time, Sultan Omar Ali Saifuddien (the present sultan's father) was careful to retain British involvement in defence and foreign affairs – a move whose sagacity was made apparent when, in 1962, an attempted coup led by Sheik Azahari's pro-democratic **Brunei People's Party** was crushed by British Army Gurkhas. Ever since the failed coup, which stemmed from Omar's refusal to convene the first sitting of the legislative council, the sultan has ruled by decree in his role as an unelected prime minister, and emergency powers have been in place. Despite showing interest in joining the new Malaysian Federation in 1963, Brunei chose to opt out rather than risk losing its oil wealth and compromising the pre-eminence of its monarchy; not until 1984 did it cease to be a British protectorate and become fully independent.

Little scrutinized by the outside world, modern Brunei charts an unruffled course, though there's no clear sense how the country plans to cope when its oil runs out in a couple of decades, and even fairly well-educated young people find it hard to find jobs. The sultanate retains close ties with the UK and, regionally, especially with Singapore. Relations with Malaysia, by no means poor, look set to become yet warmer following a 2009 pact. Details remain sketchy, but Brunei is said to have given up its claims to the **Limbang** district of Sarawak, while Malaysia conceded its claim to certain offshore oil fields, and offered to help Brunei exploit them. The fruits of the agreement are already being seen elsewhere: the two countries are jointly working on yet another Sarawakian **dam**, in Limbang, apparently to supply power to Brunei, and a new bridge has been created over the **Pandaruan River** to link Limbang and Temburong, eliminating the need for a ferry crossing.

In May 2014, to international and some local consternation, **Islamic hudud punishments** were brought in at the sultan's behest, to be introduced in three phases. In theory, the *hudud* penal code could mean people convicted of adulterous or homosexual acts being stoned to death, and thieves having a hand amputated. However, it remains to be seen whether such punishments will be used in practice, and if so how often; also unclear is the degree to which the many non-Muslim residents of Brunei, such as the Chinese community, and foreign visitors will be subject to them. However things evolve, one injunction it's as well to adhere to is the ban on consuming food and drink in public during daylight hours throughout **Ramadan**. Check government travel advice websites for updates on the situation.

ARRIVAL AND DEPARTURE
BRUNEI

By plane Bandar's airport has flights from Kota Kinabalu, Kuala Lumpur, Jakarta and Singapore, and reasonable connections with cities elsewhere in the region and further afield.

By bus Reaching Brunei by bus is easy. A couple of daily services run to Bandar from Miri in Sarawak, via the coastal towns of Kuala Belait and Seria, and from Kota Kinabalu in Sabah. Daily buses also run all the way from Pontianak in western Kalimantan.

By boat Muara, Bandar's port, is served by boats from Labuan and from Lawas in Sarawak.

GETTING AROUND

By car Brunei is small enough that you can visit most towns as day-trips from the capital. However, the bus system is indifferent, so renting a car is the ideal way to explore. It's not overly expensive, starting at B$80/day and fuel is cheap.

ESSENTIALS

Alcohol, tobacco and drugs Brunei is famously dry, though tourists are permitted to bring two bottles of liquor and twelve cans of beer for private consumption. The sultan is also very anti-smoking (although he himself smokes cigars); you are only permitted to bring one packet of nineteen cigarettes tax-free through customs (you will be liable to pay a duty of B$5 on each packet thereafter), and smoking is not permitted in any public building. Although it's not technically illegal to smoke in public spaces, you should do as the locals do and light up in a back alley. You will also see many signs in customs making it clear that being found with drugs is an executable offence.

Money The Brunei dollar (B$; also called the ringgit in Malay) has the same value as the Singapore dollar, widely used in Brunei.

Opening hours Brunei has a split weekend as far as government bodies are concerned: Fridays and Sundays are days off. Some private businesses follow government hours, while others work Monday to Friday with a half-day on Saturday.

Entry visas Most Western nationalities are allowed to enter visa-free for thirty to ninety days, although for some reason Canadians and Australians can only get fourteen days and Australians must get a visa on arrival.

Bandar Seri Begawan

BANDAR SERI BEGAWAN (known locally as **Bandar** or **BSB**) feels more like a provincial town than a capital. It is also a newish, largely postwar city, dominated by drab concrete – until comparatively recently, the seat of power and main settlement was Kampung Ayer, the picturesque water village visible from all along Bandar's river bank. The commercial centre, built on reclaimed land after the British Resident arrived in 1906, comprises a mere handful of riverside streets and is surprisingly tranquil, not to say dull; recent development has been concentrated in the suburbs.

Despite its underwhelming air, Bandar packs in a surprising amount for visitors. **Kampung Ayer** is the obvious sight, but perhaps even more memorable are the **proboscis monkeys** that live in a mangrove forest just a twenty-minute boat ride upriver from the centre. Not many tourists glimpse them, though, whereas virtually everyone heads to the **Omar Ali Saifuddien mosque** – an iconic building that turns out not to be all that spectacular up close. At their best, the city's **museums**, whether glorifying the sultanate or documenting local history and culture, are genuinely enlightening.

8

The waterfront

Following the middle-class flight to the suburbs, efforts to bring life back to the centre (thus far not entirely successful) have culminated in the revamp of the city's **waterfront** along Jalan McArthur. The 0.5km esplanade is a good place to get your bearings – from here you can see **Kampung Ayer**; a golden onion dome and white saddle-roofed building that forms part of the sultan's palace; and the tower of the **Arts and Handicraft Centre**.

PROBOSCIS MONKEYS

For many visitors, a trip to Borneo would not be complete without an encounter with a **proboscis monkey**, found only in riverine forests and coastal mangrove swamps. The reddish-brown monkey derives its name from the adult male's enlarged, drooping nose; females and young animals are snub-nosed. The role of the male's oversized member, which seems to straighten out when the animal is issuing its curious honking call, is likely to do with establishing dominance within a group and, so, in attracting a mate.

The monkeys specialize in eating hard-to-digest mangrove leaves, an adaptation that has enlarged their stomachs and left them with distinctive pot-bellies – and limited their distribution. Entirely arboreal, they're capable of making spectacular leaps across the river channels that cut through mangrove forests, arms thrown wide to catch foliage on the far side – though, in case they miss, they're also proficient swimmers, with webbed toes.

As well as the Brunei River near Bandar Seri Begawan, good places to spot proboscis monkeys include the Kinabatangan (see p.431) and Labuk Bay (see p.429) sanctuaries of Sabah, and Bako National Park (see p.332) in Sarawak.

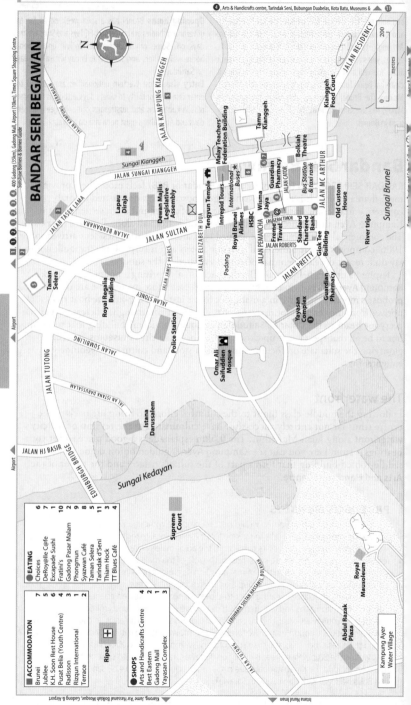

BANDAR SERI BEGAWAN

4 Arts & Handicrafts centre, Tarindak Seni, Bubungan Duabelas, Kota Batu, Museums & 13

400 Gadong (33km), Gadong Mall, Airport (10km), Times Square Shopping Centre, SunShine Borneo & Borneo Guide

JALAN RESIDENCY

Kianggeh Food Court

Tamu Kianggeh

Bolkiah Theatre

Malay Teachers' Federation Building

Sungai Kianggeh

JALAN SUNGAI KIANGGEH

JALAN KAMPUNG KIANGGEH

Guardian Pharmacy

JALAN CATOR

Bus Station & taxi rank

Tengyun Temple

Intrepid Tours

International Buses

Wisma Java

Lapau Diraja

Dewan Majlis Legislative Assembly

HSBC

Royal Brunei Airlines

JALAN PEMANCHA

Fresmex Travel

LPG/GERAI TIMOR

Standard Chartered Bank

Old Custom House

JALAN MC ARTHUR

JALAN TASEK LAMA

JALAN BENDAHARA

JALAN SULTAN

JALAN ELIZABETH DUA

Padang

JALAN ROBERTS

Giok Tee Building

JALAN PRETTY

Sungai Brunei

River trips

Taman Selera

Royal Regalia Building

JALAN JAMES PEARCE

JALAN STONEY

Police Station

JALAN SUMBILING

Yayasan Complex

Guardian Pharmacy

JALAN TUTONG

JLN AN ISTANA DARUSSALAM

Omar Ali Saifuddien Mosque

Istana Darussalem

JALAN HJ BASIR

EDINBURGH BRIDGE

Sungai Kedayan

Supreme Court

Airport

Airport

Kiarong, Jame' 'Asr Hassanil Bolkiah Mosque, Gadong & Airport

Kiarong, Jame' 'Asr Hassanil Bolkiah Mosque, Gadong & Airport

LEBUHRAYA SULTAN HASSANIL BOLKIAH

JALAN TUTONG

Royal Mausoleum

Abdul Razak Plaza

Kampung Ayer Water Village

Istana Nurul Iman

N

0   200
metres

ACCOMMODATION

Brunei	7
Jubilee	5
K.H. Soon Rest House	6
Pusat Bella (Youth Centre)	4
Radisson	3
Rizqun International	1
Terrace	2

Ripas ✚

EATING

Choices	6
DeRoyalle C@fe	7
Excapade Sushi	1
Fratini's	10
Gadong Pasar Malam	2
Phongmun	9
Syazwan Café	8
Taman Selera	5
Tarindak d'Seni	11
Thiam Hock	3
TT Blues Café	4

SHOPS

Arts and Handicrafts Centre	4
Best Eastern	2
Gadong Mall	1
Yayasan Complex	3

8

At the heart of the esplanade, the simple **Old Custom House** contains a small museum of the city's development (Mon–Thurs & Sun 8.30am–5pm, Fri 8.30–11.30am & 2–5pm, Sat 9.45am–5pm; free), though labelling is entirely in Malay. Nearby, a couple of smaller buildings with pointed white tent-shaped roofs are home to several attempts at smart **cafés**, but they've still not really become part of the city's fabric and are frequented mainly by foreigners – a charge that could equally be levelled at the waterfront as a whole. At night families arrive for a quick stroll, admiring the myriad lights of Kampung Ayer across the dark river, before scooting off elsewhere for refreshments.

Kampung Ayer Tourism and Culture Gallery

Across the water from the esplanade • Mon–Thurs & Sun 9am–5pm, Fri 9–11.30am & 2.30–5pm, Sat 9.45am–5pm • Free • ☎ 220 0874

The **Kampung Ayer Tourism and Culture Gallery** is the obvious place to start exploring Kampung Ayer. It houses the **tourist office** (see p.457), though its small museum is sadly not as interesting as the 600-year-old history of Kampung Ayer it charts. A little **observation tower** offers good views over the colourful wooden houses and back towards downtown. From here you can simply head off into the water village via assorted meandering walkways, though the maze-like character of the place and lack of signage make it difficult to identify specific sights. A few homes may have crafts for sale, and you may be lucky enough to chance upon, say, cottage industries involving rattan-weaving.

Omar Ali Saifuddien Mosque

Jalan Masjid Omar Ali Saifuddien • Mon–Wed, Sat & Sun 8.30am–noon, 1.30–3pm & 4.30–5.30pm, Thurs open to Muslims only, Fri 4.30–5pm

Though modest in size, the **Omar Ali Saifuddien Mosque** must have been a marvellous sight when completed in 1958. Topped by a 52m-high dome, it would have dominated what was then very much a small town, and is beautifully located on the edge of a circular lagoon. The decision to plonk the modern Yayasan Complex of shops just southeast has done it no favours, however, and the mosque is now at that awkward in-between age where it looks neither gleaming new nor venerable, merely a bit grimy in places. Still, commissioned by and named after the father of the present sultan, it makes

---

KAMPUNG AYER

While neighbouring Malaysia still holds a few water villages, notably in Kota Kinabalu, none can match Bandar's **Kampung Ayer** for size. Practically a small town by itself, it snakes downriver for 2km beyond the city centre and upriver for another 1km or so, as well as up the Kedayan tributary of the river to the Edinburgh Bridge. Timber houses built on stilts and piles have occupied this stretch of the Brunei River for hundreds of years, and Kampung Ayer's historical significance cannot be underestimated. A census in 1911 showed that nearly half Brunei's population lived here, including the sultan, whose long-vanished palace was a suitably souped-up wooden affair.

Today the area is home to more than 39,000 inhabitants (almost ten percent of the country's population) in 42 villages with their own shops, clinics, mosques, schools and fire services, minus fire engines, of course. They also have electricity and mains water, but many houses remain unconnected to the sewerage system, which seems not to deter the boys who swim in the river. While residents are content with their lot, insofar as they have stayed put rather than move to dry land, the authorities are intent on tinkering with Kampung Ayer. They have embarked on a project to build several dozen non-timber homes in the area, boasting solar panels and billed as eco-friendly, and they continue to extend sanitation to the villages. There's also talk of action to arrest the decline in village traditions, notably crafts; one plan is to market Kampung Ayer as an "artisanal village" to showcase what trades linger, for example silversmithing and boat-building, though it's not clear when this might be put into effect. Most tour operators (see p.457) offer half-day **boat trips** that include the water village.

tasteful use of opulent fittings – Italian marble, granite from Shanghai, Arabian and Belgian carpets, and English chandeliers and stained glass. The lagoon holds a replica of a sixteenth-century royal barge, or *mahligai*, used on special religious occasions.

Royal Regalia Building

Jalan Sultan • Mon–Thurs, Sat & Sun 9am–4.30pm, Fri 9–11.30am & 2.30–4.30pm • Free • ☎ 222 8358

In addition to a handful of uninteresting museums, downtown Bandar holds one that is simply essential – the **Royal Regalia Building**, easy to pick out as its roof is shaped like a strange domed helmet. While the name might lead you to expect a dry costume collection, it's actually a hilarious collection of regal paraphernalia whose subtext is to serve as a massive paean to the sultan. Perhaps the most significant objects are those used during his coronation, including the *tongkat aja* – a model of a human arm in gold, used to support the royal chin during the ceremony, which took place just across the road in the grand-looking Lapau Diraja building. Most visitors get an even bigger kick out of two massive **chariots**, one used for the coronation, the other for his highness's silver jubilee in 1992, the throng on the day recreated by dozens of mannequins in aristocratic Malay dress. Elsewhere there's an eccentric display of gifts the Brunei royals have been lumbered with, courtesy of blue-blooded intimates and world statesmen – replica temples made of crystal, and the like.

Tamu Kianggeh

Jalan Sungai Kianggeh • Daily dawn–dusk • Free • Bus #37

Just sixty or so years ago, Bandar still had *padian* – women traders who would hawk their produce from boats in and around Kampung Ayer, rather as women still do in Thailand's floating markets. Their role was gradually usurped by the central produce market, **Tamu Kianggeh**, alongside the canalized Kianggeh creek. The *tamu* sells everything from machetes to *midin* – nothing you can't see in markets in Sarawak or Sabah, but entertaining all the same. Friday morning is the busiest, and thus the best, time to turn up.

Arts and Handicrafts Centre

Jalan Residency, just over 5min walk east of Tamu Kianggeh • Mon–Thurs, Sat & Sun 9am–5pm, Fri 9–11.30am & 2.30–5pm • Free • ☎ 224 0676 • Bus #39

Bandar's **Arts and Handicrafts Centre** is a substantial complex where young Bruneians are taught traditional skills such as weaving, brass-casting and the crafting of the *kris*, the traditional Malay dagger. Unfortunately classes are not generally open to public view without prior arrangement, so you'll have to make do with browsing the pricey **gift shop**. The other reason to visit is to enjoy classic Bruneian food at their restaurant, *Tarindak d'Seni* (see p.460).

Kota Batu

It's fitting that Brunei's main **museums** should be a little way east of the centre at **Kota Batu**, the site of the capital when the Brunei sultanate was at its height. The area was excavated in the early 1950s by Tom Harrisson, who was instrumental in uncovering so many aspects of Sarawak's history and culture. A few old walls aside, however, this largely wooded area, close to the river, holds scant signs of former habitation.

Brunei Museum

Jalan Kota Batu, 4km east of the centre • Sun–Thurs 9am–5pm, Fri 9–11.30am & 2.30–5pm, Sat 9.45am–5pm; Ramadan daily 9am–3pm (Fri until noon); closed religious holidays • Free • ☎ 224 4545 • Bus #39

An old-school non-interactive affair occupying a charmless hunk of 1970s concrete, the

Brunei Museum has a few worthwhile sections where you could happily while away an hour or two. Skip the mediocre petroleum and natural history galleries on the ground floor in favour of the **Islamic art gallery**. While sadly this makes no attempt to put its contents into historical context, the selection of Levantine, Persian and Mughal artefacts such as kilims, illuminated Korans and inlaid boxes is exquisite at times. Most of the collection belongs to the sultan and his relations; indeed, a special display highlights a handwritten manuscript of the Koran's opening surah by the sultana herself, though the illumination around it is rather finer than the calligraphy. Upstairs, the **traditional culture gallery** is the highlight, with its dioramas of village life and some great examples of *bedil* and *meriam* – carved cannon bearing crocodile and dragon-like naga heads, their jaws forming the muzzle. The **archeology and history gallery** rewards a quick look too, offering a neat recap of Brunei's glory days at Kota Batu and its near-obliteration in the nineteenth century.

At the time of writing the museum was closed indefinitely for restoration, so it's best to call before you go.

Malay Technology Museum

Jalan Kota Batu, 4km east of the centre • Sun–Thurs 9am–5pm, Fri 9–11.30am & 2.30–5pm, Sat 9.45am–5pm; Ramadan daily 9am–3pm (Fri until noon); closed religious holidays • Free • ☎ 224 4545 • Bus #39

Right by the Brunei River, the endearingly misnamed but surprisingly good **Malay Technology Museum** focuses not on kampung-built MP3 players but on traditional lifestyles and architecture, with – despite Brunei's tiny population of indigenous tribes – some creditable ethnographic exhibits that are sorely lacking in northern Sarawak. The first hall has a thought-provoking display on different styles of kampung house and their bewildering roof shapes; another is devoted to activities such as fishing using traditional traps. Best of all is the third hall, with scaled-down replicas of a Lun Bawang longhouse, a Penan shelter and a hut for trampling sago pith to make flour, among other tribal structures. Such themes will continue at a proposed **Maritime Museum** nearby, showcasing local boat-building and so forth, though its actual opening date is anyone's guess.

Istana Nurul Iman

By the Brunei River 4km west of the centre, off Jalan Tutong • Open two days a year during the Hari Raya Aidilfitri festival marking the end of Ramadan • Bus #42, #44, #46, #48 or #56

Unless you are in town at the right time of year, the closest you're likely to get to the sultan's palace, the **Istana Nurul Iman**, is on a river trip to spot Bandar's proboscis monkeys. Even viewed from afar, the palace impresses with its scale: it's bigger than London's Buckingham Palace, the main buildings stretching for nearly 0.5km. Needless to say, it's also a monument to sheer self-indulgence, with nearly 1800 rooms – including 257 toilets – and at least 500 chandeliers. The design, by Filipino architect Leandro Locsin, tries to incorporate Islamic motifs such as arches and domes, plus a traditional saddle-shaped roof, though many might say it fails on all counts. There's said to be a secret passage connecting the palace with the sultan's former home, the considerably more modest Istana Darul Hana, also by the river about 1km closer to the centre of town.

Jame 'Asr Hassanal Bolkiah

3km northwest of the centre, on the northern edge of Kiarong suburb • Mon–Wed, Sat & Sun 8am–noon, 2–3pm & 5–6pm, Thurs & Fri open to Muslims only • Free • Bus #1 or #22

With sky-blue roofs, six golden domes and pleasant grounds with fountains, the **Jame 'Asr Hassanal Bolkiah** is a grander sibling to the Omar Ali Saifuddien mosque downtown. Built in the 1990s to mark the sultan's silver jubilee, it's also the largest mosque in Brunei, though some of the neat mosaic decoration has a slightly plastic appearance. The mosque is conveniently close to the malls and restaurants of the suburb of Gadong, 1km north, but getting there on foot means traversing some fearsome highways. If you happen to pass this way at night, look out for the evocative lighting, which gives the building an air of serenity despite the fast-moving traffic.

Gadong

5km northwest of the centre • Bus #1 or #20 runs along the main drag, right past the Abdul Razak Complex; a taxi from downtown costs B$8–10 (B$12–15 after sunset)

If you spend much time outside the centre while in Bandar, it's likely to be in the most thriving suburb of **Gadong**. The place isn't much to look at: a collection of mundane concrete blocks and traffic-clogged streets surrounding the multiple blocks of the **Abdul Razak Complex**, which includes two hotels and the **Gadong Mall**, where despite the grandiose exterior the shopping is unmemorable. Gadong is, however, a good spot for **eating**, with decent restaurants and a terrific **pasar malam** where they sell all manner of Bruneian Malay goodies (see p.460).

ARRIVAL AND DEPARTURE

BANDAR SERI BEGAWAN

By plane Brunei International Airport (☎ 233 1747) is 8km north of the city. A taxi into town costs around B$25–35, while during daylight hours buses #11, #23, #24, #34, #35, #36 and #38 (B$1) run to the bus station. Royal Brunei Airlines is on Jalan Sultan (☎ 221 2222); Bangunan Haji Ahmad, the building that holds the *deRoy@lle C@fe*, houses Malaysia Airlines (☎ 222 3074), Philippine Airlines (☎ 222 6971) and Singapore Airlines (☎ 224 4902).

Destinations Jakarta (6 weekly; 2hr 20min); Kota Kinabalu (1–3 daily; 40min); Kuala Lumpur (4–5 daily; 2hr 30min); Manila (1–2 daily; 2hr 5min); Melbourne (1 daily; 6hr 50min); Mulu (4 weekly; 30min); Singapore (2–3 daily; 2hr).

By bus All domestic buses use the bus station on Jalan Cator, while international services park on Jalan Sungai Kianggeh by a conspicuous modern glass tower. Buses to Malaysia, operated by PHLS (☎ 277 1668 or ☎ 718 3838, ⊛ phls38.com), include the Jesselton Express, which heads daily at 8am to Kota Kinabalu (7hr 30min) via Limbang (1hr 30min), Lawas (3hr), Sipitang (4hr 30min) and Beaufort (5hr 30min), and a Miri bus at 7am and 1pm (4hr). You seldom need to buy tickets in advance, but can do so either from bus conductors before departure, or from the *deRoy@lle C@fe* (see p.460). Indonesian buses run by Damri and SJS make the massive haul to Pontianak daily at 2.30pm and 4pm respectively (24–28hr). Both pass through Sarawak's main cities, but can't set passengers down in Malaysia, for which you will have to catch a bus to Miri and change if you want to continue west. Ticket agents

---

BRUNEI RIVER TRIPS

Most Bandar tour operators (see opposite) offer guided half-day trips on the Brunei River that take in **Kampung Ayer**. Unfortunately the tours tend to be pricey, starting at B$85/person, and, in Kampung Ayer at least, they show you little that you can't see on your own, though most include tea and cakes at one of the houses. Where such trips come in handy is in combining Kampung Ayer with the chance to see **proboscis monkeys**. If you were in Kuching or Kota Kinabalu, the nearest groups of the monkeys would be a long excursion away in Bako or the Garama River, so it's incredible that here in Bandar they can be found a mere twenty minutes' boat ride upriver from the centre, beyond the royal palace in a sliver of woodland and mangrove hemmed in between a residential neighbourhood and the river. The best time of day to see them is around 8am or 5pm, when it's cooler and the monkeys come out to forage.

It's perfectly possible to arrange a river trip **independently**: village boatmen hang around at the jetty area at the western end of Jalan McArthur, close to the *Fratini's* restaurant, which is also where the tour boats leave from. The boatmen won't proffer life jackets or slick commentary (and may not speak that much English), but they charge much less than a tour company: with some bargaining, reckon on around B$20 per hour for one person, and B$5 per person after that for up to eight. Note that it will take at least an hour to have a reasonable go at spotting the monkeys (depending if there's a queue to enter the mangroves) and enjoy a quick spin around Kampung Ayer. Another advantage of arranging your own trip is that you can ask to be let off elsewhere along the river later – after monkey-spotting first thing in the morning, possible places to visit include Bubongan Duabelas and the Handicrafts Centre (see p.454).

can be found above the bus station and, across the elevated concrete link, on the same level in the building on the north side of Jalan Cator.

By boat The only boats that serve Bandar itself, to and from Bangar in the Temburong district, use a jetty on Jalan Residency close to the Kianggeh food court (every 30min 6.45am–5.15pm; 50min; B$6). All international ferries use the terminal in Muara (see p.462).

GETTING AROUND

Nowhere in Bandar's compact centre is more than a 20min walk from anywhere else, but you'll probably use the city's modest **bus** system to reach outlying attractions and the suburbs.

BY BUS

Bus station On the ground floor of Kompleks Darussalam on Jalan Cator.

Routes Most domestic buses are compact, purple 22-seater vehicles, and operate only between 6am and 6.30pm. There is a bus map in the tourist office's guide, though it's only slightly useful – a coloured "line" gives a general idea where each bus might be heading, but you must note the route number for your destination and ask around in the bus station. On average there are two buses an hour on each route (popular services such as #1A to Gadong and #39 to Muara via the Kota Batu museums might run every 15–20min).

Fares and stops A standard fare of B$1 covers any journey within and even quite far out of Bandar. Outside the city centre, designated stops may be thin on the ground, but drivers halt anywhere convenient.

Intertown buses Painted in colours other than purple, a handful of buses serve Tutong (1hr) and Seria (1hr 30min), generally leaving the bus station every 1–2hr until 4pm or so. For Kuala Belait, change at Seria. While many buses head out beyond the city limits, no services run to Temburong.

BY TAXI

Ranks and companies Taxis come into their own at night, when the bus network has shut down, but are relatively rare – many people can afford cars. While there are a couple of taxi cooperatives (☎ 222 2214 or ☎ 222 6853), most drivers work independently and can only be summoned by mobile phone; hotels keep lists of favourites. In downtown Bandar, there's a taxi rank outside the Jalan Cator bus station. Taxis show up sporadically at suburban malls too, though they can be so scarce in Gadong that you may have to ask a hotel there to book one.

Fares Taxis aren't metered, so get an idea of current fares from your hotel; reckon on B$8–15 between the centre and nearby suburbs. Prices rise by fifty percent after dark.

BY WATER-TAXI

Routes and access Little speedboats plying the Brunei River, known as water-taxis, are fun for whizzing around the river, but of limited use since most of the few waterside attractions are perfectly walkable. You can attract the attention of a boatman at numerous jetties and steps leading down to the river and Kianggeh canal (by Tamu Kianggeh).

Fares The fare for any journey along the central stretch of the river is B$1.

BY CAR

Car rental Avis, at the *Radisson* hotel (☎ 222 7100); Hertz, at the airport (☎ 233 2983); Qawi in Gadong on Jalan Penghubung Berakas Lambak Kanan (☎ 265 5550).

INFORMATION

Tourist offices Brunei Tourism (ⓦ bruneitourism.travel) run offices at the airport and the Kampung Ayer Tourism and Culture Gallery (both Mon–Thurs & Sat 9am–5pm, Fri 9–11.30am & 2–5pm; closed public holidays and in the afternoon during Ramadan; ☎ 220 0874). Both supply maps and brochures, but little else. Tourism Malaysia (Mon–Thurs & Sun 9am–5pm, Fri 9–11.30am & 2–5pm,

Sat 10am–5pm; ☎ 238 1575) is on the first floor of the *Rizquan International* in Gadong (see p.458).

Internet access Most hotels have internet access and wi-fi, as does the *deRoy@lle C@fe* and adjacent rivals.

Newspapers Local English newspapers such as the *Borneo Bulletin* and *Brunei Times*, inevitably filled with news about the royal family, offer useful leads on events and new venues.

TOUR OPERATORS

Although Bandar's expensive tour operators major in rather predictable city tours, Ulu Temburong trips and river excursions, they also offer a few destinations that are awkward to visit independently, notably **Selirong Island** in Brunei Bay – a great spot for birding – and the **Bukit Peradayan Forest Reserve** on the eastern edge of Temburong (the latter is also sometimes included in Temburong packages).

Borneo Guide Unit 5, second floor, Plaza Al-Abrar, Simpang 424a, Gadong ☎ 242 6923, ⓦ borneoguide.com.

Fairly standard offerings, with two notable exceptions. The first is a day-trip out to Berambang Island in the Brunei

River estuary (B$115) for an unexpected slice of rural Brunei, including a short jungle trek to a hilltop for great views, and a visit to a water village. The other is a longhouse visit near Labi that includes a walk into primary rainforest (B$165).

Freme Travel 403b Wisma Jaya, Jalan Pemancha ☎ 223 4280, ⓦ freme.com. The usual destinations, plus trips to Selirong Island and out to the Seria oil field (see p.465).

Intrepid Tours First floor, Brunei Malay Teachers'

Federation Building, Jalan Sungai Kianggeh ☎ 222 1687, ⓦ bruneibay.net. The chance to snorkel and fish in Brunei Bay is one of their more unusual trips.

Sunshine Borneo 2 Simpang 146, Jalan Kiarong ☎ 244 1791, ⓦ exploreborneo.com. Veteran company with a comprehensive portfolio of packages, featuring such destinations as the Bukit Peradayan Forest Reserve, which they combine with visits to nearby modern longhouses for B$119, or trekking up the hill to nearby Bukit Patoi Forest Reserve for B$114.

ACCOMMODATION

Brunei not being backpacker territory, Bandar holds no great **budget** options, though the city has an adequate array of hotels. Some visitors prefer to stay outside Bandar, commuting in for the sights – certainly feasible, though it won't save you any money and you'll have to head out well before sunset if you're using public transport. The obvious out-of-town place to stay is the lavish *Empire* (see p.463), though it's possible to base yourself in **Seria** or even Bangar in **Temburong**. All hotels have wi-fi unless otherwise stated.

DOWNTOWN

★ Brunei 95 Jalan Pemancha ☎ 224 4828, ⓦ thebruneihotel.com. The nicest and best-value place in the centre, transformed from a dowdy lump of 1960s concrete into a well-run business-oriented hotel. All rooms have beautiful timber flooring and stylish modern fittings, though there's no discount for singles. Free shuttle transport to and from Gadong for the shops and night market. Rates include breakfast. B$140

Jubilee Jalan Kampung Kianggeh ☎ 222 8070, ⓦ jubileehotelbrunei.com. A dull concrete tower with somewhat cramped rooms and dated, slightly worn furniture. Weirdly, many of the supposedly en-suite bathrooms are actually just outside the rooms they belong to, though they do have bathtubs. Still, with rates including breakfast, it is inexpensive. B$85

K.H. Soon Rest House Third floor, 140 Jalan Pemanacha ☎ 222 2052. Archetypal Chinese-run flophouse, of a kind that's vanishing elsewhere. Rooms are large and have a/c, but are a bit tatty and bare, with rough cement floors, though some are en suite. Soundproofing isn't great either, and cleanliness could be better. At least the prices are good. They do actually have a six-bed dorm room, though they don't seem to like telling people. No wi-fi. Dorm B$20, doubles B$39, en-suite doubles B$45

Pusat Belia (Youth Centre) Jalan Sultan Kianggeh ☎ 222 2900. Used for student conferences, Bandar's youth centre features various dorms – single-sex, in line with

local values – that take travellers. Facilities include a small pool (B$1) and wi-fi, and there are plans for an internet café. Awkwardly, reception keeps standard office hours (Mon–Thurs & Sat 7.45am–4.30pm); at other times, call the manager using the number on display or hope to bump into a staff member. Dorms B$10

Radisson Jalan Tasek Lama ☎ 224 4272, ⓦ radisson .com. Brunei's first top-notch hotel, with a pool, spa, fitness centre and other amenities. A recent renovation has given it a new gloss, and lowered prices. Free shuttle-bus service to the shopping malls. B$150

Terrace Jalan Tasek Lama ☎ 224 3554, ⓦ terracebrunei .com. Ageing, like the *Jubilee*, but a slightly better deal, with larger rooms, an outdoor pool, and a fairly cheap multicuisine restaurant (mains B$4.50–7). Their advertising slogan, "Brunei's best value in hospitality", isn't far off. B$65

GADONG

Rizqun International Southeastern end of Abdul Razak Complex ☎ 242 3000, ⓦ rizquninternational .com. The priciest hotel in town, adjoining the Gadong Mall, with an ostentatious lobby featuring lots of marble and gaudy stained glass. Facilities include a pool and gym, and there are sometimes thirty percent weekend discounts. Not a bad deal if you get one of the regular promotional rates, which include breakfast. B$320

EATING

In a country where eating and shopping count as the main pastimes, Bandar has a good sprinkling of venues catering to both. There are inexpensive stalls downtown at **Tamu Kianggeh** and a stone's throw away at the so-called **Kianggeh food court** on Jalan Residency, the latter good for river views at dusk – however, both pale in comparison to those at Taman Selera and at **Gadong's pasar malam**. If Brunei has a national dish, it's **nasi katok**. Widely sold for as little as B$1 at stalls and in a few cheap diners, it's a more substantial answer to *nasi lemak* – featuring plain rather than coconut

OPPOSITE *EMPIRE HOTEL & COUNTRY CLUB (P.463)* >

rice, topped with a large joint of chicken or sometimes a helping of beef. Various tales explain the name (meaning "knock rice"), the most common being that hawkers devised it as a breakfast for people working night shifts, and used to knock on workplace doors in the morning to announce its arrival. Malay food doesn't dominate the culinary scene, however – there are plenty of Chinese and a few Indian options as well, plus a smattering serving Japanese and other international cuisines. A good **website** covering Brunei's restaurant scene is ⓦ lovefoodhatewaste.org.

DOWNTOWN

Choices Brunei Hotel, 95 Jalan Pemancha ☏ 224 4828, ⓦ thebruneihotel.com. The *Brunei Hotel's* coffee house is great for a Western-style breakfast – B$14.95 buys a buffet of sausage, beans, hash browns, cereals and so forth, with eggs and pancakes cooked to order, plus the usual local rice or noodle options. At other times they serve up a mixture of Western and Malaysian food. Daily 6–10.30am, 11.30am–2.30pm & 7–10pm.

DeRoy@lle C@fe Jalan Sultan ☏ 223 2519. This stands out among several cafés in the area as Bandar's most established hangout, with an extensive menu of so-so food: sub-style sandwiches, burgers and the like, free wi-fi and newspapers, plus two screens with BBC news, HBO movies and international sport. Not a bad place for breakfast – egg on French bread plus juice and coffee or tea, for example, only costs B$6. Daily 24hr.

★ **Fratini's** In a riverside block at the Yayasan Complex, Jalan McArthur ☏ 223 2555. Highly popular, *Fratini's* is an upmarket Italian chain with branches around the country. The food tends to be not bad rather than great, but the breadth of the menu compensates: a wide range of pizzas in three sizes (from B$12), plus pasta options (B$15) and more expensive mains such as sea bass with ratatouille (B$29). This riverside branch has a few tables outside with good views, and they'll deliver for free. Daily 10am–11pm.

Phongmun Second floor, Teck Guan Plaza, Jalan Sultan ☏ 222 9561. Downtown's best Chinese restaurant, predictably done out with temple-style red arches and dragons. Cantonese food is the order of the day, including dim sum in the mornings; otherwise the house specialities are braised pork leg eaten with buns (from B$20), and claypot chicken (B$14). The full menu runs to several pages, but you'll probably be given a cut-down version with no dish costing more than B$10. Daily 7am–10.30pm.

Syazwan Café 30a Jalan Sultan ☏ 233 0727. A cut above the area's other Indian Muslim *kedai kopis*, frying a full range of rice or noodle dishes to order (RM3 buys an ample portion), plus a good *nasi campur* spread, *thosai*, *murtabak*, very good *roti* and *nan* bread and even Chinese-style stir-fries. Daily 7.30am–9pm or so.

★ **Taman Selera** Off Jalan Tutong, close to the Terrace hotel. The most atmospheric downtown place for dinner, bar none, is this open-air food court, where dozens of stalls sell Malay food. *Ayam penyet* – tender barbecued chicken – is especially popular (try stall #7) and a couple of vendors sell satay and *nasi katok* too (around B$2–3.50). For

something a little pricier, head to the Mizu Seafood Village, where they have live lobster in tubs and other seafood, all sold by weight and cooked to order. Cheaper seafood stir-fries, fried rice and noodles are also available for around B$3.50–6 . Sit close to the stall you're ordering from. Daily 4.30–11pm.

★ **Tarindak d'Seni** Eastern end of the Arts and Handicrafts Centre complex, Jalan Residency ☏ 224 0422, ⓦ tarindakdseni.com. Despite the bland modern decor, this buffet restaurant serves a very impressive Malay spread; lunch costs B$15, dinner B$22; on Sundays, breakfast is B$8 and high tea B$12. Tables groan with dishes such as beef *rendang*, stir-fried *keladi* (yam greens), *ikan kicap* (fish stewed in soy sauce), all eaten with plain or *biriyani* rice. They also serve a classic Bruneian staple, *ambuyat* – sago starch, looking and smelling like congealed glue; tease it out of the bowl with chopsticks and eat it with sauces such as *tempoyak* (fermented durian). More palatably, they have Western salads and oodles of local and European cakes. Mon–Sat noon–2.30pm & 7–10pm, Sun 8–11am & 3–5pm.

GADONG

Excapade Sushi First floor, Block C, Abdul Razak Complex, north of the main drag ☏ 244 3012. Highly popular sushi chain with many branches in Bandar and around the country, thanks to reasonable prices and a menu that also includes a range of Japanese staples, such as sashimi and bento sets. Avoid the *unami*, however. Look at about B$10–20 and book ahead, especially at weekends. Daily 11am–2.30pm & 6–10.30pm.

Gadong Pasar Malam Just east across the canal from the Rizqun hotel. Many tourists trek out to Gadong for this entertaining night market. Besides a section selling fruit and vegetables, it has a few dozen stalls selling all manner of local snacks for B$1–3, including grilled chicken and fish, *kelupis* (glutinous rice, often stuffed with minced beef or prawns and steamed in the leaves of the *irik* plant) and the sweet crêpe *apam balik*. As ever with night markets, though, there's nowhere to sit. Daily 4.30–11pm.

★ **Thiam Hock** 5 Yong Siong Hai Building ☏ 244 1679. Nothing much to look at, but then the best Chinese restaurants are often like that. Revered by locals for its excellent fish head – curried, cooked in a spicy tamarind sauce, or chopped up with noodles. There's also a wide range of other seafood, plus the usual pork, veg and tofu; mornings are dominated by noodles (B$5.50), while most other non-seafood dishes start at B$8. To find the building, head south out of the Gadong Mall, for example using the exit by the Guardian pharmacy. Daily 8.30am–10.30pm. **TT Blues Café** 12 Yong Siong Hai Building ☎ 242 4527. This informal café-restaurant has big-screen soccer and is good for a cholesterol-raising mixed grill (B$10) and Western snacks, though they also have Malay options ranging from *rojak* to *cendol*, all around B$4–5. Especially busy at lunch and weekends. Tues–Sun 9am–2pm & 5–10pm, Fri 9am–noon & 2–10pm.

SHOPPING

Despite the population's healthy disposable incomes and attachment to shopping, Brunei's **malls** are disappointingly devoid of glitz – plenty of people drive across the border to **Miri** to shop, while the genuinely rich jet off to Singapore or Kuala Lumpur on a regular basis. **Opening hours** are curtailed during Ramadan, and individual shops in shopping centres keep their own hours.

Arts and Handicrafts Centre Jalan Residency ☎ 224 0676. The gift shop here is a great place to browse a wide selection of crafts, though anything really worth having – notably silverware and brocade – is priced in the hundreds of Brunei dollars. Mon–Thurs, Sat & Sun 9am–4.30pm, Fri 9–11.30am & 2.30–4.30pm.

Best Eastern Times Square Shopping Centre, Jalan Berakas, near the airport. The biggest selection of English books in town. Even here, though, any foreign titles about Brunei and its royal house – this Guide included – are likely to be impossible to find. Bus #23, #24, #36 or #38. Daily 9.45am–9.45pm.

Gadong Mall Abdul Razak development. While the sheer size of the Gadong Mall is impressive, its shops, mostly selling trinkets, phone accessories, cheap clothes and so on, are nothing special; the big name, such as it is, is the Utama Grand department store. Otherwise, it's more of a place where young people turn out to see and be seen. The paltry selection of English-language books in the ground-floor magazine shop is the best you can get anywhere close to central Bandar. Daily 10am–10pm.

Yayasan Complex South of Omar Ali Saifuddien mosque. A much earlier attempt to revive downtown Bandar than the revamped waterfront, this multibuilding mall is rapidly losing ground to its out-of-town rivals. The only outlet worth much of a look is the Hua Ho supermarket and department store. Daily 10am–9.30pm.

DIRECTORY

Banks There are several banks (Mon–Fri 9am–4pm, Sat 9–11am) downtown, notably HSBC at the corner of Jalan Sultan and Jalan Pemancha, plus Standard Chartered on Jalan Sultan.

Cinemas Your best bet is the The Mall Cineplex at Gadong Mall (☎ 242 2455, ☎ themallcineplex.com).

Embassies, consulates and high commissions Australia, DAR Takaful IBB Utama, Jalan Pemancha (☎ 222 9435); Canada, fifth floor, McArthur Building, Jalan McArthur (☎ 222 0043); Indonesia, Lot 4498, Simpang 528, Sungai Hanching Baru, Jalan Muara (☎ 233 0180); Malaysia, 61 Simpang 336, Kampong Sungai Akar, Jalan Kebangsaan (☎ 238 1095); Philippines, Simpang 336, Diplomatic Enclave, Jalan Kebangsaan (☎ 224 1465); Singapore, 8 Simpang 74, Jalan Subok (☎ 226 2741); Thailand, 2 Simpang 682, Kampung Bunut, Jalan Tutong (☎ 265 3108); UK, Unit 2.01, Block D, Complex Yayasan Sultan Hassanal Bolkiah (☎ 222 2231); US, Simpang 336-52-16-9, Jalan Kebangsaan (☎ 238 4616).

Hospital The RIPAS Hospital is near the centre on Jalan Tutong (☎ 224 2424). For an ambulance, call ☎ 991.

Pharmacies Guardian Pharmacy has outlets on Jalan Sultan and on the ground floor of Gadong Mall.

Police Central Police Station, Jalan Stoney (☎ 222 2333), or call ☎ 993.

Post office The GPO (Mon–Thurs & Sat 8am–4.30pm, Fri 8–11.30am & 2–4pm; ☎ post.gov.bn) is at the intersection of Jalan Elizabeth Dua and Jalan Sultan.

Visa extensions The Immigration Office is out towards the airport on Jalan Menteri Besar (Mon–Thurs & Sat 7.45am–12.15pm & 1.30–4.30pm; ☎ 238 3106, ☎ immigration.gov.bn; bus #1 or #24).

8

Muara district

As most of Brunei's natural attractions are in Temburong and Tutong, there's little to detain you in the capital's district, **Muara**. However, no visit to Brunei would be complete without checking out two eccentric attractions in **Jerudong** – the **Empire Hotel & Country Club** and the **Jerudong Park Playground**. Also worth a visit is **Muara Beach** and the **Bukit Shahbandar Forest Recreation Park**, a nature reserve with only the most basic facilities for visitors.

Muara

MUARA, Brunei's main port, 25km northeast of Bandar, has nothing else to recommend it other than **Muara Beach** 3km north, which boasts an adequate stretch of sand and a small food court; it's a long hot walk out here unless you want to wait for the erratic local minibus. You can wear your bikini on the beach, so long as it's under all your other clothes – everybody in the sea is fully clothed.

ARRIVAL AND DEPARTURE   MUARA

By ferry Brunei's international ferry terminal, a couple of kilometres south of what passes for the town centre, is served by bus #39 (hourly; 1hr) which stops on the main road at the green mosque, just under 1km from the terminal. The #33 minibus runs from Maura Beach via Maura town centre to the port, but it's request-only for the ferry terminal and so only really useful when departing. The latest boat departure schedules appear daily in the local English press.

Destinations Labuan (daily 7.30am, 8.30am, 9am, 1pm, 3.30pm & 4.30pm; 1hr 30min; passengers B$17, cars B$58–78); Lawas (daily 11.30am; 2hr; B$22).
By bus From Bandar, the most reliable buses for Muara are #38, which heads north to the airport and then east to Muara, and #39, which goes east to the Kota Batu museums and then north to Muara. The only bus to the beach is the #33 from Maura town centre.

Jerudong and around

The fishing village at **JERUDONG**, 15km northwest of Bandar, is a simple place where you can see the fishing boats pulled up on the beach, and sample smoked fresh fish in the wet market. Walking west along the beaches and through the car park will bring you to the **Empire Hotel & Country Club**, the big sight around here, while the **Bukit Shahbandar Park** is across the highway, and for the kiddies the **Jerudong Park Playground** is just 4km southwest.

Empire Hotel & Country Club

Close to Jerudong, 15km northwest of Bandar, off the Muara–Tutong Highway • ☎ 241 8888, ⊕ theempirehotel.com • Bus #57 may on request call at the hotel itself; if the driver refuses, get off on the highway and walk in (around 10min), or take a #55 to the fish market at Jerudong and walk in through the back entrance; a taxi from Bandar costs B$30

It might seem odd to traipse out of Bandar just to see a hotel, but then the **Empire Hotel & Country Club** is no ordinary hotel. A personal project in the 1990s of Prince Jefri, the wayward and discredited former finance minister, the complex cost US$1 billion to build and put such a drain on the state's coffers that the government had to take a stake in what had been intended as a private development.

The result, benefiting from the skills of thousands of craftsmen from assorted artistic traditions, is jaw-dropping. Just to stroll through the lofty central atrium with its 25m-high marble columns, is striking enough. Then there's the gold-plated balusters of the lobby staircase, laden with 370 tiger's eye gemstones, and the handrails coated with mother-of-pearl. Royal influence, of course, extends here; renovations can only go ahead once the designs are approved very high up. While the hotel doesn't really throw open its doors as a tourist attraction, it's vast enough that no one minds neatly dressed visitors who come to gawp and then, more often than not, eat at one of the restaurants. Very few of them smile much.

Bukit Shahbandar Forest Recreation Park

Along the Muara–Tutong highway, directly south of the Empire Hotel & Country Club • Free • Bus #57

The **Bukit Shahbandar Forest Recreation Park**, a compact area of acacia, pine and heath forest equipped with trails, carpets a hilly area with lookout points over the *Empire Hotel* complex, Bandar and the South China Sea. Marking the entrance to the park is an information centre with displays on the surrounding terrain. The trails are well signposted and popular with joggers, and there are a few rest huts for shade and shelter.

Jerudong Park Playground

Jerudong, south off the Muara–Tutong highway, 4km southwest of the Empire Hotel & Country Club • Wed–Fri & Sun 5–10.30pm, Sat 5pm–midnight • B$20, family pass B$40, foreigners must bring ID • ☎ 261 2044, ⓦ jpcc.com.bn • Bus #57

In its 1990s heyday, the **Jerudong Park Playground** was the wonder of Brunei, almost like the country's answer to the Tivoli Gardens in Copenhagen. Built by the government as an amusement park for the sultan's subjects, it was an essential stopover for visitors, the rides all totally free; famously, Michael Jackson and Whitney Houston played the park's theatre. Like all extravagances the place inevitably became uneconomic to maintain, even with Brunei's oil revenues, and it slowly descended into moribundity. Relaunched in 2014, albeit on a diminished scale, the park is worth a visit if you're in the area – but even the kids might think it a bit dated. It's most atmospheric in the evening; if using public transport, be sure to arrange a taxi in advance to collect you after the buses stop at sunset.

ACCOMMODATION AND EATING
JERUDONG AND AROUND

Empire Hotel & Country Club Near Jerudong ☎ 241 8888, ⓦ theempirehotel.com. The great thing about staying here is that while the high-ceilinged rooms, unlike the public areas, aren't exceptional for a five-star-type resort, rates can be very reasonable. A dive shop offers PADI courses, snorkelling and diving trips and watersports such as kitesurfing (☎ 261 2551, ⓦ thebananahutbrunei.com); other amenities include a golf course, spa, cinema, swimming pools and a private lagoon. **B$220**

Li Gong Empire Hotel & Country Club ☎ 241 8888, ⓦ theempirehotel.com. Housed in a separate building – look for the red lanterns outside – this is the best known of the *Empire*'s restaurants, serving halal Cantonese food, with dim sum available at lunchtime over the weekend. The crispy chicken is particularly well regarded. From B$20. Tues–Thurs 6.30–10.30pm, Fri & Sat 11am–3pm & 6.30–10.30pm, Sun 10.30am–2.30pm & 6.30–10.30pm.

Temburong district

With a population of just ten thousand, including some Iban and Lun Bawang (Murut), **Temburong district** is the wilds of Brunei. Forested and hilly, it contains Brunei's best-known attraction, the 500-square-kilometre **Ulu Temburong National Park**, with its entrancing canopy walkway. The park has limited possibilities for walks, though, so some people visit on a short day-trip from Bandar, while most opt for two-day packages.

Bangar

The starting point for all Ulu Temburong trips is the district's only town, **BANGAR**, normally reached by speedboat from Bandar (see p.457). The boats head downriver through narrow mangrove estuaries before shooting off into the open expanse of Brunei Bay and then curling back south to head up the Temburong River. It's also possible to drive here via Limbang in Sarawak, or catch the Kota Kinabalu bus from Bandar, which passes through at about 10am. The town itself is nothing to write home about; its main street, running east from the jetty to the town mosque, holds a handful of *kedai kopis* and general stores. However, it is the nearest town to the Ulu Temburong National Park, with much cheaper accommodation and tour operators that charge around half of what you'll pay in Bandar to visit it.

ACCOMMODATION
BANGAR

Bangar Government Resthouse Just off Jalan Puni on the road to Batang Duri ☎ 522 1239. A pretty, well-laid-out place two blocks behind the harbour across the main road, the *Resthouse* has just six en-suite singles and doubles as well as more expensive and comfortable chalets; they give priority to bookings by public-sector staff. Doubles **B$30**, chalets **B$80**

Ulu Temburong National Park

Park HQ daily 8am–6.30pm • Prebooked tours compulsory, park fees included in package price

Contained within the Batu Apoi Forest Reserve, which constitutes a tenth of the area of Brunei, the **Ulu Temburong National Park** undoubtedly impresses as a pristine nature area. There isn't that much to do – the only trails are simple and short – but there are some activities on offer and the park is great for peace and quiet.

Canopy walkway

The park's main attraction, the **canopy walkway**, is reached by an hour-long trek taking in two hanging bridges and a plankway, followed by a giddying climb up the stairs around a near-vertical, 60m-high aluminium structure. The view from the top, of Brunei Bay to the north and Sarawak's Gunung Mulu National Park to the south, is breathtaking. At this height (on a good day) you can see hornbills and gibbons in the trees, as well as numerous squirrels and small birds. Fifty species of birds have been sighted on the netting around the walkway, while flying lizards, frogs and snakes feed regularly at ground level.

ARRIVAL AND INFORMATION   ULU TEMBURONG NATIONAL PARK

From Bandar On a standard two-day package, the first day is spent reaching your accommodation from Bandar, and much of the second day given over to the park before you zip back to Bandar in the late afternoon. Tour operators also offer somewhat rushed day-trips at around B\$150/person.

From Bangar You may pay slightly less if you make your own way to Bangar and join a tour there, though you must still book in advance. From Bangar, van transport is laid on to the jetty at Batang Duri, 15km south. The final leg is via longboat, with dense jungle cloaking the hills on either side and birds and monkeys bustling around in the trees; though lasting less than an hour, the journey sets the tone for the park itself. You can also take day-trips from Bangar for B\$75.

Activities Besides the climb up to the canopy walkway, activities in and around the park include night walks, rafting or tubing down the river and treks to a nearby waterfall, each costing B\$10–30/person.

ACCOMMODATION

Freme Lodge Batang Duri, 30min by longboat from Temburong National Park ☎ 223 4277, ⓦ freme.com. A substantial, comfortable place (though pretty basic considering the price) with a/c dorms and a large open-air communal dining area. Rates include one night's stay, meals and transfers from Bandar. Two-day package per person B\$240

Sumbiling Eco Village Sumbiling Lama, the penultimate village before Batang Duri ☎ 242 6923, ⓦ borneoguide.com/ecovillage. Run as a joint venture with local Iban, this is a fairly simple jungle encampment with tents and three basic huts (B\$20 extra/person), though proper toilets are provided. In keeping with the eco theme, meals are eaten off leaves rather than plastic plates. Packages include a night walk in the vicinity. Rates include one night's stay, meals and transfers. Two-day package per person B\$245

Ulu-Ulu Resort Beside Ulu Temburong National Park HQ ⓦ uluuluresort.com. Run by tour operator Sunshine Borneo (see p.458), the only accommodation within the park is quite an upmarket affair, with seventeen en-suite rooms with sleek modern decor. The advantage of staying here, comfort aside, is that only resort guests can get to the canopy walkway at sunrise. Rates include one night's stay, meals and transfers. Two-day package per person (minimum two people) B\$315

Belait district

West of Muara, beyond the noticeably agricultural Tutong district, is **Belait district**, whose coastal section is oil and gas country, and has been the economic heart of the sultanate ever since the Seria oil field was established in 1931. The oil boom led directly to the rise of the region's two main towns, **Seria** and **Kuala Belait**, both still fairly sleepy, with generally ugly concrete centres that contrast with suburbs that have quite a rural feel. Inland, though, it's a much more rural story: down the 50km-long road to **Labi** are a few modern Iban **longhouses** and forest reserves to visit.

The Labi Road

No public transport, though Bandar tour operators such as Borneo Guide and Sunshine Borneo in Bandar offer trips here

More or less midway between Tutong and Seria, a turning south off the highway marks the start of the Labi Road. Just 500m on, the thick lowland forest of the **Sungai Liang Forest Reserve** can be explored by following various walking trails from the lakes. Twenty kilometres further along, at the **Luagan Lalak Forest Recreation Park**, a freshwater swamp swells into a lake with the onset of the monsoon rains. A little further on and you reach **LABI** itself, a small agricultural settlement where durian and rambutan are cultivated.

The road beyond turns into a laterite track; around 300m along, a trail off to the east leads, after two hours' walk, to **Wasai Rampayoh**, a large waterfall. Continue south on the track to reach **Mendaram Longhouse**, the first of several Iban communities here, and home to a few dozen people. Like most Iban architecture in Brunei, it's a modern structure, with electricity and running water. The people here can guide you to **Wasai Mendaram**, a small waterfall twenty minutes' walk away with a rock pool perfect for swimming.

Seria

SERIA, 65km southwest of Bandar, stands at the epicentre of Brunei's oil and gas wealth. Before oil was discovered here at the start of the twentieth century, this was nothing more than a malarial swamp, known locally as Padang Berawa, or "Wild Pigeon's Field". Once S1, the sultanate's first oil well, began to deliver commercially in 1931, Seria expanded rapidly, with offshore drilling following in the 1950s. As you approach from Tutong, you may see small oil wells called "nodding donkeys" because of their rocking motion. Around the town are numerous bungalows, constructed by petroleum companies for their employees, while on the seafront nearly 2km west of the centre the interlocking arches of the **Billionth Barrel Monument** celebrate the huge productivity of the first well. Bandar's tour operators can organize trips to oil-related sights, including the Oil and Gas Discovery Centre.

Oil and Gas Discovery Centre

750m northwest of the bus station • Tues–Thurs & Sat 8.30am–5pm, Fri 8.30–11.30am & 2–5pm, Sun 9.30am–6pm • B$5 • ⓦ bsp.com.bn/ogdc • From the bus station, head 500m north up Jalan Sultan Omar Ali, the road running west of the Plaza Seria mall, then 250m west; taxi B$15

Seria's only specific sight is the **Oil and Gas Discovery Centre**, a museum created by Brunei Shell to bolster understanding of technology in general and the petroleum industry in particular. With its interactive exhibits, it's a lot more entertaining than the similar museum not far away in Miri, though you still need more than a passing interest in oil extraction to get much out of it. It's somewhere that all Brunei school kids are forced to go at least once. There is also a small "town" where kids can zoom around in pedal cars, though it would be more apt (and fun) if the cars were petrol-driven.

ARRIVAL AND INFORMATION SERIA

By bus Seria's bus terminus is diagonally across from the bank, south of the mall.
Destinations Bandar (every 1–2hr until 4pm; 1hr 45min); Kuala Belait (every 30min–1hr; 45min); Miri

(daily, 9am & 3pm; 2hr).
Services There's a bank, HSBC, at the southern end of the drab Plaza Seria shopping mall, which dominates Seria's small centre.

ACCOMMODATION AND EATING

Hotel Koperasi Jalan Sherif Ali ☏ 322 7589, ✉ hotel _seria@brunet.bn. A dark green building just a minute's walk up Jalan Bunga Kemantin from the bus terminal, the *Koperasi* is dated in a somehow restful way, its simple rooms equipped with a/c, TV, fridge and bathroom. B$61
My Booney Below the Koperasi hotel, Jalan Sherif Ali

☏ 322 7061. This café bids to be Seria's community hangout by offering something for everyone – indeed, the menu runs to two tomes and it takes longer to read it than to eat your meal. With dishes from Chinese to Malay to Western to Indian, there's no shortage of choice, and the seafood is great value – meals B$2–5. Daily 6am–2am.

Singapore

473 Downtown Singapore

509 Central Catchment Nature Reserve

511 Kranji and Sungai Buloh

512 Geylang and Katong

514 Changi

515 The Southern Ridges and Pasir Panjang

517 Jurong

518 Sentosa

GARDENS BY THE BAY

9

Singapore

Singapore is certainly the handiest city I ever saw, as well planned and carefully executed as though built entirely by one man. It is like a big desk, full of drawers and pigeon-holes, where everything has its place, and can always be found in it.

William Hornaday, 1885

Despite the immense changes wrought upon the tiny island of Singapore, natural historian William Hornaday's appraisal is as valid today as it was in 1885. This absorbing city-state, just 1 degree north of the Equator and only 700 square kilometres in size – if all the outlying islands are included – has evolved from a colonial port into a slick shrine to wealth and consumerism.

Singapore began its rise in 1819, when the statesman Sir Stamford Raffles took advantage of the island's natural harbour and strategic position on the maritime route between China and India to set up a British trading post. The port thrived from the word go, and remains among the busiest in the world. The country's coffers were also boosted by **industrialization**, following independence and when in the 1980s Singapore grew too successful to remain a cheap sweatshop for multinationals, it maintained its competitive edge and kept the money flowing in by developing a super-efficient infrastructure and work ethic, and diversifying into technology and finance.

With its dynamism and lack of any significant welfare system, Singapore appears to be a paragon of capitalism, and enjoys a standard of living on a par with western Europe. Yet a huge slice of the economy is dominated by conglomerates that were set up by the state, which retains a controlling interest in them. At the core of Singapore's success is **paternalism**: the government manipulates the economy and society to deliver affluence, with the populace sacrificing some personal freedoms in return. There are regulations governing everything from flushing public toilets after use to jaywalking, and, less benignly, a low tolerance of **dissent**.

It's this unwritten contract that allowed kampungs and slums to be cleared and the historic parts of the city remodelled, with much of the population resettled in bland though well-planned new towns. Even today Singapore is dogged by a sense of impermanence, its modern complexes scarcely bedding down before being replaced by something even grander. But although Singapore is the most westernized of Southeast Asian cities, to dismiss it as sterile is unfair. As with Malaysia, much of Singapore's fascination springs from its **multicultural population**, the main groups being the Chinese (around 75 percent), Malays (13 percent) and Indians (9 percent). This diversity can turn a short walk across town into what seems like a hop from one country to another.

Getting a decent taste of the island – and there's plenty to see – requires at least three days. Each of the original ethnic enclaves boasts a fair amount of period architecture in the form of neatly restored shophouses, and retains its own distinct flavour: **Little India** has its garland-sellers and curry houses, **Chinatown** its calligraphers and fortune-tellers, while **Arab Street** is home to cluttered stores selling fine cloths and curios. At the core of downtown Singapore are historic public buildings and the lofty cathedral of the **Colonial District**. Old Singapore is looking better than ever thanks to belated

Sir Stamford Raffles p.477
The Singapore River p.478
Museum passes p.481
Taking Chinese tea p.501
Singapore addresses and maps p.526

Useful bus routes p.527
Organized tours p.529
Street ice cream p.540
Street theatre p.547

THIAN HOCK KENG TEMPLE, CHINATOWN

Highlights

❶ Little India Old Singapore's most atmospheric district is a sensory overload of Tamil temples, colourful saris and aromatic spice-grinding shops. **See p.485**

❷ Chinatown Heritage Centre The colour and the slums of the Chinatown of old are brilliantly recreated at this museum. **See p.492**

❸ The Buddha Tooth Relic Temple One of Singapore's newest temples is also one of its grandest, housing thousands of Buddha figurines, a sacred tooth and even its own Buddhist art museum and roof garden. **See p.493**

❹ The Baba House Singapore's answer to the fine showpiece Peranakan residences of Melaka and Penang. **See p.500**

❺ The Botanic Gardens A relaxed and distinguished park with an immaculate orchid collection and forest walks. **See p.508**

❻ Bukit Timah Reserve This pocket of primary rainforest offers a decent taste of the jungle, without the leeches. **See p.509**

❼ S.E.A. Aquarium This gargantuan affair revels in the marine life of Singapore's far-reaching maritime trade routes. **See p.521**

❽ Food Not for nothing does Singapore market itself as a foodie paradise – hundreds of restaurants serve up every style of Chinese cuisine, sophisticated fusion fare and more. **See p.534**

HIGHLIGHTS ARE MARKED ON THE MAP P.470

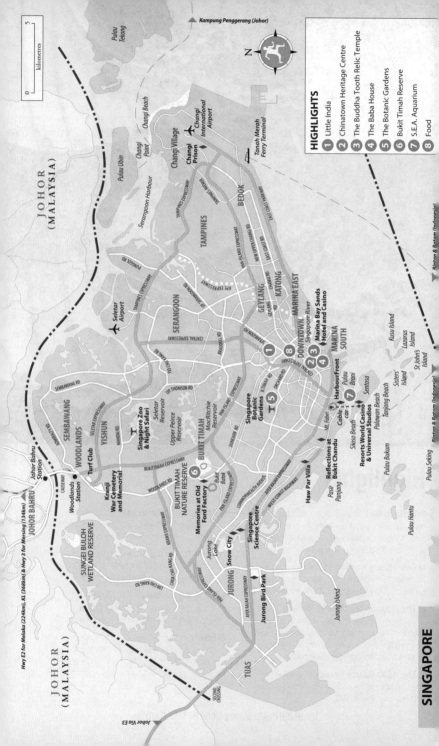

conservation work, and the country's heritage is manifest in a clutch of fine **museums**. The **National Museum** recounts Singapore's story from the fourteenth century onwards; the **Chinatown Heritage Centre** evokes the harsh conditions endured by Chinatown's earlier inhabitants; and the **Peranakan Museum** and **Baba House** celebrate Singapore's Baba-Nyonya community – just as important as that of Penang and Melaka.

There's much to enjoy by way of modern and, perhaps surprisingly, nature-oriented attractions too. The wings of reclaimed land around the mouth of the Singapore River, together forming **Marina Bay**, are the site of the striking **Marina Bay Sands** hotel and casino and the bug-eyed **Theatres on the Bay**. The latter have benefited from a huge investment in the **arts**; even on a short visit, you may well catch world-renowned performers in town. North of the city, there's primary rainforest to explore at **Bukit Timah Nature Reserve**; and the splendid **Singapore zoo**, which you can even tour at night. Should you want to venture away from the main island, the best offshore day-trip is south to **Sentosa**, the island amusement arcade that features Singapore's other casino resort.

Brief history

Little is known of Singapore's ancient history. Third-century Chinese sailors could have been referring to Singapore in their account of a place called Pu-Luo-Chung, or "island at the end of a peninsula". In the late thirteenth century, Marco Polo reported seeing a place called Chiamassie, which could also have been Singapore: by then the island was known locally as Temasek and was a minor trading outpost of the Sumatran Srivijaya Empire.

Throughout the fourteenth century, Singapura felt the squeeze as the Ayuthaya and Majapahit empires of Thailand and Java struggled for control of the Malay Peninsula. Around 1390, a Sumatran prince called **Paramesvara** threw off his allegiance to Majapahit and fled to present-day Singapore. There he murdered his host and ruled the island until a Javanese offensive forced him to flee further north, where he and his son, **Iskandar Shah**, subsequently founded the Melaka Sultanate; meanwhile, Singapore faded away into an inconsequential fishing settlement.

The country's present name is derived from one first recorded in the sixteenth century, when a legend recounted in the *Sejarah Melayu* (Malay Annals) told of how a Sumatran prince saw what he thought was a lion while sheltering on the island from a storm. He then founded a city here and named it **Singapura**, Sanskrit for "Lion City".

The British colony takes shape

By the late eighteenth century, with China opening up for trade with the West, the British East India Company felt the need to establish outposts along the Straits of Melaka. Enter **Thomas Stamford Raffles** (see p.477), lieutenant-governor of Bencoolen in Sumatra. In 1819, he stepped ashore on the north bank of the Singapore River accompanied by Colonel William Farquhar, former Resident of Melaka. At the time, swampland and jungle covered Singapore, and its population is thought to have been under a thousand. Raffles perceived the island's potential for providing a deep-water harbour, and immediately struck a deal to establish a British trading station with **Abdul Rahman**, the *temenggong* (chieftain) of Singapore and a subordinate of the Sultan of Johor.

The Dutch were furious at this British incursion into what they considered to be their territory. Raffles, realizing that the sultan's Dutch loyalties would make implementation of the deal impossible, simply recognized his brother, **Hussein**, as the new sultan. Raffles then concluded a second treaty with both Hussein and the *temenggong*. The Union Jack was raised, and Singapore's future as a trading post was set.

As early as 1822, Raffles set about drawing up the demarcation lines which can still be perceived in the layout of modern Singapore. The area south of the Singapore River was earmarked for Chinese migrants; while Muslims were settled around the sultan's palace in today's Arab Street area. In 1824, Hussein and the *temenggong* were bought

9

out, and Singapore was ceded outright to the British. Three years later, the new trading post was united with Penang and Melaka to form the **Straits Settlements**, which became a British Crown Colony in 1867.

Singapore consolidates

Thanks to its **strategic position** at the gateway to the South China Sea, Singapore grew meteorically. By 1860 the population had reached eighty thousand; Arabs, Indians, Javanese and Bugis all settled here, but most numerous of all were southern Chinese. The opening of the Suez Canal and advent of the steamship consolidated Singapore's position as a hub for international trade, a status further enhanced as the British steadily drew all of the Malay Peninsula into their clutches, allowing Singapore to profit from its hinterland's tin- and rubber-based economy.

By the 1920s, Singapore's communities were starting to find their voice: in 1926, the Singapore Malay Union was established; as was the Malayan Communist Party four years later, largely backed by local Chinese. But rumblings concerning greater self-rule were barely audible when an altogether more immediate problem reared its head.

World War II

In December 1941, the **Japanese** bombed Pearl Harbour and invaded the Malay Peninsula; less than two months later they were at the Causeway between Johor and Singapore. "Fortress Singapore" had not been prepared for an attack from the north – Singapore's artillery was pointed south, from what is now Sentosa Island. On February 15, 1942, the **fall of Singapore** was complete. Winston Churchill called the surrender "the worst disaster and the largest capitulation in British history". Three and a half years of brutal Japanese rule ensued, during which upwards of 25,000 Chinese men were shot dead at Punggol and Changi beaches as enemies of the Japanese, and Europeans were either herded into **Changi Prison** or marched up the Peninsula to work on Thailand's infamous "Death Railway".

Independence

After the war, Singaporeans demanded a say in the island's administration, and in 1957 the British agreed to establish an elected legislative assembly. Full internal self-government was achieved in 1959, when the **People's Action Party** (PAP) emerged on top in elections. Cambridge law graduate **Lee Kuan Yew**, Singapore's first prime minister, quickly sought security via a merger with newly independent Malaya (now Peninsular Malaysia). In 1963 Singapore joined with Malaya, Sarawak and British North Borneo (now Sabah) to form the **Federation of Malaysia**, but within two years Singapore was asked to leave (see p.565).

Things looked bleak for the tiny, newly independent island. But Lee's personal vision and drive transformed Singapore into an Asian economic heavyweight, and enabled his party to utterly dominate Singapore politics to this day. The media was treated in a heavy-handed fashion, and the government's attitude towards **political opposition** was even more disturbing. When the Workers' Party won a by-election in 1981, the newly elected MP J.B. Jeyaretnam found himself charged with several criminal offences, and was pursued through the Singapore courts for the next decade. In more recent times the few successful opposition candidates have, similarly, found themselves in court over apparent affronts to the government's probity.

New leaders

Goh Chok Tong became prime minister in 1990 upon Lee's retirement – though many felt that Lee still called the shots in his new role as senior minister. In 2004, Goh was succeeded by **Lee Hsien Loong**, Lee Kuan Yew's son, and on the very same day the elder Lee was named "minister mentor", a new cabinet position that gave him an official high horse from which to influence affairs. However, while the younger Lee had a sternness reminiscent of his father, Singapore was already becoming less uptight before his tenure began, and the trend continued. This new climate may be linked to the government loosening its reins in order to foster enterprise and creativity, and to lure back the many Singaporeans who have emigrated. One spin-off was a more relaxed attitude to artistic expression and also to the gay community. But the most startling expression of the city-state's evolving character was to come in the 2011 polls.

The 2011 election

On the face of it, the government's schemes had been going swimmingly in the run-up to the elections. A massive project to turn Marina Bay into a freshwater **reservoir** (to reduce dependence on Malaysian water) was completed, as was the contentious venture to build two casinos – or so-called "**integrated resorts**" – in the face of much public hand-wringing over the introduction of large-scale **gambling**.

However, the island, heavily reliant on banking, suffered its worst-ever recession in 2008, in the wake of the global financial crisis. Though it soon bounced back, losses by the state's investment arms caused some to re-examine the government's record. This came against a backdrop of ongoing challenges for ordinary people, with inflation outstripping the derisory interest offered by Singapore banks and healthcare costs rising. The government's fairly open stance on **immigration** – part of a strategy to keep Singapore attractive to global business – was a talking point too, though not out of racism, as many of the new arrivals hail from China and India just as Singapore's own citizens once did. Many Singaporeans saw migrants as taking jobs from them right across the income spectrum, and there was some resentment over the building of luxury apartments to tempt the super-rich. Even the government's much-vaunted water-management schemes came under scrutiny in the wake of more than one **flash flood** on Orchard Road, Singapore's prime shopping street.

When the island went to the polls in May 2011, the opposition took 6 out of the 87 parliamentary seats, with the foreign minister among government casualties. This was a minor political earthquake for a country where the opposition had consisted of a measly one or two seats for decades and Lee Kuan Yew gave up his cabinet post in the aftermath. While the political status quo is unlikely to change any time soon, it seems that as this city-state enters its fiftieth year of independence in August 2015, activism is no longer a dirty word for many of its citizens; they will be demanding a greater say in the country's economic and social affairs in the years to come.

Downtown Singapore

The southern part of the diamond-shaped main island is **downtown Singapore**, essentially the historic city centre. It's easy to navigate, given the excellent transport network, though individual districts are best explored on foot. You need at least two days to do justice to the main areas, namely the **Colonial District**, **Chinatown**, **Little India** and the **Arab Quarter**, though three days would be more sensible – especially if you want to have a quick look around the **Financial District** or **Marina Bay Sands**, or go shopping in **Orchard Road**.

The Colonial District

City Hall, Raffles Place, Esplanade or Bras Basah MRT

On the north bank of the Singapore River is what might be called the **Colonial District** – although locals might refer to it as the Civic District or use the names of landmarks, notably the **Padang**. This rectangular green expanse is flanked by dignified reminders of British rule, including the erstwhile Parliament House, City Hall and what's now the Asian Civilizations Museum. This being Singapore, modernity makes its presence felt amid these echoes of the past: the *Swissôtel* towers

9

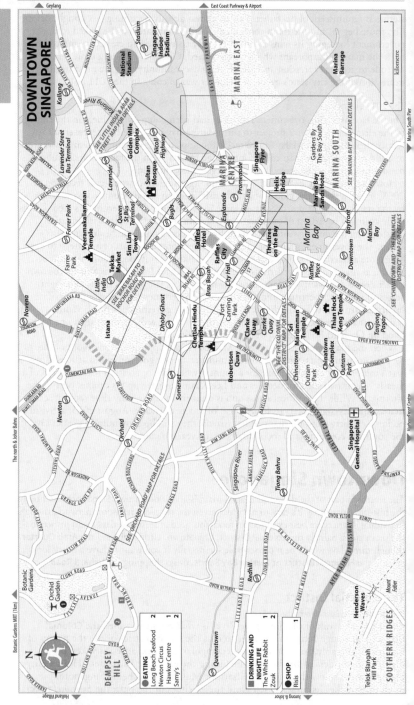

DOWNTOWN SINGAPORE

EATING
Long Beach Seafood	2
Newton Circus Hawker Centre	1
Samy's	2

DRINKING AND NIGHTLIFE
The White Rabbit	1
Zouk	2

SHOP
Risis	1

to the north on Stamford Road; to the east in the **Marina Centre** area (see p.505) sit the ultramodern Theatres on the Bay and the glorified Ferris wheel that is the Singapore Flyer; and to the south of these are the arresting *Marina Bay Sands* and the spires of the **Financial District** (see p.501). The river itself was once the epicentre of Singapore's trade boom; today, its old warehouses are all trendy nightspots. Come in September, and you'll see crash barriers and fences sprouting in both the Colonial District and Marina Centre, where the main roads form the racetrack of Singapore's night-time **Formula One Grand Prix**.

The Padang

City Hall, Esplanade or Raffles Place MRT

The **Padang**, earmarked by Stamford Raffles as a recreation ground shortly after his arrival, is the very essence of colonial Singapore. Its borders have never been encroached upon by speculators and so it remains much as it was in 1907, when G.M. Reith wrote the following in his *Handbook to Singapore*: "Cricket, tennis, hockey, football and bowls are played on the plain…beyond the carriage drive on the other side is a strip of green along the sea-wall, with a foot-path which affords a cool and pleasant walk in the early morning and afternoon." Once the last over of the day had been bowled, the Padang assumed a more social role: Singapore's European community would hasten to the corner once known as Scandal Point to catch up on the latest gossip.

The brown-tiled roof, whitewashed walls and green blinds of the **Singapore Cricket Club**, at the southwestern end of the Padang, have a nostalgic charm. Founded in the 1850s, the club was the hub of colonial British society and still operates a "members only" rule. (Eurasians, formerly ineligible for membership due to the prejudices of the time, founded their own establishment in 1883: the **Singapore Recreation Club**, at the opposite end of the Padang.)

The National Gallery (Old Supreme Court and City Hall)

1 & 3 St Andrew's Rd • ⓦ nationalgallery.sg • City Hall or Raffles Place MRT

On the Padang's west side are two of the most imposing colonial edifices on the island which, in late 2015, should be open as one even grander building – Singapore's gigantic new **National Gallery**.

On the left is the former **Supreme Court**, identifiable by its dome, topped with green lead. Built in Neoclassical style in the 1930s, it replaced the exclusive *Hotel de L'Europe* – whose drawing rooms allegedly provided Somerset Maugham with inspiration for many of his Southeast Asian short stories. It was then itself replaced in 2006 by the **New Supreme Court** behind on North Bridge Road (designed by Norman Foster, with an unmistakable flying-saucer-like upper tier).

To the right of the old Supreme Court is **City Hall**, which has witnessed momentous events in the island's history. It was on its steps, backed by grandiose Corinthian columns, that Louis Mountbatten, supreme allied commander in Southeast Asia, announced Japan's surrender in 1945. Fourteen years later, Lee Kuan Yew chose the same spot for his address at a victory rally celebrating self-government for Singapore.

Both buildings have undergone a complete refit to create the new gallery, showcasing local and regional art, plus major international travelling exhibitions. Resource centres and historical exhibits occupy some of the old courtrooms and government departments, while a roof terrace offers terrific views over much of the district.

The parliament buildings

1 Old Parliament Lane and 1 Parliament Place • Details of how to witness debates at ⓦ parliament.gov.sg • Raffles Place or City Hall MRT

A dignified white Victorian building, the **Old Parliament House** was originally the home of a rich merchant, designed by Singapore's pre-eminent colonial architect, the Irishman George Drumgoole Coleman. The bronze elephant at the front was a gift to

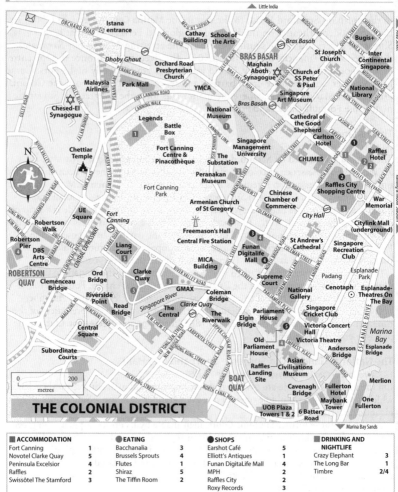

THE COLONIAL DISTRICT

ACCOMMODATION		● EATING		● SHOPS		■ DRINKING AND NIGHTLIFE	
Fort Canning	1	Bacchanalia	3	Earshot Café	5	Crazy Elephant	3
Novotel Clarke Quay	5	Brussels Sprouts	4	Elliott's Antiques	1	The Long Bar	1
Peninsula Excelsior	4	Flutes	1	Funan DigitaLife Mall	4	Timbre	2/4
Raffles	2	Shiraz	5	MPH	2		
Swissôtel The Stamford	3	The Tiffin Room	2	Raffles City	2		
				Roxy Records	3		

Singapore from King Rama V of Thailand (upon whose father *The King and I* was based) after his visit in 1871. Relieved of its legislative role in 1999, the building now holds a contemporary arts centre called **The Arts House**, including a café stocking literature, DVDs and so forth by home-grown talent. Backing onto the building is the rather soulless new **Parliament House**, where parliamentary business is now conducted, and which faces North Bridge Road.

Victoria Concert Hall and Victoria Theatre

11 Empress Place • Ⓦ vtvch.com • Raffles Place or City Hall MRT

Opposite the Singapore Cricket Club are two more fine examples of colonial architecture, the **Victoria Theatre** and, to the right, the **Victoria Concert Hall** (also called the Victoria Memorial Hall). The former was completed in 1862 as Singapore's town hall, while the concert hall was added in 1905. Having been closed for renovations lasting several years, both venues are once again being used for prestigious cultural events.

SIR STAMFORD RAFFLES

Fittingly for a man who was to spend his life roaming the globe, Thomas Stamford Raffles was born at sea on July 6, 1781, aboard the *Ann*, whose master was his father Captain Benjamin Raffles. By the age of 14, the young Raffles was working as a clerk for the **East India Company** in London, his schooling curtailed because of his father's debts. Even then, Raffles' ambition and self-motivation were evident: he studied through the night with a hunger for knowledge that would spur him on to learn Malay, amass a collection of natural history treasures and write his two-volume *History of Java*.

In 1805 he was chosen to join a team going out to Penang, then being developed as a British entrepôt. Once in Southeast Asia, he enjoyed a meteoric rise and by 1807 he was named chief secretary to Penang's governor. In 1810, Raffles was appointed secretary to the Governor-General in Malaya, quickly followed by his appointment as **governor of Java** in 1811. Raffles' rule of Java was libertarian and compassionate, his economic, judicial and social reforms transforming an island bowed by Dutch rule.

Java was handed back to the Dutch in 1816 – much to Raffles' chagrin. He was transferred to the governorship of **Bencoolen** in Sumatra, and arrived in 1818. There, he found time to study its flora and fauna, discovering the incredible *Rafflesia arnoldii* (see box, p.586) on a jungle trip. By now, Raffles strongly believed that Britain should establish another base in the Straits of Melaka. In 1819 he sailed to the southern tip of the Malay Peninsula, where his securing of Singapore early that year was a daring coup in the face of local and Dutch opposition.

For a man inextricably linked with Singapore, Raffles spent remarkably little time there. His last visit was in 1822; by August 1824, he was back in England. Awaiting a possible pension from the East India Company, he busied himself founding **London Zoo** and setting up a farm in what is now northwest London. But the new life he had planned never materialized. Days after he heard that a Calcutta bank holding £16,000 of his capital had folded, his pension application was refused; worse still, the Company was demanding £22,000 for overpayment. Three months later, on July 4, 1826, the brain tumour that had caused him headaches for several years took his life. He was buried in Hendon with no memorial tablet – the vicar had investments in West Indian slave plantations and was unimpressed by Raffles' friendship with the abolitionist William Wilberforce. Only in 1832 was Raffles commemorated, by a statue in Westminster Abbey.

During the Japanese occupation, the concert hall's clock tower was altered to Tokyo time, while the **statue of Raffles** that stands in front of it narrowly escaped being melted down. It was sent to the National Museum, where the newly installed Japanese curator valued it enough to hide it, claiming it had been destroyed. A copy can be seen staring towards the Financial District at Raffles' **landing site**, where, in January 1819, the great man apparently took his first steps on Singapore soil.

Asian Civilizations Museum

1 Empress Place, north side of Cavenagh Bridge · Sat–Thurs 10am–7pm, Fri 10am–9pm · S$8, or S$11 for joint ticket with Peranakan Museum; Fri after 7pm S$4 · ☎ 6332 7798, ⓦ acm.org.sg · Raffles Place or City Hall MRT

A robust Neoclassical structure, the **Empress Place Building** was named after Queen Victoria and completed in 1865. It has seen service as a courthouse and as government departments, but it now houses the fine **Asian Civilizations Museum**, tracing the origins and growth of Asia's many cultures, from the Middle East to China (in particular). In the small Malay World section, look out for a spectacular Kelantan *makara*, a huge goggle-eyed mongrel creature once used in Hindu rituals, while elsewhere there are Dayak masks from Borneo, *kerises* from Indonesia, Hmong garments from Laos and so forth.

A slight misfit here – though apt, given the museum's location – is the excellent **Singapore River gallery**. There are displays of sampans and other river craft, and a diorama of a timber dwelling for coolies that recalls the grim lodging houses that once featured in London's docklands. But best of all are oral history clips featuring people who once worked on and lived by the river.

9

THE SINGAPORE RIVER

Little more than a creek, in the nineteenth century the **Singapore River** became the main artery of Singapore's growing trade, and was clogged with **bumboats** – traditional cargo vessels the size of houseboats, with eyes painted on their prows as if to look where they were going. The boat pilots ferried coffee, sugar and rice to warehouses called **godowns**, where coolies loaded and unloaded sacks. In the 1880s the river itself was so busy it was practically possible to walk from one side to the other without getting your feet wet. Of course **bridges** were built across it as well, and most of them are endearingly old-fangled to look at now, apart from the massive new Esplanade Bridge at the river's mouth.

Walking beside the river today, all sanitized and lined with trendy restaurants and bars, some occupying the few surviving godowns, it is hard to imagine that in the 1970s this was still a working river. It was also filthy, occasioning a massive clean-up campaign that moved the river's commercial traffic west to Pasir Panjang within the space of a few years; it led to the river's current status as one of the leading nightlife centres of Singapore.

RIVER TOURS

You can get a view of the city at river level on tours in tarted-up versions of bumboats. There are two broadly similar options, taking in Clarke Quay, Boat Quay and Marina Bay: the **Singapore River Experience** (daily 9am–10.30pm; 3–4 hourly; S$22; 40min; ☎6336 6111, ⓦ rivercruise.com.sg); and the **River Explorer** (daily 9am–10.30pm; 2 hourly; S$22; 40min; ☎6339 6833, ⓦ riverexplorer.sg). On the former, you board at any one of several ticket booths along the route; on the latter, you must buy tickets and board at the riverside close to the *Novotel Clarke Quay* hotel. More prosaically and much more cheaply, it's also possible to ride the **river taxi** service, although you will need an ez-link card for this (see p.526).

Cavenagh Bridge

Raffles Place or City Hall MRT

Cavenagh Bridge, with its elegant suspension struts, is one of the Singapore River's historic bridges, linking the Padang with Boat Quay and Raffles Place in the Financial District. Named after Major General Orfeur Cavenagh, governor of the Straits Settlements from 1859 to 1867, the bridge was constructed in 1869 by Indian convict labourers using imported Glasgow steel. A sign still maintains: "The use of this bridge is prohibited to any vehicle of which the laden weight exceeds 3cwt and to all cattle and horses." Nowadays the bridge takes only pedestrians. From its north side you can take in a quintet of towers on the south bank: the grey-and-blue metallic sliver of the Maybank Tower, the clean, white Bank of China, wedge-shaped Six Battery Road, and finally the two UOB Plaza towers.

St Andrew's Cathedral

11 St Andrew's Rd; Visitor Centre on North Bridge Rd • Mon–Sat 9am–5pm; free volunteer-led 20min tours Mon, Tues, Thurs & Fri 10.30am–noon & 2.30–4pm, Wed 2.30–4pm, Sat 10.30am–noon • ☎6337 6104, ⓦ livingstreams.org.sg • City Hall or Esplanade MRT

The Anglican **St Andrew's Cathedral** is the most distinguished of a clutch of nineteenth-century churches north of the Padang, their steeples dwarfed by most buildings around them. Built in high-vaulted Neo-Gothic style using Indian convict labour, it was consecrated on January 25, 1862. The exterior walls were plastered using Madras *chunam* – an unlikely composite of eggs, lime, sugar and shredded coconut husks which shines brightly when smoothed – while the small cross behind the pulpit was crafted from two fourteenth-century nails salvaged from the ruins of England's Coventry Cathedral after it was razed to the ground during World War II.

Raffles City

City Hall or Esplanade MRT

Raffles City, a huge development that sits beside the intersection of Bras Basah and North Bridge roads, north of the cathedral and Padang, comprises two hotels – one of which is the 73-storey **Swissôtel** – as well as floor upon floor of offices and shops. Completed in 1985, the complex was designed by Chinese-American architect I.M. Pei – the man behind the glass pyramid that fronts the Louvre in Paris – and required the controversial demolition of the Raffles Institution, a school established by Stamford Raffles and built in 1835 by George Drumgoole Coleman. Once a year, athletes compete to run all the way up to the top floor (ⓦswissotelverticalmarathon.com); the current record stands at under seven minutes.

The War Memorial

Esplanade or City Hall MRT

The open plot east of Raffles City is home to four 70m-high white columns. They are nicknamed "the chopsticks" but are actually the **Civilian War Memorial**, commemorating those who died during the Japanese occupation. Beneath it are bodily remains, reinterred from unmarked wartime graves around the island.

Raffles Hotel

1 Beach Rd • ☎ 6337 1886, ⓦ raffleshotel.com • Esplanade or City Hall MRT

Across the way from what was, for a time, the world's tallest hotel is one of the world's most famous. The lofty halls and peaceful gardens of the legendary **Raffles Hotel**, almost a byword for colonialism, prompted Somerset Maugham to remark that it "stood for all the fables of the exotic East". If you're not staying here, the best way to glimpse the place is by dining at one of its restaurants or treating yourself to a Singapore Sling in the *Long Bar* (for the princely sum of S$32).

History of the hotel

Raffles Hotel opened for business on December 1, 1887. The hotel's heyday was during the first three decades of the twentieth century, when it established its reputation for gracious luxury – it was the first building in Singapore with electric lights and fans. In 1902, a little piece of Singaporean history was made at the hotel, according to an apocryphal tale, when the last tiger to be killed on the island was shot inside the building. Bartender Ngiam Tong Boon created another *Raffles* legend, the **Singapore Sling** cocktail, in around 1910. Over the years, the hotel has hosted many a politician and film star, but it is proudest of its **literary connections**. Hermann Hesse, Rudyard Kipling, Noël Coward and Günter Grass all stayed here, and Somerset Maugham is said to have written many of his Asian tales under a frangipani tree in the garden.

Following the Japanese takeover of the island in 1942 the hotel became a Japanese officers' quarters, then briefly a transit camp for liberated Allied prisoners in 1945. Postwar deterioration earned it the affectionate but melancholy soubriquet "the grand old lady of the East", and the hotel was little more than a shabby tourist diversion when the government finally declared it a national monument in 1987. An expensive and contentious four-year facelift and extension followed, which added a mundane shopping arcade on North Bridge Road, although it restored the original hotel's air of bygone elegance.

Hill Street

A couple of blocks west of the Padang, **Hill Street** leads south along the eastern side of Fort Canning Park to the river. The brash building at no. 47 with a striking pagoda roof is the **Singapore Chinese Chamber of Commerce**, dating from 1964, though remodelled since. Along its facade are two large panels, each depicting intricately crafted porcelain dragons flying from the sea up to the sky.

Church of St Gregory the Illuminator

60 Hill St • Daily 9am–6pm • ⓦ armeniansinasia.org • City Hall or Bras Basah MRT

One of the most appealingly intimate buildings in downtown Singapore, the Armenian

9

Church of St Gregory the Illuminator was designed by George Drumgoole Coleman and completed in 1835, which ranks it among the country's oldest buildings. The white circular interior, fronted by a marble altar and a painting of the Last Supper, includes a framed photo of the few dozen Armenians who lived in Singapore in 1917, for whom the tiny church would have been room enough. Among the handful of graves in the tranquil garden is the tombstone of Agnes Joaquim – a nineteenth-century Armenian resident of Singapore – after whom the national flower, the delicate, purple *Vanda Miss Joaquim* orchid, is named; she discovered it in her garden and had it registered at the Botanic Gardens.

Central Fire Station

Junction of Coleman and Hill streets • Galleries Tues–Sun 10am–5pm • Free • City Hall or Bras Basah MRT

The splendid red-and-white-striped **Central Fire Station**, built in 1908, sports a central watchtower that was once the tallest structure in the area, a perfect vantage point for spotting blazes early. Today it's partly given over to the **Civil Defence Heritage Galleries**, tracing the history of firefighting in Singapore. Of more interest than the displays – restored vintage fire engines and the like – are the accounts of historic fires in Singapore. At Bukit Ho Swee, in 1961, a blaze ripped through a district of *atap* huts and timber yards, destroying sixteen thousand homes. The disaster led directly to a public housing scheme that would ultimately spawn the island's numerous new towns.

Freemasons' Hall

23a Coleman St, directly behind the Central Fire Station • City Hall or Bras Basah MRT

Recently given a fresh lick of paint, Singapore's compact **Freemasons' Hall** features a proud Palladian facade bearing the masonic compass-and-square motif. The building dates from the 1870s and remains in use, although part of it is now given over to a trendy restaurant. It's worth noting that Stamford Raffles himself was apparently a mason.

Peranakan Museum

39 Armenian St, just west of Hill St • Sat–Thurs 10am–7pm, Fri 10am–9pm • S$6, or S$11 joint ticket with the Asian Civilizations Museum (see p.477); Fri after 7pm S$3 • ☎ 6332 7591, ⊕ peranakanmuseum.sg • City Hall or Bras Basah MRT

A beautifully ornamented three-storey building that started out in 1910 as the Tao Nan School – Singapore's first school to cater for new arrivals from China's Fujian province – now houses the **Peranakan Museum**. It honours a culture which, in its own way, is to Singapore, Malaysia and Indonesia what Creole culture is to Louisiana. The museum should whet your appetite for not only the Baba House (see p.500) but also the Peranakan heritage of the Katong area (see p.512).

The diversity of the Peranakans comes through in the first gallery, which includes video interviews with members of Melaka's small **Chitty** community, a blend of Tamil, Chinese and Malay. Thereafter the galleries concentrate on the **Baba-Nyonyas**, the Peranakans of Singapore, displaying their possessions – theirs was always largely a material culture – and educating us in their customs, in particular the traditional twelve-day **wedding**. Memorable displays include the classic entrance into a Peranakan home: a pair of *pintu pagar* (tall swing doors), overhung with lanterns; look out also for artefacts such as beautiful repoussé silverware, including "pillow ends", coaster-like objects used for some reason as end-caps for bolsters.

National Museum

93 Stamford Rd • Reopens late 2015; contact the museum directly for opening times and prices • ☎ 6332 3659, ⊕ nationalmuseum.sg • Bras Basah, Dhoby Ghaut or City Hall MRT

An eye-catching dome on Stamford Road, seemingly coated with silvery fish scales, marks the **National Museum of Singapore**, to give it its full title. A major redevelopment in the mid-2000s transformed the Neoclassical building into a superb modern museum that used multimedia and oral history to capture the sometimes bittersweet story of

MUSEUM PASSES

For S$20 (or S$50 for a group of five), you can buy a three-day pass valid for, and available from, the National Museum (see opposite), the Asian Civilizations Museum (p.477), the Peranakan Museum (opposite), the Singapore Art Museum (p.484), the wartime museum Reflections at Bukit Chandu (p.516), and the minor Philatelic Museum.

Singapore's rise. In 2014 the museum was abruptly put through another revamp to tie in with the island's 50th anniversary of independence celebrations in 2015, and the contents are being kept hush-hush. It's likely that the new museum will maintain its excellent multimedia emphasis, while continuing to display artefacts such as the mysterious **Singapore Stone** (all that survives of an inscribed monolith that stood near where the *Fullerton* hotel is today) and beautiful gold jewellery excavated at Fort Canning and thought to date from the fourteenth century. The previous museum did not shy away from the ambiguities of Singapore's path to prosperity, touching on the loss of old traditions and more contentious issues such as the island's postwar politics, and it's to be hoped that its replacement does the same.

Fort Canning Park

No formal hours; numerous entrances, including steps on Hill St or via the back of the National Museum • Guided walk leaflets from information point on River Valley Rd, opposite the Liang Court Shopping Centre, or at Ⓦ nparks.gov.sg • Fort Canning MRT (when open), or Bras Basah, Dhoby Ghaut or Clarke Quay MRT

When Raffles first caught sight of Singapore, **Fort Canning Park** was known as Bukit Larangan (Forbidden Hill). Malay annals tell of the five ancient kings of Singapura who ruled the island from here six hundred years ago, and unearthed artefacts prove it was inhabited as early as the fourteenth century. The last of the kings, Sultan Iskandar Shah, reputedly lies here, and it was out of respect for – and fear of – his spirit that the Malays decreed the hill forbidden. Singapore's first Resident, William Farquhar, displayed typical colonial tact by promptly erecting a bungalow on the summit. It was replaced in 1859 by a fort named after Viscount George Canning, Governor-General of India, but only a gateway, guardhouse and adjoining wall remain today. Fort Canning Park offers a welcome respite from Singapore's crowded streets and is packed with shady, mature trees (which, unfortunately, also tend to put paid to panoramic views over the Singapore River).

Pinacothèque Singapore

Fort Canning Centre, behind the National Museum • Opens mid-2015; see website for times and prices, Ⓦ pinacotheque.com.sg

The **Fort Canning Centre**, up a grassy slope from the National Museum, is a surprisingly grand former British barracks – now home to the Asian outpost of the privately run Paris art museum **Pinacothèque**. It aims to emulate its parent gallery, which has shaken up the French art world with a high-profile collection of greats such as Monet, Rembrandt and Modigliani – the gallery's owner is a Modigliani specialist – as well as temporary exhibitions with boundary-crossing appeal.

The underground bunker just above the Fort Canning Centre houses the **Battle Box**, a ticketed animatronics-based exhibition of wartime events in what was the British command centre before Singapore fell. Recently closed for a revamp, it should be open again in mid- to late 2015.

Raffles Terrace

South side of Fort Canning Park

Just left of the Fort Canning Centre, there is a *keramat* (auspicious place) on the supposed site of Iskandar Shah's grave, which attracts a trickle of local Muslims. Continue round the hill and you meet the staircase from Hill Street at **Raffles Terrace**, where there are replicas of a colonial flagstaff and a lighthouse – the hill was the site of a working lighthouse that functioned up until the middle of the last century.

9

Along River Valley Road

Fort Canning Park's southern boundary is defined by **River Valley Road**, which skirts below the park from Hill Street. At the corner with Hill Street is the **MICA Building**, with shuttered windows in bright colours. Formerly the Hill Street Police Station, it is now home to the Ministry of Communications and Information, as well as the Ministry of Culture, and its central atrium houses several galleries majoring in Asian artworks.

GMAX

Daily 2pm till late • S$45 • ☎ 6338 1766, ⓦ gmax.com.sg • Clarke Quay MRT

Hill Street meets the Coleman Bridge over the Singapore River, next to which is a theme-park-style ride called **GMAX** that looks like an alien war machine, all gantries and cables. Billed as a "reverse bungy", it's a metal-and-glass pod suspended from cables, allowing screaming thrill-seekers within to be tossed around in the air for several minutes at a time.

Clarke Quay

3 River Valley Rd • ⓦ clarkequay.com.sg • Clarke Quay MRT

Painted in gaudy colours and housing flashy eating and nightlife venues, the nineteenth-century godowns of **Clarke Quay** feel about as authentic as the translucent plastic canopy that shelters them; nearby Boat Quay (see p.499) feels homelier even when at its busiest. Further up River Valley Road is **Robertson Quay**, offering more of the same although generally quieter.

Chettiar Temple

15 Tank Rd • Daily roughly 8.30am–12.30pm & 5.30–8.30pm • Free • ☎ 6737 9393, ⓦ sttemple.com • Bus #143 from Orchard Rd or Chinatown

Just west of Fort Canning Park and close to Robertson Quay is what is still generally known as the **Chettiar Temple** (its official name being the Sri Thendayuthapani Temple). The shrine, with a large, attractive *gopuram*, was built in 1984 to replace a nineteenth-century temple constructed by Indian *chettiars* (moneylenders) and is dedicated mainly to the Hindu deity Lord Murugan. It's also the destination of every participant in the procession that accompanies the annual Thaipusam Festival (see p.488).

Bras Basah Road to Rochor Road

Bras Basah, City Hall, Dhoby Ghaut or Bencoolen/Rochor (when open) MRT

Bras Basah Road – the main thoroughfare between Orchard Road and what would have been the seafront – is so named because rice arriving on cargo boats used to be brought here to be dried (*beras* [modern spelling] *basah* means "wet rice" in Malay). The zone between it and **Rochor Road** at the edge of Little India has a transitional sort of feel, sitting as it does between the Colonial District and two of Raffles' "ethnic" enclaves to the northeast. The aptly named Middle Road, running smack through the centre of the grid, was originally meant to mark the Colonial District's northern edge.

Despite modernization, the area still boasts some long-established places of worship and is another focus for the visual and performing **arts**. City planners have turned many distinguished old properties on and around **Waterloo Street** over to arts organizations, including the **Singapore Art Museum**, and lured the country's leading institutes in the field here, among them the Nanyang Academy of Fine Arts (**NAFA**) on Bencoolen Street; the **Lasalle College of the Arts**, whose futuristic glass buildings under a translucent canopy between McNally Street and Albert Street deserve a look; and the **School of the Arts**, in an imposing new building next to the Cathay cinema.

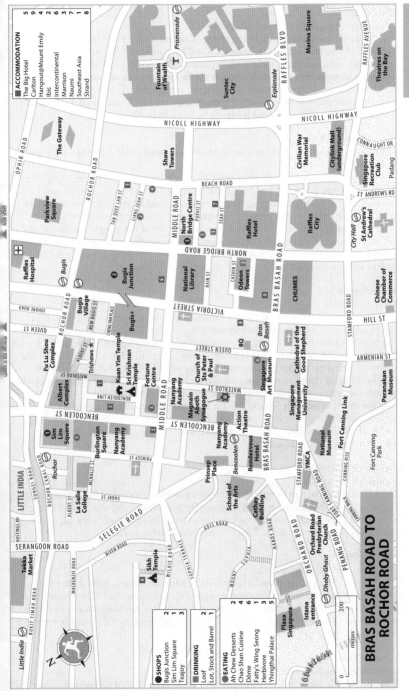

BRAS BASAH ROAD TO ROCHOR ROAD

ACCOMMODATION
The Big Hotel	5
Carlton	9
Hangout@Mount Emily	4
Ibis	2
Intercontinental	6
Marrison	3
Naumi	7
Southeast Asia	1
Strand	8

SHOPS
Bugis Junction	2
Sim Lim Square	1
Teajoy	3

DRINKING
Loof	2
Lot, Stock and Barrel	1

EATING
Ah Chew Desserts	2
Chao Shan Cuisine	4
Dome	6
Fatty's Wing Seong	1
Herbivore	3
Yinghthai Palace	5

metres 0   200

9

CHIJMES
30 Victoria St • ⓦ chijmes.com.sg • City Hall, Bras Basah or Esplanade MRT

The restored Neo-Gothic husk of the former Convent of the Holy Infant Jesus is now a complex of bars and restaurants named **CHIJMES** (pronounced "chimes"). Complete with courtyards, fountains and a sunken forecourt, it appeals particularly to expats and tourists, although for some locals it still sticks in the craw that planners allowed what had been one of the area's historic schools to be repurposed like this. A relic from the building's original role survives at the **Gate of Hope** on its Victoria Street flank, where local parents once left unwanted babies to be taken in by the convent.

Singapore Art Museum
71 Bras Basah Rd • Sat–Thurs 10am–7pm, Fri 10am–9pm • S$10, free Fri 6–9pm • ☏ 6589 9580, ⓦ singaporeartmuseum.sg • Bras Basah, City Hall or Dhoby Ghaut MRT

The **Singapore Museum** might seem to lack a *raison d'être* after the grand arrival of the National Gallery (see p.475), although the official word is that the museum will continue to focus on challenging, contemporary East Asian art. Whatever the exhibits might be, the setting in the former St Joseph's Institution, Singapore's first Catholic school, certainly impresses. The cloisters and silvery dome last rang to the sound of school bells in 1987, but many of the original rooms survive, among them the chapel (now an auditorium), whose Stations of the Cross and mosaic floor remain intact. The gallery also has an annexe, **8Q**, around the corner at 8 Queen St.

Waterloo Street
Bras Basah or Bugis MRT

Head up Waterloo Street from the Art Museum and you almost immediately come to the peach-coloured **Maghain Aboth Synagogue**, looking like a colonial mansion despite the Stars of David on the facade. The surrounding area was once something of a Jewish enclave – another building midway along nearby Selegie Road bears a prominent Star of David – though the Jewish community, largely of Middle Eastern origin, never numbered more than about a thousand. Dating from the 1870s, the synagogue can be visited, though only by prior arrangement (enquire on ☏ 6337 2189).

At the intersection with Middle Road is **Sculpture Square**, based around a tiny chapel built in the 1870s that housed the Christian Institute, where residents could debate and read about their faith. Today, its grounds and interior gallery space feature modernist works by local artists.

Sri Krishnan Temple
152 Waterloo St • ☏ 6337 7957

In 1870 the **Sri Krishnan Temple** was nothing more than a thatched hut containing a statue of Lord Krishna under a banyan tree. The present-day shrine is a good example of Southeast Asian religious harmony and syncretism in action, with worshippers from the nearby Buddhist Kwan Im Temple sometimes praying outside.

Kwan Im Temple
178 Waterloo St • Daily 6am–6.30pm • ☏ 6337 3965

The best-known sight on Waterloo Street is the **Kwan Im Temple**, named after the Buddhist goddess of mercy. The current version dates only to the 1980s – hence its rather slick, palatial appearance – and draws thousands of devotees daily; it can be filled to overflowing during festivals. Fortune-tellers and religious artefact shops operate in a little swarm just outside.

Albert Street
Northern end of Waterloo St, close to Rochor Rd

Intersecting Waterloo Street is **Albert Street**, which in the 1960s looked not unlike

Jalan Alor in Kuala Lumpur does now: lined with shophouses and stalls legendary for their street eating. Today it's been so remodelled that much of it isn't even shown on some maps. It is worth a stroll, however, if only to gaze at the zigzagging glass facades of the **Lasalle College of the Arts** near the street's northern end, or to check out the **market** that stays open into the evening around the junction with Waterloo Street, selling everything from potted plants to mobile phone cases. Albert Street is also the starting point for touristy **trishaw** excursions (see p.529).

Bugis Village and Bugis Junction

Bugis (pronounced "boogis") **Street**, the southern extension of Albert Street, was one of the most notorious places in old Singapore, crawling with rowdy sailors, prostitutes and ladyboys by night. The street was duly cleared, partly to build the Bugis MRT station and partly because it was anathema to the government. In its place today is **Bugis Village**, a bunch of stalls and snack vendors lining two covered alleyways. It's hardly the Bugis Street of old, though it does recapture something of the bazaar feel that the island's markets once had. Amid the T-shirt sellers, at least one outlet sells sex toys – once unthinkable in Singapore – and the only obvious link to the area's seedy past.

Across Victoria Street from here is another throwback to the past, the **Bugis Junction** development. Entire streets of shophouses have been gutted, scrubbed clean and then encased under glass roofs as part of a modern shopping mall and hotel, the *Intercontinental*.

Little India

Little India, Farrer Park or (when open) Jalan Besar MRT • Note that buses to Serangoon Rd return via Jalan Besar

Of all Singapore's historic quarters, the most charismatic has to be **Little India**. Indian pop music blares out from speakers outside cassette shops; the air is perfumed with incense, curry powder and jasmine garlands; Hindu women parade in bright saris; and a wealth of restaurants serve up excellent, inexpensive curries.

That Little India has kept its identity better than any other old quarter is in no small way down to the migrant Tamil and Bangladeshi men who labour to build new MRT stations, shopping malls and private villas. On Sundays they descend on Little India in their thousands, making the place look like downtown Chennai or Calcutta after a major cricket match. The district's backbone is **Serangoon Road**, one of the island's oldest roadways, dating from 1822; the account below starts from Tekka Market, next to Little India MRT, and then covers the side roads off Serangoon Road in stretches. The best time of year to visit is in the run-up to **Deepavali** (Oct or Nov) when much of Serangoon Road is festooned with festive lighting and special markets are set up in the open space beyond the Angullia Mosque (opposite Syed Alwi Road) and on Campbell Lane, which sell decorations, garlands and Indian sweets.

Tekka Market

Southwestern end of Serangoon Rd • Little India MRT

Tekka Market is a must-see, combining many of Little India's commercial elements under one roof. It's best to arrive in the morning when the wet market is at its busiest. Halal butchers push around trolleys piled high with goats' heads, while at seafood stalls live crabs, their claws tied together, shuffle in buckets. Look out also for a couple of stalls selling nothing but banana leaves, used to serve up the curry meals you'll probably enjoy at some point during your stay. Talking of food, the hawker centre here is excellent, and although the same can't be said of the mundane outlets upstairs selling Indian fabrics and household items, there are great views over the wet market to be had from above.

Buffalo Road

Buffalo Road, along the northern side of Tekka Market, sports a few provisions stores with sacks of spices and fresh coconut, ground using primitive machines. Its name, and

9

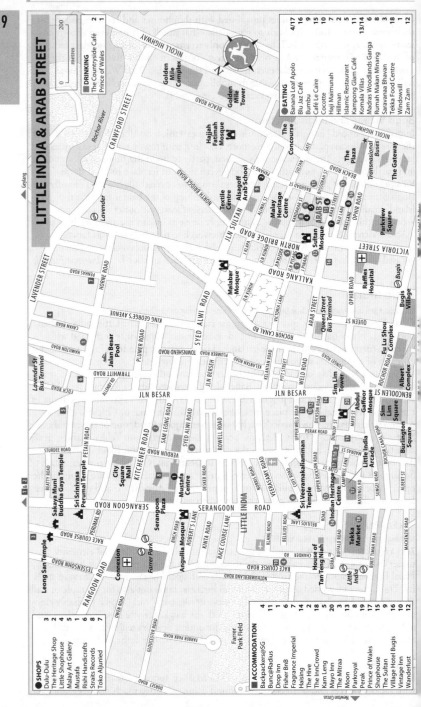

LITTLE INDIA & ARAB STREET

0   metres   200

SHOPS

Dulu-Dulu	3
The Heritage Shop	2
Little Shophouse	4
Malay Art Gallery	5
Mustafa	1
Rishi Handicrafts	6
Straits Records	8
Toko Aljunied	7

ACCOMMODATION

Backpackers@SG	4
Bunc@Radius	11
Drop Inn	1
Fisher BnB	6
Fragrance Imperial	7
Haising	14
The Hive	2
The InnCrowd	18
Kam Leng	5
Mayo Inn	20
The Mitraa	3
Moon	13
Parkroyal	8
Perak	19
Prince of Wales	17
Shophouse	15
The Sultan	9
Village Hotel Bugis	16
Vintage Inn	10
Wanderlust	12

DRINKING

The Countryside Café	2
Prince of Wales	1

EATING

Banana Leaf Apolo	4/17
Blu Jaz Café	16
Bumbu	9
Café Le Caire	15
Cocotte	10
Haji Maimunah	7
Hillman	2
Islamic Restaurant	5
Kampong Glam Café	11
Komala Villas	13/14
Madras Woodlands Ganga	6
Rumah Makan Minang	8
Saravanaa Bhavan	3
Tekka Food Centre	18
Windowsill	1
Zam Zam	12

that of neighbouring Kerbau ("buffalo" in Malay) Road, recall the latter half of the nineteenth century when **cattle and buffalo yards** opened in the area, luring more Indians in search of work and swelling the population.

Kerbau Road

Kerbau Road is notable for its meticulously renovated shophouses and for being, like Waterloo Street 1km south, a designated "arts belt", home to several creative organizations. Curiously, the road itself has been split into two parts with a pedestrianized bit of greenery in the middle. Here, at no. 37, you can't miss the gaudily restored **Chinese mansion**, built by one Tan Teng Niah, a confectionery magnate, in 1900 and now used as commercial premises. Look out also for the traditional picture framer at no. 57, packed with images of Hindu deities.

Sri Veeramakaliamman Temple

141 Serangoon Rd, just beyond Belilios Lane • ☎ 6295 4538, ⓦ sriveeramakaliamman.com • Little India MRT

Recently refurbished, the **Sri Veeramakaliamman Temple** is the most prominent shrine on Serangoon Road and just as worthwhile as the rather more famous Sri Mariamman Temple in Chinatown. The temple is dedicated to Kali, the Hindu goddess of power or energy, and beyond the gaudy lion-flanked *gopuram* is an equally gaudy *mandapam* (worship hall) housing several depictions of her with ten arms. Some have blue skin and fangs, while others show her apparently trampling on her husband Lord Shiva, recalling an episode from the Hindu scriptures.

Hastings Road to Cuff Road

Across Serangoon Road from the Tekka Market, the **Little India Arcade** is a lovingly restored block of shophouses bounded by Hastings Road and Campbell Lane. It's a sort of Little India in microcosm: behind pastel-coloured walls and green shutters you can purchase textiles and tapestries, bangles, religious statuary, Indian sweets, tapes and CDs, and even traditional Ayurvedic herbal medicines. Exiting the arcade onto **Campbell Lane** places you opposite the riot of colours of the Jothi flower shop, where staff thread jasmine, roses and marigolds into garlands for prayer offerings. The outsized building with a facade of glass hexagons at the corner with Clive Street is the new **Indian Heritage Centre**, currently under construction; it will house performance venues and some small-scale museum displays.

Dunlop Street

Dunlop Street is defined by beautiful **Abdul Gaffoor Mosque** at no. 41 (daily 8.30am–noon & 2.30–4pm), whose green dome and bristling minarets have enjoyed a comprehensive and sympathetic renovation in the last few years. Surrounded by gardens of palms and bougainvillea, its cream interior walls decorated with stars and crescent moons, the mosque features an unusual sundial whose face is ringed by elaborate Arabic script denoting the names of 25 Islamic prophets. A couple of streets along is **Cuff Road**, where a traditional spice grinder can still be seen at no. 2, though it's mainly open at weekends.

Rowell and Desker roads

Both Rowell and Desker roads mark a noticeable shift from the South Indian flavour of much of Little India: Bengali features prominently on some shops signs, and at weekends the streets are thronged with Bangladeshi migrants. However, both roads have another claim to fame – or infamy – as they have long been synonymous in Singapore with vice. Along the backs of the shophouses between the two roads is an alleyway where the doorways are illuminated at night. Here gaggles of bored-looking prostitutes sit indoors watching TV, seemingly oblivious to the men gathered outside who mostly appear inclined to merely observe them, as though treating the whole thing as some kind of street entertainment.

9

Syed Alwi Road to Petain Road

Little India takes on a more Islamic feel around **Syed Alwi Road**, across from which is the Angullia Mosque at its northern end, but the road is better known for being the hub of the shopping phenomenon that is the Mustafa Centre. Known just as "Mustafa" to locals, it's an agglomeration of department store, moneychanger, travel agent, jeweller, fast-food joint and supermarket, much of the place open 24/7. The business somehow grew from modest beginnings into a behemoth, occupying two interlinked buildings of its own, as well as part of the Serangoon Plaza on the main road. You'll probably find it more appealing than most places on Orchard Road, as you rub shoulders with Indian families seeking flown-in confectionery from Delhi, Chinese and Malay shoppers wanting durian fruit or pots and pans, even African businessmen buying consumer goods that are hard to find at home.

Sam Leong Road is home to some surviving **Peranakan shophouses** decorated with stags, lotuses and egrets. There's more Peranakan architecture a few blocks north on **Petain Road**, where the shophouses have elegant ceramic tiles reminiscent of Portuguese *azulejos*.

Sri Srinivasa Perumal Temple

397 Serangoon Rd • Daily 6.30am–noon & 6–9pm, though it may be possible to visit at other times • ☏ 6298 5771 • Farrer Park MRT

Little India more or less comes to an end at Rangoon and Kitchener roads, but it's worth continuing up Serangoon Road to see two very different temples. Dating from the late nineteenth century, though rebuilt in the 1960s, the **Sri Srinivasa Perumal Temple** has an attractive five-tiered *gopuram* with sculptures of the various manifestations of Lord Vishnu the preserver. On the wall to the right of the front gate, a sculpted elephant trumpets silently, its leg caught in a crocodile's mouth. But the temple's main claim to fame is as the starting point for the annual **Thaipusam** festival (see p.45), when devotees leave the temple in procession, pausing only while a coconut is smashed at their feet for good luck, and parade all the way to the Chettiar Temple on Tank Road (see p.482).

Sakaya Muni Buddha Gaya Temple

366 Race Course Rd • Daily 8am–4.30pm • Farrer Park MRT

Just beyond the Sri Srinivasa Temple, a small path leads northwest to Race Course Road, where the slightly kitsch **Sakaya Muni Buddha Gaya Temple** betrays a strong Thai influence – which isn't surprising as it was built by a Thai monk. On the left of the temple as you enter is a huge Buddha's footprint, inlaid with mother-of-pearl, and beyond it a 15m-high Buddha ringed by a thousand electric lights. Twenty-five dioramas depicting scenes from the Buddha's life decorate the pedestal on which he sits. It is possible to walk inside the statue, through a door in its back; inside is yet one more diorama, depicting the Buddha in death. One wall of the temple features a sort of wheel of fortune, decorated with Chinese zodiac signs. To discover your fate, spin it (for a small donation) and take the numbered sheet of paper that corresponds to the number at which the wheel stops.

Arab Street (Kampong Glam)

Bugis or Nicoll Highway MRT

Before the arrival of Stamford Raffles, the area of Singapore south of the Rochor River held a Malay village known as Kampong Glam, possibly named after a type of tree (the *gelam*) that grew there. After signing the dubious treaty with the newly installed "Sultan" Hussein Mohammed Shah, Raffles allotted the area to him and designated the land around it as a Muslim settlement. Soon the zone was attracting Malays, Sumatrans and Javanese, as well as Hadhrami Arab traders from what's now eastern Yemen, as road names such as Arab Street, Baghdad Street, and Bali Lane suggest. Now the Arab community, descended from those Yemeni traders, is thought to number around

15,000, though they are something of an invisible minority, having intermarried into Singapore society and being resident in no particular area.

Sadly, gentrification is fast diluting the Islamic and Malay character of the district – still referred to as **Kampong Glam** or just **Arab Street**. Slick upstart restaurants, many serving alcohol (to the chagrin of some locals), have displaced many old textiles stores and curry houses. Nevertheless it's worth spending at least a couple of hours wandering the area's lanes, with the **Sultan Mosque** and the **Malay Heritage Centre** being the two obvious sights.

Arab Street

The little shophouses of **Arab Street** and surrounding lanes have a cosiness and intimacy that's more Georgetown than the Lion City. Textile and carpet stores are most prominent, and you'll also see leather, basketware, gold, gemstones and jewellery for sale; the pavements of Arab Street in particular are an obstacle course of merchandise. It's easy to spend a couple of hours weaving in and out of the stores, but some traders are masters of persuasion and will have you loaded with sarongs and whatnot before you know it.

Haji Lane and Bali Lane

South of Arab Street, **Haji Lane** and tiny **Bali Lane** – the latter petering out into the wide walkway next to Ophir Road – have traditional shops rubbing up against trendy boutiques; in the evenings and at weekends DJs set up informally to spin dance music on Haji Lane. It's one of Singapore's most organic enclaves, but it's also clear that the split-personality fundamental to the area's appeal is fast swinging toward the chichi.

Incidentally, it's worth taking a brief look at the **Parkview Square** office building just across from here on North Bridge Road. Though the tower is only a decade old, its styling just screams 1930s Art Deco (à la Batman's Gotham City). When it was built, great care was taken to site it dead between the two razor-blade-like towers of **The Gateway**, the I.M. Pei-designed development one block south – for the sake of feng shui, of course.

Sultan Mosque

3 Muscat St • Sat–Thurs 9.30am–noon & 2–4pm, Fri 2.30–4pm • Free • ☎ 6293 4405, ⓦ sultanmosque.org.sg • Bugis MRT

On the eastern side of North Bridge Road (though the best views of its golden domes are from pedestrianized Bussorah Street to the east), the **Sultan Mosque** or Masjid Sultan is the beating heart of the Muslim faith in Singapore. An earlier mosque stood on this site, finished in 1825 and constructed with the help of a donation from the East India Company. The present building was completed a century later to a design by colonial architects Swan and MacLaren. Look carefully at the base of the main dome and you'll see a dark band that looks like tilework, though it actually consists of the bottoms of thousands of glass bottles.

Bussorah Street itself is home to some worthwhile souvenir outlets, though the restaurants are taking over. During the Muslim fasting month, neighbouring **Kandahar Street** is awash with stalls of the **Ramadan bazaar** from mid-afternoon, selling *biriyanis*, *murtabak*, dates and cakes for consumption by the faithful after dusk.

The Malay Heritage Centre (Istana Kampong Glam)

Sultan Gate • Tues–Sun 10am–6pm • S$4 • ☎ 6391 0450, ⓦ malayheritage.org.sg • Bugis or Nicoll Highway MRT

Between Kandahar and Aliwal streets, the colonially styled **Istana Kampong Glam** was built as the palace of Sultan Ali Iskandar Shah, son of Sultan Hussein who negotiated with Raffles to hand Singapore over to the British. Until just a few years ago the house was still home to the sultan's descendants, though it had fallen into disrepair. Then the government acquired it together with the similar, smaller yellow house in the same grounds, which belonged to the heirs of a wealthy merchant.

9

The yellow house now hosts an attempt at a posh Malay restaurant, while the istana has been dressed up as the overly slick **Malay Heritage Centre**, one of the few Singapore museums that misses its mark. The best displays celebrate the rural boat-building and fishing lifestyle of yore, plus Singapore's unjustly overlooked Malay literary and pop-culture scene of the postwar period. But there's a deafening silence on the building of new towns – a mixed blessing for all who experienced upheaval and relocation, especially for the Malays, who saw every one of their villages erased and communities broken up.

North of Sultan Mosque

The stretch of **North Bridge Road** between Arab Street and Jalan Sultan has a less touristy feel and although gentrification is evident here, too, the shops and restaurants tend to be geared more towards locals than tourists. Kazura Aromatics, at no. 705 for instance, sells alcohol-free perfumes, while neighbouring shops stock items such as the black, fez-like *songkok* traditionally worn by Malay men, and even swimwear for Muslim women.

Several roads run off the western side of North Bridge Road, including Jalan Kubor (literally "Grave Street"), which takes you to an unkempt **Muslim cemetery**, where it is said that Malay royalty are buried. Turn right here up Kallang Road to reach Jalan Sultan and the blue **Malabar Mosque**, built for Muslims from the South Indian state of Kerala and a little cousin of the Sultan Mosque, with similar golden domes. Its traditional styling belies its age – the mosque was completed in the early 1960s.

The Hajjah Fatimah mosque

4001 Beach Rd, just east of the junction with Jalan Sultan • Nicoll Highway or Bugis MRT

Beach Road's chandlers and fishing-gear shops betray its former proximity to the sea, until land reclamation created the Marina Centre district to the southeast. One quirky sight, a stone's throw from Arab Street, is the **Hajjah Fatimah Mosque**, its minaret looking strangely like a church steeple (perhaps because its architect was European). The minaret also visibly slants at six degrees to the vertical – locals call it Singapore's Leaning Tower of Pisa. The mosque is named after a wealthy businesswoman from Melaka who made her money in shipping. Her family home stood on this site until two break-ins and an arson attack compelled her to move, after which she paid for the mosque's construction, completed in 1846.

Chinatown

Chinatown, Telok Ayer, Outram Park, Tanjong Pagar or Clarke Quay MRT; buses run southwest along North and South Bridge rds and New Bridge Rd, returning along Eu Tong Sen St

Bounded roughly by Eu Tong Sen Street to the northwest, Neil and Maxwell roads to the south, Cecil Street to the southeast and the Singapore River to the north, the two square kilometres of **Chinatown** were never really an ethnic enclave – Singapore is, after all, a Chinese-majority country – more the focal point of the island's Chinese life and culture. Immigrants poured in following Singapore's foundation. The land southwest of the river became a place where new arrivals from China – mostly from Fujian (Hokkien) and Guangdong (Canton) provinces and, to a lesser extent, Hainan island – found temples, shops with familiar products and, most importantly, *kongsis* – clan associations that helped them find lodgings and work as small traders and coolies.

This was one of the most colourful districts of old Singapore, but after independence the government chose to grapple with the tumbledown slums by embarking upon a **redevelopment** campaign that saw whole streets razed. Not until the 1980s did the remaining shophouses and other period buildings begin to be conserved, though restoration has often rendered them improbably perfect. Furthermore, gentrification

OPPOSITE CHINATOWN'S THIAN HOCK KENG TEMPLE (P.498) >

9

has inevitably replaced the clan houses and religious and martial arts associations with boutique hotels, art galleries, new-media companies and bars. Getting a taste of the old ways of Chinatown now often means heading off the main streets into the concrete municipal housing estates.

Even so, as in Little India, the character of the area has had a bit of a shot in the arm courtesy of recent immigrants. As regards sights, the **Thian Hock Keng**, **Buddha Tooth Relic** and **Sri Mariamman** temples are especially worthwhile, as is the **Chinatown Heritage Centre** museum, and there's enough shophouse architecture to justify a leisurely wander.

Chinatown Heritage Centre

48 Pagoda St • Reopens late 2015, see website for opening hours and prices • ☎ 6534 8942, ⓦ chinatownheritagecentre.sg • Chinatown MRT

One exit from Chinatown MRT brings you up into the thick of the action on Pagoda Street, where the **Chinatown Heritage Centre** stands in marked contrast to the tacky souvenir stalls. Spread across three restored shophouses, the museum brings to life the history, culture, labours and pastimes of Singapore's Chinese settlers, with evocative displays and the liberal use of oral history clips.

Early on, the scene is set by a model junk, like those on which the *singkeh* (literally "new guests"), the early migrants, arrived; accounts tell of the privations they endured sailing across the South China Sea. Once ashore at Bullock Cart Water (the translation of the Chinese name, used to this day, for what would become Chinatown), settlers not only looked for work but also formed or joined clan associations, or the less savoury secret societies or triads. These connections, and every other facet of Chinatown life, are made flesh in displays like the mock-up of the prostitute's shabby boudoir and the pictures and footage of haunted addicts seeking escape through opium, their "devastating master".

The tour climaxes with a recreation of the conditions that migrants endured in Chinatown's squalid shophouses; the effect is heightened by the absence of air conditioning in this section of the Centre. Landlords once shoehorned as many as forty tenants onto a single floor; if you think it couldn't possibly happen today, spare a thought for the thousands of mainly Indian and Bangladeshi migrant workers who can be seen toiling on building sites all over Singapore. Most live in basic dormitories, and in 2008 a journalist documented 54 workers crammed into triple-decker beds in an eight-by-six-metre room.

Along South Bridge Road

Head down Pagoda Street from the Chinatown Heritage Centre and you come to **South Bridge Road**, one of Chinatown's main thoroughfares, carrying southbound traffic. At no. 218, on the corner of Mosque Street, stands the pastel green **Jamae Mosque** (also called the Chulia Mosque), established by South Indian Muslims in the 1820s. Its twin minarets appear to contain miniature windows while above the entrance stands what looks like a tiny doorway, all of which makes the upper part of the facade look strangely like a scale model of a much larger building.

One street northeast, at the junction with **Upper Cross Street**, roadblocks were set up during the Japanese occupation, and Singaporeans were vetted for signs of anti-Japanese sentiment in the infamous **Sook Ching** campaign (see p.510). That tragic episode is commemorated by a simple, signposted monument in the **Hong Lim Complex**, a housing estate that also happens to boast walkways lined with herbalists, makers of *chops* (rubber stamps), and stores selling dried foodstuffs and so forth – much more representative of the area's original character than more recent arrivals.

To top up your blood-sugar level while wandering the area, pop into the **Tong Heng pastry shop** (daily 9am–10pm) at no. 285, which sells custard tarts, lotus-seed-paste biscuits and other Chinese sweet treats.

Sri Mariamman Temple

244 South Bridge Rd • Daily 7am–noon & 6–9pm, though it may be possible to look around at other times • Free • ☎ 6223 4064 • Chinatown or Telok Ayer MRT

Singapore's oldest Hindu shrine, the **Sri Mariamman Temple**, boasts a superb *gopuram* bristling with brightly coloured deities. A wood and *atap* hut was first erected here in 1827 on land belonging to Naraina Pillay, a government clerk who arrived on the same ship as Stamford Raffles on the latter's second trip to Singapore. The present temple was completed around 1843, though it has been extended and overhauled several times since.

Inside, look up at the roof to see friezes depicting a host of Hindu deities, including the three manifestations of the supreme being: Brahma the creator (with three of his four heads showing), Vishnu the preserver, and Shiva the destroyer (holding one of his sons). The main sanctum is devoted to Mariamman, a goddess worshipped for her healing powers. Smaller sanctums dotted about the walkway circumnavigating the temple honour other deities. In the one dedicated to the goddess Periachi Amman, a sculpture portrays her with a queen lying on her lap, whose evil child she has ripped from her womb; it's odd, then, that Periachi Amman is the protector of children, to whom babies are brought when one month old.

Once a year, during the festival of **Thimithi** (Oct or Nov), a patch of sand to the left of the main sanctum is covered in red-hot coals that male Hindus run across to prove the strength of their faith. The participants, who line up all the way along South Bridge Road waiting for their turn, are supposedly protected from the heat of the coals by the power of prayer.

Eu Yan Sang Medical Hall

269 South Bridge Rd • Mon–Sat 8.30am–6pm • ☎ 6225 3211 • Chinatown or Telok Ayer MRT

Across from the Sri Mariamman Temple is the **Eu Yan Sang Medical Hall,** one of the oldest Chinese herbalist practices in the area. The smell is the first thing you'll notice (a little like a compost heap on a hot day); the second is the weird assortment of ingredients on the shelves. Besides the usual herbs and roots favoured by the Chinese, there are various remedies derived from exotic (and endangered) species. Blood circulation problems and wounds can allegedly be eased by mixtures of centipedes and insects crushed into a "rubbing liquor"; the ground-up gall bladders of snakes or bears apparently work wonders on pimples; while deer penis is supposed to provide a lift for any sexual problem.

Upstairs, the small but engaging **Birds' Nest Gallery** casts light on this most unusual of famous Chinese delicacies. Produced by swiftlets, the edible nests are a mixture of saliva, moss and grass, and emerged as a prized supplement among China's royal and noble classes during the Ming Dynasty. The birds live high up in the caves of Southeast Asia, and at Niah in Sarawak you can see their nests being harvested – arduous and sometimes dangerous work. You may also have encountered the dubious Malaysian practice of rearing the swiftlets in bricked-up town-centre shophouses, which is why the birds can be seen wheeling at dawn and dusk over many Malaysian town centres.

Buddha Tooth Relic Temple

288 South Bridge Rd • Daily 7am–7pm • Free • ☎ 6220 0220, ⓦ btrts.org.sg • No shorts, vests or non-vegetarian food • Chinatown or Tanjong Pagar MRT

The imposing **Buddha Tooth Relic Temple** is arguably the most in-your-face of Chinatown's shrines. The place simply clobbers you with its opulence – even the elevators have brocaded walls – and the thousands upon thousands of Buddhist figurines plastered up and down various interior surfaces. It also boasts its own museum and a gallery of Buddhist art.

With gently curving roofs featuring tiles and other ornaments made in Japan, the temple has its origins in the discovery, in 1980, of what was thought to be a tooth of Buddha inside a collapsed stupa at a Burmese monastery. The monastery's chief abbot visited Singapore in 2002 and decided the island would make a suitable sanctuary for

CHINATOWN AND THE FINANCIAL DISTRICT

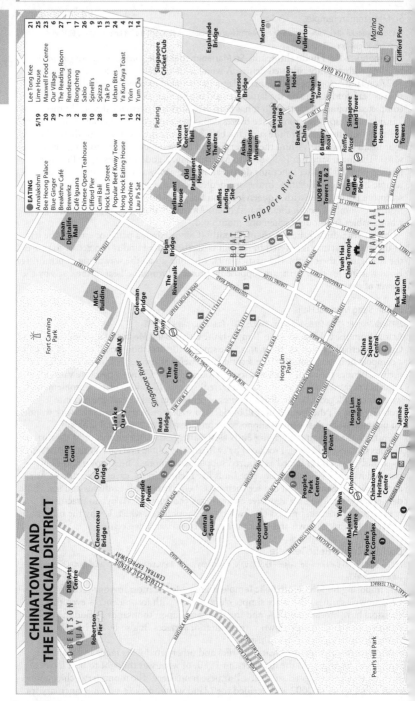

● EATING		
Annalakshmi	21	
Bee Heong Palace	5/19	
Blue Ginger	20	
Breakthru Café	29	
Brewerkz	7	
Café Iguana	2	
Chinese Opera Teahouse	18	
Clifford Pier	10	
Cumi Bali	28	
Hock Lam Street		
Popular Beef Kway Teow	8	
Hong Hock Eating House	11	
Indochine	16	
Lau Pa Sat	22	
Lee Tong Kee	21	
Lime House	25	
Maxwell Food Centre	23	
Our Village	6	
The Reading Room	27	
Rendezvous	1	
Rongcheng	17	
Sabio	26	
Spinelli's	9	
Spizza	15	
Tak Po	13	
Urban Bites	24	
Ya Kun Kaya Toast	4	
Yixin	12	
Yum Cha	14	

9

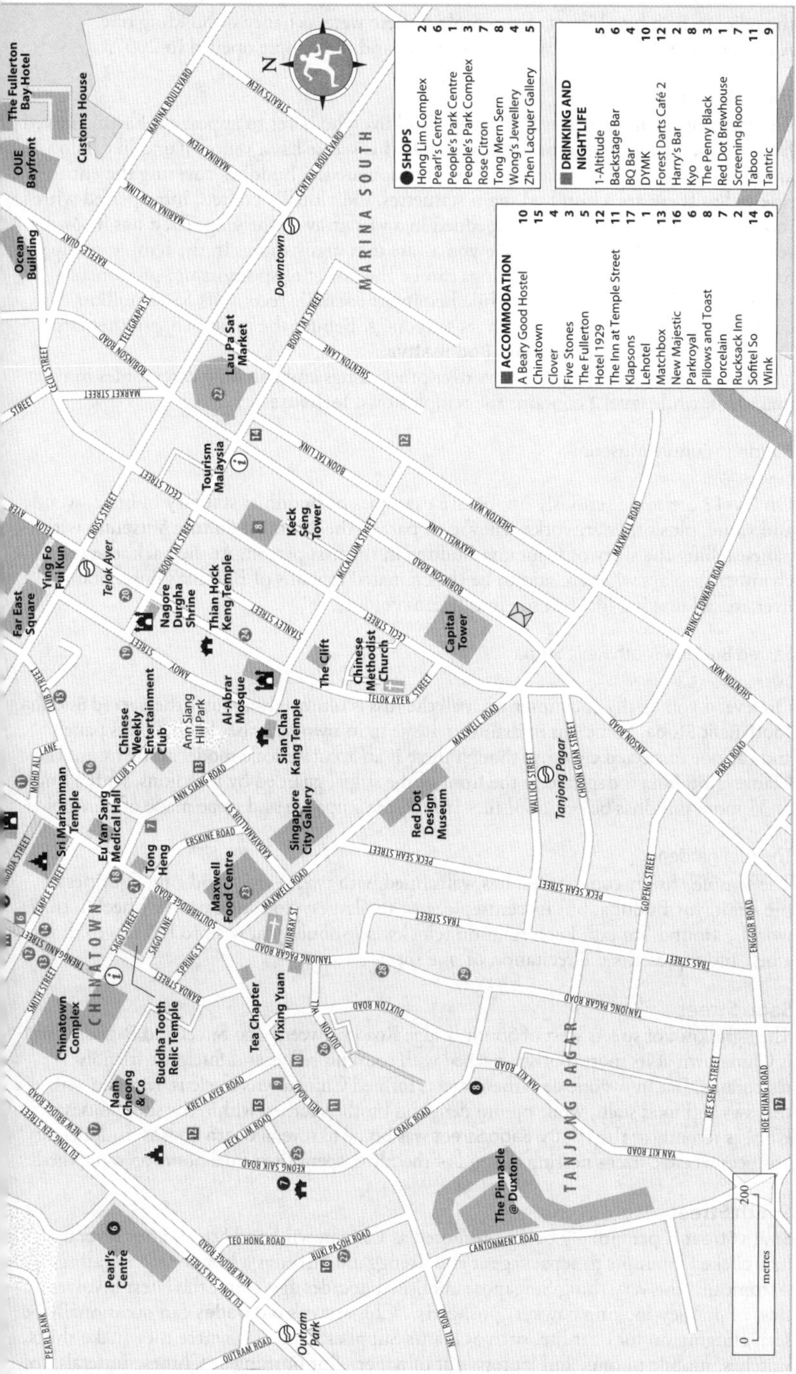

SHOPS
Hong Lim Complex 2
Pearl's Centre 6
People's Park Centre 1
People's Park Complex 3
Rose Citron 7
Tong Mern Sern 8
Wong's Jewellery 4
Zhen Lacquer Gallery 5
DRINKING AND NIGHTLIFE
1-Altitude 5
Backstage Bar 6
BQ Bar 4
DYMK 10
Forest Darts Café 2 12
Harry's Bar 2
Kyo 8
The Penny Black 3
Red Dot Brewhouse 1
Screening Room 7
Taboo 11
Tantric 9
ACCOMMODATION
A Beary Good Hostel 10
Chinatown 15
Clover 4
Five Stones 3
The Fullerton 5
Hotel 1929 12
The Inn at Temple Street 11
Klapsons 17
Lehotel 1
Matchbox 13
New Majestic 16
Parkroyal 6
Pillows and Toast 8
Porcelain 7
Rucksack Inn 2
Sofitel So 14
Wink 9
N
MARINA SOUTH
CHINATOWN
TANJONG PAGAR
The Fullerton Bay Hotel
Customs House
OUE Bayfront
Ocean Building
Lau Pa Sat Market
Downtown
Tourism Malaysia
Keck Seng Tower
Far East Square
Ying Fo Fui Kun
Telok Ayer
Nagore Durgha Shrine
Thian Hock Keng Temple
Capital Tower
The Clift
Chinese Methodist Church
Al-Abrar Mosque
Chinese Weekly Entertainment Club
Ann Siang Hill Park
Sian Chai Kang Temple
Singapore City Gallery
Red Dot Design Museum
Tanjong Pagar
Sri Mariamman Temple
Eu Yan Sang Medical Hall
Tong Heng
Maxwell Food Centre
Chinatown Complex
Buddha Tooth Relic Temple
Tea Chapter
Yixing Yuan
Nam Cheong & Co
The Pinnacle @ Duxton
Pearl's Centre
Outram Park
0
200
metres

9

the relic, to be housed in its own temple if there were a chance of building one. A prime site in Chinatown was duly secured, and the temple opened in 2007.

The main hall

The focus of the main hall is **Maitreya**, a Buddha who is yet to appear on Earth. Carved from juniper wood said to be 1000 years old, his statue has a yellow flame-like halo around it. But what really captures the attention are the Buddhas covering the entire side walls. There are a hundred main statuettes, individually crafted, interspersed with thousands more tiny figurines embedded in a vast array of shelving. Each has its own serial number and signs soon make you aware that many things in the temple are up for "adoption" – figurines and fittings can be the object of sponsorship, presumably winning the donor good karma while helping the temple recoup its S$62 million construction bill and keep up with its outgoings. Behind the main hall, another large hall centres on the **Avalokitesvara Bodhisattva**.

The **mezzanine** affords great views over proceedings and chanting ceremonies in the main hall, while **level 2** contains the temple's own **teahouse**.

Buddhist Culture Museum

Daily 9am–6pm

On **level 3** are some seriously impressive examples of Buddhist **statuary** in brass, wood and stone, plus other artworks. They're all part of the **Buddhist Culture Museum**, with panels telling the story of Gautama Buddha in the first person. At the back, the relic chamber displays what are said to be the cremated remains of Buddha's nose, brain, liver etc, all looking like fish roe in different colours.

Sacred Buddha Tooth Relic Stupa

Daily 9am–noon & 3–6pm

On level 4 you finally encounter what all the fuss is ultimately about – the **Sacred Buddha Tooth Relic Stupa**. Some 3m in diameter, it sits in its own chamber behind glass panels and can't be inspected close up, though there is an accurate scale model at the front. The Maitreya Buddha is depicted at the front of the stupa, guarded by four lions, with a ring of 35 more Buddhas below; floor tiles around the stupa are said to be made of pure gold.

The roof garden

The temple's lovely **roof garden** has walls lined with twelve thousand tiny figurines of the Amitayus Buddha, but its centrepiece is "the largest cloisonné prayer wheel in the world", around 5m tall. Each rotation (clockwise, should you wish to have a go) dings a bell and represents the recitation of one sutra.

Sago Street

The tight knot of streets west of South Bridge Road between Sago Street and Pagoda Street is Chinatown at its most touristy, packed with souvenir sellers and foreigner-friendly restaurants. But in bygone days these streets formed Chinatown's nucleus, teeming with trishaws and food stalls, while opium dens and brothels lurked within the shophouses. Until as recently as the 1950s, **Sago Street** was home to several **death houses**, rudimentary hospices where citizens nearing the end of their lives spent their final hours on rattan beds.

Smith Street

Smith Street is perennially being promoted as Chinatown Food Street, after several half-cocked attempts to repackage it and Trengganu Street as a hub for street eating – ironically, the very thing Singapore abolished decades ago – and the latest involves a slew of phoney-looking hawker "pushcarts". Chinatown's **old trades** can occasionally be seen clinging on for dear life, such as Nam's Supplies at no. 22, where they make shirts, watches, mobile phones and laptops out of paper – for burning at Chinese funerals, to ensure the deceased don't lack creature comforts in the next life. The ugly, concrete **Chinatown Complex** at the end of the street is a workaday place housing outlets selling silk, kimonos and household goods.

The Bukit Pasoh conservation area
Outram Park MRT

In the southernmost corner of Chinatown is an area packed with restored shophouses, worth a look for their beautifully painted facades, some in Art Deco style, and tilework. **Clan houses** were once the claim to fame of **Bukit Pasoh Road**, but while some have survived with their character intact, such as the Yee Clan Association at 9 Bukit Pasoh Rd, many more have morphed into boutiques or boutique hotels; the Gan Clan's building at 18–20 Bukit Pasoh Rd now rents out space to a posh restaurant. There are clan houses on neighbouring **Keong Saik Road** too, though until recently it had a more unsavoury reputation as a red-light area.

New Bridge Road and Eu Tong Sen Street

Chinatown's main shopping drag comprises southbound **New Bridge Road** and northbound **Eu Tong Sen Street**, along which are a handful of shopping malls. Try to pop into one of the barbecued-pork vendors around the intersection of Smith, Temple and Pagoda streets with New Bridge Road – as they're cooked, the thin, flat, red squares of *bak kwa*, coated with a sweet marinade, produce a rich, smoky odour that is pure Chinatown. As you chew on your *bak kwa*, check out two striking buildings across the road. On the left is the Art Deco **Majestic Theatre**, built in 1927 as a Chinese opera house by Eu Tong Sen, the wealthy businessman behind the Eu Yan Sang Chinese medicine company. Today it has been reduced to housing a few forgettable shops, but note the five images of figures from Chinese opera on its facade. Just beside it, and built a few years later, stands the former *Great Southern Hotel* (today the Yue Hwa Chinese Products Emporium), which had a fifth-floor nightclub where wealthy locals would drink liquor, smoke opium and pay to dance with so-called "taxi girls".

Ann Siang Hill

Ann Siang Hill is both the name of a little mound and of a lane that leads off South Bridge Road up a slope, where it forks into Club Street on the left and Ann Siang Road, which veers gently right. Despite being only a few paces removed from the hubbub of the main road, the hill is somehow a different realm, a little collection of gentrified shophouses with a distinct villagey feel. Packed with swanky restaurants, cafés and bars, plus the odd boutique, the area typifies the new Chinatown. At the southern end of the road, a short flight of steps leads up to **Ann Siang Hill Park**, a sliver of generic greenery whose only attraction is that it offers a **short cut** to Amoy Street.

Club Street

Scarcely any of the clan associations and guilds whose presence gave **Club Street** its name now remain. Most notable of all is the **Chinese Weekly Entertainment Club** at the end of a side street also called Club Street. Flanked by roaring lion heads, this mansion-like building was constructed in 1891 as a venue where Peranakan tycoons could socialize, and still serves as a private club today.

Singapore City Gallery
URA Centre, 45 Maxwell Rd • Mon–Sat 9am–5pm • Free • ☎ 6321 8321, ⓦ ura.gov.sg/gallery • Tanjong Pagar or Telok Ayer MRT

Town planning may not sound the most fascinating premise for a gallery, but then again, no nation remodels with such ambition as Singapore, whose planners are constantly erasing roads here and replacing one ultramodern complex with an even more souped-up development there. The latest grand designs for the island are

9

exhibited west of Ann Siang Hill at the surprisingly absorbing **Singapore City Gallery**, within the government Urban Redevelopment Authority's headquarters.

The URA has rightly been criticized in the past for slighting Singapore's architectural heritage, so it is heartening that displays on the first and second floors make reassuring noises about the value of the venerable shophouses and colonial villas that remain. But the gallery's emphasis is more upon the future than the past, amply illustrated by the vast and incredibly intricate **scale model** of downtown Singapore, with every row of shophouses, every roof of every building – including some not yet built – fashioned out of plywood. This and other models are turned out by a dedicated team whose first-floor workshop is sadly not open to the public, though you might catch a glimpse of them at work through the glass. The gallery also hosts a wraparound on the island's cityscape and temporary exhibitions concerning best practice in town planning.

Amoy Street

Amoy Street, together with Telok Ayer Street, was designated a Hokkien enclave in the colony's early days (Amoy being the old name of Xiamen city in China's Fujian province). Long terraces of smartly refurbished shophouses flank the street, all featuring characteristic **five-foot ways**, or covered verandas, so called because they jut five feet out from the house. If you descend here from Ann Siang Hill Park, you'll emerge by the small **Sian Chai Kang Temple** at no. 66. With the customary dragons on the roof, it's dominated by huge urns, full to the brim with ash from untold numbers of burned incense sticks. Two carved stone lions guard the temple; their fancy red neck-ribbons are said to bring good fortune and prosperity.

Telok Ayer Street

One street removed from Amoy Street is **Telok Ayer Street**, its name, meaning "Watery Bay" in Malay, recalling the mid-nineteenth century when the street would have run along the shoreline. Thanks to land reclamation, it's no closer to a beach than is Beach Road, but some of Singapore's oldest buildings cling on between the modern towers – temples and mosques where newly arrived immigrants and sailors thanked their god(s) for their safe passage.

The first building of note you come to if you walk up from the station is the square 1889 **Chinese Methodist Church**, whose design – portholes and windows adorned with white crosses and capped by a Chinese pagoda-style roof – is a pleasing blend of East and West. Just beyond McCallum Street, the blue-and-white **Al-Abrar Mosque** is built on the spot where Chulia worshippers set up a makeshift thatched mosque in 1827.

Thian Hock Keng Temple

158 Telok Ayer St • Daily 7.30am–5.30pm • Free • ☎ 6423 4616, ⓦ thianhockkeng.com.sg • Telok Ayer or Chinatown MRT

With ornate dragons stalking its broad, low-slung roofs, the immaculately restored **Thian Hock Keng Temple** stands in marked contrast to the gleaming glass building opposite, belonging to the Hokkien Clan Association, which manages it. For all its beauty, the temple feels marooned in a sea of commercialization. With much of Chinatown's community uprooted, it's something of a museum piece, one that schoolkids are taken to so they can glimpse life in "the old days".

Construction began in 1839 using materials imported from China, on the site of a small joss house where immigrants made offerings to Ma Zu, the queen of heaven. A statue of the goddess, shipped in from southern China in time for the temple's completion in 1842, stands in the centre of the main hall, flanked by the martial figure of Guan Yu on the right and physician Bao Sheng on the left. Against the left wall, look out for an altar containing the curious figures of General Fan and General Xie. The two are said to have arranged to meet by a river bridge, but Xie was delayed; Fan waited doggedly in the appointed spot and drowned in a flash flood, which supposedly accounts for his black skin and the grimace on his face. When Xie finally arrived, he was filled with guilt and hanged himself – hence his depiction, with tongue hanging down to his chest.

Nagore Durgha Shrine

140 Telok Ayer St • Museum daily 10am–6pm • Free

It's a testament to Singapore's multicultural nature that Thian Hock Keng's next-door neighbour is the charming brown-and-white **Nagore Durgha Shrine** to the Muslim ascetic, Shahul Hamid of Nagore. It was built in the 1820s by Chulias from southern India, as was the Jamae Mosque (see p.492), so it's not surprising that the buildings appear to be cut from the same architectural cloth.

Part of the shrine now houses an excellent small **museum** dedicated to the history of Telok Ayer Street. The few simple artefacts and photographs do a good job of unpacking the nuances of Muslim Indian identity in Singapore, a country where Hindu members of the Indian community are referred to by the part of India they emigrated from, yet their Muslim counterparts have been lumped together under the banner of their faith.

Ying Fo Fui Kun

98 Telok Ayer St, beyond the junction with Cross St • Telok Ayer or Chinatown MRT

Among the smartest of Chinatown's surviving clan houses, the **Ying Fo Fui Kun** was established in 1822 by Hakkas from Guangdong province. It has narrowly avoided being swallowed up by the adjacent Far East Square complex, but in its present orderly state, with an immaculate altar boasting gilt calligraphy and carvings, it's hard to imagine it having been the social hub of an entire community. Membership drives are launched periodically to try to stop it turning into a senior citizens' club, given that provincial dialects – traditionally used as a marker of identity among the Chinese – have been on the decline since the 1970s following an aggressive state campaign to standardize on Mandarin.

Far East Square

Far East Square is a sort of heritage development, a rather mundane collection of shops, restaurants and offices that engulfs what would have been the northernmost part of Amoy Street. Also co-opted into the complex is the **Fuk Tak Chi Street Museum** (76 Telok Ayer St; daily 10am–10pm; free). This was once Singapore's oldest temple, having been established by the Hakka and Cantonese communities in 1824; today it's a mere "street museum", its altar holding a model junk crewed by sailors in blue shorts. A diorama depicts Telok Ayer Street in its waterfront heyday, with pigtailed labourers taking part in a procession to the temple, depicted with a stage set up in front where opera performers are getting ready to strut their stuff.

Hong Lim Park

Between Upper Pickering St and North Canal Rd • Clarke Quay MRT

A few minutes' walk southwest from the Singapore River, **Hong Lim Park** is not much more than a field ringed by trees, but it's of symbolic significance as the home of **Speakers' Corner**, in its northern corner. Since its designation in 2000, citizens have, in theory, been able to speak their minds here, just as people do at its famous exemplar in central London. This being Singapore, regulations require you to register your intention to speak and prohibit discussion of religion or anything that could be deemed to provoke racial discontent. Despite this, the site's libertarian leanings have rubbed off onto the park itself, which has regained some of its historic role as a site for rallies and demonstrations – a much-needed channel for public expression after the suffocation of the 1970s and 1980s.

Boat Quay

Close to the old mouth of the Singapore River, the pedestrianized row of waterfront shophouses known as **Boat Quay** is one of Singapore's most commercially successful

9

bids at urban regeneration. Derelict in the early 1990s, it's since become a thriving hangout, sporting a huge collection of restaurants and bars. The area's historical significance may be easier to appreciate through its street names – Synagogue Street nearby, for example, was the site of the island's first synagogue.

The Yueh Hai Ching Temple

30b Philip St

The twin-shrined **Yueh Hai Ching Temple** (also called **Wak Hai Cheng Bio**) feels even more isolated than the Thian Hock Keng, nestling as it does among the towers where Chinatown shades into the Financial District. Completed in the 1850s, it is another of Chinatown's temples built on the old coastline and has been gorgeously restored. Hai Ching means "calm sea" and an effigy of Tian Hou or Mazu, the queen of heaven and protector of seafarers, is housed in the right-hand shrine; the temple was a destination for newly arrived migrants. Be sure to look up at the roof, crammed with tiny depictions of scenes from Chinese folklore and hand-painted back to their original glory as part of the temple's overhaul.

Tanjong Pagar

Tanjong Pagar or Outram Park MRT

The district of **Tanjong Pagar**, south of Chinatown, was once a veritable sewer of opium dens and brothels. Then it was earmarked as a conservation area and many dozens of shophouses were refurbished as bars, restaurants and shops, notably on Neil Road and Duxton Hill. A grander example of the area's architecture can be found right where South Bridge Road flows into Neil and Tanjong Pagar roads: here you'll easily spot the arches and bricked facade of the **Jinrikisha Building**, constructed at the turn of the last century as a terminus for rickshaws.

Tanjong Pagar's most interesting attraction is the **Baba House**, though as an architectural attention-grabber it's rivalled by the seven interlinked towers of **Pinnacle@ Duxton**, a showpiece municipal housing development on Cantonment Road, dominating Chinatown's southern skyline. One more attraction is worth a look: the **Red Dot Design Museum**, celebrating the best in product design and advertising.

Baba House

157 Neil Rd • Free, but only visitable on compulsory tours (4 weekly; book at least a week in advance • ☎ 6227 5731, ⓦ edu.nus.sg /museum/baba • Outram Park MRT (Cantonment Rd exit), or bus #174 from Orchard Rd or Bras Basah Rd to its terminus

The **Baba House** is one of Singapore's most impressive museums, partly because it isn't really a museum: what you see is a late nineteenth- or early twentieth-century Peranakan house, meticulously restored to its appearance in the late 1920s, a particularly prosperous time in its history.

Like Penang's Cheong Fatt Tze Mansion, the place is easily spotted as it's painted a vivid blue. Note the **phoenixes** and **peonies** on the eaves above the entrance, signifying longevity and wealth respectively and, together, marital bliss. Even more eye-catching is the **pintu pagar**, the pair of swing doors with beautiful gilt and mother-of-pearl inlays.

The ground floor

Beyond the *pintu pagar*, yet more exquisite inlay work is in evidence on the antique chairs in the **main hall**, used for entertaining guests. The altar here, among the last of its kind in Singapore, is backed by an exquisitely carved wood screen behind which the women of the household could eavesdrop on proceedings. Behind it is the **family hall**, with an air well open to the sky in its midst. Note the original tilework depicting roses and tulips, indicating a European influence, and the gilt bats on the walls – bats are associated with good luck thanks to their Mandarin name *bianfu*, as *fu* is a homonym for the Chinese character meaning "good fortune".

TAKING CHINESE TEA

At two Tanjong Pagar teahouses, visitors can glean something of the deep Chinese connection with tea by taking part in a workshop lasting up to an hour. Participants are introduced to different varieties of tea and talked through the history of tea cultivation and the rituals of brewing and appreciating the drink. The water, for example, has to reach an optimum temperature that depends on which type of tea is being prepared; experts can tell its heat by the size of the rising bubbles, described variously as "sand eyes", "prawn eyes", "fish eyes", etc. Both venues also stock an extensive range of tea-related accoutrements such as tall "sniffer" cups used to savour the aroma of the brew before it is poured into squat teacups for drinking.
Tea Chapter 9–11 Neil Rd ☎6226 1175, ⓦtea-chapter.com.sg. Tea-making demonstration and sampling session for S$33 per person, or an all-day (8hr) course for S$150.
Yixing Yuan Teahouse 30 Tanjong Pagar Rd ☎6224 6961, ⓦyixingxuan-teahouse.com. Hour-long workshops from S$20 per head for a group of at least five.

The upper floors

Upstairs at the front end of the house, the centrepiece of the **main bedroom** is an ornate wooden four-poster bed with gilt and red lacquer decorations, bearing carved motifs such as musical instruments and yet more bats. Your guide will almost certainly open up the **peephole** in the floor, exposing a small shaft down to the main hall. The **third storey**, a later addition, is used for temporary exhibitions.

The Red Dot Design Museum

28 Maxwell Rd • Mon–Fri 11am–6pm, Sat & Sun 11am–8pm, plus monthly Fri evening crafts market till late • ☎ 6327 8027, ⓦ museum.red-dot.sg • S$8, though free during crafts market

Housed in a bright red building, the modest **Red Dot Design Museum** focuses on the creative use of illustration and multimedia and, much more interestingly, on international product design. You'd never think stepladders, nutcrackers and shower heads could hold so much scope for ergonomic and stylistic improvement. It's at its best during the monthly crafts market, **MAAD**, when local artists and designers set up stall to showcase their work.

The Financial District

Raffles Place, Telok Ayer or Downtown MRT

If Singapore's **Financial District** (or **Central Business District/CBD**; map, pp.494–495) figures in the popular imagination at all, it would be because of the rogue trader Nick Leeson, whose antics here brought about the **Barings Bank collapse** of the 1990s – though it seems like small beer when set against the global financial improprieties of recent years. The area, south of the mouth of the Singapore River, has no specific sights but makes a reasonable prelude to Boat Quay (see p.499), Telok Ayer Street in Chinatown (see p.498), the Colonial District (via Cavenagh Bridge; see p.473) or the southern part of Marina Bay (see p.502).

Raffles Place

What is now the Financial District was swamp until land reclamation in the mid-1820s rendered it fit for building. Within just a few years, it was home to the colony's busiest business address, Commercial Square, boasting the banks, ships' chandlers and warehouses of a burgeoning trading port. The square later became Singapore's main shopping area until Orchard Road overtook it in the late 1960s; today known as **Raffles Place**, it's the heart of Singapore's high-profile banking sector.

Surfacing from Raffles Place MRT, follow the signs for Raffles Place itself to feel like an ant in a canyon of skyscrapers. To see what things look like from the top of that canyon, the place to head is One Raffles Place, the complex to the west of the square, with truly stunning views from its rooftop bar, *1-Altitude* (see p.544). The three roads

9

that run southwest from Raffles Place – Cecil Street, Robinson Road and Shenton Way – are all chock-a-block with more high-rise banks and financial houses.

Battery Road

Heading towards the river from Raffles Place, you come to **Battery Road**, its name recalling the days when Fort Fullerton (named after Robert Fullerton, first governor of the Straits Settlements) and its attendant battery of guns used to stand to the east on the site of the *Fullerton* hotel. From here, Cavenagh Bridge is just a couple of minutes' walk away.

The main attraction here, Boat Quay aside, is the elegant **Fullerton Building**, worth viewing from Collyer Quay to the east for its façade, fronted by sturdy pillars. This was one of Singapore's tallest buildings when it was constructed in 1928 as the headquarters for the General Post Office (a role it fulfilled until the mid-1990s). These days, it serves as the luxury *Fullerton* hotel, its atrium worth a peek if only to admire the enormous columns within.

Collyer Quay

Collyer Quay runs south along the western shore of Marina Bay from what was the mouth of the Singapore River, linking the Colonial District with Raffles Quay and Shenton Way further south, both of which mark the former line of the seafront. Just east of Collyer Quay, the Merlion Park is home to the **One Fullerton** development, whose bars and restaurants and nightclub look out over the bay, and to a cement statue of Singapore's national symbol, the **Merlion**. Half-lion, half-fish and wholly ugly, the creature reflects the island's maritime connections and the old tale concerning the derivation of its present name, derived from the Sanskrit "Singapura", meaning "Lion City".

Clifford Pier

80 Collyer Quay

South of the park, the Art Deco **Clifford Pier** building, long the departure point for boat trips out to Singapore's southern islands, was rendered defunct by the barrage that seals Marina Bay off from the sea. Mirroring the development at Marina South, the building, along with the **Customs House** building a minute's walk on, have been transformed into restaurant complexes, run by the company that owns the *Fullerton* hotel; part of Clifford Pier forms the entrance to the hotel's pricier new sibling, the *Fullerton Bay*.

Lau Pa Sat

18 Raffles Quay

Arguably the best place for refreshments in the Financial District is the charmingly old-world **Lau Pa Sat**, literally meaning "old market" – it was built in 1894 as a place for traders to sell produce. Also known by its original name, **Telok Ayer Market**, Lau Pa Sat has served as a hawker centre since the 1970s, except for a hiatus in the 1980s when tunnelling for the MRT required the octagonal cast-iron structure to be dismantled, then reassembled piece by piece. Aficionados of **satay** should turn up in the evening, when vendors set up in a row outside on Boon Tat Street.

Marina Bay

Bayfront, Downtown or Promenade MRT

It's hard not to be awed by the audacity of **Marina Bay**, the project that has transformed downtown Singapore's seafront over two generations. An exorbitantly ambitious piece of civil engineering, it entailed the creation of three massive expanses of reclaimed land and a barrage to seal off the basins of the Singapore and Kallang rivers from the sea. The result is a seaside freshwater **reservoir** with a crucial role in reducing Singapore's dependence on Malaysian water supplies.

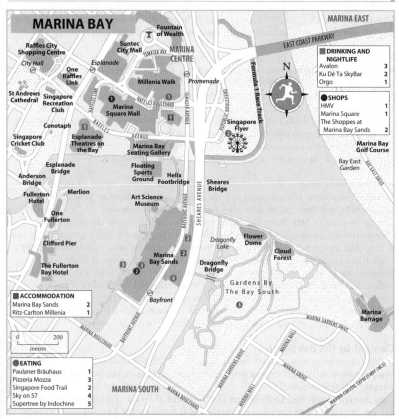

Although the bay's southern "jaw", **Marina South**, now sprouts a host of bank buildings to rival Raffles Place, the area is dominated by the **Marina Bay Sands** casino resort, with its museum and rooftop restaurants; it is inevitably the focus of any visit to the bay, along with the extravagant new **Gardens by the Bay** next door. Close to the Padang, the **Theatres on the Bay arts complex** is worth a detour for its skyline views, with more of the same available from the oversized Ferris wheel of the **Singapore Flyer**.

Marina Bay Sands

10 Bayfront Ave • ☎ 6688 8826, ⓦ marinabaysands.com • Bayfront MRT, or bus #106 from Orchard Rd/Bras Basah Rd or #133 from Victoria St
Rarely does a building become an icon quite as instantly as the **Marina Bay Sands** hotel and casino, its three 55-floor towers topped and connected by a vast, curved-surfboard-like deck, the SkyPark. The most ambitious undertaking yet by its owners, Las Vegas Sands, it opened in 2010 and quickly replaced the Merlion as the Singapore image of choice in the travel brochures. Even if you have no interest in the casino – open 24/7, naturally – the complex, which includes a convention centre, a shopping mall, two concert venues, numerous restaurants and its own museum, is well worth exploring. The hotel atrium, often so busy with people gawping that it feels like a busy train station concourse, is especially striking, the sides of the building sloping into each other overhead to give the impression of being inside a narrow glassy pyramid.

In the evening, a free laser show, **Wonder Full** (daily 8pm & 9.30pm, Fri & Sat extra show at 11pm; 15min), splays multicoloured beams from atop the hotel's towers onto

9

Marina Bay, with fountains shooting up from below. Visible from around the bay, the display isn't especially captivating unless you're at the hotel itself.

SkyPark

Observation deck Mon–Thurs 9.30am–10pm, Fri–Sun 9.30am–11pm • S$23 • Tickets and access from box office on basement 1 of tower 3, at the northern end of the complex • ☎ 6688 1057

From what would have been an impossible vantage point, high above the sea before the creation of Marina Bay, the SkyPark's observation deck affords superb views over Singapore's Colonial District on one side and the conservatories of **Gardens by the Bay** on the other. Unfortunately tickets are overpriced, and you don't get close up to one of the SkyPark's iconic features, its 150m **infinity pool**. On the other hand, there's no charge to access the area if you eat or drink at any SkyPark venue.

ArtScience Museum

At the northern end of the Marina Bay Sands complex, close to the helix footbridge that links the area with the Singapore Flyer and Theatres on the Bay • Daily 10am–10pm, last admission 9pm • Prices vary depending on the exhibition

The casino resort's **ArtScience Museum**, perhaps meant to temper the relentless obsession with consumption everywhere else in the complex, is easily spotted: its shape is supposed to represent a stylized lotus blossom, though from certain angles it looks more like a stubby-fingered hand in concrete. The museum's remit is to decode the connections between art and science, but its permanent gallery is so tiny and full of waffle as to be almost laughable. In practice it specializes in world-class travelling exhibitions, sometimes only tenuously linked to the museum's supposed theme: highlights since it opened have included artefacts salvaged from the *Titanic*, works by Leonardo da Vinci and the photographic portraits of Annie Leibovitz.

Gardens by the Bay South

18 Marina Gardens Drive • ☎ 6420 6848, ⓦ gardensbythebay.org.sg • Daily 5am–2am; conservatories 9am–9pm • Free admission; OCBC Skyway S$5; conservatories S$28; last ticket sales at 8pm • Bayfront MRT (enter via the Dragonfly Bridge) or bus #400 (3 hourly) from Marina Bay MRT to the front entrance

Two vast conservatories, roofs arched like the backs of foraging dinosaurs, are the most eye-catching feature of the southern section of **Gardens by the Bay**. Intended to be a second botanic garden for Singapore, the gardens are split into three chunks around Marina Bay; the southern area, next to *Marina Bay Sands*, is very much the centrepiece.

One conservatory houses Mediterranean and African flora, the highlight being the stands of small, bizarrely shaped **baobab** trees. The neighbouring conservatory nurtures **cloud forest** of the kind found on Southeast Asia's highest peaks, and includes a 35m "mountain" covered in ferns, rhododendrons and insect-eating sundews and butterworts.

The gardens' other big draw is the **Supertree Grove**, an array of towers resembling gigantic golf tees and sheathed in a sort of red trelliswork, from which climbers, ferns and orchids poke out. The towers don't look all that alluring from close up; more exciting is the slightly wobbly **OCBC Skyway**, an aerial walkway connecting the tops of the two tallest supertrees and providing good views over the gardens and around Marina Bay. At night the supertrees are lit up using power from their own solar cells, and take centre stage in free **light shows** at 7.45pm and 8.45pm.

Marina Centre

Promenade or Esplanade MRT, or City Hall MRT via the subterranean CityLink Mall

The large triangle of reclaimed land east of the Padang and the *Raffles Hotel*, robbing Beach Road of its beach, is officially called **Marina Centre**, though locals invariably invoke the names of the Marina Square or Suntec City malls when referring to it. This is the oldest part of the Marina Bay project, open since the early 1990s, but still jars next to the historical neighbourhoods to the west: ordinary amenities such as places of worship and schools are totally absent, and instead the area is dominated by the Suntec

Convention Centre, plush offices and hotels, and the aforementioned malls. Visitors come mostly to enjoy views of the cityscape from either the southern end of Marina Centre or the Singapore Flyer – or both.

Esplanade – Theatres on the Bay

1 Esplanade Drive • Daily 10am till late, 45min tours Tues–Sun 9am, 12.30pm & 2pm, Sat & Sun 9am • S$10 for tours, otherwise free • ☎ 6828 8377, Ⓦ esplanade.com

Opinion is split as to whether the two huge, spiked shells that roof the **Esplanade – Theatres on the Bay** project, just east of the Padang, are peerless modernistic architecture or indulgent kitsch. They have variously been compared to kitchen graters, hedgehogs, even durian fruit (the preferred description among locals), though two giant insect eyes is perhaps the best comparison.

Opened in 2002, Esplanade boasts a concert hall, theatres, gallery space and, on the third floor, **library@esplanade**, with a wide range of arts-related books and other resources. It's possible to do a guided tour of the facilities, but what lures most casual visitors are the **views**, particularly fine at dusk, across the bay to the Financial District and *Marina Bay Sands*.

Singapore Flyer

30 Raffles Ave, 10min east of Theatres on the Bay • Daily 8.30am–10pm, every 30min • S$29.50 • ☎ 6333 3311, Ⓦ singaporeflyer.com

Standing a lofty 165m tall, the **Singapore Flyer** is the same height as the summit of Bukit Timah, the island's highest natural point, and about 30m taller than the London Eye. The dollar-a-minute ride – billed as a **flight** – initially has you looking east over the Kallang district, home to the grand new Sports Hub stadium complex. Beyond the shipping lanes, Indonesia's **Riau archipelago** looks so close. Looking north, it's more exciting to pick out the golden domes of the Sultan Mosque and the shophouses of Arab Street beyond the twin Gateway buildings on Beach Road. As your capsule reaches maximum height, you might just make out the low hump of **Bukit Timah**, topped with a couple of radio masts, on the horizon beyond Theatres on the Bay.

The descent affords good views of **Marina Bay Sands** and the **Financial District**. Originally the ride began with these, but feng shui concerns meant the wheel's direction had to be reversed (apparently having the capsules ascend pointing towards the banks' towers was channelling good luck up and away from the area). The Flyer's downside is that the most atmospheric areas of old Singapore, including the remaining rows of shophouses in Chinatown and Little India, are largely obscured by clumps of towers; better views can be had from rooftop bars, notably *1-Altitude* (see p.544).

Orchard Road and around

It would be hard to conjure an image more at odds with the present reality of **Orchard Road** than the late May Turnbull's depiction, during early colonial times, of "a country lane lined with bamboo hedges and shrubbery, with trees meeting overhead". In the early part of the last century, merchants taking a constitutional would have strolled past rows of nutmeg trees, followed at a discreet distance by their manservants. Today, the area is synonymous with **shopping** – huge, often glitzy malls selling everything you can imagine line the road (see p.549).

Orchard Road begins as the continuation of Tanglin Road and channels traffic east for nearly 3km to Bras Basah and Selegie roads, near the Colonial District. The bucolic allure of the area of old survives 1km beyond Orchard Road's western end, where you'll find Singapore's excellent **Botanic Gardens**.

Dhoby Ghaut

In the **Dhoby Ghaut** area, at the eastern end of Orchard Road, Indian *dhobies* (laundrymen) used to wash clothes in the Stamford Canal, which once ran along

9

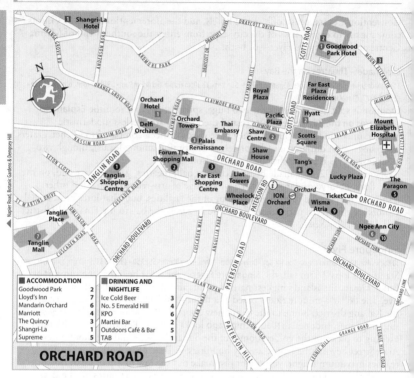

ACCOMMODATION

Goodwood Park	2
Lloyd's Inn	7
Mandarin Orchard	6
Marriott	4
The Quincy	3
Shangri-La	1
Supreme	5

DRINKING AND NIGHTLIFE

Ice Cold Beer	3
No. 5 Emerald Hill	4
KPO	6
Martini Bar	2
Outdoors Café & Bar	5
TAB	1

ORCHARD ROAD

Orchard and Stamford roads. Those days are long gone, though something of the past survives in the **Cathay building** (ⓦcathay.org.sg), home to the company behind one of Singapore's and Malaysia's oldest cinema chains. The building houses a multiplex cinema and boasts a 1939 Art Deco facade that looks better than ever after a recent refurbishment which saw its tower behind demolished and, unusually, replaced by a smaller construction.

Cathay Gallery

Level 2, the Cathay building, 2 Handy Rd • Mon–Sat 11am–7pm • Free • ⓣ 6732 7332, ⓦ thecathay.com.sg/the-cathay-gallery

The **Cathay Gallery** offers a window into the past, displaying memorabilia – costumes, promotional materials and vintage photos – of the Cathay Organization's eight decades in the movie business, including its heyday in the 1950s and 1960s, when the company made its own Chinese- and Malay-language films.

The Istana

Istana and grounds only open four or five days a year, with a nominal entrance fee (see website for details) • ⓦ istana.gov.sg • Dhoby Ghaut MRT

A 3min walk west along Orchard Road from Dhoby Ghaut MRT takes you past the **Plaza Singapura** mall, beyond which stern-looking soldiers guard the main gate of Singapore's **Istana**, built in 1869. With ornate cornices, elegant louvred shutters and a high mansard roof, the building was originally the official residence of Singapore's British governors; now it's home to Singapore's president, a ceremonial role for which elections are nonetheless contested. The first Sunday of the month sees a **changing of the guard** ceremony at the main gate at 5.45pm.

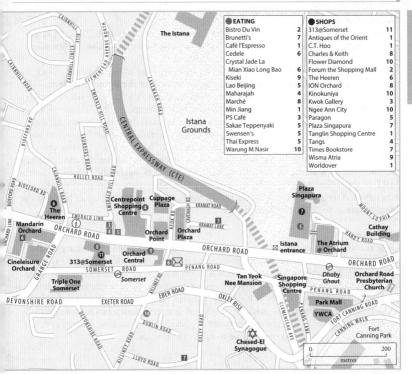

● EATING	
Bistro Du Vin	2
Brunetti's	7
Café l'Espresso	1
Cedele	6
Crystal Jade La Mian Xiao Long Bao	6
Kiseki	9
Lao Beijing	5
Maharajah	4
Marché	8
Min Jiang	1
PS Café	3
Sakae Teppenyaki	5
Swensen's	5
Thai Express	5
Warung M Nasir	10

● SHOPS	
313@Somerset	11
Antiques of the Orient	1
C.T. Hoo	1
Charles & Keith	8
Flower Diamond	10
Forum the Shopping Mall	2
The Heeren	6
ION Orchard	8
Kinokuniya	10
Kwok Gallery	3
Ngee Ann City	10
Paragon	5
Plaza Singapura	7
Tanglin Shopping Centre	1
Tangs	4
Times Bookstore	7
Wisma Atria	9
Worldover	1

Emerald Hill

Somerset MRT

A number of architecturally noteworthy houses have survived the bulldozers at **Emerald Hill**, behind the Centrepoint mall and a 5min walk west of the Istana. Granted to Englishman William Cuppage in 1845, the hill was for some years afterwards the site of a large nutmeg plantation. After his death in 1872, the land was subdivided and sold off, much of it to members of the **Peranakan** community. Walk up Emerald Hill Road today and you'll see exquisite houses from the era, in the so-called **Chinese Baroque** style, typified by the use of coloured ceramic tiles, carved swing doors, shuttered windows and pastel-shaded walls with fine plaster mouldings. Unsurprisingly, quite a few now host trendy restaurants and bars.

Goodwood Park Hotel

22 Scotts Rd • Orchard MRT

A few minutes' walk north up **Scotts Road** off Orchard Road stands the impressive **Goodwood Park Hotel**, with gleaming walls and a distinctive squat, steeple-like tower. Having started out in 1900 as the Teutonia Club for German expats, it was commandeered by the British Custodian of Enemy Property with the outbreak of war across Europe in 1914, and didn't open again until 1918, after which it served for several years as a function hall. In 1929 it became a hotel, though by 1942 it and the *Raffles* – designed by the same architect – were lodging Japanese officers. The *Goodwood Park* was later used for war-crimes trials. Today the hotel remains one of the classiest in town and is a well-regarded venue for a British-style tea.

9

Botanic Gardens

1 Cluny Rd • Daily 5am–midnight • Free, with free weekend tours of some sections plus free concerts • ☎ 6471 7138, ⓦ sbg.org.sg •
Tanglin gate: bus #7 from Arab St area or #174 from Chinatown, both via Somerset Rd, next to Orchard Rd; Bukit Timah Rd entrance:
Botanic Gardens MRT or bus #66 or #170 from Little India, or #171 from Somerset Rd

Singapore has long made green space an integral part of the island's landscape, but none of its parks come close to matching the refinement of the **Botanic Gardens**. Founded in 1859, the gardens were where the Brazilian seeds that gave rise to the great **rubber plantations** of the Malay Peninsula were first nurtured in 1877. Henry Ridley, named the gardens' director the following year, recognized the financial potential of rubber and spent the next twenty years persuading plantation-owners to convert to this new crop, an obsession that earned him the nickname "Mad" Ridley. In later years the gardens became a centre for the breeding of new **orchid** hybrids. Recent additions have extended the park all the way north to Bukit Timah Road, where the Botanic Gardens MRT station offers a route to the newest, least interesting part of the gardens; the itinerary that follows assumes the classic approach up Tanglin and Napier roads to the **Tanglin gate** at the start of Cluny Road.

Into the gardens

Once through the Tanglin gate, take a sharp right up the slope to the **Botany Centre** just ahead, a research facility where you can pick up free maps of the gardens from the information desk. Alternatively, continue straight down the path from the gate, lined with frangipanis, casuarinas and the odd majestic banyan tree, for five minutes to reach the tranquil **Swan Lake**, nearly as old as the gardens themselves. At the lake's far end, paths run through **The Dell** – originally designed as a fern garden but now delightfully overgrown and jungly – to the **ginger garde**n, packed with flowering gingers as exotic and gaudy as anything you could hope to see in the tropics.

National Orchid Garden

Daily 8.30am–7pm, last admission 6pm • S$5

A feast of blooms of almost every hue are on show at the **National Orchid Garden**. Most orchids anchor themselves on trees in the wild, so it's initially odd to see them thriving here at ground level in special beds. There's an entire section of orchids named after dignitaries and celebrities who have visited; *Dendrobium Margaret Thatcher* is a severe pink with a couple of petals twisted like pasta spirals, while *Vandaenopsis Nelson Mandela* is a reassuring warm yellowy-brown.

Be sure to visit the superb **cool house**, mimicking conditions at the tops of equatorial mountains; through its mists you'll spot some stunning **slipper orchids**, their petals forming a pouch below, as well as insectivorous **pitcher plants**. Finally, the **gift shop** stocks an incredible range of orchid paraphernalia, including blossoms encased in glass paperweights or plated with 24-carat gold (or even silvery rhodium for extra snob value).

Back to Tanglin gate

Exiting the orchid garden, head up the boardwalk to enter the central **rainforest** with a trail past numbered highlights, including a spectacular banyan tree that's a mass of aerial roots. The trail and forest end above **Symphony Lake**, where occasional concerts are staged.

By now you've seen much of the best of what the gardens have to offer, and there's not that much to be gained by continuing north. Heading back towards Tanglin gate, look out for the park's loftiest tree, a stunning 47m *jelawai* on the edge of the rainforest tract; this and several other exceptionally tall trees are fitted with lightning conductors. Close by, to the right, is one of the loveliest spots in all of Singapore, a grassy area centred upon a 1930s **bandstand**, encircled by eighteen rain trees for shade.

If you head straight on from here you should arrive back at the Botany Centre via **Holttum Hall**, a 1920s house that now hosts a **museum** of the history of the gardens, although the most striking exhibit is a modern chandelier made entirely of test tubes and lab flasks – celebrating the gardens' role in plant research. Alternatively, head downhill through the **sundial garden** to end up back at the lake.

North to Bukit Timah Road

Continue northwards from Symphony Lake, and you soon reach the **Visitor Centre** – marooned in the middle of the gardens – with a gift shop and café. Next comes the dreary **Evolution Garden**, where fake petrified trees help to illustrate how plant life has evolved over millennia. With children in tow, you might want to head to the **Jacob Ballas garden** (daily 8am–7pm), containing an enclosed water play area; otherwise, it's several minutes' walk through the **bamboo garden** to reach the MRT station. To catch a bus back into town, use the overhead bridge from the station across to Dunearn Road on the far side of the canal, where you'll find the bus stop.

Central Catchment Nature Reserve

For a taste of Singapore's wilder side, head to the **Central Catchment Nature Reserve** (informally known as the "central nature reserve"). The lush heart of the island is dominated by **rainforest** and several large **reservoirs**, and there are opportunities for **hikes** up **Bukit Timah**, the island's tallest hill. The interest isn't limited to the jungle though: close to Bukit Timah, **Memories at Old Ford Factory** is a museum housed in the building where the British surrendered to the Japanese, while the northern end of the nature reserve holds Singapore's highly regarded **zoo**, with a separate **Night Safari** section open from dusk, and the zoo's newest offshoot, the **River Safari,** presenting the animals (including pandas) and fish of rivers as diverse as the Mekong and the Mississippi.

Bukit Timah

Bukit Timah Road shoots northwest from Little India, passing leafy suburbs en route to Johor Bahru (it was the main road to the Causeway until superseded by the Bukit Timah Expressway). Some 9km on from Little India, the road becomes Upper Bukit Timah Road and arrives at **Bukit Timah** itself, often called "Bukit Timah Hill" by locals – a deliberate tautology as the surrounding district is also known as Bukit Timah.

Bukit Timah Nature Reserve

Hindhede Drive • Reopens fully from mid-2016; check website for details • Free • ⓦnparks.gov.sg • Beauty World MRT (when open); bus #171 from Somerset and Scotts rds, or #67 or #170 from opposite Little India MRT (follow signs for bus stop 1/Exit A); ask to be let off opposite Bukit Timah Shopping Centre, then use the overhead footbridge at the Courts furniture store; buses back to town leave from the stop on the left as you leave Hindhede Drive

One of Singapore's last pockets of primary rainforest can be experienced in the excellent **Bukit Timah Nature Reserve**, established in 1883 by Nathaniel Cantley, then superintendent of the Botanic Gardens. **Wildlife** abounded in this part of Singapore in the mid-nineteenth century, when the natural historian Alfred Russel Wallace came here to do fieldwork; he later observed that "in all my subsequent travels in the East I rarely if ever met with so productive a spot". Wallace also noted the presence of tiger traps, but by the 1930s Singapore's tigers had met their end (the Visitor Centre displays a photo of the last specimen to be shot on the island). **Long-tailed macaques** haven't dwindled, however; some can even be seen wandering around the houses at the base of the hill peeking in bins for food. What really impresses is the dipterocarp forest itself, with its towering **emergents** – trees that have reached the top of the jungle canopy as a result of a lucky break, a fallen tree allowing enough light through to the forest floor to nurture saplings to maturity.

Until sometime in 2016, the reserve is largely closed for its slopes to be stabilized and the boardwalks and Visitor Centre renovated. The red trail (30min) – basically a proper road leading to Bukit Timah's summit at 164m – should be accessible at weekends and

9

it was possible to reserve a place on various guide-led nature hikes in early 2015. For details of when the other three, more interesting trails curling through the jungle will reopen, and to download a trail map, see ⓦnparks.gov.sg.

Memories at Old Ford Factory

351 Upper Bukit Timah Rd • Mon–Sat 9am–5.30pm, Sun noon–5.30pm • S$3 • ⓦnas.gov.sg/moff • Bus #171 from Somerset and Scotts rds, or #67 or #170 from Little India MRT; get off when you see the old fire station on the right, then walk on for 2min

The old Ford car factory at Bukit Timah was the first of its type in Southeast Asia when it opened in October 1941. But in early 1942 the Japanese invaded, and on February 15 Lieutenant General Percival, head of the Allied forces in Singapore, surrendered to Japan's General Yamashita in the factory's boardroom. Today the Art Deco building houses a little wartime museum, **Memories at Old Ford Factory**, making good use of military artefacts, period newspapers and oral history recordings.

While the surrenders that bookended the Japanese occupation obviously get some attention, as does the life of British POWs, it's with its coverage of the **civilian experience** of the war that the museum really scores. The occupiers mounted cultural indoctrination campaigns, and displays recall how locals were urged to celebrate Japanese imperial birthdays. Stung by local Chinese efforts to raise funds for China's defence against Japan, the Japanese launched **Sook Ching**, a brutal purge of thousands These events are illustrated by, among other items, some moving sketches by Chia Chew Soo, who witnessed members of his family being killed in 1942. Not least among the privations of occupation were **food shortages**, as recalled by displays on wartime crops – speak to any Singaporean above a certain age today, and chances are they can tell you of having to survive on basics such as tapioca during those dark years.

Singapore Zoo

80 Mandai Lake Rd • ☎6269 3411, ⓦzoo.com.sg • Bus #138 from Ang Mo Kio MRT, #927 from Choa Chu Kang MRT • Private bus transfers daily and nightly from downtown run by SAEx (from various locations; ☎6753 0506, ⓦsaex.com.sg; S$6) or Safari Gate (from Suntec City Mall, Marina Centre, near Promenade MRT; ☎ 6338 6877, ⓦsafarigate.com; S$7)

On a promontory jutting into the tranquil Seletar reservoir, the **Singapore Zoo** and its offshoots, **Night Safari** and **River Safari**, consistently draw crowds, which is partly down to their "open" policy: many animals are kept in spacious, naturalistic enclosures behind moats, though creatures such as big cats still have to be caged.

The zoo

Daily 8.30am–6pm • S$28 • Combination tickets: S$64 with Night Safari, S$50 with River Safari, S$55 with Bird Park (see p.517); see website for prices of tickets that add on two or all three of these

Home to more than 300 species, the zoo could easily occupy you for half a day if not longer. A tram ($5) does a one-way circuit of the grounds, but as it won't always be going your way, be prepared for some legwork.

Highlights include the **Fragile Forest** biodome, a magical zone where you can actually walk among ring-tailed lemurs, sloths and fruit bats, and **Frozen Tundra** – a well-received new enclosure featuring, naturally enough, polar bears. The **white tigers** are a big draw too, not actually white but resembling Siamese cats in the colour of their hair and eyes. Primates are something of a strong point, too: orang-utans swing through the trees overhead close to the entrance, and at the **Great Rift Valley zone** you can espy the communal life of a hundred Hamadryas baboons, including some rather unchivalrous behaviour on the part of males, who bite females to rein them in.

Animal shows and feeding shows run throughout the day, including the excellent **Splash Safari**, featuring penguins, manatees and sea lions. There are also elephant ($8) and pony ($6) rides, plus a popular water play area called **Rainforest Kidzwalk** (from 9am; bring your children's swimming gear).

Night Safari

Daily 7.30pm–midnight, with shops/restaurants from 6pm and last admission at 11pm • S$39 • Combination tickets: S$64 with zoo, S$56 with River Safari, S$61 with BirdPark; see website for prices of tickets that add on two or all three of these

Many animals are nocturnal; the Night Safari section is so enjoyable that you wonder why similar establishments aren't more common. It's true that the Borneo-style tribal show at the entrance is tacky, and there can be long queues for the free tram tours (with commentary; 40min), but these are just niggles at what is the most popular strand of the zoo.

The trams take you around two-thirds of the site. You can forgo them altogether and simply walk around the leafy grounds – an atmospheric experience in the muted lighting. But that way you miss out on some enclosures, notably those for large mammals such as elephants and hippos, and the **Indo-Malayan trail**, featuring Asiatic black bears and an artificial waterfall. Areas you can only visit on foot include the **Fishing Cat Trail**, with the *binturong*, sometimes called the bearcat (you'll understand why when you see it); and the **Leopard Trail**, where your eyes will strain to spot the clouded leopard and slow loris.

It's worth catching the **Creatures of the Night** show (hourly 7.30–9.30pm, plus Fri & Sat 10.30pm; free), an educational affair touching on the importance of conservation and recycling, and starring otters, raccoons, owls and wolves, among others.

River Safari

Daily 9am–6pm • S$25; Amazon River Quest and River Safari Cruise each S$5 • Combination tickets: S$50 with zoo, S$56 with Night Safari, S$47 with BirdPark; see website for prices of tickets that add on two or all three of these

The zoo's latest enterprise is in some ways the most ambitious of the lot: a single park that tries to do justice to the fauna of seven of the world's great rivers and the lands they flow through. **River Safari** tries with modest success to span the divide between aquarium and zoo.

There are too many tanks for comfort at the start, presenting badgers, various alligators and crocs, catfish and other creatures of the Congo, Mississippi, Ganges, Nile and Mekong. Much better is the hangar-like **Giant Panda Forest**, housing two giant pandas and the raccoon-like **red panda**, with white ears and a stripy orange tail. The second half of the park is given over almost entirely to what's billed as **Amazonia**, and much of that is taken up by one 10min ride, the so-so **Amazon River Quest**, in which your "boat" is carried along a sluiceway past enclosures of scarlet ibises and spider monkeys, among others. Seats are limited, so book your River Safari and ride tickets online or face a long wait. Saved for last is the most humongous tank of all: the **Amazon Flooded Forest**, home to manatees, giant arapaima fish, otters and piranhas.

A proper boat ride is also on offer: the **River Safari Cruise** out on the Seletar reservoir and around the back of the zoo, where you can view elephants and other animals (15min; no need to book ahead).

Kranji and Sungai Buloh

While land reclamation has radically altered the east coast and industrialization the west, the **northern** expanses of the island up to the Straits of Johor still retain pockets of the **rainforest** and mangrove swamp that blanketed Singapore on Raffles' arrival in 1819. Though thickets of state housing blocks are never far away, something of rural Singapore's agricultural past clings on by way of the odd prawn- or poultry-farm or vegetable garden. Two attractions make it worth considering coming this far from downtown: the **Kranji War Cemetery and Memorial**, and the wetland reserve at **Sungai Buloh**.

9

Kranji War Cemetery

9 Woodlands Rd • Daily 7am–6pm • Free • ⓦ cwgc.org • Kranji MRT, then a 10min walk west and south, or bus #170 from opposite Little India MRT or Bukit Timah, or #927 from the zoo to the junction of Woodlands and Mandai rds, then a 15min walk north

Kranji War Cemetery and Memorial is the resting place of the many Allied troops who died in the defence of Singapore. Row upon row of graves slope up the manicured hill, some identified only as "known unto God". Beyond the simple stone cross that stands over the cemetery is the **memorial**, around which are recorded the names of more than twenty thousand soldiers (including personnel from Britain, Canada, Australia, New Zealand, Malaya and South Asia) who died in this region during World War II. Two unassuming **tombs** stand on the wide lawns below the cemetery, belonging to Yusof bin Ishak and Dr B.H. Sheares, independent Singapore's first two presidents.

Sungei Buloh Wetland Reserve

301 Neo Tiew Crescent • Mon–Sat 7.30am–7pm, Sun 7am–7pm; guided tours Sat 9.30am • Free • ☎ 6794 1401, ⓦ sbwr.org.sg • Bus #925 from Kranji or Choa Chu Kang MRT to the Kranji reservoir car park, then a 15min walk; on Sun the bus becomes #925C and makes a detour to the reserve

A coastal reservoir runs through the western part of Kranji, beyond which is the **Sungei Buloh Wetland Reserve**, the island's only nature park of its kind. Expanses of mangrove and mud flats are crisscrossed by embanked trails and walkways, with views across the strait to Johor Bahru. The vegetation rapidly gets monotonous, but then **birdlife** is the main reason to come. There's a reasonable chance of spotting sandpipers, egrets and kingfishers, and between September and March, migratory birds from around Asia roost and feed here, especially in the early morning. Several **hides** dot the landscape, and you can get an elevated view over the reserve from the tallest of them, the oversized-treehouse-like **Aerie**. It's worth gazing down at the creeks, too, harbouring mudskippers, banded archerfish – which clobber insect prey by squirting water at them with their mouths – and even the occasional saltwater crocodile.

Geylang and Katong

The neighbouring eastern suburbs of Geylang and Katong may seem mundane at first sight, but both have deep roots and character of the sort absent from the island's new towns. Malay culture has held sway here since the mid-nineteenth century, when Malays and Indonesians arrived to work first in the local *copra* (dried coconut kernel) processing factory and later on its *serai* (lemon grass) farms. **Geylang** retains quite a strong Malay feel today, and the shops, markets and restaurants are worth checking out for Malay food or merchandise, though there are no specific sights. **Katong** was once a beachfront district popular with the wealthy, including many of Peranakan ancestry, who built their villas here in prewar times. The area's **Peranakan heritage** lives on to some degree, and provides the main lure for visitors. You can sample what both districts have to offer by heading south from the **Geylang Serai** area, in the east of Geylang, to Katong via **Joo Chiat Road**, as described below.

Geylang Serai

Paya Lebar MRT, then a short walk south and east, or bus #2 or #51 (from Chinatown) and #7 (from the Botanic Gardens and Orchard Rd), all of which pass through Victoria St, and will drop you on Sims Ave, the main eastbound drag

Geylang has acquired a certain notoriety as something of a red-light district. Arrive by bus, and you'll spot numerous numbered lorongs (lanes) on the way, mainly to the right of Sims Avenue; brothels along them are recognizable by the coloured lights outside. But Geylang is also home to the recently rebuilt **Geylang Serai market**, very much the focus of the area's Malay life. A large, two-storey complex, it's easily spotted on the north side of Sims Avenue, with sloping roofs reminiscent of certain styles of a kampung house. The stalls are predominantly Malay, selling textiles, *kuih* (sweetmeats) and snacks such as *rempeyek*, delicious fried flour rounds encrusted with spices and peanuts.

Joo Chiat Road

Languid **Joo Chiat Road** is where Geylang shades into Katong, the latter now a middle-class residential area, though a little of the former's seediness spills over here after dark. The 1.5km stroll southeast into Katong proper at East Coast Road is hardly a chore thanks to several distractions, including some traditional businesses amid the increasingly fancy shops.

At the northern end of the road, opposite the Geylang Serai market, the **Joo Chiat Complex** looks like a drab suburban mall but feels more like a market inside. There's a notable Malay/Islamic feel, the shops selling batik, rugs and silk, Malay music CDs and *jamu* – assorted herbal remedies. Occasionally a stage is set up behind for people to partake of impromptu bouts of old-fangled *joget* dancing.

At no. 252, Chiang Pow Joss Paper Trading produces funerary paraphernalia in one of several nicely restored shophouses on the road, while Nam San at no. 261 makes mackerel *otah-otah*, a kind of dumpling. Just beyond, the immaculate **Peranakan shophouses** on Koon Seng Road (on the left) are the architectural highlight of the area, with their restored multicoloured facades, French windows, eaves and mouldings. At no. 320, peek through the 1960s louvred windows at the workaday Ann Tin Tong Medical Hall, a world away from Chinatown's slick herbalists. Teong Theng, at no. 369, sells attractive rattan furniture and accessories, popular items in Singapore homes a generation ago, but now almost totally out of favour.

9

Katong

Bus #12 from Chinatown, Victoria St and Lavender MRT, or #14 from Orchard Rd; both call at Mountbatten MRT en route

From the Koon Seng Road intersection, Joo Chiat Road runs 600m on to **East Coast Road**. The beach hinted at by that name has long since gone – pushed further south by the creation of the East Coast Park, with its leisure facilities and restaurants, on several kilometres of reclaimed land. However, the area is worth visiting thanks to a pocket of outlets celebrating its Peranakan traditions – it's not hard to find places serving Nyonya food, and there's Rumah Bebe at 113 East Coast Rd, selling clothing and jewellery (see p.550).

Katong Antiques House

208 East Coast Rd • Daily except Mon 11am–5pm • Optional tours S$15 per person • ☎ 6345 8544

East of the junction with Joo Chiat Road is the Katong Antiques House, whose owner, Peter Wee, is a veteran spokesman for the Peranakan community. He has amassed a treasure-trove of artefacts, from wedding costumes to vintage furniture and, more prosaically, old books in Baba Malay, a blend of Malay and Hokkien Chinese. By prior arrangement, he can give you a tour of the traditionally decorated shophouse, which as with all such buildings has rooms that stretch on for a surprising distance behind the narrow facade.

Changi

Tanah Merah MRT, then bus #2; alternatively, and much slower, pick up the bus from Chinatown or elsewhere downtown

Even in the 1970s, eastern Singapore still looked the way the outskirts of some Malaysian towns do today, dotted with kampungs, low-rise housing estates and tracts of wooded land or stands of coconut palms. It's hard to visualize that landscape as you head out through areas of new towns like Bedok (a quiet seaside suburb until the arrival of state housing projects and the reclamation of land for the East Coast Park) on the way to **Changi**, right at the eastern tip of the island. The main reason to head this far east is to see **Changi Museum**, commemorating the internment of Allied troops and civilians by the Japanese during World War II. In the Singaporean consciousness, the Changi district has long embodied a beachside idyll; just a bit further afield from the museum is the **beach**, for a dip or bask on a hot day.

Changi Museum

1000 Upper Changi Rd North • Daily 9.30am–5pm • Free, audioguides S$8, guided tours S$12 • ☎ 6214 2451, ⓦ changimuseum.sg • Tanah Merah MRT, then a 20min ride on bus #2

Changi Prison was the infamous site of a World War II POW camp in which Japanese jailers subjected Allied prisoners, both military and civilian, to the harshest of treatment. Those brutalities are movingly remembered in the **Changi Museum**. It was formerly housed within the prison itself, which remains in use – drug offenders are periodically executed here – but was moved wholesale just up the road when the prison was extended.

Novelist James Clavell drew on his experience of Changi in writing *King Rat*, never forgetting that in the cells "the stench was nauseating… stench from a generation of confined human bodies." No museum could possibly bring home the horrors of internment, though this one does a reasonable job of picking over the facts of the Japanese occupation and the conditions prisoners endured. Memorable exhibits include artworks by internees, with pride of place given to reproductions of Stanley Warren's so-called **Changi Murals**, depicting New Testament scenes (the originals are housed within an army camp nearby, where Warren was held). A final section features a recreation of an improvised theatre where internees put on entertainments to amuse fellow inmates, though here there's only a TV screen showing wartime footage.

In the museum courtyard is a simple wooden chapel, typical of those erected in Singapore's wartime camps; the brass cross on its altar was crafted from spent ammunition casings. The messages on its board of remembrance are often touching and worth a read (ask staff for pen and notepaper to add your own).

Changi Point and the beach

Bus #2 from Tanah Merah MRT

Beyond Changi Prison, the tower blocks thin out and the landscape becomes a patchwork of fields, often a relic of colonial-era military bases still used by Singapore's forces. Ten minutes on via the #2 bus is the coast at **Changi Point**, with a cluster of eating places and shops called Changi Village, mainly serving the beach-going public.

To reach the **beach** from the bus terminus, head on past the market and food court and bear left to the *Ubin First Stop* seafood restaurant, where you'll see a canalized inlet from the sea. The footbridge here leads to a stretch of manicured grass and trees, the prelude to a narrow strip of brownish sand fronting greenish-blue water – actually not uninviting (unless you were expecting something out of coastal Terengganu), and the sight of aircraft rumbling in low every few minutes on the Changi flight path soon ceases to be a distraction. Facilities, including showers and a camping area, are shown on a map of the so-called Changi Beach Park available from ⓦnparks.gov.sg.

The Southern Ridges and Pasir Panjang

While no less endowed with new towns and industrial estates than the east of the island, western Singapore retains a leafier, more open feel. An unusually verdant example of this is at the **Southern Ridges**, an umbrella term recently dreamed up for the coastal ridge that begins at the southern tip of the island and continues 9km northwest, under various names, to a site just beyond the main campus of the National University of Singapore. The ridge is lined by a chain of parks and general greenery, and it's now possible to do an extended walk along it using a series of ingenious footbridges and elevated walkways.

The main attractions en route are **Reflections at Bukit Chandu**, a museum commemorating the wartime defence of that hill by Singapore's Malay Regiment; and **Mount Faber**, with views over downtown Singapore and cable-car rides across to Sentosa island (see p.518). In between the Southern Ridges and the sea, **Pasir Panjang**, once a sleepy district of kampungs and still a relatively quiet residential area, is home to just one sight, the entertainingly tacky Buddhist theme park of **Haw Par Villa**.

The account below takes the Southern Ridges walk in an easterly direction, ending at Harbourfront MRT beneath Mount Faber – a sensible choice as this avoids a steep climb up the hill and allows you to finish at the massive VivoCity mall, where you can assuage any appetite and thirst worked up along the way. Haw Par Villa, the furthest site west covered here, is really an optional extra as far as the walk is concerned. One more practical point: the links between parks on the walk often offer little shade, so be assiduous about **sun protection** and bring a reasonable supply of water.

Haw Par Villa

262 Pasir Panjang Rd • Daily 9am–7pm • Free • ☎ 6872 2780 • Haw Par Villa MRT or bus #200 from Buona Vista MRT or #51 from Chinatown

Delightfully unmodernized, **Haw Par Villa** is an unexpected star among Singapore's lesser-known sights. Featuring a gaudy parade of hundreds of statues of people and creatures from Chinese myth and legend, it was once the estate of the Aw brothers, Boon Haw Aw and Boon Par Aw, who made a fortune early last century selling Tiger Balm – a cure-all ointment created by their father. Within the grounds were their villa and private zoo, but when the British began asking the owners of large animals to get

9

licences, the brothers replaced the zoo with statuary; subsequently the park acquired a new moniker, a mishmash of the brothers' names.

The main path curls up and around a hill past one hilariously kitsch tableau after another. One of the best shows titanic combat as the Eight Immortals of Taoist mythology attack the Dragon King's undersea palace. Elsewhere, look out for a curious folk-tale scene in which a deer and a goat, the latter talking into a bakelite telephone, take tea with a rabbit and a rat, who are newlyweds.

The centrepiece is the **Ten Courts of Hell**, a tunnel housing gory depictions of punishments meted out to deceased sinners. Tax dodgers and late rent-payers are pictured being "pounded with a stone mallet", prostitutes are drowned in the "filthy blood pool", to name but two; in one tableau someone appears to be being gored to death by a giant brush. Finally, the dead are shown having their memories wiped by drinking a cup of "magic tea" prior to reincarnation.

Reflections at Bukit Chandu

31k Pepys Rd • Tues–Sun 9am–5.30pm • S$2 • ☎ 6375 2510, ⓦ nhb.gov.sg • Pasir Panjang MRT, then a 10min walk north uphill

The defence of Pasir Panjang against the Japanese by the 1st and 2nd Battalion of the Malay Regiment is remembered at the tiny **Reflections at Bukit Chandu** museum. It's housed in a lone colonial building that once served as officer accommodation, though it became a food and munitions store during the war. Here "C" company of the Malay Regiment's second battalion made a brave stand against the Japanese on February 13, 1942 – two days before the British capitulation – and sustained heavy casualties.

There's nothing special about the small collection of artefacts focusing on this event, though the displays do communicate the human toll of the conflict, as well as highlighting British ambivalence about working with the Malays: the Malay Regiment was only begun as an experiment to see "how the Malays would react to military discipline", and only when they proved themselves was it taken seriously, with members sent to Singapore for training.

The canopy walk

Bear left along the ridge from the Reflections at Bukit Chandu for your first taste of the Southern Ridges trail – and a wonderful introduction it is too, for this is where the **canopy walk** begins. Soaring above the actual trail, the walkway takes you east through the treetops, with signs pointing out common Singapore trees such as cinnamon and *tembusu*, and views north across rolling grassy landscapes, the odd mansion poking out from within clumps of mature trees. After just a few minutes, the walkway rejoins the trail leading downhill to some mundane nurseries and the west gate of the desultory **Hort Park** on Alexandra Road.

From Alexandra Arch to Mount Faber

The Alexandra Road end of Hort Park is very close to one of the huge, purpose-built footbridges on the Southern Ridges trail, the white **Alexandra Arch**, which is meant to resemble a leaf but looks more like the Singapore River's Elgin Bridge on steroids. On the bridge's east side, a long, elevated metal walkway zigzags off into the distance; it's called the **forest walk**, though it passes through nothing denser than mature woodland on its kilometre-long journey east. The walkway zigzags even more severely as it rises steeply to the top of **Telok Blangah Hill**, whose park offers good views of the usual residential tower blocks to the north and east, and of Mount Faber and Sentosa to the southeast.

Proceed downhill, following signs for **Henderson Waves**, and after 750m you come to a vast footbridge of wooden slats over metal. High up in the air over broad Henderson Road, the bridge has undulating parapets – the "Waves" – boasting built-in shelters against the sun or rain.

Mount Faber

On the east side of Henderson Waves and north of the VivoCity mall • Free • ☎ 6377 9688, ⓦ mountfaber.com.sg • A stiff walk up from Harbourfront MRT

In bygone years, leafy **Mount Faber**, named in 1845 after government engineer Captain Charles Edward Faber, was a favourite recreation spot for its superb **views** over downtown. These days, you'll have to look out for breaks in the dense foliage for vistas over Bukit Merah new town to Chinatown and the Financial District, or head to the **Faber Peak**, a smart bar and restaurant complex at the very summit. The complex is also the departure point for the deluxe **cable car** to the HarbourFront Centre and on to Sentosa island (daily 8.45am–10pm; S$29 return).

To descend, follow signs for the **Marang trail**, which eventually leads down a steep flight of steps on the south side of the hill to VivoCity, with the HarbourFront Centre next door.

HarbourFront Centre and VivoCity

Harbourfront MRT

On Telok Blangah Road, the **HarbourFront Centre** is nothing more than a glorified ferry terminal from where boats set off for Indonesia's Riau archipelago (see p.526), as well as the departure point for **cable cars** heading to Mount Faber and Sentosa island. Much more worthwhile is the **VivoCity** mall, with a curious fretted white facade that looks like it was cut out of a set of giant false teeth, and housing three good food courts (in particular *Food Republic* on level 3), a slew of restaurants, a cinema and other amenities; from here Sentosa is just a 10min walk away (see p.518). The red-brick box of a building with the huge chimney east of the mall, and connected to it by an elevated walkway, is **St James Power Station**, a clubbing mecca housed in, surprise surprise, a converted power plant.

Jurong

Occupying a sizeable slab of southwestern Singapore, sprawling **Jurong** was notoriously dubbed "Goh's folly" in the 1960s when Goh Keng Swee, then Singapore's finance minister, decided it was vital to create a major industrial town here on unpromising swampy terrain. To the surprise of not just the avowed sceptics, the new town took off, and today Jurong boasts a diverse portfolio of industries, including pharmaceuticals and oil refining – in which Singapore is a world leader despite having nary a drop of black gold of its own. Jurong also has sizeable residential quarters and various leisure attractions, though only two constitute a serious temptation to make a trip here: the extensive avian zoo that is the **Jurong Bird Park**, and the **Singapore Science Centre**, with an entertaining emphasis on interactivity.

Jurong Bird Park

2 Jurong Hill • Daily 8.30am–6pm • S$25, combination tickets: S$55 with zoo, S$61 with Night Safari, S$47 with River Safari (see website for details of tickets that add on two or all three attractions) • ☎ 6265 0022, ⓦ birdpark.com.sg • Boon Lay MRT, then bus #194 or #251; heading back, you pick up the #194 from the stop where you arrived, while for the #251 you should cross to the other side of the road

Lining Jalan Ahmad Ibrahim, the **Jurong Bird Park** is home to one of the world's biggest bird collections, with nearly four hundred species. You'll need at least a couple of hours to have a good look around the grounds, though you can save a little time using the park's trams ($5).

Besides the four expansive walk-in aviary, described below, the park also has a number of worthwhile smaller enclosures, such as the hugely popular **Penguin Coast** (feeding times 10.30am & 3.30pm). Just inside the entrance, it juxtaposes half a dozen penguin species against the backdrop of a mock Portuguese galleon, designed to evoke the

9

sighting of penguins by explorers such as Vasco da Gama. Utterly different is **World of Darkness**, a fascinating owl showcase that uses special lighting to swap day for night.

The park also puts on various bird shows, the most exciting of which is Kings of the Skies (daily 10am & 4pm), in which eagles, hawks, falcons and owls show off their predatory capabilities.

The walk-in aviaries

While not the most impressive of the major aviaries, the **Southeast Asian Birds** section makes seeing local birdlife far easier than overnighting in a hide in Taman Negara; you find fairy bluebirds and other small but delightful creatures feasting on papaya slices, with a simulated thunderstorm at midday. Close by are **Jungle Jewels**, featuring South American birdlife in "forest" surroundings, and the **Lory Loft**, a giant aviary under netting, its foliage meant to simulate the Australian bush. Its denizens are dozens of multicoloured, chattering lories and lorikeets, which have no qualms about perching at the viewing balcony or perhaps even on your arm, hoping for a bit of food (suitable feed is on sale).

At the far end of the park is the **Waterfall Aviary**, long the park's pride. It boasts a 30m cascade and 1500 winged inhabitants, including carmine bee-eaters and South African crowned cranes.

Singapore Science Centre

15 Science Centre Rd • Daily 10am–6pm • S$12 • ☎ 6425 2500, ⓦ science.edu.sg • Jurong East MRT, then a 10min walk or bus #66 or #335, or a long ride on #66 all the way from Little India

Interactivity is the watchword at the **Singapore Science Centre**, on the eastern edge of the parkland around the artificial Jurong Lake. Galleries here hold hundreds of hands-on displays focusing on genetics, space science and other disciplines, allowing you to understand fire, test your ability to hear high-pitched sounds and be befuddled by optical illusions. It goes down well with the kids on school outings, who sweep around the place in deafening waves.

Omni-Theatre

21 Jurong Town Hall Rd • Films daily noon–8pm; observatory Fri 7.50–10pm • S$12 or S$19 joint ticket with Science Centre; observatory free • ☎ 6425 2500, ⓦ omnitheatre.com.sg

Just north of the Science Centre, the **Omni-Theatre** shows hourly IMAX movies about the natural world, and houses an **observatory** that does free stargazing sessions on Fridays. Being almost on the equator, Singapore enjoys views of both the northern and southern skies, though light pollution and puffy tropical clouds can put a dampener on things.

Snow City

21 Jurong Town Hall Rd • Daily 10am–6pm • S$15/hr including use of their jackets and boots, though glove rental costs extra • ☎ 6560 2306, ⓦ snowcity.com.sg.

Hi tech machines let it snow year-round in this corner of equatorial Singapore, though the slope at **Snow City** is just 60m long and less than three storeys high, leaving scope only for "tobogganing" on rubber rings.

Sentosa

Nominal S$1 admission fee • ☎ 1 800 736 8672, ⓦ sentosa.com.sg • Harbourfront MRT, then a 10min walk using the Sentosa Boardwalk footbridge from the VivoCity mall

Nearly forty years of rampant development have transformed **Sentosa** into the most built-up of Singapore's southern islands, so it's ironic that its name means "tranquil" in Malay. The island has certainly come a long way since World War II, when it was a

OPPOSITE LITTLE INDIA (P.485) >

9

British military base and known as Pulau Blakang Mati ("Island of Death Behind"). Contrived but enjoyable in parts, Sentosa today is a hybrid of so-so resort island and out-of-town theme park, promoted for its rides, passable beaches and the massive new casino resort on its northern shore, Resorts World, which also features a Universal Studios theme park, a maritime museum, a fabulous aquarium and numerous hotels.

If you want to visit, avoid the weekends and school breaks unless you don't mind the place being positively overrun, with long waits to get into the main sights.

ARRIVAL — SENTOSA

There are multiple ways to reach the island other than walking, the most popular of which is the Sentosa Express monorail. Note that all the options below include the island entry fee in the fare, and that **taxi** journeys to and from the island incur a surcharge of several dollars depending on the time of day.

By monorail The Sentosa Express operates every 5min from level 3 of the VivoCity mall (S$4). See below for details of stops on the island. Note that there is no charge to ride the monorail back to VivoCity.

By bus The #RWS8 bus shuttles between HarbourFront/VivoCity to Resorts World (regular bus hours; S$2). At weekends there are one-way night buses #NR1 and #NR6

from Resorts World to Marina Bay, the Colonial District, Clarke Quay and Orchard Rd (Fri & Sat 11.30pm–2pm; S$4.50).

By cable car The most stylish way to arrive is via the revamped cable-car system from Mount Faber via tower 2 of the HarbourFront Centre (daily 8.45am–10pm; S$29), though the harbour and city views and plush cabins aren't quite worth the outlay.

INFORMATION

An information point at the end of the Sentosa Boardwalk where you arrive dispenses free **maps** (also available at monorail stations and from ⓦ sentosa.com.sg), which are especially handy given that new venues and sights seem to replace others every few months. Alternatively, download the **MySentosa app** (Apple and Android devices).

GETTING AROUND

All transport once you've arrived on Sentosa is free.

By bus The island has three colour-coded internal buses that run on loop routes, plus a so-called beach tram running the length of the southern beaches; all routes are charted on the free island maps.

By monorail The Sentosa Express calls at Waterfront station on the northern shore (for Resorts World), Imbiah station a little further south, and Beach station on the southern shore, for the three beaches.

Resorts World Sentosa

Close to Waterfront station on the island's north shore • ☎ 6577 8888, ⓦ rwsentosa.com

The Resorts World development is visually plastic, like something out of a Silicon Valley corporate headquarters, but it boasts some of Sentosa's biggest attractions. Booking online for Universal Studios or the aquarium (if you see only one thing at Resorts World, shell out for this) is a good idea, not only to save queuing up to get in (though be prepared to queue for rides at the former), but also because tickets may sell out in advance on certain days.

Universal Studios Singapore

Resorts World Sentosa • Daily 10am–6 or 7pm • S$74, or S$100 with S.E.A. Aquarium; many rides have minimum height requirements and may not be suitable for young children

The ersatz character of Resorts World becomes rather entertaining at the **Universal Studios** theme park, where fairy-tale castles and American cityscapes rear bizarrely into view in the sultry heat. The park is divided into seven themed zones, encompassing everything from ancient Egypt – the least convincing of the lot – to DreamWorks' animated hit *Madagascar*.

Standard tickets offer unlimited rides, but there's much more to do than get flung around on cutting-edge roller coasters or, in the case of the Jurassic Park Rapids Adventure, on a circular yellow raft: museum-style exhibits unwrap the world of film production, and you can watch musical spectaculars in a recreation of Hollywood's Pantages theatre.

The Maritime Experiential Museum and S.E.A. Aquarium

9

Resorts World Sentosa; turn right from the Sentosa Boardwalk as you arrive • Daily 10am–7pm • day ticket S$38, or S$100 with Universal Studios, or S$67 with Adventure Cove, or S$18 after 4pm for people with Universal Studios or Adventure Cove tickets

Highlighting the historical sea trade between China and India and the Middle East, the **Maritime Experiential Museum** might seem a touch too cerebral for a casino development, and in the event it stoops to cheesy audiovisual trickery to entertain. It's really there to serve as a prelude to the wonderful **S.E.A. Aquarium**, showcasing the marine life of that very same maritime route.

The museum

The museum's centrepiece is a massive replica of the bow of a ship used by the Ming-dynasty emissary **Cheng Ho** (also known as Zheng He), which has a lion's head figurehead whose eyes flare red as it exhales smoke. Slightly more memorable is the **Typhoon Theatre**, where videos show Chinese actors with American accents enacting events leading up to a shipwreck – evoked with thunder and lightning, sprays of water across the audience and a final catastrophic capsizing that does something unusual to the entire room.

The most impressive exhibit is sadly marooned on pillars up near the ceiling: the **Jewel of Muscat**, a recreation of a ninth-century Arab dhow. The sailing boat was built without nails (coconut fibre binds the timbers), and was a gift to Singapore from Oman in 2010. Delivery took 68 days – under sail, of course.

The aquarium

Basement of the Maritime Experiential Museum

Awe-inspiring in its ambition and scale, the aquarium has tanks covering ten habitats, arranged in a long loop. If you see it in the intended direction – people often go the "wrong" way – you begin with a magnificent evocation of a **shipwreck** swarming with schools of Southeast Asian fish, including mottled honeycomb stingrays. The Southeast Asian theme continues in the next section, with an 8m-tall cylindrical **coral garden**, but both these tanks pale in comparison to the monster **Ocean Gallery** halfway through. Some 36m long, with walls 70cm thick, it's so vast that a restaurant and several hotel suites have their own vistas onto part of it. Here you can watch mindboggling shoals of small silvery fish moving in unison, while giant manta rays, goliath groupers and sharks sweep through. Elsewhere, look out for the fabulous collection of assorted **jellyfish**, some glowing like part of a very exotic lava lamp, thanks to coloured lighting.

Adventure Cove Waterpark

Resorts World Singapore, a 2min walk beyond the Maritime Experiential Museum • Daily 10am–6pm • Day ticket S$36, or S$67 with S.E.A. Aquarium; diving or other interactions with marine life costs extra (see website for details)

The Adventure Cove Waterpark is the priciest and the best water-themed play park in Singapore, and by no means just for kids. The magic ingredient is the presence of actual sea life: **Rainbow Reef** lets you snorkel in the presence of thousands of fish, while at **Adventure River** you float down a long channel past surreal marine-themed statues, eventually ending up inside a watery glass tunnel within an aquarium tank, where the fish gawp at you drifting by. You can also pay extra to be lowered inside a glass enclosure into the shark tank or wade in a pool filled with rays. Of the rides and slides, the star is undoubtedly the **Riptide Rocket**, a roller coaster which uses magnets to hoist passengers' dinghies on the upward legs; the lines for it get ever longer as the day wears on, so it's best tackled early.

Trick Eye Museum

Resorts World Singapore, close to the Sentosa Boardwalk • Daily 10am–9pm • S$25, or S$48 with aquarium or Adventure Cove Waterpark • ☏ 6795 2370, ⓦ trickeye.com/singapore

If you're the sort that likes sticking your head into life-size fairground figures with the faces cut out, then the **Trick Eye Museum** is practically made for you. Here you can

9

insert your head or, in some cases, all of yourself into giant tableaux and strike poses within famous Impressionist paintings, fairy-tales' scenes or any number of surreal rooms and streetscapes. It's a fad that has swept East Asia, where the museum is the tenth member of its franchise; when it opened in mid-2014, crowds queued for up to five hours just to garner those crazy snaps and, of course, associated Facebook likes.

Crane Dance

Close to the Maritime Experiential Museum • Thurs–Mon 9pm (some weeks nightly); 10min • Free

Sentosa isn't much of a night-time destination, but if you linger after sunset, you may want to catch either Wings of Time (see opposite) or **Crane Dance**. The latter features the computer-manipulated courtship of two enormous mechanical birds, standing metres from shore, accompanied by fireworks and dazzling lighting and water effects. If you're not sure whether to stick around for it, you can preview the whole shebang on YouTube.

Other Sentosa attractions

Just about every patch of Sentosa that isn't a beach, hotel, golf course or a luxury home for the super-rich is packed with rides and other diversions, ranging from a Merlion replica whose inside you can walk around to a vertical wind tunnel that replicates the sensation of skydiving by keeping a person aloft on a continuous upward blast of air. The selection here covers a few of the more interesting and sensibly priced offerings.

Madame Tussauds

Imbiah Lookout • Daily 10am–9pm (last admission 7.30pm) • S$30, or S$35 with Images of Singapore LIVE • ☎ 6715 4000, ⓦ madametussauds.com/singapore • Imbiah station

Inevitably, the **Madame Tussauds** waxwork franchise has fetched up in Singapore, its seventh opening in Asia. There are a sprinkling of local and East Asian figures, including Malaysian actress Michelle Yeoh and Chinese basketballer Yao Ming, amid the usual cast of celebrities from the worlds of showbiz and sport. Its unique feature, however, is a magical illuminated boat ride down a fake river, past miniaturized Singapore scenes such as Gardens by the Bay, an Indian temple *gopuram* and a Chinese opera, on to the neighbouring Images of Singapore LIVE.

Images of Singapore LIVE

Imbiah Lookout • Daily 10am–9pm (last admission 7.30pm) • S$15, or S$35 with Madame Tussauds • Imbiah station

Images of Singapore LIVE takes you on a journey through Singapore's history, using a mixture of life-sized dioramas, glossy multimedia effects and costumed actors. Along the way you can meet characters such as a nineteenth-century lamplighter in Commercial Square – Raffles Place as it then was – and be at the *Raffles Hotel* during a Japanese air raid in 1941, before finally taking the boat ride out to Madame Tussauds.

Luge and Skyride

Daily 10am–9.30pm • S$15 (S$10 Skyride only) • ☎ 6274 0472, ⓦ skylineluge.com • Beach station for Skyride, Imbiah station for Luge

Surprisingly good fun, the **Skyride**, akin to a ski lift, takes you up the hill behind Siloso beach, after which you ride your **Luge** – a sort of small, unmotorized go-kart – and coast down either of two long, curving tracks back to your starting point.

Megazip Adventure Park

A 5min walk west of Imbiah station • Daily 11am–7pm • ☎ 6884 5602, ⓦ megazip.com.sg

Megazip is a zip-line or flying-fox ride, in which you slide, suspended from a steel cable, from a hilltop down to an islet beyond Siloso Beach ($39). Other offerings are a mini-bungee jump ($19), an obstacle course that's all ropes and netting ($35) and a climbing wall ($19).

WaveHouse

Siloso Beach • Daily 10.30am–10.30pm • First hour S$35 or S$45 depending on "ride", S$5 more at weekends • ☎ 6238 1196, ⓦ wavehousesentosa.com • Beach station

WaveHouse does for surfing what Universal Studios does for ancient Egypt, conjuring up a semblance of the real thing using torrents of water sent along two contoured blue slopes. One generates a continuous 2m curling wave; the other is flat and suitable for beginners.

Fort Siloso

At the northwest tip of the island, beyond Siloso Beach • Daily 10am–6pm, free tours Fri–Sun 12.30 & 3.30pm (via the fort tram at Beach station) • S$12 • Beach station

Fort Siloso guarded Singapore's western approaches from the 1880s until 1956, by which time its uselessness had been already shown up by the Japanese marching in from Johor. Today, the recorded voice of one Battery Sergeant Major Cooper talks you through a mock-up of a nineteenth-century barracks, complete with living quarters, guardroom, laundry and assault course. Be sure to check out the **Surrender Chambers**, where life-sized figures re-enact the British and Japanese surrenders of 1942 and 1945, respectively. After that you can explore the complex's hefty gun emplacements and tunnels.

Wings of Time

At the start of Siloso Beach • Daily 7.40pm & 8.40pm; 25min • S$18 • ⓦ wingsoftime.com.sg • Beach station

The minority of visitors who hang around Sentosa after dusk are either heading to one of the beach bars (see p.542 & p.545) or to **Wings of Time**, a kids' fable cast as a lavish sound-and-light show, featuring pyrotechnics, lasers and live actors. Most of the action takes place on a series of offshore platforms, as well as aerial screens of water and mist, with seating right at the beach to take it all in.

The beaches

The best that can be said about Sentosa's three **beaches**, created with vast quantities of imported beige sand, is that they're decent enough, with bluey-green waters, the odd lagoon and facilities for renting canoes, surfboards and aqua bikes. For tranquillity, however, you'd probably do better at Changi Beach (see p.515): at Sentosa you have to deal with not only crowds but also the view of one of the world's busiest shipping lanes – expect a parade of container ships and other vessels all day.

Siloso Beach, extending 1500m northwest of Beach Station, is the busiest of the three, with well-established resorts and facilities, including good restaurants. **Palawan Beach**, in the opposite direction from Beach Station, is meant to be the most family-oriented and boasts a children's play area centred on a mock galleon. It also features a suspension bridge leading out to an islet billed as the "Southernmost Point of Continental Asia" – though a sign concedes that this is so only by virtue of three artificial links, namely the bridge itself, the bridge from HarbourFront to Sentosa, and the Causeway. Beyond Palawan, **Tanjong Beach** tends to be slightly quieter than the other two as it starts a full kilometre from Beach Station.

ARRIVAL AND DEPARTURE   **SINGAPORE**

Most visitors fly into **Changi Airport**, in the east of the island, or arrive by bus or train via the 1km **Causeway** that links Johor Bahru to the island (although some luxury buses use the **Second Crossing** bridge into Tuas in the west, and more may follow suit after the new Tuas Link metro station opens there). Wherever you arrive, the well-oiled public transport system, including **MRT metro trains** and an elaborate **bus** network, means that you'll have no problem getting into the city centre.

BY PLANE

CHANGI INTERNATIONAL AIRPORT

Singapore's airport (ⓦ changiairport.com), at the eastern

tip of the island 16km from downtown, is well laid out and runs like clockwork: the country in microcosm. There are three main terminals, connected by free Skytrains, with a

9

fourth scheduled to open in 2017. There are the usual exchange facilities/ATMs, accommodation booking counters representing the major hotels, and plenty of shops and restaurants. But chances are you'll not linger long – baggage comes through so swiftly that you can be heading to the city centre within twenty minutes of arrival. Connections with Malaysia and Brunei include:

Destinations Bandar Seri Begawan (1–2 daily; 2hr); Ipoh (2 daily; 1hr 30min); Kota Bharu (4 weekly; 1hr 20min); Kota Kinabalu (1–2 daily; 2hr 30min); Kuala Lumpur (KLIA; hourly; 55min); Kuala Lumpur (Subang; at least 6 daily; 1hr); Kuala Terengganu (3 weekly; 1hr 15min); Kuantan (daily; 50min); Kuching (3–4 daily; 1hr 20min); Langkawi (1–2 daily; 1hr 30min); Miri (4 weekly; 2hr); Penang (at least 8 daily; 1hr 20min); Redang (April–Oct 3 weekly; 1hr 45min).

Airlines AirAsia, Changi Terminal 1 ☎ 6307 7688; Firefly, 16–92 The Central, 6 Eu Tong Sen St (above Clarke Quay MRT) ☎ 6227 3833; Malaysia Airlines, 02–09, Singapore Shopping Centre, 190 Clemenceau Ave off Orchard Rd ☎ 6433 0208; Royal Brunei #03-11 UE Shopping Mall, 81 Clemenceau Ave ☎ 6235 4672; Singapore Airlines, #04-05, ION Orchard (above Orchard MRT) ☎ 6223 8888 (helpline is 24hr). For the numerous other airline offices, see ⓦ yellowpages.com.sg.

Transport connections Between 6am and 11pm, the easiest way to get into the city centre from the airport is on an MRT train; the station is beneath terminals 2 and 3 (change at Tanah Merah; 30min; S$2.40). Alternatively, bus #36 (same hours, roughly every 10min; S$2, no change given) heads to the Orchard Rd area via Marina Centre and the Colonial District. Transport desks at each terminal can also book you places on 24hr airport shuttle buses, which serve most downtown hotels and hostels ($9). A taxi to downtown costs at least S$20 and takes up to half an hour; there's an airport surcharge of S$3–5, and a fifty percent surcharge midnight–6am.

BY TRAIN

Malaysian trains no longer serve downtown Singapore, after a deal in 2011 in which Singapore took ownership of the KTM railway line on the island. As a result, trains now terminate just inside Singapore at Woodlands station near the Causeway checkpoint. With KTM still charging a premium for journeys that begin or end in Singapore, it's hardly worth using Woodlands station – use Johor Bahru station just on the far side of the Causeway, and cross between the two countries by bus.

WOODLANDS STATION

KTM revises its schedules often; check the latest timetables on ⓦ ktmb.com.my. At the time of writing there were three daily services to Kuala Lumpur, one of them a sleeper, one continuing through to Butterworth; and two trains daily to the interior, one of which is a sleeper that plods up to Kelantan on the east coast. With deep pockets, you could

ride the Eastern & Oriental Express to Bangkok (see p.28).

Destinations Butterworth (1 daily; 14hr); Gua Musang (1 daily; 12hr); Ipoh (1 daily; 10hr 30min); Jerantut (for Taman Negara; 2 daily; 8hr 30min); Johor Bahru (5 daily; 5min); Kuala Kangsar (1 daily; 11hr 15min); Kuala Lipis (2 daily; 9hr 30min); Kuala Lumpur (3 daily; 7hr 30min); Seremban (3 daily; 6hr 30min); Taiping (1 daily; 12hr); Wakaf Bharu (for Kota Bharu; 1 daily; 16hr).

Transport connections To reach the centre, catch bus #170 or #170X to Kranji MRT (daily 6am–midnight); #170 continues all the way down to Little India and terminates at Queen St near Bugis MRT and Arab St.

BY BUS

In the absence of a proper long-distance bus terminal, most buses terminate at, and leave from, the Beach Rd area. Heading to Malaysia, note that you don't have to buy a ticket from Singapore; it's cheaper to catch a local bus from the Queen St terminal to Johor Bahru's Larkin bus station and pick up an express bus there (with a better choice of services to the east coast, too).

Golden Mile Complex/Golden Mile Tower 5001/6001 Beach Rd Most bus companies serving west coast destinations beyond KL and also Hat Yai in Thailand are based at these two neighbouring shopping/office complexes, including: Konsortium (☎ 6392 3911, ⓦ konsortium.com.sg), Grassland Express (☎ 6292 1166, ⓦ grassland.com.sg), Sri Maju (☎ 6294 8228, ⓦ srimaju.com) and Starmart Express (☎ 6396 5681, ⓦ starmartonline.com). Any westbound bus from outside the complex will take you to the City Hall MRT station, while Nicoll Highway station is a 10min walk away.

Destinations Alor Star (2 daily; 12hr 30min); Cameron Highlands (1 daily; 10hr); Hat Yai (Thailand; 3 daily; 18hr); Ipoh (7 daily; 8hr 30min); Kamunting (for Taiping; 2 daily; 9hr 30min); Kuala Kangsar (2 daily; 9hr); Kuala Lumpur (every 1–2hr daily; 6hr); Lumut (for Pangkor; 1 daily; 9hr 30min); Melaka (9 daily; 3hr 30min); Penang (5 daily; 10hr 30min); Seremban (9 daily; 5hr); Sungai Petani (1 daily; 11hr).

The Plaza 7500a Beach Rd Transnasional (☎ 6294 7034, ⓦ transnasional.com.my), and its associated Plusliner company operate to both coasts from a basement office on the side of The Plaza facing away from Beach Rd itself. Arab St and Bugis MRT are just a few minutes away on foot.

Destinations Kota Bharu (1 daily; 13hr); Kuala Lumpur (at least 7 daily; 6hr); Kuantan (2 daily; 6hr); Mersing (2 daily; 4hr).

Queen St terminal Johor Bahru buses use this terminal near Bugis MRT, including #170 (daily 5.30am–12.30am, every 15min; 1hr–1hr 30min; S$2) and two nonstop services, the Singapore–Johor Express (every 10min; 6am–10pm; S$3.30) and the Causeway Link #CW2 service (2–4 hourly; 6am–11.45pm; same fare; ⓦ causewaylink .com.my). Hang on to your ticket at immigration so you can use it to resume your journey (on the same service, though not necessarily on the same vehicle) once you're through.

THE MRT SYSTEM

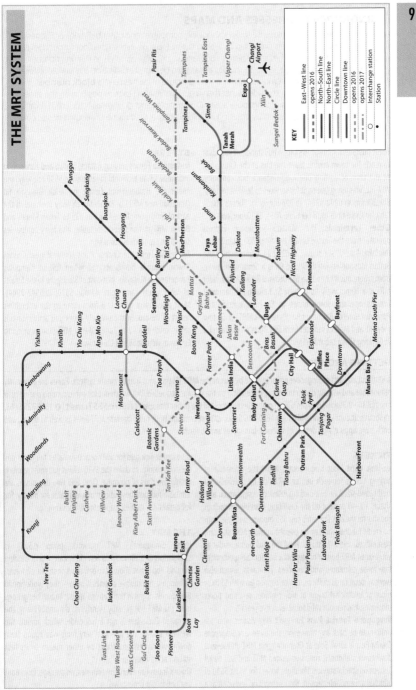

KEY

— East–West line
···· opens 2016
— North–South line
— North–East line
— Circle line
— Downtown line
···· opens 2016
-·-· opens 2017
○ Interchange station
• Station

9

SINGAPORE ADDRESSES AND MAPS

Addresses pertaining to high-rise towers, shopping complexes and other buildings are generally written using two numbers preceded by #, as in #xx-yy. Here xx refers to the floor (ground level is 01, the next floor up 02, the first basement B01, and so on) while yy refers to the unit number – thus a restaurant whose address includes #04-08 can be found in unit 8 on the building's fourth storey. All buildings within municipal housing and industrial estates have a **block number** displayed prominently on the side, rather than a number relating to their position on the street.

The best **online maps** of Singapore are at ⓦonemap.sg and ⓦ.streetdirectory.com (both also available as apps); search by entering a building name, road name or six-digit postal code.

These buses terminate at JB's Larkin bus station; if you want to reach the town centre, leave the bus at the Causeway. At the time of writing one long-distance bus company, 707-Inc, was using Queen St for services to Melaka (6 daily; 3hr 30min; ☎6292 8254, ⓦ707-inc.com). There's also a rank for share taxis to JB (☎6296 7054; S\$10/person).

Other terminals The Malacca–Singapore Express operates from the Textile Centre building, 200 Jalan Sultan (Melaka, 4 daily; 3hr 30min; ☎6292 2436). From here the Sultan Mosque on North Bridge Rd is a 5min walk away, from where bus #7 heads to the Orchard Rd area; Lavender MRT is a 10min walk up Victoria St/Kallang Rd. Starmart Express operates some buses to KL from outside the *Parkroyal Hotel* on Kitchener Rd (Farrer Park MRT) and a few more KL and Melaka services from City Plaza on Geylang Rd in Geylang (Paya Lebar MRT).

BY FERRY

Indonesia Ferries serving Batam, Bintan and Karimun in Indonesia's Riau archipelago (all around S\$30 one way) use either the HarbourFront Centre on Telok Blangah Rd (HarbourFront MRT) or Tanah Merah ferry terminal in the east of Singapore, linked by bus #35 to Tanah Merah and Bedok MRT stations. For timetables and ferry companies see ⓦsingaporecruise.com.sg.

Malaysia From the Changi Point terminal near Changi Beach, humble bumboats sail when full to Kampung Pengerang in Malaysia, just east of Singapore in the Straits of Johor (daily 7am–7pm; 45min; S\$10; ☎6542 7944). Most passengers get a taxi from there to the unexciting resort of Desaru. In the unlikely event you arrive via this route, catch bus #2 to Tanah Merah MRT station or on to Geylang, Victoria St and Chinatown.

GETTING AROUND

Just about all parts of Singapore are accessible by **bus** or the **MRT** (Mass Rapid Transit) metro system. **Fares** are eminently reasonable and usually rise in tiny steps depending on the distance travelled, but watch out for overcrowding during rush hour (7.30–9.30am & 5–7pm). Two companies run most of the public transport network: **SBS Transit** (☎1800 225 5663, ⓦsbstransit.com.sg) and **SMRT** (☎1800 336 8900, ⓦsmrt.com.sg). Both firms operate MRT lines as well as buses, and both have **apps** giving details of stations, bus routes and so forth.

TICKETS

ez-link card Most Singaporeans avoid the rigmarole of buying tickets for each bus or MRT ride by purchasing a credit-card-sized ez-link card (ⓦezlink.com.sg), which also shaves 10–40 percent off the cash fare, with bigger savings the shorter the trip. The cards cost S\$5 (non-refundable) with no credit loaded, and can be bought at most MRT stations, post offices, and 7-11 stores. Hold the card over a reader as you exit an MRT barrier or step off a bus for the appropriate fare to be calculated and deducted. The cards, which also work as debit cards in shops, can be topped up with S\$10 or more of additional credit at ticket offices or using ticket machines, and remain valid for at least five years.

Singapore Tourist Pass For short-stay visitors who are unlikely to be back any time soon, the three-day Singapore Tourist Pass is ideal. Sold at Changi Airport MRT and several downtown stations, it covers unlimited MRT and bus travel (except on special services like night buses) for S\$30, S\$10 of which is a refundable deposit. You can top it up and use it as a

standard ez-link card for additional travel after the three-day window, though to claim the S\$10 refund you must return it within five days of purchase. One- and two-day passes are available too, but these offer much less value for money. For full details, see ⓦthesingaporetouristpass.com.sg.

THE MRT

Using Singapore's MRT network (map p.525) is straightforward, although a few things are worth bearing in mind. You're not allowed to eat, drink or smoke on trains, although using mobile phones is okay – they work fine in the tunnels. Signs in the stations appear to ban hedgehogs from the MRT but actually signify "no durians". Finally, the so-called Circle line is not a full circle, which means the western side of the line is a very long way round from downtown unless you travel by other means to its first station at HarbourFront.

Hours Trains run every five minutes, on average, from 6am until midnight downtown.

Fares From S$1.40 to S$2.60 (S$0.85 to S$2.30 with an ez-link card).

LRT Three LRT (Light Rail Transit) networks connect suburban estates with the MRT. As a tourist, you're unlikely to make use of any of them.

BUSES

Routes Singapore's bus network is incredibly comprehensive and the profusion of routes can be confusing. Thankfully, central bus stops display detailed lists of destinations served by each bus, and both the SBS Transit and SMRT websites contain full route information and rather complicated journey planners – but they may not tell you about potential connections involving each other's buses.

Hours Buses start running around 6am and wind down from 11.30pm; the very last regular buses leave downtown around 12.30am. Between midnight and 2am a few Night-Rider (run by SMRT, and prefixed "NR") and Nite Owl (SBS Transit, suffixed "N") buses are available; costing around S$4.50, they are one-way services that cross the city centre and then operate as express services to their ultimate destinations, the outlying new towns.

Fares Cash fares range from S$1.30 to S$2.40 (S$0.80 to S$2 with ez-link card, and slightly cheaper again on the few buses with no a/c). Some buses charge a flat fare while a few don't take cash at all – check signage at the front of the bus. Paying cash, drop the fare into the metal chute next to the driver; change isn't given. If you have an ez-link card, you must tap the card on the reader upon entering the bus *and* at the exit door when you get off.

TAXIS

Taxis Thousands of taxis roam the streets of Singapore, so you'll hardly ever have trouble hailing a cab – except late at night or when demand soars during a tropical downpour. All are clearly marked "TAXI". On the whole, drivers are friendly, but their English isn't always good; if you're heading off the beaten track, have your destination written down, or be aware of a landmark that they can aim for. Note a rule that applies Mon–Sat 7.30am–8pm within downtown: here passengers are not supposed to flag taxis down on main roads – in practice, those served by buses – but should wait at a taxi rank (at shopping malls and hotels, for example).

Fares Unlike in Kuala Lumpur, all drivers use their meters, the fare starting at S$3 for the first kilometre, then rising 20¢ every 400m or so (classier limousine taxis are slightly more expensive). Note annoying surcharges during the morning rush hour and after 6pm: an extra 25 per cent is payable Mon–Fri 6–9.30am & 6pm–midnight, Sat & Sun 6pm–midnight, and 50 percent extra between midnight and 6am nightly. Journeys involving Changi airport or the casinos incur a surcharge of several dollars, as do phone bookings. Road usage tolls levied on journeys along expressways and within the downtown area are also factored into fares.

Taxi companies Comfort/CityCab ☎6552 1111, ⓦcdgtaxi.com.sg; Premier Taxis ☎6363 6888, ⓦpremiertaxi.com; SMRT Taxis ☎6555 8888, ⓦsmrt.com.sg. You can also book a taxi using the Uber app.

RIVER TAXIS

River taxis occupy a grey area somewhere between being a plank of the public transport system and a tourist attraction. The boats function like shuttle buses on the Singapore River, plying between Robertson Quay and Marina Bay (Mon–Fri 7am–9pm, Sat & Sun 10am–9pm; every 10–20min; S$3–4 via ez-link cards only). Operated by the two companies that run river tours, they make slightly different stops depending on whose boat you are riding (details on ⓦriverexplorer.sg and ⓦrivercruise.com.sg).

USEFUL BUS ROUTES

Handy **bus routes** are listed below. One-way systems downtown mean that services that use Orchard Road and Bras Basah Road in one direction return via Stamford Road, Penang Road, Somerset Road and Orchard Boulevard; buses up Selegie and Serangoon roads return via Jalan Besar and Bencoolen Street; and services along North and South Bridge roads and New Bridge Road return via Eu Tong Sen Street, Hill Street and Victoria Street.

#2 From Eu Tong Sen Street in Chinatown all the way to Changi Prison and Changi Beach, via the Arab Quarter and Geylang Serai.

#7 From the Botanic Gardens to Orchard Road, Bras Basah Road and Victoria Street (for the Arab Quarter), then on to Geylang Serai.

#36 A loop service between Orchard Road and Changi airport via Suntec City and the Singapore Flyer.

#56 Little India to Marina Centre via *Raffles Hotel*.

#65 Orchard Road to Little India and on up Serangoon Road.

#170 From the Queen Street terminal to JB in Malaysia, passing Little India, the Newton Circus food court, the northern end of the Botanic Gardens, Bukit Timah Nature Reserve and Kranji War Cemetery on the way.

#174 Runs between the Botanic Gardens and the Baba House in Neil Road, via Orchard Road, the Colonial District, Boat Quay and Chinatown.

9

DRIVING

Driving in Singapore Given the efficiency of public transport, there's hardly any reason to rent a car in Singapore, especially when it's a pricey business. Major disincentives to driving are in place in order to combat traffic congestion: a permit just to own a car costs more than many makes of car.

Tolls Drivers have to pay tolls to enter a restricted zone encompassing Chinatown, Orchard Rd and the Financial District, and to use many of the island's expressways. This being Singapore, it's all done in the most hi tech way using Electronic Road Pricing (ERP): all Singapore cars have a gizmo that reads a stored-value CashCard from which the toll is deducted as you drive past an ERP gantry.

Parking Generally expensive, though at least many car parks offer the convenience of taking the fee off your CashCard, failing which you have to purchase coupons from a licence booth, post office or shop.

Car rental The only sensible reason to rent a car in Singapore is to travel up into Malaysia – and even then it's far cheaper to rent in Johor Bahru. If you are still keen to rent in Singapore itself, contact Avis (ⓦ avis.com.sg) or Hertz (ⓦ hertz.com); both have offices at Changi airport.

Driving from Malaysia To drive a Malaysian car into Singapore, you need to buy a stored-value Autopass card and rent a card reader; both are available at the Causeway or Second Crossing. Thus equipped, you can pay your vehicle entry toll and road tolls in Singapore. For more details on this and other matters to do with driving in Singapore, see ⓦ lta.gov.sg.

CYCLING

Though largely flat, Singapore is hardly ideal cycling country. There are almost no bike lanes along main roads, where you'll have to brave furious traffic, though this doesn't put off the few dedicated locals and expats whom you'll see pedalling equally furiously along suburban thoroughfares such as Bukit Timah Rd. Cycling downtown isn't such a great idea though, and bicycles aren't allowed on expressways.

Parks and beaches Where bikes come into their own is in recreational areas and nature parks, which are linked by a park connector network; see ⓦ nparks.gov.sg. The East Coast Park, on the southeast shore of the island, has a popular cycle track with rental outlets along the way (expect to pay S$5–81 for a mountain bike, and have some form of ID), and you'll also find bike rental at Changi and Siloso beaches (the latter on Sentosa). Wherever you cycle, you'll need a high tolerance for getting very hot and sweaty – or drenched if you're caught in a downpour.

INFORMATION

Visitors Centres The Singapore Tourism Board (STB; helpline Mon–Fri 9am–6pm ☎ 1800 736 2000, ⓦ yoursingapore.com; app available) bills its tourist offices as Visitors Centres. Their main downtown location is smack in the middle of Orchard Rd, at the start of Cairnhill Rd (daily 9.30am–10.30pm; Somerset MRT); they also have a counter on the ground floor of the ION Orchard mall (daily 10am–10pm; above Orchard MRT), and in Chinatown at 2 Banda St, behind the Buddha Tooth Relic Temple (Mon–Fri 9am–9pm, Sat & Sun 9am–10pm).

Heritage trails Leaflets providing historical background on Singapore's older neighbourhoods and suggested walking trails can be downloaded from the "Publications" section of ⓦ ura.gov.sg.

Internet access Internet cafés are fairly thin on the ground except in Little India, where it's quite easy to stumble across one; prices start at S$2/hr. There's also a free wi-fi network, Wireless@SG/SGx, available at shopping malls and other public buildings. Unfortunately performance can be erratic, and registration – search online for various sign-up pages – may require a password to be sent to your mobile phone number, a process that itself doesn't always work. Streets in the heart of Chinatown, around Pagoda St, have their own free wi-fi for tourist use.

Listings Listings of entertainment events, restaurant reviews and so forth can be found in the fortnightly free publication *I-S* (ⓦ is.asia-city.com), available at some malls, museums. and restaurants. The "Life!" section of the *Straits Times* also has a decent listings section. Also of use to visitors are another free magazine, *The Finder* (ⓦ thefinder .com.sg), and ⓦ expatsingapore.com, both geared towards the large expat community.

Malaysia information Tourism Malaysia is at 80 Robinson Rd in the Financial District (Mon–Fri 9am–5pm; ☎ 6532 6321).

ACCOMMODATION

If one thing leaves a nasty taste in the mouth in Singapore, it's the price of **accommodation**. Room rates have spiralled ever higher in recent years, and though they appeared to plateau in 2014, even a mid-range double room in the city centre now nudges S$150 a night. On the plus side, most accommodation is well run, and budget travellers have a plethora of centrally located **hostels** and **guesthouses** to choose from, many with upmarket decor and fittings.

Most **hotels** are blandly modern, but there are plenty of **boutique hotels**, usually characterful or quirky affairs in refurbished shophouses. One thing to note is that any **hotel** advertising hourly or "transit" rates tends to be used by locals for illicit liaisons; normally only obviously seedy hotels stoop to this, though the ubiquitous and otherwise well-managed budget chains *Hotel 81* and *Fragrance* have been tainted by this in the past.

ORGANIZED TOURS

Singapore is so easy to navigate that there's little reason to do an **organized tour**, which is perhaps why the range of offerings tends to be uninspired. Many tours seem to feature transport as a key element, whether that be a dedicated tourist bus, a Singapore River boat (see p.478 for more on river trips), a novelty vehicle or the **trishaw**, which at least hearkens back to the island's past. Singapore's streets were once packed with three-wheeled cycle rickshaws, functioning like taxis, but now trishaws exist only to give tourists a spin on certain routes. In Chinatown, you may be able to negotiate a ride with freelance trishaw men around the back of the Buddha Tooth Relic Temple; alternatively, book a trip with the operator listed below.

To engage a **guide** for a more personalized look at, say, Singapore's architecture or historical districts, try the directory at ⓦ guides-online.yoursingapore.com.

DuckTours ☏ 6338 6877, ⓦ ducktours.com.sg. Tour the Colonial District and Marina Bay on an amphibious vehicle; fun for families. They also sell (overpriced) day passes on open-top, hop-on hop-off buses that circulate frequently around downtown, making it easy to see all the main sights. Daily: duck tours 10am–6pm, open-top buses roughly 9am–6pm; each $33

The Original Singapore Walks ☏ 6325 1631, ⓦ singaporewalks.com. Guided walks of historic downtown areas and Changi (the latter with a wartime focus), generally lasting 2hr 30min; around S$35 per person.

Singapore Footprints ⓦ singaporefootprints .com. Free weekend afternoon walking tours of the historic areas around the Singapore River, though note that the guides are university student volunteers and thus neither professional nor licensed, so standards will vary.

Singapore Nature Society ⓦ nss.org.sg. If your stay in Singapore is an extended one, consider taking out annual membership of this conservation group, which conducts guided nature walks, birdwatching trips and so forth.

Trishaw Uncle Booth on Queen St, close to Bugis MRT ☏ 6337 7111, ⓦ trishawuncle.com.sg. This trishaw cooperative charges S$39 for a half-hour ride around the immediate vicinity and Little India, or S$49 with Clarke Quay included. Daily 11am–10pm.

Hotel **promotional rates** are pretty much the norm and apply almost year-round, except perhaps during the Formula One race in the third week of September. At the other end of the scale, **five-star** and some four-star hotels continuously adjust their rates depending on demand. The prices here are meant to be typical starting prices, including taxes, but do not account for possible weekend variations (small surcharges at some hostels and cheaper hotels, discounts at pricey hotels geared to business travellers). Besides contacting places directly, you can also book through sites such as ⓦ agoda.com and ⓦ hostelworld.com.

LITTLE INDIA, LAVENDER STREET AND ARAB STREET

Little India proper and beyond – the zone extending up to Lavender St, reachable via Farrer Park or Lavender stations – is the best place to find budget accommodation, although hotels are hit and miss. Handily for those who end up here, there's an excellent public swimming pool near Farrer Park MRT (see p.551). The area around Arab St also has a few good places to stay.

HOSTELS AND GUESTHOUSES

Backpackers@SG 1st floor, 111j King George's Ave ☏ 6683 2924, ⓦ bpsg.com.sg; map p.486. Exceptionally plain but homelier for it, this is a simple hostel occupying part of a low-rise residential block, with a snazzy new extension in the same building. Unlike some, it doesn't have mega-sized dorms – the largest has eight beds. A reasonable choice if you want a quiet stay. Dorms S$S21

★ **Bunc@Radius** 15 Upper Weld Rd ☏ 6262 2862, ⓦ bunchostel.com; map p.486. *Bunc* is a sprawling place, its size matching its ambition to be a "flashpacker" hostel taking the concept of comfort on a budget to new heights. Beyond the sleek lobby is a warren of dorms with individual lighting fixtures and sockets for each bed (some of the beds are even built for two). There's a women-only floor and a dedicated gaming room as well. The sole private room has disabled facilities, though anyone can reserve it. Dorms S$22 (double beds S$45), private room S$150

Drop Inn 247 Lavender St ☏ 6635 9100, ⓦ dropinnsingapore.com; map p.486. Not really a boutique hostel as it styles itself, but it is tidy, sedate and family-friendly. Staff are welcoming and can take you on a free "heritage crawl" through old districts on request. Dorms S$30, doubles S$80, family room S$130

Fisher BnB 177 Tyrwhitt Rd ☏ 6297 8258, ⓦ fisherbnb .com; map p.486. Unexpectedly smart guesthouse with a ten-bed women's dorm, an eighteen-bed mixed dorm and a family room for four. The bathrooms are just one area where the decor is right up to date – the management is especially proud of the Japanese-built bidets. Dorms S̄$̄28, family room S̄$̄130

The Hive 624 Serangoon Rd (corner of Lavender St) ☎6341 5041, ⒲thehivebackpackers.com; map p.486. A large hostel where every room is named after a flower and the exterior is decorated black and yellow. Bee theme aside, there's a large lounge with a pool table, an Xbox-equipped games room and a range of dorms and rooms. Dorms S̄$̄20, singles S̄$̄40, doubles S̄$̄60

★**The InnCrowd** 73 Dunlop St ☎6296 9169, ⒲the-inncrowd.com; map p.486. Perennially excellent hostel with dorms plus a range of rooms with, unusually, their own TV. Shared showers and toilets are kept spotless, and there's a comfy lounge, cheap beer and free internet access. They run tours too, including a scooter-powered trip around the old quarters and Gardens by the Bay. Dorms S̄$̄20, doubles S̄$̄60

The Mitraa 427 Race Course Rd ☎6396 3925, ⒲mitraa.com.sg; map p.486. This bills itself as "the friendliest backpacker hostel", and friendly it usually is, as well as organized. If they're full they may be able to put you up at their *Mitraa Inn* offshoot nearby. Dorms S̄$̄25, doubles S̄$̄70

Prince of Wales 101 Dunlop St ☎6299 0130, ⒲pow.com.sg; map p.486. Justifiably popular place done out in primary colours, with a/c dorms, a couple of double rooms and cheap beer from their very own bar/beer garden. They have a similar set-up in the thick of the action at Boat Quay, on the south bank of the Singapore River. Dorm beds S̄$̄22, doubles S̄$̄60

Shophouse 48 Arab St ☎6298 8721, ⒲shophouse hostel.com; map p.486. The rooftop lounge/terrace is the standout feature at this slick, bustling hostel which, given the location, also has some predictably quasi-Arabic decor. There's a women's floor, too. Dorms S̄$̄20

Vintage Inn 60 Race Course Rd ☎6396 8751, ⒲vintageinn.sg; map p.486. A swanky affair with arrays of capsule-style beds against the wall, each with a privacy curtain. Breakfast isn't the usual toast-and-coffee affair, but local dishes such as *roti prata* or Chinese savoury carrot cake. Dorms S̄$̄25 (double beds S̄$̄55)

HOTELS

Fragrance Imperial 28 Penhas Rd ☎6297 8888, ⒲fragrancehotel.com; map p.486. Despite the drab yellow exterior, this is a cut above fellow members of the budget chain, with slick if smallish rooms, a café and rooftop swimming pool. Rates include breakfast. S̄$̄160

Haising 37 Jalan Besar ☎6298 1223, ⒲haising.com.sg; map p.486. Friendly, secure Chinese-run cheapie offering simple, a/c en-suite rooms with TV; rather boxy but not bad for the price. S̄$̄65

Kam Leng 383 Jalan Besar ☎6239 9399, ⒲kamleng.com; map p.486. The nicely renovated Art Deco exterior makes clear that this place is all about recreating the feel of a distinguished prewar Chinese hotel. It's a bit lacklustre inside

– the lobby is threadbare save for a few period objects and rooms have plain tiled or plain cement floors. At least the bathrooms are unapologetically modern. Good value. S̄$̄150

★**Mayo Inn** 9 Jalan Besar ☎6295 6631, ⒲mayoinn.com; map p.486. A partial refurbishment has given a new lease of life to this simple, good-value hotel's two dozen rooms, which now feature modern bathrooms and, in some cases, what's billed as a Japanese-style "bed" – a wooden dais with a mattress on top. S̄$̄110

★**Moon** 23 Dickson Rd ☎6827 6666, ⒲moon.com.sg; map p.486. Aiming to offer a boutique-hotel experience without straining your wallet, the *Moon* has stylishly kitted-out rooms with snazzy wallpaper, iPhone docks and strategically placed drapes – to help take your mind off the fact that many are actually windowless. Rates include breakfast. S̄$̄180

Parkroyal 181 Kitchener Rd ☎6428 3000, ⒲parkroyalhotels.com; map p.486. The classiest of the non-boutique hotels in the area, with a marbled lobby, bags of contemporary style and the usual profusion of restaurants, plus pool and gym. If you're arriving by taxi, be sure to mention the address as this is one of three *Parkroyal* hotels in town. Breakfast included. S̄$̄250

Perak 12 Perak Rd ☎6299 7733, ⒲peraklodge.net; map p.486. Set within a nicely restored shophouse and somewhat staid – probably not a bad thing given the hullaballoo of Little India. Rooms are comfy, if unremarkable, breakfast is included and there's a pleasant residents-only rest area. S̄$̄140

The Sultan 101 Jalan Sultan ☎6723 7101, ⒲thesultan.com.sg; map p.486. A pleasant, relatively low-key hotel occupying a series of tastefully refurbished shophouses. Take your pick from, among others, a handful of cosy singles plus so-called attic rooms on the top floor, which are a little quieter than the rest. Breakfast included. S̄$̄180

Village Hotel Bugis 390 Victoria St (main entrance on Arab St) ☎6297 2828, ⒲stayfareast.com; map p.486. Beyond the dated shopping centre downstairs is a modern business-class hotel, recently refurbished, with its own pool, gym and restaurants. S̄$̄270

Wanderlust 2 Dickson Rd ☎6396 3622, ⒲wanderlusthotel.com; map p.486. As at its sibling hotel, Chinatown's *New Majestic*, there's a touch of modern-art wackiness at *Wanderlust*: the "industrial glam" lobby includes barber's chairs and many rooms are colour-themed, some even equipped with guest-programmable multicoloured lighting. Facilities include a jacuzzi and French restaurant. Rates include breakfast. S̄$̄240

BRAS BASAH ROAD TO ROCHOR ROAD

The grid of streets between Bras Basah Rd and Rochor Rd (and a bit beyond, uphill from Selegie Rd) has been rendered a bit sterile by redevelopment, which has also wiped out nearly all the cheap accommodation that once packed

Bencoolen St; now it's mostly modern mid-range hotels that remain. The area remains a good choice if you can afford it, as it's within easy walking distance of the Singapore River, Little India and the eastern end of Orchard Rd.

HOSTELS AND GUESTHOUSES

★**Hangout@Mount Emily** 10a Upper Wilkie Rd ☎6438 5588, ⓦhangouthotels.com; map p.483. Owned by the company behind the historic Cathay cinema at the foot of Mount Emily, the *Hangout* is an impressive designer guesthouse with a breezy rooftop terrace that's great for chilling out in the evening. Book online for better rates, which include a simple buffet breakfast. Dorms **S$40**, rooms **S$130**

HOTELS

★**The Big Hotel** 200 Middle Rd ☎6809 7988, ⓦbighotel.com; map p.483. This excellent new hotel occupies a converted office building, which is perhaps why they chose post-industrial chic for the lobby, all artfully exposed ducting and pipes. The cheaper rooms are on the boxy side, but all are snug, soundproofed and feature pale wood floors and furniture. Breakfast costs extra. **S$175**

Carlton 76 Bras Basah Rd ☎6338 8333, ⓦcarltonhotel .sg; map p.483. Boasting a grand new extension and a redesigned lobby dominated by a spidery glass artwork suspended from the ceiling, this towering four-star hotel has elegant rooms, a pool, spa and gym – and keen rates for what's on offer. **S$360**

Ibis 170 Bencoolen St ☎6593 2888, ⓦibis.com; map p.483. If you've stayed in other hotels run by this no-frills chain, you'd probably describe them as functional, modern and just a little dull. The 7-11 shop in the lobby feels totally apt, though on a more positive note the place is well insulated from traffic noise. **S$230**

Intercontinental 80 Middle Rd ☎6338 7600, ⓦintercontinental.com; map p.483. Like the adjoining Bugis Junction mall, the *Intercontinental* incorporates some of the area's original shophouses, here converted into "shophouse rooms" with supposedly Peranakan decor, though this merely amounts to Oriental-looking vases and paintings of tropical fruit. Still, the hotel is luxurious and has all the amenities you could want, and rates can fall by a quarter at weekends. **S$375**

Marrison 103 Beach Rd ☎6333 9928, ⓦmarrisonhotel .com; map p.483. This simple hotel is surprisingly comfortable, the rooms done out in neutral hues. A very good deal, given the location and included breakfast. **S$140**

Naumi 41 Seah St ☎6403 6000, ⓦnaumihotel.com; map p.483. The slate-grey exterior doesn't inspire, but inside is a stunning boutique hotel where every room is kitted out like a luxury apartment and boasts a kitchenette. Rooms on one floor are reserved for women only, there's a

rooftop pool, and gaming consoles are available to all guests on request. **S$400**

★**South East Asia** 190 Waterloo St ☎6338 2394, ⓦseahotel.com.sg; map p.483. Behind the yellow and white 1950s facade is a reasonable hotel with functional if slightly tired doubles, featuring the usual mod cons. It's practically next door to the lively Kwan Im temple, to boot. Cheaper than most of its neighbours by some margin. **S$100**

Strand 25 Bencoolen St ☎6338 1866, ⓦstrandhotel .com.sg; map p.483. Rooms here are a little worn and nondescript, but they are more than serviceable and surprisingly affordable. There's a better-than-average breakfast for the price – you get a dish cooked to order in addition to a simple buffet of breads and cereals. **S$150**

THE COLONIAL DISTRICT

The area immediately north and east of the Singapore River only has a few places to stay, all hotels.

Fort Canning 11 Canning Walk, northern side of Fort Canning Hill ☎6559 6770, ⓦhfcsingapore.com; map p.476. Hotel facades don't come much more imposing than that of the former British military HQ fronting this plush boutique hotel. Rooms are spacious, immaculately decorated and boast bathtubs that are, curiously, often either smack in the middle of the room or out towards the window. Pools on two levels and lush gardens, too. The snag: it's a bit of a trek down flights of steps to reach Dhoby Ghaut MRT and Orchard Rd. Breakfast costs extra. **S$375**

Novotel Clarke Quay 177a River Valley Rd ☎6338 3333, ⓦnovotelclarkequay.com; map p.476. This dull tower block might seem like just another bland business-oriented hotel, but the wood-panelled lobby and tasteful contemporary furnishings give the boutique hotels a run for their money. The usual four-star amenities include pool and gym. Breakfast not included. **S$375**

Peninsula Excelsior 5 Coleman St ☎6337 2200, ⓦytchotels.com.sg; map p.476. Really two hotels fused together – as hinted at by the presence of two swimming pools at either end, one of which abuts the current lobby – and nicely modernized, unlike the 1970s shopping arcades below. Decent value, with weekend discounts too, although breakfast isn't included. **S$250**

Raffles 1 Beach Rd ☎6337 1886, ⓦraffleshotel.com; map p.476. Though the modern extension is a mixed bag, the *Raffles* remains refreshingly low-rise and still has colonial-era charm in spades, especially evident in the opulent lobby and the courtyards fringed by frangipani trees and palms. Amenities include oodles of restaurants and bars, a rooftop pool and a spa. All rooms are suites and there's a round-the-clock butler service, too. **S$800**

Swissôtel The Stamford 2 Stamford Rd ☎6338 8585, ⓦsingapore-stamford.swissotel.com; map p.476. The upper-floor rooms, restaurants and bars aren't for those

9

with vertigo, though the views are as splendid as you'd expect from one of the tallest hotels in the world, with over a thousand rooms. Perhaps even more impressive is having an MRT station (City Hall) in the basement. **S$625**

CHINATOWN AND BOAT QUAY

Chinatown runs a close second to Little India and Lavender St in its selection of guesthouses, and also boasts a good many upmarket and boutique hotels. **Boat Quay**, right on the south bank of the Singapore River, is dominated by restaurants and bars, but has two worthwhile places to stay, one of which is the splendid *Fullerton* hotel.

HOSTELS AND GUESTHOUSES

A Beary Good Hostel 66a/b Pagoda St ☎ 6222 4955, ⊛ abearygoodhostel.com; map pp.494–495. A spick-and-span hostel with ten- to fifteen-bed mixed dorms and a Wii console in the lounge. The website lists a couple of offshoots elsewhere in Chinatown, one with women-only dorms and private rooms. Dorms **S$27**

Five Stones Level 2, 61 South Bridge Rd ☎ 6535 5607, ⊛ fivestoneshostel.com; map pp.494–495. "Five stones" is what locals call the game of jacks, so it's no big surprise that most dorms at this hostel have murals illustrating a different childhood pastime. There are two doubles, too, plus an unusually cosy lounge. Dorms **S$30**, doubles **S$110**

Matchbox 39 Ann Siang Rd ☎ 6423 0237, ⊛ matchbox .sg; map pp.494–495. *Matchbox* revels in a good location on chichi Ann Siang Hill. The pod-style beds are the standout feature, each with an orthopedic mattress, reading light and power socket. There's also a splendid loft space packed with multicoloured pouffes and with old-school board games to play. Dorm beds S$40, doubles (a two-bed dorm) **S$100**

Pillows & Toast 40 Mosque St ☎ 6220 4653, ⊛ pillowsntoast.com; map pp.494–495. A friendly place with a chilled-out loft lounge and a variety of female or mixed dorms, all with at least eight beds. Not a bad choice. Dorms **S$28**

Rucksack Inn 38a Hongkong St ☎ 6532 4990, ⊛ rucksackinn.com; map pp.494–495. A mixed dorm, a female dorm and a handful of assorted private rooms, managed by friendly and informed staff. If they're full, they may well send you to their branch nearby on Temple St. Dorm beds **S$32**, doubles **S$110**

★**Wink** 8a Mosque St ☎ 6222 2940, ⊛ winkhostel .com; map pp.494–495. One of the best designer hostels in town, with hi tech capsule beds (including some doubles), each inside flower-themed rooms with colour-coded lighting to match. Facilities include an upstairs kitchen and lounge, a spacious landing where you can watch DVDs, and free use of a tablet computer for every guest. Dorms **S$50** (double beds **S$90**)

HOTELS

Chinatown 12–16 Teck Lim Rd ☎ 6225 5166, ⊛ chinatownhotel.com; map pp.494–495. Not bad for the price and location, the *Chinatown* has serviceable rooms done out in the usual neutral tones. The bathrooms can be a bit poky, but at least a basic self-service breakfast is included. **S$150**

Clover 5 Hongkong St ☎ 6653 8888, ⊛ hotelclover5 hongkongstreet.com; map pp.494–495. Functional, contemporary rooms in a six-storey building crowned by a small rooftop pool. Good value, with breakfast included. Their sister hotel, round the corner, offers slightly bigger rooms with funky murals and access to the same pool, for about ten percent extra. **S$190**

The Fullerton 1 Fullerton Square ☎ 6733 8388, ⊛ fullertonhotel.com; map pp.494–495. Nearly as impressive as the *Raffles*, with a stunning Art Deco atrium propped up on massive columns like an Egyptian temple. Rooms and bathrooms are spacious and plush. Amenities include a gym, spa and pool. **S$520**

★**Hotel 1929** 50 Keong Saik Rd ☎ 6347 1929, ⊛ hotel1929.com; map pp.494–495. Less pricey than its sibling, the *New Majestic*, this shophouse hotel looks genuinely 1929 on the outside, but the interior has been renovated to look like a twenty-first-century version of the early 1960s, all very retro chic. Rates include breakfast. **S$225**

The Inn at Temple Street 36 Temple St ☎ 6221 5333, ⊛ theinn.com.sg; map pp.494–495. Packed with old-fangled furniture for a semblance of a period feel, but the rooms are boxy and there's no breakfast. Still, you can't argue with the prices. **S$120**

Lehotel 16 Carpenter St ☎ 6534 4859, ⊛ lehotel.com .sg; map pp.494–495. A worthwhile budget offering with sterile, slightly worn rooms, the cheapest ones windowless. No breakfast. **S$120**

★**New Majestic** 31–37 Bukit Pasoh Rd ☎ 6511 4700, ⊛ newmajestichotel.com; map pp.494–495. The open-air lobby and shabby ceiling (highlighting the building's vintage status) offer the first of many surprises at this boutique hotel. Every room has been eccentrically decorated by local designers – one has seaweed simulations growing out of the wall. Other quirks include a pool with floor portholes that allow you to look down into the restaurant, just as diners can look up at you swimming by. Rates include breakfast. **S$325**

Parkroyal 3 Upper Pickering St ☎ 6809 8888, ⊛ parkroyalhotels.com; map pp.494–495. Looming over Hong Lim Park, Singapore's most architecturally striking hotel since *Marina Bay Sands* also has three towers, linked by curvy-sided rice-terrace-like structures overflowing with vegetation. The use of wood and glass throughout emphasizes the nature theme, in part by allowing plenty of sunlight in. Another garden crops up at the open-sided central tier that serves as a "wellness floor", home to the infinity pool, spa and gym. **S$400**

Porcelain 48 Mosque St ☎ 6645 3131, ⊛ porcelainhotel .com; map pp.494–495. Browns and beiges are the default colours at most Singapore hotels, but *Porcelain* bucks the trend: Ming pottery motifs in blue and white are much in evidence, giving the otherwise unremarkable, smallish rooms of this new hotel a calming quality. Breakfast not included. S$160

TANJONG PAGAR AND THE FINANCIAL DISTRICT

There are only a few hotels amid the office towers of Tanjong Pagar and the Financial District. Neither area is all that interesting to stay in, but proximity to Chinatown and the Colonial District make them worth considering.

Klapsons 15 Hoe Chiang Rd ☎ 6521 9030, ⊛ klapsons .com; map pp.494–495. What sort of hotel would house its reception within a metal sphere where the echoes make you sound as if you're chirruping like an alien? That's just one of the oddities in this designer establishment of just seventeen rooms, each with different decor; the suites boast a jacuzzi for good measure. Rate excludes breakfast. S$275

★**Sofitel So** 35 Robinson Rd ☎ 6701 6800, ⊛ sofitel .com; map pp.494–495. Almost lost amid the staid bank buildings, this is a super-cool, Karl Lagerfeld-influenced conversion of two narrow office blocks into a stylish whole. The "heritage wing" has decor like a French palace; across the atrium from it is the quirky, eclectic "hip wing", where you might find Russian dolls on the tables or wall-mounted plastic hands for hanging clothes. Breakfast costs extra. S$475

MARINA BAY

Marina Bay accommodation is synonymous with modern four- and five-star affairs, all located at the rather bland Marina Centre district next to Beach Rd, with the obvious exception of *Marina Bay Sands*.

Marina Bay Sands 10 Bayfront Ave ☎ 6688 8868, ⊛ marinabaysands.com; map p.503. Not just one of the island's most famous buildings but also the largest hotel in Singapore, with an astonishing 2500 rooms. Frankly they're no better than those in most of its five-star competitors unless you shell out for, say, one of the Straits suites, with two en-suite bedrooms, a baby grand piano and butler service – for at least S$5000 a night. Otherwise, stay here for the architecture and that infinity pool. S$575

Ritz-Carlton Millenia 7 Raffles Ave ☎ 6337 8888, ⊛ ritzcarlton.com; map p.503. Arguably king of the pricey hotels in Marina Centre, with magnificent views across to the towers of the Financial District – even from the bathrooms, where butlers will fill the bath for you. S$600

ORCHARD ROAD

You generally pay a premium to stay in the Orchard Rd shopping area, though it's hardly the most interesting part of downtown, and now that many stores have branches across town, only the sheer modernity of the district lends it any edge.

Goodwood Park 22 Scotts Rd ☎ 6737 7411, ⊛ goodwoodparkhotel.com; map p.503. Built on a leafy hillock and designed by the architect responsible for the *Raffles*, it is a genuine landmark in a cityscape characterized by transience. It still exudes the refinements of a bygone era and boasts a variety of rooms and suites, plus several highly rated restaurants and two pools. Breakfast not included. S$350

Lloyd's Inn 2 Lloyd Rd ☎ 6737 7309, ⊛ lloydsinn.com; map pp.506–507. Less than a 10min walk from Orchard Rd, what was once a motel-like ugly duckling has had a total facelift and blossomed into a sleek establishment with a roof terrace and water feature, intended for foot-dipping, taking up much of the garden. Breakfast included. S$220

Mandarin Orchard 333 Orchard Rd ☎ 6737 4411, ⊛ meritus-hotels.com; map pp.506–507. Female staff at this old favourite wear kitsch quasi-oriental uniforms, but don't let that put you off; this towering hotel with more than 1000 rooms is still at the top of its game, luxurious to a fault, and has its own high-end mini-mall, too. Rate excludes breakfast. S$350

Marriott 320 Orchard Rd ☎ 6735 5800, ⊛ marriott .com; map pp.506–507. One of the plushest hotels on Orchard Rd, occupying a pagoda-like tower rising above Tangs department store, and featuring a hot tub in every room plus the obligatory pool, spa and gym and plenty of restaurants. Some deals throw in breakfast for practically nothing. S$550

★**The Quincy** 22 Mount Elizabeth ☎ 6738 5888, ⊛ quincy.com.sg; map pp.506–507. A 10min, slightly uphill walk off Orchard Rd, this is one of Singapore's more endearing boutique hotels, melding contemporary aesthetics with comfort. Rooms come with iPhone docks and a glass-walled bathroom, and there's a pool near the top of the building. Rate includes breakfast. S$340

Shangri-La 22 Orange Grove Rd ☎ 6737 3644, ⊛ shangri-la.com; map pp.506–507. A 10min walk west of Orchard Rd, the oldest member of what's now a global hotel chain still epitomizes elegance, with 750 rooms set in an expanse of landscaped greenery. Facilities include tennis courts, gym, pool and spa. S$575

Supreme 15 Kramat Rd ☎ 6737 8333, ⊛ supremeh .com.sg; map pp.506–507. This 1970s concrete box has basic, predictably dated rooms, though they're not too cramped; rates are a steal and include breakfast. S$120

GEYLANG AND KATONG

With the range of accommodation available downtown, there are few compelling reasons to stay in the suburbs except to save a little money. Katong, with its Peranakan heritage and good restaurants, is as good a choice as any,

9

though note that some of neighbouring Geylang's seediness can spill over into Joo Chiat Rd after dark.

★**Betel Box** 200 Joo Chiat Rd ☎6247 7340, ⓦbetelbox.com; map p.513. Singapore's socially committed hostel, *Betel Box* tries to highlight the island's cultural heritage by organizing tours of interesting neighbourhoods, and has its own little resource library. A 15min walk from Paya Lebar MRT, or bus #33 from Bedok or Kallang MRT. Dorms S̲$̲2̲0̲, doubles S̲$̲8̲0̲

Champion Hotel 60 Joo Chiat Rd ☎6342 0988, ⓦchampionhotel.com.sg; map p.513. As dull as its shophouse neighbours on the outside, this suburban hotel punches above its weight on the inside, borrowing just enough chic touches from much pricier offerings in Chinatown. A 10min walk from Paya Lebar MRT. No breakfast. S̲$̲1̲1̲0̲

Santa Grand East Coast 171 East Coast Rd ☎6344 6866, ⓦsantagrandhotels.com; map p.513. One of the nicer offerings from this mid-priced chain, partly housed in a conservation building. Rooms are more than adequate, and the secluded rooftop pool is a bonus. Rates include breakfast. Bus #14 from Orchard Rd/Bras Basah Rd/Bedok MRT. S̲$̲1̲5̲0̲

SENTOSA

Staying on Sentosa isn't such a bad idea, especially if you have young children. On the downside, heading back to your hotel for a short break from sightseeing on the "mainland" is a bit of a drag unless you catch a cab.

Hotel Michael Resorts World ☎6577 8888, ⓦrwsentosa.com. The main reason to stay at Resorts World is to tap into regular packages that throw in discounted or free admission to Universal Studios and so forth. *Hotel Michael* is more interesting than the rest, with fittings, wall paintings and other decorative touches by the American architect and designer Michael Graves. S̲$̲3̲7̲5̲

Mövenpick Sentosa 23 Beach View, near Imbiah station ☎6818 3388, ⓦmoevenpick-hotels.com. A splendid hotel housed partly in former British barracks dating from 1940. All rooms have elegant contemporary fittings, but the most impressive are the pricey *onsen* suites with their own large outdoor Japanese hot tub. S̲$̲3̲4̲0̲

Rasa Sentosa Resort Western end of Siloso Beach ☎6275 0100, ⓦshangri-la.com. One of the best pre-casino-era hotels; recently refurbished and family-friendly, it boasts a large freeform pool with water slides, a "kids' club" with purpose-built play areas and activities such as treasure hunts and beach walks, plus a spa. S̲$̲6̲0̲0̲

Siloso Beach Resort 51 Imbiah Walk ☎6722 3333, ⓦsilosobeachresort.com. The central swimming pool is a stunner, its curvy fringes planted with lush vegetation and featuring a waterfall and slides; it far outshines the slightly tired rooms. Still, the resort is tranquil enough (the music from the nearby beach bars generally stops around 10pm) and rates include breakfast. S̲$̲2̲2̲5̲

Singapore Resort and Spa 2 Bukit Manis Rd ☎6275 0331, ⓦsingaporeresortsentosa.com. A swanky affair in secluded grounds above Tanjong Beach, with a spa featuring outdoor pools and imported volcanic mud that's reputedly great for your skin. S̲$̲3̲5̲0̲

EATING

Along with shopping, **eating** ranks as Singapore's national pastime. Walk along any street downtown and just about every other building seems to be overflowing with food outlets, from restaurants to corner kiosks serving snacks. It's not just local food on offer, of course: the island's restaurants truly run the gamut of Asian and international cuisine.

As in Malaysia, food is both a passion and a unifier across ethnic divides. Certain foods are largely or uniquely Singaporean: **chilli crab**, a sweet-spicy dish pioneered at long-gone rural seaside restaurants and now served all over the island; and **mee rebus**, a Malay dish of egg noodles served in a thick, spicy gravy based on yellow-bean sauce, with tofu, boiled egg and beansprouts as accompaniments – to name but two.

Costs By far the cheapest and most fun places to eat are **hawker centres/food courts**, housed either within shopping malls or in their own open-air premises, where you can eat well for S$10 a head. Old-fangled *kopitiams* (the same as *kedai kopis* in Malaysia) are also inexpensive, though increasingly uncommon downtown; the best concentrations are in Little India and the Arab St area. Prices at mid-range restaurants start at around S$20 a head, and there many upmarket places where you'll pay three or four times that, although most of these also have good-value weekday set-lunch specials. As with hotel bills, there's also the matter of the ten percent **service charge** and 7.7 percent **tax**, levied by all but the cheapest restaurants and cafés (price indications here include these surcharges).

RESTAURANTS, HAWKER CENTRES AND FOOD COURTS

Although all of Singapore's top hotels have reliable **restaurants**, it's usually more interesting to check out the many great independent establishments, several of which have evolved into chains. Some Chinese restaurants and *kopitiams* pride themselves in being *zichar* places – essentially being able to offer cooked-to-order dishes not on the menu, for roughly the same cost; it's therefore well worth asking if you're aching to try something you don't see listed.

Food courts and **hawker centres**, having started out as hygienic but faceless markets to organize the stalls that once lined the island's streets, are moving up in the world these days, not just in terms of having a/c. Singapore now boasts several food-court chains, notably *Food Republic and Food Junction*, some of whose outlets feature snazzy decor and even "curated" stalls, picked for their culinary pedigree.

CHINATOWN

Singapore's Chinatown is, of course, no Chinese ghetto and its eating places are thus pretty diverse, although the central Sago, Smith, Terengganu and Pagoda streets tend to be dominated by touristy Chinese restaurants – seldom the best in their class. For places on the south bank of the river, including Boat Quay, see p.536.

Annalakshmi #01–04 Central Square, 20 Havelock Rd ☎6339 9993, ⓦannalakshmi.com.sg; map pp.494–495. Come here for excellent Indian vegetarian dishes served up by volunteers, with no prices specified; you pay what you feel the meal was worth. Profits go to an association promoting South Indian culture. It's best to turn up for their superb buffets (at lunchtime plus dinner Fri–Sun), though note that they take a dim view of people helping themselves to more than they can finish. A branch at 104 Amoy St (☎6223 0809; Mon–Sat 11am–3pm) serves buffets only. Daily 11am–3pm & 6–10pm.

Bee Heong Palace 132–134 Telok Ayer St ☎6222 9074; map pp.494–495. Less crowded than more famous rivals for Hokkien cuisine, this nondescript modern place nevertheless serves up creditable *hae cho*, minced pork and prawn fried up like little rissoles, plus *kong bak*, pork stewed in soy sauce and stuffed into semicircular buns. Portions are decent and prices reasonable – reckon on S$45 for two, without alcohol. Mon–Sun 11.30am–3pm & 6–10.30pm Tues, Thurs–Sun.

Breakthru Café #01–02c People's Park Centre (at the back of the building), 101a Upper Cross St ☎6533 5977; map pp.494–495. A church-run caféteria might seem an odd idea, but this one gives employment to former drug addicts and people convicted of drug possession. It's a great place to refuel cheaply on rice and noodle meals and dim sum selections, (mostly under S$10), and to do a bit of people-watching: judges from the law courts opposite do lunch here and interact quite amicably with staff they may have previously sentenced. Mon–Thurs 7am–6pm, Fri 7am–5pm, Sat 7am–3pm.

Hong Hock Eating House South Bridge Rd, opposite the Jamae Mosque; map pp.494–495. Somewhere between a *kopitiam* and a small food court, this excellent place takes a multicultural approach: Chinese fare includes claypot curry fish and oyster omelette, while an Indian Muslim stall serves *nasi campur* and "tissue" *prata* – a sweet *roti* artfully folded up like a napkin. A good place to head after partying into the small hours. Daily 11.30am–7am.

Indochine Upstairs at 47 Club St ☎6323 7347, ⓦindochine.com.sg; map pp.494–495. Classy Vietnamese, Lao and Cambodian cuisine in chic surroundings sums up this chain, and their Club St venue is

no exception. The Vietnamese *chao tom* (minced prawn wrapped round sugar cane) and deep-fried Vietnamese spring rolls (in veggie and non-veggie versions) are mouthwatering starters, while the Lao *larb kai* (chicken in lime juice with salad) is one of many excellent main dishes. Mon–Fri noon–10.30pm, Sat 6–10.30pm.

★**Lee Tong Kee** 278 South Bridge Rd ☎6226 0417, ⓦipohhorfun.com; map pp.494–495. For years the speciality of this retro-styled restaurant, with old-fashioned fans and marble tables, has been Ipoh-style *hor fun*, supposedly smoother than regular tagliatelli-type rice noodles. Though you may have trouble discerning that difference, their many noodle variations are undeniably good whether served dryish or in soup (all around S$7). Also available are assorted dumplings plus their signature lime juice, usually served with a pinch of salt. Get there early for lunch, when it gets packed out. Daily Mon 11am–4pm, Wed–Sun 11am–9pm.

Lime House 2 Jiak Chuan Rd ☎6222 3130, ⓦlimehouse.asia; map pp.494–495. An impressively renovated shophouse where the lack of a/c seems entirely apt given the culinary focus on the opposite corner of the earth – the Caribbean. The menu includes standards like curried goat, but more interesting are fusiony dishes like the red snapper starter with avocado, sorrel and pomegranate (S$17) or the rib-eye steak with jerk sauce and watermelon compote (S$40). Plenty of rum-based cocktails, too, with a bar section in the back garden. Tues–Sat noon–midnight.

Maxwell Food Centre Corner of South Bridge & Maxwell rds; map pp.494–495. One of Singapore's first hawker centres and home to a clutch of popular Chinese stalls, including the well-known Tian Tian for Hainanese chicken rice, plus others that are good for satay or *rojak*. Daily roughly 7am–midnight.

★**The Reading Room** 19 Bukit Pasoh Rd ☎6220 9019; map pp.494–495. Cosy shophouse café-restaurant with barely ten tables and yes, shelves and shelves of books; some customers actually deign to read novels over their coffee. Foodwise there are light bites such as beer-battered fish and chips and Portobello mushroom burgers (both S$20) as well as plenty of tapas selections; decent cakes, too, and a full drinks list, including Kopparberg ciders. Mon–Thurs 11am–11.30pm, Fri–Sun 8am–1am.

Rongcheng 271 New Bridge Rd ☎6536 4415; map pp.494–495. One of several Sichuan hotpot places here, though not signposted in English – look out for the Chinese name in black on a red sign, next to the Japan Home shop. Hotpots require you to help yourself to the raw ingredients, then cook them in your choice of stock, boiling away on the stove at your table. You mix your own dips too, choosing from different chilli sauces, minced garlic and even tahini. Eat as much as you want for around S$20/head. Busiest in the evening. Daily 11.30am–6am.

9

Spizza 29 Club St ☎6224 2525, ⓦspizza.sg; map pp.494–495. Modern, unpretentious pizzeria with a tempting A to Z of thin-crust offerings cooked in a traditional wood oven (from S$20). They deliver all over the island, too (order on ☎6377 7773). Mon–Fri noon–2.30pm & 6–10.30pm, Sat & Sun noon–10.30m.

Tak Po 42 Smith St ☎6225 0302; map pp.494–495. Compact, competent and inexpensive Cantonese restaurant, refreshingly untouristy considering the location, with a/c inside and some tables out on the street. All the usual dim sum favourites, including *siu mai* dumplings, yam cake and excellent pork ribs with black beans, plus a wide range of *congees* (savoury rice porridges). For afters, try the baked egg tarts, which are spot on, the pastry not too flaky and the custard filling not oversweet. Around S$20/head without drinks. Daily 7am–10.30pm.

★**Urban Bites** 161 Telok Ayer St ☎6327 9460, ⓦurbanbites.com.sg; map pp.494–495. It's nothing much to look at, but serves excellent Lebanese cuisine, from a tender *kafta khashkhash* (minced lamb kebab) to home-cooking favourites like *mujadara* (rice with lentils and fried onions). You can order mezze-style or individual mains; reckon on S$30/head, minus drinks. Mon–Sat 9am–9.45pm.

Yixin 39 Temple St, no phone; map pp.494–495. Workaday vegetarian *kopitiam* that turns out dishes such as mock Peking duck (S$8), plus rice and noodle standards like *lor mee* (noodles in a tangy, gloopy sauce). A picture menu makes ordering easy. Barely signed in English, but easy to spot by the *Santa Grand Chinatown* hotel. Daily 7.30am–9.30pm.

Yum Cha #02–01 20 Trengganu St (entry via Temple St) ☎6372 1717, ⓦyumcha.com.sg; map pp.494–495. Grand dim sum restaurant with several dining rooms and a wide-ranging menu. They call their house speciality pomfret "tapino" – it's a fish hotpot for around S$50. Mon–Fri 11am–11pm, Sat & Sun 9am–11pm.

BOAT QUAY TO RIVERSIDE POINT

The south bank of the Singapore River is packed with busy restaurants and bars, at their most atmospheric in the restored shophouses of boisterous Boat Quay, though even the modern complexes can be a more enticing prospect than overpriced Clarke Quay on the north bank. All places reviewed here are right by the river or no more than a couple of streets back from it.

Brewerkz #01–05/06 Riverside Point, 30 Merchant Rd ☎6438 7438, ⓦbrewerkz.com; map pp.494–495. Popular for its highly rated beers, brewed on site, and American fare, including excellent burgers and sandwiches, plus barbecued ribs, pizzas, nachos, grilled potato skins and the like. It's on the pricey side though, with burgers starting at S$25. Busy at weekends. Sun–Thurs noon–midnight, Fri & Sat noon–1am.

★**Café Iguana** #01–03 Riverside Point, 30 Merchant Rd ☎6236 1275, ⓦcafeiguana.com; map pp.494–495. This open-fronted restaurant is adorned with a huge mural of Frida Kahlo amid assorted other Mexicana. They serve fajitas, tacos, burritos and all the other standards, with mains around S$30. The avocado ice cream makes a great dessert, and there's a vast range of tequilas and margaritas as you might expect. Can get very crowded in the evenings. Mon–Thurs 4pm–1am, Fri 4pm–3am, Sat noon–3am, Sun noon–1am.

Hock Lam Street Popular Beef Kway Teow 6 North Canal Rd ☎6535 0084; map pp.494–495. For decades this was a highly regarded stall on the now-vanished Hock Lam St, at the site of the present Funan DigitaLife Mall. The stall survives, albeit as a little shophouse restaurant, serving the same *kuay teow* noodles with beef slices or beefball dumplings, dry or with soup; servings cost around S$7. Mon–Fri 11am–8.30pm, Sat & Sun 11am–4pm.

Our Village Entrance on fifth floor, 46 Boat Quay ☎6538 3092; map pp.494–495. A hidden gem, with fine North Indian and Sri Lankan food, and peachy views of the river and Colonial District from its lamplit sixth-floor terrace. Mon–Fri noon–1.45pm & 6–11pm, Sat & Sun 6–11pm.

Rendezvous #02–72 The Central, 6 Eu Tong Sen St ☎6339 7508, ⓦrendezvous-hlk.com.sg; map pp.494–495. For decades *Rendezvous* has been dishing out its revered *nasi padang*. Its current location in a mediocre mall doesn't suit at all, but thankfully the curries have stayed the course, in particular the superb chicken korma – a mild curried stew of just the right degree of richness, derived from coconut milk rather than cream or yoghurt. A couple of curries with rice and side dishes are unlikely to cost more than S$25 a head. Daily 11am–9pm.

TANJONG PAGAR AND THE FINANCIAL DISTRICT

You're unlikely to head to these areas for the food alone, but they do boast some excellent, if often pricey, independent restaurants.

Blue Ginger 97 Tanjong Pagar Rd ☎6222 3928, ⓦtheblueginger.com; map pp.494–495. In a smartly renovated shophouse, this trendy Nyonya restaurant has become a firm favourite thanks to such dishes as *ikan masal asam gulai* (mackerel in a tamarind and lemon-grass gravy), and that benchmark of Nyonya cuisine, *ayam buah keluak* – chicken braised in soy sauce together with savoury Indonesian black nuts. Daily noon–2.30pm & 6.30–10.30pm.

Clifford Pier 80 Collyer Quay ☎6597 5266; map pp.494–495. An upmarket restaurant serving up a sort of nouvelle cuisine take on Southeast Asian street food: *laksa*, *rojak*, duck in a Thai red curry sauce, plus novel desserts like *teh tarik* ice cream and soursop sorbet. Noodle dishes cost

9

around S$20, about four times what you'd pay at a food court, but then food courts don't feature marble floors and the lofty, arched ceiling of the former boat terminal. Daily noon–2.30pm, 3.30–5.30pm & 6.30pm–midnight.

Cumi Bali 66 Tanjong Pagar Rd ☎6220 6619, ⓦcumibali.com; map pp.494–495. Bamboo sieves and flutes line the walls at this tiny, inexpensive *nasi padang* joint. Both the beef *rendang* and satay Madura, marinated in sweet soy sauce, hit the spot, and they have generous set lunches for under S$10. Mon–Sat 11.30am–2.30pm & 6–9.30pm, Sun 6–9.30pm.

★**Lau Pa Sat** 18 Raffles Quay; map pp.494–495. The food court at this historic market building offers a real panoply of Singapore hawker food, including satay – vendors set up their barbecues just outside on Boon Tat St in the evenings. Pricier outlets offer cooked-to-order seafood such as chilli crab. Open 24hr.

Sabio 5 Duxton Hill ☎6690 7562 (no reservations), ⓦsabio.sg; map pp.494–495. Spanish-owned and -run, this tiny but elegant restaurant serves delicious tapas, including excellent pan-fried calamari, tender grilled lamb cutlets and aged ham from acorn-fed pigs (hams sold by weight, otherwise most tapas S$10–20). Wash it down with their own sangria or Estrella Galicia beer. Often packed. Mon–Fri noon–10.30pm, Sat 5–11pm, Sun 11.30am–10pm.

THE COLONIAL DISTRICT

Although you can eat cheaply in the Colonial District at mundane restaurants inside malls like Funan (see p.549), the more interesting – and generally pricey – places tend to be housed within heritage buildings. Besides the restaurants below, there's also the *Tiffin Room* at the *Raffles* hotel for a blowout high tea (see p.543).

Bacchanalia Ground floor, Freemasons' Hall, 23a Coleman St ☎6509 1453, ⓦbacchanalia.asia; map p.476. One of the more lavish culinary arrivals of recent years assembles familiar ingredients in unexpected ways – if crisp pork belly with red cabbage, apple and capers grabs you, the rest of the menu probably will too. Mains start at S$35, or you can go for a two-course set lunch at S$45 – though note that everything is a not-quite-full-sized serving placed in the middle of the table for sharing. Mon–Thurs noon–3pm & 6pm–midnight, Fri noon–3pm & 6pm–2am, Sat 6pm–2am.

★**Brussels Sprouts** #01–12 The Pier at Robertson Quay, 80 Mohamed Sultan Rd ☎6887 4344, ⓦbrusselssprouts.com.sg; map p.476. This riverside restaurant specializes in – you guessed it – Belgian-inspired mussels and clams. There's a bewildering range of seasonings, from a strongly alcoholic white wine sauce to Thai tom yam, accompanied by unlimited helpings of fries (S$48). You can also choose from a plethora of fruity Belgian beers, including Lindemans and Leffe on draught. Tues–Fri 5–11pm, Sat & Sun noon–11pm.

Flutes National Museum, 93 Stamford Rd ☎6338 8770, ⓦflutes.com.sg; map p.476. An upmarket choice for modern European and fusion cuisine, with main courses starting at S$45. Best to go for the set lunch (two courses for around S$40) or, even better, the Sunday lunch of roast beef with the usual trimmings, plus dessert (S$45). There's a separate afternoon tea session Fri–Sun too. Mon–Thurs 11.30am–2pm & 6.30–10pm, Fri & Sat 11.30am–2pm, 3–5pm & 6.30–10pm, Sun 10am–2.30pm & 3–5pm.

★**Shiraz** Block A, Clarke Quay #01–06 ☎6334 2282, ⓦshirazfnb.com; map p.476. The best Persian restaurant in town, not that there's much competition, but the many Iranians among the clientele can't be wrong. Massive portions of tender kebabs and stews, all served with mounds of fluffy, aromatic saffron rice. Not cheap – main courses from S$35 – but still better value than most places in overpriced Clarke Quay, with belly-dancing most evenings just before 9pm, too. Mon–Thurs 6.30–11pm, Fri & Sat noon–3pm & 6.30pm–2.30am, Sun 6.30pm–2am.

BRAS BASAH ROAD TO ROCHOR ROAD

The area sandwiched between the Colonial District and Little India features plenty of well-established restaurants, including a good cluster close to *Raffles Hotel*. Two worthwhile food courts are also worth checking out at the Bugis Junction mall near Bugis MRT: the plush *Food Junction* on level 3, serving a good range of local street cuisine, and the Japanese-dominated one taking most of level B1, complete with plastic models of dishes and even the ice creams.

Ah Chew Desserts #01–11, 1 Liang Seah St ☎6339 8198; map p.483. Taking up two restored shophouses, *Ah Chew* confronts you with strange local sweets containing beans or other unexpected ingredients. The cashew-nut paste is not bad if you like the sound of a broth made of nut butter; also available are the likes of *pulot hitam*, made with black sticky rice. Cautiously sample a few items by ordering the small servings; most bowls cost S$5 or so. Mon–Thurs 12.30–11.30pm, Fri 12.30pm–12.30am, Sat 1.30pm–12.30am, Sun 1.30–11.30pm.

★**Chao Shan Cuisine** 85 Beach Rd ☎6336 2390; map p.483. This Teochew restaurant retains the informality it had when it was out in the suburbs – the casually dressed proprietor wanders around chatting to customers. His wife takes orders for marvellous standards such as braised goose on a bed of beancurd; oyster omelette (in two styles, crispy or regular); fish maw soup (rather gelatinous) and cold crab. Around S$30 a head, minus drinks. Daily 11.30am–2.30pm & 5.30–10.30pm.

Fatty's Wing Seong #01–31 Burlington Square, 175 Bencoolen St ☎6338 1087; map p.483. Run by an avuncular chubby cook in bygone decades, *Fatty's* was an institution on the now-vanished foodie paradise that was Albert St. Today it's a touristy restaurant that maintains the original's no-frills *zichar* approach, and also does standards such as chicken rice. Around S$20 a head without drinks. Daily noon–2.30pm & 5.15–10.15pm.

★**Herbivore** #01–13 Fortune Centre, 190 Middle Rd ☎6333 1612; map p.483. There's a cluster of vegetarian restaurants near Waterloo St's Kwan Im Temple, particularly at the Fortune Centre building, where the star is this excellent place serving tasty tempura, "chicken" teriyaki and so forth. Good-value sets (from S$20) with noodles or rice plus accompaniments like soya sashimi, pickle and salad, plus dessert. Mon–Fri 8.30am–3pm & 5–10pm, Sat & Sun 8.30am–10pm.

Yhingthai Palace #01–04, 36 Purvis St ☎6337 1161, ⊛yhingthai.com.sg; map p.483. A smartly turned-out Chinese-influenced Thai restaurant, where you can't go wrong with the deep-fried pomfret with mango sauce, Thai fishcakes or deboned chicken wings stuffed with asparagus and mushroom. Around S$40/head, excluding drinks. Daily 11.30am–2pm & 6–10pm.

LITTLE INDIA

Little India is paradise if you're after maximum flavour for minimum outlay; the first part of Serangoon Rd and its side streets, as well as Race Course Rd, are packed with inexpensive, excellent curry houses specializing in South Indian food, often dished out onto banana leaves and with plenty of vegetarian options; some places offer North Indian and Nepali dishes too. The only drawback to eating here is the dearth of worthwhile places that aren't Indian.

★**Banana Leaf Apolo** 54 Race Course Rd ☎6293 8682; map p.483. Banana-leaf-type restaurant with a wide selection of Indian dishes, including fish-head curry (from S$25 depending on size) plus chicken, mutton and prawn curries (S$14). The lunchtime "South Indian vegetarian meal" is a steal, a huge thali of rice, poppadoms, two main curries and several side ones, plus a dessert, for around S$10. There's another branch in the Little India Arcade nearby. Daily 10am–10pm.

Cocotte Wanderlust Hotel, 2 Dickson Rd ☎6298 1188, ⊛restaurantcocotte.com; map p.486. It's an obvious misfit in the area, but one that impresses with its eccentric decor and modern French cuisine using prime ingredients. They do some "communal" mains for sharing, including beef bourguignon and their signature roast chicken (S$60). Three-course weekday set lunches are good value at S$38. Mon, Wed & Thurs noon–2.30pm & 6.30–10.30pm, Fri–Sun noon–3pm & 6.30–11pm.

Hillman 135 Kitchener Rd ☎6221 5073, ⊛hillmanrestaurant.com; map p.486. This little Chinese restaurant is unaccountably popular with rowdy Japanese businessmen, though don't let that put you off. They come, as you should, for the tip-top *zichar* food. Particularly good are the claypot noodles and, for the adventurous, claypot sea cucumber – not a vegetable but a marine relative of

starfish and sea urchins. Reckon on S$30/head excluding drinks. Daily 11.30am–2.30pm & 5.30–10.30pm.

Komala Villas 76–78 Serangoon Rd ☎6293 6980; map p.486. A veteran, rather cramped vegetarian establishment with more than a dozen variations of *dosai* – what they're best at, although they have a few more substantial rice meals – just a few dollars each, plus fresh coconut water to wash it down. Branch at 12–14 Buffalo Rd (☎6293 366; open from 8am). Daily 7am–10.30pm.

Madras Woodlands Ganga 1 Cuff Rd ☎6295 3750. This simple vegetarian restaurant serves up great-value Indian buffets (Mon–Fri lunchtime S$10, weekend lunchtimes and all eves S$12), featuring several curries, rice, *nan* and a dessert, with the option of ordering à la carte as well. Daily 11.30am–3pm & 6–10.30pm.

Saravanaa Bhavan 84 Syed Alwi Rd ☎6297 7755, ⊛saravanabhavan.com; map p.486. A South Indian vegetarian franchise, based in Chennai, but with branches as far afield as New York, with all the staples from *vada* (dhal-flour doughnuts) to *dosai*, plus their popular Indian take on Chinese food: the Gobi Manchurian (curiously not on the menu) is basically a spicy sweet and sour pork with cauliflower instead of pork. Reckon on paying S$15 per person, minus drinks. Daily 9am–midnight.

★**Tekka Food Centre** Alongside Tekka market at start of Serangoon Rd; map p.486. One of the best old-school hawkers' centres on the island, always steamy hot and busy. The Indian and Malay stalls are especially good; look out for exceptional Indian *rojak* – assorted fritters with sweet dips. There's a decent selection of Chinese stalls too, but they pale by comparison. Daily 7am–late.

ARAB STREET/KAMPONG GLAM

It seems natural that Arab St should boast several Middle Eastern and North African restaurants with meze, kebabs and couscous, but many of these places are recent and rather slapdash interlopers; the mainstay of the area's dining has long been Malay and Indonesian food. Note that the more traditional venues don't serve alcohol.

Blu Jaz Café 11 Bali Lane ☎6292 3800, ⊛blujazcafe .net; map p.486. Buzzing café-restaurant stretching between Bali and Haji lanes, and easily spotted with its gaudy decor and regular live jazz. Reliable local and Western food – everything from chicken kebab to fish and chips – at affordable prices; a steak will set you back around S$25. Mon & Fri noon–1.30am, Tues–Thurs noon–12.30am, Sat 4pm–1.30am.

Bumbu 44 Kandahar St ☎6392 8628, ⊛bumbu.com .sg; map p.486. Affordable Thai and Indonesian cuisine, with a few Nyonya offerings in keeping with the Peranakan antique furniture impressively scattered all around this shophouse restaurant. Around S$25/person without drinks. Tues–Sun 11am–3pm & 6–10pm.

9

STREET ICE CREAM

A couple of generations ago, ice cream in Singapore often meant stuff sold by hawkers from pushcarts, in exotic flavours like sweet corn, red (aduki) bean and yam. This was so-called *potong* ("cut" in Malay) ice cream because it came in brick shapes and the seller would use a cleaver to slice it into slabs, to be served either between wafers or even rolled up in white bread – giving a new dimension to the term "ice cream sandwich".

The general elimination of street stalls put paid to that trade, but in recent years the ice-cream vendors have made a comeback. They're often to be seen at Cavenagh Bridge, on Orchard Road, outside Bugis MRT and at other downtown locations. The bread option complements the ice cream surprisingly well, serving as a sort of neutral sponge cake. As for the weird flavours, they're all more than palatable; you can also find red-bean ice cream on a stick in supermarkets and convenience stores, sold under the name "Potong".

★ **Café Le Caire** 39 Arab St ☎ 6292 0979, ⓦ cafelecaire .com; map p.486. This relaxed diner was the first Arabic restaurant in the area by some margin and unlike the patchy, overpriced new arrivals, is a reliable, inexpensive bet for Lebanese and Egyptian kebabs, dips and wraps. The signature dish is Yemeni harissa, a spicy stew of minced lamb and cracked wheat. For those into hubble-bubbles, they do over a dozen tobaccos. Sun–Thurs 10am–3.30am, Fri & Sat 10am–5.30am.

Haji Maimunah 11 & 15 Jalan Pisang ☎ 6297 4294, ⓦ hjmaimunah.com; map p.486. A tiny restaurant that's great for inexpensive Malay food. Mon–Sat 7am–8pm (closed during Ramadan).

Islamic Restaurant 745 North Bridge Rd ☎ 6298 7563; map p.486. The modernized premises don't hint at this restaurant's heritage: check out the photos of functions they catered for in the 1920s. *Biriyanis* are their speciality (S$8) though they also do a huge range of North Indian chicken, mutton, prawn, squid and veg curries, with good-value set meals at around S$10. Daily 10am–10pm; closed Fri 1–2pm.

★ **Kampong Glam Café** 17 Bussorah St; map p.486. Fantastic roadside *kopitiam* serving inexpensive Malay rice and noodle dishes, cooked to order, plus curries. Come not just for the food but for a good chinwag with friends over *teh tarik* late into the evening. Daily 8am–1am.

★ **Rumah Makan Minang** 18 Kandahar St, ☎ 6294 4805, ⓦ minang.sg; map p.486. A street-corner place serving superb *nasi padang*, including the mildly spiced chicken *balado* and more unusual curries made with *tempeh* (fermented soybean cakes) or offal. For dessert you might get freshly made sweet pancakes stuffed with peanuts and corn – much better than they sound. Just S$10/head for a good feed. Mon–Fri 7am–8pm, Sat & Sun 7am–5pm.

Zam Zam 697 & 699 North Bridge Rd ☎ 6298 7011; map p.486. Staff at this venerable Indian Muslim *kopitiam* have the annoying habit of touting for custom even though the place draws crowds, especially on Fridays, with its *murtabak* and *biriyani* offerings (there's even a venison

version of the latter). Avoid the house speciality drink, *katira* – it's like one of Singapore's sickly ice desserts, only melted. Daily 8.30am–10pm.

MARINA BAY

The malls and fancy hotels scattered around Marina Bay hold some decent restaurants, though few are worth going out of your way for.

Paulaner Bräuhaus #01–01 Millenia Walk, 9 Raffles Blvd ☎ 6883 2572, ⓦ paulaner.com.sg; map p.503. The cavernous ceiling with a maypole sticking up into it is impressive, as is the menu of Bavarian delights such as the bitty *spätzle* pasta, but the best reason to come is the terrific Sunday brunch spread, including superb pork knuckle, sausages and salads, and desserts like strudel and cheesecake. It's good value at S$56 with unlimited soft drinks, or S$68 with unlimited beer from their microbrewery. Mon–Fri noon–2.30pm & 6.30–10.30pm, Sat 6.30–10.30pm, Sun 11.30am–2.30pm & 6.30–10.30pm.

Pizzeria Mozza #B01–42 Marina Bay Sands mall, 1 Bayfront Ave ☎ 6688 8522, ⓦ pizzeriamozza.com /Singapore; map p.503. An excellent range of reasonably priced thin-crust pizzas starting at S$25, with plenty of salads, panini and soups, plus good desserts. Daily noon–11pm.

★ **Singapore Food Trail** Beneath the Singapore Flyer; map p.503. Arguably more interesting than the Flyer itself, this retro-style food court evokes Singapore's street-food scene of half a century ago, its stalls mocked up as pushcarts. The food can be retro too – for example satay *bee hoon*, rice vermicelli drenched in the peanut sauce normally eaten with satay, and popular in the 1970s – though it also features lots of evergreens, including oyster omelette and *popiah* (steamed spring rolls). Nothing costs more than S$10. Mon–Thurs 10.30am–10.30pm, Fri– Sun 10.30am–11.30pm.

★ **Sky on 57** SkyPark at Marina Bay Sands ☎ 6688 8857; map p.503. Here's how to circumvent that huge SkyPark admission charge – by eating at this fine restaurant featuring a harmonious marriage of Far Eastern and French cooking. Fiendishly expensive at dinner, when mains start at S$50, but okay value at lunchtime when their superb king prawn *laksa* costs S$30, or a three-course set menu is S$60. Head up via tower 1. Daily 7.30–10.30am, noon–2.30pm & 6–10.30pm.

Supertree by Indochine Gardens by the Bay ☎ 6694 8489, ⓦ indochine.com.sg; map p.503. From an eyrie atop the gardens' tallest supertree, *Indochine* serves up its usual range of sophisticated Lao, Thai and Vietnamese food, here mostly available as tapas (from S$20) or sharing platters, the best of features grilled beef, assorted spring rolls and lychee-and-pork beignets (S$100 for four). Daily 10am–1am (food from noon).

ORCHARD ROAD AND AROUND

Eating in Singapore's shopping nexus – Orchard Rd, Tanglin Rd and Scotts Rd – is almost completely about restaurants in malls and hotels, though a few venues are housed in refurbished shophouses. Most malls have food courts, and indeed two of the island's slickest are to be found here: *Food Republic* inside 313@Somerset, and *Food Opera* in the basement of ION Orchard.

Bistro Du Vin #01–14 Shaw Centre, 1 Scotts Rd ☎ 6733 7763, ⓦ bistroduvin.com.sg; map pp.506–507. Informal French restaurant that does an exceptional duck leg confit, plus standards such as escargot and French onion soup – and none of that nouvelle cuisine presentation-over-substance nonsense either. The lunch deals are reasonable value at S$40 for three courses; mains ordered à la carte cost just about as much. Daily noon–2pm & 6.30–10pm.

★ **Crystal Jade La Mian Xiao Long Bao** #04–27, Ngee Ann City ☎ 6238 1661, ⓦ crystaljade.com; map pp.506–507. *Crystal Jade* is an umbrella for several linked Chinese restaurant chains, each with a different emphasis. The mid-priced *La Mian Xiao Long Bao* outlets focus on Shanghai and northern Chinese cuisine, as exemplified by *xiao long bao*, succulent Shanghai pork dumplings, and the northwestern speciality *la mian*, literally "pulled noodles", the strands of dough being stretched and worked by hand. Daily 11am–10pm.

Kiseki #08–01 Orchard Central mall, 181 Orchard Rd ☎ 6736 1216, ⓦ kisekirestaurant.com.sg; map pp.506–507. If you come here often enough you might end up as rotund as the sumo wrestler statue at the entrance. This "mega Japanese buffet" has everything from sushi to Japanese curry pizza, via tempura, *yakitori* and (at dinner) steak, plus a sizeable dessert section. Prices range from S$24 Mon–Fri lunchtime to nearly double that Fri–Sun eves. Daily 11.30am–3pm & 6–10.30pm.

★ **Lao Beijing** #03–01 Plaza Singapura, 68 Orchard Rd ☎ 6738 7207, ⓦ laobeijing.com.sg; map pp.506–507. Styled like a classy, old-fangled Chinese teahouse, this restaurant specializes in northern Chinese fare, including Peking duck and "Chairman Mao's Favourite Braised Pork"

– suitably red in colour – plus dishes from elsewhere in China. There's also a weekend "high-tea" featuring not scones and cream but dim sum (S$20). Mon–Fri 11.30am–3pm & 5.30–10pm, Sat & Sun 11am–5pm & 6–10pm.

Maharajah 39 Cuppage Terrace ☎ 6732 6331, ⓦ maharajah.com.sg; map pp.506–507. This pleasant North Indian restaurant has a large terrace and a tempting menu that includes several tandoori options plus the unusual fish Nur Jehan – fried deboned fish with a cashew sauce. Around S$35/person without alcohol. Daily 11am–11pm.

★ **Marché** Ground floor and basement, 313@Somerset, 313 Orchard Rd ☎ 6834 4041; map pp.506–507. Never mind that Mövenpick's *Marché* restaurants are formulaic when you can have *rösti*, sausages or crêpes cooked to order in front of you, or help yourself to the superb salad bar. Daily lunch specials offer a meal and drink for around S$12, while the bakery counter does takeaway sandwiches (from S$5), bread sticks and Berliners, doughnuts with a range of fillings. Daily 11am–11pm; bakery from 7.30am.

Min Jiang Goodwood Park Hotel, 22 Scotts Rd ☎ 6730 1704; map pp.506–507. This stylish affair serves some Cantonese food and lunchtime dim sum (with a weekend afternoon dim sum buffet at S$39/head), though their spicy Sichuan specialities are the most interesting. Good choices include the prawn fried with dried chillies, Sichuan smoked duck and long beans fried with minced pork. Reasonably priced for a top hotel. Daily 11am–2.30pm & 6–10.30pm, Sat & Sun also 3.30–5.30pm.

Newton Circus Hawker Centre Corner of Clemenceau Ave North and Bukit Timah Rd, near Newton MRT; map p.474. A venerable open-air place with a wide range of food. It's noted for its seafood, for which you can end up paying through the nose; prices are on the high side for stalls anyway, as the place is very much on the tourist trail. Late afternoon until the early hours.

★ **PS Café** Level 2, Palais Renaissance, 390 Orchard Rd ☎ 9834 8232; ⓦ pscafe.sg; map pp.506–507. Marvellous though pricey restaurant set in something resembling a glasshouse and offering an inventive, constantly revised menu of fusion fare and great desserts. Mains from S$30. Mon–Fri 11.30am–midnight, Sat & Sun 9.30am–midnight.

Sakae Teppenyaki #B2–52 Plaza Singapura, 68 Orchard Rd ☎ 6337 5676, ⓦ sakaeteppenyaki.com; map pp.506–507. One of many mini-restaurants squeezed into the shopping mall's basement food court, with tables set around hot griddles all geared up to prepare teppanyaki, Japanese fry-ups of meat or seafood. Choose from various set combinations of ingredients and a chef will cook them with aplomb, and more than a dash of seasoning, in front of you. About S$20/head, excluding drinks. Daily 11.30am–9.30pm.

9

Swensen's #03–23 Plaza Singapura, 68 Orchard Rd ☎ 6837 0650, ⓦ swensens.com.sg; map pp.506–507. Wins no prizes for trendiness, but for what is essentially a chain of ice-cream parlours, the food menu is extensive – salads, pasta dishes, jumbo-sausage subs, etc. Prices are reasonable, with soups and many of the huge range of ice-cream concoctions weighing in at around S$10. Daily 10.30am–10.30pm.

Thai Express #03–24 Plaza Singapura, 68 Orchard Rd ☎ 6339 5442, ⓦ thaiexpress.com.sg; map pp.506–507. A modern chain with plenty of wood and chrome fittings and where everything is done chop-chop. The menu is packed with Thai rice and noodle standards (from S$12) plus lots of desserts. Daily 11am–10.30pm.

Warung M Nasir 69 Killiney Rd ☎ 6734 6228; map pp.506–507. Tiny but well-respected Indonesian *nasi padang* joint, with standards such as fried chicken *balado*, beef and chicken *rendang* and tofu or beans fried with *sambal*. Daily 10am–10pm.

DEMPSEY HILL

Dotted with old bungalows and the odd field, the stretch of Holland Rd 1km west of the Botanic Gardens' Tanglin Gate and 2km west of the start of Orchard Rd was originally a British army camp, which later housed Singapore's Ministry of Defence. No one quite agrees on what to call the area now that the military is long gone, but Dempsey Hill (or Tanglin Village; ⓦ dempseyhill.com.sg) is worth a look for its jumble of posh restaurants and bars, plus health spas, antique shops and so forth. The venues below are close to the main road and can be reached on foot. Buses #7, #77 and #174 head past here from Orchard Blvd.

Long Beach Seafood Block 25, Dempsey Rd ☎ 6323 2222, ⓦ longbeachseafood.com.sg; map p.474. Once you had to trek to the beaches to find Singapore's best Chinese-style seafood, but no longer, now that this beachside stalwart has set up here. The best dishes really are magic, including treacly crisp baby squid, chunky Alaska crab in a white pepper sauce, steamed *soon hock* (goby) and, of course, chilli crab. An expensive but worthwhile blowout. Daily 11am–3pm & 5pm–1am.

★**Samy's** Block 25, Dempsey Rd ☎ 6472 2080, ⓦ samyscurry.com; map p.474. Housed in a colonial-era hall with ceiling fans whirring overhead, *Samy's* is an institution that's been serving superb banana-leaf meals for decades. Choose from curries of jumbo prawn, fish head, crab or mutton, and either plain rice or the delicate, fluffy *biriyani*. There's excellent freshly squeezed lemonade or *teh tarik* – made the old-fashioned way with much ostentatious pouring – to wash it all down. You can eat well for S$20/head excluding drinks. Thurs–Mon 11am–3pm & 6–10pm.

GEYLANG AND KATONG

In line with their heritage, the suburbs of Geylang and Katong hold several inexpensive Nyonya and Malay restaurants.

328 Katong Laksa 51 East Coast Rd, at the corner of Ceylon Rd; map p.513. Just as different parts of Malaysia have their own take on *laksa*, so does Katong: here the noodles are cut into short strands for easy slurping off a spoon. Run by a brother-and-sister team, this *kopitiam* is regarded as one of the original purveyors of the dish, using seafood and without the meat of more modern variations. Daily 8am–10pm.

Guan Hoe Soon 38/40 Joo Chiat Place ☎ 6344 2761, ⓦ guanhoesoon.com; map p.513. Open in one form or another for more than half a century, this restaurant turns out fine Nyonya cuisine in home-cooked style, including *ngoh hiang*, a yummy sausage-like item in which minced prawn is rolled up in a wrapper made from bean curd, and satay *babi* – not a Malay satay, but a sweetish red pork curry. Around S$25/head. Daily 11am–3pm & 6–9.30pm.

★**Haji Maimunah** 20 Joo Chiat Rd ☎ 6348 5457, ⓦ hjmaimunah.com; map p.513. Inexpensive Malay diner serving good breakfasts (*nasi lemak*, *lontong* etc) and a fine *nasi campur* spread, featuring the likes of *ayam bakar sunda* (Sundanese-style barbecued chicken), with cooked-to-order choices such as *siput lemak sedut* (snails with coconut milk) and assorted *kuih* for afters. Tues–Sun 8am–9pm (Ramadan noon–10pm with special buffet meal).

Peranakan Inn 210 East Coast Rd ☎ 6440 6195; map p.513. As much effort goes into the food as went into the renovation of this immaculate, bright green shophouse restaurant, which offers a great range of authentic Nyonya favourites including a delectable *bakwan kepiting*, a pork meatball soup. Reckon on S$20/person, minus drinks. Daily 11am–2.30pm & 6–9.30pm.

SENTOSA AND VIVOCITY

There aren't many cheap places to eat on Sentosa, so if you're keen to keep costs down, try the VivoCity mall above HarbourFront MRT.

Bora-Bora Beach Bar Palawan Beach ☎ 6278 0838. This cheery bar has a huge menu featuring everything from vegetarian platters to banana-and-Kahlua freezes. Sun–Thurs 10.30am–9pm, Fri & Sat 10.30am–10pm.

★**Food Republic** Level 3 VivoCity. Perhaps the best example of this upmarket food court, the stalls styled to resemble something out of prewar Chinatown. The cuisine, from hand-picked stallholders, is top-notch too: try the scissors-cut curry rice – mixed rice/*nasi campur* but with the hawker slicing up the rice serving with scissors and heaping curry gravy onto it. Avoid at peak times, though, as the place will be rammed. Mon–Thurs 8am–10pm, Fri–Sun 8am–11pm.

Slappy Cakes Close to Universal Studios, Resorts World ☎ 6795 0779. A great place to bring kids for a pancake cookery class. You pick a batter (chocolate or zucchini, say), then something to add to the mix (strawberries or ham, anyone?) and then cook it at your table's griddle before topping it off with, say, pineapple jam or Greek yoghurt. It's good fun and if the results aren't quite up to scratch, well at least you won't have anyone to get cross with other than yourself (probably). One order (S$15) will make enough pancakes for two to share as a snack. Daily 8am–9.30pm.

★**Soup** #02–141 VivoCity ☎6376 9969. So-called samsui women once sailed from Sanshui, in China's Guangdong province to work on Singapore building sites. This fine little restaurant celebrates the cuisine of these redoubtable women, most famously their ginger chicken; similar to the steamed chicken in chicken rice, it comes with a gingery dip and iceberg-lettuce leaves to roll it up in. Reckon on S$25/head, excluding drinks. Daily 11.30am–10pm.

Trapizza Siloso Beach ☎6376 2662. Of the eating places on Siloso Beach, *Trapizza* stands out for its excellent pizzas and pasta dishes starting at S$20. Daily 11.30am–9.30pm.

CAFÉS AND HIGH-TEA VENUES

Western-style café chains are easy to find in downtown Singapore, though thin on the ground in Little India. The places reviewed here have only a limited selection of food, typically pastries, muffins, sandwiches and so forth, but make inexpensive spots for a Western breakfast nonetheless. Also reviewed are a couple of hotel venues renowned for that most colonial of traditions, high tea. It doesn't come cheap but it's a good excuse for a blowout – you get a lot more than just tea and scones for your money.

Brunetti #01–35 Tanglin Mall, 163 Tanglin Rd ☎6733 9088; map pp.506–507. An incredible Australian café with cabinet after cabinet of exquisite macaroons, cakes and ice creams that together come in almost as many colours as you'd find in a paint catalogue. Not too pricey – cheesecake costs S$8 – though the light meals and savoury snacks aren't such good value. Daily 8am–9pm.

Café l'Espresso Goodwood Park Hotel, 22 Scotts Rd ☎6730 1743; map pp.506–507. A legendary array of English cakes, scones and speciality coffees, not to mention chocolate fondue, for high tea – so successful they've extended it to lunchtimes at weekends. S$53. High tea Mon–Thurs 2–5.30pm, Fri–Sun noon–2.30pm & 3–5.30pm.

★**Cedele** #B1–37, Ngee Ann City, 391 Orchard Rd ☎6235 2380, ⓦcedeledepot.com; map pp.506–507. A café-bakery combo, *Cedele* serves up some of the very best sandwiches in Singapore (S$6–8) – think, say, honey dijon chicken on rosemary focaccia– and sells a vast variety of specialist breads. Some branches, like this one, also have a restaurant with soups, pies and inventive light meals such as the beetroot burger, which even non-veggies love. Daily 10am–10pm.

Dôme Singapore Art Museum, 71 Bras Basah Rd ☎6339 0792; map p.483. Slick café chain with an impressive list of coffees and teas plus light meals such as fish and chips and sausage-and-egg breakfasts. This branch stays open conveniently late. Daily 8.30am–10.30pm.

Spinelli's #01–28 China Square Central, 18 Upper Cross St; map pp.494–495. Part of a chain that's generally a safe bet for a good coffee or even a "spin" – a slushy iced coffee with flavouring of your choice. Muffins, scones, sandwiches and cheesecake too. Mon–Sat at least 9am–8pm, Sun 10am–7pm.

Tiffin Room Raffles Hotel, 1 Beach Rd ☎6412 1190; map p.476. High tea at this Anglo-Indian-themed restaurant is a genuinely scrumptious buffet of, oddly, dim sum plus servings of English scones, pastries, cakes and sandwiches – a real treat at S$70. High tea daily 3–5.30pm.

Windowsill 78 Horne Rd, 500m from Lavender MRT ☎9004 7827, ⓦwindowsillpies.sg; map p.486. Within walking distance of Arab St and Little India, this admirable specialist pie shop and café puts heart and soul into a porfolio of nine distinctive dessert pies and tarts. Concoctions like coconut lime vodka and banana-and-almond brittle are as yummy as they sound, and start at S$8 a slice. Tues–Thurs 11am–9.30pm, Fri 11am–10.30pm, Sat 10am–10.30pm, Sun 10am–9.30pm.

Ya Kun Kaya Toast #01–31 The Central, 6 Eu Tong Sen St, map pp.494–495. Now a ubiquitous chain, *Ya Kun* started out in the prewar years as a Chinatown stall offering classic *kopitiam* breakfast fare – *kaya* toast (the same as *roti kahwin* in Malaysia) plus optional soft-boiled eggs eaten with white pepper and soy sauce. Of course there's strong local coffee too, normally had with condensed or evaporated milk. Daily 7am–10pm.

DRINKING AND NIGHTLIFE

With its affluence and large expat community, Singapore supports a huge range of drinking holes, from elegant colonial chambers through hip rooftop venues with skyline views to slightly tacky joints featuring Chinese karaoke or middling bands covering Western hits. The best **bars** cluster mainly along the Singapore River and on Orchard Rd, though anywhere expats hang out won't be short of watering holes, notably Ann Siang Hill in Chinatown. There's also a bunch of glitzy and vibrant **clubs** that spin cutting-edge sounds, all minus – this being Singapore – any assistance from illicit substances. One or two venues regularly lure the world's leading DJs to play, although the scene has come off the boil in recent years.

Bar essentials Bars tend to open in the late afternoon, closing anywhere between midnight and 3am, an hour or

two later on Friday and Saturday, and may shut on Sunday; a few places are also open at lunchtime. A pint of Tiger beer

9

at a bar or club will start at around S$12 – double what you'd pay at a hawker centre – and prices can be much higher in fancier venues or for imported brews. A glass of house wine usually costs much the same as a beer, and spirits a few dollars more. During happy hour, which can last half the evening, you'll either get a considerable discount off drinks or a "one-for-one" deal (two drinks for the price of one), and some bars also have a house pour, a discounted cocktail, wine or beer on offer all night. Note that more upmarket venues, including hotel bars, often have a "smart casual" dress code, generally meaning no shorts, vests or sandals after sunset.

Club essentials Most clubs have a cover charge, if not all week then at least on Friday and Saturday; the charge almost always includes your first drink or two, and varies between S$15 and S$35 (weekends are pricier, and men pay slightly more than women). Where women get in free on ladies' night (often midweek), they have to pay for their first drink but may get unlimited refills of the "house pour" at certain times.

BARS

BOAT QUAY TO RIVERSIDE POINT, AND CHINATOWN

BQ Bar 39 Boat Quay ☎ 6536 9722, ⓦ bqbar.com; map pp.494–495. One of Boat Quay's cooler venues, thanks to the friendly staff, memorable views of the river from upstairs and diverse sounds, anything from dance to rock. Kebabs available too from a nearby outlet run by the same management. Mon & Tues 11am–1am, Wed–Fri 11am–3am, Sat 5pm–4am; happy hour until 8pm.

Harry's Bar 28 Boat Quay ☎ 6538 3029, ⓦ harrys.com.sg; map pp.494–495. A well-established joint popular with locals as well as foreigners, and with branches all over downtown. There's a range of light meals and snacks; happy hour is until 8pm. Daily 11.30am–1am; Fri & Sat until 2am.

The Penny Black 26 & 27 Boat Quay ☎ 6538 2300, ⓦ pennyblack.com.sg; map pp.494–495. Hardly a convincing evocation of a "Victorian London pub" but pleasant enough, with one table built around a red pillar box, Strongbow cider on draught, plenty of pub grub – cottage pie, ploughman's lunches, etc – and live UK football matches on TV. Mon–Thurs 11.30am–1am, Fri & Sat 11.30am–2am, Sun 11.30am–midnight.

Red Dot Brewhouse 33 & 34 Boat Quay ☎ 6535 4500, ⓦ reddotbrewhouse.com.sg; map pp.494–495. Many of Singapore's slicker bars are expat-run, but not the *Red Dot Brewhouse*, the brainchild of one local who got bitten by the homebrew bug many years ago. Among their range of beers and ales, the most radical is the Monster Green Lager, rich in blue-green algae regarded by some as a superfood. Mon–Thurs noon–midnight, Fri noon–2am, Sat 3pm–1am.

Screening Room 12 Ann Siang Hill ☎ 6221 1694, ⓦ screeningroom.com.sg; map pp.494–495. The unpretentious rooftop bar here (officially *La Terraza*,

though few people know it as that) is a convivial spot for an evening drink, with the bonus of views of Chinatown's shophouses and modern towers, plus plenty of snacks available from the restaurant below. Mon–Thurs 6pm–1am, Fri & Sat 6pm–3am.

TANJONG PAGAR AND THE FINANCIAL DISTRICT

★**1-Altitude** Levels 61–63, One Raffles Place ☎ 6438 0410, ⓦ 1-altitude.com; map pp.494–495. Whether or not this is "the world's highest alfresco bar" as claimed, the views of the Colonial District, Marina Bay and Chinatown from the roof of the One Raffles Place tower are simply stunning. It's best to drop by towards the end of your stay, when you can make sense of the cityscape and ponder the myriad changes that half a century of rapid development has wrought upon this island. Cover charge S$30; smart casual dress only. Daily from 6pm: Mon & Tues until 2am; Wed & Thurs until 3am, Fri & Sat until 4am, Sun until 1am.

Forest Darts Café 2 #01–05 Shenton House, 3 Shenton Way ☎ 6224 5631; map pp.494–495. Amid the banker-dominated bars of the Financial District is this more down-to-earth darts bar with electronic boards that save you doing lots of arithmetic. Mon–Fri 4pm–1am, Sat 6pm–2am, Sun 3–10pm.

THE COLONIAL DISTRICT

The Long Bar Raffles Hotel, 1 Beach Rd ☎ 6412 1816; map p.476. It's still just about mandatory to have a Singapore Sling amid the old-fashioned elegance of the bar where Ngiam Tong Boon invented it in 1915. Daily 11am–12.30am.

BRAS BASAH ROAD TO ROCHOR ROAD

★**Loof** Top of the Odeon Towers Extension, 391 North Bridge Rd #03–07 ☎ 6338 8035, ⓦ loof.com.sg; map p.483. This rooftop garden bar is an elegant place to chill out, with views into the back of the *Raffles* hotel opposite. There's a strong local flavour too, in the form of cocktails and bar snacks that use lots of Southeast Asian ingredients, plus a nostalgic recreation of an old neighbourhood shop selling knick-knacks. Happy hour weekdays until 8pm. Mon–Thurs 5pm–1am; Fri & Sat 5pm–3am.

★**Lot, Stock and Barrel** 30 Seah St; map p.483. Cheerful, unpretentious venue frequented by a post-work crowd in the early evening, with some backpackers making their presence felt later on, drawn partly by a jukebox featuring everyone from Sinatra to Beyoncé. Daily 4pm–3am; happy hour 4–8pm.

LITTLE INDIA AND ARAB ST

The Countryside Café 71 Dunlop St ☎ 6292 0071; map p.486. A delightfully low-key, convivial establishment, with something of the feel of a middle-class Singapore household of yesteryear, at least in its middle-of-the-road music – complemented by posters of Kenny Rogers and

Johnny Cash on the wall. Run by a friendly Indian woman, it offers five dozen different bottled beers at reasonable prices and the menu of bar snacks and food – partly Indian, partly Western – is nearly as impressive. Monday 6pm–2am, Tues–Sun 10am–2am, Fri & Sat until 3am.

Prince of Wales Backpackers Hostel 101 Dunlop St ⓦ pow.com.sg; map p.486. Below the hostel is a buzzing travellers' bar with live acoustic music or bands most nights, plus beer and cider at keen prices. Sun–Thurs 9am–1am, Fri & Sat until 2am.

MARINA BAY

Ku Dé Ta SkyBar North tower, Marina Bay Sands, 1 Bayfront Ave ⓣ 6688 7688, ⓦ kudeta.com.sg; map p.503. The bar at the SkyPark's fanciest venue is one of the best ways to bypass the 57th-floor admission fee and enjoy fabulous views over downtown Singapore. Stella and Hoegaarden on draught; no happy hour, though, and you'll need to dress fairly smartly in the evening. Daily noon– 1am; Fri & Sat until 2am.

Orgo Roof terrace, Esplanade – Theatres on the Bay ⓣ 6336 9366, ⓦ orgo.sg; map p.503. They make a big thing of their huge range of cocktails, which emphasize fresh fruit and herbs, but the views of the spires of the Financial District sell themselves. Happy hour until 8pm. Daily 6pm–2am.

ORCHARD ROAD AND AROUND

Quite a few of Orchard Rd's most interesting drinking venues occupy restored Peranakan shophouses at the start of Emerald Hill Rd, close to Somerset MRT.

Ice Cold Beer 9 Emerald Hill Rd ⓦ emerald-hill.com; map pp.506–507. Noisy, happening place where the beers are kept in ice tanks under the glass-topped bar. Shares a kitchen with *No. 5 Emerald Hill*. Sun–Thurs 5pm–2am, Fri & Sat 5pm–3am; happy hour daily 5–9pm.

★**No. 5 Emerald Hill** 5 Emerald Hill Rd ⓦ emerald -hill.com; map pp.506–507. Set in one of Emerald Hill Rd's restored houses, *No. 5* is not only an opulent feast for the eyes but also offers speciality cocktails plus great chicken wings and thin-crust pizzas. Tetley's on tap, some outdoor seating and a pool table upstairs. Mon–Thurs noon–2am, Fri & Sat noon–3am, Sun 5pm–3am; happy hour until 9pm.

KPO 1 Killiney Rd ⓣ 6733 3648; map pp.506–507. You'd never have guessed that *KPO*, with its big black sofas and slick roof terrace, was once part of the now much-reduced post office next door. It's convivial and relaxed in the afternoon, but can get raucously noisy after dark, with DJ sets some evenings. Happy hour until 8pm. Mon–Thurs 3pm–1am, Fri & Sat 3pm–2am.

Martini Bar Grand Hyatt Hotel, 10 Scotts Rd ⓣ 6732 1234; map pp.506–507. Choose from several dozen martini variations at this plush bar, ranging from their

trademark lychee martini to one that simply blends vodka with Southern Comfort. Several options are half-price before 9pm, when you can order one for a mere S$11 (it's at least double that later on). Daily noon–2am.

Outdoors Café & Bar Peranakan Place, corner of Orchard and Emerald Hill rds ⓣ 6738 8898; map pp.506–507. Pleasant alfresco place with a canopy for shade, a great spot to watch the passing trade on Orchard Rd. Erdinger on draught, plus other beers and a range of cocktails, and an extensive menu of Western and Asian mains and light meals. Sun–Thurs noon–2am, Fri & Sat noon–3am; happy hour till 7pm.

DEMPSEY HILL

The White Rabbit 39c Harding Rd, Tanglin Village ⓣ 9721 0536, ⓦ thewhiterabbit.com.sg; map p.474. This restaurant housed in a restored church has a marvellous open-air bar specializing in wine and gin – the range is staggering. A great spot for a drink away from the bustle of downtown. Sun–Thurs 6pm–midnight, Fri & Sat until 1.30am.

CLUBS

Avalon South Crystal Pavilion, Marina Bay Sands ⓣ 6597 8333, ⓦ avalon.sg; map p.503. An outpost of the Hollywood original, *Avalon* is entombed within a squat glass islet, reached by a walkway out over the water. The music extends from trance through house to general electronica, and the see-through architecture ensures all-round views of the Financial District and Singapore Flyer. Cover charges S$25–35. Wed & Fri–Sun 10pm–late.

Kyo #B1–02 Keck Seng Tower, 133 Cecil St ⓣ 8299 8735, ⓦ clubkyo.com; map pp.494–495. Groovy basement venue with progressive dance sounds by local and international guest DJs. Cover charge S$20–25. Wed & Thurs 9pm–4am, Fri 9pm–4.30am, Sat 11pm–6am.

Tanjong Beach Club Tanjong Beach, Sentosa ⓣ 9750 5323, ⓦ tanjongbeachclub.com; map pp.494–495. If you needed a reason to trek to Tanjong Beach, this would be it. Styled like a luxury beach bungalow, it boasts an incongruous infinity pool, a pricey restaurant and a bar, hosting weekly beach parties (usually Sun from 3pm) featuring guest DJs. Tues–Fri 11am–11pm, Sat & Sun 10am–midnight.

Zouk/Phuture/Velvet Underground 17 Jiak Kim St ⓣ 6738 2988, ⓦ zoukclub.com; map p.474. Launched in the 1990s, *Zouk* is one of Singapore's most successful clubs and still the best for many, though for others it's getting a little mainstream. House remains the mainstay, with guest sets from world-renowned DJs from time to time. *Zouk* also houses two smaller clubs, *Phuture*, specializing in hip-hop and R&B, and *Velvet Underground*, which has areas dedicated to lounge and dance. The cover charge depends on the night, but typically starts at S$25. Bus #16 from Somerset/Orchard MRT; ask to be let off close to the *Grand Copthorne Waterfront*

9

hotel, next door. Zouk Wed, Fri & Sat 11pm till late; Phuture Wed 10pm till late, Fri & Sat 9pm till late; Velvet Underground Wed, Fri & Sat 10pm till late.

GAY VENUES

Singapore's gay scene, though modest, is among the best in Southeast Asia, and in recent years the country has seen the annual Pink Dot rally (a gay pride event, although this being Singapore it's all tame and family-friendly; June; ⊛pinkdot.sg) grow into one of the most well-attended mass meetings on the island. That said, attitudes toward homosexuality remain contradictory. Colonial-era legislation banning sex between men, though no longer enforced, remains on the statute book despite attempts to repeal it. Despite the generally tolerant atmosphere, gay venues keep a low profile, functioning largely unhindered but scarcely using the word "gay" in advertising.

The scene centres on Chinatown and Tanjong Pagar, where there are some half a dozen bars and clubs; note that they only really get busy at weekends, and only after 10pm. Two sources of information are the Pelangi Pride Centre (a small gay library

project near Commonwealth MRT; ⊛pelangipridecentre.org) and, for lesbian events, ⊛twoqueens.me.

Backstage Bar 13a Trengganu St ☎6227 1712; map pp.494–495. Entered through a side door in Temple St (look for the discreetly placed rainbow flag), this tiny bar offers a view over the souvenir stalls of Trengganu St. Daily 6pm till late.

DYMK 41 Neil Rd ☎6224 3965, ⊛dymk.sg; map pp.494–495. Probably the friendliest gay bar in town. They tend to keep the music a tad quieter than elsewhere, making it a good place for a relaxed chat. Most of the crowd are 20- and 30-somethings. Sun–Thurs 8pm–midnight, Fri 7pm–1am, Sat 8pm–2am.

Taboo 65/67 Neil Rd ☎6225 6256, ⊛taboo.sg; map pp.494–495. Small club spinning the usual mix of house, trance and other pulsating sounds. Wed–Sat 10pm till late.

Tantric 78 Neil Rd ☎6423 9232; map pp.494–495. Pleasant enough shophouse bar with a clientele slightly more reflective of Singapore's multiethnic make-up than the largely Chinese crowd elsewhere. Daily 8pm till late.

ENTERTAINMENT

Even on a brief visit, it's hard not to notice how much state money has been poured into the **arts** community and infrastructure: prime property has been turned over to cultural organizations in areas like the Waterloo St "arts belt", and prestige venues such as Theatres on the Bay host world-class performers. Cynics might say this cultural push is mainly about keeping Singapore attractive to skilled expats, while others raise the important issue of whether world-class art can bloom where **censorship** is very much alive. Nonetheless, it would be a shame not to catch a performance of some kind if you are visiting for a few days, whether one drawing on Asian traditions or a gig by a big-name Western band.

Tickets You can buy tickets directly from venues or through agencies such as SISTIC (the largest, with outlets in downtown malls; ☎6348 5555, ⊛sistic.com.sg) and Gatecrash (☎6100 2005, ⊛gatecrash.com.sg).

Festivals Major cultural festivals include the Singapore International Festival of the Arts (calendar online; ⊛sifa .sg), running the gamut from concerts to theatre through dance and film; and the Singapore Fringe Festival (Jan or Feb; ⊛singaporefringe.com), which concentrates on theatre and the visual arts. There's also the annual Singapore Writers' Festival (⊛singaporewritersfestival .com), featuring international as well as local writers working in all four of the country's official languages.

FILM

As well as the latest Hollywood blockbusters, Singapore's cinemas show a wide range of Chinese, Malay and Indian movies, all with English subtitles. Western movies in languages other than English also pop up occasionally, as do features by a small but competent group of local directors, best appreciated at the Singapore International Film Festival (⊛sgiff.com). Cinema-going is popular here, so it's worth turning up early or booking in advance if the film is a hot new release. Tickets start at S\$10, but can cost

two or three times that for blockbuster films or screenings at the fanciest multiplexes. Be prepared for noise during shows: Singaporeans are great ones for chattering through the movie. If you intend to be in Singapore for a while, you might want to sign up to the Singapore Film Society (⊛sfs.org.sg), which puts on monthly members-only screenings and occasional mini-festivals.

MULTIPLEX CHAINS

Cathay Cinemas include: Cineleisure Orchard, 8 Grange Rd (near Somerset MRT); Cathay Cineplex, 2 Handy Rd (near Dhoby Ghaut MRT); ⊛cathaycineplexes.com.sg.

Golden Village Cinemas include: Level 7, Plaza Singapura, 68 Orchard Rd; Levels 2 & 3, VivoCity, Harbourfront; ⊛gv.com.sg.

Shaw Cinemas include: Lido 8 Cineplex, Shaw House, 350 Orchard Rd (IMAX-equipped); Bugis Cineplex, Bugis Junction, 200 Victoria St; ⊛shaw.sg.

INDEPENDENT VENUES

Alliance Française 1 Sarkies Rd ⊛alliancefrancaise .org.sg. Weekly French-language films with English subtitles. A 10min walk from Newton MRT.

National Museum Cinematheque National Museum,

93 Stamford Rd ⓦnationalmuseum.sg. The museum mounts its own laudable programme of films from around the world, including some vintage classics and free screenings.

Omni-Theatre See p.518. One of Singapore's two IMAX cinemas.

The Picturehouse Cathay Building, 2 Handy Rd ⓦthepicturehouse.com.sg. Not strictly an indie but, unlike Cathay's multiplexes, devoted to art-house films from Asia and the rest of the world.

Rex 2 Mackenzie Rd ☎6337 2845, ⓦrexcinema.com .sg. On the edge of Little India, this is one of the oldest cinemas in town, now specializing in the Tamil and Bollywood movies plus the occasional Malay flick.

The Screening Room 12 Ann Siang Hill ☎6221 1694, ⓦscreeningroom.com.sg; map pp.494–495. "Where art meets film" is the motto of this posh restaurant/bar complex, incorporating a cinema screening the relatively intellectual end of Hollywood's output, plus the odd Asian film.

THEATRE

Drama is the arts scene's strongest suit: a surprising number of small theatre companies have sprung up over the years, performing works by local playwrights that dare to include a certain amount of social commentary. Foreign theatre companies tour regularly too, and lavish Western musicals are staged from time to time.

COMPANIES

Action Theatre 42 Waterloo St ☎6837 0842, ⓦaction .org.sg. Stages work by Singaporean playwrights as well as the standard repertoire, with its own hundred-seater venue on site.

The Necessary Stage Marine Parade Community Building, 278 Marine Parade Rd ☎6440 8115, ⓦnecessary.org. Pioneering socially conscious theatre group. Their premises are out near Katong though some productions are staged downtown.

Singapore Repertory Theatre DBS Arts Centre, 20 Merbau Rd, Robertson Quay ☎6733 8166, ⓦsrt.com

.sg. English-language theatre, performing more than just the most obvious British and American plays.

Theatreworks #72–13 Mohamed Sultan Rd ☎6737 7213, ⓦtheatreworks.org.sg. Another of the pioneers of the new Singapore stage, Theatreworks were formed in 1985.

CLASSICAL AND TRADITIONAL MUSIC AND DANCE

At the heart of Singapore's healthy Western classical music scene is the Singapore Symphony Orchestra, whose concerts often feature stellar guest soloists, conductors and choirs from around the world. Dance is an another thriving art form, with several active local troupes and regular visits by international companies.

COMPANIES AND ORCHESTRAS

Chinese Opera Teahouse 5 Smith St ☎6323 4862, ⓦctcopera.com.sg; map pp.494–495. For an interesting culinary and musical experience, come here for the Sights and Sounds of Chinese Opera (Fri & Sat 7pm), a set meal followed by performances of excerpts from Chinese operas. The package costs S$40, though you can watch the opera selections alone for S$25 (includes tea and snacks; admission at 7.50pm).

City Chinese Orchestra ⓦcityco.com.sg. Chinese classical and folk music recitals, at various venues.

Singapore Chinese Orchestra Singapore Conference Hall, 7 Shenton Way, Financial District ☎6440 3839, ⓦsco.com.sg. Performances of traditional Chinese music through the year, with occasional free concerts.

Singapore Dance Theatre ☎6338 0611, ⓦsingaporedancetheatre.com. Contemporary and classical works at various venues, sometimes by moonlight at Fort Canning Park.

Singapore Lyric Opera ⓦsingaporeopera.com.sg. Western opera and operetta, at various venues.

Singapore Symphony Orchestra ⓦsso.org.sg. Performances throughout the year at Esplanade – Theatres on the Bay and other venues. Occasional free concerts at the Botanic Gardens and hour-long daytime shows for children.

STREET THEATRE

Walk around Singapore long enough and you're likely to stumble upon some sort of streetside cultural event, most usually a **wayang** – a Malay word used in Singapore to denote **Chinese opera**. Played out on outdoor stages next to temples and markets, or in open spaces in the new towns, wayangs are highly dramatic and stylized affairs, in which garishly made-up characters enact popular Chinese legends to the accompaniment of the crashes of cymbals and gongs. They're staged throughout the year, but the best time to catch one is during the Festival of the Hungry Ghosts, when they are performed to entertain passing spooks. Another fascinating traditional performance – lion-dancing – takes to the streets during Chinese New Year, and puppet theatres may appear around then, too. Chinatown and the Bugis/Waterloo Street area are places where you're most likely to stumble upon performances.

9

Siong Leng Musical Association 4B Bukit Pasoh Rd ☎6222 4221, ⓦsiongleng.com. A body dedicated to preserving *nanyin* (literally "southern sound") – the distinctive music and opera of southeast China, sung in dialect. Regular performances at various locations, with occasional shows in the exceptional temple surroundings of Thian Hock Keng.

Temple of Fine Arts ☎6535 0509, ⓦtempleoffine arts.org. This Indian cultural organization is dedicated to perpetuating traditional music and dance, and puts on occasional concerts and exhibitions.

POP, ROCK, BLUES AND JAZZ

Singapore is firmly on the East Asian gig circuit for Western stadium-rock outfits as well as indie bands, though some gigs can be marred by a rather staid atmosphere as locals can be uncomfortable about letting their hair down. Local bands do exist and some aren't at all bad, but these are more likely to perform in community centres rather than decent venues. Rivalling Western music in terms of popularity are Canto- and Mando-pop, bland hybrids of Chinese lyrics and Western pop; superstars of both genres visit periodically, to rapturous welcomes. The best music festival is Mosaic (March; ⓦmosaicmusicfestival.com), showcasing an excellent range of jazz and rock acts at Theatres on the Bay.

INDEPENDENT VENUES

Blu Jaz Café 11 Bali Lane ☎6292 3800, ⓦblujazcafe .net; map p.486. Live jazz Wed, Fri & Sat eves. Mon & Fri noon–1.30am, Tues–Thurs noon–12.30am, Sat 4pm–1.30am.

Crazy Elephant #01–03 Block E, Clarke Quay ☎6337 7859, ⓦcrazyelephant.com; map pp.494–495. Of the hotchpotch of brash venues along Clarke Quay, this bar has a tad more street cred, with live music – blues and rock – practically every night and an open-mike jam session on Sun. Some tables are by the water's edge. Mon–Sun 5pm–2am, Fri & Sat until 3am; happy hour until 9pm.

TAB #02–29 Orchard Hotel, 442 Orchard Rd ☎6493 6952, ⓦtab.com.sg; map pp.506–507. This compact venue features a nightly DJ sets plus rather poppy shows by local and East Asian acts, though a few up-and-coming Western bands stop by as well. Daily 9.30pm–4.30am (different hours on gig nights).

Timbre The Substation, 45 Armenian St ☎6338 8030, ⓦtimbre.com.sg; map p.476. Open-air bar-restaurant at the back of Singapore's oldest independent arts venue, with local bands and singer-songwriters performing original material, though it can be a little derivative. Daily from 6pm.

Timbre The Arts House, 1 Old Parliament Lane ☎6336 3886, ⓦtimbre.com.sg; map p.476. More sets by local musicians in a high-visibility riverside location. Mon–Sat from 6pm.

SHOPPING

Choice and convenience make the Singapore shopping experience a rewarding one, but the island's affluence and strong currency mean most things are priced at Western levels; Kuala Lumpur can be a better hunting ground for bargains. If you're around during the **Great Singapore Sale** (late May to late July; ⓦgreatsingaporesale.com.sg), you can find prices seriously marked down in many stores. Malls elsewhere tend to be smaller and slightly more informal; the most interesting in **Chinatown** are like multistorey markets, home to a few more traditional outlets stocking Chinese foodstuffs, medicines, instruments and porcelain. Chinatown also has a few antique and curio shops along South Bridge Rd, and more knick-knacks are on sale around **Arab St**, where you'll also find textiles and batiks, robust basketware and some good deals on jewellery. **Little India** has silk stores and goldsmiths as well as **Mustafa**, a department store that's known all over the island for being open 24/7. South of Little India, the grid of streets between **Rochor Rd** and the Singapore River is home to a few malls specializing in electrical and computer products. Elsewhere downtown, there are more malls at **Marina Centre** and **HarbourFront**, and **Marina Bay Sands** has its own mall. Shopping complexes, malls and department stores are almost all open daily from 10am–9pm, some until 10pm.

Complaints In the unlikely event that you encounter a problem with a retailer that you cannot resolve mutually, you may be able to recover your money by initiating proceedings at Singapore's Small Claims Tribunal. It only costs S$10 to have your case heard, though you will need to attend in person; see ⓦsmallclaims.gov.sg for more information.

Tax refunds On leaving the country by air or sea, tourists can claim a refund of Singapore's goods and services tax (**GST**; 7.7 percent at the time of writing) on purchases over S$100, provided the shop in question is a member of one of three tax refund schemes. You will either have to complete a form which must be signed by the retailer, and then present the goods, forms and receipts to the customs authorities when you leave, or else ask the shop to link your purchases to one of your debit or credit cards, in which case you claim the tax back by, for example, scanning a barcode at a booth at the airport. It's a bureaucratic headache; for detailed guidance, have a look at the "GST: For consumers" section of ⓦiras.gov.sg, or pick up the appropriate leaflet from a tourist office.

SHOPPING COMPLEXES AND DEPARTMENT STORES

ORCHARD ROAD AND AROUND

313@Somerset 313 Orchard Rd (above Somerset MRT) ⓦ 313somerset.com.sg; map pp.506–507. Uniqlo and Zara are the star names at this newish mall.

Forum the Shopping Mall 583 Orchard Rd ⓦ forumtheshoppingmall.com; map pp.506–507. Plenty of items to please the most pampered of spoiled children– upmarket kids' clothes, toys and so forth.

The Heeren 260 Orchard Rd; map pp.506–507. There's really only one reason to come here – it's home to the flagship outlet of Robinsons, one of Singapore's oldest department stores.

ION Orchard 2 Orchard Turn (above Orchard MRT) ⓦ ionorchard.com; map pp.506–507. Despite the impressive hyper-modern facade and a sprinkling of designer names, Armani included, by far the most popular section of this cavernous mall is *Food Opera*, its excellent food court on basement 4.

Ngee Ann City 391a Orchard Rd ⓦ ngeeanncity.com .sg; map pp.506–507. A brooding twin-towered complex, home to the Japanese Takashimaya department store and the excellent Kinokuniya bookstore, plus several jewellers.

Paragon Opposite Ngee Ann City ⓦ paragon.sg; map pp.506–507. Calvin Klein, Prada, Versace and many more at this swanky mall.

Plaza Singapura 68 Orchard Rd ⓦ plazasingapura .com.sg; map pp.506–507. Veteran mall with a bit of everything: Marks & Spencer, the Singapore department store chain John Little, sportswear and sports equipment, musical instruments, audio, video and general electrical equipment.

Tanglin Shopping Centre 19 Tanglin Rd (next to Orchard Parade hotel) ⓦ tanglinsc.com; map pp.506–507. Good for art, antiques and curios.

Tangs Corner of Orchard and Scotts rds ⓦ tangs.com; map pp.506–507. Tangs is a department store dating back to the 1950s, and the only one to have its own building on Orchard Rd, topped by a pagoda-style construction occupied by the *Marriott* hotel. The store itself sells a wide range of reasonably priced clothes and accessories.

Wisma Atria 435 Orchard Rd, opposite Tangs ⓦ wismaonline.com; map pp.506–507. A good range of middle-market local and international fashion shops, plus the Japanese department store Isetan.

CHINATOWN

Hong Lim Complex 531–531a Upper Cross St; map pp.494–495. One of several Chinatown shopping centres where ordinary people buy ordinary things – dried mushrooms, cuttlefish and crackers from provisions shops, for example.

Pearl's Centre 100 Eu Tong Sen St; map pp.494–495.

Home to some Chinese medicine clinics and a few shops selling Buddhist paraphernalia.

People's Park Centre 101 Upper Cross St; map pp.494–495. Stall-like shop units selling Chinese handicrafts, electronics, silk, jade and gold.

People's Park Complex 1 Park Rd; map pp.494–495. A venerable shopping centre that, like the Hong Lim Complex and adjacent People's Park Centre, is among the most entertaining places to browse in Chinatown because it's so workaday. Also here is the Overseas Emporium on level 4, selling Chinese musical instruments, calligraphy pens, lacquerwork and jade.

THE COLONIAL DISTRICT

Funan DigitaLife Mall 109 North Bridge Rd ⓦ funan .com.sg; map p.476. A variety of stores here sell computer and electronics equipment.

Raffles City 252 North Bridge Rd (above City Hall MRT) ⓦ rafflescity.com; map p.476. Home to a branch of Robinsons department store with a Marks & Spencer within it, plus numerous fashion chains.

BRAS BASAH ROAD TO ROCHOR ROAD

Bugis Junction Victoria St, above Bugis MRT ⓦ bugisjunction-mall.com.sg; map p.483. Mall encasing several streets of restored shophouses, and featuring the Japanese/Chinese department store BHG and a number of fashion outlets.

Sim Lim Square 1 Rochor Canal Rd ⓦ simlimsquare .com.sg; map p.483. Cameras and electronic goods – with some haggling, it can be cheaper than Funan DigitaLife Mall.

LITTLE INDIA

Mustafa Syed Alwi Rd ⓦ mustafa.com.sg; map p.486. Totally different in feel to the malls of Orchard Rd, Mustafa is a phenomenon, selling electronics, fresh food, luggage, you name it – and it never closes. Daily 24hr.

MARINA BAY

Marina Square 6 Raffles Blvd ⓦ marinasquare.com .sg; map p.503. Nowhere near as large as its sprawling neighbour, Suntec City, but better laid out and with a very diverse range of outlets.

The Shoppes at Marina Bay Sands 10 Bayfront Ave; map p.503. Beneath the iconic hotel is a hotchpotch of swish designer outlets and some quite humdrum stores.

ELSEWHERE IN SINGAPORE

VivoCity Next to HarbourFront Centre and above HarbourFront MRT ⓦ vivocity.com.sg; map p.474. A humdinger of a mall, containing a branch of Tangs department store, a cinema, a *National Geographic* outlet, three food courts (*Food Republic* is exceptional; see p.542) and many restaurants.

9

ART, ANTIQUES, CURIOS AND SOUVENIRS

Antiques of the Orient #02–40 Tanglin Shopping Centre ☎6734 9351; map pp.506–507. Antiquarian books and maps, engravings and old photos. Mon–Sat 10am–6pm, Sun 11am–4pm.

Dulu-Dulu 723 North Bridge Rd, opposite Sultan Mosque ☎6341 7743; map p.486. Ancient typewriters, brass spittoons and beaded necklaces are among the items jostling for space at this friendly Indian Muslim-run junk shop. Daily 10am–6pm.

Elliott's Antiques #02–13 Raffles Hotel Arcade ☎6337 1008; map p.476. Chinese antique furniture and art. Daily 11am–7pm.

Eng Tiang Huat 10 Lorong 24a Geylang ☎6734 3738. Oriental musical instruments plus *wayang* costumes and props. Mon–Sat 11am–6pm.

Far East Inspirations 33 Pagoda St ☎6224 2993; map pp.506–507. The classiest of several antique shops here, offering Asian furniture, porcelain lamps and vases. Daily 10.30am–6.30pm.

The Heritage Shop 93 Jalan Sultan ☎6223 7982; map p.486. An incredible range of bric-a-brac, from antique radios to beautiful enamelware tiffin carriers – little pots for cooked food, stacked and held together within a metal frame for easy carrying. Daily 1.30–8pm.

Katong Antiques House 208 East Coast Rd, Katong ☎6345 8544; map p.513. Peranakan artefacts and Chinese porcelain (see p.514). Tues–Sun 11am–5pm.

Kwok Gallery #03–01 Far East Shopping Centre, 545 Orchard Rd ☎6235 2516; map pp.506–507. An impressive inventory of traditional Chinese pottery, jade and sculpture. Mon–Sat 11am–6pm.

Little Shophouse 43 Bussorah St, near Sultan Mosque ☎6295 2328; map p.486. Well named, this small outlet boasts some fine but pricey examples of Peranakan beaded slippers (from S$300), plus replica Peranakan crockery. Daily 10am–6pm.

Malay Art Gallery 31 Bussorah St ☎6294 8051. Stocks *songket* and *kerises* from Malaysia and Indonesia. Mon–Sat 8.30am–5.30pm, some Sun 9am–4.30pm.

Rishi Handicrafts 5 Baghdad St, Kampong Glam ☎6298 2408; map p.486. Specializes in a range of baskets made from rattan, bamboo and other materials, plus some knick-knacks, too. Daily 10am–5.30pm (Sun from 11am).

Rumah Bebe 113 East Coast Rd, Katong ☎6247 8781; ⊛rumahbebe.com; map p.513. Peranakan products, including beaded shoes and handbags, costume jewellery and the traditional *kebaya* garb of Nyonyas. They also offer courses in beading and Nyonya cookery. Tues–Sun 9.30am–6.30pm.

Teajoy #01–05 North Bridge Centre, 420 North Bridge Rd ☎6339 3739; map p.483. Close to the National Library, this sells Chinese tea sets with special attention paid to oolong accoutrements. Daily noon–8pm.

Tong Mern Sern 51 Craig Rd, Tanjong Pagar ☎6223 1037, ⊛tmsantiques.com; map pp.494–495. "We buy junk and sell antiques", proclaims the banner outside this great little establishment. The owner is quite a character and can tell you all about the collection of crockery, old furniture and other bric-a-brac he has amassed. Mon–Sat 9am–6pm, Sun 1–6pm.

Worldover #01–49 Tanglin Shopping Centre ☎6836 0187, ⊛world-over.com; map pp.506–507. No need to schlep to Istanbul or Marrakesh for those *Arabian Nights* lamps you always wanted to festoon your lounge with – get them at this friendly little shop instead. Daily 10.30am–8.30pm.

Zhen Lacquer Gallery 1 Trengganu St, Chinatown ☎6222 2718; map pp.494–495. Specializes in lacquerware boxes and bowls. Daily 10.30am–9pm.

JEWELLERY

C.T. Hoo #01–22 Tanglin Shopping Centre ☎6737 5447; map pp.506–507. Specializes in pearls. Mon–Sat 9.30am–6.30pm.

Flower Diamond #03–02 Ngee Ann City ☎6734 1221; map pp.506–507. Contemporary designs as well as more traditionally styled bling, at sensible prices. Daily 10am–9pm.

Risis National Orchid Garden, Singapore Botanic Gardens ☎6475 5104, ⊛risis.com; map p.474. Singaporeans tend to view gold-plated orchids – available as brooches, pendants, earrings, even on tie clips – as clichéd, but tourists snap them up here as well as at Changi Airport. Daily 8.45am–6.30pm.

Wong's Jewellery 62 Temple St, Chinatown ☎6323 0236; map pp.494–495. Chinese-style outlet, good for jade, gold and pearls. Daily 10am–7.30pm.

FABRICS AND FASHION

Charles & Keith Several outlets, including #B3–58 ION Orchard ☎6238 1840; map pp.506–507. Singapore's answer to Malaysia's Jimmy Choo, the brothers Charles and Keith Wong design stylish, affordable women's shoes and handbags too. Daily 10.30am–10pm.

Dakshaini Silks 65 Serangoon Rd, Little India ☎6291 9969; map p.486. Premier Indian embroidered silks. Mon–Sat 10am–9pm, Sun 10am–8pm.

Rose Citron 23 Keong Saik Rd, Chinatown ☎6323 1368; map pp.494–495. Delightful French-designed bags, scarves and cushion covers in bright floral and abstract designs – and not super-pricey either. Mon–Sat 10.30am–6.30pm.

Rumah Bebe 113 East Coast Rd, Katong ☎6247 8781; ⊛rumahbebe.com; map p.513. This delightful place sells beaded shoes and handbags, costume jewellery and the traditional garb – *kebaya* and sarong – of Nyonya women. They also offer courses in beading and Nyonya cookery. Tues–Sun 9.30am–6.30pm.

Toko Aljunied 91 Arab St ☎6294 6897; map p.486. Batik cloth and *kebaya* – the blouse/sarong combinations traditionally worn by Nyonyas. Mon–Sat 10.30am–7pm, Sun 11am–5pm.

BOOKS

Singapore bookshops are reasonably stocked; all the larger ones carry a good selection of Western and local fiction and nonfiction titles, plus a range of magazines. Besides the stores listed here, there's also Select Books – mail-order-only at the time of writing – with the best selection of speciaist books on Singapore, Malaysia and the rest of East Asia (ⓦselectbooks.com.sg).

Kinokuniya Level 3, Ngee Ann City ☎6339 1790, ⓦkinokuniya.com.sg; map pp.506–507. One of Singapore's best bookshops, with titles on every conceivable subject and some foreign-language literature too, plus loads of magazines. Daily 10am–9.30pm.

Littered With Books 20 Duxton Rd ☎6220 6824; map pp.494–495. Despite its name, this indie outlet has a neatly laid out, though somewhat random, selection of literary fiction, thrillers and travel writing. Daily at least noon–8pm, slightly longer hours Fri–Sun.

MPH #B1–24, Raffles City ⓦmph.com.sg; map p.476. Veteran of the local book trade, though not as comprehensive as it once was. Daily 10am–10pm.

Times Bookstore #04–18 Plaza Singapura; ⓦtimesbookstores.com.sg; map pp.506–507. A well-stocked local chain. Daily 10.30am–9.30pm.

CDS AND DVDS

Western and Asian CDs and DVDs are widely available in Singapore, although here as elsewhere the physical trade is fast being overtopped by the download tide. For Indian releases specifically, there are a few outlets in Little India; and for Malay music, head to the Joo Chiat Complex, Geylang (see p.513).

Earshot Café Arts House, 1 Old Parliament Lane ☎6334 0130; map p.476. It is indeed a café, but happens to stock CDs, DVDs and books by Singaporean creatives. Mon–Fri 11am–8pm, Sat 11am–5pm.

HMV #02–320 Marina Square, 6 Raffles Blvd, Marina Centre ☎6733 1822, ⓦhmv.com.sg; map p.503. Your best bet for mainstream releases and with dedicated jazz and classical music sections. Daily 11am–9pm.

Roxy Records #02–15 Excelsior Shopping Centre ☎6337 7783; map p.476. A range of imported indie and other hard-to-find releases, plus some secondhand vinyl – even records of Chinese opera. Mon–Sat noon–9.30pm.

Straits Records 24a Bali Lane ☎9681 6341; map p.486. Stocking CDs by local bands, including some Malay music, plus releases by obscure US metal/thrash acts and better-known 1970s punk and reggae, some on vinyl, this minuscule upstairs shop epitomizes the mix of sensibilities at play around Arab St. Daily 3–10pm.

DIRECTORY

Banks and exchange There's no shortage of ATMs – practically every MRT station has one, as do all malls. Licensed moneychangers, offering slightly more favourable exchange rates than the banks, aren't hard to find, particularly in Little India (eg at Mustafa, see p.486) and on Orchard Rd.

Embassies and consulates The "missions" section of the Singapore Ministry of Foreign Affairs website ⓦmfa.gov .sg carries a full list.

Emergencies See p.52.

Gyms California Fitness (ⓦcaliforniafitness.com), True Fitness (ⓦtruefitness.com.sg) and Fitness First (ⓦfitnessfirst.com.sg) all operate downtown gyms, though you will need to take out membership to use them.

Hospitals The state-run Singapore General Hospital, Outram Rd (SGH; ☎6222 3322, ⓦsgh.com.sg; Outram Park MRT), has a 24hr casualty/emergency department, as do the privately run Raffles Hospital, 585 North Bridge Rd (☎6311 1111, ⓦrafflesmedicalgroup.com); and Mount Elizabeth Hospital off Orchard Rd (☎6737 2666, ⓦparkwayhealth.com).

Pharmacies Both Guardian and Watsons are ubiquitous downtown, with branches in shopping malls and even in a few MRT stations, though only the largest outlets handle prescriptions.

Phones For details of mobile phone providers, see p.58.

Police In an emergency, dial ☎999; otherwise call the police hotline ☎1800 225 0000.

Post offices The island has dozens of post offices (typically Mon–Fri 8.30am–5pm & Sat 8.30am–1pm), with the one at 1 Killiney Rd (near Somerset MRT) keeping extended hours (Mon–Fri 9.30am–9pm, Sat 9.30am–4pm, Sun 10.30am–4pm). For more on the mail system, contact SingPost (☎1605, ⓦsingpost.com).

Swimming Singapore has some of the world's best state-run swimming facilities; just about every new town has a well-maintained 50m open-air pool, open from early morning until well into the evening. The best-located downtown pool is the Jalan Besar Swimming Complex on Tyrwhitt Rd, near Lavender and Farrer Park MRT station. Charges are a mere S$1–1.50; have coins available for the ticket gates and lockers.

Travel agents The following are good for discounted airfares and packages: STA Travel ☎6737 7188, ⓦstatravel .com.sg; Sunny Holidays ☎6767 6868, ⓦsunnyholidays .com.sg; and Zuji ⓦzuji.com.sg.

Vaccinations Tan Tock Seng Hospital, across the road from Novena MRT, has a Travellers' Health & Vaccination Centre (☎6357 2222, ⓦttsh.com.sg).

Women's helpline AWARE ☎1-800/774 5935, ⓦaware .org.sg.

ORANG-UTAN

Contexts

553 History

570 Religion

574 Peoples

579 Development and the environment

583 Wildlife

587 Books

591 Language

601 Glossary

History

The modern-day nations of Malaysia, Singapore and Brunei only became independent in 1963, 1965 and 1984 respectively. Before that, their history was inextricably linked with events in the larger Malay archipelago, from Sumatra across Borneo to the Philippines.

Unfortunately, little hard archeological evidence in the region pertains to the prehistoric period, while events prior to the foundation of Melaka are known only from unreliable accounts written by Chinese and Arab traders. For an understanding of the formative fourteenth and fifteenth centuries, there are two vital sources: the **Suma Oriental** (Treatise of the Orient), by Tomé Pires, a Portuguese emissary who came to Melaka in 1512 and used his observations to write a history of the region, and the seventeenth-century **Sejarah Melayu**, the "Malay Annals", which recount oral historical tales in a poetic style. Portuguese and Dutch **colonists** who arrived in the sixteenth and seventeenth centuries supplied written records, though these tended to concern commercial rather than political or social matters. At least there's a wealth of information from **British colonial** times that, despite an imperialistic bias, gives detailed insights into Malay affairs.

Beginnings

The oldest remains of *Homo sapiens* in the region, discovered in the Niah Caves in Sarawak, are thought to be those of hunter-gatherers, dating back some 40,000 years; other finds in the Peninsular state of Kedah are only 10,000 years old. The variety of **ethnic groups** now found in both east and west Malaysia – from small, dark-skinned Negritos through to paler Austronesian Malays – has led to the theory of a slow filtration of peoples through the Malay archipelago from southern Indochina. That theory is backed by an almost universal belief in animism, celebration of fertility and ancestor worship among the various peoples.

The Malay archipelago acquired a strategic significance thanks largely to the **shipping trade**, which flourished as early as the first century AD. This was engendered by the two major markets of the early world – India and China – and by the richness of its own resources. From the dense jungle of the Peninsula and northern Borneo came aromatic woods, timber and nipah palm thatch, traded by the forest-dwelling Orang Asli with the coastal Malays, who then bartered or sold it on to Arab and Chinese merchants. The region was also rumoured to be rich in **gold**, leading to its being described by contemporary Greek writers as "The Golden Chersonese" (*chersonese* meaning "peninsula"). Although gold was never found in the supposed quantities, ornaments made of the metal helped to develop decorative traditions among craftsmen, and survive today. More significant, however, were the **tin fields** of the Malay Peninsula, mined in early times to provide an alloy used for temple sculptures. Chinese traders were also attracted by the medicinal properties of various sea products, such as sea slugs, collected by the Orang Laut (sea people), as well as by pearls and tortoise shells.

c.35,000 BC	200 AD	7th c.	c.14th c.
Human settlement at Niah in what is now northern Sarawak	Malay Peninsula comes under Indian cultural and religious influence	The Sumatran Srivijayan empire, encompassing the Malay Peninsula, rises to prominence	Srivijaya is challenged by the Majapahit empire of Java and declines

For their part, the indigenous peoples acquired cloth, pottery, glass and absorbed the beliefs of those with whom they traded. From as early as 200 AD, **Indian traders** brought their Hindu and Buddhist practices, and archeological evidence from later periods, such as the tenth-century temples at Lembah Bujang (see p.159), suggests that the local population not only tolerated these new belief systems, but adapted them to suit their own experiences. Perhaps the most striking contemporary example of such cultural interchange is the traditional entertainment of *wayang kulit* (shadow plays), whose plots are drawn from the Hindu *Ramayana*.

While trade with India developed very early, contact with **China** was initially less pronounced due to the pre-eminence of the Silk Road, further north. Only in the eighth and ninth centuries did Chinese ships first venture into the archipelago. By the time Srivijaya appeared on the scene, a number of states – particularly in the Kelantan and Terengganu areas of the Peninsula – were sending envoys to China.

Srivijaya

The inhabitants of the western Peninsula and eastern Sumatra were quick to realize the geographical advantage afforded by the Melaka Straits, which provided a refuge where ships could wait for several months for a change in the monsoon winds. From the fifth century onwards, a succession of **entrepôts** (storage ports) were created to cater for the needs of passing vessels. One such entrepôt eventually became the mighty empire of **Srivijaya**, eminent from the start of the seventh century until the end of the thirteenth, and encompassing all the shores and islands surrounding the Straits of Melaka. Its exact location is still a matter for debate, although most sources point to **Palembang** in southern Sumatra. Srivijaya's stable administration attracted commerce when insurrection elsewhere frightened traders away, while its wealth was boosted by extracting tolls and taxes from passing ships. Srivijaya also became an important centre for **Mahayana Buddhism** and learning. When the respected Chinese monk I Ching arrived in 671 AD, he found more than a thousand monks studying the Buddhist scriptures.

Political concepts developed during Srivijayan rule were to form the basis of Malay government in future centuries. Unquestioning **loyalty** among subjects was underpinned by the notion of *daulat*, the divine force of the ruler (called the Maharajah), which would strike down anyone guilty of *derhaka* (treason) – a powerful means of control over a deeply superstitious people.

The decision made around 1080 to shift the capital, for reasons unknown, north from Palembang to a place called **Melayu** seems to have marked the start of Srivijaya's decline. Piracy became almost uncontrollable, and even the Orang Laut, who had previously helped keep it in check, turned against the Srivijayan rulers. Soon both local and foreign traders began to seek safer ports, and the area that's now Kedah was a principal beneficiary. Other regions were soon able to compete by replicating the peaceable conditions and efficient administration that had allowed Srivijaya to thrive.

Srivijaya's fate was sealed when it attracted the eye of foreign rivals. In 1275, the Majapahit empire of Java invaded Melayu and made inroads into many of Srivijaya's peninsular territories. Sumatra and Kedah were raided by the Cholas of India, while the Thai kingdom of Ligor was able to extract **tributes** of gold from Malay vassals, a practice

Early 15th c.	15th c.	1511
Paramesevara, a Srivijayan prince, establishes a kingdom at Melaka, which soon flourishes as a Muslim sultanate	The Brunei Sultanate rises to prominence, exercising power over most of northern Borneo	The Portuguese capture Melaka

that continued until the nineteenth century. Moreover, trading restrictions in China were relaxed from the late twelfth century onwards, making it more lucrative for traders to bypass the once mighty entrepôt and go directly to the source of their desired products. Around the early fourteenth century Srivijaya's name disappears from the records.

The Melaka Sultanate

With the collapse of Srivijaya came the establishment of the **Melaka Sultanate**, the Malay Peninsula's most significant historical period. Both the *Sejarah Melayu* and the *Suma Oriental* document the tale of a Palembang prince named **Paramesvara**, who fled the collapsing empire of Srivijaya to set up his own kingdom, finally settling on the site of present-day Melaka.

As well placed as its Sumatran predecessor, with a deep, sheltered harbour and good riverine access to lucrative jungle produce, Melaka set about establishing itself as an international marketplace. The securing of a special agreement in 1405 with the new Chinese emperor, Yung-lo, guaranteed trade to Melaka and protected it from its main rivals. To further ensure its prosperity, Melaka's second ruler, Paramesvara's son **Iskandar Shah** (1414–24), took the precaution of acknowledging the neighbouring kingdoms of Ayuthaya and Majapahit as overlords. In return Melaka received vital supplies and much-needed immigrants, which bolstered the expansion of the settlement.

Port taxes and market regulations were managed by four **shahbandars** (harbour masters), each in charge of trade with certain territories. Hand in hand with the commodities trade went the exchange of ideas. By the thirteenth century, Arab merchants had begun to frequent Melaka's shores, bringing with them **Islam**, which their Muslim Indian counterparts helped to propagate among the Malays. Melaka's prestige was enhanced both by its conversion to Islam, making it part of a worldwide community with profitable trade links, and by territorial expansion which, by the reign of its last ruler **Sultan Mahmud Shah** (1488–1528), included the west coast of the Peninsula as far as Perak, Pahang, Singapore, and most of east coast Sumatra.

The legacy of **Melaka's golden age** reaches far beyond its material wealth. One significant development, the establishment of a hierarchical **court structure**, was to lay the foundations for a system of government lasting until the nineteenth century. According to Malay royal tradition, the ruler, as head of state, traced his ancestry back through Paramesvara to the maharajahs of ancient Srivijaya; in turn Paramesvara was believed to be descended from Alexander the Great. The ruler also claimed divinity, a belief strengthened by the kingdom's conversion to Islam, which held sultans to be Allah's representatives on earth. To further secure his power, always under threat from the overzealous nobility, the Melaka sultan embarked on a series of measures to emphasize his "otherness": no one but he could wear gold unless it was a royal gift, and yellow garments were forbidden among the general population.

The Melaka Sultanate also allowed the **arts** to flourish; the principal features of the courtly dances and music of this period can still be distinguished in traditional entertainments today. Much more significant, however, was the refinement of **language**, adapting the primitive Malay that had been used in the kingdom of Srivijaya into a language of the elite. Such was Melaka's prestige that all who passed through the entrepôt sought to imitate it, and by the sixteenth century, Malay was the most widely

c.1530	1641	1786
Alauddin Riayat Shah, son of the deposed Melaka sultan, establishes the Johor Sultanate	The Dutch East India Company seizes Melaka from the Portuguese	Francis Light establishes a port at Penang – the first British settlement in the Malay Peninsula

used language in the archipelago. Tellingly, the word *bahasa*, although literally meaning "language", came to signify Malay culture in general.

The Portuguese conquest of Melaka

It wasn't long before Europe set its sights on the prosperous sultanate. At the start of the sixteenth century, the **Portuguese** began to take issue with Venetian control of the Eastern market. They planned instead to establish direct contacts with the commodity brokers of the East by gaining control of crucial regional ports. The key player in the subsequent conquest of Melaka was Portuguese viceroy **Alfonso de Albuquerque**, who led the assault on the entrepôt in 1511, forcing its surrender after less than a month's siege. Aloof and somewhat effete in their high-necked ruffs and stockings, the Portuguese were not well liked, but despite the almost constant attacks from upriver Malays, they controlled Melaka for the next 130 years.

There are few physical reminders of the Portuguese in Melaka, apart from the gateway to their fort, A Famosa, and the small **Eurasian** community, descendants of intermarriage between the Portuguese and local women. The colonizers had more success with religion, however, converting large numbers of locals to **Catholicism**; their churches still dominate the city.

The Dutch in Melaka

Portuguese control over Melaka lasted for well over a century, until it was challenged by the Vereenigde Oostindische Compagnie (VOC), or **Dutch East India Company**, who were already the masters of Indonesia's valuable spice trade. Melaka was the VOC's most potent rival, and the company's bid to seize the colony succeeded in 1641 when, after a five-month siege, the Dutch flag was hoisted over Melaka.

Instead of trying, like the Portuguese, to rule from above, the Dutch cleverly wove their subjects into the fabric of government. Each racial group was represented by a *kapitan*, a respected figure from the community who mediated between his own people and the new administrators – often becoming wealthy and powerful in his own right. The Dutch were also responsible for the rebuilding of Melaka, much of which had turned to rubble during the protracted takeover of the city; many of these structures, in their distinctive Northern European style, still survive today.

By the mid-eighteenth century, conditions for Melaka's trade with China were at their peak: the relaxation of maritime restrictions in China itself had opened up the Straits for their merchants, while Europeans were eager to satisfy the growing demand for tea. The Chinese came to Melaka in droves and soon established themselves as the city's foremost entrepreneurs. Chinese settlement in the area and, in some cases, intermarriage with local Malay women, created a new cultural blend, known as **Peranakan** or Baba-Nyonya – the legacies of which are the opulent mansions and unique cuisine of Melaka, Penang and Singapore.

A number of factors prevented Dutch Melaka from fulfilling its potential, however. Since their VOC salary was hardly bountiful, Dutch administrators found it more lucrative to trade on the black market, taking backhanders from grateful merchants, a situation that severely damaged Melaka's commercial standing. High taxes forced traders to more economical locations such as the newly established British port of

1795	1819	1824
The British East India company captures Dutch possessions in Southeast Asia, including Melaka	Exploiting a succession dispute in Johor, Stamford Raffles negotiates the creation of a British settlement in Singapore	The Anglo-Dutch treaty leaves the British firmly in control of the Malay Peninsula and Singapore

THE BUGIS AND MINANGKABAU

Through the second half of the seventeenth century, a new ethnic group, the **Bugis** – renowned for their martial and commercial skills – trickled into the Peninsula, seeking refuge from the civil wars that wracked their homeland of Sulawesi (in the mid-eastern Indonesian archipelago). By the start of the eighteenth century, they were numerous enough to constitute a powerful court lobby, and in 1721 they took advantage of factional struggles to capture the kingdom of Johor, now based in Riau. Installing a Malay puppet sultan, the Bugis ruled for over sixty years, making Riau an essential port of call on the eastern trade route; they even almost succeeded in capturing Melaka in 1756. But when Riau-Johor made another bid for Melaka in 1784, the Dutch held on with renewed vigour and finally forced a treaty placing all Bugis territory in Dutch hands.

In spiritual terms, the **Minangkabau** (see box, p.267), hailing from western Sumatra, had what the Bugis lacked, being able to claim cultural affinity with ancient Srivijaya. Although this migrant group had been present in the Negeri Sembilan region since the fifteenth century, it was in the second half of the seventeenth century that they arrived in the Malay Peninsula in larger numbers. Despite professing allegiance to their Sumatran ruler, the Minangkabau were prepared to accept Malay overlordship, which in practice gave them a great deal of autonomy. Although the warrior Minangkabau were not natural allies of the Bugis or the Malays, they did occasionally join forces to defeat a common enemy. In fact, over time the distinction between various migrant groups became less obvious as intermarriage blurred clan demarcations, and Malay influence, such as the adoption of Malay titles, became more pronounced.

Penang, whose foundation in 1786 heralded the awakening of British interest in the Straits. In the end, Melaka never stood a chance: the company's attention was distracted by other centres such as Batavia (modern-day Jakarta), the VOC "capital", and by the kingdom of Johor.

Johor and Brunei

When Melaka fell to the Portuguese, the deposed sultan, Mahmud Shah, made for Bintan island in the Riau archipelago, just south of Singapore, where he established the first **court of Johor**. When, in 1526, the Portuguese attacked and razed the settlement, Mahmud fled once again, this time to Sumatra, where he died in 1528. It was left to his son, Alauddin Riayat Shah, to found a new court on the upper reaches of the Johor River, though the kingdom's capital was to shift repeatedly during a century of assaults on Johor territory by Portugal and the Sumatran Sultanate of Aceh.

The **arrival of the Dutch** in Southeast Asia marked a distinct upturn in Johor's fortunes. Hoping for protection from its local enemies, the court aligned itself firmly with the Dutch, and was instrumental in their successful siege of Portuguese Melaka. That loyalty was rewarded with trading privileges and assistance in securing a treaty with Aceh, which at last gave Johor the breathing space to develop. Johor was the supreme Malay kingdom for much of the seventeenth century, but by the 1690s its empire was fraying under the despotic rule of another Sultan Mahmud. Lacking strong leadership, Johor's Orang Laut turned to piracy, scaring off trade, while wars with the Sumatran kingdom of Jambi, one of which resulted in the total destruction of Johor's capital, weakened it still further. No longer able to tolerate his cruel regime, Mahmud's

1826	1841	1846
Singapore joined administratively with Penang and Melaka to form the Straits Settlements	With the Brunei Sultanate in decline, James Brooke is installed as the first rajah of Sarawak	Brunei cedes Labuan island to the British

nobles stabbed him to death in 1699. Not only did this change the nature of power in Malay government – previously, law deemed that the sultan could only be punished by Allah – but it also marked the end of the Melaka dynasty.

During Melaka's meteoric rise, **Brunei** had been busily establishing itself as a trading port of some renown. The Brunei Sultanate's conversion to **Islam**, no doubt precipitated by the arrival of wealthy Muslim merchants fleeing from the Portuguese in Melaka, also helped to increase its international prestige. When geographer **Antonio Pigafetta** visited Brunei with **Ferdinand Magellan**'s expedition of 1521, he found the court brimming with visitors from all over the world. This, indeed, was Brunei's "golden age", with its borders embracing land as far south as present-day Kuching in Sarawak, and as far north as the lower islands of the modern-day Philippines. Brunei's efforts, however, were soon curtailed by Spanish colonization in 1578, which, although lasting only a matter of weeks, enabled the Philippine kingdom of Sulu to gain a hold in the area – and thus put paid to Brunei's early expansionist aims.

The arrival of the British

At the end of the eighteenth century, Dutch control in Southeast Asia was more widespread than ever, and the VOC empire should have been at its height. Instead, it had somehow become **bankrupt**. Defeat in the Fourth Anglo-Dutch War (1781–83) lowered Dutch morale still further, and when the British, in the form of the **East India Company** (EIC), moved in on Melaka and the rest of the Dutch Asian domain in 1795, the VOC barely demurred; it was dissolved five years later.

Initially, the British agreed to a caretaker administration whereby they would assume sovereignty over the entrepôt to prevent it falling under French control, now that Napoleon had conquered Holland. By the time the end of the Napoleonic Wars in Europe put the Dutch in a position to retake Melaka, between 1818 and 1825, the EIC had established the stable port of **Penang** and – under the supervision of **Sir Thomas Stamford Raffles** – founded the new settlement of **Singapore**. The strategic position and free-trade policy of Singapore – backed by the impressive industrial developments of the British at home – threatened the viability of both Melaka and Penang, forcing the Dutch finally to relinquish their hold on Melaka to the British, and leaving Penang to dwindle to a backwater. In the face of such stiff competition, smaller Malay rivals inevitably linked their fortunes to the British.

The British assumption of power was sealed by the **Anglo–Dutch Treaty of 1824**, which apportioned territories between the two powers using the Straits of Melaka and the equator as the dividing lines, thereby splitting the Riau-Johor kingdom as well as putting the brakes on centuries of cultural interchange with Sumatra. This was followed in 1826 when Melaka, Penang and Singapore were unified into one administration, known as the **Straits Settlements**. Singapore replaced Penang as its capital in 1832.

Raffles had at first hoped that **Singapore** would act as a market to sell British goods to traders from all over Southeast Asia, but it soon became clear that **Chinese** merchants, the linchpin of Singapore's trade, were interested only in Malay products such as birds' nests, seaweed and camphor. But passing traders were not the only Chinese to come to the Straits. Although settlers had trickled into the Peninsula since the early days of

1851	1874	1881
Hugh Low makes the first documented ascent of Gunung Kinabalu	Perak becomes the first Malay state to take a British adviser or Resident after the signing of the Pangkor Treaty	The British North Borneo Company takes control over all of what is now Sabah

Melaka, new **plantations** of pepper and gambier (an astringent used in tanning and dyeing), and the rapidly expanding **tin mines**, attracted floods of workers eager to escape a life of poverty in China. By 1845, half of Singapore's population was Chinese, and likewise principal towns along the Peninsula's west coast (site of the world's largest tin field) and, for that matter, Kuching, became predominantly Chinese.

The Pangkor Treaty

Allowed a large degree of commercial independence by both the British and the Malay chiefs, the Chinese formed **kongsis** (clan associations) and triads (secret societies). The **Malays**, too, were hardly immune from factional conflicts, which frequently became intertwined with Chinese squabbles, causing a string of **civil conflicts**: in Penang in 1867, for example, the triads allied themselves with Malay groups in a bloody street battle that lasted several days.

Such lawlessness was detrimental to commerce, giving the British an excuse to increase their involvement in local affairs. A meeting involving the chiefs of the Perak Malays was arranged by the new Straits Governor, Andrew Clarke, on Pulau Pangkor, just off the west coast of the Peninsula. In the meantime, Rajah Abdullah, the man most likely to succeed to the Perak throne, had written to Clarke asking for his position as sultan to be guaranteed; in return, he offered the British the chance to appoint a **Resident**, a senior British civil servant whose main function would be to act as adviser to the local sultan, and who would also oversee the collecting of local taxes. On January 20, 1874, the **Pangkor Treaty** was signed, formalizing British intervention in Malay political affairs.

Perak's first Resident, J.W.W. Birch, was not sympathetic to the ways of the Malays; his centralizing tendencies were opposed by Abdullah when he became sultan. Fearful of a Malay rebellion, senior British officials announced that judicial decisions would from now on be in the hands of the British. This went against the Pangkor Treaty, and furious Malays soon found a vent for their frustration: on November 2, 1875, Birch was killed on an upriver visit. Only with the appointment of the third Resident of Perak, the respected Hugh Low, did the system start to work more smoothly.

Other states soon saw the arrival of a Resident, and agreements along the lines of the Pangkor Treaty were drawn up with Selangor, Negeri Sembilan and Pahang during the 1880s. In 1896, these three and Perak became bracketed together under the title of the **Federated Malay States**, with the increasingly important town of **Kuala Lumpur** as the capital.

British Malaya

By 1888 the name **British Malaya** had come into use – a term that reflected the intention to extend British control over the whole Peninsula. Over subsequent decades, the economic and administrative powers of the Malay sultans were eroded, while the introduction of rubber estates in the first half of the twentieth century made British Malaya one of the world's most productive colonies. The rapidity and extent of the British takeover in the Peninsula was unprecedented, aided by advances in communications.

1887	1890	1890s
Having launched Penang's *Eastern and Oriental* hotel two years earlier, the Sarkies brothers create Singapore's *Raffles*	Charles Brooke, second rajah of Sarawak, captures Limbang from Brunei, splitting the sultanate in two	Henry Ridley, director of Singapore's Botanic Gardens, works out how to tap rubber commercially

The extension of British power brought further unrest, particularly in the east coast states, where the Malays proved just as resentful of British control as in Perak. A set of skirmishes took place in Pahang in the early 1890s, when Malay chiefs protested about the reduction of their privileges. After one powerful chief, Dato' Bahaman, was stripped of his title by Pahang's Resident, Hugh Clifford, the Dato' led a small rebellion that soon became the stuff of legends. One fighter, **Mat Kilau**, earned a place in folklore as a hero who stood up to the British. From this time, Malays would interpret the uprisings as a valiant attempt to safeguard their traditions and autonomy.

By 1909, the northern Malay states of Kedah and Perlis had been brought into the colonial fold. In 1910, Johor accepted a British general-adviser; a 1914 treaty between Britain and Johor made his powers equal to those of Residents elsewhere. Terengganu, which was under Thai control, was the last state to accept a British adviser, in 1919. These four states, together with Kelantan, were sometimes collectively referred to as the **Unfederated Malay States**, though they shared no common administration.

By the outbreak of World War I, British political control was more or less complete. The Peninsula was subdivided into groups of states and regions with the seat of power split between Singapore and Kuala Lumpur.

The expansion of British interests in Borneo

The Anglo-Dutch Treaty did not include **Borneo**, where official expansion was discouraged by the EIC, which preferred to concentrate on expanding its trading contacts rather than territorial control. The benefits of Borneo did not, however, elude the sights of one British explorer, **James Brooke** (1803–68). Finding lawlessness throughout the island, Brooke persuaded the Sultan of Brunei to award him his own area – **Sarawak** – in 1841, becoming the first of a line of "**White Rajahs**" who ruled the state until World War II. Brooke quickly asserted his authority by involving formerly rebellious Malay chiefs in government, although the interior's tribes proved more of a problem. Subsequently Brooke and his successors proved adept at siphoning more land into the familial fiefdom.

Though the association between the British and James Brooke was informal (Brooke was careful not to encourage European contacts that might compromise his hold), trade between Singapore and Sarawak flourished. By the mid-nineteenth century, however, the British attitude had altered; they chose Brooke as their agent in Brunei, and found him a useful deterrent against French and Dutch aspirations towards the valuable trade routes. Eventually, in 1888, Sarawak, North Borneo (Sabah) and Brunei were transformed into **protectorates**, a status that entailed responsibility for their foreign policy being handed over to the British.

The legacy of James Brooke was furthered by his nephew **Charles Brooke** in the second half of the nineteenth century. Like his uncle, Charles ruled Sarawak in paternalistic fashion, recruiting soldiers, lowly officials and boatmen from the ranks of the tribal groups and leaving the Chinese to get on with running commercial enterprises and opening up the interior. **Vyner Brooke**, Charles's eldest son, became rajah in 1917; his reign saw no new territorial acquisitions, though there was a steady development in rubber, pepper and palm-oil production. The tribal peoples mostly continued living a traditional lifestyle in longhouses along the river, while the end of their practice of head-hunting was followed by some degree of integration among the area's varied racial groups.

1896	1917	1933
The Federated Malay States are created, encompassing the four states that have a British Resident, with Kuala Lumpur as capital	Vyner Brooke becomes the third and, as it turns out, last rajah of Sarawak	The first Malay-language feature film, *Laila Majnun*, is made in Singapore

By way of contrast, the **British North Borneo Chartered Company**'s writ in what became Sabah encountered some early obstacles. The company's plans for economic expansion involved clearing the rainforest, planting **rubber** and **tobacco** over large areas, and levying taxes on the tribes. Resistance ensued, with the most vigorous action, in 1897, led by a Bajau chief, **Mat Salleh**, whose men rampaged through the company's outstation on Pulau Gaya. Another rebellion by **Murut** tribespeople in 1915 resulted in a heavy-handed response from British forces, who killed hundreds.

By the start of the twentieth century, the majority of the lands of the once-powerful **Sultanate of Brunei** had been dismembered – the sultanate was now surrounded by Sarawak. But the sultan's fortunes had not completely disappeared and with the discovery of oil, the British thought it prudent to appoint a Resident. Exploitation of the small state's oil fields gathered pace in the 1930s following investment from British companies.

Development and ethnic rivalries

In the first quarter of the twentieth century, the British encouraged hundreds of thousands of **immigrants** from China and India to come to Peninsular Malaysia, Sarawak, North Borneo and Singapore. They arrived to work as tin miners or plantation labourers, and Malaya's population in this period doubled to four million. This bred increasing resentment among the Malays, who believed that they were being denied the economic opportunities advanced to others.

A further deterioration in Malay–Chinese relations followed the success of mainland Chinese revolutionary groups in Malaya. Malayan Chinese joined the **Malayan Communist Party** (MCP) from 1930 onwards and also formed the backbone of postwar Chinese movements that demanded an end to British rule and what they perceived as special privileges extended to the Malays. At the same time, Malay nationalism was gathering its own head of steam. The **Singapore Malay Union**, which held its first conference in 1939, advocated a Malay supremacist line. A year earlier, the first All-Malaya Malays Conference, organized by the Selangor Malays Association, had been held in KL.

The Japanese occupation

Landing in Kelantan in December 1941, Japanese forces took barely two months to sweep down the Peninsula and reach Singapore. The **surrender** of the British forces there in February 1942 ushered in a Japanese regime that brutalized the Chinese, largely because of Japan's history of conflict with China; at least 25,000 people were tortured and killed in the two weeks immediately after the surrender of the island by the British military command. Allied POWs were rounded up into prison camps; many of the troops were subsequently sent to build the infamous "Death Railway" in Burma.

In **Malaya**, towns and buildings were destroyed as the Allies attempted to bomb strategic targets. But with the Japanese firmly in control, the occupiers ingratiated themselves with some of the Malay elite by suggesting that after the war the country would be given independence. Predictably, it was the Chinese activists in the MCP, more than the Malays, who organized resistance during wartime.

December 1941 also saw the Japanese invade **Sarawak**, beginning with the capture of the Miri oil field. Although the Japanese never penetrated the interior, they quickly

Dec 1941	Feb 1942	September 1945	1946
Japan lands forces in Kelantan and captures Miri in Sarawak	Singapore falls to the Japanese	Japanese forces in Southeast Asia formally surrender in Singapore	Britain introduces the Malayan Union, turning Malaya into a full colony rather than a protectorate

established control over the populated towns along the coast. The Chinese in Miri, Sibu and Kuching were the main targets: the Japanese put down rebellions brutally, and there was no organized guerrilla activity until late in the occupation. What resistance there was arose from "Z Force", namely Major **Tom Harrisson** and a team of British and Australian commandos, who in 1945 parachuted into the remote Kelabit Highlands to build a resistance movement.

In **North Borneo**, the Japanese invaded Pulau Labuan on New Year's Day, 1942. Over the next three years the main suburban areas were bombed by the Allies, destroying most of Jesselton (modern-day KK) and Sandakan. Captured troops and civilians suffered enormously – the worst single outrage being the "Death March" in September 1944, when 2400 POWs were forced to walk from Sandakan to Ranau (see p.423).

In September 1945, just prior to a planned Allied invasion to retake Singapore, the **Japanese surrendered** following the dropping of atom bombs on Nagasaki and Hiroshima. The surrender led to a power vacuum in the region, with the British initially having to work with the MCP's armed wing, the **Malayan People's Anti-Japanese Army** (MPAJA), to maintain order in many areas. Violence occurred between the MPAJA and Malays, particularly against those accused of collaborating with the Japanese.

Postwar upheaval

Immediately after the war, the British introduced the **Malayan Union**, in effect turning the Malay States from a protectorate into a colony and removing the sovereignty of the sultans. Another effect was to give the Chinese and Indian inhabitants citizenship and equal rights with the Malays. This quickly aroused opposition from the Malays, the nationalists among whom formed the **United Malays National Organization** (UMNO) in 1946. Its main tenet was that Malays should retain special privileges, largely because they were the first inhabitants, and that the uniquely powerful position of the sultans should not be tampered with.

UMNO's resistance led to the Malayan Union idea being replaced by the **Federation of Malaya**. Established in 1948, this upheld the sultans' power and privileges and brought all the Peninsula's territories together under one government, apart from Chinese-dominated Singapore, whose inclusion would have led to the Malays being in a minority overall. Protests erupted in Singapore at its exclusion, with the **Malayan Democratic Union** (MDU), a multiracial party, calling for integration with Malaya – a position that commanded little support among the Chinese population.

After the Japanese surrender in **Borneo**, the Colonial Office in London made Sarawak and North Borneo **Crown Colonies**, with Vyner Brooke offering no objection. Sarawakians were torn over the change in arrangements, however: while the ruling assembly, the Council Negeri (composed of Malays, Chinese, Iban and British), had voted to transfer power to Britain, some Malays and prominent Iban in Kuching opposed the move. Protests reached a peak with the assassination in Sibu in 1949 of the senior official in the new administration, Governor Duncan Stewart. But on the whole, resentment at the passing of the Brooke era was short-lived as the economy expanded and infrastructure improved. Britain also signed a Treaty of Protection with the Sultan of Brunei, who remained the chief power in the state while Sarawak's high commissioner took on the purely decorative role of governor of Brunei.

1946	1946	1948
Despite local protests, Vyner Brooke cedes Sarawak to the British government, bringing the White Rajahs' dynasty to an end	The British North Borneo Company cedes Sabah to the British government	Malay opposition to the Malayan Union leads to its replacement by the Federation of Malaya, which respects the status of the sultans

The Emergency

Many Chinese in the Peninsula were angered when the country changed status from a colony to a federation, effectively making them second-class citizens. According to the new laws, non-Malays could only qualify as citizens if they had lived in the country for fifteen out of the last twenty-five years, and they also had to prove they spoke Malay or English.

Following the communist takeover in China in 1949, most Malayan Chinese ceased to look to China; the more political among them founded a new political party, the **Malayan Chinese Association** (MCA). Some local Chinese, however, identified with the MCP, which under its new leader, **Chin Peng**, declared its intention of setting up a Malayan republic. Peng fused the MCP with the remains of the MPAJA, and, using arms supplies that the latter had dumped in the forests, from June 1948 he launched sporadic attacks on rubber estates, killing planters and employees as well as spreading fear among rural communities. This civil conflict, which lasted until 1960, was euphemistically called **the Emergency** for insurance purposes; planters would have had their policies cancelled if war had been officially declared. At its peak, around ten thousand of Chin Peng's guerrillas were hiding out in jungle camps, using a support network of Chinese-dominated towns and villages in the interior. In many cases inhabitants were cowed into submission by means of public executions, though many poor rural workers identified with the insurgents' struggle.

Although the Emergency was never fully felt in the main urban areas, British rubber-estate owners would arrive at the *Coliseum Hotel* in KL with harrowing stories of how "communist terrorists" had hacked off the arms of rural Chinese workers who refused to support the cause, and of armed attacks on plantations.

The British were slow to respond to the threat, but once Lieutenant-General Sir Harold Briggs was put in command of police and army forces, Malaya was on a war footing. Briggs' most controversial policy was the **resettlement** of 400,000 rural

THE EMERGENCY AND THE ORANG ASLI

The impact of the Emergency on the **Orang Asli** of the interior was dramatic. All but the most remote tribes were subject to intimidation and brutality, from guerrillas on one side and government forces on the other. In effect, the Orang Asli's centuries-old invisibility had ended; the population of Malaysia was now aware of their presence, and the government of their strategic importance.

The Orang Asli had no choice but to grow food and act as porters for the guerrillas, as well as – most important of all – provide intelligence, warning them of the approach of the enemy. In response, the government implemented a disastrous policy of removing thousands of Orang Asli from the jungle and relocating them in new model villages in the interior, which were no more than dressed-up prison camps. Hundreds died in captivity before the government dismantled these settlements. By then, not surprisingly, active support for the insurgents among the Orang Asli had risen – though allegiances switched to the security forces when it became clear the guerrillas were heading for defeat. Government attempts to control the Orang Asli during the Emergency turned out to be the precursor to initiatives that persist to the present day, drawing the Orang Asli away from their traditional lifestyle and into the embrace of the Malaysian nation-state.

1948	August 1957	1959
The Malayan Community Party launches an insurgency from the jungle, which comes to be called The Emergency	The Federation of Malaya – the Malay Peninsula, minus Singapore – gains independence	Singapore gains full self-government under Lee Kuan Yew, while remaining a British colony

Chinese – mostly squatters who had moved to the jungle fringes to avoid the Japanese during the war – as well as thousands of Orang Asli. Although these forced migrations were successful in breaking down many of the guerrillas' supply networks, they alienated many Chinese and Orang Asli who had previously been sympathetic to the British.

The violence peaked in 1950 with ambushes and attacks near Ipoh, Kuala Kangsar, Kuala Lipis and Raub. The most notorious incident occurred in 1951 on the road to Fraser's Hill, when the British high commissioner to Malaya, **Sir Henry Gurney**, was assassinated. Under his replacement, Sir Gerald Templer, a new policy was introduced to win hearts and minds. "White Areas", perceived as free of guerrilla activity, were established; communities in these regions had food restrictions and curfews lifted, a policy that began to dissipate guerrilla activity over the next three years. The leaders were offered an amnesty in 1956, which was refused, and Chin Peng and most of the remaining cell members fled over the border to Thailand where they received sanctuary.

Towards independence

The Emergency had the effect of speeding up political change prior to independence. UMNO stuck to its "Malays first" policy, though its president, **Tuanku Abdul Rahman** (also the chief minister of Malaya), won the 1955 election by cooperating with the MCA and the Malayan Indian Association. The resulting bloc, the **UMNO Alliance**, swept into power under the rallying cry of **Merdeka** (Freedom). The hope was that ethnic divisions would no longer be a major factor if **independence** was granted.

With British backing, *merdeka* was proclaimed on August 31, 1957 in a ceremony in Kuala Lumpur's padang – promptly renamed Merdeka Square. The British high commissioner signed a treaty that decreed that the **Federation of Malaya** was now independent of the Crown, with Tuanku Abdul Rahman the first prime minister. The new **constitution** allowed for the nine Malay sultans to alternate as king, and established a two-tier **parliament**, comprising a house of elected representatives and a senate with delegates from each state. Under Rahman, the country was fully committed to economic expansion, with foreign investment actively encouraged – a stance that has survived to the present.

Similarly, in **Singapore** the process of gaining independence acquired momentum throughout the 1950s. In 1957, the British gave the go-ahead for the setting up of an elected 51-member assembly, and full **self-government** was attained in 1959, when the People's Action Party (PAP) under **Lee Kuan Yew** won most of the seats. Lee immediately entered into talks with Tuanku Abdul Rahman over the notion that Singapore and Malaya should be joined administratively. Tunku initially agreed, although he feared the influence of the far left in the PAP.

In 1961, Tuanku Abdul Rahman proposed that Sarawak and North Borneo should join Malaya and Singapore in an enlarged federation. Many in Borneo would have preferred the idea of a separate Borneo Federation, although the Konfrontasi (see opposite) was to make clear how vulnerable such a federation would be to attack from Indonesia. Rahman's suggestion was, however, not fuelled by security concerns but by **demographics**: if Singapore were to join the federation, the country would acquire a Chinese majority. This made the two Borneo colonies useful as a counterweight to Singapore's Chinese.

1962	September 1963	August 1965
President Sukarno of Indonesia uses military incursions – the Konfrontasi – to agitate against Sabah and Sarawak joining Malaya	The Federation of Malaya becomes the Federation of Malaysia, augmented by Singapore, Sarawak and Sabah; Brunei opts out	Singapore leaves the Federation and goes it alone as an independent country

Although Abdul Rahman had wanted **Brunei** to join the Malaysian Federation, Sultan Omar refused when he realized Rahman's price – a substantial proportion of Brunei's oil and gas revenues. Brunei remained under nominal British jurisdiction until its **independence** on January 1, 1984.

Federation and the Konfrontasi

In September 1963, North Borneo (quickly renamed Sabah), Sarawak and Singapore joined Malaya in the **Federation of Malaysia** – "Malaysia" being a term coined by the British in the 1950s when the notion of a Greater Malaya had been propounded. Both Indonesia, which laid claim to Sarawak, and the Philippines, which claimed jurisdiction over Sabah as it had originally been part of the Sulu Sultanate, reacted angrily. Border skirmishes with Indonesia known as the **Konfrontasi** ensued, and a wider war was only just averted when Indonesian President Sukarno backed down from taking on British and Gurkha troops brought in to bolster Sarawak's small armed forces.

Within the federation, further differences surfaced in Singapore during this period between Lee Kuan Yew and the Malay-dominated Alliance over the lack of egalitarian policies; many Chinese were concerned that UMNO's overall influence in the federation was too great. Tensions rose on the island and racial incidents developed into full-scale **riots** in 1964, in which several people were killed.

These developments were viewed with great concern by Tuanku Abdul Rahman in Kuala Lumpur, and when the PAP subsequently attempted to enter Peninsular politics, he decided it would be best if Singapore left the federation. This was emphatically not in Singapore's best interests, since it was an island without any obvious natural resources; Lee cried on TV when the expulsion was announced and Singapore acquired full **independence** on August 9, 1965. The severing of the bond between Malaysia and Singapore has led to a kind of sibling rivalry between the two nations ever since.

Racial issues and riots

Singapore's exit from the Malaysian Federation was not enough to quell ethnic tensions. Resentment grew among the Malaysian Chinese over the principle that Malay be the main language taught in schools and over the privileged employment opportunities offered to Malays. After the Alliance lost ground in elections in May 1969, Malays in major cities reacted angrily to a perceived increase in power of the Chinese, who had commemorated their breakthrough with festivities in the streets. Hundreds of people, mostly Chinese, were killed and injured in the **riots** that followed; KL in particular became a war zone with large crowds of youths on the rampage. Rahman kept the country under a state of emergency for nearly two years, during which the draconian **Internal Security Act** (ISA) was used to arrest and imprison activists, as well as many writers and artists, setting a sombre precedent for authoritarian practices still followed today.

Abdul Rahman never recovered full political command and resigned in 1970. That September, the new prime minister, **Tun Abdul Razak Hussein**, initiated a form of state-orchestrated positive discrimination called the **New Economic Policy** (NEP), which

May 1969	1971	1981
Deadly race riots scar Kuala Lumpur	The Malaysian government introduces its New Economic Policy, including positive discrimination in favour of Malays	Mahathir Mohamad, to become Malaysia's long-serving prime minister, takes office

THE BUMIPUTRA POLICY

Provisions in the New Economic Policy (NEP), introduced in the wake of the 1969 race riots, became known as the **bumiputra policy** as they were intended to provide a more level economic playing field for Malays, Orang Asli and the indigenous peoples of east Malaysia (*bumiputra* means something like "sons of the soil" in Malay). In terms of wealth, these communities (as well the Indians) were lagging far behind the Chinese. This was partly the result of colonial policy: the immigrant Chinese made strides as businesspeople in the towns, while the Malays were either employed as administrators or left to get on with farming and fishing in rural areas, while the Indians toiled on the railways and the plantations.

The policy has been moderated, renamed and rejigged over the years, but basically awards *bumiputras*, in particular the Malays, privileges such as subsidized housing and easier access to higher education and civil-service jobs. The *bumiputra* policy has undoubtedly achieved a reasonable degree of **wealth redistribution**, though a less laudable consequence has been the creation of a super-rich Malay elite. What's more, the policy is deeply resented by the non-beneficiaries. The Indians are especially aggrieved, having never been wealthy; the Chinese have continued to rely on their own devices in business while shunning the public sector, where they feel the odds have been stacked against them.

Despite the policy's undoubted popularity among Malays, Mahathir and his successors have questioned the wisdom of allowing the system to continue indefinitely, fearing that it has fostered complacency in the very communities it is meant to help. The difficulty for all UMNO leaders is that any meaningful retreat from the policy requires political daring. Only the opposition, which generally wants to reform Malaysian politics in a nonracial mould, has attempted to make progress in this regard, though it is just as risky an enterprise for them.

gives ethnic Malays and members of Borneo's tribes favoured positions in business and other professions. Also under Razak, a crucial step was taken towards Malaysia's current political map with the formation in 1974 of the **Barisan Nasional** ("National Front", usually abbreviated to **BN**), comprising UMNO plus the main Chinese and Indian parties and – since the 1990s – parties representing indigenous groups in Sabah and Sarawak. This multiethnic coalition has governed the country ever since.

The Mahathir era

The dominant figure in Malaysian politics since independence has been **Dr Mahathir Mohamad**, prime minister from 1981 until 2003. Even Malaysians not generally favourably disposed towards the BN credit him with helping the country attain economic lift-off; under Mahathir, industrialization changed the landscape of regions like the Klang Valley and Johor, manufacturing output eclipsed agriculture in importance, and huge **prestige projects** like the Petronas Towers and KLIA were completed. Mahathir meanwhile kept his supporters happy with a raft of populist pronouncements, including railing against the West for criticizing Malaysia's human-rights record (he claimed that by what he termed "Asian values", prosperity was valued more highly than civil liberties). Less well remembered is the fact that Mahathir's tenure also saw the extensive use of the ISA in what became known as **Operation Lalang** when, in 1987, more than a hundred politicians and activists were detained following tensions between UMNO and Chinese political parties over matters to do with

1984	1987	1997	1998
Brunei becomes independent	The Malaysia government launches Operation Lalang, a major crackdown against its critics and sectors of the press	The Asian economic crisis envelopes the region	Anwar Ibrahim, Malaysia's deputy prime minister and finance minister, is sacked by Mahathir and subsequently convicted of corruption and sodomy

Chinese-language education. These arrests were bad enough, but more durable in its effects was state action to curb press freedom. Especially notable was the government's closure of the pro-MCA English-language *Star* newspaper for several months; when it reopened, many of its senior managers had been replaced.

In 1997, the economy suffered a major setback when Malaysia was sucked into the **Asian economic crisis**, which began in Thailand and Korea. Mahathir took personal charge of getting the economy back on track, sacking his deputy and finance minister **Anwar Ibrahim** in 1998. A former student leader and once an espouser of progressive Islamic policies, Anwar had enjoyed a meteoric rise upon joining UMNO and had been groomed to succeed Mahathir, though relations between the two subsequently soured. The nation was stunned when, within a week of his dismissal, Anwar was arrested on corruption and sexual misconduct charges; a succession of mass demonstrations in his support ensued. Anwar's treatment in detention became the subject of much concern when he appeared in court on the corruption charge sporting a black eye. He was eventually found guilty – leading many observers to question the independence of the judiciary – and sentenced to six years in jail. In 2000, he was also found guilty of sodomizing his driver and sentenced to nine years in prison.

Meanwhile, Anwar's wife, Wan Azizah Wan Ismail, formed a new party, **Keadilan** ("Justice", sometimes also called **PKR**), which has contested subsequent elections in alliance with other opposition parties, including the Chinese-dominated Democratic Action Party (**DAP**) and the Islamist **PAS**.

Malaysia under Abdullah Badawi

Momentously, in 2003, Mahathir resigned and handed power to Anwar's replacement as deputy prime minister, **Abdullah Badawi**. Hailing from Penang, Abdullah (often referred to as Pak Lah) is a genial man, in marked contrast to his abrasive predecessor, and he asserted himself effectively, winning a landslide general election victory in 2004. Soon after, Anwar's sodomy conviction was overturned and he was released, though he remained barred from standing for parliament until 2008 as his corruption conviction was not quashed.

As a relatively new broom, Abdullah enjoyed much goodwill early on; it was hoped he would make good on his promises to sweep cronyism and corruption out of Malaysian politics. But as time wore on, authority seemed to ebb away from his government in the face of crises and scandals.

The first and most sensational of these was the affair of **Altantuya Shaariibuu**, a Mongolian woman who went missing in the KL area in 2006. Her remains, which had been blown to bits with explosives, were soon discovered, and it transpired that she was an associate of a defence analyst with links to **Najib Tun Razak**, Abdullah's deputy. The case created a stink around the government, and two policemen, members of an elite unit protecting politicians and other senior authority figures, were subsequently sentenced to death for her murder. Also damaging was the brief flowering of **HINDRAF**, the Hindu Rights Action Force, in 2007. Representing Malaysia's Hindu Indian community, HINDRAF was aggrieved over dubious conversions of Hindus to Islam, the demolitions of several Hindu shrines said by the government to have been built without proper approval, and the fact that Hindu Indians continue to languish near

2003	2004	2004
Abdullah Badawi succeeds Mahathir as Malaysian prime minister	Anwar Ibrahim is freed from jail having had only his sodomy conviction overturned	Lee Hsien Loong, Lee Kuan Yew's son, becomes prime minister of Singapore

the bottom of the economic pile in Malaysia, without the benefits that Muslim Indians can claim.

HINDRAF appears to have run out of steam without the government giving ground, but the episode has been one of many that has left a nasty taste in the mouth, undermining the BN's reputation for protecting the rights of all of Malaysia's ethnic groups.

The 2008 elections

In February 2008, Abdullah called a **snap general election** for the following month – when Anwar Ibrahim was still barred from standing. If the timing was maximally convenient for Abdullah, the result was anything but: the BN was duly returned to power, but on its **worst showing** since its formation in 1974. This time, the BN failed to win more than two-thirds of seats in parliament, which had hitherto afforded it the right to tinker with the constitution. To make matters worse, the opposition alliance unseated the BN in an unprecedented number of **state assemblies**, not just in largely Malay Kedah, where voters had previously flirted with PAS, but also in cosmopolitan, prosperous Selangor, Penang and Perak.

In the wake of the election, amid euphoria and recrimination, everything in Malaysian politics seemed to be up for grabs. A more clinical assessment would be that a large number of voters, not necessarily comprehending the opposition's platform but galvanized by such issues as cronyism, social and racial inequalities, rising crime and the soaring cost of fuel, were intent on firing a warning shot across the BN's bows. Perhaps the worst news for Abdullah was how badly the BN fared in the Peninsula, home to three-quarters of the population: its majority there was wafer-thin, and it took just one out of eleven seats in KL. Only victories by the BN-allied parties of Sabah and Sarawak had secured the coalition a working majority.

Testing times

Unfortunately for Abdullah, things got no better for the BN in the aftermath of the polls, as the various affairs that had come to light beforehand played themselves out like a tragicomic drama. Against this turbulent backdrop, **Anwar Ibrahim** made a triumphant return to parliament in August 2008, his wife resigning her seat so that he could stand in a by-election. Just prior to all this, however, Anwar was sensationally arrested once again on a charge of sodomy, this time involving a young aide of his. Allowed bail, Anwar took up his new role as leader of the opposition coalition, **Pakatan Rakyat**, while having to make appearances in court. Then in 2009 Abdullah Badawi stepped down, to be replaced by his deputy **Najib Tun Razak**.

In 2012, Anwar was cleared of the second sodomy charge, freeing him to play a frontline role in the impending polls, which took place in May 2013. It proved to be another watershed election, though not quite as the opposition would have liked. For the first time, the combined opposition parties won more than half the popular vote, but the first-past-the-post voting system meant the BN achieved a workable majority in the federal parliament, as well as recapturing the state assemblies in Kedah and Perak. The opposition's next significant move was an attempt to shoehorn Anwar into the

Dec 2004	March 2008	2009
Penang and Kedah in Malaysia are struck by the Indian Ocean tsunami, though with only modest loss of life	Malaysia's opposition enjoys its best general election showing since independence	Najib Tun Razak becomes Malaysian prime minister

chief minister's job in **Selangor**, the most developed state in the Federation and their one true showcase. But that was thwarted when, in March 2014, his acquittal on the second sodomy charge was overturned on a government appeal. In February 2015, the Federal Court – the highest in the land – upheld the government's appeal, and Anwar was sent to prison once again at the age of 67. He was thus removed from front-line politics for the duration of his five-year sentence and, by the electoral rules, for another five years after that.

It seems clear that Malaysia is entering ever more uncertain waters. On the one hand, the country remains a working example of a multiethnic, multicultural state. On the other, it is also a collection of little powder kegs, any one of which could spark a major conflagration at any time. Scarcely a year seems to go by without some new corruption scandal involving politicians or officials who eventually get off scot-free; the nation's finances are in a parlous state (hence the belated attempt to introduce a goods and services tax, just as oil revenues are depressed by low crude prices); and the rise of **Malay supremacist** groups is threatening to sow discord and uncertainty.

Gone are the well-meaning but ultimately fruitless reformist noises of the Abdullah Badawi era. Najib, with his patrician roots – his father was Tun Abdul Razak Hussein – has proven an ineffectual, bland leader, seemingly directionless and unable to stand up to hawkish anti-Chinese sentiment in his own party, never mind bringing the country together in the wake of the two Malaysia Airlines disasters of 2014. Although he has repealed much-hated legislation which provided for detention without trial, he has also done an about-face on a promise to do away with the **Sedition Act**, which could in principle be used to imprison anyone questioning the validity of the country's ethnic or religious policies – though the suspicion is that it will never be used against the Malay Right, and is only being kept on as a thinly veiled threat against non-Malay secularists and intellectuals. The opposition, for its part, has been more clearly exposed as a marriage of convenience between parties with some sharply contrasting views: PAS, for instance, continues to harp on about introducing harsh Islamic *hudud* punishments in Malay-dominated Kelantan, which would be a complete dealbreaker for the DAP in Chinese-dominated Penang. As for Anwar's incarceration, it has once again deprived the opposition of its only plausible prime minister in waiting. Yet the opposition could gain sympathy from Anwar's second spell as an apparent political martyr, and Anwar's wife and now politically active daughters will step into the breach to an extent. This means it's not clear that the BN stands to benefit overall.

If there is a ray of hope, it is that Malaysian **democracy** is enjoying a small renaissance. Now that the opposition has many more parliamentarians, the press is less cowed about reporting their policies, and civil rights organizations are campaigning ever more vocally, as borne out by several massive Bersih (Malay for "clean") demonstrations in KL in recent years, calling for an end to electoral fraud. Thorny issues around corruption, race and religion, long swept under the carpet in the name of economic progress, are being debated with some rancour but also more thoroughly and purposefully, which could ultimately lead to the country taking a more enlightened path.

May 2011	**May 2013**	**August 2015**
The Singapore opposition enjoys its best election showing since independence	The Malaysian opposition wins the popular vote in the general election, although the BN coalition remains in power	Singapore marks fifty years of independence in its own right

Religion

Islam is a significant force in Malaysia, given that virtually all Malays, who comprise just over half the population, are Muslim; in Singapore, where three-quarters of the population are Chinese, Buddhism is the main religion. There's a smaller, but no less significant, Hindu Indian presence in both countries, while the other chief belief system is animism, adhered to by many of the indigenous peoples of Malaysia. While the colonial period drew Christian missionaries to the region, the British, in a bid to avoid unrest among the Malays, were restrained in their evangelical efforts. Christian missionaries had more success in Borneo than on the Peninsula; indeed, the main tribal group in Sabah, the Kadazan/Dusun, is Christian, as are many or most Kelabit and Iban in Sarawak. That said, Christianity is a significant minority religion in Peninsular Malaysia and Singapore, with a notable following among middle-class Chinese and Indians.

One striking feature of religion here is that it can be a **syncretic** blend of beliefs and influences. In a region where fusion is visible in everything from food to language, it's not hard to come across individuals who profess one faith, yet pray or make offerings to deities of another, in the warm-hearted belief that all religions contain some truth and that it therefore makes sense not to put all your spiritual eggs in one devotional basket.

Animism

Although many of Malaysia's indigenous groups are now nominally Christian or Muslim, many of their old animist beliefs and rites still survive. In the animist world-view, everything in nature – mountains, trees, rocks and lakes – has a controlling soul or spirit (**semangat** in Malay) that has to be mollified. For the Orang Asli groups in the interior of the Peninsula, remaining animist beliefs often centre on healing and funeral ceremonies. A sick person, particularly a child, is believed to be invaded by a bad spirit, and drums are played and incantations performed to persuade the spirit to depart. The death of a member of the family is followed by a complex process of burial and reburial – a procedure that, it is hoped, ensures an easy passage for the person's spirit.

In Sarawak, **birds**, especially the **hornbill**, are of particular significance to the Iban and Kelabit peoples. Many Kelabit depend upon the arrival of migrating flocks to decide when to plant their rice crop, while Iban augury interprets sightings of the hornbill and other birds as good or bad omens. In some accounts of Iban beliefs, two bird spirits are involved in the creation of the Earth and sky, and the Iban themselves are descended from a bird spirit named Sengalang Burong.

Hinduism

Hinduism arrived in Malaysia long before Islam, brought by Indian traders more than a thousand years ago. While almost all of Malaysia's ancient Hindu past has been obliterated, elements live on in the popular arts like *wayang kulit* (shadow plays), the plots of which are drawn from the sacred *Ramayana*.

The central tenet of Hinduism is the belief that life is a series of rebirths and reincarnations that eventually lead to spiritual release. A whole variety of deities are worshipped, which on the surface makes Hinduism appear complex; however, a loose understanding of the *Vedas* – the religion's holy books – is enough for the characters and roles of the main gods to become apparent. The deities you'll come across most often are the three manifestations of the faith's supreme divine being: **Brahma** the creator, **Vishnu** the preserver and **Shiva** the destroyer.

Hinduism returned to the Peninsula in the late nineteenth century when immigrants from southern India arrived to work on the Malayan rubber and oil-palm plantations. The Hindu celebration of Rama's victory – the central theme of the *Ramayana* – in time became the national holiday of **Deepavali** (or Diwali; the festival of lights), while another Hindu festival, **Thaipusam**, when Lord Subramaniam and elephant-headed Ganesh, the sons of Shiva, are worshipped, is marked by some of the region's most prominent religious gatherings.

Step over the threshold of a **Hindu temple** in Malaysia or Singapore and you enter a kaleidoscope world of gods and fanciful creatures. The style is typically Dravidian (South Indian), as befits the largely Tamil population, with a soaring **gopuram**, or entrance tower, teeming with sculptures and a central courtyard leading to an inner sanctum housing the presiding deity. In the temple precinct, you'll invariably witness incense being burned, the application of sandalwood paste to the forehead, and *puja* (ritualistic acts of worship).

Islam

Islam gained its first firm foothold in the Malay Peninsula with the conversion of Paramesvara, the ruler of **Melaka**, in the early fifteenth century. The commercial success of Melaka accelerated the spread of Islam; one after another the powerful Malay court rulers took to the religion, adopting the Arabic title "sultan", either because of sincere conversion or because they took a shrewd view of the advantages to be gained by embracing this international faith. On a cultural level, too, Islam had its attractions – its concepts of equality before Allah freed people from the Hindu caste system that had dominated parts of the region. Even after the Melaka Sultanate fell in 1511, the hold of Islam was strengthened by the migration of Muslim merchants to Brunei.

The first wave of Islamic missionaries were mostly **Sufis**, representing the mystical and generally more liberal wing of Islam. In the region Sufism absorbed some animist and Hindu beliefs, including the tradition of pluralist deity worship. However, Sufism's influence declined in the early nineteenth century when the puritanical **Wahhabi** sect of mainstream **Sunni** Islam captured Mecca. The return to the Koran's basic teachings became identified with a more militant approach, leading to jihads in Kedah, Kelantan and Terengganu against the Malay rulers' Siamese overlords and, subsequently, the British.

Islam in Malaysia and Singapore today is a mixture of Sunni and Sufi elements, and its adherents are still largely comprised of Malays, though a minority of the Indian community is Muslim, too. While Islam as practised locally is relatively liberal, the trend away from tacit secularism that has swept the Muslim world in the last two or three decades, has not left the two countries untouched. There's now a better understanding of Islam's tenets – and thus better compliance with them – among Muslims in both countries.

Of course, this drift has its social and political dimensions. In Malaysia, with its history of sometimes awkward race relations, Islam is something of a badge of identity for the Malays; it's significant that the Malaysian **constitution** practically regards being Malay as equivalent to being Muslim. Thus Malaysia has seen an increase in religious programming on TV and in state spending on often ostentatious new mosques, while even in consumerist Singapore, the Malay minority is becoming more actively engaged in religion. Malaysia's religious establishment has also become more vocal, making proclamations to discourage Muslims from practising yoga (because of its supposed Hindu origins) and Muslim women from wearing short hair and trousers (because this would apparently encourage lesbianism), though such decrees have no legal weight. All of this said, for most Muslims in Malaysia and Singapore, Islam remains a matter not of dogma but of blending a personal interpretation of the religion with living in a multifaith community.

Islam and the law

One striking way in which Islam influences day-to-day affairs is that in certain areas, Muslim and non-Muslim citizens are subject to different **laws**. In Malaysia, for example, a Muslim man may avail himself of the Islamic provision for a man to take up to four wives, if certain criteria are met, but non-Muslim men are subject to the usual injunctions against bigamy and polygamy. Likewise, while it would be acceptable for an unmarried couple to share a hotel room if neither person is Muslim, it would be illegal (an act known as **khalwat**) if both were Muslim; if only one of them were Muslim, only that person would be committing an illegal act. This legal divide is reflected in the judicial systems of both Malaysia and Singapore, in which **syariah** (sharia) courts interpreting Islamic law exist alongside courts and laws derived from the British legal system.

Both Malaysia and Singapore limit Islamic jurisprudence to matters concerning the family and certain types of behaviour deemed transgressions against Islam, such as *khalwat*, or for a Muslim to consume alcohol in public. In this regard, the *syariah* courts are in many ways subservient to the secular legal framework. This also means the harsher aspects of Islamic justice, such as stoning or the cutting off of a thief's hand, are not deemed permissible; an attempt in the 1990s by the state government of Kelantan, run by the Islamist opposition PAS party, to introduce them within the state was thwarted by Malaysia's federal government. The Islamic standard of proof in a case concerning rape – requiring the victim to be able to produce four witnesses – also does not apply, since rape cases are tried within the secular system.

However, the two juridical systems are experiencing a sort of territorial dispute in the important area of **religious conversion**. It's very difficult for Malaysian Muslims to convert out of Islam as the secular courts are unwilling to uphold their choice without the involvement of the *syariah* court, which might refuse permission or, worse, wish to punish them as apostates. In this Catch-22 situation, any Muslims who take up a new faith or no faith at all can never make their choice official, and for the most part simply keep mum. Controversy has also arisen when one person in a marriage converts to Islam and then wants to use Islamic law to divorce the spouse or change the registered religion of their children, for example. The roles of the two legal systems in these situations ought to be clarified as a matter of urgency, but there has been little progress.

THE BOMOH

An important link between animism and the Islam of today is provided by the Malay **bomoh**, a kind of shaman. While *bomoh*s keep a low profile in these times of greater Islamic orthodoxy – no *bomoh* operates out of an office, and there are no college courses to train *bomoh*s or listings of practitioners in the telephone directory – the fact is that every Malay community can still summon a *bomoh* when it's felt one is needed to cure disease, bring rain during droughts, exorcize spirits from a newly cleared plot before building work starts, or rein in the behaviour of a wayward spouse. A central part of the *bomoh*'s trade is recitation, often of sections of the Koran, while – like his Orang Asli counterparts – he uses techniques such as burning herbs to cure or ease pain and disease.

Mosques

In Malaysia, every town, village and hamlet has its mosque, while the capital city of each state hosts a grandiose **Masjid Negeri** (state mosque). You'll rarely see contemporary mosques varying from the standard square building topped by onion domes and minarets, though the oldest mosques reveal unusual Sumatran or other Southeast Asian influences. Two additional standard features can be found inside the prayer hall, namely the **mihrab**, a niche indicating the direction of Mecca, towards which believers face during prayers (the green *kiblat* arrow on the ceiling of most Malaysian hotel rooms fulfils the same function), and the **mimbar** (pulpit), used by the imam.

One of the five **pillars of Islam** is that the faithful should pray five times a day – at dawn (called the *subuh* prayer in Malay), midday (*zuhur*, or *jumaat* on a Friday), mid-afternoon (*asar*), dusk (*maghrib*) and mid-evening (*isyak*). On **Friday**, the day of the communal *jumaat* prayer, Muslims converge on their nearest mosque around noon to hear the imam deliver a *khutbah* (sermon); all employers allow Muslim staff a three-hour break for the purpose.

Chinese beliefs

The three different strands in Chinese belief ostensibly point in very different directions. **Confucianism** is a philosophy based on piety, loyalty, humanitarianism and familial devotion, a set of principles that permeate every aspect of Chinese life; **Buddhism** is a religion primarily concerned with the attainment of a state of personal enlightenment, nirvana; and **Taoism** propounds unity with nature as its chief tenet.

The Chinese are seldom doctrinaire; someone who claims to be Buddhist, Taoist or Confucianist may be in practice be a mixture of all three. **Ancestor worship** is also common, as is devotion to folk deities such as **Tua Peh** (or **Pek**) **Kong**, sometimes described as the God of Prosperity.

Chinese temples

The rules of **feng shui** are rigorously applied to the construction of Chinese temples, so that each building has a layout and orientation rendering it free from evil influences. Visitors wishing to cross the threshold of a temple have to step over a kerb intended to trip up evil spirits, and walk through doors flanked by fearsome door gods; fronting the doors may be two stone lions, providing yet another defence.

Temples are normally constructed around a framework of huge, lacquered timber beams, adorned with intricately carved warriors, animals and flowers. More figures are moulded onto outer walls, which are dotted with octagonal, hexagonal or round grille-worked windows. Larger temples typically consist of a front entrance hall opening onto a walled-in courtyard, beyond which is the hall of worship, where joss sticks are burned below images of the deities. The most striking element of a Chinese temple is often its **roof** – a grand, multitiered affair with low, overhanging eaves, the ridges alive with auspicious creatures such as dragons and phoenixes and, less often, with miniature scenes from traditional Chinese life and legend. In the temple grounds you'll see sizeable ovens, stuffed constantly with paper money, prayer books and other offerings; and possibly a **pagoda** – the presence of which is, once again, a defence against evil spirits. Temples linked to individual clans may also have an **ancestral hall** displaying ranks of upright **ancestral tablets**, each representing a forebear of a clan member.

Peoples

Largely because of their pivotal position on maritime trade routes between the Middle East, India and China, the present-day countries of Malaysia, Singapore and Brunei have always been a cultural melting pot. During the first millennium AD, Malays arrived from Sumatra and Indians from India and Sri Lanka, while later the Chinese migrated from mainland China and Hainan Island. All these traders and settlers arrived to find that the region already held a gamut of indigenous tribes, thought to have migrated around 50,000 years ago from the Philippines, then connected by a land bridge to Borneo and Southeast Asia. The indigenous tribes who still live on the Peninsula are known as the Orang Asli, Malay for "the original people".

Original people they may have been, but their descendants now form a minority of the overall populations of the three countries. Over the last 150 years a massive influx of Chinese and Indian immigrants, escaping poverty, war and revolution, has swelled the population of **Malaysia**, which now stands at over 25 million. Just over half are Malays, while the Chinese make up nearly a quarter of the population, the Indians eight percent, and the various indigenous groups just over a tenth.

Brunei's population of around 380,000 is heavily dominated by Malays, with minorities of Chinese, Indians and indigenous peoples. In **Singapore**, only tiny numbers of indigenes were left on the island when Raffles arrived. They have no modern-day presence in the state, where around three-quarters of the 4.6-million-strong population are of Chinese extraction, around fourteen percent are Malay, and nearly nine percent Indian.

The Malays

The **Malays** are believed to have originated from the meeting of Mainland Southeast Asian, Taiwanese and even Papuan groups over the last 5000 years. Also known as Orang Laut (sea people), they sustained an economy built around fishing, boat-building and, in some communities, piracy. The growth in power of the Malay sultanates from the fifteenth century onwards – coinciding with the arrival of Islam – established Malays as a force to be reckoned with in the Malay Peninsula and Borneo. They developed an aristocratic tradition, courtly rituals and a social hierarchy that have a continued influence today. The rulers of Malaysia's states still wield great influence, reflected in the fact that they elect one of their number to hold the post of Yang di-Pertuan Agong, a pre-eminent sultan who holds the title for a five-year term. Although a purely ceremonial position, the *agong* is seen as the ultimate guardian of Malay Muslim culture and, despite recent legislation to reduce his powers, is still considered to be above the law. The situation is even more pronounced in **Brunei**, to which many Muslim Malay traders fled after the fall of Melaka to the Portuguese in 1511. There, the sultan remains the supreme ruler (as his descendants have been, on and off, for over five hundred years).

Even though Malays have been Muslims since the fifteenth century, the region as a whole is not fundamentalist in character. Only in Brunei is alcohol banned, for instance. Perhaps the most significant recent development affecting Malays in Malaysia has been the introduction of the **bumiputra** policy (see box, p.566).

The Chinese and Straits Chinese

Although **Chinese traders** began visiting the region in the seventh century, the first significant community established itself in Melaka in the fifteenth century. However, the ancestors of most of the Chinese now living in Malaysia – ethnic Hakka, and migrants from Teochew (Chaozhou) and Hokkien (Fujian) – emigrated from southeastern China during the nineteenth century to work in the burgeoning tin-mining industry and, later, rubber and oil plantations. A large number came as labourers, but they swiftly graduated to shopkeeping and business ventures, both in established towns like Melaka and fast-expanding centres like KL, Penang and Kuching. Chinatowns developed throughout the region, even in Malay strongholds like Kota Bharu and Kuala Terengganu, while **Chinese traditions**, religious festivities, theatre and music became an integral part of a wider multiracial culture. On the political level, the Malaysian Chinese are well represented in parliament and occupy around a quarter of current ministerial positions. By way of contrast, **Chinese Bruneians** are not automatically classed as citizens and suffer significant discrimination at the hands of the majority Malay population. **Singapore**'s nineteenth-century trade boom drew many Cantonese, Teochew, Hokkien and Hakka traders and labourers, who established a Chinatown on the south bank of the Singapore River. Today, the Chinese are the most economically successful racial group in Singapore.

One physical reminder of the Chinese presence in major cities is the presence of **kongsi** (literally "company") and **clan halls** (also called clan houses or associations). Each once functioned like a clan or regional club, providing help and protection for newly arrived migrants, who naturally tended to band together with others from the same part of China. At times they could also be a focus for community rivalry, as in the case of the Penang riots (see p.144). Many clan halls are excellent examples of traditional southern Chinese architecture, incorporating courtyards, shrines and sometimes living quarters.

THE BABA-NYONYAS

The **Baba-Nyonyas** are a Chinese subgroup with deep roots in the Malay Peninsula and a distinctive hybrid culture. It's often glibly said that they are the product of Chinese/Malay intermarriage, though this ignores the practical difficulties of marrying into a Muslim family without converting to Islam. What's more likely is that male migrants, arriving from China from at least the sixteenth century onwards, married local women, some Malay, others from the region's various communities such as Orang Asli or ethnic Thais. Eventually their descendants became a community in their own right – the menfolk known as **Babas**, the women **Nyonyas** – although confusingly the terms **Straits Chinese** and **Peranakan** are also used for them as a whole (Peranakan can also refer to other mixed-race groups, such as the Chitties of Melaka).

The Baba-Nyonyas clung on to some aspects of Chinese culture while absorbing influences from the Peninsula, most notably in terms of their dress – Nyonyas wore beautiful Malay-style batik-print clothes – and food (see p.39), but also in their language: many spoke Chinese dialects, notably Hokkien, but they also had their own Malay dialect. With the arrival of the British, they mastered English too, and this was to prove the foundation for a golden era when many Baba-Nyonyas became immensely wealthy. They were the bridge between the Western world and the *sinkeh*, the newly arrived Chinese migrants, who were eager to succeed. Many *sinkeh* married Nyonyas and the resulting family businesses flourished; choice residential areas such as Singapore's Katong were packed with Peranakan mansions.

It wasn't to last. In the interwar years, the British loosened the immigration rules to allow migrants to bring their wives with them, and some members of an older generation of migrants were, by then, giving their children a Western education. The Baba-Nyonyas became far less useful to the new blood from China and were simply outnumbered by them. They were also viewed with disdain by the mainstream community as being not properly Chinese. The Baba-Nyonya identity has now been largely subsumed into a wider Chinese one, though in recent decades their culture has at least been showcased in museums and their culinary heritage, at least, shows no signs of going away.

The Indians

The second largest non-*bumiputra* group in Malaysia, the **Indians**, first arrived as traders more than two thousand years ago, although few settled; only in the early fifteenth century did a small community of Indians (from present-day Tamil Nadu and Sri Lanka) become based in Melaka. Like the majority of Chinese, however, the first large wave of Indians – Tamil labourers – arrived as indentured workers in the nineteenth century, to build the roads and rail lines and work on the European-run rubber estates. An embryonic entrepreneurial class from North India soon followed, and set up businesses in Penang and Singapore; mostly Muslim, these merchants and traders found it easier to assimilate themselves within the existing Malay community than did the Hindu Tamils.

Although Indians comprise under a tenth of the populations of Malaysia and Singapore, their impact is widely felt. The Hindu festival of Thaipusam is celebrated annually at KL's Batu Caves by upwards of a million people (with smaller but still significant celebrations in Singapore and Penang); the festival of Deepavali is a national holiday; and Indians dominate certain professional areas like medicine and law. And then, of course, there's the food – very few Malaysians these days could do without a daily dose of *roti canai*, so much so that this Indian snack has been virtually appropriated by Malay and Chinese cafés and hawkers.

The Orang Asli

Most of the **Orang Asli** – the indigenous peoples of Peninsular Malaysia – belong to three distinct groups, within which various tribes are related by geography, language or physiological features. It's difficult to witness much of Orang Asli life as they largely live off the beaten track, though touristed communities at Taman Negara and the Cameron Highlands can be visited. To learn more about the disappearing Asli culture, the best stop is KL's Orang Asli Museum (see p.106).

Senoi

The largest group, the **Senoi** (the Asli word for "person"), number about forty thousand. They live in the large, still predominantly forested interior, within the states of Perak, Pahang and Kelantan, and divide into two main tribes, the Semiar and the Temiar. These still adhere to a traditional lifestyle, following animist customs in marriage ceremonies and burial rites. On the whole they follow the practice of shifting cultivation (a regular rotation of jungle clearance and crop planting), although government resettlement drives have persuaded many to settle and farm just one area.

Semang

The two thousand or so **Semang** live in the northern areas of the Peninsula. They comprise six distinct, if small, tribes, related to each other in appearance – most are dark-skinned and curly-haired – and traditionally shared a nomadic, hunter-gatherer lifestyle. However, most Semang nowadays live in settled communities and work within the cash economy, either as labourers or selling jungle produce in markets. Perhaps the most frequently seen Semang tribe are the Batek, who live in and around Taman Negara.

Aboriginals

The third group, the so-called **Aboriginal Malays**, live in an area roughly south of the Kuala Lumpur–Kuantan road. Some tribes in this category, like the Jakun and the Semelais who live around the lakes of the southern interior, vigorously retain their animist religion and artistic traditions despite living in permanent villages near Malay communities, and working within the regular economy.

Others

One of Malaysia's other Orang Asli tribes, the Lanoh in Perak are sometimes regarded as Semang, their language is closer to that of the Temiar. Another group, the semi-nomadic Che Wong, of whom just a few hundred survive on the slopes of Gunung Benom in central Pahang, still depend on foraging to survive, and live in temporary huts made from bamboo and rattan. Two more groups, the Jah Hut of Pahang and the Mah Meri of Selangor, are particularly fine carvers, and it's possible to buy their sculptures at regional craft shops.

Indigenous Sarawak: the Dayak

In direct contrast to the Peninsula, indigenous groups make up a larger chunk of the population in **Sarawak**, which currently stands at two million. Although the Chinese comprise 29 percent of the state's population and the Malays and Indians around 24 percent together, the remaining 47 percent are made up of various indigenous **Dyak** groups – a word derived from the Malay for "upcountry". Certain general aspects of their culture – for instance, the importance of bronze drums and reburial ceremonies – might indicate that the Dyak arrived in the region from mainland Southeast Asia around 2000 years ago.

The largest Dyak groups are the Iban, Bidayuh, Melanau, Kayan, Kenyah, Kelabit and Penan tribes. They have very distinct cultures as well as a few commonalities. Many live in **longhouses** along the rivers or on hillsides in the mountainous interior, and maintain a proud cultural legacy that draws on animist religion, arts and crafts production and jungle skills.

The Iban

The **Iban** (see p.339) make up nearly thirty percent of Sarawak's population. Originating hundreds of miles south of present-day Sarawak, in the Kapuas Valley in Kalimantan, the Iban migrated north in the sixteenth century, and came into conflict over the next two hundred years with the Kayan and Kenyah tribes and, later, the British. Nowadays, Iban longhouse communities are found in the Batang Ai river system in the southwest and along Batang Rajang and tributaries. These communities are quite accessible, their inhabitants always hospitable and keen to demonstrate such aspects of their culture as traditional dance and textile weaving. In their time, the Iban were infamous head-hunters – some longhouses are still decorated with heads taken in battle long ago.

The Bidayuh

Unlike most Dyak groups, the **Bidayuh** traditionally lived away from the rivers, building their longhouse on the sides of hills. Culturally, the most southerly of Sarawak's indigenous groups are similar to the Iban, although in temperament they are much milder and less gregarious, keeping themselves to themselves in their inaccessible homes on Sarawak's mountainous southern border with Kalimantan.

The Melanau and Kelabit

The **Melanau** are a coastal people, living north of Kuching in a region dominated by mangrove swamps. Many Melanau, however, now live in towns, preferring the kampung-style houses of the Malays to the elegant longhouses of the past. They are expert fishermen and cultivate sago as an alternative to rice. The **Kelabit** people live on the highland plateau separating north Sarawak from Kalimantan. Like the Iban, they live in longhouses and maintain a traditional lifestyle, but differ from some other groups in being Christian.

The Penan

The semi-nomadic **Penan** traditionally live in temporary lean-tos or small huts in the upper Rejang and Limbang areas of Sarawak. They rely, like some Orang Asli groups in the Peninsula, on hunting and gathering and collecting jungle produce for sale in local markets. In recent years, however, the state government has tried to resettle the Penan in small villages – a controversial policy not entirely unconnected with the advance of logging in traditional Penan land.

The Kenyah and Kayan

Most of the other groups in Sarawak fall into the all-embracing ethnic classification of **Orang Ulu** (people of the interior), who inhabit remote inland areas, further north than the Iban, along the upper Rajang, Balui and Linau rivers. The most numerous, the **Kayan** and the **Kenyah**, are closely related and in the past often teamed up to defend their lands from the invading Iban. But they also have much in common with their traditional enemy, since they are longhouse-dwellers, animists and shifting cultivators.

Indigenous Sabah

Sabah has a population of around 2.6 million, made up of more than thirty distinct racial groups, between them speaking over eighty different dialects. The **Dusun** account for around a third of the population. Traditionally agriculturists (the word *Dusun* means "orchard"), various Dusun subgroups inhabit the western coastal plains and the interior. These days they are known generically as **Kadazan/Dusun**, although strictly speaking "Kadazan" refers only to the Dusun of Penampang. Other Dusun branches include the **Lotud** of Tuaran and the **Rungus** of the Kudat Peninsula, whose convex longhouses are all that remain of the Dusun's longhouse tradition. Although most Dusun are now Christians, remnants of their animist past are still evident, most obviously in the harvest festival, or *pesta kaamatan*, when their *bobohizans*, or priestesses, perform rituals to honour the *bambaazon*, or rice spirit.

The mainly Muslim **Bajau** tribe, who drifted over from the southern Philippines some two hundred years ago, now constitute Sabah's second largest ethnic group, accounting for around ten percent of the population. Their penchant for piracy quickly earned them the sobriquet "sea gypsies", though nowadays they are agriculturalists and fishermen, noted for their horsemanship and buffalo rearing. The Bajau live in the northwest of Sabah and annually appear on horseback at Kota Belud's market (see p.411).

Sabah's third sizeable tribe, the **Murut**, inhabit the area between Keningau and the Sarawak border, in the southwest. Their name means "hill people", though they prefer to be known by their individual tribal names, such as Timugon, Tagal and Nabai. The Murut farm rice and cassava by a system of shifting cultivation; their head-hunting days are over, but they retain other cultural traditions, such as constructing brightly adorned grave huts to house the graves and belongings of the dead.

Development and the environment

Malaysia is gradually becoming more environmentally friendly, largely as a result of well-organized and scientifically persuasive organizations within the country, rather than pressures from outside, but the pace of change is slow and huge problems remain. Logging and large-scale development projects, like dams, hog the spotlight, and remain a prime focus for NGOs, but just as pressing are concerns over oil-palm cultivation and wetlands erosion, as well as the impact of environmental degradation on the lifestyles of indigenous groups.

As a small, highly built-up island, **Singapore** has few wild areas left to spoil. Nevertheless, the country maintains an area of rainforest around its central reservoirs as well as other nature reserves, such the wetland area at Sungai Buloh. Singapore's very compactness dictates that it has to be vigilant on matters of pollution, and thus the island has strict laws on waste emissions and even an island, Pulau Semakau, created entirely out of ash from incinerated refuse.

The tiny sultanate of **Brunei** has interfered least with its forest, but then, its enormous oil wealth and tiny population ensure it has little need to.

Logging and deforestation

The **sustainable exploitation** of forest products by the indigenous population has always played a vital part in the domestic and export economy of the region – for almost two thousand years, ethnic tribes have bartered products like rattan, wild rubber and forest plants with foreign traders.

Although blamed for much of the deforestation in Sarawak and Sabah, the bulk of indigenous agricultural activity occurs in secondary rather than primary (untouched) forest. Indeed, environmental groups believe that only around one hundred square kilometres of primary forest – a tiny proportion compared to the haul by commercial timber companies – is cleared by the indigenous groups annually. **Logging**, despite having slowed, is still a cause of huge grievances among the indigenous peoples of east Malaysia.

The Peninsula

Peninsular Malaysia's pre-independence economy was not as reliant on timber revenues as those of Sabah and Sarawak. Although one sixth of the region's 120,000 square kilometres of forest, predominantly in Johor, Perak and Negeri Sembilan states, had been cut down by 1957, most of the logging had been done gradually and on a small, localized scale. As in Sabah, it was the demand for rail sleepers during the 1920s' expansion of the Malayan train network that first attracted the commercial logging companies. Wide-scale clearing and conversion to rubber and oil-palm plantations in the more remote areas of Pahang, Perlis, Kedah and Terengganu intensified in the 1960s. By the end of the 1970s, more efficient extraction methods, coupled with a massive increase in foreign investment in the logging industry, had led to over forty percent of the Peninsula's remaining forests being either cleared for plantation purposes or partially logged.

Logging in west Malaysia has, however, slowed significantly in the last few decades, with environmental impact assessments being carried out before logging is allowed to proceed. One positive piece of legislation is the creation, more than a century ago, of

Permanent Forest Reserves, though it doesn't involve a watertight system: even if a parcel of land is labelled a reserve, it can still be partially logged. But at least now the work must be carried out in a sustainable manner integrating checks and impact assessments.

Sabah

Commercial logging began in **Sabah** in the late nineteenth century, when the British Borneo Trading and Planting Company started to extract timber for use as railway sleepers in China. By World War II, the larger **British Borneo Timber Company** (BBTC) was primarily responsible for the extraction of five million cubic metres of rainforest timber, and Sandakan became one of the world's main timber ports. Areas were logged indiscriminately, and the indigenous tribal groups who lived there were brought into the economic system to work on the rubber and tobacco plantations that replaced the forests.

By the early 1960s, timber had accelerated past rubber as the region's main produce; by 1970, nearly thirty percent of Sabah's forests had been logged, accounting for over seventy percent of exports. Nowadays much of the logged land is used for oil-palm cultivation (see opposite).

Sarawak

In many ways **Sarawak** seems to exemplify Malaysia's environmental policies at their worst. It's here that all the problems come into sharp focus – the forest is either being degraded by commercial logging or felled altogether for oil-palm cultivation, in the process ruining the ancestral lands of native peoples.

Having accelerated in northern Sarawak under Vyner Brooke during the 1930s, timber extraction became a major revenue earner for the state during its short postwar period as a Crown Colony and after independence as part of Malaysia. Accurate figures as to the current state of Sarawak's rainforest are notoriously hard to come by, though perhaps less than thirty percent of the primary forest cover remains, and even that can be so fragmented that it's practically useless from a wildlife conservation point of view.

In principle the indigenous peoples have so-called **native customary rights** over their ancestral forest, and can use them in court to block the government granting logging or other concessions. However, the system is fraught with difficulty, partly because such rights are based on incomplete colonial-era data as to where the various groups once lived. Besides, even where the tribes can establish their rights, they may not wish to exercise them – they may instead be more interested in what the logging companies can offer, such as new roads and schools, plus jobs in the cash economy.

Of course, logging, unlike clearing land for oil palm, does not mean the wholesale destruction of the forest: the logging companies are after hardwood trees, which they should try to remove as cleanly as possible. In practice felling may involve collateral damage to other trees, and it's notable that none of the Sarawak timber concerns has been certified under the Malaysian Timber Certification Scheme (MTCS) to indicate that they manage forests responsibly.

Meanwhile the state continues to trumpet its target of gazetting 10,000 square kilometres (eight percent of Sarawak's land area) as national parks or wildlife reserves that are off-limits to the public, plus a further 60,000 square kilometres as permanent forest reserve. Impressive though these figures may sound, it's notable that many of the newer national parks scarcely function as such, since they are sited in inaccessible areas and have barely any facilities. This haphazard creation of parks might be thought to augment their effectiveness as conservation areas, but there is no such fringe benefit – policing to stop logging or poaching is minimal. It could be argued that the parks are, in fact, a smokescreen for what's happening elsewhere in Sarawak – for example,

OIL-PALM CULTIVATION IN MALAYSIA

Malaysia is the world's biggest producer of **oil palm**, a valuable economic crop that's used as a biofuel and in food products. The industry has been a massive stimulus for employment – over half a million people are now involved in its production, and many more in various subsidiary industries. Sabah, Malaysia's poorest state, is benefiting in particular. Furthermore, land surrounding the cultivation areas has been subject to improved infrastructure: public services such as schools and hospitals have been developed, while roads are built and telecommunication networks established.

Yet the industry's speedy proliferation has had a harmful impact on the environment: critics say the land cleared for the agro-crop contributes significantly to global warming, notably greenhouse gas emissions. Palm trees are increasingly replacing native tropical rainforest and thus threatening the survival of many animal species, including the orang-utan. Communities may also have their food and water supplies cut off or contaminated, while their cash-crop farms – fruit trees and rubber plantations – are wiped out. Meanwhile, social conflict is triggered between the planters and local residents who are forced off their land.

And the industry keeps on growing: the oil's use as an alternative, "clean" biofuel has meant that demand is kept stable. While the negative impacts are ongoing, at least on some level there's increased awareness of the substantial environmental impact. The recognition is growing that a stronger sustainability policy is needed to safeguard Malaysia's rainforests and all who depend on them.

the intensive logging of the Baram River basin in the north, in areas around the Kelabit Highlands and Gunung Mulu National Park. Meanwhile land also continues to be cleared for oil palm, with a target of having 20,000 square kilometres under cultivation by 2015.

Dam-building is another big issue on the Sarawak environmental agenda. The prime example is the massive Bakun dam project, which will generate electricity for no obvious market – and is only the first in a series of dams scheduled to be built in the coming years.

While the picture in Sarawak may appear bleak, there are a few reasons for optimism: some logging companies are beginning to have their practices assessed as a first step towards gaining MTCS certification, and there is genuine commitment among some government biodiversity managers to try to reform the state's policies.

Air pollution

For the inhabitants of Peninsular Malaysia and Singapore, the environmental issue that has affected them most has not been forest depletion or land rights, but **air pollution**, particularly dust and smoke caused by forest fires – dubbed "the haze" by the local media. During a severe, prolonged episode in 1997–98, the haze was so bad that motorists were warned to keep their distance from one another, and respiratory illnesses rose alarmingly. Visibility in the Straits of Melaka, one of the world's busiest shipping routes, also dropped dramatically.

The Malaysian government originally suggested that the agricultural methods of the indigenous peoples – which involve the burning of excess vegetation at the end of growing cycles – were to blame. However, further research indicated that small longhouse communities could not have caused such extensive fires. The haze is generally blamed on Indonesian plantation companies using fire to clear large areas of forest to facilitate the planting of crops such as oil palm and acacia. The Indonesian government does not appear to have been able to change the habits of its forest developers, given that the 1997 catastrophe has been repeated, albeit to a much lesser extent, several times since, and the haze must be regarded as a threat that can plague a visit to Malaysia and Singapore with little warning.

The threat to traditional lifestyles

Although large-scale projects such as the Bakun Dam are the most prevalent threat to indigenous tribes' way of life, **logging**, whether licensed or illicit, represents a constant challenge. The effect on wildlife has an obvious impact on communities' ability to hunt, but the failure to respect native customary rights has also led to the desecration of burial places and sections of rivers used for fishing – notably in the forests around Bintulu, Belaga and Limbang. In southwest Sarawak, the Iban have had some success in challenging logging, however: a historic court case in 2001, Rumah Nor v. Borneo Pulp and Paper, led to a ruling in favour of the longhouse community, after the community's map was accepted as court evidence for ownership of land. Emboldened by this ruling, several communities have filed petitions, but in many cases the courts have not revoked the state-awarded logging concessions.

The **Penan** have arguably been the worst hit by logging, as their traditionally semi-nomadic lifestyle makes it hard for their land rights to be defined and recognized. In addition, the Sarawak state government's avowed policy since the mid-1980s has been to bring the Penan into what it views as the development process (as applied to the more settled Dyak and Orang Ulu groups for many decades), urging them to move to permanent longhouses, work in the cash economy and send their children to school. Very often, the Penan receive no notice that their land has been earmarked for logging until extraction actually begins – examples in remote areas around Belaga have been documented by the environmental group **Sahabat Alam Malaysia** (SAM). Reports from one of the remaining semi-nomadic Penan communities situated in Sarawak's Ulu Baram area reveal that loggers continue to penetrate their last reserves illegally.

Wildlife

Set well inside the tropics and comprising everything from pristine ocean to coastal mangroves, lowland rainforest and mountain moorland, the range of habitats on the Malay Peninsula and Borneo is only matched by the diversity of its fauna – over 700 species of birds and more than 200 kinds of mammals. You don't have to be an ardent nature-spotter to appreciate this: even a brief visit to any of the region's national parks – or just the FRIM forestry reserve on Kuala Lumpur's outskirts – will put you face to face with clouds of butterflies, troops of monkeys, and an incessant background orchestra of insect noise.

Despite being separated by the South China Sea, the wildlife and plant communities of the Peninsula and east Malaysia are similar, since the two were joined by a land bridge until after the last Ice Age – though the various regional wildlife reserves offer a range of experiences. On Peninsular Malaysia, **Taman Negara** provides full-on tropical jungle, a good place to see large mammals; **Fraser's Hill**, on the other hand, is better known for its birdlife. Sabah's **Sungai Kinabatangan** and **Bako National Park** in Sarawak are good for estuarine and river forest creatures, while shallow lakes at Sarawak's **Loagan Bunut National Park** are home to many different bird species, as is Brunei's **Ulu Temburong National Park**.

Even though it's now predominantly urban, with little plant or animal life, **Singapore** still holds several remnants of its verdant tropical past, particularly at **Bukit Timah Nature Reserve**, the splendidly manicured Botanic Gardens, and the **Sungai Buloh Nature Wetland Reserve** in the far north of the island. Day-trippers to Pulau Ubin, just off Singapore and easily accessible by boat from the Changi Point ferry terminal, can also see the mangrove flats of **Chek Jawa**.

Poaching and habitation loss due to deforestation mean that the future of the region's wildlife is far from assured. Fortunately, many **not-for-profit organizations**, such as WWF Malaysia (Ⓦwwfmalaysia.org), are campaigning to preserve the species and terrains most under threat.

FORESTS

Coastal mud flats are usually protected by **mangroves**, a diverse family of trees that thrive in brackish water and tend to support themselves on a platform of elevated roots that form an impenetrable barrier to exploration – and refuge for small creatures such as mudskippers, crabs and young fish.

Moving inland, the region's lowland forests are thick with **dipterocarps** (meaning "two-winged fruit"), a diverse group of trees often prized for timber. Other forest species include several palm trees (one of which, the spiky, vine-like rattan palm, is used to make cane furniture and the like); liana vines; massive fig trees (many of which support their huge trunks with buttress roots); 50m-tall *tualang*, Southeast Asia's tallest tree; and wild **fruit trees**, such as durian, mango, guava and rambutan. You'll seldom see flowers though (except fallen petals); so little light reaches the forest floor that trees and climbing plants only flower high up in the canopy. To get around this, a whole group of small plants have become epiphytes – using the trees as perches to get nearer the sunlight – including orchids and a wide range of small ferns, which sometimes cover the upper surface of larger branches.

Montane forest predominates above 1000m, comprising mainly oak and evergreen native conifers with a shrub layer of bamboo and dwarf palm. Above 1500m is **cloud forest**, where trees are often cloaked by swirling mist, and the stunted, damp boughs bear thick growths of mosses and ferns; at elevations of over 1700m, you'll find miniature montane forest of rhododendrons, the boughs heavily laden with dripping mosses, pitcher plants and colourful orchids.

Mammals

Big mammals are exciting to encounter in the wild, and several are unique to the region. Asian **elephant** are found both in Peninsular Malaysia and Borneo, though probably the best chance to see them is at Taman Negara, which is also good for **tapir** – a pony-sized relative of the rhino, with a black-and-white body and vestigial trunk.

Other mammals you might encounter include **clouded leopards** – a beautifully marked cat species with a pattern of cloud-like markings on the sides of the body – spotted **leopard cat** (around the size of a large domestic cat), and nocturnal **civet**, tree-dwelling creatures that look like a cross between a cat and a weasel. Don't get your hopes up about seeing **tigers**, now thought to number no more than 500 in the Peninsula, or reclusive **sun bears**, marked with a white crescent across their chest – though you do occasionally see their deep claw grooves in tree bark.

Another possibility in undisturbed forest on the Peninsula are *seladang* or *gaur*, a giant type of wild cattle with white leg patches, which look like ankle socks. There are also several species of **deer**: the larger *sambar*; the *kijang* or barking deer, the size of a roe deer; and the lesser and greater mouse deer.

Primates (monkeys and gibbons) are found throughout the Peninsula and Borneo. Most common are the long-tailed and pig-tailed **macaques**, which come to the ground to feed, the latter identified by its shorter tail, brown fur and pinkish-brown face. There are dusky and spectacled **langurs** too, elegant grey monkeys with white patterns that spend most of their time up in the trees – they're also known as leaf-monkeys, after their diet. The region's several gibbon species are entirely arboreal, with specially elongated forearms that allow them to swing athletically through the canopy – they tend to have very loud, wailing calls too, easily recognized. Big-nosed, pot-bellied proboscis monkeys – and Southeast Asia's sole ape, the **orang-utan** (see box, p.428) – are found only in Borneo.

One of the most unusual smaller mammals to keep eyes peeled for is the **colugo**, a bizarre forest creature that looks like a cross between a fruit bat and a squirrel. It spends the day sleeping in tree hollows, and the night gliding through the forest looking for flowers and fruits.

Birds

One fairly common bird that epitomizes the entire Malay region – and is even a totem to some Dyak tribes – is the **hornbill**. Its huge size, bold black-and-white markings, large curved beak and noisy, swooshing flight make it easily identifiable, even in thick jungle. Other forest birds include **trogons** (brightly coloured, mid-storey birds); green **fruit pigeons** – strongly coloured but strangely hard to see; **bulbuls**, vocal, fruit-eating

---

HOW TO FIND WILDLIFE

Tropical wildlife is most active at dawn and dusk, though some larger mammals forage through the night. It's surprising how even large animals can be fairly invisible, especially in forest, where low light and random vegetation can break up their otherwise recognizable outlines. Here are some tips for finding creatures, without doing anything dangerous – such as turning over logs to look for snakes:

Listen – aside from calls, many creatures make distinctive noises as they move, from the raucous crashing of active monkey troops, to staccato rustlings of mice and lizards in leaf litter.

Look – many smaller creatures spend the day hidden under leaves and in hollows and crevices in tree trunks. At night, insects – and insect-eating animals – are attracted to lights; check ranger offices, chalets and huts around national park headquarters.

Signs – footprints, scarred bark, mud wallows and flowers, fruit and torn twigs strewn along paths are all signs of animals, some of which might be feeding in the canopy above you.

Eyeshine – at night, use a torch held at or above eye level to reflect eyeshine, either from invertebrates such as crickets and spiders, or nocturnal mammals – anything from tapir to deer, mice and civets.

HORNBILLS

You should have little difficulty in identifying **hornbills**: they are large, black-and-white birds with disproportionately huge bills (often bent downwards), topped with an ornamental **casque** – a generally hollow structure attached to the upper mandible. The function of the casque is unknown; it may play a role in attracting a mate and courtship ceremonies. Ten of the world's 46 species of hornbill are found in Malaysia, many of them endangered or present only in small, isolated populations.

One of the smallest and most commonly seen species, the **pied hornbill**, can be identified by its white abdomen and tail, and white wingtips in flight. Reaching only 75cm in length, it may even be spotted in leafy suburban areas. Also widely seen, the **black hornbill** is only slightly larger and black, save for the white tips of the outer tail feathers (some individuals also show a white patch behind the eye).

Larger species include the **helmeted hornbill** and the **rhinoceros hornbill**, both over 120cm in length, mainly black, but with white tails and bellies. Although it's the symbol of Sarawak, the rhinoceros hornbill is rarely seen there or elsewhere; it has a bright orange rhino-horn-shaped casque, whereas the helmeted hornbill has a bright red head, neck and helmet-shaped casque. The call of the helmeted hornbill is notable for being a remarkable series of "took" notes that start slowly and accelerate to a cackling crescendo.

birds that often flock to feed; **minivets**, slender birds with long, graduated tails and white, yellow or red bands in the wings; and round-winged **babblers**.

Plump and brilliantly coloured, **pitas** are notoriously shy and difficult to approach, though sometimes easily found thanks to their noisy progress through leaf litter on the forest floor. Other ground-dwelling birds to look for include the shy **Malaysian peacock pheasant**, with a blue-green crest and distinctive "eye spots" along its back and long tail; the similar **fireback**; and the 1.7m-long **great argus pheasant**.

The most common birds of prey are kites, buzzards and, along the coast, fish eagles, very large white and grey birds with a wedge-shaped tail. In forest, you might encounter the **crested serpent eagle** and the **changeable hawk eagle**, often spotted soaring over gaps in the forest canopy.

Other species confined to tropical forests are **trogons**, of which five species are present at Taman Negara, and several species of **hornbill** – large, broad-winged, long-tailed forest birds, some of which have huge, almost outlandish bills.

A feature of montane forest bird flocks is the **mixed feeding flock**, which may contain many different species. These pass rapidly through an area of forest searching for insects as they go, and different observers are likely to register entirely different species in the same flock. Look for **racket-tailed drongo**, a black bird with long tail streamers; the **speckled piculet**, a small spotted woodpecker; and the **blue nuthatch**, a small species – blue-black in colour with a white throat and pale eye ring – which runs up and down tree trunks. Several species of brightly coloured **laughing thrushes**, thrush-sized birds that spend time foraging on the ground or in the understorey, also occur in these flocks.

Reptiles

Small lizards – mostly skinks – are probably the commonest **reptiles** in the region; you'll often hear their frantic scuffling among forest-floor leaf litter. Nocturnal geckos have sucker-like pads on their toes that enable them to run up walls (and even glass); they're often seen around lights, stalking any insects that settle nearby. On forest fringes, look for flying lizards, which at rest are small, bony, grey and unimpressive – until they unfold wings and glide between trees like paper darts. Fairly common, even in semi-rural parks, they're easily missed. Around water – and especially near popular picnic spots, where they can pick up scraps – you'll see heavily built **monitor lizards**, the largest of which can approach 2m.

RAFFLESIAS

The *Rafflesia* is a strange plant that parasitizes tree roots, and whose presence can only be detected when its rubbery flowers, up to a metre across, burst into bloom. Its full name, *Rafflesia arnoldii*, recalls its discovery in Sumatra in 1818 by Sir Stamford Raffles (see p.477) and his physician, the naturalist Dr Joseph Arnold, who collected a 7kg specimen and sent a description of it to the Royal Society in London. The blooms, which are the world's largest and stink of rotting meat, are pollinated by carrion flies. Each flower's central "bowl" holds around 7 litres of nectar, while the petals, as Raffles recorded, "are of a brick-red with numerous pustular spots of a lighter colour. The whole substance of the flower is not less than half an inch thick, and of a firm fleshy consistence". The flower buds have been very much in demand by *bomohs* (Malay shamen) and their Chinese *sinseh* counterparts for use in medicine, particularly as an aid to accelerate the shrinking of a woman's womb after she has given birth. There's no specific flowering season, though in any one locality the plants seem to bloom at particular times of the year. As each flower lasts only a few days, however, there's a lot of luck involved in actually seeing one; national park rangers might be able to give likely times.

Snakes – Malaysia and Borneo hold over 200 species, including poisonous cobras, kraits and pit vipers – are another common but seldom-seen creature; they tend to move off as soon as they detect your footfalls. The largest, the reticulated python, is capable of growing 8m long, though you're much more likely to see either harmless **whip snakes** (which eat insects and lizards) and green **tree snakes**.

Saltwater **crocodiles** – the world's largest, heaviest reptile – are now virtually extinct throughout Peninsular Malaysia, though numbers are increasing in Borneo. Scuba divers might encounter several species of marine **turtle**, all of whose populations are declining (see p.252); certain beaches are also famous as turtle rookeries, where you might see adults coming ashore to lay eggs above the high tide line, or young turtles hatching, digging themselves out of the sand and heading for the sea en masse.

Books

Singapore and, to a lesser extent, Malaysia have healthy English-language publishing scenes, churning out books on local history, politics, society and culture, plus a modest amount of fiction. Besides the major bookshops listed throughout this Guide, a good source for specialist titles is the mail-order-only Select Books (𝕨 selectbooks.com.sg).

In the reviews that follow, books marked ★ are especially recommended, while o/p signifies a title is out of print. As per Chinese custom, surnames are given first for Chinese authors who don't have Christian names.

TRAVEL AND GENERAL INTEREST

★ *Encyclopedia of Malaysia*. A brilliantly produced series of tomes on different aspects of Malaysia, all beautifully illustrated and – not always the case with locally published material – competently edited. The volumes on the performing arts and architecture are particularly recommended. Available as individual volumes or as a set.

Isabella Bird *The Golden Chersonese*. Delightful epistolary romp through old Southeast Asia, penned by the intrepid Bird, whose adventures in the Malay states in 1879 ranged from strolls through Singapore's streets to elephant-back rides. A free download from various online libraries.

Tom Harrisson *Borneo Jungle* and *World Within*. Tough, eccentric British anthropologist Tom Harrisson spent much of his professional life studying Sarawak's Dyak groups, especially the Kayan, Kenyah and Punan, whom he greatly

admired. *Borneo Jungle* is a lively account of his first trip during the 1930s; *World Within* the story of how he parachuted into the highlands during World War II to organize Dyak resistance against the Japanese.

★ **Agnes Keith** *Land Below the Wind*. Bornean memories galore, in this charming account of expat life in prewar Sabah; Keith's true eye and assured voice produce a heartwarming picture of a way of life now long gone. Her naive sketches perfectly complement the childlike wonder of the prose.

Redmond O'Hanlon *Into The Heart of Borneo*. A hugely entertaining yarn recounting O'Hanlon's refreshingly amateurish romp through the jungle to a remote summit on the Sarawak/Kalimantan border, partnered by the English poet James Fenton.

HISTORY AND POLITICS

★ **Munshi Abdullah** *The Hikayat Abdullah*. Raffles' one-time clerk, Melaka-born Abdullah became diarist of some of the most formative years of Southeast Asian history; his firsthand account is crammed with illuminating vignettes and character portraits.

★ **Charles Allen** *Tales from the South China Seas*. Mosaic of the final colonial decades in Malaysia, Singapore and Brunei, formed from the personal reminiscences of former estate managers, teachers, nurses, engineers, soldiers, police chiefs and District Officers. Not nearly as pro-Raj as you might expect, and the drama of everyday lives, often in inhospitable conditions, is evinced with considerable pathos.

★ **Barbara Watson Andaya and Leonard Andaya** *The History of Malaysia*. Unlike more paternalistic histories penned by former colonists, this standard text on the region takes a more even-handed view of Malaysia, and finds time for cultural coverage, too.

Jim Baker *Crossroads: A Popular History of Malaysia and Singapore*. Not as authoritative as the Andayas' history, but bang up to date and thoroughly readable.

Victoria Glendinning *Raffles and the Golden Opportunity*. An enjoyable, thorough biography of Singapore's founder Sir Stamford Raffles, though occasionally bogged down in the details of his upbringing and domestic life.

★ **Patrick Keith** *Ousted*. Most of the largely young population of Malaysia and Singapore know little of the events that saw Singapore leaving the federation in 1965. And yet, as this excellent memoir by a former Malaysian government adviser demonstrates, many of the issues that led to the rift continue to shape both countries and their mutual ties today – Malaysia is still laden with ethnically based politics, while Singapore remains the fiefdom of the PAP.

Wendy Khadijah-Moore *Malaysia: A Pictorial History 1400–2003*. If you're going to produce coffee-table books on Malaysia's history, you could do a lot worse than this well-illustrated portable museum. Don't come to it expecting trenchant commentary, though: Anwar's arrest in the late 1990s, for instance, gets a mere couple of lines.

James Minchin *No Man Is An Island* (o/p). This

well-researched, and at times critical, study of Lee Kuan Yew refuses to kowtow to Singapore's ex-prime minister and is hence unavailable in Singapore itself.

Farish Noor *What Your Teacher Didn't Tell You*. An enjoyable series of lectures on subjects that remain awkward in Malaysia, from ethnicity to sexual attitudes.

Bob Reece *The White Rajahs of Sarawak*. A handsome coffee-table book about the extraordinary Brooke dynasty.

★**C.M. Turnbull** *A History of Modern Singapore 1819–2005*. Mary Turnbull had barely completed a major update of this standard work when she died in 2008, and what a fine legacy: the new edition is lucid, thorough, nearly always spot-on in its analysis and utterly readable.

WORLD WAR II

★**Russell Braddon** *The Naked Island*. Southeast Asia under the Japanese: Braddon's disturbing yet moving firsthand account of the POW camps of Malaya, Singapore and Siam salutes courage in the face of appalling conditions and treatment; worth scouring secondhand stores for.

★**Spencer Chapman** *The Jungle is Neutral*. This riveting firsthand account of being lost, and surviving, in the Malay jungle during World War II reads like a breathless novel.

★**Agnes Keith** *Three Came Home*. Pieced together from scraps of paper secreted in latrines and teddy bears, this is a remarkable story of survival in the face of Japanese attempts to eradicate the "proudery and arrogance" of the West in the World War II prison camps of Borneo.

Eric Lomax *The Railway Man*. Such is the power of Lomax's artless, redemptive and moving story of capture during the fall of Singapore, torture by the Japanese and reconciliation with his tormentor after fifty years, that many reviewers were moved to tears.

★**Lucy Lum** *The Thorn of Lion City*. You might expect a memoir of a wartime childhood in Singapore to be dominated by the savagery of the Japanese, but that's nothing compared to the torment inflicted on the author at the hands of her manipulative and violent mother and grandmother. That it's all told with zero artifice only makes it more compelling.

CULTURE AND SOCIETY

James Harding and Ahmad Sarji *P. Ramlee: The Bright Star*. An uncritical but enjoyable biography of the Malay singer, actor and director sometimes likened to Malaysia's Harry Belafonte. More importantly, it's a window onto what seems like a different era – though only half a century ago – when Singapore was the centre of the Malay entertainment universe, and when Malay life was, frankly, more carefree than today.

Michael Heppell *Iban Art: Sexual Selection and Severed Heads* This excellent illustrated volume provides a deeper coverage of Iban art than the pretty pictures might lead you to assume, detailing the motifs and symbolism of traditional clothes, tattoos and carvings.

★**Erik Jensen** *Where Hornbills Fly*. In the 1950s, before he became a British diplomat, the author arrived in Sarawak as a callow young man with idealistic notions of learning about the Iban. He soon wound up living in longhouses in the Lemanak area (near Batang Ai), helping the Iban make the change to a settled existence without imposing upon them as a "superior" foreigner. His memoir is so intricately and tenderly observed you can only wonder why he waited half a century to write up his experiences.

Lat *Kampung Boy* and *Town Boy*. Two comic-strip albums by the country's foremost cartoonist about growing up in Malaysia during the 1950s and 60s; gentle and fun, though without any sentimentality.

★ **Paul Malone** *The Peaceful People*. A moving, accessible study of the Penan people of Sarawak and of the enormous upheavals they have been through, transitioning from hunter-gatherers to a largely settled existence in just a few decades. Along the way Malone recounts their run-ins with authority and their ambivalent, unequal relationship with the logging industry eating into their ancestral lands.

Bernard Sellato *Innermost Borneo: Studies in Dayak Cultures*. Anthropologist Sellato spent much of the 1990s with the indigenous Borneo tribes of Kalimantan, who are related to the Sea Dyaks of Sarawak. This excellent ethnographic work contains ravishing images of a traditional, isolated world that will eventually be subsumed into greater Indonesia.

★**Dina Zaman** *I Am Muslim*. A well-observed set of wry essays, with more candour than would be appropriate in this guidebook, on Islam as practised in Malaysia; form without enough substance is, sadly, often the verdict. The section on sexual attitudes is particularly recommended.

FOOD AND COOKERY

Aziza Ali *Aziza's Creative Malay Cuisine; Sambal Days; Kampong Cuisine*. For years, Aziza Ali ran the only worthwhile high-end Malay restaurant in Singapore, and her *Creative Malay Cuisine* cookbook is packed with recipes that will impress at dinner parties, though the emphasis is firmly on southern rather than east coast dishes. *Sambal Days* is quite a different beast, a memoir of a middle-class Malay childhood that soon morphs into a reverie of special

foods for just about every occasion.

★**Betty Saw** *Rasa Malaysia*. A nicely illustrated cookbook that covers dozens of the standard dishes you'll find served at food courts and in homes around the country, including various Chinese and Nyonya recipes, though very little South Indian fare. It's all organized by state, which helps give a feel for regional cuisine, though annoyingly there's no index.

NATURAL HISTORY AND THE ENVIRONMENT

G.W.H. Davison and Chew Yen Fook *A Photographic Guide to Birds of Borneo*; **M. Strange and A. Jeyarajasingam** *A Photographic Guide to Birds of Peninsular Malaysia and Singapore*; **Charles M. Francis** *A Photographic Guide to the Mammals of Southeast Asia.* Well keyed and user-friendly, these slender volumes carry oodles of glossy plates that make positive identifying a breeze.

Junaida Payne *Wild Malaysia: The Wildlife and Landscapes of Peninsular Malaysia, Sarawak and Sabah.* Coffee-table book, recently reissued, capturing forest and beach vistas of the kind that linger in the mind long after you've left Malaysia.

★**Alfred Russel Wallace** *The Malay Archipelago.* The immensely readable journal of Wallace's 1854–62 expedition to collect natural history specimens in Borneo and Indonesia, during which he independently formulated the theory of evolution by natural selection – prompting Charles Darwin to publish his landmark *Origin of Species.*

Lukas Straumann *Money Logging: On the Trail of the Asian Timber Mafia.* An unrelenting exposé of avarice and corruption at the heart of Sarawak's government and timber corporations, by the executive director of the Bruno Manser Fund, which campaigns on behalf of the state's indigenous tribes.

ART AND ARCHITECTURE

Julian Davison and Luca Invernizzi Tettoni *Black & White: The Singapore House*; **Peter and Waveney Jenkins** *The Planter's Bungalow.* Two tomes dealing with colonial "Anglo-Malay" residences, often strange hybrids of mock-Tudor and Southeast Asian elements, and sometimes raised off the ground on posts like a kampung house. Both volumes also examine the lives of those who occupied these houses, not always as wealthy as you might assume.

★ **Kang Ger-Wen** *Decoration & Symbolism in Chinese Architecture.* This beautifully photographed book focuses on temples and clan houses in Singapore, but will come in handy at any Chinese historic building in Malaysia, dissecting the meanings and stories hidden in roofing styles, vegetal motifs, altars and so on.

Peter Lee and Jennifer Chen *The Straits Chinese House.* A beautifully illustrated volume exploring Peranakan domestic artefacts and their now largely vanished traditions; an excellent memento of a visit to the Baba-Nyonya museums of Penang, Melaka and Singapore.

★ **Lim Huck Chin and Fernando Jorge** *Malacca: Voices From the Street* (self-published; ⊛ malaccavoices.com). By the architects responsible for the restoration of 8 Heeren Street (see p.273), this labour of love chronicles the evolution of Melaka, street by street, the decline of

traditional trades and pastimes, and the degeneration of some areas into a crass modernity. Printed on heavy-duty paper and illustrated with the authors' own colour photographs.

★ **Farish A. Noor and Eddin Khoo** *The Spirit of Wood: The Art of Malay Woodcarving.* Much weightier in tone than your average coffee-table book, this deals not only with the superb woodcarving produced on the east coast of the Peninsula and in southern Thailand, but also with the whole pre-Islamic consciousness that subtly imbues the woodcarver's art. Packed with great photos, too, of gorgeous timber mosques, incredibly detailed *kris* hilts and the like.

Anthony Ratos and H. Berber *Orang Asli and their Wood Art.* One of few accessible explorations of Orang Asli lifestyles and cultures, though note that only a third of this picture-heavy volume is devoted to their fantastical carvings; the rest of the photos are of Asli settlements and generic, if pretty, jungle scenes.

★ **Robert Winzeler** *The Architecture of Life and Death in Borneo.* Highly readable, illustrated study of the traditional architecture of Borneo, looking at the evolution of longhouses over the years and symbolism in building design.

FICTION

★ **Anthony Burgess** *The Long Day Wanes* (o/p). Burgess's Malayan trilogy (*Time for a Tiger, The Enemy in the Blanket* and *Beds in the East*), published in one volume, provides a witty and acutely observed vision of 1950s Malaya, underscoring the racial prejudices of the period.

James Clavell *King Rat.* Set in Japanese-occupied Singapore, a gripping tale of survival in the notorious Changi Prison.

★ **Joseph Conrad** *Lord Jim.* Southeast Asia provides the backdrop to the story of Jim's desertion of an apparently sinking ship and subsequent efforts to redeem himself; modelled upon the sailor A.P. Williams, Jim's character also yields echoes of Rajah Brooke of Sarawak.

★ **J.G. Farrell** *The Singapore Grip.* Lengthy novel – Farrell's last – of World War II Singapore in which real and fictitious characters flit from tennis to dinner party as the countdown to the Japanese occupation begins.

Marco Ferrarese *Nazi Goreng.* A noir-ish debut novel by a long-time Italian resident in Malaysia, in which a couple of Malay skinheads from Alor Setar drift from drudgery-relieving punk bands to espousing far-right Malay supremacist views, then get sucked into international drug smuggling centred on Penang. Though characterization is a bit thin at times, it's plausible enough to make for an entertaining read.

Barbara Ismail *Shadow Play.* Lightweight whodunnits seem to be taking off in Malaysia and Singapore: the latter has its Inspector Singh franchise, and now there's Ismail's Kelantan-based Kain Songket Mysteries series. It kicks off with this decent enough novel about a Kota Bharu woman who, not content with selling brocade, turns out to be surprisingly good at solving murders – though not all the allusions to Kelantan's distinctive culture are convincing.

Golda Mowe *Iban Dream*. The fabulous saga of a boy raised by apes who has to tackle a series of quests as a rite of passage. Just about every indigenous group in Sarawak makes an appearance at some point in what isn't a bad read once you get used to the mystical-fable style.

Preeta Samarasan *Evening Is The Whole Day*. Set mostly in 1950s Ipoh, this debut novel ruthlessly dissects the lives of a dysfunctional upper-middle-class Indian family, with precious few laughs to be had in a tale of infidelity, class disparities and violence behind closed doors.

★**W. Somerset Maugham** *Short Stories Volume 4*. Peopled by hoary sailors, bored plantation-dwellers and colonials wearing mutton-chop whiskers and topees, Maugham's short stories resuscitate Malaya c.1900; quintessential colonial literature graced by an easy style and a steady eye for a story.

★**Han Suyin** *And The Rain My Drink*. Han is best remembered for her autobiographical novel, which inspired the 1950s Hollywood hit *Love is a Many-Splendored Thing*, but the newly reissued *And The Rain My Drink* deserves wider attention; there is no better novel of the upheavals of the Communist insurgency and the fag-end of British rule in Malaya, informed by Han's time living in 1950s Johor Bahru.

Tan Tuan Eng *The Gift of Rain* and *The Garden of Evening Mists*. By a South Africa-based Malaysian, both these novels are deliberately paced and infused with the author's passion for Japanese culture. The first, set in Penang, focuses on the curious relationship between a Eurasian boy and his family's Japanese tenant as war breaks out, while the second follows a Chinese wartime internee during the subsequent Emergency, when she returns to the Cameron Highlands to confront her ghosts and an old Japanese acquaintance.

Language

Malay, officially referred to as Bahasa Melayu (literally "Malay language"), is the national language of Malaysia, Singapore and Brunei. Part of the Austronesian language family, it's an old tongue that became a regional lingua franca through its use in the ancient kingdom of Srivijaya and during the fifteenth-century Melaka Sultanate. Native speakers of the language are found not just in Peninsular Malaysia and northern Borneo but also in pockets of Indonesia, where a version of Malay has been adopted as the official language.

Malay is only one of many languages used in the three countries covered in this book. In Singapore, English, Mandarin and Tamil are also official tongues, with English pre-eminent as the language of government and business, while Hokkien is the most used regional Chinese dialect. In Malaysia itself, English retains an important position in business, law and government, Tamil is widely spoken among the Indian community, while Mandarin is much used by the Chinese, as are Chinese dialects such as Cantonese (especially in KL and Ipoh) and Hokkien (in Penang and on the east coast).

In practice, **English** is fairly widely understood except in rural areas and in the Malay-dominated east coast and the north of the Peninsula, where it really does pay to pick up a few words of Malay, especially since the basics are simple enough to learn. Besides, it's entertaining to get to grips with a tongue that, like English, is a ready absorber of loan words. The influence of English on modern Malay is apparent to most travellers, and with an awareness of Asian languages, it's not hard to discern the infusion of words from Sanskrit (stemming from the ancient impact of Hinduism on Southeast Asia), such as *jaya* ("success") and *negara* ("country"), as well as from Arabic, which has contributed words like *maaf* ("sorry") and many terms to do with Islam.

To pick up the language, it's best to buy a coursebook that focuses on **vernacular** Malay, as our vocabulary section does, rather than the formal language used in print and broadcasting. A good choice is *A Course in Conversational Malay* by Malcolm W. Mintz (SNP Publishing, Singapore).

Pronunciation

Malay was once written in Arabic script, but over the years this has been almost completely supplanted by a Romanized form. However, the Romanized **spellings** are prone to inconsistencies: for example, *baru*, "new", crops up in variant forms in place names like Johor Bahru and Kota Bharu, while new and old spellings of certain common words still coexist, for example *sungai/sungei*, *kampung/kampong*, and so forth.

Spelling quirks aside, Bahasa Malaysia is one of the more straightforward languages to pronounce, once you get your head round a few rules. One basic point to remember is that the consonants **k, p, t** have slightly less force in Malay than in English (to be precise, they aren't aspirated in Malay); if you emulate the sounds at the start of the Spanish words *cuatro*, *pero* and *toro*, you'd be in the right ball park. Other points of difference are listed below.

Syllable stress isn't complicated in Malay, though it can seem unnatural to English speakers. As a general rule, the stress lands on the **penultimate syllable** of a word (or, with words of two syllables, on the first syllable), hence SaRAwak, TerengGAnu. The chief exception concerns two-syllable words whose first syllable contains a short vowel (usually denoted by an "e"); in such cases, the stress sometimes falls on the second syllable – as in *beSAR* (big), *leKAS* (fast), and so forth; unfortunately, this isn't predictable.

MANGLISH AND SINGLISH

Manglish and **Singlish**, the distinctive forms of English widely spoken in Malaysia and Singapore respectively, can be as confusing to the uninitiated as Jamaican patois. They're really two sides of the same coin: in both, conventional English syntax gives way to a word order that's more akin to Malay or Chinese, and tenses and pronouns are discarded. Ask someone if they've ever been abroad, and you might be answered "I ever", while enquiring whether they've just been shopping might yield "Go, come back already". Responses are almost invariably distilled down to single-word replies, often repeated for stress. Request something in a shop and you'll hear "have, have", or "got, got". Other stock manglings of English include:

aidontch-main	"I don't mind"
betayudon(lah)	"You'd better not do that!"
debladigarmen	A contraction of "the bloody government"
is it?	(pronounced *eezeet*?) "Really?"
tingwat?	"What do you think?"
watudu?	"What can we do?", a rhetorical question
yusobadwan	"You're such a bad one!" meaning "that's not very nice!"

Suffixes and **exclamations** drawn from Malay and Hokkien complete this patois, the most notable being the Malay intensifier "lah", which seems to finish off just about every other utterance. In Malaysia you may hear the Malay question marker "kah" at the ends of queries, while Chinese on both sides of the Causeway might apply the suffix "ah", as in "so cheap one ah", which translates as "is it really that cheap?" or "wow, that's cheap" depending on the intonation; "ah" on its own can also mean "yes", especially if accompanied by a nod of the head. If Manglish and Singlish have you baffled, you might try raising your eyes to the heavens and crying either "ayoh" (with a drop of tone on the second syllable) or "alamak", both expressions denoting exasperation or dismay.

While these linguistic quirks often amuse foreigners and locals alike, both countries are worried that an apparent decline in **English standards** could affect their ability to do business globally. During the colonial era, the minority who could speak English tended to have a decent facility for the language. Now all students learn some English in school (in Singapore, English is actually the official language of education), but often they emerge with a weak grasp of the language. In Malaysia, there is an ongoing debate over English, with Malay nationalists wanting to emphasize Malay and other communities wanting English to get more prominence in the school curriculum. For its part, Singapore, a country with a history of preachy state campaigns, has seen the creation of a government-backed Speak Good English movement (ⓦ www.goodenglish.org.sg).

VOWELS AND DIPHTHONGS

a somewhere in between the vowels of c**a**rp and c**u**p, but changes to a short indeterminate vowel if at the end of a word, as in banan**a**

aa like two "a" vowels separated by the merest pause; thus *maaf* (forgiveness) is rendered *ma + af*

ai as in f**i**ne (written "ei" in older spellings)

au as in h**ow**

e as in h**er**, though in many instances (not predictable) it is like the é of saut**é**, as in *kereta* (car), pronounced *keréta;* in yet others it denotes a short indeterminate vowel

i somewhere between the **i** of t**i**n and the **ee** of t**ee**n

o as in st**o**ne, though shorter and not as rounded as in English

u sometimes short as in p**u**ll, sometimes long (eg, if at the end of a word) as in p**oo**l

ua as in d**oer**

CONSONANTS

c as in **ch**ip (and written "ch" in older spellings), though slightly gentler than in English

d becomes **t** when at the end of a word

g hard, as in **g**irl

h can drop out when flanked by vowels; thus *tahu*, "know", is usually pronounced as though spelt **tau**

k drops out if at the end of the word or if followed by another consonant, becoming a glottal stop (a brief pause); thus *rakyat* (people) is pronounced *ra + yat*

kh as in the Scottish lo**ch**; found in loan words from Arabic

l unlike in English, l is not swallowed if it occurs at the end of a word

ng as in ta**ng** (the "g" is never hard – thus *telinga*, "ear", is *te-ling-a* and not *te-lin-ga*); can occur at the start of a word

ngg as in tango
ny as in canyon; can occur at the start of a word
r is lightly trilled (though in some accents it can be

rendered like the French r of Paris); drops out at the
ends of words when preceded by a vowel
sy as in shut

Grammar

Word order in Malay is similar to that in English, though note that adjectives usually follow nouns. **Nouns** have no genders and don't require an article, while the **plural** form is constructed either by saying the word twice, if the number of objects is unspecified (thus "book" is *buku*, "books" *buku-buku*, sometimes written *buku2*), or by specifying the number of objects before the singular noun ("three books" is thus *tiga buku*). **Verbs** have no tenses either, the time of the action being indicated either by the context, or by the use of words such as *akan* (functioning like "will") and *sudah* ("already") for the future and past. The verb "to be" seldom appears explicitly, so, for example, *saya lapar* literally means "I [am] hungry". There are two words for **negation**: *bukan*, used before nouns (for example *saya bukan doktor*, "I'm not a doctor"), and *tak* (formally *tidak*), used before verbs and adjectives (as in *saya tak lapar*, "I'm not hungry"; *saya tak makan*, "I've not eaten"). Possessive constructions are achieved simply by putting the "owner" after the thing that's "owned"; thus *kampung saya*, literally "village [of] I", is "my village".

Malay words and phrases

One point to note regarding **pronouns** is that Malay lacks a convenient word for "you", all the options being either too formal or informal. In fact, the normal way to address someone is to use their name to their face, which can seem strange to English-speakers. If you don't know someone's name, then you can use *abang* (brother) or *kak* (sister) to address a person of roughly the same age as you, or *adik* to a child, or *pak cik* or *mak cik* to a much older man or woman respectively.

You'll often see the word Dato' (or Datuk) or Tun placed before the name of a government official or some other worthy. Both are honorific titles of distinction roughly equivalent to the British "Sir". Royalty are always addressed as Tuanku.

PERSONAL PRONOUNS

I/my	saya	**he/she**	dia
we (excludes the person being spoken to) or **kita** (includes the person being spoken to)	kami	**they**	mereka
		Mr	Encik *or* Tuan
		Mrs	Puan
		Miss	Cik
you (formal) or **awak** (informal)	anda		

GREETINGS AND OTHER BASICS

"Selamat" is the all-purpose greeting derived from Arabic, which communicates a general goodwill.

good morning	selamat pagi	**safe journey**	selamat jalan
good afternoon	selamat petang	**welcome**	selamat datang
good midday (used around noon)	selamat tengah hari	**bon appetit**	selamat makan
		how are you?	apa khabar?
good evening	selamat malam	**fine**	baik *or* bagus
good night (literally "peaceful sleep")	selamat tidur	**see you again**	jumpa lagi
		please	tolong
goodbye (literally "peaceful stay"; used by someone leaving)	selamat tinggal	**thank you**	terima kasih
		you're welcome	sama-sama
		sorry/excuse me	maaf

never mind, no matter	tak apalah	husband	suami
yes	ya (sometimes pronounced a bit like "year")	wife	isteri
		friend	kawan
no	tidak	person	orang
this/that	ini/itu	do you speak English?	boleh cakap bahasa inggeris?
here	sini		
there (very nearby), (further away)	situ sana	I (don't) understand	saya (tak) faham
		that's fine/allowed	boleh
what is your name?	siapa nama awak?	can you help me?	boleh tolong saya?
my name is…	nama saya…	can I…?	boleh saya…?
where are you from?	dari mana?	to have, there is/are	ada
I come from…	saya dari…	what?	apa?
…England	…England	what is this/that?	apa ini/itu?
…America	…Amerika	when?	bila?
…Australia	…Australia	where?	di mana?
…Canada	…Kanada	who?	siapa?
…New Zealand	…Zealandia Baru (or just "New Zeelan")	why?	mengapa? or kenapa?
		how?	bagaimana?
…Ireland	…Irlandia	how much/many?	berapa?
…Scotland	…Skotlandia		

USEFUL ADJECTIVES

good	bagus	enough	cukup
a lot	banyak	open/closed	buka/tutup
a little	sikit or sedikit	hungry	lapar
cheap/expensive	murah/mahal	thirsty	haus
hot/cold	panas/sejuk	tired	letih
big/small	besar/kecil	ill	sakit

USEFUL VERBS

come/go	datang/pergi	know (someone)	kenal
do	buat	like	suka
eat/drink	makan/minum	push/pull	tolak/tarik
enter, go in	masuk	see	tengok
give/take	beri/ambil	sit	duduk
have, possess	punya or ada	sleep	tidur
hear	dengar	want	mahu
help	tolong	wish to, intend to	nak
know (something)	tahu		

GETTING AROUND AND DIRECTIONS

where is…?	di mana…?	wait	tunggu
I want to go to…	saya mahu pergi ke…	turn	belok
how do I get there?	bagaimanakah saya boleh ke sana?	left	kiri
		right	kanan
how far?	berapa jauh?	straight on	terus
how long will it take?	berapa lama?	in front	di depan or di hadapan
when will the bus leave?	bila bas berangkat?	behind	di belakang
what time does the train arrive?	jam berapa keretapi sampai?	north	utara
		south	selatan
go up, ride	naik	east	timur
get down, disembark	turun	west	barat
nearby/far away	dekat/jauh	street	jalan
stop	berhenti	airport	lapangan terbang

bus station	stesen bas *or sometimes* hentian bas	ticket	tiket
train station	stesen keretapi	fare (adults/children)	tambang (dewasa/kanak-kanak)
jetty	jeti *or* pangkalan	house	rumah
bicycle	baisikal	post office	pejabat pos
boat	bot *or* bot penambang (the latter is used of small passenger-carrying craft)	restaurant	restoran
		church	gereja
		mosque	masjid
longboat	perahu *or* bot panjang	Chinese temple	tokong
car	kereta	museum	muzium
motorcycle	motosikal	park, reserve	taman
plane	kapal terbang	toilet (men/women)	tandas (lelaki/perempuan)
taxi	teksi	entrance	masuk
trishaw	beca	exit	keluar

ACCOMMODATION

hotel	hotel	I need a room	saya perlu satu bilik
guesthouse	rumah tumpangan *or* rumah rehat	I'm staying for... nights	saya mahu tinggal... malam
dorm	asrama	please clean my room	tolong bersih-kan bilik saya
room (double/single)	bilik (untuk dua/satu)		
bed (double/single)	katil (kelamin/bujang)	can I store my luggage here?	boleh titip barang?
fan	kipas		
air-conditioned	berhawa dingin	I want to pay	saya nak bayar
bath, shower	mandi		

BANKING AND SHOPPING

how much is...?	berapa harga...?	market	pasar
I want to buy...	saya mahu beli...	night market	pasar malam
can you reduce the price?	boleh kurang?	supermarket	pasaraya
I'll give you no more than...	saya bayar tidak lebih dari...	bank	bank
I'm just looking	saya hanya lihat-lihat	money	wang *or* duit
shop	kedai	moneychanger	pengurup wang

NUMBERS

0	kosong	10	sepuluh
1	satu (sometimes shortened to the prefix "se-" when used with a noun)	11	sebelas
		12	duabelas
		20	duapuluh
2	dua	21	duapuluh satu
3	tiga	100	seratus
4	empat	121	seratus duapuluh satu
5	lima	200	duaratus
6	enam	1000	seribu
7	tujuh	2000	duaribu
8	lapan	1 million	sejuta
9	sembilan	a half	setengah

TIME AND DAYS OF THE WEEK

what time is it?	pukul jam berapa?	quarter to six ("five three-quarters")	lima tiga suku
time is...	pukul...		
three o'clock	tiga	six-thirty ("six half")	enam setengah
ten past four	empat sepuluh	7am	tujuh pagi
quarter past five	lima suku	8pm	lapan malam

hour	jam	later	nanti
minute	minit	next...	...depan
second	detik	last...	....yang lalu, ...lepas
day	hari	not yet	belum lagi
week	minggu	never	tak pernah
month	bulan	Monday	hari Isnin
year	tahun	Tuesday	hari Selasa
today	hari ini	Wednesday	hari Rabu
tomorrow	esok *or* besok	Thursday	hari Kamis
yesterday	semalam *or on the east*	Friday	hari Jumaat
	coast kelmarin	Saturday	hari Sabtu
now	sekarang	Sunday	hari Ahad *or* Minggu

Food and drink glossary

The list below concentrates on Malay terminology, though a few Chinese and Indian terms appear (unfortunately, transliteration of these varies widely), as well as definitions of some culinary words used in local English.

BASICS, INCLUDING COOKING METHODS

Deciphering menus and ordering is sometimes a matter of matching ingredients and cooking methods – for example, to get an approximation of chips or French fries, you'd ask for *kentang goreng*, literally "fried potatoes". If you don't want your food spicy, say *jangan taruh cili* ("don't add chilli") or *saya tak suka pedas* ("I don't like spicy [food]").

bakar baked
bubur porridge
garpu fork
goreng fried
istimewa special (as in "today's special")
kari curry
kedai kek bakery ("cake shop")
kedai kopis a diner ("coffee shop") concentrating on inexpensive rice spreads, noodles and other dishes, while serving some beverages
kering dried
kopitiam Hokkien Chinese term for a *kedai kopis*; commonly used in Singapore
kuah gravy
kukus steamed
layan diri self-service
lemak "fatty"; often denotes use of coconut milk

makanan/minuman food/drink
mangkuk bowl
manis sweet
masam sour
masin salty
medan selera food court
panggang grilled
pedas spicy
pinggan plate
pisau knife
rebus boiled
restoran restaurant
sedap tasty
sudu spoon
sup/sop soup
tumis stir-fried, sautéed
warung stall

MEAT (DAGING) AND POULTRY

ayam chicken
babi pork
burong puyuh quail
char siew Cantonese honey roast pork

daging lembu (**sapi** in Borneo) beef
itek duck
kambing mutton
lap cheong sweetish, fatty pork sausage (Cantonese)

FISH (IKAN) AND OTHER SEAFOOD

ambal bamboo clams, a Sarawak delicacy
fishball spherical fish dumpling, rubbery in texture, often added to noodles and soups
fishcake fish dumpling in slices, often added to noodles
ikan bawal pomfret

lian bilis anchovy
ikan keli catfish
ikan kembong mackerel
ikan kerapu grouper
ikan kurau threadfin

ikan merah red snapper
ikan pari skate
ikan siakap sea bass
ikan tongkol tuna
ikan yu or **jerung** shark
kepiting or **ketam** crab

kerang cockles
keropok lekor tubular fish dumplings (an east coast speciality)
sotong squid, cuttlefish
udang prawn
udang galah lobster

VEGETABLES (SAYUR)

bangkwang a radish-like root (also called *jicama*), used in Chinese *rojak* and in *popiah* fillings
bawang onion
bawang putih garlic
bayam spinach or spinach-like greens
bendi okra, ladies' fingers
bunga kobis cauliflower
bendawan mushroom
chye sim or **choy sum** brassica greens, similar to *pak choy*
cili chilli
halia ginger
jagung corn
kacang beans, pulses or nuts
kangkung convolvulus greens with narrow leaves and hollow stems; aka water spinach or morning glory
keladi yam

keledek sweet potato
kentang potatoes
kobis cabbage
lada chilli
lobak radish
lobak merah carrot
midin jungle fern, much served in Sarawak
pak choy or **pek chye** soft-leaved brassica greens with broad stalks
petai beans in large pods from a tree, often sold in bunches
pucuk paku fern tips, eaten as greens
rebung bamboo shoots
tauge beansprouts
terung aubergine
timun cucumber
ubi kayu tapioca

OTHER INGREDIENTS

asam tamarind; also used to indicate a dish flavoured with tamarind
belacan pungent fermented shrimp paste
daun pandan pandanus (screwpine) leaf, imparting a sweet bouquet to foods with which it's cooked; used not only in desserts but also in some rice dishes
garam salt
gula sugar
gula Melaka palm-sugar molasses, used to sweeten *cendol* and other desserts

kaya orange or green curd jam made with egg and coconut; delicious on toast
kicap soy sauce
kicap manis sweet dark soy sauce
mentega butter
minyak oil
tahu tofu (beancurd)
telur egg
tempeh fermented soybean cakes, nutty and slightly sour

NOODLES AND NOODLE DISHES

The three most common types of noodle are *mee* (or *mi*), yellow egg noodles made from wheat flour; *bee hoon* (or *bihun* or *mee hoon*), like vermicelli; and *kuay teow* (or *hor fun*), like tagliatelle.

char kuay teow Chinese fried *kuay teow*, often seasoned with *kicap manis,* and featuring any combination of prawns, Chinese sausage, fishcake, egg, vegetables and chilli
Foochow noodles steamed and served in soy and oyster sauce with spring onions and dried fish
Hokkien fried mee *mee* and *bee hoon* fried with pieces of pork, prawn and vegetables; a variant in KL has the noodles cooked in soy sauce with *tempeh*
kang puan (or **kampua**) **mee** a rich Sibu speciality – noodles cooked in lard

kolok mee *mee* served dryish, accompanied by *char siew* slices
laksa basically noodles in a curried soup featuring some seafood and flavoured with the *laksa*-leaf herb (*daun kesom*); variations include Nyonya *laksa* (featuring coconut milk), *asam laksa* (Penang-style, with tamarind) and *laksa Johor* (made with spaghetti)
laksam *kuay teow* rice noodles in a fish sauce made with coconut milk and served with *ulam* (salad); an east coast speciality
mee bandung *mee* served in thickish gravy flavoured with beef and prawn (both of which garnish the dish)

mee goreng Indian or Malay fried noodles; Indian versions are particularly spicy

mee hailam *mee* in an oyster-sauce-based gravy

mee kari noodles in a curried soup

mee pok Teochew dish using ribbon-like yellow noodles, served with fishballs and a chilli dressing

mee rebus boiled *mee*; varies regionally, but one of the best is that sold in Singapore, featuring *mee* in a sweetish sauce made with yellow bean paste, and garnished with boiled egg and tofu

mee siam *bee hoon* cooked in tangy-sweet soup flavoured with tamarind, and garnished with slices of hard-boiled egg and beancurd

mee suah like *bee hoon* but even more threadlike and soft; can be made crispy if fried

sar hor fun flat rice noodles served in a chicken-stock soup, to which prawns, fried shallots and beansprouts are added; a speciality in Ipoh

wan tan mee roast pork, noodles and vegetables, accompanied by pork dumplings

RICE (NASI) DISHES AND SPREADS

char siew fan common one-plate meal, featuring *char siew* and gravy on a bed of steamed rice

claypot rice Chinese dish of rice topped with meat (such as *lap cheong*), cooked in an earthenware pot over a fire to create a smoky taste

daun pisang Malay term for banana-leaf curry, a Southern Indian meal with chutneys and curries, served on a mound of rice, and presented on a banana leaf with poppadums

Hainanese chicken rice Singapore's unofficial national rice dish: steamed or boiled chicken slices served on rice cooked in chicken stock, and accompanied by chicken broth, and a chilli and ginger dip

lemang glutinous rice stuffed into lengths of bamboo

nasi ayam Malay version of Hainanese chicken rice

nasi berlauk simply "rice with dishes"

nasi biryani saffron-flavoured rice cooked with chicken, beef or fish; a North Indian speciality

nasi campur standard term for a rice spread, served with an array of meat, fish and vegetable dishes to choose from

nasi dagang east coast speciality; a slightly glutinous rice steamed with coconut milk, and often brownish in appearance, usually served with fish curry

nasi goreng rice fried with diced meat and vegetables and sometimes a little spice

nasi kandar a spread of rice and curries originating with Indian Muslim caterers in Penang; the rice is often stored in a container made of wood, which is said to give it a distinctive flavour

nasi kerabu blue or green rice traditionally coloured with flower pigments, though these days food colourings may be used; found particularly in Kelantan, it's usually served with a fish curry

nasi kunyit rice given a bright yellow colour by turmeric

nasi lemak a Malay classic, rice cooked with a little coconut milk and served with *ikan bilis*, cucumber, fried peanuts, fried or hard-boiled egg slices and *sambal*

nasi Minang rice spread featuring dishes cooked in the style of the Minang Highlands of western Sumatra; similar to **nasi Padang**

nasi minyak rice cooked with *ghee*

nasi Padang rice spread with the dishes cooked in the style of Padang, Sumatra

nasi putih plain boiled rice

nasi ulam rice containing blanched herbs and greens

pulut glutinous rice

ROTI (BREAD) DISHES

The word *roti* refers both to griddle breads and to Western bread, depending on the context.

murtabak thick griddle bread, usually savoury stuffed with onion, egg and chicken or mutton

murtabak pisang a sweet version of *murtabak*, stuffed with banana.

roti bakar toast, usually served with butter and *kaya*

roti bom an especially greasy *roti canai*, containing a cheesy-tasting margarine

roti canai light, layered griddle bread served with a

thin curry sauce

roti John simple Indian dish, a French loaf split and stuffed with an egg, onion and sweet chilli sauce mixture; versions containing meat are occasionally seen

roti kahwin toast spread with butter and *kaya*

roti prata Singapore name for *roti canai*

roti telur *roti canai* with an egg mixed into the dough

roti telur bawang *roti canai* with an egg and chopped onion mixed into the dough

OTHER SPECIALITIES

ayam goreng Malay-style fried chicken

ayam percik barbecued chicken with a creamy coconut sauce; a Kota Bharu speciality

bak kut teh literally "meat bone tea", a Chinese soup

made by boiling up pork ribs with soy sauce, ginger, herbs and spices

chap chye a Nyonya stew of mixed vegetables, fungi and sometimes also glass noodles (aka *tang hoon*, a rather elastic vermicelli)

chee cheong fun Cantonese speciality, vaguely like ravioli, featuring minced shrimp rolled up in rice-flour sheets, steamed and dredged in a sweet-salty red sauce

chye tow kuay also known as "carrot cake", comprising a rice flour/white radish mixture formed into cubes and fried with egg and garlic; a savoury-sweet version with added *kicap manis* is also worth trying

congee watery rice gruel eaten with slices of meat or fish or omelette; sometimes listed on menus as "porridge"

dim sum Chinese meal of titbits – dumplings, pork ribs, etc – steamed or fried and served in bamboo baskets

dosa/dosai/thosai Southern Indian pancake, made from ground rice and lentils, and served with dhal (lentils); *masala dosa* features a potato stuffing, while *rava dosa* has grated carrot in the batter

fish-head curry the head of a red snapper (usually), cooked in a spicy curry sauce with tomatoes and okra

gado-gado Malay/Indonesian salad of lightly cooked vegetables, boiled egg, slices of rice cake and a crunchy peanut sauce

idli South Indian rice-and-lentil cakes, steamed

kari kepala ikan *see* fish-head curry

kongbian Chinese-style bagels, found only in Sibu

kuih pai tee Nyonya dish vaguely resembling fried spring rolls, except that the *pai tee* are shaped like cup cakes; filling is like that for *popiah*

lontong a pairing of a *sayur lodeh*-like curry with rice cakes similar to *ketupat*

oothapam rice-and-lentil pancakes; South Indian

otak-otak mashed fish mixed with coconut milk and chilli paste, then steamed in strips wrapped in banana leaf; a Nyonya dish

popiah spring rolls, consisting of a steamed dough wrapper filled with peanuts, egg, bean shoots, vegetables and a sweet sauce; sometimes known as *lumpia*

rendang dry, highly spiced coconut curry with beef, chicken or mutton

rojak the Chinese version is a salad of greens, beansprouts, pineapple and cucumber in a peanut and prawn-paste sauce; quite different is Indian *rojak*, a variety of fritters with sweet chilli dips

satar similar to *otak-otak* but made in triangular shapes; found on the east coast

satay marinated pieces of meat, skewered on small sticks and cooked over charcoal; served with peanut sauce, cucumber, raw onion and *ketupat* (rice cake)

sayur lodeh mixed vegetables stewed in a curry sauce containing coconut milk

sop ekor Malay oxtail soup

sop kambing spicy Malay mutton soup

sop tulang Malay beef-bone soup

steamboat Chinese fondue: raw meat, fish, veggies and other titbits dunked into a steaming broth until cooked

umai raw fish salad, mixed with shallots and lime, found in east Malaysia and Brunei

umbut kelapa masak lemak young coconut shoots, cooked in coconut milk

vadai South Indian fried lentil patty

yam basket Sarawak speciality: meat, vegetables and soya bean curd in a fried yam crust

yong tau foo bean curd, fishballs and assorted vegetables, poached and served with broth and sweet dipping sauces

SNACKS AND ACCOMPANIMENTS

acar pickle, often sweet and spicy

bak kwa Chinese-style sweet barbecued pork slices, eaten as a snack

budu fermented fish sauce

cempedak goreng *cempedak*, similar to jackfruit, fried in batter, allowing not just the flesh but also the floury stones to be eaten

curry puff also called *karipap* in Malay; a semicircular pastry parcel stuffed with curried meat and vegetables

kerabu not to be confused with *nasi kerabu*, this is a salad of grated unripe fruit, mixed with chilli, grated coconut, cucumber and other ingredients

keropok (goreng) deep-fried prawn or fish crackers, derived from a dough like that used to make *keropok lekor* (see p.242)

ketupat unseasoned rice cubes boiled in packets of woven coconut-leaf strips, served as an accompaniment to satay

pau or **pow** Chinese stuffed bun made with a sweetish dough and steamed; *char siew pau* contains Cantonese honey-roast pork, *kai pau* chicken and egg, while there are also *pau* with sweet fillings include bean paste, dried coconut or *kaya*

rasam sour-spicy South Indian soup flavoured with tamarind and tomato

sambal dip made with pounded or ground chilli; *sambal belacan* is augmented with a little *belacan* for extra depth of flavour

sambar watery South Indian curry served with *dosa*

tempoyak fermented durian paste, a Malay condiment

ulam Malay salad of raw vegetables and herbs

yew char kuay Chinese fried dough sticks, good dunked in coffee; not unlike Spanish *churros* in flavour and texture

DRINKS

When ordering beverages in a *kedai kopis*, there are various standard terms to bear in mind. *Kosong* ("zero") after the name of the drink means you want it black and unsugared; the suffix *-o* (pronounced "oh") means black with sugar, *susu* means with milk (invariably of the sweetened condensed variety), *ais* or *peng* means iced, *tarik* ("pulled") denotes the popular practice of frothing a drink by pouring it repeatedly from one mug to another and back, and *kurang manis* ("lacking sweetness") means to go easy on the sugar or condensed milk. A few places also allow you to order your drink *see* or *si*, meaning with unsweetened evaporated milk. It's quite possible to combine these terms, so in theory you could order *kopi susu tarik kurang manis peng*, which would be a frothy milky coffee, iced and not too sweet. Note that condensed milk is often assumed to be wanted even if you don't say *susu*.

air botol a bottled drink (usually refers to soft drinks)

air kelapa coconut water

air laici tinned lychee juice, very sweet, usually with a couple of lychees in the glass

air minum drinking water

air tebu sugar-cane juice

bandung or **air sirap bandung** a sweet drink, bright pink in colour, made with rose essence and a little milk

bir beer

chrysanthemum tea delicately fragrant tea made from chrysanthemum blossom, and served slightly sweet, either hot or cold

cincau or **chinchow** sweet drink, the colour of cola or stout, made with strips of jelly-like seaweed

jus juice (the word *jus* is usually followed by the name of the fruit in question)

kopi coffee; some *kedai kopis* offer it freshly brewed, others serve instant

kopi jantan coffee that's claimed to be a male tonic, often advertised with posters showing avuncular Malay men apparently endorsing the drink

kopi tongkat Ali similar to *kopi jantan* (*tongkat Ali* is a herb that Malays believe has aphrodisiac qualities for men)

lassi Indian sweet or salty yoghurt drink

susu milk

teh tea

teh bunga kekwa chrysanthemum

teh limau ais iced lemon tea

tuak rice wine (Borneo)

FRUIT (BUAH)

belimbing starfruit

betik papaya

cempedak similar to jackfruit

duku, duku langsat small round fruits containing bittersweet segments

durian famously stinky large fruit containing rows of seeds coated in sweet creamy flesh

durian belanda soursop

epal apple

jambu batu guava

kelapa coconut

laici lychee

limau lime or lemon

limau bali pomelo

mangga mango

manggis mangosteen

nanas pineapple

nangka jackfruit

nyiur alternative term for coconut

oren orange

pisang banana

rambutan hairy-skinned stone fruit with sweet white flesh

salak teardrop-shaped fruit with scaly brown skin and bitter flesh

tembikai watermelon

DESSERTS

agar-agar seaweed-derived jelly served in squares or diamonds, and often with coconut milk for richness

air batu campur ("ABC") another name for *ais kacang*

ais kacang ice flakes with red beans, cubes of jelly, sweetcorn, rose syrup and evaporated milk

bubur cha cha sweetened coconut milk with pieces of sweet potato, yam and tapioca

cendol coconut milk, palm sugar syrup and pea-flour noodles poured over shaved ice

cheng tng clear, sweet Chinese broth containing fungi and dried fruit

kuih or **kuih-muih** Malay/Nyonya sweetmeats, ranging from something like a Western cake to fudge-like morsels made of mung bean or rice flour

kuih lapis layer cake; either a simple rice-flour confection, or an elaborate wheat-flour sponge comprising numerous very thin layers and unusually rich in egg

pisang goreng bananas or plantains coated in a thin batter and fried

Glossary

adat customary or traditional law

air water

air panas hot springs

air terjun waterfall

ancestral hall building at clan temple housing ancestral tablets

ancestral tablet small upright object representing a departed forebear, venerated in Chinese ancestor worship

atap/attap palm thatch

Baba Straits-born Chinese (male)

bandar town

bandaraya city

bangunan building

banjaran mountain range

batang river system

batik wax and dye technique of cloth decoration

batu rock/stone

bejalai period in an Iban youth's life when he ventures out from the longhouse to experience life in the towns

belian a hardwood traditionally used to construct Sarawak longhouses

belukar secondary rainforest, essentially woodland that regrows in areas where primary forest has been disturbed or cut down

bomoh traditional spiritualist healer

bukit hill

bumbun hide

bumiputra person deemed indigenous to Malaysia ("son of the soil")

bungalow in local English, any detached house

candi temple

Cantonese pertaining to the Guangdong province of southeast China

clan association social club and welfare organization, its members drawn from Chinese migrants from a particular city or area; its premises are called a clan hall/house

coolie colonial-era term for an unskilled labourer

daerah an administrative district

daulat divine force possessed by a ruler that commands unquestioning loyalty

Dayak/Dyak a now largely obsolete umbrella term once used to denote the tribal peoples of Borneo

dipterocarp the predominant family of trees in the rainforest, comprising many types of exceptionally tall trees reaching up to the top of the forest canopy

ekspres express (used of boats and buses)

empangan dam

Foochow pertaining to Fuzhou, a city in Fujian province, southeast China

gasing spinning top

gawai annual festivals celebrated by indigenous groups in Sarawak

gelanggang seni cultural centre

gereja church

godown warehouse

gopuram pyramidal tower decorated with deities and placed over the entrance to a Hindu temple

gua cave

gunung mountain

Hainanese pertaining to Hainan Island, southeast China

halal something permissible in Islam

hill station a settlement or resort at relatively high altitude usually founded in colonial times

Hokkien pertaining to the Fujian province of southeast China, the main dialect of which is more formally called **minnan**

huay guan/kuan another term for clan association

hutan forest

ikat woven fabric

istana palace

jalan road, street

jambatan bridge

kampung/kampong village

kelong a fishing platform extending out to sea from some beaches, acting to lure fish to nets at the far end

kerangas sparse forest ("poor soil")

khalwat an offence under Islamic law, typically involving an unmarried Muslim couple being together in private

kongsi Chinese clan house/temple; has entered Malay as a word meaning "share"

kota fort

kris wavy-bladed Malay dagger

kuala river confluence or estuary

labu gourd; also used of the gourd-like ceramic bottles made as souvenirs in some parts of the Peninsula

lata waterfall

laut sea

lebuh avenue, street

lebuhraya highway/expressway

lorong lane

mak yong courtly dance-drama

makam grave or tomb

Malaya old name for the area now called Peninsular Malaysia

Mamak Indian Muslim; used particularly of restaurants run by Indian Muslims

mandi Asian method of showering by dousing with water from a tank using a small bucket or dipper

masjid mosque

Mat Salleh Malaysian slang for a white person

Melayu Malay

menara minaret or tower

merdeka freedom, in general; can specifically refer to Malaysian independence

Minangkabau matriarchal people from Sumatra

negara national

nipah a type of palm tree

Nyonya/Nonya Straits-born Chinese (female)

Orang Asli Peninsular Malaysia aborigines ("original people"); also Orang Ulu (upriver people) and Orang Laut (sea people)

padang field/square; usually the main town square

pangkalan jetty or port (literally "base")

pantai beach

parang machete

pasar market

pasar malam night market

pasir sand

pejabat Pos post office

pekan town

pelabuhan port/harbour

penghulu chieftain, leader

Peranakan Straits-born Chinese

perigi well

persekutuan federal

pintu arch/gate/door

pondok hut or shelter

pulau island

rajah prince

Ramadan Muslim fasting month

rebana drum

rotan rattan, and the rattan cane used to inflict corporal punishment

rumah persinggahan lodging house

rumah rehat older guesthouse (literally "resthouse"), now mainly privately run, though once state-owned

rumah tumpangan boarding house

samping songket worn by a man as a short sarong over loose trousers

saree traditional Indian woman's garment, worn in conjunction with a **choli** (short-sleeved blouse)

sarung/sarong cloth worn as a wrap around the lower body

sekolah school

semenanjung Peninsula

seni art or skill

shophouse a two-storey terraced building found mainly in town centres, and often featuring a facade that is recessed at street level, providing a shaded walkway that serves as a pavement

silat Malay art of self-defence

songket brocade

songkok Malay male headgear, a little like a flattish fez, made of black velvet over cardboard

storm corridor an exterior pathway with an overhead shelter throughout its length

sultan ruler

sungai/sungei river

taman park

tamu market/fair

tanjung/tanjong cape, headland

tasik/tasek lake

telaga freshwater spring or well

teluk/telok bay or inlet

Teochew pertaining to Chaozhou, a city in Fujian province, southeast China

tokong Chinese temple

towkay Chinese merchant

tuai tribal headman (Sarawak)

wasai waterfall or area with a pool (Brunei)

wau kite

wayang show, ranging from a film screening to Chinese opera

wayang kulit shadow-puppet play (literally "skin show", after the fact that the puppets are made of hide)

wisma commercial building

ACRONYMS

BN Barisan Nasional or National Front – the coalition, dominated by UMNO, which has governed Malaysia since 1974

KTM Keretapi Tanah Melayu, the Malaysian national railway company

MAS Malaysia Airlines

MCA Malaysian Chinese Association, the Chinese wing of the governing BN

MCP Malayan Communist Party

MRT Singapore's Mass Rapid Transit system

PAP Singaporean People's Action Party

PAS Parti Islam SeMalaysia, the Pan-Malaysian Islamic Party

PKR Parti Keadilan Rakyat, the Malaysian opposition People's Justice Party (usually called simply Keadilan)

SIA Singapore Airlines

UMNO United Malays National Organization

Small print and index

604 Small print

605 About the authors

607 Index

618 Map symbols

A ROUGH GUIDE TO ROUGH GUIDES

Published in 1982, the first Rough Guide – to Greece – was a student scheme that became a publishing phenomenon. Mark Ellingham, a recent graduate in English from Bristol University, had been travelling in Greece the previous summer and couldn't find the right guidebook. With a small group of friends he wrote his own guide, combining a highly contemporary, journalistic style with a thoroughly practical approach to travellers' needs.

The immediate success of the book spawned a series that rapidly covered dozens of destinations. And, in addition to impecunious backpackers, Rough Guides soon acquired a much broader readership that relished the guides' wit and inquisitiveness as much as their enthusiastic, critical approach and value-for-money ethos.

These days, Rough Guides include recommendations from budget to luxury and cover more than 120 destinations around the globe, as well as producing an ever-growing range of ebooks.

Visit **roughguides.com** to find all our latest books, read articles, get inspired and share travel tips with the Rough Guides community.

Rough Guide credits

Editors: Samantha Cook, Matt Milton
Layout: Anita Singh
Cartography: Rajesh Chhibber, James Macdonald
Picture editor: Yoshimi Kanazawa
Proofreader: Karen Parker
Managing editor: Keith Drew
Assistant editor: Sharon Sonam

Production: Nicole Landau
Cover design: Nicole Newman, Anita Singh
Editorial assistants: Rebecca Hallett, Freya Godfrey
Senior pre-press designer: Dan May
Programme manager: Gareth Lowe
Publishing director: Georgina Dee

Publishing information

This eighth edition published July 2015 by
Rough Guides Ltd,
80 Strand, London WC2R 0RL
11, Community Centre, Panchsheel Park,
New Delhi 110017, India
Distributed by Penguin Random House
Penguin Books Ltd,
80 Strand, London WC2R 0RL
Penguin Group (USA)
345 Hudson Street, NY 10014, USA
Penguin Group (Australia)
250 Camberwell Road, Camberwell,
Victoria 3124, Australia
Penguin Group (NZ)
67 Apollo Drive, Mairangi Bay, Auckland 1310,
New Zealand
Penguin Group (South Africa)
Block D, Rosebank Office Park, 181 Jan Smuts Avenue,
Parktown North, Gauteng, South Africa 2193
Rough Guides is represented in Canada by Tourmaline
Editions Inc. 662 King Street West, Suite 304, Toronto,
Ontario M5V 1M7
Printed in Singapore

© David Leffman and Richard Lim 2015
Maps © Rough Guides
No part of this book may be reproduced in any form
without permission from the publisher except for the
quotation of brief passages in reviews.
624pp includes index
A catalogue record for this book is available from the
British Library
ISBN: 978-0-24118-454-7
The publishers and authors have done their best to ensure
the accuracy and currency of all the information in **The
Rough Guide to Malaysia, Singapore & Brunei**; however,
they can accept no responsibility for any loss, injury, or
inconvenience sustained by any traveller as a result of
information or advice contained in the guide.
1 3 5 7 9 8 6 4 2

MIX
Paper from
responsible sources
FSC
www.fsc.org
FSC™ C018179

Help us update

We've gone to a lot of effort to ensure that the eighth
edition of **The Rough Guide to Malaysia, Singapore
& Brunei** is accurate and up-to-date. However, things
change – places get "discovered", opening hours are
notoriously fickle, restaurants and rooms raise prices
or lower standards. If you feel we've got it wrong or
left something out, we'd like to know, and if you can
remember the address, the price, the hours, the phone
number, so much the better.

Please send your comments with the subject line
"Rough Guide Malaysia, Singapore & Brunei Update" to
@ mail@uk.roughguides.com. We'll credit all contributions
and send a copy of the next edition (or any other Rough
Guide if you prefer) for the very best emails.
Find more travel information, connect with fellow
travellers and plan your trip on ⓦ roughguides.com.

ABOUT THE AUTHORS

Richard Lim Not to be confused with his Singapore journalist namesake, Richard Lim (plus.google.com/+RichardLim) spent many years working in book publishing, including a stint as a Rough Guides editor. Nowadays, he edits articles for magazines while taking regular time out to wander around Southeast Asia and the Middle East. He lives in London.

Kiki Deere is a freelance travel writer who spends most of the year gallivanting around the globe with a pen in hand, enjoying some of the world's most exciting and imaginative cuisines (she rates Malaysian food as among the planet's very best). She has worked on more than twenty guidebook titles including the *Rough Guide to the Philippines* and the *Rough Guide to Southeast Asia on a Budget*.

Joanna James started her career as a commodity broker in London, before effecting a daring escape to Beijing, where she did an MBA at Peking University. She now lives on a small island in Hong Kong and works as a freelance writer and photographer when she's not at the beach or making the islanders laugh with her attempts at Cantonese. Jo has previously contributed to the Rough Guides to China and Myanmar.

Charles Young has been travelling since university and, as well as working on more than a dozen Rough Guide titles, has taught English in Catalunya, run a coffee shop in Hong Kong, been a publican in South Korea and worked in the spice trade in India. He should be older than he is.

Acknowledgements

The writers would collectively like to thank Samantha Cook and Matt Milton (who edited the Singapore chapter) for unflappable editing, Rajesh Chhibber and James Macdonald for the maps and Anita Singh for fine typesetting.

Richard Lim thanks Susanah Toh from STB, Ooi Geok Ling and Janice from Penang Global Tourism, and Syuhaida and Azman Shah of Tourism Malaysia in Kedah. Thanks also to Edward in the Cameron Highlands, Lay Chun in Taiping and Ladia in Lenggong. Special thanks go to Gary (RIP), Hong and Tony in Ipoh; John Gee; Kee Beng; Louis Joseph; Joe Ng; and to my family in Singapore.

Kiki Deere would like to thank Eliane Sterchi once again for her excellent KL recommendations, without whose help this guide would not have been possible; Siti at the *Renaissance JB* for her help and assistance; the staff at Tunayama on Tioman Island for their warm hospitality; YTL for their exceptional assistance in Melaka and KL; Sharen Kiu and Eli Lum for their hospitality and great

recommendations in Melaka; Biggy in KL for being such good company and in constantly good spirits; thank you also to *Casa del Rio*; *Courtyard at Hereen*; *Regency KL*, *Anggun Boutique Hotel* and *Villa Samadhi*; and last but not least Budgie, as ever, for his wonderful support and for putting up with a partner who is always on the road.

Joanna James Many thanks to all who helped with my research, knowingly and unknowingly, voluntarily and involuntarily. In particular, thanks are due to Nicky and Barney, Shiv and Ashima in Singapore, Dexter in KL and Jessica in Kuantan – you guys are awesome! Thank you!

Charles Young Thanks go to Evangeline, Ben and company in Kuching, the guys at Ana Rais for the tasty BBQ frog, Olz and Qing Qing for being good travelling companions, all the guesthouse owners in Bario, Sapang and Master Chew in Pa Lungan, Aussie Chris in Miri, the indomitable Lucy, Tom from the jungle in KK, Ronald in Kudat, and all the people of East Malaysia who made this a joy to research and helped me out in so many ways.

Readers' updates

Thanks to the following who kindly wrote in with corrections and suggestions (and apologies to anyone we've inadvertently omitted):

Helen Akitt, Katie Burrell, Neil Charlton, Andy Conner, Neil Gokani, Yvonne Kluin, Monica Mackaness and John Garratt, Norman Skiba, Rachel Teo, Aleksandra Uzytkownik and Tim Weisselberg.

Photo credits

p.1 Maurizio Rellini/SIME/4Corners
p.2 Sylvain Oliveira/Alamy
p.4 Rod Porteous/Robert Harding World Imagery/Corbis
p.5 Mark Hannaford/AWL Images
p.9 Adrian Lyon/Alamy (t); Victor Borg (b)
p.11 cfweng/123RF.com (t); Moon Yin Lam/Alamy (b)
p.12 Bazuki Muhammad/Reuters/Corbis
p.13 Ocean/Corbis
p.14 Christian Kober/Robert Harding Picture Library
p.15 Paul Seheult/Eye Ubiquitous/Corbis (t); David Kirkland/Getty Images (b)
p.16 Christian Kober/AWL Images (t); Crystite licenced/Alamy (c); Scubazoo/Alamy (b)
p.17 James Davis Photography (t); Victor Borg/Alamy (b)
p.18 GoPlaces/Alamy (t); Robert Francis/Robert Harding World Imagery/Corbis (b)
p.19 David Poole/Robert Harding World Imagery/Corbis (t); Reinhard Schmid/4Corners (b)
p.20 Ultra.F/Getty Images (t); Andrew Watson/Getty Images (b)
p.21 Steven Morris/The Food Passionates/Corbis (tl); Peter Horree/Alamy (tr); Gianni Iorio/4Corners (bl); Thomas Cockrem/Alamy (br)
p.22 dbimages/Alamy (t); Fiona Rogers/Corbis (b)
p.23 Rainforest World Music Festival (t); Thomas Cockrem/Alamy (c); Sergio Pitamitz Collection/Alamy (b)
p.24 Thomas Cockrem/Alamy (tl); Bruno Morandi/Hemis/Corbis (tr)
p.26 Peter Adams/Corbis
pp.60–61 Atlantide Phototravel/Corbis
p.63 Simon Reddy/Alamy
p.79 Jose Fuste Raga/Corbis (t); Jon Hicks/Corbis (bl); Peter Guttman/Corbis (br)
p.107 Tibor Bognar/Corbis
pp.112–113 Gavin Hellier/JAI/Corbis
p.115 Angelo Cavalli/Robert Harding World Imagery/Corbis
p.133 Tibor Bognar/Robert Harding Picture Library (t); Peter Adams/Corbis (b)
p.153 Rob Walls/Alamy

pp.180–181 ADS/Alamy
p.183 Crystite licenced/Alamy
p.197 Getty Images (t); Marc Anderson/Alamy (b)
pp.210–211 Hugh Sitton/Corbis
p.213 Aqua Image/Alamy
p.233 Mike Sivyer/Alamy
pp.260–261 Felix Hug/Corbis
p.263 Alan Copson/AWL Images
p.283 LOOK Die Bildagentur der Fotografen GmbH/Alamy
pp.306–307 Fiona Rogers/Corbis
p.309 Jay Sturdevant/Alamy
p.329 Richard Lim
p.347 David Poole/Robert Harding World Imagery/Corbis (tl); Asia Images Group Pte Ltd/Alamy (tr); Chris Hellier/Corbis (b)
p.365 Andrew Watson/Getty Images
pp.382–383 Juan Carlos Munoz/Getty Images
p.385 Paul Kingsley/Alamy
p.395 Clownfishphoto/Alamy (t); Ozimages/Alamy (b)
p.419 Stephanie Rabemiafara/Art in All of Us/Corbis (t); Louise Murray/Robert Harding World Imagery/Corbis (b)
pp.444–445 Stefano Paterna/Alamy
p.447 MJ Photography/Alamy
p.459 Iain Dainty/Alamy
pp.466–467 Maurizio Rellini/SIME/4Corners
p.469 Travelscape Images/Alamy
p.491 Gavin Hellier/JAI/Corbis
p.519 Then Chih Wey/Xinhua Press/Corbis
p.537 Andrew Woodley/Alamy (t); Travelscape Images/Alamy (b)
p.552 Ben Queenborough/Getty Images

Front cover and spine Langkawi Bird Paradise, Langkawi © Fabrizio Romiti/SIME/4Corners
Back cover Rainforest and Kinabatangan River, Sabah © Juan Carlos Muñoz/Robert Harding Picture Library (t); Marina at night, view from the Singapore Flyer © Maurizio Rellini/SIME/4Corners (bl); Salang Village, Salang Bay, Pulau Tioman © Alan Copson/AWL Images (br)

Index

Maps are marked in grey

A

Abai 433
Abdul Rahman, Tunku 564
Abdul Razak Hussein, Tun 565
Abdullah Badawi 567, 568, 569
Aboriginal Malays....................576
accommodation.........................35
Ai River 338
Air Batang (ABC) 296
Air Batang, Tekek and 295
Air Hitam (Penang) 154
airlines, domestic......................33
Ajeng...381
alcohol................................42, 450
Alor Star/Setar............. 159–162
Alor Star........................... 160
Altantuya Shaariibuu 567
Altingsburg, Fort......................108
altitude sickness 43
ancestor worship 573
ancestral tablets.......................573
Anglo-Dutch Treaty 505, 558
animism 570
Annah Rais 336
Anwar Ibrahim.......126, 567, 568, 569
Api, Gunung 370
Arau 171
Asian Economic Crisis 567
Atkinson, Francis George........390
Ayer Hitam 304
Ayer Itam 154
Ayer Keroh 281
Azahari.......................................450

B

Ba' Kelalan 379
Baba-Nyonyas...........39, 141, 273, 480, 487, 500, 507, 513, 514, 575
Bahasa Melayu..........................591
Bajau people 437, 578
Bako National Park...... 332–335
Bako National Park............ 334
Bakun dam.................................351
Balik Pulau................................158
Balok beach 255

Balui River........................... 349, 351
bambaazon................................578
Bandar Seri Begawan.. 451–461
Bandar Seri Begawan 452
Bangar 463
Banggi, Pulau 413
banks..56
Baram Dam 380
Baram River...............349, 364, 380
bargaining...................................51
Bario 374
Barisan Nasional 566
basketry 50
Batang Ai 338–340
Batang Ai National Park 339
Batang Duri................................464
Batang Rejang 341, 345, 346
Batek people 185, 192, 196, 202, 208, 576
batik...49
Batu Bungan..............................369
Batu Caves.................................105
Batu Ferringhi 155
Batu Ferringhi 155
Batu Lawi 379
Batu Punggul 403
Bau 336
Bavanggazo 411
Bawang Assan longhouses....344
beadwork 50, 321
Beaufort 404
beer 42
bejalai 339
Belaga 349, 353
Belait 464
Benarat, Gunung 370
Bendera, Bukit 145, 154
Berawan people 319, 373
Bersih demonstrations 569
Besar, Pulau (Melaka) 283
Besar, Pulau (Seribuat Archipelago)..............................303
Bidayuh people 336, 577
Bila Bigan 379
Bilit..431
Bintulu 352–354
Bintulu 352
Birch, J.W.W...............................559
Bird, Isabella 136
bird's nests, edible..........362, 433, 493
birdlife 584
birdwatching..........104, 110, 131, 512

bloggers.......................................44
BN...566
boat-building, traditional 240
boat travel, Sarawak 314
boats 32
bobohizan 578
bomohs 572
books 587
border crossings
  Brunei to East Malaysia 450, 456
  Labuan to Brunei 409
  Malaysia to Singapore....................288
  Sabah to Brunei 388
  Sabah to Sarawak 388, 405
  Sarawak to Brunei............................358
  Sarawak to Sabah 358
  Singapore to Malaysia.......... 523, 524
  to Indonesia...........................29, 314
  to Thailand 28, 171, 222
Bornean Sun Bear Conservation Centre.....................................428
Borneo Jazz Festival 359
brassware 243
Briggs, Harold 563
Brinchang 175
Brinchang 175
British Malaya...........................559
British North Borneo Chartered Company 387, 388, 561
Brooke, Anthony.......................313
Brooke, Charles 313, 320, 449, 560
Brooke, James.........313, 315, 449, 560
Brooke, Vyner 313, 560
Brunei............................ 444–465
Brunei 448
Brunei Muara 461
Brunei People's Party...............450
Brunei Sultanate 449, 558, 561
Buddhism 573
Bugis..557
Bujang Valley.............................159
Bukit Kayu Hitam......................171
Bukit Peradayan Forest Reserve 457
Bukit Shahbandar Park............462
bumiputra policy......................566
Buntal..330
Bunut, Tasik...............................373
buses, local 31
buses, long-distance 30
butterfly farm (Penang) 156
Butterworth................................136

C

Cahaya Bulan beach.................218
CAMERON HIGHLANDS
.... **171–179**
Cameron Highlands........... **172**
Brinchang **175**
Tanah Rata......................... **174**
   accommodation 176
   arrival...................................175
   Brinchang 175
   butterfly farm 175
   departure.............................175
   eating...................................177
   hiking...................................178
   information...........................176
   Kea Farm 175
   Lavender Garden 175
   Orang Asli 176
   restaurants...........................177
   rose centre...........................175
   Tanah Rata............................173
   tea plantations.....................173
   Time Tunnel 175
   tours.....................................176
   Tringkap 175
camping........................... 36, 47
candat sotong.....................235
car rental...............................34
casinos 103, 503
caving 105, 323, 368
cellphones.............................57
ceramic jars, Sarawak.............319
chalets 36
charcoal production...............132
Che Wong people 577
Cheng Ho 273, 521
Cherating **249–253**
Cherating................................249
children, travelling with...........59
Chin Peng...............................563
Chinese (people)......................575
Choo, Jimmy...........................140
Chukai...................................248
civets....................................584
clan associations/halls/houses
...........71, 129, 143, 492, 497,
   499, 559, 575
Clifford, Hugh.................. 182, 203
climate.............................12, 50
clinics 43
cloud forest......................416, 583
clouded leopard 584
coaches 30
Coleman, George Drumgoole
.............................475, 479
colugo...................................584
Commonwealth War Cemetery
....130
Confrontation, the 313, 565
Confucianism.........................573

consulates (Malaysian,
   Singaporean and Bruneian)
....53
Cornwallis, Charles.......... 135, 140
costs......................................50
coup, Brunei...........................450
Coward, Nöel..........................479
crafts.....................................49
credit cards 56
crime...............................51, 387
Crocker Mountain Range
....401
crocodiles..............................586
culture...................................48
currency..................................55
customs, local..........................48
customs allowances 54
cycle rickshaws........................35

D

dagger, Malay 239
dam construction.....................581
Damai.....................................331
Danga Bay 288
Danum Valley Conservation
   Area 436
DAP.......................................567
Dayak....................................577
de Albuquerque, Alfonso 556
death marches................. 421, 423
deforestation..........................579
dehydration.............................42
Delok River.............................340
Democratic Action Party 567
dengue fever............................43
desserts...................................41
diarrhoea................................42
dipterocarps...........................583
disabilities, travellers with........59
diving.....................................47
dolphins............................330, 338
dress, appropriate 48
drinks.....................................41
driving....................................33
drugs, illegal............................54
Dungun.................................248
duty-free.................................50
Duyong, Pulau 240
Dyak.....................................577

E

east coast, The.............. **210–259**
east coast, The..................... **214**

East India Company, British 72,
   135, 270, 556, 387, 471, 477,
   558
East India Company, Dutch
........................122, 160, 270, 556
Eastern & Oriental Express 28
Eastern & Oriental Hotel 140
economy..................................8
electricity................................52
elephants...............................189
embassies (Malaysian,
   Singaporean and Bruneian)
....53
emergencies.............................52
Emergency, the 110, 563
Empire Hotel & Country Club
....462
employment.............................55
Endau Rompin National Park
....304
English, local usage of............591
Entikong................................314
environment, the......................579
Escape Theme Park..................156
ethnic groups.........................574
etiquette 37, 48
Eu Yan Sang 121
exchange 56
exchange rate...........................55
expressways, Malaysian 33, 85

F

fabrics 49
Fairy Cave..............................336
Farquhar, William............. 471, 481
Federated Malay States..........559
Federation of Malaya 562
Federation of Malaysia 565
feng shui.................................573
ferries, domestic 32
ferries, international
   Brunei to Malaysia 462
   Malaysia to/from Indonesia 27,
      84, 276, 441
   Malaysia to/from Thailand............28,
      167, 171
   Malaysia to/from Zamboanga
      (Philippines) 424
   Singapore to Indonesia 526
   Singapore to Malaysia...................526
festivals 45
fireflies 109, 132, 251, 330,
   404, 405, 430
flights
   domestic 33
   from Australia and New Zealand
....27
   from South Africa.....................27

from the UK and Ireland..............27
from the US and Canada..............27
regional 28, 29
food **37–41**
forest, montane........................583
Forest Research Institute of
  Malaysia 104
Formula One 65, 475
Fort Altingsburg........................108
Fort Sylvia 346
Foster, Norman........................475
Fraser's Hill 110
FRIM........................104
fruit, tropical........................41

G

Garden of Eden (Mulu)..........368
Gawai Kenyalang........................319
gay life 54, 99, 151
Gaya, Pulau 398
Gemia, Pulau 245
Genting (Tioman) 299
Genting Highlands........................103
GEORGETOWN **136–152**
Georgetown 137
Georgetown, Central
........................**138–139**
accommodation........................147
airport........................146
arrival........................146
banks........................152
bars........................150
bike rental........................147
Blue Mansion........................144, 148
bookshops........................151
Botanic Gardens........................145
buses........................136, 146, 147
car rental........................147
CAT shuttle........................136
Cheong Fatt Tze Mansion 144
city hall, former........................140
clan houses........................143
clan jetties........................144
clock tower........................137
clubs........................151
colonial district........................137
consulates........................152
departure........................146
Dewan Undangan Negeri........140
Dharmikarama Temple........................145
Eastern & Oriental Hotel........................140
entertainment........................151
Esplanade........................140
festivals, cultural........................151
Fort Cornwallis........................140
gay scene........................151
guides, specialist........................147
Hock Teik Cheng Sin Temple........143
hospitals........................152
House of Yeap Chor Ee........................141

information 147
internet access........................152
Kapitan Kling Mosque........................142
Khoo Kongsi........................143
Kipling, Rudyard........................140
KOMTAR........................145
Kuan Yin Teng........................142
Light, Francis........................140
Little India........................142
mail........................152
markets........................151
Masjid Kapitan Kling........................142
Maugham, Somerset........................140
Mor Hun club........................143
Nattukkottai Chettiar Temple........145
nightlife........................150
Padang Kota Lama........................140
Penang Museum........................140
Penang riots........................144
Peranakan Mansion........................141
pharmacy........................152
police........................152
post office........................152
puppetry........................143
reclining Buddha........................145
restaurants........................149
St George's Church........................140
Sarkies brothers........................140
shopping........................151
Sri Mahamariamman Temple 142
State Legislative Hall 140
street art........................142
Sungai Nibong bus station 146
Syed Alatas mansion........................143
taxis........................147
town hall, former........................140
train station........................146
transport........................136, 146
trishaws........................147
UNESCO, effect on Georgetown
........................141
visa extensions........................152
Wat Chaiya Mangkalaram........145
Yap Kongsi........................143
Yeap Chor Ee, House of........................141
ghazal music 284
gibbons........................584
glossary........................601
Goh Chok Tong........................472
Gomantong Caves........................433
Gopeng........................121
gopurams........................571
Grass, Günter........................479
GST........................52
Gua Charas........................255
Gua Musang........................**206**
Gua Musang 207
guesthouses........................35
Gunung Gading National Park
........................337
Gunung Mulu National Park
........................**366–372**
Gunung Mulu National Park
.... 367
Gurney, Henry........................110, 564

H

halal food 40
handicrafts........................49
Harrisson, Tom........................319, 362, 366,
  375, 376, 562
Hash House Harriers........................67
Hassanal Bolkiah........................449
hawker centres........................37
haze........................581
head-hunting........................313, 400
Headhunters' Trail........................370
health........................42
heat, coping with 42
Hesse, Hermann........................479
highways, Malaysian 33, 85
Hijjas Kasturi........................72
hiking........................47
HINDRAF........................567
Hinduism........................570
history........................**553–569**
history of Sabah........................387
history of Sarawak........................312
holidays........................56
homestays........................36, 380, 381
hornbills........................124, 134, 162,
  167, 169, 354, 373, 407, 416,
  431, 436, 570, 585
hospitals........................43
hostels........................35
hotels........................35
huay guan........................ 71, 129, 143, 492,
  497, 499, 559, 575
Hubback, A.B........................66, 70, 117
hudud........................217, 450, 569
hydroelectricity........................581

I

Iban people..........**338–340, 344,**
  577
Igan River........................341
ikat........................321
independence, Singapore........565
Indian influence........................554
Indians (peoples)........................576
indigenous groups........................576
information........................58
inoculations........................42
insurance........................54
interior, The........................**180–209**
interior, The........................ 184
Internal Security Act........................565
internet access........................54
Ipoh........................ **117–121**
Ipoh........................ 118

ISA 565
Iskandar Shah 471, 481, 555
Islam 217, 571

J

Jah Hut people 106, 577
Jakun people 576
Japanese occupation 561
Jelawang 214
Jelawang Jungle Park 208
jellyfish 43
Jerantut 185–189
Jerantut 188
Jerudong Park Playground 462
Jessel, Charles 388
Jesselton 387, 388
Jeyaretnam, J.B. 472
Johor Bahru 285–290
Johor Bahru 286
Johor sultanate 286, 557
Juara 300–302
Juara 301
Jungle Railway 201

K

Kadazan/Dusun 390, 396, 400, 578
Kalampunian Damit, Pulau 406
Kampung Ayer (Bandar Seri Begawan) 453
Kampung Peta 304
Kampung Santubong 330
Kampung Tellian 351
Kangar 171
Kanowit 344, 345, 346
Kapalai, Pulau 439
Kapas, Pulau 245–247
Kapas, Pulau 245
Kapit 346
Karak Highway (E8) 85
Karakit 413
kayaking 323, 393
Kayan people 349, 578
Keadilan 567
kedai kopis 37
Keith, Agnes Newton 423
Kek Lok Si 154
Kelabit Highlands 373–380
Kelabit Highlands 374
Kelabit people 319, 373, 577
Kelapang River trail 377
Kellie's Castle 119

Kemaman 248
Keningau 402
Kenong Rimba State Park 200–203
Kenong Rimba State Park 202
Kenyah people 349, 578
kerangas 339
kereta sapu 31
keris 239, 242
Kerteh 248
Ketam, Pulau 109
khalwat 572
Kinabalu National Park 414–420
Kinabalu National Park 415
Kinabatangan River 431
Kinarut Laut 394
Kitingan, Joseph Pairin 388
Kiulu River 400
Klang, Port 85
Klias Peninsula 393, 404, 405
kopitiam 37
Kota Belud 410
Kota Bharu 215–224
Kota Bharu 216
Kota Bharu, Around 220
KOTA KINABALU 388–398
Kota Kinabalu 389
   accommodation 393
   airport 391
   arrival 391
   bars 397
   buses 392
   car rental 392
   consulates 398
   departure 391
   fireflies 404
   hospital 398
   information 392
   Klias Peninsula 393, 404
   markets 391
   rafting 404
   restaurants 396
   Sabah Art Gallery 391
   Sabah Parks 392
   Sabah State Museum 390
   shopping 397
   Signal Hill 390
   tour operators 393
   trains 392
   transport 392
   visa extensions 398
   Wetland Centre Park 391
kris 239, 242
Kristao 275
KTM 31
Kuala Besut 225
Kuala Gandah elephant sanctuary 189
Kuala Kangsar 126–128
Kuala Kangsar 126
Kuala Kedah 161

Kuala Kinchin 305
Kuala Koh 207
Kuala Kubu Bharu 111
Kuala Lipis 203–205
Kuala Lipis 204
Kuala Litut 370
Kuala Lumpur and around 60–111
Kuala Lumpur and around 64
KUALA LUMPUR 66–104
Kuala Lumpur 68–69
Bangsar Baru 97
Brickfields and KL Sentral 82
Bukit Bintang 76
Chinatown, Colonial District and 71
Chow Kit, Little India to 73
Colonial District and Chinatown 71
Golden Triangle 76–77
KL Sentral, Brickfields and 82
Kuala Lumpur transport system 87
Little India to Chow Kit 74
   accommodation 88
   airports 83
   Alor, Jalan 94
   aquarium 75
   arrival 83
   Badan Warisan 75
   Bangsar 96
   banks 103
   bars 98
   Batu Caves 105
   Bird Park 81
   bookshops 101
   Brickfields 82
   Bukit Bintang 75
   bus stations 84
   buses, city 86
   Butterfly Park 81
   car rental 86
   Carcosa Seri Negara 80, 92
   casino 103
   Central Market 67
   Chan See Shu Yuen 70
   Chinatown 70
   Chow Kit 73
   cinemas 100
   city tours 88
   classical music 100
   clinics 103
   clubs 99
   Coliseum Bar 73
   Coliseum Cinema 73
   colonial district 66
   consulates 103
   Convention Centre 75
   Court Hill Ganesh Temple 72
   crafts 101
   cultural centres 103
   cultural shows 100

departure..................................83
E8 (Karak Highway)..............85
embassies.............................103
entertainment......................99
ferries to Indonesia.............85
gay scene................................99
Golden Triangle.....................74
guesthouses..........................88
gyms......................................104
health clubs.........................104
history....................................62
hospitals...............................103
India Mosque.........................73
information............................88
Islamic Arts Museum...........80
Jalan Alor...............................94
Jamek Mosque.......................67
Kampung Bahru....................73
Karak Highway (E8)..............85
KL Sentral..............................84
KLCC......................................74
KLIA/KLIA2............................83
Kompleks Kraf.......................75
Komuter trains.............84, 86
KTM headquarters................70
Kuala Lumpur train station...70
Lake Gardens.........................80
left luggage.........................103
Little India.............................73
live music..............................99
long-distance taxis..............85
LRT...86
mail......................................103
Malaysia Tourism Centre.....88
malls....................................102
maps......................................88
Masjid India...........................73
Masjid Jamek.........................67
Masjid Negara.......................78
MaTiC.....................................88
Maybank Building.................72
Menara KL..............................78
Merdeka Square....................66
Monorail................................86
Moorish architecture...........66
Muzium Negara......................81
Nanas, Bukit..........................78
National Mosque...................78
National Museum...................81
National Textile Museum......67
nightlife................................99
Numismatic Museum.............72
Old KL railway station.........70
Orang Asli Museum......106, 107
Orchid and Hibiscus Gardens...81
Pasar Seni...............................67
Petaling Street......................70
Petronas Towers....................74
planetarium..........................81
police...................................103
post offices..........................103
pubs.......................................98
restaurants............................92
RMP Museum..........................80
rock climbing.......................103
Royal Selangor Club..............66
St Mary's Cathedral...............67
shopping..............................101

sports facilities...................104
Sri Kandaswamy Temple.......83
Sri Maha Mariamman Temple...72
Subang airport......................83
Sultan Abdul Samad Building...66
Taman Tasik Perdana............80
TAR, Jalan..............................72
taxis, city..............................86
TBS...85
Terminal Bersepadu Selatan...85
Thaipusam.............................72
theatre................................100
Touch 'n Go cards.................86
tour operators.......................85
tourist offices.......................88
tours......................................88
train station..........................84
transport...............................85
travel agents.........................85
Tun Abdul Razak Memorial...81
visa extensions....................104
Kuala Penyu.........................405
Kuala Perlis..........................171
Kuala Selangor.....................108
Kuala Selangor Nature Park...108
Kuala Sepetang.....................132
Kuala Tahan.................189–193
Kuala Tahan........................ 190
**Kuala Tahan: day-trips and
    short trails...................... 194**
Kuala Terengganu........237–243
Kuala Terengganu.............. 238
Kuala Terikan.......................370
Kuantan.......................253–257
Kuantan.............................. 254
Kubah National Park............335
KUCHING.......................315–328
Kuching.......................316–317
    accommodation.................323
    airport..............................322
    aquarium...........................325
    arrival...............................322
    Astana...............................321
    banks................................328
    bars...................................326
    bike rental........................322
    Bishop's House..................319
    Brooke Gallery...................321
    buses.................................322
    car rental..........................323
    Carpenter Street................319
    cat statue..........................321
    caving................................323
    Charles Brooke Memorial.....318
    Chinatown..........................319
    Chinese History Museum......318
    consulates.........................328
    cookery classes.................328
    crafts.................................326
    departure...........................322
    DUN Building......................321
    ferries, to Sibu..................322
    Fort Margherita..................321
    guides, hiring....................323
    hospitals............................328
    information........................323

Islamic Museum...................320
Kampung Boyan....................322
Kuching Mosque...................320
Main Bazaar.........................317
Malay villages......................322
Masjid Negeri.......................320
massage...............................328
motorbike rental..................322
Old Courthouse complex......317
orchid garden.......................321
post office............................318
restaurants..........................325
river cruises.........................317
river trips.............................323
Round Tower........................318
St Thomas's Cathedral.........318
Sarawak Craft Council.........318
Sarawak Forestry Corporation
   323
Sarawak Museum.................319
Sarawak Steamship Company
    building............................318
shopping..............................326
Square Tower........................318
State Assembly Building.......321
Sunday market (Satok).........320
tattoo parlours.....................328
Textile Museum....................318
tour operators......................323
transport..............................322
Tua Pek Kong........................319
Tun Jugah Foundation gallery....321
visa extensions....................328
waterfront............................316
weekend market (Satok).......320
Kuching Wetland National Park
   331
Kudat....................................411
Kukup...................................285
Kundasang............................421

L

Laban Rata......414, 415, 418, 420
Labi......................................465
labu (pottery)......................126
Labuan.................................407
Labuan Bird Park.................407
Labuan Town...............407–410
Labuan Town....................... 408
Labuk Bay Proboscis Monkey
    Sanctuary.........................429
Lahad Datu...........................434
Lake Kenyir..........................243
Lalang, Operation.................566
Lambir Hills National Park......361
Lamin Dana..................351, 352
Land Dyaks...........................308
land rights.....................185, 580
Lang Tengah, Pulau..............236
LANGKAWI...................163–170
Langkawi........................... 164

Cenang and Tengah beaches 165
accommodation 168
aquarium 163
arrival 167
banks 170
bars 170
boat trips 166
cable car 165
car rental 168
Cenang beach 163
departure 167
diving 166
eagle feeding 166
Gunung Raya 167
hornbills 167
hospital 170
information 168
internet access 170
Kilim Geoforest Park 167
Kok beach 163
Kuah 163
LADA 168
Machinchang, Gunung 165
mangrove cruises 166, 167
nightlife 170
Pantai Cenang 163
Pantai Kok 163
Pantai Pasir Hitam 167
Pantai Tengah 163
Pasir Hitam beach 167
Pulau Payar Marine Park 166
restaurants 169
shopping 170
SkyBridge 165
SkyTrex Adventure 166
snorkelling 166
Tanjung Rhu 167
taxis 168
Telaga Tujuh 165
Tengah beach 163
transport 167
Underwater World 163
watersports 166
language 34, 591
langurs 584
Lankayan, Pulau 430
Larut, Bukit 131
laundries 55
Lawas 364
Lee Hsien Loong 472
Lee Kuan Yew 472, 564, 565
leeches 46
Lemanak River 340
Lembah Bujang 159
Lenggong Valley 132
leopard cats 584
lesbian life 54
Light, Francis 135, 140
Limbang division 364, 449
Limbang town 370
Lio Matoh 380
Loagan Bunut National Park 373

logging 579
Lok Kawi Wildlife Park 400
Long Akah 381
Long Belaban 379
Long Kerong 381
Long Lama 380
Long Lamai 381
Long Lellang 381
Long Medang 379
Long Murum dam 351
Long Palungan 378
Long Rapung 379
Long San 380
longhouses 36, 312, 336, 340, 344, 346, 348, 351, 361, 375, 465
Lotud 578
Low, Hugh 414, 559
Lower Kinabatangan Wildlife Sanctuary 431
Luagan Lalak Forestry Recreation Park 465
Lumut 122, 124
Lumut, Bukit (Sarawak) 353
Lun Bawang people 373, 379
Lundu 337

M

Ma'Daerah turtle sanctuary 248
Mabul, Pulau 439
macaques 584
magazines 44
Magellan, Ferdinand 387, 558
Mah Meri people 106, 577
Mahathir Mohamad 566
Mahmud Shah 555
mail 55
Majapahit Empire 554
mak yong 219
malaria 43
Malay Annals 553
Malay College 126
Malay language 591
Malay people 574
Malay road signs 34
Malayan Chinese Association 563
Malayan Communist Party 561
Malayan Democratic Union 562
Malayan People's Anti-Japanese Army 562
Malayan Union 562
Maliau Basin 443
mamak 40

Mamutik, Pulau 399
Mangkok 225
Manglish 592
mangroves 583
Manser, Bruno 381
Mantabuan Island 438
Mantanani, Pulau 410
Manukan, Pulau 399
maps 55
Marang 244
Marang **244**
Mari-Mari Cultural Village 400
Marudi 380
MASwings 33, 366
Mat Kilau 559
Mat Salleh 388, 561
Mataking, Pulau 439
Matang Mangrove Forest Reserve 132
matrilineal tradition 267
Maugham, Somerset 475, 479
Maxwell Hill 131
MCA 563
MCP 561
Medan Portugis 275
media, the 44
MELAKA **268–281**
Melaka **269**
8 Heeren Street 273
A Famosa 271
accommodation 276
arrival 275
Ayer Keroh 281
Baba-Nyonya Heritage Museum 273
banks 281
bars 280
botanical gardens 281
Bukit China 275
butterfly and reptile sanctuary 282
car rental 276
Chee Ancestral House 273
Cheng Ho Cultural Museum 273
Cheng Hoon Teng 274
Chinatown 272
Christ Church 271
crocodile park 282
departure 275
Dutch graveyard 271
hospital 281
information 276
Istana Kesultanan 271
Jonker Walk night market 272
Kampung Hulu Mosque 274
Kampung Kling Mosque 274
Kampung Morten 274
Maritime Museum 272
Masjid Kampung Hulu 274
Masjid Kampung Kling 274
Melaka Wonderland 282
Muzium Rakyat 272
Pirates Park 274
Porta de Santiago 271

Portuguese settlement...................275
restaurants......................................278
river trips...276
Riverside Walk................................274
St Paul's Church.............................271
St Peter's Church............................274
Sam Poh Kong Temple...................275
shopping..280
Sri Poyyatha Vinayagar Temple
....274
Stadthuys...270
Straits Chinese Jewellery Museum
....273
swimming pool...............................281
Taman Mini-Malaysia & ASEAN
....282
Taming Sari Revolving Tower 272
tours...276
transport..276
Villa Sentosa...................................275
visa extensions...............................281
zoo..281
Melaka Sultanate............. 268, 555
Melanau people................. 351, 577
Melawati, Bukit..............................108
Melayu (town).................................554
Mendaram longhouse.................465
menora...219
Mentawai...370
Menumbok.......................................405
Merang..226
Merapoh...205
Merbok..159
Mersing........................... 290–292
Mersing.. 291
Minangkabaus................... 267, 557
Miri 355–361
Miri 356
Miri reefs...358
mobile phones................................. 57
Moliangin Pasar, Pulau 413
money... 55
monitor lizards................................585
monkeys..584
Monsopiad Cultural Village
....399
montane forest...............................416
Moorish architecture...................... 66
mosques, architecture..................573
mosques, visiting............................. 49
mosquitoes....................................... 43
motorcycle rental............................ 34
Mountain Torq (Kinabalu) 418
MPAJA..562
Muar...284
Muara...462
mud volcanoes................... 406, 436
Mukah..351
Mukut..299
Mulu National Park 366–372
Mulu National Park............ 367
Mulu, Gunung..................................371
Murud Kecil, Gunung....................381

Murud, Gunung...............................379
Murut (Lun Bawang) people
.... 373, 379, 403, 578

N

Najib Tun Razak.............................568
Nanga Delok....................................340
Nanga Medamit...............................370
Nanga Sumpa..................................340
native customary rights...............580
New Economic Policy 565
newspapers...................................... 44
Ngemah Ulu....................................340
Ngiam Tong Boon 479
Niah National Park 361–364
Niah National Park 363
Nipah...299
North Borneo Railway 400

O

oil palm industry 581
Omar Ali Saifuddien Mosque
....453
opening hours.................................. 56
Operation Lalang............................566
Orang Asli........106, 107, 122, 134,
176, 182, 185, 563, 576
Orang Asli Museum 106, 107
Orang Laut.......................................578
Orang Ulu..................308, 349, 578
orang-utans.............335, 339, 427
outdoor activities........................... 47

P

Pa' Dalih..377
Pa' Lungan.......................................378
Pa Rupai..379
Pa' Ukat...378
Padang Besar..................................171
Padang Kemunting Turtle
Sanctuary....................................281
Padas River.............393, 400, 404
PADI courses.................................... 47
Pakatan Rakyat..............................568
Palembang.......................................554
palm oil...581
Pan-Borneo Highway 314
Pandan beach..................................337
Pangkalan Gawi..............................243
Pangkor 122–126

Pangkor, Pulau..................... 123
Pangkor Laut..................................123
Pangkor Town.................................122
Pangkor Treaty................................559
Panukaren, Pulau...........................413
PAP 472, 564
Paramesvara....................................471
Parti Bersatu Sabah.....................388
PAS 212, 217, 219
Paya..299
PBS...388
PCB (Kelantan)...............................218
Pei, I.M. 479, 489
Pekan 257–259
Pekan 258
Pelagus Rapids...............................349
Pelli, Cesar 75
Penan homestays 380, 381
Penan people..........369, 376, 381,
577, 582
Penang.......................... 134–158
Penang, Pulau 135
Penang Hill.......................... 145, 154
Penang National Park 156
Penang War Museum...................158
Penarik..225
Pengkalan Balak Turtle
Sanctuary....................................281
Pengkalan Kubor.............................222
People's Action Party 472,
564
peoples...574
Perak Man 132
Perak Tong Temple........................118
Perhentian, Pulau 227–234
Perhentian, Pulau 227
Pesta Kaamatan 578
Petronas Towers.............................. 74
Pewanis project..............................225
pewter... 50
pharmacies....................................... 43
phones... 57
Picnic with the Penan 381
Pigafetta, Antonio.........................558
Pinnacles, the.................................370
PKR...567
pollution, air...................................581
Polo, Marco.....................................471
Pom Pom, Pulau.............................439
Pontianak (Indonesia)...............314
population..8
Poring Hot Springs........................420
Portuguese colonialism 556
post... 55
pottery... 50
proboscis monkeys........ 333, 393,
404, 405, 429, 451, 456
Pryer, William..................................422
pua kumbu 50, 321, 339
public holidays................................. 56

Pulau Pangkor.......................123
Pulau Payar Marine Park.........166
Pulau Tiga National Park.........406
Pulong Tau National Park......374, 379
Punan people 349
puppetry.............................218, 219

R

race relations................................65, 565
radio 44
Raffles...479
Raffles, Thomas Stamford......471, 558, 586
Rafflesia 134, 176, 207, 337, 401, 416, 586
rafting 48, 121, 304, 336, 393, 404
rail network, Malaysian.......31
Rainforest Discovery Centre 428
Rainforest Musical Festival.....332
Ramadan 37
Ranau..421
Rantau Abang................................247
Rantau Panjang............................222
Raub 111
Rawa, Pulau..................................303
Redang, Pulau...............................235
Rejang River 341, 345, 346
religion...570
reptiles..585
Resident system.............................559
Riau Archipelago 505
Royal Belum State Park 134
Rumah Benjamin Angki 344
Rumah Ipang.................................340
Rumah Jandok................................348
Rungus people 412, 578

S

Sabah 382–443
Sabah..................................386
Sabah Agricultural Park..........403
Sabah Parks 392
Sabah State Railway 392
Sabah Tea Garden 421
Sahabat Alam Malaysia 582
St John, Spenser 366, 414
Salang..298
Salang...............................298
sales tax...52

Sandakan 422–427
Sandakan 424–425
sandflies...303
Santubong Peninsula................330
Santubong, Gunung.................330
Sapi, Pulau....................................398
Sapulut...443
Sarawak 306–381
Sarawak 310–311
Sarawak, history of....................312
Sarawak Cultural Village..........330
Sarawak Forestry Corporation 323, 333
Sarawak national parks 333
Sayong...127
school holidays 56
sea dyaks 308
sea gypsies 437
sea lice...43
Sedition Act 569
Sejarah Melayu.........................553
Selai...305
selambau (fishing).....................373
Selingan, Pulau.............................430
Selirong Island...............................457
Semang people...............185, 576
semangat....................................570
Sematan 337
Semelai people 576
Semenggoh Wildlife Rehabilitation Centre 335
Semiar people 576
Semporna.....................................437
Senoi people 185, 576
Sepilok...427
Sepilok Orang-utan Rehabilitation Centre 427
Seremban.....................265–267
Seremban 266
Seria...465
Seribuat Archipelago 302
service charges.............................52
Setiu wetlands.............................225
shahbandars.................................555
shared taxis 32
sharia...572
shophouses 10
shopping 49
Siar beach 337
SIB church 381
Sibu 341–345
Sibu 342
Sibu, Pulau 302
Sibuan Island...............................438
Sidang Injil Borneo 381
Sihan people 350
silver.......................................50, 219
Similajau National Park 354
Sinambung, Gunung................413
SINGAPORE 466–551

Singapore 470
Bras Barah Road to Rochor Road................................483
Chinatown and the Financial District.....................494–495
colonial district and Marina Centre, The 476
Downtown Singapore 474
Geylang and Katong.......... 513
Little India and Arab Street 486
Marina Bay 503
MRT system, The................525
Orchard Road 506–507
Abdul Gaffoor Mosque 487
accommodation.........................528
addresses..................................526
Adventure Cove Waterpark.........521
airlines.......................................524
airport.......................................523
Al-Abrar Mosque.......................498
Albert Street 484
Alexandra Arch 516
Amoy Street 498
Ann Siang Hill............................497
Arab Street 489
Armenian church 479
arrival...523
Art Science Museum.................504
arts festivals..............................546
Arts House.................................476
Asian Civilizations Museum 477
Baba House.................................500
Bali Lane...................................489
banks..551
Barings Bank..............................501
bars 543
Battery Road...............................502
Battle Box...................................481
Beach Road 490
beaches 515, 523
Bird Park 517
Birds' Nest Gallery 493
Boat Quay..................................499
bookshops.................................551
Botanic Gardens 508
Bras Basah Road.......................482
Buddha Tooth Relic Temple 493
Buffalo Road..............................485
Bugis Junction 485
Bugis Street 485
Bugis Village..............................485
Bukit Pasoh Road 497
Bukit Timah................................510
bumboats 478
bus stations 524, 526
buses 524, 527
Bussorah Street.........................489
cable cars 517
cafés, Western 543
canopy walk (Southern Ridges) 516
car rental 528
casinos 503, 512, 520
Cathay Building 506
Causeway...................................523
CBD 501

CDs....................................551
Central Catchment Nature Reserve
....509
Central Fire Station...................480
Changi Beach..........................515
Changi Museum.......................514
changing of the guard...............506
Chettiar Temple.......................482
CHIJMES..............................484
Chinatown.............................490
Chinatown Complex..................497
Chinatown Heritage Centre.........492
Chinese Chamber of Commerce
....479
Chinese Methodist Church..........498
Chinese Weekly Entertainment
Club....................................497
Chulia Mosque........................492
Church of St Gregory.................479
cinemas................................546
City Hall................................475
civic district...........................473
Civil Defence Heritage Galleries
....480
Civilian War Memorial................479
clan associations.....................497
Clarke Quay...........................482
classical music.......................547
Clavell, James.........................514
Clifford Pier...........................502
Club Street............................497
clubs....................................545
Collyer Quay...........................502
colonial district.......................473
consulates.............................551
Crane Dance...........................522
Customs House.......................502
cycling..................................528
death houses..........................496
Dempsey Hill..........................542
departure...............................523
Desker Road...........................487
Dhoby Ghaut...........................505
driving..................................528
DuckTours..............................529
embassies..............................551
Emerald Hill............................507
Empress Place Building.............477
entertainment.........................546
Esplanade – Theatres on the Bay
....505
Eu Tong Sen Street....................497
Eu Yan Sang Medical Hall............493
ez-link cards...........................526
fabrics..................................550
Far East Square.......................499
ferry terminals........................526
Financial District......................501
Fort Canning Park....................481
Fort Siloso.............................523
Freemasons' Hall.....................480
Fuk Tak Chi Street Museum.........499
Fullerton Building.....................502
Gardens By The Bay South.........504
Gateway, the...........................489
gay scene..............................546
Geylang................................512
Geylang & Katong....................513

GMAX..................................482
Goodwood Park Hotel...............507
Great Southern Hotel................497
gyms....................................551
Haijah Fatimah Mosque.............490
Haji Lane...............................489
Har Par Villa...........................515
HarbourFront Centre.................517
Henderson Waves....................516
high tea.................................543
Hill Street..............................479
Hong Lim Complex...................492
Hong Lim Park.........................499
Hort Park...............................516
hospitals...............................551
ice cream, local.......................540
Images of Singapore LIVE...........522
Indian Heritage Centre..............487
information.............................528
internet access.......................528
Istana...................................506
Istana Kampong Glam...............489
Jacob Ballas Children's Garden
....509
Jamae Mosque........................492
jewellery...............................550
Jinriksha Building.....................500
Joo Chiat Complex....................513
Joo Chiat Road........................513
Jurong..................................517
Kallang.................................505
Kampong Glam.......................488
Kandahar Street......................489
Katong..................................514
Katong Antiques House..............514
Keong Saik Road......................497
Kerbau Road...........................487
kongsis.................................497
Kranji War Cemetery.................512
Kwan Im Temple......................484
La Salle College......................482
Lau Pa Sat.............................502
Leeson, Nick...........................501
Little India.............................485
Little India Arcade....................487
Luge and Skyride.....................522
Madame Tussauds....................522
Maghain Aboth Synagogue.........484
Majestic Opera House................497
Malabar Mosque......................490
Malay Heritage Centre...............489
malls....................................549
maps....................................526
Marina Bay.............................502
Marina Bay Sands hotel and Marina
Centre..................................504
Maritime Experiential Museum
....521
Masjid Sultan.........................489
Masonic Lodge........................480
Megazip Adventure Park.............522
Memorial...............................512
Memories at Old Ford Factory
....511
Merlion.................................502
MICA Building.........................482
Mount Faber...........................517
MRT system............................526

museum passes.......................481
music, live.............................547
music shops...........................551
Mustafa................................488
NAFA....................................492
Nagore Durgha Shrine...............499
National Gallery.......................475
National Museum.....................480
National Orchid Garden.............508
New Bridge Road......................497
Night Safari............................511
nightlife................................543
observatory............................518
Old Parliament House................475
Old Supreme Court...................475
Omni-Theatre.........................518
opera, Chinese........................547
Orchard Road.........................505
Padang.................................475
Parkview Square......................489
Parliament.............................476
Pasir Panjang.........................515
Peranakan Museum..................480
Petain Road............................488
pharmacies............................551
Pinacothèque.........................481
Pinnacle@Duxton....................500
post offices............................551
Raffles City............................479
Raffles hotel...........................479
Raffles landing site...................477
Raffles Place..........................501
Red Dot Design Museum............501
Reflections at Bukit Chandu........516
Resorts World Sentosa..............520
restaurants............................534
Ridley, Henry..........................508
River Safari............................511
river taxis..............................527
river trips..............................478
Robertson Quay.......................482
Rowell Road...........................487
St Andrew's Cathedral...............478
St James Power Station..............517
S.E.A. aquarium.......................521
Sago Street............................496
Sakaya Muni Buddha Temple.......488
School of the Arts.....................482
Sculpture Square.....................484
Second Crossing......................523
Sentosa................................518
Serangoon Road......................485
shopping...............................548
Sian Chai Kang Temple...............498
Singapore Art Museum...............484
Singapore City Gallery...............497
Singapore Cricket Club...............475
Singapore Flyer.......................505
Singapore Recreation Club..........475
Singapore River................477, 478
Singapore Science Centre...........518
Singapore Sling.......................479
Singapore Tourist Pass...............534
Smith Street...........................496
Snow City..............................518
Sook Ching.....................492, 510
South Bridge Road...................492
Southern Ridges......................515

souvenirs......................................550
Speakers' Corner.........................499
Sports Hub...................................505
Sri Krishnan Temple....................484
Sri Mariamman Temple................493
Sri Srinivasa Perumal Temple......488
Sri Thendayuthapani Temple........482
Sri Veeramakaliamman Temple
....487
street theatre..............................547
Sultan Mosque............................489
Sungei Buloh Wetland Reserve
....512
swimming pools...........................551
Syed Alwi Road............................488
Tan Teng Niah, house of..............487
Tanglin Village.............................542
Tanjong Pagar.............................500
tax refunds..................................548
taxis..527
teahouses....................................501
Tekka Market...............................485
Telok Ayer Street.........................498
Telok Blangah..............................516
theatre..547
Theatres on the Bay....................505
Thian Hock Keng Temple..............509
tours..529
trains (Malaysian)........................524
transport.....................................526
travel agents...............................551
Trengganu Street.........................496
Trick Eye Museum........................521
trishaws......................................529
Universal Studios.........................520
Upper Cross Street......................492
vaccinations................................551
Victoria Concert Hall...................476
Victoria Theatre...........................476
VivoCity.....................517, 542, 549
Wak Hai Cheng Bio......................500
walks, guided..............................529
Wallace, Alfred Russell.................510
Waterloo Street...........................484
WaveHouse.................................523
wayangs.......................................547
Wings of Time.............................523
women's helpline.........................551
Woodlands Station......................524
Ying Fo Fui Kun...........................499
Yueh Hai Ching Temple................500
zoo..510
Singapore Malay Union................561
Singapore Sling...........................479
Singlish.......................................592
sininggazanak...........................391
Sipadan, Pulau............................438
Sipitang......................................404
Siti Nurhaliza..............................203
Snake Temple..............................157
snakes...................................43, 586
snorkelling....................................47
songket.......................................50
Sook Ching...........................492, 510
south, The......................260–305
south, The............................264

souvenirs......................................49
speed limit....................................33
sports...47
Sri Menanti..................................267
Srivijaya Empire...........................554
stalls, food....................................37
Stong, Gunung.............................208
Stong State Park..........................208
Straits Settlements............136, 558
studying..55
Subramaniam Swamy temple
....105
Sufis..571
Sukau..431
Sultan of Brunei..........................449
Sulug, Pulau................................399
Suluk people................................437
Sumbiling.....................................464
sun bears...............................428, 584
Sungai Lembing...........................255
Sungai Liang Forest Reserve
....465
Sungai Petani..............................158
Sungai Relau...............................205
Sungai Tangap longhouse.....361
Suri, Pulau...................................221
Swettenham, Frank........................65
swiftlet nests.............362, 433,
493
syariah (sharia) law.....................572
syncretism...................................570

T

Tabin Wildlife Reserve.................435
tablets, ancestral.........................573
Tahan, Gunung............................198
Taib Mahmud...............................313
Taiping........................128–131
Taiping...............................128
Tama Abu Range.........................375
TAMAN NEGARA........185–200,
205, 207
Taman Negara...................186
Kuala Tahan.......................190
Kuala Tahan: day-trips and
short trails......................194
blinds..195
camping.......................................187
canopy walkway...........................193
costs..187
fees..187
guides, hiring...............................190
hides..195
Indah, Bukit.................................194
Kuala Keniam...............................198
Kuala Koh entrance......................207
Kuala Perkai.................................198
Kuala Tahan.................................189

Kuala Tahan entrance..........189–193
Kumbang hide..............................196
Lata Berkoh.................................195
Merapoh (Sungai Relau) entrance
....205
package trips................................191
park headquarters........................190
Tahan, Gunung............................198
Tenor trail...................................198
Teresek, Bukit..............................193
Taman Negara Pulau Pinang
....156
Tambunan....................................401
Tambunan Rafflesia Reserve
....401
Tamils...576
Tanah Rata..................................173
Tanah Rata..........................174
Tanjung Aru.................................394
Tanjung Datu National Park....337
Taoism...573
tapir..584
Tasik Kenyir.................................243
Tataluan......................................403
tattoos, tribal...............................328
Tawau........................441–443
Tawau.................................442
Tawau Hills Park..........................441
taxis.......................................32, 35
TBS...85
tea plantations.............173, 421
Tebedu...314
Tekek...295
Tekek and Air Batang........295
telephones.....................................57
television.......................................44
Teluk Bahang...............................156
Teluk Chempedak.........................253
Temburong...................................463
Temenggor, Tasik.........................134
Temiar people...............185, 576
temples, Chinese..........................573
temples, visiting.............................49
Tengah, Pulau..............................303
Tenggol, Pulau.............................248
Tenom..402
Terengganu State Museum....239
Terminal Bersepadu Selatan....85
Teru River....................................373
textiles...................................49, 321
Thaipusam.......72, 106, 122, 145,
488
tigers...584
time...58
Tioman, Pulau.............292–302
Tioman, Pulau....................293
Tip of Borneo..............................412
Titiwangsa range.........................110
To' Kenali....................................217
Tok Janggut.................................215
tolls, road......................................34
Touch 'n Go...................................34

tour operators.............................. 29
tourist information.................... 58
trains, Malaysian 31, 201, 392, 404
transport....................................... 30
travel agents................................ 29
travellers with disabilities......... 59
trekking advice........................... 47
trishaws.. 35
Tropical Spice Garden..............156
Trus Madi, Gunung 401
Tua Peh Kong............................573
Tuaran...394
Tuanku Abdul Rahman Park..398
Turtle Islands National Park...430
turtles.......................156, 228, 236, 247, 248, 250, 252, 281, 301, 338, 354, 430, 586
TV... 44
Twin Otters 366

U

Ulu Baram.....................................380
Ulu Muda Eco Park...................162

Ulu Temburong National Park 464
UMNO...572
Unfederated Malay States......560

V

vaccinations.................................. 42
vegetarian food........................... 40
via ferrata 418
visas.. 52
VOC...................122, 160, 270, 556

W

Wakaf Bharu 221
Wallace, Alfred Russel 320, 509, 589
Wan Azizah 567
water, drinking 43
water village (Brunei)...............453
water village (Labuan).............407
watersports.................................. 47

wayang kulit......................218, 219
weather...........................12, 13, 50
west coast, The............. 112–179
west coast, The.................... 116
White Rajahs 313, 560
whitewater rafting 48, 121
wildlife...583
Wind Cave 336
windsurfing 48
women 49
woodcarving................................ 50
work... 55

Y

Yap Ah Loy 65

Z

Zaharevic, Ernest 140
Zamboanga (Philippines).......424
Zheng He...........................273, 521

Map symbols

The symbols below are used on maps throughout the book

▬ ▪	International boundary	⊞	Hospital	⅄	Campsite
▬ ▪	Province boundary	ℭ	Telephone	⌂	Hut/hide
▬ ▬ ▬	Chapter division boundary	☂	Public gardens	☪	Mosque
	Major road	⚐	Golf course	⛩	Buddhist temple
	Minor road	∩	Arch	⚚	Hindu/Sikh temple
	Motorway road	♉	Castle/fort	⛩	Chinese temple
	Pedestrian road	⚱	Museum	✡	Synagogue
	Railway	🏛	Monument	✦	Snorkelling
	Ferry route	⚓	Swimming pool	†	Church (regional map)
	Footpath	⊠	Gate	⊟	Church (town map)
	River	▲	Peak	▭	Market
✈	Airport	⁂	Rock	⬭	Stadium
✗	Airport (regional)	⌣	Bridge	▦	Building
Ⓗ	Helipad	☀	Hill	▭	Park
⊖	MRT station (Singapore)	◠	Cave	▭	Beach
★	Transport stop	∴	Ruin	▭	Christian cemetery
P	Parking	⌇	Marshland	▭	Muslim cemetery
◆	Point of interest	⚘	Waterfall	▬	Wall
@	Internet access	◇	Gorge	▬ ▬	Ferry route
ⓘ	Tourist office	⚜	Viewpoint	⊪⊪⊪⊪	Funicular
✉	Post office	⚐	Lighthouse		

Listings key

- ■ Accommodation
- ● Eating
- ■ Drinking/nightlife
- ● Shop

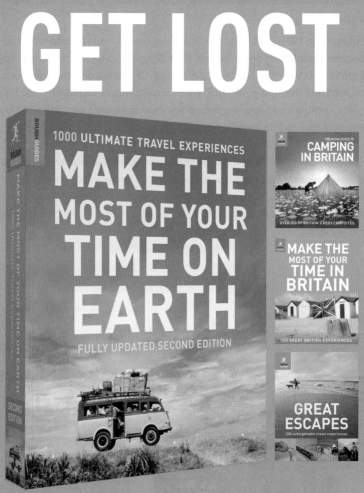

A ROUGH GUIDE TO
ROUGH GUIDES

Published in 1982, the first Rough Guide – to Greece – was a student scheme that became a publishing phenomenon. Mark Ellingham, a recent graduate in English from Bristol University, had been travelling in Greece the previous summer and couldn't find the right guidebook. With a small group of friends he wrote his own guide, combining a highly contemporary, journalistic style with a thoroughly practical approach to travellers' needs.

The immediate success of the book spawned a series that rapidly covered dozens of destinations. And, in addition to impecunious backpackers, Rough Guides soon acquired a much broader and older readership that relished the guides' wit and inquisitiveness as much as their enthusiastic, critical approach and value-for-money ethos.

These days, Rough Guides feature recommendations from shoestring to luxury and cover more than 120 destinations around the globe. Our ever-growing team of authors and photographers is spread all over the world, particularly in Europe, the US and Australia.

Rough Guides now number around 200 titles, including Pocket city guides, inspirational coffee-table books and comprehensive country and regional titles, plus technology guides from iPods to Android. As well as print books, we publish groundbreaking ebooks for every major digital device.

Visit ⓦ roughguides.com to see our latest publications.

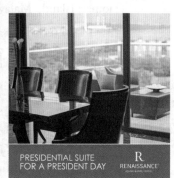